THE OTHER SIDE OF NASHVILLE

...an incomplete history & discography of the nashville rock underground, 1976-2006...

WRITTEN & EDITED BY REV. KEITH A. GORDON
(WITH A LITTLE HELP FROM SOME FRIENDS!)

!@#
EXCITABLE PRESS

New York • Nashville

The Other Side Of Nashville:

An Incomplete History & Discography of the Nashville Rock Underground

ISBN #978-0-9850084-0-6
Published by Excitable Press, a Conspiracy M.E.D.I.A company
35 Montclair Avenue • Batavia NY 14020 • Web: http://www.excitablepress.com

Author/Editor's Disclaimer:

The material in this book represents the recollections and opinions of Rev. Keith A. Gordon and may differ from those of other individuals involved in the events outlined herein. Although every effort has been made to verify the facts, dates, people and places described within these pages, no intentional misrepresentation may be implied. If you don't remember it this way, sorry...this is my story, dammit, and if you don't like it...write your own book!

If I forgot you or your band, sorry, 'cause in any project this size, there are bound to be omissions. That's why we're calling this doorstop "an incomplete history" because I know that I've overlooked *more than a few bands*, so don't be logging onto the Internet to bitch about it because after six years of trying to get bands involved in putting this thing together, I just don't care anymore...ya snooze, ya lose, ya know?

CONTENTS...

SECTIONS:

FEATURES

APPENDIXES

FORWARD / FRED MILLS

If my first encounter with Rev. Keith A. Gordon wasn't precisely one-on-one, it was still fortuitous, and by my reckoning, prescient. He and I were both reviewing bootleg CDs for a music fanzine that specialized in chronicling the illicit but then-thriving bootleg underground, and it was clear from his enthusiastic embrace of the format that rock 'n' roll in all its tattered, tarnished, boozy, drugged-out glory was paramount in his life – not to mention his evidencing a healthy disrespect for authority and a total disdain for whatever the so-called "received wisdom" of the moment might be.

I became a fan of Gordon's work, and years later the two of us find ourselves once again appearing alongside one another in the pages of a music publication. By way of full disclosure, I'm technically his editor (*Blurt Magazine*). But in actual practice it's a peer relationship first; a mutual admiration society second; and even the third component, that I'm assigning and paying him, is more of a *Him: "Just heard this amazing* [insert band name or record title]—*whattaya think about me doin' something on it?"* and *Me: "I trust your instincts, let's do it!"* dynamic than any traditional writer-pitches-the-editor-and-hopes-for-response scenario.

That's the kind of unbridled enthusiasm, and devotion to thumbing his nose at the status quo, that Gordon brings to the volume you currently hold in your hands. It's simultaneously a reference work and an alternate history of the Nashville music scene, a milieu whose story has been viewed so often through the whiskey-and-gingham tinted lens of Music Row that the very word "Nashville" instantly summons images of Hank Williams, Patsy Cline, Dolly Parton, Porter Wagoner, George Jones, Loretta Lynn and, er, Minnie Pearl, and all the attendant Grand Ole Opry tropes or *Hee Haw*-isms you'd care to mention. Which is fine, don't get me wrong; for young artists aspiring to careers in country music, and to a lesser extent, bluegrass and folk, Nashville is rightfully iconic, and it continues to produce performers gifted with enormous talent, from Zac Brown and Taylor Swift to Tim McGraw and Keith Urban (who is technically Australian, but he had to move to Nashville to make it big, and anyway, he's a helluva guitarist).

Still, Gordon, who spent a good chunk of his life in Nashville, understands that living in or moving to Nashville doesn't automatically mean that if you're a musician you have to check your rock 'n' roll credentials at the city limits and apply for membership in the CMA. Just ask erstwhile White Stripes mainman Jack White, whose career as rocker, producer and label owner (Third Man Records) has flourished since relocating to the city several years ago. Or Dan Auerbach and Patrick Carney of Akron upstarts the Black Keys, who've made Nashville their second home of late. Or even my good friends in the Ettes, a two-girl/one-guy garage rock dynamo originally hailing from L.A. who also have found the city's rock denizens extremely hospitable over the past few years, not to mention the fact that Nashville's geographic position proves fortuitous when it comes to sketching out tour routings.

Point of fact, there are as many musical wrinkles, subgenres and just plain oddballs to be found in Nashville as any other large city, outsized reputation be damned. I won't claim firsthand knowledge of Nashville, having only skirted it by highway once while driving from the east coast to the west awhile back; nor will I attempt to examine the whole "what's in the water there?" angle either – that, my friends, should be part of the reason you picked up this book in the first place. And Gordon's the man to guide you.

In sifting through these encyclopedia-styled pages, one encounters everything from punk/pop provocateurs (Government Cheese, from the late '80s/early '90s, and featuring a very young Tommy Womack, one of my heroes); to latterday, explosive – pun intended – funk/soul shouters (The Dynamites featuring Charles Walker); to contemporary singer/songwriters with a twang in the heart and superior DNA in the cells (Justin Townes Earle, whose pappy you may have also heard of); to glammy '80s hair metal (Every Mother's Nightmare); to contemporary indie pop more typically spotted in hipstervilles such a Brooklyn (Be Your Own Pet). Naturally, Jason & the *Nashville* Scorchers also are prominently featured here, along with frontman Jason Ringenberg's delightful kids-music side project, Farmer Jason, and while I can't prove it, I suspect that it was Gordon's deep love for the Scorchers that partially provided the impetus for the book project.

The Scorchers, y'see, were for many outsiders, yours truly included, the first inkling that there just might be musical life beyond the restrictive confines of the Opry. I distinctly remember getting a copy of their debut EP back in '82 and pondering both its more-than-apropos title, *Reckless Country Soul*, and the band moniker. The early '80s, recall, was when the promise of punk and new wave was finally coming into focus and underground bands everywhere were pulsing with the D.I.Y. imperative. How maverick was it, then, for a band steeped in the punk ethos to actually claim that most conservative-leaning of names – *Nashville* – as its own?

God bless 'em for that, and by the same token, God bless Gordon for setting the record straight about Nashville. There's plenty here to mull over, even *obsess* over and begin trying to track down some of the music. So have a shot, crack a beer, and kick back with the Reverend. / Fred Mills / Raleigh NC / September 2012

INTRODUCTION: FROM COWTOWN TO ROCK & ROLL MECCA

Gather 'round kiddies, the old man has a story to tell….

I know that you young whippersnappers aren't going to believe me, but at one time, Nashville had no original rock music scene. Yup, nothing but horrible Top 40 cover bands, honky-tonk country acts, and gospel singers. In the early 1970s, Music Row was dominated by slick, over-produced "Countrypolitan" sounds laden with syrupy strings and molded into a semblance of urbane pop music sellable to suburban housewives…it's a tactic used by Nashville's major labels, more or less, 'til this current day, to separate their female demographic from a bit of their grocery money.

When I moved to the rural suburbs south of Nashville in 1971 from the urban wasteland that was Erie, Pennsylvania at the time, it was a case of pure culture shock. I was fourteen years old, and had spent most of my short life living in Erie – with nine months in Cleveland, and another year in a rural area literally on the edge of Lake Erie. The lovely "mistake on the lake" that was Erie had the highest violent crime rate per capita of any city in the U.S. during my residence, and I went to elementary and junior high school with the sons and daughters of mobsters and the brothers and sisters of outlaw bikers.

Upon arriving in what was then the middle-class enclave of Brentwood, our house overlooked a pasture where cows grazed. The neighborhood kids didn't know Jimi Hendrix or Janis Joplin when they saw the giant-sized B&W posters on my bedroom walls, but they knew who Merle Haggard was. Franklin High School took some adjusting to, going to school with rednecks and farmers, preppie kids and the first African-American students that I'd met (Erie was 95% Italian Roman-Catholic, and 99.9% whitebread). Naturally, I fell in with the rockers and misfits, dope-smokers and "losers" who didn't fit into the uneasy role of jock, good student, or school band member.

When I finally got wheels, or at least found older friends that did, we went hog-wild cruising into Nashville to catch the latest concert at the tin-cup that was the Municipal Auditorium. We saw the Rolling Stones in '72 (with Stevie Wonder opening), caught Jethro Tull, Alice Cooper, Joe Cocker, Three Dog Night, and countless others. When we got old enough to sneak into bars, though, we were sorely disappointed…the Roller Coaster club off Nolensville Road had nothing but cover bands, the Villager in Hillsboro Village had a jukebox, and so on. There was plenty of beer, but little decent music to be heard outside of a full-fledged concert.

Little did I know at the time that R. Stevie Moore and his friends like Victor Lovera and Roger Ferguson were working to change the poor state of rock 'n' roll music in Nashville. The three of them were involved in a number of bands like Goods, trying to perform original rock music in a city dominated by country twang. When Moore released his independent *Phonography* album in 1976, it was the first shot in the creation of a local music scene that, 35+ years later, is thriving like no other point in the city's history.

The Other Side of Nashville is the story, of sorts, of the creation and evolution of the city's non-country music scene, from the landmark release of Moore's **Phonography** album through my departure from the Nashville area in 2006. That's 30 years, give or take, of involvement of one sort or another in the city's local rock scene…either as a fan, or as a music journalist and critic. This book is sub-titled "An Incomplete History & Discography of the Nashville Rock Underground" because, well, that's what it is. Sure, there are entries that run over into the years 2007-2010, but the bulk of this stuff concerns the three decades during which I was intimately involved with the local rock scene and the musicians that launched a revolution.

As a teen, I was music-crazed, and devoured every issue of *Rolling Stone*, *Crawdaddy*, *Fusion*, *Circus*, and especially *Creem* magazine, taking my cue from writers like Dave Marsh, Lester Bangs, and Greg Shaw, buying records that they recommended. When I discovered that I could get FREE records if I started writing about them, I saved up enough grass-cutting money to buy a copy of the annual *Writer's Digest* guide, and started sending out letters to every music-oriented publication listed in the book.

Only one magazine responded with anything but an outright rejection – *Sunrise*, "The Journal of Music & Liberation" published by the remnants of John Sinclair's White Panther Party in Illinois. While I can't say that the ghosts of the MC5 or Up! inhabited the zine, they did publish my first tentative album reviews (I was 15 years old), and I was lucky to have as my first editor the legendary rock critic Rick Johnson. Rick was my friend, mentor, and confidant, and while he was a friend of Bangs, Johnson had developed a critical voice that was entirely his own, and he encouraged me to do the same.

After *Sunrise*, I began contributing album reviews to *Hank Magazine*, published by the larger-than-life Harvey McGee (who, at one time, held the dubious distinction of being the only Nashvillian with more unpaid parking tickets than I). My next writing opportunity came via an older guy that I kind of knew in high school, Thom King, who had begun publishing *Take One Magazine*, Nashville's first "alternative" paper (*Hank* was purely music, while *Take One* included politics, arts, etc).

Take One provided an unparalleled learning experience, not only offering the opportunity to hone my writing skills with the seemingly endless supply of promo LPs available, but in all areas of media. Working with Thom, his brother John, and writer/editor Sam Borgerson, I learned to put a publication together from scratch. Typesetting, lay-out, proofreading, photography...I learned it all while working at *Take One*.

With *Take One*, we covered the fledgling local music scene, such as it was, and I remember that we reviewed the first album from Lovera's group the Smashers, covered the first performance by the Ramones in Nashville, hung out with Marshall Chapman, and basically made ourselves into a major pain in the ass with the local media and record labels.

Sadly, when I left Nashville to live in the Detroit area circa 1979-81, the local rock scene grew by leaps and bounds, mostly due to Rick Champion and Phranks 'n' Steins. R. Stevie Moore had long since left town for New Jersey, but folks like Jason Ringenberg and Dave Olney would take his place, and in the late 1970s and early 1980s, original rock 'n' roll bands like Dave Olney & the X Rays, the White Animals, Jason & the *Nashville* Scorchers, and others began to pop up.

When I returned to the Music City during the summer of 1981, I came back to what was beginning to look a lot like a thriving local rock scene to rival that which I'd been part of in the Motor City. Friday and Saturday nights were spent at Cantrell's, the Exit/In or, later, at Rooster's in the Cannery. I worked part-time at the Collector's Dream store on Elliston Place (where Rock Block Guitars would later exist), swapping my day labor for free LPs and comix, and working at a restaurant at night for beer money to be spent at the local rock 'n' roll shows.

I eventually fell in with Andy Anderson and the *Nashville Intelligence Report* crowd, writing for one of the first (and best) local music zines long before Gus Palas came to town and launched *The Metro* magazine in August 1985...by which time the local rock scene was pretty much in full bloom. Bands would pop up and disappear overnight, some of the more popular artists would sign with regional, and then national record labels, and Nashville began to take on the buzz of a real scene to rival those developing independently in Austin and Athens. As an editor, critic, columnist, and sometimes janitor for *The Metro*, I had a front-row seat for the Nashville rock explosion.

The Other Side of Nashville is a (misguided?) attempt to put my relationship with the Nashville rock scene into some sort of context, and maybe document a bit of history along the way. I understand that the ole Reverend has been a bit of a polarizing figure through the years, and I've publically feuded with the Nashville Entertainment Association, the Country Music Hall of Fame, most of the labels on Music Row, local churches, and even a group of Vandy grad scenesters that, for a brief time, took over *The Metro* while Gus was AWOL. Hell, I feuded with Palas most of all, and my later arguments with friend and editor Daryl Sanders at *The Metro/Bone Music Magazine* were the stuff of legend.

Yes, I can be a prickly asshole and a real sumbitch, but I've ALWAYS been one of the Nashville rock scene's biggest supporters. I was the first "music journalist" to write about Jason & the *Nashville* Scorchers in a national magazine (CMJ's short-lived *Progressive Media*, before they canned me for being an obstinate bastard), championed the local scene in both *Rolling Stone* magazine and *The Austin Chronicle*, and chatted up editors that I knew at publications like *Creem* and *Trouser Press* to provide Nashville bands with early coverage. I wrote about Nashville bands for Atlanta's *Tasty World*, and other regional rags, and I frequently covered the local scene during the late 1990s and early 2000s in my pop culture column in the bi-weekly *View From The Hill* community newspaper in Long Beach, California.

Contrary to what some might believe, there was a local Nashville rock scene long before the Kings of Leon, Ke$ha, Paramore, Be Your Own Pet, and other "buzz bands" burst onto the international music scene during the past half-decade. Trailblazers like Jason & the *Nashville* Scorchers, the White Animals, Afrikan Dreamland, Jet Black Factory, the dusters, the Royal Court of China, the Shakers, Dessau and, well, a lot of the bands listed in this book from the 1980s and '90s, laid the framework for today's notoriety, doing the gruntwork and convincing people in New York and L.A. that there was more to the Music City than *Hee Haw*…

Most of all, **The Other Side of Nashville** is one man's memories of the birth and evolution of a thriving, creative, hard-partying, and hard-rocking local music scene. Back in the early days, anything and everything seemed possible, and bands got together just for the hell of it, for the pure joy of playing rock 'n' roll. Any mistakes or omissions contained herein are entirely mine, as are the memories of hundreds (thousands?) of drunken nights spent reveling in the talents and vision of the rockers that built the Nashville scene.

\\ Rev. Keith A. Gordon //
Snowbound outside Buffalo NY, February 2012

"A great man with a crazy plan..." – Martin Popoff, 2010

THE REVEREND SEZ "THANKS!"
A project such as this can't happen without the help of many people. I'd like to thank the following for their support and contributions to **The Other Side of Nashville***:*

Aashid, Andy Anderson, Stephen Anderson, Dave Barnette, Pete Berwick, Jeff Cease, Chip Chilton, Doyle Davis, Troy Davis, Danny Dickerson, Tracey Dooling, Holly Duncan, John Elliott, Scott Feinstein, Donna Frost, Bill Glahn, Mike Grimes, Tommy Hash, Lisa Hays, David Henderson, Warner Hodges, Jeff Holmes, Willie Jemison, Robert Jetton, Thom King, Tom Littlefield, Robert Logue, Heather Lose, Andy Martin, Ken McMahan, Threk Michaels, Fred Mills, R. Stevie Moore, Nuno Monteiro, Steve Morley, Barry Nelson, David Olney, Gwil Owen, Gus Palas, Dave Perkins, Graham Perry, Martin Popoff, Jason Ringenberg, Mary Sack, Daryl Sanders, Mark Shenkel, Ross Smith, Allen Sullivant, Scott Sullivant, Bryan Talbot, Bernie Walters, Dave Willie, Tommy Womack, Steve Woods, Kenny Wright, and anybody else I may have forgotten over these past six years...

Interspered in the pages of the book are local concert posters, mostly from the 1980s, which were graciously provided by Allen Sullivant, curator of the **Nashville 80s Rock** website (http://www.nashville80srock.net)

The Other Side of Nashville *is dedicated to my beautiful and supernaturally-patient wife Tracey; to the musicians that have made such great music over the last three decades; and to those friends we've lost along the way:*

Aashid, Argyle Bell, Lee Carr, Chip Chilton, Drew Claesges, Jack Emerson, Chris Feinstein, Barry Felts, Stacy Fleeman, Bruce Hackemann, Ric Harman, Paul Kirby, Tim Krekel, Vince Liveri, Don Mooney, Rick Moore, Will Owsley, Brooks Phillips, Joey Rossi, David Schnaufer & Max Vague

METRO MUSIC AWARDS 1989 - 1991

Long before the local music industry decided to offer its own version of "Nashville Music Awards" as an excuse for self-congratulation and, of course, to throw a party, Gus Palas and *The Metro* magazine held three awards programs to honor the Music City's best and brightest. The awards were voted on by readers of the magazine and, believe it or not, as a non-biased counter of some of the votes, the results were right down the line. As a result, the awards tended to showcase the great diversity of the city's underground talent.

<u>1989 Winners</u>
Band of the Year: The Dusters
Musician of the Year: Kenny Greenburg / The Kingsnakes
Best Female Vocalist: Melora Zaner / Raging Fire
Best Male Vocalist: Judson Spence
Best New Band: The Stand
Hall of Fame Award: Preston Sullivan / Carlyle Records
Album of the Year: John Hiatt – *Slow Turning*
EP of the Year: The Shakers – *Living In The Shadow Of A Spirit*
Best Pop Band: The Questionnaires
Best Rock Band: Walk The West
Best Blues Band: The Kingsnakes
Best Hardcore Band: F.U.C.T.
Best Hard Rock Band: The Stand
Best Dance Band: Dessau
Best Avant-Garde Band: Grinning Plowman
Best Electric Guitarist: Kenny Greenburg / The Kingsnakes
Best Acoustic Guitarist: Oscar Rice / The Shakers
Best Bass Player: Dave Barnette / The Dusters
Best Keyboard Player: Giles Reaves
Best Drummer: Paul Simmonz / The Stand

<u>1990 Winners</u>
Band of the Year: Intruder
Musician of the Year: Arthur Vinett / Intruder
Female Artist of the Year: Jaime Kyle
Male Artist of the Year: Webb Wilder
Female Vocalist of the Year: Jonell Mosser
Male Vocalist of the Year: Jimmy Hamilton / Intruder
Best New Band: Jane, His Wife
Album of the Year: Intruder – *A Higher Form Of Killing*
EP of the Year: Rednecks In Pain – *Your Greasy Granny's Got Holes In Her Panties*
Best Pop Band: Paradise Lost
Best Rock Band: The Dusters
Best Blues Band: The Dusters
Best Hardcore Band: F.U.C.T.
Best Hard Rock Band: Arch Angel
Best Dance Band: Dessau
Best Avant-Garde Band: Alien In The Land Of Our Birth
Best Guitarist: Ken McMahan / The Dusters
Best Bass Player: Dave Barnette / The Dusters
Best Keyboard Player: Tommy Cage
Best Drummer: Kenny Earl

The Reverend at the Metro Music Awards

<u>1991 Winners</u>
Band of the Year: The Hard Corps
Musician of the Year: Bela Fleck
Female Artist of the Year: Ashley Cleveland
Male Artist of the Year: Webb Wilder
Female Vocalist of the Year: Matraca Berg
Male Vocalist of the Year: Tommy McRae / Guilt
Debut Artist of the Year: The Hard Corps
Hall of Fame Award: Aashid Himons
Album of the Year: Chagall Guevara – *Chagall Guevara*
Pop Band of the Year: Chagall Guevara
Rock Band of the Year: Every Mother's Nightmare
Blues Band of the Year: The Dusters
Hardcore Band of the Year: F.U.C.T.
Alternative Band of the Year: Jet Black Factory
Guitar Player of the Year: Arthur Vinett / Intruder
Bass Player of the Year: Victor Wooten / The Flecktones
Keyboard Player of the Year: Roger Osborne / 15 Strings
Drummer of the Year: Dave Kennedy / Walk The West

A Note on *The Metro*:
Although I've defended Gus Palas and *The Metro* elsewhere in this hefty paperweight, a word should be said about the people who actually did the heavy lifting in putting out over 100 issues of the city's best-known and longest-lasting music magazine. *The Metro* was an important stepping-stone in my own development as a writer, and I imagine that Brian Mansfield (*U.S.A. Today*) would say the same. The zine also featured talented scribes like Andy Anderson (*Nashville Intelligence Report*), Kath Hansen, Clyde Crawley, Michael McCall, Bill Spicer, Heather Lose, and many others as well as photographers like Ross Smith, James Williams, and Michael Godsey and cover artist Tim "Mercury" Shawl. Finally, don't forget longtime editors Lisa Hays and Rebecca Luxford, who made it work in spite of Gus in what were often poor working conditions...

AASHID HIMONS: THE LION OF NASHVILLE....

Although he is only remembered today by a small group of loyal fans and fellow musicians, nobody did more to support and propel the Nashville non-country music scene to the point it is today than Aashid Himons. Both as the founder of popular local band Afrikan Dreamland – whose revolutionary mix of blues, rock, and reggae earned Aashid, Mustafa, and Darrell fans worldwide – and as a solo artist as prolific as Nashville is ever likely to see, Aashid always championed local music and musicians. At the peak of their popularity, Afrikan Dreamland would pack hundreds of fans into a club, and Aashid helped many a band develop a regional following by the mere virtue of allowing them to open for Afrikan Dreamland. Aashid's prescence around town always drew a crowd, and his flirtations with different musical styles, and collaborations with many of Nashville's most talented musicians, are unparalleled.

My wife Tracey and myself spent many an evening sitting on the porch, or in the living room of our humble country shack talking with Aashid, discussing current, past, and future events. Aashid would often hold court in front of an audience of teenage computer hackers, fellow musicians, and assorted ne'er-do-wells that would visit our house full of cats, regaling us with his stories. You never knew when Aashid would drop by; he'd usually just call and say "One Heart. Is this a good time?" Sadly, my friend and brother Aashid passed away in early 2011; this obituary that I penned for the About.com Blues website, based on the bio I wrote for All Music Guide, tells Aashid's story as well as anything I've ever written. One Heart...

A rchie "Aashid" Himons, an integral part of Nashville's non-country music scene for better than three decades, passed away on Saturday, March 19, 2011 after a brief illness. Himons was 68 years old at the time of his death.

A musical innovator who fused traditional country blues with reggae and world music during the late 1970s, Aashid, as he is known to his many fans, is best known for his popular "blu-reggae" band Afrikan Dreamland, which put Himons' myriad of musical influences into play in creating an energetic and unique sound. With bandmates Darrell Rose and Mustafa Abdul-Aleen, the trio recorded six albums and would be the first reggae-oriented band to receive airplay on MTV. Himons' roots ran deep, though, and included a formative background in blues and soul music.

Himons was born in rural West Virginia in 1942, learning the piano by age 3 and the drums by 5 years old. Like many blues artists of the era, Himons sang in the church, and the talented youngster subsequently appeared on several radio and television shows, including *The Today Show* with Dave Garroway. Himons left home as a teen, hitchhiking to New York City and later joining the army.

After serving his stint with the military, Himons settled into the Washington, D.C. music scene, forming the R&B group Little Archie & the Majestics. During the 1960s, Himons would record a number of sides for various labels and with different bands, but it was a 1966 deal with Dial Records that would result in a pair of singles – "All I Have To Do" and "You Can't Tie Me Down" – that would become known as classics of "northern soul" music, and highly collectible, especially by British aficionados of the genre.

Afrikan Dreamland

AASHID HIMONS: THE LION OF NASHVILLE....

During the late 1960s, Himons worked throughout the country as a blues musician, performing coffeehouses and street corners as "West Virginia Slim." He landed in Toronto in 1969, forming the short-lived duo God & I with musician and actor Jim Byrnes. Himons' restless spirit would lead him to Mexico City, where he performed with a local blues band, but it was during a trip to the Honduras in 1972, where Himons experienced a performance by Count Ossie & the Mystical Revelation of Rastafari, that he had a musical and spiritual epiphany that led to his conversion to Rastafarianism and the creation of his "blu-reggae" style.

A hybrid of country blues, R&B, and reggae that was influenced by Count Ossie's mesmerizing Nyabinghi rhythms and the Jamaican style popularized by Bob Marley, blu-reggae would later influence contemporary blues artists like Corey Harris. Himons landed in Nashville during the late 1970s; now known as "Aashid," he formed Afrikan Dreamland with Rose and Aleem. The trio would quickly become one of the Music City's most popular bands, Afrikan Dreamland helping kickstart an original local music scene that had little to do with the city's country music tradition.

Mostly written by Himons, Afrikan Dreamland's positive lyrics preached a philosophy of peace and love, and triumph over adversity, whether caused by economic or social injustice…a thread that would carry through Aashid's entire career. Aside from their popular recordings and seemingly ubiquitous performances, Aashid and Afrikan Dreamland would use their drawing power to help young bands, and many of Nashville's early rock 'n' roll talents got their start opening for Afrikan Dreamland.

After the breakup of Afrikan Dreamland in 1987, Aashid embarked on a lengthy and varied musical journey that saw the gifted artist applying his talents to blues, gospel, country, reggae, dub, ambient, and space music. Recording both as a solo artist and with a number of bands like the Pyramid Underground, the Blu-Reggae Underground, Akasha, and Aashid & the New Dream, Himons collaborated with a number of Nashville's most adventurous musicians, talents like Tony Gerber, Giles Reaves, Ross Smith, Gary Serkin, and Kirby Shelstad, among many others. Prolific to a fault, Himons would become one of the most popular artists on mp3.com during the 1990s as his musical collaborations resulted in dozens of albums that would capture a worldwide audience for Aashid's unique musical vision.

In 1995, Aashid reunited with his former bandmates Rose and Abdul-Aleen, as well as a number of his more recent collaborators, under the Afrikan Dreamland name to release the two-CD set *The Leaders*, which further explored the blu-reggae sound. In the late 1990s, Aashid formed the Mountain Soul Band to experiment with country blues and Appalachian-inspired hillbilly music. Working again with friends like Reaves, Gerber, and Shelstad, the Mountain Soul Band also included the talents of brothers Victor and Reggie Wooten, and multi-instrumentalists Jody Lentz and Tramp, then of the Nashville trio Bonepony. This collaboration resulted in a pair of critically-acclaimed albums, 1998's studio release *Mountain Soul* and the live *West Virginia Hills*, released a year later.

Himons continued to make music during the 2000s, albeit slowed down by recurring problems with his health. The definition of the DIY artist, Himons utilized cutting-edge technology to record and edit complex, textured, and thought-provoking music on his trusty iMac computer. While not well-known outside of the Southeast, Himons nevertheless has thousands of fans worldwide that have been touched by his positive message, exciting music, and indomitable spirit.

We'd run features of one sort or another on Aashid Himons a few times in the pages of The Metro *over the course of the magazine's first five years, but it wouldn't be until 1990 when* Metro *publisher Gus Palas and myself decided to nail down a full-length interview with the local music visionary. My wife Tracey and I spent several hours talking with Aashid in an informal interview session, recording the conversation for posterity.*

I'm not sure where the tapes went – maybe Gus has 'em – but the interview yielded enough material to split into two articles of nearly 2,000 words each in length. We ran the first part of the interview in the May 1990 issue, the second part in June, and together they represent the longest and most comprehensive piece on the influential Nashville musician that I've seen in print. At one point, Aashid and I had talked about working together on a full-length biography, and we'd gone so far as to outline the book, and Aashid had dug up dozens of photos to use to illustrate his life's story. Sadly, the project never got off the ground...

PART ONE

A couple of months ago, one of the most significant artistic events in the history of Nashville occurred on our Community Access cable channel: *Aashid All Night*, a ten-hour marathon of music, random video footage, interviews, and dialogue created and compiled by the ever-popular, long-time Nashville musician, artist, and spiritual philosopher Aashid Himons. We managed to coerce Aashid away from his around-the-clock work day to sit down for a few hours and share his thoughts on both his art and *Aashid All Night*, as well as events in the world at large.

An undertaking as massive and important as *Aashid All Night* just doesn't occur, literally, overnight. A background of work and a series of events lead up to the germination of an idea. Then that idea has to be carried to fruition. Says Aashid, "I've had a television show on the Community Access channel for over two years now; it started as a talk show called *New Day With Aashid*, and I invited all of my friends…basically people who were searching for knowledge and wisdom, and we talked about whatever their expertise was. I did 28 talk shows before I got tired of the talk shows. People were asking for music, saying 'why don't you do more music?' So, in June, I changed the format. I got a video camera to shoot visuals, which I put music to. *Aashid Presents* has gotten popular; a lot of people watch it now.

Continuing, Aashid says "I walked into the Viacom station a month ago, and one of the women, Dixie Aubrey, said 'you know, you should do an all night TV show,' just off the top of her head. I started thinking 'yeah, that would be a big thing to do.' Then Elliot Mitchell walked in, and overheard it and said "you ought to call it *Aashid All Night*!' I decided that I was going to do it, but that I was going to run old footage of all the shows, mix it up, but then I decided that I couldn't do that, I had to do some new stuff, too. I started calling people and interviewing people, and getting people to play music, coming to my house and jamming with me. I put it together along with old footage. My friend Steve Carroll did the graphics and some of the animation things that were between there. Then I called and I got a lot of people to sponsor it, and underwriters. Everybody I asked said 'yes' the first time…so it was just supposed to happen."

Evidently, the proportions of the undertaking hadn't struck Aashid at that moment. He says, "It was a ten-hour show, which is a lot of footage, so I bit off more than I thought I could chew. I didn't know if I was going to get it together, about half-way through, because it was really wearing me out. I was up all night, every night…it really was "Aashid all night," Aashid up all night getting it together. I'm really low budget, because my stuff it not about commerciality, it's about communication, to communicate ideas to people, so everything I do is with people power. Somebody would say 'hey, nobody is going to be in the studio tonight, so come on in,' so that's how I get everything done. I don't have any money, but who needs money when you've got people working. When you've got people working together…that is money"

Aashid All Night was, by any standards, an unqualified artistic success, riveting many a viewer to their television until the wee hours of the morning, mesmerized by the unique mix of music, visuals, and dialogue. Says Aashid, "I've probably gotten more response from that show than anything that I've done, maybe because if you turned it on at any time during the night, you'd see it; people couldn't miss it!" Along with other local visionaries such as Tony Gerber and Allen Green, Himons was one of the first area artists to venture into mixing visuals with music. "I'm getting more done with this video music than I ever was with just music," says Aashid, "now it looks like I'm going to be able to do art and make a little bit of money, and that's unusual."

Aashid has long been identified as one of the grandfathers of the local alternative music scene, one of the artistic pioneers who, along with Darrell Rose and Mustafa Abdul-Aleen, collectively known as Afrikan Dreamland, successfully fused such

INTERVIEW: "PRESENTING AASHID"

diverse musical elements as rock, reggae, and the blues to present a new musical hybrid with which to spread their message of brotherhood. Even in those early days, Himons realized that video was destined to be the wave of the future.

Says Aashid, "In 1980, when I first got Afrikan Dreamland together, we got real popular fast. In the first year, all of the TV stations wanted us, and MTV was just then really starting, I was thinking 'the future is going to be video albums!' Nobody had even heard of a video album then, but I knew that it was going to come...so every time a television station would ask us to play, I'd say that the only way that I'd do it is if they gave me a one-inch copy of what we did, and give me the rights to use it."

"You see, they didn't think that we could do anything with it, so they said 'sure?', thinking 'a one-inch copy, what's he going to do with that, heh, heh, heh'...they didn't think that anything was going to happen. I knew, so I started piecing it together, piecing all of these little things from Channel 2, 8, 5, 4, they all had us on, and I got it and got them to sign the release form so that owned it."

Aashid continues, "so now it's 1983 and people still don't have video albums. I ran into an old friend who had gotten into video, working with Southern Productions, which is a state-of-the-art place here. The White Animals kept telling me of this guy named 'Lou,' when I realized that he was an old friend and I said 'hey, I've got to talk to him!' So I told him what was going on, and he was into my message anyway, so we put one together for hard cost."

"We put together a video called *Television Dreams*. That was when MTV was coming to Nashville looking for stuff, looking for country music. They were coming to tell people how to make better country videos; country videos used to be terrible, so they were showing them how to upgrade. They had a meeting downtown, which I couldn't go to, so I asked Mustafa, who was a member of the band, to go, He's also a lawyer, and he's always late...this time it paid off. Everybody was there already when he walked in with his dreadlocks, and the only seat left was next to the MTV people. He handed them his card and told them about the video. They wanted a video from Nashville so bad, we immediately sent it to them. Afrikan Dreamland became the first U.S. reggae band to be played on MTV."

"I took that video, and an apartheid video that we had done, and I put them together with the others and I had my first video album. Lou had been producing and directing up until then, but he was teaching me as we went along, so that when he got busy with other things, I could continue. I'm just really into learning. If you're doing something, I can watch you and I'll learn, I won't even have to bother you...that's my thing. I've learned how to edit, learned how to direct and to tell a story."

"Videos started happening and I saw that video was definitely going to be the future. If you're just playing music, you know sound, but you've got to get into the visuals and colors and lighting with video. Lighting is seriously complicated. Now I notice lighting...you start noticing how the light falls through the window, what color the light is, whether it's blue or gold. You know that light is all different colors, but it's a real subtle thing that you don't notice until you get into it and start noticing the subtleties. I had to learn a whole other realm in order to get into videos."

Of the music industry's increased reliance on and obsession with video, Aashid says "technology is really threatening to a lot of people. A lot of musicians learn their craft; they've gotten comfortable with it, then along comes technology. They took all of these years learning to play an instrument, so they say 'I don't want to mess around with this stuff.' It's really important to know how to use these things as a tool. It can detract from it, but it doesn't have to. I think that technology is a really positive thing, as far as music goes."

Popular music seems to be moving backwards, back into a more acoustic-oriented sound, a fact that hasn't escaped the awareness of Mr. Himons. "I'm starting to get into acoustic stuff," says Aashid, "that's what people want. The nineties are going to be acoustic. People are tired of going deaf, finally realizing that you do go deaf! The people who used to get right up to the speakers at shows are gone now. They've even got an acoustic program on MTV, *Unplugged*; who ever would have thought that that would happen?"

America's current flirtation with acoustic music isn't the only parallel which could be drawn with the decade of the sixties. "The nineties," says Aashid the philosopher, "are going to be real similar to the sixties, politically. It comes in thirty year cycles…people are going to be standing up for what they believe in, whatever it is. The people of Europe are moving towards democracy. We're losing all of our rights while they're getting theirs. They come and kick in your door; they don't even have to have a search warrant anymore. Used to be, they did it anyway, but you had a case against them. Now all they've got to say is 'I thought they had drugs'."

"That's all that this drug thing is, is a move towards fascism. William Burroughs said years ago that it was going to happen; he said that they were going to use drugs to install fascism in this country. So what's going on? I truly believe that, sooner or later, in order to do the things that they want to do to control people, every other one of us is going to be a policeman…that's the only way that it's going to work!"

"There's too many things that they call crimes," says Aashid, "it's just ridiculous! I think that it's really weird to lock people up for doing drugs. I can understand locking people up for the things that they do while doing drugs, but it's like the state owns our bodies. They want to own our bodies, so that they can tell us what to do."

PART TWO

"I think that it's really weird to lock up people for doing drugs, said local reggae artist, video visionary, and spiritual philosopher Aashid Himons at the end of last month's exclusive *Metro* interview."I can understand locking people up for the things they do while doing drugs, but it's like the state owns our bodies. They want to own our bodies, so that they can tell us what to do."

These controversial comments have raised the ire of many people who would prefer to remain blind to our government's continued use of deception and force to keep its servants…the public which put them in power in the first place…safely pacified and in line. Of the government's attempted control of the populace, Himons states "they're coming close to doing it now, with this mind control thing. This guy, John Stockwell, an ex-C.I.A. agent, just defected

and he's exposing all of this stuff…he was naming movies that have been put out that they placed subliminal messages in. That stuff works too, I know that it works."

"There has to be a little bit of truth in propaganda for the people to believe it, or people wouldn't even deal with it. So you get some truth, with a whole bunch of lies wrapped around it. You can't control people when they come together, though. If the black people and the white people ever came together in this country, do you know how powerful this country would be? That's the weakness in this country, and the government does it. They're doing it on purpose," says Aashid of the strain on race relations and the continuance of racism in the United States, "because that means that everyone will think that we need government. People aren't getting along, so we need them to take care of us."

"That's what this guy Stockwell says," states Himons, referring to the ex-agent who has carefully documented decades of C.I.A. misconduct and interference both here and abroad. "He said that they have agents that are people in this society that are people who just like to kill. The C.I.A. hires these people and sends them to all different parts of the world to live a life of luxury. All these people have to do is now and then kill somebody or create a disturbance that makes the government unstable, and all of their orders come out of Washington. Stockwell said that under orders from Bush (our

INTERVIEW: "PRESENTING AASHID"

President was formerly head of the C.I.A.), they killed a hundred thousand Africans in Angola, and that's when he, Stockwell, woke up because he just didn't understand. There was no reason for him to kill them except that they just wanted to keep the country unstable. This is what we do, it's our tax dollars that go to kill these people all over the world and keep countries unstable so that they will have to grow our food for us. They have to grow our bananas and all of that stuff for slave wages, because they have no choice!"

How has racism been perpetrated in this country, institutionalized to the extent that it may not ever be removed? "Racism has always been around," says Aashid, but what happens is as the economy gets worse, it'll seem as if racism is worse. Actually, it just makes people dig into themselves for something that they already have in them, anyway. It's like they don't have anything to do, they don't have any money to spend, so they can't go out and have a good time, so they've got to blame someone for the shape that they're in. They might blame the Vietnamese who have come here, or the black people, or the black people are going to blame the white people."

"Everybody wants to blame each other for everything that happens when, actually, we're all to blame for everything that happens to us because that's the way the universe works. We're all responsible and, as a black person, I have to lift the yoke of oppression off of myself because, you see, white people can't set me free. I have to set myself free."

"Black people," says Aashid, "a lot of them haven't set ourselves free. It's like if you keep a person chained up for years and years, they know just how long their chain is. You can take the chain off and they won't go further than that chain because they think it's still there. That's the way that slavery and oppression is done."

A thread that runs through all of Himons' music and video art is the need for people to band together to effect change in our society. Says Aashid, "I think that the people who want to try and change things in our society are going to have to come together and start working together. We've got to change it into something positive where we can all get along and realize that beneath these different prejudices and different likes and dislikes, we're basically all the same. We have to all do the same things and we all have the same needs...we're all basically human beings, and this is what we've got to wake up to and realize our 'oneness.' This is what I mean by 'one heart'...we are all one, we are the same and we are a collective consciousness. We all have very similar ideas and thought patterns, it's just that we handle them in different ways."

"How many times does the same idea get thought all over the world at the same time, the same day," asks Aashid. "It's that

collective consciousness, that link between us all. I can feel it, I can feel a connection between people. Christianity teaches us to be separate, it does not teach the oneness of human beings. I'm not talking about Christ's teachings, I'm talking about Christianity...they're not necessarily the same thing. Christ definitely taught the oneness, but the fundamentalists, they don't teach that because if they did then what would they do to keep everybody afraid of everybody else and keep their churches under control?"

But isn't Christianity, like all of the outlaw religions of the Western world, about nothing but control? "Yes, most religions are," says Aashid, "but I would hate to say all. Christianity teaches that the whole world's got to hear about it, so that you've got to go out and put people everywhere. So what happens is that missionaries go into the bush in Central America and South America and Africa and they teach people the Bible and they teach them to be afraid to die. Then after they have them afraid to die, they bring in the mercenaries and tell them that they're going to kill them if they don't do what they want them to."

"That's a terrible plan, the way that's done," says Himons, "but all of these people in these primal cultures are hip to it and we don't understand why we're the most hated nation in the world. We get real indignant, saying 'I don't know why they want to kill us...we've done so much for them.' You or I may not do it, but they look at us as being the ones who do it. All they know is that it's the people of the United States of America that these mercenaries are representing, people like Del Monte, United Fruit..."

"I lived with some Indians in Central America," says Aashid, "that were working on their own property for the United Fruit Company. Do you know that they wouldn't allow them to grow any food for themselves, they could only grow food for us? They could only grow bananas on their property, if they grew anything else, they were dead."

"That was us doing that, because we want Kroger to have bananas 24 hours a day so that we can go get them. Is this really how we want to be? As a nation, some people may say 'yeah,' because they don't care as long as they can get what they want...I can't live with that kind of thing."

Aashid Himons has been a part of Nashville's alternative landscape for so long that people don't remember a local scene without his presence. Aashid came to town in August of 1979, but he had visited here before. "Back in about 1966 or '67," Himons says, "I was working with Buddy Killen at Tree Music and Dial Records, so I used to come to Nashville all of the time."

Of his final move to Nashville, Aashid remembers "I had been living in Pittsburgh...that's when I started the whole

Afrikan Dreamland project, because it came into my mind to fuse blues and reggae together, so I started putting this album concept together. I had decided that I wanted to leave town and started to head to Minneapolis until I thought of how cold it gets up there, so then we decided to stop in Nashville and see old Buddy. I'd let him hear my new stuff and see what he thinks of it."

"You have to realize," Aashid continues, "that he hadn't seen me since about 1967. I had a process and wore pointed toe shoes and sharkskin suits and ties, you know what I mean… I was really weird, in bad shape. That's what he remembered, so I walked into his office in 1979 with dreadlocks and a tie-dyed t-shirt and the whole thing just freaked him out. He listened to the music and he regrouped…he said 'you know, this music has got something, but you'll never do anything with it here in Nashville.' When he said that, I decided that I'd stay here in Nashville, so I did."

Waxing serious, again, one has to wonder if the things that Aashid is battling against…pollution, racism, oppression… are too far along to fix at this stage of the game. "We don't really have the time to do anything," says Aashid, "the only way that we'll make it is if, all of a sudden, and this is possible, real possible, that we change. One thing that could do it right now is communication. We're going through serious strains right now with all of the information that we have."

"People have never had the information that we've got right here in the United States. You can switch from channel to channel to channel on TV, it doesn't make any difference whether it's true or not. You've got all of the libraries, you can just walk in and get any book. In history, it's never been like that before…that stuff, information, used to be just for the very elite. You don't have to be elite, anymore, in this country to have access to information."

With all of the configurations," says Aashid, "people can get confused by it. With TV you have stereo television, you have cable, VCRs, video disc players, satellite dishes with 200 channels; in music you have records and tapes, CDs, digital audio…it's a bit of technological overkill." Technology is also something that can be used for communication and, says Himons, "it may be what wakes us up" to a greater spirituality.

Says Aashid, "I think that spirituality always leads to…as you become more spiritual and you become more knowledgeable, you also become more compassionate and you naturally just can't see people suffer. You're going to get into politics," reflects Himons, perhaps explaining his own political bent, "because suffering is political. People are made to suffer for political reasons. You go in and try to alleviate that suffering and there are powers that are not going to like that. If

spirituality is man's relationship with himself, then politics is man's relationship with other men."

Aashid Himons is, without a doubt, a man of many talents: a compassionate man; a knowledgeable man; and the holder of many opinions. He is a poet and a prophet, an accomplished songwriter and a skilled musician; a visionary and an artist, a student and a friend. Most of all, he is a man carrying a burden, a message of universal peace and harmony. Spreading his message may not be the easiest of jobs, but it's the only job for Aashid Himons.

"Communication is the only real answer,
fear and hate just another type of cancer;
So people of the planet, come together if you please,
ignorance is a curable disease.
So wake up everybody, the time is here;
for learnin' about the truth, so you don't have no fear…"
– Aashid, "The Human Race"

CD REVIEW: AASHID'S MOUNTAIN SOUL

Aashid Himons has been a fixture of Nashville's non-country music scene for long that it's easy to take him for granted. One of the founders of the near-legendary Afrikan Dreamland in the early-1980s, Aashid has been the voice of conscious of the Music City's alternative culture for almost two decades now. Whether as a musician exploring the depths of reggae, space music or the blues, a documentary filmmaker, host of the influential *Aashid Presents* television show, or as a crusader for many causes, Aashid's multi-media talents have always been intelligent, vital and thought-provoking.

Nonetheless, Aashid's latest musical effort – the *Mountain Soul* CD – comes as a surprise in spite of his past track record as an innovator and trailblazer. A collection of country blues, hillbilly folk and other traditionally styled music, Aashid has shown us yet another facet of his immense talent with *Mountain Soul*'s enchanting performances. An African-American with his roots in the mountains of West Virginia, Himons explains the lineage of this material in the CD's liner notes. In the harsh hills of Virginia and West Virginia, Kentucky and Tennessee, African slaves often played music alongside the poor Irish and Scottish immigrants of the area. The resulting collaboration created a folk music tradition that spawned such genres as gospel, bluegrass, blues and country music.

To be honest, there aren't many musicians these days exploring the artistic milieu that *Mountain Soul* showcases so nobly. On *Mountain Soul* Aashid works alongside some of Nashville's best – and most underrated – musicians, folks like Giles Reaves, fiddle wizard Tramp and bassist Victor Wooten. Himons has created here a mesmerizing song cycle that incorporates original songs written in the authentic signature of the hills as well as a handful of timeless classics. Aashid's commanding baritone is perfectly suited to this material, whether singing a soulful, blues-infused cover of Hendrix's "Voodoo Child," the mournful spiritualism of Rev. Gary Davis' "You Got To Move" or on originals like the moving "Stranger In Paradise" or with the talking blues and nifty guitar work on "The Crazy Blues."

One of my personal favorites on *Mountain Soul* is "Mr. Bailey," Aashid's tribute to the first star of the Grand Ole Opry, harmonica wizard Deford Bailey. A talented and charismatic African-American musician from East Tennessee, Bailey's lively performances popularized the Opry radio broadcast in the thirties and helped launched the careers of such country legends as Roy Acuff and Bill Monroe. Tragically, Bailey's contributions to the Opry and American music have been forgotten. It has long been Aashid's crusade to get Bailey his long-deserved place in the Country Music Hall Of Fame, and this song is just another reminder of that glaring injustice.

Mountain Soul is definitely not an album for the casual user of music, requiring more than a three minute, radio-influenced and MTV-bred attention span. Although the album's style and often times simple instrumentation might not seem so upon first listen, these are frightfully complex songs - musically multi-layered and emotionally powerful. This is music as old as the earth itself, its origins in the blood and sweat and tears of the common people who created it. With *Mountain Soul* Aashid Himons has paid an honor to both the roots of all popular modern music and the forgotten artists who wrote it.

Mountain Soul is an artistically and spiritually enriching listening experience, a musical trip through time that will clear the cobwebs out of your ears, rekindle the fire in your heart and remind you of the reasons you began to love music in the first place. – *Alt.Culture.Guide*, 1999

AASHID
Web: www.goarchie.com

Band Members:
Aashid Himons (vocals, guitar, keyboards, percussion)

Other Musicians:
Gary Serkin (guitars) (I)

Comments: One of the most talented and imposing figures in Nashville rock history, Aashid Himons may be as close as one can get to being a force of nature. A towering 6'6" tall with leonine dreadlocks, a graying beard and a ready smile, Aashid did more to promote Nashville rock than anybody.

Aashid produced so damn much fine music over the course of his lifetime that the discography offered below is certainly incomplete and probably missing large chunks of his catalog. Info on other musicians is also limited to whatever was printed on the cassette or CD, which was often not much, but then again Aashid often times recorded everything himself.

Aashid had enjoyed a lengthy career in music before ever coming to Nashville, and has been known as "Little Archie," "Go Ayo" and "West Virginia Slim" through the years. His singles as Little Archie are particularly sought after by English collectors. Thanks to Daryl Sanders for helping compile this list.

Aashid Recordings:

I. Kozmik Gypsy (Ayo Records 1987, LP)
Side One
1. Culture Woman
2. In A Figga Of Speech
3. Apartheid

Side Two
4. The Gods And I
5. I And I Survive

II. In My Genes (Tanasi Tapes 1987, cassette)
Side One:
1. Dancing In Disguise
2. The Current
3. Indigenous Nations
4. Dream A Lot
5. Intuition

Side Two:
1. In My Genes
2. One Dream
3. Hurricane Dub
4. One Love
5. Memories

III. Blues Dancer (Soptek Records 1987, cassette/CD-R)
1. Children Of Love
2. Blues Dancer (Song For Jimi)
3. Truth Within/Baby Please Don't Go
4. Angel Of Light Pt.1
5. Listen To The Drumbeat
6. Rhythm Sauce
7. Washitaw Nation / I And I Survive
8. Angel Of Light Pt.2

IV. One Heart (Tanasi Tapes 1988, cassette)
Side One:
1. Fly
2. Addiction World
3. The Human Race
4. One Heart
5. Atlantis Is My Home
6. I Believe

Side Two:
7. Hurricane
8. Sleeper Awake
9. Aummmmm
10. Let The Minstrel Sing
11. Afrikan Lady
12. Love Song

Produced by Aashid Himons
Includes Gary Costner on guitar on "One Heart" and Richard Downs on guitar on "Atlantis Is My Home," "Aummmmm" and "Sleeper Awake;" synthesizers on "Sleeper Awake."
Also includes vocals by Bonnie Gallie, Jeanette Golter and Sue Ramsey.

CD REVIEW: AASHID'S WEST VIRGINIA HILLS

For almost two decades now, Aashid Himons has been Nashville's most adventuresome musician. Sure, there's lots of players making $1,000 a session up and down "Music Row" who claim to be able to play varying styles of music, but few of them give up their cushy day jobs to blaze any new trails. From the moment Aashid first set foot in the "Music City," however, he's done whatever strikes his fancy, whether that might be playing reggae, blues, space music or even a bit of country.

From his work with the first incarnation of the wonderfully talented Afrikan Dreamland through a solo career and various collaborations with other artists, Himons has reveled in the sheer joy of making music, commercial considerations be damned. Recently, with the release of *Mountain Soul*, Aashid sojourned back to his hillbilly roots and created an inspired collection of songs that draw upon a musical tradition almost as old as the Appalachian mountains themselves.

West Virginia Hills is a live document of many of the songs from *Mountain Soul*, performed by Himons and his "Mountain Soul Band" at Gibson's Café Milano in Nashville. Comprised of some of the most underrated musical talents that the Nashville scene has to offer, the Mountain Soul Band is up to the task of recreating these songs in a live setting. It is a testament to Aashid's talents and the respect provided him by Nashville's best musicians that Aashid can get artists of this caliber together for such a performance. (I count at least three successful solo artists on this roster as well as former members or players with artists like Lisa Germano, the Cactus Brothers, and Bonepony.)

The material on *West Virginia Hills* is a spirited mix of blues, bluegrass, roots rock and country with elements of Celtic and African music. With spiritual and musical influences that range from the highest mountaintop in Appalachia to the lowest cotton field in the Mississippi Delta, the performances here possess the soul and fervor of a church revival and the energy and electricity of a mosh pit at any punk show. Although many of the songs are originals, such as the joyful title track or the Delta-styled "Country Blues," there are also the covers expected of such a project, musical homage's to the artists who created this music: folks like Willie Dixon, Blind Willie McTell and Muddy Waters. Aashid's "The Captain's Song" is another highlight of the *Mountain Soul* album performed here live.

There are fewer and fewer artists these days willing to "walk on the wild side" and embrace styles of music that are completely without commercial potential. Some, like Bruce Springsteen's flirtation with folk music or Steve Earle's recent bluegrass project, are natural outgrowths of the artist's roots. In other instances, however, as with Aashid Himons and the members of the Mountain Soul Band, it is done out of a sheer love and respect for the music they're performing. The material presented with much skill and reverence on *West Virginia Hills* is more than a mere throwback to another era – it's also the root of all the music we enjoy today. For that alone, Aashid and the Mountain Soul Band deserve a loud "thanks!"
–*Alt.Culture.Guide*, 2000

V. Black Holiness (Soptek Records 1988, cassette/CD-R)
1. Black Holiness
2. Devachan
3. Heaven
4. The Ark
5. Be

VI. Christmas Is Love (Tansi Tapes 1989, cassette)
Side One
1. Love Is…
2. Joy To The World
3. Santa Claus Is Coming To Town
4. Silent Night
5. Jingle Bells
6. Here Comes Kwaanza
7. Little Drummer Boy
8. The Eastern Star

Side Two
9. Imani
10. Noel
11. Kuumba
12. Give
13. Christmas In Your Town
14. Christmas Is Love
15. Happy New Year!

VII. One Drum (Tanasi Tapes 1990, cassette)
Side One
1. Drum One (Medicinal)

Side Two
2. Drum Two (Transcendental)
3. Drum Plus

VIII. Mountain Soul (Soptek Records 1998, CD)
1. Country Blues
2. Stranger To Paradise
3. The Crazy Blues
4. I Bet You'll Be Dead
5. Circle Of Fault
6. Mr. Bailey
7. Nothing But A Lifetime
8. High De High, Ho De Ho
9. Voodoo Child
10. Just Another Rollin' Stone
11. Bacon Fat
12. You've Got To Move
13. Got My Mojo Working
14. The Captain's Song
15. Will The Circle Be Unbroken
16. Small Circle

Comments: A "comeback album" of sorts for Aashid, the artist trying his hand a some hillbilly and folk music.

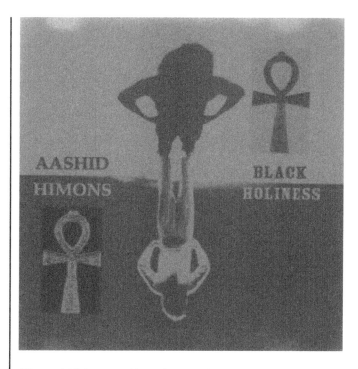

IX. Aashid @ Dawn (Soptek Records 2000, CD-R)
1. Dawn
2. Warm Winds
3. Aura
4. Nature Spirits
5. Sierra Silencio
6. Blue Lotus
7. Quest
8. Thrill Seeker
9. Golden Fountain

X. Alone In Space (Space For Music Records 2001, CD)
1. Alone With Self
2. Black Man From Soptek
3. Holiness
4. In Space
5. Tranquility
6. Ringing In The Dreams
7. Rapturous
8. Seven Marys
9. Prayer
10. Song For Amen
11. Well Done

XI. The Metaphysician (Soptek Records 2001, CD-R)
1. The Metaphysician
2. Devachan Pt. 1
3. Devachan Pt. 2

XII. Sea Of Rejuvenation (Soptek Records 2001, CD-R)
1. The Overworld
2. Holy Surf
3. Existence

4. Cosmobile
5. Manifest Destiny
6. Great Mother
7. Sondava!

Comments: Recorded with Giles Reaves (synth samplers)

XIII. Revelation Om (Soptek Records CD-R, 2001?)
1. Om
2. Blue Lotus
3. Brain To Brain
4. Ebb And Flow
5. Embrace Destiny
6. Energy Center
7. Ethereal Nature
8. Focus
9. Fore Spirits
10. Grounded Space
11. Inner Exploration
12. Mindspace
13. Position Of Comfort
14. Revelation
15. Self Knowing
16. Om

XIV. Expression & Truth (Soptek Records 2001, CD-R)
1. In The Beginning
2. Ascension
3. Izmale'
4. Expression And Truth
5. Radiance
6. Royal Feelings
7. Treeline

8. Voices Of Mu
9. Voices Of Alpha

Comments: Throughout much of the early 2000s, Aashid cranked out album after album, released on CD-R through Tony Gerber's Space For Music label, and distributed online through the now-defunct mp3.com (killed by the major labels, if you must known....). Much like his friend and frequent collaborator Gerber, Aashid embraced the new millennium and new ways (digital) of distributing music like few musicians of his time. I always got the impression that having people hear his music was more important than "monetizing" his art, and he'd never made shit for money from his work anyway, Aashid would just channel his energies into making more music.

AASHID HIMONS & GILES REAVES

Band Members:
Aashid Himons (vocals, keyboards, synthesizers, percussion)
Giles Reaves (keyboards, synthesizers, percussion)

Recordings:

I. Dubh Daiye (Soptek Records 2000, CD-R)
1. M'Daiye 1
2. M'Daiye 2
3. Drum Daiye
4. Aum (Daiye)
5. Dubh Daiye 1
6. Dubh Daiye 2

II. Eternity's Door (Soptek Records 2001, CD-R)
1. A Good Night
2. When Love Comes Through Eternity's Door
3. Step Up

III. Principles Of Peace (Space For Music Records 2002, CD)
1. Prince Of Peace

AASHID HIMONS & PYRAMID UNDERGROUND

Band Members:
Aashid Himons (vocals, keyboards, percussion) (I, II)
Giles Reaves (keyboards, percussion) (I, II)
Kirby Shelstad (midi-kat, percussion) (I)
Mike Simmons (guitars) (I, II)
Reggie Wooten (guitars) (I)
Jamie Simmons (bass) (I, II)
Paul Simmons (drums) (I, II)

I. One Love (Soptek Records 2000, CD-R)
1. From The Beginning
2. Let Your Love Come Out
3. It's You

4. Mr. Bailey
5. Across The Wall
6. The Rhythm Of Life
7. Trip
8. Eden
9. It's All Over
10. Washitaw De Dugdahmoundyah

II. Will They Ever Understand (Soptek Records 2000, CD-R)
1. Time To Begin
2. I Can Hear My Baby Calling
3. Keep On Rockin' Me
4. Misery And Pain
5. Tell Them What They Need To Know
6. Will They Ever Understand

Comments: Recorded live at 12th & Porter on February 22, 1997.

AASHID HIMONS & SONS OF AKASHA

Band Members:
Aashid Himons (keyboards, drums, percussion) (I)
Giles Reaves (keyboards, drums, percussion) (I)
Kirby Shelstad (midi-kat, drums, percussion) (I)
Mike Simmons (guitar) (I)

Recordings:

I. Kosmik Jamz (Soptek Records 2000, CD-R)
1. Many Miles
2. The Journey
3. Celtic Rhapsody

4. Urbanesque
5. Kemit
6. Rhythm Island
7. Eternal Love
8. New Birth
9. The Road Ahead

Comments: Aashid always had a knack for attracting the most talented of musical collaborators, and this Sons of Akasha line-up was probably his most accomplished. Reaves and Shelstad are skilled electronic and organic artists, adding keys and percussion, while Mike Simmons – best-known around town for his hard rock and heavy metal bands – displays the (impressive) full range of his talents here.

AASHID HIMONS & THE MOUNTAIN SOUL BAND

Band Members:
Aashid Himons (vocals, guitar, Ashiko drum) (I)
Giles Reaves (drums, percussion) (I)
Seth Ritter (banjo) (I)
Kirby Shelstad (talking drum, percussion) (I)
Bobby Taylor (harmonica) (I)
Tony Gerber (mandocello) (I)
Jody Lentz (mandolin) (I)
Tramp (fiddle) (I)
Amir Rashidd (harmonica) (I)

Recordings:

I. West Virginia Hills (Soptek Records 1999, CD)
1. West Virginia Hills
2. Country Blues

3. Little Red Rooster
4. The Captain's Song
5. Got My Mojo Workin'
6. Spoonful
7. Will The Circle Be Unbroken
8. Bacon Fat
9. Wish I Was In Heaven
10. West Virginia Hills (Reprise)
11. Voodoo Child / Sweet Mama's Door
12. Statesboro Blues
13. Why Don't You Love Me

Comments: The logical follow-up to Aashid's *Mountain Soul* CD, this collection was recorded live at Gibson's Cafe Milano on 10/10/98 with some of the best musicians that Nashville has to offer, including **Tony Gerber**, **Giles Reaves**, and Tramp of **Bonepony**, among others. (see review ➜).

AFRIKAN DREAMLAND

Band Members:
Aashid Himons (vocals, guitars, keyboards, percussion) (I-V)
Mustafa Abdul-Aleen (flute, woodwinds, percussion) (I-V)
Darrell Rose (Ashiko drums, percussion) (I-V)

Comments: Formed in 1980 by Aashid as a musical forum "from which to communicate the Rastafarian spiritual beliefs of peace, love and justice between members of all races and religions." The band's sound was a mix of reggae, island rhythms, rock & roll, R&B and the blues, which they called "blu-reggae." Aashid's socially-conscious lyrics and unique sound won them critical acclaim and a national reputation. Afrikan Dreamland performed at several anti-nuclear rallies, played behind folk singers Anne Romaine and Holly Near, and even placed a video on MTV.

The band's discography is admittedly incomplete, as Afrikan Dreamland released some of the city's earliest indie-rock vinyl, often in limited quantities, which have long since passed beyond this mortal plane. A few original LP copies float around on eBay in the $25 - $50 range, and some wag out on the west coast has taken to bootlegging Afrikan Dreamland albums and selling them for $50 as "new." The band broke-up in 1987 but reunited frequently afterwards.

I. Jah Message (Ayo Records 1981, LP)
1. Grassy Fields
2. Zion Thing (Rastafari)
3. You Got To Move
4. Kick Boot Scratch Bite
5. Labuga Land
6. The Gods and I
7. Kristina
8. Africa
9. Home To The Sun

II. Nineteen Eighty Oneness (Ayo Records 1981, cassette)

III. Dance And Survive (Ayo Records 1982, LP)
Side One
1. Welcome to Alkebulan
2. Last Chance to Dance
3. Disarmament Time
4. Dreadlock Music

Side Two
5. S.O.F.T. Stomp
6. Delivery
7. Skank It With Me
8. Protest and Survive

IV. Stateside Rasta (Ayo Records 1983, LP)
Side One
1. Stateside Rasta
2. Babylon's Burnin'
3. Guidance

Side Two
4. Id
5. Song for Deforf
6. Last Chance to Dance

V. The Leaders (Soptek Records 1995, CD)
Volume One
1. Jah Boogie
2. Grassy Fields
3. Dance & Survive
4. Ethiopia
5. Womanhood

6. The Stone
7. Come Take Me
8. The Leaders
9. Home
10. It Feels Real
11. Freedom Skank
12. Apartheid

Volume Two
13. Samba Reggae
14. Love Sounds
15. Mdaiye
16. Black Folks
17. I Touch The Stars
18. Cultural Treat
19. The Next Man's Army
20. Goin' Back Ethiopia (Fonga Alafia)
21. Baby I'm Yours
22. Abu Aha
23. USA
24. Will The Circle Be Unbroken
25. I & I Survive

AASHID
In My Genes
(Tanasi)

Black Holiness
(Tanasi)

One Heart
(Tanasi)

Tall, imposing, with natty shoulder-length dreadlocks and graying beard, Aashid Himons is a familiar sight on the streets of Nashville. As the driving force behind Afrikan Dreamland, Aashid was among a handful of pioneers that helped shape and influence the early-eighties onslaught of local bands. As a well-respected artistic entity in their own right, Afrikan Dreamland created a sound based on Jamaican reggae, American R&B, and various indigenous African musics, and their reputation for artistry, honesty, and talent was known around the world.

For various lamentable reasons, Afrikan Dreamland is no more. Himons retains the spark of creativity, though, releasing tapes such as the three considered at a prolific rate which, considering the quality of these three, is admirable indeed. *In My Genes* is, perhaps, the closest in many ways to the work of Afrikan Dreamland. Side one presents five vocal songs done in Aashid's typically impeccable reggae style. Rhythmic and nearly hypnotizing, the songs here lyrically reveal the soul of a dreamer, a man and an artist sincerely preaching the gospel of brotherhood and peace. The second side of *In My Genes* is a collection of inspired instrumental pieces, wildly syncopated African rhythms complete with birdsongs and animal cries. This is no mild, new age doodling here, but an aggressive, gutsy collection of style and substance.

Black Holiness is Aashid's "space music" album. Composed and produced by Aashid with help from Richard Downs, this tape is Himons' personal spiritual statement, a collection of four visionary pieces that are as harmonically powerful as Aashid's lyrical songs are verbally potent. Mostly missing are the drums and rhythms normally associated with Aashid's work. *Black Holiness* is instead a dark, mystical journey into the heart and soul of the composer, a creative tour de force that easily ranks beside such well-known composers as Constance Demby and Michael Stearns. Although it might not appeal to strict fans of Aashid's Afrikan Dreamland work, this tape would be instantly accessible to fans of such talents as Giles Reaves, William Linton, or Anthony Rian and, as such, would open up a new audience for Himons.

One Heart completes this trilogy and returns Aashid to his better-known vocal-style songs. The selections here are forceful, lyrical pieces in which Aashid tackles some of the weighty issues of our day such as drug abuse, racism, and sexual responsibility. The title cut, written by the beautiful and talented Bonnie Gallie, is a soulful, moving duet between her and Aashid, an anthemic cry for brotherhood that is applicable to the Christian or the Muslim as it is to the Rasta. It is the centerpiece of the album whose message is one of joyful peace and love. – *The Metro*, 1988

ACTUEL (a/k/a ACTUALS)

Band Members:
Steve Anderson (vocals, guitar, keyboards) (A1)
Gary Rabasca (bass, percussion) (A1)

Other Musicians:
Robb Earls (keyboards) (A1)
John Elliott (rhythm machine) (A1)
Yael Gaubert (bass) (A1)
Jim Marshall (drums, marimba) (A1)

Actuel Recordings:

A1. Actuel (Tiki Records 1982, 12")
Side A
1. Things

Side B
2. East To West
3. No Regrets

Comments: Too far ahead of its time, Nashville's Actuals…
later evolving into Actuel…stood alone as one of the city's
rock pioneers. The duo of vocalist/guitarist Steve Anderson
and bassist Gary Rabasca made up the band's core, pursuing
a vision of high-tech music that was unique for the states at
that time, and uniquely alien for the Music City audience.
Under the Actuel name, the band released a couple of 12"
EPs which, along with a 91 Rock benefit show appearance,
won them a loyal local following. (*See Stephen's article* ➜)

AFTERDARK

Band Members:
Price Jones (vocals, guitar) (I)
Mark MacKenzie (guitar, vocals) (I)
June "The Tune" Kato (bass) (I)
Jackie Hajacos (keyboards) (I)
Jeff "Hilton" Hayes (drums) (I)

Afterdark Recordings:

I. Afterdark (demo tape, 1990)
1. Maybe It's Time
2. Our Song
3. Afterdark
4. Something About You

Comments: Price Jones had been part of the band Dark Star
with at least a couple of Afterdark's members, and the band's
name was conceived as a play on the original ("After Dark,"
gettit?). Jones would go on to record a fine full-length solo
album, *Oooznoz.*

KENT AGEE

Band Members:
Kent Agee (vocals, guitar) (I)

Other Musicians:
Steve Brewster (drums) (I)
Gary Burnett (guitars) (I)
Shannon Forrest (drums) (I)
George Marinelli (guitar) (I)
Georgia Middleman (vocals) (I)
Jon Mock (whistle, bodhran, concertina) (I)
Russ Paul (guitars, dobro, banjo) (I)
Allison Prestwood (bass) (I)
Tammy Rogers (violin, mandolin, bazouki) (I)
Harry Stinson (vocals) (I)
Joy Lynn White (vocals) (I)
John Willis (guitars) (I)

Kent Agee Recordings:

I. Fields & Fences (self-produced CD, 2003)
1. From Now On
2. Love Is a Boat
3. Gingham Dress
4. Faithless Girl
5. Love Will Come Around
6. Omens of the End
7. Pleasant View Lane
8. Lenny
9. Rose Connally
10. The Wild Midwest
11. Lyda Rose
12. Wouldn't You
13. Ophelia

Comments: Agee was the former frontman of popular local band **Jane, His Wife**. Although that band, sadly, never released any recorded music, Agee released this single solo CD as a showcase for his fine songwriting talent. Agee has made a name for himself through the years as a songwriter, with songs recorded by folks like Joy Lynn White, Sherri Austin, Rhet Atkins and even Engelbert Humperdink.

A.K.A: RUDIE

Band Members:
Rob Hoskins (vocals, keyboards, trombone) (I-II)
Ken "Special K" Miller (guitar, vocals) (I-II)
John Pavlovsky (guitars, vocals) (II)
Al Shropshire (bass) (I-II)
Dave DePriest (drums) (I-II)
Mark "Smiley" Shenkel (sax, vocals) (I-II)
Robert Means (trombone, keyboards, vocals) (I-II)

Other Musicians:
Roland Alphonso (tenor sax) (I)
Mark Pfaff (harmonica) (I)
Obie Ewing-Roush (trombone) (I)
Frank Sass (percussion) (I)

A.K.A: Rudie Recordings:

I. Trouble Clef (self-produced 2001, CD)
1. Arte Bella
2. Come Down
3. Tales To Tell
4. Rain From The Sky
5. Trouble Clef
6. Oliver's Army
7. Is It Okay?
8. Wichita Lineman
9. Lavochka
10. Dance Hall Ruler
11. Get Off My Cloud
12. People Make The World Go 'Round
13. Rhumba Ska
14. Golden Love
15. Is It Okay? < extended >
16. Bella Dub
17. Tears From My Version

Comments: Nashville's favorite ska-punk rudeboys, A.K.A: Rudie, was formed by Rob "Rudie" Hoskins and Mark "Smiley" Shenkel, both from **Freedom Of Expression**. With an energetic Island sound that was heavier on the ska riddims but with the energy and sincerity of punk rock, A.K.A: Rudie was unlike any other local band.

A.K.A: Rudie

II. Live Inna Windows (Ready Room 2003, CD)
1. Tales To Tell
2. Lavochka
3. Cool And Deadly
4. Oliver's Army
5. Three Gifts
6. Is It Okay?
7. Trouble Clef
8. Dance Hall Ruler

Comments: Live performance from Windows On The Cumberland features the band's delightful rock, reggae and ska sound. The band went the extra mile and made this an enhanced CD so that you can put it in your computer and watch video footage of the performance. Too cool...

ALL THE QUEEN'S MEN

Band Members:
Amanda Williams (vocals, guitar)
Catherine Capozzi (guitars)
Chris Farrell (bass)
Tamara Gooding (drums)

Comments: All The Queen's Men contributed two cool funk-rock songs ("The Mirror" and "Something To Tell Me") to the *Treason Records Sampler Vol. 1* CD.

ALL $TAR

Band Members:
All $tar (vocals) (I, II)
Jody Stevens (guitar) (II)

All Star Recordings:

I. $tarlito's Way I: I Am Not Your Friend (Grind Hard/Loyalty Records 2006, CD)

II. $tarlito's Way II (Grind Hard/Loyalty 2008, CD)
Disc One: *December 15th a Star was Born*
1. Life Story…
2. Get Money (featuring Birdman)

3. I'm On It
4. $.T.A.R. Lito
5. I Feel How I Look (featuring Mike J)
6. Hatin' Ain't Healthy
7. Alphabet Soup
8. I Ain't Worried About Nothin'
9. Champagne And X
10. Gangsta-est Swag Of The Year
11. Mind Over Heart
12. I'm Shakin' It
13. Nawimtalkinbout
14. I'm A MF Star
Bonus Track: Grind Hard For The Money Remix

Disc Two: *Internal Affairs*
1. Intro
2. I'm Alright
3. 1 Leg At A Time
4. F… 'Em All (featuring Q.T.)
5. Bless…
6. Mirror Man
7. And I Love You (Whatever)
8. I'm Tryin' To Live (featuring Trouble)
9. Coming Back To You (featuring Macy Gray)
10. That Sh** Ain't Real
11. Rap Music Ruined My Life
12. Keep Doing My Thang
13. Living Will
Bonus Track: You Lyin' Remix (w/Young Buck)
Bonus Track: Ghetto Super Star

Comments: All $tar is an up-n-coming local rapper caught in the limbo of recordco politricks that have kept his major label debut from being released. This ambitious two-CD set is a kind of bootleg release, put on the street under the cover of night in an attempt to put some money in the artist's pocket ('cause his label sure ain't doin' it!).

RICHARD ALLEN & KIRBY SHELSTAD

Band Members:
Richard Allen (shakuhachi, flute, whistles) (I, II)
Kirby Shelstad (synth, vibes, percussion) (I, II)

Other Musicians:
Sam Bacco (percussion) (I)
Charles Debray (mandolin) (I)
Sam Levine (piccolo, lyricon) (II)
Mike Miller (bamboo sax, whistles) (I, II)
Mark O'Conner (violin) (II)
Tom Rhoady (congas, percussion) (I)
Michael Rhodes (fretless bass) (II)
Paul Speer (12-string guitar) (I)
Cam Williams (mountain dulcimer) (I)

Richard Allen & Kirby Shelstad Recordings:

I. Peaceful Solutions (Love Circle Music 1984, tape)
Side One
1. Merlin's Suite:
   A. The Vision
   B. Merlin's Quest
   C. The Return
2. Lori
3. Morning Prayer

Side Two
1. High In The Andes
2. Bamboogie
3. Gentle Flow
4. Just Friends
5. Shakuhachi Baby
6. Rights Of Man
7. Still Seeking

Comments: Produced by Kirby Shelstad. Interestingly enough, the woodwinds used on the album were all handmade from bamboo by Richard Allen.

II. Peaceful Solutions II (Love Circle Music 1987, tape)
Side One
1. Riverroad
2. Soaring
3. Eve
4. Avalon
5. Winter Suite:
   A. Lullabye
   B. Dreams of Peace
   C. Sleigh Ride

Side Two
1. Sailing Free
2. Childsplay
3. Speak With Angels
4. Himalayan Hiway
5. Healing Touch
6. Thanksgiving Passage

AMERICAN BANG

Band Members:
Jaren Johnston (vocals, guitar) (I, II)
Ben Brown (guitar) (I, II)
Kelby Ray (bass) (I, II)
Neil Mason (drums) (I, II)

American Bang Recordings:

I. Move To The Music (Maverick/Reprise 2007, CD)
1. Move To The Music
2. Good as Gold
3. All Night Long
4. American Ride

Comments: Formerly known as **Bang Bang Bang**, the band's red-hot momentum has slowed significantly since signing with Madonna's Maverick label. This EP was issued in October 2007, and little more was heard until the band's major label debut was released in 2010.

Another View: "Playing raucous, strutting hard rock with a classic sense of style and a contemporary sweat and swagger, American Bang are a four-piece band from Nashville who prove there's still room for rock in the world's capital of country music." – Mark Deming, *All Music Guide*

II. American Bang (Reprise Records 2010, CD)
1. Whiskey Walk
2. Wild And Young
3. Rewind
4. Angels
5. She Don't Cry No More
6. Hurts Like Hell
7. All We Know
8. Wouldn't Want To Be You
9. A Man Can Change
10. Other Side Of You
11. Roll On

Comments: Produced by veteran Bob Rock, the debut album finally comes out and fails to impress anybody with money to burn. Above-average hard rock.

Continued on page 30...

CD REVIEW: ALL STAR'S STARLITO'S WAY II

When it comes to rap music, the Reverend is credentialed, fool.

The last few years have seen an increase in popularity and commercial success for rap from "Da Dirty South," a wide-ranging albatross that includes everybody from UGK's Texas drawl and DJ Screw's syrup-drenched, snail-paced mixes to the Three-Six Mafia's Memphis thugsta rap and Atlanta's many talented representations.

Along the way, though, Cashville seemingly got left out of this "Dirty South" thing. After all, Haystack may not be Eminem, but he's a damn good rap stylist nevertheless. Other Music City rappers like Cadence or Kool Daddy Fresh have also been overlooked and/or underappreciated by the powers-that-be at the big labels. Other than Young Buck, who would have won props for his skills regardless of his G-Unit affiliation, the Music City's rap scene has been, well, dissed....

Case in point: All $tar, Cashville's Prince, Nashville's latest great hope for big league rap success. Signed to the Universal Music-distributed Cash Money label, All $tar recorded his major label debut, *$treet Ball*, three years ago and still it sits in a label tape vault, waiting for some corporate clown to decide to release the disc. The delay may have been fatal, as rap's commercial fortunes have experienced a larger-than-average sales decline in an industry where most artists are treading water while label execs sit on their shoulders and pocket as much cash and perks as they can while waiting for somebody to come along and save them.

Not satisfied with waiting, All $tar has taken it back to the streets, releasing the *$tarlito's Way: I Am Not Your Friend* mixtape in 2006, and following up this year with the critically-acclaimed *$tarlito's Way II*. A biographical concept album, of sorts, this two-CD set is an ambitious and revealing look deep into the psyche of the artist. Expressing youthful exuberance and self-doubt, the rapper's admitted work ethic ("grind it out") makes *$tarlito's Way II* both an engaging song cycle and a fine document of Nashville life outside of Belle Meade, Green Hills and West End.

The first disc, titled *December 15th a Star was Born*, kicks off with the extended six-minute diatribe "Life Story." All $tar recounts the ups and downs of his short life with stark honesty, his concise rhyme jumping from day to day in front of a sparse beat. The song relies entirely on $tar's verbal skills and tho' it might not fit on a radio playlist, it's an impressive artistic statement nonetheless. The disc includes some other gems, such as the hypnotic "I'm On It," the rapper's voice hidden beneath a constant wash of rhythm, the song an intelligent treatise on money, drugs and women.

The grandiose "Hatin' Ain't Healthy" swaggers out of the speakers with All $tar's lyrical braggadocio set against a symphonic backdrop, the words a typical "don't hate me 'cause I'm young, rich and good lookin'" rapper's boast. Fate Eastwood's lively production blows the song up to larger-than-life proportions, the muscular beats almost overwhelming the vocals. "Alphabet Soup" is a nifty lil' slice o' poetic gymnastics, utilizing the letters of the alphabet to construct each verse. Set against a Beatlesque electro-pop sample, the song is a true gauge of All $tar's verbal virtuosity.

Three bonus tracks, two unnamed, are tacked onto the end of disc one, and in many ways they foreshadow the darkness that's about to come. All $tar spits out cinematic rhymes of life in the streets of Cashville, with eerie samples and gossamer rhythms propping up his machinegun verbal delivery.

If the first disc is all about reckless confidence and the optimism of youth, the second disc of *$tarlito's Way II*, titled *Internal Affairs*, represents the flip side of the coin. These songs represent the cold, brutal truth of urban life that is often criticized by the kind of idiot cultural pundits that don't actually *listen* to rap music, much less live in the government-sponsored squalid conditions that spawned rap as an art form in the first place. This is the 21st century blues, baby, and these rhymes touch upon the fleeting nature of fame, and the wages of decades of inner-city poverty...

"I'm Alright" wallows in its conspicuous consumerism, but beneath the surface lay the rot of uncertainty and the recognition that the good times, and one's very existence itself, could end in a heartbeat. The champagne and fast cars are constantly threatened by casual violence, and your career is in the hands of people sitting atop some building a long ways away. Backed by Jody Stevens' transcendent guitar leads, "Mirror Man" is an introspective glance into the abyss of the self, All $tar's vocals struggling to rise out of the mix at times like shards of consciousness as the rapper literally speaks to himself in two voices. It's a revealing, multi-layered song with curious construction and intriguing results.

The spirited "Rap Music Ruined My Life" recounts All $tar's major label experience. As his album sits, languishing on an executive's desk somewhere, the rapper recognizes that "I'm running out of time, I'm not running out of rhymes." He's not bitter, just questioning the wisdom and the slow pace of an industry that holds his artistic fate in their hands. The dark "Keep Doing My Thang" is less an affirmation than an omen of doubt, the rapper's positive outlook dwindling with time and tragedy, his worries set to a cacophonic beat.

The disc ostensibly closes with "Living Will," the rapper seemingly coming to grips with his uncertain future as he offers a heartfelt shout-out to "the hustlers, the gangsters, the streets; the boosters, the jackers, the ones that put you to sleep," hoping that they will just remember his name once he's gone. Over some sort of sped-up vocal sample the protagonist flatlines in the ER...is he reborn or lost to time? The bonus track, "Ghetto Super Star," only partially answers the question, cleverly obscuring reality with the sheen and glamour of a chorus built from a lofty R&B sample.

There's a lot to digest on *Starlito's Way II*, and I wouldn't paint all of the songs here as impressively as I have those specifically mentioned above. In between these peaks, All $tar is often prone to dropping into gangsta rap clichés, and with so many cooks tampering with the broth (eight producers by my count), there is little thematic continuity within the soundtrack.

Regardless, All $tar is a talented lyricist and charismatic performer; given the proper resources and guidance, he could easily rise to the top of the rap game. Throw Fate Eastwood and/or Coop, the producers behind the best songs on *Starlito's Way II*, into a decent studio with a modest budget and let's see what kind of magic they might pull out of All $tar. Of course, it might have all come together already on *Street Ball*, if any of us ever get the chance to hear it... – *Cashville411* website 2008

ANASTASIA SCREAMED

Band Members:
Chick Graning (vocals, guitar, percussion) (A1-2, I-III)
Christopher Cugini (guitars, bass, mandolin) (A1-2, I-III)
Michael Lord (bass) (A1)
Charlie Bock (bass, guitar, keyboards) (A2, I-III)
Chris Burdett (drums, percussion) (A1, A2, I-III)

Other Musicians:
Michael Cella (chimes) (III)
Tanya Donelly (vocals) (III)
Eric England (harmonica) (II)
Allen Green (piano) (I)
Dave King (saxophone) (III)
Collin Tilton (saxophone) (I)
Drew Townson (vocals, keyboards) (III)

Anastasia Screamed Recordings:

Singles/ EPs

A1. Electric Liz (Killing Floor Records 1988, 12" EP)
Side One
1. Sun Celebration
2. Now
3. I Am (a horse you are)

Side Two
4. Augusta Furnace
5. D.A.

Comments: Five-song EP recorded in Boston at the fabled Fort Apache studios with noted producer and engineer Sean Slade. I believe that the band was still in transition at this point, eventually relocating completely to Nashville.

American Bang

A2. Samantha Black (Roughneck Recording 1990, 12" EP)
Side One
1. Samantha Black

Side Two
2. What Kind Of Truth Is This?
3. Sun Celebration

Comments: Three-song 12" vinyl EP includes "Samantha Black" from the band's upcoming album as well as "Sun Celebration" from their earlier EP and "What Kind Of Truth Is This?", an outtake from their Boston sessions with Sean Slade.

Albums

I. Laughing Down The Limehouse (Roughneck Recording Company 1990, CD)
1. Beautiful
2. Lime
3. Disintegrations, Yesterday
4. The Skidder
5. Violet
6. Searcher No. 9 (Song 16)
7. Tide
8. Parts Of Us
9. Tricked Into Feel
10. Shade
11. Samantha Black
12. Notown

Comments: The album that won Anastasia Screamed respect everywhere but in their adopted hometown.

II. 15 Seconds or 5 Days (Roughneck Recording Company 1991, CD EP)
1. 15 Seconds Or 5 Days
2. Buick Mackane
3. (When I Don't Think) I Can Hang On
4. Samantha Black (single version)
5. Tide

III. Moontime (Roughneck Recording 1991, CD)
1. Tornado
2. Out Of The Light
3. Stand By
4. One Deep Breath
5. She Must
6. Dead In The Grass
7. Get A Load Of That Machine
8. 15 Seconds Or 5 Days
9. Fall To Ceiling
10. Blues
11. Dead Ants

ANDREW & THE UPSTARTS

Band Members:
Andrew Roblin (vocals, guitar, banjo) (A1,I)
Anthony Isabel (vocals, bass, keyboards) (A1,I)
Jeff Stallworth (vocals, drums, percussion) (A1,I)
Tony Crow (samples) (A1,I)
Doug Moffet (saxophone) (A1,I)

Andrew & the Upstarts Recordings:

<u>Singles/EPs</u>

A1. Shiver & Shake (Upstart Records 7" vinyl)
<u>Side One</u>
1. Shiver & Shake

<u>Side Two</u>
2. Everything Hurts

<u>Albums</u>

I. Uproar (Upstart Records 1987, LP)
<u>Side One</u>
1. Forbidden Love – Radio Mix
2. Dr. Ruth
3. The Boy Who's Looking
4. Watch Out For The Humans

<u>Side Two</u>
5. Hey, Lonely Girl
6. Is Something Going On?
7. Forbidden Love – Dance Mix

Comments: Andrew & the Upstarts were considered a pop-punk band by some, a power-pop band by others, and they were all both right and wrong.

Andrew Roblin pursued an inspired blend of revved-up Buddy Holly rock with early 1980s new wave elements. Roblin, who wrote for both *Billboard* and *Music Row* magazine, fled Nashville long ago for Pennsylvania, where he fronted a bluegrass band called Andrew Roblin & the Pocono Mountain Men for a while.

APACHE UNDERGROUND

Band Members:
Drew Claesges (vocals) (R.I.P.)
Brian Hunter (guitars)
Byron Hamlett (bass)
Scott Ballew (drums)
Darren Stafford (vocals)

Comments: Apache Underground was formed by members of the John Carter Cash Band, adding Drew Claesges in place of JCC. Apache Underground pursued an undeniably rock & roll sound. Sadly, Claesges passed away in early 1991, replaced by Darren Stafford from Pink Slim.

APOLLO UP!

Band Members:
Jay Leo Phillips (vocals, guitar, keyboards) (I-II)
Mike Shepherd (bass, vocals) (I-II)
Jereme Frey (drums, vocals) (I-II)
Todd Kemp (percussion, vocals) (II)
Tony Read (vocals) (II)

Apollo Up! Recordings:

I. Light The End & Burn It Through (Theory 8 2003, CD)
1. Saw Her Standing There
2. Ticonderoga
3. #8 (I Still Love You, But I Want You To Die)
4. The Escalator Broke Down
5. Distance/Difference
6. Magnetic South
7. Like That!
8. My Real Baby
9. Some Kind Of Washington
10. Jagged Eisenhower
11. This Contract Is Patently Unfair (Where Do I Sign?)

Apollo Up!, continued on page 33....

INTERVIEW: ANASTASIA SCREAMED

It's an old story: a band without honor in their adopted hometown travel across the pond to discover audience adoration and critical acclaim. Hell, Jimi Hendrix couldn't get a parking ticket in his Seattle, Washington hometown until he conquered Britain and returned to the states as a bona fide phenomenon. Such is the case with Anastasia Screamed....

Nashville's Anastasia Screamed are largely unknown in the United States outside the circle of their loyal local cult following. Travel overseas, however, as I recently did and the buzz streetside is deafening. Britain's prestigious rock journal, the *New Music Express*, not only chose Anastasia Screamed's debut album, ***laughing down the limehouse***, as one of 1990's best, but they also chose the band as one of the best new bands of the upcoming year. A string of well-received live performances created a loyal following for the guys overseas, with a scattering of upcoming European dates certain to build upon that base.

You lucky *Metro* readers, however, don't have to hop a Concord SST over to lovely London town to catch the Music City's best known exports...you can, instead, be sue to be at the band's upcoming February 6th performance at Nashville's Exit In club. See 'em now, gang, 'cause who knows... Anastasia Screamed just might return as an authentic European phenomenon in their own right and you'll have to pay *twice as much* in order to see the next big thing their next time around.

Anastasia Screamed's roots date back to several years ago, where guitarist Chris Cugini and drummer Chris Burdett attended high school together in Boston. "We started up some pretty bad bands," remembers Cugini, "but we kept working at it." After high school, says Chris, "we were working at the same place and one day, we got on the public transportation in Boston, going to work, and we saw this scruffy-looking kid walk onto the back of the bus carrying a guitar and we just started chatting."

Continuing, Chris talks about Anastasia Screamed guitarist and vocalist Chick Graning. "We started talking about rock and we said 'why don't you come over and jam?' He said 'I'm really into hard rock,' and we thought he meant Foreigner or something like that. I said 'I don't know if this is going to work or not.' When he came down, though, we saw that we were all in the same place musically, into the Replacements, Husker Du and stuff like that."

The trio recruited temporary members from their circle of acquaintances. "We got kids that we knew that owned basses," says Chris, "we didn't have a bass player at the time, so anybody who had a bass could play in our band for a while." "We used them," says Chick, laughing. "We said at the beginning that we'd keep going until we found the right

person," says Chris, though it wasn't until the band made their move to Nashville that the right fourth member was found.

The addition of bassist Charlie Bock rounded out the band's line-up. "It wasn't really a band before then," says Chris, "just a bunch of songs and three guys playing them." Their move to Nashville came hot on the heels of their second record release, and the growth of a core audience in the Boston area...so why move to the Music City?

"There's no logical explanation for it," says Chick Graning, "and I'm not going to try and make one up. Something said 'go to Nashville' and I just moved here. There was no good reason for it." Says the band's manager, Lisa Hein, "I pressured everybody, too, because I was sick of being cold and poor. I said 'I've had enough!'" "Rent is incredibly expensive in the northeast," adds Chris.

Continuing, Chick says, "there's so many bands, too. There's really no point in trying to tour without big support because you're going to lose money, no matter what, just on expenses." "We did it a few times," adds Chris, "and we lost a lot of money. Even when there were people at the shows, which made up for the nights when just a few people showed up, we still lost money."

In retrospect, the band's sudden move to Nashville a couple of years back proved to be a wise move. Nashville's geographical location allows a working band to book weekend dates of a few hours drive in around a dozen states, and the city's still-growing alternative music scene has proved receptive to Anastasia Screamed's guitar-heavy wall-of-sound musical approach.

The band released *Electric Liz*, an impressive five-song EP, around the time of their 1988 move to Nashville. Recorded at Fort Salem, Massachusetts, Chris says that the disc "got us signed to the label that we're on now." Of their signing to London's Fire Records, Chris says "we were looking at other labels when we got a call from the guy who manages Bullet Lavolta and the Lemonheads, and he said 'there's this English label that's looking at you guys and they don't know how to get in touch. They thought that you'd broken up.' They didn't know that we were in Nashville."

"We gave them a call," continues Chris, "and they made us the best offer. They let us do what we want, gave us the money we need." "We can produce ourselves if we want to," adds Chick, citing the autonomy given the band by the label. "The other good thing about Fire Records," says Chris, "is that they are based out of London, so we get to go there as opposed to being signed to an American label. We do need to play here," he adds, "but it's a lot of fun to play over there."

The result of their signing with Fire is ***laughing down the limehouse***, an impressive debut disc that rocks the listener with an all-out aural assault of soaring guitarwork, pounding bass lines and powerful percussion which are woven into a thick, multi-layered and textural tapestry of sound which overwhelms the listener's consciousness and opens them up to Graning's hallucinogenic-tinged lyrical theater of insanity. The result is a wholly unique sound, a bastard stepchild combining the energy of the Replacements with Bob Mould's musical obliqueness to create something entirely new.

"The album is sort of a history of what we've been up to," says Chick of ***laughing down the limehouse***, "the songs that made it. For every one or two songs on the record, there's probably one that we threw away. All of the songs represent different times in the life of the band." The album, distributed in the U.S. by Dutch East India, has done quite well in England, yielding a significant hit in the single "Samantha Black" and capturing them a share of the competitive European music market.

The band has already made plans for its next album, and recently recorded a soon-to-be-released three-song single here in Nashville. "Our next stuff will be much more 'down to earth," says drummer Chris Burdett. "There will be the huge sonic-ness," adds Chick, "but there will be some other elements added as well."

Anastasia Screamed is prepared for their upcoming European dates, and the new single, to be released in time for their shows there, is certain to whet expected audience's appetites for the band's next album. I'll predict that by this time next year rolls around, the guys will have conquered Europe and will return, Hendrix-like, to gain the bit of honor that they deserve in their homeland by capturing the hearts and ears of the record-buying public as they become alternative music's "next big thing." – *The Metro*, 1990

Apollo Up!, continued...

II. Chariots Of Fire (Theory 8 Records 2006, CD)
1. Walking The Plank
2. Invisible Syllable
3. No Song
4. Cut Up
5. Situation: Hot!
6. Even If You Don't Die
7. Custom Critical
8. The Job's A Game
9. Tennessee For Victory
10. Plans

ARCH ANGEL

Band Members:
Bob Langley (vocals, guitars)
Jimmy Mullins (guitars)

Comments: Mullins came from the band Lost Axis. Bob Langley is a Christian rocker in California these days.

CRYSTAL ARMENTROUT

Band Members:
Crystal Armentrout (vocals, guitars) (I)

Other Musicians:
Eric Dail (drums) (I)
Bill Dingess (keyboards) (I)
Sam Harris (bass) (I)
Rodney Lay, Jr (vocals) (I)

CD REVIEW: CRYSTAL ARMENTROUT'S AS IT SHOULD BE

CRYSTAL ARMENTROUT
As It Should Be
(Great Escape Records)

Singer/songwriter Armentrout is a bit of a conundrum. On one hand, she brings a honeycomb-sweet upper range to her vocals reminiscent of Rachel Sweet's best work, but when she gets down and dirty, her voice takes on an earthy, sensual quality that takes one back to the blue-eyed soul of the 1970s. She is a much better guitarist than she has a right to be (yes, that's green-eyed jealousy rising to the surface), punching up every song with fiery leads and funky rhythms.

Armentrout's ecstatic vocals and dynamic fretwork breathe life into the songs on *As It Should Be*, setting her head and shoulders above the mass of *American Idol* wannabes trolling for record deals. While a legion of Clarkson clones is practicing holding a note for, you know, a really long time, Armentrout has been honing her craft, developing a unique musical style that incorporates roots rock and soulful pop with a touch of the blues. Produced with a deft hand by the Dead Rebels' Greg Walker, *As It Should Be* is an encouraging debut from a rising talent. *– Alt.Culture.Guide*, 2006

Crystal Armentrout, continued...

Kevin McKendree (keyboards) (I)
Brice Menaugh (drums) (I)
David Smith (bass) (I)

Crystal Armentrout

Eric Speece (keyboards) (I)
Greg Walker (vocals, tambourine) (I)

Crystal Armentrout Recordings:

I. As It Should Be (Great Escape Records 2004, CD)
1. If I Wanted You
2. Sweeter Than Mine
3. Geraldine
4. Clean
5. Since You've Been Gone
6. Simple Test of Faith
7. Sometimes
8. As It Should Be
9. Free
10. Bye, Bye Baby
11. Raining In My Heart
12. If I Wanted You (alternate mix)

Comments: Singer/songwriter Armentrout came to Nashville from Staunton, Virginia (home of country legends the Statler Brothers) and landed at The Great Escape store on Broadway and Division.

It proved to be a fortuitous coincidence, as she met Greg Walker, who would co-produce and help finance *As It Should Be*. Although Armentrout's talents as a singer and guitarist are more evident from her live performances, the album turned out pretty good in its own right.

ART CIRCUS

Band Members:
Arthur Circus

Art Circus Recordings:

I. *Art Circus* (Infinity Cat Records 2006, CD)
1. The World Expects Too Much Of Me
2. That's Not Punk
3. Fred Flare
4. New Jersey
5. Sellout
6. Be Your Own Pet
7. Disappear
8. I'm Watching Big Brother
9. Sidewalk
10. Boys Club
11. I'm Worried About April
12. Brick Wall
13. When Boys Lie
14. Hummer
15. Summer
16. Fred Flare (The 10th Street Remix)

Comments: Not much info available on this thinly-packaged disc, but the song "Be Your Own Pet" is allegedly where the band got its name.

ASSJACK

Band Members:
Hank Williams III

Assjack Recordings:

I. *Assjack* (Sidewalk/Curb Records CD, 2009)
1. Tennessee Driver
2. Wasting Away
3. Choking Gesture
4. Gravel Pit
5. Cut Throat
6. Smoke The Fire
7. Cocaine the White Devil
8. Redneck Ride
9. No Regrets
10. Doin' What I Want

Comments: Assjack is the hardcore/heavy metal alter ego of Nashville wildman Hank III, son of country royalty Hank Jr. (and, yes, grandson of "you know who"). Hank III played all the instruments on this Assjack debut. Hell, I'd love to have seen the faces on the staid, normally conservative Curb Records execs when they heard this album...

Another View: "Clocking in at a little over 31 minutes, this is a blast-your-face-off outing with one song bleeding very purposefully into another. With the exception of some synth noise, III has done an exceptional job of making the outing sound live – with the exception of some of the drums that sound programmed (which is fine). Standout cuts include the brutally emotional "Cut Throat" and the slamming "Cocaine the White Devil," which has the brutal power of later Ministry, the over the top volume and guitar riffing of Roach Motel, and the dynamics of Slipknot. This is a solid debut that appeals to a very particular audience. – Thom Jurek, *All Music Guide*

ATTICUS FAULT

Band Members:
Todd Evans (vocals, guitar) (I, II)
Jason Noe (guitar, vocals) (I, II)
Chris Laurent (bass, vocals) (I, II)
Paul Asciutto (drums) (I, II)

Other Musicians:
Jay Joyce (guitars, bass, keyboards) (I, II)

Atticus Fault Recordings:

I. *Atticus Fault* (Uninhibited Records/MCA 2002, CD)
1. Soundtrack
2. My First Trip To Mars
3. Too Late
4. Little People
5. Mary Mother
6. Silver Stars
7. 1000 Years

Andrew & the Upstarts — Shiver and Shake!

8. Maybe
9. Damn
10. She's A Vision
11. Angel
12. Once Around The Sun

II. Mars EP (Uninhibited Records/MCA 2002, CD)
1. Soundtrack
2. My First Trip To Mars
3. Maybe
4. Once Around The Sun

Comments: Atticus Fault has been compared, in some circles, with U2 and Coldplay, and such comparisons are apt, if only because of the band's lush, thickly-orchestrated sound. I give credit and/or blame for the band's sound more to producer Jay Joyce than to the band, which didn't seem to have developed a distinctive sound of its own.

Atticus Fault seems to have benefited more from the late 1990s major label signing spree than from any sort of local buzz, since I haven't found anybody that remembers them. I didn't think very much of them at the time, and five years later, I still don't think that they were a very good band. If they'd spent a few years of toiling away in the trenches and sharpening their tools, maybe recording a couple of indie releases, then Atticus Fault *might* have been ready for the major leagues. Otherwise, the album (and EP) sound like so much modern rock piffle….

AURA

Band Members:
D. Mahoney (vocals) (A1)
Mike Simmons (guitar) (A1)
M. Fischer (guitar) (A1)
B. Pugh (bass) (A1)
Paul Simmons (drums) (A1)
K. Earl (drums) (A1)

Aura Recordings:

A1. Aura (Yamama Records 1982, 7" vinyl)
<u>Side One</u>
1. Time To Fill

<u>Side Two</u>
2. Cross Bows
3. Natas Dog

Comments: One of Mike Simmons earliest bands, Aura walked a fine line between hard rock and heavy metal. "Time To Fill" is a prog-oriented metallic creeper with plenty o' Goth overtones and some nice Simmons guitar while "Cross Bows" is a more traditional metal romp in a Judas Priest/Iron Maiden vein. "Natas Dog" returns to an early, underutilized prog-metal sound.

AUTOVAUGHN
Web: www.autovaughn.com

Band Members:
Darren Potuck (vocals, guitar) (I)
Steve Wilson (guitar, vocals) (I)
Drew Wilson (bass) (I)
Andy Grooms (drums) (I)

Autovaughn Recordings:

I. Space (AutoVaughn Music 2006, CD)
1. One More Time
2. Stay Another Night
3. Rock Your Body
4. Hold On Tight
5. On The Radio
6. One Man Lifeboat
7. Comeback
8. We Escape
9. Everybody
10. Hell Of A Place

Autovaughn

IT COMES ON ANYHOW: STEPHEN ANDERSON

There have always been periods when the creative energies of individuals have, in a sense, overflowed and come together, creating a wave or, in some cases, a virtual tsunami with cultural changes worldwide.

I feel fortunate to have been born in 1954, which gave me the opportunity to experience more than one of these creative spikes, so to speak, and some exciting times. I was just old enough to be carried away by the music of the Beatles, Stones, Kinks, etc. and by the energy of it all. One of my best memories from those early days in Nashville was seeing the Rolling Stones, with Brian Jones still in the band. I was around 10 years of age. I had begun playing guitar at age 8 and was hooked from then on, and started writing songs around the same time

Then around 1968, I was turned onto what was happening around the world, all the music and cultural changes, an explosion, and I was determined to be part of it. At age 14, I was too young by all accounts, but I managed it by any means necessary, making it to concerts, pop festivals, and many other events. There is far too much to say about all this but the focus of this book is Nashville from 1976-1986, so I'll move ahead.

However, there are a few bands/artists that very much carried the seeds of what came later. In 1973, Iggy and the Stooges played Nashville. I think the club was called Muther's Music Emporium. It was an incredible show and made a huge impression on me.

The Velvet Underground had broken up in 1970 and Lou Reed continued solo. His first LP was released, with an unusual line-up of players but great songs. In 1972, just as his second LP *Transformer* was released, he was touring and I went to see him in Memphis, a show I'll never forget.

The other influence I gotta mention is Bowie. In fact, he was very much connected to both Iggy and Lou, largely responsible for the success of both of their solo careers. I saw him with original band the Spiders from Mars in Nashville several times but I also saw them on their first U.S. tour and only the second gig in the U.S. after NYC, I believe. It was Sept. 24, 1972, in Memphis as well, at Ellis Auditorium. Bowie's influence on the period to follow is too extensive to cover here, so I'll leave it at that.

As I've said, these bands were like precursors to what came after, so around 1977, when I connected with what was happening, with a vengeance, mainly in N.Y.C., London, L.A. and San Fran, it was like the natural next step. As always seems to be the case, the early days were the most exciting, before the media and business interests got their hands on it, watered down and assimilated it, in the interest of…what else: profit. By 'early days' I mean approx 1976-1980, although in Nashville and many cities, other than the four I mentioned, things happen a bit later. But that doesn't matter so much as the creative energy that exists and whether original ideas and sounds are happening.

For me, it's impossible to write about this period without mentioning guitarist Lenny Breau, who was a major influence on me. Although he played different music from most of the others covered here, Lenny would very much be considered part of the "other side of Nashville." He lived here off and on from 1976 until his death in 1984. There's no way to go into it properly here, but for those interested, there is a great deal online and elsewhere about Lenny, including my book *Visions: a Personal Tribute to Jazz Guitarist Lenny Breau*. I met Lenny in 1976 and he became a mentor and dear friend, like family, until his passing. No matter what music, projects, bands, etc, I was involved in, I was also spending time with Lenny and learning from him. He was certainly one of the greatest guitarists and innovators of all time on the instrument.

In addition to my interest in jazz and solo guitar, I had been writing my own kind of songs, both instrumental and with lyrics, and had a band called Nova Express, with Barney Evers on bass and various temp members. I was also playing in various contexts, both recording and live performance with various bands/artists. One of these was with musician and singer, Andy Byrd. I played on some of his original music, kind of rhythm and blues, rock, etc. and I was strictly playing as a sideman. Then around 1978, Andy was putting together a band and had financial backing and a budget with which to put the players on salary. This meant that, even if we played no gigs we got paid, a pretty deal and almost unheard of.

So I joined and we began rehearsals and soon got some gigs. I liked Andy and his wife, Katherine, and I wasn't doing it for the money only, but I was hesitant, only because the offer came just as I was connecting with some of what was happening, and discovering bands like the Ramones, Talking Heads, Television, many others. And I had so many original ideas, music of my own that I wanted to pursue. I felt like, finally there was some common ground out there and possibilities for playing and developing my music among people who at least shared some similar values, perhaps more.

In the commercial music world, sounding the same and creating via formula was considered a merit. But now there was an undercurrent of artists like myself, whose approach and views were the antithesis of that. I suppose in some ways I felt like I had found a home, where being different was actually an advantage and conceptually, it was open season.

Right as all this was happening, I got the offer to join the band, which is why I was conflicted. But it was a good gig and people (and I had almost no income then), so I did it. The name of the band was the Hots. In the beginning we were doing mostly Andy's songs, some of which were rhythm and blues and others all-out rock. During this time I was going down to Atlanta a good bit, and a favorite place was a little record shop called Wax'n'Facts in Little Five Points. I got to know the owner Danny Beard and occasionally would stay at his house while in town. Through Danny I met a number of people in bands from Atlanta and Athens, including the B-52s. Danny's girlfriend back then was Kate Pierson. I got to know Ricky Wilson best and his sister Cindy, who I dated for a minute. Ricky played a big Mosrite guitar and strung it with only 4 strings, leaving the two center strings off. I loved his playing and wrote a tune for him, "Popo" which my later band Actuals used to play live.

Danny had a small label called db records and put out their first record, a 45 of "Rock Lobster" and "52 Girls." I think he gave away probably a couple of hundred at their gigs and I actually still have one. Anyway, Wax'n'Facts was a great place in those days and usually every band came by at some point during the day, both local bands/artists and those in from out of town. Also Danny got every new release by bands from all over, many of which were impossible to find elsewhere. Of course this was pre-internet and in a sense, Wax'n'Facts was like a source of links to so much new stuff happening everywhere.

Back in Nashville, the Hots got some unexpected gigs, one of which was opening for the Cars at Municipal Auditorium. It

Actuel @ The Cannery

was fun but the sound onstage was terrible. I suppose it was a flaw in the design of the space, I don't know, but after you played a note, or drums played a beat, it would go out and then come back as an overwhelming echo or slap-back. Apparently this wasn't so detectible out front, but it was a major drag onstage. So we had to compensate somehow and I guess we managed. I wasn't much of a Cars fan, and I think the best thing for me about that gig was playing at the Municipal Auditorium. I had seen so many great shows there, like the Stones, Bowie, the Byrds, James Brown, and many others. So the history of the place made it special, but the sound sucked.

Another show we did was at The Tennessee Theatre. It was kind of a showcase with Bobby Bradford Blues Band opening. The sound there was much better and again there was history there. When I was a kid there were like 5 or 6 movie theatres downtown on the same street, the Tennessee among them, and I went to them all. So it was unusual but cool playing there.

Not long after I joined the band, I was able to bring in some songs I wanted to play, including a few of my originals. We did a Ramones tune and a couple of vintage '60s tunes I dug, including, "Red Rubber Ball" by a band called Cyrcle, from 1966. I'm not certain, but I think this was the first time any band had played a Ramones tune live in Nashville, at least at fairly big shows. But the band was still mostly commercially oriented and I was more and more anxious to put together my own thing.

We played a show at the Agora in Atlanta, with several other bands on the bill, some of which were doing some good original stuff and I met quite a few people. Danny Beard was there and my friend Andy Norman, who did art work for several bands. He also performed with the Hots on occasion, a sort of modern vaudevillian bit. Anyway, while staying in Atlanta during that weekend I made a decision to leave the band and form my own thing.

Not long after this, I moved to San Francisco, driving out with Andy Norman, who was moving to L.A. It was a great time to be in San Francisco and so much was happening. I did music for experimental film, performance art, played solo and with ensembles. I met people from some interesting bands, including Tuxedomoon, the Residents, the Avengers, etc., and played with some of them, including Patrick Miller from Minimal Man, Michael Belfer from T-moon, Snakefinger, and others.

In early 1980, I returned to Nashville for what I thought was only a brief time. Not long after I got back, I ran into a friend and musician I had worked with in the past, Robb Earls. I remember we sat in a parking lot and talked for hours and decided to try putting something together. Robb had a small but well-equipped recording studio a bit out of town, in Fairview. The first thing we did was to record 2 songs I had written with bass player Kenny Lynerd. Robb engineered as well as playing keyboards. Kenny was on bass, Boo Boo McAfee on drums and I played guitars. I did vocals on one of the songs, Kenny on the other. It turned out well; in fact, one of the tunes, "Today," was recently re-released on CD. Anyway, Robb and I soon began looking for permanent members for bass and drums, since Kenny and Boo Boo were already committed.

I think around this time some guys that often came to see the Hots formed their own band: Cloverbottom. I had become friends with Johnny and Rock and then met their drummer John Elliot. He was interested in joining our band so after that we found bassist Gary Rabasca, and we got together just to see how it went. Right from the start we connected musically and began rehearsals at Robb's cabin studio. I had a bunch of original songs and Robb did as well. It came together very quickly and we found our own unique sound right off. I proposed the name Actuals, and our first gig was at a small club called Phranks n' Steins, run by Rick Champion. Rick was a true patron and a supporter of not only our band and Cloverbottom, but of all the new stuff that was happening in Nashville.

It's always difficult to put a label on music, and especially in those days when so many different kinds of sounds were finding a place among people with similar passions for original music and ideas. Whether it was called punk, alternative, new wave, etc., wasn't and isn't of any importance. Rather it was about a great deal of creative energy flowing, available to anyone with original ideas willing to pursue them, and with no interest or desire to follow rules and restrictions imposed by the music business or any other existing system. For a lot of people, including myself, this had always been our attitude and approach, so there was perhaps some vindication, and it was an exciting time.

Even though in Nashville it was a small scene, a number of new bands began appearing, and Phranks n' Steins was pretty much the place to play and connect, etc., certainly in the earliest days. Rick had most of the local bands playing there and also began to book bands from elsewhere. Some of the local bands I remember, and those we often played with were: File 13, Cloverbottom, Civic Duty, USR, the Ratz. These are just some of the early bands I recall, there were many more from a bit later on.

Among my memories of non-local bands, there are a couple in particular. One was R.E.M. When they played Phranks n' Steins, they were just starting out and were pretty rough. We played with them twice and they were improving because they toured constantly, playing anywhere they could. One of

our gigs with them is pretty amusing and worth telling about. Our band was called Actuals of course, but we played a few gigs with a band (allegedly) from Birmingham called Slim Jim. What most people didn't know was that Slim Jim was us, along with friend Tim Wilson. We wore disguises and the music was nothing like Actuals. It was mostly screwing around, just for fun, although we did some interesting stuff.

We didn't play our regular instruments and also used found sounds and tape. I had made a tape of Wm. Burroughs doing a live reading in San Francisco, which we layered into the mix, and just all kinds of stuff, like "Freebird" backwards. We would open for ourselves (Actuals) and any other bands on the bill. So one night we played with an unknown band called R.E.M. and appeared as both Actuals and Slim Jim. The Slim Jim set was quite a performance and afterwards Michael, the singer with R.E.M., came up to me, all breathless and wide-eyed, declaring it was one of the best things he had ever heard. I got a kick out of that.

I suppose before I leave the topic of R.E.M. I should tell how we made an error in judgment, or one of our members did anyway. Bill Berry, R.E.M.'s drummer contacted us and asked us to play some dates with them on an upcoming tour. Before the rest of us could do anything about it, our drummer had turned him down. Why, I didn't know then nor do I know now. So we certainly missed an opportunity there.

We played Louisville a few times and met a band from there called Babylon Dance Band. I really dug them and we played some gigs together, both in Louisville and in Nashville. Tara Key was really a unique guitar player. She looked like a little librarian (which indeed she was) but she played like a whirling dervish. We kept in touch for many years and later she had the band Antietam with husband Tim, also from BDB. She also performed with Yo La Tengo in the film *I Shot Andy Warhol*.

A lot of students from Vanderbilt Univ were fans of Actuals and came to all our gigs. Most were law students and we often got written up in the Vandy papers. One of our best gigs was at Vanderbilt, a place on campus called 'The Good Woman Coffeehouse'. We also played the Exit-In, J. Austins, Rock City, run at one time by the somewhat bizarre couple, Jade and Luv, and other clubs. I suppose, next to Phranks n' Steins, we played the most at Cantrell's. One memorable gig there was with Atlanta band the Brains who, I think, I had met through Danny in Atlanta. Their lead singer and keyboardist Tom Gray wrote a tune called "Money Changes Everything" which I think was on their first 45. Sometime later, Cyndi Lauper had a big hit with the tune, but I always liked their version best.

I think Actuals was together about a year, during which time we played a lot but never signed with a label. We had some offers, most notably from a guy named Johnny Wright with Warner Bros. He was attracted by our version of "Ghost Riders in the Sky" and began courting us, so to speak. We did that tune entirely as a lark, just a bit of silly fun and it had little to do with what we were about conceptually. So, the fact that it was that song that they were interested in made us a bit wary, but we played along; after all, free dinners and drinks is not something to refuse. Well, when we got into meetings and it was all clear that Wright and Warners wanted to re-make us into a good little band, in some preconceived image, etc. Well, we had no interest in that, so that was it.

I think the Exit In was our last gig as Actuals. I had decided to form another band and Robb was going to do the same. I named my band Actuel, which was suggested to me by a friend who was working as a model in Paris and elsewhere. We were talking about it all and she said that a current term in France was to say like 'that's actuel', meaning that's cool or hip, etc. A slang term more or less. And it has other meanings as well, so I dug it. Robb called his band Factual. Elliot stayed with Robb, and Gary stayed as well for the time being. I moved back to San Francisco, where I had lived before, and formed Actuel. There was still a great deal

happening in San Fran and I got more involved, hooking up with most of the artists I knew from before and others. We played events in parking lots and rooftops, of which there were many. I also played a couple of clubs, Mabuhay Gardens and The Deaf Club. The latter was unique in that, during the day it was actually a place for the deaf, particularly kids. But during the night on weekends, it became a punk club. The deaf folks dug it because they could 'feel' the very loud music.

The first incarnation of Actuel was with Yael Gaubert, a girl who had moved to SF from France and played bass and cello. We were a duo but played with various others, mostly friends of hers. I had some financial backing from friends in Nashville who were great supporters of my music, most importantly Mac Linton. So the initial plan was to record an EP, an extended play 45, with 3 songs. We did one tune at Harbor Sound studio in Sausalito and the other two were finished later in Nashville.

I had to return to Nashville after a few months and had written a lot of material in the meantime. I eventually hooked up with Gary Rabasca again on bass and we played as a duo for awhile, using a rhythm machine and some taped sound. My publishing company helped rent us a house, which we used as a band house for rehearsals. Andy Norman, who was working in animation and other visual arts, also lived there. We finished the EP, with the song I did in San Francisco, "Things," on one side. The other side had two songs that I had begun here while still with Actuals, "East to West" and "No Regrets." Hugh Entrekin helped with it and we got distribution from various companies.

Mostly it went to college radio stations and soon began doing very well. I was quite surprised at the reception, it was #1 and #2 at several stations across the country and we began receiving a great deal of correspondence from DJs and others. Then we were contacted by a man named Wayne Halper, who wanted to represent us. He had worked with Grace Jones and others and was legit, so we agreed. Among other things he took the EP to France, to an event for showcasing new artists, making deals, etc. I believe it was called the Midem Festival in Cannes, France. It turned out well and soon we were contracted to do an LP for a division of CBS in the Netherlands, although it would be some time before the record was released.

In the meantime, we decided to perform as a trio and began looking for a drummer. We finally found Soren Berlev, who had moved to Nashville from Denmark, where he had been with a very successful band called Gasolin'. He was a fine player and we had a natural feel playing together. We rehearsed, played several gigs and began recording the album. Phranks n' Steins was gone, but we played Cantrell's, Exit In, Southwinds, other local venues and out of town.One show that a lot of folks probably remember was a benefit show for Vanderbilt radio station WRVU. There were several bands, including Civic Duty, Practical Stylists, and Afrikan Dreamland. It was a good night as I recall, not just the music but because everyone involved was positive and got along well, which is so often not the case with so many bands playing together. We also played other gigs at Vanderbilt (Rites of Spring, etc.) and back in Louisville with Babylon Dance Band. Some gigs in Atlanta went well, gigs with bands like Pylon and others. Danny Beard usually came and I would see Ricky Wilson if he was in town.

While recording the album, and performing we were making plans for a more extensive tour. We were getting more and more bookings along the east coast, so we decided to make a big move and base ourselves at Gary's mom's house in New York state, near the Finger Lakes. There we would have a good rehearsal space and be more centrally located, closer to major cities, especially N.Y.C. where we eventually planned to move. We had several gigs booked in N.Y.C. at The Ritz, Danceteria, Pyramid, and other smaller, more obscure places. We also were playing at Brown Univ in Rhode Island, Cambridge/Boston, and other cities in the northeast.

Our first gig was at Syracuse University in Syracuse, NY. The night before the show we were out having some drinks, etc. and before I knew it we were involved in a fight. To make a long (and painful) story short, I ended up with a broken nose, black eyes, cracked jaw and generally bashed. Gary fared better overall but his one main injury was a deal breaker. That is, he had broken one of his hands. With my injuries we could have eventually continued with the tour. But Gary couldn't play at all. His hand would take months to heal, so that was that. To say it was a huge catastrophe for us would be an understatement. All the work: a year of booking and coordinating and all the support we had had from various quarters in helping us get there was negated in a single night. Our music and sound wouldn't really have been affected but if we had to cancel the tour, which we did, then the energy and momentum we had built, which is so dependent on timing and so many intangible factors, would not survive and it seemed doubtful that the band would either.

After the medical treatments, hangovers, freak-outs, etc, we came to a decision, and really there were few options. Gary and Soren returned to Nashville with the van, but I decided to move to N.Y.C. I had a good friend there and she let me move into her place on the lower east side. I was fairly devastated and just wanted to go, so I took a bus and arrived in Manhattan, dazed and confused. I was basically unrecognizable, my face blackened with bruises, jaw cracked and all the other injuries still fresh. Had it been any other city, I would have been treated with suspicion and disdain, but instead I felt like the city embraced me. It's difficult to describe.

Slim Jim a/k/a Actuel

For example, I was living in what was at the time one of the most dangerous parts of the city, East 5th St. between Ave. B and C. I had friends that had lived in the city for years, in other areas like uptown and/or the west side, who wouldn't come to see me, said they wouldn't dare. But the guys on the street, mostly Puerto Rican, were great to me. While I was healing, I had some difficulty walking and they would even carry me up the stairs… well, stuff like that. It was now my neighborhood and I felt safe, and good. I think it served as a kind of catharsis and helped me deal with the nightmare that had happened, the crash of the band and all. I played some solo gigs in the city, some jazz and music for experimental film, played small places like No Se No, Lucky 7, The Dive, and some rooftops. Well, it's too much to go into here, but at least it was a creative time and saved me from total despondency after the band catastrophe.

Sometime later, I moved back to Nashville for various reasons and eventually started playing with Gary again. Soren had returned to Denmark, so we played some as a duo. Gary was also playing with Ed Fitzgerald in his band Civic Duty. At some point their drummer, Beat Zenerino, joined Gary and I and we reformed Actuel. I was playing solo guitar and various projects but it was nice to also be back playing those Actuel songs, and some of my favorite things by Lou Reed, Beach Boys, Syd Barrett, etc. During part of this time I was roommates with Bill Lloyd, who was just getting his own thing going. After all that had happened I had practically forgotten about the LP that was to be released overseas. It had taken longer than expected and by the time it was released, the original band had crashed, along with its momentum and energy. But the LP did quite well nevertheless, mostly in Holland, Germany, and France, as well as in Belgium. It had distribution here in the U.S. as well, but it was mainly in Europe. It was titled *Monuments* and manufactured by CBS Grammofoonplaten BV, Haarlem, Holland.

We played a few shows in Nashville as the re-formed Actuel. One of these was at the Cannery opening for a band that had been big in the late '60s/early '70s, the Guess Who. But I suppose the most memorable (and somewhat infamous) show was one that we did not long after the LP came out. It's one I would prefer to forget but, for the sake of accuracy, I suppose I will tell the tale.

Cat's Records had our LP in the store and asked us to play a show they were putting together at Cantrell's, co-sponsored by WRVU I believe. It would feature two bands, both of them trios: Actuel and a band called In Pursuit, with Jay Joyce, Emma Grandillo, and Jeff Boggs. It was a kind of showcase and there would be label reps, A&R guys, etc, in attendance, scouting for new bands for their labels, so it was a good opportunity. But to be honest, I didn't feel all that enthusiastic, at least not like I would if I had the original band and was at the level we had attained before the crash. But I was into it nonetheless and certainly appreciated the invitation, extended by Steve West, although he may have regretted it later on.

We asked Bill Lloyd to play as well. He played with us on a couple of tunes and we played with him, as his band, performing a short set of his tunes. Also joining us, on marimba, for a couple of songs was Jim Marshall, a friend and drummer who I played with over the years. Well, I wish I could say it went great but the fact is that it did not. I don't remember it too clearly, but well enough. Now it's true that I was no stranger to getting high, drinking, etc, but I almost always had it together for performances. Bill Lloyd, with myself on guitar, Gary on bass, and Beat on drums, went on first and it went well. It was fairly early and I wasn't wasted yet. But it was also my birthday, March 15th (beware the Ides of March) and maybe I felt compelled to indulge myself. But it wasn't just that. This was an important gig and normally I would be focused and on track, but I think many factors were involved in throwing things into chaos, so to speak.

In retrospect I think to a large degree it was frustration, over the timing, etc. We weren't the band we had been before. I think I was still recovering from the catastrophe of what had gone down and I just wasn't as inspired as I had been, and would be again, but not right then. Add to that the drinking and drugs (in huge excess, to be honest) and it was a recipe for disaster. Well, perhaps disaster is too strong a word, but it

was certainly not what the sponsors expected, nor wanted. I won't (and can't) describe the entire experience but, for example, at one point I instructed a man up front to go get me a drink. Now this wasn't some late night, small crowd but a packed house and a big production. So it was unheard of to do such a thing. And worse than that, the man happened to be one of the A&R guys from a label!

Well, I can tell you that none of the labels would touch us after that and after my other antics of the night, which I won't go into. I recall that about two-thirds of the way through our set I saw Steve West offstage frantically motioning for us to wrap it up! Of course that had little effect on me and we continued. Surprisingly the crowd seemed to be having a good time, it was rock 'n' roll after all, which I pointed out, and I think people just knew I was long gone and they didn't care. But the same cannot be said for the organizers, sponsors, and label dudes. So that was that and frankly, at the time I didn't care at all. In retrospect of course I do think of how it might have been if…well, screw it. Years later Jay Joyce told how that gig had been a good break for In Pursuit and I think it helped them get signed, etc. It probably helped Bill as well. But for us, well, there it is. Timing…it's a bitch!

We played a few more gigs as Actuel but, really, after the crash of the original band, my heart was never in it 100%. But I was involved in other things as always, mostly solo stuff and short-term projects with other artists, both here and in NYC.

One that happened, right at the end of 1986 or early 1987, was a series of impromptu performances at Centennial Park. We showed films, projected on the large white bandshell, and I played the soundtrack live. Andy Norman showed the films, using a 16mm projector. Also involved from the start were Jon Ausbrooks and Gary Price, both now in Austin I think. It wasn't promoted or announced but by the time we did the second one a lot of people were showing up, like friends Chris, Byron, and Matt Swanson, that were just starting a band called Clockhammer. I think I actually played on the bill with them on their first gig.

By the time we did the final show at the park, the fifth one I think, there were pretty good crowds coming. This was exactly the kind of thing I loved doing, bypassing the bullshit, business, money squabbles, power and ego plays, etc, and just getting right to it, with the energy and focus on the creative process. But then the park police shut us down. It's true we had no permit nor permission from the proper authorities, so there was nothing we could do. But it was cool, we had some great nights and it was a unique experience.

I think I entered my most creative period since that time, but we're at the end of our focused period. Except one other project that may have begun at the end of that time period was called Mosaic, which was myself, Rusel Brown (O'Brien), and Giles Reeves, with contributions from Tony Crow, Andy Norman, Matt McLendon and others. But that's a story for another time, or book.

Overall, I have good memories of those days. Nashville was never an easy or natural environment for pursuing original music, whether it be playing in a band or whatever one's creative concept may be. But sometimes we managed to twist the city's arm; to make it happen by sheer force of will, collective and otherwise. It comes on anyhow. – sda

A Note On Actuals/Actuel:

I have sometimes been asked in what ways the music of Actuel was different from that of Actuals. I suppose the most obvious factor was the instrumentation; Actuals was a quartet, with guitar, keyboard, bass, drums; whereas Actuel was a trio, with guitar, bass and drums. Of course the more important differences were conceptual. With Actuals, both Robb and I were writing the songs, and our individual ideas were, of necessity, more open to changes and adaptation by the entire band. In Actuel, this kind of process still occurred but all the songs were my own, with Gary contributing a great deal to their development.

It's always been difficult for me to describe the music itself but, in general, I think you could say that Actuel's music was more melodic and also a more minimal approach. Without keyboard or other instruments, the guitar and bass had to provide all the harmonic content. But rather than trying to fill up the space by over-playing, etc, we tried to develop a different way of playing, more like counterpoint, where the parts were woven together so to speak, rather than playing like straight chords with bass on bottom.

As I said, it's difficult to describe but I think this was one of the more unique aspects of our approach in Actuel. In Actuals, we also had a great deal of interaction between instruments, just in a different way and as a quartet we became very tight and used dynamics to great effect at times.

BE THERE!

Span·O·Life CORPORATION presents OCTOBER

PLACID FURY

30TH WELCOME TO KELLERS! THURSDAY

FRIDAY 31ST

Lovebottom

FILE 13 HALLOWEEN PARTY

How lovely can you be?

ACTUALS SAT.

NOV. 1ST

1909 west end

Phrankensteins n

320 7250

ID REQUIRED

DAN BAIRD
Web: www.danbaird.net

Band Members:
Dan Baird (vocals, guitars) (I-III)

Other Musicians:
Terry Anderson (vocals) (I-III)
Pat Buchanon (vocals) (I,III)
Keith Christopher (bass, percussion) (I-III)
Mauro Magellan (drums) (I-III)
Brendan O'Brien (guitar, vocals, keyboards) (I-III)
Benmont Tench (piano) (I,III)

Dan Baird Recordings:

I. Love Songs For The Hearing Impaired (Def American Records 1992, CD)
1. The One I Am
2. Julie & Lucky
3. I Love You Period
4. Look At What You Started
5. Seriously Gone
6. Pick Up The Knife
7. Knocked Up
8. Baby Talk
9. Lost Highway
10. Dixie Beauxderaunt

Comments: I'm not sure exactly when the former Georgia Satellites frontman made Nashville his base of operations after leaving Atlanta, but Dan has been part of the local music scene for so long we couldn't exclude him. When the Satellites broke-up following the dismal showing of their third album, 1989's fine *In the Land of Salvation and Sin*, Baird released this solo debut a couple of years later.

The album's "I Love You Period" was a surprising Top 30 hit single (hitting its stride at the dawn of the grunge explosion), allowing Baird to record a follow-up, *Buffalo Nickel*, a few years later. It certainly didn't hurt that Baird's band at the time included journeyman Keith Christopher and former Satellites' drummer Magellan, a truly scary rhythm section.

II. Buffalo Nickel (American Recordings 1996, CD)
1. Younger Face
2. Cumberland River
3. I Want You Bad
4. L'il Bit
5. Hell To Pay
6. Woke Up Jake
7. Birthday
8. Hush
9. Trivial As The Truth
10. Hit Me Like A Train

Comments: Baird had so much fun with his debut album he decided to get the gang together for one more go at the brass ring. Didn't happen, though, *Buffalo Nickel* going nowhere fast, and Dan and Keith later hooked up fellow travelers like Eric Ambel of the Del-Lords and Terry Anderson in the Yayhoos, an on-again, off-again gutbucket rock ensemble that has released two albums so far. Baird has gone on to form a couple of other bands like the Sofa Kings and Homemade Sin; tour Europe a lot; and has produced albums by a few other artists.

III. Out of Mothballs (Jerkin' Crocus 2003, UK CD)
1. Rock This Place
2. Picture On The Wall
3. Memphis
4. Any Little Thing
5. Shine A Light
6. Little Stories
7. Trouble Comin'
8. Lock And Key
9. Seventh Son
10. Shake It Wild
11. Don't Open That Door

Another View: "In a just world, Dan Baird would be a big ol' rock star, regularly setting stadium-sized crowds into a boogie frenzy with his hot-wired rootsy raunch. However, ever since the Georgia Satellites' *Open All Night* dropped off the charts, the mainstream has had little use for Baird, but *Out of Mothballs*, a collection of outtakes and rarities from Baird's archives, offers further proof that the man knows how to get on the good foot and crank out the groove for anyone who cares to listen."

"Featuring a pair of Georgia Satellites tunes cut for a best-forgotten John Stamos movie in 1990, and a handful of songs that didn't make the cut for Baird's solo albums ...*Out of Mothballs* may have been stitched together from leftovers, but nearly everything here rocks loud and proud, and it hangs together with road-worn ease just like the man's best albums." – Mark Deming, *All Music Guide*

DAN BAIRD & HOMEMADE SIN

Band Members:
Dan Baird (vocals, guitars) (I)
Warner Hodges (guitars, vocals) (I)
Keith Christopher (bass) (I)
Mauro Magellan (drums) (I)
Ken McMahan (guitars, vocals)

Dan Baird & Homemade Sin Recordings:

I. Dan Baird & Homemade Sin (Jerkin' Crocus 2008, CD)
1. Damn Thing To Be Done
2. Crooked Smile
3. Two For Tuesday
4. Runnin' Outta Time
5. Just Can't Wait
6. Lazy Monday
7. Cryin' To Me
8. I Know What It's Like
9. She Dug Me Up
10. Well Enough Alone
11. Champagne Sparkle
12. I Can Do Without You
13. Oh No, There She Goes
14. Hellzapoppin'

Dan Baird

Comments: Damn fine collection of new material featuring Scorchers' guitarist **Warner Hodges** and Baird's long-time musical foils Christopher and Magellan. A number of songs were co-written with **Tommy Womack**. Originally **Ken McMahan** held the lead guitar slot, dropping out before this album was recorded. Hard-to-find import CD, now OOP.

Another View: "*Dan Baird & Homemade Sin* is swaggering, beer-drinking, hell-raising, paycheck-spending rock & roll of the first order, and while conventional wisdom has it they don't make records like this anymore, thankfully Baird and his buddies aren't bothered by such trivialities."
– Mark Deming, *All Music Guide*

DAN BAIRD & THE SOFA KINGS

Band Members:
Dan Baird (vocals, guitars) (I)
Ken McMahan (vocals, guitars) (I)
Kyle Miller (bass) (I)
Nick Forchione (drums) (I)

Dan Baird & the Sofa Kings Recordings:

I. Redneck Savant (Blue Buffalo Records 2001, CD)
1. L'il Bit
2. Sheila
3. Dixie Beauxderaunt
4. All Over But The Cryin'
5. Dan Takes 5
6. Kind Hearted Woman Blues
7. I Dunno
8. Younger Face
9. Another Chance
10. Keep Your Hands To Yourself
11. Dancing Queen
12. Woke Up Jake
13. Myth Of Love
14. Sin City
15. Daydream Believer
16. The Twist
17. Battleship Chains

Comments: Live album recorded with Baird's band, which included guitarist Ken McMahan at the time. Recorded in Berne, Switzerland in August 2000, *Redneck Savant* features a mix of Satellites tracks and Baird solo tunes, as well as a couple of covers and McMahan's best Delta bluesman vox on "Kind Hearted Woman Blues." Hard-to-find import CD.

BANG BANG BANG

Band Members:
Jaren Johnston (vocals, guitar) (I)
Ben Brown (guitar) (I)

Kelby Caldwell (guitar) (I)
Nathan Hansen (bass) (I)
Ethan Pilzer (bass) (I)
Neil Mason (drums) (I)

Bang Bang Bang Recordings:

I. I Shot The King (self-produced CD, 2005)
1. Traffic
2. I Shot The King
3. Unstoppable
4. Turn It Up
5. American Ride
6. Cassanova Strut
7. Crazy
8. Heartbreak City
9. Self Control
10. Wish You Well
11. We Were Young
12. Fantastic World

Comments: Bang Bang Bang was formed in 2005 by a bunch of high school friends, including Ben Brown and Neil Mason of Llama. It didn't take long for the band to create a largish buzz 'round town for their own particular brand of "southern fried garage rock" that they called "bangrock."

The band played in front of local faves like the Pink Spiders and Autovaughn as well as national acts like the Black Crowes and Lynyrd Skynyrd before getting signed by Madonna's Maverick Records label and changing their name to **American Bang**. Personally, I find it kinda funny that the band's old MySpace profile has been taken over by an online pharmacy (as of this writing).

BANG SHANG-A-LANG

Band Members:
Rusel Brown (I)
Tommy Dorsey (I)
Tony Crow (I)
Marky Nevers (I)
Giles Reaves (I)

Bang Shang-A-Lang Recordings:

I. Bang Shang-A-Lang (self-produced tape, no date)
1. Love You Want
2. Scavenger Soul
3. Beg

Comments: Bang Shang-A-Lang was short-lived but important, introducing talents like Tony Crow, Marky Nevers, and Giles Reaves to the local music scene.

BARE JR.

Band Members:
Bobby Bare Jr. (vocals, guitar) (I, II)
Mike "Grimey" Grimes (guitar, vocals) (I)
Dean Tomasek (bass) (I, II)
Tracy Hackney (dulcimer, harmonica) (I, II)
Keith Brogdon (drums, percussion) (I, II)
John Jackson (guitar) (II)
Charles Wyrick (guitar) (II)

Other Musicians:
Tim Carroll (guitar) (II)
Tony Crow (keyboards) (II)
Brad Jones (keyboards) (II)

Bare Jr. Recordings:

I. Boo-Tay (Immortal Records/Epic 1998, CD)
1. Boo-Tay
2. Nothin' Better To Do
3. The Most
4. You Blew Me Off
5. Tobacco Spit
6. Faker
7. Patty McBride
8. Give Nothing Away
9. Soggy Daisy
10. Love-Less
11. I Hate Myself
12. Naked Albino
13. I Wanna Live
14. Why Don't You Love Me

Comments: One of the most stunning, out-of-left-field releases by a Nashville band, catching fans and critics alike by surprise. Bare Jr. was comprised of several local scene veterans, but the vision was clearly that of Bobby Bare Jr., and it was unlike anything we'd heard before...

II. Brainwasher (Immortal Records/Virgin 2000, CD)
1. Overture: Love Theme from Brainwasher
2. Brainwasher
3. If You Choose Me
4. Why Do I Need A Job
5. You Never Knew (I Lied)
6. Shine
7. God
8. Miss You The Most
9. Kiss Me (Or I Will Cry)
10. Dog
11. Limpin'
12. Devil Doll
14. Gasoline Listerine

BOBBY BARE JR'S YOUNG CRIMINALS' STARVATION LEAGUE

Comments: A shake-up in the band – including Mike Grimes retiring to open his record store – did little to change its sound for the second album. Heavy touring aside, Bare Jr. seemed to have been a year or two early for the alt-country "boom" and never caught on beyond a loyal cult audience. Being signed to Immortal Records couldn't have helped the band any, either…better known for nu-metal/hard rock bands like Korn and Incubus, they didn't know how to publicize a band as outré as Bare Jr. A change in distribution from Sony to Virgin certainly didn't put more CDs in the stores....

BOBBY BARE JR.'S YOUNG CRIMINALS' STARVATION LEAGUE

Band Members:
Bobby Bare Jr. (vocals, guitar) (I-III)
Kevin Teel (guitar, bass, steel guitar) (I)
Matt Swanson (bass) (I, II)
Tony Crow (keyboards) (I, II)
Paul Niehaus (steel guitar) (I, II)
Paul Burch (drums, guitar) (I, II)
Mike "Grimey" Grimes (bass) (II, III)
Andrew Bird (violin) (II)
George Chambers (sax) (II)
Duane Denison (guitar) (II)
Tracy Hackney (dulcimer) (II)

Other Musicians:
Carl Broemel (guitar, keyboards) (III)
Patrick Hallahan (drums) (III)
Jim James (vocals) (III)
Brad Jones (bass, keyboards) (III)
Carey Kotsionis (vocals) (II, III)

Ben Martin (percussion) (III)
Deanna Varagona (sax, vocals) (II, III)
Corey Younts (keyboards, vocals) (III)

Bobbt Bare Jr.'s Young Criminals' Recordings:

I. Bobby Bare Jr.'s Young Criminals' Starvation League
(Bloodshot Records 2002, CD)
1. I'll Be Around
2. Flat Chested Girl from Maynardville
3. Mehan
4. Bullet Through My Teeth
5. The Monk at the Disco
6. Dig Down
7. What Difference Does It Make
8. The Ending
9.
10. Stay in Texas
11. Paintin' Her Fingernails

Comments: Using a number of the old gang in the studio, Bobby Bare launched the Young Criminals' Starvation League, pursuing a sound slightly more country and less raucous than previously. Did it right, too, signing with Bloodshot, who have some idea of what to do with a rockin' country band. Yeah, the ninth song has no name….

II. "from the end of your leash" (Bloodshot 2004, CD)
1. Strange Bird
2. Valentine
3. The Terrible Sunrise
4. Visit Me In Music City
5. Your Favorite Hat

Bare Jr.

BARE JR.
Boo-Tay
(Immortal/Epic)

The son of country star Bobby Bare, Junior's music bears only a passing resemblance to that of his father. Sure, there's plenty of country influence here – how could you grow up in Nashville in the seventies and eighties with artists like Johnny Cash, George Jones, Willie Nelson and the like hanging around town and not soak some of it up?

For Bobby Bare, Jr. however, country is not a means to an end, but rather a flavor to add to his energetic stew of Southern rock and punkish attitude. The material on *Boo-Tay* blows away 99% of the alt-country poseurs trying to ride a rising trend to fame and fortune. As a band, Bare Jr. kick out the motherfucking jams with a vigor that surely has Hank spinning in his grave.

Boo-Tay's guitar-driven songs burn with a fervor I've only heard matched by Jason & The Scorchers and, more recently, Slobberbone, with the young Bare's wonderfully imperfect vocals often spiraling out of control like a drunken dervish while guitarist Michael Grimes tears off razor-sharp riffs like some sort of bloodthirsty predator.

Bare's songs tread familiar lyrical ground, albeit with his own peculiar individual twist, the subject matter ranging from self-loathing and lost innocence to betrayal and unrequited love. Cuts like "The Most," "Faker," "Why Don't You Love Me" and the wickedly dark "I Hate Myself" (written with Shel Silverstein) are overflowing with brilliant imagery, not-so-subtle wordplay and hard-rocking instrumentation. One of the more engaging debut discs this year, *Boo-Tay* is a welcome introduction to the talents of Bare Jr. – *Alt.Culture.Guide*, 1998

6. Don't Follow Me (I'm Lost)
7. Let's Rock & Roll
8. Borrow Your Girl
9. Things I Didn't Say
10. Your Adorable Beast
11. Beguiled Bashful Burnt

III. The Longest Meow (Bloodshot Records 2006, CD)
1. Bionic Beginning
2. The Heart Bionic
3. Gun Show
4. Back To Blue
5. Sticky Chemical
6. Uh Wuh Oh
7. Demon Valley
8. Mayonaise Brain
9. Snuggling World Championships
10. Borrow Your Cape
11. Where Is My Mind
12. Stop Crying

Comments: Produced by Brad Jones, the band recorded 11 songs in 11 hours on one Saturday in March 2006.

THE BARKING SPIDERS

Band Members:
Pat McLaughlin (vocals, guitar)
Keith Christopher (guitar)
Michael Joyce (bass)
Michael Organ (drums)

Comments: Mentioned once or twice in local music rags, the Barking Spiders played around town circa the mid-1980s.

THE BASICS

Band Members:
Tom Littlefield (vocals, guitar)
Doug Lancio (guitar)
Greg Herston (bass)
Hunt Waugh (drums)

Comments: One of the city's first and most popular bands at the time, the Basics would soon evolve into the band known as **the Questionnaires**. Their very cool song, "Born To Die," was included on WRVU's ***Local Heroes*** compilation tape.

BE YOUR OWN PET

BE YOUR OWN PET

Band Members:
Jemina Pearl Abegg (vocals) (A1-A6, I-III)
Jonas Stein (guitar) (A1-A6, I-III)
Nathan Vasquez (bass) (A1-A6, I-III)
John Eatherly (drums) (III)
Jake Orrall (bass)
Jamin Orrall (drums) (A1-A6, I-II)

Be Your Own Pet Recordings:

Singles/EPs

A1. Damn Damn Leash (Infinity Cat Records 2004, CD-R)
1. Damn Damn Leash
2. Electric Shake

Comments: British version of ***Damn Damn Leash*** was re-released by XL Recordings in 2005, adding the song "Spill."

A2. Fire Department (Infinity Cat Records 2005, 7" & CD EP)
1. Fire Department
2. Take That Walk
3. Hillmont Avenue

A3. Extra Extra (Infinity Cat 2005, vinyl 7" & CD EP)
1. Extra Extra
2. Feel Me Loud
3. Steal

A4. Let's Get Sandy (Big Problem) (Infinity Cat Records 2006, vinyl 7" & CD single)
1. Let's Get Sandy (Big Problem)
2. Early Sandy (I Got a Big One)

A5. Adventure, Pt. 1 (XL Recordings 2006, 7" & CD EP)
1. Adventure
2. Ouch
3. We Will
4. Vacation You Can Be My Parasol

Albums/EPs

I. Be Your Own Pet (Ecstatic Peace/Universal 2006, CD)
1. Thresher's Flail
2. Bunk Trunk Skunk
3. Bicycle Bicycle, You Are My Bicycle
4. Wildcat!
5. Adventure
6. Fuuuuuun
7. Stairway To Heaven
8. Bog
9. Girls On TV
10. We Will Vacation, You Can Be My Parasol
11. Let's Get Sandy (Big Problem)
12. October, First Account
13. Love Your Shotgun
14. Fill My Pill
15. Ouch

Comments: Be Your Own Pet was the alt-rock "buzz" band for much of 2006, signing a deal with Sonic Youth guitarist Thurston Moore's Ecstatic Peace label (distributed by Universal) and releasing their critically-acclaimed, self-titled debut album, scoring high-profile bookings to perform at such coveted venues as the Glastonbury and Reading Festivals in the U.K.

The members of Be Your Own Pet came together in the basement studio of the Orrall brothers, sons of noted Music City songsmith Robert Ellis Orrall. They were all students at the University School of Nashville and found out that they had shared musical tastes. They started writing songs together, playing shows at local places like Guido's Pizza and Bonga Java. Their creative efforts resulted in the home-brewed CD-R ***Damn Damn Leash***. An mp3 of a song from the EP made its way to Zane Lowe of BBC Radio One and the disc was later released by XL Recordings in the U.K. Sonic Youth's Moore was a fan after ordering the band's EP by mail and would sign Be Your Own Pet to his label.

Another View: "A joyous noisefest of clashing guitars and fractured, off-kilter vocals that delights in its naïveté and impresses with its innocence ... Pearl's voice is baby-doll cute with a hint of sexual menace."

- 50 -

THE OTHER SIDE OF NASHVILLE

II. Summer Sensation (Ecstatic Peace/Universal 2006, CD)
1. Bicycle, Bicycle
2. Girls On TV
3. Fire Department
4. Take That Walk
5. Hillmont Avenue

III. Get Awkward (Ecstatic Peace/Universal 2008, CD)
1. Super Soaked
2. The Kelly Affair
3. Twisted Nerve
4. Heart Throb
5. Bitches Leave
6. Bummer Time
7. You're a Waste
8. Food Fight!
9. Zombie Graveyard Party!
10. What's Your Damage?
11. Creepy Crawl
12. The Beast Within

Comments: Seemingly the last gasp from what was once one of Nashville's best and brightest contenders for national rock & roll prominence, BYOP has been seriously talking about going their separate ways since I penned this stuff. Too bad, 'cause BYOP coulda been HUGE!

THE BEAT POETS

Band Members:
B. Willie Dryden (guitar, keyboards, vocals) (I)
Rudie Whaling (vocals) (I)
Ivan Carling (bass) (I)
David Humphries (drums) (I)
Lee Carroll (keyboards) (I)

The Beat Poets Recordings:

I. Catch Her In The Rye (Harlequin 1990, tape)
Side One
1. Bruce
2. The original LONDON back-beat talking BLUES
3. Down in the Underground
4. Slipping Away

Side Two
5. Lolita Rock
6. Kaleidoscope Caliope
7. Under The Sun
8. La Parisienne "LIVE"
9. Sour Grape "LIVE"

BEDLAM

Band Members:
Jay Joyce (vocals, guitars) (I, II)
Doug Lancio (guitars, vocals) (I, II)
Chris Feinstein (bass, vocals) (I, II)
Michael Radovsky (drums) (II)
Giles Reaves (keyboards) (II)

Bedlam Recordings:

I. Bedlam (MCA Records 1991, CD)
1. Turnin' The Lights Out
2. Heaven
3. She Does Then She Doesn't
4. Harvest Moon
5. Drink It Down

Comments: Bedlam was, if memory serves, Jay Joyce's first band after **In Pursuit**, the talented guitarist hooking up with former **Questionnaires** members Doug Lancio and Chris Feinstein. It was the alt-rock '90s and Bedlam was noisy and shambling with elements of melodic pop. If my earlier reviews mean anything, I didn't like 'em much then, still don't think much of it all today...everybody here is much more talented than these records would suggest.

II. Into The Coals (MCA Records 1992, CD)
1. Drink It Down
2. Madhouse
3. Just About Home
4. Hiding Place
5. Carnival Lights
6. Lucky
7. Turnin' The Lights Out
8. Heaven
9. Upside Down
10. Sunday To Sunday
11. Freakshow
12. Closing Time

Another View: "Bedlam, a Nashville trio, has nothing to do with country and everything to do with alternative rock. The threesome showed a fair amount of promise on its debut album, ***Into the Coals***; the CD isn't perfect, but its strongest tracks indicated that Bedlam was a group to keep an eye on. At their best, the alterna-rockers make it clear that they have a way with a hook – "Carnival Lights," "Closing Time" and the rowdy opener "Drink It Down" are perfect examples of how infectious Bedlam can be..."
– Alex Henderson, *All Music Guide*

THE BEES (U.S.)

Band Members:
Daniel Tashian (vocals, guitar) (I-II)
Robbie Harrington (bass) (I)
John Deaderick (bass) (II)
Jason Lehning (piano, vocals) (I-II)
David Gherke (drums, vocals) (I-II)

The Bees Recordings:

I. Starry Gazey Pie (self-produced CD, 2004)
1. Destiny on the Lawn
2. Starry Gazey Pie
3. Love is a Holiday
4. Message from the Birds
5. Sea of Stars
6. It's Only Gravity
7. Letters from the Dead
8. Bring on the Clowns
9. Mrs. Wilson
10. It Was

II. High Society (self-produced CD, 2006)
1. The Country Life
2. High Society
3. Ms. November
4. Imaginary Girl
5. She is Gone
6. Catch Yer Own Train
7. Tativille
8. We'll Go Walking
9. Hard Luck Tom
10. Dream of Love
11. The Broadway Lights

BEGGAR'S OPERA

Band Members:
Decklan Young (vocals)
Blake Richards (guitars)
H.P. Toze (bass)
Chris Theiry (drums)

ADRIAN BELEW

Band Members:
Adrian Belew (vocals, guitars) (I-VI)

Adrian Belew Recordings:

I. Here (Plan 9 Records/Caroline 1994, CD)

II. The Experimental Guitar Series Volume 1: Guitar As Orchestra (Discipline Global Mobile 1995, CD)

III. Op Zop Too Wah (Passenger Records 1996, CD)

IV. Side One (Sanctuary Records 2004, CD)
1. Ampersand
2. Writing on the Wall
3. Matchless Man
4. Madness
5. Walk Around the World
6. Beat Box Guitar
7. Under the Radar
8. Elephants
9. Pause

Comments: I'm providing a cursory listing here for the underrated avant-garde guitarist Adrian Belew 'cause 1) he's frickin' great; and 2) he's called the Nashville area home since 1994, and has performed in town frequently. Born and raised in Kentucky, Belew came to Nashville in 1975 and hooked up with the popular covers band Sweetheart. He was "discovered" by Frank Zappa while playing with Sweetheart at notorious local club Fanny's and was asked by the rock legend to join his tour.

The Zappa tour brought Belew to the attention of David Bowie, who asks the guitarist to join *his* band. Belew appears on the Bowie albums ***Stage*** and ***Lodger***, which in turn led to prog-rock legend Robert Fripp asking Belew to join the re-formed King Crimson. Through the years, Belew has also lent his talents to recordings by folks like Nine Inch Nails, Laurie Anderson, and Porcupine Tree, among others. Got all that? Yeah, Belew is one of the most underrated of all the guitar gods, his talent recognized by some of the best of the rock world.

Belew has forged a significant solo career, as well, releasing better than a dozen albums on his own, as well as with the

Cincinnati-based pop band the Bears. I've only included here those discs that I'm reasonably certain that Belew made while living 'round these parts. I haven't listed any of the players he used on these records, like bassist Les Claypool or guitarist Robert Fripp, 'cause they aren't local anyway.

V. Side Two (Sanctuary Records 2005, CD)
1. Dead Dog on Asphalt
2. I Wish I Knew
3. Face to Face
4. Asleep
5. Sex Nerve
6. Then What
7. Quicksand
8. I Know Now
9. Happiness
10. Sunlight

VI. Side Three (Sanctuary Records 2006, CD)
1. Troubles
2. Incompetence Indifference
3. Water Turns to Wine
4. Crunk
5. Drive
6. Cinemusic
7. Whatever
8. Men in Helicopters v4.0
9. Beat Box Car
10. Truth Is
11. The Red Bull Rides a Boomerang Across the Blue Constellation
12. &

ADRIAN BELEW - BELL & SHORE

BELL & SHORE

Band Members:
Nathan Bell (vocals, guitar, steel guitar) (I-II)
Susan Shore (vocals, guitar) (I-II)

Bell & Shore Recordings:

I. Little Movies (Flying Fish Records CD)

II. L-Ranko Motel (Rom Records 1989, CD)
1. The L-Ranko Motel
2. Address Unknown
3. The Day Crazy Bob Ran the Dirt Track In The Nude
4. The Flint Hills of Kansas
5. Rosalinda
6. Fighting Days
7. Blue Is the Color of Regret
8. The Running Girl
9. Skull and Crossbones
10. She Must Be So Strong
11. Johnny "El Gato" Miguel
12. Radio V-I-E-T-N-A-M
13. Daddy Was No Good

Comments: I worked with Nathan a short while at Mosko's down on Elliston Place during the early 1990s, along with **Threk Michaels** and most of the gang from **Celebrity Toast & Jam**. Nathan and Susan had moved to Nashville from Iowa and Nathan got a publishing gig in town. The two played often at the Bluebird and opened for talents like Emmylou Harris and Townes Van Zandt.

Nathan worked with producer/guitarist Richard Bennett and recorded an album of songs in 1991 that was never released. Nathan and Susan retired from the music biz in 1995 to raise a family, but Nathan has recently begun playing and recording again. (Note: since neither of the albums listed above were recorded in Nashville, studio musicians are not listed here. Bell & Shore are included here because of their early '90s Nashville presence and, well, 'cause Nathan is a hell of a songwriter.)

Another View: "Nathan Bell writes gritty, incisive, story-songs filled with the details of rough lives hardened on the wrong side of the tracks. The songs reveal Bell as a lyricist worthy of ranking alongside such modern-day heroes as Guy Clark, Rodney Crowell, and Steve Earle."
– Michael McCall, *Music Row Magazine*

A Newer View: "Then as now, Bell's work had a crisp literary quality, a tough blue-collar sensibility and a terse, muscular musicality. His songs sidled alongside Richard

---

ADRIAN BELEW
Side One
(Sanctuary Records)

Latter-day King Crimson guitarist and former Zappa sideman Adrian Belew hasn't released a solo album in nearly eight years, preferring to work with Robert Fripp as part of legendary prog-rockers Crimson, and with his own band, the Bears. When he hits the studio to do a little solo work, Belew does so with a vengeance, recording three – count 'em – three solo albums for release this year. *Side One* is the first of these efforts, a magnificent showcase for Belew's original and highly unique six-string skills. To put it bluntly, Belew's jagged guitarwork has more sharp edges than a broken bottle.

Belew recruited Les Claypool from Primus and Tool's Danny Carey to accompany him on several cuts, including the Hendrix-flavored "Ampersand," composed of syncopated rhythms and angular riffs, and the funky, distraught "Writing On The Wall."

Belew's breathless vocals on the dreamy, drifting "Matchless Man" are supported by a fluid lead with a Moroccan flavor while "Madness" offers exactly that, a descent into darkness with cacophonic, swirling guitars and recurring riffs. The experimental "Elephants" uses found vocals and plodding, heavy leads approximating an elephant's cries to describe the plight of this endangered animal.

There are few vocals on the album, Belew preferring to let his guitar do the talking for him. At a mere thirty-three minutes, *Side One* may seem a bit brief, but the songs here are complex and quite intense. *Side One* is the work of an innovative instrumentalist not the least bit above experimenting with sound and composition. – *Alt.Culture.Guide*, 2004

Thompson and Lou Reed as much as Steve Earle and Mark Germino – his two most common local comparisons. Nashville seemed like it could fit: It still had the glow of the '80s, when big-time deals went to songwriters like Lyle Lovett, Mary Chapin Carpenter and the O'Kanes."
– Michael McCall, *Nashville Scene*, 2007

PETE BERWICK

Band Members:
Pete Berwick (vocals, guitar, bass) (I-IV)

Other Musicians:
Bart Alonzo (guitars) (I)
Stevie Ray Anderson (bass) (IV)
Denise Berwick (vocals) (III)
Jamie Bowles (keyboards, vocals) (IV)
Bill "The Kid" Ceas (drums) (I)
Tom Comet (bass) (II, IV)
Denny Daniels (keyboards) (III)
Patrick Doody (drums) (III, IV)
T.C. Furlong (steel guitar) (III)
Tim Good (guitars) (II, IV)
Don Griffin (guitars) (III)
Allan Hatten (harmonica) (IV)
Steve Holland (drums) (IV)
Bob Lizik (bass) (III, IV)
Billy Maryniak (keyboards) (I)
David Russell (mandolin, fiddle) (IV)
Brian Vance (guitar) (IV)
Sheldon Wheaton (keyboards) (I)
Kevin Woods (guitar) (IV)
Craig Wright (drums) (II, IV)

Pete Berwick Recordings:

I. 6 Pack Town (self-produced 1990, tape)
Side One
1. 6 Pack Town
2. I'm Only Bleeding
3. Empty Bed

Side Two
4. Fool In Love
5. Desperate Rider
6. When I'm Gone

II. Hell To Pay (Shotgun Productions 1994, tape)
Side One
1. Rebels And Cadillacs
2. I Ain't Him

Side Two
3. Hell To Pay
4. Vacancy In My Heart

III. Only Bleeding (Shotgun Records 2002, CD)
1. Must Think She Loves Me
2. Chained
3. Nuclear Boy
4. White Lines
5. Outsider
6. Only Bleeding
7. Gotta Get Out Of Here
8. Without Your Love
9. Cold Steel Gun
10. Standing At The Gates Of Hell

Comments: Recorded in Chicago, Berwick's first full-length album draws upon his Nashville experience, the artist crafting an excellent set of songs that are focused sharper than a laser, lyrically. Berwick's band included Tom Comet of **the Sluggers**.

IV. Ain't No Train Outta Nashville (Shotgun 2007, CD)
1. Rebels And Cadillacs
2. Six Pack Town
3. When I'm Gone
4. The Years We Left Behind
5. Devil Knows His Name
6. I Ain't Him
7. Ain't No Train Outta Nashville
8. Only Bleeding
9. Can't Hide The Tears
10. Rusted Ball And Chain
11. This Used To Be A Town

Comments: Berwick's sophomore effort was actually recorded first, in Nashville, during the depths of the artist's

turbulent local residence (confused? See interview ➜).

Another great set of songs, including a different version of "Only Bleeding" than on the album of the same name. The album's title cut, "Ain't No Train Outta Nashville," was used in the Peter Bogdanovich movie *The Thing Called Love* (with River Phoenix, Samantha Mathis and Sandra Bullock); local legend **Webb Wilder** also had a small part in the film.

THE BIS-QUITS

Band Members:
Will Kimbrough (vocals, guitars, piano) (I)
Tommy Womack (vocals, guitars, bass) (I)
Mike "Grimey" Grimes (bass, guitars, vocals) (I)
Tommy Meyer (drums, keyboard, vocals) (I)

Other Musicians:
Robin Eaton (percussion) (I)
Jeff Finlin (percussion) (I)

The Bis-Quits Recordings:

I. The Bis-Quits (Oh Boy Records 1993, CD)
1. Tommy's On His Own
2. Blues & Wine
3. Betty Was Black (& Willie Was White)
4. Anal All Day
5. Cold Wind

Pete Berwick

6. Cyberpop
7. 76 Bisquits
8. Smell the Taste of Love
9. The Powers That Be
10. Tennessee Valley Girl
11. Walking On A Wire
12. Yo Yo Ma

Comments: Nashville's first "supergroup" included members of **Will & the Bushmen**, **Govt. Cheese** and **Go Go Surreal**. One fondly-remembered indie album later, Kimbrough and Womack went on to significant solo careers....

Another View: "Take a Southern egghead guitar band, throw in a dash of Devo and Frank Zappa, add a pinch of Richard Thompson, and you get the delightfully off-kilter Bis-quits and their self-titled album, *The Bis-quits*." – Alanna Nash, *Entertainment Weekly*

Another View: "The Bis-Quits counted among their ranks some of the best-known and most-respected Nashville rock musicians. They quickly became a major draw and released their self-titled debut through John Prine's Oh Boy imprint. With the two-headed talents of guitarists/vocalists/ songwriters Tommy Womack and Will Kimbrough, along with bassist Mike Grimes, the musicianship is top-notch even as the garage aesthetic lends considerable charm to the outing." – Tom Demalon, *All Music Guide*

THE BLACK CROWES

Band Members:
Chris Robinson (vocals) (I)
Rich Robinson (guitars) (I)
Jeff Cease (guitars) (I)
Johnny Colt (bass) (I)
Steve Gorman (drums) (I)

Other Musicians:
Laura Creamer (vocals) (I)
Chuck Leavell (keyboards) (I)

The Black Crowes Recordings:

I. Shake Your Moneymaker (Def American 1990, CD)
1. Twice As Hard
2. Jealous Again
3. Sister Luck
4. Could I've Been So Blind
5. Seeing Things
6. Hard To Handle
7. Thick N' Thin
8. She Talks To Angels
9. Struttin' Blues
10. Stare It Cold

Comments: Yeah, yeah, I know that there's a lot of discussion and disagreement over whether or not the Black Crowes were actually a *Nashville* band, given their origins in Atlanta. Let's just agree to share them, shall we, at least for this first album which included the work of underrated Nashville rocker **Jeff Cease**. After all, this Nashville/Atlanta band practiced in the Music City (in a rehearsal hall above the *Metro* magazine offices for a while), played frequently at local joints like Sal's (shows often promoted by GVPIII), and was known then as Mr. Crowe's Garden.

Shake Your Moneymaker struck a chord with an early 1990s audience hungry for something more than '80s-era nerf metal. The Crowes pursued a roots-rock direction with more emphasis on a bluesy, R&B vibe (a la the Faces) as opposed to country styling. The Crowes would later meander close to the precipice of the jam band movement as a sort of new age Allman Brothers Band; become spokesmen for the late 1990s hemp revival; and bring an aggressive new dynamic to sibling rivalry, the brothers Robinson matched, perhaps, only by the brothers Gallagher of Oasis as fighting kinfolk in the tabloids.

In the end, the Crowes became musically irrelevant and frontman Chris Robinson married a beautiful movie starlet. Once Cease left the band, after this debut album (did he jump or was he pushed? Jeff, wisely, ain't sayin'…), the Crowes no longer had any semblance of a Nashville connection, which is why none of their other albums are listed here.

Another View: "The Crowes' deceptively sleazy debut broke the band, peaking at around six million copies worldwide, hatching cleverly unconventional (but conventional) hit after hit. *Shake Your Moneymaker* is a fairly Stonesy piece of work above all, but imaginative and wide…party rock with sincerity, class and spent decadence, although let's not forget that this could all be a little more calculated than the Scowler Brothers are letting on, given the band's roots as post-punk Paisley rockers." – Martin Popoff, **The Collector's Guide To Heavy Metal, Volume 3: The Nineties.**

True Story, Told Here For The Hundredth Time:
Back around the time that *Shake Your Moneymaker* was released, *Metro* magazine publisher Gus Palas had set up a phone interview for me with Chris Robinson of the Black Crowes for a cover story. Chris, however, had…shall we say…engaged in too much of the rock & roll lifestyle the night before, and was hungover and unresponsive to my questions. I had a splitting migraine headache at the time and finally, when I told Chris that "we didn't have to waste his time or mine doing the interview if he didn't want to," he intelligently replied with a hearty "fuck off" and hung up the phone.

Well, it wasn't the first conversation that I'd had go south, but it was one of few. In 35 years and literally 200+ artist interviews, Chris Robinson stands alongside Richard Butler of the Psychedelic Furs and the guys in Rush as the biggest dickheads that I've ever spoken with. But at least Butler bought me a few beers later and apologized, whereas Chris just had to stir up some shit. Realizing, perhaps, that he had lost his young band a cover story, he called up his manager and told him that I had been completely unprofessional and called him names and told him to "fuck off" before rudely hanging up on the fledgling rock star, bruising his tender ego.

His manager subsequently rang me up and began reading me the riot act, an interlude that I wasn't willing to tolerate. Saying something to the effect that Chris was full of shit, I told his manager that "I have the tape." You could almost hear the brakes screeching as he backed up the blame train. "You have a tape?" he asked. So I played it for him. He apologized for Chris and later sent me a nifty Black Crowes t-shirt that I later sold on eBay for a few bucks.

But, gentle reader, it didn't end there. Admonished, perhaps, by his more publicity-savvy manager on how to handle the media, Chris wasn't too happy with the experience. Perhaps forgetting who I was, Chris began talking shit around town about me and, to a lesser extent, Gus. When he came into The Great Escape one day while I was hanging around talking with Doyle Davis, Chris and I had a few words and straightened out the disagreement between us (basically, I told him that I'd stomp a mudhole in his ass if he kept talkin' smack about me).

Revisiting the Crowes' first three albums, they hold up well, better than expected, but since they were based on timeless blues-rock and R&B conventions, that's to be expected. That *Metro* magazine cover? We ended up giving it to Robin Trower. We ran a story on the Crowes later, Kath Hansen interviewing Jeff Cease, an infinitely more intelligent and talented musician to speak with....

Chris & Rich Robinson of the Black Crowes

BLACK DIAMOND HEAVIES

Band Members:
John Wesley Myers (vocals, keyboards) (I-III)
Van Campbell (drums, vocals) (I-III)
Mark "Porkchop" Holder (guitar) (I)

Black Diamond Heavies Recordings:

I. You Damn Right (self-produced CD EP, 2004)
1. Hambone
2. Leave It in the Road
3. Big Boat
4. Poor Brown Sugar
5. No Doctor
6. Down Down Down

Comments: Black Diamond Heavies is a garage-blues wrecking crew similar to the Black Keys, another recent Nashville transplant. Myers (a/k/a "Rev. James Leg") was a member of a like-minded blues-rock gang, the **Immortal Lee County Killers**, while Campbell came from the Invisibles. Holder would leave the band after this EP.

II. Every Damn Time (Alive Natural Sound Records 2007, CD)
1. Fever In My Blood
2. All To Hell
3. Leave It In The Road
4. Let Me Coco
5. Poor Brown Sugar
6. Stitched In Sin
7. White Bitch
8. Signs

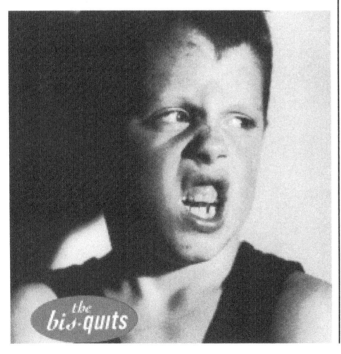

9. Might Be Right
10. Guess You Gone And Fucked It All Up

III. A Touch Of Someone Else's Class (Alive Natural Sound Records 2008, CD)
1. Nutbush City Limits
2. Everythang Is Everythang
3. Numbers 22 (Balaam's Wild Ass)
4. Bidin' My Time
5. Take A Ride
6. Solid Gold
7. Smoothe It Out
8. Make Some Time
9. Oh, Sinnerman
10. Loose Yourself
11. Happy Hour

BLIND FARMERS FROM HELL

Band Members:
Alan McDonald a/k/a Murcell Rancid (vocals, guitar)
Jeff Tatum a/k/a/ Burford St. Pilot (guitar)
Ben Northern a/k/a Nasty Bandana (bass)
Sam Baker a/k/a Punky Bandana (drums)
Hiram Q. Wattage (drums)

Comments: MTSU students playing cornpone metal with plenty of humor; a popular band in its day.

BLOOD OF THE GODDESS

Band Members:
Jeneveve (vocals, guitars, keyboards)
Dave Crocco (drums)
Chris Tench (bass)
Dave Hallum (bass)
Barton Haneberg (bass)
Jim Roberts (percussion)

Comments: Blood of the Goddess contributed two songs ("Not That Screwed Up" and "Animals") to the *Treason Records Sampler Vol. 1* CD. Also contributed the song "The Best Lovers" to *Spin Cycle*, the 1997 NeA Extravaganza CD.

BLUE MILLION

Band Members:
David Meade (vocals, guitar)
Jake Schrader (guitar)
Stephen Tallent (bass)
Scott Miller (drums)

Comments: Changing their name from "Verdant Green," Blue Million is best known for producing the talented singer and songwriter **David Meade**.

BLUES CO-OP

Band Members:
Miranda Louise (vocals)
Warren Haynes (guitar, vocals)
"Dr. John" Jaworowicz (bass, vocals)
"Smokey" Greenwell (saxophone, harmonica)
John Mattick (keyboards)
"Captain Bill" (drums)

Comments: Short-lived blues-rock band that sent **Miranda Louise** on her way to a solo career, and prompted **Warren Haynes** to later form popular blues-rockers Gov't Mule.

THE BOILERS

Band Members:
Ricky Emerson (vocals)
Paul Pearce (guitar/vocals)
Kyle Miller (bass)
Pat Benson (drums)

Comments: Song "Can't Talk To You" appeared on the *City Without A Subway* compilation (1986). They were a good band with a growing local fan base, so I'm not sure why they didn't go further than they did. Ricky Emerson was another PDQ Pizza alumnus, working the Brentwood store.

BOMBPOPS

Comments: Contributed the song "Modern Education" to *Spin Cycle*, the 1997 NeA Extravaganza compilation CD.

BOMBSHELL CRUSH

Band Members:
Michael Clark (vocals) (I)
Denny Smith (guitars, vocals) (I)
Tony Higbee (bass, vocals) (I)
Billy Baker (drums, vocals) (I)
Joey "J.D." Garner (guitar)

Bombshell Crush Recordings:

I. Bombshell Crush (self-produced 2004, CD)
1. One Five Seven A.M.
2. Get Away
3. That Actor
4. Green
5. Reality Crisis
6. Back To Me
7. What's Your Sign?
8. Only In My Head
9. Carousel
10. Long Time Comin'

Band Bio: "In a creatively bankrupt industry dominated by aging post-teen idols, grammatically challenged bling kings, and interchangeably benign faux-punk bands; where A&R men and critics alike scramble to lay claim to the next big thing, Bombshell Crush are a breath of fresh air. Playing with a reckless disregard for achieving IT status, their sound is a unique hybrid of pop, hard rock, punk, and metal."

Comments: Bombshell Crush barely lasted two turns of the calendar before disappearing from the local Nashville scene, leaving behind a single CD and a bunch of shows at local clubs, with the odd foray to Atlanta and even as far as Cleveland. The band pursued a mongrel blend of glammy punk, hard rock, and '80s nerf metal that wasn't half bad, but was hopelessly out-of-time in the jaded early 2000s.

BONAFIDE

Band Members: Bonafide (vocals)

Bonafide Recordings:

I. I Got Next (Southeast Entertainment 2005, CD)
1. 100 Barz
2. Bout Business
3. Can't Do Right

BONAFIDE - BONEPONY

4. Welcome To Cashville
5. Whats Really Good
6. Make You Move
7. It's Hard
8. Killaz & Gangstaz
9. As Good As It Gets
10. Tha Shit
11. Put My Hands On You
12. I Was
13. Hard As Us

Comments: Not much information provided in the liners, but Bonafide was an up-and-comer on the Nashville rap scene that I believe has since disappeared. *I Got Next* shows a young stylist still trying to find his voice; Bonafide ain't no 50 Cent, but he shows promise. The beats here are weak and mostly whack, but Bonafide's rhymes are creative and display a sense of imagery missing from a lot of aspiring rappers. Partnered with the right producer, here's an artist that could make some waves in an otherwise moribund gangsta rap scene.

BONEPONY
Web: www.bonepony.com

Band Members:
Scott Johnson (vocals, guitars, percussion) (I-VII)
Nicolas Nguyen (vocals, guitars, bass) (III-VII)
Kenny Wright (drums, percussion, guitar) (VI, VII)
Kenny Mims (dulcimer, mandolin, vocals) (I, V)
Bryan Ward (guitars, vocals) (I, II, V)
Tramp (vocals, fiddle, mandolin, banjo) (II-V)

Other Musicians:
Chris Carmichael (fiddle, mandolin) (IV, VII)
Ken Coomer (percussion) (II)
Jason Dunaway (bass) (III, VII)
Mickey Grimm (drums) (III, IV, VII)
Craig Krampf (drums, percussion) (IV)
Kelly Looney (bass) (IV)
Bobby Wood (keyboards) (IV)
Bob Wray (bass) (IV)

Bonepony Recordings:

I. Stomp Revival (Capitol Records 1995, CD)
1. Poor Boy Blues
2. Where The Water's Deep
3. Blue Blue Blue
4. P.S.O.B.
5. Right Time To Love
6. Soap
7. Seeds Of Peace
8. Bleeker Street
9. Shrouded In Blue
10. Travelin' Stew
11. Rebecca
12. Feast Of Life
13. Sugar On The Pill

Comments: The band's major label debut left execs at Hollywood and Vine shaking their heads in confusion. Are they a rock band? A country band? Formed by Johnson and Ward in Baltimore in 1989, moved to Nashville in 1991.

Another View: "Scott Johnson, Bryan Ward, and Kenny Mims employ mandolins, fiddles, dobros, and dulcimers on their debut album, which would seem to suggest a traditional country or bluegrass sound. But they wield their instruments as aggressively as if they were electric guitars and howl their lyrics as though they were singing punk rock, so the result is a lively hybrid of old timey and new wave."
– William Ruhlmann, *All Music Guide*

II. Traveler's Companion (Super Duper Recordings 1999, CD)
1. Mountainside
2. Antidote
3. Cowboy Song
4. The Crush
5. Knees
6. Voodoo Banjo
7. Sweet Bye and Bye
8. Fish In The Sea
9. East Texas Rhythm
10. Eyes Wide Open
11. Savanna Flowers
12. Salvation Song
13. Shine On

Comments: Mims is gone, replaced by former **Cactus Brothers** multi-instrumentalist Tramp. Capitol had rejected the band's sophomore album and drop-kicked them off the label. The guys got it together and recorded this superb effort entirely on their own, launching a decade of creativity and great music.

III. Fun House (Super Duper Recordings 2001, CD)
1. Bleecker Street
2. Blue, Blue, Blue
3. East Texas Rhythm
4. Old Song
5. Bayou Sky
6. Banks of Divine
7. I Stand Amazed
8. Everbody Sing
9. What's Inside
10. Feast of Life
11. Salvation Song
12. Sugar on the Pill
13. Heather's Wetter

Comments: As good as Bonepony's first two albums were, the band was even better on stage, so it was only logical that they release a live album to try and capture some of that performance magic. **Fun House** fits the bill, offering up a good selection of songs from the band's back catalog, with lively performances from clubs like Nashville's Exit/In; Evansville, Indiana's Duck Inn; Bowling Green's Kelly Green's; and Scranton, Pennsylvania's Montage Mountain.

Another View: "The unique sound of Bonepony has often been referred to as "heavy metal-bluegrass," but perhaps "mutant folk" might be a more apt description. The band makes a lot of noise for three players, mixing rustic instrumentation and roots music with a hard rock sound and punk rock attitude."

"They've often been (unfairly) relegated to the "jam band" ghetto with Phish, String Cheese Incident, and similar bands, but the truth is that Bonepony has more in common with the legacy of the Grateful Dead than those aforementioned artists. There is a shared love of American music styles, from Appalachian folk and old-time country to blues and bluegrass, for one thing. There is also Bonepony's tendency to experiment musically, taking these traditional musical forms out to the end of the creative gangplank to see what can be accomplished without falling into the waters below."
– Rev. Keith A. Gordon, *All Music Guide*

IV. Jubilee (Super Duper Recordings 2003, CD)
1. Für Kinder
2. Jubilee
3. Whisper
4. My Sunshine
5. Floating In A Glass
6. Mend A Broken Heart
7. Golden Riverside
8. Traveler's Companion
9. Waiting On A Train
10. Summertime Venus
11. Twenty More People
12. Small World

Another View: *Jubilee*, from the word *jubilant*, is a perfect description for the music of Bonepony. The band's three members – multi-instrumentalists Nicolas Nguyen, Scott Johnson, and Tramp – sound truly happy creating their music, a blend of acoustic/electric instrumentation and a combination of a myriad of traditional influences that make for a joyful noise indeed."
– Rev. Keith A. Gordon, *All Music Guide*

Bonepony, continued on page 65....

Bombshell Crush

CD REVIEW: PETE BERWICK'S ONLY BLEEDING

PETE BERWICK
Only Bleeding
(Shotgun Records)

Like many a troubadour before him, Pete Berwick made his way to Nashville in search of fame and fortune. Also like many artists that walked that same road, he ended up returning home years later without much fame and even less fortune. Berwick did all the things expected of an artist in the Music City, playing his songs at "writer's nights" in local clubs at night and working a day job at the car wash while waiting for his big break. He signed a songwriting deal with a storefront publisher and hooked up with a fly-by-night indie label. What seemed like a sure thing, a track placed in the River Phoenix movie *The Thing Called Love*, came to naught when his manager lacked the juice to get the song included on the soundtrack album.

After his Nashville fiasco, Berwick moved back to Chicago, older, wiser and just a little worse for the wear. He gave up music for a while, playing sporadically and writing a few songs. Luckily, the story doesn't end with this tale of dashed hopes and broken dreams. The attraction of the muse is a strong one, and I've personally never met a serious artist who could be kept away from their creative outlet for long.

Berwick gathered a group of grizzled Chicago rock-and-blues veterans to record one song in the studio; they ended up recording *Only Bleeding*, a ten-track reaffirmation of the power of rock & roll, and a fresh start for Pete Berwick. A fiercely independent songwriter and performer who has found that he doesn't need the corporate label system to make a musical statement, Berwick's fourth album is the accumulation of almost a decade of artistic trials and tribulations.

Only Bleeding showcases all of Berwick's various influences and incarnations, the songs mixing rock, country and blues in the creation of a heady musical elixir. "Must Think She Loves Me" and the hilarious "Nuclear Boy" are energetic, punk-tinged rockers while "Cold Steel Gun" is a barroom weeper complete with T.C. Furlong's delicious steel guitar and Berwick's appropriately morose vocals. With the biker anthem "Outsider" Berwick has created a new musical genre – "metallic country" – the song a defiant declaration of alienation that matches Nashville twang with tasty power chords.

The title track is a Dylanesque country blues tune with wonderful vocals, Berwick's mournful mouth harp work and well-placed piano courtesy of Denny Daniels. The album-closing "Standing At The Gates Of Hell" is a lively rocker with brilliant imagery, the story of a poor working class loser who dies and shows up "at the gates of hell" only to find that they won't let him in. It sounds a lot like Jason & the Scorchers – another obvious Berwick influence – but with Berwick's Rodney Dangerfield-like lyrics and dynamic delivery it's a wonderful pairing of roots rock and honky-tonk soul.

It's with "Gotta Get Out Of Here," the centerpiece of *Only Bleeding*, that Berwick hits that once-in-a-lifetime adrenaline O.D. where decades of rage and frustration are expressed perfectly in a three-minute rock song. In the tradition of Eric Burdon's "We Gotta Get Out Of This Place" or Bruce Springsteen's "Jackson Cage," the song is about hopelessness and dashed dreams and, in a more personal vein, the torment of being a talented musician in a land of mundane mediocrity.

When Berwick sings "I got a daytime job, teevee at night, if the boredom don't kill me, then the cigarettes might," he's expressing the fears of every factory worker, slaughterhouse grunt and service industry wage slave who suspects that there must be something more to life. For Berwick, the song itself is an act of transcendence, its performance "getting" him out of here, his tortured vocals and screaming guitar allowing the artist a brief moment of escape. It's a powerful musical moment, a solid example of why most of us started listening to rock & roll in the first place.

Berwick sees the world of human relationships and frailties with a folkie's sensitivity and writes about them with the poetic blue-collar perspective of a Steve Earle or Bruce Springsteen. A gifted songwriter and charismatic performer, Berwick is a true rock & roll survivor, an artist of integrity and vision who never even stood a chance in the industry babylon that is Nashville. *Only Bleeding* offers an eclectic mix of styles that defies industry homogenization to deliver a strong and thoroughly enjoyable musical experience for the listener. Pete Berwick has been singing his songs for a small, if faithful audience for far too long; with *Only Bleeding*, people will be forced to listen. – *Alt.Culture.Guide*, 2002

PETE BERWICK
Ain't No Train Outta Nashville
(Shotgun Records)

A few years back, legend has it, a young punk rocker followed Jason Ringenberg's trail out of Illinois and sojourned to Nashville with guitar in hand. This young man, like so many before him, was looking for fame and fortune in the Music City. He wrote the right songs, worked the right clubs and played the game like everyone told him he should but, tho' not for lack of talent or ambition, he found naught but heartache in the hallowed home of country music.

This young man found a manager, a silver-tongued fool who talked a good game but did little to advance his career. The young man recorded an album full of fine songs that nobody got to hear. After years of trying, he found himself beaten, bruised and battered, chewed up in the gears of a star-making machine that has little regard for talent, heart and soul; pissed off and pissed on, this young man left town and went back home, leaving Nashville that much darker and less interesting a place....

Like too many faithful, Pete Berwick found that there ain't no train outta Nashville. Hundreds of hopefuls flock to the Music City each year, and for every Tim McGraw or Faith Hill that finds fame, there are dozens that return home to Illinois, Oklahoma and points beyond, leaving behind their dreams and a piece of their soul. How many future Hank Williams or Patsy Clines have been denied the city's embrace after spending years traipsing up and down Music Row, how many have given up their musical ambitions in the face of indifference and corporate ignorance?

In Pete Berwick's case, there's a happy ending to the story. Unlike many who give up music altogether after suffering through the traumatic experience of trying to make it…whether in Nashville, New York, Los Angeles or wherever…Berwick refuses to go quietly into that good night. Five years ago, when the urge to create new music became stronger than the beatdown he took in the Music City, Berwick wrote the songs that became *Only Bleeding*. A powerful album that seamlessly mixed rock and country with punk attitude unlike anybody since early Steve Earle or Jason & the *Nashville* Scorchers, *Only Bleeding* was a defiant message that Berwick's Nashville experience may have left him bloodied, but definitely unbowed.

After the release of *Only Bleeding*, Berwick spent a year or so banging it out on the Midwestern circuit, playing smoky clubs and funky honky-tonks before once again retreating from music. However, the muse is hard to deny, and Pete started thinking about the "lost" album that he had recorded back in Nashville in '93, the one that nobody got to hear. Taking it down from the shelf and listening to it with fresh ears and the benefits of hindsight, Berwick decided that it was too good a bunch of songs to let go to waste, and I agree with him.

Ain't No Train Outta Nashville is a brilliant collection of hard-knock tales that reveal the Music City for the provincial small town that it remains in spite of its big city ambitions. These songs are about the lovable losers and hopeless dreamers that flee their one-horse towns every year to go somewhere, *anywhere* else in search of something that will break them free of their lives of quiet desperation. Although written a decade-and-a-half ago, these songs still resonate with truth and beauty and are just as true today, in the face of corporate homogenization and the "American Idolization" of music as they were when Pete wrote them between his shift at the car wash and "writer's night" at some Nashville club. Although the words here apply to many nameless travelers going down that same road, I suspect that they are also more than a little autobiographical.

Ain't No Train Outta Nashville kicks off with "Rebels And Cadillacs," a rowdy rave-up with scorching guitar and honky-tonk piano that brings a traditional edge to this blistering portrayal of musical hypocrisy (perhaps more so than when Pete first sang these words). He decries the MTV star "with a diamond ring and a pure silk scarf, singing his concern about the homeless man," adding "I couldn't help but notice his Acapulco tan." Over at CMT you'll find "more of the same, some talking hat with a common name, singing a song about the poor man's blues, while turning on the heel of his snakeskin boots," the singer boldly declaring that "I don't want to be no rebel in a Cadillac." With this opening song, Berwick has staked his turf, drawn a line in the sand that is pure punk attitude with Hank Williams' twang.

"Six Pack Town" is more than a place, it's a state of mind as well, the sort of place that people try to escape from to "find" themselves. Berwick's description of the town as a "stop and a half on the road from nowhere" is deceptive because although "there ain't nothing going down," it's still home, a place where people know their neighbors and care about their neighborhood. "Six Pack Town" is working class, small-town America, the kind of place that produces soldiers and singers, dreamers and madmen…the kind of place that people have a love/hate relationship with, the kind of place that never leaves you, even when you've left it behind….

"The Years We Left Behind" is one of the most brilliant and moving songs that these ears have heard in nearly 50 years of listening to, and loving music. We're every one of us getting older, and facing down a half-century of frustration, unfulfilled promise and lost opportunity brings with it the tendency to reminisce about "the good old days" that, to be honest, were mostly anything but good. Wise beyond his years, Berwick sings:

"Everywhere I go these days, it seems I always hear;
People talk about desperation, heartache and despair.
The broken-hearted dream that died, the memory from the
past; The good old days, the glory days, the love that didn't
last, And the childhood that disappeared too fast.
Sometimes at night when all is quiet, and I am all alone;
I hear the voice of yesterday through people I have known.
Some are laughing, some are crying, some of them have died.
I always thought the grass was greener on the other side,
I guess that's why I can't kiss the past goodbye…."

"Time doesn't wait for no one," sings Berwick on the chorus, declaring that "it's not patient, it's not kind; it seems to me we see the future only through our eyes so blind," concluding that "we're living in the years we left behind." Pete's insight is both poetic and bleakly realistic – we can't escape our past, no matter how hard we try, and our future is just the sum of the experience and heartache that we've lived through. None of us is unblemished by the past yet, when facing our inevitable mortality, we hang on to those memories like a life raft as the minutes tick by ever more loudly. Berwick addresses these concerns with dazzling beauty:

"When nighttime turns to morning, still I'm clinging to the past.
I want to stop the clock some times, those hands just turn too
fast. I don't want to get old; it's a shame how fast time flies.
If heaven's what we're living for, then someone tell me why,
Why no one, why nobody, wants to die?"

You'd think that after a stroke of musical genius like "The Years We Left Behind," that *Ain't No Train Outta Nashville* would flicker and burn out from lack of energy. No, Berwick has lulled us into a warm, quiet remembrance only to kick us back awake with the jolting "Devil Knows His Name," an eerie, Western-tinged tale of betrayal and escape. If the protagonist of the earlier song finds comfort and solace in his memories, the figure at the heart of "Devil Knows His Name" is trying to outrun the nightmares of his past. Washes of haunted instrumentation flow through the song like a tumbleweed until the guitar explodes and the song fades into an uncertain fate...

The album's namesake, "Ain't No Train Outta Nashville," tells the story of every hopeful songwriter and singer that ever made their way to the Music City in search of something to build a life upon. With the lyrics set to a swinging rockabilly beat, the song's truth lies beneath Berwick's tongue-in-cheek delivery, the words summing up the songwriter's experience. Describing a staggering blur of beer, cheap motels, bad jobs and dashed hopes, he sings, "I play most times for free, and sometimes I just play to eat." There's no way to escape intact, "once you're here, you're here to stay, if you're a songwriter, they just throw the key away."

The hauntingly beautiful "Only Bleeding" ties *Ain't No Train Outta Nashville* with its predecessor and it fits perfectly well on either album as both recordings, in their own individual way, are primarily about the continued chase of fame in the face of constant rejection or, worse yet, lack of recognition. Displaying the same sort of defiance as Dylan's "It's Alright Ma (I'm Only Bleeding)," Berwick's Midwestern drawl sums up the intense loneliness and the darkness felt by every songwriter and poet in the face of indifference.

The song's protagonist is an almost divine figure, shouldering the sins of everyman and offering salvation through his own pain, as expressed by this, and every other song that touches upon the bleak fate that befalls us all, from Springsteen's "Darkness On The Edge Of Town" to Joe Grushecky's "Blood On The Bricks." In the end, however, by forgiving those who would sin against him, the poet triumphs against those who would try to silence his or her words.

Fittingly, *Ain't No Train Outta Nashville* ends with the one-two punch of "Rusted Ball And Chain" and "This Used To Be A Town." Berwick searches for answers on "Rusted Ball And Chain," finding nothing but more questions. He reaffirms his commitment, however – to life, to love, to music – singing "freedom's just another word, if you ain't got a dream. Without a dream, your freedom, it just don't mean anything." And for those who doubt his efforts, he adds, "people try to put me down, and throw me off my track, but I just keep on keeping on, there ain't no turning back." Roaring down the lost highway in that ghostly Cadillac, Berwick is in it for the long run and won't be dissuaded by the obstacles that are thrown in the path of every creative person. While others would give up with a whimper, this singer carries on regardless of the weight.

In the end, the singer does escape, getting out of Nashville only to go home and discover that "This Used To Be A Town." The memories of the past have been betrayed by the unrelenting march of "progress," the kind of small-town development that tears down the past to rebuild every town in the image of every other town. "Time bulldozed it away, built a couple of malls, and they both look the same," he sings, "don't they realize the childhood that died when they tore it all down?" It's an uneasy commentary on the state of America, a sad exclamation mark on the old saying that "nothing stays the same." It's also a down song to end the album on, reinforcing, perhaps, the idea that you can't escape the past, so you may as well embrace it, protect its innocence lest somebody comes to take it away.

      The best album of 2007 was actually recorded in 1993 and, surprisingly, it was so damn far ahead of its time that it sounds as fresh, dynamic and topical today as it would have fourteen years ago; maybe more so. Too rock & roll for Nashville's taste, too country for the coasts, Pete Berwick has nevertheless been on the verge of his "big break" for almost two decades now. Luckily, it hasn't kept him from making great music. ***Ain't No Train Outta Nashville*** is proof that you can't keep a good man down, and if you ain't listening to Pete Berwick, then you ain't listening to shit...

– Trademark of Quality blog, 2007

Bonepony, continued...

V. Rare Cuts, Volume 1 (Super Duper Recordings 2002, CD)
1. Introduction
2. Mad Man Blues
3. Big Dream Blues
4. Waitin' On A Train
5. Fish In The Sea
6. Lady Madonna
7. Travelin' Stew
8. Birds Fly Away
9. Thread Of Life
10. Cowboy Song
11. Body
12. 20 More People
13. - 20. Radio IDs
21. Tramp Grunts

Comments: Collection of miscellaneous Bonepony tracks unreleased anywhere else, including radio IDs and other stuff.

VI. Feeling It (Super Duper Recordings 2006, CD)
1. Home
2. She's My Religion
3. Good News
4. Sweet River
5. Love Ain't Predictable
6. Colour Blue
7. Something Good
8. Lonely
9. Farewell
10. Feeling It
11. Park City Jam

Comments: Tired of Bonepony's grueling 200+ yearly performances, Tramp is gone, replaced by the equally-talented multi-instrumentalist **Kenny Wright**. Whereas Tramp was a great fiddle player, Wright is skilled with string instruments (guitar, mandolin) as well as drums and percussion. A breakthrough album by any measure.

VII. Celebration Highway (Super Duper 2007, CD/DVD)
1. Free (studio version)
2. Cowboy Song
3. Lonely
4. Voodoo Banjo
5. She's My Religion
6. Bayou Sky

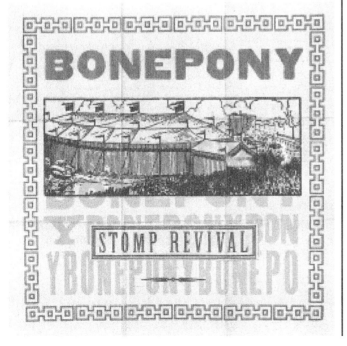

7. Something Good
8. Love Ain't Predictable
9. Half As Much Love
10. Home
11. High Cold India
12. Poor Boy Blues
13. S.O.B.
14. Soap
15. Free
16. Jubilee

Comments: *Celebration Highway* is a wonderful two-disc set that documents a live Bonepony performance at Nashville's Belcourt Theatre from March 2007. The first disc is a DVD of *"Celebration Highway" – The Film* while disc two offers an audio CD of the night's performance.

BONEYARD

Band Members:
Vince Liveri (vocals)
Steve Finney (guitar, vocals)
Terry Hudgens (bass)
Gary Uselton (drums)

Comments: Heavy metal band contributed the song "Crucified By Life" to *What's The Buzz?* 1993 compilation CD. Pretty popular around town for a while....

November 2011 Update: As we were getting ready to publish, Boneyard guitarist Vince Liveri passed away after a brief illness.

I was working with Vince on getting some more information on the band for this section, but it understandably to back seat to his personal situation. Vince was well-loved on the local scene, and will be missed...

BRADFORD BLUES BAND

Band Members:
Bobby Bradford (vocals, guitars)
Kenny Greenberg (guitars, vocals)
Jeff Cipperman (bass)
Paco Shipp (harp)
Bruce Stewart (drums)

Comments: The Bradford Blues Band was the house band at the Rock Harbor Inn over in West Nashville for years. Bobby

Bonepony

Bradford was a solid blues-rock guitarist, while Kenny Greenberg should have been a star. Harpist Paco Shipp has recorded several albums on his own.

The band contributed a song, "Any Love I Can Find," to WKDF's *Street Hits* album, but I couldn't find any other recordings for the band, which is a shame 'cause I remember seeing them perform more than once back in the early 1980s and it was always a lot of fun.

JOHN BRANNEN

Band Members:
John Brannen (vocals, guitar) (I)

Other Musicians:
Clyde Brooks (drums) (I)
Tom Gray (keyboards) (I)
Kenny Greenberg (guitars) (I)
Warner Hodges (guitars) (I)
Dave Kiswiney (bass) (I)

John Brannen Recordings:

I. Mystery Street (Apache Records 1988, CD/LP)
1. Desolation Angel
2. Primitive Emotion
3. The Drifter
4. Shadows In The Night
5. Paradise Highway
6. Dreaming Girl
7. Mystery Street
8. The Wild One
9. Searching For Satisfaction
10. Twilight Is Over

Comments: Born in South Carolina, John Brannen bounced around a lot before landing in Nashville to record this album, which *Billboard* called "a panoramic rock 'n' roll dreamscape of emotions." Working with top-notch axemen like **Warner Hodges** and **Kenny Greenberg**, as well as Tom Gray of Atlanta band the Brains, the album yielded a minor rock hit with the song "Desolation Angel."

Brannen also contributed the song "Madonna Of The Moss" to *Spin Cycle*, the 1997 NeA Extravaganza compilation CD. Brannen has since become known as a skilled outsider songwriter (i.e. he doesn't slum on Music Row) and alt-country singer.

JONATHAN BRIGHT
Web: www.jonathanbright.com

Band Members:
Jonathan Bright (vocals, guitars, bass, drums)

Jonathan Bright Recordings:

I. Radio Free Tennessee (self-produced 2004, CD)
1. Tweaking The Fine Tune
2. Ruin
3. Paralyzed
4. Shine
5. Turn Me On
6. Sleep

Comments: Jonathan Bright kicks ass! The Music City veteran has been a member of beloved local bands like **Swing** and **Vagantis** and recently started a new band called **Defense Wins Championships**. Bright maxed out his credit card and worked with producer **Jay Joyce** to record this incredible six-song EP.

Jonathan pursues a genuine '70s-styled BIG rock sound with lots of guitars and riffs like Van Halen and fat melodies like Cheap Trick, i.e. he's not ashamed to play guitar-driven hard rock the way that it was meant to be played, with intelligent lyrics and solid strong structure. Bright has also done some very cool things with video as of late, creating an uber-cool clip for "Tweaking The Fine Tune," the lead cut from *Radio Free Tennessee*, as well as a tantalizing video for Van Halen's "Hot For Teacher" that is "based on a true story."

THE BUNNIES

Band Members:
Donna Frost (vocals, guitar)
Chuck Allen (guitars)
Todd Andrews (bass)
Tony Frost (drums, vocals)
Johnny Lauffer (keyboards, vocals)
Jeff Van Allen (guitars)
Todd McAlpin (bass)
Rick Federico (bass)

The Boilers

THE BUNNIES - BURNING HEARTS - BUZZKILL

Comments: The Bunnies were the first high-profile band fronted by my old high school friend **Donna Frost** and her younger brother Tony. The band re-formed due to popular demand to celebrate its 25th anniversary, with Donna and Tony joined by guitarist Jeff Van Allen and Donna's former Paper Dolls bandmate Turina Davis.

Donna says: "We saw all of our friends like the Times (later to become Radio One) and the Resistors playing the scene and thought, why not us? We were already playing together. So we threw our hat in the ring and it was much fun indeed! We had a lot of fun in our Bunnie days, but after a few years, Tony and I wanted to go on to other things...he ended up with Richie Owens' next band, the Movement, and I ended up in the Paper Dolls."

BURNING HEARTS

Band Members:
Jean Ann Chapman (vocals)
Bruce Beyer (guitars)
Scott Borchetta (bass) (A1)
Matt Green (drums) (A1)
Kevin Montgomery (vocals) (A1)
Todd Ellis (guitars) (A1)

Burning Hearts Recordings:

A1. Burning Hearts (Melting Records 1985, 7" vinyl)
This Side
1. Can't Get Back

Other Side
2. Life Of Crime
3. Sherry's Eyes

Comments: Former SoCal punk rocker Scott Borchetta ("Scott Rage") came to Nashville in 1981 and, after several years as a bass player for touring country acts, struck out on his own and formed Burning Hearts in 1984 with Ellis and Montgomery. The best-known line-up of the band included former **Invasion of Privacy** heartthrob Jean Ann Chapman on vocals.

Borchetta eventually went into the business end of music and currently runs the indie label Big Machine Records, whose biggest star is country heartthrob Taylor Swift. As we're getting ready to publish, word on the street (well, Music Row) is that Borchetta is getting ready to cash in on his work and sell Big Machine to a deep-pocketed major label.

Another View: "Burning Hearts' three-song EP on Melting Records will melt your turntable with its high-powered, intensifying rock 'n' roll. The energy in Burning Hearts is projected by singer Kevin Montgomery, bassist Scott Borchetta, guitarist Todd Ellis, and drummer Matt Green..."
– Debbie Burrows, *The Metro*, 1986

BUZZKILL

Band Members:
Brooks Phillips (vocals, guitars)
Paul Kelvington (bassist)
Shelton Willians (drums)

Comments: Hardcore, metalcore, whatever you wanna call it from the "lets-go-crazy" halcyon days of the alt-rock 1990s, the band fronted by former **F.U.C.T.** guitarist Brooks Phillips.

Comments: "Combining the power of '70s-era metal like Black Sabbath with the passion of hardcore punkers like Big Black, Nashville's own Buzzkill is a band that successfully balances underground integrity with widespread appeal."
– *Bone Music Magazine*, January 1994

The Bunnies, circa 2010

BONEPONY
Traveler's Companion
(SuperDuper Recordings)

It's safe to say that Nashville's Bonepony is, perhaps, the most unique band that you'll ever experience. Comparisons don't do them justice when there's no band on earth that these ears have heard that sounds anywhere close to the original mix of rock, folk, country, bluegrass and blues that these guys have created. The folks at Capital Records evidently agree, dumping the band after a single fine album that the label obviously had no idea how to market. Undaunted, Bonepony founders Scott Johnson and Bryan Ward regrouped with new member Tramp on fiddle (ex-Cactus Brothers), the trio recording and releasing the excellent *Traveler's Companion* on their own SuperDuper Recordings label.

Hewing closer to traditional music forms than even many alt-country bands are willing to risk, Bonepony nevertheless rock with the enthusiasm and energy of any half-a-dozen heavy metal bands. Kicking out the jams with an unlikely mix of fiddle, mandolin, banjo, dobro and other folksy instruments and featuring excellent vocal harmonies, the raw spirit of the music serves to support the finely-crafted songs on *Traveler's Companion*. Original songs like the sweetly spiritual "Sweet Bye And Bye," the country-flavored "Savanna Flowers" or the witty and charming "Fish In The Sea" are smart, engaging affairs that tend to grow on you with each hearing, regardless of the sparse nature of the backing instrumentation.

Bonepony called upon some high-octane friends to assist in making *Traveler's Companion*, among them Lucinda Williams, Reese Wynans, Brad Jones and Wilco's Ken Coomer. The band's production works quite well, their light touch emphasizing the songs rather than any individual agenda. Since the band had complete creative control of the project, they released the disc in a package composed of industrial hemp, using soy ink for the printing, a smart choice in my book. If you're tired of vacuous pop artists and cookie-cutter FM radio rock bands, treat yourself to something different and check out Bonepony. *Traveler's Companion* is proof that you don't have to be signed to a major label to produce major league music.

BONEPONY
Feeling It
(Super Duper Recordings)

It should come as no surprise that *Feeling It*, Bonepony's fourth studio album, should open with a song like "Home." Although the band's roster has shuffled a bit through the years, revolving around frontman Scott Johnson, the current line-up of Johnson, Nicolas Nguyen and Kenny Wright represents decades of experience and tens of thousands of miles on the road. Grizzled veterans of countless local and regional bands, the trio has earned every right to be tired, fed up with the music business and worn down by the rigors of the road. Yet "Home," at once both spry and weary, is a celebration of both those left behind *and* the brotherhood of the road, "singing in a traveling band." The song offers the usual mixed genres of Bonepony's sound, an overall bluesy feel complimented by a bluegrassy stomp and strum.

Concerned with relationships – with family, with friends, with fans – *Feeling It* is an affirmation of the band's faith in the power of music. Relationships are hard to manage when you spend 100+ nights a year on the road, and the value of a family waiting for you increases with every mile traveled. Several songs here touch upon the subject, dissecting it from different perspectives. The guys are clearly reconciling the wanderlust of their chosen profession with the need for roots and romance. Whether directly addressing the issue, as with the Southern-fried funk of "She's My Religion" or the mournful, high lonesome sound of "Colour Blue," or indirectly, as with "Good News," the question rises to the forefront of the album. The wonderful "Something Good" is classic Bonepony, sparse acoustic instrumentation matched with infectious vocal harmonies in the creation of a complex love letter that would translate well to both rock and country radio (if the medium wasn't run by idiots).

The high point, in my mind, of *Feeling It* is the defiant "Farewell," a recommitment to the muse that calls all three bandmembers, a casting off of the ghosts of the past and the negative energy that would drag them down. Sung by Johnson with a deliberate hesitancy, the song brings the album full circle, where all roads lead back home. It jumps directly into the triumphant title song, the band finally succumbing to the siren of the stage, balancing family and fans with the magic of the music. It's only appropriate that the album closes with "Park City Jam," a brief yet energetic reprise of "Home" with whoops and hollers and handclaps that punctuate the joy and jubilation that is the root of *Feeling It*.

Bonepony's music, for those unfamiliar with the band, is an eclectic mix of rock, country, folk, blues and bluegrass. It's a sound as old as the Appalachian Mountains and as alien to today's trend-driven, focus-group-created-frankenrock as you could possibly be. This is music for the heart and soul, not for corporate marketing. Bonepony's sound translates well to the stage, where the acoustic instrumentation and the band's dynamic performances can spark a fire hotter than a Delta roadhouse on a Saturday night. With no disrespect to former fiddle player Tramp, the addition of multi-instrumentalist Kenny Wright to the trio was a smart move, widening the band's capabilities even as they strip these songs down to the basics. *Feeling It* will both satisfy longtime fans and earn the band new fans, the album's honesty and energy an antidote to the restless dissatisfaction felt by many music lovers.

BONEPONY
Celebration Highway
(Super Duper Recordings)

A live performance by Nashville's Bonepony is always a treat – as close to a true Bacchanalian celebration of life, love and music as you can put on in public and avoid getting arrested these days. Thus, it is only fitting that the second live album of the band's lengthy, eighteen-year career should be titled *Celebration Highway*, 'cause this hard-working trio has earned its well-deserved reputation as a live band by hitting the highway and performing some 200+ nights annually for years on end. Along these many miles, they've attracted an ever-growing audience of loyal fans every bit as rabid as those you may find at a Phish, DMB or Widespread Panic show.

Celebration Highway was recorded on both audio-and-videotape during a March 2007 performance at the Belcourt Theatre in Nashville. For this landmark show, Bonepony beefed up its normally muscular three-man wrecking crew of Scott Johnson, Nicolas Nguyen and Kenny

Wright with friends like fiddle-player Chris Carmichael, bassist Jason Dunaway and drummer/percussionist Mickey Grimm. The addition of these backing players fattens the band's typically raucous sound and allowed all of the Bonepony guys to come up front now and then to showcase their multi-instrumental talents and natural charisma. Sounding unlike any band you've ever heard, Bonepony's unique hillbilly stomp is a hard-hitting, energetic blend of Appalachian folk, roots rock, Piedmont blues, East Tennessee hill country Gospel fervor and reckless country soul.

Performing live, frontman Scott Johnson's vocals are an impressive mix of Texas twang, Mississippi Delta drawl and a fast-paced, tongue-twisting, gnarled Southern auctioneer patois that rivals the verbal skills of any street-bred rapper. Guitarist Nicolas Nguyen, a veteran of local Nashville hard rock outfits like Prodigal Suns and the Social Kings, is a vastly underrated string-bender that also holds his own on banjo, fiddle and mandolin. Drummer Kenny Wright, another familiar face around town for his work with Scarlet, Prodigal Suns and the late Max Vague's band, as well as Nguyen's partner in the Social Kings, is another of Nashville's unheralded talents, a powerful presence behind the kit but also a skilled guitarist and mandolin player. All three guys lend their voices to create joyous waves of harmony.

A two-disc set with one audio CD and a full-length DVD, the audio portion of *Celebration Highway* offers up highly-spirited performances of fifteen well-drawn Bonepony songs pulled from across the band's four studio albums. It's fitting that Johnson wears a Ramones t-shirt throughout the show, as his band brings a fervor and energy to its performances that rivals any punk band's restless edge. The Bonepony guys just give themselves up to the music, and much like true believers caught up in the holy spirit at a church revival, they just go where the music and the audience takes them.

It's the songs on which Bonepony hangs its collective hats, though, and beneath the electricity of these largely-acoustic tunes lays a deceptively complex lyrical heart. The spry, energetic "Home," from the band's recent *Feeling It* album, is a celebration of both those left behind and the brotherhood of the road, the joy of "singing in a traveling band." A high-octane hoedown, "Voodoo Banjo" is an instrumental raver that Johnson's growling vocals skate and slide across like a New Orleans jazzman hitting a high note. "Bayou Sky" is a beautiful, country-styled song with soulful vocal harmonies and enchanting string work...and I could go on and on, 'cause in truth, it's all good here. The material presented on **Celebration Highway** is road-tested, tried-and-true and will rock your stereo speakers nearly as hard as it did on the stage.

The DVD disc offers *"Celebration Highway" – The Film*, a concert documentary of the Belcourt Theatre performance intercut with band interviews. Capturing the band's explosive onstage vibe, the professionally-shot, albeit low-budget film also does a fine job of showing Bonepony's relationship and interplay with its audience. The DVD also includes bonus features like the "Day In The Life" mini-docu, a video biography of the band, and music videos for their songs "Lonely" and "Sweet River," the former an acoustic-based sagebrush-blues that expounds on the joys of bachelorhood even while bemoaning the lack of female companionship, the latter a folksy conceptual love-goes-sour tale of young parenthood and coming-of-age far too soon.

Bonepony is one of Nashville's lesser-known treasures, a talented and creative band that, while perhaps unfairly pigeonholed as an alt-country or Americana outfit, nevertheless rock with the energy and passion of any punk or metal band. *Celebration Highway* is a solid documentary, both a souvenir for the faithful fan and a fine introduction to the charms of this deserving band for any newcomer looking for honest, sincere and entertaining music. There's plenty of room under the Bonepony tent for everybody and, as Scott Johnson says, "music should lift you up," perfectly expressing the band's musical philosophy when he adds "if it doesn't make you smile, then it's missing something." With *Celebration Highway*, there's plenty for both the band and its fans to smile about.... – *Cashville411* website, 2008

INTERVIEW: PETE BERWICK

During the years that he was in Nashville, Pete Berwick worked as hard as any local rock band to get his music heard. Pete worked in a car wash on Lower Broadway during the day, haunted clubs and writer's nights after dark. Since leaving the Music City a few years ago, Pete has released a wealth of music...cowpunk, Americana, whatever you want to call it...some of it recorded in Nashville, some in Chicago, but always with his indominable spirit driving the tracks...

Well, let me ask you, we got this tape recorder going here, what got you interested in music in the first place?
Well, folk was a big influence. My brother had this old beater guitar that was handed down from my grandmother and it was kind of his guitar and I'd sneak away when I could and pound on it and he'd get pissed. My earliest influences I can remember, of course, the country music that my mother would listen to would be like...oh, what's that song...way down in the land of cotton, George Jones and that sort of thing, the old AM country stations, but then primarily Bob Dylan.

Dylan, definitely, I tried to emulate him, and then later on, John Prine. When I was about 10 or so, *Sticky Fingers* was a major influence. *Sticky Fingers*, I wore that cassette tape out when I was a kid. They had songs on there just every one of them was great, so definitely the Stones and Dylan and the old country.

My folks kind of forced piano lessons on me, so I learned those fundamentals...I hated it, but I had piano lessons from kindergarten through junior high, and I was getting pretty good at that, learning waltzes and classical and polkas, all that stuff, but I didn't give a crap about it and so as soon as I was old enough to quit piano lessons, I did, and went back to the guitar 'cause piano wasn't cool, you couldn't wear it around your neck.

I know that you ended up getting into punk...
I was really big on Lou Reed and the New York Dolls: this was before the Ramones came along and I thought Lou Reed was the coolest and, of course, there was Iggy Pop. I was very aware of the New York punk scene even though I really didn't have any of the records, somehow I knew what was happening out there. Somehow, I really can't remember whether it was through *Creem* magazine or just hearing stuff here and there, and so I was dabbling in that, trying to write punk songs, of course, very badly.

Then around 1978, I saw the Ramones for about $2 at the Ivan Hall in Chicago, it just totally fuckin' saved my life. I was like 'okay, yeah, that's right, that's what I'm trying to do, that's what I've been trying to do,' and these guys are out there doing it. It hit me the same way it did Chrissie Hyde, and the Clash, and the other fans who went and saw them and the rest is history. It was just great and I really cut my teeth on that.

Let me ask you a couple of questions kind of not really involved in the interview, but do you remember a band called the Swingers up in Chicago?With Rick DiBello?
Oh yeah. They did a version of "Leaving On A Jet Plane" and my band the Generics, we also did a version of "Leaving On A Jet Plane," and to this day I can't remember whether we did it because I heard them do it, or if it was just coincidence, but they did a punk version of "Leaving On A Jet Plane." God, I can't believe that you remember those guys.

What made you decide to go to Nashville?
I just knew I had to go, I'd been mulling over it for years. I knew that if you wanted to catch fish you, had to go to the pond. When I was younger, I think when I was about 20, I almost got in my car one day and drove to California, but I probably didn't have the gas money to make it.

I never really even considered New York, so I tried out Nashville, especially with my style of music. I thought it would be the obvious place, so it really was a no brainer...

Do you remember what year you moved down there?
I think that it was 1990, '91...it was right before the Gulf War.

So you played in different punk bands during the 1980s, and gradually evolved into what you were doing or...?
I would say around late '70s was when I started. I put together my first punk band, and I played guitar for a band called The End and we toured Wisconsin and up into Minnesota.

That band broke up, they basically broke up because the guitarist and the singer were fighting over a microphone, and I went solo and I started doing folk and cover songs. I really started writing the roots-rock stuff around 1985.

Of course, I'd heard some Jason and the Scorchers and I'd been writing stuff in that vein anyway. When I heard Jason and the Scorchers, it was to me like the first time I heard the Ramones. It was really an inspiration to keep doing it, it validated it.

The first time I heard Steve Earle sing, I thought 'I got to get my ass to Nashville' 'cause I was really beating my head trying to do this stuff in Chicago because sports bars and all these places out here, they want to hear Styx and REO Speedwagon. I'd get thrown out of clubs singing this stuff, club owners were asking 'what kind of shit is that you're doing? Where's the cover song?' I knew I had to get down there [to Nashville], so yeah, it was about 1991.

When you got to Nashville, was it everything you'd expected?
It was fun; I wouldn't trade it for anything! I really went there with a chip on my shoulder. I think every generation of

people that go down there they think they're the ones that are going to just take over the city and change the way Music Row thinks. It was everything I thought it would be, I think I got what I expected. I don't really know what my aspirations were.

One thing I did do when I got down there was I wrote my ass off. I wrote a lot of crap, but then out of the crap came a lot of good. I think it took a good five years to realize, you gotta be yourself because when you try to write for what Music Row wants, at least me personally, I write some shit....

When I was down here, it was Garth's world, you know [Garth Brooks]. That "Garth mania," I probably couldn't have picked the worst time to go down there, try to get anybody's attention. They didn't need it, suddenly everybody was selling a million records and Music Row was just having a feeding frenzy, they only wanted to sign people with hats.

What kind of approach did you take when you came to town? What did you think, how did you get started trying to make a name for yourself?
I heard a lot of advice like everybody does, got me a job at Opryland Hotel cleaning pots and pans in the kitchen and then I graduated to the car wash. I worked in some factories and stuff, tried to get a living going and then I did every writer's night I could.

It's easier to make friends in Nashville so you make some good friends, and then I started co-writing with some people. Then I put together the Nashville Underground, I tried to play every where I could with that but as you know, Nashville's not exactly full of clubs.

Do you remember who was in the Nashville Underground band?
It was Mark Stoner, I was playing drums, Danny Walker played on bass...the first guitarist they had, I can't remember his name, James something, but yeah Tim Gunn, who has played with Hege V, George Hamilton V. I spent some time on Music Row, where I really pissed away time with Bitter Creek Records. I'd go down and we'd sit around for half a day just talking about all the great things that were going to happen.

He had you on a management and a record deal?
Yeah, you know, he wanted to publish everything I wrote... fortunately I kept that from happening.

That was lucky....
Yeah. You know, it was talk, talk, talk, talk, and I could have been spending time checking out other possible contracts and I'm spending all my time with him, so the good part of my time down there it was tied up with him. He did co-produce this record with me.

He's the one that brought together the players and hooked up the studio time, I financed most of it with the money I got from "Ain't No Train Outta Nashville," from the River Phoenix movie, then he got me on that Charlie Daniels benefit down in Florida so that was one real thing he made happen. But there was just a lot of wasted time.

One thing I learned is that you have to have a plan, just go down there and start swinging wild and knocking on doors wildly and just hoping somebody sees you play somewhere. I don't know, maybe it works like that for some people, but I don't think that's my destiny.

How did you get the song in that movie, The Thing Called Love*?*
It was one of those long shots, and I think it's the reason people play these open mics, but I was doing the Bluebird Café one night, and I'd always go there reluctantly, but I felt inclined to go whenever I could.

Dermott Mulroney, the co-star with River Phoenix, was actually hanging out there. He liked the song, approached me, and I met him at the Holiday Inn over a couple beers we talked about it. He got a copy of the tape and he got it right to [director] Peter Bogdanovich and got it in the movie.

So you recorded the Ain't No Train Outta Nashville *album while you were in Nashville, how come it never came out at the time?*
We recorded it and it basically just sat on his [the manager's] desk. He ran out, he had no money…you have to package it and master it and all that, that costs thousands of dollars. I would go in there and ask 'what are we going to do now, what are we going to do now,' and I remember one day I said, 'Bo what's the plan,' and one day he just said, 'I don't have a plan.'

What he was basically waiting for was for me to finance the rest of it…I didn't fuckin' have it and if I did, you're the record company…to this day, I don't even know if the session players got paid for that. It became clear to me that it wasn't going anywhere. I didn't have the money and their staff you know, I would go in and I'd see some artwork lying around like he was going to try to put something together for a jacket, but that's the furthest I ever saw it.

Around that time, Tim Goode wanted to put together a project because he was trying to push himself as a producer, so he wanted to get me signed to the Scorchers' label. I did that project with him and Craig Wright, who played with Steve Earle and Billy Jo Shaver.

I kind of knew I had to get away from Bo because I don't know, I had aspirations that maybe I'd have luck with that project. I kind of had two things going on at the same time, a

conflict of interest you know. I just walked, I just went and said 'you know what, I want out of this deal' and it was kind of ugly. He basically swung at me and I left.

Did he ever even try to shop the album to the labels on Music Row?
He was trying to sell the project to somebody for like $1,000 or something so he could get out of town. I don't know whether he ever got a taker, though.

So what made you decide to release Ain't No Train Outta Nashville*?*
I'm patient with my recordings; I'm not one of these people that just wants to deal with two records a year. I think you can bore people with too much music, a less is more kind of thing. I'm patient with my writing and everything and so, five years later, I'm getting the bug again, I want to do another album.

I'm making a list of the songs, "Devil Knows His Name," do that one, and "Rebels and Cadillacs," and I'm thinking 'wait a second, I already have some of these songs recorded.' I almost forgot about it, to be honest with you, and I didn't listen to it, I just shelved it 'cause I was so just pissed off and frustrated…I had left Nashville and it was on the shelf.

INTERVIEW: PETE BERWICK

Of course, I kept it, I didn't just toss it and I thought 'wait a second.' I listened to it and I thought, it didn't sound dated to me, that was the test. It still sounded damn good. I listened to it again and again, and again, and I think you know what, I'm just going to put this one out, that'll save me some money.

And the songs are good. Like you said, there's no point in them going to waste.
The thing is, although there was also a version of "Only Bleeding" that we did which I totally...I've totally rewritten "Only Bleeding" because the original version on the *Ain't No Train* sessions was long, it was one verse too long, and I tweaked it through the years and that version ended up on *Only Bleeding*.

So I replaced the *Ain't No Train*'s version of "Only Bleeding" with the updated one from *Only Bleeding* and that made ten songs and I thought well, I'll make it an eleven song album, so I added "I Ain't Him" from the Tim Goode, Tom Comet, Ted Wright session and I was a little concerned with mastering and everything, but I thought the guys did a pretty good job.

So what sort of response did you get for Only Bleeding*? I know you played around a lot...*
The reviews were good, they really were, there was hardly a bad review...there were a couple clunker reviews, but most of them were very good.

I know you played around the region at that time.
Yeah, it was actually dead, I mean it was probably about a year and a half two years, close to two years we played almost every weekend, mostly biker bars and shithole dives. We played pretty relentlessly, a lot of empty rooms in a lot of cases, but we got some good gigs too.

What year did you leave Nashville?
It was towards the very end of 1995. They say it takes five years to make it in Nashville, I gave it five years.

I guess you were pretty burned out by the time you left and went back to Chicago?
I'd had it, you know, I bought seven acres out in Charlotte, just west of Dickson. Jason [Ringenberg] was living out there at the time, and he had a farm out that way and I had my mobile home moved out there and me and my wife, we just kind of like doing the "Mayberry" thing and that was a lot of fun...got to run around naked, burn things, and shoot off my guns and just kind of saw what it was like to just live in the boonies, just remove myself and didn't drive back into Nashville for any more projects.

I dissolved the band, I wasn't talking to my manager anymore. I got a job at the Nashville Wire Factory and just started living a very simple existence for a year and a half. It was kind of nice, it was kind of nice not to be chasing that carrot; I just was working, coming home, having a couple beers, watch some TV, sit out on the back porch just surrounded by woods and acreage and just reflect.

I did a lot of reflecting, God what am I going through. It was really a radical time in my life actually, I mean it wasn't, I didn't know where the fuck I was going from there, and then when I came back to Chicago for my grandmother's funeral, it was then I made the decision to move back.

Basically, a lot of it was that I was sick of being broke, I was sick of living hand to mouth. We weren't starving, but....

But you weren't getting rich, either....
No, I thought I knew if I came back, and coming back was a good move because I started earning better money, which I would need to put out my next album, which was *Only Bleeding*.

What was that like that, how did you get the itch to do that album? I remember we talked back then, and what was the lead up to that?
It never left me; it's like I became possessed with it, that was always my dream. I was back in Chicago for six years and making a living as an entertainer, doing comedy and singing telegrams and shit shows and what not, but there was something missing.

One of the things I've learned is you can start making gobs of money but – and I always wanted to kick everybody's ass who ever said this – but money does not buy happiness.

Money enables you not to have to worry about money, but just sitting around thinking, well I make a lot of money now, so I'm happy...I need it to rock, and there are these quality songs in me, but damn it, I got to put out there.

What's to say about making a record...when you perform, it's really a grind. I do hundreds of shows a year, I do about 400, between kid's shows and my music shows, and staying on top with everything I do, and it's almost like it's not real.

When you record a record...I could get hit by a truck tomorrow and at least that record is a memorial, my songs live on, and now with the computer data thing, they end up all over the freaking place, your music is going to live eternally.

I realized since 9/11 happened, that really did it for me...I thought 'what the fuck,' it shook me up like it shook up everybody, and it made me realize 'you got to do what you got to do now, there ain't no denying it.'

I saw America retreat, I saw people cancel their vacations, I saw people decide not to go out to dinner…I thought 'what a bunch of pussies, what are you doing, you should be doing just the opposite!'

It really pissed me off to see people doing this stuff. So I decided I was going to do just the opposite, I was going to go into the studio and record an album. There's this guy at the time who used to come and manage me, an old friend of mine, he was like 'oh no, no, it's not a good time for music.'

It was just all the negative voices were in the air, 'who's going to buy your album, nobody is spending now, we're going into a recession.' It really couldn't have been a worse time to do it, and that's why I decided to do it…

CACTUS BROTHERS - BOB CAMP PROJECT

THE CACTUS BROTHERS

Band Members:
Paul Kirby (vocals, guitar, harmonica) (I, II)
Will Goleman (guitar, banjo, vocals) (I, II)
John Goleman (bass) (I, II)
David Kennedy (drums, percussion) (I)
Sam Poland (pedal and lap steel guitar) (I)
Tramp (guitar, fiddle, mandolin, vocals) (I, II)
David Schnaufer (electric & acoustic dulcimer) (I)
Jim Fungaroli (steel guitar, dobro) (II)
Johnny Tulucci (drums) (II)

Cactus Brothers Recordings:

I. The Cactus Brothers (Liberty Records 1993, CD)
1. Sixteen Tons
2. Crazy Heart
3. Our Love
4. Devil Wind
5. Sweet Old-Fashioned Girl
6. Blackberry Blossom
7. The Price Of Love
8. Big Train
9. Swimmin' Hole
10. One More Night (With You)
11. Bubba Bubba
12. Fisher's Hornpipe

Comments: What began as an acoustic, more country-flavored side project of **Walk The West** members Paul Kirby and the Goleman brothers took on a life of its own as the Cactus Brothers began to appeal to both country *and* rock audiences. Signed to Capitol Nashville President Jimmy Bowen's revived Liberty Records imprint, the band received a big push and supported their end of the deal by touring constantly, playing several hundred shows each year.

II. 24 Hrs., 7 Days A Week (Capitol Nashville 1995, CD)
1. This Love's Gonna Fly
2. Lodi
3. 24 Hrs., 7 Days A Week

Music Man

Don Mooney

318 Natchez Court • Nashville, Tennessee 37211
(615) 833-7000

4. Highway Patrol
5. A Woman's Touch
6. Secret Language
7. Love Me Too
8. He Never Got Enough Love
9. You're The Reason
10. Redhead
11. Chains Of Freedom

Comments: Fast-forward a couple of years and you have an entirely different story. The legendary label exec Jimmy Bowen was either gone or on his way out; Liberty Records became just another trademark owned by EMI, and the Capitol Nashville staff had no idea of what to do with the Cactus Brothers, who obviously rocked too hard for a label dominated by Garth Brooks. They subsequently stuck the band with Randy Scruggs who, despite his family pedigree, I feel was an unsympathetic producer. Without the unique instrumental talents of Sam Poland and **David Schnaufer**, the Cactus Brothers sounded like a lot of other country-rock bands and within a few months of this CD release, the band had broken up. Tramp went on to play with **Bonepony**.

THE BOB CAMP PROJECT

Band Members:
Bob Camp (vocals, 18-string guitar) (I)
Tim VanHook (vocals) (I)
Jim McKell (keyboards) (I)
Wailin' Wood (harmonica) (I)
Mike Miller (sax) (I)
Michael "Moses" Scrivner (auto-harp) (I)
Roger Sampson (guitar) (I)
Don Mooney (guitar, keyboards) (I)
Scott Elliot (bass, vocals) (I)
Bones Lamer (percussion) (I)
Don Kendrick (drums) (I)

Bob Camp Project Recordings:

I. The Bob Camp Project (Weenie Head, no date, cassette)
Side One
1. D.U.I. Over Y.O.U.
2. December Wind
3. Paranoid Schizoid Freak
4. Venture Adventure
5. Getting' High On Socrates

Side Two
6. Can't Keep Me Down
7. Livin' Fast (On Borrowed Songs)
8. Tap Dancin' Clown
9. It Was A Party
10. Katie

THE CACTUS BROTHERS
The Cactus Brothers
(Liberty Records)

The Nashville rock & roll scene of the mid-1980s was an exciting and invigorating tonic of youthful innocence and energy, with unbridled creativity matched by awkward inexperience. One of the many bands working to define this scene and garner world-wide critical acclaim (albeit without commercial success) was Walk The West. One of the area's most popular outfits, these country-influenced rockers hung up their spurs at decade's end. Their achievements included an excellent self-titled album for Capital (which has become a bona-fide collector's item) and the creation of an innovative hybrid of country and rock which owed as much, thematically, to Johnny Cash as to the Byrds and Gram Parsons.

The nucleus of that band has been reincarnated as the Cactus Brothers, and both sides of the rock/country equation are much better for it. Their self-titled Liberty Records' debut manages to capture the intimacy and acoustic-oriented style which made the Cactus Brothers a live draw equally as popular as their predecessors ever were. This is a band awash in instrumental talent, from master dulcimer player David Schnaufer to dobroist Sam Poland, from the multi-talented Tramp to the Goleman Brothers, Paul Kirby and drummer David Kennedy...and they make the most of the talent they've got.

The music here is a hybrid of country roots and rock spirit, with covers like Merle Travis' "Sixteen Tons" and the Everly Brothers "The Price Of Love" performed in a manner unlike any you've ever heard. Traditional instrumentals such as "Fisher's Hornpipe" and "Blackberry Blossom" showcase the band's musical abilities while the originals fall somewhere in between. Whereas singer/songwriter Paul Kirby comes across like a stone cold country crooner on material like "Bubba Bubba" or "Crazy Heart," songs like "Devil Wind" and "Big Train" are strongly reminiscent of Walk The West's best stuff. All in all, *The Cactus Brothers* is a solid album, a fine introduction to a highly talented group of guys who have the vision, the skills and the hard-won experience to achieve whatever they wish. – *The Metro*, 1993

INTERVIEW: THE CACTUS BROTHERS

Introduction: As told by the story below, the Cactus Brothers were formed out of one of Nashville's most popular rock bands, Walk The West. The Cactus Brothers became much bigger than its alter ego, touring the world as the Music City's shaggy musical ambassadors and setting several milestones along the way. A super-heavy touring schedule (200+ nights annually) eventually took its toll and the band broke up, leaving behind two excellent CDs and hundreds of electric live performances. Multi-instrumentalist Tramp continued to make waves as a member of the Nashville trio Bonepony. This Cactus Brothers interview was conducted with damn near the whole band at local photographer Libba Gillum's house in Brentwood, Tennessee and originally ran in the **Tennessean** *newspaper's* **T-Bone** *entertainment insert, June 2, 1995.*

During the past few years, country music has become a big business, the hottest game in the entertainment world. Although the streets of Nashville's "Music Row" may not be paved with gold, there are a few new Mercedes parked alongside the row. Set aside for a moment, however, the platinum albums, the snakeskin boots and the ever-present Stetson hats and one thing remains: the relationship between the artist and the audience. That's what has made country music successful, and that's the way that it will always be.

Roadwork is the key to creating the bond that exists between the country artist and the fan, and there's no substitute for slogging it out on the road, night after night, playing for anyone who'll listen. Nashville's legacy was built upon the efforts of folks like Hank Williams – Senior *and* Junior – Johnny Cash and George Jones, criss-crossing America's rural landscape in busses, vans and beat-up old cars. Most of today's country superstars have paid their dues, putting their time in on the road. It should come as no surprise, then, that the next Nashville act perched on the brink of stardom is also its hardest working. The Cactus Brothers wouldn't have it any other way.

INTERVIEW: THE CACTUS BROTHERS

The Cactus Brothers have toured constantly since the 1993 release of their self-titled Liberty Records' debut, performing over 250 shows since January of that year, playing in some 40 states, Canada, Mexico and five European countries. "We've been to Europe three times in the past year and a half," says Cactus Brothers fiddle player Tramp. "Twenty-two border crossings without getting arrested," he adds, laughing. Their two dozen foreign performances during '94 places the band among some heady company, as only Willie Nelson and Garth Brooks brought country music to more overseas audiences.

With the many overseas dates that the band has played during the last couple of years, it's only natural that they would have collected a number of road stories. One event sticks out above the others, however. "It was our final show on the European slot, and Tramp sets his bow on fire," says Kirby. "I'm doing the old Blue Oyster Cult thing where I'm down to my last string and I'm riding it and the place is going berserk. We ended up hooking up with a biker gang in Norway called the Prowlers whose clubhouse was an old World War Two Nazi bunker."

The band's hometown serves to bring them a fair amount of recognition in Europe. "You say that you're from Nashville and they go..." says Tramp, giving the thumbs up sign. "It's an honor to be from Nashville," says Kirby. Adds bass player John Goleman, "we go around, we're ambassadors for Nashville. We talk it up...it's a great place to live." As a nod to its overseas status and popularity, the Cactus Brothers will be the first act from the Music City to travel to the former Soviet Republic of Estonia, the Cactus Brothers the only North American act to play the 3rd Annual Country Picnic in the Tallinn, the historic Estonian capital.

The Cactus Brothers originally began as a side project for members of the popular mid-1980s Nashville rock band Walk The West. After touring the country in support of a self-titled album for Capital Records, the band came home wanting to try something different. "We came back into town looking for some action," says Kirby. The idea of the Cactus Brothers had been born a few months previous. "Paul, John

The Cactus Brothers

and me played at a funeral, acoustically, and that was the beginning of the Cactus Brothers," says Tramp, "then everybody in Walk The West joined in."

The new band began appearing at several Nashville area clubs, playing "songs that we had written off to the side that we'd never used in the Walk The West format," says Kirby. Tramp adds, "the Cactus Brothers was a great outlet for us to play in Nashville without wearing out our Walk The West name. It was only for fun that we were doing it, but we started drawing really big crowds." More country-oriented than their alter ego, they nevertheless rocked just as hard. It wasn't long before the popularity of the Cactus Brothers matched that of Walk The West.

It was about this time that Walk The West began having problems with their West Coast label. "They were kind of looking for more pop, Duran Duran or something...I don't know what," says bass player John Goleman. "They'd hear our tapes and say 'what's this fiddle in here?' They had a lot of trouble with it."

"I hate anybody who hates the fiddle," says Tramp. "And you can quote me on that!" he adds, laughing. "Everybody kept saying, though, 'you're too country,' because we'd play stuff with country influenced vocals and lyrical content and with country instruments on top of the big beat rock and roll stuff. After the Cactus Brothers thing started taking off, started getting a lot of attention, we said 'we'll just say that we're country, we'll call ourselves the Cactus Brothers and basically do the same thing.' Then we turned around and got signed by the same label that dropped us."

The Cactus Brothers recorded their debut album with noted Nashville producer Allen Reynolds. "Reynolds really wanted to cut it live in the studio," says Kirby, and the resulting album went a long way toward capturing the band's raw live energy on disc. The critically acclaimed album spun off a number of singles and three videos, including an inspired cover of the classic "Sixteen Tons," with a video of that song winning a prestigious Bronze Award at the Worldfest video competition in Houston.

For its second album, the band wanted to present songs that were slightly less raucous than on their debut. "We tried to be a little more friendly to radio," says Tramp. Recorded with producer Randy Scruggs, the album – which has been delivered to Liberty and awaits a scheduled release date – includes the expected Cactus Brothers mix of fiery originals and well-chosen cover songs. Former John Mellencamp drummer Kenny Aronoff played drums for the band on the album, with former Stevie Ray Vaughan keyboardist Reese Wynans also contributing musically.

"For this record we went in a lot more prepared," says Goleman. "Working with Randy Scruggs, he came to a few rehearsals, and we really tried to hash it all out. We just recorded it all on a little microphone in the middle of the room and when you listen to that, you can figure out your arrangements." The album showcases a mature, confident band with an incredible chemistry. Material ranges from a splendid cover of the classic Creedence Clearwater Revival song "Lodi," complete with the sorrowful punctuation of a steel guitar and Kirby's appropriately bittersweet vocals, to the honky-tonk rave-up of "Highway Patrol" and the instrumental "Redhead," with Tramp kicking out some mean fiddle riffs and the entire band jamming funky, country-style, with just a touch of traditional Celtic sound thrown in for balance.

By not being a straight rock band like Walk The West, it's freed the band to play as they like, incorporating a myriad of influences and musical possibilities into their sound. The members of the Cactus Brothers are all talented multi-instrumentalists, providing the band with a depth and dimension unthought of by other bands. The current Cactus Brothers line-up of Kirby, Tramp and Goleman, as well as banjo player/guitarist Will Goleman, steel guitarist Jim Fungaroli and drummer Johnny Tulucci, allows the band to create whatever music they care to. "It's really a great thing for a musician, to be in this band, the versatility of the music that we get to make," says Kirby.

The new album hasn't even been released yet and the Cactus Brothers are already looking ahead to the next one. "We've got a whole lot of new songs, already," says Kirby. "Wrapping up this record gave us the freedom to write a whole bunch of new stuff." Regardless of what may happen with the upcoming album release, the band will continue to do what they've been doing for the past couple of years: go on the road and play.

"We're just grateful to be making some music," says Kirby. The band is happy to be signed to a label and to be able to be on the road. "You rarely even get one shot in this business," says Goleman, "there's so many people, especially in this town, who are trying to get to just the place that we've gotten to." Concludes Tramp, "this is our third shot. We just want to sell enough records to keep ourselves on the road, playing for people."

THE CACTUS BROTHERS
24 Hrs., 7 Days a Week
(Capitol Records Nashville)

The Cactus Brothers shook up their creative roster quite a bit for *24 Hrs., 7 Days a Week*, the band's sophomore album. Sam Poland and dulcimer wizard David Schnaufer were gone, as was drummer David Kennedy. The band added steel guitarist Jim Fungaroli and drummer Johnny Tulucci and carried on with pretty much the same sound that they had built their audience and reputation on, a high-energy blend of roots rock and traditional country.

24 Hrs., 7 Days a Week benefits from the even-handed production of fellow musician Randy Scruggs, who brought the band's natural rowdy inclinations to bear on both original material and covers alike while also managing to add a slight commercial sheen to the band's rough edges. Singer/songwriter Paul Kirby's original songs are stronger and more expressive than much of his previous material; cuts like "A Woman's Touch" and "Secret Language," a duet with Matraca Berg, mine a familiar romantic vein in a lively and lyrically intelligent fashion.

The Cactus Brothers offer a pair of red-hot covers here, delivering a spirited performance of the Creedence Clearwater Revival favorite "Lodi" while the band's honky tonk roots shine brightly on a rave-up reading of Red Simpson's classic "Highway Patrol." Producer Scruggs adds some choice six-string work to fill out a handful of songs, assisted in the studio by drummer Kenny Aronoff and keyboard player Reese Wynans.

However, it was multi-instrumentalist Tramp who was the band's secret weapon, his fiery fiddle elevating songs like "You're the Reason" and the title track above the generic country-rock finding favor in Nashville in 1995. When Tramp

leads the entire band through the rocking instrumental "Redhead" you realize that, unlike many country bands during the mid-1990s, the Cactus Brothers were no studio creation, but rather a working band of talented musicians.

24 Hrs., 7 Days a Week proved to be a swan song for the Cactus Brothers, a lack of commercial success and too many nights on the road taking its toll on the bandmembers.
– Rev. Keith A. Gordon, *All Music Guide*

CHRIS CARMICHAEL

Band Members:
Chris Carmichael (vocals, violin, viola, cello, strings)

Chris Carmichael Recordings:

I. Chris Carmichael Project (Warner Chappell Music demo)
1. It Comes And Goes
2. Cool And Baby Blue
3. Something In Common
4. Wasn't It Love

Comments: Carmichael is another of Nashville's underrated talents, a skilled catgut strangler that can play a fiddle like nobody's business. Carmichael led his own band, **15 Strings** for a while, was a member of **Prodigal Sons**, played on the lone **Social Kings** album, and has lent his talents to a score of local and national recordings through the years.

Another View: "Some might consider the violin to be an odd instrument to front a rock & roll band, but in the hands of virtuoso Chris Carmichael, it's an axe every bit as deadly as any guitar could ever be. Former frontman of the popular Nashville band 15 Strings, Carmichael is a talented multi-instrumentalist – if it's got strings, he can probably play it – a fine vocalist, and an inspired songwriter."
– Rev. Keith A. Gordon, *Bone Music Magazine*

ALISA CARROLL

Band Members:
Alisa Carroll (vocals) (I)

Other Musicians:
Sam Bacco (percussion) (I)
John Gardner (drums) (I)
Kenny Greenberg (guitars) (I)
Byron Hagan (bass) (I)
Tony Harrell (piano) (I)
Byron House (bass, keyboards) (I)
Mars Lasar (keyboards) (I)
George Marinelli (guitars) (I)
Taylor Rhodes (guitars, keyboards) (I)
Brian Sutton (guitar) (I)
Danny Torroll (guitars) (I)

Alisa Carroll Recordings:

I. Then & Now (Mysterium Records 1999, CD)
1. Ophelia
2. Mind's Eye
3. Die To This World
4. Mother's Bed
5. He's Coming Back
6. Weeds
7. Little Sister
8. Bones Of A Bird
9. Immaculate

THE CARTER ADMINISTRATON

Band Members:
Todd Anderson (guitar, vocals) (I-III)
Ryan Ervin (guitar, vocals) (I-X)
Andy Willhite (bass, vocals) (IV-X)
Todd Kemp (drums, piano, vocals) (I-X)

Carter Administration Recordings:

I. Fuck Off, I'm Listening to the Carter Administration
(self-produced EP, 1999)
1. Spare the Rod, Spoil the Child
2. Nightmares
3. You Will Not Be Unfamiliar With the Back of My Hand
4. The Bomb-Ass Singles

II. High On Voting (self-produced EP, 1999)
1. Hot Sexxx Bikini Contest
2. Chris Andrews' Babies
3. Tickle Me Emo
4. Don't You Like My Balls?
5. U Throw Like A Girl
6. Mike, Your Girlfriend Sucks
7. Shitmachine

III. Do I Still Look Good? (self-produced EP, 1999)
1. Tons of Trouble
2. Le Jeu Sens Fait

3. Kinder, Gentler Motherfucker

IV. Better Ford Start Packing, the Carter's Are Coming
(self-produced 2000, CD)
1. A.L.I.M.O.N.Y.
2. Math is Hard
3. Tickle Me Emo
4. Carter 8, Chappaquiddick 1
5. Pity List '86
6. Goin' Out
7. Gunfight at Valentine Saloon
8. Roll Mama Over
9. Complain and Complain and Complain
10. Workin' for T & A
11. Belmont Boulevard
12. 54 40s or Fight
13. EZ Duz It

V. Two Man Advantage (self-produced 2001, CD)
1. A K-Car Named Desire
2. Hey Little Brother
3. Second Helping
4. El Pinko
5. Me and My Friends
6. On the Lam
7. Carolina
8. My Vocabulary
9. Payin' the Dues

VI. All Talk, No Liver (self-produced 2003, CD)
1. Carter 8, Chappaquiddick 1
2. El Pinko
3. On The Lam
4. A Kinder, Gentler Motherfucker
5. Kentucky Is Ohio's Alabama
6. Hey, Little Brother
7. My Vocabulary
8. Second Helping

VII. World Champions of the World (self-produced 2003, CD)
1. A K-Car Named Desire
2. The Shakes
3. Tickle Me Emo
4. The REM Speedwagon
5. Workin' Overtime

VIII. Pony Up! (self-produced 2004, CD)
1. The Bomb-Ass Singles
2. Liquor Store March
3. Witchfinder General
4. It's Not Rocket Surgery
5. 54 40s or Fight!
6. Tomorrow's Whiskey Today

IX. Air Guitar Force One (Theory 8 Records 2005, CD)
1. Cocaine Summer Splash
2. Heavy Machinery
3. Oxycontinental
4. Seasoned Intimidator
5. Little Kings
6. Deuteronomy 3:16
7. Petty The Fool
8. Keep Your Wife Off My Hands
9. Emission: Impossible
10. Air Guitar Force One

X. God & Country (self-produced CD, 2006)
1. Carter 8, Chappaquiddick 1
2. Evil is the Way
3. Don't Mess With Tennessee
4. Pretend You're Invisible
5. A Kinder, Gentler M*therfucker
6. Kentucky is Ohio's Alabama

Comments: Released as a free give-away to the band's fans while they record their second album for Theory 8, *God & Country* was distributed at shows and shops like Grimey's.

CASUAL WATER

Band Members:
Holly Gross (vocals, keyboards) (I)
Kevin Tetz (vocals)
Alan Powell (guitar) (I)
Pete Winders (guitar)
Scott Kale (bass) (I)
Gus Valen (drums) (I)
Jeff Shainberg (vocals, guitar)

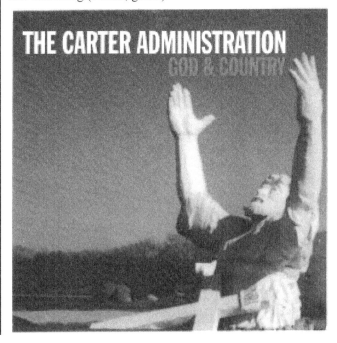

Casual Water Recordings:

I. Casual Water (self-produced 1994, cassette)
1. I Can Fly
2. So Hard To Find
3. Bigger Picture

Comments: Single-sided cassette, produced by Ed Spoto and Casual Water. An earlier Casual Water line-up, with vocalist Tetz and guitarist Winders, contributed the song "Upstairs" to the *Major Potential #1* 1991 compilation CD.

CATAWOMPUS

Band Members:
Douglas Gery (guitar, vocals) (I-IV)
Darren W. Stafford (vocals) (I-II)
Christopher Howell (guitar) (I-II)
Burton Lee (bass) (I-II)
Scott Easley (drums) (I-II)
Jason Whitmore (vocals) (III)
Ruben Garces (drums) (III)

Catawompus Recordings:

I. ...Well, It's About Time (Halcyon Music 2000, CD)
1. Ain't But Life (Too Short For That)
2. Sunday Morning
3. Jeannie
4. The Hill
5. Blush
6. Alright Alright
7. Carolina

8. Green
9. So Many Times
10. In Time
11. Ain't No Thang
12. Song Sung Yesterday

Comments: Catawompus kind of slip in at the edges of my guidelines for the book, barely qualifying as "Nashville" or "underground." Unabashedly a "Southern Rock" band, it's a safe bet that none of the city's alt-rockers have ever heard of Catawompus.

Formed by guitarist Douglas Gery in 1994 in Muncie, Indiana, the band plugged away at the Southern rock 'n' grits circuit for a few years before relocating to Nashville in '97. Since then the band has recorded three CDs and toured with the likes of the **Screamin' Cheetah Wheelies**, Molly Hatchet, Jackyl, and Great White, among others.

II. The Woodpile (self-produced CD, 2003?)
1. Forget It All
2. Hard
3. Heartland
4. Slam Bam
5. There Goes My Baby
6. Ain't But Life (Too Short For That)
7. Jeannie
8. Blush
9. So Many Times
10. Ain't Got The Blues
11. Carolina
12. Song Sung Yesterday
13. Black Hills
14. Jacobi Road
15. Nuthin' Fancy

III. The Slam Bam Jam (self-produced CD, 2003?)

IV. It's Spelled...C.A.T.A.W.O.M.P.U.S. (Halcyon Music 2005, CD)
1. Shot Of Love
2. She's The Kind Of Woman
3. Broken
4. W.O.M.P. Radio
5. Ain't Got The Blues
6. Belle Donna
7. Veins
8. Hard
9. Mean Women Blues
10. The Doctor
11. Alabama Daredevil
12. Forgive It All
13. Goodbyes

CAESAR BROWN
Web: www.caesarbrown.com

Band Members:
Tyson Lee (vocals, guitar) (I)
John Smith (guitars) (I)
Mark Sloan (guitars, keyboards) (I)
Josh Taylor (keyboards) (I)
Daniel Lewis (drums, percussion) (I)

Caesar Brown Recordings:

I. Caesar Brown (self-produced CD, 2008)
1. Music Row
2. Queen of the South
3. O Baby

Comments: The band's self-titled EP displays an uncanny mix of 1970s-styled Southern rock and classic rock vibe.

CELEBRITY TOAST & JAM

Band Members:
Jeff Keeran (vocals) (I-III)
Spot Allison (guitars, vocals) (I-III)
Don Godwin (bass, vocals) (I-III)
Ross Lester (drums) (I-III)

Celebrity Toast & Jam Recordings:

I. Vol.I (self-produced cassette)

II. Vol.II (self-produced 1992, cassette)
1. Lovesick
2. Do You Breathe
3. Everybody Loves You
4. Bloodbath
5. This Must Be The Place

Caesar Brown

Comments: Single-sided cassette distributed by the band at their frequent live shows around town.

II. Large (SureFire Records 1993, CD)
1. Cats & Dogs
2. Rock In My Shoe
3. Everybody Loves You
4. Hot
5. Do You Breathe
6. Lost Sheep
7. Brainwash
8. The Man With The Bone In His Head

Comments: I worked with several Celebrity Toast & Jam band members at Mosko's on Elliston Place, and they were a lively bunch, to be sure. They were convinced of their impending stardom, which I guess is not a bad thing for a rock 'n' roll band, and when it became obvious that Nashville was not a suitable launching pad for their inevitable success, they up and relocated lock, stock and barrel to Los Angeles.

This CD came out after the band moved and received distribution in both the U.S. and the U.K. The band was never heard from again. Allison went on to join Memphis rockers the Generics, vocalist Jeff Keeran is, as of this writing, playing with Murfreesboro's, Spike And Mallets and S.J. and the Props.

Another View: "CT&J blend together an original hybrid of pop, funk and reggae with jazz overtones, an ill-defined mix which defies categorization and grows on the listener like a large, overzealous dog…"
– Rev. Keith A. Gordon, *R.A.D!,* July 1994

CHAGALL GUEVARA

Band Members:
Steve Taylor (vocals) (I)
Dave Perkins (guitar, vocals) (I)
L. Arthur Nichols (guitar, vocals) (I)
Wade Jaynes (bass) (I)
Mike Mead (drums) (I)

Chagall Guevara Recordings:

I. Chagall Guevara (MCA Records 1991, CD)
1. Murder In The Big House
2. Escher's World
3. Play God
4. Monkey Grinder
5. Can't You Feel The Chains
6. Violent Blue
7. Love Is A Dead Language
8. Take Me Back To Love Canal
9. The Wrong George
10. Candy Guru
11. I Need Somebody
12. The Rub Of Love
13. If It All Comes True

Comments: One of a handful of Nashville bands that could have broken big internationally, Chagall Guevara had the good (mis)fortune to have been signed to the MCA label at a time when the label absolutely, positively had no frickin' idea what to do with a rock band. Band members once told me that the label had yet to release the album in England went they went overseas to tour...

CHAPEL OF ROSES

Band Members:
Chris Kelly (vocals, guitar)
Houston Greer (guitars)
Mike Rutherford (bass)
Colin Parker (drums)
Frank Yancey (bass)
Mindy Harrison (keyboards)

Comments: Chris Kelly writes about Chapel of Roses, "we did a big show w/Actuel at Roosters. It was very trendy at the time to do posters printed at Hatch Show print, so we commissioned one for the show. My grandmother had a print of woman that looked fairly Gothic to me, and I asked the Hatch Show wood cutter to make a copy of that picture. A lot got lost in translation, and the result made the poster look like the concert was featuring a Ms. Actuella Jones. Actuel's leader tried to "new wave" it up by spray painting random lines on the posters, but it was a lost cause. Fortunately, the show at Roosters was a lot better than the poster."

"We toured all over the southeast during the summer of 1985, if I remember correctly…40 watt club, 688, the usual spots during that time. We tried to release a 12 inch single w/Neo Records, but somehow that didn't really work out very well. We played a lot during the fall of '85, then I got the urge to go to college. Ka-blam! That was the end of Chapel of Roses. The rest of the fellas moved on to the band Swing."

MARSHALL CHAPMAN
Web: www.tallgirl.com

Band Members:
Marshall Chapman (vocals, guitar) (I-II)
Michael Dospapas (guitar) (II)
Robert Jetton (guitar)
Jeff Smith (guitar) (II)
Tom Comet (bass) (II)
Willis Bailey (drums) (II)

Marshall Chapman Recordings:

I. Me, I'm Feeling Free (Epic Records 1977, LP)

II. Jaded Virgin (Epic Records 1978, LP)
1. Turn The Page
2. The Island Song
3. You're The One For Me
4. I Forgot To Put The Music On
5. A Thank-You Note (Thank You, Hank)
6. I Walk The Line
7. Why Can't I Be Like Other Girls?
8. Give It Away
9. You Asked Me To

III. Marshall (Epic Records 1979, LP)

Comments: Chapman began her career as a country-rock artist with an emphasis on the "rock" side of the equation. Her three albums for Epic received critical raves, and the **Al Kooper** produced *Jaded Virgin* was picked for many year-end "best of" lists. Chapman has maintained a long career as a successful songwriter and niche performer, veering more in the country direction as the years have passed. Her early club band included Texas wildmen **Robert Jetton** and Tom Comet of the **Sluggers**. I've only listed Chapman's "rockier" first three albums here, 'though everything she does is worth hearing.

True Story: Back in 1978, the Ramones were absurdly booked into the Municipal Auditorium for a show. When the date only sold 500 or so tickets, the band found itself inexplicitly added to a Marshall Chapman showcase at the Exit/In. Chapman and her band rocked harder than they ever had to keep up with the fast-paced Ramones' sets. Meanwhile, Thom King and I and a couple other *Take One* magazine staffers (Rick & Kim Hull) were attending the show on Epic's dime, drinking beer and wine and, in the Reverend's case, later dancing with parking meters on Elliston Place. Thirty years after the fact, and I still won't talk about the party after the show, so don't ask, OK?

CHARACTER
Web: www.myspace.com/character

Band Members:
Dave Paulson (guitar) (I, II)
William Tyler (guitar) (I, II)
Eric Williams (bass) (I, II)
Ryan Norris (keyboards, guitar) (I, II)
Scott Martin (drums) (I, II)
Luke Schneider (theremin, pedal steel) (II)

Character Recordings:

I. a flashing of knives and green water (Set International Records 2002, CD)
1. detroit, 1972
2. letter from a sailor
3. colonel blimp
4. theme from "starkweather"
5. chinese skycandy
6. a flashing of knives and green water

II. we also create false promises (Fictitious Records 2004, CD)
1. what you are in the dark
2. lakeview annex
3. progressive democrat
4. passionate gun love
5. die in a woman's lap
6. while clamming in new jersey
7. don't tell winston
8. in nine
9. get handsome
10. flag is out
11. quality

THE CHERRY BLOSSOMS
Web: www.thecherryblossoms.com

Band Members:
John Allingham (vocals, guitars, harmonica) (I)
Peggy Snow (vocals, guitar, kalimba, spoons) (I)
Laura-Matter Fukushima (bass, tambourine) (I)
Allen Lowrey (drums, percussion, mandolin) (I)

The Cherry Blossoms, continued on page 88...

Marshall Chapman & band, early 1970s

INTERVIEW: CHAGALL GUEVARA

A lot has been said, some of it good, some of it not so good, about Nashville's so-called "alternative" music scene. Although it's true that the Music City has produced a number of talents, among them Jason & The Scorchers, The Questionnaires, Bill Lloyd, Aashid Himmons and Raging Fire, to name but a few, the majority of the hundred and one bands plying their trade on the streets and in the clubs of our fair city rigidly fall into a handful of tired stylistic genres of Rock and Roll.

True "alternatives" are few and far between, and are often shunned by the close-knit and elitist local music cliques. Every now and then, however, a band will come along whose fresh style, musical integrity and brash originality defies categorization and cuts across any such artificial boundaries to appeal to a cross-section of local music fans. Chagall Guevara is just such a band...

The story of Chagall Guevara is that of an "overnight-success" that only took the members a lifetime to accomplish. "We have all been kicking around the music business since the day it began," states Chagall guitarist Dave Perkins. "We've all played various, sundry roles within it which have little or no bearing on what we do today."

CHAGALL
GUEVARA
with
rockfish

FRIDAY, NOV. 15
AT 9:00 PM

328 PERFORMANCE HALL

$1.00
(18 & OVER)

THIS CONCERT
WILL BE
RECORDED
LIVE FOR
A FUTURE
MCA
RELEASE

Chagall Guevara was formed when the members, says Perkins, "met in California working on different projects and became buds, buddies...comrades, if you will, and we'd threatened or joked with each other about putting a band together. As it turned out, we all came to a juncture, a point in time where we were all available. We found ourselves by the road, hitchhiking in the same direciton, so we said, 'let's see if we can catch a ride together'." "No one would pick us up, by the way," adds guitarist Lynn Nichols, laughingly, "so it was a long walk."

The embryonic band decided to base themselves in Nashville, for a variety of reasons. Says Perkins, "I had moved from New York back to Nashville, where I had lived before I had gone to New York. I had a recording studio in my house here. So the plan unfolded that we would do it in Nashville for that and some other reasons."

Adds Nichols, "we felt like this was a good place to be outside of the music industry, away from New York and Los Angeles. Steve and I were already living in L.A. and didn't feel that it was a good environment to be in...it's not a great place to develop as a band. You're too close to the marketing aspects of the industry and many of the bands out there are affected by that."

The band had done some writing together in L.A. before moving here in February 1989, but once arriving, quickly began the task of forging a credible live band. "We wanted to play live," says Steve Taylor, the main voice behind Chagall Guevara. "Before anybody had seen us we wanted to have played a fair number of times, we wanted to feel like a live band. We weren't really interested in record company types coming to see us until we felt that the band was really together live." Another benefit was Nashville's club scene and the city's proximity to the center of the country. "In L.A.," says Steve, "where do you play unless your uncle has a thousand bucks to put the money up to play the Roxy? From Nashville, within four hours or so you have eight to ten major cities you can play in, and we felt that was important for a new band."

Chagall Guevara's first shows were in Bowling Green, Kentucky and in Nashville; they soon branched out into the Mid-South area, opening for various bands and building a loyal following of their own. "We tried to open up for a lot of bands that we thought were great bands," says Perkins, "and we got in front of some of their people and, I don't necessarily know all of the reasons, but the word just seemed to grow."

"One of the things that helped," Perkins continues, "was that the second night that we played in town, we were offered a record deal. I think that created a buzz within Music Row, and I think that, if you're a band on the street, once the labels come sniffin' around, I think that people naturally get curious and come out to see what's going on." Chagall's show-stealing appearance at the Nashville Entertainment Association's 1990 Extravaganza helped to further interest in the band.

Chagall Guevara signed with MCA Records in March of 1990. "We went through the signing thing," says Perkins, "and we got three solid offers and one that was real interested, but we told them that it was too late. We went through the agonizing roll of the dice of who to sign with and went with MCA primarily because of the people that we met there, and we felt that they didn't have anybody like us and we felt that they had their sights set on breaking bands."

The result is Chagall's recently released self-titled debut. Perkins, Nichols and Taylor, along with bassist Wade Jaynes and drummer Mike Mead, recorded the disc at Franklin's Bennett House studio. "We wanted to record the record in Nashville because we wanted to be a part of the scene, we felt it was important as a contribution from our belief in the music scene here that we take a stand to do the record here."

"Our approach on the record," says Taylor, "was to take the sonic ambiance of that house...there's a lot of big rooms, a victorian-styled mansion, and to not use the same set of digital boxes which tend to get used no matter what kind of record that you're making. So even though this is a five piece band, we did it on all forty-eight tracks in order to catch all of these different ambiances. When we actually mixed the record, we didn't use any digital reverbs at all, to try to give the record a different sound."

"It's gotten to the point where everyone uses the same tools in the recording process," says Perkins. "You listen to a really good country record, it sounds just like a good-sounding rock record, which sounds like a good-sounding Jazz record, texturally and spatially. What we wanted to do, we worked really hard on the creation of our songs, nit-picking and pulling them apart, and we wanted to carry this over into the recording of them."

Chagall Guevara, the record, is a solid, sizzling slab o' sound, as unique in its musical dynamics as it is in its style and substance. Sounding perfectly at home incorporating disparate elements of jazz, funk and soul into their compelling rock 'n' roll maelstorm, Chagall Guevara have created a sincere and exciting debut, a disc which is totally unlike anything the Music City has ever produced.

"We wanted to put something that was honestly us on tape," states Nichols. "So many bands are disappointed when they make their first record...coming out of the studio saying, 'well, it's not quite what we are live.' That happens more often than not. Since we place such a premium on playing live, we are a live band, not a computer band or a band on paper, we have the same energy, not a record that was overproduced and layered with overdubs."

The band succeeded in their goal, delivering a disc which captures the experience that is Chagall Guevara live, that is, an inspired and individualistic sound that offers the listener a choice of thirty years of musical styling. "There's a lot of different styles on the record," says Perkins. "I guess we have unspoken boundaries...I don't know that we've ever said, stylistically, that too much of that is not enough...the

point is, that in describing the songs, we tried not to paint ourselves into a corner." Every song is a three-way collaboration between Perkins, Taylor and Nichols, thus drawing upon the talent, experience and the knowledge of all three musicians.

Early response to the recording has been positive and encouraging, and a video for the disc's first single, "Violent Blue" was recently shot in a large cavern near McMinville. In attempting to be the first band to *really* break out of Nashville on a national scale, Chagall Guevara have a very good opportunity to capture the brass ring which has eluded so many other local artists. They did it their own way, with no compromises, and they did it by offering something that was completely different from anything Nashville had ever heard before...   – *The Metro*, February 1991

THE CHERRY BLOSSOMS - CHINA BLACK

Cherry Blossoms, continued...
Chris Davis (drums, vocals, kazoo) (I)
Chuck Hatcher (guitar) (I)
Taylor Martin (mandolin, ukulele, vocals, kazoo) (I)
Aaron Russell (various guitars, kazoo) (I)
Beth Matter (washtub bass, kazoo) (I)

Cherry Blossoms Recordings:

I. The Cherry Blossoms (Apostasy/Black Velvet Fuckere/
Breaking World Records/Consanguineous/Hank the Herald
Angel Recordings/Yeay! 2007, CD)
1. The Mighty Mississippi
2. Amazing Stars
3. A Love of My Own
4. Rocks and Stones
5. The Wind Did Blow
6. Rockin' Rocket Ship
7. Golden Windows
8. Clam Stand Theme
9. The Rising Tide

10. Charlie Prim
11. I'm Going to the Promised Land
12. Dolphin Song
13. Godzilla
14. Glow Jesus Glow

Comments: The Cherry Blossoms are self described as "Middle Tennessee's finest anarchic post neo-skiffle collective specializing in kazoo-exotica." Allen Lowrey, who I went to Franklin High School with, played in **Lambchop**, while Aaron Russell was a member of the **Frothy Shakes**.

Another View: "This Nashville collective long shunned the notion that music is something to be consumed, preferring the communal experience of the live show. John Allingham, Peggy Snow and/or Laura-Matter Fukushima, Allen Lowrey, Chris Davis, Chuck Hatcher, Taylor Martin, Aaron Russell, Beth Matter have been playing as the Cherry Blossoms for almost 15 years, making loose folk that sounds like a combination of Harry Smith and Sun Ra. Finally, seven years after laying songs to tape, they got around to releasing their debut album this summer (with the help of six different labels), and it's easily the most unapologetically joyous recording I've heard (and enjoyed) in some time.
– Otis Hart, *Dusted* webzine, January 2008

CHINA BLACK

Band Members:
Doc Ferszt (vocals) (I)
Elisha Hoffman (guitars, vocals) (I)
Jeff Faudem (bass, vocals) (I)
Gordon Stokes (drums, percussion, vocals) (I)

China Black Recordings:

I. A Little On The Strange Side (self-produced CD, 1993)
1. Sedrik
2. Slave
3. Screaming Out Your Name
4. Town Fool
5. Truth
6. To Be With You
7. I'm Not Your Jesus
8. Break On Through
9. Sweeter Than You Think

Comments: Back in the day you would see Doc Ferszt around town everywhere when China Black was coming up through the clubs in Nashville, especially down on Elliston Place and the West End area. The band became pretty popular in a short period of time, their rise fueled by both a dynamic live presence and this uniformly hard-rocking CD. They lit out for L.A. to find fame and fortune and were never heard from again. The *All Music Guide* web site confuses Nashville's China Black with the British techno duo of the same name, and their review of *A Little On The Strange Side* talks about songs that aren't even on the CD...and they fired me? Ferszt, Faudem and Stokes – who had first gotten together while students in Israel – would form the band Lesser God in Los Angeles after China Black broke up.

BILLY CHINNOCK

Band Members:
Billy Chinnock (vocals, guitars, keyboards) (I, II)

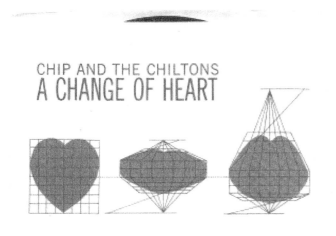

Billy Chinnock Recordings:

I. Rock 'n' Roll Cowboys (Epic Records 1985, LP)
<u>Side One</u>
1. Love Is Blind
2. Restless Hearts
3. Baby, I'm a Man
4. Somebody's Gonna Break My Heart
5. Men on the Line

<u>Side Two</u>
6. She's a Bandit
7. Down at the Bank
8. Livin' on the Edge of Heartbreak
9. Just Can't Help Who You Love
10. Rock & Roll Cowboy

II. Learning to Survive in the modern age (CBS Associated 1987, LP)
<u>Side 1</u>
1. Take No Prisoners
2. Like A Hurricane
3. Young Hearts On Fire
4. Desperate Men
5. Just A Matter Of Time
6. Last Summer

<u>Side 2</u>
7. Somewhere In The Night
8. Pretty Little Wild One
9. Another No Win Situation
10. The Boys On The Avenue
11. Since You've Been Gone

China Black

BILLY CHINNOCK - CHIP & THE CHILTONS

Comments: Bill Chinnock was a founding member of the late 1960s Asbury Park NJ music scene that spawned Bruce Springsteen, Southside Johnny Lyons, and Little Steven Van Zandt, among others. Chinnock's early bands included future E Street Band members Danny Federici and Garry Tallent.

Chinnock moved to Maine in the early 1970s and played up and down the east coast throughout the decade, before moving to Nashville in the early '80s. The two albums listed here are those Chinnock recorded while living in Nashville. Since they were largely recorded elsewhere, I haven't listed any individual musicians, although *Rock 'n' Roll Cowboys* was produced by Music Row legend Harold Bradley, and local resident John Kay of Steppenwolf played bass on the sessions.

CHIP & THE CHILTONS

Band Members:
Chip Chilton (vocals, guitars) (A1, I-II)
Greg McMillan (bass) (I-II)
"Micro" Dave Wilkins (drums) (A1, I-II)
Rick Rowe (vocals) (A1)
Bruce Bossert (bass) (A1)
Jay Jones (drums)
Derek Green (drums)

Chip & the Chiltons Recordings:

Singles/EPs

A1. A Change Of Heart (Propaganda Unlimited 1983, 7" EP)
Side 1
1. Kickstand Up
2. Woman I Know

Side 2
3. Hey Baby
4. Lagg Too

Albums

I. Where's My Cat? (self-produced 1986, cassette)
Side A
1. Next State Line
2. Last Taboo
3. Do You Really Believe
4. And The Moon Grew Smaller
5. I Like Your Sweater

Side B
6. She Said Yes
7. Woman Of The 80's
8. Don't Worry About Me
9. To Joe
10. Little Whitney

II. What's Wrong? With This Picture? (Mean Note 1987, LP)
Side One
1. Peter Gunn
2. Lori Called
3. Government Inspected
4. 8 Days To The Promised Land
5. Route 66

Side Two
6. One More Nail
7. 3 Feet Off The Floor

Chip & the Chiltons, continued on page 92...

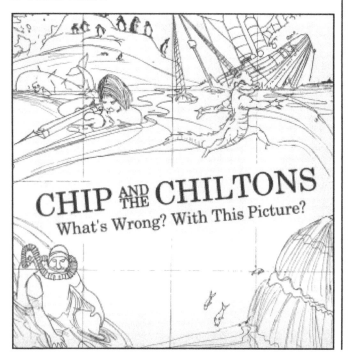

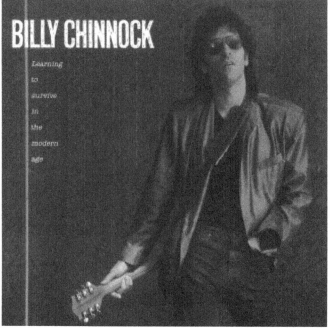

While thumbing through the current issue of *Rolling Stone*, a small but disturbing story caught my eye. Alongside the tragic tale of Boston vocalist Brad Delp's suicide was a (much) shorter piece about the death of Billy Chinnock. A rock & roll lifer whose career spanned Asbury Park, New Jersey; Nashville, Tennessee; and Portland, Maine; Chinnock sadly took his own life on March 7th, 2007 after a long bout with Lyme Disease.

Chinnock launched his career on the Asbury Park boardwalk during the late 1960s. Chinnock's Downtown Tangiers Rockin Rhythm & Blues Band included musicians like future E Street Band members Gary Tallent and Danny Federici, Vini "Mad Dog" Lopez, and David Sancious. Although Chinnock was plagued throughout his career with unfair Springsteen comparisons (much like Pittsburgh's Joe Grushecky), the fact is that both artists were products of the same era and place, subjected to many of the same cultural and geographic influences and listening to a lot of the same music. Whereas Springsteen leaned more towards early garage rock and the one-hit-wonders of '60s AM radio, Chinnock's music was influenced more by roots-rock and blues.

When A&R legend John Hammond recommended that Chinnock work on his songwriting, the artist broke away from his heavy touring on the Jersey shore rock scene and moved to Maine in 1974, where he honed his craft while continuing to perform and record. Chinnock later migrated to Nashville during the early 1980s at the prompting of musician and producer Harold Bradley. Bradley had received a cassette of his material and got in touch with Chinnock, and the two subsequently became friends. Chinnock was interested in the renewal of country influence on rock music and was impressed by the energy of the Nashville music scene, so he decided to come down and check it out for himself.

Chinnock integrated himself in the local music scene by jumping in headfirst, playing frequently at local clubs and WKDF-sponsored riverboat shows, as well as outdoor shows at Hermitage Landing. I had the pleasure of meeting and interviewing Billy for *The Metro* magazine in 1985, and witnessed firsthand his dynamic performance at that year's "Rock For The Animals" show, which included Afrikan Dreamland, Walk The West, The Paper Dolls, Raging Fire, Hard Knox, Roxx and Bill Lloyd and the December Boys – a veritable "who's who" of the mid-1980s Nashville rock underground.

While living in Nashville, Chinnock recorded two landmark albums with producer Bradley – 1985's independently released *Rock & Roll Cowboy,* and the 1987 CBS Records release *Learning To Survive In The Modern Age*, which yielded a minor hit single in the song "Somewhere In The Night." Chinnock later won an Emmy for "Somewhere In The Night," which had been used in a daytime soap opera. Chinnock later recorded a chart-topping duet with Roberta Flack which was used as the theme for *The Guiding Light* television show.

Like many non-country musicians in the "Music City," Chinnock found a great deal of frustration in Nashville and the local scene. Already a veteran of 20 years of performing and recording, he was more polished and experienced than any of the rockers playing Nashville's club scene. Although he had a loyal following – mostly blue-collar WKDF listeners – he was dismissed as too slick and mainstream by the local underground. Truth is, Chinnock's roots-rock style was easily a decade (or two) ahead of its time, and was edgier and had less "commercial potential" at that time than most of Nashville's more acclaimed "alternative" rock bands.

While I was managing a Nashville pizza delivery restaurant in the late 1980s, I noticed an order going out to Chinnock's Belmont Avenue area home. I hadn't seen Billy in a couple of years and since I was getting off work, I paid for the pizza and drove over to make the delivery and say "hello." Chinnock seemed happy to see me and we ended up talking for a couple of hours, off the cuff and mostly "off the record." He expressed a lot of anger over the way that CBS had been messing with his career…Billy had a new album in the can and was ready to have it released and launch a supporting tour. Considering that Chinnock had just won an Emmy and had the highest profile of his career, I can see why he wanted the album released. However, CBS didn't think the album "marketable" and, after a prolonged battle, dropped Chinnock from his contract.

The CBS debacle, inexcusable as it was, was not the first time that Chinnock's work had been obstructed by small-minded label executives. Signed by Paramount Records, the label released his debut album *Blues* in 1974, but shelved his sophomore effort, *Road Master*, which was produced by Tom Dowd at the legendary Bell Sound Studios in Los Angeles. To the best of my knowledge, the album has never been released. In the wake of fellow Asbury Park rocker Bruce Springsteen's success, Atlantic Records signed Chinnock to be their Springsteen and released his album *Badlands* in 1978. When *Badlands* went nowhere, the label decided to call it a day (after already recording most of a second album); Chinnock evidently got the rights to his masters back and released the 1980 album himself as *Dime Store Heroes*.

After spending the better part of the decade fighting the system, by 1990 Chinnock had left Nashville in his rear view mirror as he headed back to Maine, where he would enjoy almost 20 years of creativity and performing. 1990's *Thunder In The Valley*, released under the name "Billy & the American Suns," would be Chinnock's last major label album. He would continue to record until the end of his life, releasing material on his own indie label, East Coast Records. Chinnock also began to dabble in graphic arts and made a name for himself as a filmmaker and video producer, creating the award-winning film *The Forgotten Maine*.

Chinnock had suffered from Lyme Disease for eight years, the result of a nasty tick bite. The disease defied treatment, ravaging his immune system and leaving him in a great deal of pain. His mother, who lived with Chinnock and with whom he was very close, died ten days before Chinnock. Consumed with grief and suffering from chronic daily pain, Chinnock evidently saw no other way out than suicide. He was 59 years old, still young by today's rock 'n' roll standards.

Chinnock's sister, Caroline Payne, remembers that her brother was never envious of the success enjoyed by the artist many critics unfairly compared his work to. "I never saw him have any of that," she told the *Portland Press Herald*. "I never saw any frustration in him, any jealousy like that. He thought Bruce Springsteen was phenomenal." Although his vocals could often times sound like Springsteen's, Chinnock's music was always original, heartfelt and genuine, and over the course of a mostly unheralded career that ran almost four decades, Chinnock released 13 albums and entertained a hell of a lot of people. As usual, John Hammond was right on target when he called Billy Chinnock "the real essence of American music."

Chip & the Chiltons, continued...
8. 3rd Time's A Charm
9. Come To This
10. Little Whitney

CIVIC DUTY

Band Members:
Ed Fitzgerald (vocals, guitar) (A1)
Judi Fitzgerald (vocals, percussion) (A1)
Mark Brown (guitar) (A1)
Chuck Allen (bass) (A1)
Doug Sisemore (bass, synthesizer) (A1)
Ken Coomer (drums) (A1)

Civic Duty Recordings:

Singles/EPs

A1. Civic Duty (Telephone Records 1983, 7" vinyl)
Side A
Redwing Bird

Side B
Long Way To Heaven

Comments: For my money, Civic Duty was one that got away. Ed Fitzgerald was a brilliant songwriter and a distinctive vocalist, and the band was simply dynamic on stage. For whatever reason, though, a full-length album never happened (though evidently the songs were there – see below) and no labels ever came knocking. Civic Duty's very cool song "New China" appears on Vanderbilt's *Local Heroes* compilation tape.

CIVIC DUTY/SEVEN KEYS

Band Members:
Ed Fitzgerald (vocals, guitar) (I)
Judi Fitzgerald (vocals) (I)
Mark Brown (guitar) (I)

Chuck Allen (bass) (I)
Gary Rabasca (bass) (I)
Bob Kommersmith (bass) (I)
Ken Coomer (drums) (I)
Craig Wright (drums) (I)
Giles Reeves (drums) (I)
Beat Zenerino (drums) (I)

Civic Duty/Seven Keys Recordings:

I. One Look Back (Telephone Records 1993, cassette)
1. Afghan Feedback
2. Left Handed Gun
3. Seven Keys
4. Deep Water Down
5. The King
6. Standing At The Gate
7. White Mansions
8. My Fiery Tears
9. Big Wind
10. Gila Monster Blues
11. Darke Country Dreaming
12. Little Big Town
13. Pictures In The Sky
14. The Edge Of Love

Comments: Released as side two of Ed Fitzgerald's *Picks* limited edition cassette. Side one features solo material by Fitzgerald, recorded during various sessions and including musicians like **Dave Pomeroy** and **Al Kooper** as well as guitarist Mark Brown.

THE CLAIMSTAKERS

Band Members:
Steve Boyd (vocals, guitars) (I)
Rich Parks (guitars, vocals) (I)
Jon Bang (bass) (I)
Mike Dysinger (drums) (I)

The Claimstakers, continued on page 102...

Chip Chilton was an early and eager supporter of this book project, and provided me with plenty of photos and even some video of Chip & the Chiltons. Somewhere along the line, he decided to pen his own memories of his popular band, and asked me if I'd like this massive 7,000+ word piece for **The Other Side of Nashville**. *I agreed, and only later when I began the editing process did I realize that Chip had quite an axe to grind. In the wake of Chilton's death in February 2010, I debated whether or not I should cut this piece, and ultimately decided against it. "Six Months with Chip & The Chiltons" reflects Chip's opinion, not mine, and if anybody has any problems with Chip's words, sorry...*

Those were the days...if you think that's corny, keep reading. On Friday nights in the mid-80s, the town would be jumping. You could see Web Wilder at 12th and Porter. The Questionnaires might be at Rooster's; Freedom of Expression at the Exit/In; Government Cheese at Elliston Square. Not to mention who would be opening. Many times it would be Chip and the Chiltons, (from now on to be referred to as CATC), and many times we would not be mentioned.

I was born and raised in Nashville. My first intro to local music came at the Exit/In in 1979. I went to see David Johansen of the New York Dolls. The band that opened (which of course, was not mentioned) was Cloverbottom. These guys blew me away. They were 3 piece (hey, gotta love that, right?), loud, tight and fun. This show was broadcast live on KDF. Remember when KDF was a REAL radio station? This was the first time I had seen anything like this.

CATC (which, by the way, I did not come up with the name) first came to be and started recording around 1980. I did it a little different. Instead of playing around and then recording, I started recording and THEN started playing around. We (that would be me, Dave "Micro" Wilkins, and whatever bass player I could get) did parties at first, then bigger parties and small clubs

CHIP AND THE CHILTONS

here and there. The club's names I can't recall. From here on out, when I can't recall something, it will be referred to as ICR. At the time, I didn't have much luck breaking into the local music scene. This would soon change.

In 1985, I was delivering auto parts in Madison. I stopped at a small market to buy a Dr. Pepper. The guy behind the counter was Joey Blanton. This chance meeting would change my life. We talked bands and swapped tapes of our bands. He asked me to see his band play at 12th and Porter. Again, I was blown away. His band, The Enemy, was loose but in a tight way. They had lots of energy and good songs. Joe did most of the lead singing and song writing. I fell in fast with these guys. We ended up doing a lot of shows (and girls) with these guys. I recorded and mixed their first release in the drummer's basement on my 4-track.

Tijuana Go! was released on cassette. I got to sang back up on it. When T/G got to the dubbing stage, the other guitarist, Lee Carr quit. Joe asked me to join. Then the bass player, Eric Hubner, quit. Joe asked me to join. CATC was going great so I turned him down. This is when my relationship with Joe started to sour. It was at this point that The Enemy got a new bass player (Robert Logue) and a new guitarist (Oscar Rice) and changed their name to The Royal Court of China. Joe asked me to produce their next EP. I said I thought that Bruce Bossert, a sound man we both used and that I had done lots of studio work with, would do them a better job.

Maybe I was wrong. When I heard the first mixes of what would become *Off The Beaten Path*, they sucked. The band agreed. So they remixed it with Logue footing the bill. It still sounded sterile. I remember taking to Robert and him saying maybe they should remix, AGAIN. He said he was concerned about all the checks he was writing. Bruce Bossert, who was doing all the mixing, said a 2nd remix might make it sound 10% better. The band just didn't sound good. Blame the amps. Blame the drums. Blame the guitars. Blame the studio. But don't blame the band or the producer.

The EP, as they say, did get them a record deal. And I don't mind telling you, when they got signed, I felt low. I turned down the offer to join and now they got signed. And believe you me; Joe never let a chance go by to let me know this fact…which leads to a funny story (there are many, so get used to it). When we (me and The Enemy) were in Fuzz's (Chris, the drummer) mom's basement recording T/G, which they never paid me for which I never asked to be (but hey, you could offer, right?), we made a pact. Whoever got a deal first would help the other. Well, I guess I found out who were men of their word. After they got signed, no one in that band would even return my phone call. Around this time, to make matters more complicated, I was dating a girl that Joe had knocked up. So, against my better judgment, I was right in the middle of a very messy paternity suit. What was I to do,

leave her by the curb like everyone else had? Not my style, sorry. I will spare you the rest of this sorry story, but to say I witnessed the birth of Joe Blanton's son.

Funny story: (told you) Logue and Rice had a project called The Shakers. I recorded them the first time they cut anything. I took my 4-track to one of their garages and cut it right there; believe it or not, under a full moon. With, I shit you not, a dog howling in the night somewhere. They gave me 500 bucks for the gig. NOT!!! Never even gave me gas money. Not that I asked for it, but you know... and to top it all off, the first time they played out, they opened for CATC.

I remember Robert saying after the gig: "Chip, if you ever need a favor, just ask. I'm not kidding, just ask." Right. Tommy Smith, who owned Elliston Square at the time, came up to me while The Shakers were playing and said, "Chip, goddamn it, what the fuck is this?" What could I say? One man's trash...

The RCC's 2nd album sounded like shit as well. It just didn't capture what they were doing. The 3rd album (after a 2nd line-up change) sounded even worse. Sometimes I wonder if I had produced their first LP release, things would have been different. At least they would have sounded good. I used to get up in the morning to go to work and I would think about how things would have been if I had taken Joe up on his offer. You know, hotels, swimming pools, movie stars. Then I saw how they acted and how they treated people. Then I didn't feel as bad.

After the first gig of Joe's I went to, I left jazzed about what was happening in Nashville and wanted to throw my hat in the ring. Joe asked me if I was gonna put CATC back together and I said I wanted to. Joe said he knew of a drummer that was free and asked me if I was interested in meeting him. I said yes, and Joe set up a meeting with Jay Jones. I met Jay in March of 1985. Jay seemed hip. I gave him a tape of some CATC tunes and asked him to give it a listen. A day or two later I get a phone call from Joe Blanton asking me if I want to open for a band playing at Cantrell's in about 2 weeks. The band was called Walk the West. Joe said they were some weird band that wore western hats.

I called Jay and asked him if he liked the stuff I gave him. I also asked him if he wanted to do a gig in about 3 weeks. He laughed and said yes to both. He asked who would play bass. I told Jay I had met a bass player at a temp job I was at about a month ago who was free. I can't remember the cat's name, so let's just call him dude. Dude said he would do the gig if I gave him gas money. Dude was a metal head but would lower his skill level to play a "punk gig." The game was afoot. Three weeks later I was standing in front of the stage at Cantrell's. This was holy ground for me. Big time, here I come.

My first intro to WTW was at Cantrell's when Howie, the sound man, ex-bassist for The Piggy's, walked up to WTW and said they owed him $50 from a previous gig. Howie was a good guy and a good sound man. A pro, as it were. But you did not fuck with Howie. He would kick your ass for you, thank you very much. Howie stood close to the lead singer, whose name ICR, and said "you pay me now or no gig;" they paid him. They didn't pay me. We were to get $50 for the gig. The place was packed. We did a good show, under the circumstances. Dude came to the gig in an Ozzy shirt. And metal studded bracelets. I went to the drummer of WTW, Richard Ice, after the gig and asked for our money. He said he couldn't pay us because after they paid for sound there wasn't enough money left to pay us. What could I do? I really didn't care. I had my foot in the door and I never had to see Dude again.

I never cared for WTW much. I never cared for the Western wear thing. I had some boots one time. My ex-wife really liked them. No, that's not why I didn't like them. I was divorced long before WTW cheated me out of money. My ex, Beverley Black, was a photographer. She shot all the local bands that time. Funny story: she was shooting WTW at a gig and their lawyer came up to her and threatened to have her thrown out of Cantrell's (have you ever known anyone thrown out of Cantrell's?), and sue her if she tried to use any of the pictures. WTW had asked her to shoot them at this gig. Oh, and WTW never paid her for the film. You gotta love it!

WTW weren't much as players. I'm not saying I was at the time, but then people weren't saying we were (believe me). If they had been saying we were, I wouldn't have been agreeing with them, I think. Plus, they walked around like their shit didn't stink. You may know them and say otherwise, but that's how they treated us. One night Jay and I were hanging outside of Rooster's when Richard Ice and some woman he was with walked between us. She said "they're in CATC," meaning us. Richard said something, I don't know what, but it didn't sound flattering. Whatever it was, Jay heard it better than I did. Jay had a short fuse if you shit talked him. So Jay jumps up and walks over to Richard and asks him to repeat what he just said to his face. Richard just says "nothing" and walks – or was it prissed? – off. Like I said, didn't care much for them.

After the WTW gig, Jay said knew a guitar player he had worked with that would play bass. His name was Chris Hopkins. He could get a bass but he didn't have an amp. I had an amp he could use and gave him a tape of a few songs to learn. A few days later we got together and played a bit. It seemed to work so we decided to give it a try. We rehearsed for a couple of weeks and did a private party with The Enemy. Things went well. We kept working on our set list. I got a call from Joe Blanton that a band called Radio One needed an opening act at the Cannery up in 2 weeks. We took

the gig. The gig was on June 1st, 1985. We were tight and ready. I was 25, Jay was 22 and Chris was 17. Nashville here, we come.

The gig Radio One went well. We played good together. In 1985, we were power-pop, baby! Chris Hopkins (a/k/a "pus bag") was definitely a guitar player playing bass. He was all over the neck. He couldn't play the low end on his back. Jay thought 4 on the floor was something out of his grandfather's truck. All I did was play loud. A bassist that I worked with a few years later told a story that a friend asked him where we were playing next. He said he didn't know where but he knew it would be loud and in [the key of] A. I took it as a complement. We only played one gig with R/O. They weren't very friendly.

Our next gig was with The Boilers. We got the gig thru Joe. I don't think they knew anything thing about us. We set up and started our sound-check. We always check with this song that had three-part harmony. That way we could check everything at one time. As we were checking, I saw The Boilers standing in the back of the room. About 2 minutes into the song I saw the bass player look at the others with a look of "OH SHIT, these guys are good!" It felt good, I must say. We played many gigs with The Boilers. We opened for them, they opened for us, and it was good.

I liked those guys. ICR any names, sorry guys. The bass player was an OK guy. The singer had a good sense of humor. Never had any dealings with the drummer, but the guitar player went out of his way to prove he was dick and I don't know why. Whenever we spoke he had to indicate somehow that he was a better guitar player than me. It was true, but damn, why keep bringing it up? He was taller than

SIX MONTHS WITH CHIP & THE CHILTONS

me, but he didn't bring that up all the time. Hey, I got better-looking woman than him, but I didn't say: "hey ugly, is that you sister or your mother you're with?" We did a writer's night at Elliston Square and he sat in with us on some standards. He did his best to show he was better than me. I did the shtick I always did. I played behind my back, he did. Got on the floor and played, he did. This went on for a bit, neither we nor the crowd were laughing. He did this long, Van Halen-type solo in a 12-bar blues jam and I had had enough. I went to the microphone and said "there's no point in this," and stopped the song. I thanked him for sitting in, and he left. That was the last time I saw him play.

We played a lot. Dates slip my mind, but bands don't. We opened for The Textones from Austin TX. They were fronted by a woman who had worked with Bob Dylan. Herein lays one of my major rants. We would open for piss-ass local bands (you know who you were) and they would give us shit like "you can't sound check, just set-up and play," or "don't mess with the lights," or my personal fave, "you're too loud, turn down. You're opening, turn down." Or my all time piss-me-off, "you can't use the drum riser, set-up in front of it." We were doing a show at Music Row Showcase.

It was some piss-ass, would-be metal band we were opening for. We didn't know each other. I walked in as they were finishing their sound-check. The drummer stood up and said "do I have to tear my kit down?" The manager (what he was doing there, I don't know) said "No, CATC can set up in front." I was standing to the left of the stage behind a group of people. I said: "no they won't." The manger said "who are you?" I said "I'm Chip Chilton." He said "it's too much trouble to tear his kit down, set up in front." I said "if we can't use the riser, we won't play. So tell me what you want to do, 'cause I won't bother unloading my gear if it's a problem." It made me so mad I was ready to walk off. They looked at each other for a moment and started tearing his set down. Fuck me.

When you open for pros, you know it. The Textones sound-check went long. We didn't have much time. We were hustling to get ready. Their road manger came up and said the club wanted to open the doors because people were lining up outside and they wanted to let them in. Beer sales, ya know. He asked me how long I needed. I said 10 minutes. He kept the doors closed for 10 minutes, we sound-checked, end of story.

Here is a prime example. We opened for Will & the Bushman at MRSC; when they sound-checked, Will, the guitar player, taped all his cords down and effects to the stage, for sound-check. When they were done, Will came to me asked if he needed to move his cords and stuff. I don't remember what was said, but the end result was he left the club with all his shit still taped to the front of the stage. Could have been my

fault, who knows? So, I undid all his cords from the stage and piled them in front of his amp.

Well, when he came back, I guess you can guess what happened. He threw a big pouting hissy-fit. After the show, to show me who was boss, he wouldn't pay me our cut; a whopping $17. He just kept looking over at me like I wasn't there and kept saying "in a minute." It was 2 am and I had to be at work at 8 am. I went to the manger, Bill "Gunslinger" and told him I would be back tomorrow to get my money – all $17 of it. Will walked around with his nose so far in the air it's a wonder he didn't have a permanent neck injury.

Bill "The Gunslinger" (I have no idea), the manager at the time of MRSC, used to manage Cantrell's. I knew Bill well. When he went to manage MRSC, he said any band that played Cantrell's from now on could not play MRSC. Yeah, whatever.

Anyway, Alex Chilton was to play MRSC (no relation); we were to open. You know, Alex Chilton, Chip and the Chiltons, that kind of thing. It would be great fun. So, Sunday rolls around and I go get the paper to check the club listing for the week and guess what I see? Playing MRSC is Alex Chilton and opening is The Royal Court of China. I was pissed off. So I call the Gunslinger. Here is what he says, "the RCC boys have label interest." That was it; that was all. I guess Bill thought he would get more RCC tit if he did some good ass-kissing.

Gunslinger was trying to manage a band from NYC called The Manikenz. They were a punk-glam thing. Bill called me to do a show them. I asked Bill who would be headlining. Bill said it would be dual bill. I said OK, who would play first. Bill said CATC would. I told Bill that at this point we don't have to open for The Manikenz. We didn't do the show. I don't know how Bill put it to his boys, but they never spoke to me again. Whatever...

Never played with Will Rambeaux; weren't good enough, we were told. Weren't in that clique. Funny story: Greg, a bass player I worked with, had a day gig filling vending machines. One of his stops was where Will Rambeaux worked during the day. Apparently, Will had lost 25-cents in one of the vending machines. Will left a note on the machine saying "your machine owes me 25-cents, Will Rambeaux of the Delta Hurricanes." Gregg, left a note saying, "I'll give it to you tomorrow, Gregg of Chip and the Chiltons." Big stars at work.

Bill Lloyd was a "good" example. We did a few shows on the same bill with Bill Lloyd and the December Boys. Bill had as much, if not more success than anyone on the local scene and he always acted the same. When he was recording the first Foster & Lloyd album, I ran into him at the Gold Rush. I walked by him and he stopped me and told me what he was up to. I passed him in a restaurant one time while he was talking to some suits. He stepped out and said "hi." That's Bill.

We had a gig at MRSC opening for Bill Lloyd. Bill called me a week before the show and said he was gonna have to bump us off the ticket because his high school buddy wanted the gig and he couldn't say no. "I hope you understand," Bill said. I said no, I don't understand, but I appreciate YOU and not the club manager calling me and telling me. It's funny, but I never held it against Bill for bumping us. It's all in how you do it.

One show of the early days that stands out was The Leroi Brothers from Texas. This was really a good gig for us. The show was at Rooster's on Friday night with about 600 people there. We killed. At one of the tables up front were two guitar players that I had been in a band with about 6 years earlier. They always gave me shit about how I played and what I wanted to play. They had a front-row seat watching me play to packed house that was grooving on every note we played. With the follow spot on me, I went out in the crowd (as I often did) and got up on their table and played. It was nothing but good.

I did all the booking (for what that's worth). I had a job during the day delivering auto parts. Once a day, I had to go to town and pick a load of parts for the store. I would haul ass and get done as soon as I could so I go to different clubs and beg for gigs. I got a lot of gigs at Rooster's like this. Bill (ICR his last name) ran the place. I got along well with Bill because he was smart ass like me. He would show me his calendar for show for that month and ask me what I wanted. I would look thru and pick 2 or 3 of the best bands to open for. It was great. And I knew it.

I turned down a chance to open for The Red Hot Chili Peppers when they played at Roosters. I wanted to open for Rank and File instead. They were more popular than the Chili Peppers at the time. Then Bill pissed off Venture Booking, who handled Rank and File, and Venture pulled all their acts. RCOC opened for RHCP. Oh well...

We were having internal problems. Pusbag got drunk at a gig (it *was* an outdoor party), too drunk to play in fact, (cops shut us down early anyway). At this point in time I did not drink. Jay drank, but not when he was playing. Anything within reason, I say (well, almost), but this I would not tolerate, drunk to the point of not being able to play. I told Pusbag if he did this again, he was gone. The 3 of us agreed. They also chafed at my rehearsal regimen. We rehearsed at least 3 times a week. And rehearsal was not a party. This meant no friends, no beer. And be on fucking time; one of my other pet peeves (yes, I have many, and I know it). If I can work 8 hours, go

home and shower, load my gear up, drive across town and be on time, by God, so can you.

We were the first local original band to play at Elliston Square. Gus Palas of *The Metro* booked us there. It was my first meeting with Tommy Smith. Tommy once told me the reason they didn't put him in jail was because he would end up running the place. I went to Mike Tidwell when he first bought the Exit/In. I told him if he started booking local bands who played their own stuff, they would take care of him (meaning people would come to the shows, tell their friends it was a hip place to be and hang out and drink beer, other bands would then want to play there, blah, blah, blah). And so he did. Not us, mind you. We played there a bunch, but most of the time it was opening.

I have many fond memories of The Blind Farmers From Hell. These guys were the real deal. What you saw was what you got, and then some. We did many shows with them and had a goddamn good time. They liked to have a good time and didn't think they were better than everyone else. Pet peeve # 27.6: all the local fuckers who thought they were god's gift to the world and wouldn't smile on stage even if it meant their death. I was watching the RCOC play one night at Cantrell's. I was by the side of the stage, next to "I'm so cool I have to be defrosted twice a day" Robert Logue. When he looked the other way, I reached up and turned the volume down on his bass. He stared checking his cord, and shaking it. He went and checked his amp and was looking around for something, anything, to solve his dilemma. He looked at me with his big puppy dog eyes that said "please help me!" I just pointed to his bass where the volume knob was and pointed up with my thumb. He turned his bass up and kept playing. If he didn't know, he does now.

SIX MONTHS WITH CHIP & THE CHILTONS

We did lots of shows with Freedom of Expression. They took us under their wing, so to speak. Rob Hoskins, their lead singer and keyboard player, and I shared the sense of the absurd. Rob always wanted to produce us on some tunes, but it never came to be. I did a lot of mechanic work for FOE. I repaired their van many times. I worked on band member's cars, and girlfriend's as well. You could call it brown-nosing if you want. I called it networking. I wouldn't have done it I didn't like them. You didn't see me working on WTW's van. AND FOE paid me.

Rob and Teddy (sounds like an ice cream flavor) – Teddy was their sax player, sang back up and harmony on several tunes on CATC's *Where's My Cat?* cassette. For quite a while we would always open with the Batman theme. One night, Teddy sat in and played sax on Batman. Teddy wanted to join CATC, but I could never afford to pay him. At one point, FOE wanted me join them. Rob called me on a Thursday night and said their guitar player was quitting. We would rehearse thru the weekend and leave for Indiana on Tuesday. He said I would have to quit my job.

WOW! Why didn't he just say, "hey, you wanna play in the band?" He just assumed that I would join. I was flabbergasted and flattered. I said that I would have to think about it. First The Enemy, now FOE. I guess most people's head would have exploded from all the swelling. It made me feel good, I must admit. But it also made me nervous. I was not much of a guitar player then. (Now?) I did have people tell me my guitar tone was good and the band sounded well. I felt what we did, we did OK. But that was about it.

I think one my strengths was knowing my limitations. Not getting in over my head, so to speak (most of the time). I guess I was worried that people would find out I was a one trick pony. It was a tough decision to make. I liked doing my thing with CATC. The Enemy was more popular, and I liked playing with them as well. FOE played for a living and I could quit my day job. But, reggae was not my thing. I enjoyed playing it, but not all the time. So I did what any rocker would do. I turned them all down and stayed with my band. And this, my friends, is what separates the men from the boys.

Pusbag and Jay were not happy because they thought I was going to join The Enemy. I did play a 91 ROCK benefit with them, which Jay and P/B didn't warm up to. (CATC played it as well on another night) When I didn't fold up the CATC tent, Jay and P/B didn't say much one way or the other. Jay never said much till he had beer in him and I didn't listen then anyway. Pusbag's head had gotten so big by this point because of the attention he was getting, his whacked-out ego and his pot smoking, beer drinking, 16 year old would be hanger on friends wouldn't let him.

Trouble was on the way with Pusbag, I could see it coming. Joe, on the other hand had his ego crushed. What, someone turn down the infamous Joey Off Beat? Rob of FOE wasn't happy, but he was a pro and it didn't affect our friendship, because we were FRIENDS. Funny story (I just thought of it): I was hanging out in front of the Gold Rush one night when this guy comes up to me. He said he was a friend of the lead singer of WTW. Apparently, he knew who I was (I'm a big star, remember?). He said the lead singer was mad because of a song we wrote about WTW. We shouldn't be making fun of big time stars like them.

I asked him what the fuck was he taking about. He said the song we were doing called "I hate the west" was about WTW and we better stop playing it, or words to that effect. People called WTW "the West" for short, apparently (I didn't know this). I told this jerk that he and WTW must think, and think everyone thinks, all we do is think about WTW. The song was about the western craze that was going on that CATC didn't like. I told jerk face this. I also told him to tell his friends at WTW headquarters that they thought a lot of themselves.

Lots of bands got signed around this time. The Scorchers, not us; In Pursuit, not us; RCOC, not us; The Dusters, not us; Government Cheese, not us; The Questionnaires, not us; Screaming Cheetah Wheelies, not us. You get the picture (I hope you do by now).

I really liked (like) Web Wilder. He is a pro. He is a guitar player and guitar lover. We only played one gig with them. Funny story (again): they were showcasing at Rooster's. Bill called us at the last minute to (guess what?) open. CATC to the rescue. Again. After Webb sound checked and we were setting up, Web came up to me. It went like this:

WW: Chip, we have a label here tonight. CC: Cool
WW: I want you to play for 45 minutes. CC: O.K.
WW: Go on at 10, play 45 and that will put us on at 11. CC: O.K.
WW: No, go on at 9:50, play 45. That will put us on at 10.50. CC: O.K.
WW: No, go on at, hmmm...
CC: (says nothing)
WW: No, go on at 10... (thinking)
CC: (thinking, not knowing)
WW: Yes, go on at 10.
CC: O.K. Webb.

Nervous, I guess. Webb was one of the few REAL rock and roll bands out of Nashville who could, and can blow almost anyone off the stage. I have watched Webb jam at a friend's house and it seems to me that the man just loves to play the guitar.

1985 and '86 were good years for music in Nashville, and a lot of good bands came thru and played here. Bands that could fill up 500 and 600-hundred seat clubs. It was a great thing to be able to open for some of these bands. We played a lot in Murfreesboro and Knoxville, too. Then it happened. I knew it would. We were opening for The Flaming Lips at Rooster's. It was the dead of winter and cold as shit; we sound-checked and left. It was cold in the club, so I took my guitars with me when I left. I didn't see Pusbag when I left the club.

I got back to the club about an hour before we had to go on. I saw Pusbag playing pool with some of his scum-laden friends, but I didn't talk to him. I tuned my guitars, and put them on stage. I made out the set list and copies for everyone including Bruce, the sound man. By this time, it was time to go on. I still didn't talk to Pusbag, but at this point, this was not unusual.

He came up just as we were getting ready to go on. We hit the stage and rip into "Batman" and all is fine. 1 or 2 tunes later, I notice P/B is not as sure on his feet as he unusually is. Then he starts hitting wrong notes here and there which is not like him. We go into "Six Days On The Road," which he sings, and he is slurring words. The fucker is drunk! I couldn't believe it. We go into "Secret Agent Man," and he plays in the wrong key for about 4 bars. We do "I'm A Man," and he can hardly play his solo.

After this song I can barely contain myself. I introduce the band. I save P/B for last. I very politely introduce him and say that he has had a LITTLE too much to drink and this is his last performance with CATC. I apologize for a short set and say goodnight. I walk over to P/B and unplug MY cord from his guitar. He didn't even have a cord of his own. I start to walk off and P/B starts to give me some lip about beating me up (right), or something to that effect. I pick up my guitar stand (Fie is using mine, of course) and tell him in a very low voice if he doesn't get away from me and off the stage I will start clubbing him. He slurs something back, who knows what. Then Chip Feinstein, the light man, says stop or he will kick both of our asses. Not a pretty sight, and all on stage. I walked around as we tore down with the stand in my hand. P/B had left the club.

The singer from The F/L came up to me and asked if things were alright. I just look at him and his puffed up hair and said "no!" P/B used my amps. I hauled them to the gigs and unloaded them for him. 90% of the time, he didn't even help load the gear up. He didn't write songs or book gigs. All he had to do was show up sober and play. That was it. And the fucker wouldn't or couldn't even do that. So, per our agreement, I fired him. Jay didn't say much. Bruce, our sound man, said it didn't sound that bad out front. It sounded that bad on stage. We recorded the show, and it sound that

bad on tape. We also videotaped the show, and it looked that bad to me. Maybe I over reacted; looking back, I may have. I guess I had higher standards then. We tried for a while to replace him with no luck. After seeing the pool of talent that we had to pick from, Jay wanted P/B back. While P/B was gone, I heard him shit talking me. With what we had put into the project, much to my better judgment, let him back in. My plan was to use the piece of shit 'till I could find some else. This I kept to myself. P/B came to rehearsal and we took up where we left off. He never said he was sorry or he would do better or nothing. Nothing was said by anyone.

Our first gig reunited was headlining at Elliston Square. The place was packed. It was a very tense night for us. The crowd seemed the same way. Except for Joey Blanton. For whatever reason, he was a total ass whole the whole night. He kept yelling at us, taunting us, wanting to sit in. I had my hands full as it was. It was that night that I saw what Joe was. It was here that our friendship ended. Although I think Joe still doesn't know it. Apparently Jay's interest in CATC had ended, too. A few nights later at rehearsal in our new studio shed (which I bought with money I had borrowed from the bank and I paid back), I told the guys that FOE was gonna do a summer tour and wanted us to go out with them for about 2 weeks.

I thought this was great news. Jay takes this moment to tell he has joined another band called Order of Silence, and he is gonna quit. We were just getting ready to record what would become *Where's My Cat?* Jay said he would still record the album with us, but he was done. Needless to say, I was surprised. I said I understood he wanted to do something else but I wasn't happy that he didn't give us any notice. Well, this didn't set well with him and he got all mad and shit. He said I had fucked up. He said that I could have had someone to do the session, but not now. He packed his drums up a big huff, slammed the hatch on his car and drove off. P/B just stood there, not saying anything. Then he left.

That night I called David Wilkins, the original drummer for CATC. I had recorded with "Micro" for about 4 years. He was the best drummer I had ever worked with. He said he would do the session. I gave Micro a live tape of the tunes we were gonna do. 3 days later were setting up in my new studio to record what would become *Where's My Cat?* To show you how good/bad Pusbag was, it went just like this: Micro and I hit the studio at 7 am (that's right, AM). P/B showed up late, of course, at about 7:30. Fie and been out till 2:00 am and was hung over. He lay down on the floor while I set up the mikes and got levels. I woke him up and got a level on his bass. We tuned up and cut 9 tracks. BAM! Just like that. Pusbag did not make a mistake. He put his bass in the case and left. He was 17 years old. Micro didn't make a mistake either. Of course, all I did was make mistakes. My guitar was a scratch track, and I would dub it later. Funny story: As we were setting up, Jay came by to get something he had left in the studio. He jokingly made the remark that he should take the drums away from Micro and do it himself. I just smiled. Jay left. People are funny, aren't they?

As I worked on the tracks, we were to start looking for a drummer. I set up an audition with a drummer. I moved all the monitors and shit we needed to audition the drummer back to the studio. Then P/B called and said he could not come, we would have to do it later. I told him I had had enough; he was done, again, this time for good. He said he understood. It had almost been to the day, 6 months since we first got together. Now we were done.

Jay and I are still friendly. We used to talk every now and again until I moved recently. Pusbag was a different story. He still owed me 45 bucks for an amp I had bought for him. His bass guitar was still at my house when I gave him the boot. He called and wanted it back. I told him he would get it when he paid me the money he owed me.

Well, that night about 3 in the morning, P/B and one of his buddies try to break in my house and get it. I chased them to their car with my car. They jumped in and flew off. I drove to P/B parents' house, where he lives. I wake up his parents and tell him what he has done and why he has done it. I tell his father if somebody doesn't pay me the money I'm owed, I'm going back home and calling the police and having them (P/B) arrested.

His father asked me how much money P/B owes me. I tell him. His father reaches into his billfold and gives me the money. I go back home and get P/B's bass. When I get back to P/B's house with his bass, he was back home. I give his father the bass and tell him and his wife "your son is very talented, don't let him waste it." From what I saw of P/B later on, I guess what I said didn't mean much.

Funny story: after I had put CATC back together, we were playing at Elliston Square. After the show, P/B came up to me and stuck out his hand. I just looked at him. He looked over at one of his friends and said "the man won't shake hands." I said "you're right, you motherfucker. You tried to break into my house. You're lucky I didn't have you arrested, and luckier I didn't shoot you." He made some comment that we should go outside. I told him anytime he wanted to continue this, let me know. I walked off.

CATC went on for another 12 years. I shortened the name to The Chiltons around 1988. We headlined most of the time. It took a while, but I became a much better player (for what that's worth), and started leaning more toward blues-rock.

It's a shame that the bands that got signed during this time (1985-1990) lost their deals. Why? I heard tales that I don't have the space to tell. And since I didn't hear this stuff firsthand, I wouldn't tell anyway. I know RCOC went out of their way to piss off everyone they came in contact with. That I know. Joe couldn't keep his mouth shut, or his dick in his pants, and it cost him dearly.

The 6 months I just told you about were a wild ride I will never forget. It's funny, but the gigs I remember the best came after 1985. Probably because I headlined more and I think maybe because I became a better player. And I got much better gear to play with.

As I was doing research for this article, I came across a blog that Drew Cornutt of the RCOC had up. He talked of wanting to audition for CATC. Jay responded to this by saying that he had been in CATC when they were good. I got lots of live tapes from that period if you believe we were good. Good tunes, yes. Good players? I'll let your memory be the judge of that. It will be a lot easier on you than these live tapes will be. – *Chip Chilton*

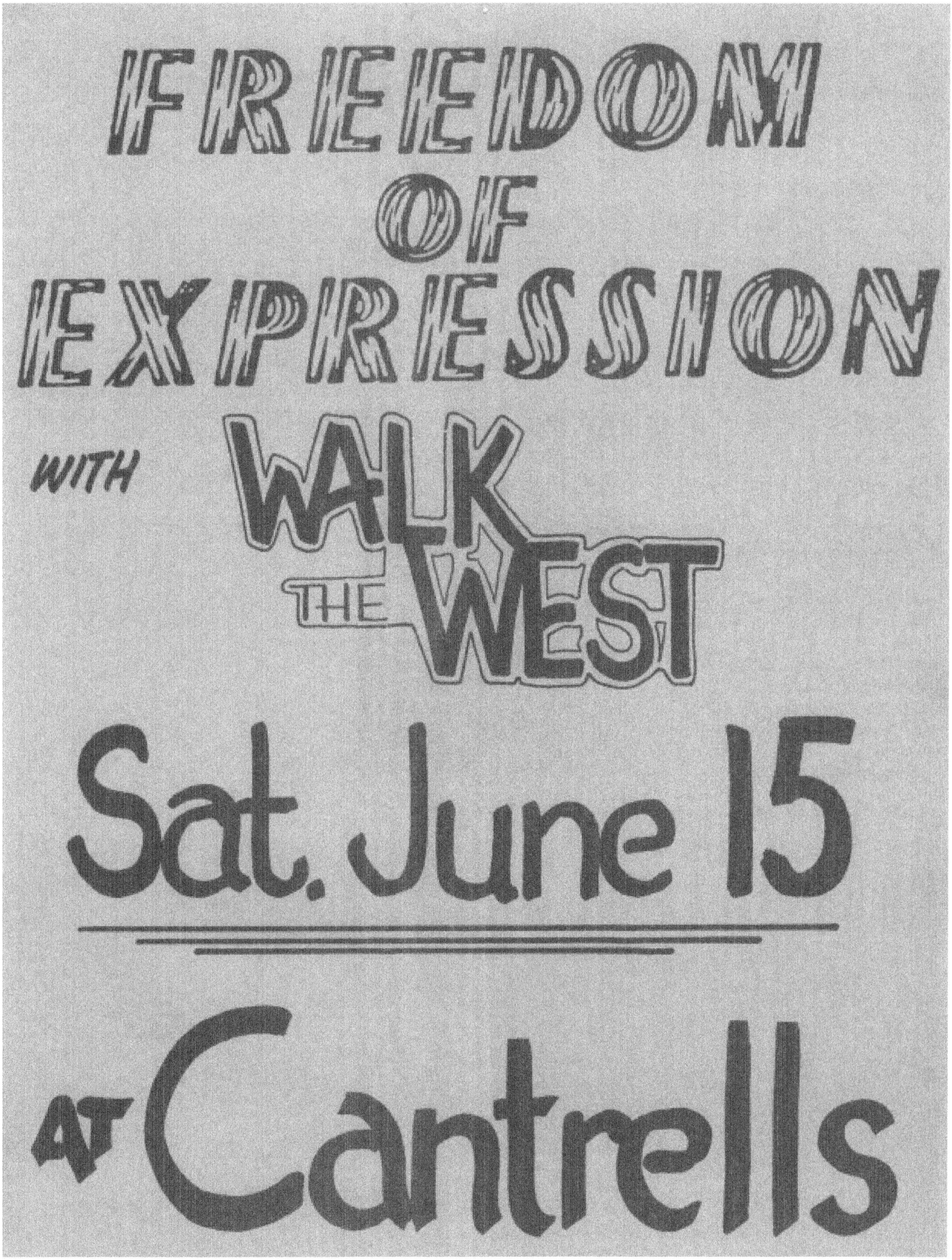

FREEDOM OF EXPRESSION

WITH WALK THE WEST

Sat. June 15

AT Cantrells

The Claimstakers, continued...

Other Musicians:
Aashid Himmons (vocals) (I)
Tim Coats (vocals) (I)

The Claimstakers Recordings:

I. Claimstakers (Staker Records 1988, LP)
Side One
1. Broken Wings
2. Wouldn't You Like To Know It
3. Aztec Plain
4. Sister's Trippin

Side Two
5. Pandemonium
6. Path Of Least Resistance
7. Western Flyer
8. One Way Road

Comments: The Claimstakers were a good band, a side project for **White Animals** members Boyd and Parks.

CLOCKHAMMER

Band Members:
Byron Bailey (vocals, guitar) (A1, I-IV)
Matt Swanson (bass) (A1, I-III)
Ken Coomer (drums) (A1, I-III)
Christian Nagle (guitar, vocals) (IV)
Mark Smoot (bass, vocals) (IV)
Chris Gallo (drums) (IV)

Clockhammer Recordings:

Singles/EPs

A1. Sun Goes Black (First Warning Records 1991?, 7" vinyl)
Side A
Sun Goes Black

Side B
Standing By

Comments: Cool collectible that came and went in support of Clockhammer's self-titled debut album. "Sun Goes Black" is from the album, "Standing By" is a non-album live track recorded at the legendary CBGB in October 1990. Kinda ironic in retrospect, but the single's back cover states "Clockhammer was, is and ever shall be" before listing Bailey, Coomer, and Swanson…don't get the joke? Read on…

Albums/EPs

I. Clockhammer (First Warning Records 1990, CD)
1. Mother Truth
2. Trial By Fire
3. Boys In Blue
4. Bridges Burn
5. Extra Crispy
6. Lament
7. Wither
8. No Show
9. Calypso
10. Sun Goes Black
11. Girl From Ipanema

II. Carrot EP (First Warning Records 1991, CD EP)
1. Standing
2. Lament
3. Shadowplay
4. Mother Truth

III. Klinefelter (First Warning Records 1992, CD)
1. Greying Out
2. Bluest Eyes
3. Standing By
4. Nullify
5. Away
6. Hollows
7. Years Of Days
8. Destination
9. Next Month
10. Drone
11. Mitch's Theme

Comments: CD produced by Paul Q. Kolderie and Sean Slade at their Fort Apache studios in Cambridge, MA, album art direction by the multi-talented **Tony Gerber**. This was the last hurrah for this line-up of Clockhammer. Depending on who you speak with, either Bailey's girlfriend was playing the role of "Yoko" in convincing the Clockhammer frontman to shed himself of the talented Matt Swanson and Ken Coomer, or else the rhythm players gave Bailey the boot for being a prick.

Either way, one of the more interesting local bands of the 1990s went the way of so many before them; by the time that Bailey put together a "new" Clockhammer a year or so later, the game was pretty much over.

IV. So Much For You (Houses In Motion 1994, CD)
1. When Words Fall
2. Laurel
3. Pyramids
4. Tangled
5. Tipping The Balance
6. Wishbone
7. Glide
8. Gemini
9. Remain
10. I've Always Known
11. Dark Grey Spaces
12. Losing A Thousand Days
13. Now Begins The Rain

Comments: I haven't heard this CD, so I can't honestly say much about it other than Bailey had assembled a new Clockhammer around himself and his cousin, Chris Nagel. First Warning had gone belly up by this time and *So Much For You* was released in Germany by the Houses In Motion.

DAVE CLOUD w/THE GOSPEL OF POWER

Band Members:
Dave Cloud (vocals, guitar, piano, horns) (I-III)

Gospel Of Power:
Matt Bach (bass, drums, guitars, casio) (I-III)
Brian Boling (drums) (I-III)
Paul Booker (guitar) (I-III)
Tony Crow (keyboards, programming) (I-III)

Other Musicians:
Matt Button (II, III)
John Elliott (programming) (I)
Dave Friedman (bass) (I, III)
Ben Martin (II, III)
Laurel Parton (II, III)
Matt Swanson (casio) (I, III)

Dave Cloud Recordings:

I. Songs I Will Always Sing (Thee Swan Recording Company/Bloodsucker Records 1999, CD)
1. I'll Run the Jack on You
2. Subliminal Face
3. Fantastic Rage
4. I'm into Something Good
5. Sleep All Day
6. Teenage Bossman
7. Eight Miles High
8. It Ain't Nothing to Me
9. Green Fields
10. Living in Your Love
11. Wild One

12. Lay, Lady, Lay
13. Sifu Bruce Lee
14. Winter Winds
15. Geronimo
16. Moonage Daydream
17. When Everyone is Gone
18. Our Love (Don't Throw it all Away)
19. Icy Cold Brew

II. All My Best (Thee Swan Recording Company 2004, CD)
1. Hey Baby! Let's Get Away
2. Get Down Tonight
3. Heatwave
4. Goin' to the Go Go
5. Cool Water
6. Save the Last Dance for Me
7. Motorcycle
8. Sing 9 and 90
9. Warmth of the Sun
10. Bugle Call with Guitar
11. Lavender Clothes
12. Young Love
13. Booty Shoe II
14. Love Jones
15. Me and Mrs. Jones
16. Puff Rider
17. You Can't Lose
18. Let's Spend the Night Together
19. Vixen...Vixen...Fox...Fox
20. Summer Holiday
21. All Day Music
22. Evil Dracula Man

III. Napoleon of Temperance (Fire Records 2006, UK CD)

Disc One
1. Vixen...Vixen...Fox...Fox
2. Puff Rider
3. Lavender Clothes
4. I'll Run the Jack on You
5. You Missed A Damn Good Chance
6. Goin' to the Go Go
7. Love Jones
8. Cool Water
9. Sleep All Day
10. Subliminal Face
11. Fantastic Rage
12. Winter Winds
13. Bugle Call with Guitar
14. Misengendered Mulatto Squandering Abeyance to Phantasmagoria
15. When Everyone is Gone
16. Sing 9 and 90
17. Motorcycle
18. Summer Holiday
19. Living in Your Love
20. Booty Shoe II
21. Save the Last Dance for Me
22. Sudden Stop

Disc Two
1. Belinda Purvis
2. Eight Miles High
3. Heatwave
4. All Day Music
5. Our Love (Don't Throw it all Away)
6. How Can You Mend a Broken Heart?
7. I'm into Something Good
8. You Can't Lose
9. Lay, Lady, Lay
10. Sifu Bruce Lee
11. Get Down Tonight
12. Warmth of the Sun
13. Young Love
14. Me and Mrs. Jones
15. Let's Spend the Night Together
16. Wild One
17. It Ain't Nothing to Me
18. Moonage Daydream
19. Geronimo
20. Icy Cold Brew
21. Green Fields
22. Teenage Bossman
23. Evil Dracula Man

Comments: Cloud's immeasurable genius was finally recognized by England's Fire Records, which released this two-CD "retrospective" as the bard's European "coming out party." With 45 tracks, *Napolean of Temperance* includes a lot of material from Cloud's first two albums as well as a smattering of new songs and his concise cover tunes.

CLOVERBOTTOM

Web: www.cloverbottom.net

Band Members:
Barry Williams a/k/a "Rock Strata" (vocals, guitar) (A1)
John Milillo a/k/a "Johnny Hollywood" (bass) (A1)
John Elliott a/k/a "El Taco" (drums) (A1)
Bryan Talbot a/k/a "Bryan D'Beane" (drums)
Rob Callahan (drums)
Jim Christopher (guitar, keyboards, vocals)
Vicki Christopher a/k/a "Kiki Silva" (vocals)
Larry Partin a/k/a "L.P." (guitars, vocals)

Cloverbottom Recordings:

A1. Anarchy In The Music City (Toolbox Records 1980, 7" vinyl EP)
Side One
1. Anarchy In The Music City
2. Life Is A Game

Side Two
3. Cottage Cheeseheads
4. Nuclear War

Comments: In early-to-late 1970s-era Nashville, the name "Cloverbottom" was a pejorative term, used to ridicule the person on the receiving end. Named for the city's notorious center for the mentally retarded, Nashville's first punk band was also one of the city's first original rock bands.

Booked by Rick Champion at the legendary Phrank 'n' Steins, the band played a few original tunes sprinkled in-between Buzzcocks and Stranglers covers. Cloverbottom's core line-up of Rock Strata, Johnny Hollywood and **John "El Taco" Elliott** recorded only one lone four-song EP, 1980's *Anarchy In The Music City*, but those four songs still kick ass almost 30 years later!

Anarchy In The Music City EP
Review by Thom King, *The Nashville Gazette*, April 1980

The long-awaited Cloverbottom EP is finally on the street. For dedicated fans of Nashville's most visible punk group, this collection of four new wave classics is a delayed Christmas present that just keeps on giving.

Containing such jewels as "Anarchy In Music City," "Life Is A Game," "Cottage Cheeseheads," and "Nuclear War," this self-produced record has captured the raw energy of Cloverbottom. Anyone who has seen this power trio live in town will be able to feel the stage presence that screams out of the grooves on this disc.

If you haven't experienced new wave music, this EP offers a quickie course. There aren't any female singers with blonde hair, or fashionable lead singers in skin tight pants. These guys didn't name themselves after a form of transportation. They took their title from the local mental institution. That alone should give you a hint of their attitude. If the name isn't enough, listen to some lines from this record:

the clutters

CLOVERBOTTOM - THE CLUTTERS

"Life is a game I ain't ready to play?" ("Life Is A Game"); "If you don't like us you can leave." ("Anarchy In Music City"); and finally, "Monotony will drive you insane" ("Cottage Cheeseheads").

Rock Strata, Johnny Hollywood and John Elliot (who has since left the band to join Actuals, no the, just Actuals) capture the raw underbelly of Nashville Punk. $2.00 and a trip to New Life Records on Charlotte Ave. will provide a primer and teaser for a new form of Nashville Music.

THE CLUTTERS
Web: www.theclutters.com

Band Members:
Doug Lehmann (vocals, guitar) (A1, I-III)
Jake Rosswog (bass) (A1, I-III)
Ali Tonn (keyboards) (A1, I-III)
Steph Filippini (drums) (A1, I-III)

The Clutters Recordings:

Singles/EPs

A1. Oh! (Wrecked 'Em Wreckords 2003, 7" vinyl)
Side A
1. Oh!
2. Reason to Complain
3. Don't Care About Me

Cloverbottom

CLOVERBOTTOM REMEMBERED...

It was spring of nineteen eighty. The first night I performed with Cloverbottom, we played four sets at forty-five minutes each, nearly everything at a hundred miles an hour. The next morning, my right wrist was so swollen up, it was almost frozen, and I couldn't imagine how I could do it all again that night. Rick Champion called and congratulated me on the previous night. He gave me a little pep talk and encouragement, and my wrist eventually loosened up.

I'd never been in a three piece band before, and it created an urgency in my playing to make as much noise as possible to fill any gaps. Mostly, it was about energy; whatever we may have lacked in virtuosity, we made up for in power, and it helped that I was already in good physical shape. We played songs by bands I'd never heard of – the Flies, Gloria Mundi, the Buzzcocks, the Stranglers, the Only Ones. It was a parallel existence – we'd roar through nearly four hours of exciting and fun music of the times, adrenaline and endorphins pumping, then I'd go home late and wind down with spacey chamber jazz from northern Europe.

A small perk for us was that Rick Champion not only was the manager for the club, but for Cloverbottom as well, so we rehearsed in Phrank 'n' Steins on Monday and Tuesday nights when the club was closed. As such, we sort of felt like we owned the place. Rock and (especially) Johnny constantly had their fingers on the pulse, and we'd get together and talk about other bands' members and more memorable show attendees.

One evening before we got started, an obviously older woman showed up, dressed in semi-formal business attire. She had a younger girl with her, and had an aura of specific purpose. Martha Kibby was serving drinks that night, and the woman refused drink offers. At some point into our first set, Martha began asking questions, trying to figure out who she was and why she was there. The woman finally told her that she was an administrator with Clover Bottom Developmental Center for retarded citizens, and she was scoping us out to see if there was any shameful mocking or disgraceful satire going on. Satisfied that there was none, other than our not-quite-literal name appropriation, she left.

There was an underlying sentiment that we could all get away with anything we wanted, and we pretty much did. Frankenstein's (it had long ceased to be referred to as "Phranks and Steins") was like the rumblings of a volcano before eruption. Terry Cantrell should be enshrined somehow; when he opened Cantrell's after the unfortunate closing of Frankenstein's, the energy took root, expanded and diversified. (*By email from Bryan Talbot*)

Side B
1. Crack Your Heart
2. Are You Ready For The Country

Albums/EPs

I. The Drew EP (self-produced limited CD-R, 2001?)
1. Back Of My Mind
2. Calling Her Name
3. Busted Dreams, Broken Heart
4. Cup Of Coffee

II. T & C (Chicken Ranch Records 2006, CD)
1. Crack Your Heart
2. Clash City Girl
3. You'll Never Be Famous
4. Rock & Roll
5. The Untitled One
6. Oh!
7. Leave It Behind
8. Nothing
9. Calling Her Name
10. I Wanna Live…
11. Polaroid

12. When Worlds Divide
13. Busted Dreams / Broken Heart

III. Don't Believe A Word (Chicken Ranch Records 2007, CD)
1. 9999 (Ways To Hate Us)
2. Radio
3. Living Thing
4. Rockaway
5. Fire
6. The Way Home
7. On Repeat
8. The Short One
9. Aww, C'mon
10. Let It Roll
11. Temperature
12. Surrender

STACIE COLLINS

Band Members:
Stacie Collins (vocals, guitar) (I, II)
Dan Baird (guitars, bass, vocals, percussion) (II)
Ken McMahan (guitars, bass) (II)
Allen Collins (bass, guitars) (II)

Cloverbottom

STACIE COLLINS - THE COMFIES

Paul Griffith (drums, percussion) (II)
Eric Borash (lap steel, guitar) (II)

Other Musicians:
Jack Irwin (keyboards) (II)
Britt Savage (vocals) (II)

Stacie Collins Recordings:

I. Stacie Collins (self-produced 2001, CD)
1. Big Freight Train
2. All She Needed
3. Set Me Free
4. I'm Tryin'
5. Time To Fly
6. When The Mornin' Comes
7. Once Upon A Time
8. Dandelion
9. Charlie
10. Blame It On Me
11. Sweet Dream
12. All My Dreams Come True

II. The Lucky Spot (Rev Records 2007, CD)
1. It Ain't Love
2. Long Gone
3. Lucky Spot
4. Sorryville
5. Show Your Mama
6. Baby Sister
7. Never Ever
8. Ramblin
9. Do You Miss Her
10. Top Of That Mountain

Comments: With musicians like Dan Baird and Ken McMahan involved, how could *The Lucky Spot* fail to be great? Bassist Al Collins, Stacie's husband, is no slacker, either, and has been playing with **Jason & the Scorchers** on their rare live performances as of late.

THE COMFIES
Web: www.thecomfies.com

Band Members:
Benjamin Adam Harper (vocals, guitar) (I)
Rafael Cevallos (guitar, vocals) (I)
Nathan Hansen (bass) (I)
Sam Smith (drums) (I)

Other Musicians:
Andrea Barrett (vocals) (I)

Stacie Collins

Dave Cloud

Keith Lowen (bass) (I)
Bill Slattery (drums) (I)

The Comfies Recordings:

I. Close To Me (Livewire Recordings 2006, CD)
1. Close To Me
2. That's What She Gets
3. Medicine
4. In My Room
5. Your Sunshine
6. Understanding 23
7. Dear Miss Anderson

Comments: The Comfies were formerly known as Harper, but had to change the band's name because of some damn Australian didgeridoo player that goes by that name. All of the band's members are seasoned scene vets, Cevallos from **the Pink Spiders**, Hansen from **Bang Bang Bang** (now **American Bang**) and Silent Friction, and Sam Smith from **Lifeboy** and **Character**.

Another View: "Something like the Posies with a dash of Superdrag's saccharine harmonies, Britpop sensibility and firm grasp of the hook." – *The Nashville Scene*

COMMA 8 COMMA 1

Comments: Contributed the song "River Collectibles" to *Spin Cycle*, the 1997 NeA Extravaganza comp CD.

COSMIC FLIGHT

Band Members:
William Linton (synthesizers) (I)
Anthony Rian (synthesizers) (I)
Mason Stevens (guitar) (I)

Cosmic Flight Recordings:

I. Cosmic Flight (Emerald Castle Music 1987, cassette)
Side One
1. Pole Star
2. Solar Eclipse

Side Two
3. Cosmic Flight

Comments: Anthony Rian is actually **Tony Gerber** (Anthony Rian Gerber to be precise), and Cosmic Flight is actually Atreeo, but trending more towards "space music" than electronic experimentation. This cassette was a defining moment in the local space/ambient music community, receiving national airplay on the award-winning *Hearts Of Space* public radio program and thus setting the stage for musicians like Linton,

Gerber, **Giles Reaves** and even **Aashid** to make the Music City a focal point of the international space music scene.

SHERRY COTHRAN

Band Members:
Sherry Cothran (vocals, guitar) (I)
Brian Reed (guitars, keyboards) (I)
Ethan Pilzer (bass) (I)
Andy Hull (drums) (I)
Jeff Roach (keyboards) (I)

Sherry Cothran Recordings:

I. Who Let The World In (Rain Records 2004, CD)
1. Carried Along
2. Blackbirds
3. Tired of Waiting For You
4. To Be Someone
5. Who Let The World In
6. The Pearl
7. Let Your Hair Down
8. Nothing Broken
9. Bunny The Rain God
10. Whipporwhill

Comments: Don't let the alleged "solo" status of this first album from singer/songwriter Sherry Cothran fool you – this is really just **the Evinrudes** by another name, albeit with a

The Clutters

slightly more pop-oriented direction. Cothran's vocals are still strong and alluring, Reed's guitarwork still underrated.

KRISTEN COTHRON

Band Members:
Kristen Cothron (vocals, guitar) (I)

Other Musicians:
Dan Baird (guitar) (I)
Pat Buchanan (guitar) (I)
Chris Carmichael (strings) (I)
Tony Harrell (keyboards) (I)
Greg Morrow (drums) (I)
Alison Prestwood (bass) (I)
Vince Santuro (drums) (I)
Ben Strano (guitar, piano, Mellotron) (I)

Kristen Cothron Recordings:

I. *Love Letters From A Fool* (self-produced CD, 2006)
1. Dangerous
2. High on the Blues
3. Last Chance Girl

Kristen Cothron

4. Love Letters from a Fool
5. Your Love
6. RSVP
7. Slow Down
8. Whenever You Come Around
9. Love is a Gamble
10. Fall

THE CREEPING CRUDS

Band Members:
Manthon (vocals) (I)
Ziggy McNasty (guitars, vocals) (I)
Jeano Roid (guitars, vocals) (I)
Phil Crudd (drums, vocals) (I)

Other Members:
Dr. Wolfie Von Wolfsbane (vocals)
Don Of The Dead (bass)
Old Dirty Boomer (drums)

Creeping Cruds Recordings:

I. *The Incredibly Strange People Who Stopped Living And Became...* (Horror Bands 2005, CD)
1. Intro
2. All Hail The Horror Host
3. Blood On The Banisters
4. I Sold My Brain
5. I Eat The Living
6. Driving Miss Zombie
7. The Ghosts Of West Memphis
8. Stomp Tokyo
9. Blood Moon
10. I, Vampire

Comments: Nashville's answer to the Misfits delivered a very cool collection of horror flick punk rock.

CROP CIRCLE HOAX

Band Members:
Justin Tidwell (bass, vocals) (I, II)
Grey Carter (guitar, vocals) (I, II)
Cole Carter (guitar, vocals) (I, II)
Tom Lord (drums, vocals) (I, II)

Crop Circle Hoax Recordings:

I. *Scope_Resolution_Operator* (Thump AV, no date, cassette)
Program A
1. Oa Oa Ah
2. When You Do
3. Nothing Nowhere
4. Tried To

5. Too Late
6. Changes Me
7. Voodoo Magic

Program B
8. 2nd Chance
9. Fail
10. Anti-Matter
11. Explain
12. I Am

II. Tour of the NATO Countries (Ambient Slutch, no date, CD)
1. Warmup Set
2. Ever
3. I Do
4. Driving
5. She Hangs The Planets
6. Head Is Wrong
7. 50%
8. Don't Know Why
9. On My Side
10. Shot You
11. Rot Away
12. Bend My Heart
13. As Much As
14. Hope To Die
15. I Don't Care
16. G-Frenzy
17. Days
18. Wait
19. Treehouse
20. Clack
21. Waste

CRUEL BLUE

Band Members:
Bob Bowden (vocals, guitars) (I)
Tony Morreale (bass, vocals) (I)
Tim Hunze (drums, vocals) (I)
Michael Praytor (keyboards) (I)

Cruel Blue Recordings:

I. Up Steep Stairs (King Yippie Music 1988, cassette)

Side One
1. Nada Song
2. On The Beach
3. Dream In Front Of Me

Side Two
4. Elizabeth's Lovers
5. Eggshells
6. Lose Me

From the Murfreesboro Musicfest 2 program (1989):
"The guitar-dominated lyricism of psychedelia, disciplined by punk's brevity and force, erupts in Cruel Blue's version of power-pop at its best."

Comments: I don't know a heck of a lot about this Murfreesboro band outside of the cassette that they sent to me or *The Metro* back in the day. In the band's first year they appeared with national acts like Men Without Hats and the Wild Seeds. I got to know Tony Morreale later when he worked for Sony Records.

CRYSTAL ZOO

Band Members:
Keith Flynn (vocals)
Jeff Anders (guitar)
Matt Sluder (guitar, vocals)
Mickey Hayes (drums, vocals)

Comments: Asheville, North Carolina band that relocated to Nashville, had some high-powered folks behind them. Allman Brothers guitarist Warren Haynes produced the band's demos, and the Crystal Zoo was managed by Doc Fields of the Creative Action Music Group.

MARY CUTRUFELLO

Band Members:
Mary Cutrufello (vocals, guitars) (I)

Mary Cutrufello Recordings:

I. When The Night Is Through (Mercury Records 1998, CD)
1. Sunny Day
2. She Can't Let Go
3. Sweet Promise of Love
4. Tired and Thirty
5. Miss You #3
6. Tonight's the Night
7. Highway 59 (Let It Rain)
8. Sister Cecil
9. Sad, Sad World
10. Rollin' and Tumblin'
11. Two Hard Roads
12. Goodnight Dark Angel

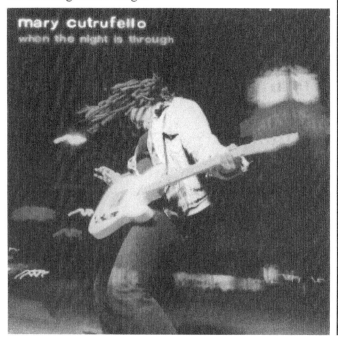

MARY CUTRUFELLO
When The Night Is Through
(Mercury)

"Heartland" rock ruled the roost during the 1980, dominating the charts and blazing a fearsome trail through the arenas and stadiums of Middle America. This roots-based style of rock 'n' roll, once practiced by folks like Bruce Springsteen, Bob Seger and John Mellencamp, has today become sadly passe. Not because there was anything fundamentally wrong with the music. The cynicism of the early 1990s, perhaps best illustrated by Kurt Cobain and Nirvana and their many clones, has given way to an entirely market-driven pop music landscape that is light, fluffy, non-controversial and, well, coldly calculated to separate the fools, er…record buying public from their hard-earned coin. There's no room at the inn for gritty, optimistic, realistic, guitar-driven rock 'n' roll…

An entirely engaging debut from an unabashed Springsteen fan, Mary Cutrufello – a young African-American woman – makes with ***When The Night Is Through*** the best case yet for the equality and liberation provided by rock music. Working in a vein that is definitely "heartland" influenced, Cutrufello belts out songs of love and betrayal, the weariness of life's burdens and the endless possibilities of two lanes of smooth blacktop like a character out of a Springsteen song.

Like most debuts, ***When The Night Is Through*** has its flaws, mostly due to Cutrufello's unchained exuberance. But when Cutrufello hits the bull's eye – such as with the bittersweet "Tired And Thirty" or the anthemic "Tonight's The Night" – she creates an emotional mix of lyrics and music that is universally appealing and overtly optimistic in the face of overwhelming circumstances. It's this lyrical ability to relate realistic common themes that made heartland rock so popular with the mass of working class fans in the first place, fans that have been ill served these past few years by vacuous pop and over-promoted, pre-fabricated trends like electronica.

Definitely out-of-step with musical trends and cultural currents, Cutrufello marches to the beat of her own different drummer. Whether she represents the first ripples in a new wave of heartland rock or is merely a musical anomaly, Cutrufello feels the passion that drove such rockers as Bruce Springsteen, Joe Grushecky or John Mellencamp to create great music.

Like she says in "Tonight's The Night": "I'm almost 22 and I'm old enough to know/'bout the fire in my heart and the fever in my soul…" It's a testament to Cutrufello's talent and charisma that she got to buck the trends and make ***When The Night Is Through*** in the first place. I'm willing to bet that we'll hear more from this young talent in the future.
– *Alt.Culture.Guide,* 1998

*G*uitarist Jeff Cease has been a fixture on the Nashville rock scene since he was a teenager in the early 1980s. Bands like the Wayouts and Rumble Circus helped define rock 'n' roll in the Music City during the 1980s, putting Nashville on the map for something more than country music. Cease spent a couple of years with the Black Crowes, playing on the Crowes' enormous 1990 debut album Shake Your Moneymaker and touring the world before parting ways with the brothers Robinson. Cease ended up back in Nashville, forming the popular Rayon City Quartet, and he continues to make a living as a professional musician...not an easy endeavor in this day and time. We spoke by phone in April 2007...

What got you interested in music in the first place?
When I was a kid, my parents were both from Memphis, so they had a bunch of Memphis music around the house...Jerry Lee, a lot of Elvis records...and I liked it. I remember we had Ike and Tina Turner and Chuck Berry. No one in my family was musically inclined at all, but my dad and mom had an acoustic guitar sitting around the house and I migrated to it and picked it up. I wanted an electric guitar, so my dad said 'well, if you learn to play three songs on acoustic, I'll buy you an electric.' So I learned to play "Wildwood Flower" by the Carter family, and then two other songs I can't remember, and then I got some kind of off-brand electric and a little amp...then it was over.

Then you were on your way, huh?
Yeah, there was no going back, and I was young, I was 10 or 11

What was the first band you guys came up with?
The first real band I was in was a little hardcore punk band called Social Tension, and we were all a weird bunch of kids! We were totally into the punk rock scene; we were totally a fuckin' American hardcore band!

We did all-ages shows; I think we probably did the first all-ages show ever at Cantrell's. We played a Sunday matinee at 3:00, and it was us and another band from Knoxville called the Arbitraries...we were doing an all-ages show and it turned into a thing, and we had great crowds on Sundays. We were probably doing five of them.

Do you remember who was in that band with you?
The singer was a guy named Robert Perry; the drummer was Jason Cook, who was an English fellow. His sister was Katie Cook, she's a host on CMT now, and the bass player was Frank Masse.

So where did you go from Social Tension, did you go to the Wayouts...?
Yeah, the Wayouts was the natural progression; it went from straight edge to the Replacements. The Wayouts...we were all in high school, we were the funniest damn band. I think we started probably the summer of 1984, we started playing together and the bass player was a guy named Bobby Green who was also in Swing and in Rayon City Quartet, who I played with later on. We met in high school and became instantly best friends, just two guys that really understood each other, we both had similar passions for music.

That was back when there was a lot more innocence in the scene and everyone was kind of in it together...
Yeah it was, everyone was friends and all the other bands were our buddies and we lived with different people who were in other bands. The Wayouts, it was only a three piece band and eventually we started adding guitar players and we just had different friends show up and play guitar. I know Chris Feinstein and Scott Feinstein both from Shadow Fifteen played with us, Gary Privett played with us, some random guy from New Jersey named Dave who we met in a bar one night...

Dave from Jersey, huh?
Yeah, he was driving through Nashville and he seemed like a nice enough guy, and he had a guitar and we had him come to practice with us and he ended up staying in Nashville for a month and played in our band for a month and we just hung out. That's all the guy did. So we were that kind of band, we attracted all these bizarre people, we were so inspired by the Replacements, it was so obvious.

What are some of your other memories of the Wayouts, what were some of your best gigs and some of your worst?
Oh man, they were all great! They were all great, and none of them were any good. The one picture I have of our band is this thing – we didn't document anything, you know – we played a thing called the Ice Cream Social at that hotel that was behind the Shoney's Inn over on Music Row...we played there with Chapel of Roses one night and I can get you a picture, it's the only picture of the three of us.

INTERVIEW: JEFF CEASE

There was another picture of us that's got four members in the band, but the reason there's four members in the band…I was going to do an interview with the girl at the school paper and I was skipping class to do an interview. I was in the bathroom on the way to the library with a friend of mine named Chris Parks and he asked "what are you doing" and I said "I'm going to go do this interview." Then he says, "man, I don't want to go back to class" so I said "come with me and we'll say you're in the band." So he did the interview with us – the guy didn't play an instrument at all, and he comes and does the interview, so we had to have him in the pictures so it's this picture of four guys.

I remember we opened for the White Animals once in Chattanooga and that was hysterical because we got there and I don't know who drove us there because I didn't have a license, I wasn't old enough to drive, but we get there and there are these beer bash things and it's like 5:00 and we're supposed to be playing like 9:00 or 10:00 and we don't know anybody, so we started drinking at 5:00. So I can only imagine how horrible we were, but that night was hilarious. We went down to Birmingham, we played down there, we would do a lot of house parties. We did a party once at the Methodist church in Brentwood and a bunch of punks showed up and they just trashed the place. We even played a toga party for a sorority and we would get drunk and play covers…we had a handful of originals that we would do but, you know, we were just being our idols…

Did you go from the Wayouts to Rumble Circus, is that what was next or...?
Yeah it took a while for Rumble Circus to develop. I kind of bashed around and did a few shows playing acoustic guitar for a while trying to figure out what I was going to do. To show you how close the Nashville scene was, I remember after we split up, our drummer went to the Marines and I was going with this girl, she didn't want me to be in a band

anymore…she ran Bobby away and that was a drag because we were best friends…of course we still are, I actually talked to him today.

Yeah, but you probably don't even remember that girlfriend anymore...
I remember she was crazy! She made an impression. I knew who she was, but she made an impression. But I remember Tom Littlefield of the Questionnaires called me, so I went over to Tom's house and sat around…you're supposed to sit on the porch and drink beer, but he just wanted to know what I was going to do. He said, "I just want to make sure you were still going to play, 'cause I think you need to play, I think you have something going on and you need to find another band."

I've known Tom for quite a while... I knew his sister before I knew him because I dated a girl from Hillsboro who was part of that circle with Tom's sister Alex and we used to have parties at their house. I was always the oldest guy around all the kids, they were in high school and I was out, so Tom was more my age. He always looked at me like "who the hell are you?" But then we met each other later for an interview and started drinking beer, and you know how that goes...
I'll tell you the first time I ever met Tom we had heard about each other, our reputations preceded us. We were at Cantrell's and I don't know how it happened but we were sitting down, we were talking, and ten minutes later we were outside in the parking lot fighting.

Yeah that sounds like Tom, too.
And then five minutes after that we were back inside drinking and laughing again.

How did you end up getting Rumble Circle together?
Well, Eric Hubner had been in some other bands, and I'm not even sure of the bands he was in. He was a bass player in Rumble Circus and we had always spoken to each other, we kind of dug each other and we would hang out. He had this singer friend of his named Jeffrey, and they were trying to start a band, so we hooked up and the three of us started writing together and we went through a couple of different drummers trying to find the right guy and we finally got the right guy in Alan and that was probably '86 that we got that going on…

We started playing and, really, I had no idea what we were doing. I didn't know what the music business was; I didn't know what a record deal was. I had no idea. I remember Chris Feinstein sitting

The Way-Outs

me down and explaining a record deal to me and they were talking over my head! So, with Rumble Circus, we got together and started working and we realized, "you know, this is really good! There are some good songs here and so we actually sought out management and ended up working with Grace Reinbold, who was working with Royal Court of China and White Lace, if you remember them.

Yeah. I have a guy from up in Canada that bothers me about once a month that is a White Lace collector...
Oh my God!

There ain't much to collect, but because of this project he found me, and he thinks that I'm going to unearth some secret store of White Lace goodies.
Maybe there's a bunch of nice denim somewhere, I don't know...

So we ended up with Grace and at one point we actually had a deal, we were signed with a label called Wing Polygram and this was right before we played the Extravaganza in '88, and we had a lot of label interest. A couple of days before the Extravaganza, we had a meeting with them and they said "consider yourself signed, consider it done." We thought, "this is great!" So we go play the Extravaganza and we walk in there incredibly cocky, I smashed my guitar, we think we have a record deal so screw those people! We didn't talk to any other label people. Two weeks later, the people from Wing called back and said, "well, we spoke out of turn, looks like it's not going to happen." We were so pissed off!

How did you get hooked up with Grace? You were looking for management and...
I think we asked her to come see us, and she liked what she saw and signed us up and we got along really well. I always liked Grace, she was really nice. She was definitely in our court, you know, she would have done anything for us and I think she did as much as she could have.

I think that's the key statement right there. I think that, being based in Nashville, that she had an uphill climb. The record labels – and I've heard this from more than one local musician – the labels looked at Nashville as being some kind of backwoods province or something.
Yeah, yeah, especially in the mid-80s...a rock band out of Nashville? Nobody was interested.

What are some of your most memorable gigs with Rumble Circus?
Rumble Circus was a hell of a band...there was a man in Knoxville, I remember we played some place, it was a three story club and the bottom of it was a bar, street level was a bar, and the middle was a bar with a showroom in it where the bands played and then the

third level up on top was an apartment where the band could stay. I remember we played the show there and it was packed out, it was insane, and after the show we'd all go up to the third floor. We'd just finished playing, we took all our gear up there and cleaned it up and we're going downstairs and have a drink and some guy comes up and punches Jeffrey in the face.

We had no idea what went wrong! So me and our sound guy Steve Dibble, we start chasing the guy up the steps and there's these sawhorses that block off each level and as we get to each level, the guy keeps running and Dibble is taking the saw horses and throwing them down the steps. We get down to the bottom and Dibble and I both jump on the guy at the same time and we all go through the club's plate glass window, and as soon as we're outside, as soon as the glass hits the ground, we looked like a western movie. It was amazing...cops were everywhere!

The owner of the club grabbed me and Dibble, takes us upstairs, the guy that hit Jeffrey got away; I don't know what happened there. We didn't get in any trouble; it was just one of those things. Then another time we played some kind of dance or party for Harpeth Hall, we did it for money so we could record. It paid us a lot of money and they made us do three sets...we weren't an original band, so we're not going to do three sets, we worked up a few covers, but the great thing about that show was every set, every single set we opened with "Give Me Some Money" by Spinal Tap! The joke went completely over the crowd's head. Years later, I was talking to Radney Foster, and he says, "man, I was at that show! My wife was a teacher and I was in college, I was at the show as a chaperone and that was hilarious."

Did you guys ever release any music locally?
Rumble Circus never did. We had a videotape that was shot and we always thought that we were going to get a deal. We

Rumble Circus

played it from that angle, we never did get anything, release anything independently which we probably should have.

We did a video for one of our songs with a film student named Knox Wyatt. He said "you guys are my favorite band, I want to do a video for class, can I do you guys?" We said "hell yeah!" I remember we played one of those things downtown like Summer Lights and somebody from MTV, the guy's name was Kevin, I can't remember his last name, he was kind of a funny guy and he was showing videos of local bands in between sets and so we got our video shown up there. We got to go up on stage, it was really cool, we were up there with the Scorchers and Royal Court of China...

How long did Rumble Circle last?
I think I left the band in late 1988 and went to Atlanta to play with the Crowes. They got a couple of other guitar players and went on for a little bit longer, I'm not sure how long.

So how did you get hooked up with the Black Crowes anyway?
They saw Rumble Circus and George Drakoulias, who ended up producing *Shake Your Money Maker*, was interested in producing Rumble Circus. He was interested in Rumble Circus, so he came out in Atlanta and saw Rumble Circus and brought some of the Crowes guys with him, and I hit it off with them. The Crowes ended up needing a guitar player so they said "why don't you come down here and play with us?" I thought about it for a while and I hung out with them when they came to Nashville and there was a particular girlfriend...I wanted to get away from in Nashville, so I thought moving to Atlanta would be a good way to do it. It just kind of seemed that Rumble Circus had run its course, so I decided to move on.

Was there any other label interest for Rumble Circus?
We talked to other people but we never came as close to anyone as we did with that Wing Polygram deal, and I don't know for what reason they backed out, but once they backed out, there were conflicts and stuff...

After you left the Crowes, is that when you went with Rayon City Quartet?
Well, actually, after I left I did a lot of things...I've jumped all around. I moved up to New Jersey for a while, I lived in Arkansas for a while, I just wanted to kind of move around the country. It was the first time in my life I actually had some money and I had real freedom. I met my wife in Arkansas, so I ended up staying there. But I talked her into moving here to Nashville, and I think the first thing I did when I got back here was to play with band called Bitter Pills with Frank Caldwell, Tony Frost, and Richard Ide.

That was fun, it was a good little pop thing, but Bobby and I – Bobby from the Wayouts – we started talking again and we

talked about music. It's just so contagious for the two of us, put us in the same room and we're going to pull out a guitar and try to write a song. We get such a kick out of playing together and our interests are so similar. So Rayon City Quartet just came out of that, just a really strong friendship. We worked the hell out of that thing, we put out one CD and it did really good. We put it out independently and we made our money back on it.

That's doing pretty good for an independent release, to break even.
It was great and we had such a good time doing it that we made a second record and about the time we finished it, we had already written a third record and we just kind of, everybody started having kids and, I think, for some reason I'm the one that wants to play all the time. I'm the guy, I'm the lifer, and not everyone is like that and I think I drove everybody else crazy.

Who else was in Rayon City Quartet?
It was Bobby, the bass player was Jack Garland, and the drummer was Jeffrey Perkins.

What did you end up doing after Rayon City?
Well, I took a little time off, I became a professional person. I did professional work and I hated it, so I put myself back out there and started doing guitar for hire. Now I'm playing country and I play with an artist named Trent Tomlinson who's on Lyric Street, it's a Disney label and I'm in his touring band, so I work a lot.

Who were some of your musical influences through the years?
I listen to so many things, I always have. I've always been very open-minded about music. The Rolling Stones are a tremendous influence on me throughout everything. Even when we were in the Wayouts, we did a couple of Stones songs. When I was in Rumble Circus I was hugely into 1960s-era garage punk, the more obscure the better. I would go to shops and seek out those viral collections of oddball, mid-60s garage bands.

If you could play with anybody, who would you like to play with?
I don't know, there's so many...I could probably take Ronnie's place in the Stones. For years, I wanted to play with [Paul] Westerberg [the Replacements]; I thought I could bring something to what he does. I'd like to play with Mike Ness from Social Distortion.

DADDY

Band Members:
Will Kimbrough (vocals, guitar) (I-II)
Tommy Womack (vocals, guitar) (I-II)
Dave Jacques (bass) (I-II)
John Deaderick (keyboards) (I-II)
Paul Griffith (drums) (I-II)

Daddy Recordings:

I. At The Woman's Club (Cedar Creek 2008, CD)
1. Glory Be
2. Cold Chill
3. I Don't Like It
4. Happy In Your Skin
5. Cousin Darryl
6. You Made Your Bed
7. I Miss Ronald Reagan
8. Nightmares
9. Martin Luther
10. Slide It In
11. Vicky Smith Blues
12. Too Much Truth
13. The Powers That Be/Ooh La La
14. Gloryland

Comments: A fine collection by two of the most talented performers in Nashville, **Will Kimbrough** and **Tommy Womack**, Daddy also includes some familiar sidemen and a strong selection of songs, performed live.

Another View: "Needing no introduction are the talented leading men of Daddy. Enter Tommy Womack and Will Kimbrough, whose partnership goes back to early-'90s Nashville; the two were beardless at the time, both pluckin' their guitars and barking in The bis-quits. Fast forward to February 18th and 19th, 2005 when these (mostly) original tracks were recorded live in Frankfort, Kentucky at the titular venue. Rumor has it the band is now banned from appearing there, but that's another story." – Robinson, *Miles Of Music*

II. For A Second Time (Cedar Creek Music 2009, CD)
1. Nobody From Nowhere
2. Early To Bed, Early To Rise
3. The Ballad Of Martin Luther King
4. Love In A Bottle
5. Wash & Fold
6. I Went To Heaven In A Dream Last Night
7. He Ain't Right
8. I Want To Be Clean
9. Hardshell Case
10. Redemption Is The Mother's Only Son

Comments: Second effort from the talented pairing of Will Kimbrough and Tommy Womack, with a skilled backing trio that compliment the chemistry and make Daddy one of the most exciting and intelligent bands on the scene today.

DANGEROUS

Band Members:
Tara Slee (vocals)
Todd Austin (guitars)
Donnie Castleman (bass)
Duke Kevorkian (drums)

THE DAYTS

Band Members:
Richie Owens (vocals, guitars) (A1)
Norm Rau/Ray (guitars) (A1)

The Dayts Recordings:

Singles

A1. I Don't Want You Around (Song Fountain Recording Co. 1982, 7" vinyl)
Side A
I Don't Want You Around

Side B
Never Wanted To Leave You

Comments: Popular Nashville band the **Resistors** – with **Richie Owens** and **Norm Rau** – moved to Los Angeles in search of fame and fortune. The band members dyed their

hair blonde, opened for folks like John Hiatt and the Bangles, and eventually came back to the Music City to tour the SE college circuit. Dunno who the other two blond guys in the band were, though...

DE NOVO DAHL
Web: www.denovodahl.com

Band Members:
Joel McAnulty (a/k/a Joel Dahl) (vocals, guitar) (I-IV)
Keith Lowen (bass, vocals) (III, IV)
Serai Zaffiro (vocals, percussion, omnichord) (I-IV)
Joey Andrews (a/k/a "Mixta Huxtable") (drums) (I-IV)
Matthew "Moose" Hungate (keyboards, vocals) (III, IV)
Mark Bond (a/k/a "Vovo Dahl") (keyboards) (I-II, IV)
Dave Carney (bass) (I-II)
Derek "Sandy" Sandidge (guitar) (I-II)
Jon Schneck (bass)
Other Musicians:
Jeff Carney (vocals) (IV)
Ian Fitchuk (vocals) (IV)
Peter Groenwald (keyboards, vocals) (IV)
Matt Slocum (pedal steel, cello) (IV)

De Novo Dahl Recordings:

I. De Novo Dahl (self-produced CD-R, 2003)
1. Top of the World
2. Waiting for My Friends
3. Mishka
4. Memphis
5. Rumors
6. Monsterproof

II. Cats & Kittens (Theory 8 Records 2005, CD)

Disc One ("Cats")
1. All Over Town
2. Jeffrey
3. Listen Up
4. I Woke Up Late
5. The Funk
6. Push Bottons
7. Ryan Patrick Huseman Darrow
8. Piggy's Adventure
9. Be Your Man
10. End of Time
11. Rub You Wrong
12. Conquest at Midnight
13. Monday Morning
14. Cowboy and the Frenchman
15. Sexy Come Lately
16. New Belief

Disc Two ("Kittens")
17. Magic
18. Sexy Mr. Falcon Jive Mister
19. Pop He Stop He
20. I Broke A Plate
21. Dinosaurs!
22. Big Ol' Buttons
23. Wanna Beer Man?
24. Target Practice
25. Rhythm PHD.
26. Turtle Italian
27. Rubber Dubbie
28. Doddy-Ball Upside Down
29. Little Conquest on the Prairie

De Novo Dahl, continued on page 120...

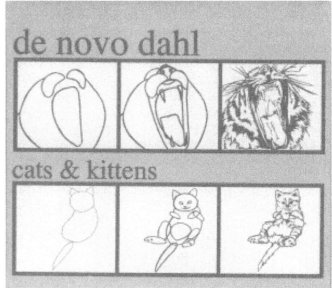

DADDY
For A Second Time
(Cedar Creek Music)

Back when you kiddies were still watching Saturday morning cartoons in your spidey PJs and eating chocolate-frosted sugar bombs by the boxful, two nice young men from Kentucky, and another from Alabama, were playing in a critically-acclaimed rock 'n' roll band called the bis-quits. Although these three gents had spun a wonderful collection of intelligent garage-pop with blues-rock overtones and a soupcon of country twang, they were soon forgotten, lost in the enormous commercial shadow of a bunch o' guys from Seattle named Kurt, Eddie, Chris and their, well, kinda grungy, flannel-clad friends.

Fast forward 16 years, and you'll find Daddy, which is, really, mathematically two-thirds of the bis-quits playing with some (talented) friends. Over the past decade-and-a-half or so, the three nice young men – Will Kimbrough, Tommy Womack, and Mike "Grimey" Grimes – have pursued various fates in and out of the music biz. Grimes played for a while with alt-country cut-ups Bare Jr. before escaping the industry's clutches only to open his much-lauded record store in Nashville (Grimey's Music on Eighth – tell 'em the Reverend sent ya!).

Kimbrough has toyed around with a critically-acclaimed solo career that has yielded four solid albums (and an EP), but his real bread-and-butter has been touring and recording as a guitar-for-hire for folks like Jimmy Buffett, Rodney Crowell, Todd Snider, and others. Womack, on the other hand, has put his experience with the bis-quits and, previously, the much beloved Kentucky cult band Govt. Cheese, to good use as a whipsmart, slightly neurotic, constantly embattled solo troubadour, also with four acclaimed studio albums (and a live disc) under his belt.

Daddy began as a one-off between friends and former bandmates, their live 2005 album *At The Woman's Club* documenting two nights' shows in Frankfort, Kentucky. As these things are wont to do, demand for Daddy and the band's growing popularity has resulted in *For A Second Time*, the official and righteous Daddy studio debut. A ten-song collection of various Kimbrough and Womack originals and a handful of collaborations between the two (and one excellent total band effort), *For A Second Time* may well be the best collection of pure music-making that you'll hear come out of Nashville this year.

As they say in Nashville, it all begins with a song – something forgotten long ago by the industry's Music Row – and Kimbrough and Womack are two of the best wordsmiths ever snubbed by the biz. Both songwriters have been around the block a time or three and suffered through the indignities

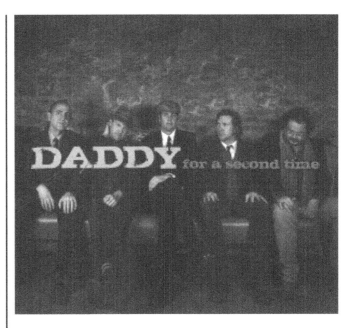

and ignorance of men in suits with corporate smiles, and their experience shines through their songs. The semi-biographical "Nobody From Nowhere," for instance, sounds like a John Hiatt outtake circa *Slow Turning*, but with Kimbrough's slinky fretwork and great harmony singing between Kimbrough and Womack. The song perfectly sums up the isolation of growing up in the rural South, where everything is miles away from anything else, and dreams of the big-time are tempered by simple pleasures.

Much of the rest of *For A Second Time* follows a similar tack, Kimbrough and Womack swapping lead vocals on songs that are built around the former's tempered optimism and the latter's wry sense of humor and joyful cynicism. "Early To Bed, Early To Rise" is Womack's advice to a younger generation, an only-slightly-tongue-in-cheek warning about the rat race from a man that has lived it firsthand. The New Orleans-tinged "Wash & Fold" possesses all the funky soul of the Meters, Kimbrough mouthing a sly come-on to a young lovely that is equal parts Ray Davies and Aaron Neville.

Of course, the Daddy guys also recognize a good song when they hear it, and their loving cover of '60s-era folkie Mike Millius' "The Ballad of Martin Luther King" provides the sort of intricate wordplay that Womack excels at spitting out. The ode to the African-American hero is especially ironic provided the band's deep-rooted Dixie sound, but these boys have always embraced equality in all things – especially music – and the song's folkie origins are amped up with squalls of harmonica, bluesy guitarwork, and more than a little introspection.

The full band collaboration "I Went To Heaven In A Dream Last Night" is a syncopated, almost stream-of-consciousness

DE NOVO DAHL - DEACON FIELDS - DECEMBER BOYS

tale of Womack's brush with the almighty that evinces a dark sense of humor, manic vocals, and more great throwaway lines and imagery than we can recount here (although "a funny thing happened on my way to the grave, I didn't burn out and I didn't fade away, my heart kept beating until the end of the ride" is a pretty damn funny line). The band backs it up with a funky-cool, twang-jazz soundtrack with lighter-than-feather cymbal brushing, scraps of honky-tonky piano, and Kimbrough's piercing six-string notes. "He Ain't Right" is another semi-autobiographical look back at childhood and what it's like to be smalltown different, the lyrics pounded home above a muscular rhythm, bee-sting fretwork, and potent, gospel-tinged keyboards.

Will Kimbrough and Tommy Womack bring the best out of each other, creatively, and with nearly two decades of friendship and shared musical history to work off of, it should come as no surprise that they're able to come up with gem after gem. The background guys in Daddy are no slouches, either, but rather talented pros able to cut loose from their day jobs and spin some fun, complex, and satisfying music behind their charismatic frontmen. Altogether, *For A Second Time* adds up to more than the sum of the individual band member's talents; Daddy the best band that you've never heard (yet). – *Blurt* magazine, 2009

De Novo Dahl, continued...

30. Piggy's Misadventure
31. Jose', You Love Me?
32. Absentee Ballad

III. Shout (Roadrunner Records 2007, CD-EP)
1. Shout
2. Sexy Come Lately
3. Dance Like David
4. Crap Your Pants Say Shout
5. Sexy Mr. Falcon Jive Mister
6. Dance Like David Bason

IV. Move Every Muscle, Make Every Sound (Roadrunner Records 2008, CD)
1. Shout
2. Heartbreaker
3. Means to an End
4. Make Some Sense
5. Be Your Man
6. Shakedown
7. Marketplace
8. Sky is Falling

Deacon Fields

9. New Hero
10. Wishful Thinking
11. Subject of the Kill
12. Been Kept Up
13. Not To Escape

DEACON FIELDS

Band Members:
John Alexander (vocals, guitar)
Lance Frizzell (guitars)
Rob Phillips (bass)
Mike Cull (drums)

Comments: Deacon Fields was a popular Murfreesboro hard rock band formed in the fall of 1986 by songwriter Frizzell. Alexander, from **F Particles** joined in the spring of 1987. I don't know of any recordings released by this band, but they opened for better-known bands like the dusters, Riff Rath, Eleven 59 and the Manikenz in Murfreesboro and Nashville. All four members were 18 years old or younger, and three were still in high school.

DECEMBER BOYS

Band Members:
Bill Lloyd (vocals, guitar, keyboards)
David Russell (guitar)
Scott Sullivant (bass, vocals)
Jim Hodgekins (drums)

Comments: Basically, December Boys was the original **Practical Stylists** band with a different name and the talents of **Bill Lloyd**, the band pursuing Lloyd's whip-smart power-pop vision. I remember seeing them at Summer Lights one year and they were great! Sadly, I don't believe that this outfit recorded anything, but if you look on YouTube or Allen Sullivants uber-cool Nashville '80s website, there's video.

DEL GIOVANNI CLIQUE
Web: www.myspace.com/delgiovanniclique

Band Members:
Jeff McKinney (vocals) (I)
Ian Wolczyk (guitar, vocals) (I)
Dave Viglione (bass) (I)
Jake Caldwell (drums, vocals) (I)
Henry Go (bass, vocals)
Casey Kinnan (drums)

Other Musicians:
Max Abrams (horns) (I)
Richard Del Favero (keyboards) (I)
Abbie Huxley (vocals)

Del Giovanni Cllique Recordings:

I. On Display (self-produced CD, 2004)
1. 212
2. Get Free
3. Push The Envelope
4. Amplify
5. Highly Combustible
6. Focus
7. Orbit
8. Stranger Things

Comments: Odd little band this, a curious mutant hybrid of funk-infused post-punk modern rock with rapped vocals. The band landed a Miller Lite sponsorship after winning a battle of the bands at 12th & Porter that was promoted by radio station 102.9 The Buzz.

First prize was $2,500 cash, free studio time, 5,000 CDs branded with the Miller Lite logo and other promotional materials, which resulted in *On Display*. The Del Giovanni Clique subsequently toured, opening for a wide range of headliners including Hoobastank, Everclear, SR-71, the North Mississippi Allstars, and Big Ass Truck.

Another View: "*On Display*, recorded at Nashville's The Spank Factory, is filled with head-bobbing hooks and jump-out-of-your-seat rhythms coupled with furious guitar riffs and thought-provoking lyrics. Hypnotically belching, "This is my freedom, my liberation, my season, my resurrection," the first track, "212," is underground anthem-worthy and a great introduction to the rest of the album.

The rocking, 311-inspired "Get Free" also fits into the "jump-up R&B" category by commanding audiences over and over again to bounce. "Push The Envelope," "Focus" and "Orbit" are more mellow and jazzy tracks, but still dripping with a high-powered freshness. The coda, "Stranger Things," reminds with a Red Hot Chili Peppers-inspired funk that

"stranger things have happened" than a white boy from Middle Tennessee trying to make a living as a rapper."
– Will Jordan, *Nashville Rage* (August 5, 2004)

DELTA HURRICANES

Band Members:
Will Rambeaux (vocals, guitar)
Dave Schultz (bass, vocals)
Craig Owens (drums)

Comments: Later become known as **Will Rambeaux & the Delta Hurricanes**. The song "White Trash," recorded with this line-up, appeared on WRVU's *Local Heroes* compilation tape. Rambeaux later released a single with a larger Delta Hurricanes band.

TOM DELUCA

Band Members: Tom Deluca (vocals, guitar)

Comments: Deluca, a talented songwriter, has had material recorded by Aldo Nova, David Allen Coe and Molly Hatchet.

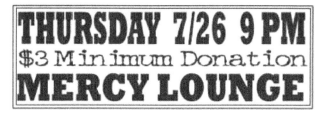

DESSAU

Band Members:
John Elliott (vocals, drums, keyboards) (A1-A5, I-III)
Skot Nelson (guitar) (A1-A3, II, III)
Mike Orr (bass, guitar) (A1-A5, I, III)
Norm Rau (guitar, percussion, vocals) (II)
Barry Nelson (bass) (A4, A5, I, III)

Other Musicians:
Steve Anderson (guitars) (III)
Paul Barker (bass, guitars, programming) (II, III)
Patrick Benson (drums) (A1)
Frank Brodlo (guitar) (A3, II)
Van Christie (programming, synths) (II)
Ken Coomer (drums) (II)
Kim Ervin (vocals) (A1)
Lynn Greer (percussion) (III)
Tom Gregory (percussion, vibes) (A2, A3)
Kevin Hamilton (guitar) (A1)
Price Harrison (vocals)
James Horn (bass) (A1)
Bill Jackson (guitars) (III)
Alain Jourgensen (guitar, programming) (A4)
Jim Marcus (programming) (II)
Jason McNinch (programming, synth, guitars) (II)
Richard Patrick (guitars) (II)
Brooks Phillips (guitar) (III)
Giles Reaves (programming, vocals, percussion) (A3)
Andy Schmidt (guitar) (A2)
Matt Swanson (programming) (II, III)
Terry Townson (horns) (III)
Luc Van Acker (guitars) (II)

Don Wallace (bass) (II)
Matt Warren (programming) (II)
Mars Williams (saxophone) (II)

Dessau Recordings:

Singles/EPs

A1. Red Languages (Dessau Limited 1985, 12" vinyl)
Side A
1. Red Languages

Side B
2. First Year
3. Crutch Of Utility

Comments: Dessau's first 12" EP was produced by Martin Hannett, most notable for his work with Joy Division, the Buzzcocks (as "Martin Zero") and New Order. Hannett was also basically the staff producer for Factory Records in his hometown of Manchester U.K. when he met Elliott.

Elliott later stood as best man at Hannett's wedding (see interview ➔) and convinced the producer, who was spiraling downwards into heroin addiction, to sit behind the board for these three songs. The collaboration worked, garnering Dessau attention from music fans that otherwise wouldn't have looked at the band twice, and it helped Hannett get back into the production game after a hiatus of several years.

What I Wrote At The Time: Elliott's musical philosophy is born of his other talent – carpentry. The band, Dessau, is named after a city in Germany where the Bauhaus style of architecture began. "The Bauhaus is a difficult style for a carpenter," he says, "it features clean lines and no crown molding and such...it's simple though sharp-edged."
– *The Metro*, September 1985

A2. Happy Mood (Faction Records 1986, 12" vinyl)
Side A
1. Europe Light
2. Imperial Hotel

Side B
3. Unshakeable
4. First Year

Comments: A mix-n-match of sessions collected by Dessau, with songs produced, variously, by **Robb Earls**, Tom Der, and others. Both "Imperial Hotel" and "Unshakeable" led the way on college radio and earned the band a label deal, even if it was a small label like Carlyle.

Dessau, continued on page 125...

It's taken thirty years, but Nashville's rock underground, well ... it ain't exactly "subterranean" anymore, innit? No, the cat's out of the bag now, and the dirt has been removed from the long dormant hopes-and-dreams™ of Nashville's non-country music scene. Bands like the Kings of Leon, the Pink Spiders and Paramore have attracted international attention while, shall we say, "artier" bands like Venus Hum have turned out well-respected records for major league labels.

'twas not always so, my little babies – not so long ago, Nashville was a truly scary place to be in a rock band, or even *write* about people who were in rock bands. It was just back at the dawn of the '90s that the editor of a national music magazine asked the Reverend, in all seriousness, if we wore "*shoes down there?*" True, this *was* the pre-millennial dark ages, but even then I distinctly recall Dave Willie sporting a really nice pair of shoes on his feet. Think of what it was like for Jason & the *Nashville* Scorchers or Webb Wilder the first time they ventured into the big city to play ... oh, the stories they could tell you.

But I digress ... those days are safely behind us, and urban sophisticates have recently realized that not only do we mostly all wear "shoes for industry" these days, but that a Nashville band doesn't have to wear Nudie suits and throw down with a fiddle to make good music (unless they want to, of course). Three distinctive Nashville bands – Be Your Own Pet, De Novo Dahl, and Umbrella Tree – recently released their sophomore efforts to no little praise and varying degrees of commercial success, helping firm up the Music City's place on the proverbial map.

Be Your Own Pet has particularly been receiving a lot of love from out-of-towners these days for *Get Awkward*, and the Reverend has seen the band mentioned favorably in publications from the British motherland to the mysterious Orient; even Tierra del Fuego seems to have joined in the chorus of praise for Nashville's next big thing. Producer Steven McDonald (of psychedelic-punk pranksters Redd Kross) – perhaps the best possible human to capture the band's shiny, guitar-heavy, noise-pop sound – returns to his seat behind the board for *Get Awkward*.

Get Awkward jumps straight into the fire with the turbo-charged "Super Soaked," an electric shake-and-bake sizzler that's straight outta the Detroit rawk songbook. Jemina Pearl's vocals are strident to a fault (as in earthquake) while Jonas Stein's rambling guitar delivers aftershocks in waves alongside the song's explosive rhythms. BYOP had to look deep in the racks at Phonoluxe for the vintage sound of "The Kelly Affair," a band-on-the-run tale of fun and hijinx in Hollywood that evokes fuzz-drenched '60s-era garage-rock with its manic riffing, clever lyrics, and John Eatherley's muscular drumming.

Although the band has matured in the year-and-a-half since its young, loud and snotty debut, *Get Awkward* has plenty of moments where every emotion is overwhelming, every perceived snub an uppercut. "Heart Throb" benefits

DE NOVO DAHL
Move Every Muscle, Make Every Sound

from whipsmart lyrics, syncopated rhythms led by Nathan Vasquez's bold bass lines, washes of razor-sharp guitar, and Pearl's manic, lovesick teen vocal gymnastics. The other side of the coin is "Bitches Leave," a cold, cold piss-off song with a nifty signature riff and snarling, spiteful vocals. The tribal Bow Wow Wow rhythms of "Zombie Graveyard Party!" are matched by Stein's sonic guitar-squawk and Pearl's effusive vocals.

Get Awkward lives up to all the hype, perfectly capturing BYOP's mix of youthful energy, cluttered instrumentation and flailing vocals. Be Your Own Pet has been compared once too often to New York's Yeah Yeah Yeahs, mainly because of the vocal similarities between that band's Karen O and Pearl's out-of-control yelp. Sorry, but YYY is soooo yesterday, treading water while looking for a lifesaver. BYOP is the sound of tomorrow, and if they make the same creative strides between *Get Awkward* and whatever their third album ends up being as they did between their debut and this one, you'll be seeing a lot more effusive comments in print and on the web about this band in the future.

Compared to Be Your Own Pet, De Novo Dahl has proved a bit more problematic for so-called "music journalists" outside of the critical zone (i.e. within 100 miles of Nashville, including Bowling Green and, of course, Murfreesboro). On one hand, the band delivers a lush, well-crafted brand of pop-influenced rock that is long on melody and short on the sort of attitude that bloggers and benchwarmers in the blue states eat up (and which the aforementioned BYOP delivers in spades).

On the other hand, however, the band dresses like refugees from Olde Nashville, clad in fancy vines like the Countrypolitan song-pimps that one used to see traipsing from Music Row to Lower Broadway to hang out in Tootsies. The hipper-than-thou literati just can't get a handle on De

CD REVIEW: NASHVILLE'S NEXT BIG THING

Novo Dahl, 'though they've spilled a lot of ink-and-electrons in the attempt. Further complicating this critical confusion is the fact that the band's *Move Every Muscle, Make Every Sound* was released by Roadrunner Records – a label better known for Nickelback and the sort of extreme metal that would make the hair on your toes curl. Thus, De Novo Dahl's commercial prospects seem questionable from the very beginning.

Regardless, *Move Every Muscle, Make Every Sound* is a simply delightful album, a wonderfully-constructed collection of throwback pop that would sound as equally at home in the early-70s as it does in the new millennium. There's nothing that's overtly retro here, or even remotely derivative, just a reckless appropriation of influences ranging from the Beatles and the Kinks to Bowie, the Move, even ELO … in short, all the right stuff at the right time.

The band has the chops to pull off such a hat trick, and De Novo Dahl covers a lot of stylistic ground with *Move Every Muscle, Make Every Sound*. The whimsical "Shout" is a lofty shooting star featuring Joel Dahl's slightly-accented Brit-punk vocals, delicious harmonies, and upbeat life-lesson lyrics. "Means to an End" mixes shoegazer sensibilities with a bit o' feedback, lush backing vocals, and an odd melody that reminds of *Revolver*-era Beatles. De Novo Dahl gets funky with "Shakedown," revisiting '70s soul with Dahl's best high falsetto, call-and-response harmonies, and a fat soundtrack of warbling synths, subtle drumwork and wa-wa guitar.

"The Sky Is Falling" revs things up with 100mph drumbeats, fast-paced vocals, roller-coaster keyboards, and an undeniable '80s new wave vibe. The somber "Not to Escape" is a melancholy dirge of many hues, Dahl's sinewy leads bursting out of the clouds of chiming keys, crashing symbols and shuffling drumbeats. "Be Your Man" is a whirling dervish of a song, the band taking a fair-to-middlin' White Stripes/Jet garage-rock concept and cranking up the intensity a notch or six. Dahl's vocals careen off the sides like a spastic pinball while a steady barrage of sound assaults your senses.

De Novo Dahl does a fine job of melding the band's disparate personalities into a single, creative whole. The band's chemistry is such that they emphasize a song's lyrics with combined efforts. Dahl's vocals are up front on most songs, but only by default … Serai Zaffiro's feminine wiles aren't far behind in the mix, offering a fine counterpoint, followed by the rest of the guys. Matt Hungate's keyboards provide color while bassist Keith Lowan and drummer Joey Andrews build a solid framework for each song.

Dahl's six-string work is understated but often elegant, and somewhat underutilized as a punctuation mark within the songs. In those moments when Zaffiro cuts loose with her omnichord, the instrument adds an alien, antediluvian, and entirely unique sound to the band's material. Add it all up, and *Move Every Muscle, Make Every Sound* is the sort of album that, while maybe not lighting up the charts right this moment, will nevertheless be "rediscovered" over and over by rock & roll archeologists for decades to come.

Coming fast down the stretch in their attempt to be Nashville's next big thing, Umbrella Tree is part of the same complex pop landscape as BYOP and De Novo Dahl, but it's there that the resemblance ends. Umbrella Tree's sophomore album, *The Church & The Hospital*, was released on their own independent Cephalopod Records label. If this charming, sometimes difficult and totally entertaining album doesn't net the band a deal, then the Reverend will eat his large-ish, size-14 Reeboks.

The Church & The Hospital is a deceptively engaging album, the songs creeping into your consciousness like some sort of purple plague. Umbrella Tree – the trio of Jillian Leigh, Zachary Gresham, and Derek Pearson – mine the same sort of art-pop vein that the old 4AD label bands once ruled with, but with a distinctly American twist. Whereas many 4AD bands brought a certain level of proper Britannic noblesse to their sound, Umbrella Tree imbues their work with an anarchistic spirit and inherent weirdness that can only come from a people that once started a war with the symbolic act of throwing a few crates of tea in the Boston harbor.

Not that Umbrella Tree isn't capable of creating songs of immense, shimmering beauty; *The Church & The Hospital* offers many such moments across its sprawling soundtrack. Leigh and Gresham intertwine their voices beneath the instrumentation, which itself is fueled by Leigh's delicate keyboards and Gresham's ethereal fretwork. Drummer Pearson is an integral part of the Umbrella Tree sound, adding blasts of bass drum or clashing cymbals when needed to poke a hole in the thick wall of sound.

There's a concept at work here, interlocking lyrical themes paired with scraps of recurring sound, sometimes operatic and other times slightly cabaret in nature. There's no single song on *The Church & The Hospital* that necessarily stands out as a radio track or quick fix for stardom. Instead the band has crafted an album as a unified entity. Taken out of context, songs like "Make Me A Priest" – an enchanting tale with lofty vocals and changing currents – or the confused, clever "Schizophrenia" would hit your ears like a hopeless hodge-podge of sound and chaos. In the company of their neighboring songs on *The Church & The Hospital*, they fit like pieces in a somewhat surrealistic puzzle, showcasing a band of no little talent and musical ambition.

None of these bands may break-out and become Nashville's "next big thing," or even the city's "first really big thing." With Be Your Own Pet, De Novo Dahl and Umbrella Tree representing the city, I do believe that we're in good hands…

(Review originally written for the Cashville411 website but never published…)

Dessau, continued...

Another View: "John Elliott, a Nashvillian who releases his work under the band name Dessau, loves icy, technological pop. On his second – and better – mini-album, he adds an aggressive, almost sinister undertone that makes this more appealing than most creations of this too-cool-for-you school of music...overall, the LP sounds remarkably focused and professional for the low budget that usually hinders such do-it-yourself projects." – *Nashville Banner*, January 1987

A3. Mad Hog (Carlyle Records 1988, 12" vinyl)
Side One
1. Skeletons By Nature
2. Thanksgiving

Side Two
3. Unshakeable Remix
4. Unshakeable Version

Comments: After a pair of impressive EPs that garnered a fair share of airplay on 91 Rock, Dessau signed with the fledgling Nashville indie Carlyle Records, the band's *Mad Hog* EP the label's inaugural release. "Skeletons By Nature" became a minor regional hit while "Unshakeable Remix," manipulated in the studio by Alain Jourgensen and Ion (Paul Barker) of Ministry, became Dessau's calling card.

Another View: "For the vinyl-head there are few moments as wonderful as the orgasmic rush of 'a find.' By this oen refers to that first head-on collision with something that has that reek of greatness to it. For this reviewer Dessau's latest EP *Mad Hog* is one such find. Hailing from Nashville TN, this group creates a vicious Warp-factor Nine mixture of noisy guitars, machine gun programming and blood-curdling vocals...tough, loud and ugly, these guys pack a wallop on a par with Chrome, Big Black or Young Gods without sounding that much like any of those bands."
– Robert Conroy, *Rockpool*, March 1988

Yet Another View: "Were Freddie Krueger to make a record, this is what it would sound like. You can almost hear him coming after you, knives and all, in "Unshakeable," which couples the beat of a horrified heart with a melange of chaotic noises underneath a set of drooling, disjointed, horrorama vocals. In fact, "Unshakeable" isn't the work of a boogie man, but rather the project of Nashville techno-rocker John Elliott in a combination with producer Alain Jourgensen (of Ministry and Revolting Cocks fame)...

Dessau's greatest virtue is that it doesn't fall into the trap of techno-crunge without passion. This record convinces you that it's even possible to dance to your worst anxieties. Fancy that." – Pat Grandjean, *The Bob*, June 1988

Say More? "Dessau serves up thick slabs of British-derived, sequencer-fueled gloom and doom stuff, buttressed by snarling guitars and heavily processed chant-vocals..." – *Option* magazine, July 1988

A4. Isolation (Carlyle Records 1989, 12" vinyl)
Side 1
1. Isolation

Side 2
2. Crowfest

Comments: It was right around here that Dessau broke out of Nashville and became an international phenomenon, due mostly to the rise of alternative dance clubs in the U.S. to match the existing clubs in Europe. Elliott's choice of the Joy Division obscurity "Isolation" was brilliant, and as produced by Jourgensen and Barker, the song kicked serious ass. The *Exercise In Tension* album would follow shortly thereafter, creating a worldwide audience for the boys from Nashville. I've bitched about Carlyle's amateurism in the past, but you have to give the label's Preston Sullivan and Laura Fraser credit...they may not have made much money, but Dessau gained a certain notoriety on a global scale.

A5. Beijing (Carlyle Records 1989, 12" vinyl)
Side A
1. Beijing

Side B
2. Europe Light Remix

Comments: Hoping that they could catch lightning in a bottle a second time, Carlyle released "Beijing" from *Exercise In Tension* as a 12-incher to follow up on the modest success of "Isolation." The song received significant radio airplay locally, but although "Beijing" was a solid song with a wicked hook, competition for deejay attention by the industrial dance bands that were popping up all over the place by this time was fierce; besides, the dancefloor crowd hadn't really tired of "Isolation" yet...

Albums/EPs

I. Exercise In Tension (Carlyle Records 1989, CD/LP)
1. Never Change
2. No Way
3. Move Seoul
4. Principal Tension
5. More Than Mao
6. Europe Light
7. Shovel
8. Isolation
9. Crowfest

10. Imperial Hotel Remix
11. Beijing
12. Europe Light Remix

Comments: Released by Nashville's Carlyle Records to a ready-made international market whose appetite had been whetted by industrial dance units like Ministry, Skinny Puppy, and Nitzer Ebb, "Isolation" and "Beijing" both became dancefloor hits, the latter striking hot with international acclaim, the former less so. On the whole, Dessau's first full-length album was an impressive effort, fusing hard rock with industrial dance rhythms in a manner not unlike Nine Inch Nails' *Pretty Hate Machine*, released the same year. Co-produced with a fine hand by **Giles Reaves**, *Exercise In Tension* put Dessau and Reaves alike on the world map.

The original vinyl album and cassette tape that I have has eight songs (#1-8); the initial Carlyle Records stateside CD release added "Crowfest" and "Imperial Hotel Remix." The CD that I have was made in Holland by "Carlyle Records Europe" and includes all twelve songs listed above. Perhaps if Carlyle had had the resources of NIN's TVT label, Elliott would be (justifiably) as acclaimed as Trent Reznor.

II. Details Sketchy (Fifth Colvmn Records 1995, CD)
1. Sun
2. (Un)Shakeable
3. Muscle
4. Chalk Line
5. Sun Burn
6. History
7. Chalk Rub
8. Old Dudes Rest

Comments: As fast as it had become popular, industrial dance music fell by the wayside with the new decade, disappearing like nerf-metal under the siege of Seattle. Disbanding Dessau, Elliott turned his studio talents toward contemporary Christian music, working with artists like Newsboys and Albertina Walker. Elliott joined former **Chagall Guevara** members Dave Perkins and Lynn Nichols in the band **Passafist**, the group's 1995 self-titled album receiving a Dove Award nomination for "Best Christian Heavy Metal Album."

Elliott would reform Dessau in 1993 with my old Franklin High School buddy, guitarist Norm Rau. Dessau released the heavier, less dance-oriented album *Details Sketchy* in 1995, collaborating with members of Ministry, Pigface, and Filter, as well as old friends like Skot Nelson and Frank Bordlo. Just as Ministry had added more guitars and moved towards a harder-edged, semi-metallic sound, the addition of Rau – a talented veteran of Nashville bands like **the Dayts** – moved Dessau in a direction that won the band a small, albeit loyal following that felt cheated by the "grunge" revolution.

In interviews done in the wake of the album's release, John expressed dissatisfaction with the CD, which was not much more than a collection of demos recorded at Die Warzau's Warzone studios in Chicago. A lot of the people advertised as appearing on the album, like Richard Patrick of Filter/Nine Inch Nails, barely appear on a single track but were used in the marketing nonetheless.

III. Dessau (Mausoleum 1995, CD)
1. Suffer
2. Thanksgiving
3. Spinning On My Head
4. Move Seoul
5. Skeletons By Nature
6. Isolation
7. Cull
8. No Way
9. Sun 90
10. Party Zone
11. Beijing
12. Unshakeable Remix

Comments: Somewhere along the line, the BMG-distributed Mausoleum label bought the rights to Dessau's back catalog. This self-titled disc for the label includes a handful of the band's best songs from the 1980s, including "Skeletons By Nature," "Isolation," and "Beijing" alongside five previously unreleased songs that had been produced by Paul Barker in 1990 and recorded at Robb Earls' Sound Vortex studios. The Barker tracks were originally slated for Dessau's second album, but Carlyle ran out of money and never released the LP.

Another View: "Usually not hip to this kind of sawed-off, minimalist industrial metal, but Dessau works in enough groove, given their dance preoccupation, turning half of these tracks catchy, fave being the familiar "Isolation" by Joy Division, which gets as much lope as a robot can muster. Nice, detached, stand-offish old Killing Joke snobbery to it, which also helps. Perfect for the all-night batcaves all those chemical people with no jobs go to."
– Martin Popoff, *The Collector's Guide To Heavy Metal, Volume 3: The Nineties*

DHARMAKAYA

Band Members:
Stacy Fleeman (vocals, guitar) (I-II)
A.J. Schaefer (guitars) (I-II)
Mike Adkins (bass) (II)
Brad Lawson (drums) (II)
Matthew Jensen (bass) (I)
Jerry Grey (drums) (I)

Dharmakaya Recordings:

I. Precious Mess (Spat! Records 2002, CD)
1. Spat!
2. Precious Mess
3. Mary Jane
4. Deepness
5. Synthetic Lies
6. Skarred (She Sold Her Hole for Rock and Roll)
7. Reach for the Sky
8. Becoming
9. Empty Cup
10. Transcendence
11. Piss and Moan

Another View: "Dharmakaya have unleashed a frenetically perfect indie-rock release that transforms the ears into a glob of glowing molten mush!" – Roger Moser Jr, *Razorcake* 2002

II. Garmonbozia (Spat! Records 2008, CD)
1. Let You Down
2. It Makes You Cry
3. Beautiful Indiscretion
4. All These Trips
5. Fallen Candle
6. Piss and Moan
7. Way Down Low
8. Seaside Suicide
9. Into the Pink

Comments: Very cool band with Spat's A.J. Schaefer on guitar and a solid vocalist in Stacy Fleeman, R.I.P.

THE DICKENS

Band Members:
Clay A. Broome (vocals, guitar, bass)
Paul Neihaus (guitars, vocals)
Dale Burton (drums)
Rex Garner (upright bass)

Comments: Paul Neihaus came from **Jerry Dale McFadden**'s band, Dale Burton played with Radney Foster.

DISARRAY
Web: www.disarrayonline.com

Band Members:
Chuck Bonnett (vocals, guitars) (I-V)
Joe "Hootch" Dotson (bass, guitar) (II, III, IV)
Jim Johnson (guitars) (I, II)
Jerry Lomax (bass, vocals) (I, II)
Chris Looney (bass) (III)
Vance Wright (bass, vocals) (V)
Shane Harmon (drums) (I, II)
Dewey Martin (drums) (III)
Tony Moseley (drums) (IV)
David Peridore (drums) (V)
Brad Trotter (drums)

Disarray Recordings:

I. Widespread Human Disaster (V.O.I.D. Records 1995, CD)

From the band's web site: Not content to spend years languishing in Nashville waiting for a "break" that might

never come, Bonnett adopted the punk rock work ethic of trading CDs, utilizing fanzine press, and self-booking tours. "We knew from the beginning that the industry would not take us seriously because we were from Nashville, so I chose to do as much as I could myself."

II. Bleed (V.O.I.D. Records 1996, CD)

III. Spreading The Death Plague (V.O.I.D. Records 1997, cassette)

Comments: Live, cassette-only release recorded at the Cannery in Nashville in December 1997.

IV. A Lesson In Respect (Eclipse Records 1999, CD)
1. Piss (Back-Stabbing Coward)
2. Forever Scorned
3. Mindless
4. Loss Of Tolerance
5. Exist To Suffer
6. Black Truth
7. Lesson In Respect (Face Down)
8. Your Fuct World
9. Failure
10. Eye Of Disgust
11. Uncontrollable Killing Addiction
12. Enslaved Race
13. Freebird

V. In the Face of the Enemy (Eclipse Records 2002, CD)
1. Depths of the Wreckage
2. To This Day

3. Voice of Reason
4. Open Wounds (self inflict)
5. Neverending Quest For Revenge
6. Path of No Regrets
7. This World
8. Powers That Be
9. I'll Be Standing
10. Burned Soul
11. Life Is Gone

Comments: Cult metal fave Disarray's tour-de-force, an album of unusual power and metallic thunder. Produced by Gwar's Dave Brockie ("Oderus Urungus"), the album caught the attention of hardcore metal fans worldwide, although these guys couldn't get arrested in Nashville...

Another View: "Hot on the heels of Brand New Sin (and even happy circumstances from Hatebreed), Disarray chime in with their fourth album, a record which slams with the metal danger of hardcore and grunge applied to old school grooves with a touch of New Orleans sound...for a power trio from Nashville, this is a momentous onslaught of sound, perfect beer-drinking metal with integrity, heft, and neck-snapping grooves...Disarray making pretty much everybody in this Southern-slammed field (except for Superjoint Ritual) sound lane and tame by comparison."
– Martin Popoff, *The Collector's Guide To Heavy Metal, Volume 4: The '00s*

DISCIPLES OF LOUD

Band Members:
Warner Hodges (vocals, guitars) (I)
Todd Austin (guitar, vocals) (I)
Kenny Ames (bass) (I)
Matt Green (drums) (I)

Disciples of Loud Recordings:

I. Let the Beatings Begin (self-produced CD-R, 2003)
1. UH-HUH
2. Wind Me Up
3. I'm Your Man
4. TICK TOCK
5. You Must Give Me Something
6. Shock to the System
7. Go Away
8. Seduction
9. Take Me Back
10. When Mercy Calls

Comments: A more hard rock-oriented band driven by extraordinary **Jason & the Scorchers** guitarist **Warner Hodges**, with Scorchers bassist Kenny Ames standing on the sideboards, and "Toddzilla" Austin riding shotgun.

DISCIPLINE

Band Members:
Robb Houston (vocals, guitar)
Leigh Maples (bass)
Jay Toole (keyboards)
Martin Kickliter (drums)

DORCHA

Band Members:
Clay Plunk (vocals)
Mike Simmonz (guitar)
Jamie Simmonz (bass)
Paul Simmonz (drums)

Comments: One of the many variations of the Simmonz Brothers; we used to call 'em "dorka" back in the day. Mike Simmons would go on to other projects, as would his brothers.

DR. NIK

Band Members:
John Cowan (vocals)
Mike Mahaffey (guitar)
Michael Jacques (bass)
Craig Krampf (drums)

Comments: Cowan came from the well-respected country band New Grass Revival; Krampf is a well-known session pro.

DREAMING IN ENGLISH

Band Members:
Tyrone Banks (vocals) (II)
Roger Nichols (guitars) (II)
Scott Thomas (guitars) (II)
Doc Downs (bass) (II)
Jeff Brown (drums, percussion) (II)
John Massey (bass)
Derek Wiseman (drums)
Drew Wiseman (keyboards)

Dreaming In English Recordings:

I. Dreaming In English (demo cassette)
1. Easier Said Than Done
2. Rhythm Of A Woman's Heart
3. Dreaming In English

II. Stuff (MOD Records 1998, CD)
1. Where's The Sun
2. Get Over It
3. Truth
4. What She Does
5. Girl I Love You…But
6. Incense
7. Revelation
8. Keep It Together
9. Sister Sunday
10. Fly

THE DRMLS

Band Members:
Jeff Allen (vocals)
Chris Camp
Dan Cook
Ralph Pace (drums)
Kirby Shelstad (synthesizers)

Drmls Recordings:

I. Spacetime (Scam Records 1986, LP)

Comments: The name is pronounced as "dremels" and for a while they were one of the most innovative bands on the local new music scene. Song "Into The Dreamlight" was included on the NEA's *What You Haven't Heard…* compilation CD.

THE DUSTERS

Band Members:
Ken McMahan (vocals, guitars) (A1, I-III)
L. David Barnette (bass) (A1, I-III)
Chris Sherlock (drums) (II, III)
Jeffrey Perkins (drums) (III)
Leo Overtoom (drums) (A1)

Dorcha

THE DUSTERS

The Dusters Recordings:

<u>Singles/EPs</u>

A1. Red Hot and Ready To Roll (Reptile 1988, 12" vinyl)
<u>Side A</u>
1. Red Hot and Ready To Roll

<u>Side B</u>
2. Look What The Cat Drug In
3. Take A Chance On Love

<u>Albums/EPs</u>

I. This Ain't No Jukebox (Reptile Records 1990, CD)
1. Phantom Of The Strip
2. The Truck Won't Start
3. This Ain't No Jukebox…We're A Rock 'N' Roll Band
4. How Could You
5. When I Knock (She Lets Me In)
6. Hellbound Train
7. Street Legal
8. What Can I Say
9. Blues Highway
10. How Much Longer

Comments: The dusters were an anomaly on the late 1980s local music scene, an unabashedly blues-oriented rock band whereas everybody else was playing nerf-metal or trying to out-alt the alt-rock bands. Fueled by **Kenny McMahan**'s fiery guitarwork and Dave Barnette's rock solid bass, the band quickly became one of the most popular outfits in Nashville and toured extensively cross-country.

II. Unlisted Number (DixieFrog Records 1992, CD)
1. Roadhouse Blues
2. Unlisted Number
3. Devil Risin' In Me
4. Rex Cycletire
5. She Cut Me Off
6. Power Over You
7. Don't The Girls All Get Prettier At Closing Time
8. Deep, Deep Scar
9. Something About You
10. Wild About My Baby
11. Red Hot & Ready To Roll
12. It Oughta Be A Crime

Comments: The dusters' second CD was released in Europe by French blues label DixieFrog Records with only limited distribution in the United States. Former dusters' drummer Chris Sherlock played on half of these tracks, new guy Jeffrey Perkins on the other half, including one of the band's signature songs, "Red Hot & Ready To Roll."

III. Dang! (DixieFrog Records 2002, CD)
1. Goin' Up Easy
2. Mexico
3. How Long
4. Red Sun
5. Killin' Time
6. Don't Love Me
7. Night Is Gone
8. She May Be Yours
9. Poison Love
10. Barn Door
11. I'm Sorry

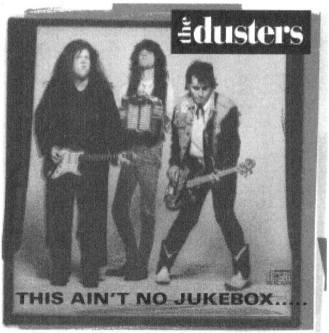

12. Cadillac Blues
13. Don't You Lie To Me

Comments: Ten years after their last album, Ken McMahan and Dave Barnette meet up by accident on historic Beale Street in Memphis. *Dang!* was the result, the band's third album and second for French based blues and blues-rock label DixieFrog.

The sound is exactly what you'd expect from the dusters, even a decade later...houserockin' blues and roots-rock, with original songs from McMahan, a couple of collaborations with **Tommy Womack**, a Chuck Berry song, and one from Kim Wilson of the Fabulous Thunderbirds, with production courtesy of McMahan's old pal **Dan Baird**.

After the dusters broke up in the early 1990s, McMahan recorded three very good albums for DixieFrog, none of which...sadly...ever received stateside distribution.

DUTCH

Band Members:
Dutch (vocals, guitar)
Rob James (guitar)
Kevin Kelp (bass)
Jerry Goldenson (drums)
Ed Commstock (keyboards)
Dave Brown (guitar)

Comments: Band contributed song "Hallelujah World" to the *Music City Rock* 1995 compilation CD.

THE DYNAMITES w/CHARLES WALKER

Band Members:
Charles Walker (vocals) (I-II)
Bill Elder a/k/a Leo Black (guitar) (I-II)
Jackson Eppley (bass) (I)
Rich Brinsfield (bass) (II)
Derrek Phillips (drums) (I-II)
Chris "Krushar" Patterson (percussion) (I-II)
Tyrone Dickerson (keyboards) (I-II)
Charles Treadway (keyboards) (II)
Jonathan Jackson (saxophones) (I-II)
Chris West (saxophones) (I-II)
Jon-Paul Frappier (trumpet) (I-II)

The Dynamites Recordings:

I. Kaboom! (Outta Sight Records 2007, CD)
1. Body Snatcher
2. Own Thing
3. Can You Feel It?
4. Come On In
5. Way Down South
6. Slinky
7. Every Time
8. Dig Deeper
9. What's It Gonna Be?
10. Killin' It

Comments: Charles Walker is an old-school soul shouter, an original that made his bones performing at Nashville's New Era club during the 1950s, and recording with noted producer Ted Jarrett. Walker left Nashville sometime during the early-

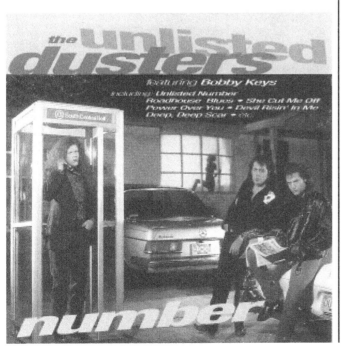

THE DYNAMITES

1960s, relocating to New York City and putting together Little Charles and the Sidewinders, an obscure soul band that held court at Small's Paradise in Harlem. Beloved by collectors of "Northern Soul," especially in Europe, Little Charles and the Sidewinders recorded sides for Chess and Decca.

Through a string of circumstances that we can all be happy about, Michael Gray – one of the curators of the Country Music Hall of Fame's wonderful "Night Train To Nashville" exhibit – introduced Grimey's co-owner/WRVU deejay Doyle "D-Funk" Davis to the charms of vocalist Walker.

In turn, Davis brought Walker to the attention of Bill Elder, local musician and producer, who was trying to put together a righteous funk band but needed an authentic singer. It proved to be a marriage made in heaven, with Walker fronting the nine-piece Dynamites.

Another View: "It's never too late to appreciate someone with vocal talents this extraordinary and here's hoping this is the start of more albums that work off this durable, retro-styled soul vibe." – Hal Horowitz, *All Music Guide*

II. Burn It Down (Outta Sight Records 2009, CD)
1. Burn It Down
2. If I Had Known
3. Somebody's Got It Better
4. Can't Have Enough
5. Do The Right Thing
6. I Got Love For You
7. Treadneck
8. Somebody Stop Me
9. (It's A) Sunny Day
10. The Third Degree
11. If You Don't Mean It
12. The Real Deal

Another View: "Nashville's retro-soul band the Dynamites has two things going for it. The first is its leader, guitarist Leo Black (real name Bill Elder), who writes new material steeped in the traditions of 1960s and '70s soul and funk, giving the group a repertoire that is familiar but not too familiar. The second is featured lead singer Charles Walker, the 65-year-old soul veteran who gives the Dynamites a direct connection to the music and time they honor. These are, however, also the elements that the Dynamites have going against them. Black's basic template is the James Brown band, but he also creates music and arrangements that recall Curtis Mayfield ("Can't Have Enough"), the smooth soul of various vocal groups ("I Got Love [For You]"), and even early-'60s Jamaican rocksteady ("The Real Deal"). But every time he brings to mind some established artist or style of the glory days of R&B, he competes with it unsuccessfully (a problem that is more apparent on record than in concert, admittedly)." – William Ruhlmann, *All Music Guide*

Known as the home of country music, Nashville had a thriving rock scene back during the mid-to-late 1980s, with bands like Jason & the Scorchers (country-punk), the Shakers (Goth-folk), Afrikan Dreamland (blu-reggae), and Practical Stylists (power pop), among many others, exploring various musical styles and stylistic fusions. One of the most popular outfits on the scene at the time was the Dusters, a no-frills blues-rock band whose hard-charging sound was fueled by frontman Ken McMahan's raging fretwork and soul-twang vocals.

At the band's early 1990s peak, the Dusters received airplay on college radio and toured steadily throughout the South, songs like "This Ain't No Jukebox...We're A Rock 'n' Roll Band" and an incendiary cover of Savoy Brown's "Hellbound Train" thrilling audiences from one side of Dixie to the other. Signed to an independent label in the Music City, the band was unable to break out of the Nashville rock ghetto in spite of a touring sponsorship from Miller Beer.

By the mid-1990s the Dusters, like so many indie rockers, were crushed by the murky sounds coming out of Seattle. McMahan launched a solo career that resulted in three acclaimed albums for the French Dixie Frog label (which had also released the Dusters' 1992 album, *Unlisted Number*) before touring as part of Dan Baird's (the Georgia Satellites) band.

In 2002, the best and brightest Dusters line-up – guitarist McMahan, bassist David Barnette, and drummer Jeff Perkins – reunited for some Nashville-area shows which, in turn, led to a return to the studio by the band to record *Dang!* with Dan Baird producing. Although the CD went out of print nearly as rapidly as it was released, it's well worth digging up for the dedicated fan of roots/blues-rock, and is currently available digitally through iTunes, Rhapsody, eMusic, and other download sites. McMahan leads his classic power trio line-up through a baker's dozen of red-hot blues-rock romps, about 90% of them original tunes, with only a sparse handful of covers thrown in for flavor.

Dang! cranks up the amps with the album-opening "Goin' Up Easy," a McMahan co-write with esteemed Music City scribe Tommy Womack, the song a steamy slab of locomotive piledriver rhythms and blistering fretwork. The menacing "Mexico," co-written with Baird, who also adds rhythm guitar (if I'm not mistaken), is the best ZZ Top song that that lil' old band from Texas never recorded, full of muscular riffs, endless swagger, and a sordid storyline that would make the Senoritas blush. The song's uber-cool false ending is complimented by a hot, brief bluesy outro.

McMahan's "Red Sun" is a funky little sucker, with a sly rhythmic undercurrent, a mind-bending recurring riff, and rolling guitar solos that are warmer than a runaway bonfire.

You'll find more than a little Delta blues spirit in the dark-hued "Killin' Time," a malevolent tale of violence and retribution with a swamp-blues vibe, a slow-burning groove, and McMahan's shimmy-shake rattletrap guitar. The discerning ear will pick up all sorts of influences here, overt and covert alike, from Robert Johnson to Savoy Brown, from John Lee Hooker to the aforementioned ZZ Top.

"Night Is Gone" offers up some of McMahan's best guitar tone, kind of a cross between Bluesbreakers-era Clapton and Stevie Ray Vaughan, the song evincing just a hint of boogie-rock within its emotional, lovestruck lyrics. McMahan's six-string work here is taut and structured but still imaginative within the rhythmic framework.

McMahan's "Poison Love" is built on a classic Bo Diddley beat, but quickly beats it into submission with a revved-up rhythm that would sound positively punkish (think Black Keys or Immortal Lee County Killers) if not for McMahan's soulful Southern workingman's twang vox and the song's femme fatale subject matter.

"Barn Door" has a heart that is pure Chicago blues, the song itself mixing its metaphors with an urban soundtrack and a storyline that has one foot in roots-rock and the other in country-blues, while another McMahan original, "Cadillac Blues," is a smoldering sample of barroom blues, wearing its heart on its sleeve with low-slung guitar licks and subtle rhythms.

One of the album's few covers, of the great Chuck Berry's "Don't You Lie To Me," throws a little New Orleans barrelhouse flavor in with Neal Cappellino's spirited piano-pounding running like the Mississippi beneath McMahan's fluid vocals and a sturdy rhythmic framework.

CD REVIEW: THE DUSTERS' DANG!

Blowing back onto the blues scene like a tornado, the Dusters have made major strides during the band's ten or so years apart. Whereas the band had been enjoyable on record, if sometimes derivative in their approach, they were never anything less than devastating while on stage, and they could never capture their live performance dynamic on tape.

As the three band members continued to grow and evolve while playing with other musicians during the ensuing years, however, they brought this maturity to the studio when making *Dang!*

McMahan's guitarplay, always the band's strong suite, has been honed to a dangerous edge through the years. The rhythm section of David Barnette and Jeffrey Perkins has developed into an explosive combination, unobtrusive when need be, a brick to your face when the situation calls for such.

But the Dusters' secret weapon may be McMahan's skilled songwriting chops, seasoned by life and experience into an impressive bit of street poetry that combines a Southern rock heart with the soul of the blues. *Dang!* proves, without a doubt, that the Dusters are bad to the bone, with a black cat moan, and a lucky mojo hand. Can you dig it?

– About.com Blues, 2010

I remember quite well the first time I saw the dusters…they were the featured performers at the first annual Metro Nashville Music Awards show. I'd heard quite a bit about these guys, the proverbial "buzz" around town, so I figured that, although having quaffed more than a few cold brews while hanging around the backstage V.I.P. room, I'd stick around and check 'em out. After the guys walked off with four awards, including the 1989 "Band of the Year" trophy, they took the stage and proceeded to smoke the place, laying into a lengthy, energetic set of their trademark rockin' blues.

If the tasty licks being presented for your aural entertainment weren't enough, with dusters' axeman Ken McMahan cranking out red-hot, razor-sharp guitar riffs and bass player Dave Barnette putting down a heavy, rhythmic foundation, well, there was a certain, well-built young lass in a skintight, low-cut, leopard-skin jumpsuit putting on her own show in front of the stage, her sensual gyrations keeping time with the music. Putting as much into the reckless abandon of her dancing as the band was putting into their music, this anonymous siren was the perfect counterpoint to the dusters' own smoky, sensual performance.

If not the most popular band in the Music City, the dusters are certainly among the top three, continuously drawing large crowds at local clubs with their patented blend of blues-infused rock and roll. The recently announced nominations for the 1990 Metro Nashville Music Awards saw the band garnering nominations in an even dozen categories, including, again, "Band of the Year" as voted by the readers of the *Metro*. They recently signed up for a second year as members of the miller Genuine Draft Band Network, and their first, full-length debut LP, ***This Ain't No Jukebox…We're A Rock 'N' Roll Band***, is due out at the end of February.

Guitarist McMahan and bass player Barnette have been playing together for years. Say Ken McMahan, "around 1984, David and I had been playing together, calling ourselves P.J. & the Dusters. We had decided that, as a band, we didn't have a definite direction. I had to decide what kind of player that I really wanted to be, what it was that I was best at. The blues thing was a natural, the blues rock and roll. We had started out a little more rockabilly…so I asked David to do it, and Leo, our original drummer. We didn't take it straight out to Elliston Square, though…we kept it in house for a long time."

Say David Barnette, "we rehearsed for six to eight months before we played out, as a three piece. The whole point of it was, 'Why go out to the clubs and have to do all that building?' Five people come out, then ten people…" Adds McMahan, "we wanted to really make an impression. We had recorded three songs on a four track and we sent them out to Mike McCall, Oermann, everyone in town. We wanted to be

as good as we could before we went out and played, and that's how we got going. We started at Elliston Square, playing Writer's Nights on Wednesdays."

"We thought at the time," says McMahan, that the only people doing the rock and roll blues were like Stevie Ray Vaughn…he was getting away with it, although he wasn't real popular at the time, so we said, "people don't really like it that much, but we'll still be playing what we want to play and have a good time, at that. I guess that there was a need for that."

The lack of a mass market for rockin' blues hasn't hampered the dusters, nor prevented them from developing a rabid cult following, not only in Nashville, but across the entire Southeast. Of the blues, Ken states, "there's a lot of movement to keep everything alive and to let everybody know about it. That's my big thing…a lot of these guys are listening to Zeppelin in college and going, 'Yeah, Killing Floor,' and they think that Zeppelin wrote it when it was really Willie Dixon who wrote it. I would like people to know these things, and that's the way we've approached it. I was listening to Eric Clapton doing "Spoonful," thinking that he had to learn it from someone…"

Adds Barnette, "one thing that we're trying to do while we're on the road…not that we're the authority, the voice of the blues…but we go out and play these clubs and bars, performing in front of a lot of college kids. Their impression of the blues is that it's just some old boring black man singing boring, slow songs about getting drunk and that kind of stuff. We're showing them that it's not boring, that it's not slow!" Says McMahan, "Johnny Winter said, and I'll take his advice any time, 'just because we play fast moving stuff doesn't mean that it's not the blues.' He definitely plays some up-tempo stuff, as we do."

"We were up in Milwaukee, at the Miller Genuine Draft seminar," says Barnette, "and Willie Dixon was the guest speaker, talking about how we have to nurture the roots of the blues. 'If you don't nurture the roots,' he said, 'then you can't bear the fruits!'…talking about how all music derives from the blues." Says McMahan, "Dixon said, 'I don't care what you're playing…rap, zydeco, reggae…you take these three chords and you put them in a twelve bar format, that's where it all came from.' He's right…that's all that rock and roll is, structurally. Blues is the original American music."

The dusters released their first effort on vinyl in 1987, a three-song EP titled ***Red Hot and Ready To Roll*** which was met with critical acclaim and a very positive response from the fans. Says Ken, "it was released on Reptile Records. We've got a great relationship with Scott (Tutt), our manager, and he produces our records…it's sort of like the Bill Hamm thing with ZZ Top…he's our manager and he knows what we

INTERVIEW: THE DUSTERS

want." Adds David, "we're trying to keep control of our music. We don't want to just be somebody's pawn…if a major label wants to talk to us, we'd love to talk, but Scott loves the band and loves our music." Says McMahan, "We don't want somebody who's going to tell us, 'you need to add a keyboard player' or 'you'll have to do these songs.' Scott likes the songs that we wrote or else he never would have approached us about working with us."

Of the EP, Barnette says, "what we originally wanted to find out when we put our the three songs, before we went and got into debt to produce a quality, full-length studio album, we wanted to put out something that we could test, put out something to get some audience feedback. An EP wasn't as expensive, with the mastering and all, and we also figured, as far as radio went, why give them eleven songs when they 're going to pick three that they're going to play and the other eight are going to be in the trashcan? So we gave them three…a blues song, a rock song and a kind of funky song." Adds McMahan, It was sort of like a business card saying 'here are the dusters…you'll be seeing a lot of them'."

Through constant touring and the power of their exciting stage show, the dusters have built a following which stretches from Pennsylvania to Texas, a following eager for the release of the dusters' long awaited LP *This Ain't No Jukebox…We're A Rock 'N' Roll Band*. Says Ken, "it seems as if everything has fallen into place now. We've been taking a real grassroots style approach, with the label and everything. Just trying to get it out to the people, establish a fan base, and then when you have a record release, you already have people who want it, whereas if we'd stayed in Nashville and only played around here, we wouldn't have anything established."

Dave Barnette continues, "we've been trying to establish 500 people in every market on this side of the Mississippi that, when our record comes out, we'd automatically have a following that's going to buy it. There's a lot of bands coming out of Nashville that don't have that fan base, so their record comes out and they're at the mercy of their record company…if the company really wants to pump the money into them and get them known, they will, if not, you just have your record come out and…"

"Ours is just a different approach," adds David. "We're not saying that it's wrong to sign with a major label, it's just that for what we wanted to do, the type of music that we're doing, that we felt that we're better off going with an independent label. The way that we look at it, we're making a living doing, probably the hardest thing that there is to do, playing in clubs. There are a lot of people not going out to the clubs these days, and there are a whole lot of people who want to go to the clubs that aren't old enough…so we're looking at it

from the standpoint that we're not working any day gigs, so if we're making a living playing clubs, then we won't have any problems."

States McMahan, "also, with the band network, the Miller Genuine Draft network, it's almost the same type thing. It's interesting that they asked us to be in that. They're trying to get out to the people, too. They have twenty-six bands, one from each region. They picked us from Nashville, Duke Tomato from Indianapolis…they could have had three multimillion dollar bands, but they chose to break new artists, to help them get established."

The dusters originally signed with the Band Network at the first of 1989, recently re-signing for 1990. Says McMahan, "we've got a one-minute national radio spot that will come out in February or March. This is going to fall together good…the record will come out and the commercial campaign, already having us on the radio with the dusters' rock and roll spot …we can say 'this song is just like that spot!' There were only six bands out of the twenty-six chosen to do the commercials, so we feel good about it."

The dusters have added a new member, drummer Chris Sherlock. Says Ken, "Leo (Overtoom) left the band last November, just before we went up the East coast. We found Chris playing with Tommy Tutone at the Grapevine and we jammed with him. He's played with a bunch of people and he understands the kind of music that we're doing, where we're coming from." The addition of Sherlock, who has studied under such drum teachers as Darryl Brown and Bernard Purdie, has added further depth and another dimension to the dusters' already hot live show.

The dusters are carrying on a tradition of American music that dates back over sixty years, a tradition perhaps begun with legendary bluesman Robert Johnson, carrying that legacy proudly into the nineties. With the new year and their forthcoming new album, it seems as if the dusters really are red hot and ready to roll. I'd recommend catching them at this year's Metro Nashville Music Awards show, where not only are they sure to walk off with their share of accolades, but they'll once again be entertaining the audience with their skilled performance…and who knows, maybe the little number in the leopard-skin will be there again to keep 'em company. Either way, it promises to be a hell of a show!
– *The Metro*, 1990?

THE 8TH GRADE
Web: www.the8thgrade.com

Band Members:
Paul Cassella (vocals, guitar, keyboards) (I)
Matt Sexton (bass)
Austin Hall (bass, drums, vocals) (I)
James Pecora (drums, vocals) (I)

Other Musicians:
Dani Amendola (strings, keyboards) (I)
Matt Hauer (guitar) (I)
Adam McIntyre (guitar) (I)

The 8th Grade Recordings:

I. The 8th Grade (Big World Productions 2004?, CD)
1. Judy in Bloom
2. Underjoyed
3. Kalamazoo
4. The Lunch Function
5. The General
6. 25 Phone Calls
7. Dying in the Hospital
8. Worst Day of Your Life
9. New State Bird
10. Dirty Deeds Done Dirt Cheap

Comments: The 8th Grade's lone album offers up pop-punk done right, balancing indie-rock and singer/songwriter conventions with punkish intensity and three-chord glee.

JUSTIN TOWNES EARLE

Band Members:
Justin Townes Earle (vocals, guitars, harmonica) (I-III)

Other Musicians:
Keith Brogdon (drums) (II)
Elliot Currie (vocals) (II)
Bryn Davies (bass, cello, vocals) (II-III)
Pete Finney (steel guitar, Dobro) (II-III)
Josh Hedley (fiddle, viola, vocals) (II-III)
Manfred Jerome (tambourine) (II)
Brad Jones (bass, keyboards) (II)
Ben Martin (drums) (II)
Travis Nicholson (vocals) (II)
Brian Owings (drums) (II-III)
Steve Poulton (guitars) (II)
Chris Scruggs (lap steel) (II)
Dustin Welch (banjo, vocals) (II)
Skylar Wilson (piano, keyboards) (II-III)
Cory Younts (harmonica, mandolin, vocals) (II-III)

Justin Townes Earle Recordings:

I. Yuma (J-Trane Music 2007, CD EP)
1. The Ghost of Virginia
2. You Can't Leave
3. Yuma
4. I Don't Care
5. Let the Waters Rise
6. A Desolate Angels Blues

Comments: Yes, Justin is the son of country-rock (or, ahem…Americana) legend **Steve Earle** and the six-song *Yuma* was his self-produced introduction to the biz. Featuring just Earle, his instruments, and his voice, the rare EP was later given away free as an incentive to buy *The Good Life* at certain indie record stores.

Another View: "The surname 'Earle' may or may not impress you. But as the title track's tragedy unfolds – it's about a 23-year old who leaps off a building ('It wasn't so much the girl/Guess it was the booze and the dope/And the way he took the weight of the world/Up upon his shoulders') – and Earle's storytelling gifts become apparent, his middle name takes on a striking resonance, too. Bottom line: You won't need a molecular biologist to help you spot this young man's musical DNA." – Fred Mills, *Harp Magazine*

II. The Good Life (Bloodshot Records 2008, CD)
1. Hard Livin'
2. The Good Life
3. Who Am I to Say
4. Lone Pine Hill
5. South Georgia Sugar Babe

6. What Do You Do When You're Lonesome
7. Turn out My Lights
8. Lonesome and You
9. Ain't Glad I'm Leaving
10. Far Away in Another Town

Comments: The young Earle's proper debut is an impressive work that rivals that of his old man at the same age.

III. Midnight At The Movies (Bloodshot Records 2009, CD)
1. Midnight At The Movies
2. What I Mean To You
3. They Killed John Henry
4. Mama's Eyes
5. Dirty Rag
6. Can't Hardly Wait
7. Black Eyed Suzy
8. Poor Fool
9. Halfway To Jackson
10. Someday I'll Be Forgiven For This
11. Walk Out
12. Here We Go Again

STEVE EARLE

Band Members:
Steve Earle (vocals, guitar, bass, harmonica, mandolin) (A1, I-XVIII, D1)

The Dukes:
Eric "Roscoe" Ambel (guitars, keyboards) (XIV-XVI)
Bucky Baxter (pedal steel, dobro) (I, II, IV-VII, XVII)
Richard Bennett (bass, guitar, harmonium) (I, II, IX)
Kurt Custer (drums, vocals) (IV, VI, IX)
Justin Earle (guitar) (X, XV)

JUSTIN TOWNES EARLE
The Good Life
(Bloodshot Records)

When you're the son of a bona fide Americana music legend, and named after one of the greatest songwriters of the genre (Townes Van Zandt), expectations are high. With his full-length debut, ***The Good Life***, Justin Townes Earle delivers everything expected of him in spades. Not content to merely mimic his dad's work, the younger Earle takes his impressive songwriting skills in a number of diverse directions. Whereas his pappy's music tends to draw more from both rock and folk worlds, the younger Earle instead goes in the other direction, pulling the best from the Tennessee and Texas hillbilly traditions.

Growing up in a musical household, Earle had the opportunity to soak in all sorts of influences, and it shows in his work. An eerily-mature songwriter that is skilled beyond his years, Earle easily weaves together story-songs in his dad's image, but with his own voice and a widely differing soundtrack. The title track from ***The Good Life*** is a delicious 1960s-styled country throwback that sounds like a classic Faron Young tune, while the heartbreaking "Who Am I To Say" is reminiscent of namesake Van Zandt's stark folk poetry.

Other songs on ***The Good Life*** showcase Earle's mastery of a diverse range of country styles. "Lone Pine Hill" is a haunting Western dirge and "What Do You Do When You're Lonesome" is a weepy Texas dancehall ballad. "South Georgia Sugar Babe" is a bluesy, Southern rock/R&B hybrid with gumbo-funk rhythms while "Lonesome And You," with its mournful steel guitar and slow shuffle, is the sort of honky-tonk country that Ernest Tubb could crank out in his sleep. "Turn Out My Lights" is a delicate, finely-crafted folk ballad…and about as close as Justin gets to sounding like his famous father.

The vocals on ***The Good Life*** are warm, certain and soulful throughout. With boundless ambition and loads of talent, Earle easily ties together strains of roots-rock, folk-blues, Tex-Mex, Western Swing and traditional country in the creation of an amazing, remarkable debut album.
– *Blurt* magazine, 2008

Stacey Earle (vocals) (V, VI, XII)
Patrick Earle (drums, percussion) (V, XII, XIV-XVI)
Dwayne "Zip" Gibson (guitar) (V, VI)
Jack "Bullett" Harris (drums) (A1, III)
Ron "Reno" Kling (bass) (A1, II, III, XVII)
Kelly Looney (bass) (IV-VII, X, XII, XIV-XVI, D1)
Mike McAdam (guitar, vocals) (II, VII, XVII)
Ken Moore (keyboards, synth) (I, II, IV, V, VI, IX, XVII)
Will Rigby (drums, percussion) (XII, XIV-XVI,)
Donnie Roberts (guitars, bass) (IV, VII)
David Steele (guitars) (X, XII)
Harry Stinson (drums) (I, II, XVII)
Craig Wright (drums) (V, VI)

Other Musicians:
David Angell (violin) (XVI)
Brady Blade (drums) (X, B3, B5)
Norman Blake (guitar, dobro, Hawaiian guitar) (VIII)
K-Meaux Boudin (accordion) (II)
Mike Bubb (bass) (XIV)
Chris Carmichael (viola) (XVI)
Pat Carter (guitar) (A1, III)
Ken Coomer (drums, percussion) (XIV)
Dennis Crouch (upright bass) (XII, XV)

Willy Domann (bass) (XV)
Casey Driessen (fiddle) (XII, XV)
The Fairfield Four (vocals) (IX, X)
Paul Franklin (pedal steel) (I)
Emory Gordy Jr. (bass, mandolin, bass) (I, II)
Tommy Hannum (pedal steel) (X)
Emmylou Harris (vocals) (VIII, X, XIV, XVI)
David Henry (cello) (XVI)
Edward Henry (violin) (XVI)
Jim Hoke (saxophone) (X)
Roy Huskey Jr. (acoustic bass) (VIII, IX, X)
John Jarvis (synth, keyboards) (I, II, IV, V, XIV)
Ray Kennedy (guitars, percussion) (IX, X, XII)
Siobhan Maher-Kennedy (vocals) (XIV)
Buddy Miller (guitar, vocals) (B3, B5?)
Rick Kipp (bass) (IX)
Doug Lancio (guitars) (XII)
Tom Littlefield (vocals) (XII)
Bill Lloyd (guitars) (IV)
Kenny Malone (drums, percussion) (XIV)
Dan Metz (bass) (XII)
Scott Miller (vocals) (X)
Greg Morrow (drums, percussion) (IX)
Steve Nathan (synth) (I)

Steve Earle

STEVE EARLE

Tom O'Brien (mandolin, vocals) (XII, XV)
Martin Parker (drums) (A1, III)
Ross Rice (drums, vocals) (X)
Peter Rowan (guitars, mandolin, vocals) (VIII)
Rick Schell (drums) (IX)
Darrell Scott (banjo, vocals) (XII, XV)
Michael Smotherman (keyboards) (X)
Lester Snell (keyboards) (V)
Garrison Starr (vocals) (XV)
Mark Stuart (guitar, mandolin) (X)
Gary W. Tallent (bass) (IX)
Benmont Tench (keyboards) (XII)
Ron Vance (drums) (XII)
Lucinda Williams (vocals) (IX)

Steve Earle Recordings:

Singles/EPs

A1. Pink & Black (LSI Records 1982, 7" vinyl EP)
Side One
1. Nothin' But You
2. Continental Trailways Blues

Side Two
3. Squeeze Me In
4. My Baby Worships Me

Comments: Limited edition EP on 7" vinyl, issued by Earle's manager John Lomax III in three pressings of 1,000 copies each. There were a couple of other early singles, but since I don't have 'em, I can't list them, and I'm not even going to attempt a complete list of all of Earle's MCA singles and 12-inchers and promo discs…I'll leave that up to the fanatical collectors. Let's

just say that Earle has been a prolific songwriter and recording artist, and leave it at that, shall we?

Albums

I. Guitar Town (MCA Records 1986, CD/LP)
1. Guitar Town
2. Goodbye's All We Got Left
3. Hillbilly Highway
4. Good Ol' Boy (Getting Tough)
5. My Old Friend The Blues
6. Someday
7. Think It Over
8. Fearless Heart
9. Little Rock 'N' Roller
10. Down the Road
11. State Trooper (live)

Comments: Like a breath of fresh air blowing across Music Row and Nashville, *Guitar Town* was Steve Earle's coming out party. The album rose to number one on the *Billboard* country chart, spawned four hit singles, and was eventually certified Gold™ for sales of 500,000+ copies. It was largely snubbed by the Nashville country music community, however, Earle too wild and too much of a crazed genius to fit in with the city's rhinestone conservatives. The live version of Springsteen's "State Trooper" was slapped on the end of the 2002 CD reissue of *Guitar Town* as a bonus track.

Another View: "He's like ten thousand footloose rock-and-rollers before him, only he's got new ways to say it."
– Robert Christgau, **Christgau's Record Guide: The '80s**

II. Exit O (MCA Records 1987, CD/LP)
1. Nowhere Road
2. Sweet Little '66
3. No. 29
4. Angry Young Man
5. San Antonio Girl
6. The Rain Came Down
7. I Ain't Never Satisfied
8. The Week of Living Dangerously
9. I Love You Too Much
10. It's All Up To You

Comments: Earle's second album was credited to Steve Earle & the Dukes, recorded between live dates with his touring band rather than Nashville studio pros. The sound was tougher, more raucous, and further distanced Earle from the Music Row tastemakers. Then again, what the hell does Music Row know? While they were busy trying to ignore Earle for being too "rock & roll," in little hamlets from Springfield, Missouri to Seattle, Washington to Denton, Texas young musicians were checking out Earle and the Scorchers and deciding that it was OK to twang-and-bang, thus sowing the seeds of the 1990s-era "No Depression" alt-country movement. Although it didn't yield a country radio hit, *Exit 0* rose to #15 on the *Billboard* country chart while "I Ain't Never Satisfied" rose to #26 on the Modern Rock chart.

Another View: "Last time you knew he was a rock-and-roller because he was a soulful wiseass, full of piss, vinegar, and super-unleaded. This time you know he's a rock-and-roller because he puts his band's name on the slug line. Whether Nashville has a contract out on him or he harbors a secret desire to become a folksinger, his will to boogie gets mired down in the lugubrious fatalism that so often passes for seriousness among self-conscious Americans. Maybe the problem with country boys who are smart enough to write their own lyrics is that they're also smart enough to read their own reviews."
    – Robert Christgau, **Christgau's Record Guide: The '80s**

III. Early Tracks (Epic Records 1987/Koch Records 1997, LP/CD)
1. Nothin' But You
2. If You Need a Fool
3. Continental Trailways Blues
4. Open Up Your Door
5. Breakdown Land
6. Squeeze Me In
7. Annie, Is Tonight the Night
8. My Baby Worships Me
9. Cadillac
10. Devil's Right Hand
11. What'll You Do About Me
12. Cry Myself to Sleep
13. A Little Bit in Love
14. The Crush

Comments: Album compiled by Epic Records from 45 rpm singles and studio tracks recorded by Earle during the early-1980s. Most of the stuff is rockabilly-flavored but clearly shows Earle's growing strengths as a songwriter. In fact, "Devil's Right Hand" would be re-recorded by Earle for *Copperhead Road* as well as covered by other artists, most notably **Webb Wilder**. Epic released the compilation in the wake of the success of *Guitar Town*, a blatant attempt to capitalize on Earle's newfound notoriety and make a few shekels on the side. Reissued on CD by Koch in 1997 with four additional tracks (#11-14), culled from Epic Records singles.

IV. Copperhead Road (Uni Records 1988, CD/LP)
1. Copperhead Road
2. Snake Oil
3. Back to the Wall
4. The Devil's Right Hand
5. Johnny Come Lately

6. Even When I'm Blue
7. You Belong To Me
8. Waiting On You
9. Once You Love
10. Nothing But A Child

Comments: *Copperhead Road* was Earle's first album to include overtly political content. The rollicking "Johnny Come Lately" was recorded with Ireland's greatest rock band, the Pogues, and compares the reception afforded WWII veterans with that experienced by soldiers returning from Viet Nam. "Snake Oil" compares then President Reagan to a traveling grifter, "Copperhead Road" takes on Reagan's "war on drugs," and "Back to the Wall" tackles the growth of poverty in America during the 1980s.

    "Nothing But A Child" was recorded with the bluegrass band Telluride, which included Sam Bush, Jerry Douglas, Mark O'Connor, and Edgar Meyer. Overall, however, the album was more rock than country, recorded in Memphis with producer Joe Hardy. *Copperhead Road* nevertheless rode the decade's "back to the country" movement to #7 on the *Billboard* country chart, also rising to #56 on the magazine's Top 200 albums chart.

Another View: "This time, it isn't only the heavy beat, loud guitars, and wild-ass vocal mannerisms that make it rock – the giveaway's the melodrama that rock set-pieces substitute for the flat inevitability of the country variety. So my prescription is simple: more Tom T., less Bruce. Meanwhile, just say his vision of history is more convincing than his vision of personal relations. Which these days is another giveaway. Grade: B"
    – Robert Christgau, **Christgau's Record Guide: The '80s**

STEVE EARLE

V. The Hard Way (MCA Records 1990, CD)
1. Other Kind
2. Promise You Anything
3. Esmerelda's Hollywood
4. Hopeless Romantics
5. This Highway's Mine (Roadmasters)
6. Billy Austin
7. Justice In Ontario
8. Have Mercy
9. When The People Find Out
10. Country Girl
11. Regular Guy
12. West Nashville Boogie
13. Close Your Eyes

Comments: Here's where it all began to unravel. By this time Earle was spiraling downward, personally and artistically, due to his overwhelming addiction to heroin and cocaine. It wasn't unusual to have Steve stumble into you at a local club, and he hung out a lot with the guys in **Guilt**, who were pursuing their own vision of rock & roll excess.

While certainly not up to the standards of his first three albums, *The Hard Way* still has a lot going for it with some strong songs like "Billy Austin" and "West Nashville Boogie." The songs "Promise You Anything" and "Esmerelda's Hollywood" were co-written by Earle and Maria McKee of Lone Justice. *The Hard Way* proved to be the last studio album recorded by Earle for five years.

VI. Shut Up And Die Like An Aviator (MCA 1991, CD)
1. Intro
2. Good Ol' Boy (Gettin' Tough)

3. Devil's Right Hand
4. I Ain't Ever Satisfied
5. Someday
6. West Nashville Boogie
7. Snake Oil
8. Standin' On The Corner (Blue Yodel No. 9)
9. Other Kind
10. Billy Austin
11. Copperhead Road
12. Fearless Heart
13. Guitar Town
14. I Love You Too Much
15. She's About A Mover
16. Rain Came Down
17. Dead Flowers

Comments: Double-album recorded live in London and Kitchener, Ontario on October 5 and 6, 1990 by Earle and the Dukes, recorded in Canada where Earle enjoyed impressive sales and rock star status. The album was released as a money-grabbing move by the label (who would soon thereafter dump Earle from the roster).

When MCA had tossed responsibility for *The Hard Way* from Nashville to its New York office, Earle found himself in artistic purgatory – too rock for Music Row's country sensibilities, too country for the Big Apple. With Earle's addictions raging out of control, the relatively meager sales of *The Hard Way* made it easy for MCA…New York *and* Nashville…to wash their hands of the troubled star.

VII. BBC Radio 1 Live In Concert (Windsong International 1992, CD)
1. Copperhead Road
2. San Antonio Girl
3. Even When I'm Blue
4. My Old Friend the Blues
5. Someday
6. The Devil's Right Hand
7. Down the Road
8. Snake Oil
9. Johnny Come Lately
10. When Will We Be Married?
11. Little Rock & Roller
12. Dead Flowers
13. My Baby Worships Me

Comments: Fans of Steve Earle didn't have a heck of a lot to crow about during the early 1990s as the artist got into a number of well-publicized (and often drug-fueled) scrapes with the law. After the relative failure of *The Hard Way*, Earle recorded an album of original material that was rejected by MCA, which chose to release the live album *Shut Up And Die Like An Aviator* instead before unceremoniously dumping Earle from the label.

This import disc, from a BBC radio broadcast, was recorded live on November 29, 1988 at The Town & Country Club. For the hardcore faithful, it was of particular interest because of the album's inclusion of the traditional Irish tune "When Will We Be Married," as arranged by the Waterboys, which had not appeared on any Earle album. There are no band members credited on the CD, but I'm guessing that it was most of the same folks what made *Copperhead Road*.

VIII. Train A Comin' (Winter Harvest 1995/E Squared Records 1997, CD)
1. Mystery Train, Part 2
2. Hometown Blues
3. Sometimes She Forgets
4. Mercenary Song
5. Goodbye
6. Tom Ames's Prayer
7. Nothin' Without You
8. Angel Is the Devil
9. I'm Looking Through You
10. Northern Winds
11. Ben McCulloch
12. Rivers of Babylon
13. Tecumseh Valley

Comments: In 1994, depending on increasingly dicey live performances to pay the bills and with addiction still eating at his soul, Steve Earle was arrested in Nashville on drug possession charges and subsequently spent a year in a rehab center. Although he had hit rock bottom, Earle came out of the ordeal with his wit, talent and ambition intact.

Earle's first album after getting clean, and his first studio effort in five years, was a stripped-down, rootsy, folk-oriented collection that includes covers of his idol Townes Van Zandt's "Tecumseh Valley" and the Lennon/McCartney gem "I'm Looking Through You." First released by Nashville's Winter Harvest label in 1995 in limited numbers, Earle later reissued the album on E Squared, the Warner-distributed label he began with **Jack Emerson**, in 1997. The tracklist shown above is from the E Squared version, which restored Earle's original sequencing for the album.

Another View: "When the vernacular flows easy or sounds that way, a rare thing, five wives and enough heroin to destroy a saner man are the kind of myth rock and roll fools are always mistaking for reality. And clean though Earle may be, he's not above or beyond embracing that myth – among his latest celebrations of romantic dysfunction is one where he all but dares the object of his obsession to call the cops… Grade: A-" – Robert Christgau, **Christgau Consumer Guide: Albums Of The '90s**

IX. I Feel Alright (E Squared/Warner Music 1996, CD)
1. Feel Alright

2. Hard-Core Troubadour
3. More Than I Can Do
4. Hurtin' Me, Hurtin' You
5. Now She's Gone
6. Poor Boy
7. Valentine's Day
8. Unrepentant
9. CCKMP
10. Billy And Bonnie
11. South Nashville Blues
12. You're Still Standing There

Comments: If *Train A Comin'* was Earle's warm-up after years sitting on (under?) the bench, *I Feel Alright* was a defiant return to form and a loud artistic statement. Lyrically addressing the cost of his addictions, lost love and friendships, and the betrayals he suffered, Earle roars through the songs like a born-again convert, jumping into the river headfirst to be baptized in the flames of his rediscovered conviction and creativity. Lucinda Williams brings her sweet tones to "You're Still Standing There," Earle uses the legendary Fairfield Four to add depth to the backing vocals, and the Carl Gorodetzky Strings, a consistent presence on 1970s-era country recordings, are here for the ambiance (I guess).

X. El Corazon (E Squared/Warner Brothers 1997, CD)
1. Christmas In Washington
2. Tanneytown
3. If You Fall
4. I Still Carry You Around
5. Telephone Road
6. Somewhere Out There

STEVE EARLE

7. You Know The Rest
8. N.Y.C. 09 Poison Lovers
10. The Other Side of Town
11. Here I Am
12. Fort Worth Blues

Another View: "Earle writes with the flair and searching eye of a great talker who's also a great reader, and he can sing with anyone…but now that he's sober he sounds drunker than ever, recalling the blurry, lost-my-dentures drawl of John Prine at his cutest. And since unlike Prine he doesn't take naturally to cute, his back-porch sentimentality can seem as unearned as any folk revivalist's; when he reflects too much, as is his current spiritual wont, he proves that the only thing softer than a tough guy's heart of gold is a populist radical's *corazon sangriento*. Grade: A-" – Robert Christgau, **Christgau Consumer Guide: Albums Of The '90s**

XI. The Mountain (E Squared Records 1999, CD)
1. Texas Eagle
2. Yours Forever Blue
3. Carrie Brown
4. I'm Still In Love With You
5. Graveyard Shift
6. Harlan Man
7. The Mountain
8. Outlaw's Honeymoon
9. Connemara Breakdown
10. Leroy's Dustbowl Blues
11. Dixieland
12. Paddy On The Beat
13. Long, Lonesome Highway Blues
14. Pilgrim

Comments: Recorded with the legendary Del McCoury Band during Earle's brief flirtation with bluegrass.

XII. Transcendental Blues (E Squared/Artemis Records 2000, CD)
1. Transcendental Blues
2. Everyone's In Love With You
3. Another Town
4. I Can Wait
5. The Boy Who Never Cried
6. Steve's Last Ramble
7. The Galway Girl
8. Lonelier Than This
9. Wherever I Go
10. When I Fall
11. I Don't Want To Lose You Yet
12. Halo 'Round The Moon
13. Until The Day I Die
14. All Of My Life
15. Over Yonder (Jonathan's Song)

XIII. Sidetracks (E Squared/Artemis Records 2002, CD)
1. Some Dreams
2. Open Your Window
3. Me And The Eagle
4. Johnny Too Bad
5. Dominic Street
6. Breed
7. Time Has Come Today
8. Ellis Unit One
9. Creepy Jackalope Eye
10. Willin'
11. Sara's Angel
12. My Uncle
13. My Back Pages

Comments: Earle's "odds 'n' sods" album includes covers of Dylan ("My Back Pages"), Kurt Cobain ("Breed"), Lowell George ("Willin'"), Gram Parsons ("My Uncle"), and the Chambers Brothers ("Time Has Come Today") as well as a handful of original tunes that didn't make Earle's regular studio albums (see review ➜).

XIV. Jerusalem (E Squared/Artemis Records 2002, CD)
1. Ashes To Ashes
2. Amerika v. 6.0 (The Best We Can Do)
3. Conspiracy Theory
4. John Walker's Blues
5. The Kind
6. What's A Simple Man To Do?
7. The Truth
8. Go Amanda
9. I Remember You
10. Shadowland
11. Jerusalem

XV. Just An American Boy (E Squared/Artemis Records 2003, CD)

Disc One
1. Audience Intro
2. Amerika v. 6.0 (The Best We Can Do)
3. Ashes to Ashes
4. (Paranoia)
5. Conspiracy Theory
6. I Remember You
7. (Schertz, Texas)
8. Hometown Blues
9. The Mountain
10. (Pennsylvania Miners)
11. Harlan Man
12. Copperhead Road
13. Guitar Town
14. (I Oppose the Death Penalty)
15. Over Yonder (Jonathan's Song)
16. Billy Austin

Disc Two
1. Audience Intro
2. South Nathville Blues
3. Rex's Blue's/ Fort Worth Blues
4. John Walker's Blues
5. Jerusalem
6. The Unrepentant
7. Christmas In Washington
8. (Democracy)
9. What's So Funny About Peace, Love & Understanding
10. Time You Waste

Another View: "Featuring a number of songs from *Jerusalem*, including "Ashes To Ashes" and "Amerika v. 6.0 (The Best We Can Do)," the album also includes musical snapshots from across Earle's storied career, from "Guitar Town" and "Copperhead Road" to the classic "Christmas In Washington." Earle rounds out the affair with a joyful rendition of Nick Lowe's "What's So Funny About Peace, Love & Understanding."

Earle's effortless blend of traditional country, roots rock, bluegrass and blues has been a major influence on the entire alt-country movement. His championing of progressive politics and causes has shown Earle to be an intelligent and informed spokesperson for a leftist view of politics shunned by the major media. Ten years after many pundits declared his career dead, *Just An American Boy* proves that Earle keeps getting better as a songwriter and performer, with lots of life left in a career that has already achieved greatness.
– Rev. Keith A. Gordon, *View From The Hill*, 2003

XVI. The Revolution Starts…Now (E Squared/Artemis Records 2004, CD)
1. The Revolution Starts...
2. Home To Houston
3. Rich Man's War
4. Warrior
5. The Gringo's Tale
6. Condi, Condi
7. F The CC
8. Comin' Around
9. I Thought You Should Know
10. The Seeker
11. The Revolution Starts Now

Comments: Here's where Earle manages to get himself on President Bush's "enemies list" (if, ahem, such a thing exists). Although Earle had been politically active for a decade and a half, and had written more than a few songs with a socio-political edge, *The Revolution Starts…Now* was a radical call-to-arms as well as a brave, ballsy move considering the Conservative backlash that targeted the Dixie Chicks (and derailed their career for a while).

XVII. Live From Austin TX (New West Records 2004, CD)
1. Sweet Little '66
2. Goodbye's All We Got Left
3. Guitar Town
4. Hillbilly Highway
5. Good Ol' Boy (Gettin' Tough)
6. My Old Friend The Blues
7. Think It Over
8. Little Rock 'N' Roller
9. State Trooper

STEVE EARLE

10. Nowhere Road
11. The Week of Living Dangerously
12. Angry Young Man
13. Fearless Heart
14. I Love You Too Much
15. San Antonio Girl
16. The Devil's Right Hand
17. Down The Road

Comments: Recorded live for the *Austin City Limits* TV show on September 12, 1986.

XVIII. Live At Montreux 2005 (Eagle Records 2006, CD)
1. Jerusalum
2. What's a Simple Man To Do?
3. The Devil's Right Hand
4. Warrior
5. Rich Man's War
6. South Nashville Blues
7. CCKMP
8. Dixieland
9. Ellis Unit One
10. Condi Condi
11. The Mountain
12. The Revolution Starts Now
13. Copperhead Road
14. Christmas In Washington

Comments: Solo acoustic set by Earle, recorded live at the 2005 Montreux Jazz Festival in Switzerland. Although a lot of Earle's songs readily lend themselves to bare-bones voice and guitar readings, the setlist for this show leans heavily towards those songs that deserve a full band treatment to make the biggest impact.

After living in and around the Nashville area for 30 years, Earle fled to the friendly, more liberal environs of NYC in 2006, moving into an apartment in Greenwich Village. In recent years Earle has flirted with acting (appearing on the gritty HBO series *The Wire*), writing poetry, and has expressed an interest in writing plays, so the city is probably the next logical step in Earle's artistic evolution. Earle's latest album, *Washington Square Serenade*, was released by New West Records in late 2007.

VIDEO/DVD

D1. Transcendental Blues Live (Artemis 2002, DVD)
1. Transcendental Blues
2. Everyone's in Love with You
3. Another Town
4. I Can Wait
5. The Boy Who Never Cried
6. Steve's Last Ramble
7. Interview

8. Lonelier Than This
9. I Don't Want to Lose You Yet
10. Wherever I Go
11. Fearless Heart
12. Halo 'Round the Moon
13. The Galway Girl
14. Copperhead Road
15. Over Yonder (Jonathan's Song)
16. All of My Life
Bonus music videos: Transcendental Blues, Over Yonder (Jonathan's Song)

D2. Just An American Boy (Artemis 2004, DVD)
A film by Amos Poe.

D3. Live From Austin TX (New West Records 2004, DVD)
1. Sweet Little '66
2. Good-Bye Is All We Got Left
3. Guitar Town
4. Hillbilly Highway
5. Good Ol' Boy (Getting Tough)
6. My Old Friend The Blues
7. Think It Over
8. Little Rock & Roller
9. State Trooper
10. Nowhere Road
11. Something About A Monday
12. Angry Young Man
13. Fearless Heart
14. Love You Too Much
15. San Antonio Girl
16. The Devil's Right Hand
17. Down The Road

D4. Live At Montreux 2005 (Eagle Vision USA 2006, DVD)
1. Jerusalem
2. What's a Simple Man To Do
3. The Devil's Right Hand
4. Warrior
5. Rich Man's War
6. South Nashville Blues
7. CCKMP
8. Dixieland
9. Ellis Unit One
10. Condi Condi
11. The Mountain
12. The Revolution Starts Now
13. Copperhead Road

BOOTLEG ALBUMS

Over the past 20+ years Steve Earle has developed a significant loyal, almost fanatical following that has done a fine job of documenting his live performances. Literally dozens of Earle shows are available, a number of which were made commercially available by notable European bootleg labels. To list all of the live Earle shows that are making the rounds of tape/CD-R traders is beyond the scope of this book, so I've just included a handful of the better-known bootleg releases as illustration of Earle's importance and influence as an American music artist. For more information, I'd suggest starting your own trading list at this web site: http://jack.mauveweb.co.uk/artists/earle/exit.shtml. Because of the nature of bootleg albums, track listings, dates, and even personnel might be suspect.

B1. The Fast Company (no label given, 1982 CD-R)

Disc One
1. Juanita
2. Bad Moon Rising
3. Lucy Dee
4. Who Do You Love?
5. Nothin' But You
6. I Fought The Law
7. Something Else
8. Honky Tonk Man
9. If You Need A Fool
10. My Baby Workships Me
11. Shake, Rattle And Roll/Flip Flop Fly

Disc Two
1. Bad Moon Rising
2. Baby Who
3. Squeeze Me In
4. Before It's Too Late
5. Continental Trailways Blues
6. Nothin' But You
7. In The Night
8. If You Need A Fool
9. Devil's Right Hand
10. Cadillac
11. My Baby Worships Me
12. She's A Rocker
13. I Fought The Law

Comments: This two-CD set documents two sets recorded live at The Fast Company bar in Hickory, North Carolina sometime during 1982 and featuring one of the earliest line-ups of the Dukes, with Zip Gibson and Jack "Bullett" Harris, two friends of Earle's from Texas. Believed to be the earliest live recording of Earle to exist, the setlist and the energetic performance have branded **The Fast Company** as an essential for any Earle fan's library.

B2. The Road And The Sky (Great Dane Records, no date given, CD)
1. Copperhead Road
2. Good Ol' Boy (Gettin' Tough)
3. The Rain Came Down

4. San Antonio Girl
5. Even When I'm Blue
6. Someday
7. Devil's Right Hand
8. Johnny Come Lately
9. Nothing But A Child
10. The Week Of Living Dangerously
11. Waiting On You
12. You Belong To Me
13. No. 29
14. My Baby Worships Me
15. It's All Up To You

Comments: Perhaps the best-known of the Earle boots, recorded live at The Cotton Club in Atlanta, Georgia on December 17, 1988 during the **Copperhead Road** tour and released by the notorious Italian Great Dane Records label. The CD was allegedly taken from a soundboard source and represents only part of the performance; a lower-quality audience recording of the entire show is also said to exist.

B3. Heavy Metal Bluegrass (Dandelion Records 1998, CD)

Disc One
1. Christmas In Washington
2. Here I Am
3. Taneytown
4. Hard-Core Troubadour
5. My Old Friend The Blues
6. Someday
7. If You Fall
8. Mystery Train, Part II
9. You Know The Rest

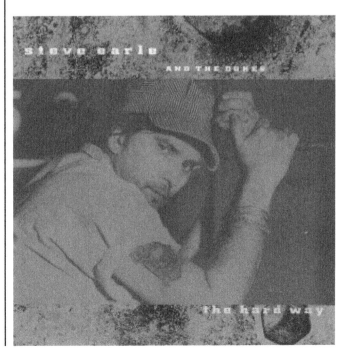

10. Windfall
11. Copperhead Road
12. Telephone Road
13. More Than I Can Do
14. Now She's Gone
15. Poison Lovers
16. Somewhere Out There
17. Billy Austin

Disc Two
1. The Devil's Right Hand
2. Nothin' But You
3. Goodbye
4. Johnny Too Bad
5. N.Y.C.
6. The Unrepentant
7. Sweet Virginia
8. Sin City
9. Johnny Come Lately
10. Valentine's Day
11. Guitar Town
12. I Ain't Ever Satisfied
13. Ft. Worth Blues
14. (Intro)
15. Ellis Unit One
16. State Trooper
17. It Takes A Lot To Laugh, It Takes A Train To Cry

Comments: Sub-titled "Undrugged in Bern," *Heavy Metal Bluegrass* was recorded during a November 1997 performance in Bern, Switzerland. This version of the bootleg omits one song from the setlist, "The Other Side Of Town" but for some reason includes four tracks (disc two #14-17) from the May 12, 1996 performance at the Barbican Centre in York, England. Available as a two-CD set containing the entire show as *Come Back Woody Guthrie*.

B4. Uncut Gems (Warner-Chappell demos 1994, CD-R)
1. Some Blue Moons Ago
2. She's So Mean
3. No. 29
4. Somethin' To Hold On To
5. Sometimes She Forgets
6. Tom Ames' Prayer
7. She Can't Break My Heart
8. When The Mornin' Comes
9. Hot Enough For Ya
10. Heatin' Up
11. Hole In My Heart
12. You Tear Me Up
13. I Won't Be Your Next In Line
14. My Old Friend The Blues
15. Promise You Anything (performed by Maria McKee)
16. I'm Not Gettin' Any Better At Goodbyes (performed by Ray Cobb)
17. The First Fool In Line (performed by Ray Cobb)
18. For Better Or Worse (performed by Ray Cobb)
19. Someone's Got To Do It (performed by Ray Cobb)
20. I'm Still Around (performed by Pebble Daniels)

Comments: Here's the story that I've found circulating about this odd bit of Earle memorabilia. During Earle's four-year, overdriven, drug-fueled exile from recording, which he calls his "vacation in the ghetto," his manager John Dotson got together with the folks from Earle's publishing company, Nashville's Warner-Chappell, and compiled a promotional CD of Earle's songs to shop around to other recording artists on Music Row.

On the surface, it was a savvy move...if Steve was barely able to tour and no label would sign him, his songwriting talent alone could help generate some income. Allegedly only 1,800 copies were created (runs of 500, 300 and 1,000 copies respectively), which seems like a lot of copies for what amounts to a glorified demo tape; nevertheless, at least one copy ended up with a bootlegger, who mysteriously re-sequenced the songs (front-loading the songs that Earle sang and moving other vocalists to the end) who ran a bunch of homebrew CD-R copies off and flooded the collector's market with them (I received a copy for review). Dunno if it helped Steve at all, but this bootleg has received widespread distribution.

B5. All American Boy (Doberman Records 2003, CD)

Disc One
1. Amerika v. 6.0 (The Best We Can Do)
2. What's A Simple Man To Do?
3. Ashes To Ashes
4. Conspiracy Theory
5. My Old Friend The Blues Intro
6. My Old Friend The Blues

7. Someday
8. Taneytown
9. The Rain Came Down
10. Harlan Man Intro
11. Harlan Man
12. Mystery Train, Part II
13. Copperhead Road
14. Guitar Town
15. Billy Austin
16. The Truth
17. Some Dreams

Disc Two
1. Hurtin' Me, Hurtin' You
2. Go Amanda
3. John Walker's Blues
4. Jerusalem
5. Transcendental Blues
6. N.Y.C.
7. The Unrepentant
8. She's A Woman
9. The Galway Girl
10. Christmas In Washington
11. Band Introductions
12. Time Has Come Today
13. Get Together
14. (What's So Funny 'Bout) Peace, Love And Understanding

Comments: Another release from the Italian Doberman bootleg label, this is an audience recording of Earle's April 6, 2003 performance from Sheffield City Hall, Sheffield England.

STEVE EARLE & THE SUPERSUCKERS

I. Steve Earle & the Supersuckers (Sub Pop 1997, CD)
1. Creepy Jackalope Eye (Earle & the Supersuckers)
2. Angel Is The Devil (Earle & the Supersuckers)
3. Before They Make Me Run (Earle & the Supersuckers)
4. Creepy Jackalope Eye (Supersuckers)
5. Angel Is The Devil (Earle)

Comments: Earle joined Eddie Spaghetti and the Supersuckers for this one-off five-song EP that has each one tackle the other's song, then team up on 'em as well as a Stones' cover. Interesting, but mostly for collectors, really.

WALTER EGAN

Band Members:
Walter Egan (vocals, guitars, keyboards) (I-II)

Other Musicians:
Ed Berghoff (guitar) (II)
Colleen Curtis (vocals) (II)
Shane Gue (keyboards, drums) (I-II)

Chris James (keyboards, vocals) (II)
Samantha Murphy (vocals) (II)
Brian Waldschlager (vocals) (I)

Walter Egan Recordings:

I. Walternative (We Records 1999, CD)
1. Let Go
2. There Goes My Girl
3. Land of the Living
4. Drawn to the Flame
5. Strange Love Affair
6. Vergin' on Tears
7. The Tide and the Sea
8. Happy Home
9. The Truth
10. Beats the Devil
11. Nobody Dreams Anymore
12. The Bias of Love
13. Get Out of the Kitchen
14. Goin' Home
15. Waitin' for Fred

II. Apocalypso Now (Gaff Music 2002, CD)
1. Far and Away
2. Love is in Your Veins
3. Ten Years Ago
4. Stubborn Girl
5. Time and the Rain
6. Only Love is Left Alive
7. Better Days
8. The Reason Why
Walter Egan, continued on page 151...

CD REVIEW: STEVE EARLE'S SIDETRACKS

STEVE EARLE
Sidetracks
(E Squared/Artemis Records)

As explained by Earle's excellent liner notes, the songs on *Sidetracks* aren't outtakes, but rather "stray tracks" that were previously unreleased or saw the light of day only on soundtrack or tribute albums. Much like Bill Lloyd's excellent ***All In One Place*** compilation album, Earle's *Sidetracks* confines these stray songs to a single package, providing extensive musician credits and song-by-song commentary. The resulting album is every bit as remarkable as any title in Earle's impressive catalog, a vital collection of original songs and inspired covers that illustrates Earle's talents as a songwriter, performer and bandleader.

Steve Earle's career has always been plagued by misconceptions, his early Nashville albums dismissed by ignorant Music Row hacks for being "too rock & roll," while mainstream rock audiences failed to embrace Earle as "too country." The truth lies somewhere in between, perhaps, but I believe that Earle is too enormous a talent to be confined by one style or genre, a fact illustrated by *Sidetracks*. A roots-music traditionalist who has had a tremendous influence on the alt-country scene, Earle has nonetheless flirted with hard rock, reggae and Celtic music as well as country, folk and bluegrass throughout the span of his nearly twenty-five year career.

"Johnny Too Bad," recorded with Knoxville, Tennessee roots rockers the V-Roys, redefines the Jamaican classic with a harder edge while the Irish-flavored instrumental "Dominick St," recorded with the Woodchoppers in Dublin, extends Earle's love affair with Celtic music. A powerful cover of

Nirvana's "Breed" showcases Earle's rowdy rock side, tho' maybe not as well as "Creepy Jackelope Eye," a lively collaboration with Eddie Spaghetti and the Supersuckers.

An alternative version of "Ellis Unit One" performed with the Fairfield Four achieves an eerie spiritual edge lacking in the solo version used in the film *Dead Man Walking*. The folkish "Me And The Eagle" stands in stark contrast to much of the material on *Sidetracks*, while a twangy, bluegrass-tinged reading of Lowell George's "Willin'" captures the spirit of the oft-covered original.

Not everything on *Sidetracks* clicks, most notably a cover of the Chambers Brothers' classic "Time Has Come Today." A technologically-crafted duet with Sheryl Crow that was recorded in Nashville with Crow in LA, the performance may have seemed a good idea at its conception, but it suffers in execution. Crow's vocal contribution is lackluster and the band fails to achieve the manic (drug-fueled?) energy of the original, although the Abbie Hoffman vocal samples are pretty neat.

This minor cavil aside, *Sidetracks* is an extremely worthwhile addition to your CD collection, a significant compilation and a revealing look "backstage" at the multi-faceted talents of Steve Earle. It's telling that by collecting his various cast-offs and rarities, Earle has cobbled together an album that still stands head and shoulders above most of the country and rock music that will be released this year. Though other artists should probably hang their heads in shame, Earle fans can rejoice in *Sidetracks*. – *Alt.Culture.Guide*, 2002

Walter Egan, continued...
9. Wanting You
10. Rain in Tennessee
11. You Pay for Love
12. You're Gonna Miss Me
13. Lullaby

Comments: Best known for his 1978 hit song "Magnet And Steel," Walter Egan has a phenomenal history as a musician and songwriter. Relocating to Nashville during the late 1990s, Egan has integrated himself into the local scene, playing around town quite frequently. These two pop-rock gems represent a small part of Egan's overall catalog, but they're the ones that he recorded while living in the Nashville area.

ELECTRIC CIRCUS

Band Members:
Noel Nutt (vocals)
Jeff Staggs (guitars)
Kent Thune (bass)
Dan Turner (drums)

Comments: Electric Circus members Noel Nutt and Kent Thune were also members of In Your Face.

ELEVEN 59

Band Members:
David Hart (vocals, guitar)
Brian Bickel (guitar, vocals)
Dave Powers (bass)
Dave Prince (drums)
Shawn Harrison (bass)
John Alexander (bass, vocals)

Comments: Another great mid-1980s Murfreesboro band, Eleven 59 played a lot around both Nashville and the 'boro. The line-up of Hart, Bidel, Powers and Price contributed the song "Want To" to the NEA's *What You Haven't Heard...* 1987 compilation CD.

JACK EMERSON

Comments: What can you say about Jack Emerson? He is arguably the most important person in the evolution of the Nashville rock scene. One of the original members of **Jason & the Scorchers**, Jack quickly reallized that the band needed some real musicians, and he bowed out to act as their manager instead.

With his old Florida pal Andy McLenon, the two men formed Praxis, an all-purpose record label and artist management company with the Scorchers as their first act. Praxis released the first multi-artist 7" EP of the Nashville rock era (*Never In*

Nashville) and the first Scorchers 7" EP (*Reckless Country Soul*) before firing the shot that would be heard around the world, the Scorchers' *Fervor* 12" EP. That disc would later be re-issued by Capitol/EMI Records and the rest, as they say, is history. A major label deal ensued and the Scorchers became "critical darlings," although their sales never matched the band's well-deserved acclaim.

Praxis was busy throughout the 1980s, handling the fledgling careers of Jason & the Scorchers, **Webb Wilder, Tim Krekel & the Sluggers**, among others. Emerson was also busy in what was called, at the time, the "college radio" indie-rock community, helping and/or working directly with artists like R.E.M., the dBs, John Hiatt, and others. Jack helped get the Georgia Satellites back together, promoting their first reunion shows and helping the band get a label deal. Major label woes and Jason & the Scorchers' bankruptcy would end up sinking Praxis.

Emerson would bounce back, though, partnering with **Steve Earle** and forming E Squared Records in 1996. With Earle as the label's keystone artist, and with distribution through Warner Music, E Squared worked with the V Roys, Bap Kennedy, and Cheri Knight, among other artists. A later deal with Artemis Records would provide the label with marketing and promotional expertise along with distribution.

Sadly, Emerson suffered a heart attack in November 2003 and died, leaving behind a solid musical legacy and a lot of grieving friends. Talking to Jack was always an uplifting experience, and he *always* had some new artist he wanted to turn you on to. It was always about the music with Jack, and while he was more professional than 99% of those in the industry, first and foremost he was always a fan. R.I.P.

Earle & Emerson

THE ENEMY

THE ENEMY

Band Members:
Joey "Offbeat" Blanton (vocals, guitar)
Lee Carr (guitar, vocals)
Erich Hubner (bass)
Chris Mekow (drums)

Comments: The Enemy put out a cassette with their crowd-pleasing, punkish "Jesus Rides A U.F.O." but damned if I can find it in my stash. One of the most popular bands on the local scene for a supernova minute, Blanton and Mekow would go on to launch Royal Court of China, Carr to Raging Fire...

Trends take a long time to come to Nashville, even longer to affect and create local participants; by the time musical styles have been filtered through the mindsets of both coasts, traveled across country and hit the great wide heartland most of us live in, the signals have been altered, the wavelength slightly changed. The resulting mutation often times produces a completely original and fresh illustration of style. Such is Nashville's the Enemy....

The Enemy is, perhaps, the Music City's hottest young band. Formed in October 1984 by guitarists Joey Offbeat (a local scene legacy, by way of the Ratz) and Lee Carr, the Enemy chose to ignore the emerging undercurrent of a country punk/C&W revival by performing a daring mixture of hardcore, power-pop, and metal-edged, drop-forged instrumentation. Trendy, unfair pigeonhole labels such as thrash or "three-chord-rock" fall before the Enemy's twin scythes of energy and humor.

"We came together rather fast," says Lee Carr, "the first night we met, introduced by a mutual acquaintance, we were at Cantrell's and just got up and played a set of Ramones' songs. Later, we all discovered that we all wanted to play the same sort of material and move in the same direction, so we began practicing, playing and working together as a band."

Carr continues, "we began by opening for everybody and their brother...bands that you wouldn't want to come out and see if you saw their name in the paper. As we developed a larger following, we started opening for better acts, such as the dB's and Alex Chilton. People would come out to see those artists and we'd get to play for them."

The bulk of the Enemy's material is made up of original songs. Says Joey Offbeat, "we've got fifty or sixty songs we can do during a show, and only a half a dozen or so are covers." Offbeat pens the lyrics and designs the skeletal structure of the songs, with the rest of the band, fellow guitarist Carr, bassist Erich Hubner, and drummer Chris "Fuzz" Mekow adding to the arrangements.

The band quickly recorded their first song, titled "I Can't Quit," which received steady airplay from Vanderbilt's 91 Rock. As encouraging as was the response that "I Can't Quit" received, it was a unique throwaway tune instead that created the band's amazing widespread local reputation...

Music City street musician Gregory Mauberret, a sidewalk serenader, prophet and prolific songwriter, penned an interesting ditty by the name of "Jesus Rides A UFO," had the lyrics printed in poster form (with the unlikely visage of pop stars Wham adorning the top of the sheet), and plastered them all over the city, on telephone poles, walls, and any object that remained stationary long enough for this wandering visionary to slap some glue onto.

"We found the lyric sheet on a pole somewhere," says Offbeat, "and Lee said 'we ought to play this...ha, ha, ha!' We did it as a joke, playing it live one night. The crowd loved it! WRVU's Adam Dread asked us to record it, so we did a four-track version that has received an amazing response."

The song caught on, becoming a sort of in-crowd favorite. "We attracted a following of nubile teenage girls," says Carr, as the band's newfound status moved them into a headlining position. Says Offbeat, "we were booked seven or eight straight weekends in various local clubs, with everybody tossing us a pessimistic 'you'll never draw crowds playing all the time.' We had so many songs, though, that we could play a different set every week without having to repeat songs. As a result, our audience grew even larger and more varied."

The Enemy will be exploding out of Nashville this summer, wandering the Southeast with their aggressive and flamboyant live show. "We'll be playing across Kentucky, Georgia, and Alabama," says Offbeat, "with occasional trips to Chicago and other Northern metro areas. We've sent out press kits and demo tapes to a lot of clubs and booking agents...we'd like to play anywhere and everywhere!" The band also had plans to release a four-song EP this fall.

"With Enemies like us...who needs friends!" is the band's motto. Talented enough to be exciting, young enough to be reckless, the electric hybrid that is the Enemy will be around to, in the words of Joey Offbeat, "have some serious fun!" Bet on it... – *Nashville Intelligence Report* #28, 1985

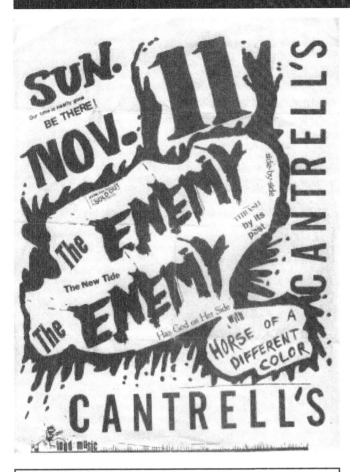

SPRING DANCE PARTY
Monday, April 25
7:00 P.M.

— at Cat's Records on West End —

Featuring...

FACTUAL

and

PRACTICAL STYLISTS

Dance into Spring at Cat's!

Rain Date: Monday, May 2

Concerts & WKDA

Bring the rock of the 80's to Nashville

THE CALL
with Special Guest
Will Rambeaux & The Delta Hurricanes

CANTRELLS
Saturday, June 4th

Show begins at 9:30

$5.00

Tickets go on sale Monday, May 23rd
at All Cat's Records

Produced by New West/Contemporary Productions

EVERY MOTHER'S NIGHTMARE

EVERY MOTHER'S NIGHTMARE
Web: www.myspace.com/emnmemphis

Band Members:
Rick Ruhl (vocals) (I – VI)
Steve Malone (guitars) (I, II)
Mark McMurtry (bass) (I, II)
Jim Phipps (drums) (I, II, VI)
Travis Hall (guitar) (III – VI)
Jeff Caughron (guitar) (III – VI)
Troy Fleming (bass) (III – VI)
Kris Beavers (drum) (III – V)

Every Mother's Nightmare Recordings:

I. Every Mother's Nightmare (Arista 1990, CD)
1. Hard To Hold
2. EZ Come, EZ Go
3. Bad On Love
4. Walls Come Down
5. Love Can Make You Blind
6. Listen Up
7. Dues To Pay
8. Long Haired Country Boy
9. Lord Willin'
10. Nobody Knows

Comments: Every Mother's Nightmare was formed by veterans of Nashville's often-maligned 1980s-era hard rock scene: Ruhl from **Hard Knox**, McMurtry from Suicide Alley and Phipps from **Justin Heat**. They were signed to Arista by the legendary Clive Davis himself, and the band's self-titled debut was pushed to the heavens by the label. Metal fans rightfully dismissed the band as "Crue lite" and the album struggled to peak at number 146 on the *Billboard* "Top 200" chart. Produced by R. Eli Ball, the band spent a lot of time traveling down I-40 between Nashville and Memphis and developed significant followings in both cities.

II. Wake Up Screaming (Arista Records 1993, CD)
1. House Of Pain
2. Closet Down The Hall
3. I Hate Myself
4. Already Gone
5. Tobacco Road
6. Slip And Fall
7. Good Die Young
8. Break Down
9. If I Had My Way
10. Bang To The Bone
11. I Needed You
12. Cryin' Shame

Comments: It could be argued that the 1980s ended with the release of Nirvana's *Nevermind*, and nerf-metal bands like

Every Mother's Nightmare were swept out with the rest of the decade's garbage. Although *Wake Up Screaming* isn't a bad hard rock album – the guys were beginning to develop their own sound by this point – musical tastes had changed and alt-rock was the new king of the hill. Arista must have flooded the country with this disc, 'cause there are literally dozens of 'em listed for sale on eBay at any given time (whereas the much-hyped debut, which you'd figure would be more prevalent, is hard-as-hell to find!)

III. Smokin' Delta Voodoo (Perris Records 2000, CD)
1. Push
2. #3
3. Delta Voodoo
4. Sympathy
5. Somehow
6. Pray
7. On Display
8. E34 (Unwritten Law)
9. Kerosene
10. Garden
11. Wait
12. Wire

Comments: When *Wake Up Screaming* failed to chart, EMN found themselves put out on the street by Arista. You have to give frontman Ruhl credit, though – while the rest of the world was trying to discover the next Pearl Jam clone, he kept the band hammering away as ersatz hard rock heroes. By 2000, Ruhl had shuffled through varying line-ups for Every Mother's Nightmare, finally settling on the crew that recorded *Smokin' Delta Voodoo* for Texas hard rock indie label Perris Records. With new players, the band's sound continued to evolve, the songs showing a bit more twang alongside the metal.

Another View: "This badly named Tennessee hair band-era roots metal act moved over half a million copies of their first two albums (combined sales) in the heyday of the do-no-wrong metal days. Back with a badly-named third album (using the word "voodoo" is as cheesy now as it was then), EMN '01 are a pretty cool cross between Tesla, L.A. Guns, Brother Cane and Jackyl, not too, too Southern, but squarely on the roots/sleaze side of L.A....a high quality band with something to say, deserving of better graphics than this cheap presentation proposes. – Martin Popoff, *The Collector's Guide To Heavy Metal, Volume 4: The '00s*

IV. Back Traxx (Perris Records 2001, CD)
1. Southern Way
2. Muddy Water
3. Seasons Change
4. Ride The Train
5. Lookin' In
6. Stoned On TV

7. Dawg
8. Sorrow
9. River
10. Outside The Circle
11. Too Far Gone
12. Bled

V. Deeper Shade Of Grey (Perris Records 2002, CD)
1. Done To Me
2. Until I Break
3. Deeper Shade Of Grey
4. See Through U
5. Carbon
6. Takes Your Breath Away
7. Hello Darkness
8. Fly Away
9. Paradise
10. Solid Ground
11. Bathe Me
12. Blind To See

VI. Live Songs From Somewhere (Perris Records 2002, CD)
1. Bathe Me
2. Walls Come Down
3. Hole Inside
4. Deeper Shade Of Grey
5. Delta Voodoo
6. Pray
7. Sympathy
8. Love Can Make You Blind
9. Bring Me Down
10. Solid Ground
11. Long Haired Country Boy
12. I'm Eighteen
13. Saturday Night Special
14. Takes Your Breath Away

Comments: The end for Every Mother's Nightmare came with the obligatory live album, this collection featuring material from all three Perris albums as well as the band's self-titled Arista debut (nothing from *Wake Up Screaming*, tho').

These live performances show more "Southern Rock" influence, the album including covers of songs by the Charlie Daniels Band, Alice Cooper, and Lynyrd Skynyrd. By this time, it was obvious that EMN was trying to wrest the "redneck metal" crown from the slightly-bent skull of Jesse James Dupree and his Jackyl cellmates.

THE EVINRUDES

Band Members:
Sherry Cothran (vocals, guitar) (I – III)
Brian Reed (guitars, keyboards, lap steel) (I – III)

EVERY MOTHER'S NIGHTMARE
Every Mother's Nightmare
(Arista Records)

A hard-rocking disc teetering shamelessly on the sonic barrier, Every Mother's Nightmare's vinyl debut puts the teeth back into metal-edged musical mayhem. A cross between nostalgic 1970s glam-metal and 1990s thrash sensibilities, *Every Mother's Nightmare*, the album, kicks out the proverbial jams with its inspired hybrid of musical influences which includes, though is not limited by, Kiss, the Babys, AC/DC, Slade, and any one of a number of true rockers who have dotted the FM radio landscape during the past two decades.

Every Mother's Nightmare represents the combined creative efforts of a foursome of well-known Music City rockers: ex-Hard Knox vocalist Rich Ruhl, guitarist Steve Malone, bassist Mark McMurtry from Suicide Alley and drummer Jim Phipps, formerly of Justin Heat. Ruhl and Phipps formed Every Mother's Nightmare a couple of years back, after the break-up of their respective bands. Moving to Memphis and hooking up with producer Eli Ball (the same guy who discovered Jason & the Scorchers), EMN were signed to Arista by the big cheese himself, Clive the D. The rest, as they say, is history.

Every Mother's Nightmare is receiving a lot of industry hype, and rightfully so. From the ringing chords of their lead-off single "Walls Come Down," to their bigger-than-life cover of Charlie Daniels' "Long Haired Country Boy," to the call-and-response power funk of "Listen Up," it is evident that this is a disc of considerable energy and emotion. Toss in their photogenic rock & roll image (just ask Joan Rivers), a couple of MTV videos and the band's own considerable talents and hard work (they've been on tour forever) and you have an equation which equals success: a valuable commodity in a hard rock field over-peopled with shallow images lacking in ability. – *The Metro*, 1990

THE EVINRUDES

Jeffrey Smith (bass) (I)
Andy Hull (drums) (I, II)
Ethan Pilzer (bass) (II
Scott Heyniger (keyboards) (I)

The Evinrudes Recordings:

I. The Evinrudes EP (self-produced CD, 1997)
1. Drive Me Home
2. Have Some Rain
3. Somebody Has To Be Pat Boone
4. Somewhere In California
5. I Can't Find Otis Redding

Comments: The Evinrudes were one of several talented husband-wife teams playing music in Nashville. This five-song EP, produced by songwriter/guitarist Brian Reed and featuring the wonderful vocals of wife **Sherry Cothran**, yielded a minor radio hit with the song "Drive Me Home" and earned the band a major label deal with Mercury Records.

II. The Evinrudes (Mercury Records 1998, CD)
1. Drive Me Home
2. Have Some Rain
3. Along The Way
4. Jimmy's On Crack (And I Don't Care)
5. Otis
6. Dick And Jane
7. Little Red Stars
8. High Street And The Universe
9. Swagger
10. Indians On The Moon

III. Somebody Has To Be Pat Boone (Flying Sparks 2002, UK CD)
1. Drive Me Home
2. Have Some Rain
3. Along The Way
4. Jimmy's On Crack
5. Otis
6. Dick & Jane
7. Somebody Has To Be Pat Boone
8. High Street And The Universe
9. Swagger
10. Somewhere In California
11. Weight Upon Your Soul

Comments: Featuring eight songs were from the band's self-titled Mercury debut, this European release earned the band a small but loyal U.K. following.

IV. Little Red Stars (A Startled Chameleon 2003, CD)
1. Sunfish
2. Good Humor Man
3. Little Red Stars
4. Bodarks Is Closed
5. Indians On The Moon
6. Dog Days
7. Raised On Sugar
8. Gypsy Moth
9. Ms. Kilbuck
10. Martin Luther Snow Day

Comments: The last hurrah for the Evinrudes came through this UK release.

THE EXCUSES

Band Members:
Jeff Skorik (vocals, guitar) (I)
Pat Meusel (bass, vocals) (I)
Chris Minnis (drums) (I)

The Excuses Recordings:

I. messin' with my good-life (Shut Yer Hole Records 1994, CD)
1. Look At Me
2. Pack My Gun
3. Bad Habits
4. Serious
5. Something I'm Not
6. So Damn Bored
7. I Got You
8. Little Christy
9. Walk A Mile
10. Why Do You Do It

Comments: Obscure early-1990s band with a cool alt-rock vibe that coulda gone somewhere with half a chance. Reminds me of the Replacements, but different.

THE EVINRUDES
The Evinrudes
(Das/Mercury)

Nashville's Evinrudes got signed on the strength of the radio-friendly "Drive Me Home," a regional hit a couple of summers ago from the band's self-produced EP. Sparking major label interest after constant airplay throughout the Southeast, "Drive Me Home" is a witty, hook-laden song that's full of clever wordplay, propelled by Sherry Cothran's sexy, breathless vocals and guitarist Brian Reed's great guitar line.

"Drive Me Home" got the Evinrudes signed, but, as shown by their big-league debut disc, the band is no one trick pony. Sure, "Drive Me Home" opens the band's self-titled intro, but there's lots of other material here to recommend that the band be given a spot in your personal music rotation. "Jimmy's On Crack (And I Don't Care)" is a rocking little slice of life, with more than a few precious observations on society's ills; "Otis" name-checks the great Otis Redding but is really a brief glimpse at the mortality that haunts us all.

Opening with a nifty bit of rhythmic voiceplay by Cothran, "Dick And Jane" is a nonsensical and whimsical sixties-styled pop song that says little but is a lot of fun to listen to. "High Street And The Universe" is another observation of our culture while "Swagger" is a delicious piece of braggadocio, the song's protagonist the baddest mofo on the block since Jim Croce's "Leroy Brown."

Guitarist Reed writes a fair tune, a little light on the instrumental side but penning lyrics chockful of humor, irony and wit and enough pop-culture references to jump-start a Trivial Pursuit tournament. Cothran's aforementioned vocals have one setting – sultry – which is entirely appropriate for the material. Overall, *The Evinrudes* is a solid effort, with more character and personality than most you'll hear these days. Give 'em a little seasoning, a veteran producer to bring out the dynamics promised by Cothran's voice and another batch of Reed's clever songs and you'd have a real Top Forty contender.
– R Squared, 1998

INTERVIEW: JACK EMERSON/E SQUARED

Introduction: Jack Emerson's influence on late 1980s southern rock is immeasurable. He formed Praxis International, an indie label and artist management company, at the age of 22 with friend and partner Andy McLenon. Praxis started with just one band – Jason & the Nashville Scorchers – but soon steered the careers of bands like the Georgia Satellites, the Questionnaires and Tim Krekel & the Sluggers. Emerson later worked with John Hiatt, Sonny Landreth, and Steve Forbert, and his support of mid-80s "college rock" bands like R.E.M. and the dB's would lead them to greater successes.

After the Scorchers broke up, Emerson moved Praxis further into the alt-country field with important early 1990s releases from Billy Joe Shaver and Webb Wilder. By 1995, however, Praxis had run its course and Emerson formed E Squared Records with friend Steve Earle. In 1999, Emerson brokered a deal between the label and Artemis Records that largely removed him from running the business side, freeing him up to pursue other projects. Sadly, Emerson died in November 2003 at the young age of 43. This interview with Emerson took place in 1996 and originally appeared in **Nashville Business In Review**.

People who claim to know a lot about these sort of things use words like "dynamics" or "synergy" when describing the inner workings of a volatile industry like the music biz. Perhaps it's time we added two new words to the industry lexicon – "experience" and "evolution," or, if you will, E^2. It's no coincidence that these two words pretty much sum up the careers of Jack Emerson and Steve Earle, the two "E's" behind the newly formed E^2 Records. Both are well-known in the local music community, Emerson as the former head of Praxis International and Earle as a critically-acclaimed performer and songwriter. Together they have created an indie label that may well rewrite the way that things are done on Music Row.

Praxis was Nashville's first independent rock & roll record label, a vital part of the Music City's early-80s, non-country music scene. Home to Jason & the Nashville Scorchers, Praxis released the band's early recordings and would act as their management through most of the decade. Along with friends and fellow Scorcher fans Andy McLenon and Kay Clary, Emerson would build a respected organization that was as professional as it was hard-working and creative.

Although the Scorchers never received the kind of commercial acceptance that they deserved, another Praxis band, the Georgia Satellites, hit it big with their first album. The success of the Satellites gained Emerson and the gang at Praxis a reputation in the industry as ace talent scouts. A subsequent deal with BMG subsidiary Zoo Records led to Praxis developing artists like Webb Wilder, Mark Germino, Sonny Landreth and Billy Joe Shaver.

Steve Earle came to Nashville in the early-1970s at the age of nineteen, a talented but struggling songwriter. Influenced by writers like Guy Clark and Townes Van Zandt, Earle developed a heady story-telling style that owed as much to rock as it did country music. Hits by several country artists with Earle-written songs led to a deal with MCA Records, Earle's first album, **Guitar Town**, taking the industry by storm. Shooting to number one on the country charts, the album won critical acclaim from sources as diverse as *Country Music* magazine and *Rolling Stone*.

Subsequent releases would showcase Earle's evolution as a songwriter, often drawing favorable comparisons with artists like Bob Dylan and Bruce Springsteen. As he incorporated heavier rock influences into his music, however, the country music establishment didn't quite know what to do with an artist of Earle's talents and vision. Earle moved to MCA's Uni Records subsidiary in New York for the last albums of his contract, a move that weakened his local industry support. Problems with drugs and alcohol hastened the decline of his career, inevitably leading to an arrest and a prison sentence for possession.

The formation of E^2 was to be part of a natural evolution for both Emerson and Earle. "After about 15 years of Praxis," says Emerson, "when we ended our Bertelsman/Zoo agreement...things had gotten a little stale. Kay was real interested in starting her own company and working out of her house. I couldn't imagine trying to run that place without her there. Andy was questioning what he wanted to do and I was questioning what I wanted to do. We were all a little burned out...so it was a natural time to close things down."

With Praxis a part of the past, Emerson was open to new opportunities. "We'd all kept in touch with Steve, because we were all really big fans." In the latter years, there "wasn't that much to keep in touch with, musically," says Emerson of Earle, "because he was going through the whole period of sobriety, working through the prison system." After Earle's release, says Emerson, "he knew that he had to stay busy...and he's always been interested in the business side, always been a producer as well as a songwriter. The more that I talked with him, the more it made sense for us to try and do something together."

After recording a well-received acoustic album for Nashville's Winter Harvest label, Earle was ready to return to his former rocking style of playing for his next album. Clean and sober for almost two years, he had stared into the abyss and emerged a stronger artist than ever. "He was looking for a solid compadre who could represent his talent at the major label side," says Emerson. "After investigating all of our possible alliances, Warner Brothers seemed to make the most sense."

The newly formed E^2 label signed a deal providing Warner Brothers the opportunity for worldwide distribution of their releases, with the exception of England, where they hooked up with Transatlantic/Castle. In return, Warner provided start-up funding for the label. Non-Warner releases will be distributed through the Alternative Distribution Alliance, a group of indie labels that works to place product in non-traditional, non-mainstream retail outlets.

E^2 has received a lot of moral support from their major label sponsors. "In essence, we've got a deal that's spread between the New York office, the L.A. office and the Nashville office," Emerson explains, citing Warner executives like Joe McKuen, Bob Merlis and Nancy Stein as being advocates of the young label. "Jim Ed Norman deserves a lot of credit," says Emerson, referring to the local label chief's recognition of Nashville's potential. "Warner Brothers understood what we wanted to do," says Emerson, "not only with Steve's records, but with the records that we wanted to make, whether Steve was producing or whatever."

The pairing of Emerson and Earle has proven to be a marriage made in heaven. "We were able to sit down and work out a complex but functional situation where Steve could help make and produce records and I'd be in the office on a daily basis to kind of glue the thing together," says Emerson. The first E^2 release was Earle's rocking ***I'm Alright***, a wonderful return to form for this talented artist. The label has also signed two new acts, Knoxville's V-Roys and Ross Rice, former member of the popular Memphis band Human Radio.

E^2 has retained control over the entire A & R process. "We have total autonomy, creatively," says Emerson, E^2 shouldering the responsibility of discovering and signing new artists, and producing their recorded efforts. "Our attitude is that if Steve and I are both over the top about something, we'll do it. If one of us is not thrilled, ready to climb over broken glass, then we won't do it." There's no pressure on the pair from anybody to crank out product, so E^2 will release fewer records than a lot of indie labels, but they'll be hand-picked by the combination management/creative team at the top of the label.

There are three things, says Emerson, that the label is looking for in an artist. "A lot of originality, which doesn't mean they don't have a good sense of the past," he says, "but rather a good sense of what they want to do, a unique sound. The second element would be songs, and not necessarily in a classic sense. With Steve, he can detect and help young writers with what they want to do, answer their questions. The third thing would be a certain timeless element. Most of the records that I listen to and that Steve listens to have been things that we enjoy as much now as when they were released."

After a record is made, says Emerson, "we get Warner Brothers and the act together, sit down and decide whether or not something is better served going out through the independent system or going out through the Warner Brothers system. What this means is that sometimes a young band that we think has a great record may spend the first six months on ADA without Warner Brothers, the machine, getting involved. If everybody agrees that's the best way to go, we may do it for two records, we may do it for three records, or we may go straight to Warner Brothers."

"We're trying to make productive use out of a strong multi-national company and still give the artist as much control as possible in terms of their own destiny," concludes Emerson. For Steve Earle and Jack Emerson, the two sides of E^2 Records, their own destinies will be built on both the sum of their previous experience and the result of their personal evolutions, a formula for success than may well become known in the future as simply E^2.

Jason & the Scorchers w/Jack Emerson (center)

INTERVIEW: JOHN ELLIOTT/DESSAU

John Elliott was another one of a handful of pioneers on the Nashville rock music scene. He was a member of such first-baby-step local bands as Cloverbottom, Actual, and Factual before moving on to Chicago for a while. Returning to Nashville, John formed Dessau just in time to ride the late 1980s industrial-dance trend to some degree of notoriety, a modicum of fame without the fortune to accompany it. His work with members of Chagall Guevara on the side-project band Passafist provided entry into the CCM (Contemporary Christian Music) market, where John produced albums for several artists...

What got you interested in music in the first place?
I grew up in Indiana, probably 50 miles north of Louisville, right in between Louisville, Cincinnati, and Indianapolis. What got me into music was seeing the Beatles on Ed Sullivan and then, in September of 1964, my dad got tickets to see the Beatles at the Indiana State Fair. So I went when I was nine to see the Beatles at an outdoor show at the fairgrounds. So that kind of got me in music and I played the snare drum, so I have to say yeah, the Beatles got me into music which, you know, I guess is a good place to start.

Were you playing in bands in junior high?
Yeah, I played in a little band in junior high and high school, we would play Grand Funk and Alice Cooper. I don't want to say that we were kind of alternative back then, but we were doing cuts off of Ten Years After's *Cricklewood Green* and we were doing the "Eighteen" by Alice Cooper, and we were doing stuff off the Grand Funk "red album," the second album. So even though it was pop music, we were kind of thinking that we were a little bit cooler than just doing a Beatles song or something.

What brought you to Nashville?
I came to Nashville with a friend of my brother, Jim – he was a roadie for the Eagles and he played keyboard for them some. He saved about $50,000 from being with the Eagles for a bunch of years and he had a dream in the summer of 1979 to move to Nashville and start a new wave band, and he was going to get a label deal because he knew all these people in L.A. That's when new wave was still, I guess, kind of new in a way, so he thought instead of trying to do that in L.A. he would go to Nashville...he rented a house out in Hendersonville, of all places, so in June of '79 I came to Nashville. I thought Nashville was the most cowboy bizarre weird place. I remember going to the Gold Rush one night and just thinking "wow, this is just weird" because in 1979, Nashville was still very pretty cowboy...

I was going up to Indiana every other weekend and one weekend I was up there, it was in August of '79 and Jim called me on a Friday morning and said "you have got to get back to Nashville as soon as possible! I went to this place called Phranks 'n' Steins and I met these people called Cloverbottom and they need a drummer and a keyboard player and I told them about you and they want to come out to Hendersonville on Sunday, two Cloverbottom guys – Rock Strata and Johnny Hollywood – and they want to jam, they want us to join their band. I got right back down there and then on Sunday, Rock and Johnny came out to Hendersonville and I was a pretty good drummer and they liked what I could do and they liked Jim, and he had gold records on his wall from the Eagles and they thought "wow, is this guy for real?" We ended up joining Cloverbottom.

We played in September, we had all the Thursdays in September at Phranks 'n' Steins and we did those four Thursdays and then all of a sudden Jim's wife – she was real L.A. and she didn't like Hendersonville – they decided they were going to move back to L.A. I said "I'm going to stay here. I'm in a band now, this is great!" I'm in a punk rock band and I'm playing...I thought Phranks 'n' Steins was great, it was cool, I was staying up all night with Scot and Johnny and they'd play me all these weird records...

What happened after Jim left Cloverbottom?
He decided that it wasn't working out and he went back to California. I had this band and I played the club for about a month or two until the first of the year, and that's when I met Steve Anderson. Steve Anderson used to come down to Phranks 'n' Steins and Rockin' Johnny worked with him because he was in the Hots, and the Hots were a pretty big band right then, they were real popular and Cloverbottom was just some kind of little garage band. Cloverbottom was able to open for David Johansen, the Ramones, and Pearl Harbor and the Explosions.

So Cloverbottom was able to open up some cool gigs, but Steve had always told me that he and Robb Earls were going to put together this band called Actual and I thought it sounded kind of cool! I met Rob and he had a studio and he did the Cloverbottom EP, so that's how I knew Rob. Around the first of the year, I got with Rob and Steve and we became Actuals, not "the Actuals," because he was, "it's Talking Heads, not the Talking Heads," and Steve was heavy into Talking Heads...that was, musically, what we were interested in, it was more new wavy...

Electronic, like in an Ultravox sort of thing...
Right, which I kind of liked...I enjoyed Cloverbottom, but I had to become a better player to play with Actuals, [that band] definitely made me a better player. Rob had keyboards and a synthesizer, and Steve was a phenomenal player and singer, so getting with him was kind of cool. Of course, Rockin' Johnny wasn't too pleased about that, but I just kind of did what I did, and then we did that thing for about a year.

Steve got burned out on doing the band and he quit, so we got another guitar player and became Factual which I thought was pretty ingenious of Robb to come up with, you know, let's change the name of the band and we'll become Factual...of course, Steve was infuriated with that because it was so close to Actual, he didn't like that at all! Rob and I were real good friends and I thought, I'll be in a band called Factual. Factual played there for a while, and I did that for probably a year or so and then I got burned out on that...

I'd been in Nashville a couple years, and I just told Rob I was just going to quit and go back to Indiana. I had no idea what I was going to do. I drove up to where I grew up and stayed up there for about a month. I was always buying this little magazine at Mosko's called *DIY*. They had what they called "scene reports" from different cities, and I didn't realize growing up that I was only four hours south of Chicago...I used to think Chicago was, you know, probably two days away to drive.

A whole world away...
Just like I never realized that, where I grew up in Indiana, I was four hours from Nashville...I thought Nashville was – I guess I could have looked on the map – but in my head, I thought "gosh, that's real far away." So I never really thought about either Nashville or Chicago growing up because where I lived in Southern Indiana it was all farms, soybeans and corn, you know, it's real rural there. It's not that Gary, Indiana, Northern Indiana, industrial kind of look.

So I was reading this paper called *DIY* and I saw that a guy out of Chicago named Cary Baker, who is now a pretty big publicist, he was writing a "scene report" called the "Chicago Scene" and he was talking about the scene up there, and it always had a phone number at the end of everybody's column. There was an L.A. reporter, New York reporter, and I just called him out of the blue from Indiana and said "hey, I'm a drummer, I've got a van, I've got drums," which was a commodity, you know, so he turned me on to a couple leads of people to call. I called up a couple different people and said "I used to live in Nashville and dah, dah, dah, I've got drums and a van" and, of course, everybody loved that. Come on up and audition, we need you.

So I went to Chicago the fall of '81 and I auditioned for a band called Algorithms and there was a girl playing violin, a guy on guitar, and a bass player, and it was pretty cool, she was kind of jazzy and she sang, and it was kind of new wave and it was weird and we played real good gigs and stuff. So I stayed with them for probably about six months...I'd always heard about this band called Stations, that they were going to get a guy named Martin Hannett to come to Chicago and produce them. I knew who he was because I used to work at Discount Records and he produced, of course, Joy Division and he produced the first U2 single, and the first Psychedelic Furs single.

So I kind of knew who Martin Hannett was and I thought "wow, Martin Hannett!" Joy Division's *Closer* was one of my favorite records, so I always heard it in Chicago by this band called Stations. One time at an Algorithms rehearsal, the girl and the guy from Stations happen to come over and visit and when they came up we all took a break, but I was still sitting at my drums. I turned the snare drum, the snare off and I started playing this little drum intro to one of the songs off of *Closer*, it's the first song and I knew it had a cool little drum thing at the front and I started playing this little drum thing just like the record and they both – this was before I even met them – they just kind of came in and they instantly came over to me and said "wow, how do you know that?" and I said "well, you know Joy Division, I love them." I didn't say anything about Martin Hannett, and they said right off, "we did a demo and Martin Hannett is going to come and we need a real drummer and would you want to join our band," so I said "yeah." The Algorithms people, they were cool on that.

It was kind of like me leaving Cloverbottom and going to Actual. They knew that it was going to be maybe a better thing for me, and this was kind of wild...the bass player in Stations at that point was Steve Albini. So I meet Steve Albini, he's 19 years old; he's a freshman at Northwestern. He's this geeky guy with weird glasses and hair, six foot something, about 100 pounds and he plays this real weird bass tone. This was way before Big Black, so I got in with those guys and we played gigs around and still everybody would ask "when is Martin Hannett coming," and we played gigs and we were real popular but finally it got kind of old just when people were asking "when is he coming?" I don't know, I don't know...like the buzz was starting to kind of die.

INTERVIEW: JOHN ELLIOTT/DESSAU

At that point, Albini just said "fuck it, he's never coming," so he quit and we got another bass player. I went back down to Indiana to do – I'm a carpenter, too – to do some carpentry work and I just said "here's my phone number, if something comes up, I'm still in your band, I'm just four hours away, give me a call." They called about two weeks later and said Martin Hannett is coming, he's really coming. So I went back up and yeah, Martin Hannett came and we went into the studio and did three songs with him. This was the summer of '82. He took the tapes, he went back to England, he was going to mix them and he was going to get us a label deal with this label called Les Disques du Crépuscule, a Belgium label. It was kind of a part of Factory Records, it was called Crépuscule and I kind of knew their stuff. They put out some oddball stuff, but he was going to get us a deal with them...

Didn't they have bands like Red Lorry Yellow Lorry or something?
No, this is kind of a little bit before them. They had a band called the Names, and they were targeting some of the Factory bands. So he [Hannett] said, "I could very easily get you on this label." Of course, he was a super heroin drug addict at that point; we'd call him every couple weeks to ask "how are the mixes going?" He'd say "I'll have them, haven't got to it yet, I'll try to do it tonight," you know, he was basically doing it. One time they got a cassette in the mail and it was wild. It was something, it was awesome, but nothing ever happened. He finally just drug addicted out and nothing ever happened with that! Steve Albini was getting ready to do Big Black, Stations were pretty big, and Hannett did come, so the next question from everybody was "when is your record coming out?"

First it was "when's he coming, when's he coming," now he came and it's "when's your record coming out?" We played for another three or four months and I got burned out with "when's the record coming out," knowing that it was never going to come out, Hannett was just blowing us off. I had a chance to come back to Nashville so I thought "fuck it, I'll go back to Nashville." So I came back to Nashville, and I realized that I didn't want to be a drummer anymore, I wanted to get a synthesizer and a drum machine and I wanted to do that because, when you're a drummer, you're just a drummer. That was like '83, so for a year or two I just made little 'boom cha cha boom,' those kind of drum machine stupid songs.

I'd kept in contact with Hannett, somehow I got his number from Station, and every six months or so I would call him and he'd act like he'd remember me and I knew he didn't know who I was. Then in the spring of 1985 he called out of the blue and said "I'm going to come to Orlando, Florida with my fiancé and we're getting married. And I want you to help us get married in Nashville." At some point I was telling him, "I have a band named Dessau and I've been recording some." He said "don't be telling me about your music shit, I'm coming to get married." But I was thinking great, Martin Hannett is going to do my record while he's in town, I had that in the back of my head. If I'm going to be the best man and I'm going to set all this up, I have to get him in the studio somehow.

So you were waiting for Martin Hannett?
Yeah, Hannett was going to come to Orlando and then he wanted to do Disney World or something for a couple days and then he and his fiancé were going to drive to Nashville. So he came and we got him married, Skot Nelson and I went down to the courthouse with him and back then you didn't even have to get a blood test, they just had to have their passports. He got to smoke a lot of pot and we got high all the time, and around 10:00 or 11:00 at night I would tell him, "I got to go down to the studio."

The first couple nights he said "okay, cool, you go do your thing and I'm just here in Nashville." After the third night, he asked "what are you all doing down there?" I said "oh, nothing, just working on some cool tracks." He said "maybe I could come down, and I said "okay." He looked at me and asked "how many digital delays can you get?" That was his quote…okay, I want to come down there, but how many digital delays can you get. So I called around and I came up with three or four of them and he loved that.

So he came down and we were working and he ended up producing *Red Language*, which was a three-song EP of mine. We had some of the tracks recorded, but we ended up doing a whole bunch more with him; he did drugs and stuff and just did that Martin Hannett thing and he ended up mixing it. He was coming for a vacation to get married and he'd been so burned out on the studio, and by '85 he didn't want to think about a recording studio, but he did. We ended up working on it and it came out pretty cool.

This was probably 1986 by then, I'd been playing around and it didn't seem like it was going to go anywhere, and then I had a chance to go to the New Music Seminar, I got one of the books that you get and when I got back, I noticed there was this label called Carlisle Records and they had an ad for an artist named Preston. They had a real ad with a phone number, so I called them out of the blue. I had a press kit that had all kinds of radio stations listed that had been playing my Martin Hannett record. I had all kinds of reviews and I had stuff in there about Steve Albini and Stations and, by then, Big Black and Steve Albini was "in" and, of course, they didn't know any of this stuff. But they saw I had something, and I played some gigs, so they said, "we want to sign you."

At that point I had already put out *Happy Mood*, my second record in 1986 with Robb Earls on his label Faction Records. So, I had a couple releases and I had a bunch of press and they said "we want you to do a record with us." I said "okay, but maybe we can start out together by doing a remix thing. I told them I know this guy named Al Jourgensen in Ministry. Of course, they didn't know anything about Ministry, but they were packing out the clubs in Chicago. So I told Carlisle then, I told them "let's do a remix because I know this guy named Al Jorgenson who does remixes." They asked "what's that cost?" I had no idea. I was able to get Al's manager, he said it was going to cost $1,500 and I thought "that's like crazy, crazy money." That just blew my mind. I went back to Carlisle and said "this guy says he'll do a remix for $1,500; he wants cash, you have to give me fifteen $100 bills that I have to drive up to Chicago, I have to give it to him before we even do anything." That's how it was going to work and they said "okay, that's not too weird." I thought that it sounded weird to me, but they were buying it.

Al always had a classic thing – "no deals, no demos, and no discounts" – he had his "three D's" and I used to think "gosh, that's weird that you would have a little mantra, a little slogan like that," but looking back, yeah...no deals, no discounts, and no demos. You weren't going to go in and do a demo and then say "I'm not sure I like it, I don't know if I want to pay you."

So he told me "I'll book the studio time if you bring the $1,500. You bring some of your gear, and you bring somebody with you." Okay, I hadn't been up there for a few years, so I called Giles Reaves. He knew Ministry, so he and I went up there and the first thing when we got there, we stayed at Al's house, and the guys from Skinny Puppy were there and I was thinking this is all kind of new for me. When we got to the house, the first thing Al asked was "do you have the $1,500?" and I did. I was so nervous carrying it I had it up under the seat of my van; I gave it to him and he was impressed. He said "okay, we'll go in the studio tonight about 1:00."

We went in, he put the tape on, and he knew the song and he said "okay, pretty cool, pretty cool." He started doing his little magic and we're sitting in the back smoking some pot and after a couple hours he looked at me and said "okay, are you ready to sing?" I said "this is a remix, you're going to just do what you do and that's it." And he said "no, no, the vocals are shit, you got to go out there and sing." I wasn't ready to sing, I was stoned, it was 3:00 in the morning in the studio, and all these Chicago guys were around, leather jackets and stuff. I'm just this Nashville guy. So he got me out there and I started singing...I probably hadn't played a gig in a year, so my voice got hoarse real fast and he says "it sounds good," so I started singing and started ad libbin' and screamin' a little bit and I love it, he's in there lovin' it, and all these Chicago guys are there egging me on. I'm taking breaks, I couldn't even talk I was so hoarse, but Al just thought the vocals were ready.

We stayed at his house that morning, and I always thought that it was wild that we would go to 5:00 or 6:00 in the morning, and then we would sleep until probably noon or 1:00. I remember getting up and using the bathroom and he'd be in the kitchen reading the paper. I guess he was used to that all-night thing; I was all hoarse and I couldn't even talk. The next night we went in the studio and we did some more stuff...I remember when he was mixing it, Jim Nash, the head guy at Wax Trax, I kind of knew him from Stations when I lived there. Nash heard this stuff and he went off on Al, asking "who is this?" Al said, "this is that guy that was the drummer for Stations with Martin Hannett" and Jim said "I want to sign these guys."

"I want these guys on Wax Trax," Nash says, "this is good stuff!" Al said, "no, they're on a label." This was 1987 and I always thought that was kind of interesting. About a month later, Al sent the tape down and we all went to Carlisle and they put it on. It was "Unshakable," and he did some real tricks on it; the vocals were all gnarly and real industrial, so I guess that's how Dessau became...I don't want to say "industrial" but, we were moving in that direction. So we came back to Nashville, we played the tape, Carlisle loved it and then they said "now you have to fill this thing out."

So we had something to play in the studio while we were working on the songs "Skeleton By Nature" and "Thanksgiving." I guess that if I'd never done "Unshakable," I wouldn't have had a reference point. I would have just been making a record that was still synth-pop with a wimpy drum machine which I thought was real cool, but maybe it wasn't. With Al having mixed this one song, we used to play it [in the studio], and we never could match it. We tried to match it, but we never could match what they were doing, but we still put it out and, of course, that was the song that DJs and everybody picked up because it was produced by Al Jorgenson, so that was the one that did well.

Dessau

So that in 1988, Carlisle said "now you've got to do a full album." We went to Sound Emporium on Belmont and I got Mike Orr and Barry Nelson in my court, they weren't on that early stuff. I knew those guys from Actual and they were at a Cloverbottom gig back in'79, so I got those guys and we became a band and we played some gigs. Carlisle gave me a little bit of money to get a drum machine so we could play live, and I started getting into that kind of screechy, screaming vocals and people seemed to like that. I never would have thought that I really was a singer, and when this kind of "scream" stuff came along I thought "I can do that."

So with Carlisle we made *Exercise In Tension*. The record hadn't come out yet, we were still working on it, and we were doing a gig in Chicago and Al and all these skinny, preppy people came and we did "Isolation" by Joy Division as a cover. I had that Martin Hannett connection, so I always liked that song, and when we were done at the end of the night, Al said "you guys need to record that song and get me to produce it." Of course, he just wanted some more money, I thought. But at that same point, the Swans had that "Love Will Tear Us Apart" single out and it was kind of a hit. So he said "record the version you guys just did live in Nashville, send me the tape, I'll do a mix of it, do my thing on it, and then you can put it on your album." I said "okay."

We recorded it in Nashville at Treasure Isle with Tom Der and Tom Hardy, and we sent it to him. He sent it back and wow, it was, man it was big, I couldn't believe how big it sounded. It was a different kind of song than "Unshakable," it was kind of slower, the drums were cooler, and he put a bunch of cool little German kind of samples of things in it." We put that on *Exercise In Tension* and we never really had "Isolation" until the very end and people instantly picked that song out of that album and said, "this is the one!" Of course, it was the one that he produced and it did sound the best because it just had Al's sound on it, and our sound was maybe not up to par yet.

"Isolation" came out and that did real well; we did a video for that and it got played on MTV and Rock America and in all those trendy dance clubs, and then we did that single called "Beijing" because that was about that Tiananmen Square. I thought that was kind of a weird, and my concept there was that these Chinese kids, they weren't ready for the Coke machines yet and all this freedom, that was a little bit too much for them. That song did pretty well, we did a video for that and I guess that's when we kind of semi-faded away; I didn't play live any more; I kind of just stayed dormant.

Then I had a chance…we toured with a band called Die Warzau, they were from Chicago, and I found out that we could go on a 30-day tour with them. We did a tour with them in 1990 and that did real well, and when we came back, there was just a blank. Carlisle was running out of money, and that's when Paul Barker came down for about a month and we tried to do a record with him, but it never worked out, so Dessau stayed dormant for a few years. Then I got a call in 1995 from a label in New York called Mausoleum, a metal label, they called out of the blue and said "we have your catalog from Carlisle Records and we want to put it out," they didn't call it the greatest hits, I don't know if I ever had a hit – not really a hit, hit – they said "we want to put out a retrospective of you and include a bunch of the Paul Barker songs because he's in Ministry and we can put a sticker on the front," and I said "yeah, yeah," because those were some good songs.

Then they said we want you to hand-pick some of the Barker songs, "Isolation" and "Beijing," put some of your stuff on there. So I was able to get the stuff off the Mad Hog EP, which was "Unshakable," and "Skeletons by Nature," "Thanksgiving"…they had never been on a CD. I was able to take stuff off Exercise In Tension and five or six of the Barker songs, and I put those on there and made it a 12 track thing and when that came out, it actually did pretty good because it had major label distribution [the CD was titled Dessau]. Who knew that by 1995, when Dessau was dead in the water, that this label would call and say we want to put out some of your stuff.

At that same point, I had moved to Chicago because Die Warzau had a studio. I called them and said "hey, you guys always said you were going to have a studio and maybe need some carpentry work," and they said "yeah, we do. Why don't you come up here, bring some of your tapes and come up here about a month." So my wife and I moved back to Chicago at the end of '94 and I got on a label called Fifth Column Records. They had a band called Chem Lab, and they had always liked my stuff from way back. I did some carpentry work for barter, did some tracks with them. Fifth Column put out that record about the same month that that BMG record came out. Of course, they didn't like that, when I told them that I had gotten a call from this label to put out my back catalog, they freaked out. They said "no, no, no, you can't do that, we have you now," and I'm said "yeah, but they want to put out my back catalog and it's BMG. I'm going to be in Wal-Mart and K-Mart" and I got a card, I finally got a card, in a record store what do you call the little divider?

Yeah, the little divider card…
Yeah, I got a card because I was on BMG and I got a RCA number, RCA 606 or whatever, and they promoted it just like it was a regular RCA BMG release. I had major label distribution. Right off they were "no, no, no" and then they thought "yes, yes, yes, this is great for us because if you get a card that means the Fifth Column release can sit right in there too." So Dessau came out and sold 10,000 copies, and the Fifth Column probably sold 5,000 but it got lots of reviews and, of course, everybody still picked up on the Ministry song. Then we moved back to Nashville…

I didn't realize you were hooked up with those Chem Lab guys.
Yeah, that's the record called Detail Sketchy that came out and it's pretty cool, we did more of the dance stuff, but I sang industrial-style vocals with them and it got me a lot of press. That record got released in Germany and it was all over in Holland and stuff where we had gone one time and it got me into Wal-Marts and K-Marts. I went into just a K-Mart in Indiana in the middle of nowhere and there's my CD!

How did you get involved with Passafist?
Before I had moved back up to Chicago, I worked with Dave Perkins on the Passafist stuff; I know there's some stuff on the Internet that says I do Christian music now. I only did some Christian music because it was Nashville and Christian music was here, and it was Dave Perkins and Lynn Nichols from Chagall Guevara, and those guys were cool.

Yeah, Passafist wasn't a Christian music project.
No. It was on R.E.X., it was kind of a Christian label, but they had Circle of Dust too, which was pretty cool. I kind of did the Passafist record with them and we got a couple Dove Award nominations and stuff so after that people were saying "you worked with Dave Perkins and Lynn Nichols," and I guess I didn't realize how kind of popular they were. So through that I was able to work with the Newsboys and Rebecca St. James and Eric Champion.

FACTUAL - FACSIMILE

FACTUAL
Web: www.soundvortex.com

Band Members:
Robb Earls (synth, vocals) (A1-2)
Skot Nelson (guitar, synth) (A1-2)
Johnny Hollywood (bass, vocals) (A1-2)
Bone Brown (drums) (A1-2)

Factual Recordings:

A1. Your Way (Faction Records 1982, 7" vinyl)
Side One
1. Your Way

Side Two
2. Think To The Beat

Comments: Robb Earls and Factual helped bring Brit-styled synth-pop to the Music City. This was a pretty revolutionary single release at the time, leading the movement towards diversity in the local scene. My copy is numbered '194' and was pressed on red vinyl…very cool!

A2. For The Song (Faction Records 1983, 12" vinyl)
Side One
For The Song

Side Two
Psychotic Romance (Remix)

Comments: Since this is listed as Faction .03 I'm guessing that I'm missing a release in-between these two. No credits on this stark black 12" vinyl, either, so we'll just pretend that everybody played on it, OK? Factual song "Got Fun" was included on WRVU's *Local Heroes* compilation tape. These days, Factual frontman Robb Earls is an in-demand producer with his own studio, Sound Vortex, in Nashville.

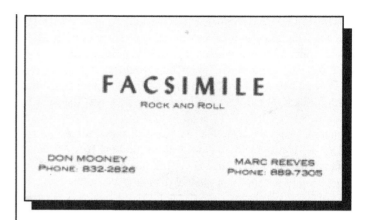

FACSIMILE

Band Members:
Don Mooney (vocals, guitar)
Mark Reeves (guitar)
Michael Lee Scinta (bass, harmonica, vocals)
Mark "Smiley" Shenkel (vocals, saxophone, guitar)
Andre Cosse (drums)
Bruce Sexton (drums)

Susan Sparks writes: A hard rocking, three piece band established in 1977 of all native Nashvillians – a rarity in this day! The name was catchy and obviously "before its time" as most people couldn't pronounce it, let alone knew what it meant (not realizing "facsimile" is the root of "fax").

Mooney and Scinta were an inseparable duo and lifelong friends from Donelson. Andre's roots in the music business came from his parents, Xavier Cosse' (manager for Chet, Boots, and Floyd) and Martha Carson (1950's Opry Star). They were later joined by another songwriter/musician, Mark "Smiley" Shenkel in 1979, lead vocals, saxophone, and guitar.

Venues: Annual local biker rallies, basement jams, battle of the bands, M.T.S.U. circuit (clubs and parties), Linwall's, and numerous clubs on lower broad, to include 3rd Avenue (?), a place with a killer stage and ran for years by a guy named Sam. Cover tunes included hits from the Rolling Stones, Hendrix, Pink Floyd, Beatles, The Who, and others too numerous to mention. It wasn't unusual to see Mooney pick out a Hendrix tune with his teeth, use the mike stand as a slide, and play awesome licks with the guitar behind his head.

Mark "Smiley" Shenkel remembers:
There were 2 strictly-rock venues in Nashville – one catered to punk, the other to metal – so Facsimile focused on getting Top 40 and country music bars to give us a try while booking the occasional gig at Springwater or the Sutler. Some establishments paid us and brought us back while others pulled the plug and kicked us out.

We were actually quite an effective combo even though we were playing a rock style that was currently out of vogue. Bikers and the classic rock crowd were our main audience and we were asked to play at some outdoor events (like Goat Fest) along with the local southern rock and top 40 bands. During a festival in Ashland City, we were perhaps too effective: the entire band was reeling from too much chemical input, and two deaths reportedly occurred during our unhinged encore rendition of "Helter Skelter." One was accidental: a fellow watching from the saddle of his tractor in the back of the field apparently passed out, fell off, and was crushed as his tractor rolled over his body. The other was the result of an assault with a tire iron while the crowd was going nuts and starting fights.

Needless to say, we were shocked when we heard the news, but didn't fool ourselves by thinking we caused the ruckus. Trouble was already brewing, and at most, our racket on stage may have helped things come to a head. Still, these events made me think hard about destructive influences, and contributed to the positive approach later applied to the original Riff Raff.

Shenkel on the band's name, sound & reputation:
The name Facsimile was suggested by guitarist Don Mooney, which was fine with us. After all, we copied some of our

favorite songs, and the word looked pretty screwy in print. Case in point: Facsimile was sometimes mispronounced "Fack Smiley."

We played mostly late-60s hard rock (Hendrix, Stones, Zeppelin, Steppenwolf, etc.), plus the occasional oddball oldie to take advantage of the sax, such as "Take 5" and "Peter Gunn." We had a few originals ironically inspired by the music of the Residents and Snakefinger. The rest of the band ridiculed me at first for listening to Ralph Records releases, then after a while they finally "got it" and went gaga over the stuff.

After finding a 1968 Telecaster in Billy Cox's (Hendrix's Band of Gypsies) pawn shop for $200, I added a guitar to my arsenal along with crude home-made percussion (smacking blocks of 2x4s together and shaking whisky bottles with pennies inside...).

The Facsimile days were wild, hazily remembered times, and destined not to last. As a recently freed ex-husband who had married at a young age, I was going hog wild with women and partying, but the rest of the band made me look relatively conservative in comparison...Facsimile fell apart after a couple of years, but later re-grouped briefly as an opener for a few Riff Raff shows.

FACSIMILE

Facsimile Moment-of-the-Weird:
During a set in downtown Nashville, I passed out in the middle of singing a long, high note and timbered forward – face first – into the middle of the dance floor. The impact woke me up, unharmed, and I leapt back to the stage in time to sing the next verse. The rest of the band apparently didn't miss a beat. Wild applause ensued.

Comments: Sadly, Chip Chilton informed me via email that Don Mooney of Facsimile had passed away on October 1st, 2007 and his aunt Beverly Hamilton let us know that Don died from complications after a car accident.

Chip Staley wrote: "When I was new in Nashville, it was Mooney and Mike McCabe who championed my cause and who led to my playing drums with both Martha Carson and Reggae/Ska band Freedom Of Expression, the latter of which changed the course of my life forever. Without him I would have never had the opportunities I still benefit from today. Mooney could sure play, his tone was equally as good, and we had some great moments together on-stage, but it's the rest that's really had an impact on me."

FAIR VERONA

Band Members:
Beth Cameron (vocals, guitar)
Doni Schroader (drums)

FAITH CARNIVAL

Band Members:
Chris Kontopanos (vocals, guitar)

Ricky Dodson (guitar, vocals)
Rick Heil (bass)
Walter Klocko (drums)

Comments: Band contributed song "The Dogs In The Distance" to the ***Music City Rock*** 1995 comp CD.

FAITH LIKE GUILLOTINE

Band Members:
Vince Buwalda (vocals)
Joe Montgomery (guitars, vocals)
Geoff Buwalda (bass)
Mark Beasley (drums)

FAITH HEALERS

Band Members:
Drake Welling (vocals)
Rob Chanter (guitar)
Bill Frazho (bass)
Tom Riss (drums)

Comments: On the Faith Healers' sound, Michael McCall sez, "melodic, atmospheric pop with an underlying social message."

FARMER JASON

Band Members:
Jason Ringenberg (vocals, guitars) (I, II)
George Bradfute (guitars, bass) (I, II)
Fats Kaplin (fiddle, banjo) (I, II)
Steve Ebe (drums) (I, II)

Other Musicians:
Phil Lee (vocals) (II)
Phillip McKennie (drums) (I)
Todd Snider (vocals) (II)
Webb Wilder (vocals) (II)

Farmer Jason Recordings:

I. A Day At The Farm With Farmer Jason (Courageous Chicken/Kid Rhino 2003, CD)
1. Get Up Up Up!
2. A Guitar Pickin' Chicken
3. Whoa There Pony!
4. The Tractor Goes Chug Chug Chug
5. I'm Just An Old Cow
6. He's A Hog Hog Hog
7. The Doggie Dance
8. Little Kitty
9. Corny Corn
10. Hey Little Lamb
11. Sundown On The Farm

Comments: "Farmer Jason" is the alter-ego of Nashville rock legend **Jason Ringenberg**, originally created to perform songs for Jason's kids. Never before has art been so selfless; *A Day At The Farm With Farmer Jason* offers up smart songs that never talk down to the kids, Jason's goofy vocals balanced by a rockin' soundtrack courtesy of friends George Bradfute and Fats Kaplin.

The album was reissued by Kid Rhino, a Warner Music label, in 2006, with Jason picking up his acoustic guitar and packin' them in at kid-friendly venues nationwide.

II. Rockin' In The Forest With Farmer Jason (Courageous Chicken/Kid Rhino 2006, CD)
1. The Forest Oh
2. Punk Rock Skunk
3. Ode To A Toad
4. Mrs. Mouse
5. Forest Rhymes
6. He's A Moose On The Loose
7. Arrowhead
8. Catfish Song
9. Opossum In A Pocket
10. A Butterfly Speaks
11. The Old Oak Tree

Comments: Farmer Jason's second kid's album lands on a major label imprint and provides a second career for the local rock icon. Billed as "grown up music for cool rockin' Mom's and Daddy-O's" (and it is) (see review ➔).

FATGNAT

Band Members:
Kevin Hogan (guitar) (I)
Mark "Smiley" Shenkel (saxophone) (I)
Joey Butler (bass) (I)
Jason Boney (drums) (I)
Jim Dye (drums)

Recordings:

I. Friend, All The Good Names Are Taken (self-produced CD, 2004)

Comments: FATGNAT is a totally unique band among a city full of them. They call it "garage jazz," and their sound is, indeed, a chaotic blend of jazz-rock fusion with a healthy dose of improvisation and plenty o' six-string mangling courtesy of Hogan.

Mark "Smiley" Shenkel talks about *FATGNAT*:
The live shows were sporadic due to our hard-to-classify

Farmer Jason

style of music (too rock for jazz clubs, too jazz for rock clubs, no vocals for the jam-band fans, etc.), and whenever we thought we found a home base for performing, something changed.

Our first FATGNAT-friendly venue, the Pub of Love, had to close temporarily when the ceiling caved in. We next played regular shows at the Radio Café until it closed (again), and then moved to the 5 Spot. Jason had moved out and left the band so he could concentrate on writing and recording with the new gear he had been amassing in his home studio.

A friend referred Brian Killian to fill the slot but he bailed after a short while and we were back to looking for another drummer – not an easy task when most of the material is in anything but straight 4/4 time (this is Nashville, not New York, yo).

We finally found a kindred spirit in the person of former Jet Black Factory pounder, Jim Dye, (referred by Dave Willie of JBF and 9PD), and FATGNAT carried on. Dye had little experience with jazz and odd time signatures, but stepped up to the plate marvelously.

FEARLESS FREAP

Band Members:
Rob Robinson (vocals, guitar) (I-III)
Jeff Stokes (guitar) (I)
Todd Tabor (bass) (I)
Ray Crabtree (drums) (I)
Mark Williams (guitar) (II, III)
Matt Logan (bass) (II, III)
Chip Murdock (drums, percussion, keyboards) (II, III)
Jerry Judd (drums) (III)

Other Musicians:
Scott Baggett (guitar, accordion, keyboards) (I)
Curtis Birch (lap steel) (II)
Bob Britt (lap steel) (II)
Tom Bukovac (guitars, bass) (II, III)
Matt Dabich (saxophone) (II)
Jim D'Arrigo (saxophone) (III)
John Glazer (keyboards) (II)
Kirk Hunt (fretless bass) (II, III)
Fats Kaplin (steel guitar) (III)
Dave Kennedy (drums) (II)
Bill Lars (trumpet) (II)
Randy Lliego (accordion) (II)
Tom Lundberg (trombone) (II, III)
Kurtis McFarland (loops) (III)
Kevin Pierce (trumpet) (III)
David Sumrall (percussion) (I)
Chris Walters (keyboards) (II, III)

FARMER JASON
Rockin' In The Forest With Farmer Jason
(Courageous Chicken/Kid Rhino)

"Farmer Jason" is more than just a nom de plume for alt-country pioneer Jason Ringenberg to create kid's music. While early Jason & the Scorchers audiences marveled at Ringenberg's whirling dervish antics, they didn't realize that it was just his unbridled enthusiasm spilling out on the stage. Ringenberg brings the same sort of reckless joie de vivre here, his second kids' album and the first under the Kid Rhino imprint.

Ringenberg is a good enough songwriter that he can pen material for kids that won't drive parents entirely crazy with repeated listens, slipping in clever asides and erudite references that sound funny enough to kids, but whip-smart to the adult listener. Farmer Jason's good-natured goofiness and nice-guy personality create a natural appeal for kids with tunes like "Punk Rock Skunk" and "Opossum In A Pocket."

The music is quite sophisticated, however, ranging from raucous country and folkish storytelling to pop-punk and rockabilly. Ringenberg is backed here by top-notch musicians like George Bradfute, Fats Kaplin and Victor Wooten while friends like Todd Snider, Webb Wilder and Kristi Rose drop by to lend their vocal talents.

If you want to provide your young 'uns with intelligent entertainment, let 'em spend some time with Farmer Jason.

– *Country Standard Time*, 2006

Fearless Freap Recordings:

I. Sucking The Existence (Rob Sum Records 1995, CD)
1. Wreck of the Ella Fitzgerald
2. This Never Made No Sense
3. Earthman
4. Sweetheart Rider
5. Strap Me In
6. Shed My Skin
7. Hey Hey Now Now
8. Spill Your Mind
9. Sucking The Existence
10. I've Got Reason
11. Miss Understood
12. Eminent Departure
13. Fearless Freap

II. Beanbag (Rob Sum Records 1996, CD)
1. Do Right Love

2. Excess Of Success
3. Here And Now
4. Beanbag
5. I Often Wonder (What It Would Be Like)
6. Wildflower
7. Always Wanting To Feel This Way
8. Phallic Steeple
9. Cake and Champagne (Wedding Song)
10. Matter Of Heart

III. Alchemy (Rob Sum Records 1998, CD)
1. Love Electric
2. Modern Day America
3. Disconnect It
4. Alchemy
5. All Over Now
6. Too Beautiful/Melinda's Song
7. Other Side of Town
8. It Ain't Easy
9. Piece Of Me
10. Isabella Umbrella
11. This Is My Life

Comments: Nashville's Fearless Freap is not to be mistaken for the Canadian band of the same name led by Bill Lawson. Rob Robinson went on to form the band Whirlybird and, of course, Ray Crabtree was a member of the infamous **White Animals**.

THE FEATURES
Web: www.thefeatures.com

Band Members:
Matthew Pelham (vocals, guitar) (A1-2, I-III)
Roger Dabbs (bass) (A1-2, I-III)
Parish Yaw (keyboards) (A1-2, I-II)
Rollum Haas (drums) (A1-2, I-III)
Mark Bond (keyboards) (III)

The Features Recordings:

Singles

A1. The New Christmas Wishbook (self-produced 7" vinyl)
Side A
1. The New Christmas Wishbook

Side B
2. The Idea Of Growing Old

Comments: Limited edition 7" red vinyl, 500 copies only available through the band's web site, digital version available from iTunes.

A2. Buffalohead (Fictitious Records 7" vinyl)

Albums/EPs

I. The Beginning (self-produced CD EP, 2001)
1. Stark White Stork Approaching
2. Walk You Home
3. Bumble Bee
4. The Beginning (Week One)
5. Two By Two

II. Exhibit A (Universal Records 2004, CD)
1. Exhibit A
2. The Way It's Meant To Be
3. Me & The Skirts
4. Blow It Out
5. There's A Million Ways To Sing The Blues
6. Leave It All Behind
7. Exorcising Demons
8. The Idea Of Growing Old
9. Someway, Somehow
10. Situation Gone Bad
11. Harder To Ignore
12. Circus

III. Contrast (self-produced CD, 2006)
1. Contrast
2. Wooden Heart
3. I Will Wander
4. Commotion
5. Guillotine

Comments: The saga of the Features provides the best evidence yet that major labels ain't worth shit. The band had a great sound, honed by several years of live performances in

Murfreesboro and Nashville. After getting a big league deal, the band managed to release *Exhibit A*, a fine album in spite of the label's influence. When the Features refused to whore themselves at the label's whim, they got booted back to indie-land. 'Tis a shame, too, 'cause these guys are *good...*

FEED FOUR

Band Members:
Jack Curry (vocals, guitar, keyboards)
Alan Powell (guitar, vocals)
Gary N. Godbey (bass, vocals)
Steve Babi (drums, vocals)

Comments: Formed around 1989 by Curry, Powell coming to Nashville (and the band) from Boston. Feed Four played *The Metro*'s 5th Anniversary Bash and had tunes played by Shannon on the deejay's *Nashville Tapes* program on WKDF.

FIFTEEN STRINGS

Band Members:
Chris Carmichael (vocals, violin)
Ken Kennedy (guitars)
Kurt Menck (guitars)
Roger Osborne (bass, keyboards)
Matt Green (drums)

Comments: Led by string-wizard **Chris Carmichael**, Fifteen Strings was kind of a highbrow hair band that included Ken Kennedy of **Lust**. They were better than they had a right to be, and certainly better than almost any Hollywood gutter rats that were popular during the late 1980s. But I'm sure that the sight of Carmichael raging on the violin scared the heebee-jeebees out of the label A&R reps, and Fifteen Strings remained a local secret.

JEFF FINLIN
Web: www.jefffinlinonline.co.uk

Band Members:
Jeff Finlin (vocals, guitar, drums, bass) (I-VIII)

Other Musicians:
Bob Angelo (pedal steel) (I)
Pat Buchanan (guitars) (V-VIII)
Tony Crow (keyboards) (I, II)
Chuck Conner (drums) (II)
Joel Diamond (keyboards) (III)
Skip Edwards (keyboards) (II)
Eric Elliott (guitar, vocals) (I, II)
Scott Esbeck (vocals) (II)
Tony Garnier (bass) (III)
Moose Harrell (guitars, lap steel, slide guitar) (I)
David Henry (strings) (VIII)
Ned Henry (strings) (VIII)
Steve Herman (trumpet) (V, VI)
Mark Hill (bass) (II, VI)
Dave Hofstra (bass) (III)
Jim Hoke (saxophone) (V,VI)
Kevin Hornback (bass, guitar) (V, VII, VIII)
Dave Jacques (bass) (I, II, VI, VIII)
Will Kimbrough (slide guitar) (VI-VIII)
Doug Lancio (guitar) (II, VI, VIII)
Randy Leago (saxophone) (V, VI)
Lij (keyboards, synth) (VII, VIII)
Mark Linebaugh (bass, guitar) (III)
Kelly Looney (bass) (I)
Phil Madeira (keyboards) (VI)
Jerry Dale McFadden (accordion) (I)

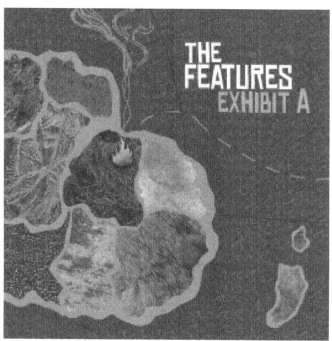

Richard McLaurin (slide guitar, synths) (III, VII, VIII)
Joe McMahan (guitar) (III)
Tommy Meyer (drums) (V-VIII)
Eric Moon (keyboards) (VIII)
John Painter (bass) (I)
Laron Pendergrass (guitar, vocals) (II, VIII)
Joe Pisapia (guitar, pedal steel) (VI)
Mark Ribot (guitar) (III)
Tammy Rodgers (viola) (II)
Larry Saltzman (guitars) (III)
Paul Slivka (bass) (VIII)
Danny Torrell (slide guitar) (II)
Dusty Wakeman (bass) (II)

Jeff Finlin Recordings:

I. *Lonely Light* (self-produced CD, 1991)
1. Corner of My World
2. You Slip Sometimes
3. Sunday's Forgivin'
4. Moonlight Mad
5. Lonely Light
6. Marathon Man
7. Law of the Land
8. I Go To Pieces
9. Silver Lining in the Clouds
10. Love Weighs Eighteen Tons

II. *Highway Diaries* (Little Dog 1995, CD)
1. Napoleon, Josephine & Me
2. West Of Rome
3. Lovers In The Street
4. Sunday's Forgivin'
5. The Promised Land
6. Hammer Down
7. Only An Immigrant
8. Come On Annie
9. Idaho

Comments: Finlin's second solo album was released on Pete Anderson's Little Dog label as the singer/songwriter moves further towards an Americana sound.

III. *Original Fin* (NBFNY Records 1999, CD)
1. Love and Happiness
2. June
3. The Perfect Mark of Cain
4. Waiting on a Flood
5. She's a Mama Now
6. Kisses From A Train
7. Weight of the Flame
8. Eighteen Tons
9. Moonlight Becomes The Dawn

Comments: Finlin would leave town prior to recording

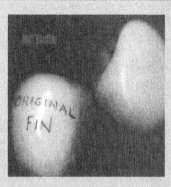

JEFF FINLIN
Original Fin
(NBFNY Records)

Wearing obvious Bob Dylan mannerisms on his sleeve like his best suit of Sunday clothes, singer/songwriter Jeff Finlin's sophomore album matches obscure imagery and oblique storytelling with sparse instrumentation. The resulting effect of ***Original Fin*** is somewhat disconcerting, as Finlin's plaintive and extremely nasally vocals struggle to keep up with his often brilliant, sometimes maddening lyrical poetry.

Finlin sounds a lot like that crazy guy in every large city, the one wandering around the streets with a sign saying "the end is near." Dominated by themes of love and betrayal, death and rebirth, the characters in Finlin's sordid little tales are always leaving – leaving bad relationships, leaving good relationships, even leaving this mortal vale.

If songs like "The Perfect Mark of Cain" or "Waiting on a Flood" seem hopelessly dark, Finlin also imbues ***Original Fin*** with the light of faith and redemption. The album closes with "Moonlight Becomes Dawn," as positive a statement of life's possibilities as you'll find in a song.

Although drawing a great deal of influence from Dylan's vocal phrasing and song structure, Jeff Finlin nevertheless forged his own identity with ***Original Fin***, delivering a thought-provoking and artistically expressive collection of songs. *– All Music Guide*

Original Fin, moving to NYC, and the album has only a cursory Nashville connection. It's a brilliant sort of Dylanesque Americana that sounds more like the Music City than New York City. ***Original Fin*** was later reissued in the U.K. in 2001 by Gravity/BMG.

IV. *Text Goes Here* (self-produced CD, 2001)
1. Law of the Land
2. Marathon Man
3. Proving Ground
4. The Hard Way
5. Way Down Town
6. Silver Lining
7. Goodbye is Just a Freight Train Coming

V. Live From Nowhere (self-produced CD, 2002)
1. West of Rome
2. Goodbye is Just a Freight Train Comin'
3. Delta Down
4. Dancing on the Downside
5. Alchemy
6. Waiting on a Flood
7. Goodtime

Comments: Recorded live at the Exit/Inn, May 2002 with friends like guitarist Pat Buchanan and bassist Kevin Hornback.

VI. Somewhere South Of Wonder (Gravity U.K. 2002 / Bent Wheel U.S. 2003, CD)
1. I Am The King
2. Sugar Blue
3. Summertime
4. Good Time
5. Delta Down
6. Which Way?
7. Alchemy
8. Miracle Along The Way
9. Where Do We Go
10. Sugar Blue Too
11. Somewhere South of Wonder

VII. Epinonymous (Bent Wheel 2004, CD)
1. Better Than This
2. Nothing's Enough
3. Postcard From Topeka
4. The Long Lonesome Death of the Traveling Man
5. Bringing My Love

6. American Dream #109
7. Forever Evergreen
8. Holes In My Hands
9. Soho Rain
10. Just Like Everyman
11. Hallelujah

VIII. Angels In Disguise (Korova Records U.K. 2006 / Rykodisc U.S. 2007, CD)
1. Better Than This
2. American Dream #109
3. Bringing My Love
4. The Long Lonesome Death of the Traveling Man
5. Postcard From Topeka
6. Soho Rain
7. Angel in Disguise
8. Forever Evergreen
9. Don't Know Why
10. Break You Down
11. Moon Man
12. Nothing's Enough

Comments: A re-release of *Epinonymous* with four different tracks, released in the U.K. by Warner Music's Korova Records.

ED FITZGERALD

Band Members:
Ed Fitzgerald (vocals, guitars) (I, II)
Judi Fitzgerald (vocals) (I, II)

Other Musicians:
Willis Bailey (drums) (I)
Eddie Bayers (drums) (I)
Steve Blazek (guitar, steel guitar) (I)
Mark Brown (guitar) (I)
Ralph Childs (bass) (I)
Jim Fey (bass) (I)
Roone Goodman (drums)
Greg Jennings (bass)
Bob Kommersmith (bass) (I)
Al Kooper (guitar, keyboards) (I)
Dave Pomeroy (bass) (I)
Tim Wilson (keyboards)
Craig Wright (drums) (I)

Ed Fitzgerald Recordings:

I. Nashville Reflex (Telephone Records 1993, cassette)
1. The Flying Dutchman
2. The Last Time
3. Oklahoma Road
4. A Finer Love
5. Straw Dogs
6. Another Sun Goes Down

7. Outlaw Blues
8. Right Between The Eyes
9. In These Hills
10. Your Imagination

Comments: Released as side one of Fitzgerald's *Picks* limited edition cassette. I have copy number 17 of 40; side two includes songs by **Civic Duty** and Seven Keys.

II. The Petrified Forest (as "J. Edward Fitzgerald") (Buffalo Way 1995, cassette)
1. Country Girl
2. Stop Breaking My Heart
3. Too Much For The Blues
4. San Antonio
5. As The Crow Flies
6. Blue Niagra
7. Gone To Gray
8. The Last Time
9. Omaha Rose
10. The Second Time Around
11. The Petrified Forest

Comments: Yes, this is Ed Fitzgerald from the legendary local band Civic Duty. Fitzgerald also placed two songs on the Rock 106 compilation *Homegrown*, with a line-up that included Greg Jennings, Tim Wilson, and Roone Goodman.

FLEMING & JOHN

Band Members:
Fleming McWilliams (vocals) (I-II)
John Mark Painter (guitar, vocals) (I-II)
Stan Rawls (bass)
Shawn McWilliams (drums) (I-II)

Other Musicians:
Todd Collins (percussion) (I)
David Davidson (violin) (I-II)
Ben Folds (drums, vocals) (I-II)
Jill McWilliams (vocals) (II)
Dennis Salee (flute) (I)

Fleming & John Recordings:

I. Delusions Of Grandeur (R.E.X. Music 1995, CD)
1. I'm Not Afraid
2. Break The Circle
3. Delusions Of Grandeur
4. Rain All Day
5. Letters In My Head
6. Love Songs
7. 6570
8. Bad Reputation
9. Hanging On A Notion

10. A Place Called Love (Intro)
11. A Place Called Love

Comments: Fleming McWilliams and John Mark Painter met while going to school at Belmont and, finding themselves simpatico as a musical couple, began writing songs together (they'd later get married). Painter made a name for himself as a session guitarist, working on the softer edge of Nashville music, from folk-country artists like Nanci Griffith to Contemporary Christian acts like dc Talk and Jars of Clay. *Delusions Of Grandeur* was originally released in '95 by the quirky little Brentwood label R.E.X. and was later remixed and reissued by Universal Music.

Another View: "*Delusions of Grandeur* is spunky, layered with rollicking wit and sophisticated sassiness. They're too sweet to be indie and too original to be mainstream, therefore Fleming & John are individualists when it comes to composing their quirky, melodic sound...when it comes to songwriting, Fleming & John refrain from typical grunge-rock riffs for more structured harmonies and crashing hooks. They are swirly and poetic when addressing love and everything that comes along with it."
– MacKenzie Wilson, *All Music Guide*

II. The Way We Are (Universal Records 1999, CD)
1. Twinkle
2. I'm So Small
3. Sssh!
4. The Pearl
5. Comfortable
6. Don't Let It Fade Away
7. The Way We Are

8. Radiate
9. Ugly Girl
10. Sadder Day
11. Rain All Day
12. Devil's Food
13. Suppressed Emotions
14. I Fall For You
15. That's All I Know
16. The Hidden Track

Comments: Friend of the band Ben Folds called Fleming & John "the Carpenter's of the 1990s with Led Zeppelin's rhythm section." With *The Way We Are* the band was bumped up to major labor status (I think that R.E.X. was long gone by now, anyway), and the resulting promotion and distribution scored Fleming & John a Top 40 hit in "Ugly Girl." Still, the band went nowhere afterwards, and last I heard they were still recording cover songs for a tribute album (admittedly cool cover tunes, tho'!).

THE FLOATING MEN
Web: www.floatingmen.com

Band Members:
Jeff Holmes (vocals, acoustic guitar) (I-XIV)
Scott Evans (acoustic bass, vocals) (I-XIV)
Jeff Bishop (drums, percussion) (I-XIII)

Fleming & John

Other Musicians:
Bill Baker (keyboards) (I)
Jeff Black (vocals, harmonica) (III, VIII, X)
Peter Bordonali (mandolin) (V)
John Byrne (dobro) (V)
Jeff Coffin (saxophone, clarinet) (VI, IX)
Chris Cottros (guitar, mandolin) (VI, VIII, IX-XI, XIV)
Larry Crane (guitar) (I)
Steve Ebe (drums) (XIV)
Caitlin Evanson (violin) (XIV)
Barry Green (trombone) (VI)
Rob Hajacos (violin, fiddle) (V)
Mike Haynes (trumpet) (VI)
Jim Hoke (tenor sax, clarinet) (XIV)
Bill Huber (trombone, tuba) (XIV)
Eva Hunter (vocals) (VI, VIII, IX, X, XI)
Billy Livsey (keyboards) (III)
Jerry Dale McFadden (keyboards) (VI)
Richard McLaurin (guitar, mandolin, dobro) (VIII)
Tony Migliore (keyboards) (V)
Andra Moran (vocals) (VI, VIII, IX, VI, X, XI, XIV)
Jody Nardone (keyboards) (VIII, IX-XI, XIV)
Neil Rosengarden (trumpet) (XIV)
Scotty Sanders (pedal steel) (V)
David Steele (guitar) (I, III, VI, V, X, XI, XIV)
Janene Stuehler (vocals) (V)
Wanda Vick (banjo, violin) (XI)
Scott Walker (harmonica) (V)

The Floating Men Recordings:

1. Tall Shadows (Meridian Records 1993, CD)
1. Where The Miracles Fly
2. A Pillar Of Stone
3. So Be It
4. Forgiven
5. So Wild
6. So Much Fire
7. Friday Afternoon
8. World Of Shadows
9. Hey Maria
10. Fade To Gray
11. A Date With A Vampire
12. Swallowed By The Night
13. Renee

Another View: "This acoustic-oriented trio offers delicate, lyrics-driven music whose surface sheen belies the muscle, passion and soul beneath the surface. In a city overflowing with gifted songwriters, the Floating Men's Jeff Holmes stands tall as a world-class wordsmith, penning tunes full of delicious imagery and artistic insight."
– Rev. Keith A. Gordon, *Bone Music Magazine*

II. Bootleg Snacks Vol. 1 (Meridian Records 1994, CD)
1. Throwing My Watch Away
2. So Wild
3. Deep Into The Night
4. The Floating Dream
5. Losing My Way
6. A Pillar Of Stone

Comments: The Floating Men take a tip from Zappa and "beat the 'leggers" with their own "official" bootleg albums, a brilliant idea for a young indie band. *Bootleg Snacks Vol. 1* is a six-song EP recorded live at the Ace of Clubs in Nashville.

III. Invoking Michelangelo (Meridian Records 1995, CD)
1. The Idle Hours
2. Wringing The Wheel
3. A Married Man
4. She Dreams About Me
5. South Carolina
6. Long Gone Tomorrow
7. Fellow Traveller
8. Don't Save Me
9. Another Maybe Someday
10. A Married Man (part II)
11. The Call Of The Wild
12. The Fire Escape

IV. Bootleg Snacks Volume 2 (Meridian Records 1996, CD)
Disc One
1. Intro
2. Butter In The Sun
3. Friday Afternoon
4. The Pain Is Over
5. The Fire Escape
6. Fade To Gray
7. The Idle Hours
8. Don't Save Me
9. South Carolina
10. Wringing The Wheel
11. It's Over
12. So Be It
13. She Dreams About Me
14. A Storm At Sunrise
15. The Call Of The Wild
16. The Call Of The Night
17. Swallowed By The Night
18. Where The Miracles Fly

Disc Two
1. Tucker Unplugged
2. Long Gone Tomorrow
3. World Of Shadows
4. Another Maybe Someday
5. The Rude Hitchhiker

6. A Date With A Vampire
7. Fellow Traveller
8. A Married Man
9. The Wilson's Jamboree
10. Calendar
11. The Town That Left Itself
12. A Rose For Emily
13. The Baptism Of Anthony
14. Swallowed By The Night (Unplugged)

Comments: Two-CD set, recorded live at the 12th & Porter Playroom on Thanksgiving weekend 1995.

V. The Song of the Wind in the Pines (Shade 1998, CD)
1. A Tall Stand Of Pines
2. Pink Champagne
3. Endless Highway
4. Over the Wateree
5. All Young Ladies
6. Devastated Divorcee
7. Gathering Souvenirs
8. Sign of Surrender
9. Dead Stallion Carousel
10. Slide Guitar Music
11. Pink Lemonade
12. The Upper Room
13. Two and a Half Hours
14. East of the Sunrise
15. The Gathering

VI. Lemon Pie (Shade 2000, CD)
1. Beer, Deli, Ice, Diesel
2. Tropic Of Capricorn

THE FLOATING MEN

3. The Fallen Edens
4. Georgia
5. Rocket To The Moon
6. Southern Woman
7. Wastin' My Time On You
8. Kingdom Of Heaven
9. Misunderstood
10. Hair Tonic And Cheap Aftershave
11. Don't Look Away
12. Floodplain
13. Lemon Pie
14. Darkness On The Edge Of Town

VII. Bootleg Snacks Volume 3: Pie Ingredients (Shade 2000, CD)
1. Rocket To The Moon
2. Cover Snippets
3. East Of The Sunrise
4. Fire Escape
5. An Intro To Pink Champagne
6. Pink Champagne
7. All Young Ladies
8. Tall Stand Of Pines
9. Call Of The Wild
10. Devastated Divorcee
11. Friday Afternoon
12. Wringing The Wheel
13. Gathering Souvenirs
14. Smokin In The Grocery Line

VIII. Bootleg IV: Live at the Belcourt Theater (Shade 2001, CD)
1. Reid's intro
2. Renee
3. Bishop audition story
4. Friday Afternoon
5. Over The Wateree
6. She Dreams
7. Me & Louise
8. Slide Guitar Music
9. Wastin' My Time On You
10. Older Men
11. East Of The Sunrise
12. Rocket To The Moon
13. Misunderstood
14. Beer, Deli, Ice, Diesel
15. The Fire Escape
16. Happy B-Day FM
17. Smokin In The Grocery Line
18. Swallowed (By The Crowd)
19. Oui Sasha! an audio liner note

Comments: Two-disc set includes additional bootleg video CD.

IX. Heroes Felons and Fiends (Shade 2001, CD)
1. Roll Down The Windows And Drive
2. Alright Chameleons
3. You Let Me Down
4. Older Men
5. New Orleans
6. Wrong Kind Of Man
7. The Usual Trees
8. Nouveau Superheroes
9. Better Days
10. Comin Home A Hero
11. Louise

X. Boot 5: Please Be Seated (Shade 2002, CD)
1. Hero
2. Roll Down The Windows and Drive
3. World Of Shadows
4. Another Maybe Someday
5. Hey Maria
6. Forgiven
7. Lemon Pie
8. Kingdom Of Heaven
9. Loser For The Evening
10. Wrong Kind Of Man
11. New Orleans
12. Alright Chameleons
13. The Usual Trees
14. You Let Me Down
15. The Idle Hours
16. The Rude Hitchhiker

XI. A Magnificent Man (Shade 2002, CD)
1. Wastelands
2. Outsider
3. Invisible Life
4. Abandoned Mansions
5. Loser for the Evening
6. No Ordinary Man
7. Bathtub Gin
8. Cheap Rags
9. Ladyfriend
10. Mere Mortal Man
11. Terrified Man
12. Poacher's Daughter

XII. Bootleg 6: The Upper Room (Shade 2003, CD)
1. Invisible Life
2. Outsider
3. Wastelands
4. Waiting For A Sign
5. Mere Mortal Men
6. Bathtub Gin
7. Girls' Night
8. Crave
9. East Of The Sunrise

10. Call Of The Wild
11. The Poacher's Daughter
12. Ol 55 (Tom Waits)
13. Remembering Paradise
14. A Long Winded Prayer
15. Unwanted

XIII. So Far So Good: The Best of The Floating Men
(Shade 2003, CD)
1. Roll Down the Windows & Drive
2. Wringing the Wheel
3. Friday Afternoon
4. East of the Sunrise
5. Georgia
6. The Usual Trees
7. Misunderstood
8. Pillar of Stone
9. The Fire Escape
10. Wastelands
11. Bathtub Gin
12. Rocket to the Moon
13. Swallowed by the Night
14. Over the Wateree
15. The Call of the wild
16. A Tall Stand of Pines (remix)
17. Where Miracles Fly (remix)

XIV. The Haunting (Shade 2004, CD)
1. Unwanted
2. Waiting for a Sign
3. Remembering Paradise
4. Girl's Night
5. The Haunting

6. Long-winded Prayer
7. Demolition Day
8. Crave
9. Dark & Cool
10. Cronies
11. Jones
12. Haunt You Down
13. Dreamland

FLUID OUNCES
Web: www.fluidounces.org

Band Members:
Seth Timbs (vocals, guitar, piano) (I, II)
Brian Rogers (guitars, vocals) (I, II)
Ben Morton (bass) (I, II)
Sam Baker (drums) (I, II)
Justin Meyer (drums) (II)
Kyle Walsh (drums)

Fluid Ounces Recordings:

I. Big Notebook For Easy Piano (Spongebath Records 1997, CD)
1. Shamrock
2. Tricky Fingers
3. Birdbrained
4. Liquorish Vampires
5. Daddy Scruff
6. Record Stack
7. Role Call

Fluid Ounces, continued on page 182...

INTERVIEW: THE FLOATING MEN

Buying a record is one thing," says Jeff Holmes, vocalist, guitarist and songwriter extraordinnaire, "but there's nothing like being in the same room as The Floating Men. I don't think that you're a real true fan until I, personally, have sweated on you. That's where the real long term bond is made."

The Floating Men – Holmes, bass player Scot Evans and drummer Jeff Bishop – have earned a reputation not only as one of the hardest-working live bands in rock and roll, but also as one of the best. A three-piece, all-acoustic band delivering intelligently structured songs, Nashville's The Floating Men have built a legion of fans the old-fashioned way: by leaving their listeners with the feeling that they got their money's worth out of the evening.

"They say that the fan of a band that they hear on top forty radio is a fan for three and a half minutes and that you have to start all over again every time that the record is played," says Holmes. "A fan that is earned by a live performance is a fan for life ... if you're a good live band. We think that we can handle that." The Floating Men are always on the road, it seems. Prior to the 1993 release of **Tall Shadows**, the band's first album, the threesome quit their day jobs and have yet to look back. They began a seemingly never-ending road show, playing an exhausting 600 dates during the following two years. "It's incredible," says Holmes, of the growing number of Floating Men fans. "With no marketing, no radio ... what press we got was great, but we didn't have anybody working it ... it was all word of mouth."

The band created a mailing list of their fans, a move that has proven to be worth its weight in gold. "We'd send that out every month, and then people on the mailing list call each other, and then they call people who aren't on the mailing list and say 'you should come see the show!' If we're playing in Asheville, North Carolina tonight," says Holmes, "there's probably somebody in Portland, Oregon going, 'hey, I've got a college roommate who lives in Asheville, maybe I should give them a call and tell them to go to that show.' So it's been just us and our fans, and they've been wonderful."

The band appreciates their fans and enjoys the support provided by them, reveling in the opportunity to go out on stage and entertain them with everything that they've got. "We'd like to try and do something like Jimmy Buffett or the Grateful Dead have done," says Holmes, "although it's obviously a totally different style of music, we want to do something like that, where it's a community of fans gathering at every show, and to remain grassroots no matter how big it gets."

The Floating Men came together in late 1990, formed from the ashes of the Little Saints, another popular Nashville band. "Scot and I had been together in another band for a number of years," says Holmes, "and when that band broke up, we started working on songs in an acoustic setting." While putting together the material that would make up their first album, the two of them auditioned a number of drummers. They discovered Jeff Bishop, a Berklee School of Music graduate, and, shortly thereafter, says Holmes, "the Floating Men were born!"

The passing "unplugged" phenomena aside, the idea of an acoustic rock and roll trio is a risky one. In an industry firmly dedicated to "business as usual," any variation from the norm is not only viewed suspiciously, but is often times a quick ticket to obscurity. What made The Floating Men decide to base their work in an acoustic vein?

"The band that Scot and I had been in had been a real loud, really complex alternative rock band," says Holmes. "When that band broke up, and we broke out the acoustic guitars and just started working on songs, we realized, first of all, that the songs were pretty good, secondly, that we could sing ... so why not make that our focus?"

"Also, it's just a totally different sound," he continues, "it's something that you don't hear everyday. We're able to do a lot of things with acoustic instruments that most people never dreamed of. We put on a rock and roll show without an electric guitar amp on stage. That surprises a lot of people."

Tall Shadows was recorded "on weekends and evenings, as our life schedules and our day jobs permitted." Although several major labels were interested in the band, they really had no idea what to do with them. "The first question that a major label executive will ask you when you meet them," says Holmes, "is 'what's your target market?' It sounds glib, but our answer was always, 'people with stereos.' Who do you eliminate? If you stood in my place every night, look at the crowd every night, there would be virtually no demographic that we could eliminate. It's a wide variety of people."

The decision was made by the band to release *Tall Shadows* on their own. "We'd been around and around with all of the majors," says Holmes, "and we decided 'to hell with them!' We were sick of waiting for them to get off of their fat asses and do something. We had great songs, we had a great following, we put on a great live show and we were about to make a great record. We were either going to be on their side or we were going to be their competition. We wound up being their competition."

In a move reminiscent of the great punk rock bands of the early eighties, they created their own indie label – Meridian Records – as a vehicle for their music. "We started it from the ground up, bootstraps up," says Holmes. "It's kind of gotten out of hand now," he adds, laughing. "We've got other titles in the catalog, we've got a great staff working for us, so we don't really need to be there anymore." *Tall Shadows*, in 1993, became Meridian's first album release.

Tall Shadows received more than its share of critical accolades. The local press were collectively stumbling over their thesauruses trying to find words of praise for the somber collection of songs. Holmes' finely-crafted stories delved lyrically into the dark underbelly of the urban underground; the music was strikingly original and refreshing, masterfully executed and without a shred of pretension. Radio airplay was minimal, but, as Holmes recollects, "we didn't really have that many records to send out to radio." On the road, fans snapped up the impressive debut disc.

Meanwhile, the band experienced the normal trials and tribulations that come with independent status. "Not having any money at all to start off with, trying to build the business from the ground up, that's been the hardest part," says Holmes. "Now that we're in the swing of things, people are buying records and we're selling tickets to our shows ... and people who buy the tickets are buying the record, and vice versa, it's begun to snowball."

The recent release of The Floating Men's second album, *Invoking Michelangelo*, finds Meridian with an important national distribution deal via DNA, the country's largest indie distributor, and a big league producer in former E Street Band bassist Garry Tallent. *Invoking Michelangelo* was recorded at Tallent's Moondog studios in Nashville.

Were there any expectations, going into the studio for this second album? "We wanted to do right by the songs, that was the main thing," says Holmes. "We wanted to catch our live feel, like we did with *Tall Shadows*, but with a little cleaner sound.

All three of us cut everything, including vocals, live in the studio. We nailed every song in one or two, three takes at the most." The contributions of a handful of studio musicians were caught live in a similar fashion, and dubbed into the mix sparingly.

The result is a vibrant record possessing an almost breathless sound, as close, perhaps, to seeing The Floating Men live as you can get outside of a club. *Invoking Michelangelo* may prove to be the best indie release of the year, a bright and beautiful collection of songs that run over with emotion, passion and intelligence. A conceptual album, it's lyrical focus is upon the uncertainties of the universal passage into adulthood.

"*Tall Shadows* was a very urban, sex and drugs, alternative lifestyle, industrial

The Floating Men

THE FLOATING MEN - FLUID OUNCES

underground kind of album," says Holmes. "I think that I've taken that same cast of characters a couple of years later, shined a little sunlight in their faces and said 'wake up.' What's happening on *Invoking Michelangelo*, throughout the record, is this ongoing struggle between one's youth and one's adulthood with all these characters. Facing the realities of adulthood, the responsibilities, the fact that your body changes – it doesn't bounce back as quickly as it used to – and yet your mind is keener than it ever was ... all those aspects of being a grown-up are very daunting to someone coming out of their twenties, especially at this time in our history."

"What I did with the record, and the way that the songs are sequenced, is to tell these stories, and let the battle rage. Then, as the big finale, which is The Call Of The Wild, track number eleven, I have the main character in that song just let go of youth, kind of symbolically, by letting this wild, young girl that he loves go because she wants to, and he can't change her." The album closes with a cut called "The Fire Escape," where the character stands reflectively on the brink of adulthood, quietly accepting a fate that none of us can escape.

After an uncharacteristic break, the band is already touring in support of *Invoking Michelangelo*. With the interest generated by their loyal fans, radio is already picking up on the disc, and initial press reviews are overwhelmingly positive. Meridian's distribution deal has gotten the disc placed into numerous new markets across the country, and demand for their live shows is at an all-time high. Although the future looks quite bright for The Floating Men, you won't find the band resting on their laurels anytime soon.

"The Floating Men are going to tour our butts off! We are going to continue to stay as close to our fans as we can," says Holmes. "There's so much more that has to be done out there. We're going to play more towns than on our last tour. That's the key to what we do, staying close to our fans." – *Bone Music Magazine*, 1995

Fluid Ounces, continued...
8. Spill Your Brains
9. Milk Moustache
10. Kept Alive By Science
11. Big Empty
12. Poor Man

II. Vegetable Kingdom (Spongebath Records 1998, CD EP)
1. Vegetable Kingdom
2. Sitting Beside Myself
3. Lend Me Your Ears
4. Stick in the Mud
5. Sucker

III. In The New Old Fashioned Way (Spongebath Records 1999, CD)
1. Lend Me Your Ears
2. Marvel Girl
3. Luxury

Fluid Oz.

4. Vegetable Kingdom
5. Eleven:Eleven
6. Drought
7. Bigger Than Both Of Us
8. Go Lucky
9. Run, Rabbit, Run
10. Comfortable
11. Ambiance
12. Have Fun
13. Downscope The Boat Captain

Comments: The Japanese release of the CD included three bonus tracks, "Sitting Beside Myself," "Stick In The Mud" and "Sucker" from the *Vegetable Kingdom* EP that weren't on the domestic release.

IV. Foreign Legion (Raygun Records 2002, CD)
1. Show On The Road
2. Poet Tree
3. Metaphor
4. Expect The Worst
5. Sugar Mama
6. The Last Thing
7. Smitten
8. Encyclopedia Brown
9. So Far, So Good
10. Stark Raving Mad
11. She Blinded Me With Science

Comments: The Japanese release of the CD by Cutti Records includes several bonus tracks: a cover of Thomas Dolby's

"She Blinded Me With Science," "Thinking Cap," "Invincible Boy" (demo) and a home recording of "City Lights" with new lyrics.

V. The Whole Shebang (Vacant Cage Records 2004, CD)
1. Paperweight Machine
2. Crazies
3. Fool Around
4. Lazy Bones
5. Big Deal (Out Of Nothing)
6. Nobody Loves You (Like You Do)
7. Hung On Every Word
8. Make It Through
9. Selma Lou
10. Tokyo Expressway
11. Destined To Be Forgotten

THE FOOD

Band Members:
R. Luther Bradfute (vocals, guitar, bass, keys) (I)
George P. Bradfute (vocals, guitar, bass, keys) (I)
Lev Spiro (drums) (I)
Greg Morrow (drums) (I)
Celeste Hauser (backing vocals) (I)

The Food Recordings:

I. Let's Eat (FNEEBFOOD Productions 1989, tape)
Side One
1. Enchilada Tuesday
2. Like A Big Dawg
3. Words Of Love (From the "Austin Sessions")
4. Day Tripper (From the "Chippunks Sessions")
5. And Your Hard Bird's Night Thing ("Chippunks Sessions")

Side Two
6. You Forgot To Put The Milk Up
7. Proud Mary (From the "Austin Sessions")
8. Horizontal Hold
9. Why Do You Keep Talking To Me When I'm Trying To Read The Paper
10. Back To The Sea

Comments: Recorded in Austin, Memphis and Nashville and produced by "Edgar M. Food." The Food was a popular local band for a brief while during the early 1990s, though this is the only recording of the band's that I am familiar with.

The Food's George Bradfute, an extremely talented guitarist, has since gone on to play with a number of people including **Webb Wilder** and **Jason Ringenberg**.

FOR KATE'S SAKE

Band Members:
Kris Wilkinson (vocals, guitar)
Rob Cheplicki (guitar)
Deanna Amis (vocals)
Chris Hall (drums)

STEVE FORBERT

Band Members:
Steve Forbert (vocals, guitar, harmonica) (I-X)

Other Musicians:
Pete Anderson (guitar) (II)
Clay Barnes (guitar, vocals) (I-VII)
Jay Bennett (guitar, keyboards) (IV)
Ernest Carter (percussion) (I)
Charlie Chadwick (upright bass) (VIII)
Roger Clark (drums) (III)
Nick Connolly (keyboards)
Ken Coomer (drums) (IV)
Danny Counts (bass) (I, V)
Anthony Crawford (guitar, bass, keyboards) (X)
Eric Darken (percussion) (IX,X)
Dianne Davidson (vocals) (III)
John Deaderick (keyboards) (IX)
Jeff Donavan (drums) (II)
Tim Drummond (bass) (VI)
Dan Dugmore (guitar) (IX)
Skip Edwards (keyboards) (II)
Paul Errico (keyboards, vocals) (I,X)
Ethan Eubanks (drums) (IX)

STEVE FORBERT

Bob Glaub (bass) (II)
Bobby Lloyd Hicks (drums) (I,V,VII,VIII)
Billy Hullett (guitar) (III,VIII)
David Jacques (bass) (IX)
Max Johnston (mandolin, fiddle, banjo) (IV)
Brad Jones (bass, harmonium) (IV)
Will Kimbrough (guitar) (VIII)
Viktor Krauss (upright bass) (IX)
Jason Lehning (piano, guitar) (IX)
Nils Lofgren (guitar) (I)
Kenny Lovelace (fiddle) (VIII)
Donna McElroy (vocals) (III)
Mark Muller (keyboards, guitar, lap steel) (IX,X)
Bobby Ogdin (keyboards) (VIII)
Shawn Pelton (drums) (IX)
Al Perkins (pedal steel, lap steel guitar) (IV)
Ross Rice (keyboards, percussion) (IV)
Tom Roady (percussion) (III)
Gary Soloman (bass) (VII)
Mark Stuart (guitar) (IX)
Bryan Sutton (guitar) (IX)
Gary Tallent (bass) (III,VIII,IX,X)
Benmont Tench (keyboards) (III)
Rob Turner (bass) (X)
Dusty Wakeman (bass) (II)
Gary White (bass) (II)

Steve Forbert Recordings:

I. Streets of This Town (Geffen 1988, CD)
1. Running On Love
2. Don't Tell Me (I Know)
3. I Blinked Once
4. Mexico
5. As We Live And Breathe
6. On The Streets Of This Town
7. Hope, Faith And Love
8. Perfect Stranger
9. Wait A Little Longer
10. Search Your Heart

Comments: Mississippi native Steve Forbert hit Nashville in 1986 after spending the first decade of his creative career wearing out the shoe-leather in the Big Apple, busking for coins in Grand Central Station, and slowly inching himself into position in a New York City club scene that was about to revolve around CBGB's. Within a couple of years, he found himself on the major/minor label Nemperer and released the charming folk-rock collection ***Alive On Arrival*** in 1978. Forbert followed up a year later with ***Jackrabbit Slim***, which yielded his first and only Top 20 hit in "Romeo's Tune."

By the mid-1980s, however, Forbert was adrift without a record deal (after delivering two more solid, if unspectacular albums for Nemperor before the label dropped him), and he

---

THE FOOD
Let's Eat!
(Fneebfood Productions)

Nutrition Information per Serving:
Serving Size.....one song
Servings per Container.....ten
Calories.....98
Carbohydrates.....11 grams
Protein.....7 grams
Fat.....0 grams
Sodium...10mg

Percentage of U.S. Recommended Daily Allowance (USRDA):
Protein.....10%
Thiamine.....4%
Calcium.....**
Phosphorus.....**
Vitamin A.....7%
Riboflavin.....9%
Iron.....12%
Ferrous Oxide.....98%
Vitamin C.....20%
Niacin.....11%
Vitamin D.....10%

** Contains less than 2% of the USRDA of these nutrients

Ingredients:
100% Grade-A rock & roll, all meat with no cereal or soy filler, with screaming guitars, throbbing bass and pounding drums, a soupcon of the blues and lots of fun, Fun, FUN! 'til daddy takes our T-bird away....

The Food's ***Let's Eat!*** Is a nutritious blend of several musical styles and influences, a tasty and filling culinary delight with which to satisfy your aural cravings without adding inches to your waistline or removing pounds from your wallet.

– *The Metro*, 1990

---

ended up where a lot of talented songwriters do – in the "Music City," Nashville.

Falling in with the city's rock community worked wonders for the artist in Stevie, and I seem to remember **Jack Emerson** of Praxis doing a little shilling for Forbert around the time of this album's release. Produced by Springsteen's E Streeter Garry Tallent, with E Street Band guitarist Nils Lofgren guesting on a tune, ***Streets of This Town*** is an inspired collection of songs.

II. *The American In Me* (Geffen Records 1992, CD)
1. Born Too Late
2. If You're Waiting On Me
3. Responsibility
4. When The Sun Shines
5. The American In Me
6. Baby, Don't
7. Change In The Weather
8. You Cannot Win 'Em All
9. Rock While I Can Rock
10. New Working Day

Comments: Forbert's best album had the label taking him west to record in L.A. with producer Pete Anderson (Dwight Yoakum, Rosie Flores) and engineer Dusty Wakeman. Forbet's lyrics have seldom shown such laser-like focus and tunes like "Responsibility" and "Change In The Weather" are mature, intelligent and, in a just world, would have received truckloads of radio airplay and accompanying sales.

III. *Mission of the Crossroad Palms* (Paladin 1995, CD)
1. It Sure Was Better Back Then
2. It Is What It Is (And That's All)
3. Is It Any Wonder?
4. Lay Down Your Weary Tune Again
5. So Good To Feel Good Again
6. Oh, To Be Back With You
7. Real Live Love
8. The Trouble With Angels
9. How Can You Change The World?
10. Don't Talk To Me
11. The Last Rays Of Sunlight
12. Thirteen Blood Red Rosebuds

Comments: Another stellar effort from the singer and songwriter, who returns to Nashville to once again work with the E Street Band's Gary Tallent and engineer Tim Coats.

Another View: "With *Mission of the Crossroad Palms*, Steve Forbert turns in an album of craftsmanlike tunes on his seventh album, including story-songs such as "It Sure Was Better Back Then" (a working man's reminiscence) and "The Trouble with Angels" (in which an ex-beauty queen robs the till to pay for her infertility treatments)… he has flowered into a distinctive, broad-based songwriter and that, in E Street Band bassist Garry Tallent, he has found a sympathetic producer able to showcase his voice and lyrics properly."
– William Ruhlmann, *All Music Guide*

IV. *Rocking Horse Head* (Paladin Records 1996, CD)
1. If I Want You Now
2. My Time Ain't Long
3. Shaky Ground
4. Dear Lord
5. Moon Man (I'm Waiting On You)
6. Don't Stop
7. Some Will Rake The Coals
8. I Know What I Know
9. Good Planets Are Hard To Find
10. Big New World
11. Open House
12. Dream, Dream

Comments: While his previous album proved that Forbert retained his songwriting chops, *Rocking Horse Head* begins the long, slow spiral downwards. Whether it was too many nights on the road or too many trips into the studio (eight now, by my count), Forbert was clearly running out of gas.

V. *Here's Your Pizza* (Paladin Records 1997, CD)
1. Stop Breakin' Down Blues
2. What Kinda Guy?/Rockin' Robin
3. One After 909
4. Years Ago
5. Everybody Does It in Hawaii
6. You're Darn Right
7. Runaway Train of Love
8. All Because of You
9. Song for Katrina
10. Honky Tonker
11. Samson and Delilah's Beauty Shop
12. You Cannot Win (If You Do Not Play)/Polk Salad Annie
13. Tribute to Ritchie Valens: His Was the Sound/La Bamba
14. Sweet Pea
15. Backin' Up Boys
16. You Cannot Win 'Em All

Another View: "Steve Forbert may have been *Alive on Arrival* (the title of his 1978 debut), but it took him another

STEVE FORBERT

19 years to get around to releasing a live album. He dug into the vaults to do it, waxing a concert he recorded with his band, the Rough Squirrels, in a small Florida club back in 1987. 'Yes there's some tape hiss here, some distortion,' Forbert admits in the liner notes, but there are also performances that 'more than make up for any technical imperfections.' For the most part, that's true, although you do have to wade through a few throwaways to get to the goodies." – Jeff Burger, *All Music Guide*

VI. Evergreen Boy (Koch Records 2000, CD)
1. Something's Got a Hold on Me
2. She's Living in a Dream World
3. Strange
4. Evergreen Boy
5. Rose Marie
6. Now You Come Back
7. Your Own Hero
8. Late Winter Song
9. Breaking Through
10. It Doesn't Matter Much
11. Listen to the Mockingbird
12. Trusting Old Soul

VII. Live At The Bottom Line (Koch Records 2001, CD)
1. Real, Live Love
2. Goin' Down To Laurel
3. Good Planets (Are Hard To Find)
4. Strange
5. The American In Me
6. Now You Come Back
7. Evergreen Boy
8. Rose Marie

9. It Sure Was Better Back Then
10. So Good To Feel Good Again
11. Oh, To Be Back With You
12. Something's Got A Hold on Me
13. She's Living In A Dream World
14. Complications
15. The Sweet Love That You Give (Sure Goes A Long, Long Way)
16. Romeo's Tune
17. Nadine/You Cannot Win (If You Do Not Play)

Another View: "Whatever period the songs come from, however, the approach is the same. Sometimes Forbert and the band rock a little harder, sometimes they ease up, but for the most part they play melodic, mid-tempo folk-rock that supports Forbert's earnest, wry lyrics, which he sings in a rusty, expressive tenor. The evenness of Forbert's music is both its chief virtue and its chief limitation: he is always pleasant and engaging, but rarely moving. In a live context, where he might be expected to kick up a fuss, he turns in tasteful recreations of his tunes. Thus, *Live at the Bottom Line* functions largely as a compilation of his music from the last five years." – William Ruhlmann, *All Music Guide*

VIII. Any Old Time (Koch Records 2002, CD)
1. Waiting On A Train
2. My Blue-Eyed Jane
3. Why Should I Be Lonely?
4. Any Old Time
5. Ben Dewberry's Final Run
6. Miss The Mississippi And You
7. Standin' On A Corner (Blue Yodel No. 9)
8. Gambling Barroom Blues
9. Desert Blues
10. Train Whistle Blues
11. My Rough And Rowdy Ways
12. My Carolina Sunshine Girl

Comments: Forbert pays tribute to the great Jimmie Rodgers with a conceptual collection of mostly-obscure Rodgers material.

IX. Just Like There's Nothing To It (Koch Records 2004, CD)
1. What It Is Is A Dream
2. Wild As The Wind
3. The Change Song
4. The World Is Full Of People
5. Autumn This Year
6. I Just Work Here
7. There's Everybody Else (And Then There's You)
8. Oh, Yesterday
9. I Married A Girl
10. The Pretend Song
11. I'm In Love
12. About A Dream

Comments: Lackluster album and, tragically, it's Forbert's first collection of new material in almost four years. The ol' boy seems to be running out of steam, and obviously the Jimmie Rodgers concept LP did nothing to re-energize him (as Springsteen's foray into Pete Seeger's songbook did for him for a while). Like Springsteen, Forbert's most robust creative days were almost 20 years ago, and now he's just treading water…

X. Strange Names and New Sensations (429 Records 2007, CD)
1. Middle Age
2. Strange Names (North New Jersey's Got Em')
3. Simply Spalding Gray
4. Man, I Miss That Girl
5. You're Meant For Me
6. I Will Sing Your Praise
7. Something Special
8. My Seaside Brown-Eyed Girl
9. The Baghdad Dream
10. Thirty More Years
11. Around The Bend
12. Romeo's Tune

Comments: Three years hasn't helped, and Forbert's best creative days are clearly behind him…and when you're re-recording earlier triumphs, as with this album's cover of "Romeo's Tune," you're probably ready to join Eric Burden on the dole queue. Sad, too, 'cause Steve has always been a nice guy and a happy family man whenever I saw him around town, which might be part of the problem…tension plus drama equals art and all that bollocks.

FOREFATHERS OF DOOM

Band Members:
Vince Liveri (vocals)
Jeff Allen (guitar)
Tony Frost (bass)
Chris Hester (drums)

Comments: For about three years this assembly of local veterans – Liveri from Arch Angel and **Boneyard**, Allen from **the Bunnies** and Tony Frost from more bands than I care to remember – was a mainstay of the Nashville hard rock scene. Before they called it quits, they had around 30 original songs, some of which can be heard on their MySpace page.

FOREVER UNGRATICAL CORINARIC TECHNIKILATION (F.U.C.T.)

Band Members:
Clay Brocker (vocals) (I-IV)
Brooks Phillips (guitar) (I-IV)
Scott (bass) (III)

Dirt Ditchfield (bass) (I-IV)
Patrick Caldwell (drums) (I-IV)
Heath Willis (drums)

F.U.C.T. Recordings:

I. Into The Aggro (1987)

II. Within (1988)

III. Forever Ungratical Corinaric Technikilation (Pak'er Records/Carlyle 1989, cassette)
Side One
1. Yet
2. Hasselator
3. Catastrophic Affliction
4. Left Door

Side Two
5. Swing
6. Technikilation
7. Mine
8. A.O.I.
9. My Define

IV. Dimensional Depth Perception (Carlyle Records 1990, CD)
1. Infectious World
2. Lost
3. Ripen
4. Technikilation
5. Suekoesng
6. My Define
7. Screen

F.U.C.T. - FORGET CASSETTES - THE FOXYMORONS

8. Infraction
9. Demeaning
10. Dimensional Depth Perception
11. Ungratical

Comments: Without a doubt, Nashville's best and favorite hardcore metal outfit, bar none. In their day, F.U.C.T. would pull 'em in from all over the south, and all ages. It helped that the band was mostly as young as its audience, and as rowdy – in my experience, lead singer Clay was up for anything at just about any time, a philosophy that unfortunately landed Mr. Brocker in prison for a few years on a bum drug charge.

Clay's fierce onstage presence and natural charisma, along with the blistering metallic onslaught of the band's songs, earned them a significant following that remembers F.U.C.T. fondly even today. Supercollider Films director Chad Rullman of Atlanta, who has made music videos for Mastodon, Nile and Neurosis among other bands, has credited F.U.C.T. as a major influence on his work. The band championed an "all ages" work ethic, and attempted to open Club Roar, an all-ages club, in the Berry Hill neighborhood of Nashville. Unfortunately, the city's draconian zoning laws were used to prevent the club from opening.

I worked security with Clay at the Cannery for shows that Gus Palas was booking. I remember him telling me that F.U.C.T. was unhappy with their deal with Carlyle Records, which also took a share of the band's live ticket sales – a kind of early "360" deal that major labels demand these days. As a result, the band would book itself out of town under different names and, as word got out among their fans, they'd usually sell out the venue and pocket the door. Sly, like a fox...

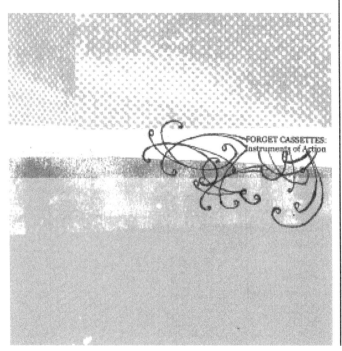

F.U.C.T. reunited for a handful of shows in 2007, sadly minus guitarist Brooks, who died a few years ago. Brocker has since turned to acting, appearing in director Ben Dixon's horror films *Shudder* and *Dark Harvest 3*.

Another View: "...a no-holds-barred leap into the abyss of otherworldly reality, thirty-plus minutes of industrial-strength rock and roll fury. Set beneath the multi-decibel mix of howling guitars, pounding drums and throbbing bass lines, you'll find vocalist Clay's twisted, painful 'King Hell' vocals kicking out some serious jams about life, morality, society and our endangered existence upon this spinning, twirling sphere that we call home."
– Rev. Keith A. Gordon, *The Metro* 1990

FORGET CASSETTES
Web: www.forgetcassettes.com

Band Members:
Beth Cameron (vocals, guitars) (I, II)
Jay Leo Phillips (bass, guitar, keyboards) (II)
Jason Milan Dietz (bass, keyboards)
Doni Schroader (drums) (I)
Aaron Ford (drums) (II)
Todd Kemp (castanets) (II)

Forget Cassettes Recordings:
I. Instruments of Action (Theory 8 Records 2003, CD)
1. German girls
2. Accismus
3. Ms. Rhythm and Blues
4. Instruments of Action
5. A Legacy's Demise
6. Like Tiny Swords
7. Bruce Wayne
8. Talking Big
9. Scales

II. Salt (Theory 8 Records 2006, CD)
1. Venison
2. Quiero, Quieres
3. The Catch
4. Nicholas
5. My Maraschino
6. Lonely Does It
7. Patience, Beth (Reprise)
8. Salt and Syncope
9. Tabula Rasa

THE FOXYMORONS
Web: www.foxymorons.com

Band Members:
David Dewese
Jerry James

THE FOXYMORONS - FREAKING APATHY - FREEDOM OF EXPRESSION

The Foxymorons Recordings:

I. Calcutta (American Pop Project 1999, CD)
1. Going Down!
2. Perfectly
3. The Duke of Gloucester
4. Almost Active
5. Reel-To-Reel
6. Bombay: A Silver Anthem
7. Hands-On Presentation
8. Broken Heart
9. Simply Enough
10. Always
11. My Shoulder Hurts
12. Something New
13. Please Be Miranda
14. Down That Road

II. Rodeo City (American Pop Project 2001, CD)
1. Left Sideways
2. August Moon
3. Baby Blue
4. Ready To Go
5. Something Out There
6. Jakarta
7. Irene
8. Nightime
9. When I Lie
10. Summer Bummer
11. Nashville
12. Untitled Bonus Track

III. Hesitation Eyes (Heatstroke Records 2005, CD)
1. Harvard Hands
2. Just Because
3. Still In Love
4. Lazy Librarian's Son
5. Between The Lines
6. Bending Back
7. This Heart Of Mine
8. Terror On The Tarmac
9. Pistol By Your Side
10. Everything Changes
11. Are You Tired
12. Hesitation Eyes

FREAKING APATHY

Band Members:
Mark Scott (vocals)
Patrick Russo (guitar)
John Baird (bass)
Scott Hertzburg (drums)

Comments: In *The Metro*, Gail Gajewski sez, "they play a cross of musical styles that include thrash, hard rock, funk, alternative and one Spinal Tap cover. You know, Faith No More, Red Hot Chili Peppers, Living Color stuff."

FREEDOM OF EXPRESSION

Band Members:
Rob Hoskins (vocals, keyboards, percussion) (I)
Don Mooney (guitars, percussion, vocals) (I)
Andy Commiskey (bass, percussion, vocals) (I)
Mark "Smiley" Shenkel (saxophone, vocals) (I)
Chip Staley (drums, vibes, percussion, vocals) (I)

Other Musicians:
Robert Means (trombone) (I)

Freedom of Expression Recordings:

I. For Lack Of A Better Word (Track 1985, 12" EP)
Side One
1. Keep It Burning
2. I Heard It Through The Grapevine
3. Stranded In Babylon

Side Two
4. Forward We Stumble
5. On The Dole
6. A Change In The Weather

The Foxymorons

Comments: One of Nashville's first reggae/ska bands, Freedom Of Expression was a popular local draw due to the band's energetic live shows, and their clever use of island rhythms in creating original songs. Hoskins, Shenkel and Robert Means would go on to form **A.K.A. Rudie**.

FREELOADER

Band Members:
Cage (vocals, guitar) (I)
Jamie (guitars) (I)
Jeremy (bass, vocals) (I)
Eric (drums) (I)

Freeloader Recordings:

I. Freeloader (self-produced cassette, 1995)
Side A
1. Steve
2. Boy Whore
3. Keyholes & Curtains

Side B
4. Fishstick
5. Beer Goggles
6. Nothin'

DONNA FROST
Web: www.donnafrost.com

Band Members:
Donna Frost (vocals, guitar) (I-III)

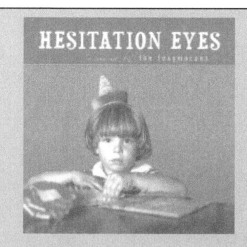

THE FOXYMORONS
Hesitation Eyes
(Heatstroke Records)

Interesting factoid: there has never been a rock band that has been signed to a deal by a Nashville label. Yup, Jason & the Scorchers, the Kings Of Leon, the Features, Webb Wilder, etc, etc, ad nauseum – not a single one of them were signed out of the "Music City." It's a bone of contention among local artists that they have to go to L.A. or NYC (or even London) to get noticed. In the case of the Foxymorons – the duo of David Dewese and Jerry James, actually – they had the double-whammy of being based in both Nashville and Mesquite, Texas.

Which, of course, led them to signing with a Philly-based label. Go figure. All the cosmic injustice suffered by Nashville rockers aside, however, *Hesitation Eyes* would be a landmark album no matter where the duo recorded it. Filled to the brim by the Foxymorons with infectious pop/rock tunes and country fringe...think Matthew Sweet, the Jayhawks, or even Velvet Crush… the Foxymorons' *Hesitation Eyes* mixes up layers of textured instrumentation, intelligent wordplay and gorgeous vocals with the odd Bob Mould-styled wash of sound to create a refreshingly new take on an old form. If they survive the stigma of being a non-country band from Nashville, the Foxymorons might make a name for themselves. – *Jersey Beat*, 2005

Other Musicians:
Jeff Allen (guitars) (III)
Tommy Allsup (guitars) (I)
J.D. Blair (drums) (I)
Gary Brotherman (bass) (III)
Ellis Clark (piano, recorder, autoharp, banjo) (III)
Chris Golden (piano, mandolin) (I)
Mark Harrison (vocals) (III)
John Heinrich (steel guitar, harmonica) (III)

Glen Rieuf (dobro, steel guitar) (I)
Fred Satterfield (drums, percussion) (III)
David Signs (keyboards, guitars, bass) (III)
Buddy Spicher (fiddle, mandolin) (I)
David Spicher (bass) (I)
Beth Travers (mandolin, vocals) (III)
Pete Wade (guitar, dobro) (I)

Donna Frost Recordings:

I. Pure And Simple (Simms Records 1998, CD)
1. My Baby Loves To Treat Me Right
2. Why Does It Feel Like Goodbye?
3. Worse Things Than Being Alone
4. Wonderful Feeling
5. Pure & Simple
6. If Only
7. Gotta Get Away
8. On My Street
9. Talk Of The Town
10. I Won't Mind That You're Not Here

Comments: As a member of **the Bunnies, the Paper Dolls** and **Mystique**, my old Franklin High School pal Donna was one of the true movers and shakers of the 1980s-era Nashville rock scene. Donna stays busy as a touring singer/songwriter these days, as well as fronting a reunited version of the Bunnies (see interview ➜).

II. Feels Like Home (Gevania Records 2001, CD)
1. Where the Sky Meets the Sea
2. Getting' Younger
3. Feels Like Home
4. Sweetest Dream
5. When I Look in Your Eyes
6. What If
7. Piece of Heaven
8. Pay Day
9. Every Night
10. Looking Glass

III. Girls Like Us (Spat! Records 2009, CD)
1. When Love Goes Bad
2. Anywhere Tonight
3. Dancing With Bruce
4. Elvis In A Tollbooth
5. Girls Like Us
6. Jacksonville
7. My Guitar Has A Long Memory
8. Hello From The Road
9. Paul McCartney
10. Payin' To Play
11. Runaway Train
12. Things Are Tough All Over
13. No Place Like Home

Freedom Of Expression

FUN GIRLS FROM MT. PILOT - FUR TRADE

FUN GIRLS FROM MT. PILOT

Band Members:
Cat (vocals) (I-III)
Donnie Kendall (guitar, vocals) (I-III)
Troy Pigue (bass) (I-III)
Chris (drums) (I-III)

Fun Girls Recordings:

I. Hi Doll! (House O' Pain 1993, 7" vinyl)
This here side
1. Rocket Cycle
2. Your Girlfriend Hates Me
3. Billy Dee Williams

That there side
4. Bad Day
5. Let's Play Pretend
6. Cookie

Comments: Formed by Cat and Donnie from the beloved punk rock outfit **Rednecks In Pain**, Fun Girls From Mt. Pilot took things one step further with the band members dressed in a grotesque parody of "drag." The sound was still whipsmart, raw punk with tongue placed firmly in cheek. Kendall and Troy Pigue were the brains behind the ultra-cool *House O' Pain* music zine and record label.

II. Lunch Box (House O' Pain 1994, 7" vinyl)
Side 1
1. Hold A Grudge
2. Girlfight Tonight

Side 2
3. Crybaby
4. Things I Hate
5. Back in the Day

Comments: Donnie and his House O' Pain cohorts were always pretty creative, and the Fun Girls' *Lunch Box* release was proof. The band's five-song 7" disc was packaged in an actual box with glued-on artwork (like an early 1970s bootleg album). Inside was a napkin, plastic fork, and the typical HO'P photocopied booklet. Each box also held a second 7" record, "select tunes from the bottom of the Fun Girls' closets" (mine was Debby Boone), and some boxes also had a piece of wrestling play money (mine was Ric Flair) that you could exchange with a band member for a Fun Girls' trading card.

III. Dairy Of A Madwoman (House O' Pain 1995, 7" vinyl)
Side A
1. Just My Luck
2. Pictures And Sounds

Side B
3. Good Goodbye
4. Monkey Flips
5. Sick Of Me

Comments: The mock Ozzy picture sleeve and parody of Osbourne's album title is just too damn precious.

FUR TRADE

Band Members:
Gwil Owen (vocals, guitar)
Stevie Wilde (guitars, vocals)
Mark Levine (bass)
Jay Mebane (bass)
Eric Shaw (keyboards)
Jeff Finlin (drums, vocals)

Comments: A popular, if short-lived group, **Gwil Owen** and **Jeff Finlin** would form **the Thieves**; later both musicians would forge moderately successful solo careers. Eric Shaw was an old pal of mine, the former assistant manager of the Shakey's Pizza in Green Hills where I spent most of the1980s (the restaurant was known as my office in some circles).

Another View: "Their specialty is forthright, driving rock 'n' roll a bit reminiscent of Dire Straits...the band insists they're not trying to imitate anyone, listing their major influences as Chuck Berry and '50s rock." – Lise Williams, *The Metro* 1986

*S*inger and songwriter Donna Frost was there for the "big bang" moment of original rock music in Nashville. As a member of such scene-making bands as the Bunnies (recently re-formed in the wake of this book project), the Paper Dolls, Mystique, and a thriving solo career that dates back nearly 20 years, Frost has definitely left her imprint on the Nashville rock scene. Donna is also one of my oldest friends, meeting in homeroom together at Franklin High School back in 1971. I think she'd agree that it's been a long, strange trip since we were both 15 years old!

What got you interested in music in the first place?
I can blame my family for that one cause my parents were singing when I was a baby, and I was traveling with them two weeks after I was born. My mom and dad traveled around, singing gospel and stuff, and my grandparents were singers, aunts and uncles and everything. It just came natural, so there was always music at our house

When I saw the Beatles on Ed Sullivan that was it, you know, it was like, "okay that's what I want to do." I started taking music lessons when I was nine on piano, then I went over to guitar when I was eleven and that was just it…I always knew that was what I wanted to do and I knew I could play and that I could sing, and that was just in me from the get go.

What was the first band you were in?
The very first band I was in was with the awesome Thom King, in Hard Stuff. It was the first actual rock band I played in, and I was with them for a few months. I think we played some frat parties and stuff and some things around Franklin, I played rhythm guitar and sang. I was all of 18. In fact, I still have the reel to reel demo tape that we did and I was singing "Somebody To Love" by the Jefferson Airplane, it was pretty funny. That was the first band I was in.

Who else was in that band, was there anybody else that did anything?
Well, Thom King was in it, of course, he did his magazines and all. Tom Rutherford was the drummer and Ken Frazier was the guitarist and there was Peter Cruz, who was the bassist. He was fresh off the boat from Germany and lived in Nashville, so that was the band at the time. We played like MTSU and UT and all that…we didn't make a lot of money, it was mostly for free beer and a few bucks. So that was my initiation into the rock world.

So where did you go from there?
We ended up forming the Bunnies…my dad was singing country at that time and I would go play with him in his bands. I traveled with him when I was in high school to go play shows. A few years after that, we became friends with the guys in Radio One and the Resistors, so my dad had put together a back-up band that was myself, my brother Tony, Johnny Lauffer played keyboards, Frank Harlow was our guitar player and Todd Andrews was on bass.

So Frank had his band the Times and then Richie Allen had the Resistors, so Tony and I, we thought "well, everybody else is doing it, we should just start a band too, so that was where the Bunnies came from. Of course, Tony and I were in there for the whole time and we had different Bunnies along the way. We had two different versions of that, Todd and Johnny didn't last past a few gigs and then Chuck Allen, we had him for a long time and Todd McAlpin and then the last version was Jeff Van Allen, a friend of Tony's from Franklin High, and Rich Frederico, so that was my first serious rock project. It was such an incredible time and so many talented people coming out of that group.

Any big events for the Bunnies? Do you remember any high points?
I think the coolest thing that happened was the night that Rick Nielson came to see us play, from Cheap Trick. They were in town, they had played a concert at Municipal and we had met them and got to be buddies. I remember one night we opened for the White Animals at Cantrell's and my brothers, they ran into Rick Nielson and he says "hey, what's going on tonight?" and they told him "we're playing down here, do you want to come?" and he said, "yeah, put me on the guest list." I'll never forget David Cannon – the White Animals manager – thought we were full of it when we told him Rick Nielson was on our guest list, and people carried on when Mr. Nielson walked in and came to watch us play. That was such a thrill to have him out there to watch us.

I think the main thing for the Bunnies, we played with a lot of bands out of Atlanta that we opened for at Spanky,'s and I think it was just the general fun of it all, just being part of something that was groundbreaking in Nashville. This was a country music town and what we were doing; some of the country music people weren't too happy about our little scene going on, but it was just exciting to be part of.

INTERVIEW: DONNA FROST

Where did you go from there?
The final version of the Bunnies we broke up in 1983 going into 1984. Tony and I were just about done with it, we said "well, this was fun," but we were both ready to move on. Paula Montondo had contacted me about joining the Paper Dolls. She said "I'm putting together an all female band." I think she lived in Ohio and moved here, and she'd had a version of the Paper Dolls, she had the name, and I think they tried to do something with it up there but it didn't really take off, so she came here. I signed on, I wanted to be part of an all-female band, you know, and so Tony went to play with the Movement with Ritchie and I left for the Paper Dolls, so that was the beginning of that little adventure.

Who was in the Paper Dolls?
Paula Montondo was the drummer and she ended up later on in the band called Sha Sha Boom, and she's also a recording engineer. Connie Butler was the guitarist and she played in Joe Loftis and the Pinks before she joined us, and then there were two bass players. The first one, Turina Mauler, I hear from her on MySpace now, she lives around here.

Joanne Pompay was the second bass player and she was with us the longest. She and her husband, they were from Florida and they had played, done the road dog thing and came here and she joined up with us; that was the Paper Dolls. I know they had a version after I left but that didn't last very long, but we had some exciting times.

What are some of your memories of the Paper Dolls?
Our very first gig was opening for 10,000 Maniacs at Cantrell's and I'll never forget Natalie Merchant sitting in the corner chanting and burning incense and stuff. We were opening for them and our guitar player Connie was in the hospital with spinal meningitis and we didn't want to cancel the gig because we were the only all-female band in town at the time.

A lot of people came out to see if we could really play our instruments, to see what the deal was. So we played that night and my brothers, they ran into Warner Hodges and said "are you coming to see Donna, are you coming to see the Dolls?" and they told him that our guitar player was in the hospital. Warner says, "do you think they'd let me play with them?" So Warner came up and played, and we played a couple of old Beatle covers with him and we just tore it up that night.

The Paper Dolls never played to an empty house, ever. Everywhere we played, people came out to see us I because we were the only all-female band playing original music in town. We had a deal with Treasure Isle and we recorded some tracks for that. There were some differences of opinion on how things should go within the band, and so I left for various reasons. I would have liked to have seen it through

and gotten a recording contract because we could have, we were a good band...

From there did you go into Mystique?
No, there's a detour. There was an interesting, quirky little band of ours called Psychic Surgery. After the Dolls broke up, I got married, and we played in a little one-off band called Alien which didn't play enough gigs to really matter, it was just a gig or two. I think it was me and my ex-husband and then Johnny Deckert of Jet Screamer and another, Bill used to play drums.

My uncle John called me and said "hey, there's this band needing a female singer/guitar player, are you interested?" I wanted to get back into a band again, I missed playing. I'd been out of it for a couple years, so I said "yeah!" I'd played in some top forty cover bands and stuff like that, but I wasn't very happy with that, so to get into an original project again was exciting to me, so I went and joined up with these boys and stayed with them for a few months and we played all over, everywhere. We released an album; Bob Oermann reviewed it and did a whole write-up on it when it came out. It was called *A Fine Line*; I have it on a cassette.

It was interesting stuff because David Cane was the guitarist and he passed away a few years ago with lung cancer...he was really good. Scott Mason was the bass player and Terry Ballard was the drummer and, in fact, Terry ended up going with me to Mystique when I left. It was cool to get back out in a band again and go travel around and do the college circuit. It was good and then we went to Mystique.

When was that?
1988

Yeah that sounds about right from the name of the band...
It doesn't hold up very well, but I laugh when I hear it. Did I really sing like that, did we really do that? Tony was playing with Triple X and I think they were winding down with that and I wanted to play with Tony again. That was the main thing I liked about that period, when Tony and I were playing together again because I just liked playing with my brother. I know he wasn't really into being in that band all the time because he was playing with Asphalt Jungle and Sixty-Nine Tribe and he'd come play with me. We had some fun times with it and, of course, we had more drummers than Spinal Tap. Nobody died, none of the drummers died, but they left and every year we had to do a new promo photo...

When Tony left the last version of Mystique, I was playing bass because I couldn't find a bass player that could do what Tony did so we decided to do a power trio thing. We had a really cool drummer named Andy Payne from Berkley, and he was our drummer. So I called the ex and I said "if it doesn't work out this time, I'm out of here, the marriage and the band." Which is exactly what I did…there were some fun times, but a lot of it just was not much fun for me at all. It was very stressful, and when you try to play music with someone you're married to, and things aren't going well, either way it's just, it's not good.

As for playing heavy metal, I don't know why, I just thought it would be fun to get into that scene and dabble with that and play around with it, but that wasn't really me. I look at those pictures now of all the bands, we all have that big hair and it's like "Oh Lord!"

The only thing you can take consolation from is in every city across the United States there was a Mystique…
Oh absolutely…that was the time wasn't it? We traveled with that band, we went from the East Coast like Myrtle Beach and we went as far as Phoenix, with the trailer all full of equipment and lights and we did the whole bit. Every time it seemed like we were getting ready to get a project out, though, we had to change band members and here we go again. I just said enough of that and decided to go on my own.

And that's when you officially launched your solo career?
When Mystique broke up it was 1993, the band lasted about five years and then in 1993 I started playing, getting out and playing writer's nights and playing some acoustic gigs. Then I was working in some country and Top 40 stuff around town to make money, with other bands and artists, and then I guess I seriously launched my solo career when I released my first CD in 1998.

I was learning the ropes about songwriters, writers' nights; the acoustic thing. I was really trying to reinvent myself and trying to find myself musically where I could do something. I had said all the stuff I had wanted to say, I didn't want to quit music…that was never, ever been even a thought. I've always loved it, I have a huge passion for it, and so I just learned the ropes and by 1998 is when I really got serious about my solo career.

What are some of the highlights of your solo career so far?
I played the Kerrville Folk Festival a couple years ago; it's a huge three-week event. There is something like 30,000 people that come to this thing every year. Peter, Paul and Mary were the headline act for the festival, which I thought was kind of neat because I liked them when I was a little kid. A lot of the places that I get to go now and play, I've gone over to England to perform, and down in the Caribbean…I've gotten to do a lot of stuff! Working on the Grand Ole Opry with Skeeter Davis was definitely a highlight because she was my idol when I was a little girl. She was the first real country/pop crossover artist with "The End of the World" and I had known her all my life, so getting to work with her was great.

I got to work with B.J. Thomas in the studio and record with him; that was fun because that was somebody else whose music I marveled at when I was a kid. Of course, getting to play with Walter [Egan] now, that's fun because I liked his music, too, back when "Magnet and Steel" came out, so that's really cool that I get to work with him sometimes. I've had some hit records overseas, number ones in the U.K. and over in Australia on the independent charts, which is cool, just different countries that my music is played in, that's always a nice thing, it really opens a lot of doors for you. Playing Janis Joplin, that was fun.

How did that come about?
I'm on this mission to try to do neat things later in life, so I got into acting in 2002 after *Feels Like Home* came out. I was out touring and all that, and then I kind of settled into this acting thing. I put together a group of songwriters to present the *Vagina Monologues* and then I got in with a couple of theatre groups and we were in this production called *Women of the Dark*, which was about the victims of Jack the Ripper, a very dark show…

Ron Cushman, who played Jack in the production, asked me "what would you really like to do in acting?" and I said that I would love to play Janis Joplin if it ever comes across, because I am a huge Janis fan. To me, there was no female vocalist ever like Joplin, and I remember when I was in junior high I'd never heard anybody sing like that and she really had a big effect on me. We did that [Janis Joplin show] for three summers…it's really a thrill to play her.

I know I don't look much like her, but when I put the feathers on and the glasses and all that, and I know her life so well that I can talk about her and be her in this fictional interview that we do in the show, it's like the fictional interview of Janis' last days and then we do the concert section where she sings. The coolest thing about the show is the cross section of people that come out because you have the old Joplin fans from the day come out to listen and remember those times, and then you have these young kids that will come to the show, who never got to see Janis live, but they're Janis fans.

Do you think that the atmosphere for indie artists has loosened up any over the past few years, and has the Internet helped or hurt?

It has helped. I definitely think so because the labels, they're not signing people, and especially when you get to a certain age like I am…let's face it, I'm not a kid…older people like me, and for a lot of people who are having trouble being heard, it has opened a lot of doors for them. The Internet has done great wonders…we didn't have all these tools available when we were starting out in the '80s, we just had to go out and hang flyers up on phone poles and send things out and hoped somebody would hear it…

I remember the NEA [Nashville Entertainment Association], they had those showcases to try and get you signed and, of course, now you don't have to worry about that because you can release your stuff yourself and sell it on the Internet and it's opened so many doors. It's definitely helped independent artists. I read an article where groups like the Eagles and Buffett and all, a lot of those old artists are going independent too because they don't have to answer to a label.

I always preach that independent is the way to go for anyone. People get too caught up in record deals, and when you lose your record deal, you're back out here with the rest of us. So you have to figure out a way to sell your music and get your name out there, and I think the Internet has been the best thing that ever happened, absolutely.

Who would you say your songwriting influences are?

There are so many to draw from, aren't there? John, Paul, George, and Ringo come out a lot in stuff that I do. I definitely would say the Beatles, of course, I guess it's the standard answer. But really, they were just the first that really inspired me. I love Lucinda Williams; she's one of my favorites; of course, Joni Mitchell, because like that era that we grew up in was when you had all those singer/songwriters like James Taylor and Paul Simon. All their stuff holds up today, and then you had to craft a song you know, and tell a story and I think those are the kind of people I have drawn from.

Bruce [Springsteen], of course I love Bruce, and something he said if you write about where you are in life and what you know, and you write about where you're at and tell a story, so that's what I'm hoping I'm doing. I've got some stories to tell and some years on my side, so I want to keep telling them.

What advice would you give young songwriters and performers?

Never give up. I know it's a cliché, but I have found that persistence pays off. The reality is that nine tenths of the people out here doing this aren't going to get signed to a major label. It doesn't matter how old you are, it's just a fact that there's some very small number that get the "Holy Grail," as we call a deal.

You just have to have a thick skin, you've got to get out there and work hard. You have to treat it as a business; it's not party all the time…drinking ten beers and jumping on the stage doesn't get it anymore. You just have to be sensible and treat it like a business and have love for what you do; you have to find a way to market yourself.

You have to find out where you fit in with the scheme of things, and in the independent market as it is, it's pretty easy to do, you just have to find your place and roll with it. Don't give up and don't let things get you down. I know people that said "if I don't get a major label deal in a year or two, I'm pitching my guitar" and I know people that did get the deal, and now they're back out playing clubs or else they sold their stuff and gave it up, just gave up their dream, and you can't do that.

If you believe in what you've got to say and if someone wants to hear it, then you should share it…you've been given a gift and you have to use it.

Within the period of a few short years, Nashville's F.U.C.T have gone from being the dream band of a pair of teen-aged high school students to being a force to be reckoned with within the Music City's thriving and creative underground music scene. Along with bands such as Clockhammer, Wishcraft, and Jet Black Factory, F.U.C.T. are helping to place Nashville on the cutting edge of the fringe of musical expression, forever erasing the city's image as the home of Country music.

"The band started in July of 1986," says F.U.C.T. bassist Dirt, "when Brooks and I got together to play some songs and form a band. We both played guitar at the time, so we hired a drummer. Then we added Clay, and we did our first show in September of '86." "Eventually," says Brooks, the band's guitarist, "our old drummer quit and we re-organized, with Patrick on drums, as a three-piece because Clay was in Arizona and California and Colorado. Dirt played bass and sang. Then Clay came back and we began evolving, as the years went by, into what we are now." Adds Dirt, "we evolved into a more streamlined band, our music became a little bit more intricate, a little more organized...it wasn't as silly as hardcore was."

As the band stands today, consisting of vocalist Clay, bassist Dirt, guitarist Brooks, and drummer Patrick, F.U.C.T. stand among the heaviest of the heavy, delivering a meaty, muscular sound that is all thrash and fury, closely akin to the sound that a Concord jet might make if shot down with a hand-held Stinger anti-aircraft missile. They bombard you with a literal wall of sound, fueled by heavy rhythms, Brooks' sonic six-string work, and Clay's snarling, growling, Mephistophelian vocals. They are powerful, emotional, energetic, and sincere...which typically translates into a loyal following.

Their lyrics are another story, however. Possible poster children for Tipper's unappreciative P.M.R.C. cronies, and a parent's worst anti-rock and roll nightmare, F.U.C.T. forsake the typical heavy metal/thrash lyrical content of party, Party, PARTY by focusing their material on positive, productive ideas and philosophies. With their lyrics, says Dirt, "we're going into the evolution of thought and the creation of thought and the creation of thought as it pertains to you and your society. We write about images in our mind, pictures. We'd like to use the lyrics separately from the music so that the lyrics will give you a picture of its own as the music supports that and branches off into more areas."

"We like to have meaning in our lyrics as well as in our music," adds Clay, "so that you can read them over and over and see something different, so that you can relate to our lyrics in a lot of different ways...you can live by our lyrics. We don't say anything wrong or bad. We say everything positive."

INTERVIEW: F.U.C.T.

F.U.C.T. developed their unique style and lyrical slant throughout the complete evolution of the band. Citing influences cutting across the complete spectrum of heavy metal, hardcore and thrash, bands such as the Bad Brains, Black Sabbath, Black Flag, Voivod, and Metallica, among others, have had a profound impact on the band that F.U.C.T. has become. Of these influences, says Clay, they were "different bands from different areas with different ideas that happened at different times which said something that was worthwhile, something that made a mark."

"Some of the bands that we listen to," says Dirt, "and some of the ideas that we are faced with now, growing up and realizing…" "You learn what works over the years," adds Brooks. "We took a lot of time to let it all sink in, a couple of years for it all to make sense." This period of self-reflection and meditation, including much reading and soul-searching, led to the maturation of the band and its art as it stands today. It also lends itself to future growth of the band. "If you stay stagnant," says Brooks, "there's no future." Says Clay, "we want to explore all of the realms of music, thought and action."

Listening to the material included on their new recording, **Dimensional Depth Perception**, one will find the band exploring, well, a theological train of thought, with their message rather spiritual in nature. While songs such as the album's title cut, "Lost," "Screen," and "Ungratical" offer an enlightened world view and more than a share of social commentary, F.U.C.T.'s material is drawn from the wellspring of concern. Says Clay, "it has a lot to do with the prophecies of God as they're written. We have these handbooks that deal directly with The Bible and we read them, check them out, and then it's all clear." Adds Dirt, "the way that they put it, it was as plain as day then…it still is, you just have to recognize it."

"I want to live in a very nice world," Dirt continues, "where everything is clean, not corrupt and dirty and sick…a world where everyone treats everyone else with respect and nobody gets walked on. That's the way that it should be." "We want to enjoy what God gave us," says Clay.

F.U.C.T.'s spiritual viewpoint isn't just mere music biz image-making, nor is it the trappings of a theological wolf in sheep's clothing…there is a heartfelt and sincere belief in a higher being, a power greater than all of the religions that have sprung up in self-centered and intolerant worship of it.

"We don't have anything to do with any organized religion or view" says Clay, "we know what's right and what's wrong and we're trying to spread the message that there's something better." "It's like salt and pepper," muses Dirt, "there's God and there's Satan and you have a choice. You do what you want."

"We all do wrong," says Brooks, "we're not saying that we don't ever do wrong. It's just that we recognize that we do wrong and try not to, and that everyone can succumb to that ignorance." With their positive message of a better society and a better world, F.U.C.T. exposes the lie that is the fabrication of so many on the religious right that consider rock and roll, especially the more emotional fringe genres such as thrash, rap, and the many variations of metal to be intellectually void and morally repugnant. These differing styles of rock music share the youthfulness of their audience and their artists in common. Bands such as F.U.C.T. reach their audience because *they are* their audience.

"We're down to Earth" says Brooks, "and we see what's going on. We're from the younger generation. We're seeing more damage and more corruption than our parents ever did, and we don't want it. Just as there's a new generation in us, there's also a new generation of ignorance."

Carrying their message directly to the streets with their razor-edged music, F.U.C.T. feel that they can make a difference, influencing a generation that, while perhaps cynical at a young age in this high-tech era of MTV, unfettered pop culture, and skewed social priorities, have more in common with their idealistic brethren of the sixties than with the angst-ridden punks of the blank generation. Of this world that they inhabit, Dirt says, "we'll do as much as we can, but we'll never change it completely…that's up to God himself." "No government, no man-made government," says Clay, "can ever change it. They'll only run it into the ground."

During their four years together as a band, F.U.C.T. has managed to build not only an impressive local following, but has begun to attract listeners throughout the central South and the Eastern states. The band has played in fifteen or sixteen states, "from the tip of Florida to New York City and everywhere in between," says Brooks.

Loyal followings in cities as diverse as Indianapolis, Indiana and Huntsville, Alabama have been built by the band's dynamic stage presence and on the strength of several demo tapes sold at the shows. A contract with Nashville's Carlyle Records has produced a nine-song cassette, known as the "green tape" and the aforementioned recent **Dimensional Depth Perception**, released on cassette and compact disc.

While they gradually expand the circle of cities in which they perform, building an audience and breaking through into the college markets via college radio, response to F.U.C.T. and their music has been encouraging. "The response has been really good," says Dirt, "people seem to like us. We appeal to them mentally, and through our music, through the edge of our music, what we say in our songs." "We're very energetic live," says Brooks, "we give them real feeling. They recognize the effort and want to participate."

One of the most frequent questions to arise about the band is the origin of their name. An acronym, F.U.C.T. stands for **Forever Ungratical Corinaric Technikilation**. Says Dirt, "the letters were invented by someone that we don't know. We just took the letters and arranged them ridiculously to make a thought-provoking word that got a little too out of hand, so we decided to slap on four big words that meant completely other things to give ourselves a new meaning and an in-depth image of what we wanted to do, what we wanted to say." Says Brooks, "it means forever ungrateful for ignorance that affects you in a negative way."

Has the band's name ever created problems in the way that they are perceived? "We had one problem, really," says Dirt, "back in the time when the Reverend Willis was running around. They used to call us the band that they couldn't mention. They couldn't spell our name because they never looked that far into it to see who we really are." Adds Brooks, "you have to look past the cover. If you look past that, you'll see something totally positive."

With their status as standing among the leaders of Nashville's underground music scene, does F.U.C.T. have any other plans for outside projects to support their message, similar to such English anarchist bands as Crass or Chumbawamba with their media projects and social programs? "We're involved in getting a club together right now," says Clay. "It'll be the first club that'll be all ages and paid for by the scene, financed by the scene, and run by the scene." Says Dirt, "we've got a show on the twenty-first of July, with four or five bands. It'll be a big benefit to officially open it up." Says Clay, "it's going to be called Club Roar."

The band is committed to their work, their message, and their audience. Young by even the standards of rock and roll, with band members ranging from nineteen to twenty-two years of age, F.U.C.T. have a potentially lengthy and prosperous career ahead of them. Their message will remain positive even while their music may change and grow. "Be aware," says Dirt, "communicate. Your actions do affect someone else whether you know it or not. You should be conscious of this affect that you can be respectful and considerate of other life on the planet. The planet doesn't belong to you, you belong to it."

Concludes Clay, "enjoy life to the fullest. You've got to respect other life around you. You want to live in it and survive, or you can destroy everything around you and slowly destroy yourself." The choice, good or evil, right or wrong, life or death, says F.U.C.T. with their music, is entirely up to you... – *The Metro*, July 1990

GREG GARING - TONY GERBER

GREG GARING

Band Members:
Greg Garing (vocals, guitars, banjo, mandolin) (I)
Andy Kravitz (drums) (I)
Mike Watt (bass) (I)
David Kahne (keyboards) (I)
Peter Rowan (mandolin, vocals) (I)

Greg Garing Recordings:

I. Alone (Paladin Records/Warner Music 1997, CD)
1. My Love Is Real
2. Safe Within Your Arms
3. Say What You Mean
4. Alone
5. Dream Too Real To Hold
6. Walk Away From Me
7. How The Road Unwinds
8. Where The Bluegrass Grows
9. Don't Cry Baby
10. All My Stars Are In Your Eyes
11. Fallen Angel

TONY GERBER

Band Members:
Tony Gerber (keyboards, guitars, synths, harp) (I-V)

Other Musicians:
Stevie "Wilde" Garner (guitar) (II)
Todd Gerber (synthesizers) (III, IV, V)
Kent Heckaman (keyboards, synths, percussion) (I, IV, V)

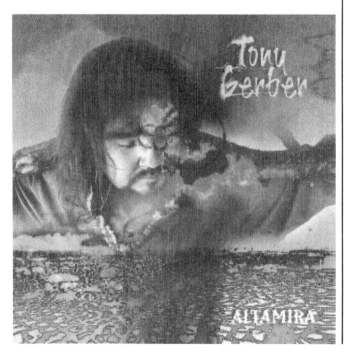

Kevin Heckaman (bass) (I, V)
Sam Jacobs (guitar) (V)
Jason Litchford (flute) (II)
Michael Manring (bass) (IV)
Rob McClain (guitar, synthesizers) (I, III, V)
Neal Merrick (percussion) (III)
Rob Mitchell (drums) (IV)
Matt Oakes (trumpet, drums) (I, IV, V)
Dariush Rad (eBow) (V)
Giles Reaves (keyboards) (I, III)
John Rose (keyboards) (I)
Kirby Shelstad (percussion) (V)

Tony Gerber Recordings:

I. Blue Western Sky (Lektronic Soundscapes 1994, CD)
1. Fair Thee Well
2. As Time Passes
3. Morning Prelude
4. The Badlands
5. Blue Western Sky
6. Morning Reprise
7. The Lunar Crossing
8. Kitt Peak
9. Frozen Waters
10. Surrounding Ground
11. After The Harvest

Comments: I first met Tony Gerber back in 1986 or '87 when we both worked at Chop Sticks Chinese Restaurant in Green Hills; I was the assistant manager and Tony was a delivery driver. We stayed friendly through the years, and I've hyped his various projects in whatever venue would allow me. Gerber is best-known as a "space music" performer, both through his solo work and via **Spacecraft**, his band of musical fellow travelers. More than that, Tony is a visionary, a classical composer who has pioneered the use of technology in making music. Often seen in the company of the like-minded talent **Giles Reaves**.

Another View: "A distinct new age attitude exists in this music, dedicated to experiencing one's environmental surroundings more than retreating into introspection. Gerber's compositional sense touches the soul softly, urging a unity with the world around us through mellow passages of peaceful tuneage."

II. Clearly Opaque (Space For Music 1999, CD-R)
1. Soliloquy
2. Dancing Wuli
3. Around Three
4. Computations
5. To The Sky
6. Don't Exit Yet
7. Slim Elephants, Small Godzillas

TONY GERBER - GERBER & ROSE - GERBER, LINTON & STEVENS

Comments: Recorded in 1987 at Al Jolson Enterprises, which had the first full MIDI studio in Nashville, set up by Gerber. A collection of experimental music composed on an early MacIntosh computer, Gerber subsequently performed these songs live at the first Space for Music festival at MTSU in '87.

III. Native Spirit (Space For Music 1999, CD-R)
1. Native Spirit
2. Wax Dancing
3. Baba's Den
4. Above The October Moon
5. Unbound Passion
6. The King's Wishing Well
7. Cathedrals
8. Caverns
9. Hans Dreaming

Comments: A collection of guitar-based instrumentals penned by Gerber over a period of ten years, some captured in the studio, others recorded live. Some nice stuff here, showcasing the wide range of Gerber's talents.

IV. Guitarscapes (Space For Music 1999, CD-R)
1. Southway
2. Survivor
3. Courtyard
4. Miles To Go
5. Mind Orbit 12
6. Merry-Go-Round
7. Descent
8. Soul's United
9. Circles
10. Longing

V. Altamira (Space For Music 1999, CD-R)
1. Prehistoric Heart
2. The Hunt
3. Altamira
4. Mountainside
5. Trek
6. Jurassic Rain
7. Above The October Moon
8. Dusk
9. Circles

GERBER & ROSE

Band Members:
Tony Gerber (keyboards, synthesizers) (I)
John Rose (keyboards, synthesizers) (I)

Gerber & Rose Recordings:

I. Airwaves (Space For Music 2000, CD-R)
1. The Lift

2. Time Totems
3. Space Bound
4. Blue Receding
5. String Theory
6. Emanating Signal
7. The Last Station

Comments: Tony Gerber and John Rose, the founding members of the ambient/space music band **Spacecraft**, actually began collaborating together musically in 1992. *Airwaves* is a 1994 recording that captures a live radio broadcast from WKMS-FM at Murray State University in Murray, Kentucky.

GERBER, LINTON & STEVENS

Band Members:
Tony Gerber (synthesizers) (I)
William Linton (synthesizers) (I)
Mason Stevens (guitar) (I)

Gerber, Linton & Stevens Recordings:

I. Cosmic Flight (Space For Music 1999, CD-R)
1. Cosmic Flight
2. Pole Star
3. Solar Eclipse

Comments: The album that made Nashville…screaming and kicking, maybe…a major hotspot in the growing 1980s "space music" universe. Tony Gerber, **Willian Linton**, and Mason Williams had all collaborated on projects before, and comprised as close to a "space music" supergroup as the Music City could boast of at the time. *Cosmic Flight* is a

THE OTHER SIDE OF NASHVILLE - 201 -

stunning collection of Eno/Cluster inspired ambient and experimental music that received heavy airplay on the syndicated NPR radio program *Hearts of Space* when it was released in 1986. Recorded digitally, but originally released on cassette, this is what the creators call "deep space."

MARK GERMINO

Band Members:
Mark Germino (vocals, guitar) (I-III)

Other Musicians:
Willis Bailey (vocals) (III)
Christine Collister (vocals) (I)
Tom Comet (bass) (III)
Phillip Donnelly (guitars, vocals) (I)
LeAnne Ethridge (vocals) (III)
Mac Gayden (guitars, mandolin) (III)
Russ Kunkel (drums) (I)
Pat McInerny (drums, percussion) (III)
Simon Nicol (guitars, vocals) (I)
Ric Sanders (violin) (I)
Peter-John Vettese (keyboards) (I)
Michael Webb (keyboards) (III)

Mark Germino Recordings:

I. London Moon & Barnyard Remedies (RCA Records 1986, CD)
1. Political
2. Oriental Drag
3. Barnyard (Rhapsody in Brown)
4. God Ain't No Stained Glass Window

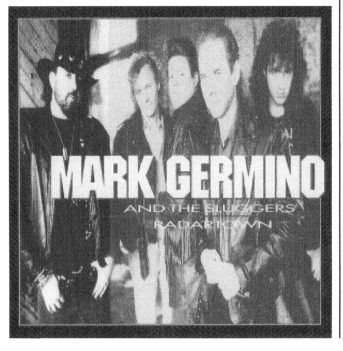

5. Sally Baker's (Low Tar) Dream
6. Broken Man's Lament
7. We Got Away
8. Immigrant Shuffle

Comments: Mark Germino moved to Nashville from North Carolina around 1974 and quickly fell in with the street poetry/alt-songwriter crowd that included talents like **Steve Earle**, Kevin Welch, John Allingham, **Dave Olney**, and Tom House. Germino began turning his carefully-constructed and verbose poetry into carefully-constructed and verbose songs, and began playing clubs at night while driving a truck during the day.

Germino scored a publishing deal in 1980 and while few mainstream Music Row hacks had the cajones to actually *record* a Germino song, a few visionaries like Johnny Cash, Emmylou Harris, and Vince Gill did so. Germino landed his label deal mid-decade after Earle had opened the door for the first wave of alt-country artists.

II. Caught In The Act of Being Ourselves (RCA Records 1987, CD)

III. Rank & File (Winter Harvest Records 1995, CD)
1. Poet's Lament
2. Fields of Man's New Order
3. Rosemary's Equilibrium
4. Rosemary's New Constitution
5. Drivin' Across America
6. Felix Tucker's Biggest Lie
7. Fire in the Land of Grace
8. Rex Bob Lowenstein
9. Very Lucky Man
10. Black Angel Cure
11. Soul of a Man
12. I'll Always Be Your Man

Comments: In between the release of his final RCA album, *Caught In The Act of Being Ourselves* in '87 and the release of the indie label gem *Rank & File* in 1995, Germino hooked up for a few years with the Sluggers (see below) for an album of real poop-punting rock 'n' roll music. This one is a fine acoustic set with Germino's typically well-written, intelligent, and erudite songs that evince more humor than a stage full o' drunken stand-up comedians.

The album also has the third – count 'em! – third version of Germino's wonderful "Rex Bob Lowenstein." After this one, Germino disappeared for over six years, turning his back on music and writing three novels. He has since come back and is touring with his unique country/rock/folk sound. Mark Germino & the Grenade Angels released *Atomic Candlestick* in 2007, but I haven't heard it and can't find a copy.

MARK GERMINO & THE SLUGGERS
Web: www.myspace.com/markgermino

Band Members:
Mark Germino (vocals, guitars) (I)
Tim Krekel (guitars, vocals) (I)
Tom Comet (bass, vocals) (I)
Michael "Spider" Webb (keyboards, vocals) (I)
Willis Bailey (drums, vocals) (I)

Other Musicians:
George Bradfute (guitar) (I)
Randall Hylton (mandolin) (I)
Suzie Katayama (cello) (I)
Walfredo Reyez (percussion) (I)
Bob Williams (guitars, mandolin) (I)

Mark Germino & the Sluggers Recordings:

I. Radartown (Zoo Entertainment 1991, CD)
1. Radartown
2. Let Freedom Ring (Volumes 4, 5 and 6)
3. Leroy and Bo's Totalitarian Showdown
4. Unionville
5. Economics (Of The Rat and Snake)
6. She's A Mystery
7. Pandora's Boxcar Blues
8. Exalted Rose
9. Burning The Firehouse Down
10. Serenade Of Red Cross
11. Rex Bob Lowenstein

Comments: *Radartown* is the culmination of Germino's better than 15 years of hard work, struggle, and flirtations with stardom, a near-perfect collection of working class blues backed by one of Nashville's best band of veteran rockers. The original "Rex Bob Lowenstein" from 1987 had earned Germino a European following and a short-lived chart position in the U.K. Here the song takes on a brilliant anarchic quality that appeals to the outlaw mentality, while tunes like "Radartown" and "Unionville" are blue collar odes to hard times. Germino's smart story-songs, like "Leroy and Bo's Totalitarian Showdown" display both his talent and wry sense of humor. Altogether, *Radartown* is one of the best rock 'n' roll albums to ever come from the mean streets of the Music City. (To help push *Radartown*, Zoo released the promotional *Economics*, a five-song CD EP with four tracks from the album, and a live version of Dylan's "Highway 61 Revisited.")

Mark Germino says: "'Rex Bob Lowenstein' cast a brilliant light on the dangers of allowing 'subscribed programming' to enter the control rooms of American radio. It was a clairvoyant, early warning of Clear Channel and things to come that would dilute and eventually eliminate a large

concluding component of the creative music process, that being, the experimental mainstream radio forum." (from Germino's MySpace page)

GHOSTFINGER
Web: www.ghostfinger.com

Band Members:
Richie Kirkpatrick (vocals, guitar, keyboards) (I)
Matt Rowland (bass, keyboards, synth) (I)
Van Campbell (drums) (I)
Matt Schaeffer (drums) (I)
Paul Niehaus (pedal steel) (I)
Berk Gibbs (turntables) (I)

Ghostfinger Recordings:

I. These Colors Run (Set International 2005, CD)
1. Animal Eye
2. Content
3. Hello Movies
4. Devil
5. Lady
6. Live My Head
7. Pretending To Die
8. Shine A Light
9. Moon
10. Rock
11. Frozen

Another View: "*These Colors Run* is an accomplishment as much as it is an album. It's a musical Mensa puzzle that Ghostfinger dared to put together. Somehow these bastard broken parts were made into songs that deconstruct convention without ever sounding confused. It's difficult to say whether there's a single song that might find its way onto a mix tape, but, like the work of Faith No More or other genre destroyers, *These Colors Run* makes for an awfully adventurous listen." – Jason Moon Wilkins, *All The Rage*

GLOSSARY

Band Members:
Joey Kneiser (vocals, guitar) (I-V)
Bingham Barnes (bass) (I-V)
Todd Beene (guitar, pedal steel, vocals) (III-V)
Greg Jacks (guitar) (III)
Kelly Kneiser (percussion, vocals) (III-V)
Matt Rowland (keyboards) (V)
Jason Manley (drums) (I, III)
J.D. Reager (drums) (IV)
Eric Giles (drums) (V)

Other Musicians:
Brian Carter (keyboards) (II, III)
Maggie Gresham (keyboards, vocals) (I)
Paul Neihaus (pedal steel) (III)
Seth Timbs (keyboards) (II)

Glossary Recordings:

I. Southern by the Grace of Location (Champ Records 1998, CD)
1. AOK
2. Only Dream
3. Transmitting A.M.

4. Bake A Cake
5. Half Mast
6. There Was A Sun Once
7. Stormy Weather
8. The Grace Of Location
9. Truth About You
10. Driving Me Home
11. Summertime
12. Soap Opera Scene
13. AKA Christmas
14. Natural Raft
15. L.A. Ambience

II. This Is All We've Learned About Living (Champ Records 2000, CD)
1. West Liberty
2. Just Be A Rampart
3. Serenade Us
4. Daydream Driving
5. Feeling Transcendental
6. One Interpretation
7. Frozen Satisfaction
8. Fast Walkin' Shit Talkin'
9. Counter Culturism
10. Wandered Off Too Far
11. The Flensing of Freeport
12. The Stars Are Alive

III. How We Handle Our Midnights (Undertow Music 2003, CD)
1. These City Lights Shine
2. Remember Me Tomorrow Night
3. Hold Me Down
4. At Midnight
5. Golden Houses
6. When Easy Street Gets Hard to Find

7. Lonesome Stray
8. The Rutherford County Line
9. Marigold Moon
10. Daylight Saving

IV. For What I Don't Become (Undertow Music 2006, CD)
1. Shaking Like A Flame
2. Poor Boy
3. Headstones And Dead Leaves
4. Time Rolling
5. Days Go By
6. American Bruises
7. The Reckless
8. Devils In The Details
9. As Far As Fear Will Take You
10. Breathe Life Into Me

V. The Better Angels Of Our Nature (Undertow Music 2007, CD)
1. Only Time Will Tell
2. Little Caney
3. Almsgiver
4. Valessa
5. Shout It From The Rooftops
6. Bitter Branch
7. Gasoline Soaked Heart
8. Nothing Can Hurt You Now
9. Chase Me Out Of The Dark
10. Blood On The Knobs

GO GO SURREAL

Band Members:
George Cohn (vocals)
Mike Grimes (guitars)
Michael Romanowski (bass)
Fenner Castner (drums)

Comments: Fondly remembered though short-lived, Go Go Surreal is best-known for their dubious tribute to actor Chuck Connors, "Ground Chuck." Mike "Grimey" Grimes would go on to **Bare Jr.** before opening his well-known indie record store.

GO JIMMY DUB

Band Members:
Les Shields (vocals) (I)
Mike ? (guitar, vocals) (I)
R. Gregory (drums, vocals) (I)

Go Jimmy Dub Recordings:

I. Where Do You Get Your Coconuts? (self-produced 1983, tape)

Side One
1. Triple X Sex
2. Other Lovers

Side Two
3. Bamboo Bay
4. JJ's Place

Comments: One of the earliest recordings from the Nashville rock underground, this funky lil' cassette featured one of my favorite whipping boys, Les Shields. I starting dating a girl (Cathy) that Les had dumped, and we made him the butt of our jokes in print for at least a couple of years (or until he joined Raging Fire). This cassette was doubly cool for its time, really, including a little lyric sheet insert. Sorry 'bout all the crap, Les…we were just kidding, really…

THE GOLDEN SOUNDS

Band Members:
Todd Evans (vocals, guitar, keyboards) (I)
Lizzie Evans (keyboards, vocals) (I)
Joshua Walker (drums) (I)
Sam Barnhart (bass) (I)
Xavia Nou (cello) (I)
Kirk Cornelius (guitars, keyboards) (I)
Madison Silvert (banjo) (I)

Golden Sounds Recordings:

I. Wings Or Horns: The Astronaut Prophecies (Meteor Sky Recordings 2006, CD)

1. Astronaut Girl
2. Oceans
3. Up And Away
4. Happy For The Good Times
5. Imposter
6. Elizabeth
7. It Stained Her Skirt
8. Lost My Potential
9. Wings Or Horns
10. Son, Don't Be Down
11. The End

GOLDEN SPEER

Comments: Wasn't this the band with the sons of Oak Ridge Boy William Lee Golden? They had expensive show posters tacked up all over town with full-color pix of the band. If not for the posters, nobody would have remembered this entirely unremarkable band; not since Whyte Lace has a vanity project caused so much negative buzz! It's a shame, 'cause the talented Marc Speer, the band's guitarist, was better than this dreck.

GOODS

Band Members:
Victor Lovera (vocals, guitars, percussion) (I, II)
R. Stevie Moore (guitars, vocals, keyboards) (I, II)
Roger Ferguson (vocals, guitar) (I, II)
Pete Spero (congas) (I, II)
Jaime Nichol (congas) (II)
Jimmy Gardner (bass) (II)

Other Musicians:
Bill Harris (drums) (I)
Bob Roundtree (guitar) (I)
Chuck Sagle (piano, vibes) (I)

Goods Recordings:

I. Herald (self-produced CD-R, 1997)
1. Please Remember
2. Guess Again
3. Man Of Me
4. I've Been Here Before
5. Jackie
6. Break Song
7. Plus Dozens More
8. Maximum/The Reply
9. Sing
10. This Is Your Lucky Day
11. Coming's End
12. Every Man Deserves The Best

Comments: A slice of early 1970s pop-rock courtesy of Mr. **R. Stevie Moore**, Goods was a Nashville rock "supergroup," of sorts, years before the Phrank 'n' Steins and Cantrells' scenes.

II. Live at Our Place (self-produced CD-R, 1997)
1. Please Remember
2. Guess Again
3. I've Been Here Before
4. My Father's Son
5. Plus Dozens More
6. Sing
7. I Figure If You Want Me
8. Christy's Moon
9. Taxis For Sale
10. Friendzy

Jimmy Gardner • Roger Ferguson • R. Stevie Moore • Victor Lovera • Pete Spero

GOODS Nashville, Tenn. Mondays 27 March 1972 Live at Our Place

11. Man Of Me
12. But Her Today
13. Everyman Deserves The Best
14. (Vic walks out)
15. (a phony Elvis)
16. I'm Here

Comments: Recorded live at Our Place in Nashville, March 27, 1972 with the Goods line-up assisted by bassist Jimmy Gardner and second conga player Jaime Nichol. Thoroughly engaging pop-rock with well-written songs penned by Moore and the underrated Lovera. If Nashville had been known for more than orchestral country tunes in the early 1970s, Goods might have had a shot at the big time.

GOVERNMENT CHEESE

Band Members:
Tommy Womack (vocals, guitars) (I-V)
Skot Willis (vocals, guitars) (I-V)
Billy Mack Hill (vocals, bass) (I-V)
Joe "Elvis" King (drums, vocals) (I-V)

Other Musicians:
Chris Becker (guitar) (IV)

Government Cheese Recordings:

I. Things Are More Like They Are Now Than They've Ever Been Before (self-produced 1985, vinyl 12")
Side One
1. This Life's For Me
2. Oh Yeah

Side Two
3. Face In The Crowd
4. Rebecca Whitmire

Comments: Debut EP from Bowling Green, Kentucky's favorite sons, Government Cheese. Produced by Byron House and recorded at High Street Studios in Bowling Green.

II. Come Back to Bowling Green…and marry me (Reptile Records 1987, vinyl 12")
Side One
1. C'mon Back to Bowling Green
2. Underneath the Water Tower

Side Two
3. Face to Face
4. Inside of You

Comments: Second four-song EP from Govt. Cheese, produced by Scott Tutt, finds the band signed to Tutt's fledgling Reptile Records label.

Go-Go Surreal

III. Three Chords, No Waiting (Reptile Records 1989, LP)

IV. Government Cheese (L.A.R. Entertainment 1992, CD)
1. Single
2. Sunday Driver
3. Before The Battered
4. For The Battered
5. No Sleeping In Penn Station
6. A Little Bit Of Sex
7. Fall In Love With You
8. Driver's Ed Films
9. Search and Destroy
10. Selling Out
11. Somewhere Between
12. Life Outside The Window
13. I Wanna Be A Man
14. Nothing Feels Good

Comments: The only Govt. Cheese CD released during the band's day, and well worth tracking down if you've never heard their unique style of pop-infused hard rock.

V. It's A Rock And Roll Party With Government Cheese (1995, vinyl 7")
Side One
1. Jailbait

Side Two
2. The Shrubbery's Dead

GRATE CHOP GRIND

Band Members:
Jamie Houston (vocals)
Don Carr (guitars)
Kevin Hornback (bass)
Steve Keller (keyboards)
Trey Bruce (drums)

GRATE CHOP GRIND - GREEN RODE SHOTGUN

Comments: Funk-rock band with **Jamie Houston** in front, performed at 1990 N.E.A. Extravaganza. Bassist Kevin Hornback also played with **Rococo**.

GREEN RODE SHOTGUN
Web: www.greenrodeshotgun.com

Band Members:
Jason Johnson (vocals) (I-III)
Shea Callahan (6-string guitar) (I-III)
David Henderson (guitars, vocals) (I-III)
John Lane (bass, vocals) (I-III)
Don Sergio (drums, harmonica, vocals) (I-III)

Other Musicians:
Brian Carter (vocals) (II, III)

David Henderson writes: "Green Rode Shotgun had about a five-six year run of getting really close to the carrot, only to have the string shortened time and time again by talentless assholes in the music industry. We were voted "best new band of 2004" by the *Nashville Scene*, and released an EP (***Persistence of Youth***), and an LP (***BANG***) to much critical acclaim (a lot of good it did to chart on CMJ!!!). We split up in '06 after much rejection from the music industry and after the singer decided to go back to school to get his masters degree."

Green Rode Shotgun Recordings:

I. Live at Exit/In (8 ohm Records 2002, CD)
1. Leaves
2. Lost Song
3. Something's Missing
4. These Days
5. She Wishes (Ronzaroma)
6. Typical
7. Anne Marie
8. A Call In A Room
9. Persistence Of Youth

Comments: Live show recorded at, well, like the title says, the Exit/In by long-time club sound guy Frank Sass. Without verification, my guess would be that the band sold this disc at shows; it's listed in the discography page of the GRS web site but I've never seen it for sale anywhere.

II. Persistence Of Youth (8 ohm Records 2002, CD)
1. A Call in a Room
2. Something's Missing
3. Lost Song
4. Persistence of Youth

III. BANG (8 ohm Records 2003, CD)
1. All the Same
2. Hopeless Crusades
3. Into the Light
4. My Will
5. Nothing is Good Enough
6. Numbers on the Wall
7. Streets of the City
8. Let it Show
9. Nothing New
10. Sideburn
11. As Pieces Fall

Green Rode Shotgun, continued on page 210....

Chances are, unless you happened to be attending college in the Southeast U.S. or lived in the region during the late 1980s, you've never heard of Government Cheese. Inspired by influences like the Replacements, Husker Du, R.E.M. and especially Nashville's Jason & the Scorchers, Government Cheese was formed in Bowling Green, Kentucky by WKU students Tommy Womack and Skot Willis (guitars and vocals). The two added a strong, stealthy rhythm section in bassist Billy Mack Hill and drummer Joe King, and promptly set out to conquer the world with their own unique brand of rock 'n roll, a curious mix of 1960s-era garage, vintage 1970s classic rock, and contemporary '80s college rock delivered without guile and with a fair amount of tongue-in-cheek humor.

The band spent the better part of a decade banging the gong, playing every smoky dive and college frat house that called on them, earning a reputation across Dixie as a rowdy and entertaining live band. While the Government Cheese story has been accounted at length in Womack's wonderful book *The Cheese Chronicles*, to date the band's musical history is largely unknown. During their day, Government Cheese released a handful of vinyl EPs and albums for Nashville-based indie label Reptile Records, while a long out-of-print CD that included much of their best material has become a sought-after collectors' item. Supported by a handful of true believers, Womack managed to raise the cash to put together the comprehensive anthology *Government Cheese 1985-1995*, a two-disc compilation that chisels into concrete the band's underrated and overlooked musical legacy.

Government Cheese were college radio staples throughout much of the Southeast during the late-1980s, and a video for the delightful power-pop ballad "Face To Face" earned frequent MTV airplay at the time. While Womack was the band's primary wordsmith, Willis and Hill contributed significantly to the band's repertoire, and the songs seemingly just poured out…for instance, longtime audience fave "Camping On Acid" sounds like Camper Van Beethoven on speed and steroids, Womack's surrealistic lyrics matched by a jumble of jangling guitars, explosive rhythms, and overall musical chaos. The hard-rocking "Fish Stick Day" was another crowd-pleaser, this live version offering up a chanted absurdist chorus, droning guitar-feedback, and King's powerful, tribal drumbeats.

Another Cheese fan favorite was "C'mon Back to Bowling Green," a rollicking slice of lovesick blue collar blues with a honky-tonk heart and electrified twang, sort of Duane Eddy meets Jerry Lee Lewis in a back-alley dive. "Single" just flat-out rocks, with plenty of ringing guitar tone, clashing instruments, lofty power-pop styled vocals, and a driving rhythm. The syncopated rhythms and folkish guitar strum behind the vocals on "No Sleeping In Penn Station" are a fine accompaniment to the song's real-life lyrical inspiration

while the metallic "Jailbait" proves that the Cheese could knock heads with any of the decade's nerf-metal cretins, raging guitars and a blistering wall-of-sound barely concealing the song's whip-smart pop-rock lyrics and gorgeous underlying melody.

The band was never afraid to take a stand on issues, either, which sometimes resulted in an unexpected response. The emotionally-powerful "For The Battered," and its dark-hued instrumental intro "Before The Battered," tackled the then hush-hush subject of domestic abuse with brutal simplicity and a menacing soundtrack of crashing instruments and noisy Sturm und Drang. Surprisingly, the disturbing revenge fantasy connected with the listeners of Nashville radio station WKDF's local music show, becoming its most-requested song.

"The Shrubbery's Dead (Where Danny Used To Fall)" is a brilliant story of the toll of alcoholism on an individual and family, Hill's lyrics bolstered by a roughneck instrumental background. The class warfare of the spoken-word ode "The Yuppie Is Dead" leads into the deeply introspective "Nothing Feels Good," a hard rock 1970s throwback (I'm thinking Starz) that speaks of the dissatisfaction of too many years on the road.

For us original "cheeseheads," the album includes a wealth of previously-unreleased material, starting with the band's raucous, off-tilt cover of Jim Carroll's "People Who Died." Delivered with punkish intensity and chaotic energy, Government Cheese manages to capture the spirit of the original while adding a menacing edge…or, as Womack says in the liner notes, "we took Jim Carroll's song and did it like the Scorchers." The band's semi-biographical "Kentucky Home" has never made it onto disc until now, a Replacements-styled triumph that speaks of growing up with

GREEN RODE SHOTGUN - BIG MIKE GRIFFIN

rock 'n' roll dreams in Podunk, U.S.A. "I Can Make You Love Me" lopes into your consciousness with a hearty bassline and wiry guitar leading into a sort of alt-rock dirge with sparse harmony vocals and an undeniable rhythm.

Government Cheese was always known for its spirited covers, which ranged from classic rock (an unreleased and raucous take of Grand Funk's "We're An American Band" is cranked out at twice the speed of the original in a white light haze) to critical faves (the Stooges' "Search & Destroy" totally demolishes the thousand and one versions done by mundane punkers, the band's reckless, ramshackle performance capturing the white heat fervor of Iggy's worst nightmares). A live cover of the Dictators "Stay With Me" retains the heartfelt innocence intended by writer Andy Shernoff while adding the Cheese's own bit of emotional longing to the mix, and a live romp through the Ramones' "The KKK Took My Baby Away" keeps about 90% of the original's breakneck pace and energy while retaining Joey's sweetness and light.

There's plenty more to like on *Government Cheese 1985-1995,* forty-three songs altogether from the best band that you never heard. If Government Cheese had hailed from Athens, Georgia like their friends R.E.M. or maybe even from Austin, Texas they might today be a household name. Instead, they remain a fond memory for a few thousand loyal fans scattered across the Southeast. The very definition of "cult band" and D.I.Y. poster children for the indie-rock aesthetic, Government Cheese flirted with the big time but never got the break they deserved...none of which makes this music any less entertaining, the songs any less brilliant, or the performances any less rocking. Although Tommy Womack has since forged an acclaimed, if modest career as an indie-rock troubadour, the music he made with Government Cheese has withstood the test of time and is ready to receive the long overdue respect it demands. – *Blurt* magazine, 2011

Green Rode Shotgun, continued...

Comments: Green Rode Shotgun was a very cool, very undervalued band that split its time between Cookeville and Murfreesboro during the early 2000s. The band featured a couple of local scene vets in guitarists David Henderson of **the Roaries** and Don Sergio of **the Features**, and both guys had previously played together in **the Preservatives** along with producer and 'Boro guy-around-town Brian Carter.

"BIG" MIKE GRIFFIN
Web: www.bigmikegriffin.com

Band Members:
"Big" Mike Griffin (vocals, guitar) (I-VIII)

Other Musicians:
John Anthony (piano) (II)
Bob Babbit (bass) (VIII)
Johnny Bird (drums) (IV-VIII)
Moe Denham (keyboards) (I, II)
Larry Emmons (bass) (I, II)
Steve Herman (trumpet) (VI)
Gregg Hoffman (drums) (I)
David Hood (bass) (III)
Clayton Ivey (keyboards) (III)
Kirk "Jelly Roll" Johnson (mouth harp) (I)
Miranda Louise (vocals) (VI)
Raymond Massey (drums) (II)
Jim "Fish" Michie (keyboards) (IV, V, VI, VIII)
Essra Mohawk (vocals) (VI)
Pat O'Connor (drums) (III)
Paco Shipp (harmonica) (V, VI)
Dennis Taylor (trumpet) (II, III, VI, VIII)

Terry Townsend (trumpet) (II, III)
Steve Vines (bass) (IV-VII)
Carson Whitsett (piano) (I)

Big Mike Griffin Recordings:

I. ...Back On The Streets Again (Waldoxy 1992, CD)
1. Workin' Is The Curse
2. Blue Looks Good On You
3. Drivin' Wheel
4. I'd Rather Go Blind
5. Delta Moon
6. Make Up Your Mind
7. I'm A Blues Man
8. You Put The Hurt On Me
9. Back On The Streets Again

Comments: "Big" Mike Griffin really is...big, that is, standing a towering 6'10" tall and weighing in at a whopping 350 pounds. Griffin's rip-roaring blues-rock sound is every bit as big as the guitarist's frame, and although he's not well-known around town, his reputation in the blues community has grown with every new album release. Plus the guy tours like a crazy, pitching his scorched-earth blues-rock sound to blues fans and bikers at festivals and clubs.

II. Gimme What I Got Comin' (Waldoxy 1993, CD)
1. Give Me What I Got Comin'
2. Been There Done That
3. Blues Will Never Die
4. I Just Can't Get Enough
5. Fifth Of Whiskey, Case Of The Blues
6. Queen Of New Orleans
7. T.V. Mama

8. Black Cat Scratchin'
9. You Got The Best Thang
10. Stretched Out

III. Sittin' Here With Nothing (Waldoxy Records 1996, CD)
1. Somebody's Been Talkin'
2. Satisfied
3. Love Is Growing Cold
4. Sittin' Here With Nothing
5. The Last Thing I Need
6. High Maintenence Woman
7. Bad Seed
8. I Am The Doctor
9. He Can't Do It
10. You Done Tore Your Playhouse Down
11. Deliver Me From Evil

IV. Harley In The Rain (Chrome Link Records 1997, CD)
1. Harley In The Rain
2. Self Defense
3. Old Maid
4. Harley Blues
5. You'll Know
6. Ain't Superstitious
7. Get Outta My Life
8. Shovel Head
9. Willin'
10. Figure Of Speach

V. Twin Brothers of Different Mothers (Chrome Link Records 2000, CD)
1. Twin Brothers
2. All About A Woman
3. Let's Have A Party (Down In Louisiana)
4. Love Will Never Die
5. Born To Ride
6. You Don't Have To Go
7. Panhead
8. Born In Chicago
9. Mean Disposition
10. Don't Let Him Ride
11. That's My Baby (In The Miniskirt)

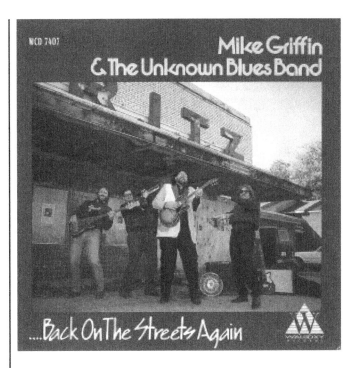

VI. Livin' Large (Chrome Link Records CD, 2001)
1. Livin' Large
2. Too Many Drivers
3. Baby Won't Ride
4. Three Hundred Pounds of Joy
5. Down In Hollywood
6. Tryin To Get Back Home
7. Oh, Pretty Woman
8. Blues for Mr. B
9. I'll Be Your Monkey
10. I Wouldn't Lay My Guitar Down

VII. Live At The Full Moon Saloon (Chrome Link CD, 2002)
1. Cool Guitar
2. Ain't Never Gonna Do
3. Electric Man
4. Highway 49
5. Somebody's Been Talkin'
6. Play With Your Poodle
7. Fifth of Whisky (Case of the Blues)

MIKE GRIFFIN
Sittin' Here With Nothing
(Waldoxy Records)
   Big Mike is a hard-core bluesman of the old school, a six-string maniac who reels off funky riffs so effortlessly and flawlessly that you just *know* that the man was weaned on Howlin' Wolf and Muddy Waters' 78s, cut his eye teeth on Willie Dixon and John Lee Hooker.
   Sittin' Here With Nothing is Griffin's third disc, a houserockin' collection of juke-joint blues that mixes smoke-flavored originals with a handful of firey covers to provide a spotlight on Griffin's immense musical skills. Griffin plays in a fluid, B.B. King-inspired style, his soulful vocals matched perfectly by Clayton Ivey's well-placed keyboard flourishes, backed by the mighty rhythm section of bassist Dave Hood and drummer Pat O'Conner. Griffin's skill and the band's chemistry work to make *Sittin' Here With Nothing* the strongest effort yet from this talented young bluesman. (1993)

8. Let's Have a Party
9. Twin Brothers (Of Different Mothers)
10. Hey Joe

VIII. Two Lane Road (Chrome Link Records CD, 2004)
1. Two Lane Road
2. She's Fine
3. To Meet The Blues
4. High Heeled Sneakers
5. Back Door Man
6. Red Headed Woman
7. It Hurts Me Too
8. The 62
9. King Bee
10. Pack It Up

THE GRINNING PLOWMAN

Band Members:
Michael Ake (vocals, guitar, keyboards) (A1, I, II)
Janet Ake (vocals, bass) (A1, I, II)
Keith Barton (guitar) (A1, I, II)
Derek Greene (drums) (A1, I, II)

The Grinning Plowman Recordings:

Singles/EPs

A1. Days Of Deformity (Carlyle Records 1988, 12" vinyl)
Side One
1. Radiator

Side Two
2. Magic House

Another View: "For a few short years, the Grinning Plowman – Nashville's favorite cult band – dominated the scene with a sound that was as avant-unusual as anything the city's dark corners ever produced. Plodding, like a stoner-rock band, with tribal rhythms and razor-sharp fretwork…kinda like the Doors-meet-Candlemass with a dash of Killing Joke. Guitarist Keith Barton tore off some meaty riffs while Janet Ake and Derek Greene kept the heart beating and vocalist Michael Ake bravely sojourned across the band's sludge-rock horizon. Another "coulda, woulda, shoulda" Nashville band, the Grinning Plowman's Carlyle label stuff stands among the best the era has to offer." – The lost liner notes for Spat's *Return To Elliston Square* CD

Albums

I. I Play Jupiter (Carlyle Records 1989, CD)
1. Radiator
2. Alone At Last
3. Magic House
4. Skyscraper
5. No More Love
6. Pretas Opera
7. Chinese Box
8. Smoke
9. Esmeralda
10. Koo-Ka

Comments: Nashville's fave cult band may have gone the way of the dodo nearly 20 years ago, but that hasn't stopped Plowman fans from haranguing the Reverend every chance they get. Seems that no matter how you describe the music of the Grinning Plowman, the band's loyal fans hear it differently, and take issue with your judgement. No matter,

The Grinning Plowman

'cause if the Plowman had been from Seattle, they would have been big…maybe not as big as Nirvana, but big nonetheless. The band broke up in 1993, and Michael Ake fell afoul of the law somehow, but a smallish clique of rabid fans have kept the flame alive all these years.

Another View: "Their sound is dark and aggressive, like a soul on fire, with the music building from a somber funeral dirge to a frenzied, dervish-like howl within the space of a few seconds. The Grinning Plowman are redefining the boundaries of music, delivering material with a Gothic feel and a vague lyrical poetry akin to Lovecraft or Crowley. This is heady stuff, exhilarating yet disquieting…"
– Rev. Keith A. Gordon, *The Metro*, August 1990.

II. Nothing Is Ever What It Is (Spat! Records 2000, digital)
1. Secret Sugar Frosting
2. Nancy's Relish Tray Demonstration
3. Hula
4. Mainframe
5. Pewter Surf
6. Functional Design
7. Monkey Speed Drome
8. Orange Room
9. Fool
10. The Wonders of Linoleum
11. Telemythos
12. Synthetic Flux

Comments: Spat! Records has, thankfully, revived the Grinning Plowman back catalog and made it all available on Amazon.com for the hardcore fans to buy as high-rez mp3 files. This digital-only LP is also available as a download, but I'm not entirely sure of its provenance. The Plowman's fans remain rabid, however, and maintain a MySpace page on the band.

THE GROOVE KRICKETS

Band Members:
Dave Baker (vocals, guitar) (I, II)
Chris Choate (bass) (I, II)
Johnny Knoch (drums) (I, II)
Mike Lester (vocals) (I)

The Groove Krickets Recordings:

I. Get Frantic (self-produced tape)

Comments: Three-song cassette, produced by Billy Cox, bassist in Jimi Hendrix's Band of Gypsies.

II. Tongue And Groove (self-produced CD)

Comments: Vocalist Mike Lester died in 1996, but the band soldiered on with guitarist Baker taking on lead vox. A popular draw on the Nashville club circuit for years, the Groove Krickets have often been overlooked when people talk about the local rock music scene. The band broke up in 2006 after over two decades in the trenches, with Baker and Knoch forming **Guns-A-Go-Go**.

GUILLOTINE

Band Members:
Robert McNair (vocals, guitar)
Jeff Barnes (guitar)
Izzy N. Sane (bass)
Andy Leffler (drums)

From the Murfreesboro Musicfest 2 program: "The notorious Guillotine feeds the local metal-starved audience massive doses of raw, intense, Power-metal from beyond the threshold of pain. Their unique sound can be described as a mixture of Judas Priest and the lightning-fast riffs of Metallica."

GUILLOTINE - GUILT - GUNS-A-GO-GO

Comments: Cool mid-1980s metal band from the 'boro, but really – "Izzy N. Sane"? You could only get away with that during the '80s metal boom, what with the imaginative band logos and skewed spelling for names. As for the purple prose that the band obviously wrote itself for the Musicfest program, that's really how the underground metal scene walks and talks, even today. Personally, I blame Martin Popoff, Canada's best-known and most prolific metal scribe…

GUILT

Band Members:
Tommy McRae (vocals) (I, II)
Chuck Allen (guitar) (I, II)
Skot Nelson (bass) (I, II)
Craig Owens (drums)
Jeff Johnson (guitar)
Paul Simmonz (drums) (II)
Harry Rushakoff (drums)

Guilt Recordings:

I. The Truth Hurts (Neo Records 1986, LP)
1. Troublemaker
2. Be Real
3. Talk To Me
4. I Wanna Know
5. Use Somebody

Comments: Guilt is one of the great lost bands of Nashville's underground rock scene. Not to be confused with the Louisville, Kentucky hardcore industrial band of the same name…speaking of which, since Nashville's Guilt had been kicking around the Southeast since the mid-80s and released a nationally-distributed CD (below) in '91, why the hell did the Louisville band name themselves 'Guilt'?

II. Thru The Night (First Warning Records 1991, CD)
1. Sundance
2. Thru The Night
3. Girl And Her Dog
4. Fast Slide Suicide
5. Waiting

Comments: This is probably the "unreleased" EP mentioned below that was recorded somewhere with **Steve Earle** at the production board. Later appeared (quietly, without fanfare) on the First Warning label. Although the indie imprint had national distribution via powerhouse major BMG, the label could never seem to muster up interest in any of their bands, and Guilt faded into obscurity (actually, they ventured out to L.A. at one point with Jeff Johnson of **Jason & the Scorchers** in tow, but the less said about all of that, the better...)

Another View: "Guilt were just as fucked up as I was and scammed me out of money constantly. Teresa signed 'em, and boy was she pissed at me about it because they really were a pain in the ass. Their record never came out." – Steve Earle, from **Hardcore Troubadour**

GUNS-A-GO-GO
Web: www.myspace.com/gunsagogo

Band Members:
Dave Baker (vocals, guitar)
Joe Gamble (bass)
Johnny Knoch (drums)

Comments: Formed from the remnants of long-running Nashville club favorites **the Groove Krickets**, Guns-A-Go-Go includes that band's Dave Baker and drummer Johnny Knoch.

Guilt

*T*ony Gerber seldom gets the credit he deserves for his contributions to the local Nashville rock scene. As "Anthony Rian," he helped bring electronic sounds to an early 1980s music scene that was based entirely on guitars. His later collaboration with William Linton and Mason Stevens, Cosmic Flight, has become a bona fide ambient "space music" classic album, receiving international radio airplay.

As both a musician and owner of the Space For Music record label, Gerber helped make Nashville one of the centers of the space music world, releasing albums by artists like Giles Reaves and Cluster's Rodelius. A talented musician, graphic artist, wood craftsman, and Internet pioneer, Gerber is a true Renaissance man. This conversation took place by phone in August 2007, as Gerber was preparing to perform a concert in the virtual world of Second Life.

How did you get involved in the world of Second Life?
I read about it in *Wired* magazine in late January of last year. So the beginning of 2006, I went and checked it out and it sounded like something I'd thought would be cool years ago, but had forgotten all about that kind of thing. I went in and I couldn't believe it. There was so much already there, everything built by the people.

Everything in [Second Life] is built by people like myself; so tonight's concert is in a forest that somebody has built. My name is Cypress Rosewood, that's my avatar name, and I live in a big tree. I'm an elf and, because I love wood, it's just part of what I do and that's kind of my persona there and so this guy designed a forest, with giant, giant trees listening to my music over and over and over. So the place looks like my music sounds, and I've actually had other people say that they didn't even know that he did that, which was pretty amazing. He created this place called the Cypress Rosewood Auditorium in my honor and I haven't performed there yet, so tonight is the first night to perform in this auditorium, but what I'm going to do after each song is I'm going to go to a different place so the audience is going to have to follow me around.

Follow you through the forest?
Yeah, and there's a campfire, I have a cave that's real primal with cave wall paintings and stuff, and I'm actually wearing Native American stuff tonight, an animal hide cape, kind of primal looking...

So you can get into it from a creative aspect, there's more than just the music, there's kind of the trappings that go with it too?
It's a metaverse...it takes everything – video, audio, art and photography, and sound and computer graphics in 3D and 2D and just everything is in there – it's a true metaverse. So basically, I'll just explain it real quick...it's Internet radio...for instance, the forest where I'm playing at tonight, that land is basically a [computer] server, so there are islands that you can buy and you build stuff, you terraform the land, whatever you want to do with it. That island is basically a server, so there's thousands and thousands, and thousands of these islands in there now, and they're huge server farms and that server is pointing to my Internet radio broadcast which, tonight, is coming from my house.

I have a 24/7 radio station I've done for a year or so now, it's space radio. If you go to my website and you click on it, you can listen to it, it runs all the time and then I pre-empt it with live concerts throughout the month. I have that schedule up on my website so if you don't actually go into Second Life, you can tune in and listen to the show on your computer and iTunes, or Windows Media, or whatever you use to play MP3 streams, you can listen to my show.

It's a whole movement that's happening...I was the first ambient space musician to go in there [Second Life] professionally and I pack out the places to max ever since the first concert, so I've become a major celebrity in there now and that's kind of interesting. There's something about my music that in that situation where you're sitting in front of your computer, it's really a good venue with the graphics and everything else that's going on. It's different than going in and listening to a rock and roll band play. It's a different experience. There's something that seems to be more intense. That's been the real exciting part about it...and you hear every individual comment from the listeners, so I'm doing a show and I hear all the audience talking amongst themselves about the show and that's real interesting.

They provide a sort of instant feedback.
Instant feedback, and you get to hear what everybody says, unlike in real life, so it's really a new form of performance.

Does that feedback impact your performance – do you know what you're going to play when you start, or does the energy of the audience kind of shape you and direct you?
There's definitely a connection of some sort, there's an energy like a real show. You get a little bit of butterflies before... there's a common element to doing a real show except I'm in my pajamas in my office and I don't have to set stuff up...

INTERVIEW: TONY GERBER

You don't have to pay for a hall or anything...
I set up the show by dragging a folder out of my inventory onto the land, and I have different stage sets already set up with instruments, and they just appear! I have a Moog and I've created other instruments in 3D, Gibson guitars and a Stratocaster, and I've also built a Space Music museum and...

All of this in Second Life?
All in Second Life! A lot of these instruments, like the Raymond Scott's Clavivox – he's part of the electronic music instrument pioneer part of my museum, so I've built one of their instruments in 3D as an example along with a picture of who it is and their name and you click on it and you get a note card that gives you a bio on who that person is and then there will be some podcast, you click on buttons to hear other things and some interviews I might do with some people in real life, but it's a huge job.

Has your popularity in Second Life helped with the record label, or has it spilled out into the real world?
No, not really, we're hardly selling any CDs and we're selling very few downloads. I'm just now starting kind of a new concept of selling the things. Although I've been selling single songs as animated music boxes in Second Life, these psychedelic Mandela-looking boxes that sit there and spin and animate, and if you click on it, it plays one of my songs or one of Spacecraft songs, or whatever is in there. I have a few of those and it's interesting, I sell them for 350 lindens – lindens is the Second Life money system – 1,000 lindens equals anywhere between $3.75 and $4.00, so 350 lindens is close to a $1.00, or $1.10, something like that, so it was kind of similar to iTunes, but you're getting a 3D graphic with it, that's kind of novel. They are actually WAV files that play in the real world, so when you click on it, anybody can hear it.

What's the status of the record label right now?
There are artists that I'm sold out of their stuff and I'm just not going to make any more. People aren't buying CDs like they were, so that's the reality...and I've been playing a lot more music and doing a lot more with my music than I was when I was running the label. I have a three year old now, I'm married, so the dynamics changed for me. Second Life has been a saving grace for me as far as music, a way for me to express myself and satisfy that part in me at a time when it's difficult for me to do anything other than be at home and be a dad.

Second Life gives you a worldwide audience, really.
It's given me a worldwide audience and connections like I haven't had for a long time. I'm meeting people in the gaming industry; it's amazing the people that I'm meeting in there. I got the book deal, which is a residual, or a sideline offshoot, and I get tips for performing. I have a show tonight, I have two shows on Sunday – one for the European audience and one for the U.S. audience, so I'm hoping to maybe make

Second Life's Cypress Rosewood (a/k/a Tony Gerber)

$120 this week in tips playing those three shows, maybe a little more. So it's actually becoming a part of our income, it's paying for groceries...

It gives you an outlet for your creative energies and maybe you can make a buck on the side...
I know there are a lot of people that aren't making anything in Second Life, but I've spent hundreds and hundreds of hours in there, I have storefronts, vending machines and all kinds of stuff in there. I'm going to write the book about it because...people have written articles and stuff, they just skim over it, they don't really come in there and see what I'm doing.

I think a lot of people are in a situation where they have to find other outlets for their music because the mainstream music machine is pretty much broken...
I'm doing performances...I did one in the dragon world, it's called *The Isle of Wyrms,* it's a girl from Canada that's created these unbelievable dragon avatars. She's probably the best designer of avatars in there, so you can buy a costume where you could become all these different dragons and she's taken it so far to where she's got like nine or ten islands now and they're all connected together. She quit her regular career and she's gone full-time in there. The concert there and the cathedral, it's a huge, massive cathedral. I did a concert in there and had about 85 people show up for that, it maxed out. The show became an album called *The Isle of Wyrms,* and then I went back and I put billboards up on the island where I did the concert and tried to sell it to the people that were at the concert, so it's kind of an interesting way of trying to sell stuff, I'm just doing different stuff like that.

Have you thought about taking any of the Space For Music albums and doing something like putting them up on eMusic, is there any interest in that or...?
Yeah there is, but quite frankly, I haven't had time to go through and get all that happening. I'd like to, and I know that John and Diane, the other two people in Spacecraft, they went through CD Baby and pushed and I told them they could, I just said you guys go with the name, you do what you can, I'll do what I can.

I'm not going to try and hog everything because I've been selling our albums for years, but we split all that, when we manufactured it we split and that's how we deal with it. They can sell theirs and they keep everything, I can sell what I have and keep everything, that's kind of how we've done it. When we do a live concert, we sell them and we just split it with everybody, however many we sell no matter whose inventory it is, that's just how we've dealt with it. They sell stuff to CD Baby, iTunes and other places that they're collecting on, and I don't have any problem with that because I can do the same thing with some of the other stuff. I have quite a few of our Spacecraft performances that aren't released that I'm going to go ahead and package and release and put out on some of those places. Right now I'm selling them directly off my site as downloads, so I get 100% of the money as far as you know, not having to split with iTunes or somebody like that.

What is the story behind the Anthony Rian/Atreeo tape you probably gave me way back when?
What's interesting about that is that the first recording I did that got some recognition and is still selling is *Cosmic Flight*, and that was with William Linton and Mason Stevens. So Atreeo was we three. We did *Cosmic Flight* as our names – Mason Stevens, William Linton, and Tony Gerber – and that tape was played on *Hearts of Space* in 1986 or '87.

That Atreeo tape was probably the first thing that I did where I was getting recognized among the people that were into electronic music. It is an amazing recording; it still is an amazing recording. I was living off 8th Avenue and we did that in the attic of this house that I lived in; it was actually recorded during a solar eclipse and we didn't even realize it, we didn't know that that eclipse was going on until after the thing was recorded. So there was some magic around the sessions.

How did you first meet up with Giles Reaves?
I actually met Giles for the first time during orientation at Belmont College. Then I worked with him for three days at Baskin Robbins in Hillsboro Village. I quit that job because I got humiliated by the manager, but Giles worked there for quite a while. Then when he was working at Castle, that was when Giles and I first recorded some stuff there.

Tony Gerber

INTERVIEW: TONY GERBER

I know that you and Giles have collaborated quite a bit through the years...
Yeah, he was part of quite a few of the Spacecraft albums.

How did Spacecraft come together?
John Rose was at my house here in Nashville and he brought some physicist...this is bizarre...this guy called him up in the middle of the night while he was doing one of his shows, he was so moved by some of the music he called up on the phone while he was driving through Lexington and wanted to meet him [Rose] for coffee at midnight after his show was over. So they met and they became a little bit friends, but it was kind of a weird deal. Then he sent John a package of some earth sounds and different physics things that he was doing with sound based on gravitational...earth's gravitation, and a set of tapes of the Voyager II sound-mapping based from the data.

John brought those up here; we opened them up and listened to them. We started taking our synthesizers, and I had a memory mode I was using and I'd program these sounds and a JD 800 Roland that was inspired by these NASA sound mappings. We thought "there's a bizarre sound, let's see if we can create some stuff that's kind of in this realm with our synthesizers." So we started recording and we said "we should just call this project Spacecraft."

That was how that started and then Chris Blaze, who was doing more of an industrial kind of hardcore, dark-sounding, using these instruments that are handmade stringed instruments, Chris joined us on those sessions and then soon after that he went to Rome, Italy, and I've hardly heard from him ever since. He didn't like the United States very much, even though he was born here but I think his dad was Italian, so he ended up living in Rome and as far as I know, he's still there. But he impacted the project because his sound, that first album you can hear, it has a harder edge.

You've been very involved in graphic arts and have worked on a lot of different local musicians' album covers, how did you get involved in that?
Growing up, I worked in print shops, so I always had an interest and I did drafting and took some commercial art classes and actually enjoyed mocking up LP covers when I was in high school, so I guess that was the writing on the wall. I helped set up a couple print shops here in Nashville, working with some people and getting them converted over to desktop publishing. Then I started Space for Media, which was a company that I had for a couple years which was a media company. That's where I started officially doing my first CD covers, which would have been around 1989. I did some larger labels in the beginning, but I always liked to work with the independent artist. I've probably done 300 or more covers since then.

HAIL TO THE KEITH
Web: www.myspace.com/hailtothekeith

Band Members:
Keith Lowen (vocals, guitar)
Zach Collier (guitar, keyboards, vocals)
Ben Patton (bass, vocals)
Sam Smith (drums)
Joel J. Dahl (vocals, percussion)
Dave Paulson (guitar)
Andrea Barrett (vocals)
Brian Fuzzell (drums)

Comments: Keith Lowen has played with a number of local Nashville/Murfreesboro bands, including **Lifeboy**, **the Privates** and **De Novo Dahl**. Hail To The Keith was started as a side project with his old Lifeboy bandmate Sam Smith, but now Lowen is said to be recording an EP of original songs for future release.

JIMMY HALL & THE PRISONERS OF LOVE

Band Members:
Jimmy Hall (vocals)
Kenny Greenburg (guitars)
Mike Joyce (bass)
Tommy Wells (drums)

Comments: Jimmy Hall moved to Nashville in 1980 to launch his solo career. After a couple of solo albums and a hook-up with British guitar legend Jeff Beck, Hall formed the R&B-oriented Prisoners of Love in 1985 with some talented folks like guitarist Kenny Greenburg of the Delta Hurricanes.

HANDS DOWN EUGENE

Band Members:
Matt Moody (vocals, bass)
Andy Wilhite (guitars)
Matt Martin
Matt Rowland
Todd Beene

Hands Down Eugene Recordings:

I. Full Blast (self-produced CD, 2005)

Another View: "With a flexible cast of musicians from the loosely amalgamated Trey Deuce collective, including proud new papa Andy Snyder (who also plays with The Bubblegum Complex), Hands Down Eugene mix the psychedelia of *The White Album* with the melodic charms of Built to Spill. Led by Ole Mossy Face bassist Matt Moody, they're a study in mellow pleasures and celebratory sing-alongs replete with a loping low end, jangling chords and the interlocking guitar riffs of Andy Wilhite. Their album *Full Blast* features a total of 29 musicians, and their live set manages to convey the sense of a communal happening – joyous, pliable and welcoming. – Steve Haruch, *Nashville Scene*

II. Madison (XOXO Records 2006, CD)
1. Denise
2. Miss Madison
3. Calloused Part
4. Full Blast
5. If It's Up To Me
6. Ticket Girl
7. Barry Short For Governor
8. Champion
9. Seeing
10. Built For Speed
11. I'm In The Way
12. Read And Disadvantaged
13. Stretch Your Eye

Comments: Guys, really, if you want people to write about you, you just can't depend on a poorly designed MySpace page for promotion…and BTW, letting your band domain name fall into the hands of spam farmers is just a sign of rank amateurism in this day-and-cyber-age.

Another View: "It's possible that the new Nashville sound personified by this band – still a little bit country, but a lot more rock 'n' roll – might have been a motivating factor for the sound of The Raconteurs. In fact, *Madison* is very reminiscent of The Raconteurs' sound, which, as with Hands Down Eugene, sounds heavily influenced by both country artists of long ago and stoner/psychedelic rock bands like Pink Floyd."

"All the longing and loneliness that remind most people of when country music was actually good are present on this record, complete with heartbreaking guitar solos, which have been absent from all genres of music for way too long. The album's lyrics are what one would expect from a band that has seen its share of bars and small towns while working hard to play music for anyone who'll listen. And with this album's unique sound, it is assured that people are going to listen." – Natalie Higdon, *Southeast Performer*, December 2006

HANK FLAMINGO

Band Members:
Trent Lee Summar a/k/a "Prank Flamingo (vocals) (I)
Eddie Grigg a/k/a "Tank Flamingo" (guitar) (I)
Philip Wallace a/k/a "Blank Flamingo" (guitar) (I)
Ben Northern a/k/a "Rank Flamingo" (bass) (I)
Stuart Stuart a/k/a "Frank Flamingo" (fiddle) (I)
Roy Watts a/k/a "Lank Flamingo" (drums) (I)
Chad Evans a/k/a "Skank Flamingo" (saxophone) (I)

Hank Flamingo Recordings:

I. Hank Flamingo (Giant Records 1994, CD)
1. Little Miss Fire Prevention
2. Baby It's You
3. When You Ran With Me
4. Tennessee Plates
5. White Lightnin'
6. Redneck Martians Stole My Baby
7. Promised Land
8. Gooseneck Trailer
9. Granddaddy's Place
10. Too Many Nights
11. Slaw

Comments: Hank Flamingo was a very popular local party band that managed to mix country twang with a R&B revue sound and rock chops. For whatever reason, I never saw these guys live and I've never heard the one album they made for Giant Records. Northern and Watts came from **Blind Farmers From Hell** to start Hank Flamingo.

Another View: "The basis of Hank Flamingo's ever-expanding following is its astounding live show, which unleashes a floating line-up if flailing Flamingoes on an unsuspecting audience. The results, as witnessed at a recent July 4 show sponsored by KDF, generate plenty of sweaty roadhouse heat: Summar, growling the blues and whipping around in suits that range stylistically from Eliot Ness to Herb Tarlek, is as maniacal onstage as he is soft-spoken and polite off. On a good night, they make the Kentucky Headhunters seem like Hohenwald hairdressers."
– Jim Ridley, *Nashville Scene* 1990

THE HARD CORPS

Band Members:
"Dirty Bob" Samuels (vocals, rapping) (I)
Ronzo "The Beast" Cartwright (vocals, rapping) (I)
"Maestro K.O." Kenny Owens (drums) (I)
"Rev Kev" Kevin Reinen (guitars, vocals) (I)
"Major Kutt" Terry Hayes (DJ, percussion, vocals) (I)
"Machine Gun" Kelly Butler (bass) (I)

Hard Corps Recordings:

I. Def Before Dishonor (Interscope Records 1991, CD)
1. Hard Corps
2. Can Can't
3. 3 Blind Mice
4. Let's Go
5. Oh Yeah
6. The Dirtster
7. The Biggamobiggamobetta
8. Make My Day
9. Back In Black
10. Bring Down The House
11. Crime Don't Pay
12. What Time Is It?
13. Why Can't We Be Friends

Comments: Wotta mess! Two producers, including Run-DMC's Jam Master Jay; four engineers; two assistant engineers – and none of the lot of 'em could capture the band's dynamic live sound to tape in the studio. The Hard Corps received a large six-figure advance, but the label saddled them with an expensive superstar producer and then under-promoted the resulting disc to death. The Hard Corps were a few years too early to ride the rock-rap wave to success, and even though Interscope was known as a rap label, they couldn't do squat with a great live band that sold out venues everywhere it went! Ronzo "The Beast" Cartwright bounced back from this debacle to form **Stone Deep**.

HARD KNOX
Web: www.myspace.com/hardknox1980s

Band Members:
Gene Hadley (vocals) (III)
Daniel Lusk (guitars) (III)
Don Murray (bass) (III)
Jay Martin (drums) (III)
Rick Ruhl (vocals)
Steve Oliverio (guitars)
Freddy Pratt (bass)
Larry Poccia (bass)
Billy Baker (drums)

Hard Knox Recordings:

I. Mark Of The Rocker (L.I.F.E.R. Records 1985, vinyl LP)
1. Get Up!
2. Mark Of The Rocker
3. Love's Out Of Season
4. Combat Alley
5. Getaway
6. Take It If You Want It
7. Love Or Money

II. All Ways End The Same (L.I.F.E.R. Records 1989, vinyl LP)
1. First Things First
2. Bad Noise
3. Cities Web
4. Ain't No Saint
5. Too Far Gone
6. Blind Me With Your Love
7. Always Ends The Same
8. All Comes Back To You
9. Make No Mistake
10. Ain't Talkin Bout No One
11. Tracks Of Danger

III. Combat Alley (Perris Records 2003, CD)
1. Get Up
2. Mark Of The Rocker
3. Love's Out Of Season
4. Combat Alley
5. Getaway
6. Take It If You Want It
7. Love Or Money
8. You're Gonna Love It
9. The Kid Gets Around
10. Nothing Ever Last Forever
11. Back Out In The Heat
12. Young And Proud

Comments: Hard Knox was a better-than-average hard rock/nerf metal band that started out in the early 1980s in Knoxville (Hard *Knox*, geddit?), moved to Fort Lauderdale, back to Knoxville, and finally landed in Nashville. Whew!

They quickly came to dominate the local hard rock scene, such as it was at the time, and after releasing two albums on their own L.I.F.E.R. label (try and find those suckers!) they hooked up with the odd little Texas-based Perris Records, home to such under-the-radar fellow travelers as…ahem, **Every Mother's Nightmare**. The *Combat Alley* CD includes the band's first vinyl album, along with a handful of demo tracks.

IV. Mark Of The Rocker (The Collector's Edition) (Fly Brothers Ent. 2007, CD)

Disc 1
1. Get Up!
2. Mark Of The Rocker
3. Love's Out Of Season
4. Combat Alley
5. Getaway
6. Take It If You Want It
7. Love Or Money
8. You're Gonna Love It
9. The Kid Gets Around
10. Nothing Ever Last Forever
11. Back Out In The Heat
12. Young And Proud
13. It's Your Turn
14. Thin Ice
15. Get Up [Demo Version]
16. Showin' That Love [1983]
17. Locked Inside
18. Don't Let It Tear You Down
19. Set You Free

Disc 2
1. First Things First
2. Bad Noise
3. Cities Web
4. Ain't No Saint
5. Too Far Gone
6. Blind Me With Your Love
7. Always Ends The Same
8. All Comes Back To You
9. Make No Mistake
10. Ain't Talkin' Bout No One
11. Tracks Of Danger

Comments: Another impossible-to-find Hard Knox compilation (or is it a wildly expanded version of the *Mark Of The Rocker* LP?) reprises the band's first two albums, and loads in a bunch of demo tracks across two CDs. Still, the relative unavailability of this set kinda renders the point moot. If you're going to put out something like this, more power to ya, but it helps if it stays in print more than, say, five minutes. When searching high and low on the 'net for these guys, *Combat Alley* is still the only Hard Knox disc I could find (and actually spend money on).

JAMIE HARTFORD

Comments: Contributed the song "Hard Hard World" to *Spin Cycle*, the 1997 NEA Extravaganza compilation CD. Also contributed the song "Good Things Happen (When You're Around)" to *The Ex-Files* 1998 NEA Extravaganza comp CD.

WARREN HAYNES

Band Members:
Warren Haynes (vocals, guitar) (I)

Other Musicians:
Greg Morrow (drums) (I)
Johnny Neel (keyboards) (I)
Michael Rhodes (bass) (I)

Warren Haynes Recordings:

I. Tales Of Ordinary Madness (Megaforce 1993, CD)
1. Fire In The Kitchen
2. Kiss Tomorrow Good-Bye
3. Movers And Shakers

The Hard Corps

4. I'll Be The One
5. Blue Radio
6. Invisible
7. Sister Justice
8. Angel City
9. Tattoos And Cigarettes
10. Power And The Glory
11. Broken Promised Land

Comments: I dunno if Haynes was living in Nashville at the time of this album's release or not, but he'd certainly paid his dues, first as a member of **Blues Co-Op** and later touring with notorious country outlaw David Allen Coe (one of my fave redneck musicians). Haynes' debut album, *Tales Of Ordinary Madness* was named after a collection of Charles Bukowski verse (my fave drunken boho poet) and featured a similar slash-and-burn, guitar-driven blues-n-hard-rock sound as Haynes' Gov't Mule band. Recorded in Atlanta with a bunch of locals, I've only listed the core band members here for brevity's sake. Haynes is, perhaps, best known these days as guitarist for the Allman Brothers Band and, as of the summer of 2009, is touring with the reformed Grateful Dead.

HAYSTAK

Band Members:
Haystak (vocals) (I-VII)
Kevin "DJ Dev" Grisham (turntables) (I-IV)

Other Musicians:
Dale Babb (vocals, guitar) (III-VI)
Charlie Barrett (guitar) (II)
Dave Davidson (strings) (II, III)
Tim Hill (keyboards) (V, VI)
Andrew Ramsey (guitar, bass) (II, III)
Shannon Sanders (vocals, horns) (I-III, V)

Haystak Recordings:

I. Mak Million (Street Flavor 1998, CD)
1. Intro
2. Go 2 War
3. Flossin'
4. Came Along Way
5. Down Yonder
6. Yeah
7. M-O-N-E-Y
8. So Dope
9. S.S. Big Pimp
10. Don't Want It
11. Ballin'
12. Desperado
13. World Wide
14. A Self-Made Man
15. Strugglin' Strivin'

Comments: Nashville had a healthy and growing hip hop scene long before Young Buck put "Cashville" on the national rap map. Big white rapper "Haystak Mak Million" (Jason Winfree), as he was known on the streets of the west side, was going to be Nashville's own Eminem, or possibly our Bubba Sparxx. Signed to Sonny Paradise's Street Flavor Records, Mak Million was produced by Paradise and Street Flavor's Kevin "DJ Dev" Grisham.

II. Car Fulla White Boys (Street Flavor/Koch Records 2000, CD)
1. Car Fulla White Boys
2. Reckon
3. Can't Tell Me Nothing
4. Dollar
5. Down South Players
6. Ride
7. Brother Like Me
8. On Trial
9. Need It Get It
10. Wish You Could See Me
11. Some of That
12. The Bottom
13. Love You Like
14. Listen

Comments: For his second album, Haystak dropped the "Mak Million" from his name and went full-tilt with a solid album of country-flavored, street-smart rhymes. Without the benefit of a recognizable novelty hit, like his friend Bubba Sparxx, Haystak wasn't going to break through to the mainstream, but *Car Fulla White Boys* sold well enough and won enough critical acclaim to get picked up and reissued on a national basis by Koch, one of the biggest players in the rap major leagues.

III. The Natural (Street Flavor/Koch Records 2002, CD)
1. Intro
2. White Boy
3. In Here
4. Dirty Dirty
5. You Got Money
6. Different Kinda Lady
7. Cool People
8. Bangin'
9. Tonight's the Night
10. Pit Bull Skit
11. Killa Man Crew
12. Fucked Up
13. Life With No Crime
14. We Get Them
15. Run Hide Duck
16. Aint Talkin' Bout' Nothin'
17. You Can't Stop It
18. Oh My God

Comments: Haystak's third album, and second for big boys Koch Records, offers more of the same…that is, po' country boy raps with a little urban zeal. By this time the limitations of Street Flavor's production duo Sonny Paradise and Kevin Grisham were quite evident. Haystak could have benefitted from more visionary production to increase his national profile. Fellow "Crazy White Boy" Bubba Sparxx added guest vocals on "Oh My God."

IV. Return of the Mak Million (Street Flavor 2002, CD)
1. First Song
2. Tote Me 2 Tha Hole
3. Monster
4. Big Boy Sh#T
5. All Alone
6. Crushed Pillow Seats
7. Come On
8. Round and Round
9. Keep Tha Lights On
10. Flamboyent
11. Back That F**k Up Off Me
12. I
13. Way's Gonna Be
14. I Fo Tha Players

Comments: By this time, the "white boy" rap craze had passed its sell-by date and Koch had dropped Haystak from its ever-revolving roster of artists. The Street Flavor machine continued to roll, however, kicking out yet another Haystak CD (probably to sell from car trunks all over Nashville, Memphis, and Atlanta).

Warren Haynes

HAYSTAK

V. Portrait Of A White Boy (40 West 2004, CD)
1. Intro
2. Fight, Write, Die
3. Dadgummit
4. Broads & Alcohol
5. Red Light
6. Hustle & Flow
7. Still You Doubted Me
8. Off Tha Wall
9. Girl
10. My First Day
11. Make Money
12. Strangest Dreams
13. Big
14. Staks World
15. Safety Off
16. First White Boy
17. Done

Comments: The first album of the "white boy" trilogy. Considering the involvement of Sonny Paradise in everything from songwriting and the publishing to album production, 40 West Records is evidently a Street Flavor label, the company benefiting from its distribution deal with Select-O-Hits of Memphis, a powerhouse in the rap world that spins records out to urban retailers across the country.

VI. From Start To Finish (40 West 2005, CD)
1. Big Ass Whiteboy
2. We Roll
3. I Ain't No Pin-Up
4. All by Myself
5. Boo Hoo Hoo

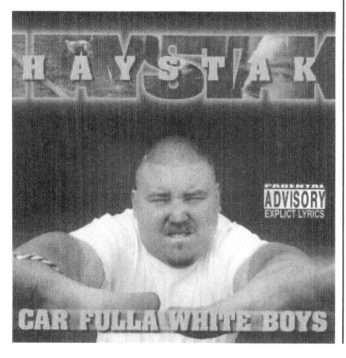

6. Keep It Southern
7. Bonnie and Clyde
8. Kick They Back In
9. Bang Bang
10. U Hard
11. My Friend
12. Whiteboy
13. Mama
14. Be Strong
15. Rollin' with Me
16. Middle of Nowhere

Comments: Part two of the "white boy" trilogy. Haystak had a small but acclaimed role in Craig Brewer's award-winning Memphis film *Hustle & Flow*.

VII. Crackavelli (40 West 2007, CD)

Disc One
1. Intro
2. Crackavelli
3. I'm Haystak
4. Bounce Through Ya Block
5. Trouble Man
6. Make You Fly
7. Track 7
8. Boss Status
9. Kindness for Weakness
10. Reloaded
11. You Soft
12. Baked
13. Fall Through the Club
14. Freak Show Skit
15. Freak Show

Disc Two
16. Welcome to Nashville
17. Nashville
18. Angels
19. My Lyrics
20. Drive
21. Excess Weight
22. Let's Ride
23. Pray for Me
24. Nothing Is Wrong
25. Respect
26. Special Kinda Girl
27. Sail On
28. Rap Money
29. Change
30. Pale Face

Comments: The third and final part of the "white boy" trilogy. You have to give ol' 'stak credit, cuz the "Crazy White Boy" is still bangin' and rhymin' almost a decade later, regardless of whether or not anybody still cares. With *Crackavelli*, an ambitious two-CD set, Haystak tries to channel his inner Tupac (or maybe Biggie).

Truth is, the man must be selling *some* CDs 'cause in a genre where the life expectancy of the average artist is half as long as Haystak has stuck around, the fact that the rapper has released seven full-length CDs puts him in impressive company. Aside from his continued solo work, Haystak has now hooked up with two other white boy rappers in the trio Paleface.

HEGE V

Band Members:
Hege V a/k/a George Hamilton V (vocals, guitar) (I)
David Thrower (guitar, pedal steel) (I)
Tim Harper (bass, vocals) (I)
Rob Ragsdale (drums) (I)

Hege V Recordings:

I. House of Tears (MTM Music Group 1987, LP)
Side 1
1. House of Tears
2. Silent Stare
3. Matter of Fact
4. Burial Ground of the Broken Hearted
5. Gone, Gone, Gone
6. Hard Way (You'll Learn the)

Side 2
7. My Decline
8. She Says
9. Grass Grows Greener
10. Ghost Town
11. She Ain't Comin' (Back No More)

Comment: Hege V was, in reality, George Hamilton V, namesake son of the country singer and Grand Ole Opry star. *House of Tears*, produced by North Carolina pop-rock genius Mitch Easter (Let's Active) falls into the melodic rock category, the younger Hamilton rebelling, in a way, against his father's trad-country roots. One of the few rock-oriented discs released by Music Row newcomers MTM (better known as a TV production company), Hege V was hamstrung by the fledgling label's feeble attempts at promotion.

HEYPENNY

Band Members:
Kevin Bevil (guitar) (I)
DJ Murphy (bass) (I)
Benjamin Elkins (keyboards) (I)
Ryan Rayborn (drums) (I)

Heypenny Recordings:

I. Use These Spoons (self-produced CD, 2006)
1. Dooley
2. Parade
3. Seem So Small
4. Let It Rain
5. Everything Is Brighter
6. Brave
7. Secreterror
8. Walnut St. Bridge
9. Radio
10. Reprise

JOHN HIATT
Web: www.thejohnhiattarchives.com

Band Members:
John Hiatt (vocals, guitar, mandolin, piano) (I-XIII)

Other Musicians:
Ken Blevins (drums) (I, VIII, IX, XIII)
Ashley Cleveland (backing vocals) (I, II)
Luther Dickinson (guitar) (X, XIII)
Cody Dickinson (drums) (X)
Pat Donaldson (bass) (II)
Davey Faragher (bass, vocals) (IV, V, VI, VII, XI, XII)
Gary Ferguson (drums, percussion) (VI)
Mac Gayden (slide guitar) (II)
Lisa Haley (violin) (V)
Michael Henderson (guitar) (II)
Ritchie Heyward (drums) (II)
Peter Holsapple (keyboards) (VI)

JOHN HIATT

David Hood (bass) (X)
David Immergluck (guitar, mandolin, pedal steel) (V, VI, VII)
Ethan Johns (guitar, mandolin) (II)
Jay Joyce (guitar, keyboards) (VIII)
David Kemper (drums) (II)
Bobby Keys (sax) (IX)
Michael Landau (guitar) (II)
Sonny Landreth (guitars) (I, VIII, IX)
Chuck Leavell (keyboards) (II)
Dennis Locorriere (backing vocals) (I, III)
Brian MacLeod (drums) (III)
Julie Miller (backing vocals) (VIII)
Patrick O'Hearn (bass) (XIII)
Bill Payne (keyboards, synth) (II)
John Pierce (bass) (III)
Michael Porter (drums) (II)
David Ranson (bass) (I, VIII, IX)
Benmont Tench (piano) (V)
Efrain Toro (percussion) (VI)
Michael Urbano (drums, percussion) (IV-VI, XI, XII)
Michael Ward (guitar) (III, IV, XI, XII)
Matt Wallace (guitar) (III)

John Hiatt Recordings:

I. Slow Turning (A&M Records 1988, CD)
1. Drive South
2. Trudy and Dave
3. Tennessee Plates
4. Icy Blue Heart
5. Sometime Other Than Now
6. Georgia Rae
7. Ride Along
8. Slow Turning
9. It'll Come To You

10. Is Anybody There
11. Paper Thin
12. Feels Like Rain

Comments: John Hiatt originally came to Nashville around 1970, scoring a publishing deal with Tree and landing hit songs with artists like Conway Twitty and Three Dog Night. On the strength of his songwriting skills, he grabbed a deal with Epic Records, which released his 1974 album *Hangin' Around The Observatory*. Hiatt followed the next year with *Overcoats* (neither of which I've covered here), but when neither album sold particularly well, he was dropped by the label, and subsequently lost his publishing deal.

Disenchanted, Hiatt moved out to L.A. just in time to be branded as an edgy, new wavy styled angry young man (a la Elvis Costello or Joe Jackson). Hiatt would release several albums for MCA Records and Geffen, finding a modicum of success, and would return to Nashville sometime in the late 1980s/early 1990s after battling alcohol and tragedy. Not sure when Hiatt landed back in the Music City, but I'm going to include *Slow Turning* in his local discography anyway, if only for the wonderful "Tennessee Plates."

II. Stolen Moments (A&M Records 1990, CD)
1. Real Fine Love
2. Seven Little Indians
3. Child Of The Wild Blue Yonder
4. Back Of My Mind
5. Stolen Moments
6. Bring Back Your Love To Me
7. The Rest of the Dream
8. Thirty Years of Tears
9. Rock Back Billy
10. Listening To Old Voices
11. Through Your Hands
12. One Kiss

Comments: Hiatt's songs have been covered by everybody from Dylan to Iggy, but his own commercial fortunes have never matched the success afforded his songwriting skills. Still, *Stolen Moments* was his best-selling album to date, inching up to #61 on the *Billboard* Top 200 chart.

III. Perfectly Good Guitar (A&M Records 1993, CD)
1. Something Wild
2. Straight Outta Time
3. Perfectly Good Guitar
4. Buffalo River Home
5. Angel
6. Blue Telescope
7. Cross My Fingers
8. Old Habits
9. The Wreck of the Barbie Ferrari
10. When You Hold Me Tight

11. Permanent Hurt
12. Loving A Hurricane
13. I'll Never Get Over You

Comments: For ***Perfectly Good Guitar***, Hiatt enlisted the help of producer Matt Wallace (Faith No More) to craft a younger, more energetic sound with the help of players like Michael Ward (School of Fish) and Brian McLeod (Wire Train). It must have helped, 'cause the album rose to #47 on the *Billboard* Top 200 chart.

IV. Hiatt Comes Alive At Budokan? (A&M Records 1994, CD)
1. Through Your Hands
2. Real Fine Love
3. Memphis In The Meantime
4. Icy Blue Heart
5. Paper Thing
6. Angel Eyes
7. Your Dad Did
8. Have A Little Faith In Me
9. Drive South
10. Thing Called Love
11. Perfectly Good Guitar
12. Feels Like Rain
13. Tennessee Plates
14. Lipstick Sunset
15. Slow Turning

Comments: Once again working with producer Matt Wallace, ***Hiatt Comes Alive At Budokan?*** – the title is a joke – ended Hiatt's run with A&M. The disc provides a finely-detailed snapshot of the previous six years, including live versions of some of Hiatt's best songs. The material is taken from several separate performances; Ward, Fargher and Urbano were called "The Guilty Dogs" for this tour.

V. Walk On (Capitol Records 1995, CD)
1. Cry Love
2. You Must Go
3. Walk On
4. Good As She Could Be
5. The River Knows Your Name
6. Native Son
7. Dust Down A Country Road
8. Ethylene
9. I Can't Wait
10. Shredding The Document
11. Wrote It Down And Burned It
12. Your Love Is My Rest
13. Friend Of Mine
14. Mile High (Thundering Through Pattenburgh)

Comments: Capitol's Gary Gersh, fresh in his position as label boss, was happy to have "stolen" Hiatt away from A&M and invested a fair amount of resources in creating and

promoting ***Walk On***. Bonnie Raitt dropped by to add vocals to a song, and Nashville's Mark Nevers helped engineer track eleven, recorded at The Castle studios in Franklin; rose to #48 on the *Billboard* Top 200 chart.

VI. Little Head (Capitol Records 1997, CD)
1. Little Head
2. Pirate Radio
3. My Sweet Girl
4. Feelin' Again
5. Graduated
6. Sure Pinocchio
7. Runaway
8. Woman Sawed In Half
9. Far As We Go
10. After All This Time

Comments: In contrast, by the time of ***Little Head***, Gersh was already on his way out at Capitol and little or no support was offered Hiatt for the album. Immergluck, Faragher, and Ferguson were called "The Nashville Queens" for this album; Tower of Power provided the horns. It all proved to be too little, too late as the rare mediocre album in Hiatt's extensive catalog peaked at a feeble #111 on the *Billboard* Top 200.

VII. Crossing Muddy Waters (Vanguard 2000, CD)
1. Lincoln Town
2. Crossing Muddy Waters
3. What Do We Do Now
4. Only The Song Survives
5. Lift Up Every Stone
6. Take It Down
7. Gone

8. Take It Back
9. Mr. Stanley
10. God's Golden Eyes
11. Before I Go

Comments: An acoustic album released through Vanguard, ***Crossing Muddy Waters*** was also licensed to eMusic for exclusive digital downloads. Hiatt was one of the first frontier major label artists to release an album digitally (a couple of years before anybody had even heard of iTunes). Didn't fare well on the pop charts, rising only to #110 on the *Billboard* Top 200 chart, but the blues community embraced the album's gritty, soul-blues-rock hybrid and pushed it up to #2 on the Top Blues Albums chart.

VIII. The Tiki Bar Is Open (Vanguard Records 2001, CD)
1. Everybody Went Low
2. Hangin' Round Here
3. All The Lilacs In Ohio
4. My Old Friend
5. I Know A Place
6. Something Broken
7. Rock Of Your Love
8. I'll Never Get Over You
9. The Tiki Bar Is Open
10. Come Home To You
11. Farther Stars

Comments: Hiatt is reunited with Sonny Landreth and the Goners for his first pure Nashville album. Mostly recorded at Woodland Studio and Jim Lightman's New Reflections Studio, ***The Tiki Bar Is Open*** was produced by **Jay Joyce**. The album performed better than his last two or three,

commercially, but not enough for the fickle Vanguard to keep Hiatt on the payroll.

IX. Beneath This Gruff Exterior (New West Records 2003, CD)
1. Uncommon Connection
2. How Bad's The Coffee
3. Nagging Dark
4. My Baby Blue
5. My Dog And Me
6. Almost Fed Up With The Blues
7. Circle Back
8. Window On The World
9. Missing Pieces
10. Fly Back Home
11. The Last Time
12. The Most Unoriginal Sin

Comments: Another new label, this time Hiatt landing at New West Records, perhaps the best-suited of all of his past suitors at understanding his unique mix of rock, country, blues, and soul. Recorded with the Goners at Blackbird Studios in Berry Hill (Nashville), this is really a showcase for Hiatt's songwriting and Sonny Landreth's inspired fretwork. Performed admirably, really, inching up to #73 on the *Billboard* Top 200 chart at a time when other artists are dropping off entirely. Why is this? Well, my theory is that while other artists are selling fewer CDs, and there are a lot fewer discs being sold overall, Hiatt's relative stability and loyal fan base still buys the same numbers of every new Hiatt album…or something like that, I guess.

X. Master Of Disaster (New West Records 2005, CD)
1. Master Of Disaster
2. Howlin' Down The Cumberland
3. Thunderbird
4. Wintertime Blues
5. When My Love Crosses Over
6. Love's Not Where We Though We Left It
7. Ain't Ever Goin' Back
8. Cold River
9. Find You At Last
10. Old School
11. Back On The Corner

Comments: Hiatt has always had at least one foot in the Stax soul sound, so it should have come as no surprise when he drove three hours west down I-40 to record ***Master Of Disaster*** in Memphis. Working with famed producer Jim Dickinson at Ardent Studio 'C', Hiatt captured on tape one of his most high-flying and boisterous albums to date.

For his backing band this time, Hiatt works with the

John Hiatt, continued on page 231...

CD REVIEW: JOHN HIATT'S BENEATH THIS GRUFF EXTERIOR

JOHN HIATT
Beneath This Gruff Exterior
(New West Records)

As a recording artist, John Hiatt has never achieved much more than cult status. He has never sold a lot of records; certainly not as many as other artists have recording Hiatt's songs. Over the course of almost thirty years, however, Hiatt has forged a career of quiet excellence, creating nearly twenty consistently solid albums and writing hundreds of remarkable songs that lesser talents will be recording for decades to come. Entering his fourth decade of writing and performing, Hiatt epitomizes the spirit of rock & roll, and if he never makes the Rock & Roll Hall Of Fame, it will be that institution's loss.

Hiatt's **Beneath This Gruff Exterior** is another fine effort on the part of the underrated songwriter and his top-notch band the Goners. For those unfamiliar with Hiatt's creative "modus operandi," he pens literate songs that are peopled with brilliant characters – losers and lovers, the lost and the redeemed. Hiatt's rough, soulful vocals are kind of like a frayed blanket, scratchy and worn but warm and familiar. The music is a mix of roots rock, Memphis soul, Delta blues, country and folk, which is why Hiatt's material lends itself so well to various interpretations. **Beneath This Gruff Exterior** showcases both Hiatt's songwriting skills and the road-worn chemistry of the Goners. Hiatt is not a bad guitarist, but he smartly steps aside and lets maestro Sonny Landreth fill his songs with whiplash slide work and a hint of bayou swamp-rock instrumental gumbo. The seasoned rhythm section of bassist Dave Ranson and drummer Kenneth Bevins keep an admirable beat beneath the festivities so that the magician Hiatt can weave his lyrical tales.

The radio-ready "The Nagging Dark" rolls along like the runaway hearts of the song's characters while "Circle Back" remembers the fleeting nature of friendships and family and the passage of time. "Almost Fed Up With The Blues," fueled by Landreth's red-hot picking, is a brilliant anti-blues blues song, the protagonist sick and tired of being sick and tired. Hiatt's imagery on "The Most Unoriginal Sin" is nearly the equal of vintage Dylan, Landreth's shimmering fretwork creating an eerie atmosphere behind Hiatt's somber vocals, the song's star-crossed lover doomed before the first chorus strikes. **Beneath This Gruff Exterior** may not be the hall-of-fame caliber talent's best album, but it doesn't fall far from the top. – *The View On Pop Culture*, 2001

CD REVIEW: JOHN HIATT'S HIATT COMES ALIVE AT BUDOKAN?

JOHN HIATT & THE GUILTY DOGS
Hiatt Comes Alive At Budokan?
(A & M Records)

John Hiatt has created a lengthy and prosperous career out of outliving other people's expectations. Originally labeled as a young punk in the vein of Elvis Costello or Joe Jackson, way back in the mid-1970s, Hiatt outlived that albatross only to be pigeonholed as a singer/songwriter. Several country hits penned for other artists threatened to stereotype this talented artist as a Music Row songmeister; a trio of brilliant albums in the late 1980s/early 1990s served to revitalize Hiatt's career and send him along the road to stardom.

Unsatisfied, Hiatt threw critics another curve, recording an uncompromising rock & roll record – *Perfectly Good Guitar* – with a bunch of young alternative types. When will they get it into their heads that Hiatt is one of those rare originals that can't be categorized. Hiatt loves the music, genres be damned.

Having more fun that he probably ever has, Hiatt now kicks out this set of fifteen cuts, *Hiatt Comes Alive At Budokan?*, softly spoofing a trend towards live albums with the Budokan label on them that were hot shit when he first hit the scene. Recorded at a series of dates last spring (none of them in Japan), this collection is a fine representation of Hiatt's dynamic live performances. Culled from shows performed at venues as diverse and different as clubs, theaters, racetracks and auditoriums, *Hiatt Comes Alive At Budokan?* showcases Hiatt's extraordinary songwriting skills on tracks like "Icy Blue Heart," "Angel Eyes," "Have A Little Faith In Me," "Tennessee Plates," and my personal fave, the rocking "Perfectly Good Guitar."

Hiatt is a soulful vocalist, pouring his heart into each cut, wrapping each song with great emotion and electricity. Regardless of the size of the forum, Hiatt's delivery is warm and personal; the backing band, The Guilty Dogs, a solid set of professionals following Hiatt's lead. *Hiatt Comes Alive At Budokan?* is not a "big sound" live disc like so many bands offer, instead it is a more subtle experience, one that plays to your heart and your mind rather than bludgeoning one into unconsciousness. In the marketplace of trends, this set may be overlooked; Hiatt transcends time, however, and cannot be refused his due.
– R.A.D! (Review & Discussion of Rock & Roll) December 1995

John Hiatt, continued...
Dickinson brothers – 2/3 of the North Mississippi All-Stars – and legendary Muscle Shoals session player David Hood. Some 31 years after launching his career, John Hiatt is still trying to bring a fresh edge to his sound and, unlike many of his peers, he doesn't seem adverse to trying new ideas.

XI. Live From Austin, Texas (New West 2005, CD & DVD)
1. Icy Blue Heart
2. Loving A Hurricane
3. When You Hold Me Tight
4. Your Dad Did
5. Straight Outta Time
6. Memphis In The Meantime
7. Something Wild
8. Have A Little Faith In Me
9. Buffalo River Home
10. Thing Called Love
11. Angel
12. Tennessee Plates
13. Slow Turning
14. Perfectly Good Guitar

Comments: Live disc documents Hiatt's December 14, 1993 appearance on public television's critically-acclaimed *Austin City Limits* program. Recorded during the tour for ***Perfectly Good Guitar*** with Ward, Fargher, and Urbano as his backing band; this tour was also documented by the 1994 ***Hiatt Comes Alive At Budokan?*** album. Part of New West's "Live From Austin, Texas" series, the DVD is the same as the CD.

XII. Live At The Hiatt (Hip-O-Select/A&M Records 2006, CD)
1. Through Your Hands
2. Child of the Wild Blue Yonder
3. Loving A Hurricane
4. When You Hold Me Tight
5. I Don't Even Try
6. Feels Like Rain
7. Something Wild
8. Perfectly Good Guitar
9. Slow Turning
10. Lipstick Sunset

Comments: Originally released in 1993 as a promo-only CD by A&M Records to hype Hiatt's ***Perfectly Good Guitar*** album, subsequently given wide release in 2006 to clean out the vaults and make a buck that Hiatt will probably never see a penny of during the rest of his career. Recorded live at The Forum, London England on December 30, 1993 with the Guilty Dogs (Ward, Faragher and Urbano) as his backing band, ostensibly the third live album culled from the same set of songs.

XIII. Same Old Man (New West Records 2008, CD)
1. Old Days

2. Love You Again
3. On with You
4. Hurt My Baby
5. What Love Can Do
6. Ride My Pony
7. Cherry Red
8. Our Time
9. Two Hearts
10. Same Old Man
11. Let's Give This Love a Try

Comments: Hiatt's latest is another solid album, the artist still managing to find interesting ways to view the world in song after eighteen albums (and counting)…

Another View: "John Hiatt's *Same Old Man* opens with the song "Old Days," in which he tells tales of life on the road, sharing stages with several aging legends of the blues, and given the grainy drawl of his vocal on the track, one can be forgiven for thinking Hiatt has begun to turn into one of the grizzled old men he's singing about. But most of the tunes on Hiatt's 18th studio album find him in considerably stronger and more nimble voice, even though the blessings and trials of maturity are a recurring theme in these 11 songs."
– Mark Deming, *All Music Guide*

HIGHSTRUNG

Band Members:
Dick Moss (vocals, guitar) (A1)
Dean Guling (bass, vocals) (A1)
Harry Mcnutt (guitar) (A1)
Oliver Klozoff (drums, vocals) (A1)

Highstrung, continued on page 233...

BOOTLEG CD REVIEW: JOHN HIATT'S 'HIATTLOGY'

JOHN HIATT
Hiattlogy
(Tendolar #TDR-116, 71:42) [bootleg CD]

SOUND QUALITY: Tracks 1-10 are a very good soundboard recording offering crisp vocals and instrumentation with volume dropping a bit across tracks nine and ten. Tracks 11 & 12 are a very good audience recording with a slight bit of hollowness, overly bright vocals and editing dropouts between songs.

COMMENTS: John Hiatt definitely falls into the category of "one of the best artists that you've never heard." The consummate songwriter and a perennial critics' favorite, Hiatt's checkered career has seen him jump from label to label in search of some degree of security and commercial success. Along the way, he's made over a dozen albums for almost half a dozen labels, created some great music, some music that was good but not great, and excelled musically in genres ranging from folk-oriented singer/songwriter material to angry "new wave" rave-ups to soulful, blues-infused rock.

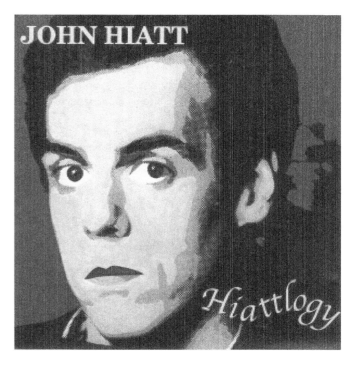

Even if you're unfamiliar with Hiatt as an artist, chances are that you've heard some of his work nonetheless – performers as stylistically diverse as Bob Dylan, Bonnie Raitt, the Neville Brothers, Iggy Pop and a slew of country types have recorded Hiatt songs, some with great chart success. Nevertheless, Hiatt remains somewhat of an obscurity, a talented and charismatic artist whose best efforts tend to bubble just under the mainstream. As such, *Hiattlogy* is one of a rare breed – a John Hiatt bootleg – of which only a handful are known to exist. The disc features a performance from what is generally considered to be the commercial and critical peak of Hiatt's career, the three-year period circa 1987-1989 that surrounds the release of his *Bring The Family* and *Slow Turning* albums.

A fine soundboard recording from a January 1989 performance in Ottawa, Canada, the entire set showcased by *Hiattlogy* is drawn from the two aforementioned albums. Hiatt's faithful legions of fans know this material like the back of their hands and it does, indeed, represent some of his best songs. Hiatt toured with the Goners during this period and this performance featuring the wonderful slide guitar of Sonny Landreth. All the material here is solid, but some songs stand out: "Memphis In The Meantime" is given a soulful, extended rendition while "Tennessee Plates" offers some particularly tasty riffage courtesy of Mr. Landreth. "Drive South" is pretty lively and "Thing Called Love," a breakthrough hit for Bonnie Raitt, is performed here with heart, though less sass than Raitt's version. Whoever edited this disc left in Hiatt's comments and intro, which adds to the listening experience.

The final four songs on *Hiattlogy* are listed as from a December 1989 performance in Germany and feature guest stars Nick Lowe and Paul Carrack. Provided Hiatt's onstage comments and given that the material is taken entirely from an earlier Hiatt album, *Riding With The King*, that was made with Lowe and Carrack, these songs are probably taken instead from a 1984 or '85 performance. The four songs are good, but the true appeal of *Hiattology* lies in the Ottawa material. For those unfamiliar with Hiatt, this collection is a good way to discover his talents. – *Live! Music Review, 1999*

Highstrung, continued...

Highstrung Recordings:

A1. Highstrung EP (House O' Pain 7" vinyl)
<u>Fecal Side</u>
1. Valerie 23
2. Pee Packs & Crapsacks

<u>Matter Side</u>
3. Average Middle Class American
4. Scabs
5. Throw It Away

HIGHWATER

Band Members:
Lewis Stubbs (guitar) (I)
Nick Govrik (bass, vocals) (I)
Chad Abel (keyboards, vocals) (I)
Angelo Merendino (drums) (I)

Highwater Recordings:

I. Second-Hand Suit (Del Rio Records 1998, CD)
1. Lose Your Mind
2. Play Me A Beat She Can Understand
3. Ready To Go
4. High Maintenance Broad
5. $100 Bill
6. High On A Hilltop
7. Meat & Three
8. Anytime (Me & My Baby)
9. Kinetic Tonite
10. Baby's Gonna Be Home Soon
11. Dancin' With Lulu

J.D. HINTON BAND

Band Members:
J.D. Hinton (vocals)
David Weyand (guitars)
Jason Dunaway (bass)
Rich Wayland (keyboards)
Craig Riches (drums)

Comments: Literal pick-up band put together when Hinton entered the Marlboro Talent Round-Up (1990) and, after one night's practice, walked off with the semi-finals win (and pocketed $7,500 and a spot in the national contest). Don't know anything else 'bout 'em and don't know how far they went, but I suspect they didn't do too much more...

HOCUS POCUS

Band Members:
Mike Easlo (vocals, keyboards)
Ken Kennedy (guitar)
Kurt Menck (guitar)
Mike Farris (bass)
John Uhlinger (drums)

Comments: Hocus Pocus was probably Nashville's best-known heavy metal band back in the day. Formed by Kennedy as **Lust** in 1979, that band eventually evolved into Hocus Pocus. Don't know if they released anything under the Hocus Pocus name as a band other than the song "Rock In Music City" from the NEA's *What You Haven't Heard...* CD compilation.

WARNER HODGES

Band Members:
Warner Hodges (vocals, guitars) (I)
Dan Baird (guitars, vocals) (I)
Al Collins (bass) (I)
Stacie Collins (harmonica, vocals) (I)
Fenner Castner (drums, vocals) (I)

Warner Hodges Recordings:

I. Centerline (Jerkin' Crocus 2008, import CD)
1. Gimme, Gimme
2. Whole Lotta Fun
3. Branded Man
4. Hell To Pay

5. I Love You, Baby
6. Time Marches On
7. How It's Gonna Be
8. Air That I Breath
9. She's Tuff
10. Harvest Moon

Comments: Erstwhile **Jason & the Scorchers** guitarist Warner Hodges steps out with his first solo album, and to quote one of his songs, it's a "whole lotta fun!" With a supporting cast that includes Scorchers' drummer Fenner Castner, underrated guitarist and bandleader-in-his-own-right **Dan Baird**, and bassist Al Collins along with the angelic voice that is his wife **Stacie Collins**, Hodges cranks-and-spanks his way through a collection of original songs; a cool Merle Haggard cover; the prerequisite Tommy Womack co-write and, yes, a Scorchers' song by **Jason Ringenberg**. Released by British rock label Jerkin' Crocus because, presumably, American labels are all hearing impaired.

WILL HOGE

Web: www.willhoge.com

Band Members:
Will Hoge (vocals, guitar, harmonica) (I-X)

Other Musicians:
Dan Baird (guitar, vocals) (I, II, X)
Pat Buchanan (guitar) (VII, X)
Sigurdur Birkis (drums) (VII, IX, X)
Chris Carmichael (strings) (VII, X)
Ken Coomer (percussion) (VII, X)
Jefferson Crow (keyboards) (VII, IX, X)
Pete Finney (pedal steel) (X)
Adam Fluhrer (guitar, vocals) (IX, X)

Audley Freed (guitar) (VII)
Doy Gardner (drums) (V, VII)
Steve Hinson (lap steel) (X)
Scotty Huff (horns) (X)
Rami Jaffee (keyboards) (X)
John W. Lancaster (keyboards) (V)
Bryan Layson (guitar, vocals) (IV, V, VII)
Tim Marks (bass) (X)
Jerry Dale McFadden (keyboards) (X)
Angela Primm (vocals) (X)
Tres Sasser (bass) (I, II, IV)
Garrison Starr (vocals) (X)
Dean Tomasek (bass) (V, VII, IX, X)
Gale West (vocals) (X)
Reese Wynans (keyboards) (X)
Kirk Yoquelet (drums, percussion) (I, II, IV)

Will Hoge Recordings:

I. All Night Long: Live At The Exit/In (self-produced CD, 2000)
1. Rock & Roll Star
2. Be Together Again
3. Ms. Williams
4. She Don't Care About Me

5. King Of Grey
6. TV Set
7. Wish
8. (I'm Pretty Sure) I'm Over You
9. All Night Long
10. Will You Still Love Me Tomorrow

Comments: Recorded live at Nashville's Exit/In club by long-time soundman Frank Sass, *All Night Long* is not listed under the discography on Hoge's web site, but is listed on Wikipedia as his independently-produced first album. No musicians are credited, but it is known that Hoge was playing with **Dan Baird** around this time.

II. Carousel (self-produced CD, 2001)
1. She Don't Care
2. Let Me Be Lonely
3. Ms. Williams
4. Your Fool
5. Heartbreak Avenue
6. Rock And Roll Star
7. Wish
8. Sweet Magdeline
9. (Pretty Sure) I'm Over You
10. Carousel

III. Almost Alone (Live At Smith's Olde Bar) (self-produced 2002, CD)
1. Let Me Be Lonely
2. Ms. Williams
3. Hey Tonight
4. Dancin' Dave And Band Intro
5. Your Fool
6. Be The One
7. Someone Else's Baby
8. She Don't Care
9. Harmonica Holder L.A. TV Blues
10. Better Off Now (That You're Gone)
11. Carousel

Comments: Acoustic CD recorded live at Smith's Olde Bar in Atlanta, Georgia.

IV. Blackbird On A Lonely Wire (Atlantic Records 2003, CD)
1. Not That Cool
2. Be The One
3. King Of Grey
4. Secondhand Heart
5. Hey Tonight
6. It's A Shame
7. Someone Else's Baby
8. TV Set
9. Better Off Now (That You're Gone)
10. Baby Girl

Will Hoge

Comments: One of Hoge's best records, and his major label debut, it was sadly underpromoted and, well, under-everything. Why the hell Atlantic signed Hoge when they obviously had absolutely no-friggin-idea of what to do with a songwriter and performer of his caliber is one of the great mystery of the ages... tho' it's not the first time that a major label has fumbled an artist's career with their juvenile and ignorant business practices.

That being said, *Blackbird On A Lonely Wire* is a great mix of melodic rockers and intelligent mid-tempo ballad-type songs, all of which possess a lot of life, a little twang, and no little energy. Atlantic could have had the next Springsteen (honest, it's that good an album), instead they dropped Hoge and got zilch in return.

V. The America EP (self-produced CD, 2004)
1. Bible vs. Gun
2. The Other Side
3. Hey Mr. President (Anyone But You)
4. The Times They Are A Changin'
5. America

Comments: Man I really love this mini-LP, which Hoge cranked out after suffering great abuse from the suits at Atlantic Records. Hoge's songwriting prescience foreshadows the late-decade financial meltdown by almost five years, and tunes like "America" and the wonderfully anti-Bush "Hey Mr. President (Anyone But You)" tackle the hard times in this land of plenty as well as the wars in Iraq *and* Afghanistan. Hoge's reading of Dylan's classic "The Times They Are A Changin'" rivals the master's for passion and energy…hell, I bought out Grimey's stash of this limited-edition EP twice and gave 'em to a bunch of friends...

VI. During The Before And After (self-produced CD, 2005)
1. Better Off Now (That You're Gone)
2. Secondhand Heart
3. Your Fool
4. Ain't No Sunshine
5. Bible Vs. Gun
6. It Doesn't Have To Be That Way
7. Ms. Williams
8. Let Me Be Lonely
9. It's A Shame
10. Not That Cool
11. She Don't Care
12. America

Comments: Live album, recorded at The Workplay Theatre in Birmingham, Alabama.

VII. The Man Who Killed Love (self-produced CD, 2006)
1. Pocket Full Of Change
2. Love From A Scar
3. Wait Til Your Daddy Gets Home

4. Woman Be Strong
5. I Got A Habit
6. The Man Who Killed Love
7. Hearts Are Gonna Roll
8. The More That I Know (The Less I Like You)
9. July Moon
10. Lover Tonight

Comments: Don't love this one as much as ***The America*** EP or ***Blackbird On A Lonely Wire*** (or even ***Carousel***)…too lackluster, too melancholy, lacking in the energy and vitality of Hoge's earlier albums. Not bad, but not as great, either….

VIII. Live In Charleston (self-produced 2006, CD)
1. Better Off Now (That You're Gone)
2. Love From A Scar
3. Sweet Magdeline
4. The Man Who Killed Love
5. Wait Til Your Daddy Gets Home
6. July Moon
7. Pocket Full Of Change
8. Hearts Are Gonna Roll
9. Southern Belle
10. She Don't Care

Comments: Limited edition live album, sold at shows.

IX. Again Somewhere Tomorrow (self-produced CD, 2007)
1. The Man Who Killed Love
2. Love From A Scar
3. Wait 'Til Your Daddy Gets Home

Will Hoge, continued on page 240...

WILL HOGE
The America EP
(self-released)

Will Hoge is cursed to be an artist of some talent in an era where talent is in little demand. Two major label releases and constant touring earned Nashville's rock & roll ambassador a small if loyal following, but did little to break him through to a mainstream audience. I don't know if Hogue's major label deal is still in place but I do know that the label did little or nothing from this scribe's perspective to promote this promising young artist.

It is no exaggeration to say that Hogue's *The America EP* is the most radical, most seditious and most courageous musical statement that will be made this year. Forget about Steve Earle's "revolution," forget about punkvoter.com and *Rock Against Bush* – the five songs offered here by Hogue are a "state of the union" address delivered straight from the American heartland. That Hogue released the disc himself is no great surprise, considering that multi-national media corporations shy away from independent thought and the sort of artistic freedom represented by *The America EP*.

In fact, Hogue did himself and his career no favor by taking a stand with these songs. After spending four years crossing the country in a van and talking to people where they played, Hogue and his band came to the conclusion that, "most hard-working Americans don't feel they have a voice." This epiphany led to the moment, says Hogue in the EP's liner notes, "that's when all of us realized that we had to make this record." In doing so, Hogue has captured everything that those of us who love rock & roll believed about the music in the first place – brash rebellion, the questioning of authority and, most importantly, championing the view of the "little guy."

"Bible Vs. Gun" kicks off *The America EP*, a letter home from a soldier caught in the middle of a battle, his religious beliefs put to the test by this ultimate example of man's inhumanity against man. In the midst of the violence, he sings, "I close my eyes and pull the trigger and kill these people I don't even know." He would gladly trade his gun for a Bible and the comfort of his faith. He asks his mother for forgiveness, praying he can still "get into heaven," but the soldier's fate is left up in the air as the song closes. Sparse instrumentation builds to a crescendo near the end, Hogue's bluesy vocals soaring above the mix.

"The Other Side" is a Springsteenesque tale of despair, an example of the extremes that people will go to when times are tight and there's no work to be found. "The Other Side" of the song holds a clever double meaning, representing both the poor man's vision of wealth and the people who enjoy "life on the other side" and the believer's faith in the afterlife. This might be the best song that Springsteen never wrote, the

protagonist a hard working man who makes one mistake, a desperate act committed in an attempt to improve his family's life. The story is told from the perspective of the man's son, who holds onto his father's dream as he sinks into his own black pool of despair. Hoge's plaintive vocals are accompanied by a martial drumbeat and gentle strings, creating a pastoral setting for an otherwise disturbing story.

The comedic "Hey Mr. President (Anyone But You)" is a roots-rock rave-up with tongue only partly in cheek. Addressed to a nameless President, Hogue points out the state of the economy, a war that is fought mainly by the poor and jobs that have gone to Mexico and concludes "anyone but you will do just fine." Name checking John Kerry, Howard Dean, even Ray Charles, the song's voice is that of dissatisfaction with the current administration.

Hogue's cover of Dylan's "The Times They Are A Changin'" is aptly chosen and timely, the singer's powerful acoustic performance sadly recalling another era and another war. Listening to it in the car the day that I bought this EP, I found Hogue's passion and commitment to the song to be energizing and inspirational, underlining the need to enact "regime change" in America.

The America EP closes with the powerful "America," an anthemic rocker with raging guitars and angry vocals. The song tells the story of an American soldier stationed in a nameless land, fighting a battle where "I'm not sure what I believe in, but I do things I can't take back." As for his mission, the soldier concludes, "Is it for freedom or oil or money/It makes no difference either way/It's just my job, I keep my head down/And hope I make it home someday."

CD REVIEW: WILL HOGE'S DRAW THE CURTAINS

The soldier returns home alive with a Purple Heart but can find no job, he's lost his family, and the nightmare of war overwhelms his attempts to sleep. "I fight these battles still waging in my head." The guitars scream and Hogue's anguished vocals cry "America, oh what can I do/America, I gave it all away for you," highlighting the sacrifices made by our men and women in uniform. It is a truly transcendent musical moment, proof that you can support our soldiers while still questioning the President's (dubious) reasons for going to war. Perhaps unconsciously, Hogue's words seem horribly prescient. Undoubtedly thousands of American soldiers will return home from Iraq during the next few years to find themselves impoverished, homeless and trying to live with the horrors that they have seen and experienced.

Hogue's *The America EP* is a minor masterpiece, perhaps the most important example of rock & roll patriotism that has ever been recorded. It's unlikely that Hogue could have released these songs under the sponsorship of a major label. *The America EP* is illustrative of the freedom and potential of taking music out of the hands of focus groups and putting it back in the hands of the artists. That few people may hear this material is beside the point and quite irrelevant. The important thing is that these songs were recorded in the first place, put out there in the world for people to discover. I salute Will Hogue for taking a stand, and you should, too. – *Alt.Culture.Guide*, 2004

WILL HOGE
Draw The Curtains
(Rykodisc)

Given the circumstances, Nashville's Will Hoge could have become just another music biz casualty. Ignorantly dropped by his major label deal after a single brilliant, shining album – *Blackbird On A Lonely Wire* – Hoge nevertheless continued to crank 'em out with alarming regularity. Studio albums, live collections for the fans, an excellent EP…better than a half-dozen, by my count, all while the artist continued to tour a couple hundred nights a year, developing a loyal fan base and finding his voice as a songwriter and performer.

Now Hoge is back playing in the major leagues, and as good as *Blackbird On A Lonely Wire* was (and continues to be a jukebox favorite 'round the Rev's home and office), Hoge's

latest effort and Rykodisc debut, *Draw The Curtains*, is hands-down an incredibly humbling collection of tunes that perfectly frame Hoge's talents as a singer *and* a songwriter. A near-perfect hybrid of streetwise rock, Memphis-styled soul and country twang, Hoge belts it out like a Beale Street busker one moment, and soars like some hard rock god of yore the next.

Draw The Curtains opens with the lovesick ballad "When I Can Afford To Lose," a gutsy move in an industry that demands up-tempo iTunes-fodder to draw in attention-deficit teens. Hoge's masterful performance here is simply amazing. Beginning with just his pleading voice and a lonely piano, Hoge amps it up with a tear-jerking, soul-stirring performance that Rev. Al Green would be proud of; if your heart isn't breaking for the singer at the end of three-minutes-plus, then there's clearly no hope for your future. Hoge follows this suburb opener with "These Were The Days," a guitar-driven rocker and another forlorn love song where the protagonist begs "give me something that I can hold onto" while desperately adding "don't let it all just get away."

There's plenty of other good stuff to hear on *Draw The Curtains* as well. The complex, textured "Silver And Gold" would sound great on the radio, a blistering, nearly-fatal cheatin' song with strikingly mournful guitarwork courtesy of Adam Fluhrer, Hoge's sharp-tongued lyrics, and Gospel-styled Hammond-bashing by guest Reese Wynans. With just Chris Carmichael's beautifully-weeping fiddle for accompaniment, Hoge stretches his rough-hewn vocals to their limits with the haunting "I'm Sorry Now," an apology, of sorts, from a man that done his woman wrong and asks, yet again, for forgiveness one more time.

"Washed By The Water" is a thinly-veiled commentary on New Orleans and the ravages of Hurricane Katrina, written from a survivor's perspective. With Wynan's elegant B3 work behind Hoge's forceful vocals, accompanied by a church-style choir and magnificent six-string work from Pat

Buchanan and Dan Baird, Hoge belts out the telling verse, "then the President came down and said things is awful sad, but ain't no words from that man gonna bring us nothing back, but in the ghosts of church bells I hear my mama say, down here we're washed by the water, the water can't wash us away." It's a powerful musical moment, delivered with heart and no little amount of passion.

Behind Pete Finney's pedal steel, Hoge delivers a magnificent tour-de-force in the album-closing "The Highway's Home," one of the top two or three "life on the road" tunes that has ever been penned by a songwriter. With brilliant language and world-weary vocals, Hoge describes himself as a "burned out junky truck stop saint" traveling down the road "with a suitcase full of empty dreams, a guitar with broken strings, a busted heart that longs to sing the blues," apologetically explaining to the love he leaves behind that he has "a mind that always leads me wrong, a head full of Hank Williams songs," concluding "I'm sorry honey, but this highway's home…." The song sums up the frustrating paradox faced by every road-worn musician and perfectly captures the endless landscape of Interstate signs, billboards and yellow lines.

The rest of **Draw The Curtains** rolls back and forth on much the same well-trodden path, Hoge delivering masterful performances of Stax-flavored lovesick soul and throwback six-string rock. Much like John Hiatt's wonderful early 1990s work, Marc Cohn's first couple of albums, and D.L. Byron's lone classic LP, Will Hoge is a romantic poet at heart, a skilled wordsmith capable of capturing complex emotions into a single phrase or verse. His lyrics are imaginative and often cut to the bone; when accompanied by his uniquely organic sound, there's simply nobody that does this kind of music better than Hoge these days. Forget about *American Idol* drones and Pitchfork-approved indie-rock clones; Will Hoge is the real deal, a rock-and-roll lifer with a hungry heart full o' soul. – *Cashville411* website, 2008

Will Hoge

Will Hoge, continued....

IX. *Again Somewhere Tomorrow* (continued)
4. Woman Be Strong
5. Bible Vs. Gun
7. Sunshine Burn
8. Someone Else's Baby
9. Rock And Roll Star
10. July Moon
11. Long Tall Sally
12. She Don't Care
13. Southern Belle
14. Lover Tonight

Comments: Recorded live at Nashville's Exit/In club in September 2006; sold through Hoge's web site and at shows. Altogether, a very professional package, from the disc's sound quality to the insert graphics. The CD provides a good selection of songs, too, ranging across the artist's many albums and presenting a diverse range of styles.

Hoge's live shows are something to see, and it speaks to the artist's commitment that when no label would touch him, he supported himself and the band by touring constantly and selling these little live gems to a (growing) appreciative audience.

X. *Draw The Curtains* (Rykodisc 2008, CD)
1. When I Can Afford To Lose
2. These Were The Days
3. Dirty Little War
4. Silver Or Gold
5. Sex, Lies And Money
6. I'm Sorry Now

7. Midnight Parade
8. Draw The Curtains
9. Washed By The Water
10. The Highway's Home

Comments: Hoge jumps back into the major label fray with the best collection of songs in his brief, albeit prolific career.

THE HOLIDAYS

Band Members:
Daniel Lusk (vocals, guitars) (I)
Johny Brian Anderson (bass, vocals) (I)
Chad Christopher (guitars) (I)
Sean McWilliams (drums, percussion, vocals) (I)
Graham Perry (keyboards, percussion, vocals) (I)

The Holidays Recordings:

I. *Hunker Down On It* (self-produced CD, 1993)
1.
2. Upside Down
3. You Do, You Don't
4. Walking Into Fire
5. Your Pleasure Is My Pain
6. Where You Been All My Life
7. Tracks
8. Break These Chains
9. Don't Say Never
10. Silent Sunshine
11. Cold Rain
12. Let It Go
13. Better Day
14. The Last Thing (I Remember)
15. Hey Whoa
16. Chicken Scratch
17.

Comments: Another one of Nashville's "here today, gone tomorrow" bands from the early 1990s, the Holidays were better than most. Three songs here were produced by **Warner Hodges**, manic axeman from **Jason & the Scorchers**. By the way, songs #1 and #17 are actually unnamed. Thought y'all would like to know that little fact.

Another View: "From the first chainsaw licks that open *Hunker Down On It* to the final ringing notes, the Holidays prove on vinyl – er, metal alloy – what fans of the Nashville band have know for years – the Holidays rock! With the release of this tasty, self-produced debut disc, the band can carry their message to the world at large. *Hunker Down On It* is a healthy combination of pop roots and raucous '70s-style rock & roll. Songs like the Southern-fried "You Do, You Don't," the gentle rocking "Your Pleasure Is My Pain" and the folkish "Break These Chains" show the band's skill at

incorporating a myriad of musical influences – from the Beatles and the Stones to Lynyrd Skynyrd or the Faces – while creating material with a distinct style and flavor."
– *Bone Music Magazine*, April 1994

HOLTZCLAW
Web: www.myspace.com/holtzclaw

Band Members:
Dober T. Pincerman (vocals) (I-V)
Supa M.C. Trickle D (guitar, vocals) (I-V)
Mark (percussion, vocals) (I-V)
Lefty Longbody (bass, vocals) (I-V)
Horatio F. Jones (vocals, percussion) (I-V)
That Damn Whore (vocals) (I-V)
Carmen D. Nominator (vocals) (I-V)
Susej (percussion, guitar) (I-V)

Holtzclaw Recordings:

I. Holtzclaw (1997, CD)

II. Double Plastic (1998, CD)

III. Greatest Hits Vol. 3 (1998, CD)

IV. Coda (1999, CD)

V. Ultimate Dance Party (Kick The Chimp Records 2003, CD)
1. Soundcheck
2. Strawberries
3. B'loney Whale
4. Pinata
5. Armed Abortion Clinic
6. Q-Tip
7. Goose Lickin' Good
8. Penguin Biscuit
9. If I Were A Kennedy
10. Cover Up My Penis
11. Heaven Or Hell
12. Holtzclaw Theme #21 & 53
13. Troy's Fanciful Kingdom
14. Ko Ko Bear
15. The Mummy
16. Green Soap
17. Albino Crotch
18. Rohypnol Girl
19. Gold, Frankincense & Myrrh
20. Richard Speck's Mantitties
21. Colorodo
22. Honest Abe
23. Sissy Izzy The Gay Elephant
24. The Sorty Of My Bling Blang
25. Serenity (The Rehab Song)

Comments: Holtzclaw's Jonathan Shockley and Travis Harmon moved from music into video in 2000, creating *The Travis And Jonathan Show* for Nashville's community access station, CATV-Channel 19. They shot only eight episodes of the satirical half-hour comedy, but video clips from the show have found new life on the Internet and attracted a cult audience. The duo have more recently achieved a degree of mainstream infamy with their Internet video series *Red State Update*, Shockley and Harmon playing Tennessee hillbillies with surprisingly erudite opinions on a wide range of subjects. *Red State Update* hit the big time when the pair were chosen to ask a question on the CNN/You Tube 2008 Democratic Presidential debate, and have since turned their redneck alter egos into something of a media sensation.

The Band's View: "Holtzclaw started as an art band/circus/monstrosity and grew from there. They played all over Nashville and Murfreesboro from '97-'99 until its inevitable self destruction. Shows typically featured nudity, fire, pyrotechs, chainsaws, piñatas, foul language, costumes, jugglers, freeform jazz, the occasional midget, drugs and alcohol and guest intros from members of the 'other' music community of Nashville. Those who saw Holtzclaw remember their experience to this day, members of Holtzclaw barely remember anything about that period of time. We had a blast, though." – Supa M.C. Trickle D

Another View: "Forget the chainsaw, the piñata, the staged audience sacrifice, and the cinematic shower of sparks and rubber snakes. What made this Murfreesboro gig by a rowdy troupe of theaterfolk-cum-art-terrorists so memorable was the oversold crowd, which stamped, hollered, heckled shouted requests, shimmied on tables, and alternated dirty dancing with fisticuffs. In short, they did exactly what an audience is supposed to do – respond to the challenge thrown down by the performer, and in turn challenge the band to kick ass that much harder." – Jim Ridley, *Nashville Scene*, 1997

HOME TOWN HEROES

Band Members:
Ann Colby (vocals)
Linda Colby (vocals)
Philip Paul (vocals)
Michael Saint-Leon (guitar)
John Snelling (keyboards)
C. J. Kowall (bass)
Bill Brewer (drummer)
Kip Ranes (drummer)

Comments: Totally unremarkable Top 40 cover band that toured the Southeast for Bobby Smith of the Let Us Entertain You booking agency. Originally known as **Phillip Paul & Patrol**, Smith recommended a merger between that band and the Colby Twins – good looking blonde twin sisters – if only to meet Paul's booking obligations. Paul left the band at the end of 1988, with the remaining members carrying on for another six months.

They're included here only because of the link between Patrol/Home Town Heroes and the **Vagrant Saints** in the form of guitarist Michael Saint-Leon and bassist C.J. Kowall, who would later join with their former Patrol bandmate Paul Snyder, forming the popular local rock band.

JAMIE HOOVER & BILL LLOYD

Band Members:
Jamie Hoover (vocals, guitar) (I)
Bill Lloyd (vocals, guitar) (I)
Dennis Diken (drums) (I)

Jamie Hoover & Bill Lloyd Recordings:

I. Paparazzi (The Paisley Pop Label 2004, CD)
1. Show & Tell The World
2. Better Left Alone
3. Screen Time
4. As You Were
5. The Buck Stops Here
6. I Can't Take It Back
7. Really Not Alone
8. Still Not Over You
9. All She Wanted
10. Walking Out
11. It Could Have Been Me
12. Fireflies

Comments: Perhaps one of the most successful musical collaborations in the power-pop realm, the mix of Jamie Hoover of North Carolina band the Spongetones and Nashville's pop genius **Bill Lloyd** proved to be sheer magic. That's Dennis Diken of the Smithereens on the cans, thus making this a power-pop trifecta!

HOPPER

Band Members:
Mike Hopper (vocals, guitars) (I)
Roger Ferguson (bass, vocals) (I)
Butch Davis (guitars, steel guitar, vocals) (I)
Mark Cudnik (drums) (I)

Other Musicians:
Gary Branchaud (bass) (I)
Paula Peterzell (vocals) (I)
Lynn Peterzell (vocals) (I)

Hopper Recordings:

I. This Is It! (self-produced CD-R, 2006)
1. This Is My Life
2. Oh What To Do About You
3. I Don't Really Care
4. Killer
5. Mix Me Up (I'm So Confused)
6. Reputation
7. Foolish Child Of God
8. It's Punk
9. Happy

10. I'm Open
11. Rammit Dammit
12. Destroy My Guitar
13. Bongo Party At Joe's Pool
14. I Only Want To Be There
15. Am I Really Here?
16. I Can't Do It For Nothing
17. Downers
18. The Public Just Eats It Up
19. Turn Around Girl
20. No Voice
21. Quits
22. Blame It On Us (The U.S.)
23. Candy Man
24. Time Won't Let Me
25. Let It All Go
26. Dollar's Worth

Comments: R. Stevie Moore sent me this one, a very cool compilation that he assembled of various studio tracks from one of Nashville's first pop-punk bands, Hopper. Bassist Roger Ferguson was in several early 1970s bands with Moore and **Victor Lovera** of **the Smashers**. Tracks #1-12 were recorded at the Acuff-Rose Studio on Franklin Road during the summer of '79. The rest were assembled from sessions at various local studios circa 1980-82.

Liner Notes: "Thus, an astonishing early post-punk rush, purportedly emanating late nites from Roy Acuff's Nashville studio, unbeknownst to the neighborhood cowboys sippin' Pabst at the local bars. This motherfuckin' disc smokes BIG rock! I couldn't believe my bleedin' ears! Musta been a hillbilly hook-up with some crystal-meth merchant nearby, I am sure! Songs are short, crisp, ballsy, defiantly devious. Drumming is so very mindblowingly solid. Mr. Hopper belts his bewilderingly bawdy banter, on top of his crack band's buzzcockian blast…" – R. Stevie Moore, 1999

THE HOTPIPES
Web: www.hotpipesmusic.com

Band Members:
Jonathan Rogers (I, II)
Dave Mengerink (I, II)
Dan Sommers (I, II)
Justin Hall (I, II)
Arthur Schoulties (I)

The Hotpipes Recordings:

I. Hotpipes (Liquid Panda Records 2006, CD)
1. If... Don't
2. Song for the Late Riser
3. Women of the World Agree
4. Much Too

5. Test Song
6. Starter Kit
7. So Bored
8. Lota Lee
9. Rattlecats
10. Downer, Quitter
11. Love In 3's

II. Future Bolt (Liquid Panda Records 2008, CD)
1. The Future is Where We Belong
2. Future Bolt
3. Brain & a Vegetable
4. You Burn or You Don't
5. Born in a Bomb
6. Thunderbolt
7. Where is the Shore?
8. I Am Better than You

THE HOTS

Band Members:
Andy Byrd (vocals, guitar)
Dale Brown (bass, vocals)
Kathryn Byrd (keyboards)
Steve Riddell (drums)

Comments: The Hots were a popular band for a short while before spinning off into other outfits. Dale Brown once came close to receiving a medieval-styled beatdown for a personal infraction that incurred the Reverend's wrath; today he's a professor at MTSU.

JAMIE HOUSTON

Comments: Few vocalists in Nashville received the push that Jamie Houston enjoyed, and yet accomplished so little. Houston also fronted the local funk-rock band **Grate Chop Grind** for a while. Considering the effort and expense that was spent promoting Houston's career, I'm kinda surprised that he never landed a major label deal.

HOW I BECAME THE BOMB
Web: www.howibecamethebomb.com

Band Members:
Jon Burr (vocals) (I)
Denis Dreck (guitars) (I)
Ricky Bizness (bass) (I)
Adam Richardson (keyboards) (I)
Andy Spore (drums) (I)

How I Became The Bomb Recordings:

I. Let's Go (self-produced 2006, CD)
1. Minute Romance
2. Killing Machine
3. Fat Girls Talkin' 'Bout Cardio
4. Secret Identity
5. Bar Song
6. Robo
7. Kneel Before Zod

Another View: "Be it a battle cry, a tersely-stated command, or the title of a Filipino television sitcom, the phrase "Let's Go!" conjures images of purpose, regardless of ethos or dogma. Hissed from William Holden's lips at the climax of Sam Peckinpah's The Wild Bunch, this epigram turned epitaph signaled the end of an era in film and art. Issued by a redoubtable General or an overzealous cheerleader, the phrase becomes emblematic of frenzy and following. For How I Became the Bomb, the phrase sure fits easily into various rhyme schemes, facilitating its ubiquitous and staggering presence on the mini-album and, thusly, it's title." – *from the band's website*

HUMAN RADIO

Band Members:
Ross Rice (vocals, keyboards) (I)
Kye Kennedy (guitar, vocals) (I)
Steve Arnold (bass, vocals) (I)
Steve Ebe (drums, vocals) (I)
Peter Hyrka (violin, mandolin, vocals) (I)

Human Radio Recordings:

I. Human Radio (Columbia Records 1990, CD/vinyl LP)
1. Me and Elvis
2. I Don't Wanna Know
3. Hole in My Head
4. These Are the Days
5. Monkey Suit
6. My First Million
7. Electromagnetisma
8. N. Y. C.
9. Another Planet
10. Harsh Light of Reality

Comments: Yeah, Human Radio was a *Memphis* band at the time that they recorded their lone CD for Columbia. However, they played in Nashville a heck of a lot back in the day, and ended up moving here in '91 in a last-ditch attempt to beat the star-making machinery. When the band broke-up in 1993 and headed back to the Bluff City, **Ross Rice** stayed behind, putting up with the session grind to feed his family. Rice later recorded a fine solo album, *Umpteen*, released in 1997 by the E Squared label.

Let's Go!

How I Became the Bomb

Jeff Holmes and the Floating Men are such an ingrained part of the Nashville rock scene that many tend to take them for granted. Still, over the course of almost 20 years and nearly as many albums, the band has consistently made interesting, vital, and intriguing music. I spoke with Jeff by phone in July 2007.

What got you interested in music in the first place?
I don't remember not being interested in music. My mom and dad said I would wake them up in the crib every morning singing, even in the crib. By the time I was old enough to know what a guitar was, every time we were in a store that had the little plastic ukuleles the kids drag around, I would have a fit and I'd have to get a new one, get one and I'd break it, and I'd get a new one next time. That started at age two. My dad played bluegrass just recreationally, and by the time I was seven, he had gotten me started playing guitar. I got into classical guitar playing, so I had a well-rounded music education.

When did you actually start playing in bands?
I was about eleven, maybe ten, and we did country and bluegrass covers. I started what has become the Floating Men in college as a twelve-bar blues band. I wanted to do real, raw blues stuff and had these dreams of becoming a lead guitar hero. I was a big fan of Johnny Winter and stuff like that back in my early teens and that carried over into college. So we got a lot of work playing raunchy roadhouse blues in those days.

Where did you go to college?
Furman University [South Carolina]. That's where I met Scott [Evans], the bass player for Floating Men, and some of the guys that wound up being in the Little Saints before that. That's how that whole continuum got started, with a blues band in college.

Unless you were in Texas, I guess that blues bands weren't particularly in demand then?
Not really, and if it had been now, you can get work as a blues band, especially in the Carolinas. Piedmont Blues, in particular, has become a big deal in this community. My older nephew goes out and interviews a lot of these guys on videotape from that part of South Carolina.

A lot of people don't realize how much blues came out of North and South Carolina.
When people talk about Piedmont Blues, Pink Anderson always comes to mind. Pink Floyd named their band after him, which has taken on a notoriety. My nephew got a chance – of course Pink's been dead for a while now – but my nephew got a chance to interview his son at the gravesite of his father. He hopped a freight train like a hobo and my nephew interviewed him on videotape at the gravesite of Pink Anderson. He handed him a guitar out of the car and said "play something for me," and he played "Rainy Night In Georgia," and it was absolutely spellbinding. He handed the guitar back to my nephew, walked back towards the rail yard, and disappeared.

What brought you to Nashville from South Carolina?
When we got out of college, we were looking for some place where we could just get work, and it was already becoming clear to us that the blues thing wasn't going to work, so we were learning covers, whatever it took to get by. I had always been into punk, so we started to incorporate some of that into our repertoire, just classic Ramones, simple things like that. We were having shit for luck in Florida getting work so we got this Nashville booking agent working for us and pretty soon it just took off. Nashville ended up being sort of central to our touring radius, so that's just where we hung our hat. I never planned it, but I married a Nashville girl and bought her a Nashville house, so now I'm a Nashville guy I guess. I still consider myself a South Carolinian in exile.

What's the story behind Little Saints, how did that band come together?
Like I said, it started out as that blues thing in college, and we were having so much trouble getting work we just started incorporating some, I guess it was called new wave at the time, some of the quirkier and poppier stuff. We started incorporating some of that into our show to get work, and it worked very well for us. But I've always been writing and built a very significant catalog of original music, so we just finally decided one day in the mid-80s to do our own music, sink or swim, and we literally stopped overnight. We played a show doing whatever we had to do to get by, covers and blues and punk, and then the next day we went out and played another show with all our own stuff, and we never looked back.

Didn't Little Saints record an album?
We made the one record that never sold well, and then we made a second record with a development deal with EMI. That record has never seen the light of day, it's still in a vault somewhere, I assume. We had the cover art and everything all ready to go and just ran out of money, the band just broke up. This was by the late '80s. Scott and I, I was already writing new

INTERVIEW: JEFF HOLMES

material from a different angle and started to spread my wings a little bit, and so Scott and I continued on and found Jeff Bishop on drums, and that became the Floating Men.

How long was Little Saints together, like four or five years?
Well, we sort of morphed. The same band was together under several different names starting as early as 1980 in college in South Carolina under a different name, and then as we morphed out of the blues thing, through the punk period and into the original stuff, it was 1989 when we broke up. So, around nine years, that's a long time.

Yeah, that's a pretty good run. The EMI thing, did that just kind of fizzle out, what was the label's perspective on it?
It was through the publishing division, it was a development deal as a writing artist. They just couldn't get me to do what they wanted me to do, to put the hay on the ground where the cows can get it.

I've always been a lot more influenced by filmmakers and novelists than I have been by the Rolling Stones and I was never going to get what they wanted. They put X amount of dollars up to do what were supposed to be demo sessions, but they were master quality demo sessions, so we got to get an album out of it. But it was absolutely just way out there, sort of abstract; they didn't have any idea what to do with it. I understand that now, but I didn't then.

What's your best memory of the Little Saints days?
I don't have many that are clear. Most of my memories are of parties, and hanging out at The Gold Rush. The band was always struggling musically, because we didn't really know what we wanted to do when we grew up as a band. We had great shows and we had terrible shows, just like everybody else. I think probably the best memory is the one that gave birth to the Floating Men; we'd just done South by Southwest in Austin and we were routed back through Houston for a day.

The album was out and fairly active and being worked reasonably well by Dave Cannon's people that we worked with, the White Animal crowd. We showed up in Houston at Velvets, it was a small room downstairs, and we had like eleven people there for that show, and four of them were journalists from local papers. One of them – I don't remember if he wrote it, or said it to me – but he said we made it look so easy he thought we were going to float right off the stage. That was the turning point for me as a writer and a musician. That's just what I thought, the whole goal of the next band is going to make it look easy, to make it float.

So you went into the Floating Men with a little bit different perspective I guess.
I'd written one or two songs, but there was no way Little Saints could play them. They were sophisticated, big-hook

pop, which was a new thing for me, but still with a depraved, Lou Reed kind of lyrical thing going on. I kind of sat on those and I thought, "I've discovered how to write big-hook pop, so the next band is going to be built around this sort of writing style and this sort of philosophy. I had done a big, loud, complicated rock show, a big stupid dumb American rock show and I was also looking to strip down and get to the real essence of the songwriting, because my songwriting had improved so dramatically. That's why Floating Men started as an acoustic act, with acoustic guitars, bass, and drums.

The Floating Men have always gone their own way and been pretty independent. Was that something that was by design, or did the nature of your music kind of make it that way?
Well, both…when we started out, we thought we had a real shot at some sort of commercial success. We spent an entire afternoon, probably five or six hours, locked up in a room in a basement on Music Row with Miles Copeland and boy, I had to wash myself after that. I actually felt skanky. I realized then that if it's all like this [the music industry], it's not going to work for me.

I tend to be a bit autocratic; I'm a nice guy but I'm sort of an alpha male too, and we don't like being ordered around. So that clearly wasn't going to work for us. We discussed things musicians don't normally discuss with labels and management, things like marketing strategies and demographics and they wound up saying "I don't know whether to hire you or sign you."

I think that we were something they didn't want, somebody that they couldn't mold. When we did our last run for *Invoking Michelangelo*, our last big nationwide tour in the mid-90s, we had broken through the New York radio market pretty significantly and had lined up literally dozens of agency people and label people and management firms and attorneys, there was a big buzz! We did one at a time and met with all of them, and the ones we liked, we scheduled things for the next day. I didn't walk away from that with any sense first of all that (a) anybody wanted to work with us because they just couldn't figure us out and because we were pretty headstrong, and (b) that I wanted to work with any of them.

From that point on, we've produced all of our own records and our fans have paid for it, and it's worked very well. It's gone from a smart rock acoustic power trio with a heroic show into a much larger extended family of musicians with a lot more sound involved, and it's become sort of an experimental laboratory for whatever pops into my head as a writer and whatever pops into the musicians' heads as really, really good musicians.

So it's been, it's just such a pleasure, and our fans love it. I never ruled out working with a label if I thought it had somebody there that wasn't a coked-up sleaze-bucket and they were making a commitment to the band for the long haul and not for the immediate gratification of a couple hit singles. That hasn't materialized and it probably never will. I've never ruled that out, but I'm not looking for it.

What was the first album that was fan financed?
I think we did two at first; *The Song Of The Wind In The Pines* and *Lemon Pie* were both sort of financed from record sales and touring, and through our relationship with Echo Music. *Heroes, Felons & Fiends* is where the fan financing really started and it was a great success and it's worked ever since.

How did that idea come up?
I think the folks at Echo Music came up with the germ of the idea and we ran with it. We were sitting there working on it, the band hadn't done more than two or three dozen dates a year since the mid-90s and there's not a lot of money in the bank, so how do we finance a record with so little money...

We'd been approached by a lot of fans saying "we play your material a lot; we can't wait until you get your stuff on an album, so if you guys need any help with money for an album let us know." We decided okay, we'll let them know, and that worked out and it's worked ever since. I'm always surprised when we say we're going to give back some tunes and does anybody want to help pay for this and they all step up, it still surprises me.

As a Floating Men fan myself, I would think that you probably have an audience that's a little smarter than usual, out of the mainstream and glad to hear some smart music.
That might be the case, yeah, there are a lot of people out there that are frustrated with radio, they're frustrated with modern pop, and they're looking for something new and we provide that.

You approach songwriting a little differently than most people, talk a little about your ideas on songwriting and what you try to do with it...
I call it blending paint on the canvas. I was a big Gregory Corso [poet] nut in college, and since I read where Allen Ginsberg called him a "wordslinger," I always loved that, and that was sort of my aspiration. I intend to let the music of the language lead the storyline rather than let a storyline or coherent idea lead or stomp on the natural rhythms and melodies of the spoken language.

There are a lot of built-in charms, it tends to be an abstract element and just a series of images and sounds in my lyrics that are as important as a storyline, or a single coherent idea or catch phrase so often used in country music. The sound of the spoken language, musically, is extremely important, and that allows me a lot of liberty to not be tied down to any single idea. It's obviously not what sells a lot of records or

Jeff Holmes & Scott Evans

songs, but it does make for very rich writing and a whole listening experience.

Writing the way that you do, separated from the clichés and expectations of commercial work, you're actually creating something that's going to have a lot more lasting power, I think, than a lot of commercial pop and rock stuff does.
Yeah, and that's a tradeoff, it's the tortoise and the hare story. You can put something out there on a Britney Spears type of level and people can comprehend the entire concept on the first listen. With our catalog, you invest some of yourself into these songs and each listening should reveal something new. These songs are pretty deep, and there's a lot in the well.

So you go back to that well over and over and always get a rewarding experience, and that's not just an aesthetic thing, it's also a commercial thing. We're the tortoises, as long as we're continuing to make rich records that people can really involve themselves in, very engaging records they can immerse themselves in, then we're always going to sell a few. We're never going to be rich, but we'll always sell a few records and that's never going to stop.

Listening to the Floating Men, I've never gotten the feeling that it's dated, that any single record obviously came from a particular time period. Your stuff tends to be like the great blues stuff, you can listen to it whenever you want, it's going to be just as relevant ten years from now as it is today, or as it was when it came out.
I appreciate that, that's one of the goals. There are a lot of reasons why that happens, and one of the reasons is that I don't own a stereo except in my car. I have an utter abhorrence for mainstream popular music, and there aren't a lot of other options. That's one of the reasons I'm writing in a cultural musical vacuum, I don't know what's going on out there, and don't give a rat's ass. I might overhear a hip-hop tune in the vehicle next to me and it will inspire something in me, and I hear a little of this and that, but I'm pretty much writing in a vacuum of self-indulgence and self-pleasure.

INTERVIEW: JEFF HOLMES

When we bring the musicians in, we tell them which rule books they can throw out which they should adhere to, and they bring their ideas too, and so you can go from Dixieland to speed-metal in the same record, or even in the same song, and somehow we try to make it work. The guys that are incredibly contemporary and are very topical, musically, they're always sort of the last big thing.

I always thought the Floating Men were never going to be the last big thing because we don't do what anyone else is doing and we may never be big, but we are the next thing. We have always completely gone our own way with absolutely no adult supervision, absolutely no label breathing down our necks, just complete artistic freedom. You can give that freedom to idiots, and you'll still get an idiotic record. You can give that freedom to the caliber of musicians that work with us and you're going to get a really interesting record every time. It might not be a great one, but it's a bet you're going to get something interesting, something you've never heard before.

I noticed from your website that you guys are going completely digital?
I get a check every quarter [for CD sales] and they take out for the packaging, and manufacturing, and shrink wrap, and shipping and handling, and for distribution networks and all that stuff...so selling digital beats the hell out of physical product right off the bat. It was two years ago when we made the decision, and we sold through the entire catalog of our first couple runs for *The Haunting*, and we've never pressed another CD. *The Haunting* continues to sell well on iTunes, so I don't see any reason to turn back now...

Jeff Holmes

You've done some solo acoustic work through the years; have you tried to bring a different perspective to that than the Floating Men when you do it? How does it differ?
I think what you get with a Holmes solo show is a little bit more in-depth with the songs. A Floating Men show is still a heroic rock and roll circus, but for me to sit down, I like to do these acoustic shows without any amplification whatsoever, and if the room is tall enough, what you get is just a person with the song and the lyrics and it gives me an opportunity to discuss a little bit about how the song came about, and I do a question and answer with the audience. It just depends on my mood every night, and every night is different and every performance of every song is different...it's very relaxed and very spontaneous.

Are we going to see Jeff Holmes solo album any time soon on iTunes?
I don't know, I've never really felt comfortable...the only things I want to say are getting said through the Floating Men. If we were to do a solo album, it would probably be a live record of me doing Floating Men songs. I've never written anything that the guys we have in our big extended family now couldn't turn into magic. They really detect my idea to make them better than I ever envisioned.

IDAHO BEACH HOUSE

Band Members:
Mark Roberts (vocals, guitars) (I)
Greg Layne (guitar) (I)
David Palmer (bass) (I)
Jay Jones (drums, vocals) (I)

Idaho Beach House Recordings:

I. Self (1992, cassette)

Comments: Idaho Beach House was a Murfreesboro-based alt-rock band whose song "Rejection" received a fair amount of airplay on WRVU. Jay Jones was drummer for **Chip & the Chiltons** circa 1985-87 and David Palmer would go on to become vocalist for **the Roaries**.

IGMO

Band Members:
Mark Pfaff (vocals, harp) (I)
Mike Grimes (guitar) (I)
Chad Mitchell (guitar) (I)
Mark Puryear (bass) (I)
Mike Webb (keyboards) (I)
Willis Bailey (drums) (I)

Igmo Recordings:

I. Ten Day Potato (self-produced CD, 1998)
1. Figure It Out!
2. Chump
3. Tomorrow Came Today
4. Dog and Pony
5. Zen
6. Bees make Honey
7. Freon
8. Sacred Cow
9. Let Me In
10. Tantric Moto-Cross
11. Dawn
12. G.I. Bill

Comments: Another fine **Brad Jones** production, Igmo included **Mark Pfaff** of **Will & the Bushmen**, Nashville man-about-town Mike Grimes, and skinman Willis Bailey of **the Sluggers**.

IMAGINE ASIANS
Web: www.imagineasians.com

Band Members:
Jeffery Neutron (vocals, guitar)
Benjamin Patton (bass)

Matthew Hungate (keyboards)
Bethany Arrington (synthesizer)
Bailey Sample (drums, percussion)

Imagine Asians Recordings:

I. imagine asians (self-produced CD EP, 2005)
1. jacquie says
2. prelude
3. daisy fuentes pictures
4. sb
5. except you
6. ana

Comments: No exact musician credits available on EP, but the band's MySpace page says that the EP features Philip Hood, Rodger Kelly, Lauren Sandidge, Mike Majett, Josh Wolter, Diana Groza, Rosie Rodanaramama'am, Arlo Hall, Ruby Amanfu, and Jeffery Neutron.

Another View: "...imagine asians make indie-minded pop that ranges from gentle, paintive songs of yearning to exuberant, nearly uncontainable bursts of melody. Rich with a sweeping palette of instrumentation, they're sweet and fun and lovely all at once." *The Nashville Scene*

IMAGINARY BASEBALL LEAGUE
Web: www.myspace.com/imaginarybaseballleague

Band Members:
Aaron Robinson (vocals, guitars)
Keith Childrey (guitars, vocals)

Imaginary Baseball League, continued...
Ben Evans (bass)
Ryan Rayborn (drums)

Comments: Murfreesboro's IBL supposedly recorded two full length albums and a pair of EPs, but I haven't seen them anywhere that I've been. They broke-up in 2005, but from the songs on their MySpace page, they had a grungy pop sound full of melody and with some interesting instrumental noodling hanging around in the background.

IMMORTAL LEE COUNTY KILLERS

Band Members:
Chet "El Cheetah" Weise (vocals, guitars) (I-III)
Jeff "J.R.R. Token" Collins (drums) (I-III)
Jeff Goodwin (keyboards) (II, III)

Immortal Lee County Killers Recordings:

I. *Love Is A Charm Of Powerful Trouble* (Estrus Records 2003, CD)
1. Robert Johnson
2. She's Not Afraid of Anything Walking
3. Weak Brain, Narrow Mind
4. Shitcanned Again
5. Goin' Down South
6. Love Is A Charm
7. Truth Through Sound
8. Rollin' And Tumblin'
9. Don't Nothing Hurt Me Like My Back and Side
10. That's How Strong My Love Is
11. What Are They Doing In Heaven Today?

Comments: The band's second full-length (I haven't included ***The Essential Fucked Up Blues***, which was definitely pre-Nashville) is a rattletrap collection of punked-up garage blues with covers of Willie Dixon, Muddy Waters,

and R.L. Burnside along with originals, including a tribute to Delta blues great Robert Johnson.

II. *Love Unbolts The Dark* (Sweet Nothing 2003, UK import)
1. "...Love Unbolts the Dark..."
2. Boom Boom (Yeah Yeah)
3. Rock and Roll Is Killing Me
4. The Dammed Don't Cry
5. Burnin' Hell
6. God Bless the Losers Who Try
7. Ain't Goin Down to Well No More
8. Said I'd Find My Way
9. Never Get out of These Blues Alive
10. Let's Get Killed
11. Devil Got My Woman

Comments: UK import album, only released in Europe, one-half live and one-half studio.

III. *These Bones Will Rise To Love You Again*
(Tee Pee Records 2005, CD)
1. Turn On The Panther
2. Revolution Summer
3. Blues
4. Boom Boom
5. Airliner
6. Stitched In Sin
7. The Damned Don't Cry
8. Wide As The Sky
9. Sonic Angel
10. Lights Down Low
11. No More My Lord

The IMMORTAL
LEE COUNTY KILLERS
II.

Comments: Former Quadrajets member Chet "El Cheetah" Weise formed the Immortal Lee County Killers in 1999 in Auburn, Alabama. After revolving through several band line-ups, he moved kit-and-kaboodle to Nashville and recruited

---

IGMO
Ten Day Potato
(self-produced)

After a long dry spell during which just about any group that knew three chords and could put up an "alternative" image was awarded a major label deal, we've finally spun things around where there are some bands out there that don't sound like Nirvana or Smashing Pumpkins. Nashville's IGMO is one of these welcome departures from the mainstream fare, a talented conglomeration of some of the Southeast's finest musicians brought together under one roof to make some honest rock & roll music.

Vocalist Mark Pfaff, a member of the legendary Will & The Bushmen, is the ringleader on ***Ten Day Potato***, fronting a superb collection of pop, rock, country and psychedelic music that borrows shamelessly from every decade from the dawn of time until today. IGMO present a new twist on the musical lessons they've learned so well, however, ***Ten Day Potato*** proving to be as refreshingly familiar as it is oddly original. In an era where many of today's "superbands" have to be taught how to play their instruments, IGMO is creating music that is as intelligent as it is invigorating. – *R Squared*, 1998 keyboardist Jeff Goodwin into the roster. The band has since broken up, and last I heard, Weise was attending M.T.S.U. Weise considered each recorded line-up of the band to be a separate entity, thus ILCK II recorded *Love Is A Charm Of Powerful Trouble* and *Love Unbolts The Dark* and ILCK3 recorded *These Bones Will Rise To Love You Again*.

Another View: "Punk-Blues with enough psychedelia for William Faulkner's ghost to feel nervous around mirrors; music of the ilck3 tastes like hot molasses spreading over a slice of Howlin' Wolf, with a side of Mc5/the Doors, an inspirational dash of John Coltrane (WWJCD?), and maybe for dessert- sundrops of pinball." – *from the band's press kit*

IN COLOR

Band Members:
Dave Zoid (vocals, guitar)
Paul Jones (bass)
Randy Ford (drums)

Comments: Dave Zoid came to Nashville from Knoxville, where he had worked with another immigrant band, **Hard Knox**, writing several of their songs. My old buddy Randy Ford had spent three years playing with **Radio One** before forming In Color with Zoid and Jones.

Another View: "In Color's music is heavily influenced by the much overlooked '70-'80 power pop invasion. They try to mix the exciting sounds of this period along with the more modern techniques of today. The end result is fun, positive music loaded with good vibes. Haunting overtones texturize their music, not making a strong angry stance, but coming through as natural aggression."
– Heather Lose, *The Metro*, February 1986

IN PURSUIT

Band Members:
Emma Grandillo (bass, vocals) (A1, I, II)
Jay Joyce (guitar, vocals) (A1, I, II)
Jeff Bogs (drums) (A1, I, II)

Other Musicians:
Mike Joyce (bass) (II)
Giles Reaves (synthesizer) (II)

In Pursuit Recordings:

Albums/EPs

I. When Darkness Falls (MTM Music 1985, LP)
Side One
1. Losing Control
2. When Darkness Falls

3. Sacrifice

Side Two
4. Witness
5. Cold World

Comments: Playing together as members of various early 1980s-era Cleveland bands, guitarist **Jay Joyce** and bass player Emma Grandillo decided to try their hand in Nashville, moving to the Music City in 1983. A 7" EP self-released by the pair as In Pursuit was poorly received, but their live shows were beginning to attract a following. A chance meeting with drummer Jeff Boggs, a Pittsburgh native who had played with Joyce and Grandillo on occasion in the Northeast, led to Boggs joining the band.

In Pursuit became the first act signed to MTM Records, a label started by the powerful television-production company named for Mary Tyler Moore by her (then) husband Grant Tinker. After tours with Mr. Mister and Starship, In Pursuit broke up when MTM was bought and shut down by British investors. Grandillo pursued a solo career as a performer and songwriter, placing songs with Garth Brooks, among others. Jay Joyce formed **Bedlam** in 1990 with **Questionnaires'** members Doug Lancio and Chris Feinstein, later joining with Feinstein to form the indie rock band **Iodine** before pursuing a career as a guitar-for-hire and successful producer.

Journalistic Disclaimer: The Reverend wrote the liner notes for the *When Darkness Falls* EP, hired by Bernie Walters, who was trying to make a real record label out of MTM.

In Pursuit continued on page 253...

THE IMMORTAL LEE COUNTY KILLERS
These Bones Will Rise To Love You Again
(Tee Pee Records)

Just a mere two years after the White Stripes won massive critical acclaim for their attempts to reinvent the blues-rock idiom with a bastard hybrid of shambling electric blues and garage rock fervor, the Immortal Lee County Killers came roaring out of Alabama with *The Essential Fucked Up Blues*. Taking the blueprint so carefully constructed by Jack White, the ILCK's Chetley Weise scribbled some notes on a brown paper bag and then proceeded to toss the White Stripes' formula into a meat grinder of distorted guitar riffs and primal, explosive percussion. Punker, bluesier and far more powerful than the Stripes' media-approved soundtrack, the Immortal Lee County Killers kicked out the jams with Son House spirit and Black Flag attitude.

A few years have passed by now, Jack and Meg became a tabloid sideshow and the bloom has fallen off the rose of punk-blues or garage-blues or whatever the hell you want to call it. R.L. Burnside is dead and many of those bands that once pursued rock & roll stardom with a washed-out, carbon-copy blues-rock sound have now become '80s new wave revival bands. Shudder. The Immortal Lee County Killers, however, are seemingly, well…immortal…the band carrying on with a new line-up and a more mature sound on album number three. Don't fear, erstwhile ILCK fans, because even though Cheetah and his crew have expanded their sound beyond the delightful musical trainwrecks of *The Essential Fucked Up Blues* and *Love Is A Charm* doesn't mean that the band has lost its way. They still hit your ears like the less-desirable business end of a shotgun blast.

If anything, *These Bones Will Rise To Love You Again* is even meaner and scarier than the ILCK's previous two albums, the band incorporating more elements of Southern soul and '60s psychedelica into the creative palette of their lo-fi aesthetic. "Turn On The Panther," for instance, includes tough-as-nails sonic distortion courtesy of Weise's over-amped guitar, Toko the Drifter's percussive drumming filling in with lightning-and-thunder intensity. Jon Spencer's "Revolution Summer" is the same sort of blues-influenced, three-chord hard rock that won the MC5 everlasting notoriety, the ILCK covering the song with a chaotic clashing of vocals and instrumentation. "Boom Boom" is the sound of the music industry imploding, a cacophonic death rattle writ larger-than-life with unrelenting percussion, manic vocals and some of the squonkiest guitar that you'll hear outside of East Village jazz clubs.

"The Damned Don't Cry" evokes the late, great R.L. Burnside, the song's martial rhythms and almost-chanted lyrics creating an air of menace, its roots in the Mississippi Hill Country and its sound straight out of Junior Kimbrough's juke joint. Even slower, more deliberate numbers like "Lights Down Low" evince a certain swampwater consistency, the song a cross between a funeral dirge and a tent revival while "No More My Lord" is a spiritual plea for relief in a Blind Willie Johnson vein. The addition of keyboardist Jeff Goodwin was definitely a good move, providing the band with another talented songwriter and complimenting the material with an instrumental style that sounds like Deep Purple's Ian Gillan, Jerry Lee Lewis, and Booker T jamming together at the Stax studios in Memphis.

For all of his bluster, drummer Toko the Drifter is capable of both tornado-force blasts and subtle, jazzy flourishes while Chet Weise is a six-string madman throwing razor-sharp riffs like ninja death stars and pounding out earth-scorching leads like bolts from the meaty paw of Zeus. Weise's understated lyrical style is short on nonsense and long on imagery, the underrated wordsmith throwing together minimalist blues-haiku that says what it needs to and then gets the hell outta the way of the general instrumental din. *These Bones Will Rise To Love You Again* is both a fine garage blues workout and an encouraging third album, displaying the Immortal Lee County Killers' evolution from a loud, badass duo with lots of heart into a loud, baddass trio with lots of heart *and* soul. *These Bones Will Rise To Love You Again* will kick you in the ass and leave you asking for another boot…and folks, it just doesn't get any better than that! – *Alt.Culture.Guide*, 2005

In Pursuit, continued...

II. Standing In Your Shadow (MTM Music 1986, vinyl LP)
Side 1
1. Standing In Your Shadow
2. Counting On Monday
3. Cold World
4. Getting Older
5. Saving Grace

Side 2
6. Laugh At The Cold
7. Only For You
8. Listen
9. Thin Line
10. Don't Stop

IN YOUR FACE

Band Members:
Noel Nutt (vocals)
Chris Hopkins (guitar)
Kent Thune (bass)
Bob Langley (drums)

Comments: In Your Face featured members of the bands Electric Circus and Langley and, according to guitarist Hopkins, the band played "controversial, commercial, funk, metal, blues, shock rock, rap 'n' roll with no rules."

INTRUDER

Band Members:
Jimmy Hamilton (vocals) (I-IV)
Arthur Vinnett (guitar) (I-IV)
Greg Messick (guitar) (II-IV)
Todd Nelson (bass) (I-IV)
John Pieroni (drums) (I-IV)
Rick Donley (drums)

Intruder Recordings:

I. Live To Die (Azra / Iron Works Records 1987 LP, reissued 1990 CD)
1. Cover Up
2. Turn Back
3. Victory In Disguise
4. Live To Die
5. Kiss Of Death
6. Cold-Blooded Killer
7. Blind Rage
8. T.M. (You Paid The Price)

Comments: Intruder's earliest incarnation began in 1984 with drummer/songwriter John Pieroni, guitarist Dave

Louden, and bassist Dave Hackley, the trio playing Black Sabbath covers in the basement. The unnamed band brought in guitarist Arthur Vinnett so that Louden could concentrate on vocals, and this line-up began performing locally as Transgresser. Members shuffled in and out, and when the smoke cleared, the line-up included vocalist Jimmy Hamilton and bassist Todd Nelson along with Vinnett and Pieroni.

The foursome recorded *Live To Die* with producer Tom Harding at Treasure Isle in Nashville after being signed to Azra, an offshoot of Dave Richards' Iron Works Records. The band admits that the label did its best to work the album, and it contributed to getting them signed to bigger indie Metal Blade. However, because Intruder wasn't part of metal's tape-trading culture at the time, they had no reputation among the underground and *Live To Die* slipped by virtually unnoticed (at the time). The LP has since become a holy grail of sorts for collectors of thrash-metal, fetching a handsome price.

II. A Higher Form Of Killing (Metal Blade 1989, CD)
1. Time Of Trouble
2. The Martyr
3. Genetic Genocide
4. Second Chance
5. (I'm Not Your) Stepping Stone
6. Killing Winds
7. The Sentence Is Death
8. Agents Of The Dark (M.I.B.)
9. Antipathy
10. Mr. Death

Comments: Intruder's debut album was a minor masterpiece of thrash-metal, largely overlooked at the time but both the

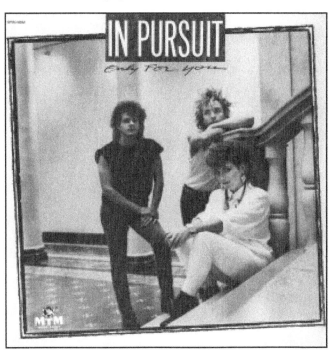

album and the band's reputation have grown over time with metal aficionados (see review ➜).

III. Escape From Pain EP (Metal Blade Records 1990, CD)
1. 25 Or 6 To 4
2. Escape From Pain
3. Cold-Blooded Killer
4. Kiss Of Death
5. T.M. (You Paid The Price)

Comments: Intruder's *Escape From Pain* EP includes three songs from the band's excellent debut disc, *Live To Die*: "Cold-Blooded Killer, "Kiss Of Death" and "T.M. (You Paid The Price)." Of the three, only "Cold-Blooded Killer" was re-recorded for the EP. Yes, that's a thrash cover of Chicago's "25 Or 6 To 4"! The band told me that *Escape From Pain* was released to give them a new recording to tour behind.

IV. Psycho Savant (Metal Blade Records 1991, LP)
1. Face Of Hate
2. Geri's Lament (When)
3. The Enemy Within
4. It's A Good Life
5. Invisible
6. Traitor To The Living
7. Final Word
8. N.G.R.I.

INVASION OF PRIVACY

Band Members:
Jean Ann Chapman (vocals) (A1)
Scott Mitchell (guitars) (A1)
Doug Sisemore (guitars) (A1)
Hajime Toniguchi (bass, keyboards) (A1)
Jeff Stallworth (drums) (A1)
Dana Belser (guitars) (A1)

Invasion of Privacy Recordings:

A1. "Show Your Emotion" b/w "Don't Walk Away" (Melting Records, 7" vinyl)

Comments: Chapman was a member of the local cover band Fibber McGhee before putting together **Invasion of Privacy**. This lone 7" single from the band has no info, or release date.

IODINE

Band Members:
Jay Joyce (vocals, guitar) (I-II)
Chris Feinstein (bass, vocals) (I-II)
Brad Pemberton (drums) (I-II)

Iodine Recordings:

I. Maximum Joy (No Alternative/TRG 1995, CD)
1. Mr. Mooney
2. Crush
3. Bells Ring
4. Turnpike
5. Superjet
6. Flyboy
7. Tainted
8. Bury Me With Her
9. Under The Same Rain

10. Pigskin
11. Rosie's Funeral

Comments: Too much talent on hand to have cranked out such a joyless exercise in futility. **Jay Joyce**'s guitar is turned up to the loudest setting, bathing the songs in feedback and distortion 'til it completely drowns out the otherwise attractive melodies while Chris Feinstein and Brad Pemberton crash-and-bang on everything in sight.

Joyce has since moved into production and his role as a guitarslinger for hire, while Feinstein and Pemberton were, most recently, backing up Ryan Adams and his giant ego as part of the Cardinals until Feinstein's tragic death.

Another View: "The appealing moments on *Maximum Joy* can easily be counted on one hand. The remainder – the vast majority of the album – falls into the sort of sub-grunge slop that burgeoned so unfortunately in the early '90s – gnarled and sludgy guitars dominate the mix, plodding through uninspired and largely inane compositions."
– Nitsuh Abebe, *All Music Guide*

II. Baby Grand (Sol 3 1998, CD)
1. Swan Dive
2. Sons of Belial
3. Dark Star
4. Monkey Disease
5. Absolute Perfection
6. Hayfield Shapmaker
7. Ten Seconds
8. Sayonara
9. Cyclops
10. Liar
11. Cucumber Cool
12. Uninvited
13. Lily

Comments: More of the same from the talented trio, creating music that was somehow both a product of and woefully behind the times. By '98, crappy boy bands and pop tarts like Britney Spears were atop the sales charts and good ole rock 'n' roll was represented by the sordid likes of Limp Bizkit, Matchbox 20, and an over-the-hill Aerosmith. Iodine may have found greater fortune in, say, 1992 but so it goes...

Intruder

CD REVIEW: INTRUDER'S A HIGHER FORM OF KILLING

INTRUDER
A Higher Form Of Killing
(Metal Blade Records)

Intruder may not have been Nashville's first, but they were definitely the city's best-known thrash band. Veterans of various local punk and metal outfits, Intruder built upon the speed-metal sound pioneered by bands like Metallica and Megadeth, adding elements of what would later become known as "progressive metal" to their unrelenting aural attack. Fueled by the phenomenal virtuosity of guitarist Arthur Vinett, the throaty growl of vocalist James Hamilton and the songwriting skills of drummer John Pieroni, Intruder built a large cult following across the United States and in Europe on the strength of their brutal live performances.

A Higher Form Of Killing, the band's second album and their first for Metal Blade Records, picks up the pace pretty much where Intruder had left off with their self-produced debut, *Live To Die*. Taking its title from the ground-breaking 1982 book on chemical and biological warfare by British journalists Robert Harris and Jeremy Paxman, Pieroni's lyrics on *A Higher Form Of Killing* mix a high-tech doom-and-gloom world view with a science-fiction landscape that has much in common with Voivod.

"The Martyr" compares Middle Eastern suicide bombers with radical Christian fundamentalists, "Genetic Genocide" touches upon DNA therapy a decade or so before its widespread use, and "Killing Winds explores the use of chemical weapons on the battlefields of Europe. The high point of *A Higher Form Of Killing*, however, is a manic cover of the Monkees' hit "(I'm Not Your) Stepping Stone," the pop/rock chestnut revved up and delivered with all the subtlety of the business end of a sledge-hammer. A strong collection of chainsaw speed-metal, *A Higher Form Of Killing* put the so-called band from "Thrashville" on the musical map alongside genre giants like Nuclear Assault. – *All Music Guide*, 2002

Whenever and wherever Invasion of Privacy play, strange and unusual events seem to occur. Electrical circuits blow up. Fuses melt down. Small fires begin burning. The level of radioactivity in the surrounding area rises to unsafe measurements. It's uncanny.

"Every time we play, something destructive happens," says guitarist Scott Mitchell. At a recent show at Vanderbilt, playing a campus frat house, the band literally brought down the house. Laughing, lead singer Jean Ann Chapman says, "during our first set, Hajime's bass amp blew up…he had to run home and get a replacement. Our second set blew the power in the house, so we had to go to a frat house next door and run all of these extension cords over to our equipment. Then the house catches fire during our third set."

Adds Scott, "halfway through our third set, we think that we're doing really good…we're playing and people are watching, dancing…all of a sudden, there's this wave of people running around the corner and out of the house. We were thinking, 'are we really this bad?' As it turns out, there was just this little fire, more smoke than anything else." Says Jean Ann, "when we were finally clear to power the system back up and play, somebody began playing the Talking Heads' "Burning Down The House." The firemen stopped for a moment and listened and started laughing, rolling on the floor. It was really funny!"

An explanation for the strange phenomena that follows Invasion of Privacy around is rather complex. Perhaps these events occur due to the power and energy of the band's live performance. Perhaps it is the head-turning beauty of lead vocalist Jean Ann, the undeniable focal point of the band. It could be any number of things. The only thing that is certain is that Invasion of Privacy is one of the more exciting and original of Nashville's local bands.

Invasion of Privacy was formed in 1983 by Chapman and original guitarist Dana Belser. Says Chapman, "we began the Invasion of Privacy concept as an outlet for performing original music. Dana was the co-founder of the band and co-wrote most of the material with me. We went to England in 1984 and did some recording in Jacobs Studio, about 40 miles north of London."

The band returned to Nashville and began taking steps to put their career in motion. "We did some recording here in town over at Castle and at Treasure Isle. We toured a bit with Jason & the Scorchers and did some shows with Will Rambeaux & the Delta Hurricanes. We played a few mid-south shows, including an opening show with Modern English."

Chapman writes the bulk of the band's material. She is quite an accomplished songwriter and performer. She originally hails from Los Angeles, where she worked as a studio

musician and vocalist. She moved to Nashville in 1980. "I was singing with people like Mac Davis and Loretta Lynn. I was writing songs and even had my own publishing company. I came to Nashville to do some session work with Loretta and just fell in love with the city."

Chapman continues, "Nashville really is a great writer's town. It's centrally located in the country, close to New York and other music cities such as Atlanta and Muscle Shoals. I looked at Nashville as the land of opportunity." About six months after her move to Nashville, Jean Ann was working with a Top 40 cover band that performed some original material, a band named Fibber McGhee. "That band evolved to one called Tomboy," she says, "and we pretty well covered the area. After that, I quit for about six months and collected myself. I was interested in putting together an original project for myself as I'd never done that before." The result was Invasion of Privacy. "I'm a lot happier with this band," she says, "because although you starve more, an original material band is more conducive to growth."

Two of the original members of I.O.P. left the band almost a month ago, including co-founder Belser. The current band, says Chapman, is better than ever. "We've only been together a few weeks," she says, "and we've just now begun to write together. We've played a few shows in the area, including several at Vandy." The sound of the band hasn't strayed much from the original concept. "We're incorporating more keyboard sounds now, whereas in the beginning we focused heavily on the guitars."

The degree of professionalism within the band is amazing. Besides Jean Ann's session work, she has achieved success as a writer, working with Warner Brothers Publishing. It was a Jean Ann Chapman song that was the B-side of the Pointer Sisters' hit version of Springsteen's "Fire." She has also had a number of songs recorded by a few European Motown acts, including a hit for Paulette Reeves, "Do It Again."

The other members of the band have equally impressive credits. Guitarist Doug Sisemore has played with country artist Gail Davies as well as rockers Danny Tate and RPM. Drummer Jeff Stallworth does innumerable recording sessions and plays in several weekend bands. Scott Mitchell does session work also, and bass player/keyboard wizard Hajime Toniguchi has performed with local favorites Afterdark and Danny Tate. The resulting combination of the five members of Invasion of Privacy is that of a smooth-running ultra-tight rock 'n' roll outfit.

Invasion of Privacy is about to release their first single, an exciting slice of '80s pop titled "Show Your Emotion," backed with "Don't Walk Away." The band will be backing up this debut vinyl with performances at Mainstreet in Murfreesboro and here in Nashville. You might just want to go down and check them out. Besides a fun show by a great rock band, who knows just what might happen? They may just burn down the house. – *The Metro*, October 11, 1985

Walk over and turn on your radio...go ahead, it won't bite! It may disgust you, though. The traits that once mattered in music, such as originality, sincerity, insight… they're not all that easy to find in popular music these days. You may have a long wait between songs. *Unless* you're listening to In Pursuit.

Illustrating that the Music City is the home of more than just country music, In Pursuit are a fresh, young band presenting an energetic brand of pop-styled rock and roll with tasteful harmonies and an emphasis on intelligent, thoughtful lyrics...not a scrap of country influence to be found.

In Pursuit is guitarist Jay Joyce, bassist Emma Grandillo (though she goes by just "Emma"...it's easy to remember and it arouses curiosity) and drummer Jeff Boggs. Together this trio creates a sound as honest and original as any to be found.

Jay and Emma hail from Cleveland, Ohio, where they played together in a number of bands. The two decided to move to Nashville two and half years ago, in order to develop original material and further their careers. "There's no writing industry to speak of in Cleveland," says Emma, "no publishers or anything like that. There are a lot of clubs to play, but we were wanting to concentrate on our writing." Upon arriving here, they came to believe, and rightfully so, that the Music City would support a talented rock band.

Drummer Jeff Boggs was added a year and a half ago, providing the then missing link in the trio's now perfect chemistry. Strangely enough, Jay and Emma had met Jeff several years previously. Says Jay, "while in Cleveland, we played in Pittsburgh (Jeff's hometown) every couple of weeks. Jeff filled in on drums for us during one of our performances there. Afterwards, we didn't see him again until we moved down here. We were playing at the Exit/In and he was in the audience." Jeff had relocated to Nashville by way of Florida and that chance meeting brought the present band together.

Although young, the median age of the band being only twenty-five, Jay, Emma and Jeff share between them over three decades of combined musical experience and training. Emma began playing guitar and taking lessons while still in grade school, the same for Jeff and his drums. Jay comes from a large family where all can sing and play some instrument.

The band put this collective experience to good use, playing frequent live dates and strengthening their already energetic and enjoyable stage show, "We've done a lot of roadwork," says Emma, "we love to play." The band has criss-crossed the Eastern United States, developing followings in cities such as Cleveland, Chicago, Cincinnati, Ohio and Athens, Georgia; "since we got together with Jeff," states Jay, "we acquired a Ford Escort station wagon and a U-Haul trailer and played pretty much wherever we could."

These performances generated several recording offers, the band choosing to sign with the newly-formed MTM Records, the same people who brought the word 'quality' to television.

Upon signing with MTM, they immediately went into the studio to record their debut album. Although the band had released a self-produced, three-song single a year or so ago, the making of this record was unique. "We had done a lot of studio work," says Jay, "making demos and developing material. But we'd never captured what we are live on record."

"This record," he continues, "comes the closest we ever have to achieving the sound we project in our live show. There's a lot of energy on this album." Adds Emma, "the songs say a lot of subtle things if you really listen. Also, since we don't really have a lead vocalist, we switch the leads around in an interplay of vocals between, and even within songs. Since we're a trio and thus limited somewhat as to instrumentation, we cover the other instruments with vocals, which gives us a unique sound."

You'll find a great deal of emphasis on lyrics within the songs of In Pursuit. Jay and Emma write the words, with the entire band working on arrangements. "We write about everyday things," says Emma, "not just the same old love songs." Life and its many aspects are represented in their creations, which will appeal to fans of all ages, from fourteen to forty-five. "We don't write for any special age group," says Emma, "we concentrate on subjects that everybody can relate to. We've seen both young and old at our shows, enjoying the music...we like breaking that barrier."

After the album is released in September, the band will be hitting the road. Says Jay, "we're talking to some booking agencies to take it out of our hands. We'd like to go out West and play, where we've never been." The group has a decided edge over their musical competition. "A lot of bands record an album," says Jeff, "and then have to hustle to get their stage show together. We developed our live performances first, and then made the record."

Adds Jay, "there will always be a difference between our live show and the records we make...like the book versus the movie. So many bands just get up on stage and play their latest album. We believe that we can make it more exciting than that!"

In Pursuit

What are In Pursuit's goals for the future? MTV? The dizzy heights of success? Gold, diamonds, and a mansion in Beverly Hills? A cameo performance on *Miami Vice*? "We'd like to become a long-term band," says Jay, "not just have one or two hit singles and die. We'd like to create a following over a period of time, an audience that respects us for that which we've accomplished artistically and will stay with us. We're not interested in a sort of contrived commerciality, though we do have a commercial sound, and it's our own sound."

Go ahead...turn on your radio. Come September, the airwaves will be just a little brighter; made that way by the energy and lyrical craftsmanship that is In Pursuit. As for those traits that so much music has forgotten...you don't have to look any further.

(By the way, in case you're wondering, the band derives its unique name from the television show ADAM 12. *As In "ONE ADAM 12 IN PURSUIT OF ..." Now you know!) – Metro magazine, August 1985*

JOHN JACKSON & THE RHYTHM ROCKERS

Band Members:
John Jackson (vocals, guitar)
Nancy Kline (vocals)
Kelley Looney (bass)
Rich Wayland (keyboards)
Jim Greasy (saxophone)
Rock Williams (saxophone)
Mickey Grimm (drums)

Comments: Jackson, formerly of power-pop darlings **Practical Stylists**, broke out on his own to form the Rhythm Rockers and play live more frequently than his former band was inclined. A fun live band with rock roots and a R&B revue sound, the Rhythm Rockers were regulars at 12th & Porter and 328 Performance Hall, as well as the Southern frat circuit for well over a decade.

They began as a covers band (tasteful covers – not Top 40 crap, but rather Van Morrison, Dire Straits and Joan Armatrading, and the obscure Atlanta funk-metal band Mother's Finest, among others), but later began penning original material to play onstage.

Another View: "The band invites comparisons to Southside Johnny and the Asbury Jukes in a vague way, but is more closely related musically to the L.A. instant-party-kit-band Jack Mack and the Heart Attack (a Jackson favorite). The sound is driving white soul, played delicately and intelligently. They are proven crowd pleasers. They can incite lifeless audiences into fits of dancing madness." – Bill Spicer, *The Metro*

JOSH JACKSON BAND

Band Members:
Josh Jackson (vocals, guitar)
Locke Sandahl (guitar, vocals)
Jason Hollis (bass)
Kris Crawford (drums)

Comments: (From Josh by email) "In addition to playing all the Nashville clubs the last few years (Exit In, 12th & Porter, 3rd & Lindsley, The End) we were honored to be named BEST LOCAL BAND & BEST NEW BAND by the 2002 *Nashville Scene* readers poll. I guess that would be our claim to fame...if we had one...I just like to rock!"

MARK AARON JAMES

Band Members:
Mark Aaron James (vocals, guitar) (I, II)

Other Musicians:
Rick Altizer (guitars, bass, percussion) (I)
David Burch (drums) (I)
Erik Halbig (guitar) (I)
Jennie Hoeft (drums) (I)
Michael Lille (guitar) (I)
Jim Roller (bass) (I)
Garry Tussing (cello) (I)

Mark Aaron James Recordings:

I. Mr. Wirehead (Wider Man Records 1998, CD)
1. Mr. WiReHeAd
2. ThE NaMe Of ThE GaMe
3. PlAyGrOuNd In YoUr HeArT
4. JuNe 17th
5. SeE If YoU CaN HuRt Me
6. GiVe A DaMn
7. Mr. BaLLAnTiNe
8. ThIs SoNg'S All AbOuT…
9. PiCk Up YoUr PrIdE
10. AuToBiOgRaPhY Of A PiSToL

Comments: Nashville is rife with talented immigrant songwriters that crank out an album or two, get thoroughly ignored by the Music Row establishment that they originally came to town to *wow*, and then they either quit the biz or eventually flee to higher ground (usually NYC).

Witness Mark Aaron James, a guy that you might have overlooked unless you happened to be hanging around when he showed up in a local club to play. He came to the Music City from Florida to attend school at Vanderbilt, played writer's nights around town, and generally suffered the fate of all pop-rock oriented songwriters in a town leaning heavily in favor of insipid pop-country schlock. James would jump from Nashville to New York City in 2002.

Another View: "No, that's not Mark Aaron James depicted on the cover of his CD, *Mr. Wirehead*. Actually that freaky cover dude with the rainbow-colored Mohawk hairstyle is a clock. And no, the Mohawk clock guy doesn't mean James does the punk rock thing, either. Rather, that image and its accompanying title track reveal James' wry sense of humor, which he also displays on such songs as "This Song's All About"... and the sobering "Autobiography of a Pistol." All this on rootsy yet modern rock that's quite Crow-like – both Sheryl and Counting Crows."
– Rick de Yampert, *The Tennessean* (February 1999)

II. Adventures With A Plastic Bag (No Alternative 2001, CD)
1. Plastic Bag
2. Happy Hour
3. After You Do
4. Rebecca Moses
5. I Might Die Without You
6. No One's As Beautiful
7. Missing You Instead
8. Up/Down
9. Little Space
10. Angie Baby.

From the artist's web site: "The year following his critically acclaimed indi [sic] release, *Mr. Wirehead*, Mark was awarded Best Local Songwriter and Best Up and Coming Band in the *Nashville Scene*'s 2000 reader's poll. In the weekly mag, owned by NYC's *Village Voice*, Mark beat out John Hyatt [sic], Lucinda Williams, Steve Earle and several other Nashville luminaries for the award. With the release of his second indi-label CD, *Adventures With A Plastic Bag*, he repeated the feat in 2001. The title song from that CD went on to make the top 100 songs of the year on Nashville's WRLT Lightening 100, gained airplay on Atlanta's 99X and was added to 126 other CMJ reporting stations, charting in 12 markets."

MARK AARON JAMES & THE BORROWED SOULS

Band Members:
Mark Aaron James (vocals, guitar) (I)
Brad Henderson (guitars) (I)
David Bennignus (bass) (I)
Kenny Zarrider (keyboards) (I)
Jennie Hoeft (drums) (I)

Mark Aaron James & the Borrowed Souls Recordings:

I. Mark Aaron James & the Borrowed Souls (Blue Star Recordings 1995, CD)
1. Hand Of The Healer
2. Radio Lines

3. Missing You Instead
4. Forbidden Love
5. Solo Duet
6. It Just Don't Matter To Me (The Apathy Song)
7. Erotic
8. Shena
9. One Step Away

JANE, HIS WIFE

Band Members:
Kent Agee (vocals)
George Bradfute (guitar)
Kyle Miller (bass)
Scott Miller (drums)
Kim Fleming (vocals)
Vicki Hampton (vocals)

Comments: One of the more popular local bands circa late 1980s/early 1990s, unfortunately Jane, His Wife never released any recordings (at least none that I'm aware of). Frontman **Kent Agee** would later release a solo CD after the band broke-up and George Bradfute would become an in-demand session player.

JASON

Band Members:
Jason Ringenberg (vocals, guitar) (I)

Other Musicians:
Dennis Burnside (keyboards) (I)
Larry Byrom (guitars) (I)

Sonny Garrish (steel guitar) (I)
Michael Henderson (guitars) (I)
David Innis (synthesizers) (I)
Craig Krampf (drums) (I)
Mike Lawler (synthesizers) (I)
Terry McMillan (harmonica) (I)
Michael Rhodes (bass) (I)
Brent Rowan (guitars) (I)
Glen Worf (bass) (I)

Jason Recordings:

I. One Foot In The Honky Tonk (Liberty 1992, CD)
1. The Life Of The Party
2. One Foot In The Honky Tonk
3. Try Me
4. Letter Of Love
5. Already Burned
6. Hardluck Boy
7. I Washed My Hands In Muddy Water
8. Feels So Right
9. Wild About Me
10. Devil's Daughter

Comments: After the break-up of **Jason & the Scorchers**, band frontman **Jason Ringenberg** recorded this misguided attempt at launching a solo career. It's not that *One Foot In The Honky Tonk* is a bad album, it's just not the work of a talent of Jason's caliber. Signed to Jimmy Bowen's Liberty Records imprint, also home to the **Cactus Brothers**, Ringenberg was put in the studio with a bunch of Music Row studio musicians to record a "country music" album. It didn't work because a) Ringenberg's unique vocal style is best-

suited to his own material, and b) producer Jerry Crutchfield didn't let Jason record many of his own songs. The players here are good – some, like guitarists Rowan and Henderson, are skilled artisans – but the material is tired and the performances largely uninspired. Jason would later find his creative voice with the self-penned, folkish country-rock of his *real* solo albums.

JASON & THE NASHVILLE SCORCHERS

Band Members:
Jason Ringenberg (vocals, guitar) (A1-3, I-XII, B1-2)
Warner E. Hodges (guitar) (A1-3, I-XII, B1-2)
Jeff Johnson (bass) (A1-3, I-IX, XI, B1-2)
Perry Baggs (drums, vocals) (A1-3, I-XII, B1-2)
Andy York (guitars, dobro, piano, vocals) (IV, XI)
Ken Fox (bass) (IV, XI)
Kenny Ames (bass) (X, XI)
Al Collins (bass, vocals) (XII)
Pontus Snibb (drums, percussion, vocals)
Jack Emerson (bass)
Barry Felts (drums)

Other Musicians:
Dan Baird (guitars, vocals) (XII)
Leon Gaer (bass) (III)
Emmylou Harris (vocals) (VIII)
Blanche & Ed Hodges (vocals) (X, XI)
Don Herron (fiddle) (X)
Robert Jetton (vocals) (A1, VII, IX)
Fats Kaplin (steel guitar, fiddle) (VIII)
Kenny Lovelace (fiddle) (III)
Jerry Dale McFadden (piano (VI, X)
Rick Richards (XI)
Donald W. Spicer (slide guitar) (III)
Jai Winding (keyboards) (III)
Link Wray (guitar) (XI)

Jason & the Scorchers Recordings:

Singles

A1. Reckless Country Soul (Praxis 1982, 7" EP)
Side One
1. Shot Down Again
2. Broken Whiskey Glass

Side Two
3. I'm So Lonesome (I Could Cry)
4. Jimmie Rodgers' Last Blue Yodel

Comments: The first blast of white light/white heat from Nashville's favorite sons caught everybody off guard, especially the growing Music City rock scene. The Scorchers' unique mix of punk fervor, country twang and heavy metal thunder was something entirely new and unexpected. I remember working at a used music/comic book shop on Elliston Place in 1982 when Scorchers manager/Praxis guy Jack Emerson brought in this EP and the *Never In Nashville* 7" EP to place on consignment in the shop.

My friend Kent Orlando and I listened to both EPs and grabbed up copies immediately. Warner Hodges once told me that even he didn't have a copy of this on vinyl. Famously recorded in **Robert Jetton**'s living room, with Jason singing in the hall, the EP was later reissued on CD by Mammoth in the wake of the label's signing of the band, with the Praxis Records logo right up front. Too cool for school, by far...

Another View: "The Scorcher's debut EP, 1982's *Reckless Country Soul*...is the sound of Joe Strummer hurling a wrecking ball through the Grand Ol' Opry. Its stand-out, 'Shot Down Again,' starts with Ringenberg screaming, 'Look out London – here come the Scorchers!' Pop-music historians of the twenty-first century will recognize this as important early evidence of the anti-eighties-hair-bands-from-England backlash." – Jimmy Guterman, **The Best Rock 'n' Roll Records Of All Time**.

A2. White Lies (Capitol EMI 1985, 12" vinyl)
Side 1
1. White Lies

Side 2
1. Are You Ready for the Country
2. Honky Tonk Blues (live)

A3. Hell's Gates (Mammoth Records 1995, UK CD)
1. Hell's Gates
2. Ruby, Don't Take Your Love To Town
3. Buried Me Like A Bone

Comments: There were other Scorchers' singles released, but I don't have 'em, so they're not listed here. This one is notable for the two non-LP outtakes from *A Blazing Grace* and because it was an easy-to-find (in Nashville) U.K. import.

Albums/EPs

I. Fervor (Praxis/EMI America 1983, 12" vinyl EP)
Side One
1. Absolutely Sweet Marie
2. Help There's A Fire
3. I Can't Help Myself

Side Two
1. Hot Nights In Georgia
2. Pray For Me Mama (I'm A Gypsy Now)
3. Harvest Moon
4. Both Sides Of The Line

Comments: Originally a five-song EP released by Praxis, this is the disc that caught the attention of the big boys and propelled the Scorchers into the major leagues. I've listed the remixed, reissued EMI America version of the EP because of the addition of the brilliant Dylan cover, "Absolutely Sweet Marie." The original Praxis release offered a different song sequence. The band's DIY-styled video for "Absolutely

Jason & the *Nashville* Scorchers

Sweet Marie" remains a fan favorite today, and has attracted tens of thousands of views on You Tube. ***Fervor*** was later reissued on CD, paired with ***Lost And Found***.

Another View: "Crossing Gram Parson's knowledge of sin with Joe Ely's hell-bent determination to get away with it, Jason Ringenberg leads a band no one can accuse of fecklessness, dabbling, revivalism, or undue irony. The lyrics strain against their Biblical poetry at times, but anyone who hopes to take a popsicle into a disco is in no immediate danger of expiring of pretentiousness. Grade: A-" – Robert Christgau, **Christgau's Record Guide: The '80s**

Yet Another View: "In late 1983, Jason Ringenberg, lead singer of Jason and the Scorchers, balanced himself on a rickety stool in the basement of a now boarded Philadelphia dive and wished aloud what he wanted his band to sound like. 'Like a religious service,' he said wistfully, 'only a lot dirtier.' This is not an attitude that brings major labels running, and Jason and the Scorchers were the great lost band of the eighties, starting great and getting better with each record, though fewer and fewer people heard them each time around. In the eighties, the music industry was simply not geared to handle an original group like Jason and the Scorchers, a ferocious hard-rock band with a strong grounding in country-and-western...if any traditional rock-and-roll band in the eighties was ahead of its time, it was Jason and the Scorchers." – Jimmy Guterman, **The Best Rock 'n' Roll Records Of All Time.**

II. Lost & Found (Capitol EMI 1985, LP)
Side 1
1. Last Time Around
2. White Lies

3. If Money Talks
4. I Really Don't Want To Know
5. Blanket Of Sorrow
6. Shop It Around

Side 2
1. Lost Highway
2. Still Tied
3. Broken Whiskey Glass
4. Far Behind
5. Change The Tune

Comments: On the strength of "White Lies," ***Lost & Found*** peaked at number 96 on the *Billboard* Top 200 chart.

Another View: "It's the punk side of country punk that takes imagination for a Nashville boy, so unlike his bicoastal brethren he throws himself into rocking out and doesn't think awful hard about words or tunes. This is rarely the most effective way to rock out. He gets by this time, but he's running on attitude, and attitude has a way of running thin. Grade: B+" – Robert Christgau, **Christgau's Record Guide: The '80s**

III. Still Standing (Capitol EMI 1986, LP/CD)
1. Golden Ball And Chain
2. Crashin' Down
3. Shotgun Blues
4. Good Things Come To Those Who Wait
5. My Heart Still Stands With You
6. 19th Nervous Breakdown
7. Ocean Of Doubt
8. Ghost Town
9. Take Me To Your Promised Land
10. Greetings From Nashville
11. Route 66
12. The Last Ride

Comments: The Scorchers' second full-length album, with the band poised on the brink of either overwhelming commercial success or permanent "cult band" status. History has shown us what happened. Jason doesn't think that this was an especially strong album, but I would beg to differ (see review ➔). No, it wasn't ***Lost & Found***, or even ***Fervor***, but there are a handful of very good songs here, and "Golden Ball And Chain" was a good choice for a single release.

The relatively short running time of the album (originally nine songs) and the label push behind the Stones' cover ("19th Nervous Breakdown") as a failed single were perhaps, in hindsight, somewhat misguided. I don't recall a single video made from this album, though I'd gladly stand corrected. The 2002 CD reissue includes bonus tracks: "Greetings From Nashville," a popular live song, and two previously unreleased tracks in "Route 66" and "The Last

Ride." *Still Standing* ended up peaking at number 91 on the *Billboard* Top 200 chart.

IV. Thunder And Fire (A & M Records 1989, LP/CD)
1. When The Angels Cry
2. Now That You're Mine
3. You Gotta Way With Me
4. My Kingdom For A Car
5. Close Up The Road
6. Lights Out
7. Find You
8. Bible And A Gun
9. Six Feet Underground
10. No Turning Back
11. Away From You

Comments: The great lost Scorchers' album, *Thunder And Fire* was a problem child from the very beginning. After leaving EMI and filing for bankruptcy, the band made its living by touring constantly. Bassist Jeff Johnson left sometime between 1986 and '89, replaced by Ken Fox, who was recruited from a classified ad. Warner brought in second guitarist Andy York and the band widened its sound significantly. The "new" Scorchers were signed to A&M and the album completed right around the time that the label was

sold to what would later become the Universal Music empire. The Scorchers were lost in the shuffle and the album was under-promoted to death. The band broke up shortly thereafter, with York and Fox forming Hearts and Minds, Warner playing with Eric Ambel (The Del-Lords) in Roscoe's Gang, and Ringenberg pursuing a solo country career.

The addition of York brought an entirely different dimension to the band's sound…a good one, in my mind…but critics weren't so kind. Many considered this to be a grab at some sort of hard rock credibility, completely disregarding the metal-edged sound of the band's previous three national releases. Jason had moved up a step in his songwriting, and worked effectively with Music City scribes like Don Schlitz, Paul Kennerley and Steve Earle. Perry – who had changed the 'S' in his name to a 'Z' for this album (Baggz) – contributes a couple of good songs, including "Six Feet Underground." Produced by Barry Beckett, *Thunder And Fire* is a prime candidate for an expanded re-release on CD.

V. Essential Jason And The Scorchers, Volume One: Are You Ready For The Country (EMI Records 1992, CD)
1. Absolutely Sweet Marie
2. Help There's A Fire
3. I Can't Help Myself

Jason & the *Nashville* Scorchers

4. Hot Nights In Georgia
5. Pray For Me Mama (I'm A Gypsy Now)
6. Harvest Moon
7. Both Sides Of The Line
8. Last Time Around
9. White Lies
10. If Money Talks
11. I Really Don't Want To Know
12. Blanket Of Sorrow
13. Shop It Around
14. Lost Highway
15. Still Tied
16. Broken Whiskey Glass
17. Far Behind
18. Change The Tune
19. Are You Ready For The Country?
20. Greetings From Nashville
21. Honky Tonk Blues (live)
22. Absolutely Sweet Marie (live)

Comments: EMI Records, in an attempt to make some money from the Scorchers at the dawn of the alt-country era, bundled *Fervor* and *Lost & Found* together on CD for the first time in a single package.

To be honest, although I loathe EMI, this was a pretty good CD. They threw in four solid bonus tracks, including the band's Neil Young cover "Are You Ready For The Country" and the **Tim Krekel** song "Greetings From Nashville" (which they also used on the *Still Standing* CD reissue) as well as two live tracks. Better yet, the release of this CD motivated Jeff Johnson to lobby the other members to get back together, which resulted in *A Blazing Grace*.

VI. A Blazing Grace (Mammoth Records 1995, CD)
1. Cry By Night Operator
2. 200 Proof Lovin'
3. Take Me Home, Country Roads
4. Where Bridges Never Burn
5. The Shadow of Night
6. One More Day of Weekend
7. Hell's Gates
8. Why Baby Why
9. Somewhere Within
10. American Legion Party

Comments: In the wake of the EMI reissue of the band's first two albums, the Scorchers got back together to play some live shows and try to make some cash themselves from the new release. They ended up having a good time, started writing some songs, and ended up working with Mike Janas at the Castle Recording studio in Franklin, Tennessee, resulting in *A Blazing Grace*. A solid comeback album, it would renew interest in the band after a five-year hiatus and would subsequently lead to bigger and better things.

VII. Reckless Country Soul (Mammoth 1996, CD)
1. Shot Down Again
2. Broken Whiskey Glass
3. I'm So Lonesome (I Could Cry)
4. Jimmie Rodgers' Last Blue Yodel
5. Help! There's A Fire
6. I'd Rather Die Young / Candy Kisses
7. Pray For Me Momma (I'm A Gypsy Now)
8. Hello Walls
9. If You've Got The Love (I've Got The Time)
10. Gone Gone Gone

Comments: One of the benefits of the Scorchers' signing with Mammoth was the long overdue CD reissue of the powerful *Reckless Country Soul* EP, with five extra bonus tracks of the same vintage. Sadly, already out-of-print, as is much of the Scorchers' back catalog.

VIII. Clear Impetuous Morning (Mammoth Records 1996, CD)
1. Self-Sabotage
2. Cappuccino Rosie
3. Drugstore Truck Drivin' Man
4. Going Nowhere
5. Uncertain Girl
6. 2+1=Nothing
7. Victory Road
8. Kick Me Down
9. Everything Has A Cost
10. To Feel No Love
11. Walking a Vanishing Line
12. Tomorrow Has Come Today
13. Jeremy's Glory
14. I'm Sticking With You

Comments: I'd personally put this one right behind *Fervor* and *Lost And Found* as one of the Scorchers' best efforts. The early 1990s "ring rust" had all been shaken off with some fast touring, the instrumental performances were powerful and focused, and the songwriting was lean and mean, including some fine collaborations between Jason and Perry and Jason and **Tommy Womack**.

The band kept their streak of great cover tunes intact with an inspired reading of the Byrds' "Drugstore Truck Drivin' Man." Unfortunately, the album proved to be a decade too late. Jeff Johnson left shortly after this to go back to his photography business, to be replaced by the more-than-capable Kenny Ames.

IX. *Both Sides Of The Line* (Capitol EMI 1996, CD)

Comments: Inferior and totally unnecessary CD reissue of *Fervor* and *Lost And Found*, sans the four bonus tracks present on the *Essential Jason And The Scorchers* compilation, which was replaced by this blatant cash grab on behalf of the Scorchers' former label. What's the matter, EMI, afraid to pay a couple of dimes more in publishing?

X. *Midnight Roads & Stages Seen* (Mammoth 1998, CD)
Disc One
1. Self Sabotage
2. My Heart Still Stands With You
3. Last Time Around
4. 200 Proof Lovin'
5. This Town Isn't Keeping You Down
6. Good Things Come to Those Who Wait
7. Blanket of Sorrow
8. Broken Whiskey Glass
9. Absolutely Sweet Marie
10. Ocean of Doubt
11. Pray For Me Mama (I'm A Gypsy Now)
12. Somewhere Within

Disc Two
1. Help! There's A Fire
2. Harvest Moon
3. If Money Talks
4. Walkin' The Dog
5. Both Sides Of The Line
6. White Lies
7. Jimmie Rodgers' Last Blue Yodel

Jason & the Scorchers, circa 2006

JASON & THE NASHVILLE SCORCHERS

8. Ezekiel's Wheels/Golden Ball & Chain
9. Going Nowhere
10. If You've Got the Love (I've Got the Time)
11. Still Tied

Comments: The culmination of nearly 16 years running of touring across the United States and around the world, the Scorchers – one of the best live rock bands of all time in my mind – finally release a live album, and a two-CD set at that. Recorded over a three-night stretch at the Exit/In club in Nashville in November 1987, this is the live album that Scorchers' fans had waited for through the years. High-octane, twangy rock & roll delivered with the passion of a tent revival and the frenzied attitude of the hottest punk band.

Guest performers here included Warner's parents Blanche and Ed Hodges. I was lucky enough to attend two of the three shows and they were both great, as were opening acts **Tommy Womack** and **Todd Snider**. The CD release was accompanied by a commercial video as well, tho' I never found a copy of the VHS tape before it went OOP.

XI. Wildfires + Misfires (Courageous Chicken/Yep Roc Records 2002, CD)
1. Absolutely Sweet Marie
2. Shop It Around
3. Lost Highway
4. Long Black Veil
5. Tear It Up (w/Link Wray)
6. If Money Talks
7. Polk Salad Annie
8. Don't Stop Doin'
9. Comin' 'Round

10. Fallen Angel
11. Too Much Too Young
12. Break Open The Sky
13. The Slow Train Never Ends (w/Blanche Hodges)
14. Window Town
15. Buried Me Like A Bone
16. Ruby Don't Take Your Love To Town (w/Rick Richards)
17. Jimmie Rodgers' Last Blue Yodel
18. Cappuccino Rosie
19. Gospel Plow

Comments: The obligatory collection of outtakes and rarities that typically signals the end of the road. This one happened because of Jason signing with Yep Roc for his solo releases, and luckily *Wildfires + Misfires* still manages to dig up a few surprises for the fans. Among the highlights: "Lost Highway" was recorded in 1984 for a King Biscuit Flower Hour broadcast, "Polk Salad Annie" was taken from a Westwood One radio broadcast, Rick Richards of the Georgia Satellites playing on "Ruby," an album outtake and the live version of "Tear It Up" with six-string legend Link Wray from the Roskilde Festival in Denmark.

That last one is particularly cool; Jack Emerson had given me a copy of "Tear It Up" back in '86, throwing it on the end of a demo cassette copy of *Still Standing* he made. The band brought me back a Roskilde t-shirt from the festival which, like all of the great t-shirts they gave me through the years, no longer fits my ever-widening frame. For a couple of years, though, I wore the hell out of that shirt. The inclusion of live performances from both the King Biscuit and Westwood One broadcasts lead me to believe that there might be more good live tape in a vault somewhere that maybe, one day, will be released.

XII. Halcyon Times (Courageous Chicken CD, 2010)
1. Moonshine Guy/Releasing Celtic Prisoners
2. Beat On The Mountain
3. Mona Lee
4. Fear Not Gear Rot
5. Mother Of Greed
6. Gettin' Nowhere Fast
7. Land Of The Free
8. Golden Days
9. Deep Holy Water
10. Twang Town Blues
11. Days Of Wine And Roses
12. Better Than This
13. When Did It Get So Easy (To Lie To Me)
14. We've Got It Goin' On

Comments: The first Jason & the Scorchers studio album since 1996 is a stunning tour de force. This is Scorchers, Mark IV as it were, with new guys Al Collins and Pontus Squib driving Jason and Warner to greater heights (see review ➜).

Jason & the Scorchers Bootlegs

B1. Rock On Germany (Courageous Chicken 2001, CD)
1. Lost Highway
2. Last Time Around
3. Are You Ready For The Country?
4. Can't Help Myself
5. If You've Got The Love, I've Got The Time
6. Shop It Around
7. Broken Whiskey Glass
8. Help, There's A Fire
9. Hot Nights In Georgia
10. Pray For Me Momma (I'm A Gypsy Now)
11. Travelin' Band
12. Change The Tune
13. You Win Again
14. Harvest Moon
15. Absolutely Sweet Marie
16. If Money Talks
17. I Really Don't Want To Know
18. White Lies
19. Around And Around
20. Honky Tonk Blues

Comments: I guess that it's OK to tell this story now. This infrequently-bootlegged performance was picked by rock historian Clint Heylin as one of the "100 Greatest Unauthorized Rock Albums Of All Time" in his book **Bootleg: The Secret History Of The Other Recording Industry**.

In a conversation about bootlegs around the time of *A Blazing Grace*, Jason admitted to me that he had bought a copy of this LP in Germany while on tour and smuggled it back home past his managers. I recommended that the band release its own bootleg albums, and this was the result, a gift to the fans from Jason and the gang...

B2. Absolutely Mannheim (Massive Attack Discs, CD-R)
1. Lost Highway
2. Last Time Around
3. Are You Ready For The Country?
4. Can't Help Myself
5. If You've Got The Love, I've Got The Time
6. Shop It Around
7. Broken Whiskey Glass
8. Help, There's A Fire
9. Hot Nights In Georgia
10. Still Tied
11. Travellin' Band
12. Change The Tune
13. This Heart Of Mine
14. Harvest Moon
15. Absolutely Sweet Marie
16. If Money Talks
17. Amazing Grace
18. Far Behind
19. Are You Ready For The Country?
20. Harvest Moon
21. White Lies

Comments: Songs #1-18 are taken from a 06/10/85 show in Mannheim, Germany while songs #19-21 are from the band's appearance at the 1986 Farm Aid II show in Austin, Texas.

Jason & the Scorchers, continued on page 279...

INTERVIEW: JASON & THE NASHVILLE SCORCHERS

Without a doubt, Jason and the Scorchers is the hottest thing to come out of Nashville since Hank Williams roamed the Southern countryside with an old guitar and a head full of dreams. Part of a growing legion of young rock rebels who deny the fashionable aspects of the art form and who readily do believe that the magic's in the music, Jason and the Scorchers combine a mixture of straight-forward rock with a measure of honky-tonk country and a dash of good ol' Bible-thumpin' gospel to produce some of the gutsiest, freshest, and most honest music being made today.

Jason Ringenberg, the Scorchers' vocalist and songwriter, came to Nashville from his parents' Illinois farm. Says Jason, "At the time, the rockabilly bands were starting to break in England, and I knew sure as hell that it was going to happen here in America. I knew that if I got the right band and got in with the right bunch of people, that I could make something that could outlast that, take a step further than that trend." The way to do this, Jason thought, was to "come to Nashville and get the young musicians that had actually grown up on the roots of American music – country and old rock and roll."

What Ringenberg found upon arriving in Nashville was quite discouraging at first. "I thought that there would be more people trying to do the same sort of thing that I was after. I was naive in that I thought there would be a real happening music scene in Nashville; but, although there *is* a music scene in town, it takes a little time to get into it. I thought that there would be eighteen clubs that you could walk into to see great bands every night – like New York City." At that time, Jason met Jack Emerson, who would become the Scorchers' manager. "He was into the same music that I was, thinking the same thoughts I was. That was two-and-a-half years ago, before rockabilly or any other new American revival broke."

After stumbling over a few obstacles, the Scorchers were born and set into a state of evolution. Says Ringenberg, "I played in a band with Jack for a while, but I knew that that band wouldn't happen. It was more or less a hobby for the other band members. That was the first incarnation of the Scorchers. We did three gigs together: one with R.E.M., one with Carl Perkins, and one opening for Nashville's Wrong Band. For the band, it was just doing something fun; for me it was getting a foot in the door."

While playing with that early band, Jason met the musicians who would make up the present day Scorchers: Jeff Johnson, Warner Hodges, and Perry Baggs. "Over the course of three months, we came together; we just coalesced. I pretty much knew from the start that this band had the potential for making it."

"All of us – especially Warner and Jeff and Perry – are rock and rollers: it's in our blood. You can look at us and see

that!" Following that rock and roll star presented the usual difficulties, though. Jason laughingly remembers, "When we all got together, everyone was sick of doing bullshit like working jobs, so we said 'the heck with it. Let's all quit our jobs and go on the road!' We were all that naive!" Two weeks later, though, Jason and the Scorchers *were* on the road; they'd quit their jobs, independently recorded their **Reckless Country Soul** EP, and left town.

At that time, says lead guitarist Warner Hodges, "Perry knew the four songs on the record and nothing else!" Jason knew of some clubs in the Midwest, and their friends in R.E.M. helped book them in a few in the Southwest. Says Jason, "We just started playing and haven't worked a day since. It's like a rock and roll dream!"

Of these early performances, Jason remembers, "Our first gigs on the road were done in real sleazy clubs where they expected us to do three-hour sets – and we knew only thirteen songs – so, we did these *long* jams. I'd sing different words, and Warner would tell jokes."

Audience response to the unique and distinctive stage show of the Scorchers was mixed and unpredictable. Of the audience, Jason remarks "They were absolutely shocked. This was before the resurgence of rockabilly – and we were three steps ahead of *that*. Jeff had a Mohawk haircut, Warner had hair down in his face, Perry had long hair to his shoulders, and I had fringe cowboy shirts and a cordless mike. People just didn't know what to think!" According to Warner, "People either loved us or they hated our guts. At first impression, they acted like we had leprosy."

In America, at that time, the Scorchers were the seminal "country-punk" band. "We were really extreme," says Jason. Since then, there have been four or five bands to come out of these same four musicians. And each one is totally different from the one which follows it five months later."

The Scorchers' mini-album, **Fervor**, was originally released in the Nashville area by Jack Emerson's independent label Praxis Records, and has recently been picked up and released nationally by EMI/America. "The Midwestern rural feeling meets the intensity of the South and you throw in a dash of good old-fashioned religion and it all comes together on **Fervor**," comments Ringenberg. "It's a very interesting album; I still listen to it myself."

Regarding **Fervor**'s sound, Jason continues, "You can see the way the band interacts, the way it has developed and matured. On **Fervor**, there are cuts recorded as long ago as fourteen months and as recently as a month ago."

As with any band that wishes to become successful, Jason and the Scorchers entered the video age. Their version of

Dylan's "Absolutely Sweet Marie" has been in light rotation on MTV for several months now. Of the taping, Jason says, "It was a new experience. We found that we came off better on film than we thought we would. I thought that, on the video, we showed a lot of charisma. The camera man on the project said that Warner should be in film…"

Warner, laughing, replies, "Maybe he heard me play guitar: 'Hey, look man, you should be in film. You need to give this music stuff up!'" Warner continues, "It's funny to me. You spend your whole life learning how to play, learning your trade as a musician, then you're thrown in front of a camera and you're told 'Now, be an actor!' It's a difficult transition to make. People may think that it's an easy thing, but everybody isn't David Bowie, proficient in every art form he wants to work in."

The need for musicians to become friendly with video is here to stay, though, as Jason realizes. "We're just going to have to make the most of it, make it a good art form."

"The only problem that I see with video," Ringenberg continues, "it that it puts a thought in people's minds as to what the song means. They can't use their imaginations to form their own interpretation of the song – particularly the lyrics. When people watched *The Lord of the Rings* on television, everyone was disappointed because they had their own thoughts as to what a hobbit looked like."

"Video presents the same problem in that the images seen on the screen – especially when the song is heard for the first time – will be implanted in their [the viewer's] minds. The video-makers are doing their [the audience's] thinking for them."

The Scorchers are currently on a major tour of the East coast in support of the EMI/America release of Fervor. According to Jason, their plans for this two-month trek are to "put on a good tour, to build a foundation with the radio stations and among the fans and the music people, and to create interest in the next album. I see this as a sort of fire and brimstone tour," Ringenberg concludes. "It will show what we are able to do and what we *aren't* able to do. It's the longest tour we've ever done, the longest amount of time we've been on the road together. We're going out to convert people into Scorchers fans."

"Most bands go out and tour *to* their fans; we're going out to win some over. Sure, we could play all the clubs that we've played and sell them out, but this is the challenge – we're looking for a wider range of people, a more varied audience. We're going to burn a path across America!"   – *CMJ Progressive Media*, May 1984

PERRY BAGGS

It is with great sadness that we report on the death of Perry Baggs, original drummer for cowpunk pioneers Jason & the *Nashville* Scorchers. Baggs was found in his Goodletsville, Tennessee apartment on Thursday morning, July 12, 2012; he was 50 years old and had suffered from severe diabetes and failing kidneys for years.

Having known Perry personally, I can say that his death is a damn shame. Baggs was always full of life and funny as hell. He was a good drummer with a lot of energy and stage presence, no mean feat considering the high-octane frontmen he played behind in Ringenberg and Hodges. Baggs was also an underrated songwriter, and he penned some of the band's best-known songs, including "White Lies" and "If Money Talks." Baggs was honored along with the Scorchers in 2008 with a Lifetime Achievement Award by the Americana Music Association.

JASON & THE SCORCHERS
Still Standing
(Capitol/EMI reissue)

I've been a rabid Jason & the Scorchers fan for a full two decades now, the band celebrating their twentieth anniversary this year. As such, it is only fitting that Capitol/EMI saw fit to reissue the band's excellent 1986 sophomore album, *Still Standing* on CD for the first time. While listening to this album for the thousandth time, however, I came to a conclusion, maybe even a mini-epiphany. Like a lot of rock & roll visionaries, listeners understood where the Scorchers were coming from or they didn't; you got 'em or you ignored them.

The Scorchers' unique blend of country twang, roots rock and punk fury didn't play well on MTV in the mid-eighties and it didn't sell many records, but it sure garnered a fair bit of critical acclaim. When the going got tough, though – as it often did during the Reagan eighties – there was nobody better at getting on stage and blowing away thoughts of your overdue car payment or impending rent than Jason & the *Nashville* Scorchers. Any night, in any venue, the Scorchers gave such cult-fave heavyweights as the Replacements a run for their money as the best damn rock & roll band in the land.

Although they were, perhaps, the most dynamic and consistent live band playing the rock & roll circuit during the mid-to-late eighties, the Scorchers' label wasn't pleased with the exposure and acclaim afforded the band's debut, *Lost & Found*. Rather than wait for the band's live performances to create word-of-mouth excitement (and sell records), the label recruited hard rock producer Tom Werman (Motley Crue) to helm the all-important second album.

The resulting production and the accompanying image "make-over" provided the band with a glossy sound and glam appearance that dismayed long-time fans. Even Werman's slick, metal-tinged production couldn't hide the Scorchers' cowtown roots, however. If *Still Standing* polished a few of the band's rough edges, it by turns emphasized Jason's manic vocals, Warner Hodges' raging fretwork and the big beat rhythms of bassist Jeff Johnson and drummer Perry Baggs.

After all these years, *Still Standing* sounds like a revelation. Jason's songwriting skills had matured nicely between the early *Fervor* EP and this second full-length LP, his masterful wordplay weaving wonderful story songs fraught with emotion and power. Rough-and-ready rockers like "Golden Ball & Chain," "Shotgun Blues" and a wild Scorchers reading of the Stones' "19th Nervous Breakdown" emphasized the band's punk mindset, Hodges whirling like a dervish, his axework underlining Jason's growing confidence in his vocal abilities. What made the band's approach work as well as it did is that the members never thought of themselves as punk rockers, not in the classic British sense of the word, at least. It was about this time that Warner, Jeff, friend Tom Littlefield of the Questionnaires and this humble scribe mixed it up with members of the Exploited outside of Nashville's legendary Cantrell's club. No, they were country punks, possessing all of the piss and vinegar of their big city counterparts; Jason, Warner, Jeff and Perry making their bones playing to hostile crowds in crappy honky-tonks and dangerous roadhouses.

To this punk attitude, the Scorchers added a country traditionalism that was as firmly rooted in Hank Williams, Johnny Cash and George Jones as any alt-country band today can claim. Jason was the son of a midwestern farmer; the remaining Scorchers were brought up in the Nashville area, Hodges playing with his parent's gospel band. When punk hit Nashville in the late-seventies, though, it hit hard, offering a stark alternative to the "countrypolitan" sound of "Music Row" in the sixties and early seventies. The Ramones' first appearance in the Music City, at the legendary Exit/Inn in 1978, would change the rules forever. Only a hundred or so people attended this mythical show, but all of them started bands, it would seem. Early-eighties Nashville shows by folks like Black Flag, the Replacements and X would spur further creativity and evolution of the growing local music scene.

The Scorchers absorbed these changing musical currents, mostly through the contributions of Johnson and Baggs, but would remain truer to their country roots than many of their west coast-based "cowpunk" counterparts. *Still Standing* manages to retain a fair share of the twang, especially on slower songs like "Good Things Come To Those Who Wait" and "Take Me To Your Promised Land."

These were not so much "power ballads," like those delivered by hair metal bands, but rather country torch songs, tortured with emotion, Jason's image-filled lyrics and potent vocal phrasing backed by a classic honky-tonk shuffle. On stage, these slower-paced songs would provide a counterpoint to the band's balls-out rockers, allowing the audience time to catch its breath. Tunes like "My Heart Still Stands With You" have aged well with time and sound as fresh today as fifteen years ago.

To the reissue of *Still Standing*, the label has added three bonus songs. The gem "Greetings From Nashville," penned by former Nashville resident Tim Krekel, is a longtime Scorchers favorite (and perhaps the only lyrical snapshot of the Southern underground of the eighties). The previously unreleased "Route 66," a live staple of the band, is provided a typical raucous treatment while "The Last Ride," an unreleased instrumental, proves for once and for all that Warner Hodges was one of the greatest six-string madmen of the eighties.

CD REVIEW: JASON & THE SCORCHERS' CLEAR IMPETUOUS...

Still Standing should have broken the Scorchers through to the mainstream, with three or four potentially big singles deserving more than the nonexistent airplay they received. Johnson would subsequently leave the band to join Nashville Goth-rockers Guilt on their sojourn to LA and the Scorchers would slightly alter their sound again with their third album, *Thunder & Fire*. The band would break-up at the end of the eighties and later get back together in 1995 for another run at the brass ring. Core members Jason Ringenberg and Warner Hodges still perform as the Scorchers today and through all of the band's trials and tribulations, they have retained an enormously loyal fan base throughout the past twenty years. If the Scorchers are, indeed, the ultimate cult band, *Still Standing* is quintessential Jason & the Scorchers. Get it and find out what all the fuss is about... – *Alt.Culture.Guide*, 2002

JASON & THE SCORCHERS
Clear Impetuous Morning
(Mammoth Records)

Seldom has a band received so much acclaim and developed such a loyal following as Jason & The Scorchers, yet never get any respect. Jason, Warner, Jeff and Perry have got to be the Rodney Dangerfields of the rock & roll world. After a hiatus of several years, the original Scorchers' line-up got back together a few years ago to record a solid collection of rock & roll tunes called *A Blazing Grace*. It went nowhere outside of their hardcore circle of fans.

Now they deliver what is arguably the finest album of their lengthy career in *Clear Impetuous Morning* and the signs are there for all to see that the effort is playing mostly to the choir, falling on those deaf ears who'd rather set down fifteen bucks for another Nirvana or Pearl Jam clone than actually grab something that would really get their adrenaline flowing. Even those nouveau country rockers over in the alt.country scene, while recognizing the Scorchers' place in their holy pantheon, don't seem to be falling over themselves to pick up a new Scorchers disc or two...

Clear Impetuous Morning finds the Scorchers mining the same country-flavored, roots-rock vein that they pioneered almost fifteen years ago. In this aspect, the band has never sounded better. Warner Hodges is an exemplary guitarist, a

legend-in-waiting on the level of Keith Richards who plays with great skill *and* flash. Hodges tears off chainsaw riffs like some kid playing air guitar in his bedroom, breathing life into each song. Jason's energetic vocal delivery is part Hank Williams, part Johnny Rotten, crooning sweet country twang on cuts like "I'm Sticking With You," kicking out the jams with reckless, joyful abandon on rockers like "Victory Road." The rhythm section of bassist Jeff Johnson and drummer Perry Baggs provide a steady beat and a strong backbone for the Scorchers performances, playing conservative foils to Jason and Warner's rock & roll crazed wild men.

Lyrically, *Clear Impetuous Morning* distinguishes itself through its maturity and wisdom. This foursome clearly aren't the idealistic youngsters that they were in 1982, and every scar that they've received through the years can be found in these songs. Jason Ringenberg, always the Scorchers main songwriter, collaborates here with some new partners. Most notable of these is Nashvillian Tommy Womack, formerly of Mid-South legends Government Cheese.

Together, they put together some of the album's hottest songs, like the new Scorchers' show-stopper, "Self-Sabotage" or "Cappuccino Rosie." A duet between Jason and Emmylou Harris on "Everything Has A Cost" proves to be a natural pairing, the two creating a haunting musical moment that is underlined by some strong six-string work from Hodges.

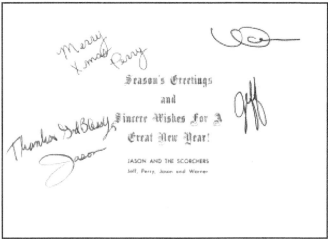

Sadly, the Scorchers seem doomed to be one of those bands who never receive a break, who never find themselves in the "right place at the right time." If the masses refuse to pick up on an album as solid as *Clear Impetuous Morning*, what's left for the band to try? As one of a handful who can truthfully say that I've been a fan of the band since the beginning, I marvel at the Scorchers ability to keep going in the face of adversity. They've suffered breaking up, getting back together again, three record labels, industry indifference, constant touring and mediocre sales for over a decade and a half. Yet they keep on rocking, cranking out some of the greatest music in the history of the genre, delivering night after night with great live performances. Like Rodney, they get nowhere near the respect they rightfully deserve. (1997)

JASON & THE SCORCHERS
Midnight Roads & Stages Seen
(Mammoth Records)

Nashville's favorite sons knocked a local audience on their collective backsides last November with the two nights of performances that make up *Midnight Roads & Stages Seen*, the Scorchers' first, and long overdue, live set. The band has long been a favorite in tape trader's circles for years, with classic vintage shows from the eighties swapped on a regular basis among an international audience. With the release of this double-disc set, Scorchers' fans across the globe finally have an authorized live set to whet their musical appetites.

For most of their career, Jason & The Scorchers have delivered solid studio albums, but it's been their live shows that have won them a hard-earned and well-deserved following among even the most hard-core rockers. Lead vocalist Jason Ringenberg's country-inflected drawl, boundless energy and manic on-stage gyrations are matched only by guitarist supreme Warner Hodges' razor-sharp riffs, instrumental acrobatics and dizzying dervish pirouettes. Drummer Perry Baggs has always been a steady keeper of the

beats while the latest addition to the line-up, bassist Kenny Ames, has meshed nicely with the founding members of the band.

Over fifteen years of performing across the United States, Canada, Europe and even "down under" have made the Scorchers a powerful live band. The chemistry enjoyed by the guys is such that, on any given night, they're the best rock & roll outfit playing anywhere – a claim not many bands could make.

If you've seen the Scorchers play live anytime during the past couple of years – or even during the past 15 years – then you're probably aware of what the band is capable of on-stage. If not, then *Midnight Roads & Stages Seen* is the album for you. Recorded at Nashville's famous Exit/In, the 23 songs chosen from two nights of shows are a veritable catalog of the Scorchers' "greatest hits." Classic cuts like "White Lies," "Absolutely Sweet Marie," "If Money Talks" or "Broken Whisky Glass" are provided an appropriate rave-up treatment.

Other more understated songs, like "Somewhere Within" (from the *A Blazing Grace* album) or Jason's collaboration with Todd Snider, "This Town Isn't Keeping You Down," are performed live here for the first time. The energy level displayed here is astounding, with every cut carefully crafted with equal parts of loving workmanship and reckless abandon.

If there was any justice in this world – which, as we all know, there's not – Jason & the Scorchers would be superstars of the biggest kind. There's seldom been a harder working group of guys in a band, nor an outfit that has managed to persevere through three record labels, bankruptcy and a brief break-up to subsequently create some of the best music of their career, as have the Scorchers. The band's influence on the current crop of alt-country hopefuls and young rockers is enormous.

Midnight Roads & Stages Seen captures the band at the peak of their career, the Scorchers still making great rock & roll almost two decades since the day they first played together.

JASON & THE SCORCHERS
Absolutely Mannheim
(Massive Attack CD-R #990167, 67:56 min) [bootleg CD]

SOURCE: Tracks 1 – 16, Mannheim Germany, June 10, 1985. Tracks 17-19, Farm Aid II, Austin TX 1986.

SOUND QUALITY: German set is a fair audience recording with significant drop-outs, clicks, fade-aways and enough hollowness and echo to make one wonder what sort of cave they recorded the songs in. Nevertheless, Jason's vocals are reasonably clear and Warner's guitar is up front in the mix. Farm Aid tracks are a fair audience recording with tinny sound, abrasive top end and a bit of distortion.

COVER: Typical Massive Attack packaging, with a B & W shot of Jason Ringenberg on the front and a pretty cool "American Gothic" styled B & W shot of the entire band on the back along with tracklist and venue info.

TRACKLIST: Lost Highway/ Last Time Around/ Are You Ready For The Country?/ Can't Help Myself/ If You've Got The Love (I've Got The Time)/ Shop It Around/ Broken Whiskey Glass/ Help! There's A Fire - Hot Nights In Georgia/ Pray For Me Mama (I'm A Gypsy Now)(incorrectly listed as "Still Tied")/ Travelin' Band/ Change The Tune/ You Win Again (incorrectly listed as "This Heart Of Mine")/ Harvest Moon/ Absolutely Sweet Marie - If Money Talks/ Amazing Grace/ Shotgun Blues (incorrectly listed as "Far Behind")/ Are You Ready For The Country?/ Broken Whiskey Glass (incorrectly listed as "Harvest Moon")/ White Lies

COMMENTS: From the dank ambience of Cantrell's and the beer-soaked stage at Phrank 'n' Steins, Jason & the Scorchers broke out of the primal early-eighties Nashville club scene to hit the world stage, their 1985 tour of Europe earning them a considerable fan base in England, Germany and points north. Although the band worked consistently throughout the eighties – in fact, demand for their live shows kept the wolves from the door when EMI bankrupted them – they never quite crossed over to the mainstream. A couple of spins of *Absolutely Mannheim* show why the Scorchers earned such a rabid cult following, however. Their audience is so loyal that a couple of years ago, the live recording sessions in Nashville for *Midnight Roads And Stages Seen* drew Scorchers fans from across the U.S., South America and northern Europe to take part in the fun.

Although the sound on *Absolutely Mannheim*, quite frankly, sucks, the performance is typical high-energy, high octane Jason & the Scorchers. Touring Europe for the first time, supporting their first full-length album *Lost & Found*, the set list here is almost identical to that on the rare *Rock On Germany* LP, an album that writer Clint Heylin considers one of the best bootlegs ever made. I've got a tape of that album, smuggled out of Germany by band members, and I believe that *Absolutely Mannheim* is even better.

The performances are both exciting, but by the time of the Mannheim show the Scorchers had been in Europe for three weeks and the live sets had really jelled. The set is pretty much normal for 1985-vintage Scorchers, the band performing most of the *Lost & Found* album mixed with cuts from the band's critically-acclaimed *Fervor* EP and a couple tunes from their original Praxis label 7" EP, *Reckless Country Soul*.

With fifteen years of retrospection, original Scorchers songs like "Shop It Around," "If Money Talks," "Last Time Around" and "Broken Whiskey Glass" are comfortable favorites; at the time they were precious cowpunk rave-ups that fused traditional country with punk energy and attitude, providing Nashville rockers with something to believe in.

Inspired covers performed here include Hank Williams' "Lost Highway" (which opened most every Scorchers set) and "You Win Again" (which would eventually be dropped from the set), Neil Young's "Are You Ready For The Country?" and Dylan's "Absolutely Sweet Marie." A Scorchers signature tune, the video for "Absolutely Sweet Marie" would introduce the band to early-eighties MTV audiences. An early version of "Shotgun Blues" from the Scorchers second album (incorrectly listed here as "Far Behind') shows the band still fine-tuning the song while the rendition of CCR's "Travelin' Band," sung by Scorchers guitarist Warner Hodges proves that Hodges should stick to his six-string wizardry.

The Mannheim set presented here is probably a couple of songs shy of complete – missing is "White Lies," the first single from *Lost & Found* and a staple of the band's performances at the time. In a summer of high points, however, the Mannheim show stands as one of the highest, the 1985 European tour peaking with an appearance in front of 40,000 people at the Roskilde Festival in Denmark where Link Wray joined the band onstage.

Whoever put this disc together made a few glaring errors in terms of song titles. Who could ever confuse "Broken Whiskey Glass," one of the band's first songs and a signature tune, with "Harvest Moon," a ballad from the *Fervor* EP (as they did here on the Farm Aid tracks)? Other songs are also misidentified, either by title or by confusing them with other Scorchers' songs.

There are also a couple of indexing errors where the band jumps from one song right into another, as with "Absolutely Sweet Marie" and "If Money Talks" with the producer/manufacturer missing it entirely. These ridiculous mistakes and generally aggravating sound quality aside, it's nice to finally see a Scorchers show on disc.

Absolutely Mannheim is an important document of one of rock's most underrated bands. With the wealth of live Scorchers' material circulating on tape, some of it of pretty decent quality, maybe we'll see more of Jason & the Scorchers on CD in the future. *– Live Music Review*, 2000

JASON & THE SCORCHERS
Halcyon Times
(Courageous Chicken/NashVegas Flash)

The Reverend remembers watching…no, witnessing Jason & the *Nashville* Scorchers tear apart a local club – Cantrell's, maybe the Exit/In – no matter, 'cause those ol' boys ripped it up like Link Wray and took that building apart brick by (figurative) brick. Nobody, and I mean *nobody* could take over a stage like Jason, Warner, Jeff, and Perry back in the day, and if you had the cajones and the stamina, they'd keep on rockin' until every last punter had dropped to the floor…

Yup, back during the early '80s in the Music City, rock 'n' roll was a man's (and a few choice women's) game, with bands fiercely rejecting the country music establishment that had hung the albatross of the cornpone *Hee Haw* image around the necks of we young soul rebels. Giants walked the dark streets and back alleys of Elliston Place and Eighth Avenue and East Nashville those days, outlaws like Raging Fire, the dusters, Shadow 15, Webb Wilder, the Bunnies, and many more who took the stage each night determined not to quit rockin' until the stinking cowtown corpse was permanently buried.

None of the musical giants of that era strode taller or played faster and louder than Jason & the *Nashville* Scorchers (the "Nashville" part was later dropped at the recommendation of some recordco dunce). They were not only the most popular band in town for a long time, one could make the arguement

that, for much of the world outside of Middle Tennessee, they were the *only* band that mattered.

The Scorchers were quite a spectacle, no matter what stage they conquered: while Jason yelped and danced and spun around like a dervish with pants on fire, Warner Hodges would play Keef to Jason's Mick, tearing otherworldly sounds out of his guitar that had been previously unheard by human ears. Bassist Jeff Johnson was the epitome of cool, holding down the rhythm, while drummer Perry Baggs was a madman on the skins, bashing the cans like Tennessee's own John Bonham while providing angelic harmony vocals behind Jason's farm-bred Illinois twang.

More importantly, at least to us on the street, the drones on Music Row and the Nashville cultural establishment *hated* the Scorchers with a passion, viewing them as either the Four Horsemen of the Apocalypse, or as the end of everything good and green and holy about the city. Legend has it that famed Nashville deejay Ralph Emery turned his nose up at the Byrds when they played the Grand Ol' Opry in 1967; a couple of decades later, the Scorchers damn near gave the poor man a heart attack.

Back on Elliston Place, however, we *knew* the future of rock 'n' roll when we heard it, and as the band began to expand its circle to the Southeast, and then Europe with one fine record after another, it looked for a moment like our predictions of Scorchers world dominance might come true…

Jason & the Scorchers, 2010

Sadly, Jason & the Scorchers never got the respect that they deserved; their records were under-promoted by the labels, or ignored in the hope that the band might just go away. Tensions grew dire within the band, members came and went, and by the time that grunge and the Seattle scene had wiped the slate clean, the Scorchers had fallen by the wayside. Although a mid-1990s Scorchers reunion would result in a pair of perfectly good studio albums and a live set that came as close as technology would allow to capturing the band's anarchic onstage energy, it seemed as if stardom just wasn't in the cards for Jason & the Scorchers.

Flash forward to 2010...the Kings of Leon are the new cocks on the walk, the first Nashville rockers to afford million-dollar homes, and it all seems so damn wrong. Sure, the local music scene still exists on some level, but every young new band seems to have its eye on the dollars and not the music, which is probably why old '80s warhorses like Royal Court of China, Shadow 15, the Bunnies, et al are drawing club crowds like it's 1985 all over again, 'cause the young 'uns wanna rock, dammit! They want none of this TMZ bullshit and celebrity band status, just rock 'n' roll to feed the soul!

Into this vacuum steps a reunited Jason & the Scorchers with *Halcyon Times*, the band's first studio album in 14 years. Messrs. Ringenberg and Hodges still captain the ship, new guys Al Collins (bass) and Pontus Snibb (drums) are on board to man the rhythm section, and various musical contributions come from fellow travelers like former Georgia Satellites frontman Dan Baird, Brit-rocker Ginger of the Wildhearts, beloved Nashville icon Tommy Womack, and former Scorchers bandmate Perry Baggs, who provides his lively harmonies to several songs.

Somewhere on his Tennessee farm ol' Jason must be hiding a damn time machine, because *Halcyon Times* sounds more like 1985 than 2010, the new album re-capturing the joyous abandon of early Scorchers' discs like *Reckless Country Soul* or *Fervor* than anything they've done since. Sure, it may not have been recorded in Jack Emerson's living room (R.I.P. Brother Jack), but *Halcyon Times*, produced by Hodges and Nashville pop-rock wunderkind Brad Jones, offers an energy and immediacy lacking in most modern recordings.

The reasons behind the crackling livewire sound of the album comes from the presence of an audience watching the band record from behind glass, and the unlikely strategy of putting Jason live in the studio, singing along with the band... something seldom done with today's Pro Tools dominated recording techniques. The result is an album that rocks like it was recorded in somebody's living room, but sounds like a well-made studio creation.

The songs on *Halcyon Times* are among the best the Scorchers have ever delivered. The breakneck rocker

JASON & THE SCORCHERS
HALCYON TIMES

"Moonshine Guy" is a paean to a certain kind of individual that, while not restricted to the South, is nevertheless a particularly Dixie-fried sort of character. With a punkish pace and intensity, Jason sings of the guy that "loves the Stones, hates the Doors/thinks the Beatles sing for girls/he's a moonshine guy in a six-pack world," his rapidfire vocals telling of the sort of last-century diehard who still yells "play Freebird" at any show he attends. A Celtic-flavored instrumental interlude in the middle, titled "Releasing Celtic Prisoners," provides just enough relief for the band to charge back in to conclude the song.

Although "Moonshine Guy" could be dismissed by some slackjaw critics as a novelty, it's really just a comic intro to a serious, joyful, and reckless set of songs that show why the Scorchers, 25 years after their debut, retain a fiercely loyal following from Lawrence, Kansas to London, England and points beyond. The collaborative songwriting efforts on *Halcyon Times* have produced some stellar results. Despite the contemporary production values, the raging "Mona Lee" sounds like vintage Scorchers with Hodges' six-string gymnastics and Jason's country soul vocals accompanied by fluid bass lines and crashing drumbeats.

The folkish "Mother of Greed" features some of Jason's best vocals, the song possessing an ethereal quality as the lyrics recount the passage of time and cash-grab progress. The Hodges/Dan Baird guitarwork here is simply gorgeous, their instruments intertwined in a beautiful melody until Hodges cuts loose with a magnificent solo. The vocal harmonies provide a gauzy, otherworldly quality to the mix. The album-closing "We've Got It Goin' On" is the sort of song that the Scorchers based their rep on, only writ large for the 21st century. With shotgun lyrics delivered at 100mph above chaotic instrumentation that echoes 1960s garage-rock intensity, Jason spits out almost stream-of-consciousness lyrics that are nevertheless intriguing: "does an empire falling ever make a sound?"; "diggin' down in the here and now 'til tomorrow is yesterday"; "blacking out on a rush of pain kind of felt like home to me". I'm not sure what it all means, but it rocks and that's good enough for me!

For all the band's protestations that they wanted to make a record that was forward-looking, the past casts a long shadow across *Halcyon Times*. The Scorchers, after all, were the great white hopes of cowpunk; the critical darlings with a cult following that were one song away from mainstream mega-stardom. Although Ringenberg and Hodges have certainly come to grips with their near-brush with infamy, somewhere deep inside them it has to chafe just a bit…on many nights, the Scorchers *were* the best rock 'n' roll band in the land, the Replacements and other pretenders to the throne be damned.

As such, *Halcyon Times* includes many subtle, and some not-so-so subtle references to days gone by, such as the inclusion of the nearly-subliminal line from "Hot Nights In Georgia" that serves as a kick-off to the second part of "Moonshine Guy." The rockabilly-tinged "Getting' Nowhere Fast" could be the band's theme song, a runaway instrumental freight train with Jason singing "we're getting nowhere fast faster than we've ever been, we're getting nowhere fast put the pedal to the metal again." In many ways, the song is a statement of defiance, and a gleeful one at that.

"Golden Days," from which the album takes its name, is a look backwards that charts the progress of a fictional protagonist through the years, meaningful lyrics matched by another solid vocal performance and a timeless pop-rock soundtrack with an infectious chorus. The darkly humorous "Twang Town Blues" is the story of the Scorchers and every other wild-eyed dreamer that landed in Nashville, or L.A., or

Jason & Warner, 2010

New York in search of fame and fortune. Telling the story of several such hopefuls with talking blues vocals resting above a menacing swamp-rock theme, the line "tonight he'll kill a six-pack just to watch it die" shouts out to Johnny Cash and Nashville's checkered musical history with eerie effect.

Co-written by Dan Baird with an eye specifically towards the Scorchers, "Days of Wine and Roses" is the story of Jason and Warner and their often complicated relationship. In many ways the song is the heart of *Halcyon Times*, Jason singing "like a soldier that doesn't know that it's time to go home, and if there's no one else to hoist the flag, well I'll go it alone" with a world-weariness that only 25 years in the music biz can bring. Warner's guitar tones are mesmerizing, bringing a bright, emotional edge to the lyrics as Jason sings "the days of wine and roses they are long dead and gone, carry on, carry on…" The song positions the Scorchers – and specifically Jason and Warner – as the veterans they are, old soldiers that refuse to go quietly into that good night.

If "Days of Wine and Roses" is the heart of *Halcyon Times*, then the pop-tinged rocker "Better Than This" serves as the album's soul. With Warner singing in a voice that is as distinctively hard rock in nature as Jason's is earthy country twang, the song delights in the unbridled joy of making music. Above a raucous soundtrack with some red-hot guitarwork, Warner sings "someday you just might find/as you're looking back in time/it gets good but it don't get better than this." No matter the band's trials and tribulations, minor successes and failures, it all fades away once they hit the stage.

Released independently by the band, *Halcyon Times* is unlikely to set the charts on fire, although it's certainly one of the best rock albums that will be released in 2010. Sensing that it might be the band's last stand – or at least their last physical CD in an increasingly digital world – the Scorchers have put together a beautiful CD package that includes great graphics, and a thick booklet full of lyrics, photos, and liner notes sure to thrill the hardcore faithful.

It's the music that counts, though, and here Jason & the Scorchers and friends have delivered in spades. The album combines the reckless energy and enthusiasm of their youth with the cautious optimism and mature talent of veteran musicians. With *Halcyon Times*, the band rocks harder and sounds better than they ever have. The Scorchers may be going nowhere fast, but they're having a hell of a time doing so...

Jason & the Scorchers, continued...

Similar in sound and sequencing to **Rock On Germany** and ostensibly taken from the same tour, this is one of the few widely-distributed Scorchers' boots. There's still other good stuff floating around the tape-trading community, and I'd personally like to see the band go ahead and release the infamous Kansas and Cat's Records Nashville shows on disc.

JAVA CHRIST
Web: www.myspace.com/javachrist

Band Members:
Josh (vocals) (A1)
Nate (bass) (A1)
Geoff (guitars, vocals) (A1)
Dave (drums) (A1)

Java Christ Recordings:

A1. Songs To Confuse Slam Dancers (House O' Pain 1996, 7" vinyl EP)
Side One
1. Gasoline
2. Suburbia

Side Two
3. Insomnia
4. Clue

Comments: Nashville's resident punk-rock maniacs were unfortunately in the wrong place at the right time.

JET BLACK FACTORY

Band Members:
Dave Willie (vocals) (I-IV)
Bob German (lead guitar) (I-IV)
Lance Frizzell (rhythm guitar) (IV)
Roy Anderson (guitar) (II-IV)
Dave Jones (bass) (I, II)
Ralph Otis Pierce (bass) (II-IV)
Jim Dye (drums) (I-IV)

Other Musicians:
Russel Brown (vocals) (III)
Robert Logue (bass, mandolin) (III, IV)
Mike Poole (keyboards) (III, IV)

Jet Black Factory Recordings:

I. Days Like These (391 Records 1987, 12" vinyl EP)
Side A
1. Real Down Ticket
2. By The Temple
3. Tonight

Side AA
1. Chelsea
2. The City Sleeps
3. Waters Edge

Jason Ringenberg, Rev. Keith & Warner Hodges

JET BLACK FACTORY

II. Duality (391 Records 1988, 12" vinyl EP)
Side 1
1. 3 Poisons
2. Interstate
3. Towards The Sun

Side 2
4. Lamplight Shining
5. Speed
6. Van Allen Belt

III. House Blessing (391 Records 1990, LP)
Side A
1. Vinegar Works
2. Indigo
3. Uncrossing
4. Look Away
5. Lumber

Side B
1. Shut Up
2. Blood Simple
3. Wind Trains
4. Mexico City
5. Bastard Sometimes
6. More Clank Than Chain

Comments: Formed in 1985 by vocalist/songwriter Dave Willie and guitarist Bob German, Jet Black Factory quickly won acclaim for their powerful live shows and a dark-hued, somber sound that won the band comparisons to the Doors and the Velvet Underground. With bassist Phil Jones and drummer Jim Dye, the band released its first recording, the

JAVA CHRIST
Songs To Confuse Slam Dancers EP
(House O' Pain Records)

Back a few years ago, I had a gig as the night manager of a local newsstand/convenience store in the university area of Nashville. As one of the few places in town that sold the notorious Jolt Cola, we had a regular weekend crowd of young punks, cybergeeks and metalheads who would buy this high-octane gutrot by the caseload. I got to know several of these customers on a casual basis, often talking music/computers/politics with them. I was old enough to be their father, but I listened to them, supported their dreams and accepted them for what they were, which was a diverse, creative lot with a lot ahead of them.

What a couple of these young Jolt guzzlers had in front of them was Java Christ, the finest young band to emerge from the Nashville scene since the Teen Idols first took the stage (which, although not really *that* long a period of time, says something nonetheless considering the large number of truly mediocre bands that come and go in the Music City in a year's time).

Thanks to the fine folks at House O' Pain, Java Christ make their vinyl debut with the 7" **Songs To Confuse Slam Dancers** EP, an altogether red-hot slab o' punk rock fun that comes with an iron-clad Reverend K guarantee: if you buy this disc from House O' Pain and don't like it, send it (in good condition, naturally) to *R.A.D!* and we'll give you yer cash back on it. Yes, it's that good.

Side One of the EP kicks off with "Gasoline," an infectious ska-tinged rocker. Layers of fuzzy guitar punctuate the tune's rock-steady rhythm, with the entire effort burning as bright as its name and subject matter. "Suburbia" opens with gonzo rock chords, flashing quickly into a fast-paced, mile-a-minute musical romp. The second side's "Insomnia" is anything but a snooze, hard and fast chords underlining a classic tale of love lost (and delivering the most effective lyrical "piss-off" since Dylan's "Positively 4th Street"). The disc closes with "Clue," another delightful ska-fest, chockful of energy and attitude.

After seeing Java Christ play live at this year's House O' Pain/Lucy's Record Shop Anti-Extravaganza show, I can say that they've got a bright future ahead of them. They're charismatic and likeable, with a solid punk ethic that just can't be beat. *Songs To Confuse Slam Dancers* is an entertaining and impressive recording debut that manages to capture enough of the band's live energy to scorch your turntable.
– *R.A.D! Review & Discussion of Rock & Roll*, 1996

six-song *Days Like This*, in 1986 on its own 391 Records imprint. The five-song EP *Duality* followed in 1987.

Ralph Pierce replaced Jones on bass, and a second guitarist, Roy Anderson, was added to the mix. The band released a full-length album, *House Blessing*, in 1990. Lance Frizzell replaced Anderson on guitar and the band's steady touring throughout the Southeast earned the album airplay on over 200 college radio stations. *House Blessing* eventually made its way onto both the *Rockpool* and *CMJ* college radio charts, which brought the band to the attention of Core executive Keith Dressel, who signed them to his Oxymoron label.

IV. The Uncrossing (Core/Oxymoron 1991, CD)
1. Fire Drum
2. Indigo
3. El Diablo
4. Look Away
5. Lumber
6. Shut Up
7. Blood Simple
8. Wind Train
9. Vinegar Works
10. Bastard Sometimes
11. More Clank Than Chain

Comments: Released by Core in 1991, *The Uncrossing* is basically *House Blessing* with a couple of new songs tacked on, and the remainder remixed for national distribution. In their own unique way, Jet Black Factory provided a Dixie equivalent to the Seattle sound. In charismatic frontman Dave Willie, the South had its own Kurt Cobain, the deep-voiced singer delivering lyrics inspired more by Kerouac and Baudelaire than by Hank Williams, and guitarist Bob German's droning six-string work providing a sonic counterpoint to Willie's intelligent wordplay. Label problems derailed the band's fortunes, however, and they broke up just as alternative rock was receiving a new lease on life courtesy of Nirvana (see interview ➔).

JETPACK

Band Members:
Sean Williams (vocals, guitar) (I-II)
Stephen Jerkins (guitar, keyboards, vocals) (I-II)
John Grimsley (bass, vocals) (I)
Pete Traisci (drums, vocals) (I)
Rob Bell (keyboards)
Landon Ihde (bass) (II)
Jeremy Lutito (drums) (II)

Jetpack Recordings:

I. Jetpack (Echomusic 2002, CD)
1. Hot Rod
2. High School Girls
3. Gloomy Jules
4. Poison
5. Lead Me On
6. I'll Beat Him Up For You
7. Padded Room
8. So Ashamed
9. These Lips O' Mine
10. Kitty Kat
11. Write These Words
12. Soaking Wet

II. The Art Of Building A Moat (Echomusic 2004, CD)
1. Mathematics
2. All Hail The Clown
3. Mrs. Flannery
4. Synthesizer
5. Destroy Your Hideout
6. Your Little Way
7. Stonehands

Comments: Due to conflicts with other bands, they had to change their name, from Jetpack to Jetpack U.K. (?), and finally to **the Nobility**.

JETT RINK

Band Members:
Max Ratliff (vocals, guitar)
"Skye James" a/k/a J. Stefan Jackson (vocals, guitar)
Dave Harrison (drums)

Comments: Little-known band from Nashville's early 1990s hard rock circuit. Ratliff and Harrison went on to form **the Keep**; "Skye James" is actually fantasy novelist J. Stefan Jackson.

ROBERT JETTON & THE ROCKIN' RANCHEROS

Band Members:
Robert Jetton (vocals, guitar) (A1, I)
Tim Good (guitars)
Tom Comet (bass) (A1)
Danny Dickerson (keyboards)
Willis Bailey (drums) (A1)

jetpack

Other Musicians:
Merel Bregante (drums) (A1)
Frank Brittingham (guitar) (A1)
Bruce Dees (guitars) (A1)
Gary Hooker (guitar) (A1)
Tim Krekel (guitars) (A1)
Don Roth (acoustic guitar) (A1)

Robert Jetton Recordings:

Singles

A1. Innocent EP (New Bohemian Records 1982, 7" vinyl)
Side A
1. When You're Holdin' Me
2. Big Mouth Blues

Side B
3. Still Around
4. The Innocent

Albums/EPs

I. Rockin' Ranchero (New Bohemian Records, no date, cassette)
1. Easy To Slip
2. It's Only Love
3. Little Troublemaker
4. Once In Love

Comments: For this four-song EP, Jetton was backed by **the Nerve**. Produced by Hank DeVito, the cassette also features Emmylou Harris and Chris Spedding. Jetton is one of the underrated talents of Nashville's rock and alt-country scenes, blowing into town from Fort Worth with his buddies Tom Comet and Willis Bailey in tow, first backing up some of Marshall Chapman's best, most rocking work.

Robert Jetton, continued on page 285...

Jetpack (pre-Nobility)

Picture this, if you will...a rock and roll band fronted by a fiercely charismatic figure, a lead vocalist with a deep, menacing baritone singing oblique and often symbolic lyrics which hint of love and betrayal, life and despair. Meanwhile, the band churns on behind him, skilled artisans weaving a musical tapestry out of the fibers of the night...

...no, they're not the next Doors, contrary to what a few uncreative critics thumbing through yellowing, brittle thesauruses might like you to believe. Any comparison between Nashville's Jet Black Factory and that almost mythological rock and roll posse are unfair. Of the label, J.B.F.'s vocalist/lyricist Dave Willie says, "I don't like it at all. That's never been deliberate on our part at all. People have a cartoon impression of what Jim Morrison sounds like and because it is a cartoon, you can plug anything into it."

Adds guitarist Lance Frizzell, "there's a new comparison now, with the Cure...I don't get that one at all. That's even harder to handle than the Doors." Comparisons aside, Jet Black Factory are an entirely original, uncompromisingly unique band in their own right, sharing more in the way of ancestry and attitude with folks like the Stooges and Velvet Underground than with over-hyped, over-merchandised matinee idols.

Formed in 1985 by Willie and lead guitarist Bob German, Jet Black Factory rapidly became one of the Music City's most popular...and unquestioningly creative bands. The duo's reasons for putting together J.B.F. were simple. Says German, "by '85, all the bands that I liked had either broken up or had gotten pretty lousy, and I just wanted to make the music that I wanted to hear."

Of the band's purpose, Willie adds, "it isn't much different today than it was then. If I wasn't doing this band, I'd be doing something else...writing, or doing something artistic to keep myself occupied. That's always been a way to blow off steam, to channel my energies in a creative way rather than in a negative or destructive way."

With the addition of drummer Jim Dye and original bassist Phil Jones, Jet Black Factory carved their own little niche into Nashville's still-expanding local music scene. Their complex and mesmerizing musical hybrid is fueled in part by German's imaginative six-string work and Willie's soaring, ethereal vocals caressing poetic lyrics. Working in a milieu outside that of any other Nashville band, they soon began to earn a rep for themselves outside of their hometown.

The band expanded upon this out-of-town respect with the release of a pair of critically-acclaimed EPs, *Days Like These* and *Duality*. These inspired recordings garnered a fair bit of college airplay, a lot of praise, and made J.B.F. the focus of a lot of well-deserved attention. Regional touring continuously

JET BLACK FACTORY • HOUSE BLESSING
SEE IT LIVE
SATURDAY JUNE 2
MIDNIGHT SUN

built the band a loyal base of fans, thus earning them status as a "cult band" for those in the know to watch.

"It was a learning experience. Actually, I prefer doing it that way," says Willie of the band's self-produced initial recordings. "We knew from day to day what was going on, where the record was, the progress of the artwork...when you do it yourself, you'll do it right, at least the way you see it."

Continuing, Willie says, "people in the industry were amazed at the response we got for those records, which are called 'vanity' releases now." German adds, "they sneer at bands who put out their own records and CDs now. It used to be that you put out your own records, that was how it was done. Now they're called a 'vanity' release. We got that expression from MTV, who refused to air any videos unless they came from a major label."

As a local scene veteran, Willie has witnessed the gradual change in the Nashville scene that he, and Jet Black Factory, helped to define. "I've been in 1,001 different groups," says Willie, who played in C.P.S. among other bands, "from hardcore bands to weirdo art-rock bands...you were together for a couple of weeks and, if you were lucky, you played one show, got some free beer, and that was the extent of it."

INTERVIEW: JET BLACK FACTORY

Continuing, Willie adds, "it used to be a lot of fun. It still is, but there used to be a real spirit of camaraderie between bands and promoters and fans…more of a sense of a scene then than there is now. The influence of a lot of outside people has made this a business rather than a lot of fun. I walk into record stores and I hear musicians talking and they're saying 'I'm a great bass player and I don't want to get into a group unless it's already signed to a major label.' You wouldn't have heard that even three years ago…that would have been insane."

In early 1990, the band released their first full-length album, *House Blessing*. Showcasing new members and a fuller, more mature sound, it provided an artistic and commercial breakthrough, of sorts, for the band. "Having the experience of two records underneath our belts," says German, "we had a lot better ideas of what we wanted to do. The songs were better, from both a songwriting and a production standpoint. We were much happier with it than with the previous two records."

House Blessing also heralded the coming of two new members of the band. With the departure of bassist Jones, J.B.F. added bassist Ralph Pierce and second guitarist Roy Anderson. Says Willie, "as soon as we got those guys in the band, it took off in a different direction, a more mature and interesting direction." With no money for promotion and little time for touring (the band members all work day jobs), *House Blessing* made quite a splash on the efforts of the band and manager Will Reynolds alone. Dozens of reviews praising the album were balanced by airplay on some 200 college radio stations. As a result, the disc charted on both the *Rockpool* and *CMJ* charts and picked up international distribution.

A glowing review of the album in *The Hard Report* brought the band to the attention of Keith Dressel, an industry executive who quickly fell in love with the band and who tried to get the band a label deal. A year later, Dressel had formed his own Core Entertainment label and, soon afterwards, signed Jet Black Factory. One of the label's first releases, J.B.F.'s *The Uncrossing* takes nine songs from the *House Blessing* LP, remixing some while adding a pair of new tunes to create a coherent whole. The hole left by departing guitarist Anderson has been filled with the addition of Frizzell. With U.S. distribution from Core, Europe handled by industry powerhouse BMG, and with distribution in Canada, Australia, and Japan as well, Jet Black Factory seem poised for international success…and, it is hoped, the identity they so richly deserve.
– *The Metro*, August 1991

Jet Black Factory

Robert Jetton, continued...
Later, Jetton was affiliated with **Tim Krekel & the Sluggers** as well as **Jason & the Scorchers**, and he's probably had more influence on the local artistry than most people realize.

JETTON & WHEELER

Band Members:
Robert Jetton (vocals, guitar) (I-II)
John Wheeler (vocals, guitar, mandolin, keys) (I-II)
Tom Comet (bass) (I-II)
Willis Bailey (drums) (I-II)

Other Musicians:
Charlie Jetton (harmonica, vibes) (I-II)
Tim Krekel (guitar) (I)
Dennis Lord (keyboards) (I-II)
Rob McCoury (banjo) (II)

Jetton & Wheeler Recordings:

I. We've Had A Few (New Bohemian 1999, CD)
1. It Might As Well Be Me
2. My Heart Plays Hell With Angels
3. The Whisky Ain't As Risky
4. Not Tonight I've Got A Heartache
5. Nothing On But The Radio
6. Too Close To Home
7. I'm Gonna Lie
8. Now That The Door Is Open
9. Something's Gonna Break
10. Last Call
11. I Can't Help Myself

II. Lyin' 'Round The Bar (New Bohemian 2001, CD)
1. I Ain't In No Hurry To Wait
2. She's Out There Cheating On Us
3. Enough To Get Over You
4. The Perfect Woman
5. I Warned You
6. Hangover Blues
7. Here Come The Wild Horses
8. Don't Go Holding Out
9. Michelle
10. What It Will Be
11. Maybe It'd Be Better (Jung Country)
12. You Can Always Leave Town
13. ('Til She Hears) Song #5

Comments: Robert Jetton hooks up with songwriting pal John Wheeler and the Sluggers to deliver two albums of smart, sadly overlooked alt-country songs that, in reality, are truer to the whiskey-soaked country spirit of Willie, Waylon and David Allen Coe than to the stinky pop-oriented swill being cranked out on Music Row like so many widgets.

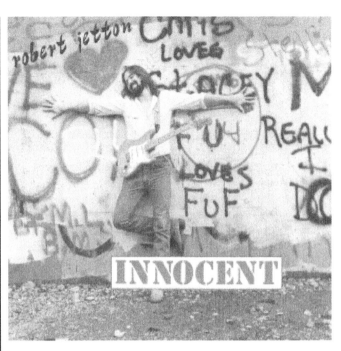

JODY'S POWER BILL

Band Members:
Ben Folds (vocals, piano)
Tom Spagnardi (bass)
Dave Rich (drums)

Comments: Formed in Nashville in 1991, the members of Jody's Power Bill had met in North Carolina played in various bands together before landing in Nashville. Folds, of course, is kinda famous these days, having done pretty good for himself in the big leagues…

JOE, MARC'S BROTHER
Web: www.joemarcsbrother.com

Band Members:
Joe Pisapia (vocals, guitar) (I, II)
Marc Pisapia (drums, percussion, vocals) (I, II)
James Haggerty (bass, vocals) (II)
Pete Langella (bass, vocals) (I)
David Mead (guitar, vocals) (I)
Dave Sheaffer (bass) (I)

Joe, Marc's Brother Recordings:

I. The Debut Of Joe, Marc's Brother (Blurge Records 1996, CD)
1. Ronelle
2. She's So Gone
3. Slow Motion
4. Mel Bay
5. This Blind Faith
6. It Still Hurts

7. Questions At The End Of The Day
8. Together
9. Feel
10. My Me
11. The Heart Of Love
12. Where Does The Time Go?

Comments: The original sound of popular mid-1990s local band Joe, Marc's Brother, was a curious blend of North and South, mostly due to the inclusion of singer and guitarist **David Mead**.

The Brothers Pisapia started out in New Jersey, moving to the Music City in 1994 to pursue their unique guitar-driven pop vision. *The Debut of Joe, Marc's Brother* was the result, one of the most overlooked gems of Music City rock history.

Another View: "…the quartet played a balls-to-the-wall brand of jaw-dropping guitar pop that found a meeting place for the Beach Boys, Elvis Costello, Cole Porter, and early Flaming Lips." – *the band's website*

II. Around The Year With Joe, Marc's Brother (Ambassador Records 2000, CD)
1. Ready To Change
2. Stand By Your Lie
3. Spinning On An Axis
4. Underwater
5. Failing In Love
6. Hide Away
7. Eraser
8. Tonight
9. Where Were You

10. Sleep My Friend
11. Closed For The Season
12. Evergreen
13. A Hate Story

Comments: Mead left the band in 1997 to launch an acclaimed solo career, leaving the remaining trio to soldier on by themselves. *Around The Year With Joe, Marc's Brother* is another fine effort, maybe slightly less good than the band's debut, but not by much.

They're still kicking around town, the members spending their time performing alongside artists like Guster and Josh Rouse while Joe, Marc's Brother is on hiatus. Still, fans can hold out hope for a third album sometime in our lives...

JOHNNY JONES

Band Members:
Johnny Jones (vocals, guitar) (I-III)

Other Musicians:
Andy Arrow (drums) (I, III)
Mary-Ann Brandon (vocals) (II, III)
Jeff Davis (bass) (II)
Billy Earheart (keyboards) (II, III)
Earl Gaines (vocals) (I)
Fred James (guitar, keyboards) (I-III)
Bryan Owings (drums) (II)
Phil Rugh (keyboards) (I)
Dennis Taylor (saxophone) (I, II)
Charles Walker (vocals) (II, III)

Johnny Jones Recordings:

I. I Was Raised On The Blues (Black Magic 1998, CD)
1. Chip off the Old Block
2. Don't Throw Your Love on Me So Strong
3. I Was Raised on the Blues
4. Can I Get an Amen
5. Groove Thing
6. Galloping Dominoes
7. Herb Stuffing
8. Sneaky Suspicion
9. Mighty Low
10. I Done Did That Already
11. Baptism of Fire

II. Blues Is In The House (Northern Blues 2001, CD)
1. A Fool Never Learns
2. Girlfriend Blues
3. I'm Gonna Love You
4. Stacked In The Back
5. I Could Be Dangerous
6. I'll Be The Judge Of That
7. Love Recession
8. Good Idea At The Time
9. Your Stuff Is Rough
10. Farm Boy
11. Why Can't We Be Alone
12. Really
13. A Rock And A Hard Case
14. The Blues Is In The House

III. Can I Get An Amen (Black Magic Records 2007, CD)
1. Don't Throw Your Love On Me So Strong
2. Chip Off The Old Block

3. Sneaky Suspicion
4. Can I Get An Amen
5. Galloping Dominoes
6. I Was Raised On The Blues
7. I Done Did That Already
8. Herb Stuffing
9. I Can't Do That
10. Ain't Nothing A Young Girl Can Do

Comments: If Johnny Jones isn't a Nashville legend, he should be. The gifted and dynamic blues guitarist has been kicking around the Music City since the early 1960s, when he fronted his band the Imperial Seven. When Jones and crew would play the New Era Club on Jefferson, a young soldier by the name of Jimi Hendrix would come down from Fort Campbell to watch and sit in, much as Jones did in Chicago when he learned to play from the likes of Muddy Waters and Howlin' Wolf.

Jones was also part of the house band for Dallas TV show *The Beat* along with Clarence "Gatemouth" Brown, and he formed another band called the King Kasuals in 1968 that played the SE soul circuit. By the end of the '70s, though, it was hard to make a living at the blues game, and Jones effectively retired from music. Lucky for us, Jones started playing again in the late 1990s, backing old R&B warhorses like Earl Gaines, Roscoe Shelton and Charlie Walker (now of **the Dynamites)**.

Sadly, the first two albums are all we currently have of Jones' brilliant studio work (as well as a live disc and another recorded with Walker, below). *Can I Get An Amen* documents a live performance from Jones' 1998 European tour in the wake of *I Was Raised On The Blues*, both of

John Wheeler & Robert Jetton

Joe, Marc's Brother

which were released by the Dutch Black Magic label. ***Blues Is In The House*** was released by the Canadian Northern Blues label and distributed stateside. If you haven't heard Jones play, you owe it to yourself to check out these discs (see review ➔). Sadly, Jones passed away in October 2009 at the age of 73 years old.

JOHNNY JONES & CHARLES WALKER

Band Members:
Charles Walker (vocals) (I)
Johnny Jones (guitar, vocals) (I)
Fred James (guitar, vocals) (I)
Jeff Davis (bass) (I)
Billy Earheart (keyboards) (I)
Andy Arrow (drums) (I)

Johnny Jones & Charles Walker Recordings:

I. In The House (Crosscut Records 2001, CD)
1. I Can't Do That
2. The Drifter
3. Slave To Love
4. Gypsy Woman
5. Finger Lickin'
6. They All Look Better In Green
7. Can I Get An Amen

Price Jones

8. Chicken Scratch
9. Storming And Raining Blues
10. Strain On My Heart
11. 99,000 Watts Of Soul Power
12. Nothing A Young Girl Can Do

PRICE JONES

Band Members:
Price Jones (vocals, guitar, keyboards) (I)

Price Jones Recordings:

I. Oooznoz (9 Dog Records 1993, CD)
1. Take The Trolley
2. Still One
3. We Women
4. Sleepin At Your Feet
5. Ya Yas
6. Hey Love
7. Missionary Ridge
8. Roller Coaster Life
9. Waiting For The Train
10. There Was A Time
11. Going To LA
12. Make Me Believe
13. Kindred Spirits

Comments: Price Jones first came to my attention as guitarist for local hard rock band Dark Star; the core of that band later split off and formed **Afterdark**. After disappearing from the scene for a while, Jones resurfaced on the phone one day with news of this excellent self-produced CD. After a short run of shows and hype around ***Oooznoz***, Price once again fell off the face of the earth (see review ➔).

JUST ROUTINE

Band Members:
Tracy Hill
Billy Stickers

JUSTIN HEAT
Web: www.myspace.com/justinheatrocks

Band Members:
Robert Leath (vocals)
Tony Padvano (guitars)
Don Murray (bass)
Jack Prince (drums)

Comments: Popular hard rock band in the vein of **Triple X** and **Hard Knox**. Justin Heat was recently reformed by vocalist Robert Leath for a reunion that, at this writing, had yet to happen.

PRICE JONES
Oooznoz
(9 Dog Records)

Nashville, the "Music City," is blessed with more than its share of great musicians and skilled songwriters. In the non-country arena, however, there have been few who have shown the persistence and drive that is a major part of Price Jones. Fewer still are those artists who can bring to their debut album nearly a decade's worth of musical experience, and the tools to do something with it, such as Jones brings to *Oooznoz*.

Reported by this scribe as "missing in action" in these pages a few short months ago, I'm glad to report that it seems as if Ms. Jones was merely busy with the details of crafting this excellent debut CD. A collection of 14 tunes which tread a stylistic ground closely akin to Kate Bush or Tori Amos, Jones, nonetheless possesses a musical identity that is entirely her own.

Skillfully handling all of the instrumentation on *Oooznoz*, save for on a handful of tracks, Jones' talents as a musician are eclipsed by her singing and songwriting abilities. Proving to be a vocalist of considerable range, style and emotion, Price's self-penned lyrics mesh perfectly with their music and delivery. Like a fine tapestry with every thread hand-placed, *Oooznoz* is a rare work of artistic integrity, Jones a still-growing young talent scoring with this major creative success. – *The Metro*, 1993

JOHNNY JONES
Blues Is In The House
(Northern Blues)

It's always a pleasure for these ears to discover a new blues guitarist, but to uncover a gem with the experience and talent of axeman Johnny Jones is unheard of these days. An old school bluesman, Jones brings the knowledge and experience of a lifetime to bear on *Blues Is In The House*, only the second solo album of his sixty-five years.

Jones spent his formative years in Chicago during the halcyon days of the fifties, playing regularly with legends like Junior Wells and Freddy King. He moved to Nashville during the sixties and rapidly became a fixture of the Music City's underrated R&B scene, leading his band the Imperial Seven through raucous performances at Nashville's infamous New Era club. Jones has played alongside Clarence "Gatemouth" Brown and Jimi Hendrix and backed up Bobby "Blue" Bland – so why, with a pedigree like this, isn't Jones better known?

Blues Is In The House serves as a fine introduction to Jones' unique playing style, part brassy Chicago blues and part funky rhythm & blues. Many of the tunes here stray off towards the bawdy side of male/female relationships; Jones delivers songs like the hilarious "Girlfriend Blues" and "Stacked In The Back" with delightful glee. It's with straightforward, Chicago-styled blues tunes like "Love Recession" or "Farm Boy" that Jones really shines, however, his Telestar guitar ringing clear and true while the backing band keeps up a steady rhythm. A remake of Jones' 1963 instrumental "Really" breathes new fire into the golden oldie while the bluesman's infectious, likeable vocals and taut six-string work propel the New Orleans-flavored "A Fool Never Learns" to new heights.

An obscure talent deserving of a greater recognition, Johnny Jones is the real deal – an imaginative guitarist, solid vocalist and skilled bandleader with roots in a bygone era. Hopefully producer Fred James won't wait too long to get Jones back into the studio to follow-up the wonderful *Blues Is In The House*.

INTERVIEW: ROBERT JETTON

Robert Jetton has been kicking around Nashville since the early 1970s, coming to the city from Texas with his pals Willis Bailey and Tom Comet who formed the rhythmic foundation of not only several of Jetton's bands, but for Marshall Chapman and Tim Krekel as well. Robert has had a front row seat as the history of the Nashville rock scene unfolded and he has more than a few stories to tell. We interviewed Robert by phone in June 2007...

How did you get started in music in the first place?
My brother, who's a fantastic harmonica player, probably one of the best I've ever known in my life, he taught me to play twelve-bar blues when I was in the third grade in Fort Worth. He taught me twelve-bar blues and Jimmy Reed stuff, and that's the first thing I learned, and from there it was on to "Gloria" and "Secret Agent Man," and I just kept moving. I never had to take lessons or anything because I was possessed, I just wanted to play, it was so fun. My buddies played, too. It was really a great situation the way we all came up and immediately got into bands, and I wound up playing with the same guys for over 30 years.

You're from Texas originally, right? I lived down there in 1976.
I'm from Fort Worth. You lived there in '76, that's funny. We were rockin' in '76! The Panther City Pickers was my band, Willis Bailey was my drummer and Tom Comet was my bass player.

So they're from Texas too?
Oh yeah, we're all from Fort Worth, we all went through high school together and we played in bands together from junior high all the way...we all came to Nashville together, and we still play together. We're all lifelong chums.

How did you end up in Nashville?
Well, here's the deal. Dave Hickey, my manager down in Fort Worth, was a real controversial character; he sent our tape to Bobby Bare. He set up this thing with Bare for us to come up and cut demos back in January of '77. And we came up and Hickey became a kind of a mentor, he was Marshall Chapman's boyfriend and producer at the time. Marshall came and sang with us on those Bare sessions at Monument Records and the next day she fired her Nashville based band and hired us to go on the road with her. She had a whole string of gigs lined up, opening for the Marshall Tucker Band and the Meters down in New Orleans, and Two Degrees, it was incredible. But we became real unpopular with the Nashville locals for a while because she fired all her local Nashville people.

You hadn't started Night Money yet I guess.
No, that was on down a ways...this was in '77. We went back to Texas and rented a karate studio and we rehearsed for six weeks with Hickey as our masochistic task master. We rehearsed eight hours a day for six weeks. He just whipped us into a frenzied shape.

At the end of my being in Marshall's band, I got a publishing deal with Merle Haggard's publishing company, and I told Marshall I was going to go do my own thing and so that was kind of right at the end, right there. When I was doing this publishing deal, they moved me out to Hendersonville. I was living in a little two room shack out there in the sticks right on the water of Old Hickory. Tom and Willis were still playing with Marshall and I think everybody was ready for a change, so we all kind of merged together again and formed the Rockin' Rancheros. Our first gig was at the Mississippi Whiskers, down on Church Street, we played there a couple times, then we hooked up with David and Becky Barrel at Phranks 'n' Steins, this was in 1978. We played as the house band at Phranks 'n' Steins for about six to eight months, and it was the most incredible place. At that point, with Hickey exposing us to the whole punk scene and everything else that was going on, we became this high energy fusion band of punk, country, and rock, doing a lot of original material and we were hitting a vein because people were right into it with us, and the place was packed every night. Jack Emerson was there every damn night.

So you went from the Rockin' Rancheros to Night Money?
The reason we started Night Money, we were a power trio – me, Willis and Tom – for a long time. It seemed like a long time, but we wanted to expand with a hot flash guitar player, and it came down to between Rob Jackson and this Jimmy O'Neal character, who had come to see us a few times to play. We found out that he was from the Moses Jones Band down in Atlanta; he was hot as a firecracker.

I don't know that I've ever known a better guitar player, but it came down between him and Rob, and we went with Jimmy. That's when we started Night Money. Jimmy was a flash guitar player, and we started playing. We were down in Texas, we were playing 300 dates a year, it was just crazy. We had a couple booking agents and we were just playing all the time.

How long did Night Money last?
It was really 1980 to '81, two years, but it was a fast burning fuse for two years. We recorded with a bunch of different producers, and some of the stuff we had in the can, it was just stupid that it didn't happen. You wouldn't believe some of the projects we recorded. Big money projects, at the best studios in town. Somebody was always after Night Money…I have an incredible collection of demos, just tons of songs that I wrote with guys in the band.

Where did you go after Night Money?
We were really burned out after a couple years with Night Money. Willis and Tom, my buddies, they went with Tim Krekel and formed the Sluggers. At one time, I was going to be the lead singer for Sluggers, but that's a whole other story. Instead I formed a band called the New Bohemians. At the time, I was signed to what they called a demo deal at CBS. I combined a bunch of projects and turned them in over at CBS, and they thought it was too raw. I wound up getting the license on the stuff and I put out an EP back then.

A lot of great things came from that. I put together the New Bohemians to support that record. It's funny, I had that name the New Bohemians for a couple years, and we played down in Dallas, got written up in like Buddy Magazine down there and all of a sudden Edie Brickell and the New Bohemians came charging out of Dallas. I had the trademark on it here in the state of Tennessee. I never pursued it, I could have, I'm

not a litigious person, but at this point I would like to sue all kinds of people.

So what happened to the New Bohemians?
I became involved with Jack and Andy (Praxis International) in a management type situation and those guys cooked up interest with Eli (Ball) and I got signed to the Nashville Music Group; it was moving quickly…

How did you get hooked up with Jack (Emerson) and Andy (McLenon)?
Jack had been such a good friend of ours ever since Phranks 'n' Steins and when he put together Jason and the Scorchers, I was showing Will, their guitar player at the time, the guitar riffs and Tom Comet was showing Jack how to play bass…

At that time it was Jason, Jack, and Perry, I guess?
Oh no, see at first it was Jason, Jack, Cheetah, and this guy named Will on guitar.

Who was Cheetah?
He was a drummer and he was kind of a fringe guy on the scene here, that guy named Cheetah. They had a gig at the Smokehouse, which later became Cantrell's – Jack, Jason, Will, and Cheetah. We were all there, there were about 15 people in the crowd, and we were all there rooting them on. They still had a lot of the same feel and energy that they had later on, even though it became increasingly rock, they still

Robert Jetton & the Rockin' Rancheros

had a lot of that punk, cow punk thing going on from the very beginning. I don't know exactly if it was Jack's vision or Jason's.

It might have been a combination of the two...
Not long after that, I was living with Steve Brantley, the guy that worked with me on the CBS project that I did, and Jack met Steve through me I guess. He brought over the band, and they had metamorphosed into Jason and Warner and Perry and Jeff. They came over and they set up in our living room, and Jason actually sang in the hall just to give it a little bit of a kind of an echo and the rest of the guys set up in the living room.

That was for the recording of the Reckless Country Soul EP?
Yeah. Steve and I were living there, and Steve had some Studer Revox eight-track which kicked ass, and Jack shows up with these guys and Perry is just a monster, he's just like an animal playing the drums, and Warner is like an animal playing the guitar. I was trying to sleep in my bedroom but I ended up singing on three of the tracks, singing all the harmonies because those guys at that time really weren't big harmony singers.

They were all pretty raw at that point.
Very raw, but so good! Later on I was up in New York and I went to a record store and there was a framed copy of Reckless Country Soul hanging on the wall for $250.

So Jack and Andy got you in with Eli Ball?
We always knew that Ely was kind of a character and he was with this Nashville Music Group. He and Wayne Halper and another fellow, they put a lot of money into it and they signed me and Pat McLaughlin. We pulled together this thing…Hank DeVito was producing and he and I worked out several songs. We brought in the Nerve and rehearsed with them, rehearsed all the songs with the Nerve and then we brought in a guy named Chris Spedding who was on the *Give My Regards to Broad Street* with Paul McCartney.

Spedding was a British guitar player and we put together that Rockin' Ranchero stuff and things were moving fast. The Nashville Music Group shut down after we spent all this money on these tapes and then Eli went to CBS and he signed me there, me and Joanna Jacobs and a bunch of people, it was a new deal kind of thing. He put together another session for me with Steve Berlin from Los Lobos and I pulled together a band real quickly with Jimmy Lester, Danny Dickerson, Kelly Loony, and Eddy Shaver and it was smoking!

It never really did anything; we recorded tracks over at this 19th and Grand Studio and they were just magic, just killer. We recorded this song called "Come On In" by a songwriter from Texas, George Green I believe his name was, but Eli

took that tape and went over and played it for the Oak Ridge Boys at MCA and they recorded it and it went to number one. Eli got fired from CBS because of that, and everything that he worked with was tainted and put on the shelf...

Didn't you subsequently put it out yourself?
I went in and got the licensing for the stuff and mixed it at Treasure Island with Hank DeVito, and I put together my record label New Bohemian Records and we put it out and I had pretty good luck with that. We toured, and played a lot of gigs on the strength of that project. We had a ton of positive reviews and worked our asses off for a few years and nothing really came of it other than having a great time and playing good music. But that kind of ran its course and the Rancheros came back together and we started banging it out at the local clubs again.

Wasn't that in the late 1980s?
Yeah. You know, Perry (Baggs) and I were roommates in the late '80s and I've seen where you've written several things about him lately. I loved Perry, he and I wrote a lot of songs together. We were roommates and we got along well, but we had our ups and downs. Perry was such a stud, he always had like a harem of women, man it was just unbelievable. He was literally like the Wilt Chamberlain of Nashville, and we got a few problems over that, but he and I really got along well, wrote songs together.

What happened with the Rockin' Rancheros?
We started rocking again and playing every Monday night at the Exit In; you wouldn't believe the people that opened for us. Every band has this thing, who has the coolest opening act? We had everybody beat, I'm not kidding, because we did every Monday at the Exit Inn and had different artists opening for us as they were coming up. Garth (Brooks) opened for us his first gig in town, basically got booed off the stage, and I paid him $25 the next day for the 30 minutes he was supposed to play in front of us, he was hilarious. R.E.M. opened for us at the Rites of Spring, and they blew my PA speakers and they promised to send me money, Stipe and Pete Buck told me they'd send money from the road to pay for my speakers.

Never saw a dime, eh?
No, never heard from them again, it's so funny now. But this string of gigs the Rancheros did was amazing because of all these different people that opened for us. Then the Rancheros played a show at 328 Performance Hall and some Warner Brothers representatives were there. They said, "we love what you do, let's do it." I went to see them the next day and I signed a developmental deal, and it was the normal record company routine, the screw the artist thing.

They said they "loved what we did," but as soon as we got in the studio, they wanted me to fire the drummer, the guitar player, and the keyboard player, change it into a whole different thing. I wanted that to work out so bad over at Warner Brothers; I stayed there for three years. But the one good thing I will say is that in that three years I wrote 75 or 80 pretty good songs. They have tons of stuff in the can, some really good stuff, but it's just been a long strange trip...

How did Jetton-Wheeler come together?
John (Wheeler) sat in with me at Douglas Corner on a show and we just clicked like crazy. We wrote 50 songs together on beer-soaked napkins at the Broadway Brew House. We started recording CDs and we were the number one CD on mp3.com for three months as soon as we started; we had a lot of positive reinforcement and we played killer gigs. It was really a high point, really fine, good stuff.

Then Wheeler, on a total fluke, recorded with a bunch of his friends a bunch of AC/DC songs on a Sunday afternoon at his house in bluegrass style, and it just took off. We were playing a gig at Douglas Corner and he put that tape on the PA system after the gig, Billy Block was in there, and the crowd just went crazy when they heard this shit. Billy came to Wheeler and said "let's do it buddy, this is going to happen." So they went through Dualtone Music and they got a whole thing going. It ended the Jetton-Wheeler thing to tell you the truth.

Was that Hayseed Dixie?
Yeah, they've recorded five records since then, and he's put a song I wrote on every record except the first one. They have a song that's playing on the Discovery Channel and Biker Build-Off, it's their theme song. They're bringing out a new record in the U.K. right now called Weapons of Grass Destruction and the song he and I wrote called "Before Your Old Man Gets Home" is the single off that record and they expect it to go gold again. I have a good relationship with Wheeler, he's a wild and crazy guy is all I can say.

Have you had any luck getting any of your other songs recorded by people in town?
I've had tons of small cuts, small to medium cuts, and a few almost busted through. I've just never really gotten that big one, even though a dozen of my good friends have all had number one songs and I've written with all of them. It's that one thing I never got, that one big song...

Never got that one big break...
Never got the big break, buddy. I love where I am now with my girls and my wife and everything. I make art, I make music, and I'm a happy guy.

Robert Jetton & the New Bohemians

THE KATIES

Band Members:
Jason Moore (vocals, guitar) (I)
Gary Welch (bass, vocals) (I)
Josh Moore (drums) (I)

The Katies Recordings:

I. The Katies (Spongebath/Elektra Records 1999, CD)
1. Powerkiss
2. She's My Marijuana
3. Noggin' Poundin'
4. Shisiedo
5. Drowner
6. Miss Melodrama
7. Girl
8. Shower
9. Ode To S.G.
10. Tappin' Out
11. Jesus Pick

Comments: "the katies were formed in 96. we played in murfreesboro a lot. we got a record deal. put out an album. played some more. lost the record deal. moved out to california and broke up. some came home. some stayed in california. three and a half years later we were all back in tennessee and we got back together. just like a frickin night time soap." – *from the band's MySpace page*

THE KEEP

Band Members:
Heidi Campbell (vocals) (I)
Max Ratliff (guitar) (I)
John Deaderick (keyboards) (I)
Dave Harrison (drums) (I)

The Keep Recordings:

I. The Keep EP (Sweat Boy Records 1995, CD)
1. Bay Of Confusion
2. Skin And Bones
3. What Happened To You
4. Straight On 'Til Morning
5. Colder Inside

Comments: "The Keep builds its eclectic musical foundation on pop, rock, and blues, with a tasty groove that's addictive. Add the haunting vocals of Heidi Campbell and Modern Rock comes of age in the visionary music of The Keep. Vision that is evident in the multi-layered meanings of the songs. Each song is a painting. The songs collectively, a tapestry crafted with artistry that weaves together the nuances of extremes in emotions..." – Internet Underground Music Archive

EDDIE KEY GROUP

Band Members:
Eddie Key (vocals, guitars, keyboards) (I)
Michael Myatt (bass, vocals) (I)
Tim Lancaster (drums, percussion) (I)

Eddie Key Group Recordings:

I. Stay Tuned (EKG Records 1985, vinyl LP)
Side One
1. Avalon
2. Burning Love
3. The Truth
4. Stay Tuned
5. Hold On You

Side Two
6. Love Life
7. You Were Right
8. Talking Out Loud
9. Down Town
10. All Night Long

KIM'S FABLE

Band Members:
Kim Collins (vocals, guitar, flute, piano) (I-III)
Chris Tench (guitar) (I-III)
Doc Downs (bass, vocals) (I-III)
Kevin Cuchia (drums, percussion) (I-III)

Other Musicians:
Caitlin Evanson (violin) (I)

Kim's Fable Recordings:

I. Breathless (Bandaloop Music 2000, CD)
1. Intro/Reach the Fire
2. Honeysuckle Girl
3. The Joke
4. Falling Thru
5. Very Deep Sea
6. Holy Dance
7. Cold Hearted
8. Common Blood
9. Mando Song
10. Shattered
11. Why Are We Here?
12. I Won't Die Today
13. Breathless...
14. hidden track

II. Dancing Under The Pale Moonlight (Bandaloop 2003, CD)
1. Blue Sky
2. Be Your Own Human
3. Wrap Around Me
4. Standing Still
5. Give a Little More
6. Atmosphere

III. Kim's Fable (Bandaloop Music 2005, CD EP)
1. Addiction
2. Mercy For The Ghost
3. Transcendental Green
4. Cradle
5. In My Way

WILL KIMBROUGH
Web: www.willkimbrough.com

Band Members:
Will Kimbrough (vocals, guitars, keyboards) (I-IV)
Tommy Womack (guitars, mandolin, harmonica) (I-III)
Mike Grimes (bass, guitar) (I-III)
David Gehrke (drums) (I, II)
Tommy Meyer (drums) (III)
Paul Griffith (drums) (IV)

Other Musicians:
J.D. Andrew (vocals) (I)
Pat Buchanan (guitars) (IV)
Chris Carmichael (violin, cello) (II, IV)
Dennis Cronin (trumpet) (I)
Mike Daley (pedal steel) (II)
John Deaderick (piano, synthesizer) (II, IV)
David Henry (cello) (I)
Ned Henry (violin) (I)
Scotty Huff (trumpet) (II)
David Jacques (bass, horns) (I, IV)
Brad Jones (guitars, bass) (I, IV)
Craig Krampf (drums, percussion) (II)
Doug Lancio (guitars) (I)
Jacob Lawson (violin) (II)
Lij (keyboards, synthesizer) (II, IV)
Jared Reynolds (bass) (III)
Kim Richey (vocals) (I, II)
Pat Sansone (piano, synthesizer) (I, IV)
Joy Tilghman Shaw (vocals) (IV)
Todd Snider (guitar, vocals) (III, IV)

WILL KIMBROUGH

Michael Webb (keyboards) (III)
Joy Lynn White (vocals) (III, IV)
J.D. Wilkes (harmonica) (IV)
Tommy Williams (drums) (III)
Craig Wright (drums, piano) (IV)
Kirk Yoquelet (drums) (III)
Adrienne Young (banjo, vocals) (III)

Will Kimbrough Recordings:

I. This (Waxy Silver 2000, CD)
1. Closer to the Ground
2. Chimayo
3. Need You Now
4. Dream Away
5. I'm on Your Side
6. Down in My Mind
7. Diamond in a Garbage Can
8. Nobody Loves You
9. We're All for Sale
10. Goodnight Moon

Comments: Singer, songwriter, and immensely-talented guitarist Will Kimbrough is better-known as a touring musician and a name in the CD liner notes of country and rock artists like Rodney Crowell, Jimmy Buffett, Kim Richey,

Todd Snider and others. For Nashville rock aficionados, however, Kimbrough first surfaced as frontman for **Will & the Bushmen**, a popular college rock band formed in Kimbrough's Mobile, Alabama hometown. After recording the band's self-titled major/minor-label debut in 1989, they moved to Nashville to record a third and final disc, *Blunderbuss*, after which they broke up.

After Will & the Bushmen, Kimbrough formed **the Bis-Quits** with friends **Tommy Womack** and Mike "Grimey" Grimes. The band released a self-titled collection of whip-smart roots-rock in 1993 for John Prine's Oh Boy Records. Between then and now, Kimbrough has worked as an in-demand guitar for hire, his solo career beginning in earnest with *This*, a fine collection of shimmering guitar-pop. Oh yeah, Kimbrough has reunited with Womack in **Daddy**, the best band that you haven't heard yet.

II. Home Away (Waxy Silver 2002, CD)
1. A Piece of Work
2. This Modern World
3. Champion of the World
4. Crackup
5. Letdown
6. War of Words
7. I Love my Baby

8. Hey Big Sister
9. Happier
10. Anita O'Day
11. You Don't Know Me so Well

III. Godsend (Waxy Silver 2003, CD)
1. Godsend
2. I Don't Have a Gun
3. I Want Out
4. Falling Apart
5. You Don't Know Me so Well
6. Philadelphia, Mississippi
7. No Land's Man
8. Too Beautiful
9. Cape Henry
10. Motorcycle Mama
11. Blue Moon of Kentucky

Comments: In between the demands of session and road work, Kimbrough squeezed out enough time to record a couple more fine collections of pop that sit squarely at the intersection of John Lennon and Alex Chilton, with just a little country twang.

IV. Americanitis (Daphne Records 2006, CD)
1. I Lie
2. Life
3. Grown Up Now
4. Pride
5. Less Polite
6. Americanitis
7. Warring Ways
8. Another Train

9. Act Like Nothing's Wrong
10. Everyone's In Love
12. Wind Blowing Change
13. Perfect Desert Blue
14. River Out of Eden
15. Let Me Say Yes
16. Rag
17. Enemy
18. Brand New Song

Comments: *Americanitis* is Kimbrough's reaction to the social and political aftermath of 9-11 and the Iraq War, his politically-charged lyrics delivered with intelligence and humility and an infectious musical mix of Beatlesque pop, roots rock and country twang. Layer on his skilled and inspired fretwork, and you have one of the most underrated albums in the Americana genre this decade (see review ➔).

TOM KIMMEL

Band Members:
Tom Kimmel (vocals, guitar) (I-II)

Other Musicians:
Eddie Bayers (tambourine) (I)
Richard Bennett (guitar) (II)
Jeanne Anne Chapman (vocals) (I)
Bill Cuomo (keyboards) (II)
Michael Joyce (bass) (I)
Kenny Greenberg (guitars) (I-II)
Vicki Hampton (vocals) (I-II)
Paul Harris (piano) (I)
Craig Krampf (drums) (II)

TOM KIMMEL - KINGS OF LEON

Mike Lawler (keyboards) (I-II)
Jonell Mosser (vocals) (II)
Dave Pomeroy (bass) (II)
Joe Vitale (drums, percussion) (I)

Tom Kimmel Recordings:

I. 5 To 1 (Mercury Records 1987, LP)
Side A
1. That's Freedom
2. Shake
3. Tryin' To Dance
4. A To Z
5. True Love

Side B
6. Heroes
7. On The Defensive
8. Violet Eyes
9. No Tech
10. 5 To 1

Comments: Born in Memphis and raised in Alabama, singer/songwriter Tom Kimmel relocated to the Music City in the early 1980s. A truly talented songwriter, Kimmel's two major label releases achieved little beyond establishing him as a potential hitmaker for other artists, and folks like Johnny Cash, Joe Cocker, the Stray Cats, and Linda Ronstadt have all enjoyed various levels of success with Kimmel songs.

II. Circle Back Home (Mercury Records 1989, CD)
1. Always
2. Swept Away
3. A Small Song
4. Skintight
5. Bon Vivant
6. Face To Face
7. Grace Under Pressure
8. On The Front Line
9. Love Is My Religion
10. Circle Back Home

KINGS OF LEON
Web: www.kingsofleon.com

Band Members:
Caleb Followill (vocals) (I-XIII)
Matthew Followill (guitar) (I-XIII)
Jared Followill (bass) (I-XIII)
Nathan Followill (drums) (I-XIII)

Kings of Leon Recordings:

I. Holy Roller Novocaine EP (RCA Records 2003, CD)
1. Molly's Chambers

WILL KIMBROUGH
Americanitis
(Daphne Records)

Will Kimbrough is one of Nashville's best-kept secrets. An in-demand guitarist that has worked with folks like Rodney Crowell, Jimmy Buffet and Todd Snider, among others, the Americana Music Association chose Kimbrough as "2004 Instrumentalist of the Year."

The biggest secret, however, isn't Kimbrough's talents as a musician (which are well documented at this point), but rather his little-known skills as a singer, songwriter and performer. Nowhere is this more apparent than with *Americanitis*, Kimbrough's third and most personal solo album yet.

Americanitis is Kimbrough's reaction to the social and political aftermath of 9-11 and the Iraq War, his politically-charged lyrics delivered with intelligence and humility and an infectious musical mix of Beatlesque pop, roots rock and country twang. Kimbrough tempers the commentary of thoughtful songs like "I Lie," "Pride" and the brilliantly subversive, Britpop-styled "Less Polite" with explorations of love and human relationships. Whereas "Act Like Nothing's Wrong" offers some timely advice and the Okie blues of "Wind Blowing Change" heralds stormy weather for America, the spry "Enemy" is a rollicking apology to romance gone wrong while "Another Train" is a raucous showcase of Kimbrough's six-string mastery.

Kimbrough has delivered his most fully realized album yet with *Americanitis*, pulling off a tight-wire act that would send lesser artists over the edge: balancing social commentary with romantic observations and making both equally entertaining. – *Country Standard Time*, 2006

2. Wasted Time
3. California Waiting
4. Wicker Chair
5. Holy Roller Novocaine

Comments: OK, by now nearly everybody is sick to death of hearing the "inspiring" story of the Followills, but here's a condensed version of it anyway. Brothers Caleb, Nathan, and Jared Followill spent their formative years travelling the SE and SW evangelical circuit with their parents, their dad a fundamentalist Christian preacher. They picked up their performance dynamic by experiencing the electricity and passion of tent shows and church revivals, but when their parents divorced, they landed in Nashville where, adding cousin Matthew, they launched the Kings of Leon, a Southern-fried, garage-rock answer to the Strokes.

Signed and primed for "overnight" success by RCA Records, the label placed the Kings Of Leon's "Molly's Chambers" in a TV ad for Volkswagon Jetta, ensuring a certain awareness of the band prior to the release of ***Youth & Young Manhood***. The versions of "Wasted Time" and "California Waiting" on this EP are different than those used on the band's debut album; "California Waiting" in particular was re-written and re-recorded. "Wicker Chair" is a non-album cut.

II. Youth & Young Manhood (RCA Records 2003, CD)
1. Red Morning Light
2. Happy Alone
3. Wasted Time
4. Joe's Head
5. Trani
6. California Waiting
7. Spiral Staircase
8. Molly's Chambers
9. Genius
10. Dusty
11. Holy Roller Novocaine

Comments: Album was produced by Ethan Johns & Angelo Petraglia, hitting #3 on the UK Album Chart and grazing the *Billboard* Top 200 at #113.

III. What I Saw (RCA Records 2003, CD)
1. Red Morning Light
2. Wicker Chair
3. Talihina Sky

IV. Molly's Chambers (Hand Me Down/BMG 2003, UK CD)
1. Molly's Chambers
2. Wasted Time (live)
3. Spiral Staircase (live)

Comments: First single from the band's debut; live tracks recorded at the Birmingham Academy, June 27, 2003.

Will Kimbrough

V. Wasted Time EP (Hand Me Down/BMG 2003, UK CD)
1. Wasted Time
2. Molly's Hangover (unreleased)
3. Joe's Head (live)

Comments: Second single from the band's debut album; live track recorded in Los Angeles. Hit #51 on the UK Singles chart.

VI. California Waiting (Hand Me Down/BMG 2004, UK CD)
1. California Waiting
2. Joe's Head (live)

Comments: Third and final single from the band's debut album; live track recorded at Birmingham Academy show, 2003.

VII. The Bucket (Hand Me Down/BMG 2004, UK CD)
1. The Bucket
2. Where Nobody Knows

Comments: First British single from the upcoming ***Aha Shake Heartbreak*** album reached #16 on the UK Singles Chart. The 10" vinyl UK version substitutes "Slow Night, So Long" in the place of "Where Nobody Knows" and includes a third song, a live version of the band's standard B-side, "Wicker Chair," recorded at the Roskilde Festival in Denmark, July 3, 2004. To make sure that the label got all of your money on this one, a 7" single of "The Bucket" was released in the UK with "Trani" as the B-side, recorded live at Bonnaroo in Tennessee, June 12, 2004.

KINGS OF LEON

VIII. Aha Shake Heartbreak (RCA Records 2005, CD)
1. Slow Night, So Long
2. King Of The Rodeo
3. Taper Jean Girl
4. Pistol Of Fire
5. Milk
6. The Bucket
7. Soft
8. Razz
9. Day Old Blues
10. Four Kicks
11. Velvet Snow
12. Rememo

Comments: Album was produced by Ethan Johns & Angelo Petraglia, hitting #3 on the UK Album Chart and #55 on the *Billboard* Top 200 Chart in the states, keeping the band's love affair with "Old Britannia" alive. CD restricted by the addition of Sunncomm copy protection by RCA's parent company, BMG.

IX. Four Kicks (Hand Me Down/BMG 2005, UK CD)
1. Four Kicks
2. Head To Toe

Comments: Second single from band's sophomore effort, reached #24 on the UK Singles Chart. A 10" vinyl version (UK) substituted a live version of "Four Kicks" from the Brussels, Belgium show (below) and a "dub mix" of "Razz."

X. King Of The Rodeo EP (Hand Me Down/BMG 2005, CD)
1. King Of The Rodeo
2. Taper Jean Girl (live in Belgium)
3. Molly's Chambers (live in Belgium)

Comments: "King Of The Rodeo" was the third and last single from the band's second album, hitting #41 on the UK Singles Chart. The live tracks are from the Brussels, Belgium show (below).

XI. Day Old Belgian Blues (RCA Records 2006, CD)
1. Taper Jean Girl
2. The Bucket
3. Soft
4. Molly's Chambers
5. Four Kicks
6. Trani

Comments: Recorded live at the AB Box, Brussels, Belgium on November 4, 2004. Several cuts were previously released on various UK CD singles. This limited edition disc was sold through independent music stores in the United States.

XII. Because Of The Times (RCA Records 2007, CD)
1. Knocked Up
2. Charmer
3. On Call
4. McFearless
5. Black Thumbnail
6. My Party
7. True Love Way
8. Ragoo
9. Fans
10. The Runner
11. Trunk
12. Camaro
13. Arizona

Comments: Like all of the band's previous work, this album was produced by Ethan Johns and band mentor Angelo Petraglia.

Initial single from the album, "On Call," was released early in the UK and hit #18 on the Singles Chart. *Because Of The Times* opened at #1 on the UK Album Chart.

Another View: "Leaning even further toward a kind of post-punk meets prog rock aesthetic than on their first two albums, Nashville-based Kings of Leon have crafted a darker, less pop-oriented and somewhat cerebral affair with 2007's *Because of the Times*. In fact, if Alan Parsons lent the Allman Brothers his spaceship, *Because of the Times* would be the resulting space odyssey. While that leads to some intriguing moments, the general move away from strong, hooky choruses to a focus on expansive, intricate and percussive arrangements may challenge casual and even some longtime fans of the band's catchy, Southern garage rock twang." – Matt Collar, *All Music Guide*

XIII. Only By The Night (RCA Records 2008, CD)

1. Closer
2. Crawl
3. Sex On Fire
4. Use Somebody
5. Manhattan
6. Revelry
7. 17
8. Notion
9. I Want You
10. Be Somebody
11. Cold Desert

Comments: Ya gotta give RCA credit for flogging a dead horse, 'cause although the Kings are bona-fide rock stars in the U.K. they have yet to move significant copies of any single album here in the U.S. Still, the band hangs in there, chipping away at stardom with each new release, developing a loyal and almost fanatical cult following stateside while retaining a certain level of "coolness" due to their British popularity and status. *Only By The Night* is showing some legs, though, resting comfortably in the *Billboard* Top Ten albums while creeping up on Gold Record sales. Oh yeah, they also won a "best performance" Grammy™ for "Sex On Fire."

Another View: "With 2007's *Because of the Times*, Kings of Leon ventured out of the garage and into the arena. Tracks like "Black Thumbnail" and "Camaro" were bold, anthemic rock songs that built upon the barnyard stomp of *Youth & Young Manhood*, and *Because of the Times* topped the U.K. charts upon its debut, officially crowning the Kings as rock & roll royalty in the process. *Only by the Night* arrives one year later, marking the band's fastest turnaround between albums; it also furthers the epic sound that *Times* introduced, flaunting a set of ringing guitars and radio-ready melodies that push the band away from the Allman Brothers' camp. If anything, much of this album takes up residence in U2's cathedral, particularly during the one-two-three punch of

Al Kooper

"Sex on Fire," "Use Somebody," and "Manhattan." Caleb Followill doesn't adopt Bono's political agenda, but the same sort of uplift exists throughout the record..."
– Andrew Leahy, *All Music Guide*

AL KOOPER
Web: www.alkooper.com

Band Members:
Al Kooper (vocals, guitar, keyboards) (I)

Al Kooper Recordings:

I. Soul Of A Man: Live (Music Masters 1995, CD)

Comments: I'm giving Kooper a mostly honorary inclusion in the book for the decade he spent in Nashville during the '90s. One of the most storied individuals in the history of rock music, Kooper's bio reads like a "who's who" and "what's what" of the rock & roll world. He recorded and performed with Dylan in the '60s; he formed not one but two legendary and groundbreaking bands (Blood, Sweat & Tears and Blues Project) that he subsequently was kicked out of by the other band members; he discovered Lynyrd Skynyrd and produced the band's first three albums, and so on.

As a singer, songwriter, musician, and producer Kooper has helped shape the sound and evolution of rock and rap (a lot of his solo work was sampled in early hip-hop recordings) through the decades. Kooper didn't record much while in Nashville, but **Bill Lloyd** appears on this album that documents Kooper's all-star 50th birthday party in NYC. If you want to know more about this underrated musician, I'd recommend you check out Kooper's fascinating bio, **Backstage Passes & Backstabbing Bastards**. After reading the book, I called Kooper the "Forrest Gump" of rock & roll in a review, and then had the poor judgement to give him a copy of said review at a book signing. He hasn't forgiven me since…

TIM KREKEL - JAIME KYLE

TIM KREKEL

Comments: I've included Krekel's info under the listing for **the Sluggers**, the band that he performed and recorded with while in Nashville. Sadly, Tim is no longer with us, passing away in his Louisville, Kentucky home in 2009 (see story ➔).

JAIME KYLE
Web: www.myspace.com/jaimekylemusic

Band Members:
Jamie Kyle (vocals, guitar, keyboards) (I)
Jimmy Lee Sloas (bass) (I)

Jamie Kyle Recordings:

I. The Passionate Kind (East West 1992, CD)
1. Kick It Down
2. Bed of Roses
3. What Am I Doing Here?
4. Bad News
5. Let It Go
6. Ragged Heart
7. No Sad Goodbyes
8. When Angels Cry
9. Baby the Rain Must Fall
10. Rescue Me

Comments: I don't really know much about Jaime Kyle save that she's an accomplished songwriter with credits that include rockers Heart and Joe Lynn Turner (!), CCR star Michael English, and country star Faith Hill – a diverse bunch by any measure. *The Passionate Kind* was released by East West, an imprint of Atco Records, itself an imprint of Atlantic Records, which is owned by…well, you get the idea. It's a sub-sub-sub-major label.

Recorded in Hollywood with mostly session players like Kenny Aronoff, Michael Thompson, and John Jorgenson, at least Kyle managed to keep her long-time bassist Jimmy Lee Sloas on board. As for the music…and I haven't heard it in probably 15 years…it's supposed to be melodic hard rock (which explains the Joe Lynn connection) with the occasional power ballad.

Kyle is still kicking around, splitting time between Nashville and L.A. and although she's released other albums, mostly in Europe, I don't have any information on any of them.

Kings Of Leon

Tim Krekel – singer, songwriter, and underrated guitarist – passed away on Wednesday, June 24, 2009 from cancer in his Louisville, Kentucky home. Krekel had been diagnosed with an abdominal tumor in March and subsequently underwent surgery, returning home in early-April. He was expected to make a full recovery, but his health took a turn for the worse over the past week.

Born and raised in Louisville in 1950, Krekel first began playing the drums before picking up the guitar. By high school, he was writing songs and performing in local bands, and during the late-60s he was leading the popular Louisville band Dusty. When two of Krekel's friends, Steve Ferguson and Terry Adams, left town to form N.R.B.Q. and scored a record contract, Krekel moved Dusty to New York City in search of fame and fortune. After gigging around the big city for a while, Krekel and Dusty returned to Louisville.

When Krekel performed with Dusty in Nashville, he landed a gig touring as the guitarist in country musician Billy Swan's band. Later Krekel came to the attention of Jimmy Buffett's manager and was hired on as Buffett's guitarist. Krekel toured and recorded with Buffett for a couple of years in the late-70s, appearing on his *Son Of A Son Of A Sailor* album, and performing with the singer on *Saturday Night Live*. His work with Buffett, in turn, led to Krekel receiving his own record deal.

Krekel's solo debut, *Crazy Me*, was released in 1979 by Capricorn Records, unfortunately just a few months before the label closed its doors. Krekel would remain in Nashville, forming the popular Music City band the Sluggers with a couple veterans of Marshall Chapman's band – hard-playing Texans Willis Bailey and Tom Comet. The trio released a single album, *Over The Fence*, for Arista Records in 1986. A few years later, Krekel and the Sluggers would back up singer/songwriter Mark Germino on his 1990 album *Radartown*.

The following year, Krekel's second solo album, *Out Of The Corner*, was released by the Italian label Appaloosa Records. Like his previous albums, it was widely acclaimed but sold few copies. Disenchanted with the music business, Krekel moved back to Louisville in 1993, but with rock 'n' roll in his blood, he couldn't stay away from the music, forming the Groovebillys. During the '90s, Tim Krekel and the Groovebillys would tour frequently throughout the Southeast, and the band released two albums, including *Underground* in 1999.

Krekel released a third solo album, *Happy Town*, in 2002 and a fourth, *World Keeps Turnin'*, in 2005. He would release his final effort, *Soul Season*, with the Tim Krekel Orchestra, in 2007. In between these activities, Krekel toured again with Jimmy Buffett, and through the years he performed alongside

Tim Krekel & the Sluggers

folks like Delbert McClinton, Lonnie Mack, Steve Forbert, Marshall Chapman, Bo Diddley, and many others.

Although he is best remembered for his skills with a guitar, Krekel also enjoyed moderate success as a songwriter. Country star Crystal Gayle had a number one hit in 1984 with Krekel's "Turning Away," and Patty Loveless hit number one in 1997 with "You Can Feel Bad," co-written by Krekel and Matraca Berg. Artists as diverse as Canned Heat, Rick Nelson, Dr. Feelgood, Kim Ritchey, Martina McBride, and Jason & the Scorchers have recorded Tim Krekel songs.

I personally had the good fortune to have met Tim Krekel in Nashville during the mid-1980s, when he was part of a group of like-minded artists that included Jason & the Scorchers, Robert Jetton & the Rockin' Rancheros, and Webb Wilder. Tim was a nice guy, and although he never caught a break from the music business, he never gave up making music. A roots-rock pioneer without realizing what ground-breaking music he was creating, Krekel was an important influence on a generation of alt-country artists.

A Louisville music institution for over 30 years, Krekel's voice and skilled guitarwork will certainly be missed by fans in his hometown as well as throughout the Southeast.
– *Originally published online by Blurt Magazine, 2009*

LADYCOP

Band Members:
Matt McKeever (bass, vocals) (A1)
Lukin Nunn (guitars, vocals) (A1)
Richard Percefull (drums, vocals) (A1)

Ladycop Recordings:

A1. LadyCop (Twitch Records 2001, 7" vinyl EP)
Side One
1. Declaration of Offence
2. Just Shut Up
3. Drug Culture Lifestyle
4. It's All Heavy
5. She Hates My Guts

Side Two
6. Narcotic Painkiller
7. Mama Mia
8. Gimp's Gimp
9. Punks In Love
10. Uh Huh Baby No

Comments: LadyCop bassist Matt McKeever used to own Off 12th, a very cool record store on a side street off, well, 12th Avenue South. I used to hang out there regularly, and gave Matt a couple of big boxes full of music and political zines for the free zine library and reading room that he wanted to include in the store. One day I drove up and the store was gone; I later found some of the zines that I had donated to Matt in the Great Escape, where he had sold them. Yeah, I bought a couple of 'em back...

KATHLEEN LaGUE

Another View: "Formerly known as The Hissy Fits, this trio deliver some of the most ferocious thrash punk heard in these parts since the heyday of FUCT and Die Vixers. The finest songs on Lady Cop's debut 7-inch, released by the local Twitch imprint and available at bassist Matt McKeever's Off 12th Records, bring to mind the best work of early '80s Northeastern hardcore bands Gang Green and Heart Attack. The main difference is that Lady Cop's snarling lyrics come off as mock aggression, an exorcism of bad vibes. And where old-school hardcore was all about putting the lyrics up front, Lady Cop bury theirs under guitarist Lukin Nunn's snarling power chords." – Ron Wynn, *Nashville Scene*, July 2002

KATHLEEN LAGUE

Band Members:
Kathleen LaGue (vocals) (I)

Other Musicians:
Tom Bukovac (guitars, keyboards) (I)
Stan Cotey (guitar) (I)
Shawn Fichter (drums) (I)
Gina Fant-Saez (vocals) (I)
Tony Nagy (bass) (I)
Michael Organ (drums, loops) (I)
Jim Thistle (drums) (I)
Richard Thomas (guitar) (I)
Kurt Wagner (guitar) (I)
Mitch Watkins (guitar) (I)

Kathleen LaGue Recordings:

I. Kathleen LaGue (Lioness Records 1999, CD)
1. Play One For Me
2. Hear My Confession
3. Drive Right Into The Sun
4. Over My Head
5. Unglued
6. Be Myself
7. Sympathy Seeker
8. Object Of My Addiction
9. Little Lies
10. Diamonds In Quicksand
11. When Will You Learn

LAMBCHOP
Web: www.lambchop.net

Band Members:
Kurt Wagner (vocals, guitar) (I-XVI)
Sam Baker (drums) (XII, XIII, XV)
Paul Burch (drums, vibraphone) (III-VIII)
C. Scott Chase (percussion) (I-VI, VIII)
Dennis Cronin (V-VIII)
Tony Crow (piano) (V, VI, VIII, XII, XIII, XV, XVI)

John Delworth (keyboards) (I-VIII, XII, XIII)
Mike Doster (bass) (I, II, V, VIII)
Steve Goodhue (drums, mandolin, banjo) (I, II, VIII)
Bill Killebrew (guitar) (I, II, VIII)
Allen Lowrey (drums, percussion) (I-IX)
Paul Niehaus (lap steel, trombone) (I-VIII, XII, XIII, XV)
Jonathan Marx (clarinet, trumpet) (I-VIII, XII, XIII, XV, XVI)
Alex McManus (guitars) (IV-IX, XII, XIII, XV, XVI)
Mark Nevers (guitars) (IV-VIII, IX, XV)
Matt Swanson (bass) (VI-VIII, XII, XIII, XV, XVI)
Hank Tilbury (glockenspiel, synthesizer) (II-IV, VIII)
Marc Trovillion (bass) (I-IX, XII, XIII, XV)
William Tyler (guitars) (VII, VIII, IX, XII, XIII, XV, XVI)
Deanna Varagona (vocals, sax) (I-IX, XII, XIII, XV)

Other Musicians:
Roy Agee (trombone) (XVI)
Matt Bach (bass) (VI)
Paul Booker (guitar) (VI)
John Catchings (cello) (II)
Bruce Colson (violin) (XV)
Ken Coomer (percussion) (VI)
David Davidson (violin) (II)
Scott Martin (drums) (XV, XVI)
John Mock (tin whistle, recorders, strings) (II)
Ryan Norris (keyboards) (XV, XVI)
Clara M. Olson (violin) (II)
Curtis Pernice (guitar) (XII, XIII)
Pamela Sixfin (violin) (II)
Marty Slayton (vocals) (XVI)
Dennis Solee (woodwinds) (XVI)
Gary Tussing (cello) (XV)
Ben Westney (cello) (XV)
Kristen Wilkinson (viola) (II)

Lambchop Recordings:

I. I Hope You're Sitting Down a/k/a *Jack's Tulips* (Merge
Records 1994, CD)
1. Begin
2. Betweemus
3. Soaky in the Pooper
4. Because You Are the Very Air He Breathes
5. Under the Same Moon
6. I Will Drive Slowly
7. Oh, What a Disappointment
8. Hellmouth
9. Bon Soir, Bon Soir
10. Hickey
11. Breathe Deep
12. So I Hear You're Moving
13. Let's Go Bowling
14. What Was He Wearing?
15. Cowboy on the Moon
16. The Pack-Up Song

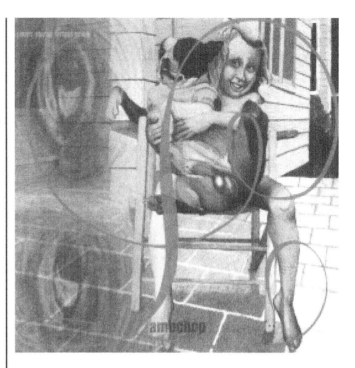

Comments: OK, I'm not going to pretend that I'm an expert
on Lambchop, 'cause I don't really know that much about them,
and own only a small portion of their CD releases. Yeah, they're
regularly called "Nashville's most fucked up country band" by
fans and critics, and their unique mix of rock, country, soul,
and jazz has found a receptive European audience even if they
remain cult favorites in the U.S. Lambchop was formed by
frontman Kurt Wagner and friends Jim Watkins and Marc
Trovillion in the mid-1980s. Originally known as Posterchild,
they began recording at Trovillion's house, releasing the results
as a series of self-produced DIY cassette tapes. As time slipped
by, they began adding members, performing at Lucy's Records,
owned by Wagner's future wife Mary Mancini. By 1992, the
band was beginning to attract attention, which earned them a
"cease and desist" letter from the lawyer for the British band
Poster Children. After rejecting such name changes as Pinnacles
of Cream and Turd Goes Black, they settled on 'Lambchop'.

II. How I Quit Smoking (Merge Records 1996, CD)
1. For Which We Are Truly Thankful
2. The Man Who Loved Beer
3. The Militant
4. We Never Argue
5. Life's Little Tragedy
6. Suzieju
7. All Smiles and Mariachi
8. The Scary Caroler
9. Smuckers
10. The Militant (reprise)
11. Garf
12. Your Life as a Sequel
13. Theöne
14. Again

LAMBCHOP

III. Hank (Merge Records 1996, CD EP)
1. I'm a Stranger Here
2. Blame It on the Brunettes
3. The Tin Chime
4. Randi
5. Doak's Need
6. Poor Bastard
7. I Sucked My Boss's Dick

IV. Thriller (Merge Records 1997, CD)
1. My Face Your Ass
2. Your Fucking Sunny Day
3. Hey Where's Your Girl
4. Crawl Away
5. Gloria Leonard
6. Thriller
7. The Old Fat Robin
8. Superstar in France

V. What Another Man Spills (Merge Records 1998, CD)
1. Interrupted
2. The Saturday Option
3. Shucks
4. Give Me Your Love (Love Song)
5. Life #2
6. Scamper
7. It's Not Alright
8. N.O.
9. I've Been Lonely for So Long
10. Magnificient Obsession
11. King of Nothing Never
12. The Theme from the Neil Miller Show

VI. Nixon (Merge Records 2000, CD)
1. The Old Gold Shoe
2. Grumpus
3. You Masculine You
4. Up with People
5. Nashville Parents
6. What Else Could It Be?
7. The Distance from Her to There
8. The Book I Haven't Read
9. The Petrified Florist
10. The Butcher Boy

Comments: With a handful of recordings for the North Carolina-based Merge Records under their collective belts, Lambchop really hit its stride with 2000's *Nixon*. The band, which fluctuates between five and fifteen active members at any given time, capitalized on its growing popularity in the U.K. with a May performance at the London Royal Festival Hall. Lambchop remains a big name in Europe, while retaining a faithful indie-rock following stateside.

Another View: "As time went on, Lambchop got a little more musically accomplished, and Kurt Wagner more inclined to write songs that were a little less of a stream-of-consciousness jumble, and a little less random. This will still strike most as a mighty odd record, though. Ostensibly much of this record was inspired by former president Richard Nixon (there is even a suggested reading list of Nixon-related books on the sleeve). But there are no direct references to him, and even any indirect ones are so oblique that you'd never make the connection if the record had a different title (or contained no reading list). Wagner's songs are less of a

Lambchop

laundry list of bringdown imagery and a tad more direct than in the past, but still suggestive of, well, the kind of voices and snatches of conversation a schizophrenic might hear and utter. The music? Yes, another incongruous clash of lush orchestrated countrypolitan music and alternative singer-songwriter rock, but the Philadelphia/'70s soul influences are pretty upfront on some tracks."
– Richie Unterberger, *All Music Guide*

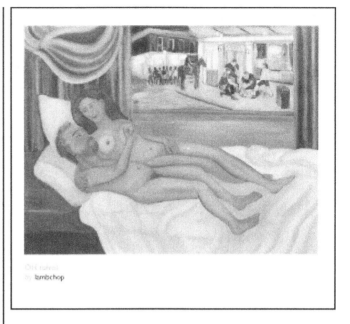

VII. The Queen's Royal Trimma (City Slang 2000, CD EP)
1. If I Could Touch the Hem of His Garment
2. Nashville Parent
3. The Old Gold Shoe
4. Give Me Your Love
5. Theöne
6. Love TKO

Comments: Limited edition CD, 1,300 copies, originally sold at the band's September 23 and 24th, 2000 shows in the U.K. Songs were recorded at Lambchop's London Royal Festival Hall concert on May 13, 2000. "Love TKO" includes members of Calexico.

VIII. Tools In The Dryer (Merge Records 2001, CD)
1. Nine
2. White
3. Cigaretiquette
4. Miss Prissy
5. The Petrified Florist
6. Each with a Bag of Fries
7. All Over the World
8. Flowers of Memory
9. Scared Out of My Shoes
10. Style Monkeys
11. The Militant (Mark Robinson Remix)
12. Up with People (Zero 7 Reprise Remix)
13. Give Me Your Love (Doppelganger Remix)
14. Love TKO
15. Or Thousands of Prizes
16. Moody Fucker

IX. Is A Woman (Merge Records 2002, CD)
1. The Daily Growl
2. The New Cobweb Summer
3. My Blue Wave
4. I Can Hardly Spell My Name
5. Autumn's Vicar
6. Flick
7. Caterpillar
8. D. Scott Parsley
9. Bugs
10. The Old Matchbook Trick
11. Is a Woman

X. Treasure Chest of the Enemy (self-produced 2002, CD)
1. The Fade Away Jumper
2. The Gettysburg Address
3. We Shall Not Be Overwhelmed
4. The Puppy and the Leaf
5. Haul Away Joe
6. Greylines In Heaven
7. Yard Work
8. Kurt Wagner's Heart Attack
9. Di Di 7
10. Flub

Comments: Collection of demos and rare studio tracks, limited edition of 1,300 sold at shows during the band's 2002 U.S. tour. A shorter EP version with fewer songs was sold during the 2001 European tour.

XI. Pet Sounds Sucks (City Slang 2002, CD)
1. The New Cobweb Summer
2. My Blue Wave
3. I Can Hardly Spell My Name
4. Flick
5. You Masculine You
6. Caterpillar
7. Bugs
8. The Book I Haven't Read
9. The Puppy and the Leaf
10. Flub

Comments: Limited edition import "tour CD," 1000 copies, sold during the band's European tour. Recorded live at the American Music Hall in San Francisco, March 2002; "Flub" is a studio recording produced by Marky Nevers.

LAMBCHOP

XII. Aw Cmon (Merge Records 2004, CD)
1. Being Tyler
2. Four Pounds in Two Days
3. Steve McQueen
4. The Lone Official
5. Something's Going On
6. Nothing But a Blur from a Bullet Train
7. Each Time I Bring It Up It Seems to Bring You Down
8. Timothy B. Schmidt
9. Women Help to Create the Kind of Men They Despise
10. I Hate Candy
11. I Haven't Heard a Word I've Said
12. Action Figure

XIII. No You Cmon (Merge Records 2004, CD)
1. Sunrise
2. Low Ambition
3. There's Still Time
4. Nothing Adventurous Please
5. The Problem
6. Shang a Dang Dang
7. About My Lighter
8. Under a Dream of a Lie
9. Jan. 24
10. The Gusher
11. Listen
12. The Producer

XIV. The Decline of Country and Western Civilization, Part 2: The Woodwind Years (Merge Records 2006, CD)
1. My Cliché
2. Loretta Lung
3. Two Kittens Don't Make A Puppy
4. It's Impossible
5. Ovary Eyes
6. I Can Hardly Spell My Name
7. The Scary Caroler
8. Your Life As A Sequel
9. Smuckers
10. Alumni Lawn
11. Burly and Johnson
12. Mr. Crabby
13. Playboy, The Shirt
14. Gloria Leonard [alternate version]
15. The Old Fat Robin
16. The Distance From Her to There [alternate version]
17. The Book I Haven't Read [alternate version]
18. Gettysburg Address

Comments: A collection of rarities, B-sides, alternate takes, compilation contributions and songs from split-singles, circa 1993-1999; also includes a new track, "Gettysburg Address." A limited edition Australian import version includes a bonus disc containing four additional tracks: "Gus," "Women," "Blur," and "Prepared."

XV. Damaged (Merge Records 2006, CD)
1. Paperback Bible
2. Prepared
3. The Rise and Fall of the Letter P
4. A Day Without Glasses
5. Beers Before the Barbican
6. I Would Have Waited Here All Day
7. Crackers
8. Fear
9. Short
10. The Decline of Country and Western Civilization

Comments: A special limited-edition version of *Damaged* included a four-track bonus disc with the songs "Pre," "Fear(re)," "Decline" and "Paperback Bible (With Drums)."

LAMBCHOP
OH (ohio)
(Merge Records)

Lambchop are a lot like one of those little puzzles that you'll find on your table at hundreds of country-styled restaurants that dot the American landscape. They're challenging, aggravating, and ultimately entertaining. Lambchop is often described as a "country" band, but only 'cause they come from Nashville…truth is, there's more soul than cornpone, more baroque romanticism than redneck angst in the signature Lambchop sound. The band's tenth album, *OH (ohio)*, presents a different perspective on the same finely-crafted portrait.

With the band's ranks held to a mere eight members (from as many as 20), this may be as minimalist a collection as you'll hear from Lambchop. Frontman Kurt Wagner conceived these songs as solo works, subsequently fleshed out to full band performances, and the result is a stripped-down, albeit still lush musical landscape that is at once both gorgeous and maddeningly hypnotic. Wagner's oblique lyrics are as inscrutable as ever, bubbling beneath the consciousness to plague your thoughts long after hearing them. Vocals, instrumentation and production all fit together perfectly, creating an interlocking musical puzzle that will keep the listener involved for hours. – *Blurt Magazine*, 2008

XVI. OH (Ohio) (Merge Records 2008, CD)
1. Ohio
2. Slipped Dissolved and Loosed
3. I'm Thinking of a Number (between 1 and 2)
4. National Talk Like a Pirate Day
5. A Hold of You
6. Sharing a Gibson with Martin Luther King Jr.
7. Of Raymond
8. Please Rise
9. Popeye
10. Close Up
11. I Belive In You

Comments: Originally conceived as a solo album by Wagner, the songs were later fleshed out with a relatively stripped-down eight-member Lambchop line-up (see review ➜).

Bootlegs

B1. Tanz-Und Folkfest (no label 2006, CD)
1. Intro
2. The Book I Haven't Read
3. Each Time I Bring It Up, It Seems To Bring You Down
4. Nothing But A Blur, From A Bullet Train
5. Low Ambition
6. Caterpillar
7. The Lone Official
8. You Masculine You
9. Up With People
10. Theöne
11. (Get A) Grip (On Yourself)

Comments: Live performance with the Dafo String Quartet, recorded 07-02-04 in Rudolstadt, Germany.

THE LAND

Band Members:
Lewis Lowrey (bass, guitar, vocals)
Allen Lowrey (drums, vocals)
Michael Rosa (guitar, vocals)
Chris Gowen (bass)

Comments: Allen Lowrey is a former Lambchop member, and I went to high school with both him and his brother Lewis. Small world, eh?

LANGLEY

Band Members:
Rick Thompson (vocals)
Bob Langley (guitars)
Chris Hopkins (bass)
P-Roy Petty (drums)

LAUGHING STORM DOGS

Band Members:
Robert Means (vocals, keyboards)
Dave Byrd (guitar, bass, vocals)
Lars Hall (guitar, bass)
Mark "Barky" Pierce (guitar, vocals)
Death Ray Cristobal (guitars, vocals)
Andrew Coleman (drums)

Comments: LSD is a popular Murfreesboro comedic rock band that has been "humping legs from coast to coast since 1986" with songs like the swinging, rockabilly-tinged "I Drink The Blood Of Elvis" and the crowd-favorite "Blow Job."

LAW OF NATURE

Band Members:
Jennifer Knight (vocals)
Chapman Welch (guitars)
Karen Estill (bass)
Jeff Starks (drums)

Comments: Band contributed song "Who Knows" to *What's The Buzz?* 1993 compilation CD.

TH' LEGENDARY SHACK*SHAKERS

Band Members:
Colonel J.D. Wilkes (vocals, harp, keyboards) (I-VI)
Mark Robertson (upright bass, bass, vocals) (I-VI)
David Lee (guitars) (III, IV, VI)
Joe Buck (guitars, strings) (I, II, V)

TH' LEGENDARY SHACK*SHAKERS

Paul Simmonz (drums) (I-VI)
Brett Whitacre (drums) (VI)
Jerry Roe (drums, percussion) (IV)

Other Musicians:
Jack Irwin (keyboards) (IV, V)
Donnie Herron (fiddle, banjo) (II, III)
Bill Huber (trombone, tuba) (IV)
Jim Hoke (saxophone, clarinet) (III, IV)
Jillian Johnson (ukulele) (V)
Nick Kane (guitars) (III)
Fats Kaplan (banjo, mandolin) (III, IV, V)
Jordan Richter (guitar) (III)
Kristi Rose (vocals) (V)
Ward Stout (fiddle) (V)

Th' Legendary Shack*Shakers Recordings:

I. Hunkerdown (Spinout Records 1998, CD)
1. The Sheriff's Ranch for Boys
2. Go Hog Wild
3. Tickle Your Innards
4. She's Gone Haywire
5. Hunkerdown
6. Back to Paducah
7. The Kentucky Song
8. Is'wanee!
9. Pitchin' A Fit
10. Rattletrap
11. The CB Song
12. Love Bug Crawl
13. That's What I Know
14. Right Behind You Baby

Th' Legendary Shack*Shakers

Comments: The debut disc from Th' Legendary Shack*Shakers, produced by Eddie Angel of **Los Straitjackets** and **the Planet Rockers** for the indie Spinout Records label, which also delivered most of the Planet Rockers' albums to an appreciative hot-rodder garage-rock audience.

II. Cockadoodledon't (Bloodshot Records 2003, CD)
1. Pinetree Boogie
2. CB Song
3. Help Me From My Brain
4. Shakerag Holler
5. Hunkerdown
6. Clodhopper
7. Bullfrog Blues
8. Blood On The Bluegrass
9. Devil's Night Auction
10. Wild Wild Lover
11. Shake Your Hips
12. Hoptown Jailbreak

Comments: Originally released by the band's own Hih-D-Hoh label in 2002, reissued with an additional song ("Hunkerdown") after LSS signed with Chicago's alt-country label Bloodshot in 2003.

III. Believe (Yep Roc Records 2004, CD)
1. Agony Wagon
2. Creek Cats
3. Where's the Devil...When You Need Him?
4. Piss and Vinegar
5. County of Graves
6. All My Life to Kill
7. Cussin' in Tongues
8. Help Me
9. Bible Cyst
10. The Pony To Bet On
11. Fistwhistle Boogie
12. Misery Train

IV. Pandelirium (Yep Roc Records 2006, CD)
1. Ichabod!
2. Sound Electric Eyes
3. No Such Thing
4. Iron Lung Oompah
5. Bottom Road
6. Somethin' In The Water
7. Jipsy Valentine
8. Thin The Herd
9. Monkey On The Doghouse
10. The Ballad Of Speedy Atkins
11. Bible, Candle And Skull
12. Nellie Bell

*Th' Legendary Shack*Shakers, continued on page 313...*

CD REVIEW: LEGENDARY SHACK*SHAKERS' SWAMPBLOOD

TH' LEGENDARY SHACK*SHAKERS
Swampblood
(Yep Roc Records)

It's been said by some that if you drive down Highway 100, south outta Nashville and through the sleepy little burg of Fairview, you'll find an old dirt road at the Hickman County line. You follow this road back through the woods 'til you find the gnarled tree where the strange chickens roost all day and night. From there, you take the gravel trail on the right, go down the hollow past Lady Sniff's shack (pay no attention to the sirens' wail that you'll hear coming from behind those walls) to arrive at the crossroads. Pick the right fork, and it'll take you down through the knotty kudzu gateway to the edge of the ole swamp…

Now, you have to be careful when going down there, 'cause much like Rudderville or Kingfield, folks 'round these parts get a might touchy if they don't know you. If you're drivin' too nice or too new of a car, the 'shiners might toss a few rounds your way thinkin' that you're a Revenue agent or some other sort of Federale. Tales say that the swamp is haunted by the ghosts of several Delta bluesmen that gave up thriving careers and settled down right here, working as farmhands in the nearby tobacco fields. On Saturday nights, they'd get together with cigar-box guitars and harmonicas and they'd sing. Somebody would drag some sort of scaly critter out of the swamp and cook it up for dinner, washing down the dubious feast with some clear, viscous, foul-tasting liquor.

If you have a mind to venture out into that neck o' the woods, I'd suggest that you first make sure that you're driving the right kind of car…nothing too flash or too Hollywood, and certainly nothing made by the flan-factories of Detroit after 1980. Maybe some sort of early-70s Mopar, like a Charger or Satellite, preferably one with a few well-earned rust holes, missing chrome and a dirty old sock stuffed in the gas nozzle. Nobody down around the swamp will look at you twice, especially if you're rattlin' *Swampblood*, the latest-and-greatest from Th' Legendary Shack*Shakers, out of your vintage quad sound-system. With the Col. J.D. Wilkes as your co-pilot across these perilous killing fields, you're assured of getting back home alive and kickin'.

Feedback-whipped howls and nancy banjo-pickin' comprise the brief instrumental "Dawn," sounding right at home surrounded by hanging vines and cypress trees. It's the perfect-fit intro to "Old Spur Line," *Swampblood*'s kick-off tune and as nasty a slice o' greasy redneck funk as you're likely to hear these days. The Colonel's vocals are slightly echoed in the mix as he spits out this cautionary tale of traveling into places that you shouldn't oughta. The band shuffles along, a minor thunderstorm behind Wilkes' haunting vocals. "Hellwater" begins with an authentic Tony

Joe White guitar lick, David Lee channeling the spirit of John Campbell as he picks out a familiar poke-salad riff and Wilkes belts out a song about the wages of sin.

Properly warmed up by this time, the Colonel and his instrumental army take *Swampblood* up a notch; "Easter Flesh" sounds vaguely Middle Eastern in flavor, with circular riffs and martial rhythms, Wilkes' up-tempo vocals bringing some sort of nasty Biblical judgment to the poor unfortunate souls who resist salvation. The title cut takes us further into the murky water than we've ever been before, the song a raucous, compelling number with manic harp work and fire-and-brimstone lyrics sung in a possessed voice. Lee's trebly fretwork fuels the song's instrumentation, a rhythmic assault that is as dense as the morning fog on the bayou.

From this point, *Swampblood* descends further into alcohol-fueled madness, each performance proudly wearing the sweat and fervor of a backwoods preacher as the Colonel puts his boys through their paces. "Cheat The Hangman" is like a runaway freighter jumping the tracks and diving headfirst into a muddy river while "Born Again Again" is an old-timey spiritual with a jug-band soul and a church-pew heart. "The Deadenin'" proves that it's not nice to fool with Mother Nature, the song an environmental anthem that has Wilkes' howlin' at the moon while the band kicks out a wily, smoke-tinted and disturbing soundtrack behind the Colonel's gnashin'-and-wailin' vocals.

There are several more gems hidden in *Swampblood*'s grooves that will tickle your imagination, like "Jimblyleg Man," an Appalachian hillbilly hoedown with spry fiddle playin' and plenty o' words about some sort of wicked sprite,

THE OTHER SIDE OF NASHVILLE

CD REVIEW: LEGENDARY SHACK*SHAKERS' BELIEVE

an imaginary evil like the chupacabra down in south Texas or West Virginia's mothman. "He Ain't Right" is a rockabilly rave-up that reminds one of Hasil Adkins. "Angel Lust" has a jazzbo sound that kicks your ears like Professor Longhair jammin' with Cab Calloway while Brett Whitacre's tribal drumbeats and tasteful fills play along nicely with Mark Robertson's muscular upright bass as Wilkes' swinging vocals take up any remaining slack. Whitacre adds the accompanying patterns behind the Colonel's mighty potent stream-of-consciousness rant "Preachin' At Traffic." *Swampblood* finishes much like it started, with the somber crosspatch "When I Die" leading into the fading hill country banjo-maul that is "Bright Sunny South."

Swampblood is Th' Legendary Shack*Shakers' fifth studio album, and if the band never evolves into world-beaters, they'll always deliver exactly what you'd expect them to: a combustible blend of roots-rock, honky-tonk country, electric blues and retro-rockabilly. Yeah, they may be a throwback to a simpler, highly-rocking time, and hopelessly out-of-step with today's musical trends. But as the Colonel says, "I dream in sepia, mono and Beta" – as defiant a statement of Luddite fist-shaking as has been committed to tape. I wouldn't expect Th' Legendary Shack*Shakers to headline the Pitchfork Festival, but if I ran into them at a cockfight, I'd buy 'em a mason jar of whatever they wanted to drink...   – *Cashville411* website, 2007

TH' LEGENDARY SHACK SHAKERS
Believe
(Yep Roc Records)

In the early 1980s, Jason & the *Nashville* Scorchers shook up the staid country music establishment with a hard-rocking blend of adrenaline-fueled punk energy and reckless country soul. Two decades later, Th' Legendary Shack Shakers have arrived to finish the musical revolution begun by Jason and his crew, tilting the city on its collective ear. Nothing could have prepared the "Music City" for the band's self-released 2002 debut – *Cockadoodledon't* – reissued a year later by Bloodshot Records. A manic collection of rockabilly, blues and country twang delivered with the intensity of a mad dervish, Th' Legendary Shack Shakers announced that it was a force to be reckoned with.

Believe proves that while they may not yet be legendary, the band sure knows how to shake the shack. Toss this slab o'

metal into your CD player and be ready for an old school tent revival to explode from your speakers. Shack Shakers frontman Col. J.D. Wilkes is ready to preach the gospel of rock *and* roll to your lonesome ears; the rest of the boys ready to save your soul with their roots rock hymnal. *Believe* opens with a train whistle, the choogling beat of "Agony Wagon" warping into an Arabic guitar line beneath a tale of a tortured soul doomed to forever ride the mythical "hellbound train." Guitarist Joe Buck adds a twangy, Dick Dale-influenced guitar riff beneath Wilkes' vocals, the lyrics delivered with all the fervor of a Southern preacher standing in the center of a Middle Eastern bazaar.

The album rolls along like a runaway hot rod fueled by whiskey and riding along a tightrope made of discarded guitar strings. "Piss And Vinegar" is a jukejoint rave-up; Wilkes' echoed vocals punching through a fog of bluesy guitars and staggered drumbeats. Driven by a Carl Perkins-styled rhythm and hazy, psychedelic fretwork, "County Of Graves" is another tragic tale, part prayer and part sermon with a drunken soundtrack. "Cussin' In Tongues" is a mutant truck-driving song, a cross between Dave Dudley and the Butthole Surfers, Pauly Simmonz' massive percussion work and Buck's stylish six-string riffing pushing the rig towards a crashing finish. If your spiritual quest is in need of some cheap thrills, let the Colonel and his boys guide you towards the path of righteousness with *Believe*.
– *Alt.Culture.Guide*, 2004

Th' Legendary Shack*Shakers

*Th' Legendary Shack*Shakers, continued...*

Comments: Includes guest appearances by fellow travelers and kindred spirits Jello Biafra and Rev. Horton Heat.

V. Lower Broad Lo-Fi (Arkam Records 2007, CD)
1. 21 Days
2. Don't Start Cry'n
3. Dump Road Yodel
4. Hip Shake
5. Bullfrog Blues
6. Yer Gonna Need Me
7. Wild Wild
8. Don' My Time
9. Rollin' In My Sweet Baby's Arms
10. Ghost Riders In The Sky
11. Devil's Night Auction
12. I Ain't Home

Comments: Live disc capturing a LSS performance from 2000 when the band was relative unknowns. Released by Alabama-based garage-rock label Arkam, which is somehow affiliated with the Florence band the Wednesdays.

VI. Swampblood (Yep Roc Records 2007, CD)
1. Dawn
2. Old Spur Line
3. Hellwater
4. Easter Flesh
5. Swampblood
6. Dusk
7. Cheat The Hangman
8. Born Again Again
9. The Deadenin'
10. Down And Out
11. Jimblyleg Man
12. He Ain't Right
13. Angel Lust
14. Preachin' At Traffic
15. When I Die
16. Bright And Sunny South

Comments: Another rockin' disc from Th' Legendary Shack*Shakers (see review ➜).

LEGENDS

Band Members:
Archie Bell (vocals)
Clifford Curry (vocals)
Maurice Williams (vocals)

Comments: Short-lived soul/R&B "supergroup" consisting of 1960s-era hitmakers Archie Bell (Archie Bell & the Drells – "Tighten Up"), Clifford Curry, and Maurice Williams ("Stay"). I think that the trio did a few shows together in the Southeast, but clashing egos prevented any sort of recording and they broke up soon thereafter...

LIFEBOY

Band Members:
William Tyler (vocals, guitar)
Keith Lowen (bass, vocals)
Sam Smith (drums, vocals)

Comments: Originally known as **Soul Surgeon**, Lifeboy's deal with Sire Records never resulted in anything beyond a single track ("Number One") included on the soundtrack to the film *Drop Dead Gorgeous* with Kirsten Dunst and Denise Richards. Interestingly enough, the soundtrack also included a track from Nashville's Tim Carroll and Knoxville band the Nevers. Lifeboy recorded a full-length album for Sire that was never released by the label, but individual tracks have trickled out through the now-defunct band's MySpace page.

Tyler plays with **Lambchop** these days, and Lowen and Smith played together in **Harper** (now known as **the Comfies**, as well as in Lowen's side project, **Hail To The Keith**. More recently, Smith has taken up the chair behind the drum set for Ben Folds.

TED LINDSAY AND THE DEMOCRATS

Band Members:
Ted Lindsay (vocals, bass) (I)
Jim Ramsey (guitars) (I)
Chip Gabbert (vocals, keyboards) (I)
Paula "Panic" Abbott (guitar, vocals) (I)
Herb Shucher (drums) (I)

Rev. Gordon & Legends

Ted Lindsey Recordings:

I. Russian Women (Ancient Mystic Records 1987, LP)
<u>Side One</u>
1. Russian Women
2. Bohiemian
3. Hot Jungle
4. Wild Night

<u>Side Two</u>
5. Walk On Fire
6. Here Comes My Baby
7. The Quiet Guy
8. Frankie The Beat
9. Whatever Baby Wants

WILLIAM LINTON

Musicians:
William Linton (synthesizers) (I)

William Linton Recordings:

I. Traveler's Tales (Linton Music 1986, cassette)
<u>Side One:</u>
1. Traveler's Tales I-V
2. Solar Wind

<u>Side Two:</u>
1. Dream Shades
2. Ocean Of Dreams
3. After The Rain
4. The Unfolding

Comments: One of the pioneers among Nashville's talented "space music" artists, Linton's 1986 album ***Traveler's Tales*** received national airplay on public radio's *Music From The Hearts Of Space* program and, along with **Tony Gerber** and **Giles Reaves**, helped put the "Music City" on the space music map.

LITTLE SAINTS

Band Members:
Jeff Holmes (guitar, mandolin, vocals) (I)
Scot Evans (bass, vocals) (I)
Randy Parsons (vocals, keyboards) (I)
Freeman D'Angelo (saxophone, flute, vocals) (I)
Grog Eisnaugle (drums) (I)

Little Saints Recordings:

I. Slapping Houses (Big Hands Records 1987, LP)
<u>Side One</u>
1. Get Inside
2. This House
3. A Rose For Emily
4. Great Big Hands
5. I Hear A Train

<u>Side Two</u>
6. The Wilson's Jamboree
7. The Baptism Of Anthony
8. Another Number Falls
9. Calendar
10. Mama Tell

Comments: Little Saints was formed in the early 1980s while the members were attending Furman University in South Carolina. Little Saints played a mix of contemporary covers (Talking Heads, the Police, R.E.M.) and original songs. Jeff Holmes would later form Nashville music institution **the Floating Men**. Check out the interveiw with Holmes (➜) for more info on the Little Saints.

LLAMA

Band Members:
Ben Morton (vocals, guitar) (I, II)
Ben Brown (guitar) (I, II)
Neil Mason (drums) (I, II)
Matthew Stewart (bass) (I)
Adam Binder (bass) (II)
Ian Fitchuk (keyboards) (II)

Llama Recordings:

I. Close To The Silence (MCA Records 2001, CD)
1. Back Where We Began
2. Three White Cars
3. Hero
4. Too Much Too Soon
5. Close To The Silence
6. All You Ever Wanted
7. Fruit
8. Chasing The Sun
9. Another Round
10. Carry Me High
11. To Believe

II. The World From Here EP (MCA Records 2002, CD)
1. Fly To You
2. Wildest Dreams
3. Waking Up
4. Serena

Comments: Originally called the Dahlia Llamas, the band changed its name when signed to MCA. Morton, Brown and Mason were "discovered" by MCA's Tony Brown while playing regular shows at Guido's Pizza in Nashville's university area; the trio was still in high school when they signed their deal. Binder and Fitchuk were added to round out the band's sound, which leaned towards a popish jam band vibe, heavily influenced by Phish and the Dave Matthews Band. Both recordings were produced by Kenny Greenberg and Matt Rollings. The incredible Bela Fleck played on the band's debut album. After Llama broke-up in 2003, Brown and Mason hooked up with former members of the Kicks (from Arkansas) and formed **Bang Bang Bang**; Morton formed the band ModernMan.

BILL LLOYD

Band Members:
Bill Lloyd (vocals, guitar, bass, keyboards) (I-VI)

Other Musicians:
Steve Allen (guitars) (V, VI)
Al Anderson (guitars) (IV)
Scott Baggett (keyboards, guitar) (II, IV, V, VI)
Dan Baird (guitar) (V)
Pat Buchanan (guitars, vibes) (IV, V, VI)
Cindy Bullens (vocals) (IV, VI)
Doug Carman (vocals) (II, IV, VI)

BILL LLOYD

Chris Carmichael (violin, cello) (VI)
Peter Case (harmonica) (VI)
Fenner Castner (drums) (II, IV, VI)
Beth Nielsen Chapman (vocals) (VI)
Rick Clark (bass) (II)
Tim Coats (jaw harp) (II)
Ken Coomer (drums) (VI)
John Cowan (vocals) (I, IV)
Marshall Crenshaw (guitar, bass, vocals) (II, IV)
Bill Demain (vocals) (IV, V, VI)
Dennis Diken (drums) (IV)
Don Dixon (bass) (VI)
Tommy Dorsey (Fairlight programming) (I)
Molly Felder (vocals) (IV, VI)
Clive Gregson (guitar) (VI)
Mike Grimes (guitar) (II)
Henry Gross (vocals) (IV)
Don Henry (vocals) (VI)
Jim Hodgekins (drums) (I)
Byron House (bass) (I-II, IV-VI)
Brad Jones (bass, guitar, vocals) (II, IV, V)
Wayne Killius (drums) (IV)
Randell Kirsch (vocals) (VI)
Al Kooper (keyboards) (II, IV)
Dennis Locorriere (vocals) (II)
Phil Madeira (keyboards, strings) (VI)
Greg Morrow (drums) (IV, V, VI)
Bob Mummert (drums) (II, V)
Marc Owens (drums) (I-VI)
Tom Peterson (bass) (IV)
Mike Radovsky (drums) (II)
Robert Reynolds (bass) (VI)
Kim Richey (vocals) (I, II, IV, VI)

Amy Rigby (vocals) (IV)
David Russell (guitar) (I)
Pat Simmons (vocals) (II)
Jody Stephens (drums) (II)
Scott Sullivant (bass) (I)
Gary Tallent (bass) (II)
Pat Terry (vocals) (II)
Greg Trooper (vocals) (IV)
Tommy Wells (drums) (II)
Rusty Young (pedal steel) (II, IV, VI)

Bill Lloyd Recordings:

I. Feeling The Elephant (DB Records 1990, CD)
1. This Very Second
2. Nothing Comes Close
3. Feeling The Elephant
4. Lisa Anne
5. All At Once You Unzipped
6. It'll Never Get Better Than This
7. I Wanna Sit And Watch The Credits Roll
8. Susan Scorned
9. This Must Be The Place
10. Everything's Closing Down

Comments: Bill Lloyd's 1986 solo debut was a breath of fresh air across the Nashville music scene. While most Nashville bands at that time were trying to rock as hard as they could, ***Feeling The Elephant*** was a masterpiece of pop-rock songwriting from the former Sgt. Arms/Practical Stylists member. Originally released by Boston label Throbbing Lobster on vinyl in 1986, later reissued on both vinyl and CD by Danny Beard's DB Records (Beard is the owner of Atlanta's uber-cool Wax-N-Facts record store). That's Bill's band the **December Boys** on "This Must Be The Place."

II. Set To Pop (East Side Digital 1994, CD)
1. I Went Electric
2. This Is Where I Belong
3. Trampoline
4. In The Line Of Fire
5. I Know What You're Thinking
6. Forget About Us
7. Alright
8. The Man Who Knew Too Much
9. Niagra Falls
10. In A Perfect World
11. The S.W.A.T. Team Of Love
12. A Beautiful Lie
13. Channeling The King
14. Out Of The Picture
15. Anything Less Than Love

Comments: Lloyd's uniformly excellent sophomore effort was recorded for strange little indie label East Side Digital. I

say strange because although they released a number of great albums by talented artists like Lloyd, Eric Ambel, the Bottle Rockets, and Chris Stamey of the dBs, their bread and butter was in releasing unusual movie soundtracks and a heck of a lot of CDs from San Francisco noise terrorists the Residents and electronc music legend Wendy/Walter Carlos.

That being said, *Set To Pop* offers up more of the whip-smart pop-rock fans had come to expect from Bill. The major league roster that Bill assembled for this album includes rock legend **Al Kooper**, Gary Tallent of Springsteen's E Street Band, Poco's Rusty Young, and Big Star's Jody Stephens as well as local talents like Brad Jones, Mike Grimes, Byron House, and Fenner Castner, among others.

III. Confidence Is High Plus 4 (Sound Asleep 1995, CD)
1. Confidence Is High
2. When Will I Ever Learn
3. When The Green Room Turns To Blue
4. Conference Call
5. Wake Up Call

IV. Standing On The Shoulders Of Giants (Koch Records 1999, CD)
1. Standing On the Shoulders of Giants
2. Cool and Gone
3. Sweet Virginia

4. Dr. Roberts Second Opinion
5. Holding Back The Waterfall
6. (Who You Gonna) Run To Now
7. Complaints
8. Don't Kid Yourself
9. This Is The Way
10. She Won't Be Back
11. Box Of Snakes
12. So You Won't Have To
13. Years Away From Here
14. Turn Me On Dead Man

Comments: Includes drummer Dennis Diken of the Smithereens and Tom Peterson of Cheap Trick; Al Kooper comes around for another go, Marshall Crenshaw plugs in his guitar, and Amy Rigby and Cindy Bullens add their wonderful backing vocals to "This Is The Way."

V. All In One Place (Def Heffer Records 2001, CD)
1. There's A Lot Of Love In This Room
2. Contact High
3. Step Inside
4. Ring Around The Moon
5. How Can We Go On
6. The Shortest Distance Between Two Points
7. Goin' Nowhere Tonight
8. Baby's Breath

Bill Lloyd and his record collection (with Scott Sullivant & Jim Hodgkins/Practical Stylists)

9. Let Her Dance
10. Work In Progress
11. The Lottery Song
12. Anytime The Time Feels Right
13. Lonely You
14. There You Are Again
15. I Don't Want To Tie You Down

Comments: *All In One Place* is a remarkably cohesive odds-n-sods collection of spare tracks taken from Lloyd's amazingly deep vault of songs. If there's a tribute album or benefit compilation that somebody is putting together, Bill Lloyd is always one of the first musicians to volunteer his songs. Other than being one of the incredibly nicest guys that I've ever met in the music biz, Bill also has great taste in music and he works well with others.

Thus we have covers of songs by Eric Carmen and the Raspberries, the Hollies, Badfinger, Harry Nilsson, Bobby Fuller and Todd Rundgren, taken from various tribute comps. There are also a number of tracks co-written with friends like **Dan Baird**, Steve Wynn (Dream Syndicate), Pat Buchanan, and **Jerry Dale McFadden**.

VI. Back To Even (New Boss Sounds 2004, CD)
1. Back To Even
2. Dancing With The Post
3. Hindon't (instrumental)
4. Dial Nine
5. Almost Taken
6. I Got It Bad
7. The World Is A Different Place Without You
8. For The Longest Time
9. Kissed Your Sister
10. We Are Two
11. Me Against Me
12. The Perfect Crime
13. A Story I Can't Tell
14. Another Side
15. Oasis

Comments: Includes backing vocals from Molly Felder and Bill Demain of **Swan Dive**.

LOGICKAL

Band Members:
Jeremy Dickens (keyboards, synth, percussion) (I)

Logickal Recordings:

I. Day By Daydream (Discrepancy Recordings 2003, CD-R)
1. Wake Up Call
2. Bad News For The Thirsty
3. In The Drink

BILL LLOYD
All In One Place
(Def Heffer Records)

Bill Lloyd is remembered by many as half of the popular country duo Foster & Lloyd, who recorded three hit albums during the late-1980s. Lloyd has always been a rocker in his heart, however, and he's enjoyed a successful career as a songwriter and session guitarist, playing with artists like Al Kooper, Kim Richey, Steve Earle and Marshall Crenshaw. His fourth album, *All In One Place*, gathers a decade's worth of Lloyd's songs from various tribute albums and compilations.

A glorious collection of pop-influenced roots rock, Lloyd joyfully interprets songs by folks like the Hollies, Badfinger, Bobby Fuller, Todd Rundgren and Harry Nilsson. He also throws in a few of his own spirited compositions, as well as songs co-written with artists like Dan Baird (Georgia Satellites), Jerry Dale McFadden (The Mavericks) and Steve Wynn (Dream Syndicate).

Think of a mix of the Beatles and the Kinks, with a slight Nashville twang, and you've nailed the pop-rock aesthetic that makes *All In One Place* an enormously charming collection of tunes. – *The View On Pop Culture*, 2003

4. Given To Dream
5. Cranky
6. Or, Gone
7. Corner's Keeper
8. Daily Reference
9. The Reach, The Tangles
10. Sybiart
11. Inserted Thusly
12. Thunderstorms

Comments: Stunningly brilliant collection of electronic music by local visionary Jeremy Dickens a/k/a Logickal.

LOJAQUE & THE FLAMING NAHDBITS!

Band Members:
Pope Lojaque the First (Aaron Lamb) (vocals)
Reverend Lemonjello "Bizzy-Balls" Jones (David Dice) (guitar)
The Naked Baby (Jason Barnett) (bass)
El King Suckular de Tiempo (Tracy Ratzloff) (drums)
Vyking bodyguard Bane The Despoiler (Derek Flynt)

Lojaque & the Flaming Nahdbits Recordings:

I. Music To Playa Hate To (Kitty Face Records)

LONE OFFICIAL

Band Members:
Matt Button (vocals, guitar) (I-II)
Ben Martin (drums) (I-II)
Sami El Amri (guitar) (I-II)
Brian Nicholls (lap steel) (I-II)

Ryan Norris (keyboards) (I-II)
Eric Williams (bass) (I-II)

Lone Official Recordings:

I. Lone Official (Set International Records 2003, CD)
1. Lament
2. Fleet Renee
3. Mystic Lady
4. Monarchos
5. Tap Dance
6. Latour
7. The Waltz
8. Scoop
9. Serena's Tune
10. Truckers Love It

II. Tuckassee Take (Honest Jon's UK 2006, CD)
1. Pony Ride
2. Fight Song
3. Stall Of The Steed
4. Amelia Earhart
5. Monarchos
6. Bacon Creek
7. Sleepy Time Down South
8. Aught Years
9. Le Coq Sportif
10. Lost My Ass
11. Country Strong
12. Pretty Waters
13. Dumb Waiter

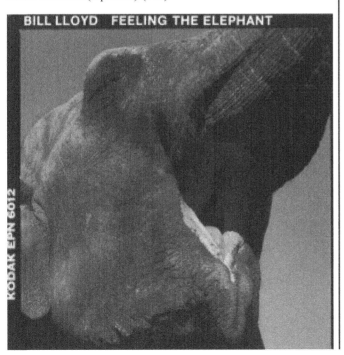

LONESOME BOB

LONESOME BOB

Band Members:
Lonesome Bob (vocals, guitar) (I-II)

Other Musicians:
Steve Allen (keyboards, guitar) (II)
Kevin Carlson (bass) (II)
Tim Carroll (guitar) (I-II)
Bill Dwyer (guitar) (I)
Dave Francis (bass) (I)
Paul Griffith (drums) (II)
Eric Holt (keyboards) (II)
Mark Horn (drums) (I)
Dave Jacques (bass) (I-II)
Fats Kaplan (piano) (II)
Phil Madiera (keyboards) (II)
Rick Schell (drums) (I-II)
Paul Slivka (bass) (II)

Lonesome Bob Recordings:

I. Things Fall Apart (Checkered Past Records 1997, CD)
1. Love Is Not Blind
2. Do You Think About Me
3. Point Of No Return
4. Waltzing On The Titanic
5. Different Shades Of Gray
6. What Went Wrong
7. My Mother's Husband
8. Heaven's Gate
9. Too Much Time

10. Someone Watching Over Me
11. The Plans We Made
12. Call My Name
13. Sleepless Nites

Comments: Produced by Lonesome Bob, album includes guest performances by Allison Moorer, Ken Coomer and Ben Vaughn (see review ➜).

II. Things Change (Leaps Recordings 2002, CD)
1. Got Away With It
2. Intro
3. Heather's All Bummed Out
4. In The Time I Have Left
5. He's Sober Now (Conversation)
6. I Get Smarter Every Drink
7. Dying Breed
8. Where Are You Tonight?
9. Dreaming The Lie
10. Weight Of The World
11. 2 Drinks On An Empty Stomach
13. It'd Be Sad If It Weren't So Funny
14. Things Change

Comments: Produced by Steve Allen and Lonesome Bob, album includes guest performances by Ken Coomer, Allison Moorer and Amy Rigby.

LONESOME BOB
Things Fall Apart
(Checkered Past Records)

Now this, this *Things Fall Apart* album from this guy Lonesome Bob, this is the way that country music was meant to be. No big-hat, tight jeans posing for photo opportunities or Music Row pop crap, this is Nashville's greatest fear: a talented and creative singer and songwriter that doesn't fit into any of their corporate molds. Boasting one of the best baritones this side of Waylon Jennings, Lonesome Bob carries on a musical tradition that has its roots in Hank Williams and Bill Monroe and runs pure through Johnny Cash, George Jones and Willie Nelson to the songs on *Things Fall Apart*. Love and betrayal, death and despair, these are some of the subjects of Bob's songs, delivered in a rocking honky-tonk style that sometimes gets a little loud and raucous while, at other times, is eloquently genteel.

Guest vocalist Allison Moorer contributes her beautiful vocals to several duets on *Things Fall Apart*. Sounding a lot like a young Emmylou Harris, Moorer's voice provides an angelic charm that counters Bob's twangy growl. A satisfying collection of tunes that will continue to grow on you with every listen, *Things Fall Apart* is the kind of country album Nashville forgot how to make. Released by Checkered Past Records, a Chicago indie that, with a roster that includes Lonesome Bob, Tommy Womack and Paul Burch, seems to have their finger on the musical pulse of Nashville better than the dozens of labels that are located here in the "Music City." – *Alt.Culture.Guide*, 1998

LOS GRINGOS

Band Members:
Steve Earle (vocals, guitar)
George Turner (guitar)
Jimmy Gray (bass)
Richard Marz (steel guitar)
Jimmy "Jimbeau" Walsh (drums)

Comments: An early band that **Steve Earle** played in upon arriving in Nashville. No known recordings of this band exist. Earle would go on to form the Dukes and make some early recordings for Epic Records, of course, before launching a moderately successful and always controversial career.

LOS STRAITJACKETS

Band Members:
Danny Amis (vocals, guitar) (I-X)
Eddie Angel (vocals, guitar) (I-X)
E. Scott Esbeck (bass) (I-III)
Pete Curry (bass) (III-X)
L.J. "Jimmy" Lester (drums) (I-IX)
Jason Smay (drums) (X)

Other Musicians:
Mike Campbell (guitar) (V)
Deke Dickerson (saxophone) (X)
Jake Guralnick (guitar) (X)
Nick Lowe (bass) (V)
"Kaiser" George Miller (vocals, guitar, saxophone) (X)

Los Straitjackets Recordings:

I. The Utterly Fantastic And Totally Unbelievable Sound Of Los Straitjackets (Upstart Records, 1995, CD)
1. Fury
2. G-Man
3. Straitjacket
4. Jetty Motel
5. Carhop
6. Caveman
7. Tailspin
8. University Blvd.
9. Gatecrusher
10. Itchy Chicken
11. Della Street
12. Calhoun Surf
13. Rampage
14. Lynxtail

Comments: Produced by notable pop/rock musician Ben Vaughn, who knows a thing or two about retro sounds, Los Straitjackets' debut album was unlike anything Nashville had heard in 30 years. Clad in Mexican wrestler masks, the four members of Los Straitjackets cranked out an exciting

Los Straitjackets

LOS STRAITJACKETS

instrumental mix of Dick Dale-influenced surf rock and Duane Eddy-styled twangy guitar with a bit of freestyle psychedelic noodling thrown in for good measure.

II. *Viva!* (Upstart Records 1996, CD)
1. Cavalcade
2. The Casbah
3. Wrong Planet
4. Lonely Apache
5. Outta Gear
6. Pacifica
7. Espionage
8. Swampfire
9. Lawnmower
10. Lurking in the Shadows
11. Brains & Eggs
12. Venturing Out
13. Tsunami!
14. Nightmare in Monte Cristo

III. *The Velvet Touch Of Los Straitjackets* (Cavalcade/Yep Roc Records 1999, CD/LP)
1. Kawanga!
2. Rockula
3. Close To Champaign
4. Hornet's Nest
5. My Heart Will Go On (Love Theme From Titanic)
6. Tempest
7. Tijuana Boots
8. Sing, Sing, Sing
9. Tabouli
10. Sterno
11. State Fair
12. All That Glitters

IV. *Damas y Caballeros!* (Cavalcade/Yep Roc 2001, CD)
1. Introduction
2. Outta Gear
3. State Fair
4. Casbah
5. Calhoun Surf
6. Itchy Chicken
7. Last Date
8. Kawanga!
9. I'm Branded
10. My Heart Will Go On (Love Theme from Titanic)
11. Squad Car
12. Rockula
13. Tempest
14. Lynxtail
15. Tailspin
16. Pacifica
17. Driving Guitars
18. Sing, Sing, Sing
19. Sleepwalk
20. Rawhide

Comments: Live album taken from summer 2000 show at The Foothill Tavern in Long Beach, California.

V. *Sing Along With Los Straitjackets* (Cavalcade/Yep Roc Records 2001, CD)
1. Black Is Black
2. Chica Alborotada a/k/a Tallahassee Lassie
3. Treat Her Right
4. I Ain't The One
5. Down The Line
6. Rey Criollo a/k/a King Creole
7. California Sun
8. I'll Go Down Swinging

LOS STRAITJACKETS
Sing Along With Los Straitjackets
(Yep Roc Records)

It's an established fact among experts in these sorts of things that Los Straitjackets have long been the coolest psychotronic surf guitar band in the known universe. Clad in Mexican wrestling masks, these mutant offspring of an unholy marriage of Dick Dale and Joey Ramone have kicked out four incredible albums of surf-garage-rockabilly instrumentals since 1995. With album number five the fantastic foursome hit upon a novel idea – why not add vocals to the songs?

They do just that on *Sing Along With Los Straitjackets*, enlisting the help of accomplished vocal technicians like Raul Malo of the Mavericks, Leigh Nash of Sixpence None The Richer, Dave Alvin, Allison Moorer, Exene Cervenka of X and many others. The result is a glorious collection of cover tunes, Los Straitjackets providing the power and various singers contributing the finesse to classic rock, pop and country material like Roy Orbison's "Down The Line," Jessi Colter's "I Ain't The One" and Scooter Davis' "The End Of The World."

Guitarists Danny Amis and Eddie Angel blaze like a house afire while beatmeisters Peter Curry and Jimmy Lester hold down the bottom line behind folks like the Rev. Horton Heat, Big Sandy and Nick Lowe. The hippest CD you could buy this year, *Sing Along With Los Straitjackets* cements the reputation of these maniac musicians as the baddest surf-rocking daddios ever! – *The View From The Hill* (California), 2001

9. La Suegra a/k/a Mother In Law
10. Bumble Bee
11. Shake That Rat
12. The End Of The World
13. A Huevo

Comments: For their fifth album, Los Straitjackets decided to shake up their instrumental schtick a bit and include – *gasp* – vocals to their songs (thus the "Sing Along With" title). It was a good idea and the results were effective; of course, when you have heavyweights like Raul Malo (of the Mavericks), Dave Alvin, Nick Lowe, Leigh Nash and Exene Cervenka (X) in your corner, how can you not score a knockout? Other guest singers include Big Sandy, Mark Lindsay (Paul Revere & the Raiders), the Rev. Horton Heat, El Vez (the Mexican Elvis) and the duo of Allison Moorer and **Lonesome Bob**, all quite charming and talented in their individual fashion.

VI. Encyclopedia Of Sound (Love Cat Music 2001, CD)
1. Furious
2. Road Rage
3. Candy Rock
4. Kaboom!
5. California Fun
6. Switchblade Stroll
7. Cactus Walk
8. Arizona Sunset
9. Country Squier [electric]
10. Country Squier [acoustic]
11. Golden Nugget
12. Heavy Bag
13. Cropdustin'

14. Cantina [electric]
15. Cantina [acoustic]
16. Sombrero
17. Onion Dip
18. Pot Liquor
19. Man From S.W.A.M.P
20. Dipsy Doodle
21. Take The 405
22. Fuzzy Nova

Comments: Lovecat Music is a legitimate label releasing mostly soundtracks and Latin albums, so I'm not sure how this disc came to be released under their imprint. The disc consists of familiar Straitjackets' jams, broken into sections under headers like "Rock & Roll Rave-Ups," "Tex-Mex" or "Psychedelic." The album isn't listed under the band's official discography on their web site. Some sources state that this album (and a second volume in 2007) weren't meant for public release but were designed for TV and movie producers so that they could choose Los Straitjackets music for their projects. I dunno, maybe they needed some quick cash and figured that they'd make a few bucks from this off-brand release.

VII. 'Tis The Season For Los Straitjackets (Cavalcade/Yep Roc Records 2002, CD/LP)
1. Here Comes Santa Claus
2. A Marshmallow World
3. Feliz Navidad
4. Jingle Bell Rock
5. Rudolph the Red Nosed Reindeer
6. God Rest Ye Merry Gentlemen
7. Frosty The Snowman

8. Christmas In Las Vegas
9. Let It Snow
10. Sleigh Ride
11. Christmas Weekend
12. Little Drummer Boy
13. The Christmas Song

Comments: The inevitable Christmas album, delivering spry instrumental versions of holiday classics.

VIII. Supersonic Guitars In 3-D (Yep Roc Records 2003, CD)
1. Squid
2. DiPinto Twist
3. Time Bomb
4. Can You Dig It?
5. San Diego Shutdown
6. Isn't Love Grand?
7. Giggle Water
8. Midnight In Salerno
9. Beach Bag
10. Jungleaya
11. Galaxy Drive
12. Tarantula
13. Dreamland

Comments: Produced by Mark Neill, album includes guest performances by DJ Bonebrake and Billy Zoom. CD includes paper glasses to look at vaguely 3-D cover art.

IX. Play Favorites (self-produced CD, 2004)
1. Out of Limits
2. Our Favorite Martian
3. Moon River
4. Bim Bam Baby
5. A Town Without Pity
6. Jack The Ripper

7. La Novia de mi Major Amigo (Girl of My Best Friend)
8. The Rise and Fall of Flingel Bunt
9. I Thought It Over
10. Telstar
11. King Of The Surf
12. Perfidia
13. Bad Reputation
14. Theme From Magnificent Seven
15. Last Date

X. Twist Party (Cavalcade/Yep Roc 2006, CD/LP)
1. Twist Party
2. Twistin' Gorilla
3. Hypno-Twist
4. Twistin' Out In Space
5. Kitty Kat
6. Foot Stomp
7. Twist 'N' Grind
8. Isn't Love Grand
9. On Tap
10. The Daddy-O
11. Domino Twist
12. Mad Scientwist
13. Chocolate Shake
14. Twistin' In The Rain
15. All Back To Drac's
16. Peppermint Twist

Comments: Always searching for a new angle to bring renewed excitement to the Los Straitjackets' sound, the masked ones kick out the jams with a collection of inspired variations on the twist dance theme. Accompanying DVD provides invaluable dance lessons, the "World Famous Pontani Sisters" burlesque troupe teaching viewers moves like the "Twistin' Gorilla" and the "Mad Scientwist."

Los Straitjackets
The Utterly Fantastic And Totally Unbelievable Sound of Los Straitjackets
(Upstart Records)

Oh boy, did the movie *Pulp Fiction* really start something, as a hundred and one surf guitar-oriented instrumental bands have begun to litter the musical landscape with commercial and critical expectations. None of these wanna-be pretenders, however, can hold a candle to the awesome flame that is Nashville's very own Los Straitjackets.

Los Straitjackets – the fantastic foursome of Danny Amis, Eddie Angel, E. Scott Esbeck and L.J. Lester, mysteriously clad in colorful Mexican wrestler's masks – kick out a fresh, hard-rocking, toe-tapping collection of fourteen guitar-driven instrumentals on *The Utterly Fantastic And Totally Believable Sound Of Los Straitjackets*. The guys throw everything into the pot, with musical influences as diverse as Dick Dale-inspired surf guitar and cheesy seventies-styled mondo movie soundtracks to jazzy lounge music and fifties retro-rockabilly.

The resulting effort is showcased on cuts like the dark, foreboding "G-Man," the rollicking chaos of "Rampage" or the bumble-bee, machine-gun staccato of "Tailspin." If you're looking for something new, get your kicks with *The Utterly Fantastic And Totally Believable Sound Of Los Straitjackets*. You'll be glad that you did!
– *R.A.D! Review and Discussion of Rock & Roll*, 1995

XI. Encyclopedia Of Sound, Volume II (Love Cat Music 2007, CD)
1. Pile Driver
2. Boa Constrictor
3. I Want Cake
4. Lookey Here
5. Just A Little Trip
6. Juke Joint Compound
7. Funky Twine
8. Blues Face
9. Susie X
10. Hindenburg
11. Gallstones
12. Apple Orchard
13. Hey Joey
14. Hooligan
15. Sloppy Joe
16. Honolulu Vice
17. Out Of The Shadows
18. Creepy Part 1
19. Creepy Part 2
20. Tennessee Cannonball
21. Off Broadway
22. Brazil Nuts
23. Miller Park
24. Color My Hair
25. At The Seashore
26. Drum Solo #1
27. Drum Solo #2

THE LOUNGE FLOUNDERS

Band Members:
Kevin Murphy (vocals, guitar) (I)
Sean Kelly (guitar) (I)

Clay Steakley (bass) (I)
Chip Jordan (drums) (I)

Other Musicians:
Tony Gerber (accordion) (I)
Jay Joyce (guitar, vocals) (I)
Giles Reaves (keyboards, vocals) (I)

Lounge Flounders Recordings:

I. Imaginary Saints (Kudzu Records/Mercury Records 1996, CD)
1. She's A Boy (...it's not their business)
2. I Am I
3. Dreaming Dangerous
4. Cross Yourself
5. Cold And Boring
6. Hijack
7. Generation
8. Captain Margot
9. Front Porch Dog
10. Too Deep Water
11. Is This The Last Of This
12. Insecurity Sometimes
13. Dutch's Dreams

LOVE CIRCLE LOGIC

Band Members:
Paul Tyson (vocals, guitar) (I)
Richard Stevens (guitar) (I)
Michael Johnson (bass, vocals) (I)
Jeff Bradshaw (drums) (I)

Love Circle Logic Recordings:

I. Love Circle Logic (Sweetfish Records 1997, CD)
1. Self
2. F.A.B. (the Flattery of A. Brockton)
3. Table
4. Naturally Go
5. Red Flags
6. Neighborhood
7. Don't Leave Me Here
8. Sunday Song
9. Stay With Me
10. Not Like Me
11. Sloe Gin Fizz

LUCK LONDON

Band Members:
Bill Baugh (vocals, guitars)
Eric Jean (guitars)
Dean Tomasek (bass)
Trent Harmon (drums)

Eric Jean Writes: "Our claim to fame (if you can call it fame) was our trash rock version of John Denver's "Rocky Mountain High". We did a few demos in AIR studio in Hendersonville, but never released a record. We opened shows for Walk the West, Jason and the Scorchers, The Georgia Satellites and Husker Du...among others I have probably forgotten, but those were the most notable.

Bill and Dean eventually went on to form Valentine Saloon after Luck London disbanded in late '87. I went on to play with V.O.C. (Victims of Circumstance) and Trent kind of fell off the face of the earth for a while. I ran into him a few years later (he was married and living in the Nashville area) and we

took a road trip to see U2 in Memphis. The trip was doomed by a broken timing belt (grrrr)."

LUCY'S RECORD SHOP

Comments: Lucy's Record Shop was *the* place to go during the 1990s for hot tunes and hotter live shows presented in an alcohol-free, all-ages environment. Originally opened during the summer of 1992 as "Revolutions Per Minute" (admittedly a cool name for a record store) by industry refugee Mary Mancini (who had worked for Elektra Records in NYC), the name of the store was soon changed to Lucy's after Mary's beloved dog, a friendly pup who roamed the store and greeted customers.

The shop offered up music that you just couldn't buy anywhere else in town (certainly not at Sam Goody's down the street), focusing on (then) underground bands like Pavement, Versus, Yo La Tengo, and fellow travelers as well as a deep selection of local tunes and zines, including a few of my misguided publications. Once Mancini hooked up with Donnie and April Kendall of *House O' Pain*, who had been booking all-ages "Migraine Matinee" shows at the Pantheon club until Gus Palas took it over, music was added to Lucy's and the shop was transformed into the local scene hotspot. Performances at Lucy's were focused mostly on local artists like Kendall's Fun Girls From Mt. Pilot or punk and metal bands like Teen Idols or Impetuous Doom, but it would soon grow to attract national acts like Guided By Voices, Unrest, and Vic Chesnutt. The Reverend even performed at Lucy's with Terminal Mycosis as part of the Fuzzy Logic Laboratories-produced "Noise" festival in March 1993 featuring Helo Kitty and others.

Mancini and the Kendalls built something more than either a record store or a performance space – they created a true community center where kids were free to be themselves without fear of criticism or hassle. A sign on the door said "No Racist, Sexist, or Homophobic Shit Tolerated," and they meant it (believe me, you *didn't* want to cross April Kendall!) and Lucy's was a place that fostered independence, free-thought, and tolerance along with a love of music. More influential than any other store or venue in Nashville rock history, Lucy's lasted five-and-a-half years, closing in January 1998. The store inspired the 1995 documentary film *Lucy Barks!* by filmmaker Stacy Goldate as well as a generation of young Nashville rockers.

Another View: "In many ways, it's a miracle Lucy's lasted this long. The tiny Church Street hangout, named for the owner's gentle, sad-eyed Weimaraner, has been an underdog in every sense. It's an independent, locally owned record store, an anomaly in an industry that saves all its perks for national chains. It books punk and independent-label rock bands in the breadbasket of country music. Most daunting of all, it caters to underage audiences, who can't buy the alcoholic beverages that keep most clubs afloat. Any one of these factors would be enough to doom most clubs…but for all these obstacles, Lucy's has been the flashpoint for a small but intensely creative local music scene – a scene that has included kids, parents, poets, skatepunks, lesbian performance artists, headbangers, and disenfranchised music fans whose high-school years are long past. Whenever movements in youth culture exploded throughout the country – grrrl power, tribalism, skacore – Lucy's brought the blast to Nashville." – Jim Ridley, *Nashville Scene*, January 1998

LUNA HALO
Web: www.lunahalo.com

Band Members:
Nathan Barlowe (vocals, guitars, keyboards) (I-VI)
Cary Barlowe (guitars) (II-VI)
Chris Coleman (bass) (II-VI)
Aaron Jenkins (drums) (II-VI)
Matt Erickson (keyboards)
Johnny MacIntosh (guitars) (I)
Mark Hill (bass) (I)
Jonathan "Lil' Jon" Smith (drums) (I)

Other Musicians:
David Henry (cello) (I)
Monroe Jones (keyboards) (I)
Matt Mahaffey (keyboards) (II)
Robert Joseph Manning, Jr. (keyboards) (II)

Luna Halo Recordings:

I. Shimmer (Sparrow Records 2000, CD)
1. Aliens
2. Superman
3. Carry Me
4. Forgiveness
5. Wait for You
6. Heaven
7. Hang on to You
8. So Far
9. Running Away
10. Beautiful
11. Complacent
12. The Way to Your Heart

Comments: The original version of Luna Halo pursued a unique vision of Contemporary Christian Music as created by Nathan Barlowe. Evidently Barlowe soon tired of a rigid CCM format that disavows rocking out and requires that you wear your faith on your sleeve.

Barlowe disbanded Luna Halo after this first album for Sparrow Records, keeping the name and reforming it a

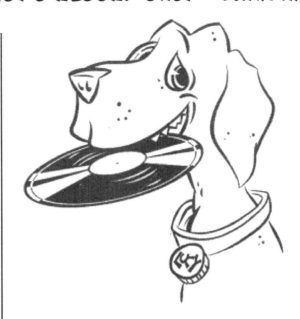

couple of years down the road with his brother Cary and an entirely new rhythm section.

II. Luna Halo (self-produced 2002, CD EP)
1. Glorious Moment
2. Closer
3. In Between
4. Collide

III. New Drug (B-Unique 2003, CD EP)
1. New Drug
2. Over the Edge
3. Half A World Away

IV. Wasting Away (B-Unique 2004, CD EP)
1. Wasting Away
2. Over The Edge
3. Bittersweet
4. Save Me

V. Tour (Warner Brothers 2006, CD EP)
1. Kings & Queens
2. I'm Alright
3. The Fool

VI. Luna Halo (American/Columbia 2007, CD)
1. Kings & Queens
2. Untouchable
3. Medicate
4. I'm Alright
5. On My Way
6. On Your Side
7. The Fool
8. Big Escape
9. Falling Down
10. English Boys
11. World On Fire

LUST

Band Members:
David Bush (vocals) (I)
Ken Kennedy (guitar) (I)
Kurt Menck (guitar) (I)
Mike Easlo a/k/a Easley (bass, drums, vocals) (I)
John Uhlinger (drums) (I)
Keith Maxwell (guitar)
Mike Farris (bass)
Jerry Cathy (bass)
Tim Morrison (bass)
Ron Keel (vocals)

Lust Recordings:

I. Lust (Lust Records 1985, 12" vinyl)
Side One
1. Hooker
2. Nites Are Lonely

Side Two
3. We're Gonna Come Gunnin'
4. Don't Say It's Over
5. You Can't Rape The Willing

Comments: Ken Kennedy, from New York City, formed Lust in Nashville in 1979, a good half-decade before the mid-1980s commercial ascent of heavy metal. As one version tells it, Lust (with Kennedy, Maxwell, Morrison and Easley/Easlo) were playing a 1980 WKDF "battle of the bands" contest and needed a more dynamic frontman than drummer Easley to sing their song entries. Recruiting Ron Keel from the band

Tabu, they went on to win the contest with what Keel later called "his first hard rock gig," recording two songs for the radio station's *Homegrown* album.

Keel fled the band almost immediately, with Morrison in tow, to form **Steeler**. Lust soldiered on for a while, releasing this lone five-song EP before evolving into **Hocus Pocus**, which would become one of the leading bands on the Nashville hard rock scene during the 1980s. Lust remains the only band I've seen that included a three-page listing of the equipment they used in their press kit. Not surprisingly, the guitarists played Gibson guitars as the band's manager – a nice guy by the name of Dwayne Powers – was a bigwig with Gibson.

Keel speaks fondly of his former band, stating on his web site that "a lot of my rock voice and persona were developed while in this band; I was formulating the vision of what I wanted Ron Keel the frontman to be: I wanted to combine the vocal prowess of Rob Halford and Klaus Meine with the showmanship of David Lee Roth and Paul Stanley, and that became a blueprint for my future efforts with all my Rock projects."

Comments: An early line-up of Lust placed two songs on the Rock 106 compilation *Homegrown*, featuring vocalist Keel, guitarists Kennedy and Maxwell, bassist Morrison and drummer Easley. Might be the only two tracks surviving with the legendary Keel rockin' the mic for Lust….

LUVJOI

Band Members:
"Big" Kenny Alphin (vocals, guitar) (I, II)
Matt Pierson (bass) (I)
Steve Brewster (drums) (I)
Adam Shoenfeld (guitars, vocals) (II)
Justin Tocket (bass, vocals) (II)
Larry Babb (drums, percussion) (II)

Luvjoi Recordings:

I. luvjOi (TBA Records/LuvjOi Records 2000, CD)
1. luvjOi
2. Discoball
3. Numb
4. Hurting Man
5. Worth The Time
6. Sad Parade
7. Acceptance
8. Electric Soul
9. Innocence
10. It's Alright
11. Rollin' Over
12. Just Like You
13. Forget To Breathe

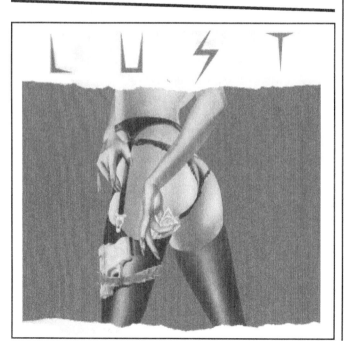

II. Volume 2 (self-produced CD, 2001)
1. Changing
2. Here In My Head
3. Screaming
4. Tragedy
5. Outside
6. Learning
7. Lover
8. Radio
9. Happy Time
10. Love
11. I Will Never Be Afraid
12. Soul Fly

Comments: LuvjOi was the homebrew rock project of country music star "Big" Kenny Alphin of the duo Big & Rich. The man wanted stardom so badly that he slugged it out in the rock 'n' roll trenches of Nashville for a couple of years.

LIAM LYNCH

Band Members:
Liam Lynch (vocals, guitar, toy piano, percussion) (I)

Other Musicians:
Todd Anderson (vocals) (I)
Josh Cheatham (double bass) (I)
Harry Finchum (violin) (I)
Aven Kepler (flute) (I)
Laurie Rosa (penny whistle, hurdy gurdy) (I)
Matthew Ryan (guitar, vocals) (I)
Chris Tench (guitar, bass) (I)

Liam Lynch Recordings:

I. Eel (self-produced CD, 1995)
1. Wax Wings
2. Try Another
3. Aphrodisiac
4. Shafali
5. Severed
6. Blind Dolls
7. Polly Jean
8. Deeper They
9. Stellar Feller
10. Morley's Car
11. Creep
12. 3 am. Long Blvd.
13. Giving It Back

Comments: Liam Lynch is the story of a talent too great to be constrained by Nashville's traditional confines. Fast-tracked as a "gifted student" in elementary school, Lynch also suffered from various neurological disabilities as color blindness, dyslexia, ADD and other stuff that led him to later describe

himself as a "watered-down idiot savant." Lynch moved to Nashville to attend school at Belmont, but cut out after three days of classes, and would later form the band **Owen's Ashes**.

After kicking around the local music scene for a while, a time that Lynch would later consider "a failure," describing it as "playing in crappy bars, going on tour, working as a dishwasher for three years," he would take a move that would eventually move him out of Nashville. Applying to Paul McCartney's brand-new Liverpool Institute for Performing Arts, Lynch was chosen as one of 40 musicians from around the world to attend the inaugural class, and only one of five to receive private guitar lessons from Sir Paul himself.

While in England, Lynch came up with the idea for the *Sifl and Olly Show*, a curious combination of sock puppets, animation, and original music that had its roots in a comedy bit created by Lynch and a couple of high school friends. The show would be picked up by MTV and become a short-lived sensation during its two seasons, and would lead Lynch into the world of music video. After directing videos by bands like the Foo Fighters, No Doubt, the Eagles of Death Metal, Tenacious D and others, Lynch would break into feature film direction with 2006's *Tenacious D in The Pick of Destiny*. As of this writing, Lynch is still making music and dabbling in video production. Oddly enough, Lynch is also a proponent of cloning technology and reportedly owns a commercially-cloned pet cat.

Somewhere in between all of this action, Lynch would sequester himself for a week in a friend's house to record *Eel*. The album is pretty much what one would expect of Lynch's innate brilliance…a finely-crafted collection of moody shoegazer rock with moments of whimsy, and no little humor.

AUDREY MALONE - MAMMY NAMMS - THE MANIKENZ

AUDREY MALONE & THE RHYTHM KINGS

Band Members:
Audrey Malone (vocals, upright bass) (I)
Mark "Smiley" Shenkel (sax, vocals, percussion) (I)
Michael Evans (vocals, guitar) (I)
Greg "Taz" Smith (drums, percussion) (I)
Brooks Hanes (vocals, violin) (I)

Audrey Malone Recordings:

I. Swingtown (Hepcat Records 1999, CD)
1. Hit That Jive
2. Memphis
3. On The Double
4. Strange
5. Swingtown
6. St. Louis Blues
7. Sin to Tell a Lie
8. Birmingham Bounce
9. Pan Handle Rag
10. Stop, Look & Listen
11. Restless
12. E.M.D.

Comments: Ultra-groovy jump blues and swing jazz band that included Nashville rock veteran Mark "Smiley" Shenkel (**Freedom of Expression** among many other bands). Frontwoman Malone was a mid-1990s arrival from Louisiana's Gulf Coast, playing in a bluegrass band before forming the Rhythm Kings. She would go on to various bands after this, both country and rock. As for the CD, it's a fine collection of covers and originals. Listen to "Memphis" and you'd swear that you're sitting in a swanky Harlem nightclub circa the 1940s, with "Smiley" blastin' the sax and Malone's sultry torch vocals lighting up the stage. Yeah, the rest of the band rocks, too, with a feverish throwback vibe that could have easily parried with any of Cab Calloway's outfits. Too cool by half...

Another View: "Tons of gasoline on it. They don't just lay there and play cocktail jazz people talk over. This is in-your-face rocket fuel – highly energized."
– H. Nelson, *In Review*, May 1999

MAMMY NAMMS

Band Members:
Bryan Porter (vocals)
Mike Crowe (guitar, vocals)
Jeff Harmon (guitar, vocals)
Bobby McGlockin (bass)
Jim Tjoflat (drums)

Comments: Very popular late 1980s/early 1990s band on the Nashville/Murfreesboro club circuit and a weekly mainstay at Sal's, Mammy Namms described their hard rock sound as "heavy groove rock."

THE MANIKENZ

Band Members:
Eddie Arace (vocals)
Lee A. Carr (guitar, vocals)
Frank Boice (guitar)
Jimmy V. (guitar)
Geor-Jo (bass)
Jim Russum (bass)
Johnny Silver (drums)

Comments: Formed in New York City in 1979, the Manikenz opened for bands like the Ramones and the Romantics while in the Big Apple, and scored an underground hit with their song "I Don't Want Romance," which received big airplay on college radio stations. The band packed up its bags and moved to Nashville in mid-1985, where they continued to terrorize local audiences for years. Lee Carr hooked up with Arace in 1988 for a brief while. I seem to remember that **Greg Walker** from The Great Escape also played with the Manikenz at one time.

MARKY & THE UNEXPLAINED STAINS

Band Members:
Marky Nevers (vocals, guitar, bass) (I, II)
Kirby Kiskadden (guitar) (I, II)
Dave Lunn (bass) (II)
Gary Privette (drums) (I, II)
Randy Bowles (drums) (I)
Tommy Dorsey (piano, horns) (I)
Tony Crow (bass, vocals) (I)
Mike Griffith (sax, piano, wind instruments) (II)

Marky & the Unexplained Stains Recordings:

I. Marky And The Unexplained Stains (Carlyle 1989, CD)
1. Junkie City
2. My Dear
3. Lift The Cup
4. Unsalvageable
5. Pleasure Island
6. R.A.D. Revolution
7. Brainwash
8. Seeing You
9. Dunce Cap
10. Keep That Shit Away

II. Nation Of Suckers (Bloodsucker Records 1992, CD)
1. Here We Come
2. Another Night Out
3. We're Going Down
4. Into The Music City
5. Become One Of Them
6. Poor Little M'Tee
7. Birdy
8. Nation Of Suckers
9. Wing Attack Plan R
10. Rollin' Down
11. Hlp Man!!!

Comments: Marky & the Unexplained Stains were a sort of Nashville underground "supergroup," with members of various bands joining together to make a joyous noise. Musically, this is rock in a vein similar to the Talking Heads, but with a little of Pere Ubu's reckless anarchistic chaos thrown in for good measure. If they hadn't been on Carlyle, a label notorious for underpromoting their bands, these guys might be thought of today in the same light as, say, the Feelies...

MARS HILL

Band Members:
Timothy James Toonen (vocals)
Mark "Q" Quatrochi (guitar)
Jeff Stangenberg (bass, vocals)
Bob Miller (drums)

Comments: Band contributed song "By Love" to *Major Potential #1* 1991 compilation CD and song "Tempted" to *What's The Buzz?* 1993 CD.

SUSAN MARSHALL

Band Members:
Susan Marshall (vocals) (I)

Other Musicians:
Eddie Blakely (guitars, vocals) (I)

Mammy Namms

DON'T PLAY INNOCENT WITH ME

SUSAN MARSHALL

Lanny Boles (drums) (I)
Mike Carlisle (guitars, vocals) (I)
Duane Eddy (guitars) (I)
Ron Frederick (percussion) (I)
Warner Hodges (guitars) (I)
Bill Hullett (dobro) (I)
Ted Lindsay (mandolin) (I)
Jerry Dale McFadden (piano) (I)
Dave Pomeroy (upright bass) (I)

Susan Marshall Recordings:

I. Don't Play Innocent With Me (Reptile Records 1986, LP)
Side One
1. Perfect Love
2. Why Can't You Tell Me Why
3. He's My Friend
4. You're Responsible
5. Don't Play Innocent With Me

Side Two
6. Special Consideration
7. Tribute To Hank Williams
8. He's All I Got
9. Miss Communication
10. I Think We're Alone Now

Comments: Not to be confused with the Susan Marshall of Memphis, this Susan lit up the mid-1980s Nashville club stages with a raging alt-country, roots-rock sound and more than a little sex appeal. Signed to Scott Tutt's Reptile Records, she recorded this with a mixed bag of seasoned studio pros and young turks like **Warner Hodges**, **Jerry Dale McFadden**, and **Dave Pomeroy**.

The album was released in France through Tutt's deal with the roots-and-blues label Dixie Frog (which has also released albums from **the dusters** and **Ken McMahan**'s solo work). Dixie Frog has also released a number of newer Marshall CDs, though no information is available through the re-vamped Reptile Records website or Marshall's (Reptile-run?) personal site, both of which are riddled with bad photos, dead links, and very little useful info.

NED MASSEY

Band Members:
Ned Massey (vocals, guitar) (I-III)
Donny Roberts (guitars) (I)
Kevin Hornback (bass) (I)
Mike Radovsky (drums) (I)
Rick Toops (keyboards) (I)

Other Musicians:
John Cowan (vocals) (I)

NATION OF SUCKERS

Michael Davis (guitar, mandolin) (I)
Steve Keller (keyboards) (I)
Ollie O'Shea (fiddle) (I)
Jeffery Perkins (drums) (I)
Bruce Wallace (vocals) (I)

Ned Massey Recordings:

I. Almost Drowned (Punch Records 1998, CD)
1. Mess
2. On a Good Day
3. I Almost Drowned
4. Smarter
5. Patrick O'Daugherty
6. Old Enough to Drink
7. Driven Away
8. Grace
9. Every Damn Dog
10. So Far Away
11. She and I

Comments: Massey originally recorded original material as frontman for the local band **Warehouse**, which seemed to be a pick-up band of local talents. He quickly jumped onto the solo tip, recording and releasing *Almost Drowned* on the now-defunct local Punch Records label. Shortly after this, Massey – a talented songwriter but an average vocalist – left town and relocated in NYC, where he's had a bit of luck as a performer, actor and playwright, most notably as a regular character on the former CBS TV series *Hack* with David Morse.

Personally, I like his material with Warehouse better, but you can't argue with Massey's drive, creativity and credentials… heck, the guy's opened for folks like Wilco, Nils Lofgren, the Smithereens, and the Neville Brothers. The other two albums are listed 'cause, well, because I have them and I felt like it, though I'm pretty sure that Ned split town before either of 'em were released. Still, I only listed musicians from the first, Nashville-made disc…

Another View: "Ned Massey's talents are undeniable. In his best moments, he offers the kind of highlights that define the glory of rock and roll." – Michael McCall, *Nashville Scene*

II. A Brief Appearance (Nick Missouri 2002, CD)
1. Strong
2. Dangerous People
3. House of Faith
4. Bosnia, 1992
5. No Accidents
6. His Wife's Crazy Dream
7. The Waiter
8. They Hijacked Jesus
9. A Lot of Time
10. A Life
11. A Brief Appearance

III. Blood Ties (Radmass Entertainment 2004, CD)
1. Blood Ties Intro
2. The Car Swerved
3. Must Be Bad
4. In The Park
5. Slave
6. Patrick O'Daugherty
7. Walking on a Wire
8. Visitation Day
9. By The Grace Of God
10. Angry Old White Man
11. Blood Ties
12. We're A Team

THE MAYONAISE FARMERS

Band Members:
Daryl Hickam (vocals)
Jon Kipp (guitars)
Ricky Duke (guitars)
Jose Alea (bass)
Brian Kees (drums)

Comments: "Citing musical influences as widely disparate as Jimi Hendrix, Voivod and James Brown, Nashville's most oddly named outfit is also one of its best. The Mayonaise Farmers bring to the table a musical sense of style that is difficult to categorize, running the gamut from bluesy rock to metallic funk to hardcore soul." – *Bone Music Magazine*, January 1994

JERRY DALE MCFADDEN

Band Members:
Jerry Dale McFadden (piano, accordion, guitar) (I)

Other Musicians:
Duane Eddy (guitars) (I)
Warner Hodges (guitars) (I)

The Manikenz

JERRY DALE MCFADDEN - PAT MCLAUGHLIN

Jerry Dale McFadden Recordings:

I. Stand And Cast A Shadow (Reptile Records 1986, LP)
1. Stand And Cast A Shadow
2. Waitin' In Your Welfare Line
3. Into The Fire
4. B-I-Bickey-Bi, Bo-Bo-Go
5. Sunset Died When the Whores Went Away
6. In The Morning
7. Country Beats The Hell Outa Me
8. Mother May I
9. This Train Is Calling My Name
10. Flames
11. Eileen

Comments: Sadly, I remember lending my copy of *Stand And Cast A Shadow* to somebody and never getting it back. Anyway, Texas native and Oklahoma transplant Jerry Dale McFadden's debut album was a rockin' example of alt-country, twangier than the Scorchers but delivered with the same reckless spirit. Scorchers' guitarist **Warner Hodges** guests, and "Country Beats The Hell Outa Me," an S&M country tune about "listening to Hank Williams while being spanked," got a lot of play on WRVU's 91 Rock. After years of doing session-and-roadwork, McFadden landed on his feet as a member of country stars the Mavericks, using his Music Row cash to collect art during his travels, later opening the TAG Art Gallery in Nashville.

Another View: "It's G-R-R-ATE! Better than a box of Sugar Corn Flakes and destined to rule the world!" – *Weasel Weekly*

PAT MCLAUGHLIN

Band Members:
Pat McLaughlin (vocals, guitars) (I-V)

Other Musicians:
Mitch Humphries (piano) (I)
Bob Mater (drums) (I)
Tony Newman (drums) (I)
Bobby Ogdin (piano) (I)
Larry Paxton (bass, vocals) (I)
Glenn Rieuf (steel guitar) (I)
Dwight Scott (keyboards) (I)

Pat McLaughlin Recordings:

I. All Right – OK! (Blue Room Records 1980?, LP)
Side One
1. I Depend On You
2. Honey Let That Train Roll
3. Long, Long, Time
4. Without A Melody
5. I'm In The Mood

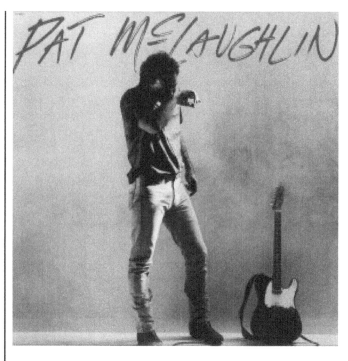

Side Two
6. Treat You Right
7. No Problem
8. Hello Birmingham
9. Wind It On Up
10. Real Thing

Comments: McLaughlin's long-lost debut album, recorded (maybe) in 1980 when the talented guitarist moved to Nashville from San Francisco, by way of Boston. I've always considered McLaughlin to be the 'Ry Cooder' of the Music City, a skilled and soulful player that is able to converse in roots-rock, blues, or country as easy as drawing breath.

Like Cooder, McLaughlin has played behind folks like Johnny Cash, Roseanne Cash, John Prine, **Al Kooper**, and the Subdudes, among many more. Unlike Cooder, though, McLaughlin is also an accomplished songwriter, with material recorded by artists as diverse as Bonnie Raitt, Taj Mahal, Nanci Griffith, Delbert McClinton, and a bunch of other folks.

II. Pat McLaughlin (Capitol Records 1988, LP)
Side One
1. In The Mood
2. Lynda
3. Real Thing
4. Wrong Number
5. No Problem

Side Two
6. Heartbeat From Havin' Fun
7. Is That My Heart Breakin'
8. Prisoner Of Love

9. You Done Me Wrong
10. Moment Of Weakness
11. Without A Melody

Comments: Extraordinary guitarist McLaughlin had to move to L.A. from Nashville to find a record deal, which says a lot about Music Row's lack of insight, foresight, and intelligence. Recorded in Hollywood with producer Mitchell Froom, the album features McLaughlin's stellar guitar work, accompanied by a slew of studio grunts like drummers Jim Keltner and Jerry Marotta, and harmonica wiz Norton Buffalo.

Another View: "This album, along with John Hiatt's **Bring The Family** and David Lee Jones' **Hard Times On Easy Street** represent a sort of new Nashville manifesto, in my mind. The message is that the walls between rock and country are breaking down faster than ever, and songwriters like these three are forging some fresh and visionary work out of the rubble." – Michael McCrickard, *Fireplace Whiskey Journal*

III. Party At Pat's (Appaloosa Records 1992, CD)
1. Down to Memphis
2. I Wish It Would Rain
3. Don't Tell Me
4. Burning Memories
5. I Don't Want No Strangers in My Bedroom
6. Imagine Me
7. Too Hard
8. A Woman and a Man
9. Hymn #122-3:21
10. Blue Moon

IV. Unglued (dos Records 1994, CD)
1. Better You Get Ready
2. Highway of the Saints
3. Night Thing [live]
4. Friendly Bird
5. Don't Tell Me [live]
6. Nothin' But Trouble
7. Knocking Around Nashville
8. Wind It on Up
9. It's Hard [live]
10. Try the Love
11. Good Woman Bad
12. Memphis
13. Long Time

V. Get Out And Stay Out! (dos Records 1995, CD)
1. Night Thing
2. Nashville
3. Days Run Together
4. Don't Tell Me
5. Down To Memphis
6. I Cried
7. I'm Ready

8. Cut Down Trees
9. Love Schedule
10. Trust Me
11. The Craze

Comments: The great lost Pat McLaughlin album, recorded for Capitol Records in 1989 but shelved by the label for reasons that were unclear and probably your typical muddy-headed major label hijinx. The album was finally released six years later by McLaughlin's own indie dos Records label. I don't get it at all – McLaughlin's self-titled debut for Capitol earned widespread critical acclaim, and in the mid-1980s the pump was primed for this sort of thing by up-n-comers like Dwight Yoakum. McLaughlin continues to make music, but I don't have any of it, and I think that he's slid further towards a more country sound.

Another View: "Once upon a time, there was a roots rocker who made music that was lean and steeped in the rock, the roll, the rhythm and the blues. It was the kind of organic, no-filler proposition that was the antithesis of the slick and packaged MTV fodder that took over the music industry in the mid-to-late '80s. He was Pat McLaughlin, and for a minute, he was the toast of the mainstream music mavens...." – Holly Gleason, *T-Bone/The Tennessean*, 1995

KEN MCMAHAN & SLUMPY BOY

Band Members:
Ken McMahan (vocals, guitar) (I-III)
Dan Baird (guitars, vocals, percussion) (I, III)
Kelly Looney (bass) (I)
Jeffrey Perkins (drums) (I, III)

KEN McMAHAN & SLUMPY BOY

Other Musicians:
Andy Brown (drums, percussion, vocals) (II)
Neal Cappellino (keyboards) (III)
Keith Christopher (bass) (I)
Jack Irwin (keyboards) (I)
Bill Lloyd (vocals) (I)
Steve McMahan (guitar, vocals) (II)
Kyle Miller (bass) (III)
Johnny Neel (keyboards) (II)
Paul Niehaus (steel guitar) (II)
Lorne Rall (bass, vocals) (II)
Eric Whorton (guitar, dobro, vocals) (II)
Tommy Womack (vocals) (II, III)

Ken McMahan & Slumpy Boy Recordings:

I. Ken McMahan & Slumpy Boy (Dixie Frog 1994, CD)
1. What's Wrong With You
2. Not Gonna Crawl
3. Wind It Up
4. Broken Glass
5. Fightin' Words
6. Hellbound Train
7. Long Gone
8. Loneliness
9. Don't Want Your Love
10. Outside Lookin' In

Comments: When **the dusters** broke up, the blues-oriented French label Dixie Frog, which had released the last dusters' album, asked Kenny Mac if he would like to record a solo disc. The result doesn't fall so far from the dusters' best work, but it also shows great growth on McMahan's part as a songwriter. Produced by **Dan Baird**, whose obsession with Savoy Brown's "Hellbound Train" is reinforced by Kenny's haunting cover of the obscure song.

II. That's Your Reality (Dixie Frog 1996, French CD)
1. Forever
2. Think I'm Gonna Leave
3. Evil Ways
4. Reality
5. Everything Turns To Dust
6. Switchboard Susan
7. On My Way
8. Only One
9. All I Feel
10. Everyday
11. Fredonia
12. Open Arms

Comments: Another red-hot-and-ready-to-rock solo set by Kenny Mac, recorded with his touring band and produced by

Ken McMahan, continued on page 339...

KEN MCMAHAN & SLUMPY BOY
That's Your Reality
(Dixie Frog – French Import)

The last time that Kenny Mac checked in here at the ConMedia world HQ, he was delivering a fine initial solo effort, *Ken McMahan & Slumpy Boy* on the French Dixie Frog label. Produced by ex-Georgia Satellite frontman Dan Baird and including the talents of folks like Stan Lynch, Terry Anderson and Bill Lloyd, the disc was a steamy slab of blues-infused roots rock.

Needless to say, even with the fine pedigree the album brought along with it, Kenny couldn't get in the back door at RecordCoAmerica, that one great major label whose A & R poseurs were too damn busy trying to find the next great alt.rock breakthrough to get their heads out of their collective behinds long enough to actually listen to some GREAT FUCKING ROCK & ROLL rather than miring themselves in martinis and misanthropy.

Now McMahan – former axeman of the much-beloved Southeastern power blues trio the dusters – has put together a permanent touring version of Slumpy Boy, knocked out *That's Your Reality*, his second disc for Dixie Frog, and is now poised to play live in your hometown. I recommend that you ring up your local neighborhood baby-sitter, draw a few dollars out of the ATM and roll on down to the club to catch Slumpy Boy 'cause, if *That's Your Reality* is any indication of what the band will be delivering live and on-stage, then we're all in for an evening of good old-fashioned rock & roll the way that it was meant to be, with lots of guitars and heavy amplification.

That's Your Reality, you see, is no wimpy "my life sucks, think I'll grow a beard" carbon-copy "alternative" crapola, no sir, this 12 song collection rocks relentlessly from start to finish. At the proper volume, it'll peel the paint off your living room walls and blow the windows out of your neighbor's house. Play it in your car stereo and it'll super-charge your engine like a set of racing cams and a tank of Turbo Blue™, melting the tar on the highway behind you.

McMahan has picked up a little more of the songwriting duties this time out, and by god, I think that the boy's got it all figured out. As good as his first solo disc was, *That's Your Reality* is even better, the material highlighting McMahan's growing ability as a wordsmith. Cuts like the rollicking "Fredonia," the introspective "Everything Turns To Dust" or the piss-off, get lost good-bye of "Reality" showcase an artistic maturity above his previous efforts.

Musically, McMahan is a vastly underrated guitarist, bringing a freshness and vitality to his material, deriving strength from his influences without ever mimicking them. Every cut here

is a fat, multi-layered, guitar-driven rocker, evoking the best of almost half a century of rock & roll history, throwing in just enough elements of country and the blues to keep it honest and interesting.

If you prefer your rock to be of the two-fisted, hairy-chested variety, if you worship at the alter of bands like Humble Pie, the Georgia Satellites, the Faces or Lynyrd Skynyrd, then *That's Your Reality* is right up your alley. With *That's Your Reality*, Ken McMahan & Slumpy Boy deliver a disc that burns like a four-alarm fire and hits like a drunken prize-fighter. – *Thora-Zine* #9, 1997

CD REVIEW: KEN MCMAHAN'S BALL & CHAIN

KEN MCMAHAN
Ball & Chain
(Dixie Frog – French import)

Ken McMahan is a friend of mine. In the interest of honesty, I have to begin any review of his work with such a disclaimer. I've gotten drunk with Ken, broken bread with him (or, in our case, shared pizza), talked about music, his career, the universe in general. He's a great guy…and with all that ethical bullshit out of the way, I can also honestly say that McMahan is one hell of a rocker, as well.

Case in point: *Ball & Chain*, McMahan's third album for the French Dixie Frog label. With each subsequent outing, Kenny's songwriting gets tighter, more structured and more interesting. His consistently invigorating six-string work improves with each album and on *Ball & Chain* he's added some interesting flourishes, musical dimensions that are absent from his earlier work. Throw in a backing band that's as tight as a fist and as scary as an I.R.S. audit and add the musical and intellectual contributions of McMahan's partner-in-crime, Dan Baird, and you've got one helluva foot-stomping rock & roll record.

With his former band, the power-blues trio the dusters, McMahan earned a well-deserved reputation across the Southeast as a fine blues guitarist. His solo stuff tends to run more towards the rock end of the spectrum, however, Kenny cranking up *Ball & Chain* with "Way Of The World," a fiery little number that sets the tone for the rest of the set. The world-weary lyrics of "Something I'll Never Know" are punctuated by a constant swamp-rock guitar riff that is literally drenched in saltwater and cypress. McMahan's traditional cover song this time out is Robert Johnson's "Kindhearted Woman," a song Kenny claims for his own with a fat, looping guitar line that creates an instrumental cadence for the vocals.

The title track is one of two McMahan co-wrote with fellow Nashville talent Tommy Womack. Opening with some nifty honky-tonk piano, the song becomes a rollicking working class anthem, a sort of "why me, Lord?" plea for the everyman. My favorite cut on the album, however, is "Wicked World." Written by Dan Baird, ex-Georgia Satellite, acclaimed solo artist and member of Nashville band Betty Rocker, Baird knows his way around a song, and "Wicked World" is no exception.

A bad-ass slice of dark-hued rock, McMahan's haunted vocals and the accompanying concertina-wire sharp guitar licks combine to make for a powerful musical moment. McMahan sounds like he's got Robert Johnson's fabled hell-hounds on his trail, his guitar howling while bassist Kyle Miller and former dusters' drummer Jeff Perkins provide a steady heartbeat to fuel Baird's tale of secular woe and spiritual despair.

Even though much of what McMahan sings about is, well, kind of depressing – stuff like lost and unrequited love, romantic betrayal and a man's burden to carry the weight of the world on his shoulders – he does so with such style and energy that you never realize the somber nature of the material. Unlike a lot of today's wet-behind-the-ears "one hit wonders," young musicians who have barely ventured outside their hometown, McMahan has experienced a bit of the world.

He's been following the dream longer than he'd probably care to admit, but what comes across in his music and on CD is the sheer, unadulterated joy of being able to play rock & roll. It's this element that's missing from contemporary music and it's something that McMahan has in abundance. *Ball & Chain* is a strong tonic, a fresh breath of life for a flaccid rock corpse in sore need of the stiff kick in the ass McMahan provides. Now, will somebody stateside please pick up this record before I have to come to your house and do something impolite? – *Alt.Culture.Guide*, 1998

Ken McMahan, continued...
McMahan and Kelly Pribble. Continuing a tradition of including an inspired cover song, this album's chosen remake is of Nick Lowe's "Switchboard Susan."

III. Ball & Chain (Dixie Frog 1998, French CD)
1. Way Of The World
2. Something I'll Never Know
3. The Long Haul
4. Outta Site, Outta Mind
5. Kindhearted Woman Blues
6. I Won't Miss You
7. Ball & Chain
8. Ten Years Ago
9. Wicked World
10. Knock Down On Your Door
11. Just Another Memory

Comments: McMahan's best effort yet (see review ➜) includes a smokin' cover of blues legend Robert Johnson's "Kindhearted Woman Blues" and a hotter reading of Dan Baird's "Wicked World." Produced by McMahan with "lotsa help" from Baird; Tommy Womack guests on the title cut. Rare copies of all these discs can still be found in shops around Nashville; as of this writing, Kenny's first album is selling as an import on Amazon.com while a Cali dealer is offering ***That's Your Reality*** for a mere $55.18!

ME PHI ME

Band Members:
Me Phi Me [La-Ron K. Wilburn] (vocals) (I)
John Michael Falasz III (guitars) (I)
CeeCeeTee [Christopher Cuben-Tatum] (bass, keyboards) (I)
Rags Murtaugh (harmonica) (I)

Me Phi Me Recordings:

I. One (RCA Records 1992, CD)
1. Intro: A Call to Arms (The Step)
2. The Credo
3. Sad New Day
4. Poetic Moment I: The Dream
5. Dream of You
6. Not My Brogha
7. Keep It Goin'
8. Poetic Moment II: The Streets
9. Black Sunshine
10. And I Believe (The Credo)
11. Pu' Sho Hands 2getha
12. Poetic Moment III: The Light
13. Road to Life
14. It Ain't the Way It Was
15. (Think) Where Are You Going?
16. Return to Arms: In Closing

Me Phi Me

Comments: Me Phi Me was the name of both the band and the rapper at the forefront of this groundbreaking outfit. Coming out of Chicago and landing, for some reason, in Murfreesboro, Me Phi Me pursued a positive message of self-esteem, intelligence and determination that was in stark contrast to the dominant, typically violent gangsta rap of the early 1990s.

Another View: "*One*, Me Phi Me's first (and only) album, established the rapper as a unique figure in hip-hop. Instead of relying on funk, soul, R&B, and rap, Me Phi Me uses folk and pop as his musical foundation, creating a new-age hip-hop that has more in common with hippies than B-boys. It's an intriguing concept — few rappers have attempted a folk-rap fusion, especially one's with neo-psychedelic overtones — but his songwriting isn't always capable of conveying his ideas." – Stephen Thomas Erlewine, *All Music Guide*

DAVID MEAD
Web: www.davidmead.com

Band Members:
David Mead (vocals, guitars, keyboards) (I-V)

Other Musicians:
Rusty Anderson (guitars) (I)

DAVID MEAD

Kenny Aronoff (drums) (I)
Butterfly Boucher (vocals) (III)
Keith Brogdon (drums) (V)
Chris Carmichael (violin, strings) (III, V)
Paul Deakin (drums) (I)
Ethan Eubanks (drums) (III, IV)
Shannon Forest (drums) (III)
Kenny Greenberg (guitars) (I)
Paul Hager (tambourine) (I)
Stephen Hague (accordion) (IV)
David Henry (cello, trombone, trumpet) (I, III, V)
Craig Herrgesell (keyboards, Mellotron) (I)
John Holbrook (Moog synth) (II)
Jim Hoke (saxophone) (V)
Jim Horn (saxophone) (I)
Lindsay Jamieson (drums, percussion) (V)
WhyNot Jansveld (bass, guitar, vocals) (IV)
Brad Jones (bass, keyboards, Theremin) (III, V)
Viktor Krauss (upright bass) (I)
Peter Langella (bass) (I)
Mike Lawler (keyboards) (I)
Jason Lehning (keyboards) (I, II)
Chris McHugh (drums) (I)
Chuck Norman (keyboards, programming) (IV)
Shawn Pelton (drums, percussion) (II)
Joe Pisapia (guitars, lap steel) (I, III)
Marc Pisapia (drums) (I, III)
Jody Porter (guitar) (II)
Anthony J. Resta (synth, percussion) (I)
Kayton Roberts (lap steel) (I)
Adam Schlesinger (keyboards, guitar, bass) (II)
Jon Skibic (guitars) (II)
Danny Weinkauf (bass) (II)

Craig Young (bass) (I)
Paul Zonn (clarinet) (I)

David Mead Recordings:

I. The Luxury Of Time (RCA Records 1999, CD)
1. Robert Bradley's Postcard
2. Sweet Sunshine
3. Touch Of Mascara
4. Apart From You
5. Breathe You In
6. World Of A King
7. Landlocked
8. Telephone
9. Everyone Knows It But You
10. She, Luisa
11. Make The Most Of
12. While The World Is Sleeping
13. Painless

Comments: David Mead's debut album was a revelation for many, surprising critics and fans alike with the artist's musical maturity and slick sense of pop sensibility. Nashville audiences, of course, were familiar with Mead through his work with bands like **Blue Million** and **Joe, Marc's Brother**, where David honed his skills playing live at local clubs. *The Luxury Of Time* was recorded in various studios, and includes a number of Nashville's best rock musicians backing Mead's finely-crafted pop-rock compositions. Michael Hanna arranged strings for many of the songs, Carl Gorodetzky's legendary Nashville String Machine appearing on "Painless." By the time of the album's release, Mead had moved to New York City in pursuit of fame and fortune.

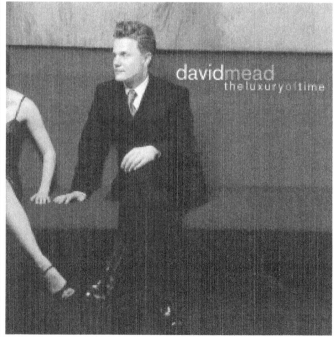

II. Mine And Yours (RCA Records 2001, CD)
1. Flamin' Angel
2. Mine And Yours
3. Comfort
4. Echoes Of A Heart
5. Standing Here In Front Of Me
6. No One Left To Blame
7. Girl On The Roof
8. Elodie
9. What's On Your Mind
10. What I Want To Do
11. Venus Again
12. Figure Of Eight
13. Only In The Movies

Comments: Mead's second major label album offers more of the same: intelligent, lush chamber-pop that is long on lyrical integrity and beautiful instrumentation, short on commercial prospects in a world still dominated by crappy boy bands and pop tarts. *Mine And Yours* was produced by Adam Schlesinger of Fountains Of Wayne, no doubt enlisted by the label to add his magic touch to Mead's already considerate songwriting skills.

III. Indiana (Nettwerk Records 2004, CD)
1. Nashville
2. You Might See Him
3. Indiana
4. Beauty
5. Only A Girl
6. One Plus One
7. Bucket Of Girls
8. New Mexico
9. Ordinary Life
10. Human Nature
11. Queensboro Bridge

Comments: Before parting ways with RCA Records after the label under-promoted his first two albums to death, Mead worked with producer Stephen Hague (New Order, OMD) in 2002 to record the tracks that would make up the *Wherever You Are* EP. That work would remain unreleased until 2005 but in the interim, Mead returned to Nashville and recorded *Indiana* with producer David Henry and the usual cast of talented local musicians.

IV. Wherever You Are (Eleven Thirty Records 2005, CD EP)
1. Wherever You Are
2. Hold On
3. Only A Dream
4. Astronaut
5. Make It Right
6. How Much

Comments: Originally recorded in 2002 with producer

Stephen Hague, these tracks were meant for an album on RCA until the label parent's merger with Sony derailed the plans of many deserving artists. The EP was finally released in 2005 by Eleven Thirty Records.

V. Tangerine (Tallulah! Records 2006, CD)
1. Tangerine
2. Hard to Remember
3. The Trouble with Henry
4. Chatterbox
5. Reminded #1
6. Hunting Season
7. Fighting For Your Life
8. Sugar On The Knees
9. Hallelujah, I Was Wrong
10. Suddenly, A Summer Night
11. Making It Up Again
12. Choosing Teams

Another View: "Four albums into a solidly workmanlike career, David Mead's ability to spin a plaintive tune and clever verse has kept him in business, albeit perennially lost in a vast sea of like-minded singer/songwriters. Always an exceptional tunesmith, *Tangerine* is the first album Mead has cut that befits an artist of his talent, with producer Brad Jones adding warm piano, swooning strings and lush harmonies to color every blank piece of compositional canvas."
– Matt Fink, *Paste Magazine* 2006

MEATEATERS KILLERS AND SUCKERS OF BLOOD

Band Members:
Mark Nevers (vocals, guitar) (A1)
Dave Lunn (bass) (A1)

MEATEATERS KILLERS & SUCKERS OF BLOOD - THE MERCENARIES

Tony Crow (vocals, juno, harp, sound thingie) (A1)
Gary Privette (drums) (A1)

Other Musicians:
Jeanie Ashmore (vocals) (A1)
Giles Reaves (juno) (A1)

Meateaters Killers Recordings:

A1. Meateaters Killers and Suckers of Blood (Bloodsucker Records 1994, 7" vinyl)
Disc One, Side One
1. Kick The Jack
2. Habitual Fuck-Up
3. Pom Pom Slaughter

Disc One, Side Two
4. Where's Tommy
5. Rat Fink
6. Bumper Sticker Man

Disc Two, Side One
1. Crime Wave
2. Some Thing After Me

Disc Two, Side Two
3. Alien Buffet
4. Somethin' Stupid

Comments: This is a pretty nifty lil' relic of the Nashville '90s…a double 7" vinyl set at 33 1/3 rpm with 10 short songs, kind of like a little vinyl EP. Featuring some of the city's better underrated talent, musicians such as Tony Crow,

Mark Nevers, and Gary Privette, Meateaters Killers and Suckers of Blood is a cross between the skewed, discordant art-rock of outfits like Pere Ubu and cool 1960s-styled pop-rock (i.e. the Beatles, if Paul was smokin' crack), with strains of punk, beach music, the Residents, the Ramones, and just about everything but the kitchen sink.

THE MERCENARIES

Band Members:
Danny Dickerson (vocals, guitar) (A1)
Kelly Looney (bass) (A1)
Jimmy Lester a/k/a Les James (drums) (A1)

The Mercenaries Recordings:

A1. "Oh Sally" b/w "You Better Surrender" (Urban Records, no date, 7" vinyl)

Danny Dickerson writes: "The Mercenaries were formed as an off shoot of John Jackson & The Rhythm Rockers. While touring with Billy Joe Shaver, our bass player Kelly Looney asked if I wanted to do some frat gigs with the Rhythm Rockers. Some time later the rhythm section formed a new band called The Mercenaries. Kelly Looney, Jimmy Lester (also known as Les James) and myself formed The Mercenaries as a three piece power pop section doing mostly my melodic rock songs but at breakneck speed. We came out about the same time as the Scorchers. We weren't as widely known as some of the other bands but some folks heard the songs and thought us the best of that crop (such as Bob Oermann the writer and Eli Ball of CBS Nashville)."

MERCY SANCTION

Band Members:
Joe Spano (vocals, guitar)
Kevin Bell (bass, vocals)
Stuart McAlister (drums)
Mark Medley (drums)

Comments: Formed in 1989, the band moved to Nashville a year later and originally recruited former **Raging Fire** drummer Mark Medley behind the kit. Contributed song "Crash" to the *Major Potential #1* 1991 compilation CD.

THREK MICHAELS

Band Members:
Threk Michaels (vocals, guitar) (I-IV)

Other Musicians:
Eddie Bayers (drums) (IV)
Dennis Burnside (keyboards) (II)
James Burton (guitar) (III)
Jimmy Capps (guitar) (III, IV)
Dianne Darling (vocals) (I)
Glen D. Hardin (piano) (III, IV)
The Jordanaires (vocals) (II-IV)
Mike Joyce (bass) (II)
Jerry McPherson (guitar) (II)
Joe Osborn (bass) (III, IV)
James Ownby (bass, keyboards) (I)
Brent Rowan (guitar) (II)
Marc Speer (guitar) (I, II)
Tommy Wells (drums) (I, II)
Roy Yeager (drums) (III)

Threk Michaels Recordings:

I. Following That Rock & Roll Star (Angel Wing 1981, LP)
Side One
1. Following That Rock & Roll Star (my epitaph)
2. Some People Say
3. Stay With Me
4. A Room For The Night
5. Down On Blue Street (everybody pays)

Side Two
6. The Man Who Never Cries (for Ricky Nelson & Smokey Robinson)
7. Coming Down To Love Tonight (Sweet Kathy Blue)
8. Nothing But A Memory
9. Just One More Song (for Karen)
10. If Love Is Like A River

Comments: Michaels entered a Nashville studio and recorded ***Following That Rock & Roll Star*** shortly after arriving in town from New York City. Using a band made up of talented friends…some of which happened to be local studio pros…Michaels crafted a pop/rock gem that was out-of-time in 1981, but would certainly resound with audiences today who thirst for an honest voice.

The Mercenaries

One of Nashville's most original artists was also one of the city's D.I.Y. pioneers. Oh yeah, Michaels had previously released three folk-styled man-with-guitar LPs while existing in NYC, catching the ear of legendary A&R genius John Hammond, Jr. (who discovered Dylan, Springsteen, Aretha Franklin, Stevie Ray Vaughan, etc.).

II. The Fallen One (Royal Records 1992, CD & LP)
1. The Fallen One (For Ricky Nelson)
2. Without You (In My Life)
3. Everyday
4. Memories Down The Line
5. Fly By Night (For Elvis Presley)
6. Yesterday Girl (For Kathy Blue)
7. Before My Life Is Through
8. Can Anyone Tell Me (Where It Went)
9. The Someday Man

Comments: Ten years after his Nashville debut, Threk managed to get back into the studio for a long-overdue follow-up to ***Following That Rock & Roll Star***. Ever the optimist, Michaels released ***The Fallen One*** on both vinyl and compact disc, managing to sell or give away almost all of 'em. The album is another fine collection of smart, literate pop/rock tunes with folkish overtones from one of Nashville's obscure and underrated songwriters (see review ➜).

III. As True As You: Songs For Ricky (Royal Records 1999, CD)
1. As True As You
2. This Lonely Girl I Love
3. My First Night With You
4. I Believe In You

5. You
6. Turn And Walk Away
7. What You're Doing To Me
8. April Fool
9. I Got A Reason To Remember
10. Have You Ever Tried To Find (It's So Hard To Find)

Comments: After flirting with his Ricky Nelson obsession with songs on his last two albums, Michaels finagled his way into historic RCA Studio B to record ***As True As You: Songs For Ricky***, his tribute to the often-maligned rock & roll pioneer. Always the dreamer, Threk denied the naysayers their doubts when he rounded up Nelson's original band, including Rock & Roll Hall of Fame guitarist James Burton, legendary bassist Joe Osborn (who has played on more #1 hit singles than any other musician), and famed sideman Glen D. Hardin to record, with the fabulous Jordanaires bringing their gorgeous vocal harmonies to bear in the background. The resulting album was pure magic (see interview ➜).

Another View: "The first track, "As True As You," sounds so much like an early sixties Rick Nelson song, you think you're hearing "Travelin' Man" for the first time. That's the best tune on the album, but there's not a clunker in the bunch (which is more than you can say for some of Rick's own albums). The love song "My First Night With You" is a special gem, as is "Have You Ever Tried To Find," a plaintive ballad that closes the disc and effectively used the Jordanaires' talents. At least two of the numbers, "You" and "I Got A Reason To Believe," have a tiny bit of country flavor to them, as did much of Rick's music.

"Michaels is not an impersonator; he's not trying to mimic Nelson's voice on this album, although he does demonstrate a similar richness and resonance. The real keys to this tribute are Michaels' songs, Hardin's arrangements and – especially – Burton's incredible guitar work and the Jordanaires' wonderful backing vocals. Any of the ten songs would have fit nicely on ***Rick is 21***, ***It's Up to You***, ***More Songs by Ricky*** or any of his other Imperial albums."
– Steve Ellingboe, *Discoveries* magazine, March 2000

IV. Lonely Always (Royal Records 2007, CD)
1. Lonely Always
2. Lonely Town
3. Song For The Lonely Seeker
4. Lonely Boy (Lonely One)
5. Lonely Just Like You
6. Lonely Dreams Of You
7. The Lonely Part Of My Heart
8. The Sound Of Lonely
9. Lonely World (Lonely All The Way Through)
10. Lonely Always (Reprise)

Threk Michaels, continued on page 349...

*T*hrek Michaels came to Nashville in the early 1980s, looking to grab the brass ring of success. In the years since, he's released a number of acclaimed albums that have gotten the singer/songwriter a lot more attention outside of the Music City than in his adopted homeland, where Music Row label execs have often feigned interest and asked for free LPs and CDs but never offered any sort of deal.

I met Threk shortly after he came to town when I was working at Duane Angel's Collectors' Dream comics and used music store on Elliston Place (where I also first met Jack Emerson). Threk and I became friends and, later, we even worked together on the notorious night shift at Moskos on the "Rock Block."

Although he's seldom performed live in town, Michaels' music has found its way around the world. Fittingly, Threk's **Following That Rock & Roll Star** *album was the first album by a Nashville rocker to be played on radio in Poland after the fall of communism, and his two Ricky Nelson tribute albums, recorded with legendary studio musicians like James Burton, Joe Osborn, and Glen D. Hardin, brought Threk's music to an entirely different audience in the early 2000s. This interview, my first of many with Michaels, was published in my* Anthem *music zine in December 1983.*

In these days and times, the world of rock music is a mega-billion dollar business. With recording income, concert merchandising, and corporate tax shelters the one-time anthem of the children's rebellion – rock and roll as typified by its early heroes: Elvis Presley, Little Richard, Chuck Berry and other pioneers – became yet another commercial wasteland, a plastic paradise, a Hollywood on wheels. In this day and age of heavy metal monsters, anti-corporate capitalists, and millionaire musicians, there are too few *real* people; far too few…

Nashville's own Threk Michaels is one of those few, a naturally friendly individual who is as at ease with fans and friends as he is with recording executives and superstars. Most of all, Threk is sincerely and hopelessly in love with this creature we call rock and roll…so much so that he has recorded, produced, and distributed his own albums, four of them to date. His most recent – **Following That Rock & Roll Star** – is a wonderful collection of roots-inspired rock music, a masterpiece of self production, a pastiche of styles and influences. He is a painter of sorts, of great vision…

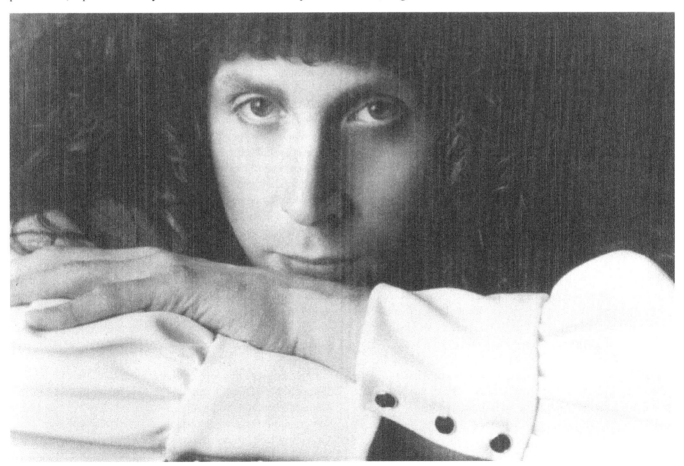

INTERVIEW: THREK MICHAELS

How did Threk Michaels get started?
"Well, I was like everybody else. The main thing you want to do when you're a teenager, you basically want to free yourself from all of the parental hassles, the school hassles…everybody I know, even now, is trying to get free from all the people trying to tell them what to do and how to do it and where to do it. Control…to me, music seemed like a way that you could get out from underneath all that control and be free."

Threk, you possess an above average knowledge of popular music; which artists have influenced you the most?
"Like most people our age, I was real little when the Beatles were big, but their impact was so big because they were on the radio and they were on television…they had a big impact because the media just took them and went crazy. Also, black music; I really listened to a lot of the Motown stuff. It wasn't individual artists as much as all of the songs on the radio which influenced me…I used to hear Marty Robbins' cowboy ballads."

How old were you when you decided that rock & roll was all that you wanted, what was the deciding factor?
"About fourteen or fifteen years of age…you start thinking you want to find a way out. You're trying to find your adolescent identity."

Like the stories that Springsteen tells about being alienated, being the odd man out?
"Exactly…Dylan had the same experience. That loneliness you feel, it's the James Dean thing, but it goes back before Dean. Since the early '50s, people have been more restless than ever…but restlessness is American. In the 1800s, everybody went west; the kid, sixteen, would say, 'I'm going to go and find an oil well or gold or something,' so the kids today are saying, 'yeah, I've got to go out and find something!'"

When did you start performing publicly?
"When I was sixteen, I quit school and got an offer from this production company forming these show groups, these real 'Las Vegas-styled' show groups."

"We had little 'Beatle' haircuts and we had to wear these jumpsuits. There were three girls and five guys, and we did "Johnny Mann" versions of "Tie a Yellow Ribbon" and other top forty hits. We played all these big hotels; we played Vegas with Tom Jones, played Vancouver, New York, Boston…all these places. I auditioned as a singer, and I played drums a little, and piano. It was like a "Mister Entertainment" type thing, because everybody was young and quite cute. We were paid well, though, transportation, we got to see America."

Where did you go from there?
"I ended up in a band called Earth Opera; we did our own album and we sold it at high school concerts. I'd started writing; I'd been writing lyrics, and the guitar player wrote the music. I started getting dissatisfied with the music we were playing, it was real mainstream rock, current material. It was fun, but it only had so much depth to it. I'd been playing guitar, though, for about a year and a half, and I wanted to write music, too…creating that separate identity I'd wanted since I was fourteen. I started listening to Dylan, Gordon Lightfoot, Jim Croce…and I started writing more reflective, mature material. I didn't want to stay seventeen forever, and I wanted to get into something, some kind of music that I could grow up with."

How did you come to record your first LP?
"I'd been writing these songs…I'd gone to New York City, looking for Dylan's ghost, basically. There were these painters down in Washington Square, and this guy asked if he could paint me and I liked it so much that I used it on the first album cover."

"About the first album, though…I had this great idea that if I recorded an album, I could take it to John Hammond, who discovered Dylan, Springsteen, and he would sign me. I would be the next big thing. I had this friend, Tommy Wells, who lives here…he plays with RPM, Gene Cotton, a great talent; he had a friend who had a studio in Detroit. So I took a Greyhound bus to the "Motor City," I slept on this guys couch and said "let's record." I sold everything I had and put the album out."

Did you get to meet John Hammond?
"I'd tried to find him, because I'd read this biography on Dylan and how John Hammond had discovered him, and all these others: Aretha Franklin, Springsteen, Count Basie…just about everyone who's mattered during the past fifty or so years. I called and he answered his own phone – no secretary. I took him a copy of the album, but I didn't get to see him that time. I called a few weeks later and he said he'd liked it. An amazing man…"

"So I moved to Nashville because I was starving in New York and I had friends here. Here in Nashville, I recorded my second album, ***Songboy Traveler***. I had written the songs in New York and I arrayed ten songs that fit together for an album. I got enough money together to press 200 copies… a real collector's item!

I immediately sent a copy to John Hammond. I spoke with him a couple of weeks later and he said he really liked it. I wanted to see him, so I said that I'd be in New York and I flew in about three weeks later and got to talk with him. He played my first album, we talked for a while and he made a call to Clive Davis. As it worked out, nothing ever happened. He did say, "Threk, there's something special about you!"

"I came back to Nashville and I thought, "this is it, I'm making progress." I waited five months and that's when I began playing on the street corners – I played down in Centennial Park with the muggers and junkies, all these people with ghetto blasters running around, and there I was with my harmonica and my guitar…so I moved from there to right in front of the Exit/In. I never stopped, never gave up hope. I went and recorded a new album titled *I Am Just a Troubadour* with a song dedicated to John Hammond. It got s small amount of airplay on Rock 106."

There's a definite evolution in your work from your early acoustic material.
"Well, I realized that the first three albums had been done acoustically, and it was coming off like an anachronism. I had taken all of my early albums to all of the record labels and I knew that I was going to have to sound more modern if I was going to get a record contract. I talked to some friends and I realized that I was going to have to have a band, so I went out and mortgaged everything that I owned and I got enough money to record with a full band."

So you formed the band 'Threk'?
"Yes…it was so hard, also; I had wanted the band that played on the LP (*Following That Rock and Roll Star*) to also play live. We've rehearsed a couple of times, but so far, it's just a concept."

Isn't producing your own albums a bit serious, not to mention expensive?
"That's no joke, it is expensive. If it's the only way I can get out what I want without compromising, then I'll continue to do it. You can get in with organizations and people who can help you if you're willing to do things their way, which means compromise…I can't do that."

What are your favorite styles of music?
"The kind of music I like most, that which I listen to most is mostly based in the American tradition: blues, some country music, folk, and certainly rock and roll. I listen to whatever combines these elements…whether it's the Band, or Odetta, or Bob Seger."

Do you think that artists and works like Springsteen's Nebraska or Little Steven and the Disciples of Soul's album will open up a more honest style of music?
"It's funny…right now, that sort of style seems like the exception to the rule. I'm dedicated to that openness and honesty and I'll do it on this level, on my own. If it's just privately-produced music, I'd rather do that than become dishonest…you've got to sleep at night with yourself."

"I don't think honesty has ever been a trend…they tried to make it into one with the folk artists, and it turned into pop, purely commercial."

What about your next album, The Fallen One?
"All of my albums have, basically, introduced Threk Michaels. The first one, *Introducing Threk Michaels*, was about my life in Greenwich Village. The next two were settled, acoustic folk. *Following That Rock and Roll Star* had a definite, harder edge. A big step, it was much more aggressive."

"The next step is *The Fallen One*. What happens when you get out there and reach for it; there's always a fall along the way as you're following that rock 'n' roll star. As you follow your vision, you stumble upon obstacles along the way…it's natural to fall. The secret, though, is that you're got to learn to deal with falling down and, more importantly, how to get back up…" – *Anthem*, December 1983

Threk Michaels, continued...

Comments: He may not be prolific, but when Threk cuts loose in the studio, the results are always worth the wait. Carrying his Ricky Nelson obsession to its logical conclusion, Michaels crafts an album of gentle throwback pop/rock based on Nelson's classic song "Lonesome Town," helped once again by Osborn and Hardin and the eternal Jordanaires. *Lonely Always* didn't garner the widespread critical acclaim that *As True As You* experienced, but those writers that "got it" really GOT IT.

Another View: "This guy has it all. The name is amazing. The cover is spectacular, as you can see. The concept of the album is flawless too. Threk is apparently a huge Ricky Nelson fan (as one should be) and *Lonely Always* is a ten-song tribute to Nelson's signature ballad "Lonesome Town.""

"Helped by the Jordanaires on backing harmonies and a suitably restrained and simple musical backing directed by former Nelson sidekick Joe Osborn and played by some smooth Nashville cats, Michaels captures loneliness under glass and studies it like a scientist, with sweet ballads like "The Sound of Lonely," "Lonely Just Like You," and the amazingly titled "Lonely World (Lonely All the Way Through)." He sounds a bit like Ricky at times, but most importantly, he sounds like he's living the material." – Tim Sendra, *All Music Blog*, 2008

Yet Another View: "With crystalline vocals that shimmer in their warmth and a cast of Nashville recording legends including The Jordanaires in the studio, Threk has put out another masterpiece that will surely outlive many of the popular albums on the airwaves today. As a tribute to Ricky Nelson's timeless album "Lonesome Town," *Lonely Always* serves as a song cycle for everyone who has ever felt lonely. Each song on the record has the word "lonely" in the title, blatantly putting forth the theme. With the vocal accompaniment of the legendary Jordanaires, Threk has captured the proverbial lightning-in-a-bottle by creating an album that would have fit just as well on WSM in the early 1960s as it does today." – Wesley Hodges, *Deli Magazine*

MOLDING

Band Members:
Eric Watkins (vocals, guitar) (I-IV)
Bobby Watkins (guitars) (I-IV)
June Kato (I-IV)
Terry Thomas (drums) (I-IV)
Cinjun Tate (guitar, vocals) (IV)

Other Musicians:
Steve Burgess (bass) (I-II)
Mike Farris (I-II)
John Wheeler (I, II, IV)
Rick White (I)

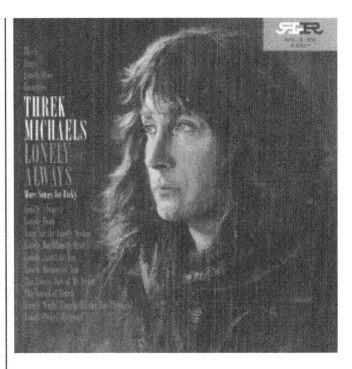

Molding Recordings:

I. Happy (self-produced 1997, CD)
1. Rock And Roll
2. Her Eyes
3. Dragon Park
4. Of Solar Squash
5. Jason LaFarge
6. One Big Drop of Water
7. Groove Me
8. Freak Me Out Frank
9. The Adventures of You and Susie
10. The Scratch Sympathy Waltz

Comments: Singer/songwriter Eric Watkins from the Birmingham band Remy Zero hooks up with his brother Bobby and drummer Terry Thomas, both from the **Screamin' Cheetah Wheelies** to form Molding. Guests include the Wheelies' Mike Farris and John Wheeler from **Jetton & Wheeler**.

II. Choose Your Own Title (self-produced 1998, CD)
1. Set Myself On Fire
2. No Reason
3. Wonderful
4. We've Got It All
5. Before You Say It
6. Heavenly Wrecks
7. Oklahoma Moon
8. Subtle Changes
9. Coffee Girls & the Suicide Shift
10. Gonna Be Alright

III. The Trilogy (self-produced 2003, CD)
1. Annie (sic)
2. Jason LaFarge
3. Wyoming
4. Phone Call
5. People Get Involved
6. I Do
7. Against The Law
8. Deadbeat Sonic
9. Song For You
10. (Phone Call)
11. Hope For The World

Comments: "One part punk, one part acoustic rockin' fun. There's something unexpected around every corner." – from the band's CD Baby page

IV. Buddha Tormented by Pol Pot (self-produced 2008, CD)
1. Woke Up Made
2. Between You and Me
3. Hell Is…
4. My Guilt and Your Body
5. Sun Tzu, Machiavelli and Iceberg Slim
6. We'll Get Through This, Baby
7. Bang
8. The War Goes On
9. Cancer Ray
10. One Foot in the Garden

Another View: "From the personal to the political, intellectual anger rock with country and punk influences that maintains the fun of raging against the dying of modern society's light." – from the band's CD Baby page

COLLIN WADE MONK

Band Members:
Collin Wade Monk (vocals, guitar) (I-III)

Collin Wade Monk Recordings:

I. Oops! I Rocked (Plug Records 1994, CD)
1. Better Than This
2. State of the Grapes
3. Hwy 62
4. I Need a Woman
5. Fallin for You
6. Color or Flavor
7. Moses
8. Pretty Powerful
9. Birth of a Child
10. Throwing Darts

Comments: Collin Wade Monk and Bongo Fury (Sam Baker, now of **Lambchop**) were one of the more interesting bands on the late 1980s/early 1990s rock scene. They put on typically high-energy shows, garnered a lot of press, and even sojourned to Memphis to record an unreleased album with famed producer and musician James Dickinson. When Baker went his way, Monk hooked up with **Will Kimbrough**, Mike Grimes, and Tommy Myer as the Ladyfingers. They auditioned for Geffen Records in L.A. but when nothing came of it, Kimbrough and Grimes formed **the bis-quits**.

Another View: "A gifted storyteller with a glib tongue and an eye for detail, Monk's songs are poetic vignettes packed with invigorating images, backed by sparse instrumentation and an almost holy rock and roll spirit…Monk's creativity and integrity serve him well…" – Rev. Keith A. Gordon, *R.A.D! Review & Discussion of Rock & Roll*, July 1994

II. winkygroovercookieprim (Plug Records 1996?, CD)

Comments: Recorded with producer Brad Jones and featuring Luther and Cody Dickinson of the North Mississippi Allstars. I don't have any other info on the disc.

III. The Astonished Gratitude of Alectrice Chevroi (MisterMonk 2004, CD)
1. Salvation!
2. House of Death
3. Now That I'm Happy
4. Stand Here All Day
5. Technicolor Town
6. Gasoline Sister
7. Little Bit of Brick
8. Touch Me Wife
9. Laugh Like That
10. Stomp on Me

R. STEVIE MOORE - RICK MOORE & THE MR. LUCKY BAND

Comments: Monk "retired" from music in 1997 in frustration and disappointment, returning in 2004 to record *The Astonished Gratitude of Alectrice Chevroi*.

R. STEVIE MOORE

Band Members:
R. Stevie Moore (vocals, guitars, keyboard, drums) (I)

Other Musicians:
Billy Anderson (bass, tambourine) (I)
Johna Lynn (vocals) (I)

R. Stevie Moore Recordings:

I. Phonography (Flamingo Records 1976, LP/CD)
1. Melbourne
2. Explanation of Artist
3. Goodbye Piano
4. Explanation of Listener
5. California Rhythm
6. I've Begun To Fall In Love
7. The Spot
8. I Want You In My Life
9. I Wish I Could Sing
10. Theme From A.G.
11. The Voice
12. Showing Shadows
13. She Don't Know What To Do With Herself
14. The Lariat Wressed Posing Hour
15. I Not Listening
16. Mr. Nashville
17. Moons
18. Welcome To London
19. You And Me
20. Wayne Wayne Go Away
21. Forecast
22. Why Should I Love You
23. Dates
24. Hobbies Galore
25. Because We're The Dig

Comments: This is where it all began. For you kids too young to remember, the Nashville music scene of the early 1970s (non-country), was an abysmal affair... cover bands, sleazy clubs with bad music, and cheap beer that cost too much. R. Stevie Moore and his friends – folks like Victor Lovera and Roger Ferguson, who played in bands like **Goods** – were the lone bright spot in otherwise dark days.

Moore released the self-produced ***Phonography*** as a 17-song, limited edition (100 copies) vinyl LP in 1976, the first D.I.Y. rock album released in Nashville (as far as I can tell). Moore later reissued ***Phonograhy*** on CD with eight bonus tracks (see review ➜). Moore opened the door; others would soon follow...

The Godfather of Nashville Rock, R. Stevie Moore

RICK MOORE & THE MR. LUCKY BAND

Band Members:
Rick Moore (vocals, guitar) (I-III)
Jimmy Nalls (guitar, vocals) (I, II)
Sammy Stafford (guitar, vocals) (II, III)
Jeff 'Stick' Davis (bass) (I)
Jerry 'Snake' King (bass, vocals) (II, III)
Tim Hinkley (keyboards, vocals) (II, III)
Michael Organ (drums) (I)
Nick Buda (drums) (II)
Mike Caputy (drums) (III)

Other Musicians:
Vicki Carrico (vocals) (I, II)
Richard Carter (percussion) (I)
Phil Dillon (guitar, percussion, vocals) (I)
Jimmy Hall (saxophone, percussion) (II)
William Howse (mouth harp) (I)
Wayne Jackson (trumpet) (I, II)
Doug Moffit (saxophone) (I, II)
Jack Pearson (guitar) (II)
Will Rhodarmer (mouth harp) (II)
Noel Roy (guitar) (I)
Joe Warner (keyboards) (I, II)
Carson Whitsett (keyboards) (I)
Reese Wynans (piano) (I)

Rick Moore & the Mr. Lucky Band, continued on page 358...

"Without deviation from the norm, progress is not possible."
– Frank Zappa

Manhattan, April Fool's Day, 1984. R. Stevie Moore is playing with his current live band, The Biggest Names in Show Business, at the Scott & Gary Show in public access TV. Now legendary, the Scott & Gary Show was a free-form, low-budget program that featured musical performances by groups who had to meet the criteria of being "fun, raw, twisted, different, intense and independent." Other guests included Half Japanese, Ben Vaughn, the Butthole Surfers (who did an historical TV debut while tripping on LSD, assuring that at least the "twisted" and "intense" premises were being taken good care of), and an unknown band of adolescents called the Beastie Boys who, off-camera, remarked prophetically that they shouldn't have to do cable TV because they would soon be big stars. But as it turned out, that wasn't the only visionary moment in the show. Another, and perhaps even stranger access of foresight occurred in the same cheap TV studio; and this time it was properly filmed.

After performing the minimal "Copy Me," with its stop and start rhythm provided by the drummer – pounding persistently on the buttons of a drum machine over the resilient melodic chorus line, "Copy me: do what I do, have what I have, be what I am" – the host, Scott Lewis, approaches Moore for a little chat. During the interview, an unusually self-confident R. Stevie, remembers his early days in Music City, USA. "Ironically, I grew up in the middle of an intense musical environment in Nashville. My father was a bass player and I was involved with all the country music. The whole story goes is that I would do these little sessions with or for my father..." But before he gets the chance to finish the story, the LP he was promoting on the show – standing neatly against the bass drum – cracks loudly. They laugh at the weird incident and after a brief comment, Moore causally concludes: "I would go home after these silly, inane country sessions and record what was in my head, which was a whole vision of '60s and '90s." "When did you start doing this?" asks Lewis abruptly, without giving time for such a preposterous statement to sink in.

Recorded during the period between1974 to 1976, *Phonography* is the sound of a brilliant young artist anonymously producing highly sophisticated pop music with primitive home equipment in a bedroom somewhere in Nashville, Tennessee. Music that still sounds fresh and inventive today, but that unfortunately remains largely unknown. While reflecting many of the sounds from the '60s and '70s, his early explorations pre-dated (both musically and aesthetically) the lo-fi and indie phenomena, which began blooming in the mid-1980s and established itself in the '90s, plus all the neo-psychedelic pop and most of the New Weird America related music of today. Many are the people who owe a secret debt to the pioneering work of Nashville's whiz kid. Not that he had any direct influence over the whole lot – something rather unlikely due to Moore's unexplainable obscurity (although he is now regarded by current acts like Ariel Pink and the Apples in Stereo as being a main source of inspiration) – he simply began doing it all by himself, more than three decades ago, right in the heart of America's country music empire.

Considered by *Rolling Stone* magazine to be one of the 50 most significant indie releases of all time, *Phonography* is merely a glimpse into the vast and eclectic world of R. Stevie Moore. He would go on to create his own fascinating sound galaxy, recording fervently at an unprecedented pace of 4 or 5 double albums per year – which now accumulates to an overflowing output of around 400 releases, and still counting. Such compulsive musical activity is as natural to him as breathing; he describes his work as being a continuous "musical diary." Moore's catalogue extends from 1968 to the present year of 2007, and if one is inclined to filter all the failed experiments and self-indulgent noodlings within, there will still be a core list of dozens and dozens of amazing double albums, containing what some people have referred to as "America's hidden musical treasure," a sort of parallel and very personal journey through the musical history of the last four decades. *Phonography* is essentially the one record that managed to surface out of Moore's deep underground obscurity to slowly establish itself as a minor cult legend.

During the *Phonography* era, R. Stevie was living a double life in-between his home-recorded iconoclasm and the country music industry he was directly related to – either by hustling songs for his father's minor publishing company or working as a studio musician for the likes of Chet Atkins and Perry Como at the RCA studio. But fascinated by the inspired creativity of artists such as the Beatles, Brian Wilson, Syd Barrett, Frank Zappa, and Brian Eno, Moore had already outgrown the southern glamour of the "Countrypolitan" sound, and would soon come to perceive it as a washed-up and limited musical form being constantly recycled by (mostly) uninspired people, who instead of attempting to create something new, were stuck in a mechanical (but highly profitable) act of repetition.

At the end of each studio session, Stevie would retreat back to his bedroom to proceed recording his audio diary. There, he set an unparalleled guideline of extreme stylistic variety, which rendered the whole of pop culture into a vast palette for the artist to use at will. His tapes featured an insanely varied lot of influences, styles and moods, all converging into a continuous sound collage; a pop wasteland of disjointed bits and pieces, where extremely well-crafted songs were interspersed with snippets of found sound, arty experimentalism, and odd, humorous skits.

R. Stevie is the perfect paradigm of someone born in the wrong place and at the wrong time. His eccentricity, both inner and outer (he sported a pronounced anglophile outlook, bleached hair, an occasional droopy mustache and big granny glasses), and the contrast it provided with Nashville's conservative mindset, made him develop a very singular sense of humor – the kind of oddball zaniness and sly sarcasm that Beck or the Ween brothers would surely relate to. Alone in his bedroom, inside the vast shell of his headphones, Stevie wandered freely into musical realms unthinkable in his native Nashville.

Besides providing a safe refuge, his eclectic recording activity and unusual musical inclinations were, to a great extent, a reaction against the strict and heavily commercialized atmosphere that surrounded him. It was through his gleeful disobedience and subversive sonic twists that Moore relentlessly poked fun at Music City's closed cultural circuit. Songs like "Topic of Same" and "I Can't Listen To Another Country Song" clearly showed how much he felt apart in his own hometown. Ultimately, he would turn his back on a potentially profitable career as a studio musician to focus instead on his unique home-recording craft.

In a way, he was dismissing the whole mediocre adult world which pressured him to grow up and become another country session musician – in his case, it would be the equivalent of a prolific writer being reduced to a short-hand typist. He was exploding with creativity and wouldn't conform to anything less than total artistic freedom. Like one of his musical heroes, Brian Wilson, Moore's music had a direct link to a sort of child-like innocence that he knew he had to preserve in order to keep producing his own brand of original music. His father, Bob Moore, didn't understand R. Stevie's weird and compulsive recording habit and, as one of Music City's most respected musicians, he probably felt betrayed and disgusted when the soon-to-be follower of the Moore legacy drifted away into what seemed to be incomprehensible regions of music and sound.

As an outsider musician in Nashville, Stevie had little or no chance of survival, his only hope was to reach outside his geographical circumscription and into wider ears. Fortunately, Moore's maternal uncle in New Jersey, Harry Palmer, understood what his unusually talented nephew was doing and provided a light at the end of the tunnel. He would play a key role in the recording artisan's future (anti) career. As MySpace would only be invented a few decades later, Moore and Palmer began plotting a way to introduce R. Stevie's music to the world.

FOR DEMONSTRATIONAL PURPOSES ONLY

"Every once in a while you'll find some recorded music that has nothing to do with trendy rock 'n' roll forms. The sound

may be unlike the way nearly every band in the studio does. The compositions are full of surprises and, again, unlike today's oh-so-standard fare. This rare type of record is seldom delivered though, so your expectations fall and you merely wait 'til out of nowhere this strange taste you've acquired is bitten suddenly on the butt (as you desired). And nevertheless you obtain a copy for yourself. And it builds within you a private sort of pride... that this relic you've found was made just for you and no one else. Mass sales are irrelevant, in this case." – HP Music, 1978

From the land of the Grand Ole Opry comes this weird and wonderful gem, an iconoclastic pop collage home-recorded by a self-taught one-man-band in his early twenties. Both raw and sophisticated, amateur and professional, *Phonography* is a dazzling journey through the inner world of a young musical wizard amazed with his own magic. The sound, as captured by R. Stevie's two inexpensive reel-to-reel tape recorders, unfolds through a series of delightful psychedelic pop songs ("California Rhythm," "I Wish I Could Sing"), weird spoken bits ("Mr. Nashville," "Lariat Wressed Posing Hour"), catchy power-pop rockers ("She Don't Know What To Do With Herself," "Why Should I Love You"), introspective sonic travelogues ("Showing Shadows," "Moons"), music hall oddities ("Goodbye Piano") and stark beautiful ballads ("I've Begun To Fall In Love," "Wayne, Wayne Go Away" and "Hobbies Galore").

A widely original work revealing an adventurous and effervescent young composer with the ability to reproduce a wildly varied range of musical gimmicks and pop hooks, and mesh them all together with idiosyncratic twists to create an all together new thing. Unlike anything anyone had ever heard before or during the mid-1970s, **Phonography** marked the birth of DIY home-recording through the voice of a unique singer-songwriter and genuine musical artist. Unfortunately, it went by practically unnoticed.

The record was the direct result of Harry Palmer's effort to help his nephew's music break away from the claustrophobic confinements of Nashville. A former member of a mild-psychedelic '60s band called Ford Theatre, Palmer was still involved in the music business – working at the time as an executive in Sam Goody's music retailer, which he would soon abandon to go to Polygram Records, and later to Atco, where he remained throughout most of the 1980s. He was one of the few people to truly recognize Moore's unique talent, and in doing so, became a sort of mentor, financing his efforts and encouraging him to do more.

Together, they founded the independent HP Music, which was to be used exclusively as a springboard for Stevie's music. But before that, Palmer took some of his nephew's most accomplished tapes to a small NY studio, where he spliced, mixed and sequenced through more than 100 songs worth of original material. The end product was a 17 track compilation that Moore named **Phonography** (a term meaning "sound writing"), which was to become his introduction to the outside world.

Moore didn't participate in the sequencing of the album, and according to himself, he didn't have to – he had complete trust in his uncle's musical expertise. "It was fully his compilation," Stevie explains, "he didn't really need my input, because I was psyched with whatever he thought was right to choose." Curiously, Palmer didn't go for the obvious mainstream approach of isolating the more accessible material from his most experimental ventures. Instead, he presented the whole pack, which he felt was essential to understand the full extension of Moore's raw talent and genius. The "weirdness" was dosed down to a series of quirky interludes (mostly spoken-word bits), which served as

links between songs. That way he would also maintain the continuous radio show format of the original tapes.

Although it's usually regarded as a sort of "best of" compilation, **Phonography** couldn't possibly contain all the highlights from that period. It was later reissued on CD with eight extra tracks, and it still doesn't cover all the great songs from that era; which is to say that the source tapes (Next, Moore or Less, Moore Often, and Returns) are well worth exploring.

After completing the final mix, Palmer pressed a limited edition of 100 copies for "demonstrational purposes only." Along with each copy they included a typed sheet that read "This is a demonstration record, presenting to you the world of R. Stevie Moore, a new and vital pop artist looking for a home in the recording industry." The year was 1976, a dark time for popular music. In the pre-punk days of arena-rock and James Taylor, not much was happening in terms of new exciting music. Stevie was confident that someone would surely recognize, if not the peculiar genius in his home-made recordings, at least the potentially radio-friendly quality of his more accessible pop songs.

Copies were distributed to record labels, music magazines and established musicians that would hopefully relate to Moore's innovative work – among them, Frank Zappa and Todd Rundgren (but as it turned out, Zappa's copy was sent to the wrong address and Rundgren never replied). **Phonography** was rejected by the industry's standards, which felt that it was probably a bit too strange to produce any mass sales. On top of that, Moore had no band, let alone a live following; and as such, he represented a risk that no label was willing to take.

But as fate would have it, a copy managed to astound New York's underground magazine, *Trouser Press*. They wrote raving reviews, declaring it a masterpiece and, consequently, Stevie began to gain some cult status among the growing new wave and punk scene. Young music writers like Kurt Loder (later a famous MTV host) and David Fricke (currently the senior editor at *Rolling Stone*) showered Moore with praises, describing him as a "seemingly bottomless well of talent" and "criminally neglected artist." Meanwhile, Palmer decided to issue a 4 song EP from **Phonography**, as HP Music's first official release.

Again, a number of copies were strategically distributed by mail to a number of selected destinations; but still, it seemed that Moore's "home in the recording industry" was far from materializing. A couple of independent distributors took small quantities, while a few others were placed in Sam Goody's stores. *Trouser Press* also became an efficient platform to help promote the EP. For a brief period it featured an ad campaign where Moore would send a free copy to anyone who phoned in. But since most people were doing collect calls, the bill soon grew out of proportion and the campaign had to be aborted. They kept using *Trouser Press* to promote the *4 From Phonography* EP, selling copies for 2 dollars each.

Poor distribution and a stroke of chronic bad luck narrowed Stevie's chances from the beginning. It seems that no success story is complete without the crucial push of luck. As history often confirms, the intersection that leads to a wider recognition is usually the result of an accidental opportunity or fruitful coincidence. Moore never had any of the above. Harry Palmer, the only connection he had with the outside music business world, didn't have the necessary funds or time to invest on a more consistent boost to his career, as he was doing all the HP promotion and public relations affairs at home as a parallel activity to his work. Since no label showed any real interest, *Phonography* was finally released by HP Music in 1978.

By far, the most enthusiastic reply came from west-coast art rockers, The Residents, who wrote an exciting fan letter to HP's headquarters. They would eventually forward *Phonography* to fellow conspirer, Chris Cutler, who guaranteed its European distribution through his British independent label, Recommended Records. That helped sow the seeds for a slow growing cult-following outside the USA, which prevented Moore from becoming totally invisible. By 1978, R. Stevie was already established in New Jersey; Harry Palmer had been successful in convincing him to leave Nashville and move up north, closer to New York's cultural pot. There, a new phase of musical maturity and impressive prolific genius took place, but that's yet another story.

SOUND WRITING

"Imaginative, eccentric, excellently played and crafted, this is a collection that has held up well and still has the ability to charm, amuse, impress and beguile." – Recommended Records

The songs in *Phonography* were crafted using only one microphone, a borrowed guitar directly plugged into the recorder, some effects pedals, a Fender bass, a drum kit that consisted of a snare, hi-hat and a card-box serving as bass drum, plus synthesizers, an out-of-tune piano and "various toy devices." As one would assume from the low budget, home-made quality of the recording, the sound is somewhat muffled, with a thin cape of tape hiss running through it. But instead of overshadowing the music, it creates a charming, alien-like texture, which adds an ethereal and fragile aura to Moore's sophisticated compositions.

In that sense, the music sounds both old and new. Stevie built innumerable layers of sound into his rudimental four-track

recorder, enriching the songs with intricate detail and underlying depth. Paradoxically, the result of accumulating so many sub-tracks gave the sound a sort of two-dimensional feel. But, as Captain Beefheart once remarked, the music still "shines like a diamond in the mud." Since the songs were created using headphones (so as not to disturb the neighborhood with his idiosyncratic pop maneuvers), it is also better appreciated at close listen – that way, one can actually get a sense of it being assembled piece by piece; a brilliant bric-a-brac tapestry of sound where you can wonder at the small details that form the amazing whole.

Because he had no mixing deck, each overdubbed instrument had to be recorded in only one take. Stevie soon learned how to take advantage of his mistakes, adopting the first commandment of Brian Eno's Oblique Strategies – "honor thy error as a hidden intention" – as his creative guideline. This element of spontaneity gave a distinct feel of authenticity to each piece, as though it couldn't have sounded any different. Moore's recording method made the process a constant battle with the unpredictable, which more than often produced new and interesting results.

One of the most picturesque examples might be the sudden bump heard in the middle of "Goodbye Piano," sounding like something falling loudly on the floor (probably an accident while recording one of the instrumental tracks). Since he had no way to turn back and correct the mistake, Stevie quickly mutters "sorry!", further reinforcing the hilarious image of a musician struggling to squeeze out one last song from his disintegrating piano. "Of course, anytime I was trying to re-record improvements of classic homemade songs in a studio, they would inevitably sound better," Stevie says, "but always lacking the genuine magic vibe of my tapes. Not easy to reproduce such deep inspired innocence creativity."

Phonography opens with a fading, dramatic synth intro that soon evolves into the epic symphonic rock of "Melbourne"– a 1970s-styled, elaborate instrumental theme – hovering over sonic canyons, as if the recording artisan was projecting his imaginary-self, far away from the dull, insipid realities of Tennessee. After landing back, the tape skips into "Explanation of Artist," where we hear Moore introduce himself while peeing in the bathroom. As the toilet flushes, the music-hall dementia of "Goodbye Piano" rolls in, and with it, the very clear notion that we're not in Nashville anymore, Toto.

Championed by the Residents as their favorite song ("It made me want to tear out my hair because it is so great, and I never tear out my hair!" wrote one enthusiastic eye-ball), "Goodbye Piano" is a delightful, cartoonish farewell to an out-of-tune piano, sung in a high-pitched Mickey Mouse-like voice over an echoey tip-tap percussion. For the song, Moore actually used an old upright piano he had to leave behind, while changing residency in 1975. As the tune grows into a delirious cacophonic mess, with piano keys flying everywhere, R. Stevie bids goodbye to his old faithful companion with the memorable line: "it was glorious knowing you the past month or two but as usual, they're sending me away because I cannot supply the money they want!"

Just as one starts to wonder where all this is leading to, the sample of an American Top 40 radio jingle pops in, and the album unexpectedly jumps to a stretch of sweet Brian Wilson-esque melodies, bringing Moore's instinctive pop smarts into full view. The first song, "California Rhythm," begins with a trembly, jerky sound (also the result of a technical misfortune but, as mentioned above, it seems as if it couldn't have sounded any different), with R. Stevie strumming his guitar and singing in a clear, melodic voice. The song comes into full-shape when the drums kick in, along with an innovative background layer of dub-like echo snares, panning from one channel to the other.

Next comes the piercing lament of "I've Begun To Fall In Love," with its poetic otherworldly beauty, sounding like something in-between the Beach Boys and the Eels. "I Want You In My Life" has a strong Macca resonance, accompanied by sprightly acoustic chords and a driving country shuffle; while the following "I Wish I Could Sing" is the point of intersection where the prog soundscapes of "Melbourne" meet the pretty wistful harmonies of "I've Begun To Fall In Love." The song begins with a reverberated field-recording of a cheerleader chant captured outside Moore's window, and then explodes into a dazzling lo-fi pop symphony. For a guy alone in his bedroom, fumbling with cheap home equipment, the complex structure and brilliant Wall of Sound-like arrangements of "I Wish I Could Sing" are a dynamic confirmation of Moore's musical genius.

"Theme from AG" is an idiosyncratic reproduction of the main theme from Andy Griffith's 1960s-era TV show – it

ends with the sound of a shutting door, and that closes the first part of the LP. Side B begins inside Stevie's room with the strange and spooky monologue, "The Voice," creating the perfect introduction to the floating, hazy psychedelica of "Showing Shadows," an introspective travelogue that transports you further down the rabbit hole, with its enchanting guitar lines and mysterious word-images: "Once upon a time there lived a fancy babe, dressed in shine and juju undertow/Just about to break within a passing day/She was showing shadows, would the morning know?"

Besides being a talented composer, Moore is also a proficient lyricist who usually favors the sounds rather than the words and their most immediate meaning; choosing instead to revel in the peculiarities of random poetical association. Another interesting aspect is the fact that most of the times, Moore sings in a convincing British accent instead of his native Nashvillean drawl, which only emerges in the spoken bits. So it's no surprise that "Showing Shadows" brings to mind another of Stevie's heroes, Syd Barrett.

Next stop is the infectious, Sparks-like "She Don't Know What To Do With Herself," which ends in a suspended mist of backwards guitar and feedback, dissolving its way into "The Lariat Wressed Posing Hour" – a comedy skit that blends Monty Python's absurdist wit with the sort of quirky, wry humor that would permeate MTV throughout the 1990s, with such cult programs as the sock puppet show, *Sifl and Olly*.

The jumpy, oddball folk of "I Not Listening" is as demented and catchy as a Ween song, while "Mr. Nashville" is an ironically prophetic dialogue between Moore and a patronizing record executive, trying to find the right words to explain why R. Stevie doesn't qualify for the music business ("Money? What exactly do you expect Mr. Nashville?").

And finally, the last track on the original edition of **Phonography**, the amazing "Moons," with its charming Magnus Chord toy organ and background echoey synth, serpentining in a whimsical motion, as the guitar tweets angular lunar notes to Moore's half-spoken vocals: "Mister Moons as you sit there enjoying your own glow, I am one of the very few souls you'd really like to know."

Stewart Mason from *All Music Guide* (also the person responsible for the CD reissue of **Phonography**), points out that "Moon's" delicate mid-part predates the sound that Stereolab would turn into a career 15 years later. In 1998, Mason re-released **Phonography** on CD (remastered by Moore), along with eight bonus tracks, through the Albuquerque-based Flamingo label.

Although the inclusion of the extra songs takes out the compact unity of Palmer's 1976 selection, they add valuable pieces to what is still regarded as "The" introduction to R. Stevie Moore. Namely, the ultra catchy, Merseybeat punk rocker "Why Should I Love You"; the staggering acoustic ballads "Wayne, Wayne Go Away" and "Hobbies Galore"; and an early 1973 version of "Dates," a pop anthem that Moore would later re-record into near perfection with the help of friend and fan, Dave Gregory from XTC.

Although the sound is still a bit embryonic, compared with the kind of work that R. Stevie would achieve in his subsequent recordings, *Phonography* is a small microcosm of its own, containing a playful and delightfully weird musical fantasy within. After 31 years, it still sounds exactly like it should – a wonderful psychedelic pop artifact from outer space, secretly home-recorded in-between country sessions in Nashville. But it's only the early beginning of an all-together fascinating musical character that would eventually get lost in the archives of history.

Both the sound and musical quality would improve immensely with his next recordings – a dark, spacey masterpiece called *A Swing And A Miss* and the irreverent *SheetRock* (both from 1977, these would be the last Nashville tapes), which showed how quickly the recording artisan had matured in his craft. And, as a devout musical buff, his already vast musical vocabulary was now widening with the advent of punk rock and new wave.

But unfortunately, if something doesn't reach enough people in its own time, it's as though it never existed. There are still a lot of historic holes remaining to be covered, and Moore is definitely one of the biggest. If one listens close enough to what he has been consistently laying down on tape since the 1970s, it becomes pretty evident that he is indeed one of the missing links between the '60s and the '90s, and that his weird access of foresight at the Scott & Gary Show in the early 1980s, was nothing short of a moment of extreme lucidity. Somewhere in suburban New Jersey sits a vast legacy of lost music to back up such an outrageous statement. – *Essay by Nuno Monteiro, written exclusively for this book, 2007*

RICK MOORE - MOTHER MERCY - MOUTHFUL OF BEES

Rick Moore, continued...

Rick Moore Recordings:

I. Slow Burnin' Fire (MRL Records 1997, CD)
1. Talk to Me Baby
2. Your Love Is Working Overtime
3. Swingin' Her Stuff
4. House Rockin'
5. Let Me Down Easy
6. Radio Station
7. Good Woman Bad
8. Muddy Water Fever
9. Chicken House Blues
10. Whole Lotta Woman
11. Make Lovin' You My Business
12. Tangled Up In Your Love
13. Slow Burnin' Fire

Comments: Rick Moore is a talented, hot-shot blues guitarist better regarded overseas than in Nashville. His stuff is a soul-blues hybrid with plenty of scorching guitar. Sadly, Moore passed away in early 2012...

II. Satisfied (MRL Records 2000, CD)
1. Satisfied Man
2. Better off with the Blues
3. Take iT Down to Memphis
4. Good Man Gone Bad
5. (I wanta) Get FuNKy
6. Hello DARKness
7. Come and go with Me
8. She's Allright
9. AcT of FAITh
10. Dark Before DAYlight
11. Memphis sTriPPer
12. Sell my monKEY
13. Fire in the Delta

III. Live In The U.S.A. (MRL Records 2002, CD)
1. House Rockin
2. Talk to Me
3. Good Woman Bad
4. Make Lovin You My Business
5. Guilty
6. Chicken House Blues
7. I Wanna Get Funky
8. Let Me Down Easy
9. Swingin Her Stuff

MOTHER MERCY

Band Members:
Mark Scott (vocals)
Matt Stamps (guitar, vocals)

Scott Shively (guitar, vocals)
Trent Golden (bass)
Todd Golden (drums)

Comments: Band contributed the song "I Why" to the *Music City Rock* 1995 compilation CD. Weren't Trent and Todd the sons of Oak Ridge Boy William Lee Golden?

MOURNING AFTER

Band Members:
Gary Privette (vocals, guitar)
Mike Orr (bass, vocals)
Barry Feltz (drums, vocals)

MOUTH FULL OF BEES

Band Members:
Brian Hardin (I)
Jeff Darden (I)

Mouth Full of Bees Recordings:

I. Mouth Full Of Bees (demo tape?)
1. Devil's Grin
2. Independence Day
3. Crazy Wheels
4. Lantern Jaw

Comments: Single-sided cassette, probably a demo tape, the only information included beyond the song titles are the names of Hardin and Darden, and phone numbers.

THE MOVEMENT

Band Members:
Richie Owens (vocals, guitar) (I)
Bob Ocker (guitar) (I)
Lerry Reynolds (bass, vocals) (I)
Lynn "Bone" Brown (drums) (I)
Edmund Turner (bass) (I)

The Movement Recordings:

I. The Movement (Neo Music Group, demo tape?)
Scene 1
1. Together We Can Survive
2. Lost Horizon
3. Back In The Cafeteria
4. I've Got Eyes

Scene 2
5. I Won't Settle Down
6. Temporary
7. Illusion of Consciousness

Comments: The Movement featured the talents of vocalist, guitarist and songwriter Richie Owens, one of the city's rock MVPs. I seem to remember this being a demo cassette that somebody handed off somewhere down the line. "Lost Horizon" also appears on the *City Without A Subway* compilation.

MR. ZERO

Band Members:
Lee Carr (vocals, guitar) R.I.P.
Grandmaster E (vocals, lyrics)
"Machine Gun" Kelly Butler (bass)
Jim Phipps (drums)

Comments: Rap/rock fusion band starring local hero Lee Carr and "Machine Gun" Kelly of similar outfit the **Hard Corps**. Unfortunately, I never heard Mr. Zero perform live since Lee and I were "feuding," or something at the time, and he had fallen in with the troika that launched the *Fireplace Whisky Journal*. I did enjoy Lee's answer to FWJ writer Randy Fox's tongue-in-cheek question about a possible Mr. Zero movie: "The Mr. Zero movie is going to be a lot like the old Elvis films. A lot of girls, the occasional busting a rhyme if even slightly provoked. On the beach, in jail, in Hawaii. Maybe even some Kung Fu action…" Rest in peace, Lee.

MUD BROTHERS

Band Members:
Erik Hellerman (guitar, vocals) (I)
Ralph Weyant, Jr. (bass, vocals) (I)
Larry Vaughn (guitar, vocals) (I)
Tim Blankenship (drums, percussion) (I)

Mud Brothers Recordings:

I. Mud Brothers (self-produced 1996?, CD)
1. Chalk It Up
2. Weatherman
3. Better Off
4. Muddy Garden
5. Nextman
6. Loosetooth
7. Planetary Waltz
8. Chattanooga Fog
9. Shadows
10. Come Dance With Me

Comments: Short-lived Nashville band kicked out a single promising CD before disappearing into the ether. They played around town a lot, though, and I used to run into guitarist Larry Vaughn a lot when he worked at The Great Escape and at Wild Oats Market. Nice guy, Larry, and a

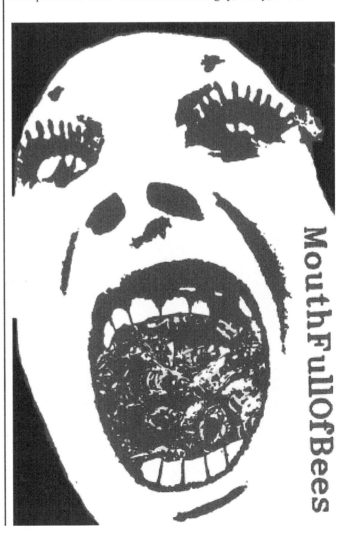

MouthFullofBees

decent CD worth picking up for pennies in the used bins 'round town (see review ➜).

DAVID MUNYON

Band Members:
David Munyon (vocals, guitar) (I)

Other Musicians:
Anthony Crawford (guitar) (I)
Warren Haynes (guitar) (I)
"Sneaky" Pete Kleinnrow (pedal steel) (I)
Craig Krampf (drums) (I)
Paul Leim (drums) (I)
Terry MacMillan (percussion) (I)
Al Perkins (dobro) (I)
David Pomeroy (bass, fretless bass) (I)
Matt Rollings (keyboards) (I)
Leland Sklar (bass) (I)
Billy Joe Walker, Jr. (guitar) (I)
Dony Wynn (drums) (I)

David Munyon Recordings:

I. Code Name: Jumper (Los Hermanos 1990, CD)
1. Maybe Over The Border
2. On The Other Side Of Harlem
3. Beijing Dreams
4. Everyday American Hero
5. Stealer Of Hearts
6. Earl's Song
7. East Of Paris
8. Me And This Old Suitcase

9. Just The Waters Rushing
10. Lost One, This Is Lost Three, Are You Lost Too?
11. Hey Benny

Comments: I met producer Greg Humphrey through the Screamin' Sirens when the notorious cowgirl punk band played in Nashville back in '85, and Greg had just moved to the Music City. In turn, Greg later introduced me to David Munyon, whose debut album Humphrey had produced. A superb songwriter, Munyon could often be found playing solo acoustic sets in various Elliston Place clubs.

For *Code Name: Jumper*, however, Munyon, Humphrey and the Hicks Brothers (Bruce and Jerry, who put up the cash) recruited some studio heavy-hitters, including bassist David Pomeroy, guitarist **Warren Haynes** (pre-Govt. Mule) and drummer Craig Krampf.

PATTY MURRAY

Comments: Former WKDF-FM deejay (1981-1987) and fervent supporter of the local rock music scene, Murray's support helped get a number of Nashville bands like Jason & the Scorchers, Will Rambeaux, and the Nerve played on the otherwise conservative, corporate FM radio powerhouse.

As the host of the weekly Sunday night "Nashville Tapes" show, Murray made a strong case for the depth and diversity of the city's rock music underground. Murray also got behind the station's Music City Queen riverboat cruises and booked local bands to appear on the boat. Sadly, Patty died in an auto

Patty Murray

accident in Florida in 1989. After leaving WKDF, she had moved to Miami and made a name for herself as a local DJ with an FM rock station. Patty's death was a shame, 'cause she was a real person in an industry dominated by egos.

MY RELATIONSHIP WITH GRAVITY

Band Members:
Chad McWherter (vocals, guitar) (I)
Cory Johnson (bass) (I)
Kevin Ferriman (drums) (I)

My Relationship With Gravity Recordings:

I. My Relationship With Gravity (Vital Records 2006, CD)
1. Impossible
2. I'm Ready
3. The Contradiction
4. Paranoid

MYSTIC MEDITATIONS

Band Members:
Mustafa Abdul-Aleem (percussion, flute)
Darrell Rose (percussion)
Michael Saleem (drums)

Comments: Formed by former 2/3s of **Afrikan Dreamland**, Abdul-Aleem and Rose added noted drummer Michael Saleem to the mix to create a truly otherworldly live experience. A local attorney, Abdul-Aleem calls the sound of Mystic Meditations "a synthesis of traditional Afrikan rhythms, fusion, reggae, new age and even some avant-garde jazz."

MYSTIQUE

Band Members:
Donna Frost (vocals)
Art Beard (guitar)
Tony Frost (bass)
Tommy Sneed (drums)

Comments: Donna Frost's late 1980s hard rock band, the sound of aqua-net and spandex…better than most of these oufits, tho' not as good as some of her other musical projects. Mystique contributed the song "Baby You Missed" to the *Major Potential #1* 1991 compilation CD.

Mud Brothers
Mud Brothers
(self-produced)

Nashville's Mud Brothers are beginning to develop a regional buzz, and rightly so. When a thousand and one bands in the Music City still want to be the industry's next heavy metal heroes, the Mud Brothers are making music that is joyful, lively and exciting. Working in the same stylistic vein as the Dave Matthews Band – that is, an open-ended, jam-oriented musical direction – the Mud Brothers have forged a sound all their own. This self-produced collection of tunes – more of a demo disc, really, than an official debut – offers up an electric mixture of Southern-fried funk, New Orleans-inspired R&B and good old-fashioned roots rock.

Several cuts stand out in this altogether solid effort: the rocking "Muddy Garden," with its tasty guitar break soaring above the mix; "Planetary Waltz's" rhetorical query is finely underlined by a fluid instrumental soundtrack and lofty vocals; or "Shadows," offering a countrified instrumental break worthy of any band from Nashville. The production by guitarist Eric Hellerman is clean and inspired in spite of the band's minuscule recording budget. The Mud Brothers make the most with what they've got, which is a lot of talent and little or no industry support. If they continue to slog it out in the clubs, the band's free-wheeling style and musical chops will end up building a well-deserved loyal following – which will definitely make the labels stand up and take notice. (1996)

NASHVILLE JUG BAND

Band Members:
Ed Dye (vocals, Dobro) (I)
Jill Klein (vocals, percussion) (I)
Dave Olney (vocals, guitar) (I)
Tommy Goldsmith (vocals, guitar) (I)
Sam Bush (fiddle, Dobro, mandolin) (I)
John Hedgecoth (jug, banjo) (I)
Dean Crum (banjo) (I)
Mike Henderson (National steel guitar) (I)
Brent Truitt (mandolin) (I)
Tom Roady (percussion) (I)
Roy Huskey (bass) (I)
Fred "Too Slim" LaBour (vocals, bass, percussion) (I)

Nashville Jug Band Recordings:

I. Nashville Jug Band (Rounder Records 1988, LP)
1. Pretend
2. Crazy Blues
3. Titanic
4. Dallas Rag
5. Racetrack Blues
6. Shortnin' Bread
7. The Women Make a Fool Out of Me
8. You Done Me Wrong
9. K.C.Moan
10. Mound Bayou
11. Don't You Love Your Daddy No More
12. Blue Moon of Kentucky
13. What's the Matter with the Mill?
14. Empty Boudoir Blues

Comments: Produced by Tommy Goldsmith, who was first a music reporter, now an editor with *The Tennessean* newspaper. Album includes songs by **Dave Olney** ("Racetrack Blues") and **Pat McLaughlin** ("You Done Me Wrong)" as well as traditional songs by Bill Monroe, Jimmie Rogers and Leadbelly.

THE NATIONALS

Band Members:
Jack Pearson (vocals, guitars)
William Howse (vocals, harmonica)
Abe White (bass)
Richard Carter (drums, percussion)

Comments: The Nationals were a traditional-styled blues band (think the Fabulous Thunderbirds) with great musical credentials. Guitarist Pearson had played with Stevie Ray Vaughan, bassist Abe White studied under jazz great Jaco Pastorius, and drummer Carter had played with Albert King and Leon Redbone.

NEIL DEAF

Band Members:
Neil Hicks

Comments: One of the Music City's more intriguing talents, Neil Hicks conceived of the "Neil Deaf" character as a catch-all for his musical projects. Contributed song "Falling Into Hand (Of Helplessness)" to the NEA's *What You Haven't Heard...* 1987 compilation CD.

NED VAN GO

Band Members:
Ned Hill (vocals, guitars, harmonica, synth) (I-III)
Eliot Houser (guitars, vocals, keyboards) (I-III)
Viva Knievel (bass) (I-III)
Ashley Mimbela (keyboards) (I-III)
Reggie Las Vegas (drums, percussion, vocals) (I-III)

Other Musicians:
Chris Hayes (backing vocals) (III)
Donnie Herron (fiddle) (III)
Kris McCarthy (backing vocals) (III)
Mark Miller (stand up bass) (III)
Michael Webb (accordion) (III)

Ned Van Go Recordings:

I. In Stereo (self-produced CD, 2001)
1. Ever Closer
2. Complicated Girl
3. Hangin' Out At Walmart

4. Wretched Town
5. Wilson
6. Don't Leave Me
7. Carnegie Hall
8. Given
9. Common Girl
10. Laid

II. Rain, Trains and The Lord Almighty (self-produced CD, 2004)
1. Back Home
2. Sweet Rebecca
3. Fade Out
4. Jennifer
5. Love Her Anyway
6. Bartender
7. Interstate
8. Ma Janet
9. Hold Down Mary
10. Laid
11. Lonely Town

III. Marry A Waitress (self-produced CD, 2006)
1. Charlene
2. Marry A Waitress
3. Factory Blues
4. Never Kissed A Girl
5. Death By Polygamy
6. The Hoedown Song
7. No Sleeping In Penn Station
8. Bedroom Wall
9. Country Girl
10. Prelude To Granny Is A Waitress
11. Granny Is A Waitress

Comments: Includes cover of Govt. Cheese's "No Sleeping In Penn Station."

From the band's EPK at sonicbids.com: Ned Van Go's members are a ragged crew made up of small town boys who are influenced by beer, desperation, good love, bad love and down home rock and roll. From breakdowns on the side of the road to causing a ruckus because of one of their songs, the boys of Ned Van Go are never boring. Their latest record "Marry a Waitress" stands out from even their earlier records because of its energy and quirkiness.

It tells stories of factory working, racism, love in prison, love in a small town and time running out on an aging musician. "Marry A Waitress" has been requested by radio stations all over the world-18 different countries, 14 stations alone in Australia, 5 in the Netherlands. Their music stands out because it can strike you as heartfelt, mean, raunchy and lovable all at once, and that's just plain hard to pull off.

NEON BUSHMEN

Band Members:
Michael Chumney (vocals, sax, keyboards) (I)
George Bretz (guitars) (I)
George Turner (guitars) (I)
Kelly Phillips (bass) (I)
Richard Furman (drums, percussion) (I)

Neon Bushman Recordings:

I. Aborigi d' Lights (Club Paradise Records 1983, LP)
Side 1
1. Love Fit
2. She's That Kind Of Girl

Side 2
3. You're A Dick
4. I Believe In Love

THE NERVE

Band Members:
Danny Rhodes (vocals, guitar)
Ricky Rector (guitar, vocals)
Michael Rhodes (bass)
Mike Lawler (keyboards)
Kirby Shelstad (keyboards)
Dale Armstrong (drums)

Comments: In-demand session musicians by day, freewheelin' jazz-fusion band by night, the Nerve never quite got their imaginative blend of rock, jazz and R&B off the ground, in spite of years of constant local gigs. Contributed song "Ain't Been Loved Enough" to the NEA's *What You Haven't Heard…* compilation CD.

NINE PARTS DEVIL

Band Members:
Dave Willie (vocals) (I)
John Troup (guitar) (I)
Rob DeHart (bass) (I)
Mark "Smiley" Shenkel (saxophone) (I)
Mark Medley (drums) (I)

Nine Parts Devil Recordings:

I. Nine Parts Devil (self-produced cassette, no date)
Side One (studio):
1. Bourbon Street
2. Confessions of a Cad
3. Disinclined
4. Rock Hudson

Side Two (live):
1. Foreign Taste
2. Wine Drunk

Comments: Nine Parts Devil was a lounge-jazz outfit with punk rock underpinnings and a chaotic art-rock heart. Citing influences as diverse as Frank Sinatra and Darby Crash, the band was founded by local veterans Dave Willie (**Jet Black Factory**), Mark Medley (**Raging Fire**), and Mark "Smiley" Shenkel (**Freedom of Expression**, **AKA Rudie**, **Facsimile**, **Riff Raff**). They played frequently at the drag bar Victor Victoria's and, by all accounts, knocked the audience down every time with their mix of "the Rat Pack, pulp novelist Jim Thompson and various '70s porn idols."

NO ART

Band Members:
Garry Privette (vocals, guitars)
Barry Felts (drums)

THE NOBILITY

Band Members:
Sean Williams (vocals, guitar) (I)
Stephen Jerkins (guitar, keyboards, vocals) (I)
Brian Fuzzell (drums, percussion) (I)
David Dewese (bass)

The Nobility Recordings:

I. The Mezzanine (Theory 8 Records 2007, CD)
1. The Mezzanine
2. Halleluiah Chorus
3. Angel's Debut

Nine Parts Devil

4. I Refuse
5. Let Me Hang Around
6. Gold Blue Sky
7. Midst of the Park
8. Skeleton Key
9. This Is What I've Wanted To Tell You
10. Riverboat
11. Worth Your While

Comments: Formerly known as Jetpack and Jetpack U.K.

Another View: "Formerly Jetpack, the band's former handle when critics dubbed them Weezer lite, the newly-christened Nobility's Sean Williams has ingested tons of mid-period Kinks and solo McCartney, regurgitating the best bits in a way that progresses rather than replicates — screaming rockers ("Skeleton Key", "Riverboat"), ballads ("Angel's Debut"), and power pop ("I Refuse") sound familiar yet new. "Halleluiah Chorus", the centerpiece and single-to-be, nicks the melodies of "Rocky Top" and "I Fought the Law", morphing into the best crazed Viking anthem since Led Zeppelin's "Immigrant Song"." – *The Big Takeover* (2007)

NOBODY'S BUSINESS

Band Members:
Kelly Franklin (vocals, guitar)
Gary Godbey (bass, vocals)
Doug Gilbert (saxophone, vocals)
Craig Boswell (trombone, vocals)
Ricky Lee (trumpet, percussion, vocals)
Eddy Joyner (piano, synthesizer, vocals)
Steve Nabi (drums, vocals)

Comments: Nobody's Business was a mid-1980s Nashville band that differed from just about anybody on the local scene in that they had a full horn section that added a brassy bottom end to their unique funk-rock sound. Formed by Ricky Lee in 1982, Belmont College student Franklin was brought in shortly thereafter to replace guitarist Chad Welling.

NOT WITHOUT WILLIE

Band Members:
Scott Barrier (vocals, guitar) (I)
Steve Eagon (guitars) (I)
Brandon Whigham (bass, vocals) (I)
Buddy Gibbons (drums, percussion, vocals) (I)

Other Musicians:
Rick Lay (percussion) (I)
Tommy McKnight (keyboards) (I)
C.J. Watson (guitar, vocals) (I)

Not Without Willie Recordings:

I. Just Call Me Bill... (Crystal Marsh Publishing 2002, CD-R)
1. Now & Then
2. What You've Done
3. After Effects
4. Smoke to Clear
5. Above It All
6. Bikki Bikki
7. I Feel It Too
8. Keep Me in Mind
9. Good Guys
10. Natural Fears
11. Heavy Water

Comments: Buddy Gibbons was the drummer on one of **Max Vague**'s earliest bands, now living in L.A. and giving lessons for cash when he isn't bringing his chops to bear behind folks like jazz guitarist Stan Lassiter.

The Nobility

INTERVIEW: BARRY NELSON

*B*arry Nelson is another one of those Nashville VIPs who has kicked around in a number of seminal bands on the scene. From Young Gray Ruins and Shadow 15 to Dessau and beyond, Barry has been there to add his understated musical skills to the mix. I spoke with Barry by phone in April 2007.

How did you get interested in music in the first place?
Growing up, of course, I was into music and AM radio and bought records. When I moved to Nashville, my brother got into some bands and I was always around it when I was younger. Finally, one day I just picked up a bass and joined Young Gray Ruins and kind of learned to play on the fly.

When did Young Gray Ruins get started?
We started in the summer of '82 and we played a lot; opened for the Gun Club at Spanky's, which was a big highlight for us. A friend of mine put together a CD of it, and so we played around that fall and that spring recorded some songs at MTSU where I was actually in school. MTSU had the recording facility, so a lot of bands recorded down there. I knew a lot of people who were in the [music business] program, so we could get free time and stuff. We recorded some songs, four songs, that spring and played some shows. We played the alternative jams that January, the one that was always opposite the Charlie Daniels jam...

I think Bill quit because he was going to go to school and in nine months, we had ran our course. We had written a lot of material. I've recently put together a 17 or 18 song Young Gray Ruins CD of all our stuff. By that spring, Shannon had met Chris Feinstein, so she went with him and sort of became paired. Then Sam, our singer quit...we thought about trying to get a new singer for Young Gray Ruins, but we didn't. After Shannon met Chris, we went and played with him and, at that point, we just decided we'd go ahead and go with him and split Young Gray Ruins up. We were only together for about nine months, and Shadow 15 started in May of '83. The three of us jammed a few times, and we knew Chris had a brother Scott who was interested in being a singer...we had some tunes worked up and he came in and started singing and we just kind of took it from there.

Did Young Gray Ruins release anything, like a cassette or anything like that?
We never did...we had the tracks, we were thinking about trying to put together a little four song EP and before that could get going, we broke up. I still have the recordings, but we never put out anything officially.

Shadow 15 played that summer in a show at Cantrell's, so we played out and we were lucky to open for some cool bands that came through over the next year, 1983 to '84. We got to hang out with the Replacements, and with Rain Parade, we opened for them one time at Rooster's, I think it was in '86. They had become friends with Laurie George, they had sent a record to her, I guess through Praxis. She was also kind of Shadow 15's manager; she helped us with gigs and with stuff.

That spring of '84, we went into the studio, the Quadraphonic studio over there on Music Row. Chuck Allen had a friend that was an engineer there and got us free time. That was a cool little studio, that's where Neil Young recorded his famous stuff...we did eight songs and made an eight-song cassette. We made copies, sold them at Cats Records...I think we sold a couple hundred at Cats. We had that tape out and continued to play live.

That next year, probably the spring of '85 or so, we decided we wanted to release a record. We took some of the tracks from the Quad thing and got with Tom Der. He's a real cool guy, he always helped the bands out, so we took the tapes from Quad and took them to Studio 19 where he worked, and beefed up some of the tracks. We did some of the vocals and recorded a couple extra tunes, and the four songs we put on the EP, we were going to release it ourselves. Then we went to Jackson, Mississippi and played down there and met Tim Lee from the Windbreakers.

We became friends with him, so when it came time to put out the record, he had the Big Monkey label that he had put the Windbreakers stuff out on. We just called and asked "can we put it out on your label" and he said "sure." So we ended up putting it out on an established label, his Big Monkey Records label and we put out a four-song EP. Then we mailed it out to all the magazines and radio stations, got the press kit together, did that whole routine. We got a good response from the record, some good airplay on the radio, had a lot of good mail from people. About that time was when Chris found a drumming gig with the Questionnaires...that was Scott's brother and I guess it's no secret, by that time Shannon and Chris were a couple and had been together through most of Shadow 15. So we were a pretty close unit. When he left, that was quite a blow to us at the time. We had just put out the record, just got the 8x10s done, crap like that. So we had to regroup, take a deep breath and get a new drummer... a guy from Birmingham that we had met and known through Carnival Season. His name was Richard Pryor, he was a great drummer, so we got him on board and plodded on and that summer of '86 played shows with him and by the time the record came out, we were drawing good crowds...we could pack the Exit In at the time, 400 or 500 people, and back then the deal was you got 90% of the door and you just had to pay the sound man $60 and pay the opening band. We were charging $5 so, with 400 people, we were getting 90% of $2000, which was a great deal. They don't do that for the bands anymore. So we got a good local following, but we never got a record deal.

You never got much interest from the labels?
We'd get some interest, nothing serious you know. I don't know how much we were concerned about that, we just had to play the music, have fun, and travel around. We knew we could record...it's easy to record in Nashville, you can always just hire some people and we figured we would make our money and save our money and put out the record ourselves. By that time, we were playing regularly and we were able to put the money back into the band for traveling.

In '87 we recorded with Richard at Treasure Isle, we recorded four songs that were sounding really good. But after Chris left, it wasn't the same, the camaraderie wasn't there...Richard was still living in Birmingham for the first bit, and Chris left, being Scott's brother and my friend and Shannon's boyfriend, it was just a mess. Shannon thought we were just ready to go, so we all just mutually parted. We had two shows left so we decided we would go do the shows and be done. So we all left amicably and actually made some good money from those last two shows.

Where did you go from there?
We started a band called Giant, which was a couple of years before that metal band. We played a show at Ellison Square and got a good review but, obviously, we weren't making money as a new band and we crumbled pretty quickly after three or four months.

When did you get hooked up with Dessau?
It was right after Giant broke up, after a nice little break, that spring of '88. John Elliott, who I had known all those years, he played in Cloverbottom and Actuals and he already had Dessau for a couple of records. Dessau was pretty well established, and my brother [Skot] played with them, Mike Orr had already played with them and rejoined. So at the time when I joined the band, there was me, Mike and John, and...little known fact...Kurt Wagner from Lambchop, he played with us for about the first four or five months when I was in Dessau, which is kind of funny now that he's the Lambchop guy.

Definitely two opposite ends of the musical spectrum there...
He played pedal steel through a distortion pedal, it was fun...we had some fun times going out of town with him, but he left to do his Posterchild thing, which became Lambchop. We did the Dessau thing for a couple years and recorded that one album for Carlyle. It was John's band, but we enjoyed playing in it. He had a pretty good following by the time we joined, so we did some tours, got to go to Holland and play. Carlyle had some deal with a label in Holland, so we went over there to play and had some good times. When it came time to record the second album, he got that guy from Ministry. The second album was going to be done by Paul Barker, and Mike and I had sort of warn out our welcome by that time and it became clear that John was going to get with Paul and do the record, so we jumped ship by then and that was the end of that...

After Dessau, did you play with any other bands?
When I quit Dessau, it was the summer of '90, so we had done Dessau for two years. Mike and I quit at the same time and actually took a two-year break, which I was glad to do because I'd been going for eight years. In the summer of '92 I got together with some guys that had a band called Pelt City. We played, we practiced...all the guys worked at Multi Bobs and we practiced upstairs. We recorded our stuff; we have an eight-song cassette release that we put out. At some point, we decided we would change our name to Canteen, so Pelt City became Canteen. We actually put the cassette out again with the new Canteen name, mailed out some stuff, got some good label interest at Alias Records, and then Grass Records which was an affiliate of BMG. We had both of them making offers, small offers to do a record, which was what we wanted at the time. We had to play out of town and on the eve of making a decision, which way we were going to go with the label, the three guys that I was playing with decided they wanted to bail. They didn't want to commit to some sort of weird deal...back then, any time you signed a deal, it was always confusing and lengthy, seven records and crap like that...

I'm not sure what their thought process was because they eventually ended up starting another band and signing to Grass. They put a record out on Grass and I can't remember the name of the band, but it didn't do anything and they broke up shortly thereafter. Unfortunately for them, I was the older, experienced guy who knew how to run the show and make the tour go good, make sure we got paid and all that crap. So when I was gone, they fell apart, it was a disaster.

THE OBSCURE - DAVID OLNEY

THE OBSCURE

Band Members:
Mike Gogola (vocals, guitars) (I-II)
Doug Tewksbury (guitars, keyboards) (I-II)
Brian Wieck (bass, vocals) (I-II)
Dan Sloan (drums, vocals) (I-II)

Other Musicians:
Max Abrams (sax) (II)
Brian Carter (guitars, vocals) (II)
Mike Longenecker (keyboards) (I)
Dave Megyesi (drums) (II)
Curt Sydnor (keyboards) (II)

The Obscure Recordings:

I. The Politics of Person (A.D. Records 2000, CD)
1. Paradox
2. The Human Condition
3. Give Up
4. Those Commie Bastards!
5. The American Scene
6. Forget About Jane
7. Anthem

Another View: "The homemade seven-song CD *The Politics of Person* finds The Obscure working in the steel-gray colors of fellow Michigan rock legends The Stooges and The MC5. Fuzzy riffs, jittery rhythms, and unhealthy doses of volume distinguish The Obscure's initial recordings, which come at the listener in pulsating waves of reverberating sound and caffeinated energy, not to mention sudden bursts of garage-y funk and Sean Connery samples, all of which are just cool as hell..." – Noel Murray, *Nashville Scene*, April 2000

Yet Another View: "The Obscure CD titled *The Politics of Person* is a radioactive exploration of punk, electrosurf, and psychedelic rock. Imagine Man or Astroman doing a cover of *The Godfather* theme song." – Venus Envy, *In Review*, 2000

II. Laugh Like A Whip, Look Like A Dagger (A.D. Records, 2002, CD)
1. Surviving Marilyn
2. Dearborn
3. Slow Catastrophe
4. Living In Sin
5. Beautiful Girls
6. Year Of The Snake
7. Give Me Some Love Sometime
8. On Top Of The World
9. Help Me Out
10. If Only
11. Thundercloud
12. Telephone As Trigger

Comments: After four years of plugging away at the music biz, both in Detroit and Nashville, **the Obscure** called it quits after this excellent CD, just when they were really beginning to make inroads locally. So it goes. Singer/songwriter Mike Gogola ended up moving to Houston, where he recently recorded an album as the Copyright Infringement, and he also played with the band Casino.

DAVID OLNEY
Web: www.davidolney.com

Band Members:
David Olney (vocals, guitars, harmonica) (I-XIX)

Other Musicians:
David Angell (violin) (X)
Monissa Angell (violin) (X)
Richard Bailey (banjo) (XVIII)
A.C. Bushnell (fiddle) (X)
Natalie Chenault (vocals) (XIV)
Bobby Daniels (vocals) (XVIII)
David Davison (violin) (X)
Robb Earls (keyboards) (XIV, XVI)
Carole Edwards (vocals) (XIV, XVI)
Leah Eneas (vocals) (XIV)
Mike Fleming (bass, banjo) (X, XIV, XVI)
Thomas Goldsmith (guitar, keyboards) (XIV)
John Hadley (vocals) (XVI)
Mike Henderson (guitars) (XIV)
Jim Hoke (clarinet, pedal steel) (XVIII)
Bill Huber (tuba, trombone) (XVIII)
Jack Irwin (keyboards, clavinet, percussion) (XVIII)
Michael Johnson (guitar) (XVI)

Thomm Jutz (guitars, bass, synthesizer) (XVI, XVII)
Anthony Lamarchina (cello) (X)
Pat McInerney (drums, percussion) (X, XIV, XVI)
Ken Moore (piano) (X)
Marianne Osiel (oboe) (X)
Gwil Owen (guitar) (XVI)
David Pomeroy (bass) (X)
Deanie Richardson (mandolin, fiddle) (X, XIV, XVI)
Dave Roe (bass) (XVIII)
Forrest Rose (bass) (X)
Steve Runkle (vocals) (X)
Mark "Sergio" Webb (guitars) (XVII)
Danita Wilson (vocals) (XIV)
Craig Wright (drums, percussion) (XVIII)
Cindy Wyatt (harp) (X)

David Olney Recordings:

I. Eye Of The Storm (Philo/Rounder Records 1986, CD)
1. Saturday Night and Sunday Morning
2. I Keep My Fingers Crossed
3. Theresa Maria
4. A Dangerous Man
5. If It Wasn't for the Wind
6. Steal My Thunder
7. Who Knows Better Than I
8. Titanic
9. Queen Anne's Lace
10. My Baby's Gone
11. Eye of the Storm
12. Ain't It That Way

Comments: After this one, Olney hooked up with the **Nashville Jug Band** for an album in 1988 before jumping back into solo work.

II. Deeper Well (Philo/Rounder Records 1989, CD)
1. Deeper Well
2. Women Across the River
3. Brand New Skin
4. Jerusalem Tomorrow
5. If Love Was Illegal
6. King of Soul
7. Poor Clothing
8. If My Eyes Were Blind
9. Way I Am
10. Illegal Cargo
11. Lonesome Waltz of the Wind
12. You Are Here

III. Roses (Philo/Rounder Records 1991, CD)
1. Lee's Highway/Bamaloo
2. Luckiest Man
3. Lean and Hungry Years
4. Last Fair Deal

Dave Olney, 1975

5. Millionaire
6. Rex's Blues
7. Rose Tattoo
8. Love's Been Linked to the Blues
9. That's Why She's With Me
10. Don't Keep It a Secret
11. Roses

IV. Top to Bottom (Appaloosa 1991, import CD)
1. Jama Ball
2. Big Cadillac
3. You Can Count On Me
4. That's My Story
5. Nothing Matters But You
6. Hey Now
7. Downtown
8. Alone
9. Frankie and Johnny
10. Smoke on Ice
11. Evil Twin
12. Where Do the Good Times Go

V. Border Crossing (Corazong 1992, CD)
1. Running From Love
2. Blue Days, Black Nights
3. Message to Garcia
4. Little Bit of Poison
5. Wait Here for the Cops
6. Two Kinds of Love
7. Sister Angelina
8. Theresa Maria
9. Latin Lover
10. I Love My Wife Blues
11. What Would I Do Without Your Love?
12. Barcelona
13. Old John

DAVID OLNEY

VI. Ache of Longing (Corazong Records 1994, CD)
1. Soldier of Misfortune
2. Such a Simple Thing
3. Only You
4. Ache of Longing
5. Crazy Fool
6. Farewell Sedalia
7. Love Can Be That Way
8. Lucky Star and Mr. Moon
9. Lelia
10. The Man on the Flying Trapeze
11. Just a Little Rain
12. Barrymore Remembers

VII. Live In Holland (SCR Productions 1994, CD)
1. Poor Clothing
2. A Little Bit of Poison
3. Rex's Blues
4. Big Cadillac
5. That's Why She's With Me
6. Jerusalem Tomorrow
7. Walk Downtown
9. What Would I Do Without Your Love
10. My Family Owns This Town
11. Ache of Longing
12. Rose Tattoo
13. Hymn of Brays
14. Millionaire
15. Vincent's Blues

Comments: Olney alone with his acoustic guitar in an intimate live setting, which places an emphasis on the lyrics of his story-songs as well as Olney's world-weary cracked-glass vocals.

VIII. High, Wide and Lonesome (Philo/Rounder Records 1995, CD)
1. Walk Downtown
2. You Gotta Hold On Me
3. Caterpillar
4. Another Place, Another Time
5. My Family Owns This Town
6. Brays
7. Raw Bone
8. Ruby Ann
9. In Your Eyes
10. Flood of '93
11. Blue Grey Eyes
12. Vincent's Blues

IX. Real Lies (Philo/Rounder Records 1997, CD)
1. House Rules
2. Barrymore Remembers
3. Camille
4. Robert Ford & Jesse James
5. I'll Fall in Love Again
6. Basketball
7. Baseball
8. Leaf in the Wind
9. Thirty Coins of Gold
10. Death, True Love, Lonesome Blues and Me
11. Sunset on Sunset Boulevard
12. Border Town
13. It Won't Be Me No More

X. Through A Glass Darkly (Philo/Rounder Records 1999, CD)
1. 1917
2. Dillinger
3. Avery County
4. J.T.'s Escape
5. Little Bit of Poison
6. The Suicide Kid
7. Snowin' on Raton
8. C'mon Through Carolina
9. Ice Cold Water
10. Race Track Blues
11. The Colorado Kid
12. That's All I Need to Know
13. Lilly of the Valley
14. Lay Down Your Kingdom
15. Barabbas
16. Dogwoods

XI. Ghosts in the Wind: Live At La Casa (Barbed Wire Records 1999, CD)
1. Two Kinds of Love
2. Sister Angelina
3. Luckiest Man
4. Shaken But Not Stirred

5. Running From Love
6. If It Wasn't for the Wind
7. Jerusalem Tomorrrow
8. Message to Garcia/Soldier of Misfortune
9. That's My Story
10. If My Eyes Were Blind
11. Barrymore Remembers
12. Love's Been Linked to the Blues
13. Evil Twin
14. Charleston Knife/Who Do You Love?
15. Contender

Comments: Live album featuring performances from 1992, 1993 and 1994, recorded during the La Casa Music Series in Bloomfield Hills, Michigan.

XII. Omar's Blues (Dead Reckoning 2000, CD)
1. Omar's Blues #1
2. If It Wasn't for the Wind
3. Delta Blue
4. My Wild Youth
5. Solid Gone
6. Omar's Blues #2
7. If I'd Have Known I Couldn't Do It
8. Bathsheba Blues
9. Absalom
10. Omar's Blues #3
11. Fast Eddie
12. Lazlo
13. Paris Incident
14. The Hat and the Cane

David Olney

Comments: Pretty cool concept album inspired by *The Rubaiyat of Omar Khayyam*, which was written in the middle ages. Olney's Omar's Blues offers a trilogy of song cycles set in various time periods: Biblical times, 1950s-era New England, Paris, the Mississippi Delta, and early Hollywood.

XIII. Women Across the River: Live (Strictly Country Records 2002, CD)
1. Saturday Night and Sunday Morning
2. Roses
3. Bathsheba Blues
4. Women Across the River
5. Deeper Well
6. If It Wasn't for the Wind
7. If Love Was Illegal
8. Titanic
9. I'll Fall in Love Again
10. Message to Garcia/Soldier of Fortune
11. 1917
12. If I'd Have Known I Couldn't Do It
13. Barrymore Remembers
14. Solid Gone

XIV. The Wheel (Loudhouse Records 2003, CD)
1. Wheels
2. Big Cadillac
3. Voices On The Water
4. Chained And Bound To The Wheel
5. Stars
6. Now And Forever
7. God Shaped Hole
8. Revolution
9. Now I Start
10. Stonewall
11. Boss Don't Shoot No Dice
12. Precious Time, Precious Love
13. The Girl I Love
14. All The Love In The World
15. Round

XV. Illegal Cargo (Strictly Country Records 2004, CD)
1. 30 Coins of Gold
2. Running from Love
3. Illegal Cargo
4. Voices on the Water

DAVID OLNEY

5. If My Eyes Were Blind
6. Robert Ford and Jesse James
7. Lean and Hungry Years
8. All of the Love
9. Contender
10. Lazlo
11. Camille
12. Dillinger
13. God Shaped Hole
14. Snowin' on Raton

Comments: Collection of live performances from Europe.

XVI. Migration (Loudhouse Records 2005, CD)
1. The Song
2. Speak Memory
3. Lenora
4. No One Knows What Love Is
5. My Lovely Assistant
6. Light From Carolina
7. All The Same To Me
8. Ace Of Spade Blues
9. Oh Lord
10. Birds
11. Upside Down

Another View: "David tells marvelous stories, with characters who cling to the hope of enduring love…saints and charlatans, gypsies and thieves, the ordinary and extraordinary. Here even the birds raising their voices in song reach for something unattainable, but David knows that the reaching is everything." – Emmylou Harris

XVII. Lenora (Strictly Country Records 2006, CD)
1. Speak Memory
2. Birds
3. My Lovely Assistant
4. I Washed My Hands in Muddy Water
5. The Song
6. No One Knows What Love Is
7. Two Kinds of Love
8. Jerusalem Tomorrow
9. Lenora
10. Chained and Bound to the Wheel
11. Vincent's Blues
12. Upside Down/Gonna Wait Here for the Cops
13. Revolution

Comments: Recorded live in Holland during Olney's 2004 and 2005 tours, the singer/songwriter accompanied by guitarists Thomm Jutz ('04) and Mark Sergio Webb ('05).

XVIII. One Tough Town (Red Parlor 2007, CD)
1. Whistle Blow
2. Sweet Poison
3. Who's The Dummy Now?
4. Little Mustang
5. No Lies
6. Oh Yeah (Dead Man's Shoes)
7. Snake Song
8. Panama City
9. Sweet Potato
10. See How The Mighty Have Fallen
11. One Tough Town
12. Postcard From Mexico
13. Rainbow's End

XIX. Live At Norm's River Roadhouse, Volume 1 (Deadbeet Records 2008, CD)
1. Intro/Whistle Blow
2. Upside Down
3. Wait Here For The Cops
4. Sweet Poison
5. Panama City
6. Postcard From Mexico
7. Intro of Band
8. Titanic
9. Oh Yeah
10. One Tough Town
11. Ukelele Waltz
12. Who's The Dummy Now?
13. Sunset On Sunset Boulevard
14. Snake Song
15. Kubla Khan
16. Lee's Highway
17. The Highway's Coming

David Olney, continued on page 376...

Dave Olney's entry into music was much like that of many a young man and woman during the 1960s. "It was something that I could do," he says, "and there weren't a whole lot of those things. The times were pretty weird, the wild '60s, and that was the thing that I could count on." Born in Rhode Island, Olney began his career playing guitar, eventually moving to North Carolina to attend college.

"I got into music really serious when I was in North Carolina," he remembers, "and a friend of mine, Bland Simpson, went up to New York and got some interest up there, so he called me up to play in the band. We did a record, but nothing much happened, so we were back in North Carolina." That band, named Simpson, would record a single album with Rick Derringer and Olney on guitars, Bland Simpson on piano, and Eric Weissberg on fiddle.

"I went down to Atlanta to be in the Atlanta Children's Theater," says Olney. "I was writing songs, and at some point it seemed the time to make a move, musically, and Nashville was the closest place. I knew a couple of people, so I had a couch to crash on. That was in 1973." Olney arrived in the Music City at the tail end of the "cosmic cowboy" phase of outlaw country music. "Waylon Jennings was hitting big, so it was still going on. I always thought that the gas crunch of '73, the first gas crisis, kind of shut things down. I don't think the business felt like it could take chances on the crazy people. You couldn't waste a lot of money on somebody that was interesting, which was too bad."

Arriving In Nashville

The local music scene had barely begun when Olney re-located to Nashville. "I'm not sure I could describe the 'big scene'," says Olney, "because I was just trying to make my way. I found this place, Bishop's Pub, which is now the Tin Angel, at 34th and West End…they had an open stage where you could go in and play and pass the hat. So I glommed onto that, and built my days around going over there and playing. I learned a lot about how to deal with an audience, and all that kind of stuff. Mostly, if I wrote a song, I had a place to go and put it out in public and see if it worked."

"As far as rock 'n' roll," Olney remembers, "I was bussing tables over at a place called Jock's, later on Mario's, and it was Muhlenbrinks for a while…every now and then, John Hiatt had a rock 'n' roll band, and he'd play there, and somewhere around that time there was a band called Peace & Quiet, and they played sort of a soft rock kind of thing. Other than that, there just wasn't any rock 'n' roll, basically. It was kind of an era where writing the songs was the big thing, not so much the performance of them."

"There were others…Marshall Chapman was playing at Steak & Ale or something like that, but I was unaware of it at the

time," he says, "I just knew my little corner that I worked." By 1977, Olney had put together his first band. "I thought it was going to be a country band," he says, "it was odd, because I couldn't rehearse with the band all together in one room. It turned out that I could only rehearse with them separately, so I didn't know what it was going to sound like until we played our first gig, which was out at Rock Harbour [in West Nashville]."

Dave Olney & the X-Rays

"Bobby Bradford, of the Bobby Bradford Blues Band…they had a really good following, and the band was more important than people give them credit for…it was his club, and we played out there. They had a dog that was wandering around, and I remember getting ready to play the first song, and I stepped on some dog shit that was on the stage. I didn't know, and we started to play and I was smelling this outrageous smell…I just said 'stop, this is not the way I'm getting this thing off the ground'…so we cleaned it up and started again. We had a fiddle player in the band, and I started jumping around and rockin' out, so the fiddle player quit immediately and it was a rock 'n' roll band from then on."

Thus was born Dave Olney & the X Rays, one of the great unsung bands of the early Nashville rock scene. "There weren't but three or four people in the audience," he remembers, "there really wasn't a scene or anything." The band performed frequently around town, though, gradually evolving as members came and went. "Jimbo Walsh was playing drums," says Olney, "Steve Runkel was playing bass…Steve was playing in a band called the Contenders, but I guess that they had already bitten the dust. Granny

INTERVIEW: DAVID OLNEY

Grantham also played bass during that period, they were both kind of in and out, but Walsh played drums, and Steve Clark played guitar. Somewhere down the line we got Kenny Moore to come up from North Carolina to play keyboards."

"Rounder had expressed some interest in me as a folk artist," says Olney. "They heard the band and thought that it was interesting, so they were in the background, early on. There was an exodus from the band; Steve Clark left, Jimbo left, the band ended up being Tommy Goldsmith on guitar, John Owen on bass, Rick Rowell on drums, Kenny Moore on keyboards, and me...that was the band that ended up getting the Rounder Record deal."

The Nashville Jug Band

Another project that Olney got involved with during the 1980s was the Nashville Jug Band. "Ed Dye would put these shows on, I believe that he did them at Springwater...which was developing into the center of the universe, which is kind of peculiar, but there you go...and Ed was bartending there. He'd but together these bluegrass throw-together things with whoever was in town, and there were these incredible people...there was Sam Bush (of New Grass Revival), Roy Huskey, Jr., just some really good players. Pat McLaughlin was in there, and I just kind of wheedled my way in, playing second-rate harmonica."

Although Olney's sound is generally characterized as folk music, there's a lot more happening there, with elements of rock, country, even blues influence seeping in around the edges. The title track of Olney's **One Tough Town** album, for instance, sounds like a scratchy 78rpm antique. "It was pretty much a conscious effort to get a sound from back in the '20s," says Olney. "To me, the '20s and '30s was pretty much a high water mark for American music. Radio got started in the '20s, and popular music was jazz...it's hard to imagine that now. It hadn't even broken down into categories, really...I'm not even sure that jazz musicians called themselves jazz musicians. What's country now, those people were doing whatever songs were being whistled on the street, and there was a lot more cross-germination."

Olney's Influences

One of the things that makes Olney's songwriting as rich and smart as it is are the myriad of influences he incorporates into his work. "As far as musicians, Jimmy Reed...my older brother would bring these records home of people I'd never heard of, and I remember Jimmy Reed struck me," he says. "From folk music, it seems almost embarrassing now to say Peter, Paul and Mary, and Joan Baez was very good. Dylan kind of re-invented the whole thing. Beyond all that, for my generation, rock 'n' roll was background music for our lives.

Ray Charles, I remember how much he moved me, and Roy Orbison."

Olney's influences go beyond musicians, however. "As for non-musicians, I remember reading a poem by Robert Browning, "My Last Dutchess," which was this dramatic monologue of this guy talking about his ex-wife, basically, and he is giving you information that he doesn't know he's giving you. You realize that he drove her to kill herself, and that really intrigued me, that you could create this character in a song and tell a story."

Townes Van Zandt

Olney's storytelling style was heavily influenced by the great Texas songwriter Townes Van Zandt. "I was living in Atlanta in '72, and I got very little work playing," he remembers. "I stumbled onto this job, playing in Athens, Georgia this one night opening for this guy, Townes Van Zandt, who I didn't know anything about. I'd written a few songs, maybe four or five at that time, but I they were efforts to sound like somebody else, basically. I didn't have a direction, and then I hear those songs that night, and it was mind-boggling to me. Everybody's heard "Pancho & Lefty" enough that it's hard to remember how amazing it was to hear that song the first time. Really, the only other model was Bob Dylan, and you weren't going to 'out Bob Dylan' Bob Dylan."

"At the time, Townes' lyrics were very abstract, it really wasn't the way it was going, and the images were completely understandable."Pancho & Lefty," you can understand the song, yet the story is just so weird that I said 'OK, that's the way to go.' He had a huge influence on my writing," says Olney. "I didn't get to know him until after I moved to Nashville, and then I went down to play in Houston and he was down there. I hung around for a week, and he was just so crazy I thought 'I can't keep up with this guy.' I consciously didn't get to know him because I couldn't physically keep up with him, and the people around him, he was the center of their world. I wanted to keep my options open. It wasn't until 1976, when he came to town and I got to know him and he was a good, funny guy whose writing I just really admired. I never knew him as well as Guy Clark or Steve Earle; I'd say that our friendship was based on music."

One Tough Town

One Tough Town, Olney's latest album, mines new territory for the artist. "I'm very proud of the other CDs that I've done," he says, "I had a crew of people and a place that I've always used, and it came around, it was time to record, but I couldn't motivate myself to do it...I just wasn't all that excited about it. I knew Jack Irwin a little bit, I knew he had a studio, and I went and did some demos and said 'this feels good.' So I went to him and told him that I had an idea of using different instrumentation, and then I asked 'do you have people to do this?' He said 'yes,' and the only rule that I had was that I didn't want to know who they were. You're not likely to tell somebody who is a pretty good friend, 'can you play differently?' I had it in mind that I wanted a kind of '20s and '30s sound."

The resulting album offers material that sounds dated, and other stuff that sounds like cutting edge rock. "When stuff is done well, it always sounds contemporary," says Olney. "When you do it well, you want to hang it on your wall." **One Tough Town** also represents a change in Olney's songwriting style. "My process has changed a lot…I used to write everything myself, now I do a lot of co-writing, especially with John Hadley. I just kind of noodle around on the guitar, get some kind of lick going, or some lyrical phrase will pop into my head and I'll just not start writing the song, I'll wait until John gets around and say 'here, I have this.' Basically, somewhere early in writing the song I'll say, 'this is something I can do,' and at that point I'll steer it in a certain direction."

"Other songs, they just come out whatever way they're going to come out. As far as words and music, I try not to write too many words down because I'll over-write. Once you have a melody, you have some restrictions, form-wise, it acts as an editor." Olney's choice of Nashville as a home base had its effect on his songwriting as well. "I always thought that the fact that I came to Nashville, which was based strictly on that it was the closest place to come to…the other choices were New York or L.A. I'm glad I came to Nashville because it's a pretty conservative view of songwriting and I think that it's worked well for me. I'm going to think of things that are pretty outside, and it's good to have something that keeps it from getting too off the charts."

While he hasn't become rich, or even famous, Dave Olney is well-respected in the industry and has won his share of critical acclaim. It seems that he's long since accepted his role as artist. "I used to be pissed-off about not being more famous," Olney says of his career. "But I got to see the world in an intimate kind of way, and that's OK."

DAVE OLNEY & THE X-RAYS - ON COMMAND

DAVE OLNEY & THE X-RAYS

Band Members:
Dave Olney (vocals, guitars) (I-II)
Tommy Goldsmith (guitar, vocals) (I)
Granny Grantham (bass) (II)
Kenny Greenberg (guitars) (II)
Ken Moore (keyboards) (I)
John Owen (bass) (I)
Rick Rowell (drums, vocals) (I, II)

Other Musicians:
Steve Gibson (guitar) (I)
Bobby Ogdin (keyboards) (I)

Dave Olney & the X-Rays Recordings:

I. Contender (Rounder Records 1981, LP)
Side One
1. Yes Indeed
2. Oh My Love
3. Will To Survive
4. Love And Money
5. Wait Here For The Cops

Side Two
1. Contender
2. Destiny
3. Steal My Thunder
4. When I Get Over You
5. She Bound To Go

Comments: Before he became Nashville's folk-rock poet

laureate, Olney fronted popular local rockers the X-Rays. Olney & the X-Rays played at Phrank 'n' Steins and other popular dives circa 1979-82, the band important rock pioneers on a barely-sentient local scene (see interview ➔).

II. Customized (Boulevard Records 1984, LP)
Side One
1. That's When You're Rockin'
2. If My Eyes Were Blind
3. Mayday
4. Monkey Chant

Side Two
1. Going Going Gone
2. Customized
3. Running From Love
4. Thirty Coins Of Gold

ON COMMAND

Band Members:
Mike Raber (vocals) (I)
Dallas Thomas (guitars) (I)
Jay Phillips (guitars) (I)
Soda (bass) (I)
Adrian Leonard (drums) (I)

On Command Recordings:

I. On Command (Set International 2004, CD)
1. A Rare Treat
2. Party Hot
3. Burned Alive & Punched in the Face
4. Eat Shit & Die, Motherfucker
5. Forced Entry
6. Fuck with Disdain
7. Expect a World of Shit
8. March of Willy T.
9. …and the Devil Stands at Attention
10. I Like Chocolate

Comments: On Command pull out all the stops to convince the listener that they have 'tude, and plenty of it to spare. Gratuitous use of four-letter words aside (really, didn't *fuck* and *shit* lose their shock value for boho-rockers back when Lenny Bruce was using them in his act?), On Command isn't a half-bad punk band. On the surface, this is standard hardcore-tinged punk fare, with angry vocals, clashing guitars and explosive rhythms. Thomas and Phillips are a notch above your typical three-chord bashers, however, a real chemistry between the two creating a blitzkrieg of sonic waves and crackling energy. Raber delivers your typical HC vox, more bark than bite, but the six-string twins, along with bassist "Soda" and drummer Leonard are creating some fairly sophisticated sounds beneath the punk rock fury.

ORDER OF SILENCE

Band Members:
Graham Perry (vocals, keyboards, guitars)
Marty Crutchfield (guitar, drums)
Brad Cole (guitar)
Ernie Aguilar (guitars, keysboards, bass)
Gavin Johnson (bass, guitar)
Eric Hubner (bass)
Rolff Zweip (drums)
Jay Jones (drums)

Comments: Primarily a vehicle for the songwriting skills of Graham Perry, former **Chapel of Roses** and **Permanent Wave**, the third incarnation of the band contributed the song "Lemme Get You Down" to the NEA's *What You Haven't Heard...* CD. See Perry's history of the band below for the complete story...

ORDER OF SILENCE HISTORY

1977
Graham Perry meets Martin Crutchfield at the creek at the end of Rolling Fork Dr. in West Nashville. Graham is fishing for crawdads and Martin is riding motorcycles with two notorious neighborhood bad kids. Graham gets nervous and calmly asks, "does anyone know what time it is?" Martin looks at his arm and says, "it's two hairs past a horse's ass." Graham says, "I guess it's time for me to leave then," and walks away.

1981
Graham Perry joins unnamed band at Battle Ground Academy as lead singer. Martin Crutchfield played drums in a rival band that included Warner Hodges, future lead guitar player for Jason and the Nashville Scorchers.

1982
Graham Perry (lead vocal, elec. guitar) joins Permanent Wave. Other members included Chris Kelley (drums), Tommy Oliphant (bass)

1985
Graham Perry joins Chapel of Roses as cellist. Chapel of Roses lineup included Chris Kelley (lead vocal), "Preach" (bass – I never knew his real name), a guy named Collin (drums), and someone else whom I don't recall. I think this band was the last band to play Cantrell's before it closed but I'm not sure. Off hand, I can't remember when Cantrell's closed. Whenever it was, the band I was in was the last band that played there.

Graham Perry (lead vocal and electric guitar) leaves Chapel of Roses and forms Order of Silence based on the musical style of the latter. This was the first of 3 incarnations of Order of Silence. The remaining lineup included Gavin Johnson (bass, guitar), Brad Cole (lead guitar), Rolff Zweip (drums), and Ernie Aguilar (guitars, keys and bass). Johnson was the former bassist for Mary K and the Cosmetics, Zweip ran a cartage company in Nashville, and Aguilar went on to play bass for Sammy Kershaw.

1986
Graham Perry (lead vocal, electric guitar) forms second incarnation of Order of Silence after first disintegrates. New members included Jay Jones (drums), formerly of Chip and the Chiltons, Eric Hubner (bass), and some guy named Sean (lead guitar). Hubner went on to form Rumble Circus with Jeff Cease (who was with the Black Crows) and later formed Thurn & Taxis. The incarnation of OOS won the Hillwood Battle of the Bands over rival Chip and the Chiltons and received a great deal of airplay on WRVU. This band opened for local icons like Will Rambeaux and the Delta Hurricanes. A "band drama event" ended this incarnation. Somewhere there is a video of a live performance of this incarnation.

ORDER OF SILENCE - GWIL OWEN

1987

Graham Perry (lead vocal, electric guitar) records "Lemme Get You Down" and submits it under the name Order of Silence to the NEA cd *Nashville: What You Haven't Heard*. Joins with Martin Crutchfield of the Delta Hurricanes to write and record new songs for a third incarnation of Order of Silence. The live band that played the NEA showcase for the cd included Perry (lead vocal, electric guitar) and Crutchfield (lead guitar) as the band core while the remaining members included that Collin guy from Chapel of Roses (drums) and Gavin Johnson from the 1st incarnation of OOS (bass). Martin and Graham begin recording and co-writing off and on through the 1980s and 90s.

The NEA showcase spawned several legendary stories. One involved Perry's ex-girlfriend who unexpectedly showed up to the show. After the girlfriend she was with asked Perry to play a song for his ex, he declared, "I'd like to play a song for my ex-girlfriend. It's called, *"Get Out of My Life!"* The band quickly broke into the song. Perry's ex proceeded to smash a bathroom mirror at the Cannery where the gig was held, beat up the 3 girls Graham was with, broke Autumn's manager's nose, and smashed a gumball machine as she was being carried out. A music exec told Martin, "Wow! You guys are like rock-n-roll stars. You got girls fighting over you and shit!"

1988

Graham Perry forms Greek Life Aquarium with Jo Horincewich (bass). Their home recorded album *Hell in Water* receives college radio airplay all over the U.S. Jo returns to New Jersey after only a few shows.

1989

Graham Perry releases a second Greek Life Aquarium single "Don't Eat The Cow!" gets a rave review by Robert K. Oerman and does well on its college radio release.

1991

Martin Crutchfield and Graham Perry form Liquid Gypsy, a recording project that lasts until 1994. Graham plays for another band called the Holidays during this time too. After personal tragedies, Perry moves to Atlanta with his recently acquired family.

Graham is now in a Memphis Americana band called Tucson Simpson which has released two records since 1999. Perry has released solo records including Hophead "Bad Daze" and Graham Perry "Perryphernalia." He has also recorded on other records including Martin Crutchfield's self-titled cd and Van Duren's *Open Secret*. – courtesy of Graham Perry

GWIL OWEN
Web: www.gwilowen.com

Band Members:
Gwil Owen (vocals, guitar) (A1, I-IV)

Other Musicians:
Jeff Black (vocals) (IV)
Brydget Carrillo (vocals) (III)
Tony Crow (keyboards, strings) (III, IV)
Bill Dwyer (guitar) (III)
Molly Felder (vocals) (IV)
Richard Ferreira (bass, keyboards) (IV)
Jeff Finlin (drums, percussion) (A1, III)
Paul Griffith (percussion) (IV)
Moose Harrell (guitar) (A1)
Steve Herrman (trumpet) (III)
Jim Hoke (saxophone, flute) (IV)
Brad Jones (keyboards) (III)
Will Kimbrough (guitar) (III, IV)
Bob Kommersith (bass) (A1)
Rick Lonow (drums) (IV)
"Southside" Johnny Lyon (harmonica) (III)
Devon Malone (cello) (IV)
Allison Moorer (vocals) (III)
Dave Olney (vocals) (IV)
Tammy Rogers (viola, violin) (III)
Rick Schell (drums, percussion, vocals) (III)
Paul Slivka (bass) (III)
Garry Tallent (bass) (III)
Dennis Taylor (saxophone) (III)
Joy Lynn White (vocals) (III)
Jason Williams (bass) (A1)

Gwill Owens Recordings:

<u>Singles</u>

A1. "Messed Up Thing" b/w "Tennessee Hi-way Blues" (Diesel Only Records 1991, 7" vinyl)

Comments: Former frontman for **the Thieves**, Gwil Owen released a handful of these 7" country-rock jukebox singles during the early-1990s for the Diesel Only label. A talented songwriter, Owen has recorded himself rather sporadically through the years, but he's done quite well as a wordsmith. A song that he co-wrote with Allison Moorer, used in the film *The Horse Whisperer*, earned an Academy Award nomination; a collaboration with Kevin Gordon was recorded by Keith Richards and Levon Helm. Owen has also had songs recorded by Toni Price, Irma Thomas, and Sonny Burgess, among many others.

<u>Albums</u>

I. Phoenix (self-produced tape, 1991)
1. Haunted House
2. Happy Endings
3. Memphis Hotel Room
4. '67 Chevy
5. The Hard Luck Serenade
6. Your Heart Is A Cadillac
7. Messed Up Thing
8. It Might Just Be Your Eyes
9. Haley's Comet
10. Stay

II. Last Man on the Moon (self-produced tape, 1993)
1. Coney Island Whitefish
2. The Kiss of Death
3. 98.6°
4. I'd Rather Be Lucky
5. The Last Man On the Moon
6. El Camino
7. No Ammunition
8. The Limitations of Love
9. Near-Sighted Angel
10. Texas Truck

III. Magnetic Heaven (Earnest Whitney Entertainment 1999, CD)
1. Tears Are My Business
2. Magnetic Heaven
3. Lonesome Wind
4. Hey
5. Eleanor
6. Something
7. Pull the Plug
8. Augusta

GWIL OWEN — Messed Up Thing b/w Tennessee Hi-way Blues

9. Sunflower
10. The Thief
11. Long Hard Road

Comments: Very cool, very strong album. I really like the wordplay on "Tears Are My Business" and the title track. "Something" is a great song, I like the vibe created by Tony Crow's wistful string arrangement. Altogether, a nice mix of lyrics, music, and performance.

IV. Gravy (Rambler Records 2008, CD)
1. Gravy
2. Mississippi Moonrise
3. Funky
4. One of These Lonely Days
5. Faith
6. Cadillac
7. Peace & Love
8. What I'm Puttin' Down
9. My Love For You
10. Reach Out
11. What I'm Puttin' Down (demo)

GWIL OWEN & THE THIEVES

Gwil Owens & the Thieves Recordings:

I. Gwil Owen & the Thieves (Bug Music demo cassette, no date)
1. My Silver Tongue
2. To Wish Upon A Star
3. Ask Any Mirror
4. Too Much

Comments: Don't know for sure if this demo tape of songs predated the band's lone album, or came after. See the main listing for **the Thieves**.

OWEN'S ASHES

Band Members:
Liam Lynch (vocals)
James Tench (guitars)
Michael Taylor (guitars)
Barton Haneberg (bass)
Ron Hiss (drums, percussion)

Comments: "Nashville's Owen's Ashes has been creating a buzz locally on the strength of their raucous rock & roll sound, which is best described as equal parts white light and sheer sonic overkill. Together, the five members of Owen's Ashes create a six-string driven rock & roll storm that is grungier than Seattle, more metallic than L.A. and rocks harder than the entire East Coast." – *Bone Music Magazine*, January 1994

OWSLEY
Web: www.owsleymusic.com

Band Members:
Will Owsley (vocals, guitar, bass, piano) (I, II)
Millard Powers (bass, mini-moog) (I, II)
Chris McHugh (drums, percussion) (I, II)
Jonathan Hamby (keyboards, synth) (I, II)

Other Musicians:
Tom Bukovac (guitar, bass) (II)
Spencer Campbell (bass, strings) (I)
John Catchings (cello) (I)
Gordon Kennedy (guitar, vocals) (II)
Phil Madeira (keyboards) (I)
John Painter (strings) (II)
Bob Parr (bass) (I)
Simon Petty (harmonica) (II)
Michael Rhodes (bass) (II)

Jimmie Lee Sloas (bass) (II)
Keith Thomas (strings) (II)

Owsley Recordings:

I. Owsley (Giant Records 1999, CD)
1. Oh No The Radio
2. I'm Alright
3. Coming Up Roses
4. Good Old Days
5. The Sky Is Falling
6. Sentimental Favorite
7. Zavelow House
8. Sonny Boy
9. The Homecoming Song
10. Uncle John's Farm
11. Class Clown

Comments: Multi-instrumental talent Will Owsley came to Nashville from Anniston, Alabama to pursue a career in music. Among the first gigs earned by the talented guitarist was backing up **Judson Spence**, touring with the singer and appearing in his MTV videos. Introduced to Millard Powers by before-the-fame Ben Folds, the two formed power-pop band the Semantics with drummer Zak Starkey, son of Ringo Starr.

When that band broke up, Owsley landed with Amy Grant as her touring guitarist (which he still does), and subsequently spent most of the 1990s playing behind folks like Grant and Shania Twain. In between tours and during downtime, Owsley pursued his own purebred pop vision, building a home studio and recording his self-titled debut album with a few friends over the course of four years.

Giant Records released the album in 1999, but instability at the label (it was finally absorbed by parent company Warner Music in 2001) as well as Giant's overall inability to break a new artist outside of the R&B/hip-hop world would bode ill for the talented young Mr. Owsley. He would later receive a Grammy™ nomination for his engineering work on his debut.

Another View: "Left to his own devices, Owsley prefers to paint lush pop-art pictures with an ELO-by-way-of-Fountains-of-Wayne brush, adding a few day-glo dollops of XTC ("Oh No the Radio") for good measure. Despite the occasional misstep into the pedestrian lane ("Good Old Days" sounds like watered-down Semisonic, and lines like "One day you'll be able to forget the sadness/Get into the gladness" are syrupy enough to clog an artery), he makes a promising, if not picture-perfect, leap."
– Jonathan Perry, *Boston Phoenix* (1999)

II. The Hard Way (Lakeview Entertainment 2004, CD)
1. Be With You
2. Rise

3. She's The One
4. Dude
5. Down
6. Matriarch
7. Undone
8. The Hard Way
9. Dirty Bird
10. Rainy Day People

Another View: "But a harder heart pulses beneath the gloss; where George Harrison's guitar arpeggios would yawn across the spectrum in languorous splendor, Owsley's slice like showers of tiny razors. The most obvious contemporary comparison is to another local hero, Ben Folds; but where Fold builds his songs on piano and irony, Owsley maintains innocence in his lyrics and sprinkles more varied sonic spices into the mix. Each is a pillar in the pantheon, one strengthened by shadow, the other bathed in a beckoning light." – Robert L. Doerschuck, *Nashville Scene* (2004)

OWSLEY
The Hard Way
(Lakeview Entertainment)

It's mighty hard for the pop-oriented rocker to make a living in Nashville – just ask Bill Lloyd, Will Kimbrough or Josh Rouse, pop aficionados all. That hasn't deterred Will Owsley from plying his trade in the "Music City," however. A better-than-average axeman in a city overflowing with six-string wizards, Owsley has managed to survive nicely on session work and tours with folks like Amy Grant and Shania Twain. In his heart, though, he's closer to Paul McCartney and Neil Finn than to Hank Williams and Merle Haggard. His critically acclaimed debut album, released by Giant in 1999, was recorded in Owsley's living room over the period of four years; it took the talented singer/songwriter about the same amount of time to deliver his sophomore effort, *The Hard Way*. Fans of the pop/rock aesthetic should be thrilled to rediscover this underrated talent, no matter how long the wait…

The Hard Way is unabashedly polished, carefully constructed songs complimented by lush instrumentation with just the slightest bit of chaos seeping in around the edges. Owsley's pop craftsmanship is akin to fellow travelers like Ben Folds or Ben Kweller, Beatlesque flourishes accompanied by influences from folks like Crowded House, Todd Rundgren and Paul McCartney's solo work. Songs like "Be With You" or "Down" are guitar-driven delights, sharply written and precisely performed with a harder edge than the piano pop of Folds or the folkish radio-rock of Sheryl Crow.

An accomplished tunesmith with an eye for detail, Owsley's skilled wordplay emboldens his observations on romance and relationships with authority. Owsley's artistic palette is a wide one – "Dude" sounds like an inspired cross between Oasis and Coldplay while "Rainy Day People" includes swirls of psychedelic guitar and trippy harmonies like Jellyfish. Wherever the music takes him, Owsley always manages to imprint familiar sonic territory with his own unique signature.

There's a lot to like about *The Hard Way*. If modern rock radio wasn't so obsessed with the same marketing schemes that plague pop culture as a whole these days, there would be room for artists like Will Owsley (and Josh Rouse, etc) to have their voices heard. Until that wonderful day when talent overshadows image, there's comfort to be had in knowing that true believers like Owsley continue to create beautiful music for a small, appreciative and loyal audience. – *Alt.Culture.Guide*, 2005

REMEMBERING WILL OWSLEY

Singer, songwriter, and underrated guitarist Will Owsley, whose few recordings were released under his last name, reportedly took his own life on Friday, April 30, 2010. Owsley was a long-time member of Contemporary Christian artist Amy Grant's band, lending his guitar talents to the singer's recordings and stage show for over sixteen years.

A truly skilled multi-instrumentalist, Owsley came to Nashville from Anniston, Alabama sometime during the 1980s to pursue a career in music. One of Owsley's first gigs was backing singer Judson Spence, touring as his guitarist and appearing in his MTV videos. Owsley was introduced to singer Millard Powers by mutual friend Ben Folds, and the pair formed the power-pop band the Semantics, with Folds playing drums on the band's early demos. Zak Starkey, son of Ringo Starr, would take over the drum stool and the trio recorded a single album, *Powerbill*, in 1993 for Geffen Records.

For reasons known only to the powers-that-be at Geffen, *Powerbill* was never released in the U.S. and the Semantics broke up in disappointment. CCM superstar Grant had gotten a hold of a promotional copy of the LP, however, and subsequently asked Owsley to join her band. Stranger still, the Semantics album would be released in Japan a few years later, where it would become a smash hit, moving over 20,000 copies and, once out-of-print, becoming a coveted collector's item in both Japan and the United States.

In between tours with Grant, Owsley pursued his own purebred pop vision, building a home studio and recording his self-titled debut album *Owsley* with a few friends over the course of four years. Giant Records released the album in 1999, but instability at the label, as well as Giant's overall inability to break a new artist outside of the R&B/hip-hop world, bode ill for the talented young Mr. Owsley. He would later receive a Grammy™ Award nomination for his engineering work on his debut. The album would also bring him to the attention of super-producer Mutt Lange, who would subsequently hire the guitarist to appear with his wife, country superstar Shania Twain, on a number of television appearances and high-profile live performances.

Undeterred by his ill experience with Giant Records, Owsley began recording his sophomore album, *The Hard Way*, shortly after the release of his debut. Released in 2004 by the independent Lakeview Entertainment label, *The Hard Way* won almost universal critical acclaim. Robert Doerschuck, writing in *The Nashville Scene*, said "the most obvious contemporary comparison is to another local hero, Ben Folds; but where Fold builds his songs on piano and irony, Owsley maintains innocence in his lyrics and sprinkles more varied sonic spices into the mix."

In the former *Alt.Culture.Guide* webzine, this writer said "*The Hard Way* is unabashedly polished; carefully constructed songs complimented by lush instrumentation with just the slightest bit of chaos seeping in around the edges. Owsley's pop craftsmanship is akin to fellow travelers like Ben Folds or Ben Kweller, Beatlesque flourishes accompanied by influences from folks like Crowded House, Todd Rundgren and Paul McCartney's solo work."

It is a measure of Owsley's instrumental talent that he was enlisted to play in the studio behind a diverse range of artists through the years, from Christian performers like Grant and Michael W. Smith, to country stars like Vince Gill and Rodney Crowell, to pop performers like the Jonas Brothers. Although he wasn't very well known by a mainstream audience, Owsley was a talented songwriter and musician, and his presence in popular music was certainly felt. William Owsley III leaves behind a wife and two children.
– *Blurt* magazine, 2010

PAPER DOLLS

Band Members:
Tiny Butler (lead guitar, vocals)
Donna Frost (rhythm guitar, vocals)
Turina Marler (bass, vocals)
Paula Montondo (drums)
Joanne Pompei (bass, vocals)

Comments: Nashville's first all-girl rock band (I think) included **Donna Frost** and Turina Davis, both of whom are playing with the reformed **Bunnies**.

Donna Frost writes: "We formed in 84...I had heard there was an all female band forming and at the time it was Paula and Sherry Keeling...who worked at Cat's...who was going to be the lead singer...but we changed direction on where we were going and Sherry was not in the band by the time we got it together to play shows. The BUNNIEs were ending, so I was looking for another band. We played a lot of shows in that two year period, to packed houses all over town...our very first show was opening for 10,000 Maniacs at Cantrell's...Tiny was hospitalized with spinal meningitis at time, and we played the show three piece...Warner Hodges guested with us on two songs. I still have the cassette tape!

We recorded some tracks at Treasure Isle for a spec deal with Tom Harding and Tom Gregory. I left the band in '85...there was another version after I'd left, so I'm not sure who those two members were."

PARADISE LOST

Band Members:
David Privett (vocals) (I)
Allan Phelps (guitars, vocals) (I)
Mark Seely (bass, keyboards) (I)
David Howard (acoustic drums) (I)

Paradise Lost Recordings:

I. Paradise Lost (MCA Records 1989, cassette)
Side One
1. Scheme Of Things
2. Shelter
3. Dark Horse
4. Light The Dark Sky
5. Someday
6. Dream Of Love

The Paper Dolls

Side Two
7. Ashes And Gold
8. Cities In The Night
9. On My Way Back Home
10. Riding Elevators
11. In The End

Comments: No, not the British doom-metal legends, Nashville's Paradise Lost were one of the great lost bands of the city's late 1980s hard rock scene. Privett bounced around a number of bands, and he had the charisma and pipes to go somewhere, but when they signed with MCA, they may as well have invited the Reaper to their next practice session...

PARAMORE

Band Members:
Hayley Williams (vocals) (I-II)
Josh Farro (guitar, vocals) (I-II)
Jeremy Davis (bass) (II)
Zac Farro (drums) (I-II)
Jason Bynum (guitar, vocals) (I)
John Hembree (bass) (I)

Paramore Recordings:

I. All We Know Is Falling (Fueled By Ramen 2005, CD)
1. All We Know
2. Pressure
3. Emergency
4. Brighter
5. Here We Go Again
6. Never Let This Go
7. Whoa
8. Conspiracy
9. Franklin
10. My Heart

II. Riot! (Fueled By Ramen 2007, CD)
1. For A Pessimist I'm Pretty Optimistic
2. That's What You Get
3. Hallelujah
4. Misery Business
5. When It Rains
6. Let The Flames Begin
7. Miracle
8. crushcrushcrush
9. We Are Broken
10. Fences
11. Born For This

Comments: While just about anybody who was betting on "Nashville's next big thing" post-2001 had the **Kings of Leon** to win and **Be Your Own Pet** to place, Paramore came running along the rail to make the race a three (now two)-

way. Fronted by the flaxen-haired Williams, and despite the "Paramore is a band" controversies of 2007/2008 the foursome remains a favorite of the teen Warped Tour crowd and, as of late 2009, with a new album on the horizon, may yet take the ribbon in a photo-finish (see review ➜).

PASSAFIST

Band Members:
Dave Perkins a/k/a "Waco Caruso" (guitar, vocals) (I)
Lynn Nichols a/k/a "Reno Caruso" (guitar, vocals) (I)
John Elliott (programming, vocals) (I)
Michael Saleem (percussion) (I)
Mustafa Abdul-Aleen (percussion) (I)

Passafist Recordings:

I. Passafist (Rex Music 1994, CD)
1. Emmanuel Chant
2. Glock
3. Christ of the Nuclear Age
4. Love-e900
5. Appliance Alliance
6. Street Fighting Men
7. The Dr. Is In

Comments: One of the most intriguing and entertaining obscurities of the Nashville rock underground features **Dave Perkins** and Lynn Nichols of **Chagall Guevara**, John Elliott of **Dessau**, Mustafa from **Afrikan Dreamland** and Michael Saleem (just read the review, OK? ➜).

PDQ PIZZA

Comments: Locally-owned pizza chain (hey Billy!) was also a haven for Nashville-area rockers. I trained at the store on Nolensville Road in 1987, working with Eric Shaw of **the Fur Trade** and Dennis Bottoms, who would sing with the Marshall Tucker Band for a while. I was assistant manager of the Stewart's Ferry store before moving to West End to help clean it up. As manager of the Green Hills and (returning to) the West End store, I had the pleasure of working with local musicians like Jimmy Johnson of **Strange Tongues**, Houston Greer of **Swing**, **David Meade**, Kevin Hornback and Brad Pemberton (now playing behind Ryan Adams with the Cardinals), among others.

As both a P.D.Q. General Manager and, later, Senior General Manager supervising two stores, I was known as a soft touch for free pizza by local musicians. I fed my buddy **Threk Michaels** on a regular basis, and coughed up pizza for Gus Palas more than once. Even out-of-town bands got in on the scam, and I remember giving a couple of free pies to the guys in California metal band Dr. Know, whose lead singer was TV kiddie star Brandon Cruz, who would grow up to imitate Jello Biafra in a facsimile of the Dead Kennedys.

PEACE CRY

Band Members:
Mike Phillips (vocals) (I)
Wendi Phillips (bass) (I)
Terry Newton (guitar) (I)
Bryan Whitton (drums) (I)

Peace Cry Recordings:

I. "Live" (self-produced cassette, 1990)
1. No Rest For The Redman
2. Naked Ground
3. Help Me
4. Open My Heart
5. War Room

Comments: Recorded live to two-track tape at House Of David, November 3, 1990. Produced and engineered by Eric Elliot and Tom Hitchcock. For a too-brief time, Peace Cry was an extremely popular band on Nashville's club circuit.

With a hard rock sound not dissimilar to Rage Against The Machine, frontman Mike Phillips would pace the stage like a cornered panther, shouting out songs while wife Wendi would play some of the meanest bass riffs you've ever heard. Newton was a pretty good guitarist and the band put on a dynamic live show, drawing 300-400 people to even a weekday show.

For a while, after Gus Palas had fled town, Mike and Wendi booked shows at the Cannery before finally merging their efforts with promoter Mark Willis of New Sound Atlanta. Mike also played a few shows with the **Intruder** guys before disappearing from the scene altogether. Mike was a great self-promoter, and hyped his band incessantly. With the right

PASSAFIST
Passafist
(R.E.X. Music)

Whether or not Passafist and their self-titled, seven-song EP end up becoming a full-time project or remain a mere footnote in the impressive musical careers of Dave Perkins and Lynn Nichols, it's a milestone in the history of the local scene. Perkins and Nichols are best-known for their work with one of the best bands to spring out of our scene, Chagall Guevara. For this effort, the pair – dubbing themselves the "Caruso" twins, in the best glimmering tradition – have rounded up a handful of the city's best nontraditional talent and put together a hard rocking disc that sounds like a bludgeon, yet cuts like a knife.

Dessau frontman John Elliott lends his distinctive and effective growling vocals to the disc, while Michael Saleem and Mustafa contribute their underrated talents as well. It's the Caruso twins, however – Waco and Reno – who steal the show, whether it's kicking out the jams with an inspired cover of the Stones' "Street Fighting Man," pounding out the wickedly pointed industrial drone of "Glock," or closing with the socio-political implications of "The Dr. Is In," with its *Dr. Strangelove* samples and jazzy, hypnotizing rhythms. It's an effort that would do any regional music scene proud and it deserves a wider audience. *– R.A.D!* Review & Discussion of Rock & Roll, 1994 break, and a sympathetic producer, I always felt that these guys could have been big, especially if they'd been able to hang on until the mid-1990s hard rock revival.

DAVE PERKINS

Band Members:
Dave Perkins (vocals, guitars) (I)
Richard Price (bass) (I)
Byron House (bass) (I)
Mel Watts (drums) (I)

Other Musicians:
Ashley Cleveland (vocals) (I)
John Elliott (drums) (I)
Paul Griffith (drums) (I)
T.J. Klay (harmonica) (I)
Craig Krampf (drums) (I)
Jimmy Nalls (guitar) (I)
Odessa Settles (vocals) (I)
Reece Wynans (keyboards) (I)

Dave Perkins Recordings:

I. Pistol City Holiness (Lugnut Records 2009, CD)
1. Break
2. Going Down
3. Cherryfish & Chicken

Paramore

4. Revival
5. Long Eleven Road
6. Bottles and Knives
7. Train at Night
8. Flown
9. Tiger Texas
10. Devil's Game
11. Preacher Blues
12. Mercy in the Morning

Comments: Dave Perkins was a member of the talented, beloved band **Chagall Guevara** and the brains behind industrial sound terrorists **Passafist**. A noted producer in the CCR world, Perkins also released a Christian album of his own once upon a time. With *Pistol City Holiness*, the gifted songwriter and guitarist rediscovered his blues mojo… (see interview and review ➜)

MARK PFAFF

Band Members:
Mark Pfaff (vocals, guitars, bass) (I)

Other Musicians:
Bill Brookhart (guitar) (I)
Mike "Rat" Connell (drums) (I)
Eric Dover (guitar, vocals) (I)
Walter Egan (guitar, vocals) (I)
Craig Headen (guitar) (I)
Chris James (keyboards, vocals) (I)
Brad Jones (bass, vocals) (I)
Will Kimbrough (keyboards) (I)
Richie Parks (guitar) (I)
Mike Purcell (guitars, bass, keyboards) (I)
Mike Webb (piano) (I)
Patrick Wilson (guitar) (I)
Warren Wolf (guitar) (I)
Kirk Yoquelet (drums) (I)

Mark Pfaff Recordings:

I. Grapes Of Pfaff (self-produced CD, no date given)
1. If You Love Me
2. Happy But Sick
3. Bless Me Father
4. Percy
5. Shot In The Head
6. Holly Would
7. Scared
8. Sit Down My Love
9. Just A Little Bit More
10. Too Bad
11. I Will Comfort You
12. Ollie Vee
13. Hello, Jimi

Comments: Produced by Pfaff and recorded at a number of Nashville-area studios, including Brad Jones' Alex The Great and the Castle in Franklin. Pfaff was a member of the beloved 1980s-era outfit **Will & the Bushmen** with **Will Kimbrough** and, later, of **Igmo** with Willis Bailey of **the Sluggers** and Nashville's favorite music retailer, Mike "Grimey" Grimes.

PHILLIP PAUL & PATROL

Band Members:
Philip Paul (vocals)
Michael Saint Leon (guitars)
John Snelling (keyboards)
C. J. Kowall (bass)
Bill Brewer (drummer)
Frank Geraude (bass)
Hoppie Vaughn (bass)
Paul Snyder (drums)

Comments: Phillip Paul & Patrol were a semi-popular Top 40 touring band during the early-to-mid 1980s, notable mostly as a valuable training ground for Saint-Leon, Kowall and Snyder, who would go on to later form popular local rockers **Vagrant Saints**. First, however, Paul & Patrol would merge with another Top 40 cover act, the Colby Sisters, and tour for a year as the **Home Town Heroes** to fulfill several contractual obligations.

THE PINK SPIDERS

Band Members:
Matt Friction (vocals, guitar) (I-III)
Jon Decious (bass) (I-III)
Bob Ferrari (drums) (I-III)

Other Musicians:
Raf Cevallos (keyboards, synth) (II)
Jonathan Morrell (cello) (II)

The Pink Spiders Recordings:

I. The Pink Spiders Are Taking Over! (Spat! Records 2004, 7" vinyl)

II. Hot Pink (CI Records 2004, CD)
1. Stereo Speakers
2. Teenage Graffiti
3. Knock Knock
4. Sham On
5. Going Steady
6. Hollywood Fix
7. Modern Swinger
8. Talk Hard
9. Chicago Overcoat
10. Little Razorblade
11. Soft Smoke

Peace Cry

THE PINK SPIDERS - PLACID FURY - THE PLANET ROCKERS

Comments: The Pink Spiders' first full-length album; a bonus track called "The Chase" is available on the Spat! Records LP version of the album, but not on the CI Records CD release. I love the seriously retro style of the CD cover, right down to the wear marks like it's an old vinyl record album. Too cool...

III. Teenage Graffiti (Suretone Records/Geffen Records 2006, CD)
1. Soft Smoke
2. Saturday Nite Riot
3. Modern Swinger
4. Hollywood Fix
5. Little Razorblade
6. Back To The Middle
7. Nobody Baby
8. Hey Jane
9. Still Three Shy
10. Adalae
11. Easy Way Out
12. Pretend That This Is Fiction

Comments: Depending on your perspective, the major label signings of the Pink Spiders and the **Kings of Leon** was either the best thing or the worst thing to happen to a still fragile Nashville rock scene. The hype heaped on these two bands is amazing. The Spiders' sound is edgy pop-punk, captured here on their big league debut by producer Ric Ocasek, formerly of the Cars, who knows a thing or two about both chart-topping new wavish pop and making the little girls swoon (hell, stringbean *married* a supermodel!).

From this curmudgeon's perspective, though, the early 2000s major label feeding frenzy in Nashville will lead to nothing but tears and will set what is left of the "local scene" back a decade. Back when **Jason & the Scorchers** and **Royal Court Of China** were signed, most local rockers looked upon it as inevitable (in the case of the Scorchers) or an aberration (RCOC). Few local musicians back in the day started a band to get signed to a deal; they did it to make music. The current crop of local bands *expects* to get a label deal and have been brainwashed into believing that it's their birthright by their managers, their lawyers, and the labels. As such, there is more of a "me first" mentality among many Nashville bands these days...

Late note, mid-2009: dropped from their label deal and with two-thirds of the band quitting in disgust, Matt Friction has regrouped the Pink Spiders with new members and is taking another stab at success. Given their harmless radio-ready sound and teenage-girl appeal, I figured that they would have gotten farther than they did the first time around, but instead they've become just another Music City major label casualty, which kind of reinforces the above argument, doesn't it?

PLACID FURY

Band Members:
Frank Harwell (vocals, guitars)
Richie Owens (bass, vocals)
Johnny Lauffer (keyboards, vocals)
Al Casey (drums)

Comments: Placed two songs on the *Homegrown* compilation album put out by Rock 106 in the early ages of the local scene, circa 1980. Harwell would go on to form **Radio One** and Owens would be an integral member of several bands, most notably **the Dayts** and **the Movement**.

THE PLANET ROCKERS

Band Members:
Sonny George (vocals, guitar) (I-VI)
Eddie Angel (guitar) (I-VI)
Mark W. Winchester (bass) (I-IV, VI)

The Planet Rockers, continued on page 395...

DAVE PERKINS
Pistol City Holiness
(self-produced)

Singer, songwriter, and guitarist Dave Perkins is, perhaps, best known as one of the creative forces behind the early-1990s rock band Chagall Guevara. Some may remember him as one of the architects responsible for mid-1990s industrial alt-rock terrorists Passafist, whereas others may know him as the producer behind such successful CCR bands as the Newsboys. Whether he's playing guitar behind Jerry Jeff Walker or singing with Amy Grant, Perkins' talent has always risen to the top.

One of Perkins' greatest loves has always been the blues, however, and with the release of Pistol City Holiness the artist rediscovers the vibrancy, electricity, and excitement that got him into music in the first place. Influenced and inspired by blues greats like Muddy Waters and Howlin' Wolf, and blues-rockers like Cream and Peter Green's Fleetwood Mac, Perkins has delivered in *Pistol City Holiness* a stunning collection of ambitious blues-rock tunes that was almost a decade in the making.

Pistol City Holiness opens with a squawk and a holler, the muddy Delta grit oozing from Dave Perkins' serpentine fretwork, his vocals gruff and supple and soulful all at once. Although the song has inherited the spirit of a hundred juke-joint jams, its underlying funky swagger, metal-edged guitar, and contemporary poor man's lyrics clearly stamp it as a fine example of 21st century electric blues, the song swinging wilder and harder than a blacksmith's hammer.

The album's lone cover, Don Nix's classic Memphis blues standard "Goin' Down," is provided a tune-up under the hood and a fresh coat of paint up top. With roaring, whiskey-soaked vocals driven by Perkins' brutal six-string assault, T.J. Klay's rampaging harpwork, and a fine bit of nearly-hidden piano-pounding courtesy of former Double Trouble keyboardist Reece Wynans, Perkins and his manic mechanics hot rod "Goin' Down" from its turbocharged, flat-track origins into some sort of interstellar, space-ace speed machine.

Perkins gets down-and-dirty with the powerful "Long Eleven Road," the song itself a showcase for Klay's tortured harpwork. With a wiry guitar riff that chases its tale in circles, Perkins' best black cat moan vocals, and Klay's timely blasts of soul, the song is a hard luck tale of a factory ghost town where little is left but sin and degradation. With a true Delta vibe that reminds of Son House's most apocalyptic visions, "Long Eleven Road" is a potent modern American fable of hopelessness and misfortune.

If "Long Eleven Road" is the story of hard luck men and long suffering women facing another brutal work week, "Bottles and Knives" is a rollicking and curious mix of Chicago and New Orleans blues music that signals the arrival of the weekend. With the entire band playing helter-skelter, Wynan's flailing ivories are matched by Perkins' joyful, ramshackle guitar solos.

Perkins' humorous lyrics are pure genius – "bottles and knives flyin' all around this place, we're gonna leave here darlin' before I lose my pretty face" – the song's protagonist claims that his girl ain't happy goin' out on Saturday night unless he gets into a fight. It's 1930s blues jukin' reality set to music, delivered with reckless abandon (and highly-amped instruments).

Blues guitarist Jimmy Nalls sits in for "Devil's Game," the former Sea Level fretburner adding some tasty acoustic notes behind Perkins' greasy slide guitar runs. The song's languid pace is deceptively framed by an underlying rhythm that moves at the speed of kudzu growing, blasts of ice-cold sax complimenting the red-hot notes of Klay's harmonica and Perkins' flame-thrower guitar. Lyrically, the song is a Southern Gothic dirge of sore temptation and the wages of sin, punishment meted out in an aching limbo that again evokes the blessed ghost of the mighty Son House.

Perkins' "Preacher Blues" is a blistering, raw blues-rock rave-up with noisy, buzzing rhythms, blustery vocals, and whipsmart lyrics that reference Robert Johnson and his fabled hellhounds. The song is probably also the best showcase on *Pistol City Holiness* for Perkins' phenomenal six-string skills, the two-and-a-half-minute rocker virtually humming and crackling with the electricity generated by the guitarist's rattling leads.

The album closes with the explosive "Mercy in the Morning," a full-tilt, anarchic, stomp-and-stammer that throws dynamite in the water in the form of scorching guitarwork, darts of gospel-tinged and honky-tonk piano, powerful drumbeats, and shots of machine-gun harp notes that dive-bomb your ears like a horde of angry hornets.

Those of us that have followed Dave Perkins' lengthy career as sideman, band member, producer, and solo artist have never been surprised by the artist's immense talent, deep musical knowledge, and ability to perform well in nearly any musical genre. Nothing could prepare the listener for the nuclear-strength fall-out of *Pistol City Holiness* that cascades from your speakers. Perkins has created a masterpiece that fuses Mississippi Delta and Chicago blues tradition with a hard-rocking, guitar-driven blues-rock sound that fans haven't heard since Stevie Ray Vaughan burst onto the scene.

Although it's hard to find, go out and beg, borrow, or steal a copy of *Pistol City Holiness*… – *About.com Blues*

INTERVIEW: DAVE PERKINS

Nashville-based singer, songwriter and guitarist Dave Perkins is best-known as one of the talented musicians behind the critically-acclaimed 1990s alt-rock band Chagall Guevara. That band's lone 1991 album has become the stuff of legend and earned all those involved in its creation status as "cult favorites." Perkins had better than a decade of experience in the trenches under his belt before helping form Chagall Guevara, however, beginning his career as a blues musician and solo artist, and later making a living as a guitar-for-hire for such a diverse range of artists as outlaw country legends Guy Clark and Jerry Jeff Walker, bluegrass great Vassar Clements, and pop chart-topper Carole King.

After a prolonged hiatus, Perkins has returned to music and released his first solo effort in nearly 25 years with the blues-rock barn-burner *Pistol City Holiness*. The acclaimed album was a labor of love for Perkins, a fact that has struck a chord with every listener that has heard *Pistol City Holiness*. Recording the album was no snap judgment for Perkins, but rather an effort that began over a decade ago.

Dave Perkins' Pistol City Holiness

The creation of Perkins' *Pistol City Holiness* album actually began a decade ago. "What had happened at that time," says Perkins, "was that I was going through one of those times that you're sick of the music business. It was one of those things where I was tired of record companies figuring new and old recycled ways to not make good on a lot of hard work and good ideas. It was just frustration with the business, and I had decided that I was going to take a couple of courses at Vanderbilt Divinity School."

"I started doing that and I really got into it," he remembers. "I got into it so much that I thought, 'wow, this is going to be my life from now on, I'm going to do religious studies.' So the idea came that I was going to do one more music project, and I'm going to do the kind of music that I came in doing," says Perkins, referring to the album's blues-rock sound. "That was the genesis of that project. It sounds a little terminal, but it was actually a joyful place to get, to shake off years of industry-mindedness and say 'I'm going to make a record of the stuff that I love the best and I'm going to do it with the people I love making music with'," he remembers.

In the Studio

"We started the project, and we got a few tracks recorded," Perkins says, "and we had started to play live. Richard, the bass player at that point in time, was living with Lucinda Williams, and was in her band when Lucinda's record, *Car Wheels On A Gravel Road*, just began to take off. He said 'we're going to run out and do this tour for four weeks, then we'll be back'…well, he didn't come back for almost two years. That was kind of the end of the band mentality for that moment. I ended up finishing a Master's Degree and got offered a fellowship at Vanderbilt to come back and do a doctoral, a PHD."

Sadly, fate would intervene in the recording of the album. "I was diagnosed with multiple myeloma," Perkins remembers. "That started a hellacious year of surgeries, and treatments, and I'm grateful to be able to say that I'm now doing very well. In the course of going through all that stuff, I went back to music-making heart and soul, that's all I wanted to think about. Slinging that guitar and writing songs, reading about music, listening to music, and watching music DVDs, so for months while I was in treatment…I wasn't good for much else…my head got back into music-making."

Preparing for the Worst

"For a while there we were not sure what was going to happen for me," says Perkins, "so I began the process of getting my house in order, so to speak. Getting all of my music, all of my masters, consolidated and localized so that my wife would know where everything was. In the course of doing that, I re-discovered the tracks that became the basis for *Pistol City Holiness*. I got inspired when I heard those tracks, so I finished the recording on those, and then wrote the other half of the record and recorded that while I was undergoing treatment. Some days all I could work was literally 20 minutes a day, but I spent months working on it and finished it up."

Fortunately, fortune would end up smiling on the beleaguered bluesman. "Something wonderful happened," says Perkins, "my friend Shane Wilson, who is an excellent mix engineer here in Nashville, asked about the blues stuff that I had played him years ago, and I told him that, interestingly enough, I was working on it. He said that he wanted to mix it, so having him come alongside turned it into a community project, and it kept on going. Other people got in on the action and volunteered their musicianship, and art direction, and it became a really beautiful experience for me, and turned out, in a lot of ways, to be the most honest musical project that I've done to date because it taps into my musical DNA like nothing I've done."

Blues Born of Turmoil

"Like all good blues records, it was born out of some pretty intense turmoil," says Perkins of *Pistol City Holiness*. "I just let all of that existential angst; I gave it full vent through the music. I chose not to dwell on the particulars too much, but to let the darkness of the times drive the musical spirit in ways…you get these odd moments of freedom when you're living under a death sentence."

The songs on *Pistol City Holiness* unleash a storm of passion and emotion, each performance backed by a jagged blues-rock soundtrack. "Even though it's an electric record for the most part, I never really had a taste for the country blues," says Perkins, "although I was a tremendous blues consumer, it wasn't on that side of things. That's the stuff that I was listening to, and reading about, and soaking up on DVDs during that whole time of being sick."

"On a spiritual level, I was tapping into the religious blues of people like Son House and Fred McDowell, and even the more superstitious stuff like Robert Johnson…that kind of strange courtship of religion and spirituality." Much like those early bluesmen, Perkins' songs came out of a place of tension and conflict. "I see both of those forces and qualities in my life," he says, "living in tension with theologies and philosophies and worldviews…that stuff became devotional music to me. I found, for me, living in a place of tension, that's the holy place, I think, and that's kind of where the title of the record comes from."

Christian community

"I had a very brief stay there [in the CCR community]," says Perkins. "When I moved back to Nashville from having centered in New York City for a pretty good while…in my early days, there wasn't a contemporary religious music movement. I got my first breaks playing with people like Jerry Jeff Walker, bluesgrass great Vassar Clements, Guy Clark, and Carole King…a long list of things that kind of led from one thing to another. Then I had my own band in New York that was my first real serious band. When we disbanded, we moved back to Nashville and that's when I found out about the Christian music business."

"The way that I found out about it is that I had three friends," he remembers, "one was Bonnie Bramlett, another was Rick Cua, who I knew from a band called the Outlaws, and then a guy named Joe English that I knew from a band that started in upstate New York, but came down to Macon, Georgia

Dave Perkins

where I was, named Jam Factory. He, of course, was in Paul McCartney & Wings. I knew all of these guys from the life that I knew in music, and they told me that they were making Christian rock records, and I had no idea what that was."

Working with Steve Taylor

"When I came back to Nashville, a couple people asked me to write songs with them, and all of a sudden it was 'will you produce my record?' I did that for a period of about three years, and one of those records that I produced was on Steve Taylor, a record that he did called *I Predict 1990*. In the course of doing that, I came to appreciate Steve's talent, and in doing the record with him under the pressure of working with an artist that was really big in that market, and feeling the label constraints of 'the record has to do this or do that,' there wasn't any kind of warm and fuzzy, I began to see that Steve was bumping his head on what was a very low ceiling creatively."

"He finished out his record deal," says Perkins, "and I produced the record, and a year later he tells me that he's looking for a mainstream deal. I had done a record that came out through A&M on a little label called What Records, that was financed by Word Records. Word was a gospel label, but they were trying to have an outlet in the mainstream, so they put together What Records and signed three artists, and I was one. We all got records out on A&M, but Word decided to pull the plug on What and I was without a deal, Steve was without a deal."

"We decided to try something, so we began envisioning this band," Perkins says, "we started putting songs together, and

INTERVIEW: DAVE PERKINS

pretty soon the guy that had been our A&R guy, Lynn Nichols, was also out of a job, so he was in L.A. and we contacted him. We decided right off the bat that we were not going to do something that was particular to the Christian market, so we decided to start from scratch, and not play off Steve's notoriety. We decided that we'd all gather in Nashville, we'd start the band, and like any good band does we'd come up honestly through the clubs, and we'd start out just being the opening act for bands that had already established their popularity. That was our model, and that's what we started doing, opening up for anybody that would have us in Nashville and the area around…Birmingham, Bowling Green, a few other places."

The Innocence

"For the three years that I was producing records for that market, it seemed that I was doing a lot of work," remembers Perkins. "I had my frustrations with working in the Christian music business on artistic levels. One thing that I will say about it is that I got to make some lifelong friends there, and I got to work with some people that were world class talents, so I consider it to be one of the positive, constructive seasons that we all pass through in our lives."

"I never did make the kind of music that really could be successful in a big way in that market, I always found myself working with artists that were conflicted, trying as artists to work out their worldview as songwriters and musicians…a lot of that music wasn't as confessional and devotional as the kind of stuff that really does sell well in that market. That was my fatal flaw in the Christian market, my vision for making the art was not fully in line, but it was good."

Before he left the CCR world, however, Perkins recorded what would be his solo debut album, *The Innocence*. Although acclaimed, sometimes belatedly, by the critical community, the album never broke through in the hidebound Christian market. "Sonically, it sounds great," says Perkins, "and for the time it was really adventurous. Like most other musical things that I've had my hands on, it got a tremendous response from people that like to listen to and write about music. But my bank account didn't reflect [the critical acclaim]…"

"It was me in my Anglophile days. I went to England in 1978 with a Guy Clark tour and wound up staying for a while and soaking in what was left of the punk movement which, at that time, people said was done. There was still plenty more to come, and that had a real impact on me and I really consumed a lot of English new music…new wave and punk…so if you listen to the record you still hear my Southern roots, but it's barely affected. It speaks the language convincingly, the record definitely had a spiritual discussion going on, but it was not necessarily easy to get to…it was much more of a mainstream record than one for the religious market."

Chagall Guevara

Perkins would put together Chagall Guevara with Steve Taylor and Lynn Nichols, and as alt-rock critical darlings, these seasoned music veterans became cult favorites. The mishandling of their self-titled debut album by the label, though, robbed the band of momentum and would eventually split them up. "It was…I don't want to use the word 'devastating' because we all got up, brushed ourselves off, and went on in our various ways of getting by, but it was one of the most frustrating experiences that I've had as a music maker because everybody came to the party. The response to the record was what a lot of people dream about. We got such great response, everybody seemed to get it for what it was, and so to have it served up to a label on a silver platter and have the label prove to be completely unable to translate that into any kind of forward motion was really frustrating."

"It wasn't just the reception of the record," says Perkins. "One of the things that was the most heartbreaking was that we actually got to make the record that we wanted to make, that we envisioned. We did not compromise on it, it was exactly what we set out to do – it was the band's vision. We had a wonderful A&R team, we had a great co-producer in Matt Wallace, and all of those people recognized the potential for greatness in the band, and they didn't want to mess with it, so that allowed us to make a record that we were proud of and that we could replicate spot-on…there wasn't a lot of trim added, it was pretty much how the band sounded. So it was hard to let go for all those reasons."

"We signed with MCA because they had just taken on a bunch of people from Columbia that had worked with bands that were similar to us, and we knew that they knew how to get it out to the people. We set about doing the record, and the day that we delivered the record to MCA, the head of marketing quit. Of course, that's like being in battle and the battle is raging and all of a sudden the General decides that he's going to go home…there was nobody to break the record, to organize all of the label's various departments to do their part."

A Collaborative Effort

"We had signed with a major management firm in L.A. that, when things got tough, they proved to be ineffective," Perkins remembers. "They had a lot of major artists that were a lot easier to deal with because they had years of momentum behind them…but in terms of what I learned for it, the process of working creatively in that band was that we had some really strong personalities in the band, we had at least three guys that were used to being their own boss, and had visions that were sometimes divergent in terms of what the trajectory of the band was going to be, what the audience of the band was going to be, aspects of lyric and music writing."

"A lot of those things, the record came together much like the making of a diamond…a lot of heat and a lot of pressure. We all fought for our ideas because we all believed in them. We got that record done, and I know that I for one…and I think that we all felt the same way…once we were able to take a step back and look at it, the sum of its parts was greater than the individual parts. The things that became my favorite parts of the record were other people's ideas."

"That was a major educational moment for me about the sociology of making music in a group. Since that time, I've worked to not hold quite as tightly to my own ideas and to look for the genius in other people's suggestions and contributions. I'm still real proud of that record, and it has an underground audience out there that amazes me…I hear from people all the time."

Nashville in the 1990s

"That was such a fun time for the Nashville music community," Perkins remembers. "I think that Nashville now has become…it still has its unique qualities, but because of the democratization of the music business, the underground scene has aspects of being like everyplace else. Back then, though, the contradictions of what was going on in the rock clubs around town, what Nashville was always known for, it was so extreme and there was so much creativity in terms of non-country music," Dave says of the early-90s rock scene.

"Here's a recollection on my part…in February of 1990 we started working on Chagall Guevara songs out in L.A. When we decided that we were going to go for it, we decided that Nashville was the place that we were going to do it, the place where we were going to make our stand. The guys that were living in California started thinking about moving to Nashville and they decided 'let's check it out, let's see what we're getting ourselves into,' so they came to town and it happened to be the same weekend that 91 Rock had their annual benefit show and we went to that and I remember the Shakers, the Grinning Plowman, Dessau, Walk The West…there were a half-dozen bands and we stayed the whole night, and at the end of the night the guys from L.A. went 'this is the place that we have to come'."

Passafist

After the break-up of Chagall Guevara, Perkins would fall into an equally cultish project called Passafist. "It started with me recording a song that was on the record called "The Christ of the Nuclear Age." I was sitting in the office of a friend of mine, a music publisher, and he said 'do you ever do any dance music?' I said 'not really, I listen to a lot of industrial music'…at that time Ministry was on my play list, Skinny Puppy. My friend said 'there's a movie being made over in London, a re-make of an old '30s horror noir flick called *Devil Doll*, and they're looking for a song for the movie. You want to take a shot at writing something for it?'."

"A few nights later, I was at a rehearsal at S.I.R. and I heard all this racket coming out of one of the rehearsal rooms and all this kind of industrial noise. I cracked the door, and there standing in the middle of the huge rehearsal space was John Elliott. He has all his stuff coming at around 200dB through the sound system in there and we re-introduced ourselves and we started a conversation that led to him coming in and doing the programming for that song for me."

INTERVIEW: DAVE PERKINS

"It was such a blast working with him…at the time, I was producing a record for this company called R.E.X., they had a folk label called Storyville and I was producing one of their artists." Perkins says. "I wound up playing these people the song and they said 'we'd love to put this out on the R.E.X. label.' I said 'alright, why not?' That was the genesis of it."

"I felt like I wanted other people involved with the project, creatively, so I got my friend Lynn Nichols from Chagall Guevara to come in, it was John Elliott from Dessau, and Lynn and me and we put the record together on a shoestring budget and had a tremendous amount of fun with it. That one doesn't live with the same kind of life force that Chagall Guevara does, but it has its adherents. I hear from people about it, and a lot of time they're from Germany or Scandinavia."

Perkins' Musical Roots

"I grew up in a musical family," Perkins says. "My mother was a fine singer who won a national voice competition when she was in high school and she received scholarship offers and wound up at the Curtis Institute of Music in Philadelphia, where she met my dad. That's where he was from, my father was a really fine keyboardist; starting at age 16 he played the interlude music at what was then the biggest radio station in Philadelphia. So I grew up in a family of music makers, so I was tuned into music."

"I heard rock 'n' roll and I was a goner," he remembers, "it caught my rebellious spirit. One of the big turning points for me; I had become a real folk music consumer. In 1965, I bought an Elektra compilation called *Folk Songs '65* and I was totally unprepared for cut one, side two, which was the Paul Butterfield Blues Band playing "Born In Chicago." I heard that harmonica…that was probably the most life-changing moment, musically, that I can recall."

"There was something about the sound, something about the spirit of the music, and something about the sound of that harmonica," says Perkins. "I make no bones about it, as a guitar player, the thing that I've chased all my life is not another guitar player, but Paul Butterfield's playing."

"I wanted to play guitar and make it sound and feel like that harmonica. What was cool, later on, when I lived in Woodstock I became friends with Butter and opened up shows for him, so that was a fulfillment of a magical moment."

With *Pistol City Holiness*, Perkins has come full circle, and satisfied his need to make honest, sincere, and powerful music. "My first professional sensibilities in music-making were in blues and blues-rock, and that's what I've come back to…but my journey has been wildly diverse, between here and there." – *About.com Blues*, 2009

The Planet Rockers, continued....

Bill "Thunder" Swartz (drums) (I-IV, VI)
Matt Radford (bass) (V)
Brian Nevill (drums) (V)

The Planet Rockers Recordings:

I. Coming In Person (No Hit Records 1991, UK CD)
1. Trouble Up The Road
2. Big Wheel
3. Tennessee Woman
4. Big Daddy
5. One's All The Law Will Allow
6. Spin My Wheels
7. Gotta Rock
8. Truck Driver's Rock
9. Yes I Do
10. Troubled Times

Comments: First album from rockabilly legends the Planet Rockers features wildman Sonny George on vox and axeman Eddie Angel rockin' the fretboard. Unlike the glut of mid-to-late 1980s-era faux-rockabilly outfits making a grab for the brass ring in the wake of the Stray Cats' unlikely MTV-fueled success, the Planet Rockers were the stone cold real thing.

George's whiskey-soaked vocals evince just the right amount of twang and Angel's Link Wray-inspired, sci-fi-meets-spaghetti-western-and-surf-n-turf-at-the-SoCal-swap-meet-guitar-grunge is never less than inspired. Angel, of course, would don a Mexican wrestling mask and later provide '50s-spirited six-string jams for **Los Straitjackets**.

II. Invasion Of The Planet Rockers (Sunjay1992, CD)

III. 26 Classic Tracks (Spinout Records 1997, CD)
1. Trouble Up The Road
2. Big Wheel
3. Tennessee Woman
4. Big Daddy
5. One's All The Law Will Allow
6. Spin My Wheels
7. Gotta Rock
8. Truck Driver's Rock
9. Yes I Do
10. Troubled Times
11. Rampage
12. Thunder Road Rock
13. Come On
14. Gravy Train
15. Thunder
16. Knock Out The Lights
17. King Fool
18. Lonesome Traveler
19. Outta Gear
20. Runnin' Man
21. Billy Thunder
22. There'll Be No More Crying The Blues
23. Pink Dominoes
24. Hot Seat
25. Run Chicken Run
26. Got The Bull By The Horns

Comments: Compilation released by Spinout Records includes the out-of-print *Coming In Person* CD and live tracks from the Twist & Shout show.

IV. A Night At The Twist & Shout (Spinout Records 1998, UK CD)
1. Wiggle Walkin' Baby
2. Tennessee Woman
3. Runnin' Man
4. Lone Wolf
5. Run Chicken Run
6. Fire Of Love
7. Big Boss Man (Run, Don't Walk)
8. Trouble Up The Road
9. Rock N' Roll Guitar
10. Gotta Rock
11. Troubled Times
12. Rockin' Daddy
13. C'mon (Rock With Me)
14. Hot Seat
15. One's All The Law Will Allow
16. Wigglin' Blonde
17. Stranger Dressed In Black
18. Rampage
19. Get Off My Back
20. Spin My Wheels
21. Yes, Juanita's Mine
22. Got The Bull By The Horns

Comments (from the Spinout Records web site): The Planet Rockers were just beginning – and this was their first gig outside Nashville – when this was recorded in April, 1990 at the Twist & Shout in suburban Washington D.C. The excitement, energy and rawness that the band captured in this peak performance is worth checking out.

V. Hillbilly Beat (No Hit Records 2000, UK CD)
1. One More Drink
2. Best Dressed Beggar In Town
3. Like A Rollin' Stone
4. Swamp Gal
5. Rockin' Mama
6. Down And Out
7. Batteroo
8. Caffeine Nicotine & Alcohol
9. Don't Knock What You Don't Understand
10. Ain't Nobody Gonna Take My Place
11. Treadin' Water
12. Down The Line
13. Hillbilly Beatnik
14. Run Don't Walk
15. Gotta Travel On
16. No More Crying the Blues

VI. Live – On The Rampage (No Hit Records 7" vinyl)
1. Rampage
2. Run Chicken Run
3. Hot Seat
4. Got The Bull By The Horns

Comments: Four-song 7" vinyl EP with small LP-sized hole.

POPPYTRAIL

Band Members:
Pamela Truex (vocals) (I)

Poppytrail Recordings:

I. Nectar (Misery & Co. 1993, CD)
1. My Lobotomy
2. Twigs
3. Revolution at the Mall
4. Myself, Myself
5. The Pearl (The Death of Country Music)
6. Sky Blue Pink
7. From a Lawless Place
8. Tending the Still
9. Ramona

Another View: "Fueled by the enigmatic Ms. Pamela's distinctive and unique musical vision, Poppytrail's debut disc, titled *Nectar*, is an inspired collection of pop tunes run amok. Intelligent lyrics, tongue-in-cheek humor, a great deal of imagination and a fine sense of satire propel Nectar into that creative otherworld where genius resides. Country music, teenage narcissism and the foibles of society are all grist for Poppytrail's musical mill, with the steady, seventies-influenced new wavish pop soundtrack lending a slightly askew tilt to it all. Cuts like "Revolution At The Mall" and "From A Lawless Place" should be on everybody's personal playlist, Nectar providing a refreshing jolt of talent and reality." – *R.A.D! Review & Discussion of Rock & Roll*, July 1994

POPULAR GENIUS

Band Members:
Andrew Bissell (vocals, guitar) (I)
Scott Van Dusen (guitar, vocals) (I)
Luke Easterling (bass, vocals) (I)
Ryan Stout (drums, percussion) (I)
Christi Matuszak (saxophone, glockenspiel) (I)

Other Musicians:
Jeff Gilkinson (cello) (I)
Jay Hagy (tuba) (I)
Adam Troxler (saxophone, trumpet, French horn) (I)

Popular Genius Recordings:

I. how to be popular (Popular G Music 2004, CD)
1. Surprised
2. Apologize
3. Carrie Anne
4. Spoiler
5. Stay Awake
6. Should've Known
7. Fun is Fun
8. Summer Anthem
9. Are You Listening?
10. Gravity
11. Don't Write This Down

PORCELAIN

Band Members:
Val Strain (vocals, guitar) (I)
Dan Strain (guitars, bass, keyboards, percussion) (I)
Jon Knox (drums, percussion) (I)
Jeff Quimby (drums, percussion) (I)

Porcelain Recordings:

I. Porcelain (Wowee Records 1998, CD)
1. Shy
2. Climb Out
3. I Was Wrong
4. Ugly
5. It's Not Too Late
6. Always The One
7. Ice On The Snow
8. Wanted Your Kiss
9. Honey
10. Erase
11. I Forgot
12. Reason
13. Something Good
14. Oh Girl
15. Fall Asleep

Comments: The husband and wife team of Dan and Val Strain made a minor splash in the local music scene with the release of Porcelain's self-titled CD. The band's lofty pop sound and Val Strain's warm vocals set the band apart from everybody else in Nashville. Changed their name to **Sparkledrive** when they found a couple other bands named Porcelain, subsequently signed a contract with Aware Records (distributed by Sony) and released a single album. You'll still find them listed as "Porcelain" on the web, though, even on Aware's web shop.

PRACTICAL STYLISTS

Band Members:
David Russell (vocals, guitar) (A1-3, I)
Scott Sullivant (vocals, bass) (A1-3, I)
Jim Hodgkins (drums, vocals) (A1-3, I)
Bill Lloyd (vocals, guitar)
John Jackson (guitar, vocals)

Practical Stylists Recordings:

<u>Singles/EPs</u>

A1. "Ralph" b/w "Swing Your Arms Around" (White Triangle Productions 1983, cassette)

A2. "General Beat" b/w "My Bed"
(Pyramid Records 1983, 7" vinyl)

Comments: For a while the "General Beat" single outsold everything at Cat's Records on West End, which is where

PRACTICAL STYLISTS

anybody who knew anything about what was going on bought their music.

Another View: "Superb, sensational, excellent, amazing, breath-taking, energetic, danceable, riveting – I could get out my thesaurus and go on and on. Nashville's premier pop band has done it again. "General Beat" is a great rave-up that shows off this band's considerable talents – Scott's voice is in fine form as his bass and Jim's drumming propel the band onward and upward; David's guitar comes through loud and clear to punctuate the melody. The flip, "My Bed," is a bit more deliberate and studied, but maintains the energy we've come to expect from the band. Snappy packaging and a fab pic of the guys make this a must have. If there was any justice in the music business, Practical Stylists would already be signed to a major label and this single would be climbing the charts, but for now I guess they'll have to content themselves with the praises of their many fans until the record company executives realize they've got the next big thing right here under their noses. Let's hope that's not too long. – Andy Anderson, *Nashville Intelligence Report* 1983

A3. Practical Stylists (Pyramid Records 1984, cassette)
1. With Me Now
2. The Big Time
3. A Day Without You

Comments: With two cassette and a 7" single released over the course of around a year, Practical Stylists were one of Nashville's big bands circa 1984. Pursuing a pure, unvarnished power-pop sound, the trio of David Russell, **Scott Sullivant** (see interview ➔), and Jim Hodgkins were dynamic live performers that could always be depended upon to draw an audience in any club. When Russell went off to attend college, Sullivant and Hodgkins soldiered on, enlisting singer/songwriter/guitarist **Bill Lloyd**, who came to town from Bowling Green (where he was the frontman for a similar power-pop band called Sgt. Arms). I don't remember the Lloyd-fronted Stylists recording anything; second guitarist **John Jackson** would join the band later. Even later, Lloyd and the three original Practical Stylists members would form the **December Boys**.

Albums

I. Post_script (Spat! Records 2008, CD)
1. Swing Your Arms Around
2. Ralph
3. My Bed
4. General Beat
5. She's Got Lots
6. Terry's Voice
7. In My Dream
8. Rights

Practical Stylists: Jim Hodgkins, Bill Lloyd, Scott Sullivant, & John Jackson

9. R. A. Wilson
10. All Around Us
11. You Never Call
12. Some Fun
13. Crowded Room
14. Shake Some Action
15. E=Mc2
16. Know What I Know
17. 800 Number

Comments: After twenty-something years, Nashville's first and best-loved power-pop band finally gets the love they deserve with the *Post_script* CD. A retrospective collection that includes all of the band's studio tracks (represented by tracks #1-8) and cool, rare live recordings (#9-17). Practical Stylists shoulda been one of the big ones (see review ➔).

THE PRESERVATIVES

Band Members:
Brian Carter (vocals, guitar)
David Henderson (bass)
Don Sergio (drums)

Comments: The Preservatives came together when **the Roaries** disbanded and that band's David Henderson hooked up with Don Sergio from **the Features**. In an email, Henderson writes, "Brian Carter is a notable producer/engineer in the Murfreesboro area, known for many of the early Features' recordings, as well as a lot of the other Spongebath Records acts...Don Sergio was the other guitar player in The Features before quitting and leaving Matt to his own devices on the guitar...I was the guitarist for The Roaries. The Preservatives played mostly material from Carter's repetoire of songs, as well as a few well chosen Ray Charles and Elvis tunes...we still get together from time to time and play (Alley Cats last fall for Ben Morton's return from Iraq party – he was the bass player for Fluid Ounces), but expired officially in 2000."

TONI PRICE

Comments: Born in New Jersey and raised in Nashville, Toni Price began singing with country bands around town shortly after graduating from high school; Price later reinvented herself as a blues belter after moving to Austin, Texas in 1989.

It was during the Music City gigs that she met **Gwil Owen**, who would subsequently write many of the songs included on Price's debut album, *Swim Away* (Antone's/Discovery, 1993), which was recorded in Austin with a number of Texas legends, including Doyle Bramhall and Tommy Shannon.

Practical Sylists w/Bill Lloyd

PRIVATE LIVES

Band Members:
Dennis Welling (vocals, guitars)
Rob Chanter (vocals, guitars, keyboards)
Bill Frazhe (bass)
Tom Riss (drums, vocals)

Comments: Private Lives formed in Detroit but relocated to the Music City in late-1986, but not before raising a bit of a ruckus in their former hometown. The band's controversial first single was a song called "Don't Let Go" that addressed several suicides of Detroit-area musicians and club owners. Their second single, "Reaction To Words," received airplay on WRVU. Chanter would go on to other things; dunno about the other guys in Private Lives.

THE PRIVATES
Web: www.theprivates.net

Band Members:
Dave Paulson (vocals, guitar) (I-IV)
Ryan Norris (keyboards) (I-IV)
Keith Lowen (bass) (I-IV)
Rollum Haas (drums) (I-IV)

The Privates Recordings:

I. The Privates (self-produced 2003, CD)
1. We Are Really Rocking Now, Haven't We?
2. Karate and Explosions
3. Cha Cha Cha
4. I'm a Koala and I'm Cold
5. I'll Be an Indian
6. H.R. Geiger Counter
7. The New Urban Car
8. Chariots of Fire
9. Pocari Sweat

Comments: The Privates are a loose-knit conglomeration of talents from other area bands, Norris performing with **Lambchop**, Lowen with **De Novo Dahl** and Haas with **the Features**. Frontman Paulson has recently (2006-07) been sitting in on second guitar with **the Pink Spiders**.

Another View: "When not touring as supporting members of acts as varied as The Pink Spiders and Lambchop, respectively, the members of this Nashville-based quartet apply their fierce musical technique to singer-guitarist Dave Paulson's byzantine pop songs. Most of the cuts on the band's debut clock in under three minutes, but each sharply arranged number covers a surprising range of territory, careening from caffeinated hook to caffeinated hook with more energy and inventiveness than a barrelful of Arctic Monkeys." – *The Big Takeover*

II. Louder Than Lightning (self-produced CD-R, 2005)
1. CGCGCGFEA
2. Tangelo
3. Song 2
4. The Mighty Ducks Are Back!
5. If I Should Call Your Name

III. Barricades (Mean Buzz Records 2006, CD)
1. Atrium
2. Despite The Snake
3. One Piece
4. Heart's Got A Hole
5. Barricades
6. Surprise
7. Mr. Christmas
8. I'm Telling
9. On Your Mark
10. Sea To Sea
11. My Shoes

IV. Motion (Theory 8 Records 2009, CD)
1. You Never Take Me Dancing
2. I'll Be Honest
3. Motion
4. The Breeze
5. Put The Hurt On 'Em

THE PUPPETS

Band Members:
Gene Scream (vocals, guitars)
Chip Staley (bass, vocals)
Hank Spooner (drums)

PURPLE GIRAFFE

Band Members:
Billy Stickers (vocals)
Jeff Johnson (guitar)
Richie Owens (guitar)
Greg Herston (bass)

Private Lives

INTERVIEW: SCOTT SULLIVANT OF PRACTICAL STYLISTS

*A*long with guitarist David Russell and drummer Jim Hodgkins, bass player Scott Sullivant was one of the original members of Practical Stylists, Nashville's answer to the power-pop trend of the late 1970s and early '80s and, for a couple of years, one of the most popular bands on the local club circuit. The band was criminally-overlooked by the major label machine at a time when they viewed Nashville as nothing but Hee Haw and country music. 'Tis a shame, too, 'cause Practical Stylists had solid songwriting, sharp melodies, and enough charisma to match up with power-pop fellow travelers like the Shoes, 20/20, Dwight Twilley, or anybody else...

After Practical Stylists had run its course, Scott and Jimmy formed Smokeless Zone, offering an interesting variation on the PS sound that netted a modicum of acclaim, the two musicians later forming the December Boys with former bandmates David Russell and Bill Lloyd. One of the Music City's true rock 'n' roll pioneers, Scott remembers those heady days in this July 2007 interview...

What got you interested in music in the first place?
I was just a huge Beatle fan. Jimmy Hodgkins was my best friend growing up, and David...we all went to the same school. Jimmy and I were in our first band together when we were in first grade; we had to pay $10 to join it. We always loved music; Jimmy was a huge music fan. He was always a real inspiration for me, he had older sisters and they were really hip, so he was always shoving stuff my way. I guess he's probably my musical mentor, to be honest. He always steered me down the right path, he turned me on to the Cars and the Clash and the Jam when I was open to that. I really followed the Beatles and other various and sundry pop stuff, I loved music and was around people that loved music...

We got old enough to start putting together bands for talent shows; we did that and started playing friend's dances and things like that. The original band that ended up being Practical Stylists was actually my college roommate Dave Foy – he used to work for the White Animals – we started that band and it was Jimmy and David, and then there was a girl named Robin Irwin who actually ended up being Robin Lee who went down the country path and had one hit, "Black Velvet," at the same time that that other girl [Alannah Myles] did.

That was the band, we did cover songs and played proms and school dances and things like that. After doing that for a while, Jimmy, David and I, we got sick of doing other people's music and started writing songs and we're definitely a closet garage band. Somehow, Bruce Fitzpatrick heard about us and he called and asked if we'd like to open a show down at Spanky's. We only had six songs, we learned three or four more cover songs and we did some gigs with the Times.

When did Practical Stylists become a working band?
Around 1981...Jimmy and I were in college at Belmont in 1980. At that point, we were still just kind of doing the cover band stuff, but talking a lot about doing our own music and listening to bands like Hots. I used to go see them, I loved the Hots, they were truly an inspiration to me. I was absolutely thrilled when Andy Byrd sought us out and wanted to produce some of my music.

Were you all ever involved with the Phranks 'n' Steins scene?
No, Phranks 'n' Steins was gone by the time we started playing. There was Spanky's, and Cantrell's, but we really cut our teeth at Spanky's.

How did the band progress from there, from your first shows?
We actually progressed pretty fast. I guess that we got a little bigger than our repertoire and, as a result, probably spent a little too much time opening for people cause it's really all the material we had. We just went out and we played pretty much everywhere we could play. When we started, there weren't a huge amount of bands there. Then the bigger name bands like the Scorchers...I remember when Jason called and asked if we'd get on the bill with them, which was probably was a real big push for us.

Andy Byrd sought us out and got us thinking about doing a recording, so we started talking with him. We worked with him and Mark Brown on that project, a single. We recorded that at Silverline/Goldline, it was just a writer's house and we recorded on a little eight-track machine. Andy was terrific; he ended up producing a lot of stuff later on in the country world. Mark Brown, he's still involved in the music industry around here. His brother Dale played bass in the Hots.

We did all of our stuff within a couple years, really. We flashed pretty hard and fast and I'd attribute that to not being afraid to break down whatever paradigms were already in place for original bands at that time. We opened for the White Animals once, we had our fair share of 16 to 30 year old girls from then on out coming to our shows because…if we opened for the White Animals, we were all of a sudden "cool."

Yeah, I don't know why the White Animals were considered a teen band by so many people on the scene…
I think most people saw them more as a cover band that did frat parties and things like that. That's what their reputation was among my peers, and there wasn't a lot of respect for that. Quite honestly, the only reason we opened for them was because Barry, who was my roommate, called me about once a week and asked me if we'd do it and we finally just said "yeah, what the heck, we'll do it." It was a pretty good paycheck, they always packed it out, and they were guaranteeing more than we usually pulled on a headlining night.

That first Practical Stylists cassette, do you remember what songs were on that?
Yeah it was "Swing Your Arms Around" and a song called "Ralph." "Swing Your Arms Around" got on a compilation album out of a college station in Georgia and got a lot of airplay down there, so we used to play down in Georgia a lot.

Then you had a 45 single that you did next?
We were on a couple of compilation albums, *The City Without A Subway* and then some other college compilation

Scott Sullivant

albums. Then we did that 45, which did really well, it got a little bit of distribution. We were actually putting together material and saving money after doing an EP next, and that's when we flamed out…our guitar player quit, which hurt real bad.

Was that when David went to school?
Actually, he joined the Navy. He saw *Officer And A Gentlemen*; I don't know…we were really flirting with success. We were doing little short tours around, a few dates with the Bongos, we opened for the Bangles a couple times, then we were doing some bigger shows. We had a publishing company that was coming after us, wanting to sign for a publishing deal which was our first step…the only problem was, they wanted us to write songs for somebody else, which is actually a pretty funny story.

That happened right after we did a show with the Bangles and I remember they called, it was Dick James Publishing, and they had us come in and we sat around and watched all these videos for bands like Tears for Fears and bands they had worked with. They were talking about how they'd all first signed a publishing deal then they turned them into stars and they wanted to do the same thing with us. They wanted to sign us on a publishing deal to write songs for the Bangles and then, maybe, we'd pursue our own life as artists. We were just cocky enough that we said "the Bangles, we just blew them off the stage, why do we want to write songs for them" and we told them no. I think they got Prince instead, so…that's how that story goes.

Did the band ever get any label interest for what you were doing?
We always had fleeting interest, but nothing serious. Phil Graham was the head of BMI at that time and he was always real good for the local scene, he was pushing people up to New York but it was really, really hard to get any interest around here. All you could hope for was to get enough of a live scene going where you could get people's attention.

How long was it after David left before you all hooked up with Bill Lloyd?
Well, we immediately hooked up with Bill. Bill had already been to a couple of our shows and sought us out, he had just recently moved to town. He was absolutely interested and it was a different sound, a little more jangly than what we were used to, but we got together, and actually our last show with David was either a Modern Music Mania or one of the 91 Rock benefits, David did the show with us and then Bill came up and we all did like three or four songs together.

So it was a smooth transition then…
A smooth transition, and then we started working up stuff and Bill wasn't comfortable handling all the…he was more comfortable with the idea of bringing in another guitar

player. We toyed around with the idea of me switching to guitar and getting another bass player, and that didn't work, so we tried out several people. There were a lot of local people who wanted to try out, but nothing really worked and somehow or another, we got John Jackson's name and brought him. He was an awesome guitar player but, unfortunately, he was a real asshole. So that didn't last very long and pretty much killed anything that was left with the band's desire. We put a bunch of time into it and it just didn't work out. That's the short history there, but really it was only a matter of three years, two to three years...

How long was it after the demise of Practical Stylists before you guys hooked up with Bill in the December Boys?
Bill went and did his own thing, and David went off and did something else again, I think he went to school, but David wasn't back in the picture yet. David came back in the picture when December Boys came around. Jimmy and I first went out and did Smokeless Zone...

It was basically just one record, but we did a lot of sitting around and writing really weird stuff and trying to reproduce some demos. We did that for a while, actually got some pretty bizarre interest out of that and got on a couple of compilation albums, but that was maybe a year, something like that. I can't remember exactly how the December Boys all came together, but by the time it did, we were excited about the idea of playing together again. I was excited about the idea of just playing back-up in a band without having to be the singer; it was intriguing to me.

Wasn't David in December Boys, too?
Yes he was. I think what really tempted everybody's taste buds was that show we did where we got Bill up on the stage and played with us, and it really rocked! David's a great guitar player, and Bill is a great guitar player, both of them together was just outrageous! We went ahead and progressed with that whole thing, I think it was 1985 or so when the December Boys thing happened.

Did the December Boys ever release anything?
We are on some of Bill's earlier solo albums; we're on a couple of those cuts.

After the December Boys, did you all get Practical Stylists back together?
After the original band played out and Bill was back doing his thing, we had an incarnation of Practical Stylists. David and we all got back together briefly with another guitar player out of Brentwood that was a Van Halen type guy, his name was Matt Stamps. We got back together and played a few shows as the December Boys...that was before we got with Bill. There was that whole period, Jimmy and David and I getting back together and playing and decided we didn't

Practical Stylists

want to do the three-piece, so we brought in this guitar player which didn't work, we ended up getting rid of him.

He was a good guitar player, but it wasn't the right mix and we just kept playing together and that's how we got hooked back up with Bill. Bill needed a band, we had been playing and that's what that was. That was a very short-lived thing. Then after that, I think we may have actually played a few shows as the December Boys, but after the December Boys, there never was any more Practical Stylists.

After all that, what did you do in terms of music?
I set up a little studio in my house and started recording just my songs and started shopping. I tried my craft as a songwriter and I shopped country and pop stuff...I've got boatloads of tapes of songs and song ideas, and a few finished songs. I worked, and went and got a job and got married, and started having babies and kind of moved on...

THE QUESTIONNAIRES

THE QUESTIONNAIRES

Band Members:
Tom Littlefield (vocals, guitar) (I, II)
Doug Lancio (guitar) (I, II)
Chris Feinstein (bass, vocals) (I, II)
Hunt Waugh (drums, percussion) (I, II)
Giles Reaves (keyboards, synth) (II)

The Questionnaires Recordings:

I. Window To The World (EMI America 1989, CD)
1. Window to the World
2. Fool's Parade
3. Beautiful Sideshow
4. Here Comes Trouble's Friend
5. Red Tears
6. Yesterday's Lie
7. Laugh
8. Teenage Head
9. Too Far Gone
10. Shake It Down

Comments: The Questionnaires' debut album was recorded with producer Pat Moran at Rockfield, Wales UK. Personally, although I thought that the album was one of the best released that year, it nevertheless didn't truly capture the band's live sound.

As for back story, the Questionnaires came out of the **Basics/Basic Static**, which was one of the city's most popular bands during the early-to-mid-1980s. Tom Littlefield

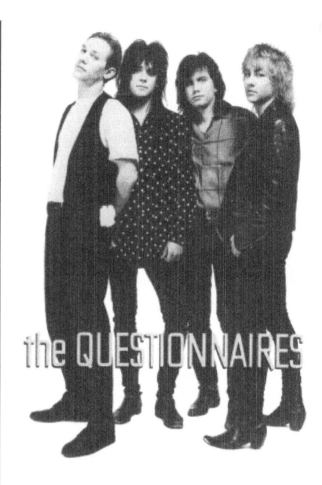

was/is a hell of a songwriter, and a hell of a lot of fun to drink beer with (see interview ➜).

II. Anything Can Happen (EMI America 1991, CD)
1. Killin' Kind
2. Trust Me
3. In The Back Of My Mind
4. Sad And Beautiful World
5. Anything Can Happen
6. Doing The Best You Can
7. Too Much Of Nothing
8. Tell Me Lies
9. Easier Said Than Done
10. Welcome Home
11. Georgia Rain
12. Yeah, Right!

Comments: The follow-up to the Questionnaires debut album was a much better recording, coming closer to capturing the band's live sound and inherent qualities. It's funny – I wrote the band's bio for the **All Music Guide** web site and if you look at the listing for *Anything Can Happen*, it shows a R.E.M. album. Go figure…

INTERVIEW: TOM LITTLEFIELD / THE QUESTIONNAIRES

Tom Littlefield of the Questionnaires is the kind of guy you'd enjoy sitting and drinking a beer with. Well-informed, opinionated, talkative, Littlefield is a walking encyclopedia of popular culture, a true connoisseur of everything from Saturday morning cartoons to rare rock records. It is only fitting that Littlefield should be at the helm of the most promising, not to mention the oldest of Nashville's new bands.

The oldest of Nashville's new bands? No, that's no contradiction in terms. Although the Questionnaires is a new name, the faces you might remember from the ever-popular Basic Static. Basic Static was formed in late 1982 by Littlefield and Questionnaires member Greg Herston. "Greg and I put the band together with Lynn Greer, who is now playing with Rowdy Yates, and Russell Beasley," says Tom. "Russell quit before we ever played a gig. We met Doug Lancio and saw him play and he joined the band."

The band ran into a few obstacles, however. Says Tom, "after we had played three or four shows, including opening for Bow Wow Wow, Greg broke his hand and Lynn decided to quit the band. We took a long hiatus because we didn't want to replace Greg. We added powerhouse Hunt Waugh on drums, and when Greg's hand got better, we played around for about a year." The band broke up due to personal conflicts although they had achieved a large following, opening for such national acts as the Fixx, X, and the Romantics. Says Littlefield, "I just got sick of it all, so I went and got a job. I worked for nine or ten months and then started to get the fever again; I wanted to play." The band re-formed again, with a slightly different direction. "We really want to make our living playing music," states Tom. "We haven't made any radical changes…we're really an extension of Basic Static…the 1985, streamlined, cushion-seated model. We're trying to improve on our material, make it more entertaining but thought-provoking."

The sound of the Questionnaires is straight-forward, pop-flavored, no-frills rock 'n' roll. Hidden beneath the beat, though, are relevant and intelligent lyrics, tightly-edited and closely-cropped for a greater impact. No mindless teen idols, these guys, but consummate artists presenting their work to the greatest number of listeners available, using the tools they possess. Littlefield writes the bulk of the band's material. The grandson of jazz great Woody Herman, Tom's creations illustrate the diversity and variety of his influences, which run the gamut from Hank Williams to Motown to the Beach Boys.

No question about it: the Questionnaires are a damn fine rock 'n' roll band. – *The Metro*, 1985

THE QUESTIONNAIRES
Windows To The World
(EMI/Capitol)

Windows To The World is the Questionnaires' debut album, but as any fan who has seen Tom Littlefield's immense songwriting skills displayed via previous bands such as Basic Static and the Basics knows, it is no overnight effort. Littlefield is one of Nashville's rock 'n' roll originals, plugging away for over a decade as he honed his skills and assembled, in the Questionnaires, as fine a pop/rock outfit as one may find anywhere. Fellow Music City rock veteran Hunt Waugh provides the heartbeat upon which bassist Chris Feinstein and guitarist Doug Lancio build the intricate melodies and instrumental backing for Littlefield's vocals and lyrics.

The result is a strong, powerful and highly original debut that has been a decade in the making. There's not a bad song on the disc, with Littlefield and the guys pulling from thirty years of rock 'n' roll history to create an album that is at once both familiar and fresh. Mature, entertaining, and intelligent, *Windows To The World* may very well be the best first album from any group this year (or for several years, for that matter). – *The Metro*, 1989

THE RACONTEURS

Band Members:
Jack White (vocals, guitars, keyboards) (I)
Brendan Benson (vocals, guitars) (I)
Jack Lawrence (bass, vocals) (I)
Patrick Keeler (drums, percussion) (I)

Other Musicians:
Dean Fertita (clavinet) (I)
Dirk Powell (fiddle) (I)

The Raconteurs Recordings:

I. Consolers Of The Lonely (Third Man Records 2008, CD)
1. Consoler of the Lonely
2. Salute Your Solution
3. You Don't Understand Me
4. Old Enough
5. The Switch and the Spur
6. Hold Up
7. Top Yourself
8. Many Shades of Black
9. Five on the Five
10. Attention
11. Pull This Blanket Off
12. Rich Kids Blues
13. These Stones Will Shout
14. Carolina Drama

Comments: Yeah, I expect to catch some shit over this one, but I call it legit! Besides, like the mutant LSD parade-float on the front cover of this one says, "Tennessee, Michigan,

Ohio," the home states of the musicians involved. Since Jack White moved to Nashville after the first Raconteurs album, I didn't count that one, but ***Consolers Of The Lonely*** is definitely in the ballpark, recorded at Bluebird Studios in Nashville with the new Music City immigrant at the forefront. Brendan Benson is well-known to indie rock fans; Lawrence and Keeler are the backbone of the underrated Cincinnati rock band the Greenhornes.

Another View: "At the very least, this bubbling blend of bizarro blues, rustic progressive rock, fractured pop, and bludgeoning guitars is a finger in the eye to anyone who dared call the band a mere power pop trifle, proof that the Raconteurs are a rock & roll band, but it's not just the sound of the record that's defiant. There's the very nature of the album's release: how it was announced to the world a week before its release when it then appeared in all formats in all retail outfits simultaneously; there's the obstinately olde-fashioned look of the art work, how the group is decked out like minstrels at a turn-of-the century carnival, or at least out of Dylan's ***Masked and Anonymous***. Most of all, there's the overriding sense that the Raconteurs are turning into an outlet for every passing fancy that Jack has but will not allow himself to indulge within the confines of the tightly controlled White Stripes...." – Stephen Thomas Erlewine, *All Music Guide*

RADIO ONE

Band Members:
Frank Harwell (vocals, guitar) (I)
Nathan Rotter (guitar) (I)
Mark Gibson (bass, guitar) (I)
Ricky Donley (drums) (I)
Randy Ford (drums)

Radio One Recordings:

I. Person To Person (Absolute Records 1987, LP)
Side One
1. One By One
2. You'll Be Sorry
3. Person To Person
4. Don't Keep Me Waiting
5. Forever

Side Two
6. I Need Her
7. Tell Me Why
8. She's Going
9. Come On Over
10. What About Me

Comments: Another great pop-oriented band of rockers...is it something in the water from the Cumberland that creates all these guys? I gave Radio One a positive mention in **The Rolling Stone Review 1985** book, pointing out (then drummer) Randy Ford's "sonic boom beat." The band released one solid album (pre-Ford), lost some members to become a trio, and later disappeared altogether. Contributed song "Don't Keep Me Waiting" to the NEA's *What You Haven't Heard…* 1987 compilation CD.

RADIX

Band Members:
Mike Yancey (vocals)
Danny Hargrove (guitars)
Robert Langley (guitars)
Mike Farris (bass)
Kenny Earl (drums)

RAGING FIRE

Band Members:
Melora Zaner (vocals) (I-II)
Michael Godsey (guitar) (I-II)
Mark Medley (drums) (I-II)
Les Shields (bass) (I)
Lee A. Carr (bass) (II)

Raging Fire Recordings:

I. A Family Thing (Pristine Records 1985, LP)
Side One
1. A Family Thing
2. You Should Read More Books

Side Two
3. 4 Tears (Church Street)
4. Beware A Man With Manners

Comments: Raging Fire was originally formed as "Ring of Fire," but I seem to remember that name conflicting with another band, thus the name change (which I think was ultimately for the better). Formed by scene veterans Mark Medley and Michael Godsey (**Committee For Public Safety**) and Les Shields (**The Ratz, Go Jimmy Dub**), with one-of-a-kind incendiary vocalist Zaner, Raging Fire was managed by man-about-town Rick Champion. The band had a great sound, unique in the city's scene (see review ➔), and seemed primed for the big time.

II. Faith Love was Made of (Neo Records 1986, LP)
Side One
1. Narrow Sky
2. More Than This
3. Drinking With Ghosts
4. A Knee-Jerk Response
5. Watching Ruby Fall

Side Two
6. Locusts Sing
7. The One You Hate
8. You & Me
9. After Loving One Man In East Texas

Comments: Man, it sure looked like it was going to happen for Raging Fire, but sadly it was not meant to be (see Mark Medley's memories of the band ➔).

WILL RAMBEAUX & THE DELTA HURRICANES

Band Members:
Will Rambeaux (vocals) (A1)
Kenny Greenburg (guitars) (A1)
Michael Rhodes (bass) (A1)
Marty Crutchfield (drums) (A1)

Will Rambeaux Recordings:

A1. "Jenny Drives A Mustang" b/w "Baby Put Your Gun Down" (Monza Records 1985, 7" vinyl)

Comments: At the urging of rock legend Roy Orbison, Will Rambeaux came to Nashville in 1982 from Lafayette, Louisiana by way of New York City. Although Will had the voice, the looks and the songs, his development deal with CBS Records would never lead to a label deal. Too bad, 'cause Will's songs were definitely good enough to succeed on the pro level, and today they'd be considered 'primo' high-octane Americana (see interview ➔).

Another View: "Debut vinyl offering from Will Rambeaux, one of Nashville's finest singers and songwriters, finds him and the Delta Hurricanes in fine form. The two great Southern roots rockers on this 45 are ace efforts and will be familiar to anyone who's seen Will crank it out live. "Jenny

Radio One

Drives A Mustang" features blastin' guitars over a chugging bump 'n grind rhythm and a great party beat. The other tune here, "Baby Put Your Gun Down," is pure delight. It just cooks and seethes with screaming guitar work, Will's impassioned vocals, and fantastic lyrics…." – *Nashville Intelligence Report #27*, 1985

THE RATZ

Band Members:
Joey Offbeat a/k/a Joe Blanton (guitar, vocals) (A1)
Les Rat a/k/a Les Shields (vocals, bass) (A1)
Randy Rodent (bass, vocals) (A1)
Bone Brown (drums) (A1)

The Ratz Recordings:

A1. "Call It Quits" b/w "Mental Block" (On Rotating Records 1981, 7" vinyl)

Comments: The late 1970s punk revolution didn't pass by Nashville, it just took a while for the city to catch up with the rest of the world. Following in the footsteps of **Cloverbottom** and Committee For Public Safety, the Ratz pursued a high-energy punk-rock sound, and were one of the first original bands of the 1980s. Les Rat, nee Shields would go on to **Go Jimmy Dub** and later **Raging Fire**, while Joey "Offbeat" Blanton would form **the Enemy**. Bone Brown kicked around with a number of bands. Cool 45rpm relic of the dawning of the Nashville rock underground.

Another View: "Brevity may well be the soul of wit – something is, at any rate, and we might as well call it brevity

since it rarely responds to, say 'Marvin' – but it can also be one rabid hamster of a handicap to your idiot savant record reviewer. Case in point: "Call It Quits" b/w "Mental Block," a single put out by local band The Ratz. On one hand, "Call It Quits" – the 'A' side – is an unassuming lightweight: quick, professional and nothing you haven't heard before (solid bass by Randy Rodent, though). Not bad by any means, but I doubt you'd hop into the bath with your favorite electric appliance if you missed it on the radio. Still, that's half the record-shot! (See what I meant about brevity, folks?) Ah, but the 'B' side – "Mental Block" – now there's the animal rock 'n' roll in all its vulgar glory, surly and swaggering, a paranoid fever in jackboots. The first time I played it, it leveled my speakers flatter than Tokyo after a fast Godzilla shuffle; second time, my stereo rolled over onto its side, breathed feebly and bled…" – Kent Orlando, *Grab!* 1991

NORM RAY/RAU

Comments: Another old high school buddy of mine, I taught him everything he knows about playing the guitar…no, not really, but I was there in the beginning and always respected Norm's talents. He kicked around in a number of bands, most notably **the Dayts** and **Dessau**; these days he's playing those good old blues with the bar band Two-Bit Eddie. Norm's dad was an accomplished sax player, a long-time staple of the early-morning *Ralph Emery Show* and once played with blues-rock guitarist Johnny Winter back in Texas. Norm's dad was also nice enough to get me a trash can to barf in one night after drinking a fifth of Jack and crashing on his living room couch.

True Story: While in high school together (while he was still known as "Norm Ray"), a small group of us were able to pull off a student-written play, a television satire called *All Rights Reversed*. After the *Saturday Night Live*-inspired skits, we had two musical segments. First at bat were **Donna Frost** and pianist Pete Carney (also one of the play's co-writers along with Bill Spicer, future scribe for *The Metro*, and yours truly), who charmed the audience with their folkish set. Then Norm came out with his guitar and a backing band (who I don't remember), he sidled up to the microphone and proceeded to exclaim, in best rock star manner, "we came here tonight to rock! If you didn't come here to rock, then get the fuck out!" Come Monday morning, we all got suspended for a week for Norm's hijinx. Ah, high school during the '70s…

RAYON CITY QUARTET

Band Members:
Robert Greene, Jr. (vocals, guitar) (I)
Jeff Cease (guitars) (I)
Jack Garland (bass, vocals) (I)
Jeffrey Perkins (drums) (I)

Rayon City Quartet Recordings:

I. Blue Suit And Tie (self-produced CD, 1999)
1. Wires and Numbers
2. Cool Again
3. Second Life
4. Lose A Little Skin
5. 32nd Avenue
6. Sidekick
7. Lover's Leap
8. West Coast Ways
9. Allison Part 2
10. I Could Never
11. Rose Colored Love

Comments: Rayon City Quartet included local MVP Jeff Cease (**Rumble Circus**) and Jeff Perkins of **the dusters**.

GILES REAVES

Band Members:
Giles Reaves (keyboards, synthesizers, percussion) (I-VI)

Other Musicians:
Rusel Brown (samples) (II)
Larry Chaney (guitars) (II)
Tony Crow (piano, bass) (II)
Tommy Dorsey (keyboards, percussion) (II)
Tony Gerber (keyboards) (III)
Aashid Himons (percussion, keyboards, synths) (III, IV, VI)
Jay Joyce (guitar) (III)
Rob McClain (guitar) (III)
Kirby Shelstad (bass, guitars, keyboards) (III)
Dave Turner (drums, percussion) (III, V)

Giles Reaves Recordings:

I. Wunjo (MCA Master Series 1986, LP)
Side One
1. Wunjo (Joy)
2. Sowelu (Wholeness)
3. Uruz (Strength)

Side Two
1. Eihwaz (Defense)/Kano (Opening)
2. Odin (The Unknowable)

II. Nothing Is Lost (MCA Master Series 1988, LP)
Side One
1. Velvet Shade
2. That's All I Can Remember
3. Nothing Is Lost
4. The Second Circle
5. Weightless Falling

Side Two
1. Here And Now
2. A Veil Of Tears
3. The Widow Sky

Comments: Released by MCA's acclaimed "Master Series" label that featured albums by talented instrumentalists like Larry Carlton, Albert Lee, Jerry Douglas, Edgar Meyer and John Jarvis. Pretty gutsy for a major label to release stuff like this that had absolutely no chance of selling many copies, but label chief Tony Brown had the juice (and a fat cushion of album sales) at the time to experiment a little with the label's fortunes.

III. Sea Of Glass (Hearts Of Space 1992, CD)
1. Evolutions
2. Twilight
3. Reverie
4. Aurora
5. After The Falls
6. Submerged
7. Suspended…On A Sea Of Glass

IV. Sacred Space (Space For Music 2000, CD)
1. Toward the One
2. Fire in the Stone
3. Darkness into Light
4. Akasha
5. Sacred Space (Sirius)
6. Great Mystery
7. Into Immensity

Giles Reaves, continued on page 413...

INTERVIEW: WILL RAMBEAUX

You know Will Rambeaux...or you should. He's the handsome devil in the trademark denim jacket that you'll spot around town. If you speak to him, you'll find him to be friendly, gracious and a tad on the quiet side...unless you get him started talking about his music. Then he'll get excited. The same sort of excitement that has unleashed a silent storm within the Nashville music scene as quietly, with little fanfare and no gimmickry, Rambeaux and the amazing rock 'n' roll outfit the Delta Hurricanes have created a large local (and regional) following with their raucous, rocking live shows and eclectic blend of roots inspired rock, Southern country soul, and Cajun spice.

Rambeaux, a native son of New Orleans, came to Nashville almost three years ago by way of New York City. "I came here on gut instinct," says Will. "I was told that Nashville was not the place to be a rocker. I figured, though, that wherever rock 'n' roll was least likely to rear its ugly head, that's where it would happen!" The subsequent growth and maturity of Nashville's local music scene since Rambeaux's arrival has proven his assumption correct.

"A vital street scene has developed in Nashville," says Will. "The best bands in the country are right here, even if most of them are undiscovered." If the truth is to be told, Music City rockers such as Jason & the Scorchers, the White Animals, Walk the West, and Will Rambeaux and the Delta Hurricanes have caused critics on both coasts to sit up and take notice.

Like many a struggling artist, Rambeaux had problems putting together a band, finding the proper combinations of

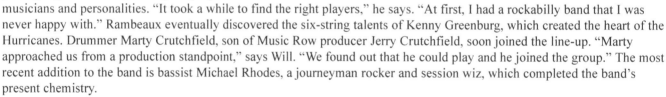

musicians and personalities. "It took a while to find the right players," he says. "At first, I had a rockabilly band that I was never happy with." Rambeaux eventually discovered the six-string talents of Kenny Greenburg, which created the heart of the Hurricanes. Drummer Marty Crutchfield, son of Music Row producer Jerry Crutchfield, soon joined the line-up. "Marty approached us from a production standpoint," says Will. "We found out that he could play and he joined the group." The most recent addition to the band is bassist Michael Rhodes, a journeyman rocker and session wiz, which completed the band's present chemistry.

The Delta Hurricanes recorded and released a single a few months back, the ground-scorching "Jenny Drives A Mustang" b/w "Put Your Gun Down." The response to this seven-inch slab of rock energy was universally positive. It was the third best-selling single this summer at Cat's Records' West End store, no mean feat if you consider the glut of commercial pap released this year, and it received accolades in the industry trade papers. "We had no great expectations," says Will. "We just went into the studio and cut a few tracks. We had decided on a single as our best effort. A lot of bands on an indie basis put out a four-song EP with two strong and two weak songs. We wanted to get people interested on the basis of two strong songs, and it worked."

The band discovered praise in some strange and unlikely places. "We found ourselves written about in little magazines, fanzines and cultural forums across the country," says Will, "which was weird and totally unexpected." Even a few big-leaguers took notice: "When Robert Palmer of *The New York Times* said he liked the single, we all thought 'Oh, God, we'd better start practicing!'," laughs Rambeaux.

The Delta Hurricanes received their reputation the old-fashioned way – they earned it with constant live performances and a fresh, original sound. Says Rambeaux, "I'm trying to bring zydeco and Cajun influences into a rock structure." The band's unique rock roots flavor has often been cited. "We're not really a roots band," says Will. "We don't interpret it that way. We don't want to sound like the radio sounded 30 years ago...we want to sound like the radio sounds today."

Nonetheless, the Delta Hurricanes possess a distinct affinity for early rock style and tradition. The originality of the Hurricanes' material is created by the odd mix of talent and taste within the band. Rambeaux's love of country music and ethnic folk material often clashed with drummer/producer Marty Crutchfield's hard urban, almost metal influence. Says Will, "Marty is probably the youngest producer working to be mentioned in *Billboard* and he certainly brings a contemporary studio edge to the band. I have this weird historical view, though, and Marty oftentimes has no idea of what I'm talking about. We're both strong-willed, hard-headed people, so in the studio it usually ends up with me saying 'I'm going to do this!' and Marty saying "I'm going to do *this!*' We put them together, and the result is the Hurricanes' sound.

Adds Crutchfield, "we don't really understand how the mix happens, but that's the way to create something that hadn't been heard. Throw in the influences of guitarist Kenny Greenberg, who Rambeaux calls "the best rock guitarist playing today" ("Kenny listens to everything and can play it all!" says Will), and the veteran professionalism of Michael Rhodes and the result is not only rocking but refreshing as well.

Currently, the band is working on another single, which hopefully will be released this winter. They continued to perform whenever possible, even opening recently for Lone Justice in Atlanta. Maybe they'll venture into the Northeast, taking their silent storm to new and even larger audiences. Their future looks good. You can bet the farm on this: Will Rambeaux and the Delta Hurricanes, one of the Music City's most talented and promising bands will continue to do that which they do best…just ask Will about it.
– *The Metro*, October 25, 1985

In the wake of Committee for Public Safety's disbandment in September 1983 childhood friend and fellow MTSU art student Michael Godsey and I began working up songs with a Vanderbilt co-ed named Melora Zaner (Michael had met her at Cantrell's) in the basement of her dorm on the Peabody campus. The idea was an organic cross between X, the Gun Club, the Scorchers, and Siouxsie and the Banshees with a dash of hardcore speed punk.

By January 1984, we had about four or five songs together when Michael and I ran into my old roommate Les Shields in a Murfreesboro dime store. We told him they were looking for a bassist upon which Les volunteered. Being the most experienced musician and music businessman of all of us, Les became an invaluable leader in launching the band in terms of road and business management (he eventually introduced us to Rick Champion) and later the recording and release of the *A Family Thing* EP. Les also contributed lyrics to some of Raging Fire's best songs including "Church Street" and "Everything Is Roses."

In the spring of 1984 we began rehearsing in a mini-warehouse in Murfreesboro and by March had about 10 songs. Needing a band name, I suggested one night we name the band 'Ring of Fire' after the Johnny Cash hit. Everyone agreed and we decided to play our first gig in the public room of Melora's dorm -– back then it was called Confederate Hall, today its known as Memorial Hall.

We played the show to a group of enthusiastic friends on a Friday night in April. We were pretty raw but overall audience response intensely positive and excited. The word got out fast and that same night Bruce Fitzpatrick called to ask us to play Cantrell's the following night and so we did. Response the following night was also very upbeat. Two gigs in and we were being asked by promoter Glenn Hunter if we wanted to go to Chicago and open for the Cramps. We did so in late May 1984 and were even mentioned in the newspaper review of the show.

The success of Ring of Fire continued to grow over the course of that summer. We opened for the hardcore Effigies in Chicago that July and then toured Indiana, Michigan, Ohio, and Kentucky. In August we found out that Tom Gray, formerly of Atlanta's The Brains had done two things: he had a significant cut called "Money Changes Everything" on Cyndi Lauper's million selling debut LP, and he had a new band called "Ring of Fire" that had already garnered national media attention.

I wanted to completely change the band's name, but it was decided too much time and money had already been invested on Ring of Fire so something similar was needed. I suggested "Raging Fire" and the name stuck. Looking back, we were just getting started. Raging Fire made its debut on September

2, 1984 opening for the Gun Club.

Rick Champion formally became our manager in the fall of 1984 and we continued to tour the Midwest from Indianapolis to Pittsburgh and the southeast from New Orleans to Raleigh. We opened for Rank and File, The Red Hot Chili Peppers, the Replacements, and of course the Scorchers. All of us were still attending college on top of this!

In October of 1984 we went to Memphis to record songs for a vinyl release, but the sessions at Memphis State produced no usable tracks and so we came back to Nashville and worked with Mike Poole at the ATV music demo studio (credited Penny Lane Recorders) on 16th Avenue. There we finally mixed and recorded *A Family Thing*. Les had already done a 45 record with The Rats and it was he that really pushed hard for the 12" EP format. We were also inspired by Scorchers success with *Reckless Country Soul* and *Fervor*. Michael did the back cover photo and I eventually did all the record graphics as a class project at school though, for some reason, I purposely left myself off the credits.

It took forever but the record was finally completed, released, and mailed to college radio in April of 1985 by our own label Pristine Records. Thanks goes out to Gigi Gaskins who executive produced the record by loaning us the money for the project.

The EP was very successful locally, but we could never get the distribution or the funding to really get the record out nationally. But we continued to tour in the summer and fall of 1985 and were confident a larger company would come along to finance a nationally-distributed LP. Biding our time, we submitted the song "Everything is Roses" to the WRVU record *City Without A Subway*. "Roses" is a song about Les's mixed emotions from being a struggling rock 'n' roller. It was during this time that he decided to use his recently earned MBA to make a living and announced his resignation from Raging Fire. We were sad to see him go and wished him the best, but the band was never the same.

Former The Enemy bassist Lee A. Carr was chosen to replace Les, and Lee played the bass on the *City Without A Subway* cut of "Everything Is Roses." *Subway* was released in the spring of 1986 on Nashville's Neo Records. Shortly thereafter Richie Owens (of Neo Records and The Movement) offered to record and release a Raging Fire LP on Neo.

Recording in a converted semi truck trailer on a gravel lot at the intersection of 16th Avenue and Demonbreun Street, producer Jeff Johnson and engineer Richie Owens directed the recording of what became *The Faith Love Was Made Of* during the sweltering summer of 1986. This record was much

darker than the debut EP and emphasized the raw hard rock elements of Raging Fire's live show that had been honed from playing in clubs.

Unfortunately, we were once again unable to get the record national distribution and had to self finance the last phases of the printing and pressing when Neo ran out of money. We made up our minds that we would not settle for anything less than a major label contract, and that is what we pursued for the next three and a half years.

Next: Raging Fire 1987-1990

In the Spring of 1989, *College Music Journal* called RF "One of Americas best unsigned bands . . ." and despite flirtations from MCA, Geffen, and especially RCA, this was as far as we got.

Today critics call RF proto-grunge, and it's true the late versions of RF sound a lot like Pearl Jam with a female singer – only Pearl Jam didn't exist yet. Wonder what would've happened if we had stayed at it until alternative rock finally broke in 1991? – *Mark Medley, August 2009*

Giles Reaves, continued...

V. Kaleida Visions (Space For Music 2001, CD)
1. Tunnel of Visions
2. Mandalic Delight
3. Iridescence
4. Rhythm of Light
5. Prismatic Balls
6. Flying Colors
7. Revolution Shimmer
8. Sparkle Vortex
9. Illuminosity

VI. The Deep End (Space For Music 2003, CD)

Comments: Giles Reaves, in my mind, was one of the true musical geniuses in the Music City. As a musician, engineer, and producer the talented Reaves' fingerprints can be seen all over the evolution of Nashville's rock scene, from the early 1980s through the new century. As a solo artist, Reaves has pursued his own particular brand of Eno-inspired "space music," and has become one of the best-known artists in the rather small pond of electronic composition. Giles has often collaborated with two other local visionaries, **Tony Gerber** and **Aashid Himons**.

GILES REAVES & JON GOIN

Band Members:
Giles Reaves (keyboards, drums, percussion) (I)
Jon Goin (guitars, bass, keyboards) (I)

Giles Reaves & Jon Goin Recordings:

I. Letting Go (MCA Master Series 1989, LP)
Side One
1. New Beginnings
2. Dream Flight
3. Letting Go

Side Two
4. Shadow Boxing
5. Journey to the Highlands
6. Sunday Afternoon
7. Blue Sky Daydream
8. Night After Night

Comments: Reaves and guitarist Jon Goin hook up to deliver one of the better instrumental efforts in the MCA Master Series. Both men are dedicated to their craft, and the interplay of their instruments is fascinating. Dunno why label chief Tony Brown ever funded the "Master Series," since it's waaayyy outside of the Music Row world, but I'm glad that he did (if only for a little while). This audiophile LP was pressed on "KC 569 Blend premium virgin vinyl." Cool...

THE REDLINERS

Band Members:
Mid-Life Marvin (vocals, guitar) (A1, I)
Jon Micro (vocals, drums) (I)
Ryan O'Rear (drums) (A1)

The Redliners Recordings:

Singles/EPs

A1. Pop, Grunge, Whatever (Dee Minus Records, 7" vinyl)
Side A
1. Just Tonight

Side B
2. Fakes

Albums

I. Either Way We're Screwed (Spat! Records 2003, CD)
1. So Negative
2. Heroes
3. Technokill
4. Pest
5. Abandoned
6. Just Tonight
7. The Sad Life
8. Toxic
9. 10 Foot Fence
10. It's Just Me

REDNECKS IN PAIN

Band Members:
Cat (vocals) (I)
Sean Denton (guitar) (I)
Donnie Kendall (bass) (I)
John DePriest (drums) (I)

Rednecks In Pain Recordings:

I. Sick Semen (self-produced cassette, 1989)
Side A
1. John's First Time
2. Stabbed In The Back
3. Won't Be Abused
4. Third Floor
5. Quick To Judge

Side B
6. You
7. The Fetus
8. Tearing Down The Walls
9. Cyanide
10. Attitudes

Comments: Ah, Rednecks In Pain (a/k/a R.I.P.) were one of the first real punk bands of note in Gnashville, led by the fearless Donnie Kendall, who would also perform with **Fun Girls From Mt. Pilot** and, with his wife April, book all-ages shows at the Pantheon, and later at Lucy's Records. Oh yeah, Donnie also published the rockin' *House O' Pain* zine. Although R.I.P.'s music was unvarnished goodtime punk with typical bad-taste lyrics, the band's socially-conscious

vibe led to them taking a stand in favor of all-ages shows and against the censorship of a local TV preacher.

THE RELATIVES

Band Members:
Robert Hale (vocals, guitar)
Mark Taylor (guitars)
Dave Rollins (guitars, vocals)
Jimmy Horner (bass, vocals)
Clint Eastwood Hill (drums)
Lawrence White (drums)

Comments: What did the Relatives sound like? In *The Metro*, Clyde Crawley sez "a combination of simple pop lyrics of the 60's and metal guitar sounds of the 70's influxed with the clever alternative intelligence of the 90's, but many standard rock and roll barriers have been surgically removed. It is high energy and very danceable."

THE RESISTORS

Band Members:
Richie Owens (vocals, guitars)
Norm Rau/Ray (guitars, vocals)
Lawrence Shipstone (bass)
Richard (drums)

Comments: One of Richie Owens' better and best-loved local bands, the Resistors would become **the Dayts** and relocate to L.A. in search of fame 'n' fortune. Yeah, they came back...

ANTHONY RIAN / ATREEO

Band Members:
Anthony Rian a/k/a Tony Gerber (keyboards/drums) (I)
William Linton (keyboards) (I)
Mason Stevens (guitar) (I)
Beat Zenerino (drums) (I)

Anthony Rian/Atreeo Recordings:

I. Teleworks / Stellar Movements (demo cassette,1986)
Side One
1. Airefare
2. Teleworks
3. Painz
4. Sky Voices
5. The Green Man
6. Fireworks

Side Two
7. Translucent Doors
8. Spectral Flights
9. Solar Eclipse

Comments: "Anthony Rian" is actually **Tony Gerber**, a well-known and respected figure in the Nashville music and art community and one of the guiding forces in bringing electronic, ambient and "space music" forms to Nashville. ***Teleworks*** was one of the first musical projects that Gerber did after moving to Nashville and it includes **William Linton** on one song and Beat Zenerino on another. Atreeo was Gerber with Linton and guitarist Mason Stevens; ***Stellar Movements*** is more of a collaborative work. This self-produced demo cassette featured Anthony Rian on side one, Atreeo on side two.

<u>ROSS RICE</u>

Band Members:
Ross Rice (vocals, keyboards) (I)

Other Musicians:
Pat Buchanan (guitars) (I)
Fenner Castner (drums) (I)
Steve Ebe (drums) (I)
Kevin Hornback (bass) (I)
Brad Jones (bass, mandolin, keyboards) (I)

Ross Rice Recordings:

I. Umpteen (E Squared 1997, CD)
1. Gone
2. Another Time
3. To See All
4. Wide Awake
5. Next to Nothing
6. Anything You Say
7. Dance Lessons
8. Dig Down Deep
9. Off My Mind
10. Miss July
11. On Earth Again

Comments: Rice, of Memphis rockers **Human Radio**, stuck around Nashville and worked the studio treadmill long after the majority of the band hightailed it back to the Bluff City. He released this overdue and underrated solo debut in '97 on Jack Emerson's E Squared Records, but it sadly went nowhere (much like the label did).

<u>RICH HIPPIES</u>

Band Members:
Warren Haynes (vocals, guitar)
Dennis Robbins (guitar, vocals)
Mickey Hayes (bass, vocals)
Tommy Irwin (steel guitar)
Mark Deaver (drums)

TAG
NASHVILLE'S INTERNET VICE GUIDE
thetag.net
DEBAUCHERY DEBUT
WITH
RAYON CITY QUARTET,
AUDRA & THE ANTIDOTE,
SIDESHOW BENNIE,
NINE PARTS DEVIL,
'DANCERS', BOOZE, CIGARS & MORE!
FRIDAY JAN. 28
THE GAS LITE
167 8th AVE NORTH

RICH HIPPIES - RIFF RATH - JASON RINGENBERG

Comments: Dunno what these guys sounded like, but I'd have liked to have heard 'em! **Warren Haynes**, of course, kicked around town in a number of bands and is currently the fretburner behind Gov't Mule as well as a member of the Allman Brothers Band and, during the summer of 2009, he toured with surviving members of the Grateful Dead as "The Dead." Haynes originally came to town during the late 1970s to play with country outlaw David Allen Coe's touring band, urged on by Mickey Hayes.

Best I can tell, Rich Hippies was formed by Haynes and Hayes at the end of their tenure with Coe. Dennis Robbins had been a member of Detroit rockers the Rockets before moving to Nashville to become a successful Music Row songwriter. I guess they had their fun, but I don't know of any recorded evidence that exists of the band…too bad!

RIFF RAFF/RIFF RATH

Band Members:
Mark "Smiley" Shenkel (vocals, guitar, saxophone) (I)
Mike Crowe (bass, vocals) (I)
Phil Harris (drums, vocals) (I)
Bruce Sexton (drums) (I)

Riff Raff/Riff Rath Recordings:

I. Ate Demos (Tapes That Go Doink 1987, cassette tape)
Side One
1. You Ain't Goin' Nowhere
2. Feed The Flames
3. Don't Believe I'm Leaving
4. Gonna Get U Off

Side Two
5. Go Tell Your Mama
6. Norwegian Wood
7. Solie
8. Tear It Up

Comments: Collection of band demos and a red-hot live version of the rockabilly classic "Tear It Up." Mark "Smiley" Shenkel, of course, is a local MVP who has played in a number of bands (and a heck of a nice guy!).

JASON RINGENBERG

Band Members:
Jason Ringenberg (vocals, guitar) (I-IV)
George Bradfute (guitars, dobro, mandolin, keyboards) (I-IV)
Fats Kaplin (violin, accordion, pedal steel) (I-IV)
Fenner Castner (drums) (II, IV)
Steve Ebe (drums) (III, IV)

Other Musicians:
Eddie Angel (guitars) (III, IV)
Gary Bennett (guitar, vocals) (II)
Luther Bradfute (synthesizers) (III, IV)
Paul Burch (guitars, bass, piano, drums) (II)
Steve Earle (vocals) (II, IV)
Eric Elliott (guitars, vocals) (IV)
Stace England (vocals) (IV)
Molly Felder (vocals) (II-IV)
Jeff Finlin (drums) (IV)
Mickey Grimm (drums, tambourine) (II-IV)
Ed Hammel (Hammel On Trial) (guitar) (II)
Moose Harrell (guitars, lap steel) (IV)
Don Herron (fiddle, steel guitar) (II)
Arty Hill (guitar, vocals) (IV)
Dave Jacques (horns) (III, IV)
John Latini (pedal steel) (III)
Phil Lee (trumpets) (IV)
Les James "Jimmy" Lester (drums) (III)
Jay McDowell (upright bass) (II)
Jerry Dale McFadden (piano, vocals) (IV)
Chuck Meade (guitar, vocals) (II)
Greg Morrow (drums) (III, IV)
Jim Roll (guitars) (III)
Kristi Rose (vocals) (II-IV)
Shakespeare's Riot (Tom, Gary, Dave & Jason) (IV)
Todd Snider (vocals) (II, IV)
Rob Stanley (vocals) (II)
Marc Trovillion (bass) (II)
Heather Twigg (violin) (IV)
William Tyler (guitars) (II)
Kurt Wagner (vibraphone) (II)
Webb Wilder (vocals) (IV)
The Wildhearts (Ginger, CJ, Danny & Stidi) (II, IV)
Shaw Wilson (drums) (II)

The Woodbox Gang (Alex, Hugh, Ratliff, Greg & Dan) (IV)
Tommy Womack (vocals) (II)

Jason Ringenberg Recordings:

I. A Pocketful Of Soul (Courageous Chicken 2000, CD)
1. Oh Lonesome Prairie
2. Whispering Pines
3. Under Your Command
4. Trail of Tears
5. For Addie Rose
6. A Pocketful of Soul
7. Hay Baling Time
8. The Last of the Neon Cowboys
9. The Price of Progress
10. Merry Christmas My Darling
11. I Never Knew You
12. The Last Ride

Comments: Ringenberg, the once and future frontman of **Jason & the *Nashville* Scorchers**, reboots his solo career with an excellent self-produced album that plays upon his strengths, i.e. Jason's songwriting talents and ability to maximize the passion and emotion of the words through his idiosyncratic vocal phrasings. With instrumentation from two of Nashville's most underrated musicians – Bradfute and Kaplin – Jason's friendly songs masterfully mash together folk-influenced lyrics, country twang and roots rock to great effect (see review ➜).

II. All Over Creation (Courageous Chicken/Yep Roc Records 2002, CD)
1. Honky Tonk Maniac From Mars (w/Hammell On Trial)
2. I Dreamed My Baby Came Home (w/Kristi Rose & Fats Kaplin)
3. Bible And A Gun (w/Steve Earle)
4. Too High To See (w/Tommy Womack)
5. James Dean's Car (w/Todd Snider)
6. Camille (w/Swan Dive)
7. One Less Heartache (w/the Wildhearts)
8. Mother Of Earth (w/Kristi Rose & Fats Kaplin)
9. Don't Come Home A Drinkin' (With Lovin' On Your Mind) (w/BR549)
10. Sun Don't Shine (w/Paul Burch)
11. Erin's Seed (w/Lambchop)
12. Last Train to Memphis (w/George Bradfute)

Comments: Jason's "duets" album finds him working with a diverse variety of guest singers, from folk-punk songwriter Ed Hammell (Hammell On Trial) and British sleaze-rockers the Wildhearts to hometown folks **Tommy Womack**, **Todd Snider** and **Lambchop**. As usual, the multi-talented Bradfute and Kaplin are backing Jason up, and his songwriting – already his strong suite – has become more focused and mature. This is the sound of an artist coming into his own.

Jason Ringenberg

III. Empire Builders (Courageous Chicken/Yep Roc Records 2004, CD)
1. American Question
2. Rebel Flag in Germany
3. Rainbow Stew
4. Tuskegee Pride
5. She Hung the Moon (Until It Died)
6. Link Wray
7. Chief Joseph's Last Dream
8. New-Fashioned Imperialist
9. Half the Man
10. Eddie Rode the Orphan Train
11. American Reprieve

Comments: *Empire Builders* displays further refinement of the unique Jason Ringenberg sound, an original mix of folk, rock and country (see review ➜). Eddie and Jimmy from **Los Straitjackets** drop by for a song (the appropriately rocking "Link Wray") while usual suspects Bradfute and Kaplin contribute their individual talents in support.

IV. Best Tracks And Side Tracks 1979-2007 (Yep Roc Records 2008, CD)

Disc One
1. Shop It Around
2. The Life of the Party
3. Bible and a Gun (w/Steve Earle)
4. Camille (w/Swan Dive)
5. Punk Rock Skunk
6. One Less Heartache (w/the Wildhearts)
7. She Hung the Moon (Until It Died)
8. Rainbow Stew
9. For Addie Rose
10. Born to Run
11. The Price of Progress
12. Prosperity Train
13. A Pocketful of Soul
14. Eddie Rode the Orphan Train
15. Link Wray (w/Los Straitjackets)
16. Tuskegee Pride
17. Half the Man
18. Chief Joseph's Last Dream
19. Broken Whiskey Glass (w/the Woodbox Gang)
20. Last Train to Memphis

Disc Two
1. Lovely Christmas (w/Kristi Rose)
2. Moose on the Loose
3. The Sailor's Eyes
4. Cappuccino Rosie (w/Arty Hill)
5. Mom's 70th Birthday Song
6. Help There's a Fire (Shakespeare's Riot version)
7. Buckminster Fuller We Need You Now

8. Who's Gonna Feed Them Hogs?
9. Paradise (w/R.B. Morris, Tom Roznowski & Janas Hoyt)
10. Jimmy Rodgers' Last Blue Yodel (w/the Wildhearts)

Comments: It's not often that an artist receives a career retrospective after only three albums, but then not every artist is Jason Ringenberg. This two-disc set does a superb job of summing up Jason's career at this point, including a few rarities, a few oddities, and a couple of previously-unreleased collaborations. Every song here is a jewel.

THE ROARIES
Web: www.myspace.com/roariesmusic

Band Members:
David Henderson (vocals, guitar)
David Palmer (vocals, guitar)
Troy Daugherty (guitars)
Mike Saindon (bass)
Matt Bach (drums)

ROCKFISH

Band Members:
Shawn Martin (vocals)
Anthony Guerriero (vocals)
Phil Makes (guitar)
Michael Romanawski (bass)
Chris DiCroce (drums)

Comments: Rockfish recorded a couple of tapes, with at least one produced by Wade Jaynes of **Chagall Guevara**. However, I have not been able to locate anything by the band although their songs were being played on both WRLT and WKDF-FM. Not to be confused with the more recent band from Grand Haven, Michigan.

ROCOCO

Band Members:
Allen Terrell (vocals, guitar) (I)
Kevin Hornback (bass) (I)
Jeff Hayes (drums) (I)
Richard Smith a/k/a HAWK (harmonica, percussion) (I)
Eric Magness (saxophone) (I)
Bart Sharp (trumpet) (I)

Recordings:

I. Photograph My Dreams (self-produced LP, 1986)

Comments: Six-song EP released by the band in 1986; I couldn't find any other information. A couple of years after

Rococo, continued on page 421...

JASON RINGENBERG
A Pocketful Of Soul
(Courageous Chicken Records)

Soul is an intangible concept – some folks has got it, some ain't – but anybody who thinks that an old country boy can't have soul is just plain mistaken. Take Jason Ringenberg, for instance. Grew up on a hog farm in Illinois, been plying his trade these past twenty years or so as frontman/songwriter/ bottlewasher for the finest posse of rockin' cowpunks that this humble critic has been proud to make acquaintance with. Not for nothing did Jason & the Scorchers name their first basement-brewed recording *Reckless Country Soul* and now Jason steps out on his own in the year "Y2J" with a fine solo effort called *A Pocketful Of Soul*.

To resubmit my original theory, if you think that a country boy can't have soul then you've never heard Mr. Ringenberg's delightful twang wrap around a set of lyrics. Technical singers are a dime a dozen down on "Music Row" and I'm looking for the guy supplying the dimes. Jason, on the other hand, is a soulful singer – technically proficient but with too much honky-tonk in him to mimic the bland pop styling demanded by Nashville's major label establishment. As raw as an icy wind blowing across a barren wheat field, Jason imparts every song on *A Pocketful of Soul* with a delightful country soul that is as authentic as it is unique. To hear Ringenberg sing "For Addie Rose," for instance, written for his young daughter, is to stare into the heart of the artist. Any damn singer can entertain your ears, but it takes soul to hit you in the gut.

There are no pretensions to be found on *A Pocketful Of Soul*, no delusions of grandeur or multi-platinum fantasies. This is a homegrown musical project, a wonderful aside from Jason's work with the Scorchers. This is country music as it used to be, created by the artist instead of committee, committed to excellence rather than demographics. Jason's critically acclaimed songwriting skills have never been questioned, tho' he's reserved some of his most personal observations for *A Pocketful Of Soul*. The aforementioned "For Addie Rose" is for every father who has ever watched his daughter grow up. The chilling "The Price Of Progress" is certainly influenced by one of the greatest tragedies of the modern age, the loss of the family farm. "The Last Of The Neon Cowboys" is a thinly-veiled tale of too many nights on the stage while Jason's cover of the long-lost Guadacanal Diary gem "Trail Of Tears" is afforded a, well, soulful reading.

Although there are some electric instruments hereabouts, *A Pocketful Of Soul* is an acoustic-oriented collection of songs, performances captured by an analog 16 track recorder and sent out into the world with no heavy production, bells or whistles. Ringenberg rounded up talented former Webb Wilder sideman George Bradfute and multi-instrumentalist Fats Kaplin to help him pick on an assortment of guitars, mandolin, dobro, steel guitar, accordion and violin.

The focus here is on Jason's vocals, however, and the damn fine songs that this talented wordsmith still manages to crank out after two decades of writing. *A Pocketful Of Soul* is a rarity – a strong solo effort from an artist known primarily for his work with a band. It is also an anomaly, a country record that is true to the spirit of the ghosts of Hank, Ernest and Lefty, living proof that Jason R. still has a few tricks up his sleeve. (2001)

CD REVIEW: JASON RINGENBERG'S EMPIRE BUILDERS

JASON RINGENBERG
Empire Builders
(Courageous Chicken/Yep Roc Records)

When "Little" Steven Van Zandt toured Europe during the early 1980s with his Disciples of Soul band, he saw the sad results of Reagan administration foreign policy. Speaking with the people he met in the towns that he played, Van Zandt became politicized, a philosophical transformation that resulted in a brace of overtly political albums. The culmination of Little Steven's left-leaning political evolution was the Sun City project, a direct artistic assault on South Afrikan apartheid.

Americana music pioneer Jason Ringenberg comes from quite a different background than the Jersey-born-and-bred Van Zandt. The son of an Illinois hog farmer, Ringenberg is more of an "aw shucks" populist than a tree-hugging leftist, and neither his previous solo work or his tenure as frontman for Jason & the Scorchers reveal little of his politics. While touring Europe and Australia in support of his *All Over Creation* solo disc, Jason found himself questioned and criticized over American policy and the actions of the current administration. It proved to be embarrassing and frustrating and it opened the artist's eyes to a radically different perspective than that shown by Fox News.

The result of Jason Ringenberg's politicization is *Empire Builders*, his third solo rock album and strongest effort to date. The songs written for *Empire Builders* try to make sense of America's place in a post-911 world and collectively evince a more critical view of the country. There is no flaming rhetoric or paint-by-numbers polemics on *Empire Builders*, nor is there any flag-waving jingoism. What you will find, however, is a cautious and considered artistic response to current events. The album opens with "American Question," Jason thoughtfully asking "can we export dignity, respecting those who disagree" over Jim Roll's taut recurring riff, the song a minimalist response to an American foreign policy of "bomb-em-and-Big-Mac-em."

Several other songs on *Empire Builders* also touch on 21st century manifest destiny. "New-Fashioned Imperialist," a jaunty satire of CEO stereotypes, is sung over the oompa riffing of Dave Jacques' tuba while "American Reprieve" is a continuation of the opening cut, delivered as the kind of jazzy tone poem that you might expect from an artist like Ed Hammel, not good old Jason. "Rebel Flag In Germany" laughingly criticizes the "Confederate" mindset that is so prevalent in the south, including his adopted home of Tennessee. Jason's embarrassment over seeing a rebel flag on a barn in Germany is equaled only by his shame at the fact

that the flag – a symbol of racism and slavery no matter what the southern heritage Neanderthals claim – still flies on flagpoles and pick-up trucks across the south.

Ringenberg balances out his social commentary with humanistic tales such as "Tuskegee Pride," Jason's love of history resulting in the masterfully crafted story of a World War II African-American pilot. The song remembers the racism that these brave soldiers and their families endured even while fighting for freedom for their children and grandchildren. It is a reminder that we still have a long way to go with the issue of race in this country. "Half The Man" is a loving tribute to his father, while a rocking remembrance of guitarist Link Wray pays homage to the criminally overlooked rocker (with a little help from Los Straitjackets axeman Eddie Angel).

All the songs on *Empire Builders* are presented in the twangy folk/rock/country hybrid that has become Jason's signature sound. Former Webb Wilder sideman and longtime Jason foil George Bradfute lends his considerable six-string skills to most of the songs and Fats Kaplin fills out the sound with some tasty pedal steel guitar.

After twenty-something years on the old rock & roll highway, Jason continues to grow and mature as a performer and a songwriter. Ringenberg doesn't claim to have all the answers on *Empire Builders*, but he does ask some mighty damn good questions... (2009)

Rococo, continued....

this Terrell would head out to L.A. and use his full name, Charlie Allen Terrell, forming a band known simply as "Terrell." A record deal with Irving Azoff's Giant Records would follow, and *On The Wings of Dirty Angels* would be released in 1990.

Since then, Terrell has found some success as a roots-rock/blues singer, recording three more albums as "Terrell" for the Virgin Records' blues imprint Point Blank, and a pair of independently-released albums as "Charlie Terrell" with his band the Vibe Assassins.

Smith, who had originally followed Terrell to Los Angeles before eventually settling down in Georgia with his family, succumbed to his long-running heroin addiction, dying of an overdose in 1998. I worked with Hornback at the legendary **P.D.Q. Pizza** on West End Avenue in 1989.

ROOTS ROCK ACTION FIGURES

Band Members:
R.S. Field (vocals, guitar, bass, piano) (I)
Kenny Vaughan (guitars, vocals) (I)
Scott Baggett (bass, guitars, keyboards, vocals) (I)
Les James Lester (drums, percussion, vocals) (I)

R.R.A.F. Recordings:

I. Calling Dr. Strong (Paladin Records 1998, CD)
1. Check Up From The Neck Up
2. How Long Can She Last
3. One Of Those Nights
4. Twangeaux
5. No Great Shakes
6. The Rest Will Take Care Of Itself
7. Calling Doctor Strong
8. Friendly Little Game
9. Powerful Stuff
10. Heart She Can't Beat
11. Long Story Short
12. Secret Heart (1982)

Comments: *Calling Dr. Strong* was one of the most criminally-neglected albums released by a Nashville band. It didn't help that their label, Paladin Records – also home to fellow traveler **Steve Forbert** – didn't have the resources to spread the gospel about this excellent group of musicians. Fronted by the uber-talented R.S. "Bobby" Field...producer, musician, songwriter, and regular **Webb Wilder** collaborator... RRAF included local scene veterans Kenny Vaughan and Scott Baggett, along with former Beatneck and future **Los Straitjackets'** drummer Les James Lester.

JOSH ROUSE

Band Members:
Josh Rouse (vocals, guitar) (D1, I-VIII)

Other Musicians:
Roy Agee (trombone) (II)
Steve Allen (keyboards) (I, II)
Paul Burch (vibraphone) (II)
Chris Carmichael (strings) (V, VII)
Dennis Cronin (trumpet) (II, IV)
John Deaderick (piano) (II)
David Gehrke (drums, percussion) (I, II, IV)
Mike Grimes (bass) (IV)
James Haggerty (bass) (V, VII)
David Henry (bass, cello) (I, II, IV)
Ned Henry (guitar) (I, II)
Jim Hoke (flute, saxophone) (V)
Neilson Hubbard (vocals) (I)
Darren Jesse (drums) (IV)
Brad Jones (bass, organ, vibraphone) (II, V, VII)
Tim Keegan (vocals) (V)
Will Kimbrough (guitars) (II)
Craig Krampf (percussion) (II)
Roger Moutenot (guitars, keyboards) (IV)
George Nicholson (keyboards) (I)
Al Perkins (pedal steel) (VII)
Curt Perkins (keyboards, vibraphone) (V)
Joe Pisapia (guitar) (V, VII)
Marc Pisapia (drums, percussion) (IV, V, VII)
Graham Spice (trumpet) (I)
Daniel Tashian (vocals) (V, VII)
Jason Moon Wilkins (bass) (I, II)

JOSH ROUSE

Josh Rouse Recordings:

I. Dressed Up Like Nebraska (Slow River/Rykodisc 1998, CD)
1. Suburban Sweetheart
2. Dressed Up Like Nebraska
3. Invisible
4. Late Night Conversation
5. Flair
6. The White Trash Period Of My Life
7. A Simple Thing
8. A Woman Lost In Serious Problems
9. Lavina
10. Reminiscent

Comments: Josh Rouse was born in Nebraska in 1972 but as a child he moved around a lot, living in California, Utah, Wyoming, South Dakota, Georgia, and Arizona. Whew! He recorded this album in Nashville prior to relocating to the city, but as it includes a number of local talents, I've included it here. From around 1998 through 2005, when Rouse would leave town, he released a handful of critically-acclaimed albums that cemented his reputation as a gifted songwriter, storyteller, and stylist.

II. Home (Slow River/Rykodisc 2000, CD)
1. Laughter
2. Marvin Gaye
3. Directions
4. Parts and Accessories
5. 100M Backstroke
6. Hey Porcupine
7. In Between
8. And Around

9. Afraid To Fail
10. Little Know It All

III. Bedroom Classics, Vol. 1 (Bedroom Classics 2001, CD)
1. Miserable South
2. A Night In
3. A Song to Help You Sleep
4. Sad Eyes
5. Sunshine
6. Michigan

Comments: Six-song EP released in a limited edition of 750 copies by Rouse on his own Bedroom Classics label.

IV. Under Cold Blue Stars (Slow River/Rykodisc 2002, CD)
1. Twilight
2. Nothing Gives Me Pleasure
3. Miracle
4. Christmas With Jesus
5. Under Cold Blue Stars
6. Ugly Stories
7. Feeling No Pain
8. Ears To The Ground
9. Summer Kitchen Ballad
10. Women and Men
11. The Whole Night Through

V. 1972 (Rykodisc 2003, CD)
1. 1972
2. Love Vibration
3. Sunshine
4. James
5. Slaveship
6. Come Back
7. Under Your Charms
8. Flight Attendant
9. Sparrows Over Birmingham
10. Rise

Comments: Rouse really made the critics stand up and take notice with this paean to the soft-rock sounds of the early 1970s. Yeah, it's a little wimpy for my tastes, but the songcraft is unparalleled, and the collaboration of Rouse and producer Brad Jones perfectly captures both the vibe and the sound of the era.

Another View: "Josh Rouse's *1972* gives away the game in the first line of the first song, the exquisite title track, when he name-checks Carole King. The record is going back in time and it is going to have fun doing it. Rouse's records have always been highly literate and highly musical, but they have never been fun like this, and make no mistake, *1972* is a fun record. Rouse sounds as loose as a goose and the songs reflect that. Not always lyrically, as some of the songs touch on such non-fun subjects as loneliness, repression, and bitterness, but definitely musically. To that end, Brad Jones' production is spot-on perfect — not an instrument is out of place and the whole record has a jaunty bounce and a lush dreaminess. *1972* is coated with sonic goodness: fluttering strings, piping horns, cotton-candy sweet flutes, funky percussion, handclaps, and great backing vocals. Rouse and Jones find inspiration in all the right places: in the laid-back groove of Al Green, the California haze of Fleetwood Mac, the dreamy melancholia of Nick Drake, the sexy groove of Marvin Gaye, and the wordy lilt of Jackson Browne or James Taylor." – Tim Sendra, *All Music Guide*

VI. The Smooth Sounds Of Josh Rouse (Rykodisc 2004, DVD/CD)
1. Michigan
2. Princess On The Porch
4. Knights Of Loneliness
5. I Just Want To Live
6. A Well Respected Man
7. Kentucky Flood
8. Pittsburgh
9. Me Gusta Dormir
10. Scenes From A Bar In Toronto
11. Smile

Comments: CD portion of two-disc DVD/CD set released by Rykodisc in 2004 offers a collection of rarities and B-sides hand-chosen by Rouse from his bedroom stash.

VII. Nashville (Rykodisc 2005, CD)
1. It's the Nighttime
2. Winter in the Hamptons
3. Streetlights
4. Caroliña
5. Middle School Frown
6. My Love Has Gone
7. Saturday
8. Sad Eyes
9. Why Won't You Tell Me What
10. Life

Comments: After the break-up of Rouse's marriage, he lit out for Spain, but not before recording this excellent love letter to his former hometown. Rouse continues to record, often times in Nashville with producer Brad Jones, but subsequent albums aren't included here 'cause he's clearly no longer a part of the local music scene. Sorry...

Another View: "*Nashville* reunites Rouse with producer Brad Jones and the two have concocted a sound even bouncier and dreamier than the already impossibly dreamy and bouncy *1972*. There are hints of all the styles Rouse references on *1972* but here they are integrated into his sound more smoothly. Jones adds all kinds of varied keyboards, strings, guitar sounds, bits of sonic trickery and atmosphere

to that sound which leads to each song sounding similar but also quite different. The production and sound are half the game and Rouse doesn't let his half down, as his songs are incredibly strong on *Nashville*." – Tim Sendra, *All Music Guide*

VIII. Bedroom Classics, Vol. 2 (Bedroom Classics 2005, CD)
1. Neighbor-hoods
2. The Last Train
3. Oh, I Need All of the Love
4. Soul'd Out
5. Daylight Savings Time

Comments: Second of Rouse's self-released collections of demos and outtakes, limited edition discs sold through the artist's web site and at shows.

Video/DVD

D1. The Smooth Sounds Of Josh Rouse (Rykodisc 2004, DVD)
1. Comeback (Light Therapy)
2. Love Vibration
3. Sunshine (Come On Lady)
4. Under Your Charms
5. Slaveship
6. 1972
7. Rise
8. Feelin' No Pain
9. Miracle
10. Under Cold Blue Stars
11. Late Night Conversation
12. Directions
13. Flight Attendant

Comments: DVD portion of two-disc DVD/CD set released by Rykodisc in 2004 captures Rouse on stage, New Year's

JOSH ROUSE & KURT WAGNER - ROXX

Eve 2003 in Nashville. DVD also includes documentary film, *The Many Moods Of Josh Rouse*, by director Matt Boyd.

JOSH ROUSE & KURT WAGNER

Band Members:
Josh Rouse (vocals, guitar) (I)
Kurt Wagner (vocals, vibraphone) (I)

Other Musicians:
Dennis Cronin (trumpet) (I)
Sharon Gilchrist (upright bass) (I)
David Henry (cello) (I)
Curt Perkins (keyboards) (I)
Malcolm Travis (drums) (I)

Josh Rouse & Kurt Wagner Recordings:

I. Chester (Slow River/Rykodisc 1999, CD EP)
1. Something You Could Always Tell
2. That's What I Know"
3. Table Dance"
4. 65"
5. I Couldn't Wait

Comments: Critically-acclaimed five-song collaboration between Rouse and friend Kurt Wagner of Nashville band **Lampchop** emphasizes both musician's strengths and reveals few weaknesses (see review ➔).

Another View: "…The follow-up to Josh Rouse's acclaimed debut is even more promising than its predecessor: for the five-song *Chester*, Rouse sought out lyrics from the great

Kurt Wagner, the mastermind behind Nashville freakshow Lambchop, and the result is a gorgeously understated record that plays beautifully to the strengths of both artists.

Despite the seeming schism between the two, Rouse's bright, chiming songs fit Wagner's darkly surreal vignettes like a glove, at times (as on the superb opener, "Something You Could Always Tell") even co-opting Lambchop's orchestral touches to stunning effect…" – Jason Ankeny, *All Music Guide*

ROXX

Band Members:
Rob Pracht (vocals)
Tim Gentry (guitar)
Jerry Hutchison (bass)
James Smith (drums)

ROYAL COURT OF CHINA

Band Members:
Joe Blanton (vocals, guitar) (I-II)
Chris Mekow (drums, vocals) (I-II)
Robert Logue (bass, mandolin) (I-II)
Oscar Rice (guitars) (I-II)
Jeff Mays (guitar) (III)
Drew Cornutt (bass) (III)

Royal Court of China Recordings:

I. Off The Beat'n Path (On Desperation Records 1986, LP)
Side 1
1. The Lottery
2. Take Me Down
3. I'm Not At Home

Side 2
4. Forget Me Nots
5. Television Gone
6. Off The Beat'n Path
7. Heart Full Of Soul

Comments: After the break-up of popular Nashville rockers **the Enemy**, frontman Joe Blanton and drummer Chris Mekow got together with Robert Logue and Oscar Rice to form the Royal Court Of China. The band's recording debut was a seven-song EP that did a great job of introducing the band's strengths. Notorious record collector Jello Biafra of the Dead Kennedys once offered me $50 for my copy of *Off The Beat'n Path*. This EP would lead to the band being signed to A & M Records.

II. Royal Court Of China (A & M Records 1987, LP)
Side 1
1. It's All Changed
2. The Last Day
3. Do You Feel The Same
4. Tye
5. Trapped In Waikiki

Side 2
6. Forget It
7. Hope
8. Tell Me Lies
9. My Babylon
10. Townsend, TN
11. Man In Black

III. Geared & Primed (A & M Records 1989, CD)
1. Geared & Primed
2. Half The Truth
3. It Came Crashing Down The Staircase
4. Six Empty Bottles

5. Mr. Indecision
6. Tijuana Go!
7. Dragon Park
8. So, Yer Love Is True
9. This Time Around
10. Take Me Down

Comments: *Geared & Primed* is what I like to call RCOC's "L.A." album. The band underwent a roster shake-up between their first A&M album and this second and last one, with Logue and Rice leaving to form **the Shakers**. Manager Grace Reinbold moved the band to Los Angeles where they unabashedly tried to jump on board the Guns 'N' Roses bullet train. Unfortunately, that train had long since left the station and this album went nowheresville despite some positive reviews. The Nashville community mostly hated it and looked upon RCOC's defection to the left coast as a betrayal.

Listened to recently, with fresh ears, *Geared & Primed* isn't a half-bad album. Sure, this isn't the Royal Court Of China that Nashville fans fell in love with, but then neither were the Shakers. Joey Blanton's songcraft had further improved for this disc, and his twangy pop-metal holds up well compared with many bands from the late 1990s (mostly due to Chris Mekow's explosive drumming). Brush with fame: the video for "Half The Truth" was directed by Sam Raimi (*Spider-Man*) and includes a cameo by actor Bruce Campbell, a childhood friend of Raimi's.

Another View: "Confusion evaporates as The Royal Court Of China greedily pluck power chords from the sky and turn honky tonk bar rock into sleazy L.A. club rock…great voice on that Joe Blanton guy: Billy Idol sings Chris Isaak and John Doe; throaty Elvis smoke over chunky, resonant rhythms that don't commit to any one style. The result: roots metal by way of roots, rather than an always contrived vice versa…a charming slab from one of the unsung." – Martin Popoff, **The Collector's Guide To Heavy Metal, Volume 2: The Eighties**.

RUCKUS

Band Members:
Bob Bearden (vocals, guitars)
Tim Cherry (bass)
Joe Gleaves (drums)

RUMBLE CIRCUS

Band Members:
Jeffrey Williams (vocals)
Jeff Cease (guitars)
Erich Hubner (bass)
Alan Johnstone (drums)

Comments: See interview (➔) with **Jeff Cease** for details about this underrated band.

RUSSIAN ROULETTE

Band Members:
Carl Cooper (vocals, keyboards)
Mike Rosa (guitars, vocals)
Tom Knight (bass)
Paul Norman (drums)

MATTHEW RYAN

Band Members:
Matthew Ryan (vocals, guitar, piano, synth) (I-XI)

Other Musicians:
Bucky Baxter (pedal steel, violin) (VII)
Brian Bequette (guitars) (IX, X)
David Bianco (percussion) (VII)
Thad Cockrell (vocals) (X)
Kris Donegan (vocals) (X)
Jim Ebert (vocals) (I)
Park Ellis (harmonica, percussion) (III)
Chris Feinstein (bass, vocals) (II, VII)
Jeff Finlin (drums) (I)
David Henry (cello, guitar) (I-III, VII, IX)
Ned Henry (violin) (II)
Neilson Hubbard (keyboards, guitar, vocals) (IX)
Aaron Hurwitz (accordion) (I)
Ethan Johns (drums, percussion) (II)
J.J. Johnson (drums, percussion) (VII)
Jay Joyce (guitar) (I)
Ray Kennedy (harmonium, percussion) (III)
Will Kimbrough (guitar, piano) (II)
Craig Krampf (drums) (I, III)
Doug Lancio (guitar, mandolin, synth) (I, II, VII, X)
Steve Latanation (drums, percussion) (VII, IX, X)
Carl Meadows (piano) (II)
Richard McLaurin (keyboards, pedal steel) (II, III)
Eamon McLoughlin (violin, vocals) (X)
Billy Mercer (bass) (IX)
Johnette Napolitano (vocals) (II)
Dave Pirner (trumpet) (II)
Mark Pisapia (drums) (IX)
David Ricketts (guitar, bass, keyboards, synth) (I, II)
Mark Robertson (bass, vocals) (VII)
Josh Rouse (vocals) (II)
Pat Sansone (piano) (II)
Trina Shoemaker (vocals) (II)
Paul Slivka (bass) (I)
Matt Slocum (cello) (VII)
Garrison Star (vocals) (IX)
Clay Steakley (bass) (III, IX)
Kevin Teel (guitar) (VII)
Aaron Till (violin) (VII)
Molly Thomas (violin, piano) (VII, IX, X)
Lucinda Williams (vocals) (III)
Tom Williams (drums) (II)
Kate York (vocals) (IX, X)

Matthew Ryan Recordings:

I. May Day (A&M Records 1997, CD)
1. Guilty
2. Watch Your Step

3. Irrelevant
4. The Dead Girl
5. Chrome
6. Lights Of The Commodore Barry
7. Disappointed
8. Beautiful Fool
9. Railroaded
10. Dam
11. Comfort
12. Certainly Never

Comments: Pennsylvania native Matthew Ryan moved to Nashville from the troubled working class enclave of Chester, south of Philadelphia, in 1993. Influenced by such a mixed bag of artists as the Clash, the Replacements, and Bob Dylan, Ryan taught himself guitar at the age of 17, and began writing his dark-hued songs shortly thereafter. As Ryan describes them on his website, his songs "tend to be about girls, socio-political issues, people on the edges, breakups, brotherhood, hate, love, fighters and hope."

May Day, his debut, is a masterpiece-in-waiting of brilliant performances and songwriting, drawing almost universal acclaim but, sadly, selling few copies as the grunge era gave way to the candy-coated, late-decade gloss of boy bands and pop divas (*sigh*).

Another View: "Drawing on such influences as Bruce Springsteen, Tom Waits, and John Cougar Mellencamp (not to mention Bob Dylan and Leonard Cohen), folk-rocker Matthew Ryan showed a lot of potential on his debut album...Ryan's voice is rough and has a very lived-in quality that proves most appropriate on such tales of loss, disappointment, and hurt as "Watch Your Step," "Chrome," and "Lights of the Commodore Barry." There isn't a lot of hope or optimism here; Ryan obviously didn't hesitate to let some of his darker feelings flow when he went into the studio to record this album, which is as pessimistic as it is soulful, moving and personal." – Alex Henderson, *All Music Guide*

II. East Autumn Grin (A&M Records 2000, CD)
1. 3rd Of October
2. Heartache Weather
3. I Hear A Symphony
4. Me & My Lover
5. Sunk
6. Sadlylove
7. I Must Love Leaving
8. Ballad Of A Limping Man
9. Time & Time Only
10. The World Is On Fire
11. Still Part Two
12. Worry

III. Concussion (Waxy Silver 2001, CD)
1. Drift
2. Rabbit
3. Happy Hour
4. Too Soon to Tell
5. Devastation
6. Autopilot
7. Chickering Angel
8. Night Watchmen
9. Somebody Got Murdered
10. Shake the Tree

IV. Dissent From The Living Room (self-produced 2002, CD)
1. The Little Things
2. Such a Sad Satellite
3. Fd29yrblues
4. After the Last Day of a Heat Wave
5. Demoland, Part 1
6. Emergency Room Machines Say Breathe
7. No Going Back
8. The Ballad of So and So
9. Anymore
10. Happy for You
11. Into the Sourdays
12. Demoland, Part 2
13. Elise Is the 13th Disciple?

Comments: In between labels, Ryan recorded this collection of demos in his home studio and offered it on CD-R to fans through his website.

MATTHEW RYAN

V. Hopeless To Hopeful (self-produced 2002, CD)
1. Rain, Rain, Rain
2. Song for Sons
3. Veteran's Day
4. I'm an American
5. Everybody Always Leaves
6. I Can't Steal You
7. This Side of Heaven
8. Postcard to Useless
9. Little Drummer Boy
10. From the Floor

Comments: Another home recording released on CD-R for the hardcore faithful. Used to be, a guy that had the obvious charisma, personality, and songwriting skills of a Matthew Ryan would be kept on by a record label as a proof of the company's commitment to "art." These days talent doesn't mean squat (unless you're signed to a committed indie label), and if you don't bring in the shekels with your first, or second album (if they let you get so far), you're releasing material to your fan base entirely on your own.

Although I respect the D.I.Y. creative avenue…heck, a lot of the artists in this book have done it themselves…it limits the ability to increase your audience and, thus, the income you need to keep on making great music. In short, Matthew Ryan should be signed to a major label where, like a Leonard Cohen, Neil Young, or Bob Dylan (all holdovers from an earlier era), he could write and perform and follow his muse wherever it takes him without worrying about putting beans on the table, ifyouknowwhatImean…

VI. Happiness (One Little Indian 2003, UK CD)
1. Rain Rain Rain
2. Veteran's Day
3. Something In The Night
4. Fd29yrblues
5. Cut Through
6. The Ballad Of So And So
7. I'm An American
8. I Can't Steal You
9. After The Last Day Of A Heatwave
10. Emergency Room Machines Say Breathe
11. Song For Sons
12. Such A Sad Satellite

VII. Regret Over The Wires (Hybrid Recordings 2003, CD)
1. Return To Me
2. The Little Things
3. Trouble Doll
4. Long Blvd.
5. I Can't Steal You
6. Caged Bird
7. Come Home
8. I Hope Your God Has Mercy On Mine

9. Nails
10. Sweetie
11. Every Good Thing
12. Skylight

VIII. These Are Field Recordings (self-produced 2004, CD)
Disc One
1. One Day the Everclear
2. Fathers and Compromise
3. The World Is on Fire
4. Railroaded
5. Return to Me
6. Sweetie
7. I Must Love Leaving
8. Irrelevant
9. Autopilot
10. Trouble Doll

Disc Two
11. The Little Things
12. Still Part Two
13. Sadlylove
14. Heartache Weather
15. I Can't Steal You
16. Chrome
17. I Hope Your God Has Mercy on Mine
18. I Hear a Symphony
19. Dragging the Lake
20. This Side of Heaven
21. Bone of Truth

Comments: Two-disc collection of odds 'n' ends, mostly unreleased demos and live tracks, released independently by Ryan. Couldn't find any other information on the set and it's not listed on his website for purchase (which is a shame, 'cause I'd buy the sucker!) Around this time Ryan began talking with his old buddy Neilson Hubbard about some sort of musical collaboration. The two talents formed the band **Strays Don't Sleep**, which released its debut album in 2005 (more about which under the band's listing).

IX. From A Late Night High Rise (2 Minutes, 59 Seconds 2007, CD)
1. Follow The Leader
2. And Never Look Back
3. Babybird
4. Gone For Good
5. Providence
6. Misundercould
7. Everybody Always Leaves
8. All Lit Up
9. Love Is The Silencer
10. Victory Waltz
11. June Returns For July
12. The Complete Family

Comments: Ryan's enchanting "Follow The Leader" was used very effectively in the "House Training" episode of the hit Fox network TV show *House*.

Another View: "On *From a Late Night High Rise*, Matthew Ryan continues the folk-tronica explorations that he experimented with on his previous outing *Regret Over the Wires*. This disc opens with some eerie electronic whirls before a fragile sounding piano introduces "Follow the Leader." The haunting soundscape matches the song's sense of dislocation as Ryan raspily intones: "If you ever really wanna get lost/then follow me." The entire album finds Ryan chasing ghosts, the past, and missed opportunities. These songs grew out of two tragic events: the death of a close friend and the imprisonment of his brother. His grappling with grief can be heard throughout this soul-searching album…" – Michael Berick, *All Music Guide*

X. Matthew Ryan Vs. The Silver State (00:02:59 Records 2008, CD)
1. Dulce Et Decorum Est
2. American Dirt
3. Meet Me By The River
4. It Could've Been Worse
5. Hold On Firefly
6. Jane, I Still Feel The Same
7. Killing The Ghost
8. They Were Wrong
9. I Only Want To Be The Man You Want
10. Drunk And Disappointed
11. Closing In

XI. Dear Lover (The Dear Future Collective 2010, CD)
1. City Life
2. Dear Lover
3. Some Streets Lead Nowhere
4. We Are Snowmen
5. Your Museum
6. P.S.
7. The Wilderness
8. Spark
9. The World Is...
10. The End Of A Ghost Story

Comments: Also released in an acoustic version; I don't have this one, thus no details on musicians. Sorry...

Another View: "Previously available online, *Dear Lover* is now in independent record stores — a great new excuse to discover a writer who pens love songs as tough as Jim Thompson novels. 'If this is it for worse or better, I swear you'll have to come get her,' Ryan sings, as though trying to stare down death. Some rockers must scream when they plumb emotions at this depth. Ryan rarely has to raise his voice above a raspy whisper. – Brian Mansfield, *U.S.A. Today*

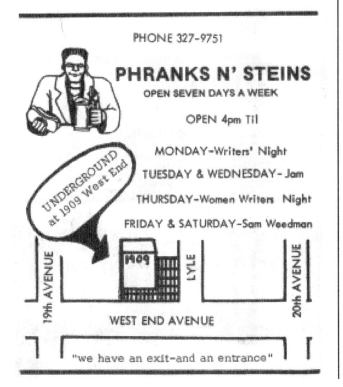

INTERVIEW: JASON RINGENBERG

Jason Ringenberg came to the Music City searching for fame and fortune and, while riding down the "lost highway," would become one of the best-known and influential musicians to emerge from the Nashville rock underground. As a founding member of Jason & the Nashville Scorchers, who arguably helped invent, or at least define the "Americana" genre, to his moderately-successful solo career...even his alter-ego as "Farmer Jason," the children's artist...Jason has continued to make great music while entering his fourth decade in the business. He's a heck of a nice guy, too, a true anomaly in an industry known for eating people's souls for brunch. I spoke with Jason by phone in July 2007, one of nearly a dozen interviews the two of us have done through the years...

What brought you to Nashville in the first place?
It was purely to get into music, to get into the music world. I was living in southern Illinois at the time and Nashville just seemed close...I could drive there, for one thing, and I just got this instinctive pull to do it. I'd never been there in my life. I'd never been to Nashville and I decided to do it, and I hopped in my van and took off, did it.

Just came to town and figured you were going to start up a band?
That's precisely how it was. I didn't have enough money when I started to pay my electric bill deposit. I didn't even have power for a month; I just lived in my PA and my guitars and stuff, that's really all I had in life.

How did the band come together? Who was the first person you met in town?
The first person was Jack [Emerson], for sure, that was almost immediately when I got into town. I went out to Springwater and I don't even know how I heard about this place, No Art was playing, Gary Salsa's band and I saw Jack there and struck up a conversation. He said, "I play a little bass, why don't we do a little band and I'll help you get started and we'll see where it goes."

So he did, we put a little band together with some friends of his....Barry Felts on drums, Jack was on bass, and a guy named Will Thomason was on guitar. We opened for Carl Perkins for our first gig. The second gig was opening for R.E.M. at Cantrell's because Jack knew R.E.M. That sort of morphed into what became Jason and the Nashville Scorchers.

So that was the original Jason and the Nashville Scorchers?
Yeah that's the first one, we did three gigs – Carl Perkins, R.E.M. and then we opened for No Art. Then we did another, and then Jack backed off to become Jack Emerson, basically. Jeff took over bass and he brought in Warner because Will left to finish school, he was studying to be an attorney. We did one gig with Barry Felts on drums, Warner Hodges on guitar and Jeff on bass and Barry just hated it. He hated Warner's stuff, they were like oil and water those two, and so Barry quit and then Warner brought in Perry and that became the band. The first gig with Perry – which is usually when we say the Scorchers started – was around 1981.

I seem to remember you telling me once that you played in places with chicken wire...
We really did, it was crazy...we were playing incredibly nutty places. We were on that sort of western and southern punk-rock circuit at the time...they called it new wave or whatever, but it had a bunch of like-minded people all over the country who would do that sort of thing in every town, and we were plugged into that. Aside from that, we were also doing really crazy shows, wherever we could get money, and some of them were actually quite violent. We were lucky to escape several times by not ending up in the hospital.

I remember some of those days, it seemed like Warner and Jeff were pretty ready to jump into it with just anyone...
Yeah, they were, they didn't back down from anybody and most of the time though it seemed like I ended up in the middle of it, facing down the barrel of a gun...sometimes literally...and somehow I was able to avert major problems. Just a few times it was really crazy.

Once in Knoxville, Jeff got mouthy with some sort of redneck guy, and I think he hit him or something, but he was a little guy and so all this little guy's friends were coming after Jeff and they all showed up, just like they appeared out of nowhere right behind the club when we were loading our gear. We're sitting there with all our amps out...we had a little 1971 Ford Econoline getting ready to load it, and luckily Jeff wasn't there. They said "where's the dude with the pink Mohawk, we want to kill him?" It was me, Warner, and Douglas standing there, facing about 15 guys who wanted to kill somebody about this. They started kicking over the amps and stuff and luckily, we just sort of talked them out of it. That was about as close as we ever came to probably getting killed. The guys were packing heat and they had knives...it was pretty dangerous, pretty scary. But that's how it was in those days; it was a more violent time, I think.

What are some of your best memories of the Scorchers' years?
The band, for me, was always a very intense experience. So I always filter it, for every great memory there's an equal amount or more of bad ones. I think probably gigs that stick in my mind, certain shows, landmark shows that sort of changed our lives, the record release show for *Fervor* at the Exit In when we sold out the room, that was a big night. The Marquee Show in London in 1984…those kind of things are what I remember most. Off stage, it was a pretty miserable experience. We fought a lot, very different people, a lot of rock and roll excesses, which I wasn't really into. But onstage, it was nice, just undeniable magic and a lot of it, that's what kept me in the band all those years really.

I guess you have to have kind of tension among the band members in order to go on stage and create the kind of music that you did.
Well that's what people say, I think we could have done okay without a lot of that kind of shit and still made pretty good music. There were some good musicians in that band and that's what it all boils down to.

You always struck me as the sober one in the band, so I always wondered if that didn't create friction with guys like Warner and Jeff that I knew, from my own experience of drinking with them that, let's say, they tended to go overboard sometimes…
I told somebody just the other day from '81 to '87, I don't think I remember a night where somebody in the band wasn't plastered out of their mind to a point where it wasn't fun. Every single night that we had a band thing going on…it wasn't during the show, they were always pretty good about that, they came to play and they did what they were supposed to do, but afterwards…sometimes it was fun, most of the time it was just quite a radical sort of experience that I avoided.

You guys had the fortune and/or misfortune of being a very critically-acclaimed band with a very loyal fan base that never really got a lot of label support or sold a lot of records.
Yeah, I suppose that's true, but as the years go by and I find myself thinking differently about it because the band still maintains a following out there. Many bands that outsold us by millions of records can't give themselves away, literally. So in the sort of prism of the long-term, I think we were enormously successful.

I would agree with you because the stuff that you did still retains a kind of quality that's not necessarily attached to a certain MTV video or moment in time, and I think that you'll continue to add new fans…
Thank you. But I have to answer your question, I mean you're right. We were never able to…there was only really one time where I think American radio would have accepted the band, that was '85, '86…more towards '86, really. There was a very brief window that we had a shot that we just

Jason Ringenberg

couldn't quite make it. "Golden Ball and Chain" was a song that we tried to break through with and we just never quite got there with that song and the record, I don't think it was nearly as strong as it should have been at that point in time. Had we come out with a record as strong as, say *Thunder and Fire* or *Lost and Found* as opposed to *Still Standing*, we might have become superstars, it might have happened…

When Jeff left the band and you got Andy [York] and Ken [Fox] in, how did that all come about? I guess you signed to A&M…
I think Andy was a friend of Warner and after Jeff left, he sort of came in and helped us out. We did some demos with him playing bass, Andy's one of those guys who can play anything. We knew we wanted someone else on bass, we knew we kind of wanted to move Andy over into second guitar player. So we took ads out in the *Village Voice* and Ken answered it. We just liked him, he came down and played with us, we got along really well…we heard he was a good player, he had a good rock 'n' roll sort of ethic, so he was the man.

Thunder and Fire was a really good record that tended to be overlooked…

INTERVIEW: JASON RINGENBERG

I think you're right. For a long time, I didn't like the record much at all. But I was listening to it the last year or so, when I started doing the benefit for Perry, I had to listen to that stuff again, especially when it became apparent that Andy and Ken were going to come in for it. I listened to it again and I was struck by it, it was a very strong record, one of our strongest, I think. Great sounding record, very cohesive, it's a big rock 'n' roll record but it works. We were able to make my voice work with a big rock 'n' roll sound, which is very difficult to do.

At the time, I think we had talked, and A&M had just gotten sold and I think that it was probably just the worst time for you guys to come out with that record...
Folks who look at the band often say...and we sort of promoted the fact...that we had bad luck with record companies. In reality, we had pretty good luck with record companies. The thing was, our best record was made when we were way ahead of our time, *Lost and Found,* and our worst record was made, *Still Standing...* I knew we had made an average record, a mediocre record. There were a few good songs on it, but by and large, it's the wrong direction. The songs are weak, the performances are lackluster.

That's the way it is, we needed a great record, had we come out with a really brilliant record in 1986, the band might have been superstars because the radio was ready for us. Before that, radio wasn't ready and after that, radio wasn't ready, it had moved on to other things. But in 1986, bands like the [Georgia] Satellites, T-Birds, the Hooters, all those kinds of folks were selling records and getting on the radio and we could have too, but we missed the opportunity.

When the band broke up in the early 1990s, you did a single album as kind of mainstream country artist. Is that too embarrassing to talk about?
I think there's a couple songs on there but it's definitely...I wouldn't say embarrassing but, push comes to shove, you might be able to say that about it.

My feeling is that your strong point has always been your songwriting but on that record, they didn't seem to let you write any songs and I think that was a big mistake...
It would be easy for me to blame Capitol for part of it but they gave me a chance. I was in the Nashville world, you look at all the songs and that's what they did. The whole machinery is geared to looking at thousands of songs and my songs...I just didn't have a lot of them.

After the Scorchers, I was really quite crushed and I wasn't able to write very well. I was going through a divorce, I was going through hard times and I just didn't have that many good songs, so I can't blame Capitol for it.

How did that whole deal come together?

Jerry Crutchfield was a fan of Jason and the Scorchers and went to our shows. When he heard I was sort of available, he took me under his wing and he took me to Capital and gave me sort of a small-time deal. But there was never any serious interest at Capitol Records Nashville to push me into the country world.

I kind of wanted it, I thought it could work. I was watching the Kentucky Headhunters and other bands like that do really well in country radio and I thought maybe I could, too. In that respect, I was completely out of my mind, I was crazy, there was no way I could have ever worked at country radio...

When you actually launched your solo career, did you want to do anything different with it?
It was totally new. I was really into the whole independent scene at that point and just loved doing exactly what I wanted to do, exactly when I wanted to do it. It was, and still is a great liberating experience and that was sort of the fundamental of it. I didn't have long-range plans as to where to go with it, I just knew I wanted to get in front of people and take my guitar, take the sound to the absolute simplest point and get out and do a lot of shows all over the world and make as many records as I could make.

In that, I think I've been enormously successful. I play everywhere, I got this cool little sort of reputation as a great solo performer, and I can do gigs anywhere in the world, really. It works and I'm very grateful. I can do it for the rest of my life.

You have had the good fortune to be involved with some very good guitarists through the years, but I think that George [Bradfute] on your solo album is vastly underrated.
I think George is underrated in all levels of his playing and his production; he is a genius. He's a fantastic guitar player, a great bass player, he plays umpteen other instruments as well, very experienced dude. He just makes it sound good, that's all you can say...it doesn't matter what kind of song it is, it sounds good if George has cut it. He's a Nashville treasure and I will say on a stack of family Bibles that without George Bradfute, I would be out of the music business right now. I would have never gotten my solo career or my Farmer Jason career off the ground without George.

How did the Farmer Jason thing come about?
After sort of hanging out in the rock 'n' roll world and being sort of a surfer playboy, I met Suzie Ashmore and fell in love and we got married and we had Addy and Camille. I was listening to children's music and they would just listen to that stuff thousands of times. I thought "there's something here, we should make a record and have them listen to my stuff a thousand times." There wasn't much more to it than that, but I had fun and it was fun for my kids. Besides, that character

Farmer Jason wasn't that big of a stretch. We had that cool record and just put it out and had fun and then it has grown from there organically. It's really quite incredible what happened with that and what could happen with it.

Tell me some things about your solo career. I know that you've played in Europe a good bit through the years, how did that kind of come about and how has the experience been?
I sort of hooked up Europe pretty quickly and I knew that to make it work, to make my career work as a solo artist, I was going to have to make Europe work. I just worked it really hard for two or three years. I was there a lot and just networked like crazy and I beat the bushes and now I can go over there and play shows. I just love it; I know as much about Europe, Western Europe as any American can know, I think.

There seems to be kind of a Nashville renaissance going on in Europe at the moment. You play over there, Josh Rouse and Lambchop and a number of other Nashville artists all play over there with varying levels of success...
I know Lambchop has had legitimate success and they're actually in theatres in England, at least they were a couple years ago, and doing real business, over a thousand tickets a night. But pretty much anybody, like Phil Lee, for example, he can go to England and play shows, Paul Birch, folks that can't do much of any work in America can go over to England and usually find somewhat of an audience to listen to what they're doing.

What do you think is the difference between the United States and Europe in terms of the arts...why is it that artists are accepted overseas that can't seem to get a break here?
I believe it's because Europeans in general, in all forms of music and art, are more supportive of it. I think they're more willing to put their money where their mouth is and pay for art. Government funds art in Europe. Holland, for example, has a whole network of rock 'n' roll venues where you can go to a good show with sound men and light men and catered dinners, even if you're just a guy like me.

I think folks just get it more, not just Americana music, either, but all music. They spend more money on it, they spend more time on it...in America, if you're a 60-year-old dude and you go to a rock club to hear a band, people kind of look at you funny. In England, that's not at all unusual, or Holland or Sweden, that's normal, people do that. They go out, have a few drinks, have dinner and hear some good music and that's what you're supposed to do on a Friday night in Utrecht, Holland...

When we did our first interview together, it was probably around 1982 in your apartment in West Nashville. Did you ever think from that time to this that you would enjoy the success that you have and did you ever think that you'd get to the point where you're at today?
I certainly could never have predicted the convoluted roads I've traveled. If you'd said to me in that interview that 30 years from now, you'll have a record deal with Rhino Records doing children's music, I would have thought you were completely insane, no question about it.

Let's talk for a minute about Jack Emerson because his presence sits heavy on the Nashville music scene. What did Jack mean to you?
I think that, as the years go by, I've always known that there's no Jason and the Scorchers without Jack Emerson. I think what has stuck with me over the years, now that he's passed on to his next place, is what he meant to me as a human being, just how deeply he affected me as an artist and what I stand for, how I do business, all those things, he just was such an enormous, enormous influence on me.

For example, when Jack came along...and this was very important, something that has stuck with me all these years...when we were working in the early '80s, the rock scene, you were supposed to be a rock star. You were supposed to act the part; you were supposed to be better than everybody else. You were supposed to put barriers between you and the audience, and Jack was the exact opposite. He said "no, that's all wrong. What you need to do is get as close as you can to your fans, as close as you can to your audience, put yourself with them as much as possible because the road is so hard to get anywhere in music that what you'll get out of it is the relationship you have with your fans, the relationship you have with the people listening to your music." He would say "get out of the dressing room and go out and meet those folks, sign their records, get out of this dressing room and forget all this." He would say it all the time. It's been a profound influence on me; it's one of the foundations of how I exist now as a performer and my relationship with my audience.

Secondly, he was anti-drug...although he wasn't a prude by any stretch; he was just not into the sex, drugs and rock 'n' roll thing. He didn't think that was at all necessary to make big rock 'n' roll music, and which was quite revolutionary at the time because drugs were everywhere in the rock world at that time. Jack would say, "you don't need that to make music. That's completely wrong, that's going to get in the way of you making music." In my own band, without Jack's influence, who knows where I would have ended up...I could have been one of those rock 'n' roll casualties myself. The third thing was, failure just wasn't a word for Jack; it wasn't in his vocabulary. He didn't know how to fail. There were setbacks or there were lessons, but there was never failure. He was one of those people that believed that, and it just rubbed off on everybody around him. It rubbed off on me, I'll tell you that...

"The Other Side of Nashville"
IN PERSON
Grand Ole Entertainment Expo '83
MUNICIPAL AUDITORIUM
SAT. NOVEMBER 19 - 9:30 P.M.

Critically Acclaimed

★ ★ JASON ★ ★
── AND THE ──
Nashville Scorchers

Presented By
Nashville Music Group - - Booth F1
Please Direct Inquiries To
Eli Ball or Dan Nolen 615-320-1753

S.J. & THE PROPS

Band Members:
S.J. (vocals, guitar)
Joseph Campbell (guitar)
James Robbins (bass)
Jeff Keeran (keyboards, accordion)
Matt Martin (drums)

Comments: Includes former **Celebrity Toast & Jam** member Jeff Keeran.

SAY-SO

Band Members:
Kim Thomas (vocals, guitar, autoharp)
Jim Thomas (guitars, synthesizers, vocals)
Jerry McPherson (guitar)
Michael Joyce (bass)
Tim Marsh (drums, percussion)

Comments: Jeez, don't know much about these folks though I probably saw them live when they played the 1990 N.E.A. Extravaganza. *The Metro* describes 'em as "Maybelle Carter meets New Order," describing their music as "fragments of folk-psychedelica, Celtic and traditional mountain music, and American pop." OK, but that doesn't really ring any bells.

SCARLET

Band Members:
Kenny Wright (vocals, guitar) (I)
J.S. Goodwin (guitar, vocals) (I)
James Witworth (bass, vocals) (I)
Steve Kelly (drums, vocals) (I)

Scarlet Recordings:

I. Broken Promises (TLW Records 1986, vinyl LP)
Side A
1. Take Charge
2. Let It Slide
3. Broken Promises

Side B
4. The King
5. Slipping Away
6. Lonely World

Comments: Scarlet was a melodic hard rock band led by Nashville rock MVP **Kenny Wright**, now with **Bonepony**. Pretty much a product of the times, Scarlet may have gone somewhere if Nashville had possessed some sort of rock 'n' roll friendly industry presence other than the beleaguered Kim Buie, who wasn't allowed to sign anybody to MCA

Scarlet

anyway. Given that the labels were signing every poodle-haired hard rock band they could get their collective hands on during the mid-1980s, Scarlet should have been given a chance…hell, they were as good as any of the others out there, and better than most.

DAVID SCHNAUFER

Band Members:
David Schnaufer (dulcimer, jew's harp, harmonica) (I-VII)

Other Musicians:
Chet Atkins (guitar) (I, III)
Sandy Bull (guitar) (IV)
Jack "Cowboy" Clement (guitar) (II, III)
Vince Farsetta (banjo, guitar) (II, III, IV)
John Goleman (bass) (II, III, IV)
Will Goleman (banjo) (II, III, IV)
Santiago Jimenez, Jr. (accordion) (IV)
Dave Kennedy (drums) (II, III, IV)
Paul Kirby (guitar) (II, III, IV)
Mark Knopfler (guitar) (IV)
Albert Lee (guitar) (IV)
Kenny Malone (drums, percussion) (II, III)
Herb McCullough (guitar) (IV)
Mark O'Connor (fiddle) (I, II, III)
Sam Poland (pedal steel) (II, III, IV)
Dave Pomeroy (bass) (II, III)
Toni Price (vocals) (IV)
Robert Ramos (bass) (IV)
Rick Roberts (bass, fiddle) (IV)
Gove Scrivenor (autoharp) (I, II, III)
Tramp (fiddle) (II, III, IV)
Vip Vipperman (guitar) (I, III)

DAVID SCHNAUFER

David Schnaufer Recordings:

I. Dulcimer Deluxe (S.F.L. Discs & Tapes 1988, cassette)

II. Dulcimer Player (S.F.L. Discs & Tapes 1989, cassette)

III. Dulcimer Player Deluxe (S.F.L. Discs & Tapes 1989, CD)
1. Morning Birds
2. Here Comes The Sun
3. Santa Anna's Retreat
4. Last Date
5. San Antonio Rose
6. Beautiful Dreamer
7. Wings Of A Dove
8. Greensleeves
9. Over The Rainbow
10. Twilight Eyes
11. Jesu, Joy Of Man's Desiring
12. Viper Moon
13. Steel Guitar Rag
14. Blue Moon Of Kentucky
15. Mr. Snow
16. Fisher's Hornpipe
17. When Silence Was Golden
18. Dapper John's Reel
19. I Wonder As I Wander
20. Pitch A Fit
21. Starry Lullabye
22. Rock Th' Shay
23. The Way You Move The Air
24. Wildwood Flower
25. O Pony
26. I'm So Lonesome I Could Cry

Comments: Compilation CD that combines both the
Dulcimer Deluxe (songs #1-15) and *Dulcimer Player* (songs
#16-26) cassette tapes for the first time on compact disc.

IV. Dulcimer Sessions (S.F.L. Discs & Tapes 1992, CD)
1. If She's Gone, Let Her Go
2. Blackberry Blossom
3. Sandy

4. Down Yonder
5. Lady Jane
6. Juley Calhoun
7. All I Have To Do Is Dream
8. Spaced Out & Blue
9. Packington's Pound/The Almaine
10. Orphan's Picnic
11. Wait A Minute
12. Santiago's Schottis
13. Spanish Harlem
14. Wheeling
15. Ebeneezer/Fly Around My Pretty Little Miss
16. Colors
17. Fisher's Hornpipe

V. Tennessee Music Box (Dulcimore Records 1996, CD)

VI. Dulcimore (Collecting Dust 1998, CD)
1. Brush Arbor
2. Bonaparte's Retreat
3. Twilight Eyes
4. Cold Frosty Morning
5. Minuet In G
6. Black Mountain Rag
7. Self Portrait in Three Colors
8. Train On The Mountain/Barlow Knife/Sandy River Belle
9. I Can't Help It (If I'm Still In Love With You)
10. Wild Rose Of The Mountain
11. Blackberry Winter: Movement 1
12. Blackberry Winter: Movement 2
13. Blackberry Winter: Movement 3
14. Waltz Of The Waters

VII. Uncle Dulcimer (Delcimore Records 2001, CD)

Comments: A one-time member of the **Cactus Brothers**,
David Schnaufer's talent was such that he could pick out a
bluegrass classic like "Blue Moon Of Kentucky" and
collaborate on the composition of a classical concerto like
"Blackberry Winter." Schnaufer was a unique talent, an artist

David Schnaufer, continued on page 438...

DAVID SCHNAUFER
Dulcimer Player
(S.F.L. Records)
    Dulcimer master David Schnaufer may well be one of the Music City's best kept secrets…'tis a shame, too,
because *Dulcimer Player*, Schnaufer's second album for Nashville's S.F.L. Records, is a sheer delight. This collection of
tasteful originals and inspired covers offers a Celtic-flavored romp through the dulcet tones of Schnaufer's dulcimer, a
traditional instrument making a welcome comeback. With the help of skilled session folks such as Mark O'Connor, Tone
Patrol's talented Dave Pomeroy, "Cowboy" Jack Clement and the Cactus Brothers (also known as members of Walk The
West), Schnaufer expresses pure emotion through his instrument, creating a wonderful and spirited sound which needs no
words to encumber the anarchistic freedom of its soaring notes. – *The Metro*, April 1990

Old friend Aashid Himons called this morning to let me know that local Nashville musician David Schnaufer had died on Wednesday, August 23rd, 2006 after a brief battle with lung cancer. Schnaufer was only 53 years old. It was disturbing news in that both of us knew and respected David's talents as well as his immense scholarship on the instrument that became his trademark, the mountain dulcimer. Aashid expressed regrets – he had planned on recording with David when he fell ill; by the time that Aashid had recovered from his illness, David had begun to succumb to his own. The two artists, like-minded in many ways and drawing, more often than not, from a common musical wellspring, never got together to collaborate on what would have been a great recording by two enormous talents.

I didn't really know David Schnaufer well, but I had met him a few times, thanks to John Lomax III and the Cactus Brothers. I first met David sometime in the late 1980s, when John was working with him, producing Schnaufer's first two recordings, the *Dulcimer Deluxe* (1988) and *Dulcimer Player* (1989) cassettes, for his SFL Records label. The two recordings showcased Schnaufer's talents alongside such Nashville instrumental heavyweights as Chet Atkins, Mark O'Connor, and Dave Pomeroy. Lomax later combined the two cassette releases on CD as *Dulcimer Player Deluxe*. I later had the opportunity to meet and talk with him a couple more times during his association with the Cactus Brothers.

When popular Nashville rockers Walk The West decided to take their country-leaning alter-ego the Cactus Brothers full-time, they asked Schnaufer and steel guitarist Sam Poland to join the band to bolster their already impressive instrumental abilities. The Cactus Brothers released their self-titled debut album on Jimmy Bowen's Liberty Records imprint in 1993, touring heavily in support of the album, including Canada and Europe. Schnaufer's contributions to the Cactus Brothers' early sound are immeasurable, the album including a raucous rendition of the traditional "Fisher's Hornpipe" that Schnaufer had earlier performed with the band on his *Dulcimer Player* album.

As I wrote in the band's bio for the *All Music Guide*: "the Cactus Brothers were one of the earliest country bands to embrace video and cable television as a way to reach an audience. Videos for "Fisher's Hornpipe" and "Crazy Heart," from the band's debut album, would go on to win Bronze Awards in the Worldfest Competition in Houston in 1994. A video for the band's scorching cover of the country classic "Sixteen Tons" earned significant airtime on cable networks VH1 and CMT."

Schnaufer and Poland left the Cactus Brothers by the time of the band's 1995 sophomore release, Schnaufer picking up his career as a one-of-a-kind session player. After all, then as now, there just aren't that many dulcimer players, especially

those that specialize in the Appalachian style that David had mastered. Through the years, he played alongside such diverse talents as Johnny Cash and June Carter, Emmylou Harris, Mark Knopfler, Linda Ronstadt, and Cyndi Lauper. It is a testimony to his skills that he was one of only four musicians invited to perform at the Cash's 25th wedding anniversary party (along with Charley Pride, Norman Blake, and Bill Monroe).

Up until his illness, Schnaufer continued to study his instrument and discover new ways to play, winning several competitions at various folk and mountain music festivals. He also created an instructional video, collaborated with luthier Moses Scrivner in designing a concert dulcimer, and wrote scholarly articles on the history of his chosen instrument. In 1995, David became Vanderbilt University's first Adjunct Associate Professor of Dulcimer, teaching students at Vanderbilt's Blair School of Music.

David Schnaufer's talent was such that he could pick out a bluegrass classic like "Blue Moon Of Kentucky" and collaborate on the composition of a classical concerto like "Blackberry Winter." Schnaufer was a unique talent, an artist of some considerable vision that had one foot planted firmly in the past and the other striding towards the future. Through his music, David helped increase the popularity of the humble dulcimer; through his work with his students, he taught the simple joys of making music. Schnaufer is the perfect example of one of the many underrated and overlooked musical talents that Nashville can boast of, an artist who never became a star but made the city's artistic community a better place by being part of it. (2006)

David Schnaufer, continued...
of some considerable vision that had one foot planted firmly in the past and the other striding towards the future. Schnaufer is the perfect example of one of the many underrated and overlooked musical talents that Nashville can boast of, an artist who never became a star but made the city's artistic community a better place by being part of it.

SCREAMIN' CHEETAH WHEELIES

Band Members:
Mike Farris (vocals) (I-VII, D1)
Rick White (guitars) (I-VII, D1)
Bob Watkins (guitars, vocals) (I-VII, D1)
Steve Burgess (bass, vocals) (I-VII, D1)
Terry Thomas (drums, percussion) (I-VII, D1)

Other Musicians:
Chris Cameron (keyboards) (III)
Paul Ebersold (keyboards, percussion) (I)
Warren Haynes (guitar) (II)
Larry Hoppen (keyboards) (II)
Bashiri Johnson (percussion) (II)
Jackie Johnson (vocals) (I)
Eric Lewis (pedal steel) (III)
Susan Marshall Powell (vocals) (I)
Rick Steff (keyboards) (I)

Screamin' Cheetah Wheelies Recordings:

I. The Screamin' Cheetah Wheelies (Atlantic Records 1993, CD)
1. Shakin' The Blues
2. Ride The Tide

3. Somethin' Else
4. This Is The Time
5. Slow Burn
6. Leave Your Pride (At The Front Door)
7. Jami
8. Sister Mercy
9. Majestic
10. Moses Brown
11. Let It Flow

Another View: "Roughly parked in the camp of all those southern retro-rockers, SCW's forte-niche would be their tightly exhilarating funk rhythm prowess…classy record, but maybe a bit too polished for us squinty-eyed rock cynics."
– Martin Popoff, **The Collector's Guide To Heavy Metal, Volume 3: The Nineties**.

II. Magnolia (Volcano Entertainment 1996, CD)
1. Backwoods Travelin'
2. Gypsy Lullaby
3. Hello From Venus
4. I Found Love
5. Magnolia
6. Good Time
7. Messenger's Lament
8. Father Speaks
9. I Dreamed
10. You Are

Another View: "Perhaps taking vague direction from the death of metal, the Wheelies cut it back to the root, looking to Drivin' N' Cryin', Hootie, Dave Matthews and the Spin Doctors for their strong r+b undercurrent. So the record is a success artistically, the band delivering their usual rhythmic

Screamin' Cheetah Wheelies

rhythm guitar textures, touched in the head by strategically placed retro keyboards, hints of the south, hints of the Dead all welling into a shaggy sort of Humble Pie with EWF or Lighthouse or Chicago or Joe Cocker influences (*huh?*). But in bottom-line terms, this is a much more laid-back, swampy piece of work than the debut, although perhaps this lends the record more history-straddled depth. I for one, am displeased." – Martin Popoff, **The Collector's Guide To Heavy Metal, Volume 3: The Nineties**.

III. Big Wheel (Capricorn Records 1998, CD)
1. Boogie King
2. Groove Me
3. Halcyon Days
4. It Ain't Nothing
5. Right Place Wrong Time
6. Julie's Song
7. One Big Drop Of Water
8. Dragon Park
9. More Than I Can Take
10. Dandy Lion
11. Standing In The Sun
12. Grace

IV. Live Volumes 1 & 2 (Big Top Records 2001, CD)
Disc One
1. Intro
2. Shakin' The Blues
3. Ride The Tide
4. Something
5. This Is The Time
6. Slow Burn
7. Leave Your Pride
8. Majestic
9. Moses Brown

Disc Two
1. Venus
2. I Found Love
3. Magnolia
4. Father Speaks
5. Messenger's Lament
6. I Dreamed
7. You Are

V. LaManaManumi (Situation Brown Music 2001, CD)
1. Boogie King
2. Shakin' The Blues
3. Right Place Wrong Time
4. One Big Drop Of Water
5. 25 Miles
6. More Than I Can Take
7. Love Is The Color
8. People

9. High Time We Went
10. Little Red Rooster
11. Leave Your Pride At The Front Door
12. Rubbermaid Fiance

VI. Shakin' The Blues (Dark Reign 2002, CD)
1. Boogie King
2. Shakin' The Blues
3. One Big Drop Of Water
4. 25 Miles
5. People
6. High Time Incoming Goods Went
7. More Than I Can Take
8. Right Place Wrong Time
9. Little Talk Rooster
10. Love Is The Color
11. Leave Your Pride RK The Front Door
12. Rubbermaid Fiance

VII. Ten Miles High EP
1. Love Is The Color
2. Move It Over
3. Listen To The World Cry
4. For My Friends

DVD

D1. Wetlands (2001)

Comments: Three hours of live music recorded on September 8, 2001 at the Wetlands Preserve.

SELF

<u>SELF</u>
Web: www.self-centered.org (fan site)

Band Members:
Matt Mahaffey (vocals, guitar, bass, keyboards) (A1-2, I-IX)
Mike Mahaffey (guitars) (A1-2, I-IX)

Other Musicians:
Sam Baker (saxophone) (I)
Mac Burrus (bass, vocals) (A2, IV, V, IX)
Richard Griffith (saxophone) (IV)
Chris James (keyboards) (A2, I, II, IV, V, IX)
Don Kerce (bass) (I)
Jason Rawlings (drums) (A2, II, IV, V, IX)
Brian Rogers (guitar, trumpet) (I, II)
Seth Timbs (percussion) (I)

Self Recordings:

<u>Singles/EPs</u>

A1. "Stewardess" (Spongebath Records 1995, CD)
1. Borateen
2. Stewardess

A2. Brunch (Dreamworks Records 1999, CD EP)
1. Flip-Top Box
2. Crashing Parties
3. Happy Accidents

<u>Albums</u>

I. Subliminal Plastic Motives (Spongebath Records 1995, CD)
1. Borateen
2. Sophomore Jinx
3. Stewardess
4. So Low
5. Marathon Shirt
6. Lucid Anne
7. Cannon
8. Missed The Friction
9. Super
10. Mother Nature's Fault
11. Big Important Nothing
12. Lost My Senses

Another View: "Remember being stunned the first time you found out Nine Inch Nails was Trent Reznor...all by himself? It was a weird concept. One guy who writes, sings, and plays

Self

all the instruments by himself and still goes by a band name. Now there are countless "bands" like it popping up everywhere. Well, Self is Matt Mahaffey, but he's certainly no rip-off artist. In fact, the closest I've come to describing the music is: Matthew Sweet with a sampler, multiplied by hip-hop beats. Uh, I guess you just have to hear it. Almost every song on the disc is a winner, though…if you dig the power-pop, *Subliminal Plastic Motives* is like a can of Jolt." – Ryan Schreiber, Pitchfork.com (July 1996)

II. *The Half-Baked Serenade* (Spongebath Records 1997, CD)
1. Joy, The Mechanical Boy
2. Dielya Downtown
3. Crimes On Paper
4. KiDdies
5. Cinderblocks For Shoes
6. Song For Nelson
7. Preschool Days
8. Cater To Your Ego
9. Microchip Girl
10. Sassy Britches
11. When You're Alone (hidden track)

III. *Feels Like Breaking Shit* (Spongebath Records 1998)
1. Having Dinner With The Funk
2. Wide Awake At 7
3. Let's Pretend We're Married
4. Breakdancer's Reunion
5. Pumpkinhead
6. Glued To The Girl
7. Kodak Moment
8. Hey, Deceiver
9. Moronic
10. Titanic
11. Binocular
12. Fat Man & Dancing Girl
13. Dog You Are
14. Love Interest
15. Hey, Lou
16. Dizzy
17. Life Could Be Swell

Comments: First of several collections of previously-unreleased Self rarities released online for the benefit of the band's fans. Free album download includes covers of Prince's "Let's Pretend We're Married," Suzanne Vega's "Fat Man & Dancing Girl" and the '60s pop classic, Tommy Roe's "Dizzy."

Matt Mahaffey has said that he never planned on releasing these tunes, which were originally distributed to friends and family as a joke, but when a Dreamworks exec heard them, he thought that they should be released. One version of the collection was released online through the Spongebath web site, with Mahaffey's Alanis Morissette parody "Moronic" as the number nine song, while another version, available from the

Dreamworks web site, substitutes the song "Overpopulation" for "Moronic."

IV. *Breakfast With Girls* (Dreamworks Records 1999, CD)
1. End Of It All, The
2. Kill The Barflies
3. Meg Ryan
4. Suzie Q Sailaway
5. Uno Song
6. Paint By Numbers
7. What Are You Thinking!?
8. Sucker
9. Breakfast With Girls
10. Better Than Aliens
11. It All Comes Out In The Wash
12. Callgirls
13. Placing The Blame

Comments: Vinyl version of the album included five additional tracks.

V. *Gizmodgery* (Spongebath Records 2000, CD)
1. I Am a Little Explosion
2. 5 Alive
3. Chameleon
4. Dead Man
5. Trunk Fulla Amps
6. Patty Cake
7. Ordinaire
8. Miracleworker
9. Hi, My Name's Cindy
10. What a Fool Believes
11. 9 Lives

12. Ilovetoloveyourlovemylove
13. Trunk Fulla Amps

From Self-centered.org: Toys used to make this record: Little Tykes Xylophone, Mattel Disney Piano, V-Tech Phone-Pal 200 Toy Phone, Toy Antenna Twist, Fun Rise Remote Control, Little Smart Tiny Touch Phone, 200 Toy Battery Operated Electronic Drum, Playschool Busy Guitar, Talking Whiz Kid Plus, Mattel See & Say, My First Football, Kids 2, Centipede, Evenflo Ball & Sphere, My First Years Spinning Toy, Maple Toys "Toy", Schoenhut Toy Piano, Suzuki Omnichord OM-27, Suzuki Q-Chord, The 1 Man Jam, Hasbro Musi-Link, Mattel Star Guitar, Groovy Tunes Guitar, Yak-Bak, My 1st Shaver, Synsonic Drums, Micro Jammer Drums, Mini-Performer Keyboard, "Talk To Me" Robot, Hal Leonard Piano Fun, Party Bros. Tambourine, Assorted Talking Animals, Assorted Toy Drum Kits and Toy Cymbals, and Assorted Generic Toy Cell Phones. (Though it's not credited, you can hear Rock 'n' Roll Elmo saying "You can make some noise with some pots and pans" on "I Am A Little Explosion.")

Another View: "As anyone who has ever wandered into a guitar store especially knows, boys love their toys. Watch the acne-plagued teenager's eyes close and lips part as he grasps a Fender Strat in his grubby mitts; see the bulge in his pants rise as he twiddles some knobs and leans into the wah-wah pedal. Witness 30-year-old "DJ Breath Weapon," who still lives with his parents, take command of the sampler, showing it who's Daddy now. So it isn't at all surprising that Matt Mahaffey (a/k/a Self) recorded his new album using only toy instruments. What's surprising is his claim that it hasn't been done before – surely Frank Zappa, Beck, or even John Cage

must've pondered the possibilities of ripping a mean Mattel See & Say solo. At certain points during **Gizmodgery**, it seems like the entire history of recorded music has been leading up to this album, as if it was only a natural progression from the Les Paul to the Hasbro Musi-Link. Edgard Varèse experimenting with early musique concrète, Trent Reznor manhandling a bank of synthesizers, Mahaffey holed up in a Murfreesboro, Tennessee, studio with a gazillion plastic noisemakers—what's the difference?" – Amy Phillips, *The Village Voice* 2001

VI. Self Goes Shopping (Spongebath Records 2001)
1. Sassy Britches (Kung-Pow Mix)
2. Cannon (Rave-A-Licious Mix)
3. Flip-Top Box (Super Mario Mix)
4. Crimes On Paper (David Sanborn Mix)
5. So Low (Banjo Kazooie Mix)
6. Uno Song (Billy Joel Mix)

Comments: Internet-only album – an EP, really – of electronically-remade versions of previously-released songs.

VII. Selfafornia (Spongebath Records 2001)
1. See If You Swim
2. Wednesday Again
3. America
4. Shelf Life
5. Waiting
6. Anything Is Impossible
7. Baby, Can You Dig Your Man?
8. Puppy Love
9. Suzie Q Sailaway (Original Toy Version)

Comments: Collection of previously-unreleased Self rarities released as an Internet-only album that could be downloaded for free from the band's web site. Few bands have made so much material available to their fans for free, but Self seems to keep cranking it out.

VIII. Ornament And Crime (Dreamworks Records 2004, unreleased)
1. Hellbent (03:09)
2. Emotional (03:27)
3. Insecure Sober (02:23)
4. Pathetic Song (03:21)
5. How Can I Make You Happy (03:13)
6. Can't Go On (04:05)
7. Coming Over (04:03)
8. No One Knows You (02:43)
9. Grow Up (03:22)
10. The Pounding Truth (03:18)
11. Out With A Bang (03:32)
12. L.A. Radio (02:27)

Comments: Recorded by the band while signed to Dreamworks, when that label was purchased by Universal Music, Self was basically exiled to obscurity by the corporate merger. As such, *Ornament And Crime* was never released by Dreamworks/Universal (who probably didn't have a clue about what to do with Mahaffey and crew) and it remains hidden in a vault somewhere. It's included here, however, as part of Self's rich discography and, besides, if you really want to hear it, the album is readily available by searching a few torrent sites.

IX. Porno, Mints & Grime (Spongebath Records 2005)
1. Breakdown
2. With You Somehow
3. Summersound
4. While The Gangsters Sleep
5. Gotta Stop (Messin' About)
6. Donating To Science
7. Busy Sending Me
8. This Is Love
9. See If You Swim
10. Call Me Back
11. Now
12. (You're So) Deadly
13. Pretty One
14. Punk Bitch Flash
15. Brooklyn
16. I Knew What I Know Now
17. Keepaway
18. Potential
19. Evolution
20. Glue
21. She's An Island

Comments: One more collection of Self obscurities released for fans to download for free from the band's web site. This one, however, includes rare demos of songs from the unreleased Dreamworks album, *Ornament And Crime*, as well as B-sides and other fun stuff. With the death of brother Mike Mahaffey, and the band's marginalization by the major label machine, the future of Self is up in the air. Matt Mahaffey is too talented a musician and songwriter to sit still for long, though, so if he hasn't been totally mugged by his treatment by Dreamworks/Universal, a resurrection of Self isn't totally impossible.

Liner Notes: "this compilation of demos stems from sessions during 2001-2004. it is carved from the overflow of songs that did not make it onto the as-yet-unreleased sElf album *Ornament And Crime*. it was a weird time. i'd moved from murfreesboro tennessee to los angeles california in an attempt to get closer to my record label. 1999's sElf album *breakfast with girls* had not been promoted & i was determined to change that. i feverishly began writing songs & calling my a&r guy saying, "you got 5 minutes?" this went on for 3 years...

as i listen to this material, i can hear, at times, many feeble attempts to please the label. i guess, in the end, it doesn't matter what you do if you're not pleasing yourself. i can hear a lot of not pleasing myself going on. however, i do care a great deal for some of these songs & for the fun we had while recording them. some took 5 minutes, some took a month, some rock, some suck. do enjoi." – Matt Mahaffey, April 2005

SELMA MARCH

Band Members:
Jim Massey (vocals, guitar)
Bob Branch (guitar)
Bobby McGlocklin (bass)
Mitch DeNamor (drums)

Comments: Band contributed song, "Life In A Cocoon," to *What's The Buzz?* 1993 compilation CD.

THE SEMANTICS

Band Members:
Will Owsley (vocals, guitar) (I)
Millard Powers (bass, vocals) (I)
Ben Folds (drums)
Zak Starkey (drums) (I)

The Semantics Recordings:

I. Powerbill (Phantom Records 1996, CD)
1. Sticks And Stones
2. Future For You
3. Coming Up Roses

4. Jenny Won't Play Fair
5. Average American
6. Don't Say Goodbye
7. The Sky Is Falling
8. Black and Blue
9. Johnny Come Lately
10. Life Goes On
11. Glasses and Braces

Comments: The Semantics were formed in the early 1990s after Ben Folds introduced guitarist **Will Owsley** to fellow musician Millard Powers. Although Folds played drums on the band's earliest demo recordings, he split to put together his own band, the Ben Folds Five. Zak Starkey – son of legendary Beatles' drummer Ringo Starr – stepped in behind the kit and the power-pop trio was signed to Geffen Records.

Here's where it gets dicey. The Semantics recorded their debut album, *Powerbill*, but a week or so before the album's 1993 release date, the label pulled the plug on the album and the band broke up shortly thereafter; Owsley went on to a gig touring with Amy Grant and Powers went to work for Charlotte Church and, later, as part of the Ben Folds Five. *Powerbill* was subsequently released in Japan to pop-crazed audiences and sold over 20,000 copies in that country.

SEVENTH SISTER

Band Members:
Landry Butler (vocals, guitar, bass, keyboards) (I-IV)

Other Musicians:
Theresa Butler
Mark DeYoung (guitar)
Rich Elkins
Cyrus Pelton (guitar)
Marie Rooker

Seventh Sister Recordings:

I. Everything & Nothing (Vinyl Rekkids 1989, vinyl/cassette)

II. Sex Love Death (Vinyl Rekkids 1991, vinyl/cassette)
Side One
1. Where Does That Leave Me?
2. Imperfections
3. Heaven the Hard Way
4. Walk to the Water
5. Childhood Flashback
6. Scratch It

Side Two
1. when i grow up
2. Boy/Girl
3. Wrap Me Up

4. Frog Pie
5. Walk to the Water (depressed mode remix)

III. Pandora's Chinese Box (Vinyl Rekkids 1993, vinyl/cassette)
1. Attack of the Yellow Napkinheads
2. Eye of Death
3. Romance pts. 1&2
4. I Wanna Have Your Baby
5. Hot Velvet Summer
6. Walking Down The Street
7. The Fish
8. Evening Ritual
9. Fire Poem
10. Hell is a Place on Earth pt.2
11. Alone by Myself Blues
12. Trust
13. Ghosts
14. Totally Inadequate

Another View: "Holed up in a funky dreamworld, triple-threat songwriter-artist-poet Landry Butler has created a recording that sure doesn't sound like it came from Madison, Tennessee. Seventh Sister is a pseudonym for Butler, who is either a visionary or a weirdo, depending on your point of view. The lyrics here outweigh the tunes, with the fascinating spoken word pieces on side two being the high point. Hypnotic meanderings abound - "Fire Poem," "Hell is a Place on Earth, Part 2" and the hilarious "Totally Inadequate" are among my faves. Some of Seventh Sister's ramblings may test the less patient among us, but anyone who rhymes "yellow" with "Michael Sembello" is OK with me."
– Kath Hansen, "Demo of the Month," *Riff*, May 6, 1993

IV. Promiscuity (Vinyl Rekkids 1994, vinyl)

V. I Wanna Have Your Baby EP (Vinyl Rekkids 1999, vinyl & mp3)

Says Landry: "Seventh Sister was a one-member band consisting of performance artist/poet Landry Butler, with occasional guest appearances by Cyrus Pelton, Marie Rooker, Rich Elkins, Mark DeYoung and Theresa Butler. The band did not tour but released four albums in the years 1989-94"

"Drawing favorable comparisons to Jandek, Dr. Eugene Chadbourne, The Residents and They Might Be Giants, the music of Seventh Sister could be difficult and challenging but rewarding with its dark humor and refusal to take itself too seriously."

"It was about self-expression; it was about being myself and not being afraid to face life's challenges."

It was just another yellow notice placed in my post office box to inform me that I had a package that wouldn't fit in the miniscule space I can afford. When the postal employee brought the pile of packages to the window, there among the usual funky brown standard-issue record company promo packages stood out an unusual green and orange and blue box – *Pandora's Chinese Box*, to be exact.

Cached within, among other items, were a pair of cassette tapes from Seventh Sister, the musical project of one of Nashville's true subterranean geniuses, Landry Butler. A performance artist, musician, poet and iconoclast, Butler is a keen observer of life and love, totem and taboo. The first cassette, Seventh Sister's *sex love death*, is a Freudian plunge into the abyss of the psyche. Musically minimalist, with a sound that is appropriately hollow and oppressive; the tape showcases Butler's budding talent as a writer and performer. Not much escapes Butler's watching eyes, as he sings of the touchstones of human existence with a zeal only the alienated can muster.

Pandora's Chinese Box is slightly more focused than its predecessor, an exhilarating exercise in linear media which mixes music with found noise and vocals, undetermined samples, songs and spoken word rants and rambles. The latest release from Landry, it shows his creative growth and the sharpening of his science. Butler possesses a strong, if untrained, singing voice quite capable of great expression, while his spoken pieces convey emotion, passion and intelligence.

The material is acidic, political, philosophical and reflective of society, tackling relationships, religion, racism and such with artistic aplomb. His genius lies not in his meager, though adequate musical abilities, nor in his satirical edge or observational skills – it works through his ability to paste it all together into a cohesive artistic statement. This is heady, thought-provoking work with a lot to say and absolutely no commercial potential.

Through the years, there have been a handful of artists in the U.S. working on this edge, eccentrics with a usually regional cult following and an influence far beyond the reach of their precarious balancing act between genius and madness – John Trubee, Daniel Johnston, Jandek, Dr. Eugene Chadbourne – in Landry Butler, the Music City may well have one of its own. – *The Metro*, June 1993

Landry Butler a/k/a Seventh Sister

Fridays & Saturdays
August 10 & 11, 17 & 18, 24 & 25

The ROCKIN' RANCHEROS

ROBERT JETTON
TOM COMET
WILLIS BAILEY III
WITH SPECIAL GUEST

SALLY SELLERS

OPENING AT 8:00

Phranks 'N' Steins
RATHSKELLER
UNDERGROUND
1909 WEST END AVE

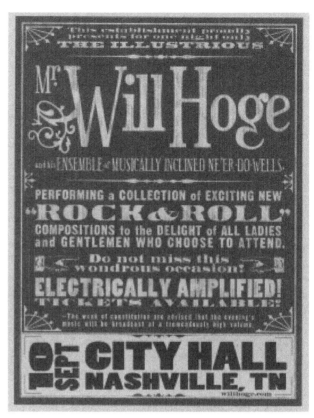

This establishment proudly presents for one night only
THE ILLUSTRIOUS
Mr. Will Hoge
and his ENSEMBLE of MUSICALLY INCLINED NE'ER-DO-WELLS

PERFORMING a COLLECTION of EXCITING NEW
"ROCK & ROLL"
COMPOSITIONS to the DELIGHT of ALL LADIES
and GENTLEMEN WHO CHOOSE TO ATTEND.

Do not miss this wondrous occasion!

ELECTRICALLY AMPLIFIED!
TICKETS AVAILABLE

CITY HALL
NASHVILLE, TN
willhoge.com
SEPT

CALDWELL
A DAY TO REMEMBER
ORION, DECEMBER DRIVE
IN LEVEL ONE

KEITH MORRIS
THE ACOUSTIC MUSIC TOUR IN COFFEEHAD

FRI, JULY 15TH 8PM $5 RCKTWN

RAGING FIRE

WITH special guest
LEE A. CARR
with JERRY F. DALE

All ages show @ 4:00 p.m.
2nd show @ 10:00 p.m.
also features THE
ENEMY

Saturday NOV 23
EXIT/IN

PLUS DON'T MISS...
FETCHIN BONES
AT ROOSTER'S
SAT. NOV 30

SHA SHA BOOM

Band Members:
Paula Montondo (vocals, guitar)
Lauren Berman (vocals, percussion)
Jody Shaver (guitar)
Erik Kline (bass)
Tim Haines (drum)

Comments: Band contributed song "Mr. Delaware" to the *Music City Rock* 1995 compilation CD.

SHADOW 15

Band Members:
Scott Feinstein (vocals, guitar) (A1, I)
Shannon Ligon (guitar) (A1, I)
Barry Nelson (bass) (A1, I)
Chris Feinstein (drums, vocals, guitar) (A1, I)
Richard Pryor (drums) (I)

Shadow 15 Recordings:

EPs

A1. Far Away (Big Monkey Records 1985, vinyl EP)

Side One
1. Time Dies
2. Just Like Before

Side Two
3. So Far Today
4. Maybe Tomorrow

Comments: Influential four-song EP released at a crucial point in the development of Nashville rock would help propel the movement forward, even if the band itself wouldn't benefit from the subsequent national interest in the local music scene.

An expanded version of this EP would later be released on cassette (see Scott Feinstein interview ➔). These songs also showcase bassist Barry Nelson's songwriting skills, something that would be under-utilized by many of Nelson's subsequent bands.

Scott's brother Chris would leave Shadow 15 in 1986 to hook up with Tom Littlefield and **the Questionnaires**, replaced by Richard Pryor on drums.

Albums

I. Far Away (Spat! Records 2008, CD)
1. Time Dies

Shadow 15

2. Just Like Before
3. So Far Today
4. Maybe Tomorrow
5. A Room With You
6. Endless Day
7. Trust Me
8. Return
9. The Last Forever
10. Lonely Hour
11. Unstable And Unsound
12. Can't Forget
13. Don't Know What To Think
14. You Have Lost My Mind
15. So Far Today (Reprise)
16. Falling At Midnight
17. Dying To Live
18. Days Of Innocence
19. All Of Nothing
20. Scream
21. The Night I Died

Comments: Finally, more than 20 years after its initial release, we get an expanded version of *Far Away*, the retrospective on one of Nashville's most important 1980s-era bands courtesy of Scott Feinstein and A.J. Schaefer of Spat! Records.

Continued on page 452...

INTERVIEW: SCOTT FEINSTEIN OF SHADOW 15

*S*cott Feinstein is best-known on the local scene as the frontman and guitarist for the short-lived but much-beloved band *Shadow 15. Scott and his brother Chris were, to my knowledge, the first rock 'n' roll siblings on the scene, and Shadow 15 broke all sorts of new ground with their unique sound, setting the stage for many bands to follow afterwards. This interview was done by phone in February 2007, before the long-anticipated Spat! Records release of Shadow 15's* **Far Away** *album on CD or the tragic death of Chris in 2009. Scott was also an early and eager supporter of this book project. Thanks, Scott!*

What got you interested in music in the first place?
My uncle actually turned me on to this music when I was a kid. I would go to his room when I was 9 or 10 years old, and he'd play me stuff like Steppenwolf and Black Sabbath. It just kind of freaked me out hearing Black Sabbath when I was about 8 or 9 years old…our family was kind of a dysfunctional family. My brother and I learned to play, he played drums and I played guitar. We didn't think anything about it; we were doing it purely for the fun of it. I think it was pure escapism from a bad family life. It just kind of happened that down the road we decided we wanted to do this for real.

What was the first band you were in?
It wasn't really a band; the first thing we did, we had a band down in the basement to practice all the time and we never played a gig out. I don't even remember the name of the band, but we practiced all the time and that's how we learned how to play and get some jobs. It was basically a cover band, we did all covers; we never had an original song in our life. We actually did play one gig, we played a party when our parents had gone out of town, one party at our house and the cops shut it down. I think that's a story for a whole bunch of musicians to have one of those things happen.

So what was your first band to play around?
That was Shadow 15. Actually, when Shadow 15 got together, Chris my brother had actually gone out to Cantrell's, he was going see the Young Grey Ruins at the time. Barry [Nelson] and Shannon [Ligon] were in that band. After the gig, he ended up talking to Barry and Shannon, and they told him that their band was breaking up and Chris just happened to mention, "well, I'm a drummer, so would you like to jam?" So they got together and started jamming at our house. I wasn't even in the band at the time. I was upstairs in my room listening to them, thinking that sounds really cool, that'd be fun. I played guitar but I never sang in my life. Barry came up one day and said "hey, we need a singer and a second guitar player, would you like to do it." "Sure, why not." I've never done it. This is what my brother and I had been practicing to do, so we started practicing and playing. So that was the first band I went out and played with.

Do you remember what your first gig was?
It was at Cantrell's, around '83, because we played from '83 to '87. I don't know the date for sure. Barry is the archivist for this band and he could probably tell you the exact date. We made recordings of almost every show we ever did. That's what we're compiling now. The original EP we did, the four-song EP, we're going to put that out with some demos we did with our second drummer Richard Pryor, and live stuff, to make it more of an album instead of an EP. So we thought after twenty years, why not digitize the stuff and put it on CD? At first, it was for ourselves just so we could have it, then we thought we'll make up a couple, maybe a few people might even be interested in hearing it. Mostly friends who have been asking for years, saying, "I don't have your EP anymore, do you have it digitally?" So it started that way.

How did you come around to recording the first EP?
The first thing we ever recorded was a project for someone at Belmont College, when they were doing the Music School down there; we recorded two or three songs. I have no idea what they were, or where they're at. Once we got the recording bug, we went back into the studio and decided we were going to record, so we recorded about eight songs. Four of them were the songs that ended up on the **Far Away** EP. Once we got that out, we got this cassette and were selling that at Cat's on West End, out of a little display. A friend of mine was an art student and he made a little display for me. Once that went pretty well, we decided to put out an EP.

We took the four songs from the eight songs we recorded on the cassette and put it on the EP. Between that and the compilation **City Without A Subway**, which we had one song on, that's all we ever released. So that's why we're looking forward to doing this stuff now. We have a four-song demo with our second drummer, named Richard Pryor, after my brother left, which nobody's ever heard and you can tell it's going in a different direction, 'cause I had written four songs. I was more influenced by Bob Mould from Husker Du and the Descendents and stuff like that. These next four songs will sound a little different because if you ever heard our stuff and how everything was kind of lick-based, everything had a lick; it was a bit more raw, a little bit more like the Husker Du sound.

What are some of your memories of playing around town during that period?
It was about '83. You know, what was so cool about it, was the camaraderie of all these different bands. It was like a place for you to fit in, it was like the misfits taking care of the misfits. No matter what kind of music you played, punk, hardcore ska, or whatever it was…when you played a gig, somebody from one of those bands or the entire band perhaps would show up to support you or support the scene. I have no idea how that is now, but I'm sure it's a lot more splintered than it was back then.

From what I saw, that "all for one" dynamic started to change in the '90s...
Yeah, I would go to see bands in the '90s and it was completely different. The bands I saw, they were kind of elusive…the metal bands would stay with the metal bands and the punk bands would stay with the punk bands and they were just different clubs that did their thing. But at the time, even metal bands, and Goth, and this, that and the other would show up at your shows, and it was really cool, and we'd do the same thing. We'd go to the shows…I just loved the camaraderie, so I really remember that so much.

The first time I played a show, I was so nervous; I had never done anything like that in my life. I thought the coolest thing was, when I was younger, I was a big fan of Kiss and stuff like that, and there was that mystery involved in those bands. Then when punk happened, it kind of broke down the barriers, and we were able to see beyond that stuff. You got to play the clubs and you saw that there really wasn't any mystery involved. We were just normal people, the audience was just normal people, and we could interact as one.

Did Shadow 15 attract any label interest from anybody?
We did, when we played an [NEA] Extravaganza and we actually got some interest from RCA. It was very limited. It was only for a short period of time. But after the show, they showed some interest and talked to us for a short period of time. Then it just kind of faded away. But we released the EP on Big Monkey Records, Tim Lee of the Windbreakers, that's his label. He saw us in Mississippi where he lived and liked us. It was just one of those hand-shake deals; there was no contract, nothing. We just did it on the fly. That was about the only label interest we ever received, but not long after that, 1985-86, we end up changing drummers and that only lasted about a year and a half. All that other stuff kind of went away…I think if we had stuck together a little bit longer, we probably would have gained some interest.

Did you get to tour with anybody? What are some of your most memorable shows?
The best show we ever did, or the most fun show we ever did, was when we opened up for the Replacements at Cantrell's. We had tried to open up for Husker Du when they

played here, but they were touring with the band Christmas, and they didn't want another opening band, but man, I tried so hard. I lobbied like crazy to open for those guys. I just wanted to be backstage and meet Bob Mould...he was an idol of mine.

We toured the South quite a bit, just basically Atlanta, Birmingham…playing with different bands like Carnival Season from Birmingham. Basically, we became really good friends with Carnival Season; we played with them quite a bit. Later on down the road, we toured with Clockhammer. That was a great time because we were all good friends, but nobody had ever heard of the bands. Back when you would tour in the '80s, it was like do it yourself, promote yourself. It was really hard to promote yourself in Nashville when you're coming to play from "Bumfuck, Mississippi." So you get there and there'd be like 20 people at the show, tops. But it was a blast to play for those people, to tour around, we had so much fun. I think most of the memories were in hotel rooms and in restaurants, after the shows.

After Shadow 15 broke up, what did you end up doing then?
I started a band called Sideshow, it was with Brad Pemberton on drums, who now plays with Ryan Adams. And Earl Beasley, I don't know if you know him, he's a bartender here in town.

I was always lucky that I played with some fantastic drummers. My brother was probably the best rock drummer at the age of 16 when we started playing Cantrell's. That was one of the secrets about us at Cantrell's, my brother was 15 or 16 the very first time we played a show at Cantrell's. We told them he was eighteen years old so they would let him in.

Then at one of the shows we were playing when he turned eighteen, Barry from the stage made a mistake and said "we just want to wish Chris a happy birthday, a happy 18th birthday," and we just knew that the management turned to us like "you Motherfuckers, I can't believe you have been fooling me this many years!" It was like "oh, shit!"

What happened with Sideshow?
We played for probably about a year, toured around and…what happened was we were playing full time with the band and none of us were making any money and all of us had really crappy jobs, so I ended up getting a gig as a guitar tech. I've been working on guitars for years. I got a chance to go out with a few different people. First I got to go out with Lisa Germano, and a few other people like the Questionnaires around town, and bands that were local. Then I got a call from John Hiatt. So I was the guitar tech on tour for John Hiatt at the time when he had Sonny Landreth on guitar.

Sonny is such a great guitarist…
Oh, yeah, and he's such a great guy! I have this story, on the very first show we ever played at Center Stage in Atlanta, he had a slide that he'd had for years, at the very first show, right when they walk on stage, I'm going back to get them and I trip over a wire and I break his slide…and of course I was completely freaking out, it's my first tour and I broke this guy's slide. He was completely cool with it, like "shit happens, don't worry about it." So I always think so much about that…he's just one of the best guys I have ever met. After that, I ended up working for Webb Wilder for about four years, through a few different bass players…

Yeah, Webb changes band members pretty frequently…
Yes, he sure did, but I got to go with Donny Roberts at the time…he was a great guitar player as well. He was like my roommate for all those four years. I did that for a while, and while I was on the road, Brad and them, they weren't sitting around waiting for me. Brad ended up playing with my brother and Jay Joyce in their first band, Bedlam. It was a four-piece band and they recorded at the Castle. Then they went to a three-piece and that was Iodine. When I came back to town, I changed my band name to Flimsy. I played with them for a short period of time. Brad was very busy with other projects, so we just called it a day. Since then, I've just been writing and thinking about recording some other stuff. I've got some things on my site that are basically demos. I keep saying I'm going to record stuff, but I keep getting older and older, I'm 42 now and I'm getting older, and older, and I don't want to wait until I'm 50 to record all these songs…

I got discouraged there for a period of time. Because I got married, I thought I had to have a full time job…I started working in the music business, for Capitol Records, for about eight years. The music business is not for me, it just absolutely sucks, the business side of it. It was so discouraging that when I came home from work I didn't even play guitar. The last thing I wanted to do was be around music…I didn't even listen to music…I didn't play music. That was eight years of my life that was just basically wasted. Now, after I have been gone from there the past three years, it's coming back. I've been slowly practicing and playing and writing and stuff like that.

You got a birds-eye-view of the industry…
Oh, my god! I kind of knew how it was anyway, but once you're really in it every day and you see these people who are just…I literally was in a sales meeting once where the director of sales actually was talking about selling to people through Wal-Mart, and he said we're actually trying to sell to the lowest common denominator. And that was a quote and that just stunned me…that's what they were thinking of their fans, that their demographic was the lowest common denominator. The IT guys I worked with at Capitol Records – this is just when Napster and everything was happening – we were all thinking "this is a Godsend to the record industry because it's another promotional outlet," because all they had was radio and newspaper to really promote their music…

And radio was going downhill…
Exactly! We would try to push three or four artists a year and you might get one hit single that would go Gold, tops. If you got lucky, you'd have one Platinum album a year. Of course, we had Garth Brooks on the label. He paid for all of our failing artists. That's when Napster was happening and we were excited, maybe it's illegal, but it's another forum for these guys to really look at and say "hey, this is another way we can use for promotion." And the COO actually came to us once while we were trying to give them a presentation about the Internet and the possibilities of downloads and such, and he actually said "I'm sorry, but it's never going to happen on the Internet." To this day, I would just love to come back to this guy and ask "how about that time you said it was never going to happen on the Internet?! How are you doing now?"

How would you like Shadow 15 to be remembered?
I hope we opened some minds a little bit because we blended a bunch of different styles together. We were fans of bands like Husker Du, Social Distortion, AC/DC, Motorhead, hardcore punk, metal…we were all over the place in music. One minute we'd be in the van listening to Patsy Cline, the next minute we'd be listening to the Wipers. I hope we opened some doors in people's minds to the fact that you didn't have to play just one genre. We were playing this music, and we had hair down to our asses, but you'd still get these hardcore guys that would come to your show, and punk guys, and they would be in to your music. It kind of showed that you didn't have to be a certain style or look a certain way or, the whole mindset. I hope that people respect it and I hope when we put this CD out that they'll listen to it again and hope that the songs are kind of timeless.

Bass player Chris Feinstein, an unsung hero of the Nashville rock scene during the 1980s and '90s, passed away on Tuesday, December 15, 2009 in New York City at the too-young age of 42 years. The cause of his death was an interaction between prescription drugs and over-the-counter cough medicine.

Feinstein's supportive bass rhythms provided the foundation for many of the Music City's earliest rock bands. Chris formed the influential early 1980s band Shadow 15 with his brother Scott, playing drums on some of the band's first recordings. Switching over to bass, Chris would join the Questionnaires, performing on both of the band's EMI Records album releases in 1989 and '91.

During the early 1990s, Chris would enjoy a lengthy musical collaboration with guitarist Jay Joyce: first in the band Bedlam with former Questionnaires' bandmate Doug Lancio, which recorded a pair of albums for MCA Records; then in Iodine with future bandmate Brad Pemberton for two albums on different independent labels.

Shadow 15

In the early 2000s, Feinstein became part of the Nashville supergroup the Cardinals with drummer Pemberton and guitarist Neal Casal, touring behind alt-country artist Ryan Adams. The Cardinals recorded three albums with Adams, including 2007's *Easy Tiger* and 2008's *Cardinology*, as well as the *Follow The Lights* EP in 2007.

Feinstein's talents were much in demand in the studio, as well, and through the years Chris contributed to albums by artists as diverse as rapper Fat Joe, alt-country diva Patty Griffin, and singer/songwriters Tim Finn, Matthew Ryan, and Albert Hammond, Jr. of the Strokes. Chris also contributed his experience and vision as a producer to a number of artists, most notably working with Moby.

A multi-instrumental musician that was often overshadowed by the charismatic frontmen that he played behind, Chris Feinstein was undeniably an integral element in the evolution of rock music in Nashville, a talented and important member of several crucial bands that helped put the Music City on the map as more than the home of country music and gospel. As an ambassador of the local music scene, Chris brought an honest little bit of Nashville to audiences across the world. He will be missed…

THE SHAKERS

Band Members:
Rebecca Stout (vocals) (A1, I)
Oscar Rice (guitar, percussion) (A1, I)
Robert Logue (mandolin, percussion) (A1, I)
Ken Coomer (drums, percussion)
Greg Garing (guitar, fiddle, banjo)

Other Musicians:
Tramp (fiddle) (A1, I)
Dave Willie (vocals, I)

The Shakers Recordings:

EPs

A1. Living In The Shadow Of A Spirit (Carlyle Records 1988, EP)
Side One
1. Living In The Shadow Of A Spirit
2. Queen Of The Haunted Dell

Side Two
3. The Healing Hymn
4. Hymn To Kate

Comments: Oscar Rice and Robert Logue were members of **Royal Court of China**, but when that band drifted towards becoming a nerf-metal caricature, the two split for the greener creative pastures of their side project, the Shakers. In Rebecca Stout they found a kindred soul and a unique voice that complimented the duo's original folk-rock leanings.

Truth is, professionally and musically, the Shakers were playing on an entirely different field than most other local bands, and they would have fit just as easily with '60s-era British bands like the Strawbs or the Incredible String Band as they did in late 1980s Nashville.

Living In The Shadow Of A Spirit is an inspired four-song conceptual EP that lyrically explores the "Bell Witch" phenomenon that occurred in Adams, Tennessee circa 1817-1820. With haunting, sparse instrumentation and Stout's incredible, ethereal vocals, these songs have held up better than most from the era, based as they are on a timeless musical tradition and imaginative story-telling.

Albums

I. Songs From Beneath The Lake (Carlyle Records 1990, CD)
1. Songs From Beneath The Lake
2. Beside The Little River
3. The Rain Song
4. King Of The Cave Fish
5. Damballah – Wedo
6. The Cold Song Of The Deep
7. Prayer For The Snake
8. Snowdrops
9. Dog In The Street
10. City Of Strange Delight
11. Old Drums
12. Stand Up

Another View: "The Shakers' first full-length album finds the band hitting their stride artistically and musically. Stout's voice has developed into the expressive tool I'd suspected that it could be, capable of soaring from a seductive whisper to passionate heights within the space of a heartbeat, caressing the chimerical lyrics that have always been the band's strong suit. The material is more fully developed musically, as well, with Logue and Rice providing subtle and effective backing to this sparsely accompanied poetry."
– *The Metro*, August 1990

From the Shakers' MySpace Page: "Formed in 1986, The Shakers grew out of a desire to do a quickie side project based on the Tennessee legend of the Bell Witch. Oscar Rice and Robert Logue were members of rapidly rising Nashville rock group The Royal Court of China at the time, playing maximum volume shows in Nashville's rock clubs. But after the two met vocalist Rebecca Stout in a small club (at one of the Georgia Satellites' earliest Nashville shows), plans for the quieter Bell Witch project began to take shape.

Debuting on Nashville's club scene in the summer of 1986, the trio quickly gained a following and things began to grow beyond

The Shakers, continued on page 458...

*R*obert Logue has been an integral part of not one but two legendary Nashville rock bands in the Royal Court of China and the Shakers. Aside from being a talented musician, Robert is also an impressive artist and poet with an eye for the macabre. Robert was also one of the first supporters of this project, graciously providing access to his large collection of Metro *magazine back issues...thanks!*

How did you get interested in playing music in the first place? I was always just drawn to music since I was a kid and borrowed my big sister's Elvis records and Jackson Five records, and stuff like that. In 1974 I got to see Elvis in concert and I loved it! I think in 1976 I saw Skynyrd and that was my first sort of long-haired, dope smokin'...my first experience of that whole side of life, that culture, and it was just electric. I was just a typical right-brained kid in school who really didn't have a clue what he was going to do. I'd entertained the thought of being a writer, this that and the other, and finally met Oscar Rice, who was obsessed with the guitar and was pretty good at it, and who was equally impractical and romantic. He was a year younger than me, but my senior year we hatched a plan that we were going to get a band together. Of course, we were met with discouragement all around, but you can't tell a kid that age anything. I went on to college for a year while he was in his senior year in high school, and the next year I dropped out. We spent the next couple years playing with drummers, trying to find a singer, and then finally hooked up with a band.

Was this when you hooked up with Joey, or was this a band of your own?
Our first real band was the Royal Court of China. We played with Chris Mekow, we saw him in another band in Hendersonville and sort of swiped him from that band. We played for a few months but we couldn't find a singer we liked. So Chris in the meantime met Joe Blanton, he met him in the bathroom at Cantrell's or something, so he took off and started playing with Joe, understandably, because we didn't have any gigs or anything going. They put the Enemy together, and so we sort of hung around the periphery of that band and eventually Lee Carr, who was the guitar player in the Enemy, I think, he wanted a little more of the spotlight, he wanted to be a little more out front, so he left to get his own band. Oscar and I started playing with him a little bit and that went on for a month or two, and we kicked around names and had some pretty unfruitful rehearsals. In the meantime, Chris Mekow started calling us saying "hey, we need a bass player and a guitar player with the Enemy," so that's how that came about.

You all changed the name of the band to the Royal Court of China?
Yeah, because we were friends with the Enemy, but musically it was what Oscar and I were interested in doing. We wanted pop guys and so we didn't want to continue on with the Enemy, but on the other hand we were just hungry to be in a band. They had some shows still booked that they needed to play, so we finished out the year and those gigs with the Enemy. Then we changed the name and played our first gig as the Royal Court of China opening for Walk the West.

So things happened pretty fast for you all as Royal Court of China. When did you record Off the Beat'n Path *and how did that come about?*
We recorded that off and on probably from the fall of '85 until January '86. We really had just gotten together for a month or two when we started recording that stuff and it sounds like it. We were trying to find a direction and it's kind of then on the record. We did a lot of rockabilly sort of stuff in the beginning, we all liked rockabilly. I think we weeded that stuff out because it seemed to become apparent as time went on, there was a certain sort of format, a direction of songwriting that would suit the band better which was more sort of...it was weird because it was a R.E.M. smashed together with Stevie Ray Vaughan kind of thing. Oscar was a big blues guy. I went to a Christian school and everybody else listened to Journey and Loverboy, and Oscar, this guy is listening to Muddy Waters and Johnny Winter. As far as rock and roll, we liked Guadalcanal Diary and stuff like that but we were still classic rockers and blues heads, too.

It always seems to me that you and Oscar were more of the folk/blues kind of orientation and Joey and Chris were more rock and hard rock.
Yeah, that's a fair explanation, although Oscar and I really liked hard rock too. We loved Ritchie Blackmore and Deep Purple and Jimmy Page, of course, was my guy. We were into that classic hard rock. We were never punkers; we got it, we liked it alright but...any band that didn't have a really good guitar player that we found interesting, we just weren't particularly interested in the band. For both of us, punk...it had the excitement, the rebellion, and the attitude but, at the same time, it wasn't musically interesting enough for us to get as in thrall with it as, say, Joe and Chris were.

How did you all get hooked up with A&M?
Everything happened really quickly. In the beginning, we were giggin' with anybody that would have us. I remember one night we opened for the Manikenz at 12th and Porter and then packed all our gear up and drove over to Music Row Showcase

to do our own show there. I think there were about three guys there and the bartender, after five or six songs, said 'guys, why don't we just call it a night.' We went through a few months of that and just trying to open for people and trying to get noticed. Towards the end of the summer, you couldn't get in the door at our shows, and I don't know exactly what happened.

A proverbial buzz started on the streets and by the end of the year, the gigs were packed. We hooked up with [band manager] Grace Reinbold sometime in the summer. Chris and I went down to see her and she wanted to work with us. She took our record *Off the Beat 'n Path*, which we still had sitting in boxes, and she put her staff on it, and they shipped all these records back out to college radio and got on the phones and worked the record. It started charting around the country, in different regions, and that attracted the interest of A&M.

Actually, the Scorchers kicked the door down, but also at that same time R.E.M. had just left IRS and was going to Warner Music and, as you remember, there was just a big buzz in this part of the country, in Nashville and Athens. It's funny, to look back now, you ask how it came about, and Grace took credit for it. Jim Zumwalt tried to take credit for it, and he tried to kill the deal, and a lot of behind the scenes, ugly stuff was going on at the time. But as far as I know, Grace made phone calls and talked to these people, and Grace arranged for David Anderle to fly in and see the band. The really cool thing about that gig, it was a year to the day since we changed our name to the Royal Court of China, we made a big deal out of that and everything. The show was packed, and Anderle turned around to Grace during the first song and said "I want them." That's what you dream of…

Yet, it got better…we had something like fifteen labels that requested meetings with the band. We met with two or three of them, and I can't remember now who we met with, and someone went to Capital but we really liked Anderle, he was just sort of laid back. He was from L.A., he'd found the Doors and sort of worked around that whole Byrds and Doors scene, the Los Angeles in the '60s. He was really nice and personable and he offered us more freedom. We were trying to drive a hard bargain and he was just laid back about it and was into letting us try to do it our way. He told us what he wanted to hear, and that's the way we went.

What do you remember about the recording of the first A&M album?
It was fast; we recorded it in something like a week. We were impatient; I look back now and we could have done that so much better. We were just impatient, but we got in at Woodland Studios, we had met with a few producers. Our original choice, we wanted Jimmy Page to produce it. We flew to New York, met with his attorney and he said, "Jimmy

is working on his own record right now," at the time he was working on *Outrider* and he said "I can get you John Paul Jones." Stupidly, being the uncompromising putzes we were, we said "no, no, no, no, it's got to be Jimmy Page."

So we didn't get Jimmy Page, but we got his lawyer. His attorney said, "I'd like to work with the band." We flew back with him working with us, and we met with a couple other producers, but nobody seemed to be on the same page. Finally, Anderle said "go in the studio and cut a song and we'll see how it goes, if I like what I hear, then…" We had asked, just let us produce it. There again, that's how cocky we were, "let us produce this." They agreed to give us a trial run and we went in with the first cut, "It's All Changed," and he came in and said "okay, sounds good, go for it." We just pretty much went in and cut it live and then went back and did some guitar overdubs and that was it. We were in the Woodland Sound Studio in Nashville.

How was the response to the album when it came out?
Locally, there was a great response. There was a lot of hype about it; Grace was always a great hype machine. She was always taking out ads, I'm sure you remember that from *The Metro*. You have to really give her credit for that, too, for getting attention on us and getting the buzz going. She was always one who believed in publicity and hype, and getting it out there.

So, yeah, it went great here; we were getting a lot of air play on KDF at the time and we did a record release show, which was packed and went great, and we had a big party afterwards. Then it was time to go out to the rest of the country, who hadn't heard of us. That was just like it would be for any band. It was great fun, but it was also frustrating at times because people didn't know who we were, and there was the usual record company problem where you get to a town and your records are not on the racks in the stores, and you're not getting the airplay that you're supposed to be getting.

Some places were better than others. It was all just learning for us, but again we were impatient, we were always just pushing, pushing, we wanted bigger tours. We wanted to open for name bands, we thought "nobody knows who we are; let's tour with somebody that can get us in front of more people to get the word out." We did some of that, we did smaller clubs too, we did them both.

Who did you end up touring with?
While I was there, we toured with the Kinks, which was great. We did three or four shows in the Midwest, but those were the first ones we did. For me, personally, I sort of had a flashback moment…I remember in Minneapolis, the first date, I was sitting in the dressing room and you could hear the Kinks playing out on the stage and there was this little

electric heater in there. It was a flashback in high school, I used to lie on the floor in my room next to this little electric heater listening to a live Kinks' record and I thought, "wow, how far we've come." We also opened for REO Speedwagon and the Hooters.

Some odd pairings there...
Well, the booking agency, wherever they have an open date, they stick you; it's not always real well planned out. We did this thing called the Fourplay tour, a six-week tour, and it was a lot of fun. It's another one of those things, I fought tooth and nail against doing it, but looking back now, it was crazy. What happened, four labels, each one picked one of their recently-signed bands that needed the publicity and they booked a whole package tour. They rented two big buses, two bands on each bus, and each label chipped in $30,000 and whatever. Coors sponsored it...we ran into shit with that, too...but we just toured all around the country like that. That was a lot of fun.

Who were you paired with, do you remember?
Three other bands you probably haven't heard of, Northern Pikes. Will and the Kill, which was Will Sexton's band, and an English band called Hurrah. They were all guitar bands and we had a friendly competition going on between everybody.

When did you and Oscar make the decision to leave the band?
There was friction going on, there was always friction in that band. That band was really all Chiefs and no Indians and there were just a lot of internal circumstances. It was a recipe for separation, a lack of communication, and there were already sort of two camps in the band. What brought it to a head was, we had started doing the Shakers, and we really just thought it as a side project. I wanted to do this Bell Witch record; I had the idea a couple years before, this kind of folksy, acoustic Tennessee record around the Bell Witch. We'd met Rebecca Stout and written some songs and then the Shakers, to our surprise, started building a following around town.

The other two guys were really threatened by that. We had no intention of making that our main focus, we looked at it like the Royal Court was our bread and butter and the Shakers was this cool thing we'd do on the side when we're in town and when we can. I think the fact that they were living across town from us, they assumed that all the time we weren't spending with them we were rehearsing with the Shakers, which wasn't true. At the end of the year we said, "we want to do an EP," just press 1,000 copies and sell them around town. Grace had said okay and set up the studio time.

Well, the other guys were agitating with A&M behind our backs, complaining about it, all this cloak and dagger

Royal Court of China, 1987

stuff...looking back, it all seems so preventable and silly but, at the time, everything was drama and a big deal. Eventually, we were presented this ultimatum, you can choose between the Shakers and the Royal Court of China, but you can't do both. I think there was a combination of strong-arm tactics of making us not do the Shakers and also this sort of, maybe on some level they wanted us to leave, I don't know. Whatever the case, we thought about it for a weekend and so we came back and said "fine, fine, fuck you." And that was the way it ended.

Was there any pressure from the label for Royal Court to change the sound?
Not when we were in it, that case was never made to us. In fact, David Anderle, who signed the band, he moved to head of the soundtrack division, so he wasn't really our A&R guy. They brought in Steven Laboske, who hadn't signed the band and so I don't know if he liked the band or not but, for whatever reason, no.

Anderle was a great fan of Oscar Rice, you know, at the time hanging out with him. He liked Oscar because Oscar was doing this sort of stuff that reminded him of Clarence White and the Byrds and that whole scene that he had come from. I really think a lot of that [the band's changing sound] was Joe, who wanted to go that route.

INTERVIEW: ROBERT LOGUE

I know the band's sound changed so drastically, that's why I asked. You can play the first record and the second record and, other than Joey singing, you can't necessarily tell it's even the same band.
Some of those songs that were on there [the second album] had been bandied about while we were in the band, like "Half the Truth," which is one we didn't particularly want to do, but ended up being our single. It came out pretty good, actually, looking at it now. There was one called "This Time Around" that we really liked, and we were going to do that with us in the band and I thought that would be really cool. I wasn't personally knocked out with what they did later. Vic Maile came in to produce, great credentials (Motorhead), but I didn't like the sound of the next record very much.

So how did you guys get hooked up with Carlisle Records?
They came and asked us right when we were leaving Royal Court, there was some publicity around that and they heard about it and they came and said they wanted to put the Bell Witch record out. We looked at it really as like a transitional thing because our plans, at the time, were to get back to a major. We said "sure" and jumped at it.

We knew a record like that was not going to go on a major so we thought "well, we can just bide our time at Carlisle." That was probably another error; we should have taken it as more of an opportunity than we did. Labels are labels, big or small, they're still labels.
So you followed up the EP with a full length album?
We recorded the Bell Witch record like January 1st, New Year's Day, and they got the record, it came out in the fall of '88, September I think. Then we went right in the studio in October and November of '88 and recorded a full-length acoustic record of *Songs From Beneath The Lake*. That promptly got tied up with squabbling because they wanted us to sign for more records, and Grace Reinbold was saying "don't do it, no don't do it."

We'd split with Grace, but she came back on board long enough to say "no, don't get tied to them, yadda, yadda," so we were getting it from both sides. That record didn't come out until the spring of 1990, it slowed things down. In the meantime, we had started playing with Ken Coomer and started doing electric stuff as the Shakers.

You were doing shows around town with Ken?
Yeah, we started the NEA Extravaganza in '89, I think was our first show with Ken. It was kind of that Dylan thing, they did the electric thing, and the Shakers' fans did not like that we were doing electric and we met some resistance and lukewarm reviews for that...

Where did the Shakers go from there?
There were just a lot of frustrating years, in different ways. Musically, we liked so much different music and we couldn't

quite decide on a specific direction. We cut some heavy, heavy electric stuff with the Shakers, believe it or not. I don't know what you'd call it, sort of heavy gothic guitar stuff, but we were also still doing acoustic sets. Some fans liked the electric songs and some wanted the acoustic, and we were just all over the place with that.

In the meantime, we had a deal lined up with Epic that we thought was a done deal and it fell apart at the 11th hour, and that really took a lot of wind out of everybody. Then we did a Royal Court reunion in '92 when the Shakers were at a low point. I think they [RCOC] had just broken up out in L.A. and limped back to town, so we all wound up together, and that lasted about six months...

You had mentioned in an e-mail about some new Shakers material?
Yeah, this is funny; we got together in the beginning twenty years ago with the purpose of writing some songs about the Bell Witch, to do a little Bell Witch record. Now we've been broken up for thirteen years and we're getting back together to write another record about the Bell Witch.

What did you do in between the ill-fated Royal Court of China reunion and now? Have you been playing any music?
The Shakers were still going and we caught a sort of second wind with the Shakers. By the time we decided to go back and do the Royal Court for a while, we started playing the Blue Sky Court and suddenly, "bam," the shows are packed again. So we caught a second wind and found a little different format for the sound.

In 1993, we met this guy named Greg Garing who, at the time, had just been playing KOA campgrounds and playing fiddle in Jimmy Martin's band. Nobody knew who he was, and he moved in next door to Rebecca Stout. So he joined and that really kicked us into gear again. He left in the fall of '94 and we played a couple more shows and, at that point, we were just worn out. So we pulled the plug on it and everybody just went in their own directions...

How did you get into the art thing?
I've always drawn; I'm one of those guys that does a little bit of everything and was always conflicted. Am I a musician who writes, am I a writer faking it at music? Finally, I decided "don't think about it, just do all of it." I had a friend from Seattle named Ashleigh Talbot who's a really amazing Victorian lowbrow artist, as she calls it. At that time, I was spending time in Seattle, I really liked it in Seattle, I liked to go up there a lot.

She was from there and had moved here and I hung out with her a lot and she sort of turned me on to a lot of stuff that I wasn't aware of yet. This was in 1995, the Jim Rose Circus and a lot of sideshow stuff and it was through her that it dawned on me that I'd always loved Victorian stuff, but I'd never thought a lot about it. The Shakers definitely had a Victorian vibe to it. She draws posters; she has a website if you're checking around, check out madametalbot.com.

She was just drawing posters and illustrating different stuff. She'd collaborate with William Burroughs and she did the banners, the big stage banners and the T-shirts for the original Jim Rose Circus, and they've done a lot of bizarre shit like that. That got me inspired, and also a guy I met at work named Richard Cook; he's the guy that I actually partnered with on the typography.com stuff, a genuine, true, crazy artist if ever one was born.

I would credit those two with getting me back drawing. I'm certainly not in a league with either one of those guys, but it doesn't matter, you just do it. Richard and I put this thing together a couple of years ago to sell our artwork and also to get out there and have a good time. We do horror conventions and belly dance shows and tattoo shows, we just have a great time meeting interesting and bizarre people.

How did your book of poetry come about?
A lot of people write poetry and they never show anybody, they put it in the drawer and I'm one of those media whores that if I do something, whether it's drawing or writing or music, I want to put it out there, run it up the flagpole and see it. I'd actually been writing for years, these poems, this is some 25 years of poetry. The first ones in the book I wrote them when I was just a kid in high school, naive romantic high school kid, all the way up until this past year and so it's sort of just like a little anthology of my stuff. It sort of shows an evolution.

I guess what spurred me to do it is that I have a 2 ½ year old daughter now, and I lost my sister last year and I'm about to lose my dad shortly…when you get older and you have a kid, you think about mortality. I thought that if something happened to me, I want to leave my daughter something so she knows who daddy was. So I did it for my daughter. It's dedicated to my daughter and to my late sister and it was just a fulfillment of a dream on the one hand, I'd always wanted to write books, I always wanted to hold a hard copy book that had my name on it that I'd written, and so it's combined with wanting to leave my daughter something.

THE SHAKERS - SHAMALAM - THE SHAZAM

The Shakers, continued...

the original parameters of a Bell Witch project. By 1987 the Royal Court of China had signed with A&M Records, but the Shakers were also filling clubs and drawing media attention in town. In early 1988 with tensions flaring inside the Royal Court, Rice and Logue left the band and the deal to concentrate on the Shakers full-time. Later that year the original Bell Witch project finally came to fruition with the release on indie label Carlyle Records of "Living In the Shadow of a Spirit", a four-song EP of songs dealing with the macabre legend.

In 1990 Carlyle Records released the full-length acoustic CD "Songs From Beneath the Lake". During this time the Shakers added Nashville drum ace Ken Coomer to the line-up and began playing as an electric/acoustic band. Later that year the Shakers signed a demo deal with Epic Records, but a full-fledged deal fell apart at the 11th hour. In 1993, an old-time music avatar named Greg Garing joined the band and remained throughout most of 1994. The Shakers played to a large and enthusiastic regional cult following but never released another record before going separate ways in late 1994."

SHAMALAM

Band Members:
Richard DuBois (vocals, guitar)
Tracy Blair (guitar)
Collin (bass)
Dave Thibodeau (drums)

Comments: Another fine Murfreesboro band, comprised of veterans of the 'boro rock scene.

THE SHAZAM

Band Members:
Hans Rotenberry (vocals, guitar) (I-VII)
Jeremy Asbrock (guitar, banjo, vocals) (III, IV, VII)
Mick Wilson (bass, vocals) (I-VI)
Mike Vargo (bass, vocals) (VII)
Scott Ballew (drums, vocals) (I-VII)

Other Musicians:
Rob Danner (piano) (IV)
Astrid Grace (vocals) (IV)
Brad Jones (keyboards, vocals) (III, IV)
Grover Lavender (fiddle) (III)

The Shazam Recordings:

Albums/EPs

I. Shake 500 (self-produced cassette, 1994)
1. OH NO!!
2. Generation Zzzz…
3. Where do we go
4. out of the blue
5. OKay
6. Blew it
7. only Bones
8. Everything
9. ME & YOU
10. where do we go PT II

Comments: Self-produced demo tape created by the band that would lead to their label deal with Copper Records.

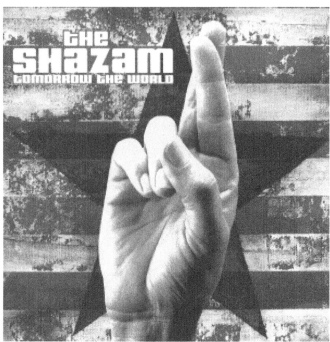

From the Shazam web site: "probably worth a whole pile of money, this is the savage young Shazam bashing out some of the tracks that would evolve into their fantastic debut album, and some that would be lost in the mists of time..."

Interestingly enough, song ten on the tape, "where do we go PT II" was reproduced as the song "Florida" on the band's debut album.

II. The Shazam (Copper Records 1998/Not Lame 2001, CD)
1. Let's Away
2. Oh No!
3. Blew It
4. Megaphone
5. Where Do We Go
6. Hooray For Me
7. Cynic
8. Engine Red
9. C'mon Girl
10. Rollercoaster
11. Deep Low
12. Florida
13. Sleepy Horse
14. Everything
15. I Hate That Song
16. Out of the Blue
17. Generation Zzzz

Comments: Debut album from the Shazam was originally released on 1998 by Copper Records, later reissued by ultra-cool power-pop label Not Lame with four bonus tracks (#14-#17). The band's sound is definitely informed by the decade of the 1970s, a mix of psychedelia, hard rock, and glam inspired by folks like the Move, the Sweet, and even a bit of Cheap Trick.

III. Godspeed The Shazam (Not Lame Recordings 2000, CD)
1. Super Tuesday
2. Sunshine Tonight
3. The Stranded Stars
4. Sparkleroom
5. Some Other Time
6. RU Receiving
7. Chipper Cherry Daylily
8. Calling Sydney
9. City Smasher
10. Sweet Bitch
11. A Better World
12. Gonna Miss Your Train

Another View: "Taking cues primarily from early Cheap Trick and Electric Light Orchestra, the Shazam mold hard rock that, initially, sounds out of place on the Not Lame label, which focuses entirely on power pop. However, on repeat listens it becomes obvious why this group is so often lumped

The Shazam

in with fine pop acts; their hooks are remarkably strong and melodic. While they're clearly out of step with the times (The music here is entirely steeped in the late '70s, and while it may have sold millions then, it is unlikely to go past "cult" status now), *Godspeed the Shazam* is an excellent hard rock pleasure." – Jason Damas, *All Music Guide*

IV. Rev9 (Not Lame Recordings 2000, CD)
1. On The Airwaves
2. Wood And Silver
3. Okay?
4. Periscope
5. Month O' Moons
6. Take Me
7. Revolution 9

Another View: "Clever guys Hans Rotenbury and pals follow up their perfect reinvention of the power pop genre on *Godspeed the Shazam* with something altogether deeper, trippy and experimental. *Rev 9* embraces more disparate '60s and '70s influences, with occasional paisley pop jangle reminiscent of '60s-loving '80s geniuses the Rain Parade, but to call this mini-album retro is impossibly hard. Avoiding post modern irony, elements of the past, present, and future are tackled with Shazam." – Jon "Mojo" Mills, *All Music Guide*

V. 2000 Miles From Budokan (Not Lame Recordings 2001, CD-R)
1. Airwaves
2. Sunshine Tonight
3. Okay
4. Calling Sydney

5. Sweet Bitch
6. Where Do We Go?
7. Chipper Cherry Daylily
8. Some Other Time
9. RU Receiving
10. The Stranded Stars
11. Hooray For Me
12. Super Tuesday
13. Megaphone
14. Oh No!
15. I Hate That Song
16. Engine Red
17. Sparkleroom

Comments: Live recording from a February 2001 show somewhere, someplace that was later released as an "authorized bootleg" and sold to the band's fans through the website and at shows. Says Hans about the show, "molten-lava hot rock-n-roll action;" due to poor sound quality (severe bootleg), this is a disc for the hardcore faithful only.

VI. Tomorrow The World (Not Lame Recordings 2003, CD)
1. Rockin' And Rollin (With My) Rock 'n' Roll Rock 'n' Roller
2. We Think Yer Dead
3. Gettin' Higher
4. Goodbye American Man
5. Fallin' All Around Me
6. The Not Quite Right Kid
7. Squeeze The Day
8. Turnaround
9. New Thing Baby
10. Not Lost Anymore
11. You Know Who
12. Nine Times

Another View: "Well, if the White Stripes are the equivalent of the Animals and the Strokes are the new Rolling Stones, then the Shazam are the garage rock movement's answer to the Beatles, or at least the Move. *Tomorrow The World* (Not Lame Records), the trio's third album, offers up a dozen Brad Jones-produced, guitar-driven and energetic pop/rock tunes. Guitarist/vocalist Hans Rotenberry brings a classic vibe to these songs, the Shazam sounding like the entire British Invasion as filtered through Motown soul and West Coast psychedelica, creating songs full of memorable hooks and bouncy riffs that will have your daughter and her friends humming for hours.

Championed by British music magazine *MOJO*, no less an authority than Steve Van Zandt, host of Little Steven's Underground Garage radio show, has declared The Shazam "one of the best things that I've heard." Who am I to argue with Springsteen's guitarist and Tony Soprano's hit man?" – Rev. Keith A. Gordon, *View From The Hill*, 2002

Another View: "*Rev. 9* suggested that the Shazam had brought the artier, psychedelic strands of their music to their logical conclusion, concluding that EP with an "interesting" epic but not-very-rock & roll cover of the Beatles' "Revolution 9" (do Beatles fans even play through that song without hitting "skip"?). But a funny thing happened between 2000 and 2002 – rock & roll, played loud and loose, became popular again. The Shazam always were a funny fit for the pop underground – sure, they write hooks, but they are really a decidedly retro arena rock band through and through – so it was no stretch to see them take an adventurous step toward joining the garage rock revival — and in the process get some increased attention." – Jason Damas, *All Music Guide*

VII. *Meteor* (50 Foot Records 2009, CD)
1. So Awesome
2. Don't Look Down
3. NFU
4. Disco At The Fairgrounds
5. A Little Better
6. Dreamcrusher Machine
7. Always Tomorrow
8. Let It Fly
9. Hey Mom I Got The Bomb
10. Latherman Shaves The World
11. Time For Pie

Comments: After a lengthy hiatus from the scene, presumably to make a living, Hans and his merry pranksters return with what might be their best album yet.

Another View: "While most contemporary power pop acts seemingly subscribe to the notion that all cultural progress came to a halt after the release of Big Star's *Radio City*, the Shazam are one band not afraid to pledge allegiance to the bigger pop/rock sounds of the late 1970s and early '80s, and on their fifth album, *Meteor*, they've literally put their money where their mouth is by hiring Reinhold Mack (professionally known simply as Mack) to produce. Mack was behind the controls for albums by Queen, Billy Squier, Sparks, and Electric Light Orchestra in the '70s and '80s, and here he gives the Shazam the sort of big, punchy, and polished sound that by all rights would have made them radio fodder had it been recorded at a time when radio still cared about rock & roll." – Mark Deming, *All Music Guide*

Yet Another View: "I've usually been able to enjoy the music of The Shazam without paying much attention to the lyrics. Sometimes cryptic, sometimes nonsensical, they pale in comparison to the music. The band always leveraged their love of guitar-oriented powerpop like The Move and The Who to create albums full of huge sounding, hook-laden rock songs. With. Big. Dumb. Riffs. *Not that there's anything wrong with that.*" – Bill Holmes, *Blurt* magazine

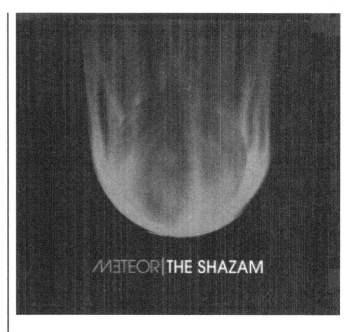

Bootlegs

B1. *Tonight Valencia, Tomorrow The World* (no label 2004, CD)
1. On The Airwaves
2. Nine Times
3. Rockin' And Rollin' With My Rock And Roll
4. Sunshine Tonight
5. Fallin' All Around Me
6. Stranded Stars
7. RU Receiving
8. Hooray For Me
9. Turnaround
10. Megaphone
11. Super Tuesday
12. Where Do We Go From Here
13. Blew It
14. Engine Red
15. Calling Sydney
16. Gettin' Higher
17. Goodbye American Man
18. Sweet Bitch
19. Jeremy Broke The Amp
20. A Better World
21. Some Other Time
22. Let's Away

Comments: Live show in Spain, recorded in 2003 at Sala Matisse by Altatension, a non-profit association that brings bands to Valencia, Spain. Converted into a bootleg and circulated in collector's circles and via P2P networks.

KIRBY SHELSTAD

Band Members:
Kirby Shelstad (vocals, keyboards, percussion, synths) (I)
Sam Bacco (gongs, percussion) (I)
Larry Chaney (guitars) (I)
Beth Nielsen Chapman (vocals) (I)
Jackie Welch (vocals) (I)

Kirby Shelstad Recordings:

I. Mother Of The Buddas (Love Circle Music 2003, CD)
1. The 21 Praises To Tara
2. The Heart Sutra
3. Manjusri Namasamghitti
4. Dedication

Comments: A frequent collaborator with **Tony Gerber** and **Giles Reaves**, multi-instrumentalist Shelstad is one of Nashville's space-music pioneers.

THE SHINDIGS

Band Members:
Don Felts (vocals)
Tom Appleton (guitar)
Jody Shaver (guitar)
Lance Dodson (guitar)
Eric Miller (guitar)
Jason Callahan (bass)
Angela Williams (bass)
Dean Bratcher (drums)

Comments: Contributed song "Love Somebody" to the *Major Potential #1* 1991 compilation CD. Contributed song "Telegrams And Flowers" to 1993's *What's The Buzz?* CD.

PACO SHIPP

Band Members:
Paco Shipp (vocals, harmonica) (I)

Other Musicians:
Jamie Hartford (guitar) (I)
Robin Henkel (dobro) (I)
Rick Lonow (drums) (I)
Mike Loudermilk (guitar) (I)
Joe McMahan (guitar) (I)
Dave Pomeroy (bass) (I)
Doug Randall (piano) (I)

Paco Shipp Recordings:

I. The Tip Of The Tongue Is A Dangerous Place To Hang Your Reputation (Earwave Records 2004, CD)
1. Evolution
2. Think For Yourself
3. Tip Of The Tongue
4. Big Fins and A Ragtop
5. Smoker's Lament
6. Straight No Chaser
7. Believe Me
8. Scratch
9. Good Life
10. Grease It A Little
11. Georgia On My Mind

Comments: Collection of blues and roots-rock from veteran harpslinger Shipp, a former member of the **Bradford Blues Band** in the 1980s as well as Jamie Hartford's band more recently. After a spell in L.A., Shipp calls North Carolina home these days.

SILVER JEWS

Band Members:
David Berman (vocals, guitar) (I-III)
Cassie Marrett/Berman (vocals, bass) (I-III)

Other Musicians:
Bobby Bare, Jr. (vocals) (II)
Tim Barnes (drums) (II)
Tony Crow (piano, keyboards) (I-III)
Pete Cummings (bass) (II)
Duane Denison (guitar) (II)
Mike Fellows (bass) (I, II)
Brian Kotzur (drums) (II, III)
Paz Lenchantin (bass) (II)
Steve Malkmus (guitar) (II)
Bob Nastanovich (drums, percussion) (II)
Paul Niehaus (pedal steel) (I)
Peyton Pinkerton (guitars) (III)
John St. West (II)
William Tyler (guitars) (I-III)
Azita Youssefi (keyboards) (II)

Silver Jews Recordings:

I. Bright Flight (Drag City Records 2001, CD)
1. Slow Education
2. Room Games and Diamond Rain
3. Time Will Break the World
4. I Remember Me
5. Horseleg Swastikas
6. Transylvania Blues
7. Let's Not and Say We Did
8. Tennessee
9. Friday Night Fever
10. Death of an Heir of Sorrows

Comments: Silver Jews – primarily the creative outlet for the genius of David Berman – had three albums for Drag City under its belt before Berman moved to Nashville. Formed in 1989 by Berman along with Pavement's Steve Malkmus and Bob Nastanovich, Silver Jews was often thought of as a Pavement side project or splinter group (Pavement drummer Steve West has also performed with the band).

By the time of Berman's move to Nashville, the band was firmly in his control, pursuing his unique vision. I've only included those albums that Berman has recorded since becoming part of the Nashville music scene.

II. Tanglewood Numbers (Drag City Records 2005, CD)
1. Punks In The Beerlight
2. Sometimes A Pony Gets Depressed
3. K-Hole
4. Animal Shapes
5. I'm Getting Back Into Getting Back Into You
6. How Can I Love You If You Won't Lie Down
7. The Poor, The Fair And The Good
8. Sleeping Is The Only Love
9. The Farmer's Hotel
10. There Is A Place

III. Lookout Mountain, Lookout Sea (Drag City 2008, CD)
1. What Is Not But Could Be If
2. Aloysius, Bluesgrass Drummer
3. Suffering Jukebox
4. My Pillow Is The Threshold
5. Strange Victory, Strange Defeat
6. Open Field
7. San Francisco B.C.
8. Candy Jail
9. Party Barge
10. We Could Be Looking For The Same Thing

SIGNS OF LIFE

Band Members:
Chris Faulk (vocals, guitar, keyboards)
Tony Miracle (guitar)
June Kato (bass)
Todd London (percussion)
Rob Mitchell (percussion)

SIMMONZ

Band Members:
Mike Easlo (vocals)
Mike Simmonz (guitar)
Jamie Simmonz (bass)
Paul Simmonz (drums)

Comments: Popular hard rock/metal band 'round the Nashville scene, the talented brothers Simmonz have played with a number of local bands. The band had to change their name to **the Stand** once another band, called "Simonz," was found in France, of all places. Later became known as **Dorcha**.

THE SINCERITY GUILD
Web: www.thesincerityguild.com

Band Members:
Jeremy Childs (guitar, bass, electric piano) (I)
Ryan Burleson (guitar) (I)
Brett Miotti (bass) (I)
Aaron Ford (drums, percussion) (I)
Ryan Parrish (guitar)

Other Musicians:
T. Read (guitar) (I)

The Sincerity Guild Recordings:

I. What It's Like On The Inside (Theory 8 Records 2004, CD)
1. The Keeping Room (Part I)
2. Leslye's New Hairdo

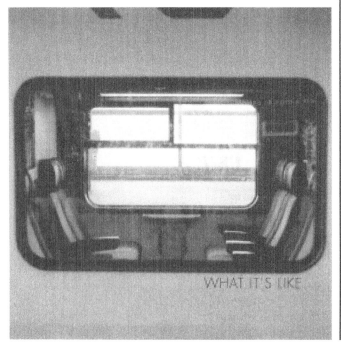

3. "When I Release The Captives Before Your Eyes"
4. "...That The Bones You Have Broken May Rejoice"
5. The Ballad Of Radioman
6. Tokens Of Deliverance
7. "Where To Now, Moses?"
8. "You Have Been Weighed In The Balances And Found Wanting"
9. Triumph Of The Ugly Duckling (Part II)
10. **

SIR REAL

Band Members:
Michael Webb (vocals, keyboards)
Timmy B (guitar)
Tom Comet (bass)
Scott Easley (drums)

Comments: Band contributed song "Hideaway" to ***What's The Buzz?*** 1993 compilation CD.

SIXPENCE NONE THE RICHER

Band Members:
Leigh Nash (vocals) (I-II)
Matt Slocum (guitar, cello, keyboards) (I-II)
Dale Baker (drums, percussion) (I-II)
Rob Mitchell (drums, percussion) (II)

Other Musicians:
David Davidson (violin) (I, II)
Chris Donohue (bass) (I)
Peter Hyrka (violin) (I)
Phil Madeira (keyboards) (I)
Jerry Dale McFadden (keyboards) (II)
John Mark Painter (mellotron, trumpet) (I)
Al Perkins (pedal steel) (I)
J.J. Plasencio (bass) (I)
Antoine Silverman (violin) (I)
Kris Wilkinson (viola) (I, II)

Sixpence None The Richer Recordings:

I. Sixpence None The Richer (Squint Entertainment 1998, CD)
1. We Have Forgotten
2. Anything
3. The Waiting Room
4. Kiss Me
5. Easy To Ignore
6. Puedo Escribir
7. I Can't Catch You
8. The Lines of My Earth
9. Sister, Mother
10. I Won't Stay Long
11. Love

Comments: Squint Records was the label formed by former **Chagall Guevara** frontman Steve Taylor, a talented and visionary crossover from the Contemporary Christian Music world. That's where Taylor met Nash and Slocum, whose Sixpence None The Richer released a couple of indie records on the CCM side of the street during the early 1990s. This self-titled effort resulted in a minor hit in "Kiss Me," which put the band on the pop-rock map after it was released as a single a couple of years after the album. Used in an episode of the *Dawson's Creek* TV show, "Kiss Me" would receive radio airplay in ten countries. The band would enjoy a second hit later in 1999 with a cover of the La's "There She Goes," from the movie soundtrack for the dismal film *Snow Day*.

Another View: "After toiling in relative obscurity in the Christian pop ghetto for several years, Sixpence None the Richer suddenly exploded on to the pop charts in 1999 on the strength of "Kiss Me," an utterly irresistible slice of swoony guitar pop that, once heard, is impossible to shake loose from the brain and could well turn out to be this generation's "I Wanna Hold Your Hand." – Rick Anderson, *All Music Guide*

Another View: "If you hold your breath and are very good, maybe 'Kiss Me' will prove a fluke. Maybe in the end it'll only be the innocent invitation to making out a deserving teen subdemographic craved. But don't tell yourself stories about biz or fundamentalist plots. Christians not proselytizers, they're an indie-rock success story who come by their limpid sound more organically than the Sundays or the Innocence Mission, both of whom they sincerely admire. Leigh Nash's clear little voice, like a young Natalie Merchant without the neurotic undertow? Her own. Matt Slocum's classed-up minor-key arrangements, like an acoustic Radiohead without the existential foofaraw? His own. They hope to create pretty, well-meaning stuff like this in perpetuity, for the sheer joy of it. Which means they could be nauseating urban skeptics for years." Grade: C+
– Robert Christgau, **Christgau's Consumer Guide: Albums Of The '90s.**

II. Divine Discontent (Reprise Records 2002, CD)
1. Breathe Your Name
2. Tonight
3. Down and Out of Time
4. Don't Dream It's Over
5. Waiting on the Sun
6. Still Burning
7. Melody of You
8. Paralyzed
9. I've Been Waiting
10. Eyes Wide Open
11. Dizzy
12. Tension Is a Passing Note
13. A Million Parachutes

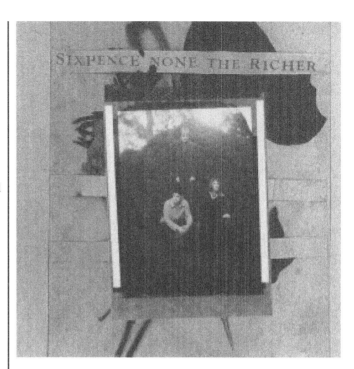

Comments: Mostly recorded a couple of years before its initial release after the band signed with Warner Music's Reprise imprint, *Divine Discontent* tried to keep the momentum provided by the band's hits "Kiss Me," and "There She Goes" in 1999. Squint was having cash flow problems, though, mostly due to its distributor, which delayed the album's release past a viable "sell by" date. Drummer Rob Mitchell joined in 2001, replacing Dale Baker, although both appear on these tracks; *Divine Discontent* itself is a mix of older and newer recordings. Sixpence None The Richer would break-up in 2004, with Matt Slocum forming the Astronaut Pushers and Leigh Nash going solo; the band would reunite in 2008, however, releasing a now-OOP EP and a Christmas album.

SIXTY-NINE TRIBE

Band Members:
John Sheridan (vocals, guitars) (A1, I)
Price Harrison (guitars, vocals) (A1, I)
Tony Frost (bass) (A1)
Mitchell Duvall (bass, vocals) (I)
Rolff (drums) (A1)
Hunt Waugh (drums) (I)

Other Musicians:
Mark Harrison (guitar, vocals) (A1)
Nancy Kline (vocals) (I)
Miranda Louise (vocals) (I)
Joe McGlohan (saxophone) (A1)
Ken Moore (keyboards) (A1, I)

Sixty-Nine Tribe Recordings:

Singles/EPs

A1. Bikers (Feralette Records 1987, 12" vinyl)
Side One
1. Bikers

Side Two
2. Summer Years

Albums

I. "...last supper relief" (Stoneage Records 1985, vinyl LP)
Side One
1. Out w/Girls
2. Do The Dog
3. Elvis Up The Nile
4. Upper Room

Side Two
5. Poisen Girls
6. P.E. Teacher
7. Cycle Girls

Another View: "Musically, 69 Tribe call to mind the late sixties/ early seventies Detroit punk/metal bands, first and foremost Iggy and the Stooges. A lot of the tunes on *...last supper relief* would have sounded right at home on *The Stooges* or *Funhouse*, but 69 Tribe are far from being just a retread band. They've taken that basic garage sound of the psychedelic/punk era documented on *Nuggets* and *Pebbles* and filtered it through a post-'76 consciousness to emerge with an intense, exciting sound of their own." – Andy Anderson, *NIR* 1985

SLAVEJACKET

Band Members:
Jerry Campbell (vocals)
Mike Franks (guitar)
Sam Mitchell (bass)
Michael Page (drums)

Comments: Band contributed song "Linda's Down" to *What's The Buzz?* 1993 compilation CD.

SLEEPMODE

Band Members:
Asher Rogers
Michael Carminati

Comments: Rogers was the frontman for the **Smartest Monkeys**; with Carminati the duo perform what they call "experimental pop."

THE SLUGGERS

Band Members:
Tim Krekel (vocals, guitar) (I)
Tom Comet (bass, vocals) (I)
Willis Bailey (drums, vocals) (I)

Other Musicians:
Warner Hodges (guitar) (I)
Terry Manning (keyboards) (I)
Dave Sutherland (guitar) (I)

The Sluggers

The Sluggers Recordings:

I. Over The Fence (Arista Records 1986, vinyl LP)
<u>Side One</u>
1. Over the Fence
2. Perfect Man
3. Written in the Wind
4. Live Wire
5. As We Believe

<u>Side Two</u>
6. I Can't Help Myself
7. Jack in a Box
8. Storm of Love
9. In That Magic Moment

Comments: Tim Krekel & the Sluggers, as I remember they were originally known, were another of Nashville's underrated mid-1980s bands. Featuring Krekel's engaging vocals and considerate, literate songwriting skills and a rhythm section as good as anybody in the biz, the band's single album for Arista went nowhere…not surprising, really, given that the label didn't know what the hell to do with **Stealin Horses**, either. Krekel would return to Louisville, where he made a lot of great records. You can find copies of this cool slab o' roots-rock goodness on eBay for a song...

THE SMARTEST MONKEYS

Band Members:
Asher Rogers (guitar, vocals, keyboards) (I)
Matt Sebastian (guitar, bass, vocals) (I)
Cody Man (bass) (I)
Gabe Pig (drums) (I)

The Smartest Monkeys Recordings:

I. The Smartest Monkeys (ERM Records 2003, CD)
1. TSM
2. Fatter Pipes
3. Cavemen to Honey
4. Prozak Winter
5. Clock In
6. Dirty Robe
7. Campout Song
8. Sarcastic Cowboy

Comments: Formed in 1992 by Hollywood transplant Asher Rogers and Matt Sebastian, the Smartest Monkeys recorded this CD and placed among the six finalists in Disc Makers' 2003 Independent World Series Southeast Showcase before disappearing entirely from the local scene. It's a shame, too, 'cause the CD was pretty good, a noisy mix of Nirvana, Bad Brains and 101 different hardcore punk bands, with each song's underlying melodies viciously attacked by discordant

guitars and crashing rhythms. Asher Rogers is now making "experimental pop" music as ½ of the duo called **Sleepmode**.

SMASHERS

Band Members:
Victor Lovera (vocals, guitars) (I)
Fagan Arouh (guitars, vocals) (I)
Gypsy Carns (bass, guitars, vocals) (I)

Other Musicians:
Tony Newman (drums) (I)
Taylor Rhodes (keyboards, percussion, vocals) (I)
Michael Snow (keyboards) (I)

Smashers Recordings:

I. Smashers (Kat Family Records 1981, vinyl LP)
<u>Side A</u>
1. Gleason
2. I Needed That
3. Took A While
4. Once Is Not Enough
5. Danger

<u>Side B</u>
6. Rock Rock
7. High School Action
8. Rock & Roll Neighborhood
9. Clown Of Mine
10. First Boy At The Dance
11. Chantra
12. All In A Day

SMASHERS - SMOKELESS ZONE - TODD SNIDER

Comments: One of the earliest bands on the Nashville rock landscape to record, in truth, songwriter Victor Lovera had been kicking around the Music City since the early 1970s, hanging out with **R. Stevie Moore** and performing in a number of bands during the decade. The band and their self-titled album would be reviled by local punks, but it's really a rather engaging slice of period pop-rock that, had Lovera been British, would have busted wide open during the early 1980s "New Wave" years.

Another View: "…the Smashers are local boys trying to make good, so I'll be charitable: in terms of muscle, these guys make the Bay City Rollers look like the Clash. Maybe I'm being a trifle unfair, but when the most imposing songs on an album (in this case, "High School Action" and "Rock & Roll Neighborhood") come out of my speakers sounding uncomfortably like warmed-over Boston – or worse, Andrew Gold – the fact that these guys are doubtless playing in earnest just doesn't make the nut." – Kent Orlando, *Grab!* 1981

SMOKELESS ZONE

Band Members:
Scott Sullivant (vocals, guitars) (A1)
Jim Hodgkins (drums) (A1)

Smokeless Zone Recordings:

A1. "(We Should Be) Together" (Pyramid Records 1986, 7" vinyl)

Comments: Excellent pop/rock 45rpm vinyl featuring 2/3 or 1/2 or whatever of the **Practical Stylists** in Sullivant and Hodgkins. Dunno why they only did one song here, but since's its pretty damn good, I'm gonna let 'em slide…

TODD SNIDER

Band Members:
Todd Snider (vocals, guitar, harmonica) (I – IX)

Other Musicians:
Pat Buchanan (guitar) (IV)
Paul Buchignani (drums, percussion) (III-IX)
Chris Carmichael (fiddle, strings) (V)
Tim Carroll (guitar) (VII)
Marshall Chapman (vocals) (I)
Keith Christopher (bass) (IV, IX)
Ashley Cleveland (vocals) (I)
Peter Cooper (bass, vocals) (VIII, IX)
John Deadrick (piano) (VII)
R.S. Field (percussion) (V)
Lloyd Green (pedal steel guitar) (VIII, IX)
Paul Griffith (drums, percussion) (V, VII, VIII)
Jim Hoke (horns) (IV, V)
Peter Holsapple (harmonica, dobro, mandolin, piano) (IV, IX)
Peter Hyrka (guitar, mandolin, violin) (I)
Wayne Jackson (horns) (IV)
David Jacques (bass, trombone) (V, VII, VIII)
Jacqueline Johnson (vocals) (III)
Robert Kearns (bass) (VIII)
Nicole Keiper (percussion) (IX)
Ray Kennedy (guitar, percussion, dobro, keyboards) (IV)
Siobhan Kennedy (vocals) (IV)
Will Kimbrough (guitar) (II-V, VII, VIII)
Doug Lancio (guitar) (I, V)
Tom Littlefield (vocals) (I, II, IV)
Mark "Hoot" Marchetti (vibes) (I)
Joe Mariencheck (bass, vocals) (I, II, III)
Eric McConnell (bass, drums, steel guitar) (VII-IX)
Joe McLeary (drums) (I-III)
Terry McMillan (percussion) (I)
Billy Mercer (bass) (VIII)
Edgar Meyer (double bass) (I)
Josh Miller (percussion) (VII)
Johnny Neel (keyboards) (IV)
Mike Plume (guitar) (V)
Suzan Powell (vocals) (III)
John Prine (vocals) (V)
Jared Reynolds (vocals) (V)
Kim Richey (vocals) (V)
David Roe (bass) (VII)
Rivers Rutherford (piano) (IV)
Eddy Shaver (guitar) (I)
Melita Snider (vocals) (VIII)
Joey Spampinato (bass) (IV)
Rick Steff (keyboards) (III)
Harry Stinson (vocals) (I)
Molly Thomas (fiddle) (VIII)
Michael Utley (keyboards) (I, II)
Libby Welbes (vocals) (VIII)

Jason Wilber (guitar, dobro, mandolin, bouzouki) (V)
Tommy Womack (guitar, vocals) (VIII, IX)
Craig Wright (piano, drums, percussion) (VII-IX)
David Zollo (piano) (III, VIII)

Todd Snider Recordings:

I. Songs For The Daily Planet (Margaritaville Records/MCA 1994, CD)
1. My Generation (Part 2)
2. Easy Money
3. That Was Me
4. This Land Is Our Land
5. Alright Guy
6. I Spoke As A Child
7. Turn It Up
8. Trouble
9. Alot More
10. You Think You Know Somebody
11. Somebody's Coming
12. Joe's Blues
13. Talkin' Seattle Grunge-Rock Blues

Comments: Todd Snider is a musical genius, and I'll brook no argument over that fact. A Music City immigrant by way of Memphis; Austin, TX; Portland, OR; and points west, Snider was discovered plying his trade in Memphis by Keith Sykes, of Jimmy Buffett's Coral Reefer Band. Sykes got tapes of Snider to his boss, who in turn signed the young singer/songwriter to a deal on his fancy new Margaritaville label (distributed by MCA/Universal).

Songs From The Daily Planet was Snider's erstwhile debut, a fine collection of material that runs the gamut from humorous novelties ("My Generation," "Alright Guy") to the deadly serious ("You Think You Know Somebody"), from twangy alt-country to roots-rock (fine distinction, that) and even hipster jazz. Oddly enough, it was the album's "hidden track," the Dylanesque talking-blues of "Talkin' Seattle Grunge-Rock Blues," that was thrown on at the last minute that garnered Snider the most attention.

II. Step Right Up (Margaritaville Records/MCA 1996, CD)
1. Elmo and Henry
2. I Believe You
3. Side Show Blues
4. Enough
5. T.V. Guide
6. Hey Hey
7. Moon Dawg's Tavern
8. Prison Walls
9. Horseshoe Lake
10. It All Adds Up
11. Tension
12. Late Last Night

13. 24 Hours a Day
14. Better Than Ever Blues Part 2

Comments: With his second Margaritaville/MCA album, Snider formally introduces his backing band, "The Nervous Wrecks." Consisting of guitarist **Will Kimbrough**, bassist Joe Mariencheck and drummer Joe McLeary, the Wrecks were also Snider's touring band.

Another View: "Picking up where he left off with his exceptional debut *Songs for the Daily Planet* Todd Snider continues his ragged-but-right blend of folk, country and rootsy rock & roll on this 14-song release. At times brilliant, Snider's songwriting talent is still intact, as is his passionate voice and the superb instrumental backing by his band the Nervous Wrecks." – Jack Leaver, *All Music Guide*

III. Viva Satellite (MCA Records 1998, CD)
1. Rocket Fuel
2. Yesterdays And Used To Be's
3. The Joker
4. I Am Too
5. I Am Two
6. Out All Night
7. Guaranteed
8. Can't Complain
9. Positively Negative
10. Once He Finds Us
11. Godsend
12. Comin' Down
13. Never Let Me Down
14. Doublewide Blues

Comments: Margaritaville went belly-up, MCA took over Snider's contract, and the result was the so-so *Viva Satellite*. Sure, there are some great songs here – "Rocket Fuel" is a blast, "Doublewide Blues" is a lot of fun – but overall this is Snider's most scattered and rickety album of the first three.

IV. Happy To Be Here (Oh Boy Records 2000, CD)
1. Happy To Be Here
2. Forty Five Miles
3. Long Year
4. D.B. Cooper
5. Lonely Girl
6. Keep Off The Grass
7. All Of My Life
8. Betty Was Black (And Willie Was White)
9. Ballad Of The Devil's Backbone Tavern
10. Just In Case
11. What's Wrong With You
12. Missing You
13. Back To The Crossroads

Comments: Snider landed on his feet, signing with John Prine's Oh Boy Records imprint. With a boss sympathetic to the artistic side of record-making, Snider may have traded greater distribution for a certain amount of creative control. The result was three excellent studio albums and a live disc that would all boost Snider's rep as a talented songwriter and performer.

V. New Connection (Oh Boy Records 2002, CD)
1. New Connection
2. Vinyl Records
3. Rose City
4. Beer Run
5. Easy
6. Crooked Piece of Time
7. Anywhere

8. Stuck All Night
9. Statistician's Blues
10. Class Of '85
11. Broke
12. Close Enough To You
13. Waco Moon

VI. Live – Near Truths And Hotel Rooms (Oh Boy 2003, CD)
1. *Ladies and Gentlemen...*
2. Tension
3. D.B. Cooper
4. Lonely Girl
5. *Hello...Sorry*
6. Beer Run
7. *Reading On The Plane, Writing On The Phone*
8. Statistician's Blues
9. Waco Moon
10. I Can't Complain
11. *The Story Of The Ballad Of The Devil's Backbone Tavern*
12. The Ballad Of The Devil's Backbone Tavern
13. Easy Money
14. Talking Seattle Grunge Rock Blues
15. Long Year
16. *Typing Gibberish*
17. Side Show Blues
18. *Any Requests?*
19. I Spoke As A Child
20. Doublewide Blues
21. *Letter From Australia*
22. Broke
23. Beer Run

Comments: Solo acoustic live album – the between-song spoken word/conversational pieces are in italics.

Todd Snider, continued on page 474...

TODD SNIDER
Step Right Up
(MCA Records)

Todd Snider hit a minor lick on the charts a year or so ago with his debut album, mostly on the strength of a single humorous cut that parodied the parody that the Seattle scene has become. Snider's band, in the song, was so "hip" and "alternative" that they didn't even play. It was a marvelous piece of work, hitting closer to the mark than many in the alt-rock world might like. For *Step Right Up*, his sophomore effort, he's put together a solid collection of songs, performed by a fine band that includes Nashville talent Will Kimbrough. I have to wonder aloud, however, if there's anything here that is going to get heard above the din and hype of current releases by folks like Dave Matthews and that Hootie guy.

Not that *Step Right Up* is a bad, or even mediocre disc. It's a crackerjack collection, showcasing Snider's incredible wit and impressive ability to turn a phrase. The music is a healthy mix of country and rock that may be just too much of each and not enough of either to receive significant radio airplay and promotion. Cuts like "Elmo And Harry," "Enough" or the deceptively funny "T.V. Guide" remind me of nothing so much as a more countrified Elliott Murphy. Snider's lyrics shoot from the hip, but are delivered from the heart and appeal to the intellect. A real talent, Snider has backed himself with an electric and energetic live band in the Nervous Wrecks. Hopefully *Step Right Up* will find a home somewhere inbetween the playlists of Triple-A and Americana formats, for it would appeal to fans of both. – *R Squared*, 1996

TODD SNIDER
East Nashville Skyline
(Oh Boy Records)

Todd Snider is one of Nashville's best-kept secrets, our very own "cult artist" who may be too eccentric, too honest and too talented to break through to a fickle mainstream weaned on boy bands, American "idols" and Music Row schlock. Snider is too often categorized as a "novelty" act because he infuses his folkish story songs with humor and wit, reducing funny-cause-they-could-be-true songs like "Beer Run" or the satirical "Talking Seattle Grunge Rock Blues" to comedic status without recognizing the skill it took to weave these tales. The same critics cavalierly dismiss Snider's more serious efforts without listening to the tears and pain behind such well-crafted tunes as "You Think You Know Somebody" or "Crooked Piece Of Time."

Considering Snider's entire oeuvre (and I have heard it all), it's time, perhaps, for a bit of rock critic heresy: Snider is this generation's Dylan. Snider's rootsy blend of rock, folk, blues and country echoes that of rock's greatest scribe. If Todd's lyrics fall short of the weighty measure of "Spanish Boots Of War" or "Blowin' In The Wind," well, those songs have been written. The Viet Nam War and the '60s are history (although Iraq may sadly provide inspiration for anti-war songs for years to come) and two generations have passed since Dylan spawned hordes of imitators. The "grunge" generation's spokesman has attitude, wit and humor to go alongside the pathos and insight, Snider drawing inspiration from other such troubled wordsmiths as Billy Joe Shaver and Kris Kristofferson much as they did from Dylan.

It's been ten years since the release of Snider's excellent debut, *Songs For The Daily Planet*, which spawned a minor hit with the album's hidden track, "Talkin' Seattle Grunge Rock Blues." During that time, Snider has suffered from problems with drugs and alcohol, spent a night or two in jail and played hundreds of live shows. He's suffered the deaths of friends and the whims of a (major) label's attempts to turn him into a rocking, Paul Westerberg-styled singer-songwriter. It's really after signing with John Prine's Oh Boy Records that Snider has blossomed as an artist and performer. Even with an enthusiastic support system behind his work, personal demons have continued to plague Snider, landing him in rehab and struggling to overcome his addictions. *East Nashville Skyline*, Snider's sixth studio album, reflects these trials and tribulations. It represents Snider's finest musical effort yet and represents an exciting new chapter in the artist's life.

As such "Age Like Wine" is an appropriate opening song for this new chapter. Snider pays homage to Billy Joe Shaver's "old timer, five-and-dimer" while admitting to himself that "it's too late to die young now." It's a reflective piece, the 37-year-old Snider now trying to "age like wine," stating that "I thought I'd be dead by now," perhaps sadly concluding "but I'm not." The following tale of mistaken arrest is biographical, "Tillamook County Jail" recounting an unwanted stay at one of Oregon's finest institutions. "Play A Train Song" is one of Snider's best compositions, a tribute to a fallen friend, the kind of rowdy, charming East Nashville born-and-bred scoundrel that you'd have to have known at some time in your life to truly understand. The minimalist "Sunshine" is about suicide and redemption while "Incarcerated" is a Memphis-styled rocker that evokes Jerry Lee in a story of somebody done somebody wrong.

Sometimes Snider's best performances are with some other artist's songs, such as Fred Eaglesmith's haunting "Alcohol And Pills." With guitarist Will Kimbrough's relentless fretwork behind Snider's mournful vocals, this tribute to music's fallen heroes – from Hank and Elvis to Gram Parsons, Jimi and Janis – hits too close to home for Snider, who has barely escaped a similar fate. Eagelsmith's chorus, "you'd think they might have been happy/with the glory and the fame/but fame don't take away the pain/it just pays the bills/and you wind up on alcohol and pills" sums up rock music's tragedies as well as could be done. A cover of Shaver's "Good News Blues" is a rowdy, bluesy raver that, as Snider writes in his liner notes, should make Shaver "dozens of dollars" in royalties; the song's true worth is as a tribute to one of country music's overlooked songwriting geniuses.

Snider's "The Ballad Of The Kingsmen" is a gem. It starts out with the story of "Louie, Louie" and evolves into an inspired rant on the religious right, Conservative politicians, Marilyn Manson and the doubtful effects of rock music and pop culture on young adults when war is broadcast on TV nightly. A hippie at heart, Snider's hilariously satirical "Conservative, Christian, Right-Wing Republican, Straight, White, American Males" puts the artist directly at odds with the mainstream zeitgeist and our current, unelected leadership. While Snider pokes fun at both sides of the political equation, he admits that he is "so liberal, I have love for conservatives."

The most telling moments on *East Nashville Skyline* come near the end. "Nashville" is a love song, of sorts, to Snider's adopted hometown, the "Nashville you don't hear on the radio" as he says in the liner notes. After wandering the country, from Oregon to California to Texas to Tennessee, Snider landed on the other side of the Cumberland River in historic and often troubled East Nashville. Perhaps his wandering days have come to an end, Snider singing that "there ain't nothing wrong with Nashville, nothing wrong with picking country songs down in Nashville, Tennessee." Snider's reading of the pop classic "Enjoy Yourself" closes the album, perhaps an affirmation of Snider's own struggles, the singer reminding his listeners (and himself) to "enjoy yourself, it's later than you think."

Assisted by his long-time partner-in-crime, Will Kimbrough (another of Nashville's criminally overlooked talents), Snider has produced the most solid and enduring album of his career. If fame and fortune haven't necessarily followed his efforts during the past decade, Snider can take solace in the fact that he nevertheless has a loyal and growing audience. Thanks to supporters like radio broadcasters Bob and Tom, who regularly feature Snider on their syndicated morning program, Snider also has a national forum for his lively music and a future that can only get better.

East Nashville Skyline represents an important new chapter in Snider's career that, with a little luck and the artist's talents, will continue another decade and beyond... – *Alt.Culture.Guide*, 2004

TODD SNIDER
Peace, Love And Anarchy (Rarities, B-Sides And Demos, Vol. 1)
(Oh Boy Records)

Singer/songwriter, humorist, social commentator and minor genius, Todd Snider is, perhaps, a man out of time. His effortless mix of rock, folk, country and blues would not have sounded out of place, say, during the 1965-75 acoustic songwriter-oriented era. Much like his former label boss John Prine, Snider tends to mix words, emotions and the occasional "big thought" all together on his lyrical palette, setting it all down on a musical canvas with broad strokes.

Unfortunately, while Snider's approach might have worked during a time when Dylan-inspired wandering troubadours as musically diverse as Prine, Warren Zevon, Bob Frank, Jackson Browne, Arlo Guthrie and Eric Anderson could successfully record for a major label, these days the bar is set a little higher. You have to move "product" to keep a deal, and Todd Snider is a little too original, a little too eclectic to stick around the majors for long.

During the '90s, Snider recorded three albums for Jimmy Buffet's MCA-distributed boutique label, Margaritaville. Although these albums displayed moments of staggering brilliance (songs like "You Think You Knoew Somebody" or "Rocket Fuel") and great humor ("Alright Guy," "My Generation, Pt. 2"), when Snider's sales failed to exceed his critical acclaim, he found himself out on the street. Those MCA-era albums have been distilled into *That Was Me: The Best Of Todd Snider 1994-1998*, a fine introduction for those unfamiliar with vintage Todd.

At the dawn of the new century, Snider found a kindred spirit in John Prine and signed with Prine's label, Oh Boy Records. During this decade, we've watched as Snider's art has matured and deepened over the course of three solid studio albums for Oh Boy, and although the acclaim has gotten louder and Snider's audience has gradually increased (albeit at a snail's pace), the artist himself, maybe driven by ambition, decided to leave a comfortable indie home to once again climb onto the lower rungs of the major label game, releasing *The Devil You Know* in 2006 for Universal's New Door Records imprint.

As such, Snider's *Peace, Love And Anarchy* is the obligatory departing collection of "rarities, B-sides and demos," culled from his time at Oh Boy Records. Although there are few revelations here – and sparse liner notes offer little in the way of documentation – there *are* a few gems hidden just beneath the surface. An acoustic version of "Nashville," seemingly a demo from Snider's *East Nashville Skyline*, works perfectly well without full instrumentation, while "Missing You," a demo from 2000's *Happy To Be Here*, is a little too rough around the edges to fit comfortably.

CD REVIEW: TODD SNIDER'S PEACE, LOVE & ANARCHY

A talented songwriter with a penchant for clever phrasing, Snider has had several of his songs recorded by other singers, and a few of these are represented by Snider's demo versions of the songs on *Peace, Love And Anarchy*. Personally, I'd like to see what Snider's longtime musical foil Will Kimbrough could do in the studio with a full band version of "I Feel Like I'm Falling In Love," originally recorded by Jack Ingram. Ingram also recorded Snider's "Barbie Doll," a bluesy song that displays Snider's intelligent wordplay. The demo for "Deja Blues," recorded by legendary country outlaw Billy Joe Shaver, is a twangy acoustic number that would also sound good with a full band behind it.

As with any collection of this sort, *Peace, Love And Anarchy* includes a couple of clunkers in the mix. Snider's cover of Jerry Jeff Walker's "Stoney" is so lifeless that it barely registers, and it sadly includes accompaniment by not one, but two local Nashville journalists – Peter Cooper and Nicole Keiper. Cooper's fingerprints are also all over "Some Things Are," a decent song and a better performance, but with listing vocals that range from a folkie whisper to a bluesy growl, it's not one of Snider's better moments. Now I don't begrudge Cooper, the Nashville *Tennessean* newspaper's frontline music journalist, his opportunities as a musician, but as the overall producer for *Peace, Love And Anarchy*, surely he could have found some Todd Snider songs in the vault that didn't involve his own (unremarkable) performances?

It is with the musical "rarities" and not with the demos, however, that the treasures of *Peace, Love And Anarchy* are revealed. "Old Friend" is a fine country-flavored duet, of sorts, between Snider and Jack Ingram, with traditional country instrumentation (dobro, mandolin, steel guitar) provided by Peter Holsapple (The dB's). Holsapple also appears on "Combover Blues," a humorous song that should become an anthem for middle aged rockers everywhere. "East Nashville Skyline" is a love letter to Snider's adopted neighborhood that should have been included on the album of the same name, while the mostly spoken-word "From A Roof Top" offers non-natives a bird's-eye view of historic East Nashville.

Closing the album, "Cheatham Street Warehouse" is a full-blown rocker, the kind of highly-personalized story-song that Snider does as well, if not better, than anybody. With a band featuring Tommy Womack on guitar, drummer Craig Wright and pedal steel wizard Lloyd Green, the song is a lo-fi delight, Snider's soulful vocals barely struggling above the mix while the band bashes and crashes with ramshackle delight. Overall, the good and grand here outweighs the simply mediocre, making *Peace, Love And Anarchy* a solid collection with many songs that will appeal to Snider's loyal fans. For newcomers, however, I'd recommend any one of Snider's Oh Boy albums as the place to start familiarizing yourself with this talented and underrated performer. – *Trademark of Quality* blog, 2007

TODD SNIDER - JILL SOBULE

Todd Snider, continued...

VII. East Nashville Skyline (Oh Boy Records 2004, CD)
1. Age Like Wine
2. Tillamook County Jail
3. Play A Train Song
4. Alcohol And Pills
5. Good News Blues
6. The Ballad Of The Kingsmen
7. Iron Mike's Main Man's Last Request
8. Conservative Christian, Right-Wing Republican, Straight, White, American Males
9. Incarcerated
10. Nashville
11. Sunshine
12. Enjoy Yourself

Another View: "Regardless of any opinions concerning his music, each successive release from singer/songwriter Todd Snider should be looked upon as a precious gift. His continuous battles against various addictions and depression have had him down for the count on several occasions, prompting speculation that his latest release could be his last. Snider is not oblivious to this situation and freely discusses it in *East Nashville Skyline*'s opening ditty, "Age Like Wine." A short summation of his life and career thus far, he recognizes that it's "too late to die young now," and concedes with a sly wink that "I thought that I'd be dead by now...but I'm not." – Aaron Latham, *All Music Guide*

VIII. The Devil You Know (New Door Records 2006, CD)
1. If Tomorrow Never Comes
2. Looking For A Job

3. Just Like Old Times
4. Carla
5. You Got Away With It (A Tale Of Two Fraternity Brothers)
6. The Highland Street Incident
7. Thin Wild Mercury
8. The Devil You Know
9. Unbreakable
10. All That Matters
11. Happy New Year

Comments: Snider jumps back into the major label fray, leaving Oh Boy and signing with Universal's New Door imprint. New Door was an interesting proposition – the label basically existed to sign artists that had formerly been signed with a Universal-related label (Margaritaville in Snider's case), the label's most notable success being a instrumental Peter Frampton CD before U-music closed it down...

As for *The Devil You Know*, at first listen I though that it was a sub-par Snider effort, not nearly up to the level of quality of his previous works. I initially blamed it on the major label atmosphere, which tends to suck the life out of even the most-motivated artist. On second listen, the album isn't nearly as bad as I thought, but it isn't as good as it could have been, either.

IX. Peace, Love And Anarchy (Rarities, B-Sides And Demos, Vol. 1) (Oh Boy 2007, CD)
1. Nashville
2. Feel Like I'm Falling In Love
3. Missing You
4. Barbie Doll
5. Old Friend
6. Combover Blues
7. I Will Not Go Hungry
8. Stoney
9. Some Things Are
10. Deja Blues
11. Dinner Plans
12. East Nashville Skyline
13. From A Rooftop
14. Cheatham Street Warehouse

Comments: As the sub-title says, this is a collection of "Rarities, B-Sides and Demos" from one of Nashville's better songwriters. Produced by Peter Cooper – yes, that Peter Cooper – *Tennessean* newspaper music journalist, who also performs on a couple of tracks. Nicole Keiper is also a writer for the *Tennessean*. WTF? Is Todd sucking up to the critics for better reviews? Who knows? See the review (➜)

JILL SOBULE

Band Members:
Jim Sobule (vocals, guitar, bass, keyboards) (I-V)

Other Musicians:
Robert Barone (vocals) (I, II, IV)
J.D. Blair (percussion) (I)
George Bradfute (guitars) (II, IV)
Louis Brown (tuba, cornet) (II, IV)
Chris Carmichael (violin, cello) (I-V)
Charlie Chadwick (bass) (III, IV)
Susy Davis (vocals) (I)
Bill DeMain (piano, vocals) (V)
Dennis Diken (drums) (V)
Steve Earle (guitar, vocals) (II, IV)
Robin Eaton (vocals, bass, harmonica) (I-V)
Molly Felder (vocals) (III, IV)
Mac Gayden (banjo) (I)
Mark Goldenberg (guitars) (II, IV)
Mickey Grimm (drums, percussion) (II-V)
David Henry (cello) (V)
Jim Hoke (clarinet, flute, harmonica) (II, IV, V)
Byron House (double bass) (I, II, IV)
Brad Jones (bass, keyboards, mandolin, vocals) (I-V)
Will Kimbrough (guitar) (V)
Wayne Kramer (bass) (I)
Viktor Krauss (bass) (I, II, IV)
Kenny Malone (drums) (I)
Jerry Dale McFadden (accordion) (I)
Eric Moon (keyboards) (I)
Roger Moutenout (synthesizer) (II)
Al Perkins (pedal steel) (II, V)
Michael Rhodes (bass) (III, V)
Ross Rice (piano, drums) (I, II, IV, V)
Kirby Shelstad (drums, percussion) (I)

Jill Sobule Recordings:

I. Jill Sobule (Lava Records/Atlantic 1995, CD)
1. Good Person Inside
2. Margaret
3. (Theme From) The Girl In The Affair
4. Karen By Night
5. Houdini's Box
6. Trains
7. I Kissed A Girl
8. The Jig Is Up
9. Resistance Song
10. Supermodel
11. The Couple On The Street
12. Vrbana Bridge
13. Now That I Don't Have You

Comments: The self-titled Jill Sobule album was actually the talented singer/songwriter's sophomore effort, a follow-up to her engaging 1990 debut album, *Things Here Are Different*. This disc yielded a minor hit single with "I Kissed A Girl," and garnered some airplay for "Supermodel." Subsequent albums never lived up to the commercial expectations of this one, but

JILL SOBULE
Things Here Are Different
(MCA Records)

In a summer nearly saturated with impressive debut albums, part-time Nashvillian Jill Sobule's *Things Here Are Different* stands apart from the pack like a fine Italian crystal goblet, or a high-priced Picasso. An inspired collection of self-penned tunes which illustrate Sobule's considerable way with words, the material found within these grooves is lyrically smart, musically complex and highly literate…no mean feat in an age of pop music which relies more on the rhythm than the substance.

Things Here Are Different opens with "Living Color," a subtle, textured song which features Sobule's distinctive, haunting vocals. An evocative piece which soars from a listful smile to a tear and back again within a few minutes, "Living Color" sets the stage for much of what is to follow. Songs such as "Gifted Child," "Golden Cage," and the title cut showcase the work of a measured and gifted songwriter drawing upon a wealth of influences, including personal experiences and heartaches.

Sobule has been characterized as a part of the "new wave" of female artists heavily influenced by folk music, including such chart-topping groundbreakers as Tracy Chapman and Suzanne Vega. I'd put her more in the class of a Kate Bush, a strong female poet who just happens to use a folk-tinged pop music medium in which to weave her amazing and mesmerizing tapestry of sound and emotion. Expect to hear more of Jill Sobule in the future. – *The Metro*, August 1990

JILL SOBULE - SOCIAL KINGS

Sobule has continued to make good music. Some might consider this another questionable inclusion, but during the early 1980s, Sobule hung around Nashville quite a lot, and even if she's considered a New York City artist these days, she continues to record with some of Nashville's best talent.

II. Happy Town (Atlantic Records 1997, CD)
1. Bitter
2. Happy Town
3. Barren Egg
4. Half a Heart
5. When My Ship Comes In
6. Clever
7. I'm So Happy
8. Little Guy
9. Underachiever
10. Love Is Never Equal
11. Soldiers Of Christ
12. Attic
13. Sold My Soul
14. Super 8

III. Pink Pearl (Beyond Records 2000, CD)
1. Rainy Day Parade
2. One Of These Days
3. Lucy At The Gym
4. Claire
5. Mexican Wrestler
6. Heroes
7. Mary Kay
8. Somewhere In New Mexico
9. Guy Who Doesn't Get It
10. Someone's Gonna Break Your Heart
11. Loveless Motel
12. Rock Me To Sleep

IV. I Never Learned To Swim: Jill Sobule 1990-2000
(Beyond Records 2001, CD)
1. Stoned Soul Picnic
2. When My Ship Comes In
3. Resistance Song
4. Houdini's Box

5. Claire
6. Big Shoes
7. Bitter
8. Mexican Wrestler
9. Margaret
10. Heroes
11. Karen By Night
12. I Kissed A Girl
13. Love Is Never Equal
14. Pilar (Things Here Are Different)
15. Smoke Dreams

Comments: A "greatest hit" retrospective that includes material from Sobule's first five albums.

V. Underdog Victorious (Artemis Records 2004, CD)
1. Freshman
2. Jetpack
3. Cinnamon Park
4. Tender Love
5. Underdog Victorious
6. Under the Disco Ball
7. The Last Line
8. Tel Aviv
9. Joey
10. Nothing Natural
11. Angel/Asshole
12. Strawberry Gloss
13. Thank Misery
14. Saw a Cop

SOCIAL KINGS

Band Members:
Kenny Wright (vocals, drums, percussion, programming) (I)
Nicolas Nguyen (vocals, guitar, bass, keyboards, synth) (I)

Other Musicians:
Chris Carmichael (violin) (I)
Michael Corbett (programming) (I)
John Downey (bass, backing vocals) (I)
Josh Ketchmark (acoustic guitar, backing vocals) (I)

Social Kings Recordings:

I. Social Kings EP (BiGG Records 1996, CD)
1. She's My Religion
2. She Can't Decide
3. Yesterday People
4. I Am Reborn
5. Speak Your Mind
6. Potential
7. Think About It

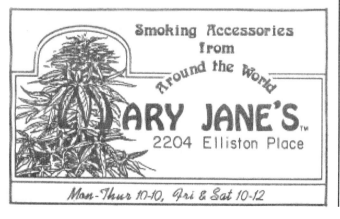

Comments: Social Kings was basically local scene veterans **Kenny Wright** and Nicolas Nguyen – 1/2 of **Prodigal Sons**, really – that performed most of the material on this CD.

This was an underrated disc upon its release and both Wright and Nguyen would later move onto other projects, most notably Wright's collaborations with **Max Vague** and, later, to **Bonepony** to reunite with guitarist Nguyen.

SOUL SURGEON

Band Members:
William Tyler (vocals, guitar)
Keith Lowen (bass, vocals)
Sam Smith (drums, vocals)

Comments: Contributed the song "Complicated" to *The Ex-Files* 1998 NeA Extravaganza compilation CD. Later changed their name to **Lifeboy** and signed a deal with Sire.

SOULSKIN

Band Members:
Matthew Marth (vocals)
Jason Hamilton (guitars)
Chris Stone (bass)
Robert Burdick (drums)

Comments: Band contributed song "A Dog, God, & An Idiot" to the *Music City Rock* 1995 compilation CD.

SOUND & SHAPE

Band Members:
Ryan M. Caudle (vocals, guitars, keyboards) (I)
Jerry L. Pentecost (drums, percussion) (I)

Other Musicians:
Avery Gardener (bass, cello) (I)
J. Patrick Reyes (guitar) (I)

Sound & Shape Recordings:

I. Where Machines End Their Lives (Smith Seven Records 2006, CD)
1. The Son Of Sunshine and All The Little Freedoms
2. The Goddess In The Garden
    I. Enter: Mother Sunshine
    II. The Child Speaks
3. Feed Me To The Spiders
4. Lovers Drink For Free
    I. Watching Through The Keyhole
    II. There Is Safety In Slumber
    III. The Narrow Curve
    IV. The Long Trip Home

5. His Station and Four Aces
6. The Dancers
7. The Plea
8. Under The Rose
9. September
10. Soldiers!, Oh! Soldiers
11. Telegram (or The Fall Of Father Sunshine)
    I. Sunrise Through The Mouth Of The Cave
    II. Narration: The Story
    III. The Fall
    IV. Sunset Through The Mouth Of The Cave

SPACECRAFT

Band Members:
Tony Gerber (vocals, guitar, synthesizers) (I-IX)
Giles Reaves (synthesizers, percussion) (III-IX)
Diane Timmons (vocals, flute, synthesizers) (I-IX)
John Rose (vocals, flute, dulcimer, synthesizers) (I-IX)
Chris Blazen (koto, sampler) (I, V)
Josie Phelan (electric cello) (VIII)

Spacecraft Recordings:

I. Spacecraft (Lektronic Soundscapes 1997, CD)
1. Planetary Orbit
2. Zero, One
3. Topo Scan
4. Transmission
5. Voyager One
6. Satellite Dispatch
7. Destination: Infinity

Comments: Nashville's very own "space music" supergroup features the inspiring talents of **Tony Gerber** and **Giles Reaves**, along with such esteemed electronic and avant-garde musicians as John Rose, Diane Timmons, and Chris Blazen. This is ambient and electronic music with brilliant textures and skilled instrumentation; not exactly rock 'n' roll, but

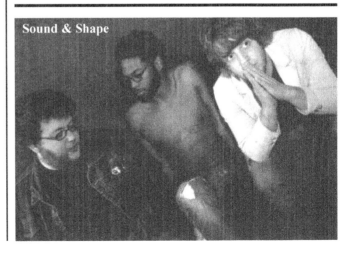
Sound & Shape

SPACECRAFT

definitely part of Nashville's music underground, and as far from Music Row as you're likely to tread...

Another View: "This music reflects a direct inspiration from excitement shared by space enthusiasts, astral thinkers, and the common man, who have achieved a galactic state of consciousness in these latter days of the 20th century." (from the Spacecraft web site)

II. Hummel: Live (Lektronic Soundscapes 1998, CD)
1. The Summon
2. Explorations In Space
3. Galileo
4. Hummel
5. Dialogues Of Energy
6. Astrollenium
7. De Profundis
8. Domes Of Light

Comments: A live performance from the Hummel Planetarium at Eastern Kentucky University, with the music directing movements of laser light refracting across the dome, which really would have been pretty neat.

III. Earthtime Tapestry (Lektronic Soundscapes 1999, CD)
1. Earthtime Tapestry
2. Living World
3. Dreams of One
4. Elder's Mourning
5. Migrations
6. Cycles
7. Beyond
8. Stepping Lightly

9. Seed
10. Thread Of Continuity
11. Homage To Gaia

Comments: Using Albert Schweitzer's "reverence for life" philosophy as a benchmark and inspiration, Spacecraft put together their best album to date. *Earthtime Tapestry* was chosen as "Electronic Album of the Year" by *New Age Journal* and the title cut was used in the film *Vanilla Sky*.

IV. Kaleida Dreams (SpaceForMusic.com Records 1999, CD)
1. Displaced
2. Full Moon Flowers
3. Sense of Wonder
4. Echoes
5. Blue
6. Restless
7. Poyo Rising
8. Inner Light
9. Eclipse
10. Joy Revisited
11. Uplifted
12. Illusions

Comments: A rare studio album from Spacecraft, Kaleida Dreams is the soundtrack for a computer animation by award-winning animator Dave Turner. The band created the music for the CD while watching the video on a large screen.

V. Twentieth Century Mix: Best Of (SpaceForMusic.com Records 2000, CD)

Comments: Includes material from the band's first four CDs.

VI. Musical Meditation For World Peace
(SpaceForMusic.com Records 2000, CD)
1. Musical Meditation (32:29)

Comments: Spacecraft performed this piece at the Unitarian Universalist Church in Nashville as part of the Symposium 2000, World Peace Through Reverence For Life international conference.

VII. Summer Town (SpaceForMusic.com Records 2001, CD)
1. Summer Town (54:57)

Comments: Recorded live at The Farm commune in Summertown, Tennessee during the Unityfest 2000 celebration. During the morning concert, over 150 people did their daily yoga and meditation exercises, a fitting use for the ambient, meditative and mesmerizing performance.

VIII. Cybersphere (SpaceForMusic.com Records 2001, CD)
1. Creative Acceleration
2. Anima-Machina
3. Fragile
4. Tunnel
5. House of Gaudi
6. Blue Planet Blue
7. Interlude
8. Cloud Traveling
9. The Pink Sides of Echoes
10. Reach Out

Comments: Cybersphere documents two different Spacecraft performances at the Renaissance Center in Dickson, Tennessee.

IX. Inside The Inside (SpaceForMusic.com Records 2002, CD)
1. Appalachia
2. Madden's Farm
3. The Nameless One
4. Center of the Earth
5. Plateau People
6. Future Ages
7. Venusian Bathysphere
8. Materializing
9. Return

Comments: Recorded live in the St. Mary's Cathedral in Philadelphia, Spacecraft's second visit to the venue; released as part of The Gathering Concert Series.

SPARKLEDRIVE

Band Members:
Val Strain (vocals, guitar, keyboards) (I)
Dan Strain (vocals, guitar, keyboards, programming) (I)

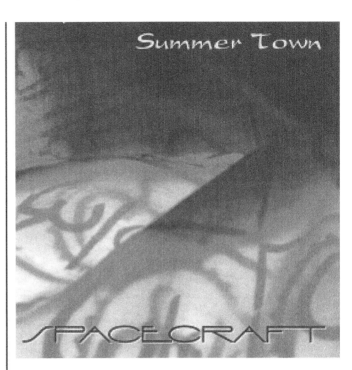

Clint Harris (bass, vocals) (I)
Adam Farley (drums) (I)

Other Musicians:
David Browning (keyboards, Mellotron) (I)
Dan Needham (drums) (I)
Jon Knox (drums) (I)
Jeff Quimby (drums) (I)
Ty Smith (drums) (I)
Sol Snyder (bass) (I)
Matt Walker (drums) (I)

Sparkledrive Recordings:

I. Sparkledrive (Aware Records/Sony 2001, CD)
1. Baby Hold On
2. Let Go
3. Come Give Me Love
4. Easier To Hide
5. Climb Out
6. Wanted Your Kiss
7. Ugly
8. Shy
9. Pick Up Sticks
10. Maybe That's Why
11. I Was Wrong

Comments: Sparkledrive, like the band **Porcelain** before it, was pretty much a musical showcase for the talented husband and wife team of Dan and Val Strain. This album shows an ethereal pop sound that makes good use of Val's dreamy voice and solid songwriting skills. This is melodic pop with a hip edge. Best I can tell, Farley didn't play a beat on this album as the credits show five other drummers (!). After Sparkledrive broke up, I believe that the Strains moved over to the CCM community.

When I was doing my Project Iraq & Roll in 2005, extorting promo CDs from the major labels to send to troops in Iraq, Dan called me and said that he had a garage full of these Sparkledrive CDs he'd send me. Never heard from him again, and never received the CDs, either...

SPEED LIMIT

Band Members:
Todd Albert (vocals, keyboards)
Mike Simmons (guitar)
Jimmy Griffith (guitars)
Brian Pugh (bass, vocals)
Paul Simmons (drums, vocals)

Comments: Band placed song "I Want You To Know" on the WKDF-FM compilation album *Street Hits*.

JUDSON SPENCE

Band Members:
Judson Spence (vocals, guitar, bass, synthesizer) (I-IV)
Jody Spence (drums, percussion) (I-IV)
Spencer Campbell (bass, percussion) (I-IV)

Other Musicians:
Dann Huff (guitars) (I)
Monroe Jones (keyboards) (I)

Judson Spence Recordings:

I. Judson Spence (Atlantic Records 1988, CD)
1. Yeah, Yeah, Yeah
2. If You Don't Like It
3. Everything She Do
4. Love Dies In Slow Motion
5. Attitude
6. Hot & Sweaty
7. Down In The Village
8. Dance With Me
9. Higher
10. Take Your Time
11. Forever Me, Forever You

Comments: Judson Spence came to Nashville in 1982 to record his first album, *Kidstuff*, and would later move to the city in '87 from Pascagoula, Mississippi. The quality of Spence's songwriting on *Kidstuff* led to his first Music City publishing deal. Spence became well known in Contemporary Christian circles and had cuts recorded by

CCR artists like Amy Grant and Bob Carlyle as well as country folk like Wynonna and Trisha Yearwood. Perhaps Spence's biggest moment as a songwriter came when Cher recorded his song "The Power" for her *Believe* album, which sold a truckload of copies.

Meanwhile, after gigging around Nashville constantly and ingratiating himself with the local music scene, Spence signed a proper deal with Atlantic Records and flew out to L.A. to record his self-titled major label debut, which was released in 1988 (since the album was recorded primarily with West Coast session players, I haven't listed most of the musicians here). Spence's unique blend of soft-rock, R&B and funk appealed to audiences and *Judson Spence*, the album, yielded a Top Thirty hit single with "Yeah, Yeah, Yeah" with a video for the song airing on MTV in moderate rotation. Spence later walked off with Nashville Music Awards for "Best Male Singer," "Soul Artist of the Year" and "Funk Artist of the Year" in *Metro* magazine's 1989 reader's poll.

It would prove to be a wild, if short, ride for Spence. He appeared in the Nicolas Cage movie *Firebird*, toured as Debbie Gibson's opening act (remember, she was a big seller then), performed on three continents and had songs appear on a number of movie soundtracks. Spence recorded his second album, co-produced with Don Gehman (John Mellencamp, Hootie & the Blowfish), only to have it rejected by Atlantic (??!). Spence filed bankruptcy to get out from under his deal.

II. PainFaithJoy (Bold Records 1996, CD)
1. Here Come the Jud
2. Goin' Down

3. Free
4. Do You Feel Like Me?
5. Anything is Possible
6. Temptation
7. High Above It All
8. Like A Rolling Stone
9. To Love Is To Live
10. We Are Blessed

Comments: After leaving Atlantic and faced with starting over, Spence sank into depression and escaped to Central America, where he performed humanitarian work in the Honduras, El Salvador, and Guatemala. Returning to Nashville, he teamed up with his brother Jody and friend Spencer Campbell and recorded *PainFaithJoy* in his parents' home in White House, Tennessee. The album brought him to the attention of Bernie Leadon, of the Eagles, who was the head of the newly-formed Pioneer Music Group.

III. I Guess I Love It (Pioneer Music Group 1999, CD)
1. Bossanovanight
2. Sputnik (I Wanna Live on the Moon)
3. New Day Dawning
4. Loved by Somebody
5. Jungle
6. Do You Dream?
7. NYC
8. Doin' the Best I Can
9. I Guess I Love It
10. Fields of Evergreen

Comments: Pioneer Music Group was underwritten by the Pioneer Electronic Corp of Japan and would be based in Brentwood, Tennessee and run by Bernie Leadon. Spence was one of a handful of artists signed by the label, a literal diamond among a whole lotta coal 'cause Pioneer signed some real dogs, like Full On The Mouth. Unfortunately, the label was evidently on shaky ground from the beginning and one day the company's employees showed up to work and found the doors locked and the company gone. Needless to say, *I Guess I Love It* received no promotion, no push and therefore accomplished nothing but provide the talented Spence with another harsh music biz lesson.

IV. The Velvet Kitten Sessions (Bold Records 2003, CD)
1. Everything Your
2. Mother & Child
3. Freedom Road
4. Fire
5. Rusty Chevrolet
6. Little Man
7. It's You I Adore
8. Standing Tall
9. Can You Feel Me?
10. The Last March

Comments: Spence released two self-produced albums in 2003; *The Velvet Kitten Sessions* features Spence's usual mix of rock, funk and soul while *Opus Dei*, which is not listed here, is a gospel-themed album recorded in Colorado. Spence signed a deal with Universal South and recorded an album to be released sometime during 2007, but the label cut Spence from its roster early in the year and, in an all-to-familiar replay of his Atlantic Records experience, the album has disappeared into major label purgatory.

C'mon now, people – Spence's songwriting skills have been on display on albums selling tens of millions of copies, and his lone widely-distributed solo effort scored a hit single. Why won't a label sign this guy and make a star out of him? Hell, he doesn't sound like anybody else, and while you and I might look upon this as an asset, narrow-minded labels evidently view it otherwise...

SPIDER VIRUS

Band Members:
Jerry Campbell (vocals, guitar, keyboards) (I-II)
Hunt Adams (guitar) (I)
Freddy Ervin (guitars, vocals) (II)
Eric Reed (bass) (I-II)
Tracy Coss (drums) (I-II)
Chike Page (drums, vocals) (II)

Spider Virus Recordings:

I. Electric Erection (Ng Records 1997, CD)
1. Millionaire Magicians
2. Wiseguys

3. Devils Dog
4. Werewolf Ears
5. Your Jody
6. Angels
7. How'd You Get So Real
8. Eye Dog
9. I Wanna Learn How To Dance
10. The New America
11. Zero The Hero
12. Sometimes You Feel Like A Nut
13. California Tan
14. Reachdown
15. Hate To Know She Breathes
16. T For Toni

Comments: A series of self-produced single releases brought the band to the attention of Steve Albini, who produced this debut album for the soon-to-be-gone Ng Records label.

II. Radio Invaders (Offtime Records 2001, CD)
1. Keeping Your Dreams Alive
2. Your Daddy Is Thru
3. Here's Where It Ends
4. Young Turks
5. I Haven't Been Seen
6. Illy Monster
7. 25
8. Midnight In Albuquerque
9. Get Out Of The Car
10. That Sums Up The Life
11. I Hope You Find Yourself
12. Summertime Is Here Again
13. I Haven't Been Seen

14. Get It All Wrong
15. You Know We Will

Comments: On this CD, Spider Virus reminds me somewhat of the Replacements. Even when they're not rolling down the tracks with the same sort of ramshackle, trainwreck-waiting-to-happen three-chord rock sound, Spider Virus chases after a "devil may care" perspective that combines hardcore punk and '80s-styled college rock.

SPOONFED

Band Members:
Eric Page (vocals) (A1)
John Kiefer (guitars) (A1)
Michael Eng (bass) (A1)
Mark Covert (bass) (A1)
Tap ("elf beats," percussion) (A1)

Spoonfed Recordings:

A1. "Easier Than You" b/w "A Day" (Betina Records 1996, 7" vinyl)

Comments: Hendersonville rockers – dunno if they ever did anything else. Found this groovy white-vinyl 45 single in a big box at The Great Escape one afternoon...

THE STAND

Band Members:
Gus Palas (vocals) (I)
Michael Simmonz (guitars) (I)

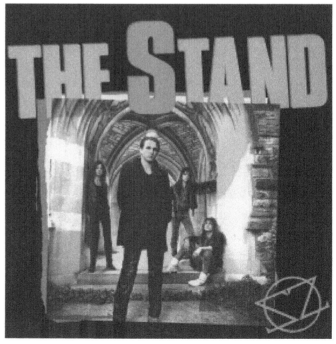

Jamie Simmonz (bass) (I)
Paul Simmonz (drums (I)

The Stand Recordings:

I. The Stand (Pak'er Records/Carlyle Records 1988, vinyl LP)
Side One
1. Nuclear Waist
2. Graduation Day

Side Two
3. All The Wrong Reasons
4. If You See Kay

Comments: Palas, publisher of *The Metro*, hooked up with the talented Simmonz brothers for this short-lived band. They got around, I'll give 'em that, performing in France and hitting the S.E. club circuit with a vengeance in support of this four-song EP. Not a bad example of period hard rock, as these things go, but sadly, by the late 1980s the market was glutted with similar bands like the Sea Hags, Love/Hate, the Four Horsemen, and even Nashville's own **Every Mother's Nightmare**, so the Stand would have had to really stand head and shoulders above everybody else to be heard – something they'd never accomplish on the local indie Carlyle Records. It would all be moot, however, because grunge was coming up hard and fast on the horizon, and would sweep Hollywood Boulevard clean of all these Crue-clones and G'n'R doppelgangers.

GARRISON STARR

Band Members:
Garrison Starr (vocals, guitar, percussion) (I)

Other Musicians:
Pat Buchanan (guitar, mandolin) (I)
Chris Carmichael (strings, violin, viola) (I)
Ken Coomer (drums) (I)

Mike Grimes (guitar) (I)
Mickey Grimm (percussion) (I)
David Henry (cello) (I)
Andy Hubbard (drums) (I)
Neilson Hubbard (percussion, keyboards, guitar, vocals) (I)
Lindsay Jamieson (drums) (I)
Brad Jones (guitar, bass, mandolin, vocals) (I)
Betsy Lamb (viola) (I)
Al Perkins (pedal steel)
Ross Rice (bass, drums, keyboards, tympani) (I)
Matthew Ryan (vocals)
Pat Sansone (keyboards, bass, percussion, guitar, synth) (I)
Mindy Smith (vocals) (I)
Kate York (vocals) (I)

Garrison Starr Recordings:

I. The Sound of You and Me (Vanguard Records 2006, CD)
1. Pendulum
2. Let Me In
3. Sing It Like a Victim
4. Pretending
5. Big Enough
6. Beautiful in Los Angeles
7. Kansas City, Kansas
8. Black and White
9. Cigarettes and Spearmint
10. No Man's Land
11. We Were Just Boys and Girls

Comments: It's a measure of respect for Starr's work that the credits on her albums look like a veritable "who's who" of Nashville's best musical talent.

II. The Girl That Killed September (Media Creature 2007, CD)
1. Unchangeable
2. Understood
3. Byhalia Road
4. 40 Days

THE STAND
The Stand
(Pak'er/Carlyle Records)

The Stand (formerly Simmonz) are ready to burn Nashville into cinder and ash with the upcoming release of their debut, a four-song EP that's a supersonic, multi-megaton blast, certain to scorch earth, demolish the competition and rock yo' head. From the crashing first chords of "Nuclear Waist," a purty lil' love song, thrashing straight into "Graduation Day" ("Did you think your education was through?" Indeed…these guys are here to teach yer ears a thing or two, bay-bee!).

The Stand roll into "All The Wrong Reasons" (a switchblade in the heart) and finish up with a song that Tipper's sure to spin for her kiddies, "If You See Kay." With this disc, the Stand serve up steamy helpings o' no-frills, no-mercy, no-kidding primal hellstorm fury, throwing a knock-out punch like Tyson in the first and delivering the right, rockin' goods while those other wimps are still trying to get it up. Make your stand... – *Metro Magazine*, 1988

5. Stay Home Tonight
6. Spectacle
7. Little Lonely Girl
8. Goldrush Heart
9. The Girl That Killed September
10. Fireworks
11. Brightest Star

STEALIN HORSES

Band Members:
Kiya Heartwood (vocals, guitar) (I-II)
Kopana Terry (drums, vocals) (I-II)
Kelly Richey (guitars)
Kevin Ray Clark (guitars, vocals) (II)
Tim Gilliam (guitars, mandolin, fiddle) (II)
Steve Kirkpatrick (bass) (II)

Other Musicians:
Kevin Dukes (guitar, mandolin) (I)
Bob Glaub (bass) (I)
Danny Kortchmar (guitars) (I)
Russ Kumkel (drums) (I)
Steve Lukather (guitars) (I)
Mandy Meyer (guitars) (I)
Mike Porcaro (bass) (I)
J.R. Robinson (drums) (I)
Leland Sklar (bass) (I)
Waddy Wachtel (guitars) (I)
Jai Winding (keyboards) (I)
Neil Young (harmonica) (I)

Stealin Horses Recordings:

I. Stealin Horses (Arista Records 1988, CD)
1. Turnaround
2. Where All The Rivers Run
3. Rain
4. Harriet Tubman
5. Walk Away
6. The Well
7. Gotta Get A Letter
8. Dyin' By The Gun
9. Tangled
10. Ballad of the Pralltown Café

Comments: This LP could have been a trainwreck of the worst sorts if not for the talents of Kiya Heartwood and Kopana Terry, which transcended corporate bullshit to deliver a strong debut album. If memory serves me well, the Kentucky band originally recorded this album with producer Jozef Nuyens at the Castle in Franklin. When Stealin Horses – really just Heartwood and Terry at this point – were signed to Arista, the label made them re-record the entire thing in L.A. with producer Greg Ladanyi and a slew of laid-back session types. Still, because of Heartwood's unnaturally strong songwriting chops, the album works (see review ➜).

After the band's self-titled album was released, Heartwood and Terry were paired with guitarist Brian Bonham and bassist Jon Dumo from British new wave pop band Roman Holiday, and the foursome subsequently toured behind bands like the Smithereens, the Del-Lords, and the Lemon Drops. Although Clive Davis and his Arista Records label had wanted to get into the "alternative rock" thing in the worst sort of way (remember, during the late 1980s, Whitney Houston was the label's biggest star), they had no idea how to handle Heartwood's heartfelt folk-rock sound. When the label dropped Stealin Horses in 1990 after under-promoting and totally misunderstanding the debut album, the British pretty boys took the first fast boat back to jolly old England with whatever cash they made.

II. Mesas and Mandolins (Waldoxy Records 1991, CD)
1. This House
2. If You Want to be Lovers
3. It's Not Magic
4. Distillery Hill
5. Beginners Mind
6. 1968 (a good day for robbin' trains)
7. Cross J Fourth Of July
8. Broad Form Deed
9. About You
10. Blue Moon of Kentucky

Comments: Stealin Horses carried on after the departure of the Brit-boys, with Heartwood and Terry recruiting their friend, guitarist Kelly Richey, to play with them. By this time, the Lexington, Kentucky band had relocated to Nashville and played around town a lot, especially at Douglas Corner. The trio of Heartwood-Kopana-Richey spent a year together while Heartwood worked on new songs, but unfortunately they never recorded together. When Richey left the band to pursue a solo career in early 1991, Heartwood and Terry packed up and moved to Oklahoma.

In Oklahoma, the Stealin Horses pair hooked up with guitarist Kevin Clark, bassist Steve Kirkpatrick, and multi-instrumentalist Tim Gilliam to record *Mesas and Mandolins*. The album is included here because of the band's local roots and because a lot of these songs were developed and performed in Nashville. Recorded in Lexington, which, like Bowling Green, falls into the larger sphere of Nashville rock (in my estimation). Released by the Jackson, Mississippi label Waldoxy, better-known for blues and R&B releases. When this album went nowhere, Stealin Horses broke up.

Heartwood returned to Nashville to record a straight country album, *True Frontiers*, for Waldoxy in 1993. A misguided attempt to wring a few more dollars out of a talented songwriter (see Jason's *One Foot In The Honky Tonk*), the album strayed too far from Heartwood's natural roots-rock and folk sound. Heartwood later hooked up with Miriam Davidson to form the successful folk duo Wishing Chair in 1995. Terry re-joined her former bandmate in Wishing Chair a couple years later. As for Richey, these days she's a bad-ass blues guitarist with a handful of solo albums under her belt.

STEELER (NASHVILLE VERSION)

Band Members:
Ron Keel (vocals) (I)
Michael Dunigan (guitar) (I)
Tim Morrison (bass) (I)
Robert Eva (drums) (I)

Steeler Recordings:

I. American Metal: The Steeler Anthology (Cleopatra Records 2006, CD)
1. Cold Day In Hell
2. Take Her Down
3. American Metal
4. Out To Get You
5. Ready To Explode
6. Hot On Your Heels
7. On The Rox (live)
8. Backseat Driver (live)
9. Victim Of The City (live)
10. Yngwie Is God (Guitar Solo From Hell) (live)
11. Band Introduction (live)
12. Excited (live)

13. Dying In Love
14. Last Chance To Rock
15. Metal Generation
16. Serenade

Comments: After helping **Lust** become one of the most popular bands on the city's young hard rock scene, Ron Keel left with bassist Tim Morrison to form Steeler with Dunigan and Eva. They played around town for a few months during 1981 before heading out to Los Angeles to pursue stardom. Steeler's indie single, "Cold Day In Hell," received some L.A. airplay and the band headlined shows above opening acts like Ratt and Metallica.

Somewhere between Steeler's 1981 move to L.A. and the 1982 recording of their self-titled debut album, the original (Nashville) band members fell by the wayside. Steeler could have become just another rock & roll footnote, a generic heavy metal band that is remembered only because Shrapnel Records owner and producer Mike Varney enlisted little-known (at the time) guitar wiz Yngwie Malmsteen to add some razzle-dazzle to tracks the band had already recorded.

It was the beginning of the era of the "guitar hero," however, and although Yngwie quickly went on to bigger and better things, his brief presence helped to make Steeler one of "those bands" that is fondly remembered in spite of itself. The ever-ambitious Keel, chafed by the constant roster changes, dumped Steeler and started his own band, simply called "Keel," in 1984. Over the next five years, Keel would become a second-tier metal star, selling millions of records.

Steeler, continued on page 490 ...

INTERVIEW: STEALIN HORSES

Faithful followers of *The Metro*…the ones who quote Brian Mansfield in arguments with their parents, the ones who read Scott Ritenour's record reviews to their English Lit teachers, those chosen few who actually met Gun Palas in a darkened bar one night…these loyal readers will recall that last month I left home, much to my parent's dismay, to find Stealin Horses.

Well, folks, I'm back…

That month on the road was a long and fruitless one as these now ragged boots wandered across the heartlands and highways of this vast land of ours. From Portland to Poughkeepsie, from Detroit to Dallas…in search of that shadowy, elusive entity known as Stealin Horses.

Imagine my surprise in returning home to find the band here, in Nashville, opening up for the Smithereens in another smash sell-out Go West show at the Cannery…right next door to *The Metro*'s corporate office complex. My sojourn ended in my own back yard; ignoring the heat and a drought of near-Biblical proportions, fellow traveler Bill C. and myself left a trail of broken-down cars and confused motorists in our wake as I raced towards my destiny and an interview with Stealin Horses' guitarist/singer/songwriter Kiya Heartwood.

Stealin Horses, if you readers are still unaware, is one of the hottest rock & roll outfits to hail from the Southeast since the Scorchers kicked ass and the Satellites rocked their way into the Top Ten. What Stealin Horses has in common with those local faves, aside from an abundance of talent, is a desire to be the best, an overwhelming sincerity, and a genuine love of what they're doing.

"This is all I ever wanted to do," says Heartwood, "play in a rock & roll band. I was fourteen years old and I started writing songs before I even realized that I was doing it." Kiya's early experience was as a drummer, playing in a number of bands although, she says, "I kept writing songs, so I kept having to come up front and sing them. Pretty soon, I had so many songs – 20 or so – that I got up enough nerve to make a tape. The guys that worked on that tape with me became Radio Café."

Radio Café played the Midwest/Southeast circuit for several years, recording and releasing an independent EP titled First World in 1985. Current Stealin Horses drummer Kopana Terry became a part of Radio Café after answering a classified ad in the Lexington Herald. "Kopana auditioned and beat out eight guys for the job," says Heartwood, "she and I hit it off right away. She's really dedicated, really wants to be in a band, wants to do it for a living."

When the decision came to pursue music as a full-time vocation, Kiya and Kopana were left alone as the remaining members of the band, lacking their commitment, dropped out. Says Kiya, "the other guys, they were old enough that they didn't want to leave Lexington, they didn't think that success was possible…they left for a lot of reasons. We changed our name to Stealin Horses." The name comes from an American Indian trial ritual of maturity and courage.

Offered a production deal by Franklin, Tennessee's Castle Studio, the band was in the midst of "paying their dues." Remembers Heartwood, "we were starving…we couldn't even get a gig in Nashville! We didn't know how to get a record deal. Living in Lexington, we were isolated." A tape was sent around to the labels, opening up a rare bidding war. Performing several showcases in Nashville, over a dozen labels were interested in signing the talented band from Kentucky.

"We were really fortunate," says Kiya, "we got to pick the label that we thought would be the best for us. We just wanted to be ourselves, we didn't want anybody saying 'Oh, you can't do this, everything has to sound alike.' When you see our show, you'll see that I'm not a model, we're not a gorgeous band…we didn't want to get made up and sold as something that we're not. That's completely against our nature." To this end, says Kiya, "Arista was the best choice for us."

The band recorded their debut album twice, first in Nashville and again in Los Angeles. The first record, says Heartwood, "didn't come out the way we wanted it to." With Arista's support, Stealin Horses went West to work with producer Greg Ladanyi (Don Henley, Jackson Browne) and a host of L.A. session players. The result, says Heartwood, was great. "It's our record…it's good!" The trick in working with session superstars such as Waddy Wachtel was, says Kiya, in "making it not sound like a Southern California record. Everyone was real receptive. I would play the songs on an acoustic guitar, explaining what the songs were about and why they had to sound a certain way. We all had a lot of respect for each other and it worked well."

Stealin Horses, the album, is a strong, emotional blend of musical styles, a surprisingly mature debut disc. Its ten tracks, all written or co-written by Heartwood, are lyrically intense, offering up imagery and sophistication matched by only a handful of current songwriters. Citing as influences on her writing "all the great songwriters, from Woody Guthrie to Hank Senior," as well as Springsteen and John Cougar Mellencamp, Kiya says "they all take short story techniques and use them in writing songs, creating a sort of narrative poetry. You have to cram a lot of information into each line."

In support of the album, Stealin Horses has been touring constantly since its release, playing this summer's "One For The Sun" show here in Nashville, as well as opening shows for the Smithereens, the Del Lords, and the Lemondrops. "We love playing," says Kiya, "so we're going to tour until they won't let us tour anymore!" Their energetic, rocking live show clears up a lot of misconceptions about the band created by their name and where they come from. "We get a lot of grief, coming from Kentucky," Heartwood states, "a lot of people say 'Oh, they're a country band,' or 'Oh, it's just a bunch of girls.' I'd like to see somebody say that after seeing us play!"

Continuing, Kiya says "it's difficult for us to get an audience as we don't fit into any preconceived categories. We're not a Southern band from Athens, we're not a heavy metal band, we're not country…" Although elements of all these styles can be found in Stealin Horses' music, they are, above all, a rock & roll band. That the band is from the South, or that it contains two women is irrelevant. One listen to the band, either live or on vinyl, is all it takes to get hooked…

Besides Heartwood and Terry, the band includes guitarist Brian Bonham and bassist Jon Dumo, former members of the British band Roman Holiday. "We auditioned people for the band," says Kiya, "and these guys were the greatest! Jon and Brian are serious, treating Stealin Horses like I treat Stealin Horses. They know that nobody gives you something for nothing and how hard you have to work to be successful." Speaking of the future, Heartwood adds, "when it comes time to record the next album, we'll be able to take a whole *band* into the studio, with everyone contributing, everyone singing."

Stealin Horses…Kiya and Kopana, Jon and Brian…proved to be everything I had hoped for when I began my search a month ago. The band's magically hypnotic stage presence, fierce primal rock & roll energy, and original style are only hinted at on disc. As fine as their album is (easily one of the year's best), one must see them live to experience that which this not-so-humble critic has found in only a handful of bands…the rockin' and rollin' real thing, dammit! You owe it to yourself to discover Stealin Horses. You'll be glad you did. – *The Metro*, August 1988

Stealin Horses

INTERVIEW: STEALIN HORSES

Sometimes an artist will develop a vision that, in turn, creates a burning desire, a desire that transcends all else. Whether it's a passion to paint the perfect portrait or mold the ultimate sculpture or write the most beautiful song, such a vision prevents the artist from doing little else in life, and often leaves the artist unfit, really, to do much else.

Rock & roll is a lot like that...a burning in the belly that drives one to obsession. It's that drive, a damning need to "rock out" that creates basket cases and millionaires, poets and prophets. It's this "call of the wild" which propels Kiya Heartwood...

Heartwood is the driving force behind the band Stealin Horses. Through many long miles, trials and tribulations, Stealin' Horses has emerged stronger than ever with a new line-up and a rockin' new album. Not the "ultimate" Stealin Horses disc – not yet – but the next step on that long road for the talented Heartwood and companions.
"This is all I ever wanted to do," says Heartwood, "play in a rock & roll band. I was fourteen years old and I started writing songs before I even realized that I was doing it." Kiya's early experience was as a drummer, playing with a number of bands before finally recording a tape of her own material with a band that became known as Radio Cafe. It was out of this band that Stealin' Horses was born.

Based at that time, in the late-80s, in Lexington, Kentucky, Stealin' Horses basically consisted of Heartwood and drummer Kopana Terry, and many different people who played along. On the strength of Kiya's songwriting skills and the band's live performances, they signed a deal with Arista Records and, in 1988, a self-titled debut album was released.

Response to that record was encouraging, and the band – Kiya and Kopana and a couple of haircuts that the label stuck them with – toured as openers for the Smithereens and the Del Lords. It moved somewhere in the neighborhood of 200,000 copies or so and, with the band's constant touring, helped to develop a loyal Southeastern cult following. It is here that the trials begin, seeing the band entrapped in all sorts of legal hassles, bankruptcy and, eventually, being dropped by Arista.

"We couldn't record for a year," says Heartwood, "so we just decided to start over." The band reformed as a trio with a talented Kelly Ritchie on guitar, "but that didn't work out," says Kiya. "So we started looking for people to try and do the Stealin' Horses that we didn't do with the Arista album. I wanted to have a band before we got signed this time, because that was a mistake before...we had sold an idea of a band without really being a band."

Heartwood and Kopana left both their Lexington homes and their Nashville base and moved west, to Tahlequah, Oklahoma. Here, in new surroundings, Heartwood continued to pursue her vision. "I decided that I wanted to have a multi-instrumentalist who was coming from a bluegrass or a traditional country background; to have a metal-kind-of guitarist and a pop/alternative bass player and have everyone be able to sing."

"That's what we've got now," Kiya adds, "but it took forever. You have to get these people who don't play the same kind of music, who like each other but don't like the same music to like my music and to want to play it. So, it took awhile..."

The eventual line-up includes guitarist Kevin Ray Clark, multi-instrumentalist Tim Gillian and bassist Steve Kirkpatrick as well as Heartwood and Kopana. Kiya also considers soundman Jimi McDuffie to be an essential part of the band. A soundman and a musician, Kiya says, "he's really responsible for what Stealin' Horses sounds like."

"After we had finally found them," says Kiya of the band, "we went into the studio in Lexington. I borrowed money from everybody that I knew, friends and family...I sold everything, got rid of my car. Got to where I was living on $200 to $300 a month and spent all of the money on the record."

The result is **Mesas And Mandolins**, the second Stealin' Horses album and, some would say, the first real S.H. disc. "We sold it to Tommy Couch's label, Waldoxy," says Kiya. "I've known him a long time. He knows how to do things right and he stays out of the artist's way. I wanted a deal that was the opposite of everything we had done in 'majorland': artistic control, art control...he doesn't tell us how to dress or what songs to do. So we'll either fall on our butts or do really well. Either way, it's up to us."

Mesas And Mandolins expands upon the talents and material presented on the debut Stealin Horses disc and takes them in a new direction. The new band provides a chemistry that was missing from the first release, a musical professionalism and, at once, a looseness that only comes from playing together and sharing a love for what you're doing. The ten songs – nine Heartwood originals and one cover, "Blue Moon Of Kentucky" – showcase Kiya's immense songwriting skills as well as the growth and maturity that only life can bring. There's a greater social consciousness evident here, as illustrated by material such as "Broadform Deed" and "This House", but there's also great love, and passion and, most of all, great rock & roll.

Stealin' Horses has managed to retain a large share of its original audience. "We've played constantly," says Kiya, "touring a circuit which stretches from Texas and Oklahoma to Kentucky and Tennessee." With recent trips westward and northward, "we're making the circuit wider. We see all of the people who bought the Arista album all the time and we haven't stopped playing those songs. With a five-piece band, they sound full, whereas on the Arista thing I was singing with myself. With the band, we'll have all five people singing, or we'll do a cappella or a bluegrass song, or whatever." The new band offers a depth and diversity Stealin' Horses had never had.

Through it all, however, it is the vision and the drive of Kiya Heartwood (with support from her constant companion, Kopana Terry) which has fueled Stealin' Horses. Someday, one way or another, Stealin' Horses will be big. They'll deliver one of the greatest albums of rock & roll. And you will of read of them here, first. – *The Metro*, 1991

STEALIN HORSES
Stealin Horses
(Arista Records)

Dear Mom & Dad:

I know that it was a great shock to come home and find out that I'd packed up and left. I've gone in search of Stealin' Horses, the hottest rock & roll outfit to ever hail from Lexington, Kentucky. Ya'see, ever since I heard Stealin' Horses self-titled Arista Records debut, I've been deeply and hopelessly in love. Stealin' Horses, as you should know, are basically Kiya Heartwood and Kopana Terry, two gorgeous and veeerrryyy talented women who write such bittersweet songs of love and betrayal, fear and endless dreams that from the opening chords of "Turnaround," the album's first single, through the power-pop melody of "Gotta Get A Letter" to the anthemic "Ballad of the Pralltown Café," I knew that these were the girls for me!

So I'm going to roam the dusty, hot blacktop of America 'til I find them. I know that they've got to be playing somewhere, touring this great land, bringing their energetic, hard-driving brand of rock & roll; well-written, Dylanesque lyrics and beautiful, near-flawless harmonies to the hundreds of small towns that dot the landscape. I'm sure that they wouldn't mind having a world-renown rock critic such as myself documenting their career (after all, look what Dave Marsh did for Bruce Springteen). I'm going to give my heart to Stealin' Horses.

It's time for my bootheels to be wandering...

Your son, Keith

Dear Son:

Good riddance! After thirty years, we thought you'd never leave!

Mom & Dad

– *Metro Magazine*, 1988

STEELER - STELLA - STIKKI WIKKIT

Steeler, contiued...

By the 1990s, when the musical winds of change blew out the old metal bands in favor of grunge, Keel was back pursuing other projects, including a stint as "Ronnie Lee Keel," country singer. Most recently Keel fronted Iron Horse, a "country metal" band, and he put Keel back together in 2009 to record a new album with the veteran metal band.

As for the Steeler compilation album *American Metal*, only the first six songs – a collection of singles and demos – feature the original Nashville line-up of the band. The live tracks are bootleg-quality performances notable only for Malmsteen's six-string presence. The remaining tracks are by the band that recorded *Steeler* in 1982.

STELLA

Band Members:
Curt Perkins (vocals, guitar, mellotron)
Charles Wyrick (guitar)
Preach Rutherford (bass)
Alan Johnstone (drums, percussion)

Stella Recordings:

I. Ascension (Beggar's Banquet 1997, CD)
1. Song In D
2. The Word
3. Bright Morning
4. Ascension
5. Azure
6. Rites Of Day
7. California
8. The Sun
9. Aporia
10. Blissmark
11. Razor

Another View: "Nashville's Stella was a prototypical early emo band mixing post-grunge distortion and heavy riffs (on first listen, the opening "Song in D" doesn't sound much different from Pearl Jam) with Curt Perkins' wailing, rending-of-garments vocals. Unfortunately, Perkins' lyrics are along the lines of that guy in 11th grade honors English who kept picking fights with the teacher over imagined slights to his embryonic genius...unsurprisingly, the best songs are the ones on which lead guitarist Charles Wyrick takes some of the spotlight away from Perkins, like on the tumbling "Word," which features the album's only real fist-pumper of a chorus, or the closing ballad "Razor," which features an elegant, crystalline guitar solo. The playing is uniformly competent, but the songs are only fitfully memorable at best..."
– Stewart Mason, *All Music Guide*

STIKKI WIKKIT

Band Members:
Mark Cerreta (vocals)
Mark Capps (guitar, vocals)
Brian T. Maus (guitar, vocals)
Scott Regal (bass, vocals)
Tim Crowder (drums, vocals)

Comments: Contributed song "Nancy Rocker" to the *Major Potential #1* 1991 compilation CD.

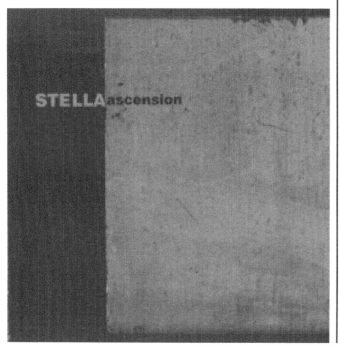

STONE DEEP

Band Members:
Ronzo "The Beast" Cartwright (vocals) (A1, I-IV)
Glen Cummings (guitar) (A1, I-IV)
Tim Brooks (bass, vocals) (I, IV)
Sam Tucker (bass, vocals) (II)
David Howard (drums) (A1, I-II, IV)
David DePriest (drums) (IV)

Other Musicians:
"Machine Gun" Kelly Butler (bass) (A1, IV)
Ruben Garzas (drums) (IV)
Terry Hayes (vocals, turntables) (IV)
Loko (vocals, turntables) (A1)
Kurtis McFarland (vocals) (IV)
Kenny Owens (drums) (IV)

Stone Deep Recordings:

Singles

A1. "Gangs and the Government" b/w "Mr. Sunray"
(Secession Records, 7" vinyl)

Albums

I. Stone Deep (Tillman Music Group 1997, CD)
1. Imperfection
2. Whoville
3. Mighty Oaks
4. Red Sea
5. Yin Yang
6. Revolution

Comments: After **Hard Corps** crashed and burned due to a disastrous major label deal, Ronzo "The Beast" Cartwright bounced back with Stone Deep. This six-song EP adds more of an R&B vibe to the (already stale) rap-rock formula, resulting in a surprisingly spry, energetic and soulful collection of songs. For a while, Stone Deep was one of the most popular outfits in Nashville, but they never seemed to catch a break. Guitarist Cummings came to the band from Scatterbrain, an underrated Long Island, NY band.

II. Kung Fu Grip (Secession Recordings, cassette)
Side 1
1. What's Going On?
2. Billy

Stone Deep

STONE DEEP - STOP THE CAR - REBECCA STOUT

3. Betterday
4. Hands
5. Circle

Side 2
6. Annie
7. Sometimes
8. All In Your Head
9. Whatcha Say?

III. Hump and Hum (1999)

IV. Engage (Irregular Records 2000, CD)
1. Babyfood
2. Gangs and the Government
3. Baby, When I Think About You
4. Mister Sunray
5. Finger To The Forty
6. Yin/Yang
7. Mighty Oaks
8. Animal
9. Whole Lotta
10. Money Makes The World Go Round
11. Whoville
12. Imperfection

Other Appearances: Stone Deep contributed three songs to the *Treason Records Sampler Vol.1*.

STOP THE CAR

Band Members:
Melissa English (vocals)

Mark Utley (guitars, vocals)
Vincent Hammerstein (bass)
Troy Davis (drums)

Comments: An alt-rock band compared to the Cure, Stop The Car relocated from Evansville, Indiana to Nashville in early 1989; they later performed at the 1990 N.E.A. Extravaganza.

REBECCA STOUT

Band Members:
Rebecca Stout (vocals)
Victor Wooten (acoustic upright bass)
Regi Wooten (guitars)
Rob DeHart (electric upright bass)
J.D. Blair (drums)
Derek Green (drums, shakers)
Graham Spice (trumpet, electric piano)
Josh Rouse (trombone)
Dam Immel (upright acoustic bass)

Comments: Stout, of **the Shakers**, launched her solo career with three songs on the *Treason Records Sampler Vol. 1* CD. Stout's "Icarus' Revenge" also appears on *The Ex-Files* 1998 NeA Extravaganza compilation CD.

REBECCA STOUT & THE CIRCUS INEBRIUS

Band Members:
Rebecca Stout (vocals, percussion)
Sharon Gilchrist (upright acoustic bass)
Rob DeHart (bowed upright electric bass)
Derek Green (drums)

Stone Deep

Graham Spice (trumpet)
Art Ruangtip (trombone)
Percy Person (keyboards, percussion)
Nicole Watkins (vocals)
Eliot Wilcox (electric guitar)

Comments: About Rebecca Stout & the Circus Inebrius, Daryl Sanders says, "one of the most innovative bands in the history of Nashville. Electric guitar was secondary with the rhythm built around drums, acoustic upright bass and bowed electric upright bass. The full line-up behind Rebecca also included keys, trumpet, trombone, electric guitar and big vocs. Nine pieces in all." Daryl's not kidding…the songs he sent me show a use of horn similar to improvisational jazz, with a strong underlying rhythmic structure driven by the inspired use of dual upright bass. Very cool, very avant-garde, the Circus Inebrius probably would have been more at home in New York City or Chicago than Nashville..

STRANGE TONGUES

Band Members:
Jimmy Johnson (vocals, guitars, bass)
Hal Ramer (guitars)
Joe Polenzani (drums)

Strange Tongues Recordings:

I. Little Dramas (Communique Records 2001, CD EP)
1. So Serious
2. Little Dramas
3. Get Lucky
4. Take Care

Comments: I had the good fortune of working with Jimmy Johnson at PDQ Pizza in Green Hills back in 1988-89 when he was ½ of an incredible country music duo with Connie Bell. Jimmy was a great songwriter with an easy lyrical style and a firm grasp of the traditional country sound, but Jimmy had too much integrity and attitude to play Music Row politics, so the duo never got signed.

Upon hearing this rock-oriented project, I had to change my opinion of Mr. Johnson – the man is simply fookin' brilliant! Strange Tongues showcased Jimmy's songwriting prowess along with an intricate and mesmerizing rock soundtrack (see review ➔). Jimmy and I lost touch with each other when the band went over to Scotland to play a few years ago; I hope to hear from him again 'cause he's just too damn talented not to be making music in some fashion.

Rebecca Stout

STRAYS DON'T SLEEP - STREETS OF ICE

Another View: "The band draws on rock's most primal instincts to convey a down 'n' dirty sound that's passionate, witty and unflinchingly honest...free of computer bytes or loop-de-loop effects, the trio weds a wicked, back-to basics sound with a pulpy, bare-knuckled look at what's true and what's false." – Michael McCall

STRAYS DON'T SLEEP

Band Members:
Matthew Ryan (vocals, guitars, synth, keyboards, bass) (I)
Neilson Hubbard (vocals, guitars, synth, keyboards) (I)
Brian Bequette (guitars, bass, accordion) (I)
Billy Mercer (bass) (I)
Steve Latanation (drums, percussion, vocals) (I)

Other Musicians:
Doug Lancio (guitars, percussion) (I)
Jeff Patterson (tambourine) (I)
Garrison Starr (vocals) (I)
Clay Steakley (bass) (I)
Kate York (vocals) (I)

Strays Don't Sleep Recordings:

I. Strays Don't Sleep (Hybrid Recordings 2005, CD)
1. Love Don't Owe You Anything
2. Pretty Girl
3. Martin Luther Ave
4. Night Is Still
5. For Blue Skies
6. Spirit Fingers
7. April's Smiling At Me
8. Cars And History
9. Falling Asleep With You

Comments: Featuring the talents of **Matthew Ryan** and Neilson Hubbard, along with a host of friends, Strays Don't Sleep was the result of Ryan and Hubbard wanting to collaborate together on an album. Originally released in the U.K. to great acclaim and more than a few sales, the album would see subsequent stateside release by the band. Sadly, no major label had the vision or the balls to pick up this enchanting album and give it a shot in a marketplace crowded with droning noise and cut 'n' paste bands.

STREETS OF ICE
Web: www.jackwilliamsmusic.com

Band Members:
Miranda Louise (vocals)
Jack Williams (vocals, guitar)

Comments: Jack Williams is an interesting cat, and it's a shame that he never made a bigger splash in Nashville during

STRANGE TONGUES
Little Dramas
(Communique Records)

Nashville artist Jimmy Johnson tried for years during the '90s to break through the barriers of the label establishment in the "Music City," but even the carefully-crafted country songs he wrote failed to sway the feeble intellects of the average major label A&R rep. With his band, **Strange Tongues**, Johnson has taken a widely divergent tack, rocking the house with the same passion and intelligence that he brought to his country-oriented material.

The band's *Little Dramas* EP clocks in at just shy of a quarter-hour, but the four songs here are filled with so much life and energy that you'll just hit the 'repeat' button on your box and forget about it. Songs like "So Serious" and "Take Care" are textured with shades of rock, pop, jazz and country styles. The songs are driven with marvelous guitar interplay between Johnson and Hal Ramer, drummer Joe Polenzani providing a strong rhythmic backbone to Johnson's soulful, rough-hewn vocals. The oblique lyrics throw out scattershot imagery that will have you scratching your head until an epiphany of understanding hits you between the ears.

As refreshing and original a band as you'll find among the indie ranks these days, Strange Tongues deserve to break out of the Nashville rock ghetto and achieve a wider following. – *The View On Pop Culture*, 2001 his brief tenure. Between 1959 and 1987, the year he formed Streets of Ice, Williams performed alongside such musical legends as Harry Nilsson, Mickey Newbury, John Lee Hooker, and Big Joe Turner as a touring guitarist. Williams fronted a number of rock bands during this time, often backing vocal groups like the Del Vikings and the Platters.

As a songwriter, Williams' songs have been recorded by everybody from Mickey Newbury and the Oak Ridge Boys to Uriah Heep (?!!). From jazz-playing beatnik poet to cosmic cowboy and roots-rocker, to his current incarnation as an acoustic folkie, Williams has survived 50 years in the music biz. Miranda Louise worked as a backing vocalist for folks like bluesman A.C. Reed, Stevie Ray Vaughan, Bonnie Raitt and many others, and has recorded a number of solo blues-rock albums. Louise and Williams were backed by a number of local musicians, but there's precious little info available.

STREPNOVA

Band Members:
Joe Montgomery (vocals, guitar)
Wayne Mehl (viola, guitar)
Fred Greene (guitar)
Bill McLaurine (bass)
Jim Dye (drums)

Comments: Strepnova consisted of several Nashville-area rock veterans, with Montgomery and Dye both formerly of **Jet Black Factory** and Greene and McLaurine from **Word Uprising**. Joe Montgomery emailed me with info on the band and says "our songs "Winter Kills," "Pushed," "St. Jim" and our version of the Velvet's "I'll Be Your Mirror" received consistent airplay on 91 Rock." Thanks, Joe!

STUPID AMERICANZ

Band Members:
Rusty (vocals) (A1)
E.B. (guitars) (A1)
Philly (bass) (A1)
Timmy (drums) (A1)

Stupid Americanz Recordings:

A1. Lost Cause (House O' Pain 1991, 7" vinyl EP)
Side One
1. Zombies From The Stratosphere
2. Hateful End
3. Lost Cause

Side Two
4. Insania!
5. Carrot Stix & Cold Beer
6. Rag His Ass

Comments: Beer-fueled hardcore punk from the Stupid Americanz, courtesy of the good folks at House O' Pain…think Murphy's Law and you'll be in the right ball park. The band also had a couple of demo tapes that it sold by mail order (and at shows), but I don't have 'em.

SUBURBAN BAROQUE

Band Members:
Allen Green (keyboards)
Lewis Lowrey (vocals, bass)

Comments: Suburban Baroque was one of Nashville's true "ahead of their time" bands, Green and Lowrey creating exciting, electronic-based music before just about anybody. I seem to remember that the band put out a cassette that I once had but have lost somewhere down the line. Green was also one of Nashville's first zinesters, publishing the local music zine *Grab!* circa 1981-82. Among the zine's writers were Green, my buddy Kent Orlando, Curtis "C Ra" McGuirt, and Rick Champion. After Suburban Baroque, Green melded electronic music with performance art under the Mind's Eye Performance Group, often working with **Tony Gerber**. Green moved to Atlanta sometime during the early 1990s – I ran into him once in Little Five Points – and continued pursuing his own artistic vision.

From YouTube: "Once upon a time in Nashville, there was a slighty geeky, slighty artsy band called Suburban Baroque. The core of the band was keyboardist Allen Green (now Welty-Green) and bassist/vocalist Lewis Lowrey. After their second drummer moved away, they invested in a

"Drumulator" beat-box and did the duo thing for awhile, until they came across guitarist Franklin Wilkinson & Lewis' brother Charles stepped in on percussion."

"These are the least "cringe worthy" tracks (hey! it was the 80s!) from two video projects they did with director Seth Ritter and Nashville's Community Access Television. The first, "Surreal Estate," was a studio shot, with multi-image slide projections chroma-keyed behind them. The other was "Just Looking," a live performance in 100 Oaks Shopping Mall (in keeping with the "suburban" concept). The sound from the live shoot proved unusable so mighty efforts were made to synchronize the live footage with a studio soundtrack. It mostly succeeds..." (AgMedia)

SUEDE TATTOO

Band Members:
Matt Orozco (vocals)
Josh Rouse (guitar, vocals)

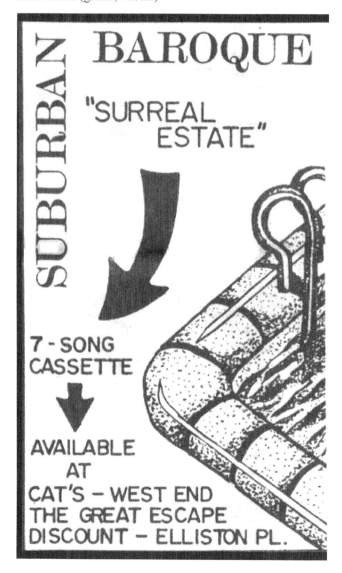

Kaley Junkins (guitar, vocals)
Charles Irwin (bass)
David Gehrke (drums)

Comments: Contributed song "One Time Jezebel" to the *Major Potential #1* 1991 compilation CD. **Josh Rouse**, of course, would go on to build an acclaimed solo career.

SUNSET A.M.

Band Members:
Barry Felts (vocals, guitar)
John Bruton (guitars)
Tony Frost (bass)
Randy Ford (drums, vocals)

From the band's MySpace page: Sunset A.M. was a Nashville based power pop band from 1991-1993 (too short lived). Started as demos recorded by Barry Felts (Jason & the Nashville Scorchers, No Art, File 13, Triple X & Burning Hearts) & guitarist John Bruton. Everyone would come to John's house and put down parts for fun. Randy Ford on drums and vocals (The Times, Radio One & In Color) & bassist Tony Frost (the Bunnies, the Movement, Triple X, Asfalt Jungle, 69 Tribe, Snakehips, Bitter Pills, Forefathers of Doom, etc). Took it to the stage and played many venues around Nashville including the Exit/In before disbanding in 1993.

SURFING THE COALDUST

Band Members:
Jack Garland (vocals, guitar)
Tim Eastwood (vocals, guitar)
Drew Cook (bass)
Chuck Turner (drums)

Comments: Band contributed song "She Knows What She Wants" to the *Music City Rock* 1995 compilation CD.

SWAG

Band Members:
Doug Powell (vocals, guitar, harmonium) (A1-2, I)
Robert Reynolds (vocals, guitars) (A1-2, I)
Tom Petersson (bass) (A1-2, I)
Jerry Dale McFadden (vocals, keyboards) (A1-2, I)
Ken Coomer (drums, percussion, vocals) (A1-2, I)

Other Musicians:
Chris Carmichael (strings) (A2, I)
Jim Hoke (harmonica) (I)
Scotty Huff (vocals, trumpet, guitar) (A2, I)
Brad Jones (bass) (A2, I)
Bill Lloyd (guitar, vocals) (I)
Kenny Vaugh (guitar) (I)

Swag Recordings:

Singles, EPs

A1. Sweet Lucinda (Diesel Only 1998, 7" vinyl)
Side One
1. Sweet Lucinda

Side Two
2. Every Little Truth

A2. Different Girls (Super Baby 2000, 10" picture disc vinyl)
Side One
1. Lone
2. Different Girl

Side Two
3. When She Awoke
4. Louise

Albums

I. catch-all (Yep Roc Records 2001, CD)
1. Lone
2. I'll Get By
3. Near Perfect Smile
4. Please Don't Tell
5. When She Awoke
6. Louise
7. Different Girl
8. You
9. Eight
10. Trixie
11. Tide
12. She's Deceiving

Comments: One of a handful of Nashville "supergroups," the veteran musicians that made up the short-lived band Swag included members of the Mavericks, Wilco, and Cheap Trick.

When **Jerry Dale McFadden** and Robert Reynolds toured together with the Mavericks, they'd talk about the diversity of music that was on the radio when they were kids, and Swag began as a loosen-knit collection of friends in a good-natured attempt to recreate a sort of music that they all loved. The "Music City" band Swag should *never* be confused with the British electronic outfit of the same name.

Another View: "This ersatz "supergroup" was created by members of such country-leaning outfits as the Mavericks and Wilco as well as pop chart-toppers like Sixpence None The Richer and Cheap Trick. The resulting collaboration, titled *Catch-All* (Yep Roc Records), is a delightful blend of sixties-influenced, British invasion-styled rock with

Beatlesque harmonies and top-notch songwriting courtesy of talents like Jerry Dale McFadden, Robert Reynolds and Doug Powell and guests like Bill Lloyd."

"Think of the Who, the Zombies, Badfinger and the Beatles and you're in the right artistic ballpark. If you're lucky you might still score an original print of this CD, sure to become a collector's item. Due to a legal misunderstanding, three cuts on *Catch-All* with Cheap Trick's Tom Petersson will be replaced with Swag songs featuring Todd Rundgren, certainly no slouch in the pop/rock department himself."
– Rev. Keith A. Gordon, *View From The Hill* (2001)

SHARI SWEET

Band Members:
Shari Sweet (vocals, percussion) (I)

Other Musicians:
Tom Bukovac (guitars) (I)
Adie Grey (vocals) (I)
Wayne Killius (drums) (I)
Michael Rhodes (bass) (I)
Ross Rice (keyboards, guitar, vocals) (I)

Shari Sweet Recordings:

I. Believe (self-produced CD, 2000)
1. Leave the Light On
2. Dog Daze
3. Going Crazy
4. Better Together
5. Wrong

SHARI SWEET - SWING

6. Slither
7. Dream About You
8. Simply Huge (Ode to Mitch)
9. Anger
10. Doin' Fine
11. Don't Want to Talk

Comments: I met a Shari Sweet back when she was in high school circa mid-1980s, but I'm not sure that the singer is the same girl. Both are gorgeous, however, and this one enlisted a great team to help her put together this album.

Sweet's sound is pop-oriented with a slight twang on some tunes, a little rock 'n' roll on others. Sweet also contributed song "Whittling My Life In The Wood" to the *Music City Rock* 1995 compilation CD.

SWING

Band Members:
Bobby Greene (vocals, guitar)
Jonathan Bright (vocals, guitar)
Houston Greer (guitar)
Mike Rutherford (bass)
Colin Parker (drums)

Comments: Early 1990s band with great potential featured the talented **Jonathan Bright**, guitarist Houston Greer (another PDQ Pizza alum), and bassist Mike Rutherford. Dunno why these guys never got signed to somebody, and all I know of them was a three or four song demo tape recorded for their publisher.

Swing

Boy howdy, 'dem Nashville punks surely hated them some Southern rock, didn't they?! Back in the day, say 1983 or '84, as the local rock scene was beginning to form in some primordial tarpit of influences as disparate as the Clash, the Ramones, XTC, and the Sex Pistols, Nashville's young soul rebels were as adamant in their dislike of Southern rock as they were of the corporate Music Row establishment.

We all have to rebel against something, I guess, and for teenaged Nashville in the early 1980s, the tendency was to rail against the commercially declining Southern rock movement in much the same way that punks in cities like London, New York, and San Francisco in 1977 rejected what they saw as the bloated rock aesthetic of the decade.

It made a lot of sense, really...by 1984, to pick an entirely arbitrary point along the fluid rock 'n' roll timeline, what few Southern rockers that were left had long since risen out of the beer-drenched trenches of regional juke-joints and honky-tonks and were reaching for, unabashedly, the brass ring of record sales and big payday arena gigs playing in front of tens, if not hundreds of thousands of people. Charlie Daniels, the one-time godfather of Southern rock, had begun his inevitable slide towards country music dotage, Lynyrd Skynyrd had been dead and buried for years, and even the Rossington Collins Band – formed by the unlucky survivors of the plane crash that robbed the world of the genius that was Ronnie Van Zandt – had fallen by the side of the autobahn.

So, yes, what Southern rock had evolved into by the early-to-mid-1980s was worthy of scorn and derision, but I suspect that it was as much generational as it was a musical thing, although nobody could ever mistake bands like CPS, the Ratz, Cloverbottom, or even Jason & the Scorchers for something as mundane as Southern rockers. To drive the point home, Nashville's rock underground even organized multi-band "Alternative Jams," scheduled up against Charlie Daniels' annual "Volunteer Jam" blow-out, and if the punks received little or no notice for their efforts beyond the couple hundred people that attended their show, they seemed to like it that way.

In the minds of many, Southern rock came to its skid-marked end on October 20, 1977 in a muddy Mississippi field near the Louisiana border when a chartered plane carrying Lynyrd Skynyrd frontman Ronnie Van Zandt, guitarist Steve Gaines, and his sister, backing vocalist Cassie Gaines came crashing to earth, killing the three of them and injuring other band members. The Reverend was 20 years old at the time, several years older than many of the local musicians that would disdain Southern rock just a few years later, and unless you had grown up during the heyday of the genre, you couldn't possibly understand the anger and sorrow that accompanied this tragedy.

The night the plane went down, we all got shitfaced drunk, and I saw young women (and more than a few men) crying tears of grief as we all bonded over the end of an era. It didn't matter which Nashville bar you went to for days after the plane crash, as they were all filled with grieving patrons and Lynyrd Skynyrd would be playing on the jukebox or stereo. The only other time I've seen a musician's death have such a widespread cultural impact is when John Lennon was shot down by a brainwashed mutant in December 1980.

Something that so many of those rebelling against what they perceived was the scourge of Southern rock never understood is that the genre itself was a rebellious response to the slick, shiny, studio-produced pop-rock of the 1960s. The first generation of Southern rockers wanted to dirty up the sound a bit, injecting a healthy dose of blues into a mix of hard rock, Memphis (and Muscle Shoals) soul, and honky-tonk country. Nashville; Macon, Georgia; and Jacksonville, Florida were the most important cities in the Southern rock universe, and the genre can be said to have begun in 1969 with the release of the Allman Brothers Band's self-titled debut album. Guitarist and songwriter Duane Allman, if you didn't know, was born in Nashville...

It took a couple of years for Southern rock to establish itself, but the enormous success of the Allman Brothers' *At Fillmore East* album in 1971 would help launch a thousand ships. Charlie Daniels had already been kicking the can around the Music City for a few years, doing session work for folks like Bob Dylan, Ringo Starr, and Leonard Cohen when he formed the Charlie Daniels Band in 1972. A year later, Lynyrd Skynyrd would release its debut album, a top 30 hit fueled by constant AOR airplay of songs like "Tuesday's Gone," "Gimme Three Steps," "Simple Man," and what is possibly the most over-played song of all time (with apologies to "Stairway to Heaven"), the dreaded "Free Bird." In short order, bands like Wet Willie, the Outlaws, Black Oak Arkansas, ZZ Top, and the Marshall Tucker Band began to pop up like kudzu vines across the South.

For five years, between 1972 and 1977, Southern rock vied on the charts and in the arenas with artists like Deep Purple and Led Zeppelin, admirably holding its own with a throwback sound that, curiously, incorporated a lot of antique, or at least

THE SCOURGE OF SOUTHERN ROCK

wizened musical roots while still managing to sound fresh and contemporary. For those of us who grew up on the stuff while in junior high or high school (FHS class of '75! Woo!), Southern rock was simply part of the soundtrack to our teen years, along with the prog-rock of Yes and King Crimson and the hard rock of Alice Cooper and Bad Company...what is now known as the "classic rock" era. Punk rock and heavy metal had yet to be "invented," although you could hear the DNA blueprint for both genres being written in the sound of the New York Dolls, the Dictators, and like-minded fellow travelers at the time.

During the half-decade commercial peak of Southern rock, a lot of great music was released (see our "Milestones In Southern Rock" list below). Charlie Daniels' annual musical celebration, the Volunteer Jam, grew from the relatively-cramped confines of the War Memorial Auditorium in Nashville to attracting ten thousand fans to the Municipal Auditorium each year. Although Southern rock had passed its creative sell-by date by 1979, it was still a commercially viable business for the major labels, and that year's Volunteer Jam – held in January 1979, long before Nashville's young punks had begun their protest against the event – culminated in the emotional reunion of the surviving Lynyrd Skynyrd members performing "Free Bird" with Daniels and band, and other guests. I was there, and there wasn't a dry eye in the house...

By 1984, however, our arbitrary jumping off point for the Nashville rock underground, Southern rock *had* become the zombie corpse that the Alternative Jam was protesting. Second generation bands like .38 Special, Molly Hatchet, and the Johnny Van Zandt Band continued to score modest chart hits well into the '80s while even early Southern rockers like ZZ Top or the Marshall Tucker Band had shed the influences that had made them special in the first place, becoming MTV darlings (the former) or a countrified pop band (the latter), more like REO Speedwagon or Night Ranger than truly dangerous or innovative. Those who survived the early 1980s, like the Allman Brothers Band or Elvin Bishop, retreated deeper into the blues, where they still sit today.

Still, for all the pointless Sturm und Drang displayed by the Nashville rock underground in the early 1980s, Southern rock remains a scourge to this day, albeit an influential one. Local (and regional) bands like Every Mother's Nightmare and the Georgia Satellites had as much Southern rock vibe about them as any band from the '70s, while the "jam band" phenomenon of the 1990s drew as much inspiration from the extended live performances of Lynyrd Skynyrd and the Marshall Tucker Band as they did the Grateful Dead. It's safe to say that bands like the Black Crowes (Allman Brothers), Gov't Mule (ditto, along with a helping of Skynyrd), Jackyl (Black Oak Arkansas), Black Stone Cherry (Molly Hatchet), and much of the Americana music of the 2000s wouldn't exist in the same form without Southern rock, if they existed at all.

In defining the Southern rock aesthetic, music historian Martin Popoff wrote in his timeless *Southern Rock Review*, "It helps if you have long hair and beards and past-expiry bellbottom blue jeans. Cowboy hats are optional; they really are." For those of us who came of age during the Southern rock era, that sums it up about perfectly...and we never understood what all of those young 'uns were bitching about in the '80s, anyway. Boy howdy!

Milestones In Southern Rock
(Here are a dozen influential Southern Rock albums that any serious collector would consider to be essential listening...)

Allen Collins/Lynyrd Skynyrd

Allman Brothers Band – *At Fillmore East* (Capricorn Records, 1971)
Allman Brothers Band – *Eat A Peach* (Capricorn Records, 1972)
Charlie Daniels Band – *Fire On The Mountain* (Kama Sutra Records, 1974)
Gregg Allman – *Laid Back* (Capricorn Records, 1973)
Lynyrd Skynyrd – *Pronounced Leh-Nerd Skin-Nerd* (MCA Records, 1973)
Lynyrd Skynyrd – *Second Helping* (MCA Records, 1974)
Marshall Tucker Band – *A New Life* (Capricorn Records, 1975)
Marshall Tucker Band – *Where We Belong* (Capricorn Records, 1974)
Richard Betts – *Highway Call* (Capricorn Records, 1974)
Rossington Collins Band – *Anytime Anyplace Anywhere* (MCA Records, 1980)
The Outlaws – *The Outlaws* (Arista Records, 1975)
ZZ Top – *Tres Hombres* (Warner Brothers, 1973)

Other '70s era Southern rock bands worth checking out include the Atlanta Rhythm Section, Barefoot Jerry, Black Oak Arkansas, Blackfoot, Dixie Dregs, Hydra, Molly Hatchet, Nitzinger, Point Blank, Potliquor, Sea Level, Wet Willie, the Winter Brothers Band and later Southern rock-inspired outfits like the Black Crowes, the Georgia Satellites, and Gov't Mule...

The tenth anniversary of Charlie Daniels' Volunteer Jam took place in Nashville, Tennessee on Saturday night, February 4th, 1984 before a sold-out crowd of some 10,000 rabid fans. Living up to Daniels' predictions, this year's Jam, an eight-hour music marathon, was the biggest and best ever, featuring some 50 performers throughout the night.

Originally a celebration of the Charlie Daniels Band's first sold-out hometown concert, Daniels had invited several musical compadres to "stop by and do some jamming." This first Jam saw sets by members of the Allman Brothers Band and the Marshall Tucker Band, with over 100 radio stations nationwide airing one-hour tapes of the event.

The second jam saw the first year's 2,400 party-goers join 10,600 of their friends in the larger Murphy Center at the Middle Tennessee State University, a long-anticipated show which sold out weeks in advance of the event. Fans were not disappointed by the evening, which was documented in the first full-length motion picture to feature Southern rock, appropriately titled *Volunteer Jam*. It featured a guest list which included, among others, Alvin Lee of Ten Years After, Jimmy Hall of Wet Willie, and several members of the Allman Brothers Band.

Subsequent Volunteer Jams were moved to Nashville's Municipal Auditorium, with an annual advance sell-out becoming not a prediction but a reality. The event transformed itself from a regional cultural event into a nationally-renowned party. Mail orders for tickets were received from as far away as New York and California. Concert-goers trekking in from Mississippi, Louisiana, and Florida weren't an unusual sight, and the music presented on stage rarely let them down.

Over the years, Volunteer Jam fans have seen and experienced a wide range and variety of talent, with such entertainment and musical names as Sea Level, Bonnie Bramlett, Roy Acuff, Ted Nugent, Billy Joel, Delbert McClinton, Quarterflash, George Thorogood, Papa John Creach, Carl Perkins, Link Wray, and the legendary James Brown gracing the stage.

Over the past decade, the Volunteer Jam has garnered its share of accolades and attention. A PBS documentary was filmed at Jam number five; the yearly event has been featured on several syndicated radio broadcasts, including airing on the King Biscuit Radio Network; and it has spawned three Epic Records album releases. The Jam has also become a civic affair, inspiring both Mayoral and Gubernatorial proclamations.

With a celebrated background such as this, the Tenth Anniversary Jam was, needless to say, anxiously awaited by both the fans and the media. Invitations to guest artists were

Rev. Gordon & Charlie Daniels, WKDF studios, January 1979

mailed out by Daniels and his promotion company, Sound Seventy, months early and if Daniels knew who was going to appear, he wasn't letting anyone else in on the secret. This year's affair was to be broadcast worldwide by the Voice of America in Europe and the Armed Forces Radio Network, and broadcast across the state of Tennessee by the six stations in the Volunteer Jam Radio Network; and the show was going to be videotaped for a two-hour television special to be produced by Dick Clark Productions and syndicated by Multi-Media in approximately 200 television markets.

Unlike previous Jams, which featured the aristocracy of Southern rock alongside a smattering of mainstream rock talent, this year's Tenth Anniversary starred the greatest talent that the Music City has to offer. Acts like Ronnie Milsap, Crystal Gayle, Rodney Crowell, Emmylou Harris, and Tammy Wynette were interspersed with the two rocking "jam sessions" held during the night.

One of the mystiques of the Jam is that no one in the audience knows in advance who is going to perform until they actually hit the stage, so fans screamed with delight at surprise appearances by *Real People*'s Byron Allen, MTV's Allan Hunter, and those laughing merry-makers, the Jump 'N The Saddle Band of "Curly Shuffle" fame. Rock music's perennial teen-ager Dick Clark also received an enthusiastic welcome from the crowd.

After sets from the Winters Brothers Band, the Nitty Gritty Dirt Band, and Grinderswitch, the Charlie Daniels Band started its set with Charlie's trademark battle-cry, "Ain't it great to be alive and livin' in Tennessee!" The set developed – about half-way through – a serious case of "fiddlin' fever" as Daniels introduced six-year-old Memphis native La-Konya Smithee, who belted out the area's theme song, "The South's Gonna Do It Again" and duo-fiddled with Daniels. Other Jam fiddlers who appeared during the set included Louise

VOLUNTEERS OF AMERICA

Mandrell, Roy Acuff, Papa John Creach, and classical violinist Eugene Fodor. The Grand Ole Opry's Boxcar Willie, Carl Perkins, and the Jordanaires also performed throughout this jam.

Blues wunderkind Stevie Ray Vaughn, who garnered critical acclaim for his work on David Bowie's **Let's Dance** album and on his fine debut LP released last year, led his Double Trouble Blues Band through a scorching set, showcasing Vaughn's original and flavorful solo guitar stylings. The audience roared and rocked through Vaughn's set, which contrasted yet blended with the evening's general country theme.

Other rocking sets included those of Steve Walsh (formerly of Kansas) and his new band Streets; the Marshall Tucker Band's Toy Caldwell and Paul Riddle performing their Southern standard "Can't You See;" and a mini-jam performance by a band made up of Dickie Betts and Butch Trucks (the Allman Brothers Band), Jimmy Hall (Wet Willie) and Chuck Leavell (of Sea Level fame). Daniels came back on stage shortly after 1:00 AM to lead everybody through the second "jam session" and into the Jam finale.

The Tenth Anniversary Jam finished, as is tradition, with Daniels and many of the evening's previous performers massing on stage and singing "The Tennessee Waltz." As the weary and hoarse revelers left the auditorium early Sunday morning and wandered into the Nashville city streets, fans on the opposite side of the Atlantic were awakening to the staggered broadcast of music, mayhem and goodwill, featuring the talent of Nashville's (and America's) most shining entertainers.
– *CMJ Progressive Media*, March/April 1984

TABLOID PRESS

Band Members:
Richard Block (vocals, saxophone, guitars, keyboards)
Andy Thompson (guitars, vocals)
Dean Norman (bass, vocals)
Scott Brown (keyboards)
Bruce Tanksley (drums)
Kelly Wike (guitars)
Dan Miller (drums)

From the Murfreesboro Musicfest 2 program (1989):
"The quartet's style is a blend of British pop and American funk with an emphasis on melody, harmonic structure, and meaningful lyrics as well."

DANNY TATE

Band Members:
Danny Tate (vocals, guitars, keyboards (I-II)

Other Musicians:
Lenny Castro (percussion) (II)
Chad Cromwell (drums) (I-II)
Bela Fleck (banjo, percussion) (I)
Warren Haynes (guitars) (I)
Gurf Morlix (guitars) (II)
Michael Rhodes (bass) (I)
Eddy Shaver (guitars) (I)

Danny Tate Recordings:

I. Danny Tate (Charisma Records 1992, CD)
1. Someday
2. How Much
3. Lead Me to the Water
4. Save a Little Love
5. Six Senses
6. Paradise Lost
7. Winds of Change
8. Feel Like a Woman
9. No Place to Hide
10. The Fever
11. Romance
12. The Taste of Your Tears
13. Angel, Fly

Comments: Danny Tate's self-titled debut offers up plenty of the slick, slightly-twangy pop/rock songwriting that the singer would perfect with *Nobody's Perfect*.

II. Nobody's Perfect (Charisma Records 1995, CD)
1. Do It All Over Again
2. Nobody's Perfect
3. The Other Road
4. Dreamin'
5. Where the Sun Goes Down
6. Stayin' Alive
7. Blind Desire
8. The Price of Love
9. Muddy Up The Water
10. Still a Fool

Another View: "This 1995 release by notable songwriter Danny Tate delivers all the pop, soft rock, and commercial country hooks one familiar with Tate's considerable history of crafting hits would expect. After spending most of the '80s and '90s penning songs for artists as diverse as Rick Springfield and Lynyrd Skynyrd, Tate struck out on his own in 1992 with his competent self-titled debut, and this follow-up, *Nobody's Perfect*, has Tate in even finer form. With a cast of excellent musicians backing him up that includes Dusty Wakeman, James Christie, and even Dwight Yoakam, Tate glides through his typically rich, purely crafted pop/country-rock. Each track is focused, yet natural and relaxed, but the one standout has to be the sincere "The Price of Love," which boasts a remarkable chorus even by Tate's high standards..."
– Jason Anderson, *All Music Guide*

More Comments: Born in Arkansas, Danny Tate was the son of a Southern Baptist minister, and would be moved as a teenager to become a lay minister himself. Tate had his own congregation at the age of 18 in Stephens, Arkansas but after graduating from Washita Baptist University with a degree in music theory, Tate moved to Nashville in 1980 to pursue his rock 'n' roll dreams. The singer/songwriter fell into a bed of roses when his publishing deal with the Welk Music Group resulted in a Top Ten hit single when Rick Springfield covered Tate's "Affair of the Heart" in 1983.

Tate re-located to L.A. to pursue stardom, and although he never scored that elusive record deal, he did sign a new publishing deal with Island Music. Crapping out in Los Angeles, he jumped to New York, where he would sign to Charisma Records before the label was absorbed by Virgin Records. His self-titled debut album was released in 1992, with *Nobody's Perfect* following in 1995. When family problems intervened, Tate moved back to Arkansas to take care of his elderly and ill mother.

During his years in the wilderness, Tate found little in the way of success as a recording artist, but other artists mined for gold in his song catalog. Tim McGraw, Jeff Healey, Travis Tritt, and Lynyrd Skynyrd are among those that recorded, and found some success, with Tate's songs. Although he had been dropped by Virgin Records, Tate found a new career in the early 2000s in recording music for use by programs like *Entertainment Tonight*, the *Ellen DeGeneres Show*, and others, a lucrative field of music particularly suited to Tate's talents.

DANNY TATE

Regardless of my feelings about his music (I found it overly derivative and not very well performed – sort of like a Bon Jovi country album), as of this writing, the guy is going through a personal hell that would force me to personally shoot some stupid sumbitch. Allegedly because of his addiction to crack cocaine, Tate's brother David, shopping around until he found a sympathetic judge, had Danny declared mentally "unfit," resulting in a court-ordered conservatorship with…guess who…taking control of Danny's finances and, basically, his life. Tate's struggles with drugs and alcohol are well-known in the local music community, but he's never been arrested, never been hospitalized from an overdose, never done anything that would seemingly call for the de facto suspension of his personal rights.

Tate has seen his original $600,000 savings account reduced by better than half through legal and other fees and his brother has taken possession of the recording studio and equipment that he uses to make a living, as well as Tate's dwindling royalty checks. After a court-ordered stint in Vanderbilt's psychiatric ward, his doctors expressed disbelief that he had been declared mentally "disabled." Prior to Vanderbilt, the only testimony presented to the court was from a child psychiatrist admittedly unschooled in addiction.

After reading Brantle Hargrove's excellent article in the *Nashville Scene*, it's obvious to the knowledgeable reader to see that Tate is getting a hell of a raw deal. Whether or not he is honestly a junkie, he's a high-functioning junkie, paying his own way in society and making a living with his music. That's more than I could say about a lot of booze-addled wife-beaters and junkie assholes in Nashville and elsewhere.

DANNY TATE
Nobody's Perfect
(Charisma Records)

If anybody ever represented the lack of that "vision thing" we speak about in this issue, it would be Danny Tate. Ol' Danny passed through Nashville a few years back, headed out of Memphis for fame and fortune.

Unlike a lot of local bands who busted their humps for years to scrape up enough cash to make a disc, Tate took a chunk o' change from a "Mud City" lawyer and recorded his (subsidized) debut album. On the strength of a single, smarmy cut, "Sex Sells," which became a regional hit, Tate landed an undeserved major label contract.

As the story has it, Tate's first big break went bust, and not being able to ascertain whether he was a muscian or a model, Danny boy made his way to L.A., became the lung cancer poster child for Dakota cigarettes, and now resurfaces, some years later with yet another label deal and *Nobody's Perfect*. An early contender for the worst disc of 1995, *Nobody's Perfect* adds stylistic schitzophrenia to Tate's musical crimes.

Just as he's tread an uninspired and indecisive career path, *Nobody's Perfect* shows that Tate is unable to figure out whose chops he wants to rip off as well. Is it Springsteen ("Do It All Over Again"), Chris Isaac imitating Roy Orbison ("Dreamin'") or John Mellencamp ("Stayin' Alive") that Tate wants to emulate?

In the long run, nobody *really* cares save for his manager and label. Pete Anderson's usual admirable production job is lost on this collection of losers, and the contributions of musicians like Dusty Wakeman, Lenny Castro, and Skip Edwards is a waste of time *and* talent.

Note to Charisma A & R staff: give me a call sometime and I'll gladly tell you about some real talent out of Nashville, artists like Threk Michaels, Max Vague, Bill Lloyd, or Pete Berwick who bring with them a spark of originality and their own musical identities. To even mention that Tate once stood the same ground as these artists is an insult to both them and Nashville. But then, nobody's perfect...certainly not Danny Tate. (1995)

TEEN IDOLS

Band Members:
Matt Benson (vocals) (A1)
Keaton Sims (vocals) (A2)
Keith Witt (vocals) (A3, II, III)
Kevin Sierzega (vocals)
Phillip Hill (guitar) (A1-A3, I-VI)
Janell Saxton (bass) (A1, A2)
Roxsan Biggerstaff (bass) (A3)
Heather Tabor (bass) (II, III)
Chris Trujillo (drums)
Steve Saxton (drums) (A1)
Wes White (drums) (A2, A3)
Matt "Drastic" Yonker (drums) (II, III)

Teen Idols Recordings:

<u>Singles/EPs</u>

A1. Old Days Old Ways (House O' Pain 1993, 7" vinyl EP)
<u>Side A</u>
1. Teen Theme
2. Old Days Old Ways

<u>Side B</u>
3. Valentine

A2. Nightmares (House O' Pain 1994, 7" vinyl EP)
<u>Side A</u>
1. Look To Me
2. Nightmares
3. I Regret It

<u>Side B</u>
4. Anybody Else
5. Outta Style

A3. Let's Make Noise (House O' Pain 1996, 7" vinyl EP)
<u>Side A</u>
1. 1989
2. Losin' My Mind
3. Everybody Knows

<u>Side B</u>
4. Let's Make Noise
5. Everything
6. She's A Poser

<u>Albums/EPs</u>

I. Teen Idols (Honest Don's Records 1997, CD/LP)
1. Come Dance With Me
2. Let's Make Noise
3. One Pill Hill

4. Porno Shop
5. I'm Not the One
6. Run Away Again
7. Lovely Day
8. Drag Strip
9. Tuff Guy
10. When I Hear Your Name
11. Breakin' Up
12. 1989
13. Peanut Butter Girl
14. Anybody Else

II. Pucker Up! (Honest Don's Records 1998, CD)
1. Pucker Up
2. Her Only One
3. Test Tube Teens
4. Insanity Plea
5. Skinflynt
6. She's A Poser
7. 20 Below
8. Cynical Fool
9. Historian
10. Virtual Loser
11. Been So Far
12. Big Girl Now
13. Now And Then
14. My Lesson

III. Full Leather Jacket (Honest Don's Records 2000, CD)
1. Midnight Picture Show
2. Every Day Is Saturday
3. Forever In My Dreams
4. King Just For A Day

5. The Voice
6. Genuine Whiskey Man
7. Rebel Souls
8. Band Wagon
9. How Long
10. West End Road
11. Camera Shy
12. I Don't Want Her
13. Coming Down
14. The Team

IV. It Found A Voice (Honest Don's Records 2000, split-CD)
1. Monsters Walk the Earth (Teen Idols)
2. Losin' My Mind (Teen Idols)
3. Human Punching Bag (Teen Idols)
4. 20 Below (Teen Idols)
5. Song for My Friend (Spread)
6. Red Zone (Spread)
7. Trouble (Spread)
8. I Don't Say Goodbye (Spread)

Comments: Extended Play CD split with Japanese punk band Spread, Teen Idols had the first four songs on the EP, which sold bucketloads (20k+) in Japan.

V. Nothing To Prove (Fueled By Ramen 2003, CD)
1. Backstabber
2. Nothing To Prove
3. Another Time
4. Read Between The Lines
5. The Longest Walk
6. Waiting For You
7. Together Again

Temporal Pain

8. Clueless
9. Dignity And Pride
10. Something Old, Something New
11. Turning the Tide
12. I Can't Think

VI. The Dysfunctional Shadowman EP (Asian Man 2003, split-CD)
1. Backstabber (Teen Idols)
2. Dysfunctional (Squirtgun)
3. Shadowman (Teen Idols)
4. Chemical Attraction (Squirtgun)

Comments: Another of many split discs that Teen Idols did with other bands, this four-song EP with Squirtgun.

TEMPORAL PAIN

Band Members:
Mark Swann (bass, drums, guitar, keyboards, TV, tape splicing, vocoder, vocals) (A1)
Slim Johnson (eBow, guitar, vocals) (A1)
Greg Walker (drums, vocals) (A1)

Temporal Pain Recordings:

A1. more to come... (Ltd/Ltd. Products 1982, flexidisc)
1. Brainstorming
2. JC
3. Waves Hit
4. Losing It
5. Baptist Girls
6. I'm Dead

A Short Bio On Temporal Pain (from Mark S): Temporal Pain's three members met at Belmont College and Cantrell's music bar in 1979, formed the record company Ltd/Ltd. Products (BMI) and recorded several hours of industrial cartoon noise punk. Recordings were made on a Teac 3440, portable cassette recorder and a Scully 8 track. Mixes were done at Belmont and home studios.

Temporal Pain's sound has been compared to early Chrome mixed with telephone static while under dental anesthesia. Ltd/Ltd. Products released a Temporal Pain 6-track vinyl flexidisc* EP in 1982 called 'more to come'. Cassette only releases were distributed in 1983.

Rough Trade, Wayside Music, Innersleeve, Constant Cause, and a few other companies distributed the flexidisc, and *OP magazine* (the leading magazine at the time that focused on underground alternative/DIY music) included the flexidisc in their 'T' issue. See Wikipedia for *OP* and *OPtion magazines*' influence on the pre-digital DIY music culture of the 1980's. Occasionally the flexidisc pops up on eBay or Gemm.

Photos of Temporal Pain were taken in Nashville at Woodbine Cemetary and a tunnel at a construction site. TP never performed live but members have performed in other traditional rock bands (Gothic Logic, Dead Rebels, Ed Fitzgerald and Civic Duty), in the respective cities Memphis, Los Angeles, and Nashville.

TP members currently occupy themselves studying philosophy in between Netflix deliveries, selling medical supplies, mellowing out on the Cumberland Plateau, pitching the smash hit 'Baptist Girls' to European car manufacturers for TV commercial background music, and working on the Temporal Pain MySpace page to feature releases by other artists on the Ltd/Ltd. Products label such as Fuchsia Kalimongers, DullBoy Palace, and The Electric Salamanders.

* Flexidiscs were manufactured from 1960 to 2000 by the Eva-tone Soundsheets Company in Clearwater, Florida.

Another View: "This is truly bizarre stuff, make no mistake about it. I mean it, really strange noises here. Lots of interesting stereo effects (great on headphones!) but not much melody. I think Knoxville's Temporal Pain are quite creative for this type of "music" and miles above our own Minimalogic." – *Nashville Intelligence Report #8*, 1982

TERMINAL MYCOSIS

Band Members:
Terminal Mycosis (synthesizer, percussion) (I, II)

Terminal Mycosis Recordings:

I. Terminal Mycosis (Potter's Wheel Records 1990, cassette)
Side One
1. Viet Kane
2. FFFM
3. Mosque Fires

Side Two
2. Factronix
3. Shards In Wax

II. Nine Of Cups (Potter's Wheel Records 1991, cassette)
Side One
1. Bells In A Dark Hallway
2. Prophet Africannes
3. Teratogens (Industrial Dub Mix)
4. Maltese Subway

Side Two
5. Yawbus Esetcam
6. (Xim Bud Lairtsudni) Snegotaret
7. Sennacirfa Tehporp
8. Yawllah Krad A Ni Slleb

Comments: The enigmatic "Terminal Mycosis" was actually Bill Claypool, my old roommate, brother, and partner-in-crime (along with the esteemed Willie the J). Fascinated by industrial music by folks like Throbbing Gristle, Nurse With Wound, etc, Claypool created incredible electronic soundscapes with lo-fi technology (see reviews ➜).

THEE PHANTOM 5IVE

Band Members:
Jeff Knutson (guitar) (A1, I)
Z. Matthews (guitar, keyboards) (I)
Retodd (bass) (A1, I)
Neal Harpole (drums) (A1, I)
Blair (guitars) (A1)

Other Musicians:
Danny Amis (bass) (I)
Jennifer Halenar (violin, keyboards, hula hoops) (I)
Wade Storie (guitar) (I)

Thee Phantom 5ive Recordings:

Singles

A1. ...Lift off to Kicksville (5ive O Sonic Sound , 7" vinyl EP)
Side A
1. Pressure
2. Out Favorite Martian

Side B
3. Surf Softly
4. (We Built A) 501 (Caddy)

THEE PHANTOM 5IVE - THESE ARE HOUSEPLANTS

Albums

I. Do The Doomdom ...and other hi-rise hymns! (Misprint Records 1998, CD)
1. Road Rage
2. Cincinnati Rag
3. 4-Bolt Main
4. 2,000 lb. Bee
5. Nuages
6. Banzai Pipeline
7. Hypoxia
8. DoomDom
9. Surf Softly
10. Cuban Getaway
11. Randy Lynn Rag
12. Buoy 5
13. Ginza Lights
14. Crash
15. Show Stoppah
16. Jeopardized

Comments: Given all the brouhaha (most of it deserved) over **Los Straitjackets**, it seems as if people overlooked the fact that Nashville had another uber-cool surf-rock band, Thee Phantom 5ive.

THESE ARE HOUSEPLANTS

Band Members:
Forrest York (guitars, synth) (I-III)
Colin York (vocals, keyboards) (I-III)
Abe White (bass) (I)
Sam Baker (drums, bass, vocals) (I, III)
Scott Brown (keyboards, synth) (I)
Jon Grimson (fretless bass, Chapman stick) (II)
Hilary Finchum (violin, vocals) (II)

Thee Phantom 5ive

Bruce Tanksley (drums, samples) (II)
Evan York (programming) (I)
Seth Timbs (keyboards, guitar, vocals) (III)

These Are Houseplants Recordings:

I. These are These are Houseplants (self-produced CD, no date)
1. Complete The Circle
2. Love That Isn't
3. Sunshine Anytime
4. It Couldn't Happen
5. Something's Missing
6. Sleep
7. If You See Me Again
8. The Owl Dance
9. Chemical Factory
10. Who's To Say

TERMINAL MYCOSIS
Nine Of Cups
(Potters Wheel Records)

    I crossed paths with this mysterious and pseudonymous recording several months ago, awestruck by its simplicity and disturbed by its dark, brooding ferocity. A cassette-only recording of eight songs, *Nine Of Cups* explores an experimental side of music where even angels fear to tread, an industrial-styled psychotic portrait of pain containing scraps and snippets of found vocals (was that Adolph Hitler...or Ronnie Reagan?), odd instrumentation, distorted guitarwork and demented percussion. At once both fascinating and repulsive, *Nine Of Cups* is a cacophonic cry into the abyss. The question raised by such an artistic statement, however, is whether its creator...the anonymous "Terminal Mycosis"...is mad, or is society?
– *The Metro*, April 1990

TERMINAL MYCOCIS
None To Share
(Potters Wheel Records)

    Nashville's Terminal Mycosis has returned with he/she/its second effort, a thick, complex and multi-layered grouping of five compositions. *None To Share* rests somewhere in the musical netherworld between industrial music and cyberpunk theory, blending magick and ritual with found vocals, technological sound, synthesizer-produced rhythms and odd, unidentified random instrumentation to create a dark and disturbing hybrid too heady for many folk. Fans or followers of Psychick TV, Arcane Device or the Hafler Trio would enjoy this; many others would simply dismiss it without knowing exactly what it is: the abyss of the soul glaring back at the listener.
– *The Metro*, November 1990

11. One Way World
12. Do You See

II. Sidereal Time

III. These Are Houseplants (Mid-Co Music Group, no date, cassette tape)
1. Pseudo Heart
2. Sunshine Anytime
3. If You See Me Again (You Won't Know Me)
4. My Vacation
5. I'll Wait For You
6. Secret Place
7. Chemical Factory
8. Who's To Say
9. It Couldn't Happen
10. One Way World

Comments: It's kind of hard to put your finger on These Are Houseplants…the recordings I have offer up precious little information, and most of what I have is from the Band's MySpace page.

From the Band's MySpace Page: "These are Houseplants made three records and had different members for each one. The first was called *These are These are Houseplants* and featured Scott Brown on keyboards, Abe White on bass, Sam Baker on drums. Colin on lead vocals and she also wrote the melodys and lyrics. ..Forrest.. played guitar and samples and wrote the music. *Sidereal Time* featured Jon Grimson on Chapman Stick which is a bass and guitar type stringed thing played with two hands like a keyboard. He also played fretless bass. Hilary Finchum played violin and sang backup. Bruce Tanksley played drums and again Colin and Forrest on vocals and guitar . The third and last record was simply called *These are Houseplants* and featured Seth Timbs on piano, acoustic guitar and backing vocals. Sam Baker on drums and bass and again Forrest and Colin.

THICKET GROVE

Band Members:
Julie Long (vocals)
Jessie Long (guitar, vocals)
Steve Ross (guitar)
Paul Henley (bass)
Josh Taylor (drums)

Comments: Band contributed song "Rich Man's Plight" to the *Music City Rock* 1995 compilation CD.

THE THIEVES

Band Members:
Gwil Owen (vocals, guitar) (I)

Bart Weilburg (guitar) (I)
Kelley Looney (bass) (I)
Jeff Finlin (drums, percussion, vocals) (I)
Tony Crow (keyboards) (I)

The Thieves Recordings:

I. Seduced By Money (Bug Music/Capitol 1989, LP/CD)
Side One
1. Everything But My Heart
2. All The Lines Are Down
3. Black Lipstick
4. Girl Of My Dreams
5. When I Wake With Someone New

Side Two
6. From A Motel 6
7. Pick A Number
8. Pendulum
9. Seduced By Money
10. Cassidy Knows

Comments: Born out of local band **Fur Trade**, the Thieves featured the songwriting skills of **Gwil Owen** and solid musicians like Kelley Looney and **Jeff Finlin**, who is no slouch in the songwriting department himself. Signed to the newly-formed Bug label (Bug Music was a successful music publishing company) and distributed by Capitol Records, the Thieves managed one sparkling shot at fame and glory in *Seduced By Money*.

Another View: "Nashville's Thieves deliver pop music the way that it's meant to be, big and powerful and with a mean bite on this, their major label debut. Songwriter and vocalist Gwil Owen possesses a clever way with a word, with songs like "From A Motel 6," "Black Lipstick" and "Girl Of My Dreams" holding their own with such acclaimed pop wordsmiths as Nick Lowe, Don Dixon, or the album's producer, Marshall Crenshaw. Everything else falls in line, musically and performance-wise, making this a first effort worth bragging about. *Seduced By Money* deserves to be a big hit…let's hope it is." – *The Metro*, 1989

THIRD EYE

Band Members:
Lance Harrison (guitar, keyboards) (I)
Dave Bastin (guitar) (I)
Michael Praytor (vocals, bass, keyboards) (I)
Robert Means (keyboards) (I)
Jerome Rothacker (drums) (I)

Third Eye Recordings:

I. Who Watches The Watchmen? (self-produced cassette, 1988)
1. Not My Idea Of Freedom
2. Saucers
3. Psychic Vandals
4. Who Watches The Watchmen?

THURN & TAXIS

Band Members:
Erich Hubner (bass, guitar, vocals) (I)
Curt Perkins (guitar, vocals) (I)
Jeffrey Sparks (guitar, harmonica, vocals) (I)
Alan Johnstone (drums, percussion, vocals) (I)

Thurn & Taxis Recordings:

I. toning up for donkeyboy (bigolbutt Records 1992, cassette)
1. Someone Else's Fire
2. 18 hrs.
3. Ginger Ginger

4. Begin
5. A Lot of People
6. A is First

Comments: All songs are repeated on side two of the tape. Thurn & Taxis was formed by Sparks and Perkins while they were exchange students in France. Back in Nashville, they added **Rumble Circus** members Hubner and Johnstone.

CORTNEY TIDWELL

Band Members:
Cortney Tidwell (vocals, keyboards, guitar) (I-III)
Todd Tidwell (guitar, bass, percussion) (I-III)
Ryan Norris (keyboards, synthesizer, guitar, banjo, drums, percussion) (I-III)

Other Musicians:
Adam Bednarik (upright bass) (III)
James DiGirolamo (keyboards) (II)
Matt Glassmeyer (clarinet, percussion) (III)
Joseph Hudson (piano) (II)
Jonathan Marx (clarinet) (II)
Wyatt Mims (bass) (II)
Lex Price (guitar) (II)
Luke Schneider (steel guitar, bass) (II, III)
Brian Siskind (steel guitar) (II)
Sarah Siskind (acoustic guitar) (II)
Aaron Thompson (bass) (II)
Kurt Wagner (vocals) (II, III)
William Tyler (bouzouki, guitar) (II, III)

Cortney Tidwell Recordings:

I. Cortney Tidwell (Sissy Bragg Records 2005, CD)
1. Mama from the Mountain
2. Drink Up
3. Hand 2 Tell
4. The Light
5. So I'll Go out and Meet My Love
6. Fever Queen

Comments: You don't get much more Nashville than singer/songwriter Cortney Tidwell. Born in the Music City and a graduate of McGavock High School, Tidwell is the daughter of country singer Connie Eaton, who had a string of hits through the 1970s. Her dad works in A&R on Music Row, and her grandfather was a country musician in the 1950s and '60s. Her take on traditional country is similar to that of **Lambchop**, i.e. experimental and slightly avant-garde (by Nashville standards, at least...). Tidwell's influences are the best – folks like Johnny Cash and Townes Van Zandt – and the talents of husband Todd Tidwell help provide the music with a certain gravitas. This six-song self-titled debut EP was released by Nashville indie Sissy Bragg Records.

II. Don't Let The Stars Keep Us Tangled Up (Ever Records U.K. 2007, CD)
1. Eyes Are at the Billions
2. Pictures on the Sidewalk
3. Missing Link
4. I Do Not Notice
5. Lala
6. Don't Let Stars Keep Us Tangled Up
7. New Commitment
8. Society
9. Our Time
10. Illegal
11. The Tide

Comments: Touring with former Pavement member Lou Barlow as his opening act, Tidwell came to the attention of the British label Ever Records, who readily signed the talented singer/songwriter and released *Don't Let The Stars Keep Us Tangled Up* to widespread critical acclaim. Appropriately, Kurt Wagner of Lambchop sings a duet with Tidwell, while the band's William Tyler adds some guitar.

II. Boys (City Slang Records 2009, CD)
1. Solid State
2. Warusii
3. Son & Moon
4. Being Crosby
5. Oslo
6. So We Sing
7. Palace

Cortney Tidwell

8. Bad News
9. Oh, China
10. 17 Horses
11. Oh, Suicide

Comments: It's obvious that American labels wouldn't know musical talent these days if it came up and bit 'em on their collectively bloated behinds. Tidwell signed with the very cool German label City Slang for her sophomore effort, recorded with much the same talented crew as her debut, the album featuring duets with Wagner and My Morning Jacket's Jim James (boy, does that cat get around!).

Between her first and second album, Tidwell toured with folks like Andrew Bird and **Silver Jews**, and performed with Martha Wainwright and Grizzly Bear...now will somebody give the girl a U.S. record deal???

TIGER RADIO

Band Members:
Kelly Fernandez (vocals, guitar)
John Sayer (guitar)
Dave McAllister (bass)
Eric Nowinski (drums)

From the Murfreesboro Musicfest 2 program: "Their music takes a poignant look at current issues and attitudes and presents them in the form of memorable, hook-laden songs that really pack a punch."

TIGERS CON QUESO

Band Members:
Casio Con Queso a/k/a Seth Graves (vocals, guitar) (I)
Josh Con Queso (bass) (I)
Steve Con Queso a/k/a Steve Cross (drums) (I)

TOMORROW'S WORLD

Band Members:
Tracy Hill (vocals, keyboards)
Norm Rau/Ray (guitar)
Victor Smith (bass, keyboards, vocals)
Russ Hill (vocals, keyboards)
Shadow Man (piano)
Gerard Hamilton (drums)

Tomorrow's World Recordings:

I. A2340 (self-produced cassette)
1. The You And Me
2. Mother
3. Highlands
4. Cinderella & Dalemere
5. All Alone
6. Time Crys
7. Oh No
8. Life In Dreams
9. What Do Ya' Want
10. Exit Left

Comments: Song "All Alone" appears on *City Without A Subway* compilation, produced by Richie Owens

TONE PATROL

Band Members:
Dave Pomeroy (bass) (I)
Larry Chaney (guitars) (I)
Kirby Shelstad (MidiVibes) (I)
Sam Bacco (percussion) (I)
Kenny Malone (drums) (I)

Other Musicians:
Wayne Roland Brown (didjeridoo, flute) (I)
Sam Bush (mandolin) (I)
Bill Miller (flute) (I)

Tone Patrol Recordings:

I. Thin Air (Earwave Records 1997, CD)
1. Part 1
2. Part 2
3. Part 3
4. Part 4
5. Part 5
6. Part 6
7. Part 7
8. Part 8
9. Part 9
10. Part 10
11. Part 11

Comments: Dave Pomeroy is a talented bassist with a subtle hand on the instrument and a thriving career as a session professional. Tone Patrol was a collaboration between Dave and some of his buddies, and an engaging album.

From the Band's CD Baby page: "Combining melodic improvisation, deep rhythmic grooves, and unusual sonic textures, Tone Patrol has created a new hybrid they call "momental music", ("modern instrumental music" and "music of the moment").

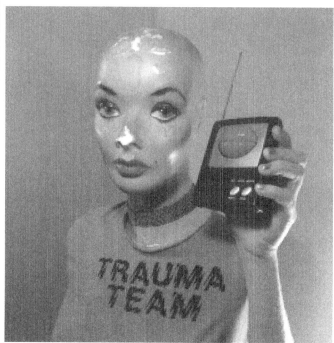

In keeping with Earwave's tradition of unique album concepts, *Thin Air* is a 45 minute continuous "audio journey" made up entirely of collective improvisations recorded digitally in live performance over a four year period. These spontaneous compositions have been edited and crossfaded into one another, creating one long flow of music."

TRAUMA TEAM

Band Members:
Laurel Parton (vocals, guitar) (I)
John Hudson (guitar) (I)
Chad Harrison (bass) (I)
Allen Lowrey (drums) (I)

Trauma Team Recordings:

I. Trauma Team (Solutions Records 2004, CD)
1. Parade
2. Rub Her Right
3. Someone I Used To Love
4. Lousy Memory
5. Issues
6. Lame Excuses
7. Realm
8. Dirty Eat Shit Looks
9. #1 Fan
10. Oven
11. Silver
12. Look Them Over
13. What's Your Limit?

Comments: Trauma Team vocalist Laurel Parton is the daughter of award-winning songwriter Candice Parton and a cousin of country music legend Dolly Parton.

Another View: "Thrashing out like some Rosemary's Baby progeny combining Romeo Void, Sonic Youth and The Stooges, this scrappy quartet led by rocking Laurel Parton is the stuff CBGB dreams are made on." – *Nashville Rage*

Trauma Team

TRIPLE X

Band Members:
Barry Felts (vocals)
Jeff Mays (guitar)
Tony Frost (bass)
Tom Gregory (drums)

Triple X Recordings:

I. The Lion

II. Picture This!

Comments: Triple X was formed by Barry Felts of **No Art** and Jeff Mays, who recruited bassist Tony Frost of **the Bunnies** (among many other bands), and drummer Tom Gregory. Local scene booster and WKDF-FM DJ **Patty Murray** called Triple X, "the South's best unsigned heavy metal act." Sadly, I have no information on the two records.

TONE PATROL
5.19.89
(Earwave Records)

For those of you who caught Tone Patrol's wonderful performance at *The Metro*'s Second Annual Nashville Music Awards show, then you're already familiar with this talented quintet. For those of you who sadly missed the affair, this tape – recorded live at Nashville's Douglas Corner – would serve as an excellent introduction. Stepping out from their various roles as session players, Tone Patrol's Dave Pomeroy, Kenny Malone, Biff Watson, Larry Chaney and Sam Bacco placed their creative skills together to deliver an energetic and mesmerizing performance, captured here in all of its beauty and grace. Tone Patrol performs an original and unique blend of jazz, rock and so-called "New Age" music, instrumental tapestries delicately woven by the combined skills of the musicians, played to perfection in the spirit of the performance. I'd suggest catching these guys their next time out…and after you see them live, you'll search high and low for a copy of this tape (as well you should). It's creative efforts such as this which serve Nashville's image as the "Music City" best. – *The Metro*, April 1990

TURBO FRUITS

Band Members:
Jonas Stein (vocals, guitar) (I, II)
Wes Traylor (bass) (II)
Zack Martin (drums) (II)
Max Peebles (bass) (I)
John Eatherly (drums) (I)

Turbo Fruits Recordings:

I. Turbo Fruits (Ecstatic Peace Records 2007, CD)
1. No Drugs to Use
2. Murder
3. Volcano
4. Know Too Much
5. The Run Around
6. Pockets Full of Thistles
7. 20th I Was Blue
8. Tennessee, Baby
9. Fight This!
10. Poptart
11. I'm Excited
12. Devo Girl
13. Crybaby
14. Ramblin Rose
15. The Ballad

Comments: Jonas Stein started Turbo Fruits as a musical side project while a member of **Be Your Own Pet**, bringing along drummer John Eatherly from that band. Adding bassist Max Peebles to the trio, they used the Pet's label connections with Sonic Youth's Thurston Moore to release this self-titled album on his Ecstatic Peace label stateside in 2007; it was released in the U.K. by Ark Records the previous year after

the band performed at the Leeds and Reading festivals over the summer of 2006.

II. Echo Kid (Fat Possum Records 2009, CD)
1. Want Some Mo'
2. Naked With You
3. Trouble!
4. Mama's Mad Cos I Fried My Brain
5. On The Road
6. Hold Me
7. Get Up Get On Down (Tonite)
8. Sadie
9. Broadzilla
10. My Stupid Heart
11. Lotta Lotta Ladies
12. Dear Moses

Comments: After Be Your Own Pet broke up in late 2008, Stein revised his Turbo Fruits line-up with Wes Traylor and Zack Martin and signed the band to the notable Oxford, Mississippi roots 'n' blues label Fat Possum Records. Sometime during all of this, Turbo Fruits found time to appear in the Drew Barrymore-directed, Ellen Page-starring film *Whip It!*, performing with fellow Nashville singer and songwriter Landon Pigg and placing a song on the movie's soundtrack alongside indie-and-alt-rock darlings like the Raveonettes, the Ettes, and Mgmt.

Another View: "The band replaces that carefree, bordering on careless feel – which was part of Turbo Fruits' charm – with more polished production values and more melody. "Naked with You" and "On the Road" filter tunes that could be lifted from '50s and '60s rock through '70s punk and glam, while "Sadie" has some of the Strokes' easygoing strut to it. At times, Turbo Fruits' sound and energy are more appealing than the actual songwriting, though the literally revved-up "Want Some Mo'," "My Stupid Heart," and "Get Up Get on Down (Tonite)" have equal amounts of enthusiasm and personality. Even if they're not as rambunctious here as they were on their debut, Turbo Fruits' exuberance carries *Echo Kid* over most of its rough spots." – Heather Phares, *All Music Guide*

THE TURN IN

Band Members:
Brian Miles (vocals, guitars)
David Brown (bass)
Casey Sanders (drums)

UMBRELLA TREE

Band Members:
Jillian Leigh (vocals, keyboards) (I, II)
Zachary Gresham (vocals, guitars) (I, II)
Derek Pearson (drums, percussion) (I, II)

Other Musicians:
Matt Slocum (cello) (I)

Umbrella Tree Recordings:

I. What Kind Of Books Do You Read? (Cephalopod Records 2006, CD)
1. Beetle in Trouble
2. Wisemen
3. Poltergeist
4. The Bird & The Fish
5. Trainstorms
6. Bats in the Belfry
7. Billy Goats Don't Eat Trash
8. Donnybrook Fair
9. A Horse That Will Come When I Whistle
10. Turpentine
11. A Story About Sasquatch

II. The Church & The Hospital (Cephalopod Records 2008, CD)
1. The Monk & The Nun
2. 1054
3. A New Job with the Police – A German Song
4. Smells/Bells
5. Make Me a Priest
6. Jellyfish Evaporate
7. Nursing the Patience
8. Schizophrenia
9. In the War I Play a Nurse – A French Song
10. Tooth on the Floor
11. The Youngest Apples

Comments: One of Nashville's most interesting young bands.

UMLAUT

Band Members:
Todd Gerber (synthesizers, computer, other instruments) (I)

Umlaut Recordings:

I. The Alchemist (Space For Music Records 2001, CD)
1. Nothing in a Body True
2. Every Essence is Immortal
3. Every Thing that is Made is Corruptible
4. Every Essence is Changeable

5. Every Body is Changeable
6. That Which is Unchangeable is Eternal
7. That Which is Always Made is Always Corrupted
8. What is Man? An Unchangeable Evil
9. All Upon Earth is Alterable
10. Time is the Corruption of Man
11. Reason in the Mind
12. Malice is the Nourishment of the World

Comments: Umlaut is Todd Gerber, brother of musician and Space For Music label founder **Tony Gerber**, and a member of local band **Dinah Shore Jr**. Experimental electronic music with a definite edge...

UNDER SHADE

Band Members:
Jason Cole (vocals, guitar) (I)
Rob Dickey (bass, vocals) (I)
Steve Dickey (drums, vocals) (I)
Ruben van Pelt (piano, keyboards, vocals) (I)

Undershade Recordings:

I. Nightly Cricket Revival (self-produced CD, 2005)
1. Yeah
2. The Steady
3. The Sun Came Out For You
4. Umbrella Love
5. Pay
6. No One Else
7. Come Away
8. Easier

9. I Know
10. Exit
11. Come Into View

Another View: "Quirky arrangements and prodigious musical talent…Under Shade is one of the most hard-hitting, dynamic, acoustic groove bands working, and their career is heating up with the release of their full length album *Nightly Cricket Revival*. – *Nashville Scene*

UNDER THE BIG TOP

Band Members:
Ron Downey (vocals, guitar)
Doli Stepniewski (bass, vocals)
Steven Rowe (keyboards, vocals)
Timothy Marsh (drums, vocals)

Comments: Downey spent most of his life in Europe and New Zealand, Marsh came to the U.S. from Canada, and the two put together Under The Big Top in the Music City.

UTOPIA STATE

Band Members:
M. Jamahl Dement (vocals, bass, keyboards) (I-II)
Juan Garrett (vocals, drum machine) (I-II)
Corey McKissack (vocals, keyboards, synthesizer) (I-II)
Reavis Mitchell (vocals, guitar, keyboards, drum mach) (I-II)
Sean "E.D." Myers (vocals, bass, keyboards) (I-II)

Other Musicians:
Lemar Carter (drums) (II)

Nioshi Jackson (drums) (II)
J.T. Jones (bass) (II)
Kamau Mason (vocals) (II)
David McLauren (guitar) (II)
Reagan Mitchell (sax) (I)
Cleveland Morland (vocals) (I)
Mark Nash (guitar) (I)
Moe Raw (guitars) (II)
John Robinson (keyboards, synthesizer) (II)

Utopia State Recordings:

I. Where Yall From? (Shika-Down Sounds 1998, CD)
1. The Landing Of Muga
2. S.P.A.C.E.
3. Whichwayizup?
4. Autumn Day (On Jefferson)
5. Blow Yo Mind
6. Summshitthree3
7. Alone-N-Thazone
8. Tha Sax Thang
9. Gitchoownfunk
10. E.B.S.
11. Tha Key
12. 4th Dimensional (Chocolate Sistas)
13. You Can't Hide
14. Death Of Sam
15. Summshitfour4
16. Celestial Journeys

II. Foallayall (Shika-Down Sounds 2001, CD)
1. Foallayall
2. Juspimpin'
3. War On Us
4. War On Drugs
5. No Surprise
6. Po-Po
7. Keep Pushin'
8. Blaktro
9. Blakness
10. Saucy Shit
11. E.B.S.
12. Revolution (Of The Mind)
13. Beat Box Break
14. Krabz
15. Prizon Mind
16. Land Of Freedom
17. Are-U-There
18. Superstarr

Comments: Nashville's best rap outfit preached a positive message with its lyrics while delivering an energetic party-styled hip-hop sound. Sadly, they got little play beyond Jefferson Street in a late 1990s, stuck as they were in a world dominated by gangsta rap.

VAGRANT SAINTS

Band Members:
Michael Saint-Leon (vocals, guitar) (I-II)
C.J. Kowall (keyboards, vocals) (I)
Paul Snyder (drums, percussion, vocals) (I-II)
Kit Dennis (bass, vocals) (II)

Other Musicians:
Steve Brantley (bass) (I)
Gary Hooker (guitar) (I)
John Snelling (keyboards) (I)
Joe Warner (keyboards) (I)

Vagrant Saints Recordings:

I. ...Vagrant Saints (Jake Barnes Music 1997, CD)
1. Sidewalks End
2. My House Is Leaning
3. Give Up The Ghost
4. Bachelor Pad
5. Little Bit A Slack
6. Chickie Run Redux
7. Brand New Man
8. I'll Take The Fifth
9. Before The Judge
10. Easy Mark

II. Mammon's Little Baby (Ray Hicks Music 2003, CD)
1. Shanty Tramp
2. Tailspinner
3. Gutter Boy
4. Talkin' It Up
5. Big Cigar
6. Too Far Gone
7. Snake Eyes
8. Big Bad Love
9. Baby's In Movies
10. Coffee Cup Kicker
11. Bring Out The Beast
12. Teenage Booze Hound

From the band's CD Baby web page: ...Creeping up from the depths of Georgia, crawling across the desert from LaLa-Land, and down through the rust belt...via the swamps of Louisiana, the skyscrapers of Manhattan and various points of heaven and hell in between, these guys eventually collide, congeal and fester in a lean-to shack on the outer edges of Music-Cityville USA. With some amplifiers and an extension cord they begin the process, working it up through the gut to the mind and out the mouth, fingers and feet to the ears of a frantic, numbed but still searching public...

"Hey man, what kind of music do you guys play?"

Well, uh, if you take some Stones and mix in a little Elvis C....; no, imagine that Albert Collins' illegitimate son had run away from home and joined Little Feat and...Some fans call it 'thinking man's rock & roll'...or was that drinking man's rock & roll? There's only one way to know for sure.

They've spoken the word on stages throughout the south, and on their first album, Vagrant Saints have spelled it out in a rhythmic sanskrit, a wormsview sonic photograph, a primal holler from the blue collar...experience the revelation...Vagrant Saints.

Another View: "Nashville rock trio with a funky groove and plenty of twang. Guitarist Michael Saint-Leon sings about the upside of lovin', gamblin', drinkin' & losin' in his friendly, shantytown drawl. Co-songwriter Paul Snyder adds vocal color and impresses on the drums. Standout is bassman Kit Dennis, best remembered up here in Boston for performances with his seminal underground band, The Infliktors (*Live at the Rat 1977*). If you dig groovy bass, then Kit Dennis' lowdown fretwork with the Vagrant Saints is well worth the price of the CD."

"These rebel dudes make it all sound so easy with well honed chops and amusing lyrics. Recorded at The Switchyard in Nashville. It looks like the group handled all the production themselves and the sound is full flavored and sharp throughout. Cover art by Boston photographer Mike Mayhan (*Subway News*) looks great. I am a sucker for any album cover that features a hot babe sitting in front of a big dressing table mirror with the band's name scrawled across it in lipstick..." – Mach Bell, *Boston Groupie News*, 2004

MAX VAGUE

MAX VAGUE

Band Members:
Max Vague (vocals, guitar, keyboards) (I-VI)
Steve Green (guitar, bass, vocals) (II, III)
Ross Smith (bass) (III-V)
Robert Kamm (drums) (III)
Buddy Gibbons (drums) (IV)
Kenny Wright (drums, guitar, vocals) (V, VI)

Other Musicians:
Michael Bondelli (guitar/drums) (I)
Drew Faulkner (harp) (I)
Steve Glaser (harp) (I)
Maria Del Rey (backing vocals, cello) (I)
Bill Hearn (drums) (II)
Dan Philips (vocals) (II)
Jim Schaller (guitar) (I)
Mitchell Sigman (guiatar, bass, keyboards) (I)
Laura Vague (backing vocals) (I)

Max Vague Recordings:

I. Love In A Thousand Faces (Metrolord Records 1992, CD)
1. Love In A Thousand Faces
2. You Won't Get Me
3. The Wheels Are In Motion
4. Don't Run Away
5. Dream
6. Hypocritical
7. How Do You Feel?
8. JRH
9. So It Goes

10. Tall Glasses
11. There's A Place
12. Changes In The Air
13. I Stay
14. In One Room

Comments: Although recorded in L.A., Max moved to Nashville shortly afterwards and plugged the album tirelessly, forming a band shortly after his arrival and hitting the local clubs. Because most of Vague's creative work was done in Nashville and because of his commitment to the local music scene, I've included this first CD in the "official" discography.

II. S.O.S. The Party's Over (Metrolord Records 1993, CD)
1. Fire
2. S.O.S.
3. Crying
4. Home
5. Imagination
6. Lie
7. Strange
8. Believe
9. Up
10 Life
11. Mind
12. Rose
13. S.O.S. (Minimalist Ultra Pumpin' Anti-Industry Groove Scene Dance Mix)

III. The Field (Metrolord Records 1995, CD)
1. Fever Dream
2. The Face In Your Window
Max Vague, continued on page 518...

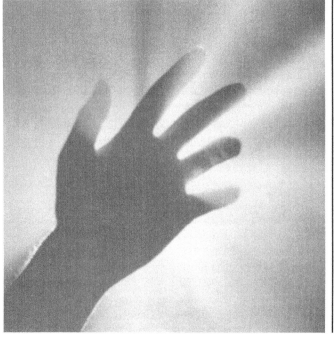

It is with great sadness that we report the death by suicide of an old friend and one of our favorite musicians, **Max Vague**. A multi-talented musician and producer as well as an enormously skilled graphic artist, Max was a leading figure in the Nashville rock music scene for over a decade. Although relatively unknown to the music world outside of the southeastern U.S., Max nevertheless recorded and released six albums without any label resources and, with various bands, toured the region relentlessly.

Max's musical career began back in the early 1980s in Monterey, California. He taught himself to play keyboards and, known by his birth name — William Hearn — played with a number of popular local bands, including Bill Hearn and the Freeze. In 1984 he packed his bags and headed to Los Angeles where he supported himself as a freelance graphic artist and musician, writing the scores for several documentary films, including a special on the GM Sunraycer. While in LA he changed his name to "Max Vague" and began an incredibly prolific period of songwriting and recording. In 1992 Max recorded his first album, *Love In A Thousand Faces*, moving later that year to Nashville with his debut disc tucked beneath his arm.

Max made an immediate splash in the Music City. This critic, writing about *Love In A Thousand Faces* in Nashville's *Metro* music magazine, said "the songs presented here — hard-edged pop/rock replete with melodic experimentation — evoke a variety of influences: the Beatles, Peter Gabriel, many electric British folkies, but are freshly original and completely uncategorizable." Shortly after arriving in Nashville, Vague recorded his sophomore effort, *S.O.S. The Party's Over*. Produced in his home studio, Max contributed nearly all of the instrumentation for this solid collection of songs. "Imaginative, colorful and intriguing, the songs on S.O.S. are like a puzzle box whose solution awaits discovery," I wrote in December '93 in *R.A.D! Review And Discussion of Rock & Roll*. Support for Max came from unlikely places, such as from NASA Space Shuttle Captain Michael Baker, who carried Max's CDs with him on two trips into space, subsequently mentioning Vague when interviewed by MTV's Tabitha Soren for the cable network's *Week In Rock* show.

Over the course of the next twelve years, Vague recorded and released four more critically-acclaimed albums, each more musically complex and rewarding than the previous. With *The Field* CD, released in 1995, Max began recording with a full band that included guitarist Steve Green, bassist Ross Smith and drummer Robert Kamm. Two years later Vague recorded the *Timing* LP with Smith and drummer Buddy Gibbons. It was with the addition of Music City rock veteran Kenny Wright to his band, however, that Max would hit his creative peak, the trio of Vague, Smith and Wright recording the powerful *Kill The Giant* album in 1998. Together, these three toured the southeast and drove home Vague's immense talents to appreciative audiences. Max's work received airplay on local and regional radio stations and accolades poured in from publications like the industry trade paper *Cash Box*, *Bone Music Magazine* and the *Nashville Scene* alternative newsweekly.

In 2002, Vague returned to the studio to record the self-titled *maxvague* CD, his darkest and most personal effort yet. A solitary figure in the studio, Max carefully crafted the songs, playing nearly all the instruments while engineering and producing the album himself. Of *maxvague* the album, this critic wrote, "there's no denying the power of his music, Vague's gift of artistic expression and his instrumental prowess making him the most consistently interesting and intriguing artist working in the American underground today." A masterful collection of songs, the album nevertheless went largely unnoticed by the mainstream and alternative press alike.

After the release of this self-titled album, Max retreated from music somewhat, supporting himself as a graphic artist. He never stopped writing songs, however, and before his death had nearly completed work on what would have been his seventh album, titled *Drive*. Max and Kenny contributed a track, "Oh Well, Okay" to the memorial CD *A Tribute To Elliot Smith*, released earlier this year by **Double D Records**. Max had found new love, was beginning a new company and was seemingly looking towards the future when he came to the decision that he had accomplished everything that he had set out to do.

Sometime in the early morning of August 13th, Max took his own life at the too-young age of 44, leaving behind his fiance Danni, his mother Gay Cameron, his sister Lynda Cameron and brother Jim "Spyder" Hearn. At a memorial service held at **The Basement** club in Nashville on Sunday night, August 28th, a packed room of family, friends and fans heard Max's siblings Lynda and Jim share their memories of their brother. Former bandmates Ross Smith, Kenny Wright and Steve Green also spoke as did Ben Mabry, one of Max's oldest friends and biggest fan and the Rev. Keith A. Gordon, who presided over the memorial service. Mike "Grimey" Grimes, co-owner of **Grimey's Music** and booker for The Basement graciously provided the club for Max's memorial. – *Alt.Culture.Guide*

MAX VAGUE

Max Vague, continued...
3. Shine Your Light
4. Epiphany
5. Storm Gathering
6. Almost Believe
7. They're Coming
8. The Trade
9. Perfect World
10. Never You
11. Rapture
12. Answers
13. Lay In The Field
14. I'm O.K.

Comments: After recording most of *S.O.S.* on his own, Vague put together a real band to record and perform with, starting with guitarist Steve Green and bassist Ross Smith. Drummers would come and go from the band until the arrival of **Kenny Wright**, a seasoned Music City rock veteran.

IV. Timing (Metrolord Records 1997, CD)
1. Timing
2. Genetic
3. Paralyzed
4. Regret

5. Cold As This Machine
6. Lie
7. Crying
8. The Night Is Gone (It's Over)
9. Crack In The Sky

V. Kill The Giant (Metrolord Records 1998, CD)
1. Island
2. Where Did You Go
3. (Paul)
4. Rebound
5. Wheels Are In Motion II
6. Love In A Thousand Faces II
7. Pictures
8. Aware
9. Dull
10. Wait
11. Radio Breaks
12. Face In Your Window II
13. Kill The Giant
14. You're Not Alone
15. Animal

Comments: The seminal line-up of Vague's many bands, with Ross Smith and Kenny Wright. This trio became the

Max Vague Band

best-known version of Max's work, building a loyal fan base in the region through live shows and recording, in my mind, the best of Max's albums, *Kill The Giant*.

VI. maxvague (Eleven Records 2002, CD)
1. Lights Out
2. Break It Down
3. 321212
4. Sometimes
5. Up2
6. Trans
7. Wish
8. The Power
9. Spirits Run The Shoreline
10. Light&Cold
11. Deeper

Comments: Vague's best album and, sadly, his last as he would take his own life. Max was a long-time friend of mine from way back in the Mosko's days with **Threk Michaels** and the **Celebrity Toast & Jam** guys. The tragedy of his death was magnified by the fact that the progressive elements of his unique sound had begun to attract attention from a handful of European labels (see reviews ➔).

VALENTINE SALOON

Band Members:
William Jewel (vocals, harp, guitar) (I)
Henry Meyer (guitar) (I)
Dean James (bass) (I)
Billy Baker (drums) (I)

Valentine Saloon Recordings:

I. Super Duper (Pipeline Records 1992, CD)
1. Mind Bomb
2. Cadillac King Revolver
3. Smothered In Daisy
4. Under My Skin
5. Flying Machine
6. Mrs. Jones
7. Soak
8. Sentimental Girl
9. Private Revolution
10. Why I Like It
11. Firin' Line
12. Tangerine

II. Under My Skin EP (Pipeline Records 1992, CD)
1. Under My Skin
2. Mind Bomb
3. Mrs. Jones
4. Funhouse
5. Soak (Total Saturation Mix)

Valentine Saloon

MAX VAGUE
S.O.S. The Party's Over
(Metrolord Records)

Nashville is a hotbed of Rock & Roll talent, but not in the way that one might think. Outside of the so-called "alternative" throngs – bands trying to chase the trend of the moment – are a handful of musicians who are taking risks, ignoring the popular currents and following their own artistic vision. One such artist is Max Vague...

A Music City immigrant by way of Los Angeles, Vague brought with him some curious baggage, such as artistic integrity, a distinct musical style and the tools and ability to bring his vision to fruition. Vague made a splash earlier this year with the pop-flavored *Love In A Thousand Faces*, his impressive debut CD. Hot on the heels of that musical triumph, Vague closes 1993 with the release of *S.O.S. The Party's Over*.

Musically, S.O.S. draws from a veritable wellspring of influences: Peter Gabriel, Eno, Pink Floyd...all pulled together into a cohesive musical whole. Vague provides nearly all of the instrumentation here, creating a lush, complex landscape that is a wonder in its beauty, awe-inspiring in its diversity and breathtaking in its scope. Upon this soundtrack, Vague has embroidered his lyrical poetry.

Imaginative, colorful and intriguing, the songs on *S.O.S.* are like a puzzle box whose solution awaits discovery. Whereas some of the cuts are more straightforward in their understanding – the title cut's theme of modern alienation, for example – others, such as the haunting "Home" (with its fatalistic refrain, "we slide into obscurity with drugs and MTV, we know too much, we can't survive, they'll never let us out alive, our only option is to hide and let them roll on by") require a bit more thought. The rose-colored glasses on the disc's cover may provide Vague with a different take on life, but even they can't hide the political reality presented in cuts like "Believe" ("we focus on the sleight of hand in some foreign land and when our minds return we've forgotten what we've learned...").

Vague is one of the most exciting artists working in rock today, an uncompromising musician and songwriter following his own muse through a commercial no-man's land, consequences be damned. As good as his debut disc may have been (and make no mistake, it is quite impressive), *S.O.S. The Party's Over* is miles ahead of that effort, showing a remarkable artistic evolution and maturity. That Vague pulls off these recorded hat tricks with just a little help from his friends (MetroLord being his own, self-financed imprint) is even more remarkable yet. But then, the guy's too damn good for a major label...they wouldn't know how to handle something this original. – *R.A.D!* December 1993

MAX VAGUE
The Field
(Metrolord Records)

Rock & roll has fielded its share of starry-eyed dreamers, insane geniuses and dedicated fools throughout the past four decades. Said artists have covered just about the entire gamut of available subject matter, from the usual lyrical staples like life, love and intoxicants to topics too disgusting for even these jaded ears. Precious few poets have really turned their eyes to the skies, however, and wondered aloud what might lie beyond this earthly dimension. The few who have usually tend to dance on the fringe of commercial acceptance, tagged forever with "cult favorite" status. For every Peter Gabriel, there's also a Roky Erikson or Nik Turner.

Whether Max Vague is a madman or a genius is not up for me to say. I suspect that there's a little of both residing in the man and artist – a certain musical genius, to be sure, but also a little foolishness for thinking that an album as lyrically vital, intelligently introspective and musically daring as *The Field* could find a receptive ear among the great gurus of radio and records. *The Field* is Vague's third album, following an impressive debut, *Love In A Thousand Faces*, and 1993's excellent *S.O.S. The Party's Over*. Vague is, perhaps, Nashville's most daring and adventurous artist. Although the home of country music, rhinestones and twanging guitars holds the promise of many rock & rollers who tend to walk on the proverbial edge – talents like Self or the Floating Men – Vague is not content to merely balance frightfully, preferring instead to crawl out and see just how far he can get on that branch before it snaps in two. With three albums under his belt, he's yet to take a tumble...

A concept album twenty years past its prime and a good decade ahead of its time, *The Field* is a masterful collection, a song cycle that tells an unusual and haunting story about alien abduction. That it's a true story, told by an individual close to the band and filtered through Vague's mighty songwriting pen, makes *The Field* and its songs all that much more powerful. There are a lot of familiar musical elements that *The Field* shares with its predecessor, *S.O.S. The Party's Over*, but they serve as a connecting lifeline rather than a simple rehashing of material. *S.O.S.* is, indeed, an introduction to *The Field*, the two serving as bookends to frame a fantastic story.

The Field begins with a disconcerting "Fever Dream," a low rumbling and jangled chiming leading almost immediately into "The Face In Your Window." Punctuated by a constantly repeating, wire taut guitar riff, "The Face In Your Window" launches the cycle, with our protagonist beginning their unearthly sojourn. From this point, the songs roll right by, a captivating, seemingly seamless composition made up of fourteen songs that sit separate and yet are melded together by a shared storyline and recurrent musical signatures. Among *The Field*'s many moments, several nevertheless stand out.

"Epiphany" is an ethereal cry for sanity, the traveler captured by their own fear and growing sense of distance. "I will make it out of this 2x6 foot box," sings Vague, the line opening and closing the song with a distinct sense of terror and determination. "The Trade" illustrates the abductee's feelings of persecution and paranoia, with repeated abductions from childhood through adulthood not uncommon, creating in the individual a sense of disconnection and uncertainty: "Why do you keep coming back to me, haven't you had enough?" sings Vague in harsh, distorted vocals. "What is this preoccupation with me, haven't I suffered enough?" The disconnected "Rapture," with its echoed, dreamlike chorus of "we fall" repeated endlessly, creating a sense of floating while a gently strumming guitar supports Vague's lofty vocals.

By the closing of *The Field*, Vague has brought our traveler full circle, through a myriad of thoughts and emotions, to a final confrontation with themselves. "I'm O.K." is a reaffirmation of life and purpose, a four minute musical struggle for identity in a psychological sea of confusion. "You sucked away my energy, you took the things that made me really me," sings Vague, "you roughed me up against my will, now tell me who the fuck I'm supposed to be."

By the closing of the song, and the album, however, our protagonist has faced their demons and won, delivering a hearty lyrical 'piss-off' to those forces in the universe, both mundane and otherworldly, that seek to rob us of our dignity and individuality: "no compromise, no pity, no self help, no revelations from now on," Vague triumphantly delivers, just above the razor-sharp and repetitive riff that runs through the song and appears throughout *The Field*. "I made it all come out the day I faced your eyes and then refused to run. So you can take your fucking lights and your tables and your eyes and go away."

Musically, *The Field* mixes the familiar influence of a half a dozen artists – I won't insult the artist by making comparisons – you'll just have to get the disc and figure it out for yourself. I will say that there's plenty to discover musically hidden beneath these lyrics, the multi-layered and complex soundtrack of *The Field* yielding something new with every listen. The music is mesmerizing, an alluring combination of deceptive electric ambiance and passionate rock & roll fury. The guitars are thick and omnipresent in the mix, the percussion understated and purposeful while a consistent bass line supports the entire process. The band that Vague put together for *The Field* is top notch, with all of the players – guitarist Steve Green, drummer Robert Kamm and bassist Ross Smith, a seasoned Nashville veteran of local

legend Aashid Himmons' various bands – have an undeniable chemistry and a cohesion that belies their brief time together. A relative neophyte in the studio, Vague has grown as a producer over the course of three albums; his work on *The Field* is quite impressive given its complexity and dimension.

The Field is a carefully-crafted piece of art, a heady tale of trial and redemption told through the eyes of an alien abductee. Although Vague has created a specific story, he has also unwittingly delivered a wonderful metaphor for life itself, the traveler of *The Field* representing every single one of us who views life from the outside looking in, with all of the attending uncertainty, doubt and psychic obstacles that accompanies such alienation (whether chosen or imposed).

Released under Vague's own MetroLord Records imprint, *The Field* is a triumph of form over fashion, of honesty and sincerity over trite trendiness and musical pretension. At some time over the course of the past few years, I stated publicly that Max Vague was too damn good to get signed by a major label, too unique to receive significant radio airplay. I stand by that statement today. It still remains to be seen whether or not anyone will prove me wrong. Until then, I can only sum up *The Field* thus: *fucking brilliant*! (1996)

CD REVIEW: MAX VAGUE'S MAXVAGUE

MAX VAGUE
maxvague
(Eleven Records)

This one came out some time ago – over a year, to be exact – but the Reverend has refrained from writing about it until now. It's not that your humble scribe couldn't put his finger on it, it's just that after reviewing nearly every Max Vague album extant, from 1991's *Love In A Thousand Faces* through 1998's *Kill The Giant*, this critic had run out of superlatives and adjectives to use in describing Vague's work. I have long asserted that Vague is the most exciting and interesting musician working in Nashville over the past decade (only the talented and chameleon-like Aashid Himons comes close).

While other local artists/bands have been chasing trends or working in established (i.e. commercial) musical genres, Vague has continued to push the envelope, to expand his sound with various musicians, studio techniques and artistic experimentation. Yet, outside of a loyal cult following, Max gets no respect from the industry "powers-that-be" in the "Music City." These mindless authority figures that should be bowing at his feet and offering praise to the gods that Nashville has an artist as willing to bare their soul as has Vague over the course of five albums.

Vague's self-titled sixth album does not fall short of his previous work. Although he has once again expanded his sound – towards a more atmospheric vibe – the songs are all vintage Vague. A vastly underrated guitarist, Vague coaxes and coerces tones from his stick that these ears have never heard, complimenting his impressive fretwork with imaginative keyboard/synth work and sparse percussion. Unlike his last few albums, which were created with a small band including drummer Kenny Wright, Vague plays all the instruments this time around (save for a lone guitar from Wright on one song).

As per usual, Vague produced the album in his home studio, the last true lone wolf of "D.I.Y." perhaps, Vague eschewing label involvement to better capture his unique musical vision. Also per usual, Vague's production on maxvague is immaculate, his seamless layering of vocals and instrumentation in the painting of each track a fine example of self-independence that should have the recording industry quaking in their boots. If the labels can't control the production and dumbing-down of an artist's vision, how will they control the commercial process? Vague is a rebel and a pioneer and if he never records another record, he can be proud of what he has accomplished.

So what about the songs on *maxvague*? You could term them prog-rock or art-rock or psychedelic rock or any one of a number of useless labels and you'd be both right and wrong. Vague's unique vision is informed by the likes of Peter

Gabriel, Brian Eno, Pink Floyd, the Beatles – a veritable melting pot of artist influences, filtered through an amazing creative mind. Although Vague's oblique, poetic lyrics are often times quite maddening, defying interpretation, they provide hours of food for thought and are supported by a complex, deeply-emotional soundscape.

In the wake of Vague's divorce, an identity crisis, artistic meltdown and romance renewed, much of maxvague the album deals with the mind, the fragile instrument that is the wellspring of emotion, creativity and thought. Woven throughout these songs are many questions that we could all ask of ourselves. "break it down" asks "am I cracking up? am I already there?" before concluding that "I can't connect or redirect or make sense of this mess."

Vague's personal anguish comes to the fore, the artist singing "nobody will ever understand the way this feels," pointing out that emotion is truly personal and none of us ever really understand what is going on inside somebody else's heart and mind. The album-opening "lights out" features a swirl of sound that recycles a common riff from half-dozen previous songs, Vague's muted vocals almost lost in the mix. The song "break it down" features the clever use of a main vocal supported by sparse instrumentation and a multi-tracked underlying vocal that runs throughout the song.

With the cautious "321212" Vague is careful not to reveal too much, not to his audience or to friends and lovers, singing "you will never know my name, you will not see me again" over and over, denying any human connection and retreating behind a mask of emotion. The artist's alienation is profound, choking on his emotions with "sometimes," a taut, fuzzed-out guitar lead supporting the chorus "sometimes I can't get my breath," the important, insightful comment "life's a cruel teacher" hidden away in the middle of the song, almost lost amidst dense instrumentation. Clues to Vague's state of mind are scattered through the lyrics, enlightening bits of codes that defy deciphering: "I wish I was a better man." "Call me unpredictable." "All it would take is a little patience to get me through this complacence." "I'm in awe of the power, it's got me on my knees."

It is love that throws a life preserver to the drowning man, pulling him out of depression and confusion and desperation and providing a light in the darkness. The album closes with "deeper," an affirmation of being that has the protagonist fighting the feelings swelling up inside, "the door is locked, so I walk around" leads into "I'm not going there again." In the end, despite his best attempts, "you turn around and all I see" is how maxvague closes, the song cycle coming full circle, the singer traveling through a personal hell to emerge out of the darkness an older and, hopefully wiser man.

The album is also about the choices we make and the consequences that we suffer. Max Vague is a friend of mine, and although I can't say that I've always agreed with the choices that he has made through the years, he has always pursued his own vision and followed his own counsel, no matter the personal cost. There's no denying the power of his music, Vague's gift of artistic expression and his instrumental prowess making him the most consistently interesting and intriguing artist working in the American underground today. The album maxvague is an important, vital addition to the artist's canon, and a CD that should not be overlooked by any listener desiring an intense and personal musical experience. – *Alt.Culture.Guide*, 2005

MAX VAGUE
Timing
(Metrolord Records)

With *Timing*, his fourth release, Max Vague has pulled a few new musical twists out of the seemingly endless bag of tricks of his, mixing healthy portions of Britpop influence with his usual ethereal progressive fare. With more melodies and livelier song structure added to his trademark musical marksmanship, Vague has developed into a world class tunesmith.

The title track, however, might well be his finest moment. With its sneering throwaway line "you've come this far, you might as well swallow," the song is a near-perfect accounting of the struggle an artist faces in retaining their integrity as well as a wickedly satirical look at an industry that devours lives and creativity alike.

Originally conceived as an eight song EP, Vague and bassist Ross Smith flew off the deep end into insanity, ending *Timing* with a twenty-eight minute instrumental opus. Dark, eerie, provocative and deceptively mesmerizing, "Crack In The Sky" serves as an excellent bookend to *Timing*, carrying the listener beyond the dreams spun with the preceding songs, sojourning into the dreamland from whence they came. – *Thora-Zine*, 1997

VARIOUS ARTISTS: "OUR SCENE SUCKS"

VARIOUS ARTISTS

Singles/EPs

A1. Nashville – Coming Fire (Vorgo Pass 1994, 7" vinyl)
Side A
1. Fun Girls From Mt. Pilot – "When I See You Again"
2. Teen Idols – "One Day"
3. Ballpeen Hernia – "Hell On Wheels"

Side B
4. Uncle Daddy – "Vacation"
5. Thee Phantom 5ive – "Banzai Washout"
6. Mount – "Shotgun Dream"

Comments: Cool little EP was a precursor, of sorts, to what Donnie and April Kendall would be doing with House O' Pain in a very short time. EP features a wide range of music on this local rock sampler, from **Thee Phantom 5ive**'s surf-rock to the **Teen Idols**' pop-punk and the **Fun Girls**' hell-bent raw punk fury.

A2. Never In Nashville (Praxis Records 1981, 7" vinyl)
This Side
1. Factual – "Wound in Time"
2. No Art – "English Boys"

That Side
3. USR – "We The People"
4. Cloverbottom – "Battery"

Comments: The voice of a new Nashville rock underground hits the street with a loud roar with *Never In Nashville*, the first release from Jack Emerson and Andy McClenon's fledgling Praxis Records label. **Cloverbottom**, of course, was Nashville's first punk band of note, while **Factual** brought electronic art-rock to the Music City. No Art and USR would yield members to other band, but they're no less important to the city's rock 'n' roll history.

A3. Our Scene Sucks (House O' Pain, 7" vinyl)
Side This
1. Floor – "Stop It"
2. Lethargic – "Wolfman"

Side That
3. Teen Idols – "Shadowman"
4. Cannibal Holiday – "Self Absorption"

Comments: One of House O' Pain's first local comps, I love the whole "our scene sucks" misanthropy. HO'P was more than a cool punkzine, they were also a very cool record label that helped document the depths of Nashville's rock underground, and created minor punk stars in the **Teen Idols**.

A4. Our Scene Still Sucks (House O' Pain, 7" vinyl)
This Side
1. Brown Towel – "Sissy Fit"
2. Situation No Win – "How The Other Half Lives"
3. Junkie War Stories – "Like To Kick"

The Other Side
4. The Vibes – "New School"
5. Process Is Dead – "New England"

Comments: Another great House O' Pain compilation, I love

VARIOUS ARTISTS: "3600 SECONDS OF CULTURE"

the rock aesthetic pursued by the HO'P folks, and that a lot of these bands would be "here today, gone tomorrow," sometimes existing for a single show or recording. Of the five bands here, Process Is Dead is the only one that I remember...

Albums

I. 3600 Seconds Of Culture (unknown cassette, around 1989)
Side One
1. Wishcraft – "Big Crunch At Prairie Lunch"
2. Wishcraft – "Echo Song"
3. 15 Minutes – "Broken Glass Jar"
4. 15 Minutes – "Escape"
5. Ming Dynasty – "Candle Flame"
6. Ming Dynasty – "Hide"

Side Two
7. Koyaanisqatsi – "Love One"
8. Koyaanisqatsi – "African Acidation"
9. Catherine Said So – "Man In A Top Hat"
10. Catherine Said So – "Caps And Stems"
11. F.U.C.T. – "Mine"
12. F.U.C.T. – "Lost"

Comments: I received a copy of this cassette from my friend Elliott back at PDQ Pizza on West End in 1989 or '90. Best I can remember, this was produced at Hillsboro High School in Green Hills under the aegis of their music business program. I'm only really familiar with a couple of the bands, and I seem to think that Brooks of **F.U.C.T.** might have gone to school at Hillsboro. Anyway, F.U.C.T. and **Wishcraft** were both pretty popular bands at the time, which may have also been when F.U.C.T. tried to open an all-ages club in Berry Hill.

II. Alive At JC's (Cicatelli Enterprises 1986, cassette)
Side One
1. Funktion – "Man in the Moon"
2. Funktion – "A Tear for Crystal"
3. Funktion – "Parker's Mood"
4. Apollo – "Run For Cover"
5. Apollo – "Middle of the Night"

Side Two
6. Apollo – "The Red Baron"
7. Rush Hour – "Mystery"
8. Rush Hour – "Freedom Jazz Dance"
9. Rush Hour – "Love and Happiness"

Comments: Yeah, so it's not exactly "rock" – it's jazz and funk and funky jazz, actually – but these bands do fit into my loose guidelines for inclusion (non-country, played locally), so here 'tis! Former music biz exec Jack "JC" Cicatelli quit his high-paying label gig, moved his family to Nashville and

VARIOUS ARTISTS
3600 Seconds of Culture
(Culture)

This compilation, privately issued by the students of Nashville's Hillsboro High School, holds some of the best young local talent that these jaded ol' ears have heard in quite a while. Not quite an hour of music, with two songs each provided by six bands, *3600 Seconds of Culture* offers a rich diversity of style and substance.

3600 Seconds of Culture opens with Wishcraft, a metal/thrash/hardcore outfit that pours out notes like so much molten slag. "Big Crunch At Prairie Lunch" and "Echo Song" are bass-heavy dirges fairly bristling with mean energy and murky, muddy vocals buried beneath an atomic blast of sound.

15 Minutes follows, offering up a couple of tasty cuts featuring Trey Beasley's Morrisey-styled vocals and a European techno-pop flavored sound with hard-edged guitars and dense, overpowering production.

My personal faves on *3600 Seconds of Culture* are Ming Dynasty, who close the first side with a pair of dreamy, exotic numbers in "Hide" and "Candle Flame." This talented trio, fueled by Greg Frahn's fluid, shining guitarwork and Lindy Rogers' mature, ethereal vocals are an act that more should be heard from.

Side two begins with Koyaanisqatsi performing one of Bach's more baroque chamber pieces, sliding gracefully into their enjoyable two-man synth and percussion show. Catherine Said So offer a shade of balance to the side contributing a couple of funky, rocking Velvet Underground-influenced pieces in "Man In A Top Hat" and "Caps And Stems," murky, rhythmic pieces with hidden lyrics and a soul of their own.

Forever Ungratical Corinaric Technikilation (F.U.C.T.) shut down the comp and rock down the house with their two cents worth o' tunes, a dynamic duo of wicked hardcore numbers that sear and burn their way into your innocent, virgin subconscious.

All in all, a fine way to spend what is not quite really "3600 seconds" with a handful of bands that should already be making a name for themselves on area stages.
– *The Metro*, 1988

VARIOUS ARTISTS: "CITY WITHOUT A SUBWAY"

opened up a jazz club/restaurant called, well, JC's. Located on a side street in Green Hills (methinks a sports bar resides in the location now), JC's offered great food, urban atmosphere, and some cool jazz.

Jack tended bar with a New York attitude and his wife worked the kitchen with some delicious recipes and prompt service. As for the bands here, Rush Hour was a popular local draw at the time, a big band anomaly amidst the growing ranks of punk rockers on the scene. Funktion also played live a lot, and featured two break-out stars in keyboardist Micky Basil and guitarist Stan Lassiter. I don't remember Apollo.

III. Area6 15 (Discrepancy Recordings 2003, CD)
1. Satellite City – "Playground Rainstorm"
2. Deltasleep – "Imipolex Shroud"
3. Mere Mortals – "Meet The Press"
4. Soulos – "Arson"
5. Mr. Natural – "Personal Space"
6. Logickal – "She's Village Sunshine"
7. Callisto – "Untitled 1930"
8. Fognode – "Bangalore (Not So Live)"
9. Jensen Sportag – "Miss Violet's Unscheduled Darkroom Liason"
10. Sculophonics – "Starmon"

Comments: Sub-titled "A compilation of Nashville's Finest Electronic Music," *Area6 15* offers a rare look into a musical sub-genre that is typically overlooked by the average music fan. Compiled by local musician Jeremy Dickens (a/k/a Logickal), the disc offers some of the cream-of-the-crop of local electronic-oriented artists. Some of these folks are involved with better-known, major label bands: Tony Miracle of **Venus Hum** is Satellite City, and that band's Kip Kubin is Callisto; while others are more notorious – Jensen Sportag has become pretty well known on the electronic scene while Mr. Natural's John Sharp has recorded with Chris Blazen of **Spacecraft** among other notables in the field. Not strictly a rock album, but about as far underground and out-of-the-Nashville-mainstream (i.e. non-Music Row) as you'll find.

IV. City Without A Subway (Neo Records 1986, LP)
Side One
1. Raging Fire – "Everything Goes"
2. The Movement – "Lost Horizon"
3. Tomorrow's World – "All Alone"
4. Shadow 15 – "The Last Forever"
5. In Pursuit – "No Way Out"

Side Two
6. The Questionnaires – "Boomtown"
7. Webb Wilder – "One Taste Of The Bait"
8. Will Rambeaux & the Delta Hurricanes – "Lous'iana Law"
9. The Boilers – "Can't Talk To You"
10. Bill Lloyd – "This Very Second"

Comments: Well-conceived sampler of the city's diverse range of musical talent, **City Without A Subway** was compiled under the aegis of Vanderbilt's "91 Rock," WRVU-FM and released by local indie Neo Records. The bands chosen represented a good cross-section of the mid-80s scene and the album featured a very cool original cover painting by folk artist Rev. Howard Finster. A lot of the usual suspects were involved in the album's creation, including Clark Parsons, Regina Gee, Laura Mitrovich, Mark Medley, and artist Tim "Mercury" Shawl. Back cover notes courtesy of Michael McCall, then with the (now defunct) *Nashville Banner* newspaper.

V. Freedom Sings (First Amendment Center 2000, CD)
1. Ken Paulson – "Introduction"
2. Greg Trooper – "Ohio"
3. Jonell Mosser – "Annie Had a Baby"
4. John Kay – "The Pusher"
5. Dan Baird – "Street Fighting Man"
6. Bill Lloyd – "Good Rockin' Tonight"
7. Tommy Womack – "Eve of Destruction"
8. Kevin Welch – "Wasteland of the Free"
9. Rodney Crowell – "Okie from Muskogee"
10. Beth Nielsen Chapman – "Society's Child"
11. Radney Foster & Bill Lloyd – "In the Ghetto"
12. Don Henry, Kim Richey & Bill Lloyd – "Where Have All the Flowers Gone?"
13. Tammy Rogers – "Blowin' in the Wind"
14. Chip Taylor – "Bigot's Graveyard"
15. Kim Richey & Don Henry – "Beautiful Fool"
16. Stone Deep – "Fight the Power"
17. Steve Earle – "Christmas in Washington"
18. Freedom Sings Performers – "This Land Is Your Land"

Comments: Sorry if you missed this one (now sadly out-of-print), 'cause it's one of the better comps to come out of the local scene. A benefit for the First Amendment Center of the Freedom Forum, an organization that fights censorship in its many forms, the disc documents a 1999 performance at The Bluebird Café in Nashville. Many of the songs performed have been suppressed, censored and/or challenged one way or another by ignorant yahoos. Yeah, it's got a lot of alt-country and folk artists among the performers, but it also has very cool performances by **Dan Baird**, **Bill Lloyd**, **Tommy Womack**, **Steve Earle** and rock-rappers **Stone Deep**. **Will Kimbrough**, Mike Grimes and Fenner Castner lend their instrumental talents to tracks from Greg Trooper, Tommy Womack and Kevin Welch.

VI. Hear Rock City / Tennessee Tracks (NEA 1988, cassette)
Side One
1. The Deal – "Brave New World"
2. Raging Fire – "A Desire Scorned"
3. Gabriel's Message – "Do You Know Me"
4. The Stand – "Muscle"
5. Sahara – "High Adventure"
6. Alex Greene – "Shattercane"
7. Group Therapy – "Time After Time"

Side Two
8. Everyman – "One Good Reason"
9. Jamie Houston – "Temptation Overload"
10. Hocus Pocus – "Ready For The Rough"
11. Rumble Circus – "Passing Phase"
12. Robb Houston – "Dream State"
13. The Bluebirds – "I'm Your Man"
14. Feed 4 – "Love Me For Me"

Comments: The first of many misguided attempts by the Nashville Entertainment Association to "promote" Nashville bands. Of the fourteen bands included on this tape, eight were part of the Nashville scene and two of those – Feed 4 and Gabriel's Message – well, nobody that I've spoken with knows who the heck they were. Most of the rest of these bands were part of the Ardent Recordings stable, the result of a ham-handed attempt by the NEA to climb into bed with Jody Stephens (which is why they added "Tennessee Tracks" to the tape's name, I guess). On the other hand, any tape that includes **Raging Fire**, **Rumble Circus** and **Jamie Houston** can't be all bad...

I shouldn't start ranting about the NEA, but here is my two cents on this worthless, puissant organization: during the 1980s and '90s, it is my opinion that the Nashville Entertainment Association did more to harm the city's non-country music scene than it ever did to help it. Sure, some (few) bands benefited from the NEA's attempts at "promoting" the scene, and the early NEA Extravaganza shows – before they began adding such well-known

"Nashville" artists as Robyn Hitchcock or Graham Parker – were fine showcases for the city's musical diversity. When they began promoting musicians from Memphis, Little Rock, Louisville and Birmingham – Alabama *and* England – the NEA lost any credibility it had with me.

Throughout this era, the NEA board was largely dominated by Music Row hacks and never had more than a handful of people involved that actually knew diddly-squat about the local music scene. Of those people sitting on the NEA board *that were* involved with the scene – you know who you are – they largely pursued their own personal agendas and favored their cronies and those artists that regularly kissed their collective asses. As such, many deserving local artists were ignored or actively held back by an organization that was more self-involved than objective. So why didn't we start our own organization to promote local rockers? Some good people like Debbie Burrow and Nashville Rocks tried, but without the resources provided the NEA by the industry and local government, it was never going to work (and, sadly, it didn't).

VII. Homegrown (Picalic 1980?, LP)
Side One
1. Lust – "Hooker"
2. Bethart – "Electric Boys"
3. Placid Fury – "All The Time"
4. Ed Fitzgerald – "Johnny Panic"
5. Sexy (feat. Aleda Pope) – "Come Home"

Side Two
6. Lust – "Speed Demon"
7. Placid Fury – "Hold Me Close"
8. Ed Fitzgerald – "Living With A Tiger"
9. Sexy (feat. Aleda Pope) – "Hot Shot Of Lovin'"
10. Bethart – "Blow Up The Band"

Comments: *Homegrown* was released by WKQB-FM, Rock 106, which was a very cool local radio station for about 15 minutes circa 1979-80. Rock 106 had great deejays like Dave Walton, Lee Stevens, Lisa Richards, and the best of them all, my old buddy Moby (as well as personalities like the one-of-a-kind Hunter Harvey, R.I.P.). The station beat up WKDF-103 (then the dominant rock & roll station in town) like a rented car, driving from zero to the top o' the heap in the radio ratings in little more than a year after their format change to a rock-oriented playlist.

For whatever reason, the station's ownership pulled the plug after only a couple of years, changing formats to something significantly wimpier than what Rock 106 was blasting out on the FM airwaves. In doing so, they lost Moby, the station's most popular jock, a local boy (Crossville) and Belmont College student that had worked for a while at KDF before jumping ship to WKQB-FM. Moby worked in Tampa

VARIOUS ARTISTS: "LOCAL HEROES"

for a while, before landing in Houston in 1981. Over the next ten years, Moby was #1 in his time slot in the ratings with stations in Houston, Dallas, and Atlanta, where he currently lives. In 1991, Moby made a change to the country side of radio, launching his syndicated "Moby In The Morning" show, which is currently broadcast by almost a dozen stations across the Southeast.

As for the *Homegrown* album, well, you have ten songs from local stalwarts like **Lust**, **Placid Fury**, and **Ed Fitzgerald** as well as a couple of lesser-knowns in Gary Bethart and Sexy (featuring a terrible vocalist named Aleda Pope). Truthfully, fully half of the ten songs here majorly suck. The two Sexy tracks are simply horrible, overwrought commercial rock with bluesy overtones, Pope shouting hoarsely above a mediocre soundtrack…shudder.

The two Lust cuts aren't half bad, with "Speed Demon" being the best of the two, and are notable mostly because they feature vocalist Ron Keel, in between Lust and **Steeler**. Fitzgerald's two songs are pretty lousy, displaying none of the talent he would bring to his work with **Civic Duty** and later solo work. The Placid Fury songs run 50/50 with the popish "All The Time" standing out. Gary Bethart wasn't a half-bad guitarist, but he didn't have enough juice to pull off these solo performances (using only outside drummers).

All in all, the *Homegrown* album is a snapshot of a fledgling Nashville rock scene that had barely begun to stir in 1980. I've seen this LP going for big bucks ($100+) on European music collectors' websites, priced entirely on the basis of the two rare Keel/Lust tracks. Go figure…

VIII. Local Heroes (Vanderbilt Student Communications 1983, cassette)
Side One
1. Civic Duty – "New China"
2. Bill Lloyd – "Feeling The Elephant"
3. Tim Krekel & the Sluggers – "Live Wire"
4. White Animals – "Don't Care"
5. Wrong Band – "I Live In My Car"
6. Jason & the Nashville Scorchers – "Hot Nights In Georgia"

Side Two:
1. Practical Stylists – "She's Got Lots"
2. The Basics – "Born To Die"
3. Delta Hurricanes – "White Trash"
4. Factual – "Got Fun"
5. Afrikan Dreamland – "The New Circle"

Comments: The first shot of true self-awareness by Nashville's local music scene, *Local Heroes* was produced by Mark Mainwaring and Tommy Franklin of Vanderbilt's WRVU-FM student-run radio station. It's one of my favorite compilations of Nashville rock, a perfect snapshot of the young scene at the time, perfectly illustrating the diversity (pop, rock, reggae) of the city's underground. All profits from the tape were donated to the Nashville Crisis Call Center.

IX. Major Potential #1 (Major Label Records 1991, CD)
1. The Shindigs – "Love Somebody"
2. Mars Hill – "By Love"
3. Rob Chanter – "Only You Know For Sure"
4. Warm Dark Pocket – "Iron Door"
5. Lark Watts – "Paper Bag"
6. Mystique – "Baby You Missed"
7. Zip Holland – "Running From The Law"
8. Lost Dogs – "Two Way Street"
9. Casual Water – "Upstairs"
10. Mercy Sanction – "Crash"
11. John Manion – "Too Close To The Edge"
12. The Lounge Flounders – "Wonder"
13. Andrew Green – "L.M.G."
14. Stikki Wikkit – "Nancy Rocker"
15. Suede Tattoo – "One Time Jezebel"
16. Aashid & the New Dream – "I And I Survive"

Comments: A lot of people, myself included, still like to criticize former *Metro* magazine publisher Gus Palas, and usually for good reasons. However, in his own unique way, GVPIII did a lot to promote the local music scene. Even if his intentions weren't always altruistic – he usually thought that he was going to make a buck off the deal – he nevertheless helped put the Nashville rock scene on the map.

The *Major Potential* CD was a collaborative effort between Palas and local producer/promoter Kevin "KC" Chopson, an attempt to launch a series of compilation discs to showcase Nashville musical talent in a way that the NEA never could, or would, attempt. Although there are a couple of intruders on this first disc – Zip Holland was from Atlanta – and several of the bands were managed by KC at the time, you can't go wrong with **Mystique**, **Warm Dark Pocket**, **Casual Water**, the **Lounge Flounders**, and **Aashid**, who is represented here by a rare live performance from the 1991 Summer Lights Festival.

X. Music City Blues, Vol. One (Music City Blues 1998, CD)
1. Dean Hall & the Loose Eels – "Waitin' at the Railroad"
2. Delicious Blues Stew – "I Got Trouble"
3. Amy Watkins – "You Can Look (But Don't Touch)"
4. Herbert Hunter & the Champions – "You Can Make It If You Try"
5. The Bagdaddys – "Let Me In"
6. The Blues Boyz – "Blamin' It On The Man"
7. Mississippi Millie & the Mud Stompers - "Handful of Trouble"
8. Stacy Mitchhart & Blues U Can Use – "You Ain't Gotta Be Poor (To Have The Blues)"
9. Jim Gibson Band – "Too Late"

10. Bobby Messano & NBO – "Holdin' Ground"
11. Joe Silva & New Blue – "Kentucky Woman"
12. Michael Holloway – "I'm In Love With That Girl"
13. Ty Houston & Black Cat Bones – "Reflections"
14. Celinda Pink & the Cellar Dwellers – "I've Earned the Right to Sing the Blues"

Comments: Released by the Music City Blues Society, this 1998 collection offers a peak behind the scenes of one of Nashville's best kept secrets – the city's growing blues scene. Some of these artists have earned followings as large as any rock band in Nashville, and Stacy Mitchhart and Celinda Pink in particular have been popular club draws for quite a while. The performances here were recorded live at the Bourbon Street Blues and Boogie Bar. (www.musiccityblues.org)

XI. Music City Rock CD, Issue 1 (MCR Records 1995, CD)
1. Mother Mercy – "I Why"
2. Doug Hall – "I Got You"
3. Sha Sha Boom – "Mr. Delaware"
4. Surfing The Coaldust – "She Knows What She Wants"
5. Shari Sweet – "Whittling My Life In The Wood"
6. Soulskin – "A Dog, God, & An Idiot"
7. Thicket Grove – "Rich Man's Plight"
8. The Thompsons – "Window"
9. Brymer – "Barney The Clown"
10. The Faith Carnival – "The Dogs In The Distance"
11. Dutch – "Hallelujah World"

Comments: With local scenesters like Leslie Hermsdorfer, Debbie Burrow, Denise Dillard, Michael Johnston, Christie Taylor and WKDF's Morgan involved, this collection was bound to be truly representative, reflecting the diversity and evolution of the local scene by the mid-1990s.

XII. Nashville Homegrown (Hunger Records 1985, LP)
Side One
1. The White Animals – "Seasons Change"
2. Mark Germino & the Folk 'n' Roll Band – "Hangin' The Moon Where The Sun Don't Shine"
3. Tom Kimmel – "True Love"
4. Will Rambeaux & the Delta Hurricanes – "Baby Put Your Gun Down"
5. Rococo – "Photograph My Dreams"
6. Neopolitan – "Listen To The Rain"

Side Two
7. John Scott Sherrill & the Wolves In Cheap Clothing – "Ain't She Fine"
8. Civic Duty – "Rose Colored Eyes"
9. Timberline – "High School Nights"
10. The Prisoners of Love – "Deaf, Dumb, Crippled and Blind"
11. The Nerve – "Ain't Been Loved Enough"
12. The Nashville Bluegrass Band – "Up Above My Head"

Comments: Interesting benefit compilation with proceeds going to fight hunger through Second Harvest Food Bank in Nashville, and the Church Worlds Relief for African Famine. Twelve bands do a pretty good job of presenting the local rock world as it existed in 1985, with the **White Animals**, **Will Rambeaux & the Delta Hurricanes**, **Civic Duty**, and the **Nerve** all active rockers on the scene. Germino had yet to hook up with the Sluggers, Kimmel was criminally underrated, and the Prisoners of Love was a "supergroup" of sorts with singer Jimmy Hall from Wet Willie and guitarist Kenny Greenburg of the Delta Hurricanes. I'd heard of John Scott Sherrill but don't know anything else, and I dunno squat about Timberline…never heard of them before, didn't hear from them after…and the Nashville Bluegrass Band? Puh-leeze!

XIII. Nashville Rock Vol. 1 (Nashville Rock Records 2006, CD)
1. Destroy By Design – "Explicit"
2. Totem Soul – "Place in the World"
3. Creeping Cruds – "Meat and Three"
4. Josh Jackson – "Misunderstood"
5. Cretin Grims – "Fuck em All"
6. Jeano Roid Experience – "Fried Chicken"
7. Disarray – "Better Days (That Have Never Come)"
8. The Exotic Ones – "The Boogie Man"
9. The Mighty Shrill – "Outta Line"
10. Guns A Go Go – "Just Another Lover"
11. Noisecult – "Blood Feast Tonight"
12. J. Paul – "Wetter Water"
13. Thousandfold – "Driftwood"
14. Say Uncle – "Bored of the Lie"
15. Axe Victim – "Panic World"

16. Chest Rockwell – "Y'all Are Dude"
17. FRB – "Freak Flag"
18. Shrinking Violet – "Cycle Ender"
19. Dying Man – "No Time For Long Goodbyes"
20. Ready Empire – "Insane"
21. Floor – "Tough"
22. Mind Splitter – "House of High Hopes"

Comments: A great compilation disc of punk, gutter-rock and heavy metal tracks that is representative of the harder edge of Nashville's rock scene, circa 2006. Released by the good folks at Nashvillerocknet.net, a great local online watering hole, and compiled by Jeano Roid of **the Creeping Cruds**, *Nashville Rock Vol. 1* is one of the top two or three local music comps that's been released to date.

XIV. Return To Elliston Square 1979-1989 (Spat! Records 2008, CD)
1. Cloverbottom – "Nuclear War"
2. Actuals – "Today"
3. The Ratz – "Mental Block"
4. The White Animals – "Don't Care"
5. Factual – "Your Way"
6. Young Grey Ruins – "School's End"
7. Practical Stylists – "General Beat"
8. The Enemy – "Jesus Rides A U.F.O."
9. Shadow 15 – "So Far Today"
10. Government Cheese – "The Shrubbery's Dead"
11. The Shakers – "Eire"
12. Raging Fire – "The Morning In Her"
13. Dessau – "Never Change"
14. The Movement – "Lost Horizon"
15. Warm Dark Pocket – "All The Time"
16. Jet Black Factory – "Three Poisons"
17. Walk The West – "Backside"
18. F.U.C.T. – "Yet"
19. Clockhammer – "Mother Truth"
20. Alien In The Land Of Our Birth – "Box"
21. The Grinning Plowman – "Radiator"
22. Word Uprising – "One The Fast Way"

Comments: A.J. and the gang at Spat! Records did a great job with this look back towards the early days of Nashville's thriving rock scene. Just about everybody that was anybody back in the day is represented here, or at least those that Spat! could get. When asked, I wrote some nifty liner notes for the release, but they didn't have enough room to use 'em…oh well. Hopefully this one does well enough to prompt a second volume...

XV. Soaking In The Center Of The Universe (Spongebath Records 1998, CD)
1. Self – "It All Comes Out In The Wash"
2. Self – "Placing The Blame"
3. The C-60s – "Remote Control"

4. The C-60s – "Jerri Curl"
5. Fl.Oz. – "Record Stack"
6. Fl.Oz. – "Milk Mustache"
7. Count Bass-D – "I'm Better"
8. Count Bass-D – "Art For Sale"
9. Fleshpaint – "Empty Rooms"
10. Fleshpaint – "Seen It On The Radio"
11. The Features – "D-Con (Radio One)"
12. The Features – "Anti-Gravity Class Of '93"
13. The Katies – "Hairclip"
14. The Katies – "Noggin Poundin'"
15. The Roaries – "Easy"
16. The Roaries – "Day Dreamer"

Comments: For a short while, Murfreesboro's Spongebath Records was the "center of the universe" as far as Nashville-area rock went, with bands like **Self**, **Fl.Oz.**, **the Features** and **the Katies** all making a big noise. This second CD sampler offers two songs each from the young indie label's incredibly diverse roster. Great cover, but why no liner notes on a "promotional" CD?

XVI. Spin Cycle (Sound Impressions 1997, CD)
1. The Evinrudes – "Have Some Rain"
2. Backwaters – "A Room In Your House"
3. Bombpops – "Modern Education"
4. Stone Deep – "Imperfection"
5. Brannen – "Madonna Of The Moss"
6. Liz Hodder – "Grace Kelly"
7. comma 8 comma 1 – "River Collectibles"
8. Rahsaan Salandy – "13,000,000 Miles"
9. Kim's Fable – "Reach The Fire"
10. Jamie Hartford – "Hard Hard World"
11. Igmo – "Sacred Cow"
12. Who Hit John – "Claim To Fortune"
13. Cassandra Vasik – "Turn To Stone"
14. Jeff Coffin – "And Why Not?"
15. Tommy Womack – "Sally Jesse James"
16. IAYAALIS – "Da Sally Walker"
17. Roscoe Shelton – "Sometimes I Get Bitter"
18. Blood of the Goddess – "The Best Lovers"
19. John Sieger – "Rock Ability"
20. Kelli Owens – "I Don't Want To Be Your Girlfriend"

Comments: A collection of local artists appearing at the 1997 NEA Extravaganza, put together by Preston Sullivan and David Sullivan, with help from Daryl Sanders. Although the NEA's annual event had taken on the distinct odor of a corpse by the mid-1990s, this collection ain't half-bad. You have your usual suspects included here – **the Evinrudes**, **Stone Deep** and Jamie Hartford – as well as a couple of dark horse contenders in **IGMO** and **Who Hit John**, and a bold, ballsy choice in old-school school soulman Roscoe Shelton (thanks Daryl!). There are a couple of real stinkers, but overall *Spin Cycle* is a fairly strong collection of local talent.

Listening to the disc with fresh ears and the luxury of distance, I had forgotten that **John Brannen** is a damn good a songwriter. Brannen's "Madonna Of The Moss" is a reminder that he easily stands alongside scribes like **Mark Germino** or **Steve Forbert** as a rockin' wordsmith. That Brannen never broke out beyond Nashville is simply criminal.

Bombpop's hard-edged pop sounds great on "Modern Education;" comma 8 comma 1 pursue an intriguing electronic-based form with distorted guitars and robotic vocals; and Kim's Fable delivers the enchanting "Reach The Fire" with beautiful, haunting vocals and lush instrumentation. Out of the 20 tracks here, easily half of the artists had the chops to play in the majors; to my knowledge, only a couple of 'em ever got a chance, which is a damn shame, and kinda counter to the NeA's goals, innit?

XVII. Street Hits…The Record Album (KDF-FM 103 1980, vinyl LP)
Side One
1. Flip Anderson – "Loser's Shoes"
2. Munchkin – "Need More Rock And Roll"
3. Southern Komfort Band – "Cookin' In Your Town"
4. Speed Limit – "Want You To Know"
5. Current Energy – "I Am"

Side Two
6. South Paw – "Take Hold"
7. Bradford Blues Band – "Any Love I Can Find"
8. Suzee Waters – "Better Get A Grip On Yourself"
9. Benjamin/Waters Band – "Out Of Control"
10. Barry McKay & the Bullets – "A Man Like Me"

Comments: Released by dominant AOR radio station WKDF-FM, *Street Hits* bills itself as "Nashville's First Album Featuring All Local Talent." Dunno whether this or Rock 106's *Homegrown* (see above) came first, but judging from the talent included here, I'd wager that KDF was the first to bring up water from the well. Outside of the **Bradford Blues Band**, who have performed locally for years, most of these bands made little of a splash on the still embryonic local scene. Flip Anderson's band yielded guitar god Kenny Greenberg, who also found time to hang around with Bobby Bradford, and **Speed Limit** may well have been Mike Simmons' first band. Other than these guys, there's nothing else to see here, so move along...

XVIII. The Best Of Nashville (Sonny's Pop Records 1995?, promo cassette)
Side One (New Rock, Vol. 2):
1. Shazam! – "Engine Red"
2. Iodine – "Mr. Moony"
3. Still – "Too Old"
4. Fearless Freep – "Sucking The Existence"

SPAT! RECORDS PRESENTS

Return To Elliston Square
1979-1989

5. Vagantis – "When You Wake Up"
6. Stone Deep – "Hands"
7. Surfing The Coaldust – "The Holy Place"

Side Two (Triple A, Vol. 2):
1. Beau Haddock – "Distant Hills"
2. Laurie Webb – "Easy"
3. Be – "Six-Chambered Heart"
4. The Evinrudes – "Bodark's Is Closed"
5. Tim Carroll – "Open Flame"
6. Marianne Osiel – "Strange Girl"
7. The Keep – "Tell The Driver"

Comments: "Sonny's Pop Records Radio Samplers are Not For Sale, Not For Profit, Promotional Use Only tools for assisting local Nashville and regional artists get more exposure through radio airplay. CD versions of these samples are serviced to the appropriate local Nashville radio stations." That's what it says in the liner notes to this odd little cassette that I found for a quarter at Phonoluxe. Split into the "New Rock" side and the "Triple A" side, this was evidently the second tape in the series. Much like what the NEA Extravaganza devolved into by including "regional" artists, I don't think that including Be (from Arkansas) or several others really helped promote the local scene.

XIX. The Ex-Files (Sound Impressions 1998, CD)
1. Collapsis – "Automatic"
2. The Evinrudes – "Drive Me Home"
3. Owsley – "Coming Up Roses"
4. Jamie Hartford – "Good Things Happen (When You're Around)"
5. Gumwrapper Curb – "You're The Girl"

VARIOUS ARTISTS: "THE EX-FILES"

6. Alisa Carroll – "Little Sister"
7. Far Too Jones – "Look At You Now"
8. The Sci-Fi – "Jupiter Boy"
9. Kevin Johnson & the Linemen – "Miss Lonely Hearts Out On The Town"
10. Willie Wisely – "Bygones"
11. Nothingface – "Pacifier"
12. Rebecca Stout – "Icarus' Revenge"
13. Grand Street Cryers – "Through The Fields"
14. Aashid & the Blu-Reggae Underground – "Love Is Everything"
15. Trish Murphy – "Scorpio Tequila"
16. Soul Surgeon – "Complicated"
17. Phil Lee – "Last Year"
18. Irresponsibles – "Over You"
19. Kelli Owens – "2's & 3's"

Comments: Another year, another NEA Extravaganza compilation disc…ho hum…really, by this time, what was really the point? Especially when the NEA tended to champion the same acts year after year in the Extravaganza line-up. While the Evinrudes' "Drive Me Home" is a great song and shoulda been a bona-fide radio hit, how many of these NEA comps did they really have to appear on? After all, they had their deal in place by 1997.

As for alt-country pin-up boy Jamie Hartford, his fingerprints are always all over these things. Hartford's country-rock snoozefests just don't make for exciting listening, and I can rattle off half-a-dozen artists without breaking a sweat that do this kind of thing a hell of a lot better. What's up, did Hartford have naughty pix of Jim Zumwalt or something?

THE MUSIC OF THE 1998
NEA EXTRAVAGANZA

On the other hand, this year's selection committee (which included Jack Emerson and Daryl Sanders) did include pop genius **Will Owsley**, whose "Coming Up Roses" is a simply mesmerizing pop/rock triumph. Alisa Carroll's "Little Sister" is a powerful, fascinating Southern Gothic ballad with kudzu draped over every word. **Rebecca Stout** remains one of the city's most underrated talents, and her "Icarus' Revenge" is a hot-blooded gaze across a smoky bar. Soul Surgeon's "Complicated" is a rocking slice of youthful enthusiasm, with great guitarwork from William Tyler.

Kudos to the inclusion of **Aashid** this time around, as the big man has often been overlooked as the dominant Nashville talent he had been for 25 years. "Love Is Everything" from Aashid & the Blu-Reggae Underground is a great representation of the man's art, a spirited combination of hypnotic blues and reggae rhythms with Aashid's distinctive baritone vocals and solid instrumental jamming that "livelied" up the clubs back in the day.

Unfortunately, the good folks at the NEA had long since forgotten their mission to promote local music by this time, and *The Ex-Files* compilation is lousy with foreigners, even if some of them are quite fetching. Florida's Gumwrapper Curb imbues "You're the Girl" with a powerful, trembling emotionalism; they later changed their name to Virginwool and released an album through Atlantic. North Carolina's Collapsis, which featured members of regional faves like Queen Sarah Saturday and Dillon Fence, flexed a brash, mid-decade alt-rock sound on "Automatic," with a cool recurring riff driving the song.

Far Too Jones was another North Carolina band kicking out a distinct pop/rock sound with a Southern twang, Kevin Johnson is a talented, DC-based Americana singer/songwriter, and Nothingface was a DC-area metal band. They're all good-to-great in their own ways, but do they belong on a Nashville music compilation? The Reverend says "nay nay!"

XX. The London Side of Nashville (Pollyfox Records 1982, LP)
Side One
1. The Raves – "Answering Box"
2. The Hots – "Strangers"
3. Factual – "Dance Of The Izods"
4. Adonis – "Love Don't Work The Way You Want It To"
5. Sunshine Adams – "Video Window"
6. Russian Roulette – "Don't Waste My Time"
7. Paradox – "Electric Sofa"
8. The Most – "Dream Girl"

Side Two
9. The Raves – "Bet You're Lonely Too"
10. The Hots – "Whose Side Are You On"

11. Factual – "Sleep On The Edge"
12. Adonis – "Young Love"
13. Sunshine Adams – "Cut To The Chase"
14. Russian Roulette – "Don't Stare Into The Sun"
15. Paradox – "One Step At A Time"
16. B.B. Gunne – "Life In The Big City"

Comments: Odd little compilation album that beat *Local Heroes* by a year with an energetic mix of rock, pop, and "new wave" (London by way of Bucksnort). Sadly, little information provided for any of the bands included, and I have no idea who some of these folks were. **The Hots**, **Factual**, Russian Roulette, and the Most (Les Shields) were reasonably well-known 'round town, and I think that Sunshine Adams were producer Neil Jefferies' band. I thought that the Raves were from Alabama, and Adonis was a horrible mainstream rock band. I did have a great time one night with the Adonis guitarist's girlfriend, though, and then later ran into the two of them at the Electric Cowboy Pop Festival…awwwk-ward! Love Factual's "Dance Of The Izods," though!

XXI. Treason Records Sampler Vol. 1 (Treason Records 1998, CD)
1. Rebecca Stout – "The Liberator"
2. Stone Deep – "Rainy Day Women #12 & 35"
3. Blood of the Goddess – "Not That Screwed Up"
4. Jennifer Niceley – "When I Lay Myself Down"
5. All The Queen's Men – "The Mirror"
6. Rebecca Stout – "Dog"
7. Stone Deep – "Baby When I Think About You"
8. Blood of the Goddess – "Animals"
9. Rebecca Stout – "Icarus' Revenge"

10. All The Queen's Men – "Something To Tell Me"
11. Stone Deep – "Baby Food"

Comment: Correct me if I'm wrong, but I think that Treason Records was the label that former *Bone* music magazine editor and man-around-town Daryl Sanders launched in the late 1980s. From this sampler compilation, Daryl had some damn fine artists lined up, and Rebecca Stout and Stone Deep should have been enough to make the label work. I have to assume that a lack of funds sank the project but, like usual, Daryl's taste in music is impeccable.

XXII. What You Haven't Heard…Nashville Rock (NEA 1987, CD)
1. Hocus Pocus – "Rock In Music City"
2. The Drmls – "Into The Dreamlight"
3. Johnny Cobb – "Into The Light"
4. The Nerve – "Ain't Been Loved Enough"
5. These Are Houseplants – "Sunshine Anytime"
6. Audience – "Heartache"
7. Radio One – "Don't Keep Me Waiting"
8. Neil Deaf – "Falling Into Hand (of Helplessness)"
9. Order Of Silence – "Lemme Get You Down"
10. Neecie Alexander – "Gone Away"
11. Jamie Houston – "Premonition"
12. Eleven 59 – "Want To"
13. Dessau – "Imperial Hotel"
14. The Grinning Plowman – "Where The Buffalo Roam"

Comments: I ranted about the NEA above, but this compilation actually predates the feeble aforementioned *Hear Rock City* cassette and honestly offers a better selection of local bands than anything that the NEA did before (or

since). However, the organization's corporate ties were a little too obvious – the rear CD insert tray doesn't list the bands included on the disc but rather offers an ad for LaserVideo duplication, and the back of the CD booklet has an ad for Copies Unlimited.

Once you delve into the booklet, you'll find Robert Oermann's hilarious "Brief Overview Of Alternative Music In Nashville" essay that name checks such red-hot local "rockers" as Marshall Chapman, Blue Jug, Gene Cotton, Tracy Nelson and White Duck (?), and refers to Bob Dylan, Ringo Starr, Neil Young and Elvis Costello as "new country artists who have recorded in Nashville." Bob never did get out much, but at least he does end his piece with a roll-call of real Nashville rockers like **Walk The West**, **Royal Court of China**, **Bill Lloyd**, **Webb Wilder** and others. On the other hand, Mike McCall's liner notes provide a quality balance to Oermann's delusions.

XXIII. What's The Buzz? Major Potential #2 (Major Label Records 1993, CD)
1. Mouth Full Of Bees – "Devil's Grin"
2. Sir Real – "Hideaway"
3. The Shindigs – "Telegrams And Flowers"
4. Kevin Tetz – "Carry Me"
5. Law Of Nature – "Who Knows"
6. Rob Chanter's Kiss Fit – "Heart Keeps Calling"
7. Mars Hill – "Tempted"
8. The Lounge Flounders – "Head Machine"
9. Flat Mass – "Cringe"
10. Selma March – "Life In A Cocoon"
11. Good Karma Day – "Dreaming Season"
12. Slavejacket – "Linda's Down"
13. Boneyard – "Crucified By Life"
14. Video Opera – "The Art Song"

Comments: This is a much more representative document of the local music scene at a single point in time than anything that the NEA managed to sludge together by committee through their many years of trying.

VEGAS COCKS

Band Members:
Steve Woods (vocals) (I)
Viva (guitars) (I)
Marcus Alan Brown (guitars) (I)
Tres Vegas (bass) (I)
Chris Mekow (drums) (I)

Vegas Cocks Recordings:

I. The Vegas Cocks (demos 1993, cassette tape)
1. Right On
2. Outside

3. Love Box
4. Motherless Child
5. Piss Poor Paul
6. On My Way To Alright
7. Camille

Comments: "With a sound that owes as much to the acid-drenched psychedelica and bluesy guitar orgies of '60s bands such as Cream, Blues Magoos, or Moby Grape as it does to '80s metal and hardcore punk, the Vegas Cocks are one of the Music City's most exciting and interesting bands." – *Bone Music Magazine*, January 1994

VELCRO PYGMIES
Web: www.velcropygmies.com

Band Members:
Cameron Flener (vocals) (I-IV)
Blake Baumeier (guitars) (I-III)
Jimmy Mullin (bass) (II-III)
Chris Eddins (drums) (II-IV)
Angel (guitar) (IV)
Jason Reed (bass) (IV)
Rob Bazell (drums) (I)
Joe Straub (bass) (I)

Velcro Pygmies Recordings:

I. 3? (BFE Records 1993, CD)
1. Love Machine
2. No Beverly Hills
3. Mona Lisa
4. Far And Away

5. Trash The Night
6. Goin' Down
7. Temptation
8. Tattoo Angel
9. Hit And Run
10. Dr. Love
11. We Ain't From Athens

Comments: Hard rock and pseudo-metal from the lunkhead school. I don't remember anything about these guys except for the name, and don't seem to have ever seen them play live...no surprise since this kind of thing isn't really my cuppa. Don't even know how long they hung around the Music City, since they seem to be based in Louisville, Kentucky these days. They have six albums to their name, but I only have two (well, three...see below) and could only find info on a couple more...the band's website sucks. The Pygmies continue to crank out '80s-styled rock 'n' roll here in the new millennium, playing the college fratboy circuit, so they must have found an audience *somewhere*...

Another View: "The Velcro Pygmies are everything that's right about rock n roll. Loud, fast, larger than life, and in your face. Big lights, foul language, tight pants and the occasional boob. They've been compared to the likes of Van Halen, Poison, Bon Jovi, and Air Supply (They've got a sensitive side too). If you like "Big Rock" this is the band for you. If you are more into the "Hippie" thing don't waste your time...you'll hate them." – from the band's website

II. Dice (BFE Records 1996, CD)
1. Who Cares
2. Rockin' In A Hard Place
3. (Seems Like) The Whole World Is In My Way
4. Sweet Marie
5. When It Hurts (It Hurts Like Hell)
6. What's In It For Me
7. Baby Can't Wait
8. True Love
9. Cam and George
10. Undeniable
11. I Think I Love You
12. Undeniable Re-mix

Comments: Two disc set that I found cheap at whatever that funky lil' used music store near Belmont circa 2006 was called. Dice is on disc one, while disc two is the band's earlier album *3?* in its entirety...

III. Life Of The Party (BFE Records 2002, CD)
1. Life Of The Party
2. Mona Lisa
3. We Ain't From Athens
4. Far And Away
5. Love Machine

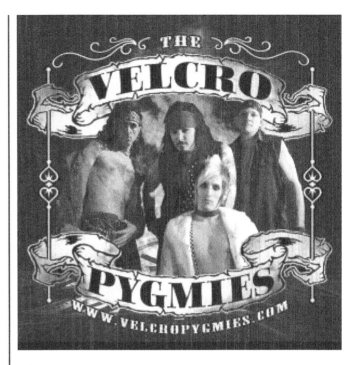

6. No Beverly Hills
7. When It Hurts (It Hurts Like Hell)
8. Twisted
9. Cam and George
10. Undeniable
11. All I Want Is You
12. I Want To
13. Tattoo Angel
14. Pussywhipped

Comments: Fourth or fifth album from the South's answer to Poison serves up more '80s glammy nerf-rock, tho' "Far and Away" sounds a lot like early Cult. The band reprises several songs from *3?* here, which makes me wonder how creative they really are...two-disc set includes DVD.

IV. American Muscle (BFE Records 2006, CD)
1. Sweet Miranda
2. Rich Bitch (All Over You)
3. Building Up To Feel So Good
4. Don't Call It Love
5. Ready To Go
6. The Punchline of Pretty
7. Beauty In A Box
8. The Best It Ever Gets
9. Get Away
10. Sweet Home Alabama

Comments: A new record, probably a good decade past its sell-by date and, judging by their photos, the band is looking a little long in the tooth these days. They're not in any of Popoff's books, so they haven't really made a splash on the metallic horizon over their two decades of rockin' the road...

VELCRO STARS

Band Members:
Shane Spresser (vocals, guitar) (I-II)
Keith Pratt (vocals, guitar) (I-II)
Rebekah Spresser (keyboards) (I-II)
Danial Norman (bass) (I-II)
Jonathan Brock (bass)
Andy Sport (drums) (I-II)
Aaron Distlet (drums)
Tyler Coppage (drums)

Velcro Stars Recordings:

I. 7 Songs for the Kidd at Heart (self-produced CD, 2006)
1. Rebekah Pop
2. Heart Disease
3. Seize the Day
4. Cascade
5. Shock & Awe
6. Just Where My Time Goes
7. Kid(d) Song

II. Hiroshima's Revenge (Grand Palace 2007, CD)
1. Same Every Day
2. Hiroshima's Revenge
3. All That I Do
4. Not So Easy
5. Hole in the Sky
6. Cascade
7. B-Side of Love
8. Brand New
9. Pretense
10. Just for the Night
11. Another Winter
12. Cinnamon Jewz
13. Distraction
14. Like a Storm
15. Pavilion

Another View: "The Velcro Stars are one of the most interesting, original, and level-headed bands to come out of Murfreesboro in a long time. Their songs are simplistic and well arranged, and bring with them hints of Pavement, Blake Babies, and Superchunk." – Nashvillezine.com

Yet Another View: "Murfreesboro's Velcro Stars make catchy, head-bobbing indie rock that surely would have landed them on the Spongebath label back in the '90s along with stylistically similar Boro band The Features, if they had been around back then. Actually, the Velcro Stars' song 'Just Where My Time Goes' has one of those great singalong codas that have made The Features' shows so fun for so long. Viva la fun rock." – *Nashville Rage*

VENUS HUM

Band Members:
Annette Strean (vocals) (I-VI)
Tony Miracle (guitar, bass, synthesizer, vocals) (I-VI)
Kip Kubin (synthesizers, computer) (I-VI)

Venus Hum Recordings:

I. Venus Hum (Mono-Fi 1999, CD)
1. Sonic Boom
2. Montana
3. Wordless May
4. Honey
5. Hummingbirds
6. Illumine
7. Run Annie Run
8. Break Me Out
9. Let the Dance Begin
10. Wooly Snow
11. King of the Hill
12. Find Yourself
13. Sonic Boom

Comments: I've seen them described in various places as a "cloud pop" band, whatever that is, but Venus Hum's debut is a clever combination of electronic pop (think Depeche Mode or Stereolab) and shoegazer vibe with a hint of electro-Goth (think the Cure). Now out-of-print, this disc demands serious cheddar from buyers on the collector's market.

II. Switched-On Christmas (Mono-Fi 2000, CD EP)
1. Let it Snow
2. Suzy Snowflake
3. Silent Night
4. St. Mary's Lake
5. Silver Bells
6. The Christmas Song

Comments: The band recorded this six-song EP exclusively for their 'Christmas Spectacular' show of 2000 in Nashville. The limited-edition disc was given away to fans that attended the show, though now the songs are available on iTunes.

III. Hummingbirds (Mono-Fi/BMG 2002, CD EP)
1. Hummingbirds
2. Alice
3. Run Annie Run
4. Illumine

Comments: Released as a precursor to the MCA label debut under the band's Mono-Fi logo but distributed by Universal. This CD EP features two songs ("Run Annie Run" and "Illumine") from the band's out of print first album. Not to be confused with the 10" vinyl EP by the same title that was released in the U.K. with differing songs.

IV. Big Beautiful Sky (MCA Records 2003, CD)
1. Hummingbirds
2. Montana
3. Soul Sloshing
4. Wordless May
5. Alice
6. Lumberjacks
7. Beautiful Spain
8. The Bells
9. Springtime #2
10. Honey
11. Sonic Boom
12. Bella Luna

Comments: The band's major label debut was released simultaneously in the U.S. on MCA Records and by BMG in the U.K. A magnificent collection of timeless electro-pop, *Big Beautiful Sky* cemented the band's cult audience.

V. Songs For Superheroes (Mono-Fi 2004, CD EP)
1. Fighting For Love
2. I Have to Save the World

3. William's Last Day At Work
4. Sister
5. My Heart
6. Fighting For Love Video

Comments: An odd little beastie, this one…the lead song, "Fighting For Love," was written with J.J. Abrams, the creative mastermind behind the recent hit movies *Cloverfield* and *Star Trek* and TV shows like *Alias* and *Lost*. Abrams discovered Venus Hum on iTunes and was so knocked out by the band that he got in touch and asked if they wanted to take his *Alias* theme song and do something with it; VH responded by using elements of that song and built a new song out of it. Two songs here were written for the *Tomb Raider* movie (with Angelina Jolie) but were subsequently not used in the film.

VI. The Colors In The Wheel (Nettwerk Records 2006, CD)
1. Turn Me Around
2. Segue #1
3. Yes And No
4. Segue #2
5. Birds And Fishes
6. Do You Want To Fight Me?
7. Genevieve's Wheel
8. You Break Me Down
9. Segue #3
10. Surgery In The City
11. Pink Champagne

VENUS HUM - VICTOR - VIDEO OPERA - V.O.C.

12. 72 Degrees
13. Segue #4
14. Go To Sleep

Comments: After an incredibly tough couple of years, Venus Hum bounced back with a new label deal and arguably the most mature and creative album of their admittedly short career. After they got bounced from both their U.S. and U.K. label deals because of typical major label bullshit, the rigors of the road strained the band's close-knit relationships.

When vocalist Strean developed painful vocal nodes, it seemed that the band was over. The trio went on hiatus, allowing Strean to recover her voice and, with therapy, she learned to sing again; Miracle returned to his hometown of Cincinnati and recorded an experimental album as Satellite City; and Kubin pursued his interests in filmmaking, creating music videos.

VICTOR

Band Members:
Victor W. Davis (vocals) (A1)

Victor Recordings:

A1. "Amerikan Dread" b/w "Amerikan Dread (N.Y.C. Dub)" (Dread Beat, 7" vinyl)

Comments: Produced by **Aashid Himons**, and released by the **White Animals**' Dread Beat label, Victor was a blu-reggae acolyte, of sorts, putting out this one fine 45rpm slice

of vinyl before disappearing (as far as I know) from the local scene. No date on the record, but I'm guessing mid-1980s. Wally Bangs, writing on his Soulfish Stew website, thinks that it came out in 1986.

VIDEO OPERA

Band Members:
Mark Prince Lee (vocals)
Rayne Rierson (bass)
Stonie Neel (keyboards)
Trent Sain (drums)

Comments: Band contributed song "The Art Song" to *What's The Buzz?* 1993 compilation CD.

V.O.C.

Band Members:
Fuzzy Roberts (vocals)
Joe Freeman (guitars)
Squire Lilly (bass)
Dan Langford (drums)

Comments: Hard rock/heavy metal band with blues roots in the vein of early Led Zeppelin.

The WHITE ANIMALS

* * * * PRESENTS * * * *

'Summer Nights of Love'

AT

The EXIT IN

NASHVILLE, TENNESSEE

Thur. · Fri. · Sat. July 17·18·19

9:00 P.M.

ADVANCE ADMISSION $4.00 ★ AT DOOR $5.00

THURSDAY ★ SPECIAL TEEN NIGHT
with... The KNOWLEDGE
ALL AGES WELCOME!

★ FRIDAY ★
ROYAL COURT OF CHINA

★ SATURDAY ★
The HO HO MEN

SLO ROLL
LONESOME TOWN DRIFTERS
HILLBILLY CASINO

SATURDAY · MARCH 19
THE END ★ $5 COVER
2219 ELLISTON PL. DOORS at 9

ELECTRIC HOLIDAY FREAKOUT

Mordred Lane
Cantrell's
Saturday 21

EJ'S PRESENTS

ONE FREE BEER
WITH FLYER

SURGE

blues reunion

FRI & SAT
OCT 18 & 19
ROCK N BLUES

WALK THE WEST

WALK THE WEST

Band Members:
Paul Kirby (vocals, guitar) (I)
Will Goleman (guitar) (I)
John Goleman (bass) (I)
Richard Ice (drums) (I)

Walk The West Recordings:

I. Walk The West (Capitol EMI Records 1986, vinyl LP)
Side One
1. Living At Night
2. Backside
3. Too Much Of A Good Thing
4. Precious Times
5. Lonely Boy

Side Two
6. Sheriff Of Love
7. Think It Over
8. Solitary Man
9. Calvary Hill
10. Do You Wanna Dance

Comments: At the height of their short career, the popularity of Nashville's Walk The West rivaled that of EMI labelmates **Jason & the Scorchers** on the Southeast club circuit. Walk The West was formed in 1984 by vocalist and guitarist Paul Kirby, childhood friends John Goleman and Will Goleman, and drummer Richard Ice. The band's rise in popularity echoed that of other similar mid-1980s Nashville artists like **Will Rambeaux** and the Delta Hurricanes, leading to a major

label deal. The result was the band's lone, self-titled album in 1986.

The band's country-rock hybrid received a modicum of critical applause but failed to reach a national audience in a field dominated by cowpunks like the Beat Farmers and hometown heroes the Scorchers. In the end, the band members found it easier to switch than to continue fighting the stigma of proving themselves as a rock band in the home of country music. Kirby and the Golemans would form the **Cactus Brothers** as a twangier side project, eventually taking the plunge and abandoning Walk The West and pursuing country stardom full-time in 1989. Still, the band's debut stands strong as a mid-1980s example of post-punk country-rock, rivaling period releases from contemporaries like Rank & File, the Long Ryders, and the True Believers.

Last Minute Update: Just heard from Donna Frost, and verified by the *Nashville Scene*, that Walk The West/Cactus Brothers frontman Paul Kirby died of cardiac arrest in September 2011. Says *Scene* scribe Jim Ridley, "in recent years, Kirby was still making music, including recordings with former Walk The West drummer Richard Ice."

Paul performed a couple of weeks before his death at a Walk The West reunion at the Exit/In's 40th anniversary party. Kirby was only 48 years old, and should be remembered as one of Nashville's premiere musical talents...

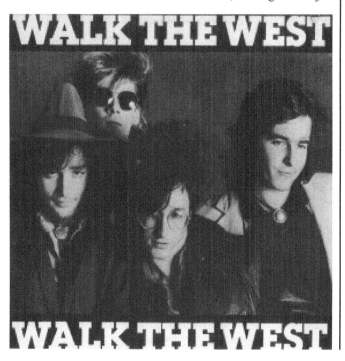

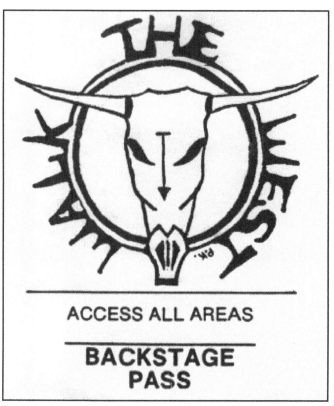

ACCESS ALL AREAS

BACKSTAGE PASS

WALLSTREET

Band Members:
Rob Pracht (vocals)
Tim Gentry (guitars)
Dave Colding (bass)
Jay Peyton (drums)

Comments: Wallstreet was formed by Rob Pracht and Tim Gentry, formerly of **Roxx**.

WANABAM

Band Members:
Tyrone Banks (vocals)
Roger Nichols (guitar)
John Massey (bass)
Drew Wiseman (keyboards)
Derek Wiseman (drums)

Comments: Formerly known as The Big House, changed their name to Wanabam in 1991.

WAREHOUSE

Band Members:
Ned Massey (vocals, guitar) (I)
Michael Davis (guitar, vocals) (I)
Kevin Hornback (bass) (I)

Rick Neel (keyboards, vocals) (I)
Jeffrey Perkins (drums) (I)

Other Musicians:
George Bradfute (guitar) (I)
Vinnie Santoro (drums) (I)

Warehouse Recordings:

I. On A Good Day (self-produced CD EP, 1995)
1. On A Good Day
2. I Almost Drowned
3. So Far Away
4. The Car Swerved
5. Magazine Shop
6. She And I

Comments: Ned Massey is a decent songwriter but fair-to-middlin' vocalist that led this conglomeration of local scene vets in the recording of this six-song EP. Certainly entertaining, but Massey would soon jump towards a solo career and, without pause, the bright lights of NYC, where he's found a modicum of success...

WARM DARK POCKET

Band Members:
Robb Earls (vocals, guitar, synthesizer) (A1)
Marilyn Blair (vocals, synthesizer) (A1)

Walk The West

Warm Dark Pocket Recordings:

A1. Warm Dark Pocket (Faction Records 1986, 12" vinyl)
<u>Side One</u>
1. Door Inside
2. Pressure Zone

<u>Side Two</u>
3. The Other Side
4. Shadows Burning

Comments: After **Factual**, Robb Earls continued to explore the possibilities of electronic music with Warm Dark Pocket.

WARSAW GHETTO

Band Members:
Allen Williams (guitar, programming, mix)
Clint Koch (programming, vocals)
Kathy Gregory (backing vocals)
Stephanie Jacobs (backing vocals)
Nunu Bassaldra (backing vocals)

Warsaw Ghetto Recordings:

I. Warsaw Ghetto (self-produced cassette, 1992)

Comments (from the band): Warsaw Ghetto was formed by Allen Williams and Clint Koch in the fall of 1991. Allen Williams had been involved with promotions at Reptile Records and Clint Koch has been in a local band, Kickback. Over several bottles of vodka they forged a sound that abused all emerging audio technologies available at the time.

Warm Dark Pocket

WATCHING THE DETECTIVES

Band Members:
Chip Staley (vocals, guitar)
Chance Chambers (guitar, harmonica, vocals)
Scott Nason (bass, vocals)
Jennifer Jared (percussion, vocals)
Joe Polenzani (drums)

WATERMELON ROAD

Band Members:
James Whelan (vocals, guitar) (I)
Amanda Whelan (vocals, piano) (I)
Zak Godwin (guitar) (I)
Rich Baker (bass) (I)
Shawn McWilliams (drums) (I)
Jeff Finlin ("more drums") (I)

Watermelon Road Recordings:

I. Mermaid & Roosters... (Impala Records 1991, CD)
1. It's Okay To Love Jesus
2. Everybody's Right
3. Chocolate Saints
4. Summer Makes A Lover
5. The Trouble With You
6. Fashion Tragedy
7. Springville
8. Mary
9. Jamie
10. 25 Years Ago
11. Media Street
12. Let It Roll Away
13. Red River Valley

Comments: The husband and wife team of James and Amanda Whelan initially made quite a splash on the local scene during the early 1990s, but where they disappeared to I don't know. Looked for them on the 'nets, found a video that might be Jim Whelan on YouTube, but nothing concrete....

LARK WATTS

Band Members:
Lark Watts (vocals)
Paul Pearce (guitar)
Glenn Mayo (bass)
Bob Mayo (drums, guitar)

Comments: Contributed song "Paper Bag" to the *Major Potential #1* 1991 compilation CD.

LARK WATTS & RATTLESHAKE

Band Members:
Lark Watts (vocals, guitars)
Dave Keefer (guitars)
Michael Lampton (bass)
Paul Stine (keyboards)
Rankin Roth (drums)
Lyria King (vocals)
Kim Beasley (vocals)
Robert Means (keyboards)
Mark Shenkel (guitars, saxophone)

Lark Watts & Rattleshake Recordings:

I. Lark Watts and Rattleshake (self-produced cassette, no date)
Side One
1. Painless
2. Night Falls

Side Two
3. 4th of July
4. Put Down the Gun

Comments: Watts kicked around Nashville for a lot of years with different bands and musical directions. Whereas his solo work was more acoustic folk/Americana sounding, Lark Watts & Rattleshake had a soulful, R&B flavored, Memphis soul-styled sound.

This four-song cassette tape, with no date, probably came to me as a demo tape, but it's pretty damn good. Another talented Nashville rocker denied by the major label machine...

WEATHERSPOON

Band Members:
Brian Hoppes (vocals, guitar) (I)
Josh Lowe (guitars) (I)
Justin Lowe (drums, vocals) (I)
Seth Waltenbaugh (bass, vocals) (I)
Chris Wilkins (guitar)

Weatherspoon Recordings:

I. Til The Neighbors Call Again (self-produced CD EP, 2003)
1. 3 6 5
2. Calling April
3. Figured Out
4. Running Away
5. Falling Back
6. Intro
7. Last Date

Comments: Formed back in '94 when the guys were still in high school, Weatherspoon came to the attention of country great Floyd Cramer, who became the band's manager and producer. Weatherspoon worked on demo recordings with Cramer until his death in 1997, breaking up in 1999 so that the members could attend college. The band reformed as a foursome in 2002 and recorded the six-song EP *Til The Neighbors Call Again*, including Cramer's hit song "Last Date" as a tribute to their early supporter.

Another View: "Interestingly, Weatherspoon's sound is a cagey blend of the old and the new. There's a pronounced first-generation British invasion tinge to the songs, but there's also a modern edge and feel in lead vocalist Brian Hoppes' delivery and the lyrics and subjects addressed in such numbers as "Calling April" and "Figured Out." Hoppes doubles on rhythm guitar, smoothly interacting with lead guitarist Josh Lowe, Justin's cousin. Bassist Seth Waltenbaugh adds the final component, with Waltenbaugh and Justin Lowe's capable rhythmic backgrounds ranging from relaxed to frenetic."
– Ron Wynn, *Nashville City Paper*, 2004

WHITE ANIMALS

WHITE ANIMALS

Band Members:
Kevin Gray (vocals, guitar) (A1, I-VIII)
Steve Boyd (vocals, bass) (A1, I-VIII)
Rich Parks (vocals, guitar) (A1, II-VIII)
Tim Coats (keyboards, "dreadmaster") (A1, II-VIII)
Ray Crabtree (drums) (A1, I-VIII)

Other Musicians:
William D. Collins (guitars) (I)
Mike Dysinger (bongos) (I)

White Animals Recordings:

Singles

A1. White Animals (Dread Beat Records 1983, 7" vinyl)
Side One
1. Don't Care

Side Two
2. Boots Again And Again And Again

Albums/EPs

I. Nashville Babylon (Dread Beat Records 1981, vinyl LP)
Side One
1. Old Jazzmaster
2. For Your Love
3. Only Sorrow

Side Two
4. Tobacco Road
5. I Need Somebody to Love Me
6. I Need You So

II. Lost Weekend (Dread Beat Records 1982, vinyl LP)
Side One
1. Constant Attention
2. These Boots Are Made For Walkin'
3. Girls
4. Secret Agent Man
5. When I Get Home

Side Two
6. Love Fades Away
7. Move
8. The General's Theme
9. Lester Chambers
10. Boots Again
11. Such A Long Time

Comments: After independently releasing the very-cool *Nashville Babylon* six-song EP/LP, with a handful of

originals mixed with unique covers of the Yardbirds and the white trash anthem "Tobacco Road," the White Animals followed with the longer, more dubtastic *Lost Weekend* album.

Featuring what would become one of their signature songs in a mesmerizing cover of Nancy Sinatra's "These Boots Are Made For Walkin'," there are a bunch of good pop/rock performances here like "Constant Attention" and "When I Get Home." At the dawn of the '80s, the White Animals were one of Nashville's few original rock bands as well as one of its most popular.

III. Ecstasy (Dread Beat Records 1984, vinyl LP)
Side One
1. Ecstasy
2. Goodnight And Goodbye
3. Gloria

Side Two
4. Dreamland
5. Don't Care
6. This Girl Of Mine
7. You Started Something
8. For Lovers Only

Comments: Entering into the mid-1980s with a pair of long players under their belts, the White Animals suddenly found themselves in the middle of the rapidly-evolving, fast-changing Nashville scene with short-lived bands coming and going on an almost nightly basis. The White Animals were already scene greybeards by '84, but they did good with this third album, delivering a pair of local faves with "This Girl

Of Mine" and the catchy, can't stop singing "Don't Care," which mostly made people forget all about those damn walkin' boots.

Another View: "This new album from Nashville's premier frat/bar/party band contains a lot of the expectable, but shows the White Animals continuing to expand and refine their sound as they move away from being just a 60's cover band." – *Nashville Intelligence Report #8*, 1982

Yet Another View: "Despite the off name and kalimba intro, I figured these Nashvillians for an especially one-dimensional bunch of popsters after happy songs like "This Girl Of Mine" and "You Started Something" provided exactly what they promised. But eventually, wondering about the "Gloria" remake and the psychedelic blues, I realized that one-dimensionality is...not the point, but the payoff. Somehow these guys sincerely inhabit a very '60s-ish reality; their message isn't some kind of distanced commentary on their musical material, it's the material itself. They say they like soul, too, and I believe them. Grade: B+" – Robert Christgau, **Christgau's Record Guide: The '80s**

IV. White Animals (Dread Beat Records 1986, vinyl LP)
Side One
1. Help Yourself (Take What's Left)
2. It's A Jungle
3. Big Shot
4. Don't Wanna Hear That Song
5. Caught Up In The Dread

Side Two
6. She's So Different
7. Not Another Love Song
8. I Can't Wait
9. Old-Fashioned Day
10. Tristan's Woe

Comments: With their fourth effort, the White Animals jettison the covers, sojourn to Memphis, and record with producer and David Byrne sidekick Busta Jones in what was seen by many as a blatant attempt to attract major label attention. As a band resume goes, this self-titled album ain't half-bad, but much of the band's charm was seemingly lost on Jones, and although cover songs had become an important part of the Animals' milieu, they previously had only served as an introduction to the band's fast-improving original songwriting. Still, gotta love "Caught Up In The Dread," a welcome nod and a wink to the band's long-time fans.

V. Live (Dread Beat Records 1986, vinyl LP)
Side One
1. You Started Something
2. (I Gotta) Move
3. Seasons Change

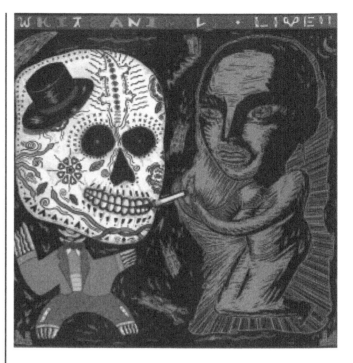

4. Constant Attention
5. Ecstasy
6. Don't Throw Your Love Away
7. I Can't Wait

Side Two
8. Don't Care
9. This Girl Of Mine
10. Love Fades Away
11. Brown-Eyed Girl
12. Not Another Love Song
13. Goodnight And Goodbye

Comments: The White Animals close out '86 with this nifty live LP that mostly captures the band's electric onstage performances and includes a handful of fan favorites like "Don't Care," "Constant Attention," and "This Girl Of Mine."

VI. In The Last Days (Dread Beat Records 1987, vinyl LP)
Side A
1. Don't Treat Me Like A Dog
2. You Bring the Best Out In Me
3. Last Five Years
4. You Don't Know
5. Rock On

Side B
6. A Lonely View
7. She's Gonna Break It
8. Could You Be Loved
9. I Thought That
10. A Prison Song

WHITE ANIMALS

Comments: More of the same, and by now it seems like the band is spinning its wheels and not going anywhere in particular. Sure, there are a bunch of good original songs, and covers of David Essex's "Rock On" and Bob Marley's "Could You Be Loved" for fans to hang their hats on. Still, after almost a decade in the trenches, the White Animals had seen their popularity begin to erode in favor of younger, fresher bands while contemporaries like **Jason & the Scorchers** and latecomers like **Royal Court of China** were being wined, dined, and signed by labels in New York and Los Angeles.

This had to burn the band and their hard-working (but blustery) manager Dave Cannon, and while I've enjoyed a couple of public shouting matches with drummer Ray Crabtree on the subject, there was at least a perceived animosity on the part of the White Animals towards other (higher profile) local bands at the time. They'd go their separate ways after this and disappear for much of the 1990s.

VII. 3,000 Nights In Babylon (Dread Beat Records 1997, CD)
1. Tobacco Road/Need Somebody To Love Me
2. Constant Attention
3. These Boots Are Made For Walking
4. Girls
5. Move
6. Don't Care
7. This Girl Of Mine
8. You Started Something
9. Ecstasy
10. Goodnight And Goodbye
11. Help Yourself
12. Big Shot

13. Don't Wanna Hear That Song
14. Caught Up In The Dread
15. Not Another Love Song
16. Don't Treat Me Like a Dog
17. Gloria

Comments (from the band's web site): "The White Animals were formed in Gawd-a-mighty Nashville, Music City U.S. of A. around 1978. The local live music of that day offered a limited selection of flavors: Top-40, "Black", and "Beach" as well as the obligatory rite-of-passage exposure to Bluegrass and large quantities of beer. Oh yes, there was other music around: "country" [still with few exceptions, a haven for hacks and failed rockers], and "Christian" [a haven for white hacks and failed rockers]. The notion arose that going into a small underground [literally] pub to hear beat versions of *Rubber Soul* Beatles and obscure Byrds album cuts, complete with harmony and some originals sprinkled in would be a good thing. Our motto was "Semper Fi-Jam" which sorta means "turning insurance salesmen into cavemen" Our dream was to wed traditional "punk" or garage-band elements with the D.I.Y. spirit of the times and create a unique "Neo-Classical" rock and roll sound. Along the way, we managed to corrupt an entire generation of young people, have more fun than 10 Frank Sinatras, and make wonderful friends and amazing memories to last a lifetime. Here is the music that fueled it all..."

VIII. White Animals (Dread Beat Records 2001, CD)
1. Future Girl
2. Broken And Lonely
3. Little Hollywood
4. I Can't Give U Anything
5. Let's Say We Didn't
6. Not So Long Ago
7. Elusive
8. Wish It Was You
9. The Last Days Of May
10. Shot Down
11. Kitty

Comments: One last shot at fame after a handful of reunion shows. Although the band members have long since established significant careers outside of the music biz – Gray as a medical doctor, Crabtree in public relations, etc, they still have the itch and after shaking off the rust they recorded this follow-up CD to have some fun and remind fans of their continued relevance.

Dunno why the White Animals never really broke out of the Nashville rock ghetto – they had two self-produced music videos that received steady MTV airplay, they packed 'em in at college campuses and clubs across the Southeast, and they toured with some moderately big names during the 1980s. The band blames its lack of national success on their lack of "hipness" as perceived by the "cultural cognoscenti," but I ain't buying that pig, boys…lack of "hip" may get your record drubbed by the drones in the alternative media (including yours truly), but it don't mean squat to most club owners counting ticket sales, and certainly not to record label execs with dollars in their eyes.

No, there was something else going on there, and the White Animals didn't achieve their potential either because of some fatal flaw on the part of the band, or because of the sometimes overbearing, Peter Grant (Led Zeppelin) management style of Dave Cannon, but whatever it was, the band ain't talkin' about it, even at this late date. After all, even Milli freakin' Vanilli got a major label deal during the 1980s…now that I've raised the ire of every single remaining White Animals fan in Nashville and beyond (and ensured a nasty email from Ray Crabtree), let me say that I always *pulled* for the band, back in the day, and if ever there was a candidate for a deluxe CD reissue series, the White Animals catalog is it (especially the first three albums).

Another View: During the summer of 2011, I met a White Animals fan at the CD Exchange store in Rochester, New York. The guy had found a couple of White Animals LPs in a pile of albums being tossed away by his college radio station in the early 1990s. He quickly fell in love with the band, and was genuinely enthused to find somebody else who was familiar with the White Animals. Evidently he ran across another WA fan online, who burned him a copy of one of the above CDs. Shows how long the band's reach was during the 1980s (and into the '90s), and what the major labels missed by not giving them a chance back in the day.

THE WHITE ROSE REBELLION

Band Members:
Tom Hockensmith (vocals)
Micah Horton (guitars)
Jeff Zeuhlke (bass)
Matt Fisher (drums)

WHO HIT JOHN

Band Members:
Pat Meusel (vocals, bass) (II)
Chuck Tate (guitars, piano, vocals) (II)
Sam Powers (guitars, piano, vocals) (II)
Dean Bratcher (drums, percussion) (II)

Who Hit John Recordings:

I. Who Hit John (self-produced, 1993, cassette)
1. Ornament
2. Pro's From Dover
3. Memory

4. Taste Battery
5. No Hands Down Winner
6. The Clipper
7. No Grand Disguise
8. When Mark's Angry
9. Coke Bottles

Comments: The band also contributed the song "Claim To Fame" to ***Spin Cycle***, the 1997 NeA Extravaganza compilation CD. I don't have the tape so I can't list players…

II. Hey Buffy (Not So Permanent 2000, CD)
1. Smile Together
2. Giving a Twist a Turn
3. Fan Club
4. Claim to Fame
5. Avoid the Fold
6. Don't Lie to Me
7. Incomplete
8. Somebody
9. Mona Lisa
10. Ballad of What Will Never Be
11. Means So Much

Another View: "In the ever-widening world of guitar-driven, powerful pop/rock, Nashville's Who Hit John have produced a record most definitely to be reckoned with. Solid, skillfully executed and never less than tuneful, the eleven songs presented here touch all the requisite musical bases (ie: Big Star's "Don't Lie To Me" plus "The Mona Lisa", a song Cheap Trick should cover FAST) but never stop short at building something new and quite original upon such totems." – Gary Pig Gold, In Music We Trust

WHYTE LACE - WILD FRONTIERS - WEBB WILDER

WHYTE LACE

Band Members:
Jace Tyner (vocals)
Matt Myatt (guitars)
Walt Anthony (guitars)
Jamie Klass (bass)
Billy Sayre (drums)

Comments: At once both one of Nashville's most loathed *and* most notorious hard rock bands, mention Whyte Lace to any of us 1980s-era old timers and you're going to get a reaction. Funny thing, tho', at this late date (March 2010), interest in the band is probably higher than it was 20 years ago, mostly 'cause they remain a largely unknown quantity. I receive several emails weekly from hard rock collectors seeking Whyte Lace demo tapes and a casual search of the Internet will dig up comments about the band on a dozen message boards.

So, exactly what *was* the story behind Whyte Lace? According to a 1987 interview with Kath Hansen in *The Metro* (yes, *that* interview), the band's roots were in L.A. when a band by the name of Destroyer evolved into Whyte Lace and subsequently moved to Nashville. It was Tyner's father, Don Tyner, who made his money in real estate, who managed the band and dropped all the coin on their white limo, practice space, full-color show posters and, well, that hair. Whyte Lace did record a demo tape that included their songs "R.O.C.K.," which is described by Hansen as "an anthemic, fist-punching, chord-banging cruncher"; the melodic "Just One Kiss"; and the "schmaltzy" tune "Dreamgirl." Dunno if they ever played any real gigs

together, outside of industry showcases that were (*surprise*) financed by dad.

Other Whyte Lace facts: the band practiced eight hours a day (how much of that was spent teasing their hair?), they took Dale Carnegie motivational courses, and Myatt was a graduate of the Guitar Institute of Technology. Sorry, but I just can't take 'em seriously…none of this helped them get a record deal which, in 1987 and given the style of music that Whyte Lace professed to play, should have been the band's birthright. I still catch shit from people over the band's full-color *Metro* cover article, as I'm sure other former scribes from the rag do…still, I've never heard a note from them, so I can only point to Whyte Lace as one of the Nashville rock music scene's more interesting phenomena…them, and Golden Spear, that is...

Another View: "Jace's lyrics are hackneyed, clichéd, stupid, childish, unimaginative, and they don't even have any meter, either…less outrageous than Kiss, less ballsy than Bon Jovi…" – anonymous, *Weasel Weekly*, July 1987

WILD FRONTIERS

Band Members:
Jan Heath (vocals, guitar)
Tommy Dorsey (synthesizers)
Mike Kisler (stick, bass)
Giles Reaves (Linn drum)

WEBB WILDER

Band Members:
Webb Wilder (vocals, guitar) (I-VIII, D1)
Denny "Cletus" Blakely (bass, guitar, vocals) (I, II, VII)
George "The Tone Chaperone" Bradfute (guitar, bass) (III-VIII, D1)
Tom Comet (bass) (VI, VIII, D1)
R.S. "The Ionizer" Field (guitar, drums, vocals) (I-VII)
Les James Lester (drums) (I-VIII, D1)
Donny "The Twangler" Roberts (guitar, vocals) (I-III, VII)
Kelly Looney (bass) (IV, V)

Other Musicians:
Scott Baggett (bass, keyboards) (III, V, VII)
Bucky Baxter (pedal steel guitar) (VI)
Tony Bowles (guitars) (VIII, D1)
Steve Conn (keyboards, accordion) (V-VI)
Jimmy Crespo (guitar) (III, VII)
Jerry Douglas (lap steel) (II, VII)
K.K. Falkner (vocals) (V)
Hugh Garraway (saxophone) (II, VII)
Kenny Greenberg (guitar) (III, VII)
David Grissom (guitar, vocals) (II, V, VII)
Steve Herrman (trumpet) (VI)

Jim Hoke (saxophone) (II-III, VII)
Thomas Johnson (Theramin) (V)
Craig Kampf (drums) (III, VII)
Al Kooper (keyboards) (III, VII)
Sonny Landreth (guitar) (III, VII)
Jim Liban (harmonica) (I, VII)
Bill Lloyd (guitar) (III, VII)
Carl Marsh (bass) (II, VII)
Greg Morrow (bass) (III, VII)
Rick Price (bass) (III, VII)
Billy Prince (bass) (I, VII)
Rick "Casper" Rawls (guitar) (V)
Jared Reynolds (vocals) (VI)
Rich Ruth (bass) (III)
Dennis Taylor (saxophone) (VI)
Willy Weeks (bass) (II, VII)
Carson Whitsett (keyboards) (I, VII)
Wally Wilson (piano) (I, VII)
Glen Worf (bass) (III, VII)

Webb Wilder Recordings:

I. It Came From Nashville (Landslide Records 2004, CD)
1. How Long Can She Last (Going That Fast)
2. Horror Hayride
3. I'm Burning
4. Is This All There Is?

5. Devil's Right Hand
6. Move On Down The Line
7. One Taste Of The Bait
8. I'm Wise To You
9. It Gets In Your Blood
10. Poolside
11. Ruff Rider
12. Keep It On Your Mind
13. Rock 'n Roll Ruby
14. Samson & Delilah's Beauty Shop
15. Cactus Planet
16. Dance For Daddy
17. Adam Dread Intro
18. Rock Therapy
19. Who Is Webb Wilder
20. Hole in my Pocket
21. Webb Wilder Credo
22. Pretty Little Lights of Town
23. Inner Space Rap
24. Rocket to Nowhere
25. Steppin' Out
26. Webb's Theme

Comments: The mighty Webb Wilder, the "Last of the Full Grown Men," came to Nashville with his buddy R.S. "Bobby" Field from Hattiesburg, Mississippi in order to conquer the music industry. Wilder and Field played together

Whyte Lace

in a short-lived band called the Viewmasters and Field also played with the Howlers (later to be known as blues-rockers Omar & the Howlers). Wilder put together the original Beatnecks with guitarist Donny Roberts, bassist Denny Blakely, and Field on drums (later replaced by Les James Lester, also of **Los Straitjackets**).

The album that introduced the world to the talents of the mighty Webb Wilder was released on vinyl in 1986 by indie Racket Records (in a "limited edition" of 1500 copies) and again in 1993 by Watermelon Records, Wilder's label at the time. Credited to "Webb Wilder and the Beatnecks" and produced by Field (a/k/a "The Ionizer"), *It Came From Nashville* masterfully and recklessly mixed roots-rock, blues, country and R&B into an entirely original musical gumbo.

The album was reissued on CD for a second time in 2004 by Landslide as "The Deluxe Full-Grown Edition" with ten newly-discovered "bonus" tracks from the same live 1986 Exit/In show that was the source for performances on the original LP release. (See review ➔)

Another View: "Wilder is about as country as Olivia Newton-John. He's got one of those pencil-necked voices like he not only went to college (which lots of real men and good old boys do these days) but maybe even prep school. His Steve Earle cover beats his Hank Williams cover, and his best song is about hanging out by a pool with a rule against dogs. And I almost don't care. Any Nashvillean who can honestly urge all his 'patrons in the teen and sub-teen demographic to pursue happiness at every opportunity' gets slack from me. Grade: B" – Robert Christgau, **Christgau's Record Guide: The '80s**

II. Hybrid Vigor (Island Records/Praxis 1989, CD)
1. Hittin' Where It Hurts
2. Human Cannonball
3. Do You Know Something (That I Don't Know)
4. Cold Front
5. Safeside
6. Wild Honey
7. What's Got Wrong With You?
8. Ain't That A Lot Of Love?
9. Skeleton Crew
10. Louisiana Hannah

Comments: Wilder's association with **Jack Emerson** and Andy McLenon at Praxis led to a major label deal with Island Records, which subsequently under-promoted this album to death. It has some great songs on it, though, like "Hittin' Where It Hurts" and "Human Cannonball." Produced, like much of Wilder's recorded milieu, by R.S. Field.

III. Doo Dad (Zoo Entertainment/Praxis 1991, CD)
1. Hoodoo Witch
2. Tough It Out
3. Meet Your New Landlord
4. Sittin' Pretty
5. Big Time
6. Sputnik
7. Run With It
8. King Of The Hill
9. Everyday (I Kick Myself)
10. The Rest (Will Take Care Of Itself)
11. Baby Please Don't Go
12. I Had Too Much To Dream (Last Night)

Comments: Wilder's jump to Zoo Entertainment, a BMG-distributed label, resulted in another solid album and more great songs in tunes like "Hoodoo Witch," "The Rest (Will Take Care Of Itself)" and "Big Time." Inspired covers of "Baby Please Don't Go" and the Electric Prunes' classic "I Had Too Much To Dream (Last Night)" rounded out a hard-rocking, entertaining album. **Bill Lloyd** and **Sonny Landreth** make guest appearances, as does the legendary **Al Kooper**.

IV. Town & Country (Watermelon Records 1995, CD)
1. Stay Out Of Automobiles
2. Nashville Bum
3. Slow Death
4. (I'm A) Lover Not A Fighter
5. To The Loving Public (spoken)
6. Honky Tonk Hell
7. My Mind's Eye
8. Too Many Rivers
9. Goldfinger
10. Hissy-Fit (spoken)
11. Talk Talk
12. Streets of Laredo (The Cowboy's Lament)
13. Short On Love
14. I Ain't Living Long Like This
15. Original Mixed-Up Kid
16. Rockin' Little Angel

Comments: Perhaps the most eclectic "covers" album in the history of rock & roll, featuring Wilder's unique readings of material from Waylon Jennings ("Nashville Bum"), the Flamin' Groovies ("Slow Death"), the Music Machine ("Talk Talk"), Rodney Crowell, and Mott The Hoople, among others.

V. Acres of Suede (Watermelon Records 1996, CD)
1. The Olde Elephant Man
2. No Great Shakes
3. Loud Music
4. Fall In Place
5. Flat Out Get It
6. Soul Mate
7. Scattered, Smothered and Covered
8. Tell Me Why Charlene
9. Why Do You Call?
10. Carryin' The News to Mary
11. Lost In The Shuffle
12. Rocket To Nowhere

Comments: The last Webb Wilder album for almost a decade, Wilder and Field take one last stab at grabbing the brass ring with incredible songs like "No Great Shakes" and "Scattered, Smothered and Covered." It was to no avail, however, since Watermelon went belly up shortly after the album's release, taking with them any possibility of promotion and tying up Wilder's releases for the label in limbo for years afterwards (see review ➔).

Webb Wilder

VI. About Time (Landslide Records 2005, CD)
1. Down On The Farm
2. I Just Had To Laugh
3. You Might Be Lonely For A Reason
4. Miss Missy From Ol' Hong Kong
5. If You're Looking For A Fool
6. Tell The World
7. Jimmy Reed Is The King Of Rock'n'Roll
8. Scattergun
9. Battle Of The Bands
10. Old Copper Penny
11. Mary Lou
12. Move It
13. The Only One
14. Little Boy Sad
15. Scattergun (instrumental)

Comments: After a hiatus of nine long years, Webb Wilder – The Hillbilly God of Rock 'N' Soul – ventured back into the studio with longtime foil R.S. Field to record this pretty cool "comeback" album (see review ➔).

VII. Scattered, Smothered and Covered: A Webb Wilder Overview (Varese Sarabande 2005, CD)
1. How Long Can She Last (Going that Fast)[1]
2. Horror Hayride[1]
3. Poolside[1]
4. One Taste of the Bait[1]
5. Ruff Rider[1]
6. Is This All There Is?[1]
7. Scattered, Smothered, and Covered[3]
8. Flat Out Get It[3]
9. Stay Out of Automobiles[2]

10. Slow Death[2]
11. Fall in Place[3]
12. Loud Music[3]
13. The Webb Wilder Credo
14. Honky Tonk Hell[2]
15. My Mind's Eye[2]
16. Rocket to Nowhere[3]
17. I Ain't Living Long Like This[2]
18. Carryin' the News to Mary[3]
19. No Great Shakes[3]

Comments: Not many Nashville rockers have hung around long enough to have an honest-to-god "best of" collection issued, but here it is, a Webb Wilder "overview" that takes a long look at a small part of the big man's musical genius. ***Scattered, Smothered and Covered*** collects tracks from the *It Came From Nashville* [(1)], *Town & Country* [(2)] and *Acres of Suede* [(3)] albums – basically, Webb's independent first album (which was reissued on CD in 1993 by Watermelon) and the other two Watermelon label releases. Unfortunately, it includes none of the brilliant material from the long out-of-print major label albums…someday, maybe, someday…

VIII. Born To Be Wilder (Blind Pig Records 2008, CD)
1. Tough It Out
2. Stay Out Of Automobiles
3. Baby Please Don't Go
4. You Might Be Lonely For A Reason
5. One Taste Of The Bait
6. Human Cannonball
7. If You're Looking For A Fool
8. Sputnik
9. Big Time

10. No Great Shakes
11. Miss Missy From Ol' Hong Kong
12. Poolside
13. How Long Can She Last
14. Louisiana Hannah
15. I Just Had To Laugh

Comments: Essentially the set documented by the ***Tough It Out*** DVD, recorded live in Birmingham, Alabama in 2005 for a PBS TV special. The CD is identical to the audio bonus disc packaged with the DVD…not my favorite Webb Wilder performance, but Webb's manager and others have told me that the situation was one of stopping, restarting and redoing songs to get them on tape rather than just letting WW and crew rip through 'em, as is their hallowed tradition.

D1. Tough It Out (Landslide DVD, 2006)
1. Flat Out Get It
2. If You're Looking For A Fool
3. I Just Had To Laugh
4. Sputnik
5. One Taste Of The Bait
6. Big Time
7. You Might Be Lonely For A Reason
8. Human Cannonball
9. Poolside
10. The Rest Will Take Care Of Itself
11. Down On The Farm
12. No Great Shakes
13. Miss Missy From Old Hong Kong
14. Louisiana Hannah
15. How Long Can She Last
16. Stay Out Of Automobiles
17. Tough It Out
18. Baby Please Don't' Go

Comments: Wilder's first DVD is a lackluster set of otherwise rockin' songs, performed for a PBS television special in Birmingham, Alabama in August 2005 by some of Webb's best musical collaborators. Packaged with an audio CD of the show. Now will somebody just throw up a couple of cameras and let WW and the Beatnecks perform the way that God intended?

WILL & THE BUSHMEN

Band Members:
Will Kimbrough (vocals, guitars, keyboards) (I-IV)
Sam Baylor (guitars, bass, vocals) (I-IV)
Mark Pfaff (bass, harmonica, vocals) (I-IV)
Bryan Owings (drums) (II-III)
Mike Connell (drums) (I)
John Etheridge (drums) (I)

Will & the Bushmen, continued on page 561…

WEBB WILDER AND THE BEATNECKS
It Came From Nashville (Deluxe Full-Grown Edition)
(Landslide Records)

Brothers and sisters, I want to share the good word about Webb Wilder and the Beatnecks and their magnificent debut *It Came From Nashville*! This will make the third time since 1987 that the Reverend has reviewed this particular album. Not surprisingly, in a corporate music world dominated by airheaded, lip-syncing Barbie dolls and angry male fashion models with out-of-tune guitars, *It Came From Nashville* holds up remarkably well. In fact, much like fine wine, this version – the album's third incarnation (vinyl, CD w/bonus tracks, CD w/more bonus tracks) – has only gotten better with age.

For you poor souls who have never experienced the greatness of the man known to legions as "WW," this is where it all began, a humble introduction to a Wilder world. Roaring into the Music City like a drunken tornado sometime during the mid-80s, WW quickly assembled a top-notch musical hit squad, a finely-tuned machine of rock & roll salvation helmed by the man behind the throne, Bobby Fields. Although a vinyl recording is a poor substitute for the magnificence that is WW in person, *It Came From Nashville* did a pretty doggoned good job of capturing the spirit – the zeitgeist, if you will – of the man from Mississippi. Wilder, Fields and crew masterfully mixed roots rock, country and blues with elements of psychdelica, swamp rock and surf music. Imagine Hank Williams, Robert Johnson and Screamin' Jay Hawkins sharing a beer at the crossroads in a midnight jam session and you'd come close to the sound of *It Came From Nashville*.

Friends, Webb Wilder and the Beatnecks hit Nashville like a double-shot of whiskey with a six-pack chaser. Along with Jason & the *Nashville* Scorchers, WW and his posse allowed a bunch of cornpone punk rockers to break loose and embrace the reckless country soul of their ancestors. After eighteen years, the songs on *It Came From Nashville* still rock like a house afire! From "How Long Can She Last," Fields' ode to youthful indiscretion, to the original album-closing instrumental rave-up "Ruff Rider," these songs are muscular, electric and 100% high-octane rock & roll. An inspired cover of Steve Earle's "Devil's Right Hand" showcases both Wilder's sense of humor and his deep, friendly baritone in this tragic tale. "One Taste Of The Bait" speaks of the dangers of love while "Is This All There Is?" is a kiss-off to failed romance on par with Dylan's "Positively 4th Street."

The original CD reissue bonus tracks are included here, a motley bunch of spirited covers that illustrate Wilder's range and tastes. From a raucous rendition of Johnny Cash's "Rock 'n Roll Ruby" to a swinging reading of Steve Forbert's

"Samson And Delilah's Beauty Shop," these are all keepers. Fields' instrumental "Cactus Planet" provides a rollicking good time while "Dance For Daddy" is a down-and-dirty, leering rocker with scrappy guitarwork. The six new live tracks included here were culled from a vintage 1986 Nashville performance at the world-famous Exit/In and include rarities like the rockabilly-flavored "Hole In My Pocket" and an early version of fan favorite "Rocket To Nowhere."

If *It Came From Nashville* introduced the world to its rock & roll savior, the album also marked Bobby Fields' emergence as a songwriter of some skill and knowledge. These songs have held up so well over time because they are rooted in the deep tradition of rock, blues and country that was forged by pioneers like Elvis, Hank and Chuck. Unfortunately, the world has turned so much that these men have mostly been lost in the haze of pre-fab pop stars and soft drink advertising. Even a prophet like WW is without honor in his own country, although a loyal cult of followers continues to keep the flame burning. Rescued from the abyss of obscurity, *It Came From Nashville* is an important document of a time when giants roamed this planet and men were unashamed to follow the *Webb Wilder Credo*:

"Work hard…rock hard…eat hard…sleep hard…grow big…wear glasses if you need 'em." Amen….
– *Alt.Culture.Guide*, 2004

CD REVIEW: WEBB WILDER'S ACRES OF SUEDE

WEBB WILDER
Acres Of Suede
(Watermelon Records)

Webb Wilder has been kicking around the Southeast for about a decade now, wowing a loyal audience with an inspired musical blend of roots rock, R & B, country and raving psychobilly. He's done the major label thing, made a couple of passes through Europe, released a handful of critically-acclaimed records while touring the states constantly and still can't get a decent shot at the "big time." His latest effort, the wonderful *Acres Of Suede*, may not get Wilder noticed by a fickle, trend-oriented music-buying public, but it's a damn fine record nonetheless.

A stylistically diverse collection of tunes delivered with heaping portions of sincerity and passion, *Acres Of Suede* offers a musical soundtrack provided by a loose-knit collection of talented Nashville-area musicians which includes six-string wizard George "The Tone Chaperone" Bradfute and moonlighting Los Straitjackets' drummer Les James Lester. With long-time Wilder co-conspirator R.S. Field sharing production duties and collaborating on 11 of the album's 12 songs, the table is set for a typically wonderful WW musical experience.

Acres Of Suede delivers on every expectation, a dozen rollicking tunes that run the stylistic gamut. *Fall In Place* is as poetic a tale of the diminished beauty of the South as has ever been written, delivered by Wilder in a gentle baritone while accompanied by K.K. Faulkner's soft, melodic backing vocals. *Flat Out Get It* is a rockabilly-styled rave-up, while *Why Do You Call?* offers a tale of unrequited love from a different perspective. *Scattered, Smothered and Covered* offers a tale of seduction gone awry, mostly spoken lyrics backed by a steady repetitive riff, the choruses punched up with a sort of mid-sixties Mersey Beat sound. *Lost In The Shuffle* evokes memories of Stevie Ray, being a fine representation of Texas barroom blues. *Acres Of Suede* closes with the psychotronic *Rocket To Nowhere*, a classic swamp-rocker filled with trembling guitars and pounding drums that propel Wilder's deep, mesmerizing vocals to new heights.

While not exclusively a "Southern Artist," Wilder nonetheless brings all of the fervor of a tent revival to his albums, drawing upon the cultural depth and musical heritage of the old South in creating his trademark sound. Wilder's entire persona, the self-created and near-legendary "Last of the Full-Grown Men" is, indeed, an alter-ego unique to the South. The last of the boarding house residents, a rootless wanderer who knows every blue plate diner, greasy spoon and thrift store in town, Wilder's character is the sort that never gets married, never has children, is always polite and seems to travel through life on a plane apart from we mere

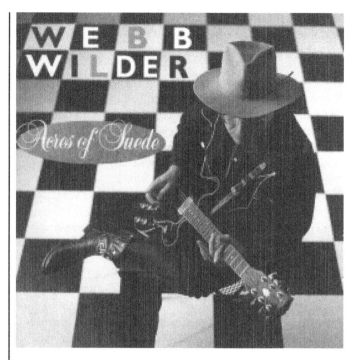

mortals. Although every aspect of this character may not be an accurate representation of Wilder himself, with every passing season it becomes more so.

It's a powerful image, one perfectly suited to the music that Wilder performs and obviously cherishes. In the end, Wilder's biggest asset – the persona that allows him the luxury of life as a performer – may also be his greatest liability, mainstream audiences unyielding in their lack of acceptance of Wilder's charm and ability. He must either reconcile himself to eternal cult status and critical acclaim, and thus continue his considerable career on that basis, or throw in the towel altogether. For those of us who can see beyond the mask to the artist underneath, we certainly look forward to more from this underrated talent.
– R Squared, 1996

CD REVIEW: WEBB WILDER'S ABOUT TIME

WEBB WILDER
About Time
(Landslide Records)

It's been nearly nine years since Webb Wilder last came 'round these parts with a new phonograph recording and we've all been that much poorer for his absence. Heck, during the great one's hiatus we've suffered through nu-metal, modern rock, Britney Spears, boy bands and Geo. Bush – a veritable cultural famine of Biblical proportions. You don't have to tie up that noose and throw it over the rafters just yet, bunkie, 'cause our year is about to get a whole lot "wilder" and this scribe can only exclaim that it's "about time!"

Rounding up his "A" Team of veteran players, studio monsters like guitarist George Bradfute, bassist Tom Comet and drummer Jimmy Lester, Webb Wilder has again hooked up with his long-time partner in crime, the "Ionizer," R.S. Field to record *About Time*. As comeback albums go, it's really like ol' Webb never left; you can't really call these grooves a "return to form" because Wilder has never abandoned his pure, untarnished vision of rock & roll with a touch of country and blues. Sure, Wilder spices up the brew now and then with some fine brasswork courtesy of Dennis Taylor and Steve Herrman, the band sounding like some R&B revue of old. Overall, old time fans of the "last full-grown man" won't be disappointed by the track selection found on *About Time*.

For those of you unfamiliar with Webb Wilder, or those who only know him through his XM satellite radio program, *About Time* will hit you like that first kiss in the backseat of your daddy's jalopy. The songs on *About Time* stand as tall as the singer, a fine combination of roots rock and Southern fried influences. "Scattergun," for instance, is a somber, Marty Robbins-styled old west tale of tragedy while "Battle Of The Bands" is a '50s-flavored rockabilly rave-up with rollicking horns and swinging rhythms. "I Just Had To Laugh" is a typical, old-school Field/Wilder lyrical collaboration about the trials of romance, offering plenty of clever wordplay, Wilder's magnificent baritone and some mesmerizing fretwork from Bradfute.

"Miss Missy From Ol' Hong Kong" is a roadhouse rocker with Steve Conn channeling the spirit of a young Jerry Lee on the ivories. As Wilder speaks of Missy's many attributes, the rest of the band teeters on the edge, blowing the roof off the mutha with instrumental interplay as tight as a fist and honed to a surgical-edge by 1,001 nights spent performing on the road. Wilder reworks Tommy Overstreet's early-70s country classic "If You're Looking For A Fool" with a heartbreaking, bittersweet tone that is punctuated by Bradfute's sadly weeping guitar. Kevin Gordon's excellent "Jimmy Reed Is The King Of Rock And Roll" is provided a

bluesy, ethereal reading that brings to mind John Campbell's voodoo king, knee deep in the swamp, howling at the moon while Hank's ghost-driven Cadillac careens around a corner, down Broadway and away from the Ryman.

There's more, but you're just going to have to pick up a copy of *About Time* for yourself and discover the mystery, the madness and the magic of the man called Wilder. Giants standing proudly above lesser talents, Webb Wilder and the Nashvegans deliver in *About Time* a tonic for our troubled days and times. Welcome back, boys!
– *Alt.Culture.Guide*, 2005

THE OTHER SIDE OF NASHVILLE   - 557 -

INTERVIEW: WEBB WILDER

Not too long ago, I picked up a zine – I don't remember its title, but the rag was reviewing several other zines – and one zine got a positive review based mainly on the fact that they had run a piece on Nashville's own Webb Wilder, "Last Of The Full-Grown Men." I thought that it was pretty cool that Wilder – a cult favorite if there's ever been one – was being considered the new standard of what was cool and what wasn't in today's pop culture. "That's great to hear," says the man, himself, "that's the kind of stuff that encourages you that there will be some sort of steamroller of momentum."

For Wilder, who has recorded five albums and toured the globe at least twice during almost a decade and a half, every word of encouragement is a welcome one. Although possessing a loyal following, Wilder's energetic and unique blend of pop, roots rock, blues and country has thus far failed to find an audience with mainstream listeners. Coupled with a distinctive baritone voice and a charismatic stage persona that is part nineteen-fifties B-movie Private Eye and part self-styled psychedelic shaman, Wilder creates the most consistently entertaining and listenable albums on the musical horizon today.

Not that Wilder ever had a chance to be anything but a rock god. "I was into it right out of the womb," says Wilder of his decision to become a musician. "My aunt, who is a dear lady named Montressa Wilder, says that I sang before I talked. I don't think that I'm a musically gifted person, but I've always loved music and always had rhythm and songs and words in my head and an affinity for show business and make-believe."

"I was into music before the Beatles," says Webb, but the Beatles and the British Rock invasion was so good, so significant, so appealing to me as the only fourth grader who already had records. That really kicked me into high gear. Before that, I was interested in Elvis and Rickey Nelson, Hank Williams and the Everly Brothers. That's what was there in the Ben Franklin Dime Store in the suburbs of Hattiesburg, Mississippi. There were country music shows on television, the Ed Sullivan Show and variety shows that featured music...a local show called McCaffrey's Showtime that sometimes had people that were so horrible that they were wonderful."

It wasn't until much later in life, however, when Wilder hit the thirty year milestone, that he decided to dedicate his life to both kinds of music – rock *and* roll. "I had stopped and started a lot of regular straight jobs that I had washed out of because I was more interested in music." He ended up in Nashville. "The band that I was in at the time was a band called the Drapes, and we were based out of Hattiesburg, which isn't a good place to be based out of if you're serious about going somewhere in the music business," recalls Wilder. "One of the things that our band had aspired to do was to relocate to a music center."

"We had a female singer, Suzy Elkins, who was a little older, married; her husband had a good career at the time as a helicopter pilot, working for the oil companies offshore. New Orleans seemed like the place that made the most sense for him to go to. I couldn't dig the idea of going there, so we didn't go anywhere, and later broke up for different reasons. I had lived in Nashville in 1974 and '75, and I had lived in Austin around '77. I like Austin a lot, but I knew one guy here who is in the business, and the business is here, and although I didn't want to pursue, necessarily, a mainstream straight country thing, there was more than that here. I figured that I'd probably end up in a 'van band' routed out of Nashville, and it was a better place to route out of...which all certainly turned out to be true."

Since coming to Nashville, Wilder has developed a knack for attracting good musicians who, unfortunately, later go onto bigger and better things. Musical contributors to Wilder's albums include guitarists Sonny Landreth and Kenny Greenburg and bassist Rick Price; his regular band has included talents like drummer Les James Lester (Los Straitjackets) and bassist Kelly Looney (Steve Earle). What is it about his music that enables him to enlist some of the region's best players?

"I do think that I've had some pretty good musicians," says Wilder, "and some of them have gone on to some pretty good things. I wish that I could say that they've gone on to wonderful things, like getting rich. I think that it's fun for them to play...I don't think that it's because I'm such a musical wellspring. Unfortunately, there's a whole lot of square music out there, and those are some of the gigs that people have to get. I think that my thing is anything but square and I think that musicians like to play it. In the last few years, there's been a good measure of premeditated spontaneity, because sometimes we just go off into stuff that we don't know – which is probably more fun for us than for the audience."

"I had such a stable line-up for a long time that I really had come to believe that was what you had to do," says Wilder. "I've run through a lot of people not because they quit or I fired them, but because by the time I got around to needing them, they had previous commitments. I've gone through a lot of bass players it seems like, lately, and they were all great. I'm on my third guitar player (George Bradfute) and he's great, and I'm on my third drummer and he's great, also."

After a couple of late-eighties / early-nineties major label releases, Wilder later resurfaced on Austin's acclaimed indie Watermelon Records label. How did he end up on the Texas label? "I guess this is the biggest faux pas in the world to say," exclaims Wilder, "but it's true – we have the same lawyer, which is supposed to be suicide. We had the first album, *It Came From Nashville*; sadly, it had wound up, for various reasons other than demand, oddly enough, going out of print. They were interested in reissuing it and have done so, and that was the beginning of our relationship with them. We dug it and it wasn't like people were beating down our doors, and they were there to make some records for us, so we did."

Recently, Wilder has taken his lone wolf, hard-boiled image into the literary world. In an extension of his private eye persona seen on the Night Flight videos, Webb Wilder P.I. is the protagonist in a wonderful and entertaining double-sided, two story book titled **Webb Wilder And The Molemen**. How did Wilder end up on the pages of a mystery novel?

"I wish that I had a concise answer for that – I almost don't know," says Wilder. "I first worked with Shane Caldwell, who is one of the two authors of the book, when Bobby Field and myself cast him in the role of Carlsbad Deveraux in our *Horror Hayride* film, which came out later on the **Cornflicks** video on BMG. I had met Steve Boyle before that, casually, and he is and was a video director, among other things. Somehow, we all came together."

"Steve had wanted Shane and I to do some video vignettes, short promos for the Hard Rock Cafe to play in their inside programming. Steve puts together these long tapes, music videos with things between them. We did some short, goofy things for that and he had the idea that it would be cool to put a package together and try and develop a Webb Wilder television series...the Molemen idea came out of that, and Shane and Steve went and wrote the script for that and, later, The Doll, and then they thought that we might attract attention for these ideas by putting them in the classic pulp novel form so that the average person could read it. It seemed like kind of a companion to the film noir film, anyway, so there you have it. They had a bunch printed up and there you go."

The response to **Webb Wilder And The Moleman** has been encouraging, the book selling most of its first printing and attracting favorable comments from both Wilder fans and hard-core mystery readers. "We did a signing, and sort of reading/mini-concert thing at Davis-Kidd here in Nashville and it was incredibly well attended. We've had various responses to it. People have pointed out that it's rife with misprints and typos, which is true, but response has been good."

Outside of a loyal cult audience, Wilder is mostly unknown, even after five albums, to the American music-buying public. He has also earned significant followings across Europe and in Canada. It is in France, though, where he has found his greatest popularity, a fact that mystifies even Wilder. "I talk better than I sing, and I'm certainly no Eric Clapton on the guitar," says Wilder. "I've been thinking about that. Country music, for instance, is not big in France. The reason for this is that a large part of what's happening in country is the lyrics. Therefore, it's more popular in countries that speak the English language. We have some great lyrics to some of our songs, but the beat is more important that the lyrics in some others, and I think that must be it. There's enough sizzle that they go for the steak, enough beat that they like it. They really prefer speaking French, but they like American stuff and they get some of the lyrics, but they like stuff that's – and I hate this word – 'packaged' as classic iconography. Maybe I'm inherently that, I don't know."

Continuing, Wilder asks, "but then, why is it popular in Chicago? We get airplay there and people know about it." There are also other Webb 'hotspots' across the country. "The most pronounced ones, due to the exposure, are in Chicago, where WZRT, a big-time station, who have treated every release as though it were a big deal whether it was or not. Austin, Houston, Dallas, have done pretty good, Jackson, Mississippi, even L.A. – believe it or not – has done pretty well. There are fans everywhere; it's just 'how many of them?' you know?"

INTERVIEW: WEBB WILDER

On his albums and during live performances, Wilder has frequently dipped into his encyclopedic knowledge of musical history to unearth choice musical nuggets to cover. In 1995, with his current band the Nashvegans, Webb decided to record an entire album of classic obscure rock and country covers. "It bought us more time to finish the originals," says Wilder of the **Town & Country** album, "and we wanted to do it. We knew that it would be fun, and it was. It was about seven seconds ahead of its time," he adds. "I'm not going to say that it is the best one," of his albums, says Wilder, "but it was the most fun. We've been fortunate that when we picked the most over-worked song, people loved it and said that we had one of the best versions, which was *Baby, Please Don't Go*. On this album, we picked our own weird collection of songs."

Wilder adds, "we had made the deal with Watermelon – you know, small labels have small budgets, and money isn't everything, but it can help you make a better record. You can spend more time or buy better stuff or whatever. To get the budget up, we had said 'how about a 2-for-1 thing?' so we got a 'one' budget that was bigger than a 'two' would be....I wish that I knew how to answer questions where I just didn't have to tell the truth, because nobody does, and it usually comes back on you. That's the truth, though, and we knew if we made two and we made the one with the original songs on it second, we could get them written." That album of original tunes was released a year later as the critically-acclaimed *Acres Of Suede*.

Who would Webb Wilder play with on his next album, if he could play with anyone? "I do have the fantasy sometimes that it would be cool to play and not sing and try to be as good a guitar player as I can be. Somewhere on the Internet, is an answer to a question like 'if I could put together a great band, who would it be?' In my case, it would be Ian McLagan, James Burton and all these people. It would be fun to play with different people. It was fun to play with Al Kooper on **Doo Dad.** It would be cool to work with Rick Danko, I'd be playing rhythm guitar and he'd be playing bass, or Duck Dunn. Be Steve Cropper for a day and play with the MGs. The thing is, though, is that he's better at being Steve Cropper than I am, so I don't have those fantasies as much as I once did."

"My latest fantasy – and this is another time where I'm being honest and I don't why – is that someone famous would stand up and say 'Webb Wilder is good.' I don't think that I have that, where a name brand rock & roller has come out for me in some sort of way. It may never happen, but it would feel good..." – *R Squared*

Will & the Bushmen, continued...

Will & the Bushmen Recordings:

I. Gawk (Waxy Silver Records 1999, CD)
1. Numbers
2. All In The Family
3. Feeling Around
4. Academia
5. Faith In Love
6. Bus Stop
7. Neil Young
8. 500 Miles
9. Typical World
10. Like Laughing
11. Dear Alex
12. Walking Alone
13. Even Wheelville
14. She's No Angel

Comments: *Gawk* was originally released on cassette by the band in 1985 and reissued on vinyl two years later. **Will Kimbrough** brought the band's excellent debut to CD on his Waxy Silver label in 2000, adding four bonus tracks.

II. Will & the Bushmen (SBK Records 1989, CD/LP)
1. House Of Mirrors
2. Book Of Love
3. Typical World
4. Blow Me Up
5. 500 Miles
6. Kimberly Stews
7. Three Girls From Detroit

8. Doubts
9. It's Gonna Be Alright
10. Like Laughing

Comments: After releasing *Gawk* in their Birmingham, Alabama backyard, Will & the Bushmen were persuaded to move to Nashville where more of a music scene was percolating in the late 1980s. Signed to SBK Records, a Capitol label imprint, the band entered the studio with noted producer Richard Gottehrer. The band's self-titled debut received rave reviews but suffered as SBK seemed to shuffle its available promotional dollars towards…*gulp*…Vanilla Ice and the *Teenage Mutant Ninja Turtles* movie soundtrack.

III. Suck On This EP (SBK Records 1989, CD)
1. Suck On This
2. Dear Alex
3. Moosehead
4. Can't Turn Back the Clock
5. Shake Some Action

Comments: Live 5-song EP released by SBK to promote the band's self-titled LP.

IV. Blunderbuss (Core Entertainment/SBK 1991, CD)
1. D.C. To Moscow
2. So Close
3. Dabble On
4. The Blunderbuss
5. Month of Sundays
6. Never Another Mother
7. Sgt. Surrender
8. Moosehead
9. Can't Turn Back The Clock
10. Laugh About It Later
11. The Very Last Time

Comments: The band's third proper album, the recording of *Blunderbuss* was paid for by SBK, but the label licensed it to independent label Core Entertainment. Funny story – Core founder Keith Dressel originally launched the label in Atlanta, later moving to L.A. to be closer to the heart of the music biz. After the city's Rodney King riots, however, Keith told me that when he saw a couple of guys running down the street in front of his office carrying a couch, he knew that it was time to move again.

Core relocated to Nashville, where the label had some success with folks like the Vigilantes of Love, Ed-E Roland (later of Collective Soul) and Nashville's own **Jet Black Factory**. **Will Kimbrough**, of course, would go on to a critically-acclaimed solo career, a productive creative partnership with Tommy Womack in both **the bis-quits** and **Daddy**, and his full-time gig as one of the best guitar-pickers in Nashville that actually pays the bills.

HANK WILLIAMS III

HANK WILLIAMS III

Band Members:
Hank Williams III (vocals, guitar, drums) (I-V)
Jason Brown (standup bass) (I, II)
Joe Buck (standup bass, accordion) (III, IV)
Zach Shedd (standup bass) (V)
Randy Kohrs (dobro, guitar) (II-IV)
Shawn McWilliams (drums) (II-V)

Other Musicians:
Chris Carmichael (fiddle) (II, IV)
Tim Carter (banjo) (III, V)
Billy Contreras (fiddle) (IV-V)
Charlie Cushman (banjo) (IV, V)
Joe Fazzio (drums) (III)
Paul Franklin (steel guitar) (I)
Andy Gibson (steel guitar) (III-V)
Travis Gillespie (harmonica) (III)
Danny Herron (fiddle, banjo) (III, IV)
Johnny Hiland (guitar) (III-V)
Rod Janzen (guitar) (III)
Dale Krover (drums) (I)
Daniel Mason (banjo) (V)
Andy McOwen (fiddle) (IV)
Greg Morrow (drums) (I)
Kayton Roberts (steel guitar) (I, II)
Brent Rowan (guitar) (I)
Gary Sommers (fiddle) (IV)
Michael Spriggs (guitar) (I)
Bob Wayne (guitar, bass, vocals) (IV)

Hank Williams III Recordings:

I. Risin' Outlaw (Curb Records 1999, CD)
1. I Don't Know
2. You're The Reason
3. If The Shoe Fits
4. 87 Southbound
5. Lonesome For You
6. What Did Love Ever Do To You
7. On My Own
8. Honky Tonk Girls
9. Devil's Daughter
10. Cocaine Blues
11. Thunderstorms and Neon Signs
12. Why Don't You Leave Me Alone?
13. Blue Devil

Comments: Better known as "Hank III," Hank Williams III – the son of Hank Jr. and grandson of the country music legend – could have taken the easy way out, riding along on the good family name and cranking out the sort of Music Row pabulum that's become the norm these days.

Hank 3

To his credit, Hank 3 is a little too wild and unpredictable to fit into today's country marketing mold. As influenced by punk rock and heavy metal as he is by classic country twang – he's played with former Pantera frontman Phil Anselmo's band Superjoint Ritual as well as his own hardcore band **Assjack** – Hank 3 is like a horse bucking his rider, and his signing to the ultra-conservative, ultra-traditional Curb Records was sure to result in a wild 'n' wooly relationship.

Indeed, Hank 3 disowns this debut album as too influenced by the label and while I haven't heard this one, it includes only a handful of original compositions, so it's safe to say that Hank was horsewhipped into making this one in a safe-as-milk manner, more Music Row than Lower Broadway, if you catch my drift...

Another View: "Hank Williams III's debut album ***Risin' Outlaw*** presents 13 tracks that show Williams' affection for authentic, rough around the edges country..."
– Heather Phares, *All Music Guide*

II. Lovesick, Broke & Driftin' (Curb Records 2002, CD)
1. 7 Months, 39 Days
2. Broke, Lovesick & Driftin'
3. Cecil Brown
4. Lovin' & Huggin'
5. One Horse Town

6. Mississippi Mud
7. Whiskey, Weed, & Women
8. Trashville
9. Walkin' With Sorrow
10. 5 Shots Of Whiskey
11. Nighttime Ramblin' Man
12. Callin' Your Name
13. Atlantic City

Comments: Hank 3's sophomore album is more up to snuff than his doubting, doubtful debut, probably because he produced the disc himself in his home studio and contributed a dozen new original tracks instead of relying on country honk songwriters.

III. Straight To Hell (Curb Records 2006, CD)
Disc One
1. Medley: Satan Is Real/Straight to Hell
2. Thrown out of the Bar
3. Things You Do to Me
4. Country Heroes
5. D. Ray White
6. Low Down
7. Pills I Took
8. Smoke & Wine
9. My Drinkin' Problem
10. Crazed Country Rebel
11. Dick in Dixie
12. Not Everybody Likes Us
13. Angel of Sin

Disc Two
1. Louisiana Stripes

Comments: Between the release of 2002's ***Lovesick, Broke & Driftin'*** album and this one, Hank 3 fought constantly with his label. Curb had refused to release the artist's ***This Ain't Country*** album, which created more than a little friction between the country rebel and the conservative Curb Records (founder Mike Curb was the former Lt. Governor of California under Governor Ronald Reagan). Hank 3 even went so far as to sell "Fuck Curb" t-shirts on his popular website. The result would be a solid, often spectacular collection that walks the line between honky-tonk country and rock 'n' roll. The set's "bonus disc" includes the incredible sonic collage "Louisiana Stripes," a nifty bit of studio gimcrackery that layers in found dialogue, heavy echo and reverb, scraps of noise, and a plethora of odd sound effects.

Another View: "There's a pure and soulful musical vision at the heart of ***Straight To Hell*** no matter how much Hank III lashes out against the confines of current country music and messes with the form, and that's what makes him most valuable as an outlaw – there's lots of long-haired dope-smoking rednecks out there, but not many that can tap into the sweet and dirty heart of American music the way Hank III does, and ***Straight To Hell*** proves he's got a whole lot to say on that particular subject." – Mark Deming, *All Music Guide*

IV. Damn Right, Rebel Proud (Sidewalk Records 2008, CD)
1. The Grand Ole Opry
2. Wild & Free
3. Me & My Friends
4. Six Pack Of Beer
5. I Wish I Knew
6. If You Can't Help Your Own
7. Candidate For Suicide
8. H8 Line
9. Long Hauls and Close Calls
10. Stoned & Alone
11. P.F.F.
12. 3 Shades of Black
13. Workin' Man

Another View: "Hank Williams III is an outlaw. Just ask him, he'll tell you...actually, you really don't need to bother, because Hank III goes out of his way to tell us about his whiskey guzzling, dope smoking, hell raising ways on nearly every track of his fourth album, ***Damn Right, Rebel Proud***. While Hank made it clear on ***Risin' Outlaw*** and ***Lovesick, Broke & Driftin'*** that he had no use for the watered-down formula pablum that oozes out of Nashville these days, it wasn't until 2006's ***Straight To Hell*** that he made a record that really honored the hard-wired spirit of a guy who played bass with Superjoint Ritual when he wasn't singing pure, unfiltered honky tonk country. ***Damn Right, Rebel Proud*** picks up where ***Straight To Hell*** left off, and like that album it's enthusiastically offensive enough that Curb Records has declined to put their name on it..." – Mark Deming, *All Music Guide*

V. Rebel Within (Curb Records 2010, CD)
1. Gettin' Drunk and Fallin' Down
2. Rebel Within
3. Lookin' For A Mountain
4. Gone But Not Forgotten
5. Drinkin' Ain't Hard To Do
6. Moonshiner's Life
7. #5
8. Karmageddon
9. Lost In Oklahoma
10. Tore Up and Loud
11. Drinkin' Over Mama

Comments: Knowing that his days with Curb were numbered, the rage and fury subsided somewhat, especially since the label had finally released his long-overdue Assjack album. *Rebel Within* is pure party-time honky-tonk, and while it shows a few signs of Hank's metallic leanings, it's also probably his most country-oriented release since his sophomore album. With the artist moving out the door in a hurry, leaving nothing but a shadow, Curb also released the long-lost *This Ain't Country* LP in 2011 as *Hillbilly Joker*.

While some might question the inclusion of Hank III amidst Nashville's non-country rockers, I feel that as an artist, Hank 3 represents the ultimate repudiation of the Music Row aesthetic. Yeah, his country pedigree is unassailable, and his music is often more twang than bang, but the guy has fought against the Music City establishment throughout his career in an effort to express himself honestly...

Another View: "More than one writer has noted that Hank III sounds a lot more like his grandfather Hank Williams than his dad Hank Williams, Jr. ever did, and he writes the kind of melodies that suit his weathered, soulful twang just right; *Rebel Within* captures a tone of bad luck and trouble with a grace and gravity that's manna from heaven for fans of 100-proof roadhouse music. However, while Hank III knows booze and heartbreak are country's two greatest themes, he seems to have leaned a bit too far into the "gettin' loaded" part of the equation; there's more booze, pot, heroin, cocaine, and other consciousness-altering substances on *Rebel Within* than you'll see in an entire season of *Intervention*, and by the end of the album, you'll probably wish someone would send Hank III and his cast of characters into court-ordered rehab..." – Mark Deming, *All Music Guide*

WIRED HITCHCOCK

Wired Hitchcock Recordings:

I. Wired Hitchcock (demos, no date, cassette tape)
1. The Best Laid Plans
2. In Restless Dreams
3. Clay

Hank 3

WISHCRAFT

Band Members:
J.P. Dodson (vocals)
Mark Aufdenkamp (guitars)
David Harvard (guitars)
Jon Murray (bass)
David Clark (drums)

The View from the Band: "There are actually two sides to our music. On one hand, we've got an unrestricted style that includes elements of punk, thrash and psychedelia. On the other, we are very tight, rhythmic and structured." – John Murray, *The Metro*, May 1990

TOMMY WOMACK

Band Members:
Tommy Womack (vocals, guitars, harmonica) (I-V)

Other Musicians:
George Bradfute (guitars) (I, II)
Fenner Castner (drums) (II-V)
Smith Curry (pedal steel) (V)
John Deaderick (keyboards, drums) (V)
Robin Eaton (vocals, percussion, banjo) (I)
Audley Freed (guitars) (V)
John Gardner (drums) (V)
Lisa Oliver Gray (vocals) (II, III, V)
Mike Grimes (bass, guitar) (I, II)
David Henry (tambourine, cello, vocals) (III)
Dave Jacques (bass) (III)

Jay Johnson (bass) (V)
Brad Jones (bass, keyboards, vocals, percussion) (I-III)
Will Kimbrough (guitars, piano, vocals) (II-III, V)
Doug Lancio (guitars) (I)
Tom Littlefield (vocals) (V)
Bill Lloyd (guitars) (III)
Ken McMahan (guitars) (III-IV)
Tommy Meyer (drums, vocals) (I)
Al Perkins (slide guitar, banjo, dobro, pedal steel) (I, II)
Ross Rice (bass, keyboards, percussion) (I-III)
Will Rigby (drums) (III)
Paul Slivka (bass) (IV, V)
Nathan Womack (guitar) (V)

Tommy Womack Recordings:

I. Positively Na Na (Checkered Past Records 1998, CD)
1. A Little Bit Of Sex
2. Skinny & Small
3. Sheila's On The Road
4. She Ain't Speakin' To Me
5. Sweet Hitchhiker
6. Positively Na Na
7. Christabella Wilson
8. I Drank Too Much Again
9. Johnny Bought A Ring
10. Whatever Happened To Cheetah Chrome?
11. I'll Give You Needles

Comments: Tommy Womack was frontman for **Government Cheese**, perhaps the most popular rock band to ever come out of Bowling Green, Kentucky, and a staple on the local Nashville music scene. After the band broke up, Womack

couldn't bottle up the muse, so he went on a long, strange solo trip that is still going strong better than a decade later. *Positively Na Na*, Tommy's debut album, was produced by Brad Jones and Robin Eaton at Jones' Alex The Great studio in Nashville. The album-opening "A Little Bit Of Sex" is a Womack song from the Govt. Cheese era.

II. Stubborn (Sideburn Records 2000, CD)
1. Rubbermaid
2. Up Memphis Blues
3. Christian Rocker
4. The Urge To Call
5. I Don't Have A Gun
6. Going Nowhere
7. Dreams And Golden Rivers
8. She Likes To Talk
9. Willie Purdue
10. Tellin' You What You Want To Hear
11. Berkeley Mews
12. For The Battered
13. They All Come Back For More

Comments: Working again with Brad Jones and Robin Eaton on the boards, Womack's second album finds him angrier, yet more focused and maturing as a songwriter. "For The Battered" is the album's obligatory Govt. Cheese song, a very tough and potent song about domestic abuse; "Berkeley Mews" is a cover of a great, underrated Kinks song written by the legendary Ray Davies. (See review ➜)

TOMMY WOMACK - WORD UPRISING

III. *Circus Town* (Sideburn Records 2002, CD)
1. Tough
2. The Highway's Coming
3. Fake It 'til You Make It
4. You Could Be At The Beach Right Now, Little Girl
5. Everything With You
6. We Can't Do This Anymore
7. Sleeping With Cecilia
8. My Name Is Mud
9. You Can't Get There From Here
10. Nancy Dunn
11. The Replacements
12. Circus Town

IV. *Washington D.C.* (self-produced CD, 2003)
1. Betty Was Black (& Willie Was White)
2. Going Nowhere
3. The Highway's Coming
4. I Don't Have A Gun
5. You Could Be At The Beach Right Now, Little Girl
6. Nancy Dunn
7. A Little Bit Of Sex
8. My Name Is Mud
9. Tough
10. Up Memphis Blues
11. We Can't Do This Anymore
12. Fake It 'til You Make It
13. Skinny & Small
14. Sweet Hitchhiker

Tommy Womack

Comments: Credited to "The Tommy Womack Band," which in this case includes guitarist **Ken McMahan**, drummer Fenner Castner, and bassist Paul Slivka. This is a 54-minute live radio performance, recorded at the XM Satellite Studio Two during October 2002. The song selection represents a veritable history of Womack's musical career, from Govt. Cheese to his solo work. Well worth searching for...

V. *There, I Said It!* (Cedar Creek Music 2007, CD)
1. A Songwriter's Prayer
2. If That's All There Is To See
3. Nice Day
4. 25 Years Ago
5. Too Much Month At The End Of The Xanax
6. I'm Never Gonna Be A Rock Star
7. I Want A Cigarette
8. I Couldn't Care Less
9. Alpha Male & The Canine Mystery Blood
10. Fluorescent Light Blues
11. A Cockroach After The Bomb
12. Everything's Coming Up Roses Again
13. Nice Day (reprise)

Comments: The amazing "comeback" album (see the review for details ➔); that's Tommy's son Nathan with a guitar solo on "Too Much Month At The End Of The Xanax." Let's face it, Womack is perhaps the most beloved musical underdog on the Nashville scene, and he certainly deserves the kind of (long overdue) indie-rock adoration that is too often heaped by the Pitchfork crowd on artists that aren't fit to shine Tommy's shoes.

WORD UPRISING

Band Members:
Fred Greene (vocals)
Dave Jones (guitars)
Bill McLaurine (bass)
Mark Beasley (drums)

Comments: They only lasted about a year, but had they stuck around, Word Uprising had the talent and songs to go somewhere beyond Elliston Square. Another band o' veterans, including **Faith Like Guillotine** drummer Mark Beasley and **Jet Black Factory**'s David Jones (on guitar), with MTSU students Fred Greene (vox) and Bill McLaurine (bass), Word Uprising quickly built a local buzz with a buzzing mix of screaming NWOBHM fretwork and blasting

Word Uprising, continued on page 576...

TOMMY WOMACK
Stubborn
(Sideburn Records)

After listening steadily to Tommy Womack's debut album, *Positively Na Na*, constantly for over a year I've finally figured it out, put my finger on Womack's place in this great rock & roll whatsis. The recent arrival of *Stubborn*, Womack's brilliant sophomore effort, reinforces my conclusion: Tommy Womack is the new Harry Nielsen! Now, now, stay with me here – much like that maligned and often-overlooked pop genius, Womack is capable of performing in a number of musical genres, from rock and blues to country and everywhere in between. Both artists write great songs with slightly skewed lyrical perspectives, and both have a keen eye for skilled sidemen. Whereas Nielsen would enter the studio with various Beatles in tow, Womack records with the cream of Nashville's underrated rock music scene, talents like Will Kimbrough, George Bradfute, Mike Grimes, Ross Rice and Brad Jones. Womack may have a more southern-fried perspective than Nielsen, but the parallels are obvious.

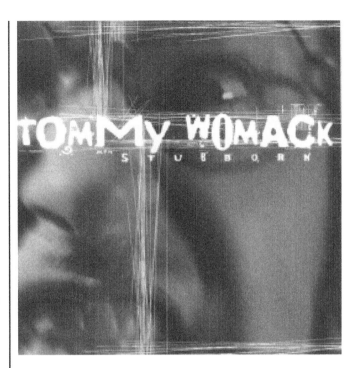

Womack's *Stubborn* opens with the chaotic "Rubbermaid," a short stream-of-consciousness rant similar to Captain Beefheart or John Trubee, backed by syncopated drums and flailing harmonica. It jumps from there right into "Up Memphis Blues," an energetic rocker with a blues edge that includes some tasty slide guitar courtesy of Al Perkins. "Christian Rocker" is a hilarious interlude with fantastic imagery dropped in between lines while "I Don't Have A Gun" is an angry blues tune featuring appropriately tortured vocals from Womack and some southern rock styled six-string work from Womack and George Bradfute. "For The Battered," a song from Womack's old band and Southeast legends Govt. Cheese, is recycled here as an electric blues with some wicked, dark-hued slide guitar from Will Kimbrough supporting the story. It's the most powerful musical statement that I've heard on domestic violence and I still get chills every time the asshole girlfriend-beater's karma catches up with him. *Stubborn*'s lone cover is of the Kink's "Berkeley Mews," a somewhat obscure Ray Davies gem offered here in a fairly straight-forward rendition that says as much about Womack's sophisticated musical tastes as it does about his ability to pull the song off on record.

Most critics, when writing of Womack, praise his songwriting abilities, pointing out the numerous characters that live in his songs. They're really missing Womack's strongest skill, however – any hack can people their songs with junkies, whores and ne'er-do-wells of various stripes (listen to any heavy metal lately?). Womack's strength is in his composition of memorable lines, clever and intelligent lyrical bombs often thrown into the middle of songs to infect the listener's consciousness days after hearing a song. Witness some of the poetic explosives hidden in the songs on

Stubborn: "I'd crawl back in the womb right now if Jesus would show up and point the way." "Gonna find me a woman who won't fall apart on the witness stand." "I want to be a Christian rocker but the devil's got all the good drummers." "She was a Presbyterian in a porno picture, tossing her values aside." "You can all go straight to hell, you'd better cut and run, get on your knees and thank the lord that I don't have a gun." It's a skill that separates Womack from the mundane "Music Row" factory writers in Nashville even as it marginalizes him from the whitebread world of radio and mainstream music. It also shows his Southern heritage as religious tradition and rock & roll yearnings clash for the soul of the songwriter with the resulting imagery creating some of rock's best rhymes. Among southern rockers, only Jason & the Scorchers' Jason Ringenburg and, perhaps, Alex Chilton match Womack word for word.

The material and performances on *Stubborn* sound more confident, Womack's talents sharply honed by a couple of years of live shows and collaborations with other artists. A gifted storyteller, an amazing songwriter and an energetic performer, Womack is one of Nashville's best and brightest. Although an indie rocker in style and attitude, Womack's work deserves the widest audience possible, distribution and promotion that only a major label could provide – if any of the corporate A&R geeks could get their collective heads out of their respective boss' rear ends long enough to listen. Personally, as long as Womack gets to keep making records like *Stubborn* I'll be happy enough.
– *Alt.Culture.Guide*, 2000

CD REVIEW: TOMMY WOMACK'S THERE, I SAID IT!

TOMMY WOMACK
There, I Said It
(Cedar Creek Music)

In a city filled to the brim with musical talent, Tommy Womack often gets overlooked. I first met Womack two decades ago when he was the frontman for late-80s cult band Govt. Cheese, a unique hard-rocking outfit that came roaring out of Bowling Green, Kentucky like the ghost of Hank Williams riding astride a Nipponese superbike with flaming tailpipes! The band's momentary flirtation with stardom inspired Womack's tale of rock & roll woe, **The Cheese Chronicles**, the best book about life on the road ever written (sorry Jack Kerouac!)

After the demise of Govt. Cheese, Womack immigrated to Nashville to pursue his musical career in earnest. Womack landed a gig as one-third of the Bis-Quits, a groovy little band that included the talented Will Kimbrough and future music retail exec Mike "Grimey" Grimes, the collaboration yielding one great roots-rock album on John Prine's Oh Boy record label. Womack would then launch his solo career, almost a decade ago, with the brilliant debut album *Positively Na Na* in 1998.

The life of an indie rocker is a tough one, though, especially when, like Tommy Womack, your main attribute is that you don't fit in. Womack has always been too country, too rock & roll, too serious, not serious enough, too wordy, too stubborn, getting older…just not marketable by today's "standards." Never mind that he's always made brilliant, entertaining music with highly personal lyrics that nevertheless appeal to many people that recognize the characters in the songs from the same streets we all walk together, if separately.

After 2002's *Circus Town*, shortly after his fortieth birthday, Womack hit rock bottom. As he writes in the liner notes to *There I Said It!*, "one morning in March '03, God came across my teeth with a skillet of White Light Truth. Whomp! I was toast at forty and destined to die poor." Womack had a meltdown, of sorts, the sort of life-paralyzing crisis-of-confidence that drops the strongest of men to their knees and into spirals of mind-crippling depression. Months passed by and those close to Womack began to worry; more than one "friend-of-a-friend" got in contact and asked me to talk to Tommy. We swapped emails back and forth, even talked on the phone once or twice, but I doubt that my words of encouragement did little more than add to the chorus of friends and admirers urging Tommy to "feel better."

Truth is, the personal hell that Womack was going through was something that few people will ever experience. He thought he saw his career circling the drain, his future uncertain, a divine voice saying, as he writes, "you had yer shot, thanks a lot," leaving him older and broke with a family

to support and the kind of dreams that tear one apart. Over the following three years, Womack recovered somewhat, got a crappy job like most of us, hating it like most of us and still, always, playing music. It was the music that, in the end, pulled him through, lending a voice to his fears and emboldening him to carry on.

The result of Womack's trials and tribulations is *There, I Said It!*, his fourth studio and fifth album overall, a mind-staggeringly brilliant collection of songs that literally open a window to the artist's soul. In many ways *There, I Said It!* reminds me of Joe Grushecky's equally powerful 2004 album *True Companion*. At the same time that Womack was living through *his* crisis, Grushecky was looking into his *own* abyss. Over fifty, overshadowed by the accomplishments of his peers, Grushecky came to the conclusion that he may never make it big in rock & roll but, "I still got a long way to go."

This is Tommy Womack's story, however, and *There, I Said It!* is his masterpiece. The songs here recount the last several years of his life, biographical tales with great humor and insight and a little sadness. "A Songwriter's Prayer" is a brilliant lead-off, a somber ode from a wordsmith to a higher power asking for just one good song, something to hang your hat on and build a career around. Delivered with pious vocals, mournful pedal steel and a haunting melody, the song is both tongue-in-cheek and deadly serious, with "we got to get out of this place" urgency.

Written about his son Nathan, "Nice Day" takes a look at life from the high side of 40, a winsome kind of tune that concludes, at the end of the day, that life is good when you have your family around you. The country-flavored "25

CD REVIEW: TOMMY WOMACK'S THERE, I SAID IT!

Years Ago" is a semi-biographical honky-tonk tale of the search for stardom by three hopefuls, spiced up with twangy steel and Womack's upbeat vocals, the story of everybody that has ever come to Nashville (or L.A. or New York) chasing a dream.

"I'm Never Gonna Be A Rock Star," from which *There I Said It!* takes its title, is a lilting, jazzy tune with Womack's soulful, fluid vocals and muted yet lush instrumentation. The song's reflective self-confession is both cathartic and one last shot at those who would try and bring the artist down. "My hair may go, but the dream remains," the protagonist sings, getting older every day while his musician friends have forged moderate careers of one form or another, "buddies on tour buses, takin' that ride, while I'm gettin' older with an itch inside." This reflective song parallels Joe Grushecky's "Strange Days," a realization that while every artistic effort through the years may not have been for naught, the lack of recognition – if not fame and fortune – is a bitter pill nonetheless.

The bluesy "Too Much Month At The End Of The Xanax" is a bleak reflection on modern life, its otherworldly, electronically-altered vocals punching their way through a cloud of tortured electric guitars and discordant rhythms. It's a style that Womack has always excelled at, self-referential talking blues paired with a hard rocking soundtrack that could just as easily been a Govt. Cheese song if it wasn't *so damn personal*. By the time you reach "I Couldn't Care Less," a rollicking pop-rock rave-up inspired by the tired 9to5 that Womack endured during his "blue period," things are starting to look up. Gigs are coming his way, and Womack delivers a lyrical coup de grace with more attitude and bile than any punk band I've been witness too, allaying his friend's fears with "I feel alright, suicide is overrated, I've killed and lied, or at least I've mutilated."

The centerpieces of *There I Said It!* are the epic stream-of-consciousness masterpiece "Alpha Male & the Canine Mystery Blood" and "A Cockroach After The Bomb." Both songs evince the sense of humor that has always driven Womack's best material, but they are also both songs that pack up the past in a box and put it on the shelf, saying goodbye to a time that none of us will ever again enjoy, much less revisit except in memory. "Alpha Male" is a wonderful recollection of a misspent youth and encroaching middle age that many of us can relate to (especially those of us whose age and experience parallels Womack's). He sees a band poster while walking to work, bringing back memories of the day 20+ years ago when all of us would run out to see a show by any band that sounded even half-intriguing, a poster on a telephone pole an invite to a night of beer, women and rock & roll. Tying the past to the present and facing his own growing obsolescence, Womack admits that "can't be a has-been when you never was."

"A Cockroach After The Bomb," a semi-shuffle with lively vocals and spry piano work courtesy of producer John Deaderick, is the yin to the yang of "Alpha Male." The song begins by expressing an angst that no 20-something-year-old young pup could ever understand, confessing, "I get up every morning and I go to a job where I've thrown up on the john. I worry about who's mad at me and spend a lot of time wishing I was gone." He remembers his previous life, in a gang with a band, "I used to be somebody, I was a star, it takes a lot of guts to fall this far," concluding that "I'm a cockroach after the bomb, carrying on…"

It's with this refrain, however, that Womack touches the album's truth, that in spite of the darkness, those that feel the muse are compelled to follow, to "carry on" no matter the price, and as Steve Forbert once sang, "you can not win if you do not play the game." The singer asks, "what if Jimi's lighter hadn't lighted, what if Monet was just near-sighted, I'll go to my grave knowing I took me a chance, I'm a cockroach after the bomb carryin' on." The song is a call to arms for all of us last-crop-baby-boomers stuck in a cubicle or middle management with a mortgage and obligations who still harbor delusions of creativity that our parents warned us against pursuing. It's fitting that the album's next-to-last song is "Everything's Coming Up Roses Again;" Womack writing in the liner notes that "this record started with a prayer and ends with its answer."

The song's waltz-like demeanor and wistful vocals belie its message – that as long as you're breathing, you can still follow your dreams. "I may be a 44-year-old office boy," writes Womack, "but I'm the office boy that did Leno!" You're never too old to sing that song, write that story, paint that picture, and thus sayeth Springsteen, "throw away the dreams that break your heart." You've got one life to live, and as *There I Said It!* slides to a close with the wiry, guitar-driven instrumental "Nice Day (reprise)," you get the sense that Womack, like Grushecky at the end of *True Companion*, has found some degree of peace in family, friends and, of course, his music.

In a city filled to the brim with musical talent, Tommy Womack has often been overlooked. Age and experience has broadened his lyrical palette, however, the songs on *There, I Said It!* among the best he's ever written. A skilled songwriter and charismatic performer, Womack peppers his songs with musical scraps of roots-rock, Americana, blues and hard-rock. Ironically, initial acclaim for this album, and the positive response afforded it by nearly everybody that has heard it, could end up reviving a career that Womack thought was on life support. By any measure, *There, I Said It!* is the work of an artist yet to hit his peak, an emotionally moving song-cycle that defies the industry gatekeepers and rocks with élan, guts and intelligence.
– Trademark of Quality blog, 2007

CD REVIEW: TOMMY WOMACK'S NOW WHAT!

TOMMY WOMACK
Now What!
(Cedar Creek Music)

With his acclaimed, semi-autobiographical 2007 album *There, I Said It!*, Nashville-based singer-songwriter Tommy Womack partially resuscitated a career that was going nowhere in a hurry. Brimming over with self-doubt, stark personal realizations, and boldly defiant statements, the album bared Womack's soul in a way that many self-absorbed indie-rockers could only pretend to offer. The songs on *There, I Said It!* were funny, sad, angst-ridden, frustrating, witty, and emotionally-charged. The album seemed, at the time, to provide a final punctuation mark to the brilliant artist's tumultuous career.

Fate had a different hand to deal Womack, however, and enough listeners connected with his confessional story-songs to thankfully write another chapter to this story. In the five years since the release of *There, I Said It!*, Womack teamed up with fellow wordsmith and underrated six-string maestro Will Kimbrough as Daddy, the duo joined by some friends to record 2009's acclaimed *For A Second Time*. Now, a half-decade after receiving his second (third?) shot at the brass ring, the former Government Cheese frontman has delivered the wonderful, wry, and playfully entertaining *Now What!*

With *Now What!*, Womack continues in a musical vein similar to that he pursued on *There, I Said It!*, with a few notable exceptions. Again, the singer is the main protagonist in his own finely-crafted stories, but while Womack's witty lyrics remains front and center, he takes a few more chances here musically than ever before, and with exciting results.

The album opener, "Play That Cheap Trick, Cheap Trick Play," is pure power-pop magic with personalized lyrics that blend an infectious melody with lyrical snapshots of domestic life mixed with the seemingly endless gigs of the itinerant musician, all delivered with an undeniable élan.

"Bye & Bye" is a stark, deliberately-paced autobiographical ballad that tells a familiar story for the hopeless romantics in the audience, a random encounter with an old love that sets the mind to wandering and wondering what might have been. Womack's perfectly-wistful vocals are laid atop a gently-strummed guitar, accompanied by John Deaderick's subtle keyboard flourishes, the lyrics themselves brilliantly insightful while crashing back to earth with an inevitable conclusion. "I'm Too Old To Feel That Way Right Now" is the flip-side of that encounter, more ruminations on love and lust that are plagued by an uneasy slide into middle age angst and grudging acceptance.

Womack's flirtations with the demon alcohol are the stuff of legend amidst the sheltered Nashville rock scene, rivaling stories of the Reverend's own tilting at that particular windmill for tall tales shared by wagging tongues across suburban fences. The singer's "On & Off The Wagon" wins the competition hands down, the song's twangy, Lambchop-styled, fractured alt-country soundtrack matched only by its clever, melancholy wordplay.

Singing of his battle with the bottle as Bill Huber's tuba staggers prominently behind the vocals, Womack tosses off sharply-phrased passages like "sometimes I like the wagon, sometimes I like to walk"; "I've learned to know my limit, I've learned to pass it by"; and "I'm smart as a whip, I'm dumb as wood" as part of a wild mea culpa that is rooted firmly in the country tradition by Jim Hoke's weeping pedal steel guitar.

By contrast, Womack's spoken word rant "90 Miles An Hour Down A Dead-End Street" is a continuation of the previous album's wonderfully wry "Alpha Male & the Canine Mystery Blood," both autobiographical raps delivered with more than a little Hunter S. Thompson-styled gonzo spirit. In this case, Womack's dialogue is accompanied by a lone brassy drumbeat, the singer tossing off stream-of-consciousness thoughts like a 21st century Bukowski while telling his sordid tale.

Prefacing the rant with the introductory "went to Indy, in the rain, to a club that was never going to have me again, a bottle of Chianti in the passenger seat, driving 90 miles per hour down a dead-end street," Womack delivers such lyrical bon mots as "I work for myself and I still get fired"; "now I just drink, except when I don't, and you're either going to get a good show or you won't"; and the sparkling nihilism "I've done everything I could to kill myself and take other people with me," with tongue only partially in cheek.

Lest one think Tommy Womack as just another hipster with a penchant for lyrical self-immolation, he blows up that misconception with the low-slung rocker "I Love You To Pieces." Womack's playful, oblique lyrics here are matched by a mid-tempo soundtrack that blends the Southern-fried funk of Dan Baird and the Georgia Satellites with the reckless, bristling rock 'n' roll of the Replacements, offering up plenty of greasy fretwork and blasts of harmonica.

The introspective "Wishes Do Come True" is an acoustic ballad that benefits from Lisa Oliver-Gray's subtle backing vocals echoing Womack's own, while "Over The Hill" is a trademark Tommy Womack construct, tilted slightly towards Tom Waits territory with an oddly discordant guitar strum and lilting vocals sliding uneasily across the tinkling piano keys and squalls of tuba.

Less a sequel than a bookend to the desperate "Hail Mary" pass that was *There, I Said It!*, Womack's *Now What!*

imagines a career beyond the soul-destroying 9 to 5 dead-end the singer saw himself trapped in for the rest of his miserable existence. Displaying a disarming optimism amidst the introspective double-clutching and romantic daydreams than previously, *Now What!* offers up more of what Tommy Womack does best – working class blues from the street-view seats of the restless American dream. – *Blurt* magazine, 2012

TOMMY WOMACK
Positively Na Na
(Checkered Past Records)

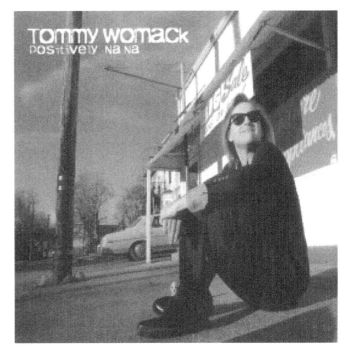

A long-time fixture of the Nashville area music scene – first as a member of the legendary Bowling Green, Kentucky band Government Cheese and later as a part of Will Kimbrough's vastly underrated Bis-quits – Womack finally gets to flex his muscle and show off his stuff with a solo album. With *Positively Na Na*, Womack scores an artistic bull's-eye.

Positively Na Na is a solid collection of country- flavored pop tunes that evince the same sort of quick wit and black humor that Womack showed in *The Cheese Chronicles*, his memoirs of life on the road with Government Cheese and possibly the best book ever written about rock 'n' roll. Womack works with one foot firmly in the sort of roots rock practiced by Bruce Springsteen and Tom Petty and the other foot in the same honky-tonk country that influenced folks like Jason & the Scorchers. Possessing a knack for story-telling, Womack pens intelligent, self-referential lyrics, the songs often dangling more than a few pop hooks from their infectious choruses. Stand-out tracks on *Positively Na Na* include "Skinny & Small," the rightful revenge of every junior high non-jock; and Womack's ode to lost rockers, "Whatever Happened To Cheetah Chrome?"

With a band that includes Nashville pop maestro Brad Jones (who also co-produced the disc), guitar wizard George Bradfute and the multi-talented Ross Rice, Womack pulls off with *Positively Na Na* that most difficult of tricks: a debut album that is as smart, likeable and entertaining as its creator. Far too talented for major label suits to recognize, Womack remains one of Nashville and the indie world's greatest secrets. – *Alt.Culture.Guide*, 1998

INTERVIEW: TOMMY WOMACK

*T*ommy Womack first came to our attention as the wild frontman singing and playing guitar in the gang that was Government Cheese, Bowling Green's finest musical export. Recording for the Nashville-based Reptile Records, and touring constantly on the Southeast club and college circuit, the Cheese made quite a name for themselves with intelligent, clever lyrics and music that approached levels of anarchy only exceeded by the Replacements.

After the demise of Government Cheese, Womack penned The Cheese Chronicles, the best book, hands-down, about life in a touring rock 'n' roll band, and after a short-lived collaboration with Will Kimbrough and Mike Grimes as the Bis-Quits, Womack launched a solo career that has been long on acclaim if somewhat short on the fame that this erudite wordsmith deserves. After a year or so of trying to match our schedules to perform this interview, I hooked up with Tommy by phone in October 2012...literally days before sending this book to the printer!

How did you get interested in music in the first place?
Kiss. Well, it started before that when I first heard the Beatles sing "Hard Day's Night" on the radio, that really galvanized me. I saw the Monkees on television and that had me miming at home with the records quite a bit. I always liked rock 'n' roll. I remember hearing "Blue Suede Shoes" by Johnny Rivers and really being taken with that. Also, "Rockin' Pneumonia and the Boogie Woogie Flu," that was a big one for me.

And then Kiss...when I was in eighth grade, Kiss just turned my head around. I kind of graduated from Kiss to Cheap Trick, and from Cheap Trick to the Kinks, and then Bruce Springsteen came down the pike. I went to college, and all of a sudden a whole world opened up, everything from the Sex Pistols to Elvis Costello and Bob Dylan and on, and on, and on.

When did you actually start playing music?
I bought a guitar for $18.00. It was a Stella guitar, $18 and 18 frets. I bought it from a girl up the street in May or June of 1978 and set about learning how to play it. I learned almost everything on my own looking through a Mel Bay "Learn Guitar" book. That's where I learned my first chords. I remember tape recording "Louie, Louie" off the radio and playing along with that.

That happened about a year after I got the guitar, but once I got that guitar, I just carried it around all the time...all the time for years and years and years, if I was doing anything I was playing the guitar. I just played the guitar all the time. I got a Yamaha acoustic, I bought it off a fellow on the same floor at my dormitory in college, my freshman year at college in 1981 and then I started playing that Yamaha all the time. My first electric guitar was a Kalamazoo, which is a low-budget Gibson. Made by the people at Gibson, it was a white SG. I got that my senior year of high school and I found I could plug it in to the back of my stereo. There was a microphone/guitar input on the back of the stereo and it would come through the eight-track channel and the turntable channel was right next to the eight-track channel, so if I put the knob half way between them, I got the guitar coming out of one speaker and the record coming out of another. I remember one of the big records I learned how to play along with was the Dictators' first record, *Go Girl Crazy*. I discovered them before I discovered the Ramones. I always liked their stuff, and it's really simple, it's easy to pick up on...every song seemed to be three chords...the key might change, but just three chords over and over again.

When did Government Cheese come about?
I graduated college in December of '84, and me and Scott Willis had been messing around trying to start a band for about six months up to that point. Graduated in December of '84 and New Year's Eve day, I got a job at a brand new Lee's Famous Recipe Fried Chicken in Bowling Green and started working there. We set about right away January of 1985 forming Government Cheese, and we played our first gig in January, it was a fraternity party. That's how it started. I had a Telecaster by then, and I was still just playing all the time. I was getting to where I could play pretty fast, and within a year of being in Government Cheese, I was playing pretty well.

I guess you have outlined most of the tall tales about Government Cheese days in your book, would you have anything that you would like to reveal?
Well...our manager goes the whole book without smoking dope. That was his biggest occupation and I picked up that bad habit from him. I'm sober now, but I have smoked a whole lot of dope in my time and I'm not sayin' that he's the cause of it, but I know what barber shop I was in when I got my hair cut.

What prompted you to write The Cheese Chronicles?
I knew I had to start writing. I started off as a writer before I got into the guitar. I was writing short stories by 7th grade, and I had a college professor writing me and trying to recruit me, because he saw my short stories in tenth grade of high school. I

am a more talented writer than I am a musician. I make no bones about that at all. All my musician qualities are learned behavior, but I'm a good writer from birth. I've got some innate understanding about how words ought to go together. I don't have that with music.

In music, I'm not much of a singer, I'm an okay guitar player, but I can write. I've channeled that in to both books and lyrics and I know enough about music now to pull it off pretty well. I came out of Government Cheese and I remember coming home from my honeymoon thinking, I've got to do a book. That was December of '92. I was thinking, "man, everybody tells me I'm a great writer, I've got to come up with a book. What should it be?" I just started writing. I figured the only real story I had was the Government Cheese story, so I started writing on it. About three years later, it came out. It's done pretty well for me. It's made me a lot of friends.

It's a good book, it's a lot of fun, and for a lot of people it probably gives them the best inside look at an indie touring rock band that they have ever had...
Yeah, I've heard that from people, that it really gives a good clear picture of what it's like. Also, you don't have to know anything about rock 'n' roll to get into it…I explain every step of the way what a PA system is, what a guitar is, what a monitor is, what mixing a record is. You don't have to know anything going into it. I wrote it so that my mom could understand everything that happened without there being any jargon that she wouldn't understand what it meant. Even though my mom was appalled at the profanity, at least she could understand it. That's just rock 'n' roll. There are some times that profanity is necessary… it's like garlic, you can't use too much of it, but sometimes profanity is the only way to express an emotion.

You put out a novel a few years ago?
Yeah, it's a Civil War novel set in the South. It's about a closeted gay confederate soldier and his sister back home, and they write letters back and forth to each other, and he eventually rises up to the rank of captain and forms the only all-gay confederate regiment to fight in the civil war. They get done away with at Gettysburg; they get stuck in the middle of Pickett's Charge, sent across the field to get mowed down. That's how they wiped the whole regiment off the history books.

I have done readings for my book and people ask me how I did my research and how I found out about that, and I have to caution them, "whoa! This is bullshit. This is called fiction." I take every effort to make it look like it really happened. It's gotten good response from the people who read it. It never had a PR person or a marketer like *The Cheese Chronicles* did, so not a lot of people know about it. I just sell it at gigs

and people like it. People think it's a fun read. It's nothing too heavy, it's just a fun read.

Are you working on a new book?
For 365 days. It started on my birthday last year and I've been writing on it every day, it's going to end on my birthday this year when I turn 50 on November 20th.

How did you start your solo career and what were your thoughts at the time?
The Cheese Chronicles came out in September of '95 and I thought I was just going to be a writer from then on…the Bis-Quits had broken up the year before, I had just been working at a book store and I would come home at night and drink wine and smoke pot and work on the book. When the book came out, I thought "I'm just going to be an author from now on." I'd had two bands that were good and had almost made it to some precipice, but it's over, right? I'm just going to be a writer from now on.

I was pretty comfortable with that and then Brad Jones called me from out of the blue and wanted to talk. He wanted to cut some demos on me on spec; if they got picked up by a label, then Brad would get a piece of the publishing. So the recording sessions were going to be free. He remembered some of the songs I'd written from the second Bis-Quits record that wound up not getting made, and he liked the songs, and he liked me…so we were in the studio and cut five tracks and that became the beginning of the *Positively Na Na* record. It was like Michael Corleone…just when I thought I was out, they pulled me back in.

So it's not like I tried to get back in to the music business, it came and got me in the form of Brad. We finished *Positively Na Na* over about a year and a half period of occasional session work, and it didn't come out until 1998. It came out about two days after my son was born. So my whole world got spun around in two different ways. The record came out and it got some great reviews, but I didn't play very much behind it, I didn't have a booking agent, and even if I did, I was one of the primary caretakers of my son. I'm glad I didn't have gigs set now, because I would have missed him as a baby.

Positively Na Na came out in '98 and then Checkered Past Records kind of folded the next year, I think. I got a deal with Sideburn Records, which was a much smaller label without a PR department or anything. In 2000, I cut *Stubborn*, and in 2001 the Washington D.C. record came out. Then in 2002 the *Circus Town* record came out. Both of those were on Sideburn and they disappeared without a trace. *Stubborn* is on Spotify now (or Rhapsody, or one of those). Maybe *Circus Town* is, too. You can at least still get *Stubborn* and *Circus Town* on iTunes; you can't get *Positively Na Na*. I can't track down the people that own it so that I can get it back and put it out myself. At least most of my records are in print. It's no different than Jason and the Scorchers not being able to put out their own back catalog or anything like that. It happens to us all.

Then I kind of dropped out of it for awhile…in 2003, I had to go to work full time because my wife got fired from her state job. I got a job at Vanderbilt the next day which was a hell job. I was in a hostile work environment working for this lady that hated me, from September 2003 until September 2004. I was sick every day going into work, I didn't know where my life was going, I was considering suicide…it was bad! I was drinking a whole lot…and I thought my recording career was done. I'd been having panic attacks for all of 2003, crying attacks…those many years of marijuana abuse caught up with me and bit me in the ass.

My lunch was going to the back of the building and smoking cigarettes and drinking diet drinks for an hour. I was getting skinnier by the day. I had no use for writing songs anymore; I was dead in the water. But the songs were coming to me and I would write them in my head, there at the back of the building smoking cigarettes on lunch break, and they turned into the songs on *There, I Said It!* Then I got some financial backing to make that record. That was the start of Cedar Creek Records and that record took off for me.

That was the start of 2007 and finally I kind of busted through. I got in the *No Depression* Top 50 of the Year, *USA Today*'s Top 30 of the year, Top 10 of the Year from *The Tennessean*, and I got on the cover of *The Nashville Scene*, and things just sort of took off for me. Five years later, I came out with the *Now What* record, last February. It's gotten great notices. If that's being successful, to have good press and radio play, then I guess I'm successful now. The pay is not so great, but I think there's a lot of that going around. I should also mention that in 2005, two years before *There, I Said It!*, the first Daddy record came out, which was my band with Will Kimbrough.

How did Daddy with Will Kimbrough come about?
Ever since the Bis-Quits had been over, we have been doing gigs as a duo. We have done tons of gigs as an acoustic duo. We had always been talking about it for years that we were going to form an electric band with our dream list of guys: Dave Jacques, Paul Griffith, and John Deaderick. We'd all worked with those three.

Dave Jacques plays bass for John Prine; Paul Griffith is one of the greatest drummers in the world, he's played for everybody; and John Deaderick is an incredible keyboardist who produced *There, I Said It!* and *Now What* and he has played with the Dixie Chicks and Michael MacDonald, and now he plays with Alison Krauss.

Tommy Womack

Those are the three back-up guys in Daddy…we knew these were the guys we wanted to get together. We wanted to call the band Daddy and we knew we wanted it to be something we could play electric guitar together because Will and I just have a real good way of playing together. It really works out well. That became the Daddy band and we released *At The Women's Club* in 2005 and *For A Second Time* in 2009. I don't know if there will be another Daddy record…I know Will wants to get a solo record out, he hasn't had one in five years, so he's kind of chomping at the bit to do that.

I see down through the years you've done song writing with a lot of different people, how has that experience been?
Co-writing is arduous but necessary. It's a way to get a song written in a day with another person where you have two people that agree whether a song is good or not. Which you don't always have when you write them alone, but it's a bit nerve-wracking. You have to sit down with somebody with a guitar, looking at each other and feeling like an idiot. Having to be clever on cue…it's a pain in the ass. It's arduous, but the results can be rewarding a lot of the time…not all of the time, but a lot of the time. I have come up with some good

stuff with Tom Littlefield, come up with some good songs with Jason Ringenberg, and Warner Hodges and Dan Baird have come up with good songs.

Let me ask you about that second Bis-Quits album you referred to that never came out. What happened with that?
Will abdicated from the group in August or September of '94, he came back from a vacation after thinking long and hard and he didn't want to do another year of playin' for the door and sleepin' on the floor. The band was pretty fractious too, the drummer and the bass player, Tommy Myer and Grimey, just fought like cats and dogs, all the time. Will and I had come from bands where we were the eccentrics and now we're in a band where we're the voices of reason. I think it was half Will financially not wanting to go another year struggling, and practically not wanting to put up with bullshit any more.

You were on John Prine's Oh Boy label, was that a decent experience or was that just kind of a grind?
Well, businesswise it was not so great, but every other way it was heavenly because I'm from Kentucky, I'm from Hopkins County which is right next door to Muhlenberg County. I've been a John Prine fan since way back. I first saw him in 1981 in Bowling Green. I'm from Kentucky, where if you don't like John Prine your taxes go up. He is just the guy! And I was suddenly on his label…and we're on a first name basis…and we're doing the occasional gig with him…and it was just heaven! To this day, I'm a big deal to some people in my home town just because they know I know John Prine. I didn't have to do anything else beyond that. I know John Prine. I was on his label.

How has the response been to Now What?
The press has been good, the sales have been okay and the radio play has been good…not incredible…just good. I don't blame radio for not playing me anymore than it does because I never give them a record that all the songs sound similar enough to where they can figure out how to program it for radio. I tend to do a rock song, a country song, then blues, then rockabilly, then a pop song…all my records are a mixed bag.

So they don't want to play "99 Miles An Hour Down A Dead End Street" during afternoon drive time?
No! I think the only one a bunch of Americana stations could find to program was "On And Off The Wagon." That was pretty straight-up, shit-kicker country. But after that, they didn't have anything else to follow up on. I think my records just confuse radio programmers, because they're like, "what's he doin'? Settle on a style, guy!" I can't blame them for that. I don't have any grudge; I understand why they feel that way. It just creates an obstacle in my pathway towards getting heard by more people.

Where would you like your solo career to go from here?
Making a living…if I could just make a living, I'd be happy. I make part of a living, but I still work day jobs. I still have to do that. With my music and my day jobs and my wife's salary, we just barely get by. We're hanging onto the bottom edge of the middle class by the fingernails. If I could just get to where I was making a living…and I don't know if I'm going to get there, I don't know how much longer this singer/songwriter thing is going to go. The economy is terrible, gas prices are through the roof, and I don't draw flies.

Most of my audience is 35 or older. All my songs on the last two records have been about parenthood and middle-age struggles…and my fans now are people of that age who relate to it, but if I go play a gig in their hometown, they're not likely to come to the gig because either they can't get a baby-sitter or they can't afford it or they just don't want to get out at night because they want to be in bed by 10. That's sort of a reality I deal with, so it's difficult for me to get gigs on the road where I can attract people, and it's difficult to make it pay because I can't get very good guarantee because I can't guarantee anybody is going to show up. I kind of go from gig to gig…okay, I still have another gig, so I've still got a career for the next three weeks or so, we'll see if another gig comes up. Of course we're booked way out farther than three weeks but, you know…

Word Uprising, continued...

cap drumbeats that would leave your head ringing (in a good way). They wanted to fuse '70s-style hard rock with '80s alt-pop and, for a while, they did just that.

THE WORSTIES

Band Members:
Anna Worstell (vocals)
Jesse Worstell a/k/a "Worsty" (guitars, vocals)
Jairo Ruiz (bass)
Caleb Dolister (drums)

KENNY WRIGHT

Band Members:
Kenny Wright (vocals, guitars, dobro, drums, theremin) (I)

Other Musicians:
Richie Albright (drums) (I)
Joe Bidewell (guitars, harmonica, keyboards, accordion) (I)
Brett Bryant (piano) (I)
Chris Carmichael (violin, vocals) (I)
Anthony Crawford (guitars, bass, keyboards, vocals) (I)
Daniel Depietro (bass, fretless bass) (I)
Scott Johnson (vocals, harmonica, hand claps) (I)
Ted Russell Kamp (bass) (I)
Nicolas Nguyen (guitars, violin, cello, dobro) (I)
Tony Paoletta (pedal steel) (I)
John Pavlovsky (guitars) (I)
Jim Thistle (drums) (I)
Kurt Wagner (bass) (I)
Michael Webb (keyboards) (I)
Bryan Wolski (bass) (I)

Kenny Wright Recordings:

I. Family Album (Super Duper Recordings 2008, CD)
1. Little Bohemian
2. That's My Girl
3. On The Other Side
4. Blue Monday
5. Left Of Me
6. Honky Tonk Heroes
7. See Them Going
8. For You
9. Song About Ohio
10. Knock Me Over
11. Rapture
12. Precious Child
13. Have It All
14. Shame On You
15. Honky Tonk Heroes (long version)

Comments: Longtime local scene MVP Kenny Wright has performed with a veritable "who's who" of Nashville bands, from hard rockers **Scarlet** and **Prodigal Sons** to **Max Vague** and, most recently, with **Bonepony**. A multi-instrumental talent, Wright's skills have always been in demand because he's just *that* damn good! *Family Album* is his first solo disc, with Wright assisted by such great musicians as his Bonepony bandmates Nguyen and Johnson, Chris Carmichael, Joe Bidewell, and many others (see interview ➔).

WRONG BAND

Band Members:
Ric Harman (vocals, bass) (A1)
Craig Powers (guitar)
Mike Rosa (guitar) (A1)
Dwayne "Dr. X" Rice (keyboards) (A1)
Andy Martin (drums)
Jeff Danley (drums) (A1)

Other Musicians:
Michael Rhodes (bass) (A1)

Wrong Band Recordings:

A1."I Live In My Car" b/w "Wrong Song" (What Records 1983, 7" vinyl)

Comments: Popular early 1980s pop/rock outfit fronted by singer Ric Harman, released just this one single, got a lot of 91 Rock airplay for "I Live In My Car" (see article ➔).

Ric Harman & the Wrong Band Remembered

Back in the early years of the exploding Nashville rock scene, one of the greatest things about the ongoing local music revolution was that, unlike Seattle, Austin, or even Athens, the Music City scene was truly diverse. From the blu-reggae of Afrikan Dreamland and the rockin-dub of the White Animals to the punk country of Jason & the Scorchers and pop bands like the Practical Stylists, there were a lot of different sounds for the music lover to check out around town.

One of the most underrated of the bands on the scene during the early-80s was the **Wrong Band**. Fronted by the photogenic Ric Harman on bass and vocals and including Craig Powers and Mike Rosa on guitars, Dwayne "Dr. X" Rice on keyboards, and Andy Martin on drums (later replaced by Jeff Danley), the Wrong Band had a solid seven-year run in the region. The band's edgy new-wavish song "I Live In My Car" was in constant rotation on WRVU-FM and they played shows across the Southeast.

Ric Harman passed away from lymphoma on June 5th, 2007 at the young age of 52, his short bout with cancer evidently doing nothing to diminish his creative spirit and zest for life. Ric had accomplished a lot after the various members of the Wrong Band went their separate ways, even if much of it was outside my sphere of awareness. A native Nashvillian and the son of noted session drummer Buddy Harman, who had played with Elvis Presley, Patsy Cline and others, Ric moved to New York City after the band broke up.

During the eleven years that he lived in NYC, Ric pursued his passions for performing and the visual arts, becoming a mime and stage magician, and he did some acting both on stage and on TV. Ric toured the country with his own cooking show sponsored by Proctor & Gamble during the early 1990s, and he made a name for himself as a professional photographer and graphic artist. He returned to Nashville a year or so ago and worked for Nashville's gay and lesbian newspaper *Out & About* as a photographer and columnist. Ric, in the guise of his alter-ego "Cosmo Shitay," wrote a regular column for *Out & About* that may well prove to be his lasting legacy.

The Wrong Band's Andy Martin had told me that he was organizing a band reunion with all of the original members, which would have been great. Listen to "I Live In My Car" or "Wrong Song," I think that you'll agree that although the production may be dated, the songs themselves have a timeless presence and rock just as much today as they did in 1983. Sadly, the band reunion won't take place without Ric Harman, a talented man of many interests that left a lasting impression on the local Nashville rock scene.

(Thanks to Andy Martin for the info on Ric's life and times...)

INTERVIEW: KENNY WRIGHT

Kenny Wright is one of the true "most valuable players" on the Nashville rock scene. A skilled multi-instrumentalist, he first came to prominence as a member of the popular 1980s-era "hair metal" band Scarlet, subsequently forming Prodigal Sons with his friend and constant bandmate Nicolas Nguyen. Nick and Kenny later formed Social Kings, the pair releasing a single acclaimed album. Kenny also toured and recorded with local rocker Max Vague until his death, and these days plays alongside Nguyen in the popular trio Bonepony.

What got you interested in music in the first place?
I guess it's just one of those things that you're born with. I've been interested in music as long as I can remember and my dad, he wasn't a professional, but he was a really good player. My grandparents were professional musicians, so I guess I got it from them. My earliest recollection of life had something to do with music, so I guess that is how I got the bug.

What was the first instrument you picked up?
There was always a guitar lying around the house because that was my dad's primary instrument, so that was definitely my first. I always had a guitar within reach and that was what I gravitated towards originally. He always had a lot of harmonicas lying around the house too, so I always fiddled around with those.

When did you pick up drums?
I always wanted to play drums, but they're loud. My dad was always saying that you can't entertain anybody with drums, but if you play guitar you can sing a song. With drums, it's just...I always wanted to play, so when I first started playing in bands, I would always play drums, whenever we'd have a break I'd go over and start playing the drums, and even though I didn't own a set, by the time I was probably 13 years old, I was a pretty competent drummer.

I had bands that I played guitar in and sang, and I had a couple of bands that I played with for school that I played drums. So I was allowed to play drums in my bands at school and play guitar and sing with my bands outside of school. So I did it like that, and it wasn't until probably 1992 or 1993 that I just kept having a hard time finding drummers for band projects that I was in. That's basically how it started, I made the switch-over to drums because I got a lot more opportunities...

Who would you say your musical influences are?
I don't know what's influenced the way I write songs, I just love so many artists and so many different kinds of music, sometimes I don't think about it until I listen back to something that I wrote or something that I recorded and I think "wow, I think I got that from so and so." I grew up around my house listening to things like folk and country like Waylon Jennings, Gordon Lightfoot, Willie Nelson, George Jones, Glen Campbell, Johnnie Cash...I loved all that stuff, and I still do. As I got a little older, I started exploring pop music and I figured out the Beatles and the Monkees...I saw the Monkees on TV and it just blew my mind. I thought "wow, who wouldn't want to be in a band then you get to live together and travel all over?" In the mid-70s, when I finally heard Kiss, that changed the way I thought about a lot of things. I sort of started really sucking it all in and it was Led Zeppelin and Queen and Black Sabbath...

What's the first band that you really got involved with?
I started conceptualizing bands when I was 10 years old. I was always into music, but when I started getting into the '70s rock stuff like Kiss, I had decided what I was going to do...I started thinking about bands and putting hypothetical bands together with friends. I probably did my first gig in 1982, I had a band called Parasite; we were basically a straight-up, metal-type thing. We weren't very good...actually, we weren't good at all. We played around and we were persistent at it but then we changed members, but hung onto the core of the band, which was me and the drummer, Steve Kelly. We put out our own record as Scarlet in 1986, and that was the first band that I really started to see any success with.

We were still not very good, but we were certainly light years ahead of what we were doing in 1981. We saw some success on radio that year; we played a lot of good gigs. We opened up for Lita Ford and some other bands like that. I remember getting some interest from Columbia, and we talked to Craig Krampf about possibly producing us, but ultimately, I don't think I personally was ready for that. It's not like I was a good enough player, I don't think my voice was good enough to really have done anything. That was back where some of these metal bands, they were horrible; I don't see how they got anything going on. It's probably a good thing that nothing did come of that, because I'd probably be working at Taco Bell.

How did you end up making the Scarlet record?
Back then, that was when all the local bands, that's what everybody felt like you had to do. Lust came out with a record, Burning Hearts came out with an EP, Triple X came out with a record, and we just felt like that's the next thing you do. If you

don't have a record deal, you get your package out there and so we got a little money together, my dad loaned us some money to record…loaned, I should say he gave us the money to record.

We ended up going to the Sound Shop with John Mills who Robert Eva had done some work with…Robert Eva sort of produced it, and John Mills engineered it. Mills had done Jeff Beck and Hall and Oates, so we thought we were happening.

We went and hammered out that record, got it all recorded, mixed, mastered, pressed, and released in three weeks or something like that. I don't think that we actually made any money on it, but we had a good run there for about a year on that record.

Where did you go after Scarlet?
Well, the original line-up changed and I ended up getting Nick, and we held onto the Scarlet thing for a long time. We played for quite a while and then, grunge came in and our kind of stuff just wasn't going on anymore, so we started looking for other things to do. Nick and I stuck together. We had a bunch of little bands with different people, guys that had been around Nashville forever, but nothing that lasted very long.

We formed a band called Casanova and that was actually a real good band but you could see the handwriting on the wall that it wasn't going to last very long. After that, Nick and I, we hooked up with Chris Carmichael and did the Prodigal Sons. Other than Bonepony, that's the band I'm probably the most proud of. We were musically the best band I'd been in and to be able to play with those guys, and do all that we did, I'm real happy about that time…that was a good band.

Did you all ever do any recording?
We did a four-song EP, we didn't release it, but it was real good. It definitely could have used a sympathetic mix…back then, we cut everything on two-inch tape and the funds were low, so we did everything as fast as possible. A lot of my recording career, up until the last couple years, everything was done very quickly because we were always looking at the clock, but we did record a four-song thing and that was pretty much it.

We played around here for just over a year and did real well. We were packing the Cannery, packing Main Street, and pretty much every place we played we did real well. But everybody wasn't in the right place at the right time, and Chris ultimately decided he just didn't want to do a band thing anymore, or at least in fronting a band. He ended up going on the road with Kathy Mattea and David Ball, and some people like that, but now he's pretty much off the road altogether, he just does scoring.

After that, Nick and I put that Social Kings thing together and we had a hard time keeping a band together. We couldn't find a good bass player that would stick with us and we needed a second guitar player that was confident…more like a utility guy, we just couldn't find that. We realized after a while that we were just sinking time and money into a project that really wasn't going to get off the ground.

It's after that you got hooked up with Max Vague…
I was doing a gig with a hockey player that played for a farm team in Pensacola, Florida and he was kind of the heartthrob there. He was a musician and I hooked up with that guy and did a few shows in Pensacola. Max came down with a mutual friend and we sort of struck up a friendship and not long after that, I ended up playing with him. We went into the studio immediately after I joined the band and recorded **Kill the Giant**.

You and Max played around, played a bunch of shows there for a while…
We hit practically every night spot in town and some of them aren't there anymore. But we did, we played a lot and had a different line-up, it seemed like, almost every time. I played drums in that band and I also played guitar for a good two years. We recorded a lot of stuff; after **Kill the Giant**, he and I started on this album called **Entropy** which was almost finished; I have all of that that I would love, at some point, to put together. I don't think that will ever happen, but I have a whole album's worth of material that we did and then Max wanted to change gears for whatever reason…there would be some catalyst that would happen in his life, and he decided that wasn't his musical direction any more. He would ultimately drop whatever it was, regardless of how long we spent on it, and that was the case with that.

But near the end, he was coming back around and we were performing some of those songs live. We had even gone into the studio and recorded a whole record of, basically, us playing live in the studio with minimal overdubs, and a lot of it was that material. I think eventually it would have gotten out, he was talking about releasing some of it on an album called **Speakerhead**, but he changed his mind about the title. I still wanted to release the album, I'd like to think of it as **Entropy** because that was the original title for it, and he had some nice artwork that he put together that I still have. I think it would make a nice little package for the hardcore fans of his out there that are still interested in what he did and, hopefully, someday I'll be able to see it released…

After Max's death, I guess that Nick got you involved with Bonepony?
While I was playing with Max, I also had a band called Moody that Nick and I started together. Then Nick got the call to join Bonepony.

INTERVIEW: KENNY WRIGHT

At one point, I was playing with seven bands at one time and on different instruments. Tramp from Bonepony had a situation where he got an opportunity to play with Hank Williams Jr. and he couldn't make one of the Bonepony gigs, so they asked me to fill in for him.

After that, it got to be a regular thing. I would come out maybe once a month and do a gig or two with them, maybe go on the road with them for a few days. I did that for several years and then Tramp finally said he was going to be leaving the band, they called me up immediately and asked me if I would join, so that's how I got that gig.

We have a lot of fun, that's sort of what it comes down to, how much you enjoy doing it because we don't operate on the level of the Eagles or someone, where everybody has their own jet and we all fly to the gig...we're in a van for 30 hours at a time together sometimes, and if you can't get along, you're not having any fun. We're certainly not making the kind of money that would make us stick together under any kind of unpleasant circumstances, so we're having a great time. We have a great following, and that's another thing we're real fortunate about.

Has Bonepony had any record labels sniffing around?
Yeah, we've had some interest...while we were recording the record; we had a couple of labels that were interested in it. But we make a big part of our income by selling merch and we needed a new product, so we went ahead and pressed it ourselves. I think the labels that were interested at that point sort of balked because we went ahead and put it out without running it past them first.

Kenny Wright

I wish I could say that people are banging at our doors and we're just trying to sort through and find out who's the best for us, but that's not the case. We have had a lot of positive reaction from people that I feel will lead to something good. I don't know that we'll ever get a huge deal with Capital or Warner Brothers, but I do think that there are labels with big distribution that could be a home for us.

The band has already been through that deal where you get a label and then you get pushed to the side. That's the reason *Soul Survivor* didn't do any better than it did...they gave up on it before they even had a chance to do anything, so we don't want that again. We'd rather get a little bit more personalized attention and maybe a little bit less money thrown at us in the front, a little bit more attention on the back end. That's what we're hoping for...

*D*ave Willie was one of Nashville's original punk rockers, a founding member of Committee For Public Safety, possibly the city's first hardcore punk band. He's best remembered as the frontman for the popular Jet Black Factory – a band that, I've long maintained, could have vied with Nirvana or Soundgarden in the alt-rock arena if they'd achieved a deal with a larger record label. I spoke with Dave by phone in July 2007.

What got you interested in music in the first place?
It was a form of escape...I got into doing pop and then punk rock, and the rest was my downfall.

What was the first band you were in?
The first band I was in was the Committee for Public Safety, probably in 1982.

I guess the Nashville music scene was just getting started around that time.
By '82, Phranks 'n' Steins had already sold. The scene was based primarily out of Cantrell's, and Springwater had a couple of shows. There was a club called Spanky's which Bruce Fitzpatrick was booking, and they did a couple of shows. Phranks 'n' Steins was history; by then the scene had been around for a while. I remembering thinking that it had been around for a long time, but obviously it had only been around for just three or four years at tops.

Where was Spanky's?
Spanky's is another club now; it's been a million and ten different things. It was in an office building on Broadway; it was the Liquid Lounge or something like that for a while. I think there's a Japanese Steakhouse on the first floor, it was just one of those weird little places. There's a funeral home right next to it...

Yeah, I think I know where you're talking about...
It was kind of a skanky little place, I always thought it was kind of odd that they would have music there. But a lot of good bands played there...I remember the Butthole Surfers played there and actually we had our first and last...we did one show there and then we were banned after one gig...

You were banned from the club?
As I remember, a urinal was broken or toilet smashed and they thought that I did it. I don't think I did...it's the kind of thing that I might have done, but on that particular occasion, I didn't. I'm sure they didn't like the music to start off with, but the fact that something got broken...

That's funny, because I got banned from Shakey's in Green Hills for almost exactly the same infraction. Somebody thought that I'd torn the urinal off the wall...
Well, back then I went out of my way to look as unpleasant as possible, the whole punk rock thing...the shaved head, my leather jacket was ripped, Confederate flag held together with safety pins, so even if I didn't break a urinal, hey I broke the urinal...

How long did CPS last?
We lasted a little over a year. It was kind of a high school band and the whole thing was kind of weird. When I first went into the music scene in Nashville, just the exposure to it was this incredible revelation. It's everything I said I wanted...I never played many sports and I never had that many friends, and I never belonged to any group. Then you go to a club and it was like everybody got along, everybody was weirdoes, everybody was a little off...everybody went out of their way to be free thinkers and a little eccentric or whatever, and I thought "thank God." It was a remarkable place to be, the land of mismatched toys, and everybody got along and the scene was so small. I remember Gigi Gaskin used to issue this weird social register with everybody's name. I mean literally, the scene was so small that she had this little social register. It was like two sheets of paper folded over horizontally, with everybody's name, phone number, and address...

Where did you go from CPS?
CPS lasted for about a year and I guess it took about a year of jerking around, trying to form bands, and then I formed Jet Black Factory in, I'm guessing, '85.

Did CPS ever do any recording?
We did some recording at MTSU; it was a student done deal and it was not very good. We recorded with Allen Green, Allen really hated us.

INTERVIEW: DAVE WILLIE

That doesn't surprise me, knowing the sort of music he did like...

Yeah, he absolutely fucking hated us, hated us as a band and hated us as individuals. We were really intrigued by that because although a lot of people probably hated us, nobody would have ever come up and say "you guys suck." Anyway, he made us a really good deal on the recording, and he was a pretty good sport about it. We did some four-track recording and it was what it was, you know, four kids trying to learn how to play their instruments...

CPS was a great time and we were able to pull a lot of bands into town...Black Flag came to town and after that, a lot of bands started playing here, which was a real big thing for us. When I first got into music, I thought I would never see these bands, and I did. Seeing them is one thing, but as you're playing with them, it was just remarkable. A little hardcore scene developed which was certainly our goal, to polarize the scene...

You guys got to open for Black Flag?

Yeah, Black Flag on their *Damaged* tour, played Nashville and then met everybody. We opened for another SST Band and we had our punk rock haircuts and leather jackets and we were waiting in the freezing cold at Cantrell's. We'd heard their record, but we never had seen a photograph of them. So we're sitting there, and there's a bunch of homeless guys there, and there's some other homeless-looking guys back there reading comic books. We're waiting around for them to show up, we have our punk rock faces on and, well, these guys are late. Come to find out, they had been there the whole time, they were the long-haired guys in the back reading comic books...they were fucking incredible, they were a great band and put on a really sweltering show.

How did you get Jet Black Factory together?

The guitar player was a roadie for Children of Noise, who were around for a year or two, and I was good friends with those guys. When they disbanded and some of them moved back to Knoxville, I made a friendship with Bob German and he and I started the project...

So what was the evolution of the band? I know that the JBF accomplished a lot more than CPS...

JBF was more of an ideological thing...we were pissed off, and we wanted a manifestation of our anger, which was CPS. Jet Black Factory was a musical project; we were serious about what we wanted to do and what it should sound like. Bob and I, we evolved this idea of how we should approach the songwriting...

One of the real advantages we had back then was 91 Rock and, early on, we got quite a bit of airplay on 91, which was incredible. Because of the amount of airplay on 91, that manifested itself as really good crowds, really good shows

early on. We were lucky enough to hook up with Mike Poole, who was a producer...none of us had any money, so Mike gave us a lot of free studio time. If the record ever did anything, he would get some money off of it...of course, he never saw penny one, but we were really lucky to have run across Mike...

So did you all do one album on your own, and then the one for Core Records?

We did three records on our own...the final record was pretty much a re-release of our third record. We tacked on two additional songs, and that was the Core release.

Did JBF open for any notable bands?

No, we really didn't...we started early on headlining and we toured pretty thoroughly through the Southeast. We had a pretty good following and radio airplay in Knoxville, we actually had incredible college radio airplay throughout the country.

The college radio was good, and our records were distributed through Dutch East India, so we got not great, but not bad record sales throughout the Southeast, in St. Louis, Carbondale, Illinois. We did one big tour up north, and the final show was at CBGB's. We were supposed to play in front of a bunch of record executives, and I forget what night of the week it was, but it was a Jewish religious holiday, so we basically played for nobody. We shared a bill with two or three other local New York bands and our $300 guarantee turned into $30. It was a long ride home with our tail between our legs...

When did JBF break up?

It would have been I think '90 or '91...

What did you do after that?

I went back to school at MTSU. My entire life, I was just so into music, from bands I was in, and I was an audiophile, listening to music continually. That was my life; the entire world was categorized by music. But when I got out of JBF, I was just so burned out, I literally didn't listen to music or play music, didn't want to talk about music. I was doing a lot of art work, a lot of print work...I was out of Nashville and away from the whole scene, and it was nice having a reprieve of maybe two years where you just do some crafts and I kind of got music out of my blood for a little bit. Then John Troup and I formed Nine Parts Devil after that, out of a desire to keep playing and do something a little different.

Weren't you involved with Tag magazine? How did that come about?

At the time, there was a huge adult scene in town, remember back in those days every street had four or five adult bookstores, massage parlors...there was so much of that stuff. I was looking at the sports section of the newspaper and there would be advertisements and I thought "yeah, there are all these adult places in town, and they really have no place to advertise." So I was thinking, if I could do a parody of a men's magazine, have it be edgy and have those people finance it...

We did some writing and put it together and we did an internet version, which got a lot of good reviews. We had a great time, but we couldn't get the ads we wanted. So we did a print version of it, and we were able to sell advertisements and put out more and more copies...over time, we did try to drop a lot of the adult people, and it became a men's magazine. We tried to make it more like a news tabloid...

How long did you put out Tag?
Four or five years...the weird thing is, when we did the internet version, we had lots of press on it, lots of people wrote about us. But when we became a print entity, it was tough; there was no mention of *Tag*. They would periodically mention fundraisers or events, but they no longer wrote about the magazine.

Well, you were competition then...
You know, not really...we're talking about a magazine that continued to lose money but that's the only thing I can figure, is that a professional magazine was not going to be happy to support us. The coup of coups for *Tag*, though, is when we did an article on [Printer's Alley stripper] Heaven Lee...

We were into this weird Nashville history stuff, and we wanted to do a piece on Heaven Lee. We would interview a lot of lawyers and politicians, and we went to this guy that ran a cabaret, a transvestite forum, on Murfreesboro Road. He was an advertiser and we were talking to him and he said, "you know, there's a rumor that she was a man." He says "I want to show you guys something," he pulled us to his office and he had photographs of a pre-operation Heaven Lee. Straight in from Cuba, Heaven Lee was, in fact, a man, until the time he became a transsexual...

What other musical projects have you been up to?
My girlfriend and I are doing a band called the Gold Diggers. She was actually in a swing band back in the '90s, more punk rock guys just improvising jazz. Anyway, she got into this network and did a lot of big shows and swing dances. She asked me "do you think you'd be interested in doing this with me," and it took a lot of coaxing. I'll tell you this, it's the first time I've ever received any money for doing a band. I never made a penny while I was with any other band, and now it's ego-free and it's fun. We do shows periodically in Nashville, we do lounge versions of punk rock songs...

CPS: Dave Willie, Mark Medley, Pat Albert & Michael Godsey

GREG WALKER BIO

Although known primarily for his work with acts in the rock 'n' roll and punk genres (with Cheetah Chrome of Dead Boys fame being the best-known example), Greg Walker's 30-year music career encompassed a large variety of styles and roles (which included forays into blues, jazz-rock fusion, progressive rock, avant-garde noise-rock, and commercial pop as a multi-instrumentalist performer, producer, promoter, and record label A&R rep).

Born in Nashville, Walker was surrounded by music from the beginning. His father, Gary Walker, was a key player in the music industry from the 1950s-1970s, starting out as an artist and songwriter, then later continuing his career by being involved in virtually every phase of the business at one point or another (as a song plugger, producer, studio owner, manager, and record company owner). Greg's mother, Peggy Boone Walker (a direct descendant of Daniel Boone), was being groomed to be a concert pianist (having won several state contests in her home state of Missouri) at the time that she married Walker and the two moved to Nashville. (The Walkers have been more well-known to the general public in recent years as owners of The Great Escape, a five location, Nashville-based retail chain which specializes in records, comics, used DVDs and other pop culture memorabilia.)

During his formative years, Greg worked with and/or was directly influenced by a variety of musicians who would have long and notable careers in the Nashville music scene. His first guitar instructor was Paul Worley, who would later go on to become one of music city's most powerful figures, as producer and record label head. While attending Hillsboro High School, Walker worked in various musical line-ups with players including Mike Doster (who would go on to play bass for B.B. King for over a decade) and Dale Brown (bassist and keyboard player for early Nashville new wave pioneers, the Hots).

By the time he graduated from high school, Walker had already learned to play all the basic rock instruments (guitar, bass, drums, and keyboards) and was making recordings that featured him performing all the parts. He had also experimented with several different musical styles, including folk rock, blues/hard rock, classical (he took piano in this style in high school and received private instruction in classical guitar from John Knowles), and jazz/rock fusion.

After becoming a student at Belmont College, Walker continued to explore more complicated musical directions; this phase peaked when he joined two other like-minded cohorts in their previously-existing outfit Prime Source (which would be best described as a combination of Gentle Giant and Jethro Tull that also included brass); the new lineup of this group had lofty ambitions: in addition to the progressive and renaissance-influenced composing and performing that the group was undertaking, they also happened to all be multi-instrumentalists whose songs were designed to allow the members to switch instruments frequently. (While with the group, Walker contributed guitar, bass, drums and synthesizer to various recordings that were made.) It was also while in college that Walker met avant-garde composer Mark Swann (who, in addition to being extremely accomplished on his main instrument, bass, was also experimenting with the use of half-speed recording, collages, tape-generated noise, etc. while doing his own original material.)

With the insinuation of punk rock and new wave into the mainstream, Walker's musical direction was due to change yet again, however: after purchasing the albums *Never Mind The Bollocks* (Sex Pistols) and *Are We Not Men? We Are Devo!*, both he and another fellow Prime Source member decided that it was time to pursue a simpler, more rock-oriented style; although the group attempted to modify their previous direction to incorporate these changes, the end result was its eventual disintegration. (At one point, during a hiatus from Prime Source activities, Walker became inspired to record an album's worth of British invasion covers in the current punk rock style, playing all the instruments himself.)

Walker's next effort at performing with a live act following Prime Source's breakup was with Modern Emotions, a new wave band that initially began in the summer of 1980 as a power trio in search of a vocalist, consisting of Walker on bass, Jennifer Thompson on guitar, and drummer Chuck Ore (who had been involved in "new music" projects that centered around the Cantrell's scene). Walker ended up leaving this project after disagreements about the future direction of the band: Thompson and Ore wanted to add synthesizer (played by Skot Nelson, a staple of the Nashville punk/new wave scene, best known for the Steve Earle-produced and, originally, Jeff Johnson-created project, Guilt) and saxophone while Walker wanted to keep the raw, three-piece guitar-based sound. (Modern Emotions only lasted for a few months after Walker left, but proved to be a fan favorite at the Alternative Jam concert that they appeared at that year.)

Disillusioned with his program of study at Belmont ("they basically taught us all the technical knowledge you could possibly learn in one semester, then decided to mold us into country club musicians from that point on") and lacking a regular band to perform with, Walker began to pursue filmmaking in 1981 along with Mark Swann. Although film was the main focus for the following year, many musical projects were still to arise. Walker began spending most of his nights at Cantrell's, the main club in Nashville where the burgeoning local punk/new wave scene was developing, and watching the performers at this venue on a regular basis proved to be a source of great inspiration. (He came up with the idea for his dream project during this period: the ultimate punk/power pop band which would combine the raw power of the Sex Pistols with the vocal harmonies of the Beatles, and the psychological and sociologically observant lyrics of the Who; this project never materialized, but he spent many years conceiving and attempting to implement this concept, and even once tried to recruit Bill Lloyd as a drummer for it, after seeing him performing on this instrument at a session at Belmont's Turnley Studio during Lloyd's first few months in Nashville.)

During the spring of 1982, Walker met Slim Johnson, who had built a recording studio in the house that he was renting; Walker recorded an electronic music piece with Johnson for a class that he was taking in the subject, then shortly afterward laid down tracks for the first song he'd written for his intended power pop project, performing all the parts himself. A tape of the song was submitted to a contest that was being sponsored by KDF, the legendary AOR radio station that dominated the Nashville FM market for many years.

Walker moved in with Johnson shortly after (during the summer of 1982) and the two collaborated on various recording projects over the next 2-3 years. One of the first sessions Walker and Johnson did together was co-producing demos on 19-year old future Indigo Girl, Amy Ray (who worked with Walker at The Great Escape during the year that she attended Vanderbilt University.) Johnson and Walker also began working with Mark Swann on a series of recordings, which were to eventually be released by the Limited/Limited record label under the name Temporal Pain.

An EP, *"more to come"* (in flexi disc format, manufactured by Evatone Soundsheets) was released by Temporal Pain in 1982; free copies of it were distributed in *OP* magazine (the leading – and possibly, at the time, the only – fairly widely-distributed magazine which focused on "underground/ alternative/DIY" music), where it received rave reviews. (The publication later changed its name to *Option* and continued to exist in this incarnation for several years before eventually folding.) Shortly after, the Temporal Pain flexi was picked up for distribution by Rough Trade.

Although promo photos were shot for the band and live performances were planned, this was never to take place, because Swann was constantly searching for a new musical direction; although more recordings were made under the Temporal Pain name, the three also began working on other projects with musical styles which differed significantly from the sound of this first group (some of which, including Dull Boy Palace, were eventually released on a cassette sampler by Limited/Limited the following year).

Greg Walker

Becoming bored with filmmaking ("because it was ten times harder than playing music"), Walker diversified his focus between 1983-1985 by taking up journalism, writing articles for both well-known local magazines such as *Anthem* (the current publication of Reverend Keith A. Gordon at that time) and more nefariously-distributed undergrounds.

He also continued working as a studio musician sporadically, with the main project of note being an album he recorded in 1984 with avant-garde pop musician Nudge Squidfish (whose main concept was combining traditional styles such as rock, pop, and country with musique concrete which he referred to as "object music"); Walker contributed piano, synthesizer, eBow guitar and kick drum to the album (the kick drum sound being produced by tapping on the back of a canvas painting), and one of his original compositions, "Getting' Ready For You," was recorded for the collection.

When the company that he worked for at the time purchased a small comic shop in Bowling Green, KY in August of 1987, Walker relocated there a few months later to run the newly acquired retail operation. Having not played live in almost seven years (all projects during this time had been studio-oriented), and having recently developed an obsession for blues, Walker decided that the best way to re-enter the live scene would be to put together an outfit with an authentic Chicago blues sound.

Delta City Depot, the band created for this purpose (with Walker on guitar), achieved this objective admirably, but only lasted for two live performances because of internal tensions; a few months after the group's demise, however, Walker joined a half-cover band (Inside Trak) that the group's bass player, Jeff Davis had gotten involved with. (Davis would later go on to be a part of future Nashville acts such as The Cowards, which featured Ned Hill of Blue Cha Cha's and Ned Van Go renown, and El Fandango, Davis's continuing solo project.) This would in turn lead to the formation of the pair's all-original band that they would use to seriously pursue a music career for the next three years.

This new outfit, dubbed the Lunacats, combined the songwriting talents and lead vocals of Davis (and occasionally Walker) with tight harmonies, high-energy improvisation (with Walker's guitar work recalling Led Zeppelin, the Doors, Jane's Addiction, etc.) and a stylistic range that encompassed folk, blues, punk, psychedelia, and traditional rock 'n' roll. (Like many bands of the era, the blanket term "alternative" was usually what was used to describe the group's sound.)

The Lunacats played continuously for over three years, building a substantial following in the mid-south with strong live performances and a cassette-only release that the band had recorded themselves. The pressures created by constant roadwork, however, and disagreement about the future direction of the band resulted in the breakup of the Lunacats in the spring of 1994, and Walker spent several months working on recordings of solo material and investigating the possibility of relocating to another college town which had a vital music scene.

In December of 1994, Walker got a call from John Albamont, former drummer of the Manikenz (a band from New York that Walker had previously met and befriended back in 1985, going so far as to become part of their road crew), inviting him to a New Year's party which was to take place at his house. During the party, Walker and other former members of the group had an impromptu jam and Walker was contacted again shortly after, with an offer to play bass with an all-punk cover band (oriented toward the original era which formed in New York in the mid-late 1970's) that the ex-Manikenz members were forming. L.A.M.F. (named after the first Johnny Thunders And The Heartbreakers album) made its live debut on May 3rd, 1995 and immediately began to receive both popular and critical acclaim, which included a rave review in the *Nashville Scene* from top music writer Michael McCall and airplay on a four-song EP they had recorded from then DJ Adam Dread.

A few months after joining L.A.M.F., Walker got a phone message from one of his bandmates that simply stated, "Cheetah Chrome is at Exit/In." Because of Chrome's legendary status in both punk and rock 'n' roll circles (having been a founding member of the Dead Boys and Rocket From The Tombs, whose compositions "Ain't It Fun" and "Sonic Reducer" were covered by Guns 'N Roses and Pearl Jam, respectively), and because of the fact that L.A.M.F. were currently covering songs by The Dead Boys, Walker assumed the message to be a joke, and didn't bother to return the call.

A short time later the same evening, however, he was contacted again and, as it turned out, some of his fellow band members were indeed at that moment at the Exit/In, enjoying Chrome's company.

Walker immediately headed to the club to meet Chrome, and the following week the two ended up running into each other again at the same location; Walker gave Chrome a ride back to the motel that he was residing in at the time (during a temporary trip he had made to Nashville to do demos with someone he had known previously), and the two ended up staying up until dawn, playing and singing together. ("He actually knew "Halo Of Flies" by Alice Cooper all the way through, which he ended up playing and I ended up singing on.")

Chrome moved to Nashville shortly thereafter, and having hit it off immediately with L.A.M.F., it was arranged for the two acts to do a show together, which also featured Nashville singer/songwriter Tim Carroll (who was currently collaborating with Chrome on new material). Only a few months after this, L.A.M.F. made the decision to disband (in December of 1995, almost exactly one year after the initial jam session which prompted their formation), and Chrome asked former members Walker (bass), Albamont (drums), and Jimmy V (guitar) if they'd like to become his backing band. The three readily agreed, and immediately began rehearsing together.

After performing a well-received Nashville live debut show, the band soon went to work on making a Cheetah Chrome solo album in New York, which was slated to appear on the newly-formed CBGB Records (owned and operated by the owner of the iconic club of the same name, Hilly Krystal, who had been both the Dead Boys' and Chrome's personal manager since discovering and signing the legendary punk outfit in the mid-1970s). Promotional plans for the album also included a possible tour of Europe and an opening slot with Pearl Jam (whose lead guitarist, Stone Gossard, claimed Chrome as his favorite guitarist).

Recording sessions began at Applehead Studio, a rustic studio located in the woods of Woodstock, New York which was owned by Michael Lang (one of the founders of the original Woodstock Festival in 1969); Applehead had previously hosted such acts as the Band and Jimi Hendrix's Band Of Gypsies in the late 60's/early 70's. Genya Ravan, who had recorded the debut legendary Dead Boys album in 1977, handled production. (Ravan had also previously had a notable career of her own, having been a part of the first all-female self-contained band Goldie and the Gingerbreads, as well as having released several solo albums and producing various other acts throughout the years.)

The initial sessions for the album went extremely well, and everyone who was involved in its production was convinced that record would be extremely successful upon release. The album, however, ended up getting shelved because of various problems that occurred with the label.

Walker and his ex-L.A.M.F. bandmates continued working with Chrome intermittently over the next four years; the outfit did a series of dates in several U.S. cities that included New York (CBGBs), Chicago, Detroit (which yielded a live album that was released in 2000 on D.U.I. records), Atlanta (where Syl Sylvain of the New York Dolls both opened and functioned as a guest member of the band), and Nashville (perhaps the band's best performance was a smoldering show at The End, which was part of the NEA festival in February of 1997). This line-up of the band, however, eventually ended because of family obligations on the part of Albamont and Jimmy V in the spring of 2000.

Although the Cheetah Chrome project was Walker's first priority, he had also begun playing guitar with two more acts during the final year of this incarnation of the Chrome outfit: F. F. Goose and Lance Palmer. F.F. Goose was a band that combined hardcore and old-school punk rock, led by Michael Raber and Adrian Leonard (who are probably best known in Nashville for the critically acclaimed unit On Command; Raber has also been responsible for several years for booking Springwater, one of Nashville's oldest "dive bar" venues, while Leonard went on to drum for The Mattoid, an idiosyncratic fan favorite on the local scene). Lance Palmer was a developing artist in the rockin' country genre whom Walker met when he moved into the residence next door to him in the spring of 1999.

As the first lineup of the Nashville-based Cheetah Chrome band began winding up its activities, Walker began to consider the idea of relocating again. After talking about the possibility of moving to New York with F.F. Goose, a more concrete opportunity arose when Lance Palmer made the decision to move to Los Angeles; without hesitation, Walker agreed to accompany him. After laying down tracks for the upcoming F.F. Goose album and doing one show with the new Cheetah Chrome band – which included Pat Albert (who had played in Nashville's first hardcore band in the '80s, Committee For Public Safety, among others) and Matt Bach (a multi-instrumentalist best known as drummer for David Cloud and Trauma team) – Walker moved to Los Angeles with Palmer in January of 2001.

Walker and Palmer struggled for almost two years in L.A. to find the right combination of players to form a band, with Walker alternating between playing guitar and bass during live shows (depending on who the duo had hired to fill in their lineup at the time). After meeting and forming a close bond with producer Dusty Wakeman (who owned Mad Dog Studios, where recordings had been made for Dwight Yoakum, Lucinda Williams, and others) at a Gram Parsons festival in Joshua Tree California (during which they

Greg Walker

participated in a private memorial ritual at Cap Rock, the site in the desert where Parsons was cremated, with Wakeman and Polly Parsons, Gram's daughter), the two recorded an impressive three-song project with Wakeman in order to capitalize on the buzz that the two had created in Hollywood that centered around Palmer's all-original song, "Rocker Chick" (which inspired local investors to be part of furthering the duo's career).

The final results of the recordings were good enough to prompt Walker's father, Gary Walker, to offer Palmer a publishing deal. (After founding and operating The Great Escape for over 25 years, Gary had been working on getting back into the music business on at least a limited basis again for some time prior to this.) Shortly afterward, Palmer and Walker found the right combination of players to form a permanent band, which Palmer christened the Dead Rebels (at this point Walker switched back from guitar to bass), which included Marco Menigan (Liz Phair) on drums and Jason "Slim Gambill" (Lady Antebellum) on guitar.

After doing a series of successful live shows, the band immediately began recording demos at West Beach Studios (a studio owned by commercial punk/hard rock act The Offspring which was formerly called The Producer's Workshop in the 1970's, and hosted Fleetwood Mac during the tumultuous recording of their *Rumours* album, among other projects).

In October of 2003, Great Escape Records was formed by the retail organization of the same name, and Walker was called on to co-produce the first record to be released by its flagship artist, Crystal Armentrout, a completely self-contained artist who was a writer, vocalist, accomplished guitarist, and multi-instrumentalist who could play 15+ instruments.

In addition to co-producing and playing on the album, Walker began to take on all duties associated with any small record label after the album's release in 2004: promoting, managing, booking, etc.

After continuing to attract attention in Hollywood (which included an offer to have their music placed on several MTV television programs), the Dead Rebels made the decision to begin recording a full-length album in summer of 2004, which took place at the legendary Cherokee Studios; during the recording process, the studio's owners (The Robb Brothers) became excited enough about the band that they decided to get involved in their career, and a series of promotional ventures involving the band were set in motion (including a pilot for a reality show being shot, an offer to place a song by the band in the *Smokey And The Bandit* movie which was currently being made, and a film in which the band had a starring role.)

Upon completion of and release of the record, the Dead Rebels undertook a coast-to-coast U.S. tour in March of 2005 to promote it; Walker continued to do double-duty by both performing with the band and functioning as a representative for Crystal Armentrout and Great Escape Records (which climaxed in a Nashville show that Walker booked, featuring both artists). After returning from the tour, the Dead Rebels were offered a record deal by the newly formed upstreaming label Quarter 2 Three (created by The Robb Brothers and Music Connection's Bernard Bauer, who had championed the band's existence for months in a series of articles written in that publication).

Walker, however, decided to retire from the music business the following year, and moved back to Nashville in October 2006, where he still currently resides. Although he participated in an L.A.M.F. reunion in 2007, Walker's focus since the move has been primarily on running The Great Escape retail chain.

YOUNG GREY RUINS

Band Members:
Sam (vocals)
Shannon Ligon (guitars)
Barry Nelson (bass)
Chaz Orr (drums)
Bill Smartt (sax)

Comments: Writer and musician Allen Green (**Suburban Baroque**), in the pages of Andy Anderson's *Nashville Intelligence Report*, described the music of Young Grey Ruins as "Psychedelic Furs gone garage or Ziggy Stardust gone punk…take your pick." Allen wasn't far from the mark, as this long-lost band's sound was fresh, original and unlikely, mixing three-chord overdrive with new wavish pop and blasts of sax in a shot for underground cred. YGR was short-lived, tho', playing local dives (even opening for the Gun Club), and is mostly remembered for sending guitarist Shannon Ligon and bassist Barry Nelson to our beloved **Shadow 15**.

THE YOUNG NASHVILLIANS

Band Members:
David Lefkowitz (vocals, milkcan) (I-III)
Jerry Lefkowitz (vocals, bass, guitar) (I-III)
Paul Lefkowitz (vocals, Casio MT-40) (I-III)
Jon Shayne (vocals, bass, keyboards, sax) (I-III)
Brad Smith (guitar, bass) (I-III)
Todd Wells (drums) (I-III)
Norman Yamada (vocals, keyboards, violin) (I-III)

Young Nashvillians Recordings:

I. Metropolitan Summer (Dread Beat 1982, LP)

II. The Young Nashvillians Are Here! (BNA Records 1983, EP)

III. The Sad Smiles Of The Young Nashvillians
(Kattywampus Records 1997, CD)
1. Young Nashvillians
2. Special Things
3. Jumper Cables
4. Vanderbilt in France
5. Green Hills
6. Shoney's Ice
7. Siren
8. Something We're Working On
9. To and Fro
10. Sugar Shack
11. Reverse Psychology
12. Flip Flop
13. Take the Tumble

Young Grey Ruins

14. Look at Me
15. Ironic Twist
16. Young Nashvillians (reprise)
17. Amelia
18. Eagle Man
19. Thanks but No Thanks
20. Wednesday
21. Follow That Girl
22. 20/20
23. Jumper Cables
24. Dance with Lance

Comments: The Young Nashvillians were, hands down, the most entertaining local rock band of the '80s! While other bands made great music and included serious (and talented) musicians among their ranks, the Young Nashvillians was never about anything other than F-U-N! Formed in 1982 as a summer project by the various members, a four-track tape of the band's songs that had been recorded in Shayne's basement made its way to Kevin Gray of the **White Animals**.

Gray subsequently released the tape as the *Metropolitan Summer* LP on the Dread Beat label during the summer of 1983. The Young Nashvillians opened several shows for the White Animals around that time. Several songs from the album received regular airplay on Vanderbilt's WRVU and the response of the young, growing local rock scene to tunes like "Jumper Cables," "Vanderbilt in France" and "Green Hills" was overwhelmingly positive.

The guys got back together the following summer and recorded *The Young Nashvillians are Here!* EP in a Music Row recording studio, played around town a bit, and then drifted off to college, jobs and adult life. The two vinyl discs were compiled on CD as *The Sad Smiles of The Young Nashvillians*, songs #1-16 from *Metropolitan Summer* and songs #17-23 from *The Young Nashvillians are Here!* (which is why I didn't list them separately above). The bonus track "Dance with Lance" was recorded by Paul Lefkowitz and Jon Shayne in 1989 and the CD compilation was released

THE YOUNG NASHVILLIANS

in 1997 by Jerry Lefkowitz on his Minneapolis-based Kattywampus label, the original recordings remixed by Shayne.

What did the Young Nashvillians sound like? Imagine Jonathan Richman, early-60s pop, late-60s garage rock, '80s-era new wave, Devo and maybe Elvis Costello all thrown in a blender. The band's songs are loose and edgy, lyrically wordy and full of local references, and a heck of a lot of fun. The guys knew that they weren't very good musicians and reveled in their rank amateurism, but their approach pre-dated and foreshadowed better-known but similar bands like the Dead Milkmen, Ween, Weezer, and They Might Be Giants.

While most of the band went into "real" jobs after school, some of them went into music. Jerry Lefkowitz launched Kattywampus Records, which doesn't seem to be around anymore. Norman Yamada is a well-respected avant-garde musician and composer in New York City who has worked with folks like guitarist Marc Ribot and pianist Anthony Coleman. Brad Smith is a well-known music biz attorney around town and a heck of a nice guy!

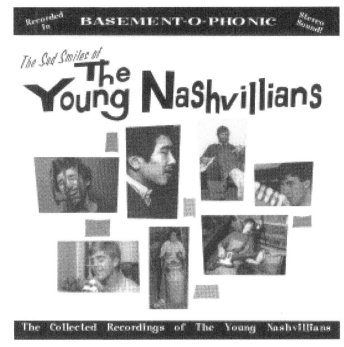

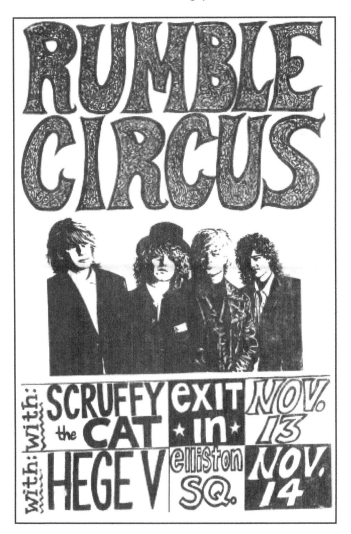

What was the first music zine in Nashville? That honor, without a doubt, goes to *Hank Magazine*, published by man-about-town Harvey Magee. *Hank* focused on "cosmic cowboy" songwriters that had flooded the town during the early 1970s, as well as Southern rockers like Charlie Daniels and the Marshall Tucker Band. *Hank* covered other strains of music – for example, this humble scribe placed a Johnny Rivers album review in the zine during my senior year of high school – but Magee's zine was really an unheralded forefather of *No Depression*, featuring artists like Don Schlitz, Marshall Chapman, and Guy Clark.

Then there's Thom King's *Take One Magazine*, which was really more than just a music zine. Thom, who I kind of knew from Franklin High School, launched the zine in 1977 with an eye towards serious journalism...like an early *Nashville Scene*, with a better balance of local news, thought-provoking articles, and entertainment coverage. I came on board somewhere around issue number three or four, after running into Thom at Shakey's Pizza in Green Hills and asking for a gig writing album reviews.

By the end of the year, Thom and I were pretty much running the rag on our own, with help from his brother John and writer Sam Borgerson. *Hank* had pretty much disappeared by 1977 and *Take One* picked up the slack in music coverage. We were the first publication in town to talk about the Ramones and the punk revolution of '77, and if we publicized Nashville's "first" rock band, the Smashers, we redeemed ourselves with coverage of Cloverbottom. Thirty-plus years later, Thom and I still talk about the trials and tribulations of publishing *Take One*.

During the waning days of *Take One*, I disappeared to Detroit for a couple of years (1979-80) and reveled in the ultra-cool punk rock scene exploding in the Motor City. A funny thing happened while I was gone, though – Nashville developed a rock scene of its own. Working out of a beer joint/hot dog stand by the name of Phranks 'n' Steins, Rick Champion provided a forum for original bands like Cloverbottom, the Actual, and others to play. Allen Green's short-lived *Grab!* music zine documented this growing scene in 1981/82, with great writers like Kent Orlando, Curtis "C Ra" McGuirt, Glenn Hunter, and Champion himself. The zine had an irreverent wit, and the couple of copies that I still have of *Grab!* offer stories on Factual and the Wrong Band as well as reviews of records by the Ratz and the Smashers.

After Green started his own band – the way-ahead-of-their-time Suburban Baroque – *Grab!* fell by the wayside and Nashville was without a real local music zine for a while. I published copies of my own zine *Anthem* on a sporadic basis, and covered some local bands, but most of *Anthem*'s meager circulation went to places like England, Germany, and Poland as well as to L.A. and NY and Chicago through mail swaps with other zinesters.

Enter Andy Anderson and the *Nashville Intelligence Report*. I can't remember when, exactly, Andy began publishing *NIR* but his zine picked up where *Grab!* left off. Andy was excited about the local music scene, and the zine featured many of the same writers that had populated *Grab!* Somewhere along the line I got involved with the project, and Andy published the zine for several years, championing local bands but also covering national artists like Katrina & the Waves and Los Lobos.

When Andy went home for a year (Knoxville, I think), Rick Champion took on the mantle as publisher, and *NIR* carried on without missing a beat. When Andy returned, he took back over from Rick and published *NIR* until after Gus Palas came to town and launched the more commercially-oriented *The Metro* music magazine. Andy stopped publishing NIR and ended up doing some writing for *The Metro* during the late 1980s. Andy was a good writer with a real fanboy's enthusiasm for, and an immense knowledge of the music; he fled the local scene during the dark days of the mid-1990s, relocating to New York City, before landing in North Carolina.

Let's clear the air before we begin discussing *The Metro*. Gus Palas was an asshole of the first degree, a manipulating conman whose promises never lived up to the reality. Over the seven years or so that Gus published *The Metro*, he ripped off, pissed off, and disappointed a hell of a lot of people. As *The Metro*'s main contributor throughout its run – the zine's music editor and resident critic, as well as photographer, graphic artist, and all-around whipping boy – nobody (and I mean nobody) got ripped off by, or pissed off at good ol' Gus more than the kindly Reverend. After all, I stood shoulder to shoulder with Palas through thick and thin, defended him at the risk of my own reputation, and went out on a limb for the rag more than once.

It all started during the summer of 1985. At the urging of Bernie Walters (the madman and visionary that tried to get the Rock & Roll Hall Of Fame to locate in Nashville), I received a phone call from Gus Palas. Bernie had told him that I was the "go-to" guy around town, the one writer that he needed on the staff of his new magazine. I bought into Gus's vision of a local music magazine and offered my dubious expertise to get the thing off the ground. *The Metro* got off to a rocky start, with Gus overestimating the meager (unpaid) staff's ability to crank out a zine every two weeks, and overestimating the amount of ad revenue the publication would pull in. From a gloomy basement office in an alleyway off Belmont Boulevard, we published the first half-dozen or so issues of *The Metro* in a cocaine-fueled haze.

Over the next seven years, Gus would keep the rag going by hook or by crook, publishing on a shoestring budget, frequently changing office spaces when unpaid rent would prompt a "midnight move." When local typesetters would no longer work on the rag without cash in advance, Gus scraped up the money to buy some Mac computers and do the lay-out and design in-house. He ran the magazine out of seedy offices (Melrose, Music Row), a nightclub (The Cannery) and his own apartment. Somehow, Gus got *The Metro* on the street more often than not.

There was a period, around 1985/86 or so, when Gus was off playing rock star with the Simmons brothers and their band the Stand. During this year, Gus abdicated his role in the magazine to a bunch of Vandy kids, pretty much duplicating the same error that Thom King had made with *Take One Magazine* a decade earlier. During his absence, this writer was marginalized by the new staff and the magazine took off in a different direction, with a more "artistic," hipper vibe. Palas returned from his hiatus in mid-1987 and took over the reins of *The Metro* from the Vandy grads that were running it.

When this group of disgruntled former staffers was shown the door in a power play between them and Palas, they started up the short-lived *Fireplace Whiskey Journal*. Launched in the spring of 1988 by former *Metro* editor Kath Hansen along with writer Tom Wood, his girlfriend (now wife) Nicki Pendleton, Regina Gee, and local musician Lee Carr, *Fireplace Whiskey Journal* drew the line in the sand. You were either for Gus Palas or you were against him.

In the zine's first issue, Wood fired off the salvo "In Defense Of The Metro," a sarcastically-titled editorial criticizing Palas for poor business decisions, his inability to keep a strict publishing schedule and...horror of horrors...for wasting ink on bands like Metallica. This writer shot off a response to Wood's smug editorial, defending Palas and *The Metro* (and, by extension, my own work). The *Fireplace Whiskey Journal*'s ruling council refused to publish my rebuttal piece in "their forum," which, of course, prompted another response on my part. Why dredge up ancient history over two publications that no longer exist? Because I was right, dammit, and they were wrong!

As I wrote at the time, "all of the creative efforts of every Nashville musician, poet or painter won't add up to shit if nobody outside of Davidson County is exposed to them. To this end, *The Metro* has served to represent Nashville culture to the world...not totally, nor flawlessly, but as adequate and balanced a forum as is possible in what is an advertiser-supported publication." I concluded my tirade with, "like it or not, Gus Palas has done more to promote local talent of **ALL** kinds, from alternative acts to heavy metal and all who stand in between, than the whole lot of prancing, posing, pseudo-intellectual rich kids and snobbish Vandy grads slumming for a semester or two down on Elliston Place." And, in retrospect, this was true. Yes, we put Bon Jovi on the cover of the very first issue, in August 1985, but we also put cult L.A. cowpunk band the Screamin' Sirens on the cover of issue number two.

Throughout the history of *The Metro*, I personally wrote stories on local talent like Dessau, the Dusters, In Pursuit, F.U.C.T., Jet Black Factory, Jason & the Scorchers, Webb Wilder, Threk Michaels, Chagall Guevara, and Aashid Himons, among many others. We also pursued stories of national importance, and provided important coverage to artists like R.E.M., Billy Bragg, Faith No More, Mojo Nixon, the Ramones, and King's X. *The Metro*'s eclectic editorial direction often provoked grumbles among local scenesters that we gave coverage to our friends, or that you could buy your way into the rag which, in one sorry instance (the unfortunate Whyte Lace incident) proved true. However, on my part, I wrote about bands that I liked, or those that contacted the magazine and asked for a story, and I was never paid a dime by Gus or anybody else (tho' Tom Littlefield and Kenny McMahan did buy beer on a few occasions).

The Metro became a force to be reckoned with around its fifth anniversary, shortly after Gus had hooked up with Lisa Hays and Lisa became the rag's de facto managing editor. A ground-breaking interview with Tipper Gore at the height of the PMRC controversy prompted an outraged Jello Biafra to pull out a copy of the magazine on Oprah Winfrey's national TV show, flashing *The Metro* on screen and quoting from the interview. This led to my interview with the Dead Kennedys frontman and more national attention. We became one of the first publications in the country to write about Living Colour, Sepultura, and Stealin' Horses. We published Andrew Eldritch's favorite Sisters of Mercy article and championed free speech in Nashville's punk underground. The magazine sponsored three "Nashville Music Awards" bashes and could boast of readers from across the country and in Europe.

In the end, though, Gus was a pretty shabby businessman and there was never enough money to support *The Metro*. Although the magazine had always attracted talented writers – folks like Rebecca Luxford, Brian Mansfield (now a long time *USA Today* writer), Bill Spicer, and old school scribes like Andy Anderson, Thom King, and yours truly – *The Metro* went dark sometime late-1991/early-1992. When Gus resurfaced after a ten month hiatus, it was to sell what was left of *The Metro* to WRLT-FM, Radio Lightning, which published it for a few months and changed the name (and editorial focus) to follow the interests of the station.

Okay, so here's how it really went down. It was the fall of 1991, October or November methinks. *The Metro* was on its last legs. Palas had pissed off, burned and mislead enough people around town that there was no haven left for his little music rag. We had set up an interview with underground musician Eugene Chadbourne – who remains one of the most interesting artists plying their trade in the American underground today – and tied it to an EC show that Gus was allegedly promoting at the Cannery. It was a slam dunk, really: Chadbourne interview in the paper, a live show a week or so later, and to top it off, a friend of mine agreed to cover Eugene's meager $500.00 guarantee. Gus didn't even have to part with any coin, just put on the show...

Chadbourne called me when he rolled into town and I met him in Green Hills. We left his rental car in a lot that I knew would be safe for overnight storage (having left my car there in a drunken Cantrell's stupor many a night) and ran down to Pizza Perfect to have some dinner. Now, the Reverend was already mighty suspicious, since Palas hadn't returned any of my calls that week, and an issue of *The Metro* with my Eugene Chadbourne interview was nowhere to be found. A deal was a deal, though, and I had already handed off my buddy Eric's five C-notes to Eugene, so, as they say, the show must go on!

Eugene and I arrived at the club around 7:00 PM (for a 9:00 PM showtime) to find the windows darkened and the parking lot strangely devoid of cars. Gus had supposedly arranged for Walk The West, who had met Eugene in Austin, to open the show and I figured that the lot would be full of that popular local band's fans. No such luck. We threw some rocks against the one window that was lit, waking the club's "security guard" from his slumber. The night watchman, a buddy of Gus's that was crashing at the club, had no knowledge of any show going on that night, and he was right.

I called up several friends, including the one that had paid Eugene's guarantee, and we all agreed to meet out at his house. There, Chadbourne pulled out his trusty songbook and beat-up guitar and proceeded to put on a private show for 13 listeners, right from the comfort of Eric's couch. Unfortunately, Nashville didn't know what it was missing, 'cause Eugene rocked the house and we all had a grand old time.

Flash forward several months to the spring of 1992. *The Metro* had been AWOL since the Chadbourne fiasco and local music fans, accustomed to a monthly...more or less...music zine were getting edgy. A number of people approached the Reverend and asked what it would take to start up a new rag. "Money" was always my answer, and when Mark Willis of New Sound Atlanta (who had taken over booking the Cannery in Gus's absence) and Mike Phillips of local band Peace Cry agreed to help underwrite the venture via advertising, R^2 (or *R Squared*, for "**R**ock & **R**oll") was born. Pan Doss at the Pantheon club jumped on board, as did Steve West at 328 Performance Hall, and off we went....

The first issue of R^2 hit the streets in June 1992, a quarter-fold tabloid with local rocker Threk Michaels and alt-metal legends King's X on the cover. I had lined up a pretty strong staff of writers, most of them former *Metro* scribes, including Brian Mansfield (who wrote a great Will & the Bushmen piece) and my old *NIR* buddy, Andy Anderson (who contributed a piece on the Ellen James Society and interviewed the Replacements' Chris Mars). We had articles on international artists (Midnight Oil), regional artists (Atlanta's Stonehart) and local artists (Michaels, Stealin' Horses). Clint Brewer, who would become the editor of the *Nashville City Paper*, contributed a cool Widespread Panic article, and Andy and I scratched out a bunch of album reviews, including discs by the Ramones, Body Count, the Beastie Boys and Jason Ringenberg's first solo album, *One Foot In The Honky Tonk*.

It took a lot of work to get that first issue of R^2 off the ground, and after collecting all the advertising monies due, we broke even, if I remember correctly. Aside from the writers who were paid a pittance for their contributions, folks like Mike Phillips and his wife Wendi, Mark Willis and his new Sound Atlanta staff (especially Roxanne), Nancy Camp

and Pam Cross in Atlanta, and Nashville's Randy Ford and Donny and April Kendall (*House O' Pain*) were all instrumental in getting the zine on the street. Thanks to Willis, we had distribution in Nashville, Atlanta, Roanoke VA, and Myrtle Beach SC. The zine had great content and if the lay-out looks a little dated and undergroundish as I look at it today, it was, by all measures, a minor triumph.

With little or no money left after producing issue numero uno of R^2, Mike Phillips and I began badgering our advertisers (Go West Presents, the Pantheon, Deja Vu, 527 Mainstreet in the 'boro and, of course, New Sound Atlanta) to place ads in issue number two. Andy and Brian and myself started cranking out copy when, who should reappear on the local scene but Gus Palas! As we were hitting up advertisers for commitments for our second issue, we often found that Gus had been there first, talking shit and trying to undercut us.

Seems that Gus was trying to resurrect *The Metro* after a hiatus of nine months or so, and the only way that he could do it was by running down those of us who had supported him through the years. We heard reports of Gus saying that I didn't know how to put together a magazine (actually, I taught *him*), that we had second-rate writers (Brian Mansfield has since published several books and has written for *U.S.A.*

Today for over a decade) and so on. It was a dirty campaign and a lot of potential advertisers were on the fence.

The Reverend, veteran of biker bars and early Internet flame wars, was ready for the fight when, unfortunately, my father died unexpectedly. After working security for New Sound Atlanta at the Cannery on a Friday night, I spoke with my father early Saturday morning before going to bed. I was awakened by my mom who said that they had rushed dad to the hospital. By the time I could drive from Franklin to Nashville, dad had died...and all the piss and vinegar that I had worked up for a feud with Palas drained right out of me. At that moment, I didn't really care about R^2 or *The Metro* or much of anything except my family.

Unbeknownst to all of us, behind the scenes, Gus was negotiating to sell *The Metro*. Maybe he knew that he couldn't beat us (after all, R^2 had his best writers and most of his advertisers) or maybe he was just trying to cash out and split town. Either way, he somehow convinced Ned Horton and Radio Lightning to buy *The Metro* for a reported $10,000 and bring the zine in-house. I'll never understand why Ned didn't just start his own music zine through the radio station rather than pay Palas (after all, *The Metro* was nothing more than a couple of crapped-out computers by this time, and Gus hadn't published an issue in over nine months).

I found out about the sale of *The Metro* when Gus called me to offer his condolences for the loss of my father and to make an offer to buy out the second issue of R^2; seems like they didn't have any material to publish a new issue of *The Metro*, so Gus convinced Ned to pay me $500 or something like that for the contents of *our* second issue. Since it didn't appear that I was going to be able to get another R^2 on the street anyway, I agreed to the purchase, paid my people, and made peace with Gus. In the process, I was drafted onto the staff of the "new" *Metro*, although it wouldn't be long until changes were in the air...

Palas had sold the bloated carcass that was *The Metro* to Radio Lightning to use as a sort of in-house music magazine. Station manager Ned Horton had some great ideas for the rag, and no little amount of vision, but he knew right from jump street that he had to do something about the magazine to make it more professional if he was going to sell it to advertisers. He spent a crapload of money on new Apple computers and all the software needed to make a magazine look nice, and then he went out and found a couple of guys to use all this new gear.

Ned hired Daryl Sanders and Jody Lentz from Athlon Sports. Unlike Gus and, really, even myself, these guys came from a higher level in the publishing biz. Athlon was a mega-bucks company, publishing annual sports guides for S.E.C. and NFL football and such, magazines with glossy color covers

and lots of advertising. I knew Daryl briefly from the good old days of *Take One Magazine*, where he had worked with Thom King before I came along, and he was to take the editorial reigns of *The Metro*. Jody was an accomplished graphic artist that could make a Mac sing, and his redesign of the rag made it look cool, clean, and professional.

Daryl and Jody rounded up a staff, including some very fine writers like Jason Moon Wilkins, Holly Gleason, Brett Ratner, Audese Green, Warren Denney, and even my old pal Andy Anderson, as well as the Reverend, to fill up the pages of *The Metro* each month. Under the new editorial regime, and in keeping with the radio station's eclectic mix of musical genres, the scope of *The Metro* expanded to include coverage of reggae, world music, jazz, blues and the new "jam band" genre. Sometime in mid-1993, *The Metro* became *Bone Music Magazine* and Gus Palas found himself gently pushed out the door.

Initially, the Reverend contributed CD reviews to *Bone*, and since I was one of the few staffers that was plugged into the Nashville music scene, I got to cover local bands as well. If the '80s offered great local bands like Jason & the Scorchers, Webb Wilder & the Beatnecks, Walk The West, the White Animals and Afrikan Dreamland, the decade to follow would see an explosion of talent. Clockhammer, Max Vague, the

Floating Men, Price Jones, Chagall Guevara, and many more would also create cool and challenging music during the 1990s.

It was Daryl Sanders who officially dubbed me "The Reverend" and began running my byline as Rev. Keith A. Gordon, claiming that since I was always preaching about music, the media, politics and such, and since I was an ordained minister, I should therefore be called "The Reverend." I began writing a column for *Bone* called "Dancing On The Edge" that covered music, zines, counter-culture and something called "the Internet." It was *Bone* publisher Ned Horton who declared that "nobody wants to read about the Internet," and therefore the magazine (and my column) should be sparing in its coverage of the fledgling technology.

With Sanders and Lentz at the helm, assisted by people like Kris Whyte (now Whittlesey, editor of *All The Rage*) and guided by Horton, *Bone* expanded with regional editions in a number of cities, including Atlanta, which were sponsored by local radio stations. A small four-page insert called *T-Bone* was produced for *The Tennessean* newspaper, featuring artist interviews and CD reviews. By 1995, *Bone Music Magazine* was a bona fide regional phenomenon covering the best mainstream and alternative music. Ned even discovered the Internet, and the Reverend was allowed to cut loose with a cover story that year about "music on the Internet."

A year later, however, the bottom fell out for *Bone*. The zine was losing "affiliates" across the country, reducing the number of editions that were produced (and the income received from those other radio stations). The Internet was providing music news faster than a monthly magazine, and Ned later admitted that he had underestimated the growth in popularity of the 'net as a new media outlet. Neither Ned nor the radio station had anything to counter the 'net, and it hurt the magazine.

In May 1996, Horton was asked to resign his position by the station's owners due to a difference in management philosophy. Local businessman David Tune took over as station manager and soon discontinued both *Bone* magazine and something called "Bone TV" that ran one or two shows on a local station. The new *Metro/Bone* magazine had managed to squeeze out almost four years before falling beneath the reaper's blade.

There have been a number of zines published in Nashville during the years, both music-oriented and otherwise. The Reverend published sporadic zines such as a resurrected *R Squared* and *R.A.D! (Review And Discussion of Rock & Roll)* on a limited basis during the late 1990s before launching the ***Alt.Culture.Guide*** music webzine in 2000. There was KP's *Rock & Read* zine, which evolved into *Shake Magazine*,

published by local musician Chris James. The local scene was never *Shake*'s main focus, although Chris and writers like Steve Morley wrote about some interesting music.

The Nashville punk underground was covered admirably for years by Donnie and April Kendall and their lively *House O' Pain* zine, but that publication eventually ran its course as well. After the *Fireplace Whiskey Journal* went belly-up, Lee Carr published several issues of the funny, scathing, and often brilliant *Weasel Weekly* zine, and later Dave Willie got together with some folks and published the culture zine *Tag*.

With the explosion of local rock 'n' roll talent like the Kings of Leon, Paramore, and others, it's a wonder that no young entrepreneur has decided to launch a new Nashville music zine. Then again, maybe the era of zines has long passed, with the web and music blogs taking up the cause. When I look back at the halcyon times of the Nashville music zine, circa 1977-1997, I have to say that it was a hell of a run...

APPENDIX B: LIFE, THE UNIVERSE & THE METRO

This was written, only slightly tongue-in-cheek, for the second anniversary issue of The Metro *in August 1987. If I only knew then what I know now...who'd have thought that* The Metro *would make it two years, much less enjoy its fifth anniversary in 1990, to finally peter-out somewhere between year six and seven?*

Gus sold the remnants of the rag to Radio Lightning in 1992, a deal brokered by Ned Horton, who became the publisher, bringing on Daryl Sanders as editor and eventually changing the name to Bone Music Magazine. *For all the criticism leveled at Palas, however, one fact remains true – nobody else has published a magazine focusing on Nashville's non-country music scene longer that Gus and* The Metro, *and many have tried in the years since. Even today, with the Nashville rock scene thriving as never before, with a highly-regarded national reputation, there is no publication like* The Metro *to champion the scene...and 'tis more the shame.*

Left unsaid in this article was how it took mountains of cocaine and gallons of beer and booze to cobble together a new issue every two weeks. Still, we accomplished quite a bit on a shoestring budget and little or no institutional support in the early years...

A long, long time ago in a galaxy far, far away... (Naw, that won't work...it's been used before).

Once upon a time, in a magic kingdom lived a... (Though none the worse for the wear, it's somehow inappropriate).

Let's try this one more time...

Gus Palas had a dream...not just your garden-variety, earthshaking, wet-the-bed kinda dream, but a vision of great magnitude and magnificence. He was going to start publishing a music magazine...and not just any kind of music mag. GVPIII was going to create a rag that featured Nashville's fledgling rock and roll performers in its pages, the local scene mixed, editorially, with coverage of the growing indie/college radio performers and the ever-changing world of big-league pop music. Throw in a dash of soul, a soupcon of jazz, and a healthy dose of "new-kid-on-the-block" brashness, mix well and serve: *The Metro.*

When I first met Gus back in the summer of '85, he told me of his dream. I, for one, thought that he'd spun this fantasy after a late-night snack of spicy anchovy burritos...and you know what kind of dreams that will produce! But whereas I dream of Sybil Danning in a Jacuzzi filled with butterscotch pudding, Gus whipped up some ridiculous ideas about founding a publishing empire.

Go figure...

Shrugging my misgivings, I got involved with *The Metro* in those long and hot early days before the first issue. After all, I'd been involved with speculative publishing projects before, from Thom King's groundbreaking *Take One* magazine, Nashville's first alternative rag, to the *Nashville Gazette*, to a host of other magazines, tabloids, and one-sheeters. It's not often that one gets a chance to participate in another's dream, and even if Gus was an odds-challenging loony-toon, well, I possess more than my own share of genetically-mutated mental illness myself.

The first issue of *The Metro* hit the stands on or around August 16th, 1985 and featured yet-to-become superstar Jon Bon Jovi and local talents In Pursuit on the cover. That first issue was mild, if not calculated. We tossed in the Music City's longest-lived rockers, the White Animals, along with a handful of record reviews and some local news. Sixteen pages chock full o' fun, and it only took us a couple of months of protracted labor after several months of pregnancy to give birth to the monster. On the seventh day, we looked at it, and it was good.

Then we all went out and got obscenely drunk...

That next morning, Gus was rattling our cages and rudely shook us from our collective stupors. "Time to work on Number Two!," he screamed, or something to that effect (memories are foggy after much time and abuse). "Well, isn't this a fine kettle of fish," we, the staff, thought. "We *slave* and *sweat* to put out the first issue and now this clownhole Palas actually wants us to begin work on a second one?" Surely, though, with the experience garnered from the mistakes of the previous endeavor, we'd be able to whip together a second *Metro* in little or no time at all...

Right enough, that second issue was a breeze. Sort of like trying to change a tire while utilizing a pair of toothpicks in place of the jack. Not unlike squeezing toothpaste *back into* the tube.

Not any easier...

After the proper two-week gestation period, the second issue of *The Metro* hit the streets, and what a King Hell mutant baby it was! The honeymoon was over kiddies, we were here to kick your rears and open your ears. We began writing rock and roll history in those pages, as we not only became the first publication in the known universe to slap the beautiful Screamin' Sirens on our cover in an exclusive pre-tour interview (they played Nashville a couple of days after the issue appeared, creating a legion of Music City Sirens Love Slaves with their charm and talent). *The Metro* was also the first rag to review John Cougar Mellencamp's breakthrough album, *Scarecrow*. We threw in features on Nashville faves Jason and the Scorchers and Bill Lloyd's phenomenal Sgt. Arms band and went home feeling good about the job we'd done.

With the third issue, we changed from the digest format that we'd used on the first two in favor of a larger, tabloid style that allowed us to offer you, the reader, more features, more reviews, and more news than any other rock rag in the Southeast. We set yet another pair of dual milestones with that one as we introduced you to both Webb Wilder and the Georgia Satellites in features by Bill Spicer and myself. Webb has become somewhat of a local legend, and is soon to be an international smash (could it be any other way?); and although we were the first magazine in the U.S.A. to discover the Satellites (after their historical reunion show at the sadly defunct Cantrell's), the rest of the world now knows them after a Number Two single and a Top Ten, Gold-selling debut album. The Satellites' success led to tours with Bob Seger and Tom Petty...and placed another feather in our caps.

From that time on, *The Metro* became a staple in Nashville. Sure, the issues were still hard to produce and, as some weeks proved to be longer than others, I was often accosted in public with cries of "Hey, Gordon ya scumbag, when's the next *Metro* gonna be out, huh??" After taming these anxious readers with a large and pointy stick, I assured them that the next issue would be in their hot little hands soon enough. And it always was, give or take a week or two...

That first year of *The Metro* saw an evolution in rock and pop music as college radio grew from a cultish, big-school plaything to a major force in presenting new talent. During those weeks and months, the pages of *The Metro* remained on the cutting edge of creativity, not content to follow the trends and cover the established and old-hat, but rather create the trends and discover tomorrow's superstars, yesterday. *The*

Metro boldly treaded where no publication had feared tread before, offering interviews and features on the likes of Motley Crue, Omar & the Howlers, Love Tractor, Amy Grant, Heart, Robyn Hitchcock, Rosanne Cash, the dB's, Green On Red, NRBQ, and countless others, long before you read about them elsewhere.

And, oh those record reviews...where else but in *The Metro* could one find the diversity of style and taste that would include coverage of such mainstream acts as Jon Butcher, Stevie Wonder, Rush, ZZ Top, and Elton John with such off-the-beaten path talent as Billy Bragg, Julian Cope, Mofungo, Kate Bush, Lou Miami, Mojo Nixon, Eugene Chadbourne, the Smithereens, etc, etc. We unearthed the Meatmen! We found Adolph Hitler living in Argentina! WE DISCOVERED THE BEATLES!! (Oops, sorry...I got a little carried away. I'm much better now.)

From that very first issue, *The Metro* has attempted to accurately reflect and support Nashville's talented and ever-growing local music scene. From those early days when a mere handful of bands were playing an equal number of clubs, we've seen the local scene evolve from an embryonic idea to a minor aggravation to those who would keep Nashville pure, country, and mediocre to a fully-bloomed, nationally-recognized hotbed of creative radicalism.

APPENDIX B: LIFE, THE UNIVERSE & THE METRO

For every local talent scarfed up by the major labels, from Jason and the Scorchers to the Sluggers, immigrants like John Hiatt, the Georgia Satellites, and Billy Chinnock there are a dozen and one as-of-yet unsigned talents like Threk Michaels, the Questionnaires, and Raging Fire. We've tried to cover them all, from In Pursuit to Afrikan Dreamland, from Bill Lloyd to Webb Wilder, from the Royal Court of China to Walk The West and beyond. Above all, we've tried to be Nashville's music magazine, and if that means turning you on to the talents of Dessau, Will Rambeaux or John Jackson, so be it.

The Metro has never been afraid to take a bold editorial stand, however popular or unpopular it may prove to be. We've taken great pains to foster originality and creativity, not just publish press releases and ad copy opinion. When the Missus of Tennessee's erstwhile Presidential candidate, Tipper (and her cohorts), attempted to castrate rock lyrics, we spoke loudly in opposition to any form of censorship. *The Metro* came out, in print, against the evil apartheid regime of the white-minority ruled South Africa, and stated its disdain, in no uncertain terms, towards racism in any way, shape or form, both within the music industry and beyond. We supported Bernie Walters in his attempts to have the rock and roll museum located in Nashville…and provided valuable coverage to the Nashville Entertainment Association's Music Extravaganzas and the annual Summer Lights festival.

The second year of *The Metro* proved to be as ground-breaking and seminal in influence as the first. Among other gems, the magazine published pieces on the Psychedelic Furs, George Carlin, Otis Blackwell, the local jazz scene as represented by Café Unique and JC's, profiles of Mickey Basil, Stan Lassiter, a historical remembrance of the Byrds' Gram Parsons, and exclusive coverage of Bubba Skynyrd's takeover of KDF.

As *The Metro* enters its third year, the magazine continues to grow in vision and importance. We've switched from bi-monthly, increased circulation and distribution, and are no longer the unproven kid in diapers. *The Metro* has passed the audition and has become one of the longest-lived and influential publications of its kind, with copies finding their way into hands across the United States and the world, receiving a fair amount of international acclaim and accolades from such far-strewn locals as Germany, Poland, and France. *The Metro* celebrates its second anniversary with this issue, even though the odds are still against its survival…

…and your humble writer is still along for the ride. 'Cause it's not every day that you get to participate in someone else's dream…and even if two years at the helm of a gang of assorted loonies, artistic thugs, and creative malcontents may have warped his sense of reality only slightly, I'm still betting that Gus can pull it off. And even if he doesn't, it'll be a hell of a ride!

Won't you join us?

Keith A. Gordon
Somewhere on Lower Broad
August 1st, 1987

APPENDIX C: LEFTOVER RECORD REVIEWS

Over the course of putting the book together, I ran across a number of reviews...most of 'em old, some freshly-written...that I had originally overlooked but wanted to include. They're reprinted here pretty much as they originally ran, with the exception of a few corrected mistakes in spelling either by myself or by the typesetter. The language is sometimes embarrassing in its hyperbole, but it all brims with youthful enthusiasm for the music. Enjoy!

ANASTASIA SCREAMED
Electric Liz
(Killing Floor)

Their recent relocation from Boston to Nashville is a plus for the Music City, with Anastasia Screamed pumping some much-needed adrenalin and hormones into the feeble local hard rock scene. With the possible exceptions of Dessau, the Stand, Intruder, or F.U.C.T., there aren't many area bands that kick out the jams like these Beantown boys.

Electric Liz, their debut EP, is a massive dose of unbridled energy, white noise and white light; a muscular slice of primal rock 'n' roll passion, the guitars ringing like Quasimodo's nightmares and the heavy rhythm section pounding like a heart attack-inducing orgasm. Good, tasty stuff, not recommended for the meek, the cowardly, or fans of "safe" AOR fodder. – *The Metro*, 1989

DAN BAIRD
Love Songs For The Hearing Impaired
(Def American)

Songwriter and frontman Dan Baird "fired" himself from the Georgia Satellites after their wonderfully complex and darkly emotional third album and struck out on his own. That he should hit the often-traveled trail of the journeyman

Love Songs For The Hearing Impaired

should certainly come as no surprise. The Satellites were always just a group of inspired journeymen at heart, as loose as a pick-up band in a one-night jam session, as tight and cohesive a unit as any well-practiced bar band could be.

Baird's solo debut draws upon the same influences and inspiration as did the band's best work – the Stones, Chuck Berry, the Faces; all musical pioneers who defied the expectations of their time and defined an art form.

Love Songs For The Hearing Impaired is no-frills, straight-ahead, gut-level, guitar-driven rock 'n' roll. A vastly underrated songwriter in a Woody Guthrie/Hank Williams "keep it simple but convey a lot of thought" vein, Baird has always had a flair for penning both lyrical and musical hooks, and he provides both here in quantity. Tunes like "The One I Am," "Jule+Lucky," "Seriously Gone," and the grammatically-correct "I Love You Period" are meat-and-potato tunes for fans who like their rock unpretentious and undiluted. From Baird, no less is expected. – *R.A.D! Review & Discussion of Rock & Roll Culture*, November 1992

THE DUSTERS
This Ain't No Jukebox...
(Reptile Records)

Nashville blues-rockers check in with their first full-length disc, which turns out to be well worth the wait. A collection of ten earth-scorching tunes, it's obvious that the dusters took their time and did it right. Although long-time fans of the band will recognize such live favorites as "The Truck Won't Start" and "This Ain't No Jukebox...We're A Rock 'N Roll Band," other cuts shine as well. The dusters' cover of Savoy Brown's "Hellbound Train" smokes the original, achieving in three to four minutes what the original took thirteen to accomplish; "Phantom Of The Strip," "Street Legal," and "Blues Highway," all dusters' originals, bristle with bluesy energy and rock and roll fury. Ken McMahan's growling, guttural vocals are well-matched to his searing guitar style, while Dave Barnette's solid bass lines and drummer Chris Sherlock's pounding rhythms round out the (still maturing) dusters sound. *This Ain't No Jukebox...* is the album that George Thorogood should have made, as a new generation of white boys pick up the blues-rock torch. – *The Metro*, 1991

STEVE EARLE & THE DUKES
The Hard Way
(MCA Records)

With Springsteen on hiatus, Seger over the hill, and Mellencamp off making movies, Steve Earle seems to have taken up the mantle of the "working man's" champion with a vengeance. Earle's songwriting skills have never been sharper than here on *The Hard Way*, his brilliant follow-up to the impressive Copperhead Road album.

Earle's lyrics are tougher and leaner and sharper than ever before, his music tight, dark, and rocking. Earle has peopled this album with characters as disturbing, troubled,

THE OTHER SIDE OF NASHVILLE — 601 —

and real as Springsteen's *Nebraska*, documenting their trials and tears on record with a skill and grace the equal of any songwriter.

If John Hiatt is the South's poet laureate of song, then Earle must surely be his darker counterpart, the troubled troubadour, romantic at heart, forever destined to walk down the other side of the tracks and chronicle the life he sees there. – *The Metro*, September 1990

MARK GERMINO & THE SLUGGERS
Radartown
(Zoo Entertainment)

Here is a perfect example of the whole being much more than the parts. I always found the Sluggers to be a solid, if unremarkable band; the addition of rock poet Germino, however, creates something else entirely: a critical and commercial contender. Germino's songwriting skills are the equal of any high-priced wordsmith in the Music City, his entertaining and thought-provoking story-songs drawing on the country and folk storytelling traditions to build a true rock 'n' roll legacy. The Sluggers rock harder here than I've ever heard them.

Radartown would appeal to fans of the Springsteen/ Petty/Mellencamp school while holding its own with the brash young guitar bands of the college radio circuit. (P.S. The CD gives you a bonus, the hilariously funny, biting satire of "Rex Bob Lowenstein," the best song about the airwaves since "Radio Radio"…check it out!)
– *Radical Pizza*, 1991

GUILT
Thru The Night
(First Warning Records)

Long-time Nashville cult-heroes deliver a strong five-song, twenty-minute EP with Thru The Night. Lovingly produced by Steve Earle, the disc showcases the band's impressive, innate abilities (which are often overshadowed by the cult of personality that has evolved around the band). The music is somber, passionate Goth-rock, heavily influenced by the works of Bauhaus, Sisters of Mercy, and Joy Division while retaining a metal-influenced edge.

Guitarist Chuck Allen's six-string soars at times, providing some honestly thrilling moments, while Skot Nelson's bass playing is an important part of the mix, throbbing with visceral delight. Toss in vocalist Tommy McRae's primal vocals and one will find Thru The Night to be an excellent intro to one of the Music City's longest-lived and exciting bands. – *Radical Pizza*, 1991

IN PURSUIT
When Darkness Falls
(MTM Records)

When Darkness Falls, as the first pop/rock release of the Nashville-based MTM Records, places a heavy burden on the shoulders of the musicians known collectively as In

Pursuit. MTM holds a heavy rep in the entertainment industry as a producer of quality television programming appealing to an intelligent audience…and they'll be expected to uphold the same high standards and quality in the recordings they release.

When Darkness Falls fulfills all expectations, succeeding on every level. In Pursuit rises to the implied challenge to create an inspired gem of '80s-styled pop music. The five songs on this mini-album are compact, complex vignettes, tales of modern life. Bassist Emma provides lead vocals on the majority of the cuts, showing an impressive range of emotion and style. In Pursuit's instrumentation is sparse, placed handily behind the vocals in the mix, 'cause, after all, the lyrics are the message.

My faves? Well, the title cut, a nifty little made-for-radio hopper, grabs my ears and "Sacrifices," which features guitarist Jay Joyce's understated though effective vocals, shows a great interplay of vocals and instruments…and Jeff Boggs' drums are always on cue. In Pursuit's *When Darkness Falls* is a quality creation just waiting for a quality audience. – *The Metro*, 1985

INTRUDER
Psycho Savant
(Metal Blade Records)

Intelligence, talent, desire, insight and straight-up balls…Intruder is, without a doubt, the finest thrash outfit on the planet today, bar none. With the impending release of *Psycho Savant*, their third LP (with a fine EP also under their belts), the rest of the world will soon discover what Nashville area Intruder fans already know all too well: Intruder kicks ass! *Psycho Savant* showcases the band at its fierce best, opening with a literal kick in the teeth called "Face Of Hate," an eye-opening look at the ignorance and hatred of past generations which still wreaks havoc in society today. The rest of the disc is equally powerful and poetic. Beneath the lightning-quick riffs which fall from Arthur Vinnett's six string like so many drops of acid rain, Jimmy Hamilton's growling vocals and the pounding rhythm section of guitarist Greg Messick, bassist Todd Nelson, and big-beat drummer extraordinaire John Pieroni, lies the heart of the band's success: their impressive social awareness.

Though the music will appeal to any fan of loud and fast thrash metal, Intruder's lyrical penchant for real-world concerns and their ability to relate their insights in words sets them above the current wave of thrashers. Songs like "Geri's Lament (When)," "Traitor Of The Living" (about the government's Mount Weather facility), and "Final Word" will appeal to one's intellect as well as your rock and roll soul. Muscular, aggressive and thought-provoking...need I say more? – *The Metro*, 1991

JASON & THE SCORCHERS
Thunder and Fire
(A & M Records)

Jason & the Scorchers are, arguably, the best-known of Nashville's brash young bands, an outfit with a critically-acclaimed past and an infinitely-open future. *Thunder and Fire* is their first album for A & M Records, and their first effort with the new band. Folks, they've never been better.

This is a mature and fully-realized work: Jason's songwriting collaborations breathe new life into the Scorchers' material; Warner's guitar playing gets better and better; and the additions of bassist Ken Fox and skilled multi-instrumentalist Andy York round out the sound of the band, allowing them more diversity and providing a fuller, bigger feel to the songs. Drummer and co-writer Perry Baggz is like Old Faithful, an often (unfortunately) overlooked and underrated percussionist who manages to balance the entire chaotic crew.

The result is an album, Thunder and Fire, that is certain to become the band's biggest. Artistically impressive, musically powerful, lyrically fresh and exciting, the Scorchers made the album that they wanted to, and it shows. The boys may have gotten older, but they've not gotten softer...if anything, they've become more passionate, more committed with age. – *The Metro*, 1989

JET BLACK FACTORY
duality
(391 Records)

Don't ask me why I like this band. I can't figure it out. I hate this kind of stuff: the dark vocals of those suicidal Goth-rockers, the jangly guitars of every band south of the Mason-Dixon line who bought their local R.E.M. franchise. It's all too bloody serious. Just give me some Chuck Berry riffs and a couple of "na-na's" and I'll go home, thank you.

But these guys are different. Dave Willie's hoarse, brooding vocals have an energy that keeps them from getting mired in Goth-muck. Bob German's guitar vocabulary isn't limited to wimpoid jingle-jangles. He is perfectly capable of snarling, and knows when nothing short of a wall of sound will do. Jim Dye and Dave Jones form a taut and understated rhythm section. Though there's nothing here with the driving force of "Water's Edge," from JBF's last effort, songs like "Interstate and Speed" present dreamlike images in a swirling vortex of guitars and urgent vocals.

Producer Mike Poole deserves mention, for this six-song EP is as well-crafted as anything the big boys put out. Somebody ought to give him a zillion dollars so he can get about the business of saving rock & roll from itself. So roll over, Chuck Berry, and tell NRBQ the news, 'cause this one's going to be on my turntable for a while. – *The Metro*, 1988

JET BLACK FACTORY
House Blessing
(391 Records)

Nobody was watching, even though it should have come as no surprise. While everyone was involved with and enthralled by a dozen and one other bands, Nashville's Jet Black Factory quietly became one of the more creative forces to be found in the city. On the heels of two successful and widely acclaimed EPs, *House Blessing* is Jet Black Factory's first full-length album and their most mature and engaging creative effort to date.

Dave Willie's voice has grown into a magnificent instrument; dark, haunting vocals caressing the somber, oblique poetry that is the band's lyrical forte. Bob German's six string work perfectly compliments the material while the remainder of the band skillfully manipulates the texture and tone of the material. Treading a stylistic ground which owes as much to the Velvet Underground as it does Joy Division or R.E.M., Jet Black Factory has delivered a debut LP, of sorts, which is sure to make the coastal trend-setters sit up and take notice. – *The Metro*, April 1990

ROBERT JETTON
Rockin' Ranchero
(New Bohemian Records)

Take Robert Jetton's *Rockin' Ranchero* f'instance...if what you crave is well-produced, spirited rock & roll (with a heavy dose o' country funk tossed in for good measure), then this is the recording for you, bunkie. Opening up with an excellent cover of Lowell George's Little Feat classic, "Easy To Slip," Jetton smoothly moves into a tasty Tim Krekel tune, "It's Only Love," delivering it with appropriately bittersweet vocals and pleasantly subdued instrumentation. A guitar-heavy, Creedence-inspired rocker, "Little Troublemaker," kicks in, adding a bit of balance; rolling into the grand finale, a Jetton original titled "Once In Love," a rockabilly-tinged honky-tonker that'll get the

APPENDIX C: LEFTOVER RECORD REVIEWS

adrenalin flowing an' those toes-a-tappin'. An artist mining a rich and diverse talent, Jetton is a fellow to keep your eyes (and ears) on in the future. – *The Metro*, 1988

THE SHAKERS
Songs From Beneath The Lake
(Carlyle Records)

I must admit that I'd never been much of an admirer of the Shakers. After seeing them live a half a dozen times and listening to their debut EP, Living In The Shadow Of A Spirit, equally as often, I found Rebecca Stout's voice to be, far too often, shrill and uncompromising; Oscar Rice and Robert Logue's backing instrumentation to be meandering and uninspired.

I must also admit that I've had a change of heart. Songs From Beneath The Lake, the Shakers' first full-length album, finds the band hitting their stride artistically and musically. Stout's voice has developed into the expressive tool I'd suspected that it could be, capable of soaring from a seductive whisper to passionate heights within the space of a heartbeat, caressing the chimerical lyrics that have always been the band's strong suite.

The material is more fully-developed musically, as well, with Logue and Rice providing subtle and effective backing to this sparsely accompanied poetry. Gone are the excesses and flaws of immaturity, Songs From Beneath The Lake showcasing a band brimming with talent and creativity, exploiting both to their fullest measure. As a former detractor, I now stand a believer. Bravo! – *The Metro*, 1990

SOCIAL KINGS
Social Kings
(BiGG Records)

Drummer Kenny Wright has long been a fixture of Nashville's local rock scene, playing in a handful of bands that, although never hitting the "big time," have nonetheless served as the blueprint for the local hard rock scene. The formation of Social Kings – a partnership between Wright and kindred musical spirits guitarist Nicolas Maxime Nguyen and violinist Chris Carmichael – could well spell a new day for this journeyman artist and, perhaps, forge a new direction for Nashville's long-suffering hard rock heroes.

Social Kings' self-titled, seven-song debut EP is an energetic and joyful mix of diverse musical styles and influences. Evoking strains of such disparate musical antecedents as British pop and Southern funk, *Social Kings* is a solid effort, an unrestrained collection of songs untainted by industry pressures or peer expectations.

Released by the band themselves on their own BiGG Records imprint, *Social Kings* is one of the more encouraging, honest and sincere indie rock albums released this year. These guys are playing the kind of music they *want* to, not what will fit into some conceptual mold.

With a gospel fervor and a deep groove, "She's My Religion" jumps into a sort of Southern-styled, blue-eyed

funk worthy of Robert Palmer. The engaging ballad "I Am Reborn" opens with the notes of Carmichael's virtuoso violin, leading into a loving tale of redemption offering delicate harmonies and Wright's soft, sincere vocals. "Yesterday People" carries with it a heavy John Lennon influence, incorporated into an energetic musical groove featuring minimal instrumentation and tasteful percussion while "Speak Your Mind" lends a new wavish Britpop feel to one of the most effective declarations of freedom that these ears have heard, bluntly proclaiming "ask not what your country can do 'cause they don't care about you." "Think About It" is the disc's best cut, aiming well-placed lyrical barbs at poverty, racism, politics and cultural trends, delivered with strong vocals and imaginative instrumentation.

There are a couple of minor caveats I have to aim at the EP: the production is slight, often underplaying Wright's and Nguyen's likeable vocals and the band's solid lyricism. The band's song construction should bring Nguyen's fine guitar playing to the forefront, playing off of Wright's solid, strong percussion performance. Otherwise, *Social Kings* is a lot of fun, a tentative first step by a collection of top-notch Nashville area musicians with minds of their own, a certain musical vision and the experience and skills to pull it off. I certainly look forward to hearing more from Social Kings in the future... – *Thora-Zine*, 1996

VARIOUS ARTISTS
Alive At JC's

What's the matter, Bunkie...bored to tears over the same old nifty fifty as heard over your "all-of-the-hits-all-of-the-time!" radio station? Heavy metal misogyny, hard rock histrionics, and empty-vee got you down? Well, cheer up...because in Green Hills, tucked away on Bandywood

Comments: Another important, oft-overlooked early '80s punk rock band, the Electric Boys lit up local clubs for a short while before yielding the bulk of its talent to **Jason & the *Nashville* Scorchers**.

JADE

Band Members:
Cindy Shelton (vocals)
Nancy Jones (keyboards, vocals)
Kevin Reinon (guitar, vocals)
Jim Summers (bass)
Joey Hicks (drums)

Another View: "There's a new color on the Nashville music scene, Jade! Jade is 2 girls and 3 guys who deliver hard driving pop music..." – *The Metro*, September 1987

PEACE AND QUIET

Band Members:
Ric Steele (vocals)
Chris Leuzinger (guitar, vocals)
Spady Brannon (bass, vocals)
Dwight Scott (keyboards, vocals)
Teener Krawczyn (drums)
Vic Mastrioanni (drums)

Comments: Formed by Ric Steele in 1969 in Miami, the original incarnation of Peace and Quiet enjoyed some regional success in the Florida area before breaking up in 1973 and later reforming in Nashville a year later. While the band banged away at trying to get a label deal, they paid the rent by serving as country diva Crystal Gayle's touring band.

Peace and Quiet also backed up the legendary Jack Clement. According to scribe John Lomax, the band's sound was a mix of rock, reggae, soul, blues, country, pop, and R&B and they knew over 600 songs, and also wrote original material. As far as I know, they never recorded an album.

PHASE SELECTOR SOUND

Band Members:
Joshua Elrod
Craig Allen

Phase Selector Sound Recordings:

I. Disassemble Dub (ROIR Records 1999, CD)
1. Sinewave
2. MSP 2004
3. Sci Fi Dub
4. LK Pryr
5. Lefty's Choice
6. Dubstep
7. Factory Present
8. Subpart J.
9. Refraction
10. Honey Dub
11. Jackson Park
12. Moving Coil
13. Meditation
14. Halo and Snake
15. Version

Another View: "The partnership of Joshua Elrod, a former Nashvillian living in New York, and Craig Allen, a Nashville graphic designer, Phase Selector Sound has created a stunning collection of dub reggae tracks that draws on the complex and multileveled history of the music while staying ever mindful of the technologically savvy present-day..." – Jonathan Marx, *Nashville Scene*, October 1999

THE JACK SILVERMAN ORDEAL
Web: www.jacksilvermanordeal.com

Band Members:
Jack Silverman (vocals, guitar)
Viktor Krauss (bass)
Tyson Rogers (keyboards)
Roy Agee (trombone)
Derrek Phillips (drums)

APPENDIX D: LAST MINUTE ADDITIONS

From the Band's Website: "Purveyors of everything from crime jazz to '70s blaxploitation-style soundtracks to scary circus music to sitcom theme songs, The Jack Silverman Ordeal mine a musical terrain far left of the typical Music City fare…the band's eponymous debut weaves together infectious grooves, haunting melodies, stellar ensemble playing, a healthy dose of tongue-in-cheek musical humor, and of course Silverman's singular guitar work – a blend of lyricism, dissonance, haunting melodies, tongue-in-cheek musical humor and imaginative improvisation that avoids (or at times lampoons) the rote clichés of the six-string canon."

SPRING CHICKENS

Band Members:
Bobby Stewart a/k/a "Methyl Ethel" (vocals)
Keith O'Neil (guitar, vocals)
Matt Benson (vocals, bass)
Chris Trujillo (drums)
Jonathan Borg (drums)
Phillip Hill (bass, vocals)
Greg Harmon (drums)

Comments: Originally known as "Methyl Ethel & the Spring Chickens," the band evolved from Bunny Yum. Matt Benson and Phillip Hill would find a modicum of fame and acclaim by founding **Teen Idols**.

From the Band: Spring Chickens included only one original Bunny Yum member and ultimately evolved into an entirely different band, with an entirely different sound. As Bunny Yum we opened for such acts as Neurosis, Ultraman, and Offspring; as Spring Chickens, we opened for ALL, Moral Crux, Birth DFX, Trusty, and Born Against.

TAYLOR & STONE

Band Members:
Jim Taylor (vocals, guitar) (I)
Gerry Stone (vocals) (I)
Rusty Nix (guitar)
Dale Brown (bass, vocals) (I)
Cheri Thomas (keyboards)
Jon Tapp (drums)

Recordings:

I. A Million Light Beers Away… (Friday Nights At Home Records 1979, LP)
Side One
1. A Million Light Beers Away
2. Hey Honey Do You Wanna Dance?
3. Hung Over And Hung Up On You
4. The Ballad of Thelma Lou
5. Wondering When The Hurtin's Gonna End

Side Two
6. She Gives Me A Feeling
7. Falling Out of Love
8. Some Coffee And A Heartache To Go
9. Where Are They Now?
10. Catchin' The Morning Train

Comments: Damn, don't know how I missed this one, either, considering that Taylor & Stone keyboardist Cheri Thomas is an old friend. Anyway, the story here is that singers and songwriters Jim Taylor and Gerry Stone recorded *A Million Light Beers Away…* with producer Gene Kennedy and a slew of Music Row session guys like Buddy Spicher and Charlie McCoy at Bradley's Barn in Mt. Juliet, Tennessee. The band members listed above served as the Taylor & Stone touring band, with Dale Brown eventually forming **the Hots**. Why is all this important? Taylor & Stone were a good decade ahead of their time, blazing alt-country sounds that were too weird for Nashville circa 1979, although **Robert Jetton** and **David Olney** were sitting in the dugout waiting for their turn at bat. Draw a straight line from the Byrds and Gram Parsons to **Steve Earle** and **Jason & the *Nashville* Scorchers** and you'll stumble across Taylor & Stone along the way…

THE WAY-OUTS

Band Members:
Jeff Cease (vocals, guitar)
Bobby Greene (bass)
Jamie Gillum (drums)

Comments: Another of those popular early (and formative) bands, Scott and Chris Feinstein (**Shadow 15**, etc) often played with the Way Outs on stage. Check out the **Jeff Cease** interview (➜) for more info on this early Nashville band.

THE WHAT FOUR

Band Members:
Jason Phelan (vocals)
Chad Harrison (guitar)
John Hudson (bass)
Chris Lassiter (drums)

Comments: Another "ahead-of-its-time" Nashville band benefits from the digital revolution, the What Four's 20-song collection *The What Four Anthology* available for purchase on iTunes.

Another View: "Every town has a band that released too few records and was heard by too few people – yet those who did carry those songs tucked away like love letters. In Nashville, such a band was the What Four, whose mid-'90s garage-pop gems would have fit right in on a children-of-*Nuggets* box set." – Jim Ridley, *Nashville Scene*

Most of these interviews were originally published in The Metro *magazine back in the 1980s, before it became* Bone *magazine and the coverage of local bands often took a back seat to national artists. Almost half of the interviews were done exclusively for this book (* new), most of them recorded during 2007. Because I had gotten rid of a lot of my old copies of* The Metro, *etc, Robert Logue graciously provided me access to his collection of local music zines back in 2006 before I left town so that I could get copies of those interviews, album reviews, and other info that I lacked. Thanks, Robert!*

APPENDIX F: MISSING IN ACTION

This is a list of those bands and artists that, despite my best efforts, managed to elude my attempts to find out something substantial enough about them to include them in the book.

ADONIS
ALIEN IN THE LAND OF OUR BIRTH
ALL WE SEABEES
ALTERED STATESMEN
AN ARIATIC SILENCE
ANOTHER ROBOT SUNSET
APOC DEATH
ASFALT JUNGLE
SAM ASHWORTH
ASS CHAPEL
AUTUMN RAIN
BABY STOUT
BAD FRIEND
BALLISTIC WHIPLASH
THE BANG UP
BAZOOKA JOE
BEDWETTER
BELOVED CHILDREN
BIG SIR
BLUE O' CLOCK
BROKEN CHAINS
BUBBLE GUM COMPLEX
CINDY BULLENS
THE C-60S
CADENCE
CAESAR'S GLASS BOX
CHILDREN OF NOISE
CHUCK ALLEN EXPERIENCE
COUNT BASS-D
THE CROWD
CYOD
DAILY PLANET
JOHN DAVIS
THE DAY GLOW GODS
DEADSUN
DEATH COMES TO MATTESON
DEPTH CORE BLUE
DIG MANDRAKES
DINAH SHORE, JR.
THE DISCIPLES OF LO-TECH
DRAIN THE LOBSTER
THE ELECTRIC BOYS
ELEVENS UP
EUREKA GOLD
F PARTICLES
FEABLE WEINER
FLASHCUT PINUPS
FLESHPAINT
FREON DREAM
THE FRIENDLIES
THE FROTHY SHAKES
GIRLS IN ACTION

GOSTBIT
HANDS OFF CUBA
HELO KITTY
THE HISSY FITS
ROBB HOUSTON
IDLE JETS
IMMORTAL CHORUS
IMPETUOUS DOOM
IVY'S VINE
JACK
JAKE LEG STOMPERS
JAP SNEAKERS
JOHN HINCKLEY & THE JRS.
JOHNNY PANIC & THE BIBLE OF DREAMS
THE JONES
KEATING
KICKSTAND
KID GORILLA
LESLIE Q.
LIGHT OF POLARIS
JEREMY LISTER
LOOK WHAT I DID
LOPPIBOGIMY
LOVEBUCKET & SLAPPHAPPY SUPERFLY
LUCKY GUNS
LYLAS
THE MAGIC WANDS
MEAN TAMBOURINES
MEDICINAL PORPOISES
MERCED
MILKSHAKE
MILLARD POWERS
ESSRA MOHAWK
THE MOST
MOTHER/FATHER
MR. POTATOHEAD
MY DISGRACE
NEIGHBORHOOD TEXTURE JAM
NO FAT CHICKS
NUMBSKULL
OLE MOSSY FACE
OVERZEALOUS
PARTY GOBLIN
PELT CITY
P.M.S.
POET NAMED REVOLVER
POSTERCHILD
P.O.W.'S
PSOMNI
THE PROTOMEN
PSYCHIC SURGERY
PSYCHO DAISY

QUASINGTON
RADON DAUGHTER
THE RAVES
RED CARPET RATS
THE REDOUBTS
ROCKIN' FOOT CLUTCH
SALIENT
SCATTER THE ASHES
SCOUT
SERATONIN
THE SHAKES
SIT AWHILE WITH ED
SLACK
SNAKEHIPS
SOCIAL CIRCLE
SPIKE AND MALLETS
SPIRITUAL FAMILY REUNION
STARING AT THE SUN
TREY STEIN
SUICIDE ALLEY
SWAN DIVE
THE SWAYS
THORNTON
THE TIMES

TIP & MITTEN
TOMMY ROT
TONY DANZA TAP DANCING EXTRAVAGANZA
TRANSYLVANIA COWBOYS
THE TURNCOATS
UPC
VAGANTIS
VAHALLA
VELVET FOG
VERDANT GREEN
WELL AWAY
WHOLE FANTASTIC WORLD
WILD DOG DAZE
ROWDY YATES
ZERO HOUR

BOOKS

• Alden, Grant & Peter Blackstock, editors. **No Depression**. Dowling Press, 1998.

• Christgau, Robert. **Christgau's Record Guide: The '80s**. Pantheon Books, 1990.

• Christgau, Robert. **Christgau's Consumer Guide: Albums Of The '90s**. St. Martin's Griffin, 2000.

• Guterman, Jimmy. **The Best Rock 'n' Roll Records Of All Time.** Citadel Press, 1992.

• Popoff, Martin. **The Collector's Guide To Heavy Metal, Volume 2: The Eighties**. Collector's Guide Publishing, 2005.

• Popoff, Martin. **The Collector's Guide To Heavy Metal, Volume 3: The Nineties**. Collector's Guide Publishing, 2007.

• Robbins, Ira. **The Rolling Stone Review 1985: The Year In Rock**. Rolling Stone Press, 1985.

• St. John, Lauren. **Hardcore Troubadour (The Life and Near Death of Steve Earle)**. Fourth Estate, 2004.

NEWSPAPERS & PERIODICALS

• Anderson, Andy. "Bill Lloyd – The Guy With Four L's." *The Metro*, May 30, 1986.
• Anderson, Andy. "Jack Emerson Talks." *Nashville Intelligence Report* #6, 1982.
• Anderson, Andy. "Practical Stylists." *Nashville Intelligence Report* #6, 1982.
• Anderson, Andy. "Sixty Nine Tribe." *Nashville Intelligence Report* #27, 1985.
• Anderson, Andy. "Smokeless Zone." *Nashville Intelligence Report* #27, 1985.
• Anderson, Andy. "The Young Nashvillians." *Nashville Intelligence Report* #20, 1984.
• Anderson, Andy. "Unmasked! The Music Behind Los Straitjackets." *T-Bone/The Tennessean*, April 21, 1995.
• Anderson, Andy. "Webb Wilder." *The Metro*, September 1991.
• Anderson, Mark. "The Resurrection of Steve Earle." *Punk Planet* #45, September/October 2001.
• Anonymous. "Whyte Lace $$$$." *Weasel Weekly*, July 1987.
• Bachleda, F. Lynne. "Success On Her Own Terms." *Riff*, November 1992. (Jonell Mosser)
• Battlefield, Kat. "John Hiatt Goes to Church." *The Metro*, July 1993.

• Beale, Matt. "De Novo Dahl: Knocking It Down and Starting Over." *Performer Magazine*, November 2007.
• Blackstock, Peter. "Back To His Life's Work After A 'Vacation In The Ghetto'." *No Depression* #3, Spring 1996. (Steve Earle)
• Boin, Cindy Lampner. "15 Minutes: Human Radio." *The Metro*, November 1988.
• Burrow, Debbie. "Burning Hearts." *The Metro*, December 20, 1985.
• Burrow, Debbie. "Dr. Nik." *The Metro*, December 1991.
• Burrow, Debbie. "Every Mother's Nightmare." *The Metro*, November 1990.
• Burrow, Debbie. "Guilt." *The Metro*, May 1991.
• Burrow, Debbie. "Lust." *The Metro*, December 20, 1985.
• Burrow, Debbie. "Radix Is Steppin' Out." *The Metro*, March 7, 1986.
• Burrow, Debbie. "The Royal Court Of China." *The Metro*, February 21, 1986.
• Burrow, Debbie. "Wallstreet." *The Metro*, January 1991.
• Callahan, Duana. "Shadow 15." *Nashville Intelligence Report* #22, July 1984.
• Callahan, Duana. "Will." *Nashville Intelligence Report* #22, July 1984. (Will Rambeaux)
• Carter, Dawn. "Raging Fire." *The Metro*, March 21, 1986.
• Carter, Dawn. "Triple X." *The Metro*, October 25, 1985.
• Champion, Rick. "Basic Static." *Nashville Intelligence Report* #20, 1984.
• Champion, Rick. "C.P.S. The Committee For Public Safety." *Nashville Intelligence Report* #14, June 1983.
• Champion, Rick. "Scorchers Speak Out." *Nashville Intelligence Report* #26, 1985. (Jason & the Scorchers)
• Coes, "Uncle" Keith. "Intruder." *The Metro*, August 1987.
• Cookston, Deb. "Bowery Boys Invade Nashville." *The Metro*, December 20, 1985. (Manikenz)
• Cornell, Rick. "An Old Dylan Rocks His Horse Head To A New Sincerity." *No Depression* #6, December 1986. (Steve Forbert)
• Crawley, Clyde. "15 Minutes: Dangerous." *The Metro*, October 1990.
• Crawley, Clyde. "15 Minutes: Feed Four." *The Metro*, September 1990.
• Crawley, Clyde. "15 Minutes: Laughing Storm Dogs." *The Metro*, October 1990.
• Crawley, Clyde. "15 Minutes: Marky and the Unexplained Stains." *The Metro*, May 1990.
• Crawley, Clyde. "15 Minutes: The Relatives." *The Metro*, September 1990.
• Crawley, Clyde. "15 Minutes: Third Eye." *The Metro*, April 1990.
• Crawley, Clyde. "15 Minutes: Under The Big Top." *The Metro*, September 1990.
• Crawley, Clyde. "15 Minutes: Wishcraft." *The Metro*, May 1990.
• Crawley, Clyde. "Apache Underground." *The Metro*, March 1991.

- Crawley, Clyde. "Clockhammer." *The Metro*, April 1990.
- Crawley, Clyde. "Jane His Wife." *The Metro*, December 1989.
- Crawley, Clyde. "The Crystal Zoo." *The Metro*, October 1990.
- Crawley, Clyde. "The Dickens." *The Metro*, January 1991.
- Crawley, Clyde. "These Are Houseplants." *The Metro*, September 1990.
- Crawley, Clyde. "Under The Big Top." *The Metro*, February 1991.
- Dellinger, Mike. "Raging Fire." *Tasty World* #4 (Atlanta), 1984.
- Duncan, Vanessa. "15 Minutes: The Manikenz." *The Metro*, July 1988.
- Ferreira, Christine. "Screamin' Cheetah Wheelies Makin' Tracks." *Bone Music Magazine*, December 1993.
- Fischer, Blair. "Toy Soldiers: Self Begin A Childish Exploration." *Rolling Stone Magazine*, January 8, 1999.
- Fisher, Elizabeth. "Nine Parts Devil prove lounge music isn't just for strangers in a hotel bar." *Sidelines* (MTSU), October 16, 1995.
- Fox, Randy. "Mr. Zero: Gangsters from Gallatin?" *Fireplace Whiskey Journal*, September 2, 1988.
- Frank, Alison. "Little Saints." *The Metro*, November 22, 1985.
- Frank, Alison. "Think On Your Feet/Freedom of Expression." *The Metro*, January 17, 1986.
- Friskics-Warren, Bill. "The Scorch Will Rise Again." *No Depression* #6, December 1996. (Jason & the Scorchers)
- Fuson, Phil. "Honky-tonk Heroes Of The Western World." *No Depression* #2, Spring 1996. (BR5-49)
- Gajewski, Gail. "Dancin' In The District Debuts In June." *Bone Magazine*, June 1993. (Lark Watts & Rattleshake)
- Gajewski, Gail. "15 Minutes: Lark Watts." *The Metro*, June 1993.
- Gajewski, Gail. "Metro Express" column. *The Metro*, September 1990.
- Gajewski, Gail. "Metro Express" column. *The Metro*, January 1991.
- Gajewski, Gail. "Metro Express" column. *The Metro*, June 1991.
- Gajewski, Gail. "Metro Express" column. *The Metro*, July 1991.
- Gajewski, Gail. "Metro Express" column. *The Metro*, September 1991.
- Gajewski, Gail. "Metro Express" column. *The Metro*, October 1991.
- Gajewski, Gail. "Metro Express" column. *The Metro*, December 1991.
- Gee, Regina. "The Movement." *Nashville Intelligence Report* #27, 1985
- Gerson, Loren. "Actuel." *Nashville Intelligence Report* #11, 1983.
- Gerson, Loren. "Dayts." *Nashville Intelligence Report* #7, 1982.
- Gerson, Loren. "Practical Sylists." *Nashville Intelligence Report* #17, 1983.
- Gerson, Loren. "Will Rambeaux & the Delta Hurricanes." *Nashville Intelligence Report* #15, 1983.
- Gerson, Loren. "Young Grey Ruins." *Nashville Intelligence Report* #9, 1983.
- Giuffrida, Meg. "The Nerve." *The Metro*, January 12, 1987.
- Gleason, Holly. "Pat McLaughlin Gets Even." *T-Bone/The Tennessean*, March 10, 1995.
- Gordon, Keith A. "1984 In Review." *Anthem* zine, 1985
- Gordon, Keith A. "Absolutely Searing!" *CMJ Progressive Media*, May 1984.
- Gordon, Keith A. "Anastasia Screamed." *The Metro*, February 11, 1991.
- Gordon, Keith A. "Animalized" *The Metro*, August 16, 1985. (White Animals)
- Gordon, Keith A. "Bone Music Magazine: Rest In Peace." *R Squared*, March 1997.
- Gordon, Keith A. "Burning Down The House." *The Metro*, October 11, 1985. (Invasion of Privacy)
- Gordon, Keith A. "Cactus Brothers: New Ambassadors of Country Music." *T-Bone/The Tennessean*, June 2, 1995.
- Gordon, Keith A. "Catch Fire With Webb Wilder." *The Metro*, June 16, 1989
- Gordon, Keith A. "Chagall Guevara." *The Metro*, February 1991.
- Gordon, Keith A. "Dessau: Bauhaus & Rock'n'roll." *The Metro*, September 27, 1985.
- Gordon, Keith A. "Illusions, Delusions and Insanity: The History of the Alternative Press in Nashville." *The Metro*, August 1988.
- Gordon, Keith A. "In Pursuit Of...Excellence." *The Metro*, August 1985.
- Gordon, Keith A. "In Search Of Stealin Horses." *The Metro*, August 1988.
- Gordon, Keith A. "Innocence Is The Last Rebellion..." *R Squared*, June 1992. (Threk Michaels)
- Gordon, Keith A. "Jet Black Factory." *The Metro*, August 1991.
- Gordon, Keith A. "No Questions Here." *The Metro*, October 25, 1985. (The Questionnaires)
- Gordon, Keith A. "Power And Passion." *The Metro*, August 16, 1989. (Dessau)
- Gordon, Keith A. "Rambeaux: Silent Storm." *The Metro*, October 25, 1985. (Will Rambeaux)
- Gordon, Keith A. "Red Hot 'N Ready To Roll." *The Metro*, February 1990. (The Dusters)
- Gordon, Keith A. "Rock The Animals." *The Metro*, September 1985. (Billy Chinnock)
- Gordon, Keith A. "Stars of Tomorrow – NEA Extravaganza '94." *Bone Music Magazine*, January 1994.
- Gordon, Keith A. "Stealin Horses." *R Squared*, June 1992.
- Gordon, Keith A. "Tales of a Six-String Madman." *The Metro*, May 1993. (Warren Haynes)

• Gordon, Keith A. "The Continuing Saga of the Georgia Satellites." *Play*, January/February 1990. (Dan Baird)

• Gordon, Keith A. "The Scorchers: Still Standing." *The Metro*, October 13, 1986.

• Gordon, Keith A. "Theology & Thrash." *The Metro*, July 1990. (F.U.C.T.)

• Gordon, Keith A. "Threk Michaels." *The Metro*, January 1991.

• Gordon, Keith A. "Webb Wilder: The King of Country, Sultan of Rock & Roll." *R Squared*, March 1997.

• Gordon, Keith A. "When Angels Cry: Scaling Mount Olympus With Jason and the Scorchers." *The Metro*, October 1989.

• Gordon, Keith A. "With Enemies Like This..." *Nashville Intelligence Report* #28, 1985. (The Enemy)

• Gordon, Keith A. "Volunteers of America." *CMJ Progressive Media*, March/April 1984. (Volunteer Jam)

• Gordon, Rev. Keith A. "Blue Western Sky: Tony Gerber's Heaven & Earth." *Bone Magazine*, March 1995.

• Gordon, Rev. Keith A. "Jason & the Scorchers: Nashville's Favorite Sons." *T-Bone/The Tennessean*, February 3, 1995.

• Gordon, Rev. Keith A. "Nashville Scene Report." *The Austin Chronicle*, March 16, 1990.

• Gordon, Rev. Keith A. "The Road Goes On." *Bone Magazine*, May 1995. (The Floating Men)

• Gordon, Rev. Keith A. & the *Bone* Staff. "Stars of Tomorrow – NEA Extravaganza '94." *Bone Magazine*, January 1994.

• Gordon, Keith A. & Jon Rich. "Grassroots, Rhythm and Rhyme." *The Metro*, September 27, 1985. (Afrikan Dreamland)

• Gordon, Keith A. & Tracey Dooling. "Presenting Aashid, Part One." *The Metro*, May 1990.

• Gordon, Keith A. & Tracey Dooling. "Presenting Aashid, Part Two." *The Metro*, June 1990.

• Green, Allen. "Anarchy Again!" *Nashville Intelligence Report* #19, 1984.

• Green, Allen. "Factual." *Grab!*, January 15, 1981.

• Green, Allen. "Factual." *Nashville Intelligence Report* #16, 1983.

• Green, Allen. "Gostbit." *Nashville Intelligence Report* #28, 1985.

• Green, Allen. "Oh crap! I got the Wrong Band!" *Grab!*, Oct/Nov. 1981

• Green, Allen. "White Animals." *Nashville Intelligence Report* #15, 1983.

• Hansen, Kath. "A Bunch Of Tommyrot." *The Metro*, January 12, 1987.

• Hansen, Kath. "A Wistful Look Back at the Skinhead." *Fireplace Whiskey Journal*, June 2, 1988.

• Hansen, Kath. "Guilt Guilt Guilt Guilt Guilt." *The Metro*, March 23, 1987.

• Hansen, Kath. "Luck London." *The Metro*, March 23, 1987.

• Hansen, Kath. "Only For You." *The Metro*, February 9, 1987. (In Pursuit)

• Hansen, Kath. "The Grinning Plowman on the Killing Floor." *The Metro*, March 1987.

• Hansen, Kath. "The Movement Forward." *The Metro*, May 25, 1987.

• Hansen, Kath. "The Royal Court of China: Mood is Everything." *The Metro*, February 23, 1987.

• Hansen, Kath. "Tom Deluca." *The Metro*, October 13, 1986.

• Hansen, Kath. "Whyte Lace: See Your Own Future Yesterday!" *The Metro*, July 1987.

• Hargrove, Brantley. "Court-Ordered Hell." *The Nashville Scene*, January 20, 2010. (Danny Tate)

• Hench, David. "Maine rock 'n' roll icon Bill Chinnock dies at 59." *Portland Press Herald*, March 9, 2007.

• Hinz, Karl. "15 Minutes: Go Go Surreal." *The Metro*, November 1988.

• Kaye, Roger. "Debut shows Nightmoney has potential for big future." *Fort Worth Star-Telegram*, June 16, 1980.

• Keilich, Larissa. "Eleven 59." *The Metro*, August 1986.

• Keiper, Nicole. "Paramore Watches Itself Grow On The Road." *The Tennessean*, June 18, 2006.

• Keiper, Nicole. "Zero To 60 In A Pink Blur." *The Tennessean*, August 20, 2006 (Pink Spiders)

• King, Thom. "Anarchy In Music City." *The Nashville Gazette*, April 1980. (Cloverbottom)

• King, Thom. "How I Spent Over $100,00 To Get Some Free Records: A Partial History of Nashville's Take One Magazine." *The Metro*, August 1988

• Krantz, Dana. "Rumble Circus – Live at the Dreambowl." *The Metro*, February 1988.

• Levine, Mike. "Victor's Home Cooking." *Electronic Musician*, June 2008 (Victor Wooten)

• Lomax III, John. "Dave Olney." *Hank* magazine, August 1976.

• Lomax, John. "Peace and Quiet: Rockers In Countryland." *Hank* magazine, May 1977.

• Lomax III, John. "Song City Serenades." *The Nashville Gazette*, July 1980. (Nightmoney, Dave Olney)

• Lose, Heather. "A Day In The Life Of Jimmy Hall." *The Metro*, August 18, 1986.

• Lose, Heather. "In Color." *The Metro*, February 21, 1986.

• Lose, Heather. "Playing Twenty Questions With Chip & The Chiltons." *The Metro*, August 1986.

• Lose, Heather. "Roxx & Rolling Into The Future." *The Metro*, August 18, 1986.

• Lucey, Dennis. "Contenders." *Hank* magazine, May 1977.

• Luxford, Rebecca. "15 Minutes: Eleven 59." *The Metro*, June 1988.

• Luxford, Rebecca. "15 Minutes: Robert Jetton." *The Metro*, September 1988.

• Magee, Harvey. "Marshall Chapman Exposed." *Hank* magazine, August 1976.

• Mansfield, Brian. "If You Don't Like It, It's Not His Problem." *The Metro*, November 1988.

• Mansfield, Brian. "The Bears Rise and Shine." *The Metro*, June 1988.

• Mansfield, Brian. "Will & the Bushmen." *R Squared*, June 1992.

• Mainwaring, Mark Brian. "Ed Fitzgerald Returns!" *Nashville Intelligence Report* #6, 1982.

• McCall, Michael. "Bell's Jar (Singer-songwriter Nathan Bell returns to Nashville with a wider view)." *Nashville Scene*, November 22, 2007

• McCall, Michael. "Rising Ranchero." *Nashville Banner*, March 25, 1988. (Robert Jetton)

• McCrickard, Michael. "The Pat McLaughlin Story." *Fireplace Whiskey Journal*, July 3, 1988.

• Menconi, Debbie. "Burning Hearts." *The Metro*, January 12, 1987.

• Menconi, Debbie. "Triple X." *The Metro*, January 12, 1987.

• Minnigh, Bruce. "Mystic Meditations." *The Metro*, August 1991.

• Minnigh, Bruce. "The Shindigs." *The Metro*, January 1991.

• Moore, Tracy. "Back To The Drawing Board." *Nashville Scene*, Sept. 7, 2006. (The Features)

• Moore, Tracy. "Private Parts." *Nashville Scene*, November 23, 2006. (The Privates)

• Morris, Edward. "Market Forces." *Nashville Scene*, May 9, 1995. (Andrew & the Upstarts)

• Moses, Michael. "Former Ben Folds collaborator Owsley Pays His Dues." *Rolling Stone*, April 8, 1999.

• Murray, Noel. "Free-For-All: Local Musicians Unite For Fun-Spirited Side Project." *Nashville Scene*, March 8-14, 2001. (Swag)

• O'Brien, Kathleen. "The Amazing Grace of Jason and the Scorchers." *Tasty World*, 1985?

• Oermann, Robert K. "Grinning Plowman reaps songs they have sown in EP." *The Sunday Tennessean Showcase*, December 27, 1987.

• Oermann, Robert K. "Robert Jetton rescues his record from the limbo of label bureaucracy." *The Sunday Tennessean Showcase*, April 3, 1988.

• Owens, Tiffany. "Mary, Mary, Quite Extraordinary." *Experience Hendrix*, March/April 1999 (Mary Cutrufello)

• Parsons, Clark. "Will & the Bushmen." *Fireplace Whiskey Journal*, August 5, 1988.

• Parsons, Randy. "15 Minutes: The Boilers." *The Metro*, July 1988.

• Peisner, David. "American Regal." *Spin* magazine, October 2008. (Kings Of Leon)

• Perry, Jonathan. "Swag: Cheap Tricks." *Boston Phoenix*,
• April 26-May 2, 2001

• Philbrook, Erik. "Founding Member of the Jersey Shore Music Scene is Back with a New Album." *ASCAP Playback Magazine*, June 2004. (Billy Chinnock)

• Phillips, Amy. "Boy Toys (Gizmodgery Review)." *The Village Voice*, February 23, 2001. (Self)

• Ponce, Linda. "Trio went East hoping to prove West noteworthy." *Fort Worth Star-Telegram*, February 4-5, 1981. (Nightmoney)

• Ratner, Brett. "The Intoxicating Stomp of Bonepony." *T-Bone/The Tennessean*, May 26, 1995.

• Rian, Anthony. "The Artistic Value of Suburban Baroque." *Nashville Intelligence Report* #24, October 1984

• Ridley, Jim. "Band Du Jour: Mammy Namms." *First Impressions*, January 1990.

• Ridley, Jim. "City Of Nights." *Nashville Scene*, December 18, 1997 (Holtzclaw)

• Ridley, Jim. "Country Boys Can Survive." *Nashville Scene*, September 20, 2007 (Red State Update)

• Ridley, Jim. "Devil May Care." *Nashville Scene*, June 15, 1995. (Nine Parts Devil)

• Ridley, Jim. "Flamingo Express." *Nashville Scene*, July 12, 1990. (Hank Flamingo)

• Ridley, Jim. "Shamalam: All The Hip Facts You Need." *The Metro*, May 4, 1987.

• Rivers, Cindy. "Making Beautiful Music Together." *Ink 19*, August 1998. (The Evinrudes)

• Sanders, Daryl. "Al Kooper: Soul of a Man." *T-Bone/The Tennessean*, February 17, 1995.

• Shenkel, Mark. "Blind Farmers plowing into local music scene." *The Sunday News Journal*, March 2, 1986.

• Smith, Clark. "Blues Co-Op Brings Blues To Music City." *The Metro*, March 21, 1986.

• Spicer, Bill. "Fur Trade." *The Metro*, January 12, 1987.

• Spicer, Bill. "John Jackson & the Rhythm Rockers Keeping Busy." *The Metro*, December 6, 1985.

• Spicer, Bill. "The Full Grown Man Theory." *The Metro*, September 1985. (Webb Wilder)

• Spicer, Bill. "This Is Not A Jazz Band." *The Metro*, February 1986. (Rococo)

• Staley, Chip. "Patty Murray: Nashville's Rock And Roll Mama." *The Metro*, April 4, 1986.

• Steber, Bill. "MTSU band on the move." *Sidelines*, March 5, 1985. (Freedom Of Expression)

• Sweeney, Jeff. "Say Cheese!" *The Metro*, November 11, 1985. (Govt. Cheese)

• Tennille, Andy. "The Dynamites: Soul Explosion." *Harp* magazine, November 2007.

• Tilford, Bryan. "Self Interview" *Ink 19*, November 2000.

• Walker, Steve. "Breaking Up Is Hard To Do..." *Shake Rattle & Roll*, March 1993 (Human Radio)

• Washington, T. Lee (a/k/a Keith A. Gordon). "The Fallen One." *Anthem*, July 1985 (Threk Michaels)

• Webb, Robert. "15 Minutes: The Faith Healers." *The Metro*, June 1990.

• Wilkins, Jason Moon. "Ghostfinger These Colors Run" CD review. *All The Rage*, December 13, 2005.

• Williams, Lise. "The Fur Trade." *The Metro*, February 7, 1986.

• Williams, Wheat. "Road Report: Jerry Dale McFadden of the Mavericks." *Keyboard* magazine, December 1996.

• Wilson, Pete. "Celebrating a simpler, happier hometown with the Young Nashvillians." *Nashville Scene*, July 31, 1997.

• Wilson, Scott. "Nashville Bridges: Young Music Row bands such as Llama cross over into rock." *The Pitch* (Kansas City), June 14, 2001.

• Wood, Gerry. "Nashville Is Rolling With Rock Again." *Billboard* magazine, July 1987(?)

• Wood, Tom. "Jimmy Hall and the Prisoners of Love." *The Metro*, January 12, 1987.

• Wood, Tom. "Rambeaux for real." *Fireplace Whiskey Journal*, July 3, 1988. (Will Rambeaux)

• Wood, Tom. "Steve Earle." *Fireplace Whiskey Journal*, October 7, 1988.

• Wilff, Andalucia. "Aashid Himmons: New Horizons." *The Metro*, February 1988.

• Wynn, Ron. "Right Fan Brings Success." *Nashville City Paper*, January 23, 2004. (Weatherspoon)

• Yampert, Rick de. "Holtzclaw shocks Music City rock." *The Tennessean*, date unknown – probably 1997.

• Uncredited. "Factual." *Nashville Intelligence Report* #4, 1982.

• Uncredited. "Local Hero: Mike Simmons." *The Metro*, February 23, 1987.

• Uncredited. "Ring Of Fire." *Nashville Intelligence Report* #22, July 1984.

• Uncredited. "Thrashers!" *The Entertainer*, September 1, 1987. (Deacon Fields)

• Uncredited. "Whos' News: Jade." *The Metro*, September 1987.

BAND BIOGRAPHIES

Dan Baird (Geffen Records)
Bare, Jr. (Epic Records)
Dessau (Carlyle Records)
The Dusters (Reptile Records)
Every Mother's Nightmare (Arista Records)
Steve Forbert (Paladin Records)
Fleming & John (Universal Records)
The Floating Men (Meridian Records)
Freedom of Expression
Glossary
Grinning Plowman (Carlyle Records)
The Hard Corps (Interscope Records)
John Hiatt (Capitol Records)
Hot Action Cop (Lava Records)
In Pursuit (MTM Records)
Intruder (Metal Blade Records)
Jason & the Scorchers (EMI Records)
Jet Black Factory (391 Records)
Will Kimbrough (Waxy Records)
Tim Krekel & the Sluggers (Arista Records)
Jamie Kyle (Atco Records)

Legendary Shack Shakers (Yep Roc Records)
Lust
Manikenz
Me Phi Me (RCA Records)
Peace Cry
Practical Stylists
The Questionnaires (EMI Records)
Raging Fire (Pristine Records)
Will Rambeaux
Giles Reaves (MCA Records)
Riff Rath
Royal Court of China (A&M Records)
Matthew Ryan
Self (Spongebath Records)
Sparkledrive (Aware Records)
Stealin Horses (Arista Records)
Stone Deep (Secession Records)
Swag (Yep Roc Records)
The Thieves
Max Vague
Valentine Saloon
Vegas Cocks
Warm Dark Pocket
Webb Wilder (Landslide Records)
Wrong Band

PHOTO CREDITS

• Locker photo page 3, courtesy Holly Duncan
• Rev. Keith A. Gordon photo page 7 by Tracey Dooling
• Afrikan Dreamland photo page 9 by J. Clark Thomas, courtesy Ayo Records
• Aashid photos pages 12, 13 & 15 by Ross Smith
• A.K.A.: Rudie photo page 25 courtesy Mark Shenkel
• American Bang photo page 30 courtesy Reprise Records
• Crystal Armentrout photo page 34 by Kristina Krugg
• Actuel photo page 38 courtesy Stephen Anderson
• Actuel/Slim Jim photo page 41 by Anita French
• Dan Baird photo page 46 by Michael Wilson, courtesy Def American Records
• Bare Jr. photo page 48 by Jay Blakesberg, courtesy Immortal Records
• Black Crowes photo page 57 courtesy Warner Music
• Bonepony photos pages 66 & 70 courtesy Bonepony
• The Bunnies photo page 68 courtesy Donna Frost
• Pete Berwick photos pages 73 & 75 courtesy Pete Berwick
• Cactus Brothers photo page 78 by John Lee Montgomery III, courtesy Kinetic Management & Liberty Records
• Marshall Chapman photo page 85 courtesy Robert Jetton
• China Black photo page 89 by Mark Morrison
• Chip & the Chiltons photos pages 93 - 97 courtesy Chip Chilton
• Cloverbottom photos pages 106 & 107 courtesy Cloverbottom
• Stacie Collins photo page 108 by Staci McQueen
• Dave Cloud photo page 108 by Mark Swanson

- Kristen Cothron photo page 110 courtesy Kristen Cothron
- Way-outs photo page 114 courtesy Jeff Cease
- Rumble Circus photo page 115 by Billy Wade, courtesy Jeff Cease
- Dorcha photo page 129 by Beth Gwinn, courtesy Carlyle Productions
- Steve Earle photo page 139 by Michael Wilson
- Dessau photo page 164 courtesy Carlyle Records
- Facsimile photo page 167 courtesy Mark Shenkel
- Farmer Jason photo page 169 by Rusty Rust, courtesy Kid Rhino
- Fleming & John photo page 176 by Eva Muller, courtesy Universal Records
- Floating Men photo page 181 courtesy Meridian Records
- Freedom of Expression photo page 191 uncredited, courtesy Tyler House Talent
- Donna Frost photo page 193 courtesy Donna Frost
- F.U.C.T. photo page 197 courtesy Carlyle Records
- The Grinning Plowman photo page 212, courtesy Carlyle Records
- Guilt photo page 214 by Carol Fonde, courtesy First Warning Records
- Tony Gerber photo page 217 by Mark Pleasant
- Hard Corps photo page 222 by Michael Lavine, courtesy Interscope Records
- Warren Haynes photo page 223 courtesy Megaforce
- Will Hoge photos pages 235 & 239 courtesy Ryko Records
- Jeff Holmes & Scott Evans photo page 247 by Tracy Tanner 2009, courtesy Jeff Holmes
- Jeff Holmes photo page 249 by Tracy Tanner, 2009
- Intruder photo page 255 by Lisa Zhito, courtesy Metal Blade Records
- In Pursuit photo page 259, courtesy MTM Records
- Jason & the Scorchers photo page 263 by Tom Sheehan, courtesy EMI America Records
- Jason & the Scorchers photo page 265 by Peter Nash, courtesy EMI America Records
- Jason & the Scorchers photo page 267 by Darin Back
- Jason & the Scorchers Christmas card page 273 courtesy Praxis International (cool, ain't it?)
- Jason & Warner photo page 279 by Tracey Dooling (I'm really as tall as these guys, maybe it's the *Animaniacs* hat making me look shorter, ya think?)
- Jetton & Wheeler photo page 287 courtesy Robert Jetton
- Rockin' Rancheros photo page 291 courtesy Robert Jetton
- New Bohemians photo page 293 courtesy Robert Jetton
- Kings of Leon photo page 302 courtesy RCA Records
- Tim Krekel & the Sluggers photo page 303 by Steve Harbison, courtesy Praxis International
- Legendary Shake*Shakers photo page 310 by Matt Slocum
- Rev. Gordon & Legends photo page 313 by Amy Busse
- Bill Lloyd & Practical Stylists photo page 317 by Rev. Keith A. Gordon – *never before published!*
- Mercenaries photo page 342 courtesy Danny Dickerson

- Threk Michaels photo page 345 by Alan Messer, courtesy Threk Michaels & Royal Records
- Rick Moore photo page 358 by Alan Messer, courtesy MRL Records
- Nine Parts Devil photo page 364 courtesy Dave Willie
- The Nobility photo page 354 by Phil Thornton
- David Olney photos pages 369 & 371 courtesy Mary Sack
- Peace Cry photo page 387 courtesy Mike Phillips
- Dave Perkins photo page 391 courtesy Dave Perkins
- Practical Stylists photo page 398 by Bill Kalinowski, courtesy Pyramid Records
- Practical Stylists photo page 399 by Rev. Keith A. Gordon
- Scott Sullivant photo page 402 courtesy Scott Sullivant
- The Questionnaires photo page 405 by Ron Keith
- Will Rambeaux photo page 410 by Casey Lutton
- Jason Ringenberg photo page 417 by Brydget Carrillo
- Self photo page 440 by Mitch Tobias, courtesy Spongebath Records & Zoo Entertainment
- Seventh Sister photo page 445 courtesy Landry Butler
- Royal Court of China page 455 courtesy Robert Logue
- Shazam photo page 459 by Daniel Coston
- The Sluggers photo page 466 by Peter Nash, courtesy Arista Records & Praxis International
- Stealin Horses photo page 487, courtesy Arista Records
- Stone Deep photos pages 491 & 492 by E. Heather Lose
- Rebecca Stout photo page 493 by Libba Gillum
- Allen Collins photo page 500 by Rev. Keith A. Gordon
- Rev. Gordon & Charlie Daniels photo page 501 by Thom King, courtesy *Take One* magazine
- Temporal Pain photo page 506 courtesy Mark Swann
- Max Vague Band photo page 520 courtesy Max Vague
- Whyte Lace photo page 551 by Alan Messer
- Webb Wilder photo page 553 by Ruth Leitman, courtesy Zoo Entertainment & Praxis International
- Webb Wilder photo page 559 by Wyatt McSpadden, courtesy Watermelon Records
- Webb Wilder "Corn Flicks" photo page 560 by Ed Colver, courtesy Zoo Entertainment & Praxis International
- Tommy Womack photo page 574 by Gregg Roth
- Wrong Band photo page 577 courtesy Mark Franklin & the Wrong Band
- Kenny Wright photo page 580 courtesy Kenny Wright
- Committee For Public Safety photo page 583 by Andy Crowell, courtesy Dave Willie
- Greg Walker photos pages 585 & 587 courtesy Greg Walker

Individual CD and LP covers courtesy the respective record labels and/or bands

The Other Side of Nashville cover art by the great Tim "Mercury" Shawl

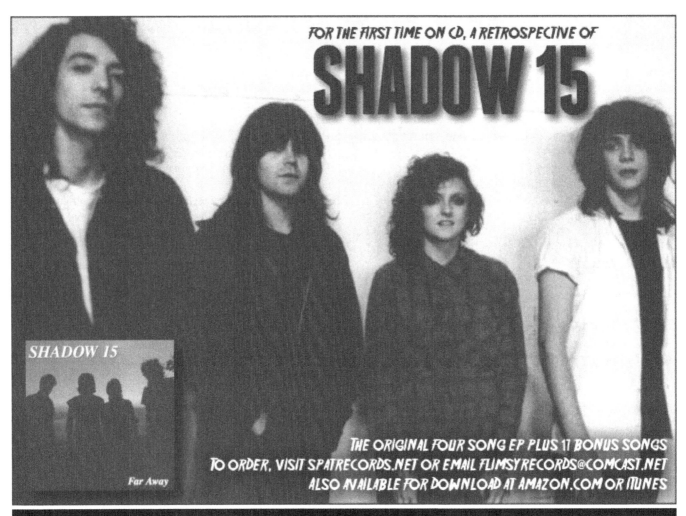

To finish up production on **The Other Side of Nashville**, I had to turn to Kickstarter to raise funds to pay Tim Shawl for his wonderful cover art, cover the cost of tape transcriptions, and a bunch of other stuff that I needed a little help with. The folks below stepped up and donated the money to finish the book, albeit a little slower than either my donors or myself may have liked. Thanks to everybody for their support!

CONTRIBUTING DONORS
Maureeen McLaughlin
Tamelyn Feinstein
Bernard Walters

SUPPORTING DONORS
Pete Berwick
Landry Butler
Jerker Emanuelson
Gayle Escamilla
Robyn Gilliam
Allison Green
Kristine Hughes
Vickie Jacobson
Fred Mills
Craig Reeves
Ira Robbins
Connor Tifarra
vonwegen121

ESSENTIAL DONORS
William Claypool
Glenn Hughes
Don Kendall
Gwil Owen
Mike Poole
Michael Principe
Nathalie

BAND DONORS
Scott Feinstein
Donna Frost
The Dusters

TRULY ROCKIN' DONORS
Dave Marsh
Jeff Ousley

HALL OF FAME DONORS
Tom Der
markmark

CPSIA information can be obtained at www.ICGtesting.com
Printed in the USA
LVOW022317180213

320699LV00003B/22/P